ESSENTIAL MATHEMATICS

FOR THE AUSTRALIAN CURRICULUM

YEAR 9

>> Additional resources online

DAVID GREENWOOD | SARA WOOLLEY
JENNIFER VAUGHAN | JENNY GOODMAN

CAMBRIDGE **FIRST**

CAMBRIDGE
UNIVERSITY PRESS

CAMBRIDGE UNIVERSITY PRESS
Cambridge, New York, Melbourne, Madrid, Cape Town,
Singapore, São Paulo, Delhi, Tokyo, Mexico City

Cambridge University Press
477 Williamstown Road, Port Melbourne, VIC 3207, Australia

www.cambridge.edu.au
Information on this title: www.cambridge.org/9780521178655

First published **2011**
Reprinted **2012 (thrice)**

Edited by Marcia Bascombe
Cover design by Denise Lane at Sardine Designs
Designed by Mary Clarke at Mason Design
Typeset by Aptara Corp
Printed in Singapore by C.O.S. Printers Pte Ltd

National Library of Australia Cataloguing in Publication data

  Essential mathematics for the Australian curriculum Year 9
  / David Greenwood ... [et al.].
  9780521178655 (pbk.)
  For secondary school age.
  Mathematics—Textbooks.
  Mathematics—Study and teaching (Secondary)—Australia.
  Education—Australia—Curricula.
  Greenwood, David Michael, 1970-
510

ISBN 978-0-521-17865-5 Paperback

Additional resources for this publication at www.cambridge.edu.au/GO

Cover: 2011 Used under license from Shutterstock.com/ Stewie74
Images: Bernegger_Manuale/Wikimedia Commons, **p. 159**; NEW LINE CINEMA / THE KOBAL COLLECTION, **p. 192**; © Michael B.
Fritz, **p. 235**; ©James Gurney 2006 **p. 380**; CDC/ Dr. Ray Butler, **p. 324**; NASA/courtesy of nasaimages.org/, **p. 355** (bottom); **All other photos**: 2011
Used under license from Shutterstock.com.

*Every effort has been made to trace and acknowledge copyright. The publisher apologises for any accidental infringement and welcomes information
that would redress this situation.*

Table of Contents

Strand and substrand

Measurement and Geometry

Geometric reasoning

Number and Algebra

Patterns and algebra

Using a CAS calculator 8.5:

Expanding and factorising (website)

About the authors

David Greenwood is Head of Mathematics at Trinity Grammar School in Melbourne and has 17 years experience teaching maths from Years 7 to 12. He has run numerous workshops in Australia and overseas in the use of technology for the teaching of maths and has a keen interest in the development of the Australian Curriculum with particular interest in the sequencing of content and the proficiency strands.

Sara Woolley was born and educated in Tasmania. She completed an Honours degree in Mathematics at the University of Tasmania before completing her education training at the University of Melbourne. She has taught mathematics in Victoria from years 7 to 12 since 2006.

Jenny Goodman has worked in comprehensive state and selective high schools in NSW since 1994 and has a keen interest in teaching students of differing abilities, from the gifted and talented students to those with learning difficulties. She currently teaches at Sydney Technical High School. She was awarded the Jones Medal for Education and the Bourke Prize for Mathematics from Sydney University.

Jennifer Vaughan has taught secondary mathematics for 30 years in NSW, WA, QLD and New Zealand, and has tutored and lectured mathematics at Queensland University of Technology. Jennifer currently teaches at Ormiston College, Queensland.

Introduction and how to use this series

Development of this series started in 2008 with an analysis of state curricula, in parallel with the work of ACARA. The manuscripts were drafted to this analysis, ACARA documents and feedback provided by the states. Revisions were made to each curriculum release including Version 1.0 published in December 2010 and other updates in 2011. Future versions will be covered in (1) printable supplements published on the companion website, (2) online electronic versions revised immediately and (3) regular reprints of the books.

As the Australian Curriculum specifies minimum content to be covered, the series includes some topics which are necessary pre-requisites for specified content and which have always been covered by individual state curricula. The series also includes logical extensions in a range of topics. Both these categories are indicated in the teaching program, which also maps the content to version 1.0. To help schools manage the transition, curriculum grids are also available mapping the content to existing state syllabuses and curricula.

Through these approaches the series is founded on a reliable teaching structure and sequence which can confidently be used to manage differentiated learning in the classroom with the minimum of preparation. For more information see the companion website.

Guide to the textbooks in this series

Features:

Australian curriculum: strands and content descriptions for chapter (also available in a grid)

What you will learn: an overview of chapter contents

Chapter introduction: use to set a context for students

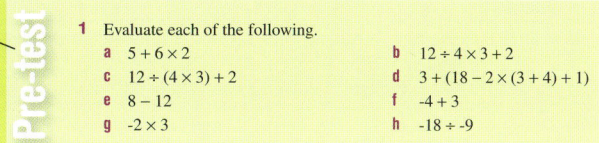

Pre-test: establishes prior knowledge (also available as a printable worksheet)

1 Evaluate each of the following.

 a $5 + 6 \times 2$ **b** $12 \div 4 \times 3 + 2$

 c $12 \div (4 \times 3) + 2$ **d** $3 + (18 - 2 \times (3 + 4) + 1)$

 e $8 - 12$ **f** $-4 + 3$

 g -2×3 **h** $-18 \div -9$

Guide to the textbooks in this series (continued)

Topic introduction: use to relate the topic to mathematics in the wider world

HOTmaths icons: links to interactive online content via the topic number, 1.6 in this case (see next page for more)

Let's start: an activity (which can often be done in groups) to start the lesson

Key ideas: summarises the knowledge and skills for the lesson (digital version also available for use with IWB)

Examples: solutions with explanations and descriptive titles to aid searches (digital versions also available for use with IWB)

Exercise questions categorised by the four **proficiency strands**

and **enrichment**

Questions are linked to examples

The **calculator icon** appears where students are advised to use their calculator to solve the problem

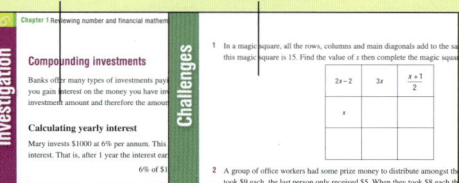

Investigations: inquiry-based activities

Challenges

1.6 Percentages and money

We use percentages for many different things in our daily lives. Some examples are loan rates, the interest given on term deposits and discounts on goods.

We know from our previous studies that a percentage is a fraction that has a denominator of 100. 'Per cent' comes from the Latin word *per centum* and means 'out of 100'.

Let's start: Which is the largest piece?

Four people receive the following portions of a cake:

Key ideas

- **Ratios** are used to compare related quantities.
  - The ratio of a to b is written $a : b$.
  - Ratios in simplest form use whole numbers divided by their highest common factor.
  - Ratios are written to compare quantities expressed in the same units.
- The **unitary method** involves finding the value of one part of a total.
  - Once the value of one part is found then the value of several parts can easily be determined.
- A **rate** compares related quantities with different units.

Example 11 Simplifying ratios

Simplify these ratios.
a $38 : 24$ **b** $2\frac{1}{2} : 1\frac{1}{3}$ **c**

SOLUTION	EXPLANATION
a $38 : 24 = 19 : 12$	The HCF of 38 and 24 is 2 so di

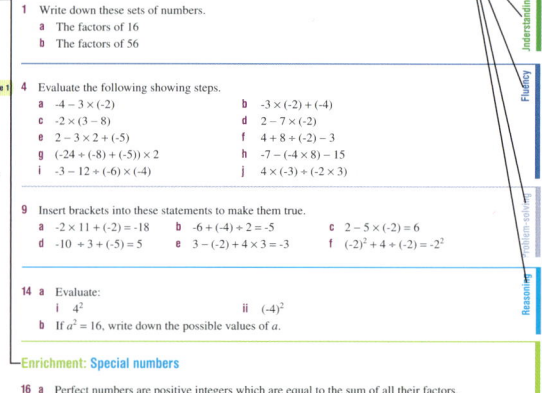

Exercise 1A

1. Write down these sets of numbers.
   a The factors of 16
   b The factors of 56

Example 1   4. Evaluate the following showing steps.
   a $-4 - 3 \times (-2)$ **b** $-3 \times (-2) + (-4)$
   c $-2 \times (3 - 8)$ **d** $2 - 7 \times (-2)$
   e $2 - 3 \times 2 + (-5)$ **f** $4 + 8 \div (-2) - 3$
   g $(-24 \div (-8) + (-5)) \times 2$ **h** $-7 - (-4 \times 8) - 15$
   i $-3 - 12 \div (-6) \times (-4)$ **j** $4 \times (-3) + (-2 \times 3)$

9. Insert brackets into these statements to make them true.
   a $-2 \times 11 + (-2) = -18$ **b** $-6 + (-4) \div 2 = -5$ **c** $2 - 5 \times (-2) = 6$
   d $-10 \div 3 + (-5) = 5$ **e** $3 - (-2) + 4 \times 3 = -3$ **f** $(-2)^2 + 4 \div (-2) = -2^2$

14. **a** Evaluate:
    i 4^2 **ii** $(-4)^2$
    b If $a^2 = 16$, write down the possible values of a.

Enrichment: Special numbers

16. **a** Perfect numbers are positive integers which are equal to the sum of all their factors, excluding the number itself.

Chapter summary: mind map of key concepts & interconnections

Two Semester reviews per book

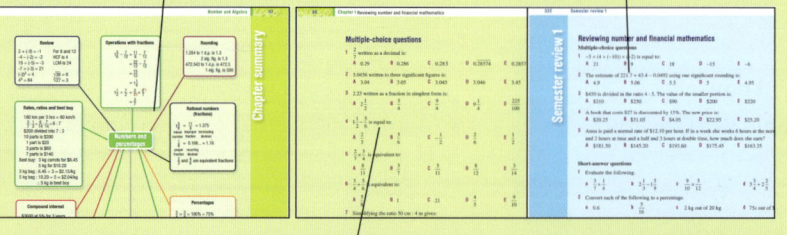

Textbooks also include:
- Complete **answers**
- **Glossary**
- **Using technology** activities

Chapter reviews with **multiple-choice, short-answer** and **extended-response questions**

Online components and associated websites

 **INTEGRATED PROGRAM**

The *Essential Mathematics/Cambridge HOTmaths* integrated program offers the best of textbook and interactive online resources for the Australian Curriculum.

When used with student accounts, the integrated program links students and their teachers to the full range of *Cambridge HOTmaths* resources for use in the classroom and at home. The integrated program can also be used with teacher accounts for in class demonstrations using IWBs or data projectors.

The integrated program is linked from icons throughout the text and topic numbers in the textbooks. See the integrated program document on the *Cambridge HOTMaths* tab in the *Essential Mathematics* resource on *Cambridge GO* (see below).

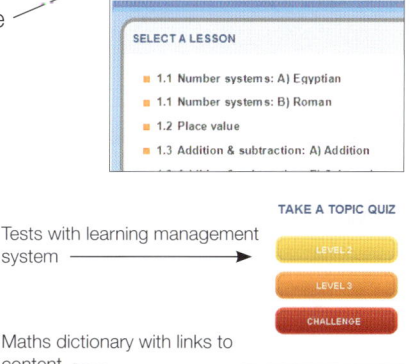

The integrated program is accessible from the drop-down course menu on *Cambridge HOTmaths*, organised by the textbook chapter and topic/lesson structure.

All HOTmaths features are included in the program, eg:

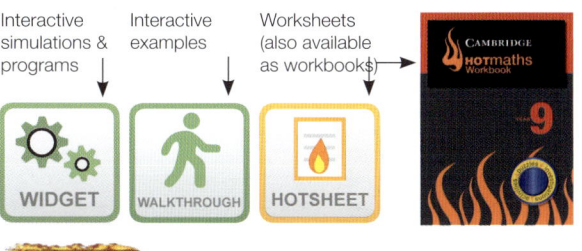

Interactive simulations & programs

Interactive examples

Worksheets (also available as workbooks)

Tests with learning management system

Maths dictionary with links to content

 ← Practice quizzes with competitive scoring option

www.cambridge.edu.au/hotmaths

Cambridge GO — YOUR GATEWAY ONLINE

Use the unique access code found in the front of this textbook to activate these resources.
For more information on how to access these resources, see over.

Free additional student support resources are available online at *Cambridge GO* and include:
- the PDF Textbook – a downloadable version of the student text, with note-taking and bookmarking enabled
- revision notes formatted for smartphones and PCs
- teaching programs and curriculum grids
- additional calculator, spreadsheet and ICT activities
- updates to address syllabus changes and amendments.

www.cambridge.edu.au/GO

Details of teacher editions and online resources are available at www.cambridge.edu.au/education

This textbook is supported by online resources...

YOUR GATEWAY ONLINE

Digital resources and support material for schools.

About the free online resources...

Free additional student support resources are available online at *Cambridge GO* and include:

- the PDF Textbook – a downloadable version of the student text, with note-taking and bookmarking enabled
- extra material and activities
- links to other resources.

Available free for users of this textbook. Use the unique access code found in the front of this textbook to activate these resources.

www.cambridge.edu.au/GO

Access your online resources today at www.cambridge.edu.au/GO

1. **Log in** to your existing *Cambridge GO* user account
OR
Create a new user account by visiting:
www.cambridge.edu.au/GO/newuser

- All of your *Cambridge GO* resources can be accessed through this account.
- You can log in to your *Cambridge GO* account anywhere you can access the internet using the email address and password with which you're registered.

2. **Activate** *Cambridge GO* resources by entering the unique access code found in the front of this textbook.

- Once you have activated your unique code on *Cambridge GO*, it is not necessary to input your code again. Just log in to your account using the email address and password you registered with and you will find all of your resources.

3. **Go** to the My Resources page on *Cambridge GO* and access all of your resources anywhere, anytime.*

* Technical specifications: You must be connected to the internet to activate your account. Some material, including the PDF Textbook, can be downloaded. To use the PDF Textbook you must have the latest version of Adobe Reader installed.

For more information or help contact us on 03 8671 1400 or enquiries@cambridge.edu.au

FORECLOSURE

Chapter **1**

Reviewing number and financial mathematics

What you will learn

Global financial crisis

The global financial crisis of 2008 and 2009 was one of the most serious financial situations since the Great Depression in the 1930s. Prior to the crisis, US interest rates were lowered to about 1%, which created access to easy credit and 'sub-prime' lending. House prices in the US rose about 125% in the 10 years prior to the crisis. When the housing bubble burst, house prices began to fall and lenders began foreclosing on mortgages if borrowers could not keep up with their repayments. At the beginning of the crisis, US household debt as a percentage of personal income was about 130%. As house prices collapsed, financial institutions struggled to survive due to the increased number of bad debts. The crisis expanded to cause negative growth in the US general economy and in other countries. In Australia, our sharemarket All Ordinaries Index collapsed by 55% from 6874 in November 2007 to 3112 in March 2009.

Pre-test

1 Evaluate each of the following.

 a $5 + 6 \times 2$ **b** $12 \div 4 \times 3 + 2$

 c $12 \div (4 \times 3) + 2$ **d** $3 + (18 - 2 \times (3 + 4) + 1)$

 e $8 - 12$ **f** $-4 + 3$

 g -2×3 **h** $-18 \div (-9)$

2 Write $\dfrac{11}{5}$ as:

 a a mixed number   **b** a decimal

3 Evaluate:

 a 3^2 **b** $\sqrt{25}$ **c** $(-4)^2$ **d** 2^3

4 Determine which is larger, $\dfrac{3}{4}$ or $\dfrac{7}{9}$:

 a by rewriting with the lowest common denominator

 b by converting to decimals (to three decimal places where necessary).

5 Arrange the numbers in each of the following sets in descending order.

 a 2.645, 2.654, 2.465 and 2.564

 b 0.456, 0.564, 0.0456 and 0.654

6 Evaluate each of the following.

 a $4.26 + 3.73$ **b** $3.12 + 6.99$ **c** $10.89 - 3.78$

7 Evaluate.

 a 7×0.2 **b** 0.3×0.2 **c** 2.3×1.6

 d 4.2×3.9 **e** $14.8 \div 4$ **f** $12.6 \div 0.07$

8 Evaluate each of the following.

 a 0.345×100 **b** $3.74 \times 100\,000$

 c $37.54 \div 1000$ **d** $3.754 \div 100\,000$

9 Find the lowest common denominator for these pairs of fractions.

 a $\dfrac{1}{3}$ and $\dfrac{1}{5}$ **b** $\dfrac{1}{6}$ and $\dfrac{1}{4}$ **c** $\dfrac{1}{5}$ and $\dfrac{1}{10}$

10 Evaluate each of the following.

 a $\dfrac{2}{7} + \dfrac{3}{7}$ **b** $2\dfrac{1}{2} - \dfrac{3}{2}$ **c** $\dfrac{2}{3} \times \dfrac{3}{4}$ **d** $\dfrac{1}{2} \div 2$

11 Find:

 a 50% of 26   **b** 10% of 600   **c** 9% of 90

1.1 Integer operations

Throughout history, mathematicians have developed number systems to investigate and explain the world in which they live. The Egyptians used hieroglyphics to record whole numbers as well as fractions, the Babylonians use a place value system based on the number 60 and the ancient Chinese and Indians developed systems using negative numbers. Our current base 10 decimal system (the Hindu–Arabic system) has expanded to include positive and negative numbers, fractions (rational numbers) and also numbers that cannot be written as a fraction (irrational numbers), for example, π and $\sqrt{2}$. All the numbers in our number system, not including imaginary numbers, are called real numbers.

Let's start: Special sets of numbers

Here are some special groups of numbers. Can you describe what special property each group has? Try to use the correct vocabulary, for example, factors of 12.

- 7, 14, 21, 28, …
- 1, 4, 9, 16, 25, …
- 1, 2, 3, 4, 6, 9, 12, 18, 36.
- 1, 8, 27, 64, 125, …
- 0, 1, 1, 2, 3, 5, 8, 13, …
- 2, 3, 5, 7, 11, 13, 17, 19, …

Markets used number systems in ancient times to enable trade through setting prices, counting stock and measuring produce.

- The **integers** include …. , -3, -2, -1, 0, 1, 2, 3, …
- If a and b are positive integers
  - $a + (-b) = a - b$ For example: $5 + (-2) = 5 - 2 = 3$
  - $a - (-b) = a + b$ For example: $5 - (-2) = 5 + 2 = 7$
  - $a \times (-b) = -ab$ For example: $3 \times (-2) = -6$
  - $-a \times (-b) = ab$ For example: $-4 \times (-3) = 12$
  - $a \div (-b) = -\dfrac{a}{b}$ For example: $8 \div (-4) = -2$
  - $-a \div (-b) = \dfrac{a}{b}$ For example: $-8 \div (-4) = 2$

- **Squares and cubes**
  - $a^2 = a \times a$ and $\sqrt{a^2} = a$ (if $a \geq 0$), for example, $6^2 = 36$ and $\sqrt{36} = 6$
  - $a^3 = a \times a \times a$ and $\sqrt[3]{a^3} = a$, for example, $4^3 = 64$ and $\sqrt[3]{64} = 4$

- ■ **LCM, HCF and primes**
  - The **Lowest Common Multiple** (LCM) of two numbers is the smallest multiple shared by both numbers, e.g. the LCM of 6 and 9 is 18.
  - The **Highest Common Factor** (HCF) of two numbers is the largest factor shared by both numbers, e.g. the HCF of 24 and 30 is 6.
  - **Prime numbers** have only two factors, 1 and the number itself. The number 1 is not a prime number.
  - **Composite** numbers have more than two factors.
- ■ **Order of operations**
  - Deal with brackets first.
  - Do multiplication and division next from left to right.
  - Do addition and subtraction last from left to right.

Example 1 Operating with integers

Evaluate the following.

a $-2 - (-3 \times 13) + (-10)$

b $(-20 \div (-4) + (-3)) \times 2$

SOLUTION

a
$$-2 - (-3 \times 13) + (-10) = -2 - (-39) + (-10)$$
$$= -2 + 39 + (-10)$$
$$= 37 - 10$$
$$= 27$$

b
$$(-20 \div (-4) + (-3)) \times 2 = (5 + (-3)) \times 2$$
$$= 2 \times 2$$
$$= 4$$

EXPLANATION

Deal with the operations in brackets first.

$-a - (-b) = -a + b$

$a + (-b) = a - b$

$-a \div (-b) = \dfrac{a}{b}$

Deal with the operations inside brackets before doing the multiplication. $5 + (-3) = 5 - 3$.

Exercise 1A

Understanding

1 Write down these sets of numbers.
  - **a** The factors of 16
  - **b** The factors of 56
  - **c** The HCF (Highest Common Factor) of 16 and 56
  - **d** The first 7 multiples of 3
  - **e** The first 6 multiples of 5
  - **f** The LCM (Lowest Common Multiple) of 3 and 5
  - **g** The first 10 prime numbers starting from 2
  - **h** All the prime numbers between 80 and 110

2 Evaluate the following.
  - **a** 11^2
  - **b** 15^2
  - **c** $\sqrt{144}$
  - **d** $\sqrt{400}$
  - **e** 3^3
  - **f** 5^3
  - **g** $\sqrt[3]{8}$
  - **h** $\sqrt[3]{64}$

3 Evaluate the following.

a $5 - 10$ b $-6 - 2$ c $-3 + 2$ d $-9 + 18$

e $2 + (-3)$ f $-6 + (-10)$ g $11 - (-4)$ h $-21 - (-30)$

i $2 \times (-3)$ j -21×4 k $-11 \times (-2)$ l $-3 \times (-14)$

m $18 \div (-2)$ n $-36 \div 6$ o $-100 \div (-10)$ p $-950 \div (-50)$

Example 1

4 Evaluate the following showing your steps.

a $-4 - 3 \times (-2)$ b $-3 \times (-2) + (-4)$

c $-2 \times (3 - 8)$ d $2 - 7 \times (-2)$

e $2 - 3 \times 2 + (-5)$ f $4 + 8 \div (-2) - 3$

g $(-24 \div (-8) + (-5)) \times 2$ h $-7 - (-4 \times 8) - 15$

i $-3 - 12 \div (-6) \times (-4)$ j $4 \times (-3) \div (-2 \times 3)$

k $(-6 - 9 \times (-2)) \div (-4)$ l $10 \times (-2) \div (-7 - (-2))$

m $6 \times (-5) - 14 \div (-2)$ n $(-3 + 7) - 2 \times (-3)$

o $-2 + (-4) \div (-3 + 1)$ p $-18 \div ((-2 - (-4)) \times (-3))$

q $-2 \times 6 \div (-4) \times (-3)$ r $(7 - 14 \div (-2)) \div 2$

s $2 - (1 - 2 \times (-1))$ t $20 : (6 \times (1 \times 2) \div (-12) - (-1))$

5 Find the LCM of these pairs of numbers.

a 4, 7   b 8, 12   c 11, 17   d 15, 10

6 Find the HCF of these pairs of numbers.

a 20, 8   b 100, 65   c 37, 17   d 23, 46

7 Evaluate the following.

a $2^3 - \sqrt{16}$ b $5^2 - \sqrt[3]{8}$ c $(-1)^2 \times (-3)$

d $(-2)^3 \div (-4)$ e $\sqrt{9} - \sqrt[3]{125}$ f $1^3 + 2^3 - 3^3$

g $\sqrt[3]{27} - \sqrt{81}$ h $\sqrt[3]{27} - \sqrt{9} - \sqrt[3]{1}$ i $(-1)^{101} \times (-1)^{1000} \times \sqrt[3]{-1}$

8 Evaluate these expressions by substituting $a = -2$, $b = 6$ and $c = -3$.

a $a^2 - b$ b $a - b^2$ c $2c + a$ d $b^2 - c^2$

e $a^3 + c^2$ f $3b + ac$ g $c - 2ab$ h $abc - (ac)^2$

9 Insert brackets into these statements to make them true.

a $-2 \times 11 + (-2) = -18$ b $-6 + (-4) \div 2 = -5$ c $2 - 5 \times (-2) = 6$

d $-10 \div 3 + (-5) = 5$ e $3 - (-2) + 4 \times 3 = -3$ f $(-2)^2 + 4 \div (-2) = -2^2$

10 How many different answers are possible if any number of pairs of brackets is allowed to be inserted into this expression?

$-6 \times 4 - (-7) + (-1)$

11 Margaret and Mildred meet on a Eurostar train travelling from London to Paris. Margaret visits her daughter in Paris every 28 days. Mildred visits her son in Paris every 36 days. When will Margaret and Mildred have a chance to meet again on the train?

12 a The sum of two numbers is 5 and their difference is 9. What are the two numbers?

b The sum of two numbers is -3 and their product is -10. What are the two numbers?

13 Two opposing football teams have squad sizes of 24 and 32. For a training exercise, each squad is to divide into smaller groups of equal size. What is the largest number of players in a group if the group size for both squads is the same?

14 a Evaluate:
   i 4^2 **ii** $(-4)^2$

b If $a^2 = 16$, write down the possible values of a.

c If $a^3 = 27$, write down the value of a.

d Explain why there are two values of a for which $a^2 = 16$ but only one value of a for which $a^3 = 27$.

e Find $\sqrt[3]{-27}$.

f Explain why $\sqrt{-16}$ cannot exist (using real numbers).

g -2^2 is the same as -1×2^2. Now evaluate:
   i -2^2 **ii** -5^3 **iii** $-(-3)^2$ **iv** $-(-4)^2$

h Decide if $(-2)^2$ and -2^2 are equal.

i Decide if $(-2)^3$ and -2^3 are equal.

j Explain why the HCF of two distinct prime numbers is 1.

k Explain why the LCM of two distinct prime numbers a and b is $a \times b$.

15 If a and b are both positive numbers and $a > b$ decide if the following are true or false.
   a $a - b < 0$ **b** $-a \times b > 0$ **c** $-a \div (-b) > 0$
   d $(-a)^2 - a^2 = 0$ **e** $-b + a < 0$ **f** $2a - 2b > 0$

Enrichment: Special numbers

16 a Perfect numbers are positive integers which are equal to the sum of all their factors, excluding the number itself.

    i Show that 6 is a perfect number.

    ii There is one perfect number between 20 and 30. Find the number.

    iii The next perfect number is 496. Show that 496 is a perfect number.

  b Triangular numbers are the number of dots required to form triangles as shown in this table.

    i Complete this table.

Number of rows	1	2	3	4	5	6
Diagram						
Number of dots (triangular number)	1	3				

    ii Find the 7th and 8th triangular numbers.

  c Fibonacci numbers are a sequence of numbers where each number is the sum of the two preceding numbers. The first two numbers in the sequence are 0 and 1.

    i Write down the first 10 Fibonacci numbers.

    ii If the Fibonacci numbers were to be extended in the negative direction, what would the first four negative Fibonacci numbers be?

Fibonacci numbers have many applications in nature, such as in the structure of an uncurling fern frond.

1.2 Decimals and rounding

Numbers with and without decimal places can be rounded depending on the level of accuracy required. When using numbers with decimal places it is common to round off the number to leave only a certain number of decimal places. The time for a 100 m sprint race, for example, might be 9.94 seconds.

Due to the experimental nature of science and engineering, not all the digits in all numbers are considered important or 'significant'. In such cases we are able to round numbers to within a certain number of significant figures (sometimes abbreviated to sig. fig.). The number of cubic metres of gravel required for a road, for example, might be calculated as 3485 but is rounded to 3500. This number is written using two significant figures.

For road construction purposes, the volume of sand in these piles would only need to be known to two or three significant figures.

Let's start: Plausible but incorrect

Johny says that the number 2.748 when rounded to one decimal place is 2.8 because:
- the 8 rounds the 4 to a 5
- then the new 5 rounds the 7 to an 8.

What is wrong with Johny's theory?

Key ideas

- To round a number to a required number of **decimal places**:
  - Locate the digit in the required decimal place.
  - Round down (leave as is) if the next digit (**critical digit**) is 4 or less.
  - Round up (increase by 1) if the next digit is 5 or more.

  For example:
  - To two decimal places, 1.543 rounds to 1.54 and 32.9283 rounds to 32.93.
  - To one decimal place, 0.248 rounds to 0.2 and 0.253 rounds to 0.3.
- To round a number to a required number of **significant figures**:
  - Locate the first non-zero digit counting from left to right.
  - From this first significant digit, count out the number of significant digits including zeros.
  - Stop at the required number of significant digits and round this last digit.
  - Replace any non-significant digit to the left of a decimal point with a zero.

  For example, these numbers are all rounded to 3 significant figures:
  $2.5391 \approx 2.54$, $0.002713 \approx 0.00271$, $568\,810 \approx 569\,000$.

Example 2 Rounding to a number of decimal places

Round each of these to two decimal places.

a   256.1793   **b**   0.04459   **c**   4.8972

SOLUTION   **EXPLANATION**

a $256.1793 \approx 256.18$ The number after the second decimal place is 9, so round
                                          up (increase the 7 by 1).

b $0.04459 \approx 0.04$ The number after the second decimal place is 4, so round
                                          down. 4459 is closer to 4000 than 5000.

c $4.8972 \approx 4.90$ The number after the second decimal place is 7, so round
                                          up. Increasing by 1 means 0.89 becomes 0.90.

Example 3 Rounding to a number of significant figures

Round each of these numbers to two significant figures.

a   2567   **b**   23 067.453   **c**   0.04059

SOLUTION   **EXPLANATION**

a $2567 \approx 2600$ The first two digits are the first two significant figures.
                                          The third digit is 6, so round up. Replace the last two
                                          non-significant digits with zeros.

b $23\,067.453 \approx 23\,000$ The first two digits are the first two significant figures.
                                          The third digit is 0, so round down.

c $0.04059 \approx 0.041$ Locate the first non-zero digit, i.e. 4. So 4 and 0 are the first
                                          two significant figures. The next digit is 5, so round up.

Example 4 Estimating using significant figures

Estimate the answer to the following by rounding each number in the problem to one significant figure
and use your calculator to check how reasonable your answer is.

   $27 + 1329.5 \times 0.0064$

SOLUTION   **EXPLANATION**

$27 + 1329.5 \times 0.0064$

$\approx 30 + 1000 \times 0.006$ Round each number to one significant figure and evaluate.
$= 30 + 6$ Recall multiplication occurs before the addition.
$= 36$

The estimated answer is reasonable.   By calculator (to one decimal place):
                                          $27 + 1329.5 \times 0.0064 = 35.5$

Exercise 1B

1 Choose the number to answer each question.
   a Is 44 closer to 40 or 50?
   b Is 266 closer to 260 or 270?
   c Is 7.89 closer to 7.8 or 7.9?
   d Is 0.043 closer to 0.04 or 0.05?

2 Choose the correct answer if the first given number is rounded to 3 significant figures.
   a 32124 is rounded to 321, 3210 or 32100
   b 431.92 is rounded to 431, 432 or 430
   c 5.8871 is rounded to 5.887, 5.88 or 5.89
   d 0.44322 is rounded to 0.44, 0.443 or 0.44302
   e 0.001 967 1 is rounded to 0.002, 0.001 97 or 0.001 96

3 Using one significant figure rounding, 324 rounds to 300, 1.7 rounds to 2 and 9.6 rounds to 10.
   a Calculate $300 \times 2 \div 10$.
   b Use a calculator to calculate $324 \times 1.7 \div 9.6$.
   c What is the difference between the answer in part **a** and the exact answer in part **b**?

Example 2

4 Round each of the following numbers to two decimal places.
   a 17.962   **b** 11.082   **c** 72.986   **d** 47.859
   e 63.925   **f** 23.807   **g** 804.5272   **h** 500.5749
   i 821.2749   **j** 5810.2539   **k** 1004.9981   **l** 2649.9974

5 Round these numbers to the nearest whole number.
   a 6.814   **b** 73.148   **c** 129.94   **d** 36 200.49

6 Use division to write these fractions as decimals rounded to three decimal places.
   a $\dfrac{1}{3}$ **b** $\dfrac{2}{7}$ **c** $\dfrac{13}{11}$ **d** $\dfrac{400}{29}$

Example 3

7 Round each of these numbers to two significant figures.
   a 2436   **b** 35057.4   **c** 0.060 49   **d** 34.024
   e 107 892   **f** 0.002 45   **g** 2.0745   **h** 0.7070

8 Round these numbers to one significant figure.
   a 32 000   **b** 194.2   **c** 0.0492   **d** 0.000 641 3

Example 4

9 Estimate the answers to the following by rounding each number in the problem to one significant figure. Check how reasonable your answer is with a calculator.
   a $567 + 3126$ **b** $795 - 35.6$ **c** 97.8×42.2
   d $965.98 + 5321 - 2763.2$ **e** $4.23 - 1.92 \times 1.827$ **f** $17.43 - 2.047 \times 8.165$
   g $0.0704 + 0.0482$ **h** 0.023×0.98 **i** $0.027 \div 0.0032$
   j 41.034^2 **k** 0.078×0.9803^2 **l** $1.8494^2 + 0.972 \times 7.032$

10 An electronic timer records the time for a running relay between two teams A and B. Team A's time is 54.283 seconds and team B's time is 53.791 seconds. What would be the difference in the times for teams A and B if the times were written down using:

  a   1 decimal place   **b**   4 significant figures

  c   2 significant figures   **d**   1 significant figure

11 $28.4 \times 2.94 \times 11.31$ is calculated by first rounding each of the three numbers. Describe the type of rounding that has taken place if the answer is:

  a   900   **b**   893.2   **c**   924

12 150 m of fencing and 18 posts are used to create an area in the shape of an equilateral triangle. Posts are used in the corners and are evenly spaced along the sides.

    Find the distance between each post. Write your answer in metres rounded to the nearest centimetre.

13 A tonne (1000 kg) of soil is to be equally divided between 7 garden beds. How much soil does each garden bed get? Write your answer in tonnes rounded to the nearest kilogram.

14 Should 2.14999 be rounded down or up if it is to be rounded to one decimal place? Give reasons.

15 A scientific experiment uses very small amounts of magnesium (0.0025 g) and potassium (0.0062 g). Why does it make sense to use two significant figures instead of two decimal places when recording numbers in a situation like this?

16 Consider the two numbers 24 and 26.
  a Calculate:
    i $24 + 26$
    ii 24×26
  b Find the sum (+) of the numbers after rounding each number using one significant figure.
  c Find the product (×) of the numbers after rounding each number using one significant figure.
  d What do you notice about the answers for parts **b** and **c** as compared to part **a**? Give an explanation.

Minute amounts of reagents are commonly used in chemistry laboratories.

Enrichment: nth decimal place

17 a Express $\dfrac{2}{11}$ as a decimal correct to 8 decimal places.
  b Using the decimal pattern from part **a** find the digit in the:
    i   20th decimal place
    ii 45th decimal place
    iii 1000th decimal place.
  c Express $\dfrac{1}{7}$ as a decimal correct to 13 decimal places.
  d Using the decimal pattern from part **c** find the digit in the:
    i   20th decimal place
    ii 45th decimal place
    iii 1000th decimal place.
  e Can you find any fraction whose decimal representation is non-terminating and has no pattern? Use a calculator to help.

1.3 Rational numbers

Under the guidance of Pythagoras around 500 BCE, it was discovered that some numbers could not be expressed as a fraction. These special numbers, called irrational numbers, when written as a decimal continue forever and do not show any pattern. So to write these numbers exactly, you need to use special symbols such as $\sqrt{2}$ and π. If, however, the decimal places in a number terminate or if a pattern exists, the number can be expressed as a fraction. These numbers are called rational numbers.

This is $\sqrt{2}$ to 100 decimal places:

1. 41421356237309504880016887
24209698078569967187537694
80731766797379907324784 62
10703885038753432764 15727

Let's start: Approximating π

To simplify calculations, the ancient and modern civilisations have used fractions to approximate π. To 10 decimal places, $\pi = 3.1415926536$.

- Using single digit numbers, what fraction best approximates π?
- Using single and/or double digit numbers, find a fraction that is a good approximation of π. Compare with others students to see who has the best approximation.

Key ideas

- An **infinite** decimal is one where the decimal places continue indefinitely.

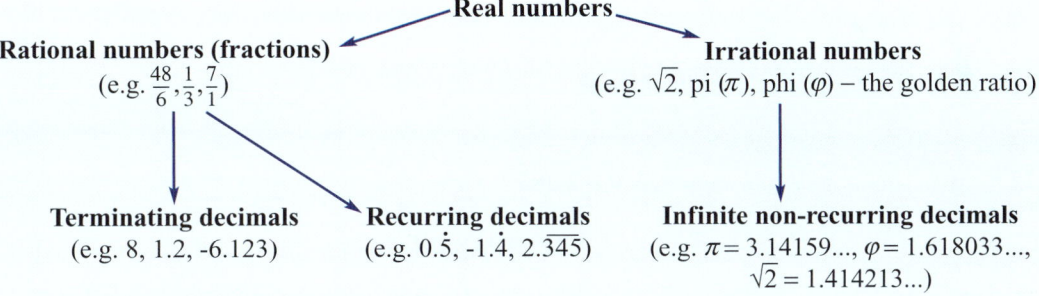

- **Equivalent fractions** have the same value.

  For example: $\dfrac{2}{3} = \dfrac{6}{9}$

- A fraction can be simplified by dividing the **numerator** and **denominator** by their highest common factor.

- If $\dfrac{a}{b}$ is a **proper fraction** then $a < b$.

  For example: $\dfrac{2}{7}$

- If $\dfrac{a}{b}$ is an **improper fraction** then $a > b$.

  For example: $\dfrac{10}{3}$

- A **mixed number** is written as a whole number plus a proper fraction.

  For example: $2\dfrac{3}{5}$

- Fractions can be compared using a **common denominator**. This should be the lowest common multiple of both denominators.
- A dot or bar is used to show a pattern in a recurring decimal number.

For example: $\dfrac{1}{6} = 0.16666.... = 0.1\dot{6}$ or $\dfrac{3}{11} = 0.272727.... = 0.\overline{27}$

Example 5 Writing fractions as decimals

Write these fractions as decimals.

a $3\dfrac{3}{8}$ **b** $\dfrac{5}{13}$

SOLUTION

a $\begin{array}{r} 0.375 \\ 8\overline{)3.^30^60^40} \end{array}$

$3\dfrac{3}{8} = 3.375$

b $\begin{array}{r} 0.3846153 \\ 13\overline{)5.^50^{11}0^60^80^20^70^50} \end{array}$

$\dfrac{5}{13} = 0.\overline{384615}$

EXPLANATION

Find a decimal for $\dfrac{3}{8}$ by dividing 8 into 3 using the short division algoritm.

Divide 13 into 5 and continue until the pattern repeats. Add a bar over the repeating pattern.

Writing $0.\dot{3}8461\dot{5}$ is an alternative.

Example 6 Writing decimals as fractions

Write these decimals as fractions.

a 0.24 **b** 2.385

SOLUTION

a $0.24 = \dfrac{24}{100}$

$= \dfrac{6}{25}$

b $2.385 = \dfrac{2385}{1000}$ OR $2\dfrac{385}{1000}$

$= \dfrac{477}{200}$ $= 2\dfrac{77}{200}$

$= 2\dfrac{77}{200}$

EXPLANATION

Write as a fraction using the smallest place value (hundredths) then simplify using the HCF of 4.

The smallest place value is thousandths.

Simplify to an improper fraction or a mixed number.

Example 7 Comparing fractions

Decide which is the larger fraction of the following.

$\dfrac{7}{12}$ or $\dfrac{8}{15}$

SOLUTION

LCM of 12 and 15 is 60.

$\dfrac{7}{12} = \dfrac{35}{60}$ and $\dfrac{8}{15} = \dfrac{32}{60}$

$\therefore \dfrac{7}{12} > \dfrac{8}{15}$

EXPLANATION

Find the lowest common multiple of the two denominators (lowest common denominator).
Write each fraction as an equivalent fraction using the common denominator. Then compare numerators (i.e. 35 > 32) to determine the larger fraction.

Exercise 1C

Understanding

1 Write these numbers as mixed numbers.

a $\dfrac{7}{5}$
b $\dfrac{13}{3}$
c $\dfrac{48}{11}$
d $\dfrac{326}{53}$

2 Write these numbers as improper fractions.

a $1\dfrac{4}{7}$
b $5\dfrac{1}{3}$
c $9\dfrac{1}{2}$
d $18\dfrac{4}{13}$

3 Simplify by cancelling.

a $\dfrac{4}{10}$
b $\dfrac{8}{58}$
c $4\dfrac{20}{120}$
d $-72\dfrac{125}{1000}$

4 Write down the missing number.

a $\dfrac{3}{5} = \dfrac{\square}{15}$
b $\dfrac{5}{6} = \dfrac{20}{\square}$
c $\dfrac{3}{7} = \dfrac{9}{\square}$
d $\dfrac{5}{11} = \dfrac{\square}{77}$

e $\dfrac{\square}{4} = \dfrac{21}{28}$
f $\dfrac{\square}{9} = \dfrac{42}{54}$
g $\dfrac{3}{\square} = \dfrac{15}{50}$
h $\dfrac{11}{\square} = \dfrac{121}{66}$

Fluency

mple 5a **5** Write these fractions as decimals.

a $\dfrac{11}{4}$
b $\dfrac{7}{20}$
c $3\dfrac{2}{5}$
d $\dfrac{15}{8}$

e $2\dfrac{5}{8}$
f $3\dfrac{4}{5}$
g $\dfrac{37}{16}$
h $\dfrac{7}{32}$

mple 5b **6** Write these fractions as recurring decimals.

a $\dfrac{3}{11}$
b $\dfrac{7}{9}$
c $\dfrac{9}{7}$
d $\dfrac{5}{12}$

e $\dfrac{10}{9}$
f $3\dfrac{5}{6}$
g $7\dfrac{4}{15}$
h $\dfrac{29}{11}$

Example 6   **7**   Write these decimals as fractions.

    a 0.35   **b** 0.06   **c** 3.7   **d** 0.56

    e 1.07   **f** 0.075   **g** 3.32   **h** 7.375

    i 2.005   **j** 10.044   **k** 6.45   **l** 2.101

Example 7   **8**   Decide which is the larger fraction in the following pairs.

    a $\dfrac{3}{4}, \dfrac{5}{6}$ **b** $\dfrac{13}{20}, \dfrac{3}{5}$ **c** $\dfrac{7}{10}, \dfrac{8}{15}$ **d** $\dfrac{5}{12}, \dfrac{7}{18}$

    e $\dfrac{7}{16}, \dfrac{5}{12}$ **f** $\dfrac{26}{35}, \dfrac{11}{14}$ **g** $\dfrac{7}{12}, \dfrac{19}{30}$ **h** $\dfrac{7}{18}, \dfrac{11}{27}$

9   Place these fractions in descending order.

    a $\dfrac{3}{8}, \dfrac{5}{12}, \dfrac{7}{18}$ **b** $\dfrac{1}{6}, \dfrac{5}{24}, \dfrac{3}{16}$ **c** $\dfrac{8}{15}, \dfrac{23}{40}, \dfrac{7}{12}$

10   Express the following quantities as simplified fractions.

    a $45 out of $100

    b 12 kg out of 80 kg

    c 64 baskets out of 90 shots in basketball

    d 115 mL out of 375 mL

11   These sets of fractions form a pattern. Find the next two fractions in the pattern.

    a $\dfrac{1}{3}, \dfrac{5}{6}, \dfrac{4}{3}, \square, \square$ **b** $\dfrac{6}{5}, \dfrac{14}{15}, \dfrac{2}{3}, \square, \square$

    c $\dfrac{2}{3}, \dfrac{3}{4}, \dfrac{5}{6}, \square, \square$ **d** $\dfrac{1}{2}, \dfrac{4}{7}, \dfrac{9}{14}, \square, \square$

12   The 'Weather forecast' website says there is a 0.45 chance that it will rain tomorrow. The 'Climate control' website says that the chance of rain is $\dfrac{14}{30}$. Which website gives the least chance that it will rain?

13   A jug has 400 mL of $\dfrac{1}{2}$ strength orange juice. The following amounts of full strength juice are added to the mix. Find a fraction to describe the strength of the orange drink after the full strength juice is added.

    a 100 mL   **b** 50 mL   **c** 120 mL   **d** 375 mL

The chance of rain could be expressed as a decimal, a fraction or a percentage.

14 If x is an integer, determine what values x can take in the following.

a The fraction $\dfrac{x}{3}$ is a number between (and not including) 10 and 11.

b The fraction $\dfrac{x}{7}$ is a number between (and not including) 5 and 8.

c The fraction $\dfrac{34}{x}$ is a number between 6 and 10.

d The fraction $\dfrac{23}{x}$ is a number between 7 and 12.

e The fraction $\dfrac{x}{14}$ is a number between (and not including) 3 and 4.

f The fraction $\dfrac{58}{x}$ is a number between 9 and 15.

Problem-solving

15 $a\dfrac{b}{c}$ is a mixed number with unknown digits a, b and c. Write it as an improper fraction.

16 If $\dfrac{a}{b}$ is a fraction, answer the given questions with reasons.

a Is it possible to find a fraction that can be simplified by cancelling if one of a or b is prime?

b Is it possible to find a fraction that can be simplified by cancelling if both a and b are prime? Assume $a \neq b$.

c If $\dfrac{a}{b}$ is a fraction in simplest form, can a and b both be even?

d If $\dfrac{a}{b}$ is a fraction in simplest form, can a and b both be odd?

Reasoning

Enrichment: Converting recurring decimals to fractions

17 Here are two examples of how to convert recurring decimals to fractions.

$$0.\dot{6} = 0.6666.....$$
$$\text{Let } x = 0.6666.... \quad (1)$$
$$10x = 6.6666... \quad (2)$$
$$(2) - (1) \quad 9x = 6$$
$$x = \frac{6}{9} = \frac{2}{3}$$
$$\therefore 0.\dot{6} = \frac{2}{3}$$

$$1.\overline{27} = 1.272727....$$
$$\text{Let } x = 1.272727.... \quad (1)$$
$$100x = 127.2727.... \quad (2)$$
$$(2) - (1) \quad 99x = 126$$
$$x = \frac{126}{99}$$
$$\therefore 1.\overline{27} = \frac{126}{99} = 1\frac{27}{99} = 1\frac{3}{11}$$

Convert these recurring decimals to fractions using the above method.

a $0.\dot{8}$ **b** $1.\dot{2}$ **c** $0.\overline{81}$ **d** $3.\overline{43}$

e $9.\overline{75}$ **f** $0.\overline{132}$ **g** $2.\overline{917}$ **h** $13.8\overline{125}$

1.4 Operations with fractions

Operations with integers can be extended to include rational and irrational numbers. The operations include: addition, subtraction, multiplication and division. Addition and subtraction of fractions is generally more complex than multiplication and division because there is the added step of finding common denominators.

→ ### Let's start: The common errors

Here are incorrect solutions to four problems involving fractions.

Fractions are all around you and part of everyday life.

- $\dfrac{2}{3} \times \dfrac{5}{3} = \dfrac{2 \times 5}{3} = \dfrac{10}{3}$

- $\dfrac{2}{3} + \dfrac{1}{2} = \dfrac{2+1}{3+2} = \dfrac{3}{5}$

- $\dfrac{7}{6} \div \dfrac{7}{3} = \dfrac{7}{6} \div \dfrac{14}{6} = \dfrac{\overset{1}{2}}{6} = \dfrac{1}{12}$

- $1\dfrac{1}{2} - \dfrac{2}{3} = 1\dfrac{3}{6} - \dfrac{4}{6} = -1\dfrac{1}{6}$

In each case describe what is wrong and give the correct solution.

Key ideas

- ■ To add or subtract fractions, first convert each fraction to **equivalent fractions** that have the same **denominator**.
  - • Choose the lowest common denominator.
  - • Add or subtract the numerators and retain the denominator.
    For example: $\dfrac{1}{2} + \dfrac{2}{3} = \dfrac{3}{6} + \dfrac{4}{6} = \dfrac{7}{6} = 1\dfrac{1}{6}$
- ■ To multiply fractions, multiply the numerators and multiply the denominators.
  - • Cancel the highest common factor between any numerator and any denominator before multiplication.
  - • Convert mixed numbers to improper fractions before multiplying.
  - • '**of**' means multiply.
    For example: $\dfrac{1}{3}$ of $24 = \dfrac{1}{3} \times 24$.
- ■ The **reciprocal** of a number multiplied by the number itself is equal to 1.
  - • For example: the reciprocal of 2 is $\dfrac{1}{2}$ since $2 \times \dfrac{1}{2} = 1$.

      the reciprocal of $\dfrac{3}{5} = \dfrac{5}{3}$ since $\dfrac{3}{5} \times \dfrac{5}{3} = 1$.
- ■ To divide a number by a fraction, multiply by its reciprocal.
    For example: $\dfrac{2}{3} \div \dfrac{5}{6} = \dfrac{2}{\underset{1}{\cancel{3}}} \times \dfrac{\overset{2}{\cancel{6}}}{5} = \dfrac{4}{5}$
  - • Whole numbers can be written using a denominator of 1.

Example 8 Adding and subtracting fractions

Evaluate the following.

a $\dfrac{1}{2} + \dfrac{3}{5}$

b $1\dfrac{2}{3} + 4\dfrac{5}{6}$

c $3\dfrac{2}{5} - 2\dfrac{3}{4}$

SOLUTION

EXPLANATION

a $\dfrac{1}{2} + \dfrac{3}{5} = \dfrac{5}{10} + \dfrac{6}{10}$

$= \dfrac{11}{10}$ or $1\dfrac{1}{10}$

The lowest common denominator of 2 and 5 is 10. Rewrite as equivalent fractions using a denominator of 10.
Add the numerators.

b $1\dfrac{2}{3} + 4\dfrac{5}{6} = \dfrac{5}{3} + \dfrac{29}{6}$

$= \dfrac{10}{6} + \dfrac{29}{6}$

$= \dfrac{39}{6}$

$= \dfrac{13}{2}$ or $6\dfrac{1}{2}$

Change each mixed number to an improper fraction.

Remember the lowest common denominator of 3 and 6 is 6. Change $\dfrac{5}{3}$ to an equivalent fraction with denominator 6 then add the numerators and simplify.

Alternatively, $1\dfrac{2}{3} + 4\dfrac{5}{6} = 1\dfrac{4}{6} + 4\dfrac{5}{6}$

$= 5\dfrac{9}{6}$

$= 6\dfrac{3}{6}$

$= 6\dfrac{1}{2}$

Alternative method: add whole numbers and fractions separately, obtaining a common denominator for the fractions $\left(\dfrac{2}{3} = \dfrac{4}{6} \right)$.

$\dfrac{9}{6} = 1\dfrac{3}{6}$

c $3\dfrac{2}{5} - 2\dfrac{3}{4} = \dfrac{17}{5} - \dfrac{11}{4}$

$= \dfrac{68}{20} - \dfrac{55}{20}$

$= \dfrac{13}{20}$

Convert to improper fractions then rewrite as equivalent fractions with the same denominator.

Subtract the numerators.

Example 9 Multiplying fractions

Evaluate the following.

a $\dfrac{2}{3} \times \dfrac{5}{7}$

b $1\dfrac{2}{3} \times 2\dfrac{1}{10}$

SOLUTION

EXPLANATION

a $\dfrac{2}{3} \times \dfrac{5}{7} = \dfrac{2 \times 5}{3 \times 7}$

$= \dfrac{10}{21}$

No cancelling is possible as there are no common factors between numerators and denominators.
Multiply the numerators and denominators.

b $1\dfrac{2}{3} \times 2\dfrac{1}{10} = \dfrac{{}^{1}\cancel{5}}{{}_{1}\cancel{3}} \times \dfrac{\cancel{21}^{7}}{\cancel{10}_{2}}$

$= \dfrac{7}{2}$ or $3\dfrac{1}{2}$

Rewrite as improper fractions.
Cancel common factors between numerators and denominators and then multiply numerators and denominators.

Example 10 Dividing fractions

Evaluate the following.

a $\dfrac{4}{15} \div \dfrac{12}{25}$

b $1\dfrac{17}{18} \div 1\dfrac{1}{27}$

SOLUTION

EXPLANATION

a $\dfrac{4}{15} \div \dfrac{12}{25} = \dfrac{4}{15} \times \dfrac{25}{12}$

$= \dfrac{{}^{1}\cancel{4}}{{}_{3}\cancel{15}} \times \dfrac{\cancel{25}^{5}}{\cancel{12}_{3}}$

$= \dfrac{5}{9}$

To divide by $\dfrac{12}{25}$ we multiply by its reciprocal $\dfrac{25}{12}$.

Cancel common factors between numerators and denominators then multiply fractions.

b $1\dfrac{17}{18} \div 1\dfrac{1}{27} = \dfrac{35}{18} \div \dfrac{28}{27}$

$= \dfrac{{}^{5}\cancel{35}}{{}_{2}\cancel{18}} \times \dfrac{\cancel{27}^{3}}{\cancel{28}_{4}}$

$= \dfrac{15}{8}$ or $1\dfrac{7}{8}$

Rewrite mixed numbers as improper fractions.

Multiply by the reciprocal of the second fraction.

Exercise 1D

1 Find the lowest common denominator for these pairs of fractions.

a $\dfrac{1}{2}, \dfrac{1}{3}$ **b** $\dfrac{3}{7}, \dfrac{5}{9}$ **c** $\dfrac{2}{5}, \dfrac{1}{13}$ **d** $\dfrac{3}{10}, \dfrac{8}{15}$

e $\dfrac{1}{2}, \dfrac{1}{4}$ **f** $\dfrac{9}{11}, \dfrac{4}{33}$ **g** $\dfrac{5}{12}, \dfrac{7}{30}$ **h** $\dfrac{13}{29}, \dfrac{2}{3}$

2 Convert these mixed numbers to improper fractions.

a $2\dfrac{1}{3}$ **b** $7\dfrac{4}{5}$ **c** $10\dfrac{1}{4}$ **d** $22\dfrac{5}{6}$

Understanding

Understanding

3 Copy and complete the given working

a $\dfrac{3}{2}+\dfrac{4}{3}=\dfrac{\square}{6}+\dfrac{\square}{6}$

$=\dfrac{\square}{6}$

b $1\dfrac{1}{3}-\dfrac{2}{5}=\dfrac{\square}{3}-\dfrac{2}{5}$

$=\dfrac{\square}{15}-\dfrac{\square}{15}$

$=\dfrac{14}{\square}$

c $\dfrac{5}{3}\div\dfrac{2}{7}=\dfrac{5}{3}\times\dfrac{\square}{\square}$

$=\dfrac{\square}{6}$

Fluency

mple 8a

4 Evaluate the following.

a $\dfrac{2}{5}+\dfrac{1}{5}$

b $\dfrac{3}{9}+\dfrac{1}{9}$

c $\dfrac{5}{7}+\dfrac{4}{7}$

d $\dfrac{3}{4}+\dfrac{1}{5}$

e $\dfrac{1}{3}+\dfrac{4}{7}$

f $\dfrac{3}{8}+\dfrac{4}{5}$

g $\dfrac{2}{5}+\dfrac{3}{10}$

h $\dfrac{4}{9}+\dfrac{5}{27}$

mple 8b

5 Evaluate the following.

a $3\dfrac{1}{4}+1\dfrac{3}{4}$

b $2\dfrac{3}{5}+\dfrac{4}{5}$

c $1\dfrac{3}{7}+3\dfrac{5}{7}$

d $2\dfrac{1}{3}+4\dfrac{2}{5}$

e $2\dfrac{5}{7}+4\dfrac{5}{9}$

f $10\dfrac{5}{8}+7\dfrac{3}{16}$

6 Evaluate the following.

a $\dfrac{4}{5}-\dfrac{2}{5}$

b $\dfrac{4}{5}-\dfrac{7}{9}$

c $\dfrac{3}{4}-\dfrac{1}{5}$

d $\dfrac{2}{5}-\dfrac{3}{10}$

e $\dfrac{8}{9}-\dfrac{5}{6}$

f $\dfrac{3}{8}-\dfrac{1}{4}$

g $\dfrac{5}{9}-\dfrac{3}{8}$

h $\dfrac{5}{12}-\dfrac{5}{16}$

mple 8c

7 Evaluate the following.

a $2\dfrac{3}{4}-1\dfrac{1}{4}$

b $3\dfrac{5}{8}-2\dfrac{7}{8}$

c $3\dfrac{1}{4}-2\dfrac{3}{5}$

d $3\dfrac{5}{8}-2\dfrac{9}{10}$

e $2\dfrac{2}{3}-1\dfrac{5}{6}$

f $3\dfrac{7}{11}-2\dfrac{3}{7}$

ample 9

8 Evaluate the following (recall $6=\dfrac{6}{1}$).

a $\dfrac{2}{5}\times\dfrac{3}{7}$

b $\dfrac{3}{5}\times\dfrac{5}{6}$

c $\dfrac{2}{15}\times\dfrac{5}{8}$

d $\dfrac{6}{21}\times1\dfrac{5}{9}$

e $6\times\dfrac{3}{4}$

f $8\times\dfrac{2}{3}$

g $\dfrac{5}{6}\times9$

h $1\dfrac{1}{4}\times4$

i $2\dfrac{1}{2}\times6$

j $1\dfrac{5}{8}\times16$

k $\dfrac{10}{21}\times1\dfrac{2}{5}$

l $\dfrac{25}{44}\times1\dfrac{7}{15}$

m $1\dfrac{1}{2}\times1\dfrac{1}{2}$

n $1\dfrac{1}{2}\times2\dfrac{1}{3}$

o $2\dfrac{2}{3}\times2\dfrac{1}{4}$

p $1\dfrac{1}{5}\times1\dfrac{1}{9}$

9 Write down the reciprocal of these numbers.

a 3

b $\dfrac{5}{7}$

c $\dfrac{1}{8}$

d $\dfrac{13}{9}$

Example 10 **10** Evaluate the following (recall the reciprocal of 8 is $\frac{1}{8}$).

a $\dfrac{4}{7} \div \dfrac{3}{5}$

b $\dfrac{3}{4} \div \dfrac{2}{3}$

c $\dfrac{5}{8} \div \dfrac{7}{9}$

d $\dfrac{3}{7} \div \dfrac{4}{9}$

e $\dfrac{3}{4} \div \dfrac{9}{16}$

f $\dfrac{4}{5} \div \dfrac{8}{15}$

g $\dfrac{8}{9} \div \dfrac{4}{27}$

h $\dfrac{15}{42} \div \dfrac{20}{49}$

i $15 \div \dfrac{5}{6}$

j $6 \div \dfrac{2}{3}$

k $12 \div \dfrac{3}{4}$

l $24 \div \dfrac{3}{8}$

m $\dfrac{4}{5} \div 8$

n $\dfrac{3}{4} \div 9$

o $\dfrac{8}{9} \div 6$

p $14 \div 4\dfrac{1}{5}$

q $6 \div 1\dfrac{1}{2}$

r $1\dfrac{1}{3} \div 8$

s $2\dfrac{1}{4} \div 1\dfrac{1}{2}$

t $4\dfrac{2}{3} \div 5\dfrac{1}{3}$

11 Evaluate these mixed-operation problems.

a $\dfrac{2}{3} \times \dfrac{1}{3} \div \dfrac{7}{9}$

b $\dfrac{4}{5} \times \dfrac{3}{5} \div \dfrac{9}{10}$

c $\dfrac{4}{9} \times \dfrac{6}{25} \div \dfrac{1}{150}$

d $2\dfrac{1}{5} \times \dfrac{3}{7} \div 1\dfrac{3}{14}$

e $5\dfrac{1}{3} \times \dfrac{13}{24} \div 1\dfrac{1}{6}$

f $2\dfrac{4}{13} \times \dfrac{3}{8} \div 3\dfrac{3}{4}$

12 To remove impurities a mining company filters $3\dfrac{1}{2}$ tonnes of raw material. If $2\dfrac{5}{8}$ tonnes are removed, what quantity of material remains?

13 When a certain raw material is processed it produces $3\dfrac{1}{7}$ tonnes of mineral and $2\dfrac{3}{8}$ tonnes of waste. How many tonnes of raw material were processed?

14 In a $2\dfrac{1}{2}$ hour maths exam $\dfrac{1}{6}$ of that time is allocated as reading time. How long is the reading time?

The concentration (proportion) of the desired mineral within an ore body is vital information in the minerals industry.

15 A road is to be constructed with $15\dfrac{1}{2}$ m³ of crushed rock. If a small truck can carry $2\dfrac{1}{3}$ m³ of crushed rock, how many truckloads will be needed?

16 Regan worked for $7\dfrac{1}{2}$ hours in a sandwich shop. Three-fifths of her time was spent cleaning up and the rest serving customers. How much time did she spend serving customers?

17 Here is an example involving the subtraction of fractions where improper fractions are not used.

$$2\frac{1}{2} - 1\frac{1}{3} = 2\frac{3}{6} - 1\frac{2}{6}$$

$$= 1\frac{1}{6}$$

Try this technique on the following problem and explain the difficulty that you encounter.

$$2\frac{1}{3} - 1\frac{1}{2}$$

18 a A fraction is given by $\dfrac{a}{b}$. Write down its reciprocal.

   b A mixed number is given by $a\dfrac{b}{c}$. Write an expression for its reciprocal.

19 If a, b and c are integers simplify the following.

a $\dfrac{b}{a} \times \dfrac{a}{b}$

b $\dfrac{a}{b} \div \dfrac{b}{a}$

c $\dfrac{a}{b} \div \dfrac{a}{b}$

d $\dfrac{a}{b} \times \dfrac{c}{a} \div \dfrac{a}{b}$

e $\dfrac{abc}{a} \div \dfrac{bc}{a}$

f $\dfrac{a}{b} \div \dfrac{b}{c} \times \dfrac{b}{a}$

Enrichment: Fraction operation challenge

20 Evaluate the following.

a $2\frac{1}{3} - 1\frac{2}{5} \times 2\frac{1}{7}$

b $1\frac{1}{4} \times 1\frac{1}{5} - 2\frac{1}{2} \div 10$

c $1\frac{4}{5} \times 4\frac{1}{6} + \frac{2}{3} \times 1\frac{1}{5}$

d $\left(1\frac{2}{3} + 1\frac{3}{4}\right) \div 3\frac{5}{12}$

e $4\frac{1}{6} \div \left(1\frac{1}{3} + 1\frac{1}{4}\right)$

f $\left(1\frac{1}{5} - \frac{3}{4}\right) \times \left(1\frac{1}{5} - \frac{3}{4}\right)$

g $\left(2\frac{1}{4} - 1\frac{2}{3}\right) \times \left(2\frac{1}{4} + 1\frac{2}{3}\right)$

h $\left(3\frac{1}{2} + 1\frac{3}{5}\right) \times \left(3\frac{1}{2} - 1\frac{3}{5}\right)$

i $\left(2\frac{2}{3} - 1\frac{3}{4}\right) \times \left(2\frac{2}{3} + 1\frac{3}{4}\right)$

j $\left(4\frac{1}{2} - 3\frac{2}{3}\right) \div \left(1\frac{1}{3} + \frac{1}{2}\right)$

1.5 Ratios, rates and best buys

Fractions, ratios and rates are used to compare quantities. A lawn mower, for example, might require $\frac{1}{6}$ of a litre of oil to make a petrol mix of 2 parts oil to 25 parts petrol, which is an oil to petrol ratio of 2 to 25 or 2 : 25. The mower's blades might then spin at a rate of 1000 revolutions per minute (1000 revs/min).

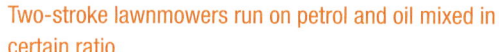

Two-stroke lawnmowers run on petrol and oil mixed in a certain ratio.

Let's start: The lottery win

$100 000 is to be divided up for three lucky people into a ratio of 2 to 3 to 5 (2 : 3 : 5). Work out how the money is to be divided.

- Clearly write down your method and answer. There may be many different ways to solve this problem.
- Write down and discuss the alternative methods suggested by other students in the class.

Key ideas

- **Ratios** are used to compare quantities with the same units.
  - The ratio of a to b is written $a : b$.
  - Ratios in simplest form use whole numbers that have no common factor.
- The **unitary method** involves finding the value of one part of a total.
  - Once the value of one part is found then the value of several parts can easily be determined.
- A **rate** compares related quantities with different units.
  - The rate is usually written with one quantity compared to a single unit of the other quantity.
    For example: 50 km per 1 hour or 50 km/h.
- Ratios and rates can be used to determine **best buys** when purchasing products.

Example 11 Simplifying ratios

Simplify these ratios.

a   38 : 24   b $2\frac{1}{2} : 1\frac{1}{3}$ c   0.2 : 0.14

SOLUTION

a   38 : 24 = 19 : 12

EXPLANATION

The HCF of 38 and 24 is 2 so divide both sides by 2.

b $2\dfrac{1}{2} : 1\dfrac{1}{3} = \dfrac{5}{2} : \dfrac{4}{3}$

Write as improper fractions using the same denominator.

$\qquad = \dfrac{15}{6} : \dfrac{8}{6}$

Then multiply both sides by 6 to write as whole numbers.

$\qquad = 15 : 8$

c $0.2 : 0.14 = 20 : 14$

Multiply by 100 to remove all the decimal places and simplify.

$\qquad = 10 : 7$

Example 12 Dividing into a given ratio

$300 is to be divided into the ratio 2 : 3.
Find the value of the larger portion using the unitary method.

SOLUTION

EXPLANATION

Total number of parts is $2 + 3 = 5$

Use the ratio 2 : 3 to get the total number of parts.

5 parts = $300

1 part $= \dfrac{1}{5}$ of $300

Calculate the value of each part.

$\qquad = \$60$

Larger portion $= 3 \times \$60$

Calculate the value of 3 parts.

$\qquad\qquad = \$180$

Example 13 Simplifying rates

Write these rates in simplest form.

a 120 km every 3 hours

b 5000 revolutions in $2\dfrac{1}{2}$ minutes

SOLUTION

EXPLANATION

a 120 km per 3 hours $= \dfrac{120}{3}$ km/h

Divide by 3 to write the rate compared to 1 hour.

$\qquad\qquad\qquad\quad = 40$ km/h

b 5000 revolutions per $2\dfrac{1}{2}$ minutes

$\quad = 10\,000$ revolutions per 5 minutes

First multiply by 2 to remove the fraction.

$\quad = \dfrac{10\,000}{5}$ revs/min

Then divide by 5 to write the rate using 1 minute.

$\quad = 2000$ revs/min

Example 14 Finding best buys

a   Which is better value?
  5 kg of potatoes for \$3.80 or 3 kg for \$2.20
b   Find the cost of 100 g of each product then decide which is the best buy.
  400 g of shampoo A at \$3.20 or 320 g of shampoo B at \$2.85

SOLUTION	EXPLANATION
a **Method A.** Price per kg.	
5 kg bag.	
1 kg costs \$3.80 ÷ 5 = \$0.76	Divide each price by the number of kilograms to find
3 kg bag.	the price per kilogram.
1 kg costs \$2.20 ÷ 3 = \$0.73	
∴ the 3 kg bag is cheaper	Then compare.
Method B. Amount per \$1.	
5 kg bag.	
\$1 buys 5 ÷ 3.8 = 1.32 kg	Divide each amount in kilograms by the cost to find the
3 kg bag.	weight per \$1 spent.
\$1 buys 3 ÷ 2.2 = 1.36 kg	
∴ the 3 kg bag is cheaper	Then compare.
b Shampoo A.	
100 g costs \$3.20 ÷ 4 = \$0.80	Alternatively, divide by 400 to find the cost of 1 g then
Shampoo B.	multiply by 100.
100 g costs \$2.85 ÷ 3.2 = \$0.89	Alternatively, divide by 320 to find the cost of 1 g then
	multiply by 100.
∴ shampoo A is cheaper	

Exercise 1E

Understanding

1   Write down the missing number.

  a $2 : 5 = \boxed{} : 10$ **b** $3 : 7 = \boxed{} : 28$ **c** $5 : 8 = 15 : \boxed{}$ **d** $7 : 12 = 42 : \boxed{}$

  e $\boxed{} : 12 = 1 : 4$ **f** $4 : \boxed{} = 16 : 36$ **g** $8 : \boxed{} = 640 : 880$ **h** $\boxed{} : 4 = 7.5 : 10$

2   Consider the ratio of boys to girls of 4 : 5.
  a   What is the total number of parts?
  b   What fraction of the total are boys?
  c   What fraction of the total are girls?
  d   If there were 18 students in total, how many of them are boys?
  e   If there were 18 students in total, how many of them are girls?

3 A car is travelling at a rate (speed) of 80 km/h.
  a How far would it travel in:
    i 3 hours?   **ii** $\frac{1}{2}$ hour?

    iii $6\frac{1}{2}$ hours?
  b How long would it take to travel:
    i 400 km?   **ii** 360 km?
    iii 20 km?

Odometers in cars record the distance travelled.

4 Find the cost of 1 kg if:
  a 2 kg costs $8   **b** 5 kg costs $15   **c** 4 kg costs $10

Example 11

5 Simplify these ratios.
  a 6 : 30   **b** 8 : 20   **c** 42 : 28   **d** 52 : 39
  e $1\frac{1}{2} : 3\frac{1}{3}$ **f** $2\frac{1}{4} : 1\frac{2}{5}$ **g** $\frac{3}{8} : 1\frac{3}{4}$ **h** $1\frac{5}{6} : 3\frac{1}{4}$
  i 0.3 : 0.9   **j** 0.7 : 3.5   **k** 1.6 : 0.56   **l** 0.4 : 0.12

6 Write each of the following as a ratio in simplest form. Hint: convert to the same units first.
  a 80c : $8   **b** 90c : $4.50   **c** 80 cm : 1.2 m
  d 0.7 kg : 800 g   **e** 2.5 kg : 400 g   **f** 30 min : 2 hours
  g 45 min : 3 hours   **h** 4 hours : 50 min   **i** 40 cm : 2 m : 50 cm
  j 80 cm : 600 mm : 2 m   **k** 2.5 hours : 1.5 days   **l** 0.09 km : 300 m : 1.2 km

Example 12

7 Divide $500 into these given ratios using the unitary method.
  a 2 : 3   **b** 3 : 7   **c** 1 : 1   **d** 7 : 13

8 420 g of flour is to be divided into a ratio of 7 : 3 for two different recipes. Find the smaller amount.

9 Divide $70 into these ratios.
  a 1 : 2 : 4   **b** 2 : 7 : 1   **c** 8 : 5 : 1

Example 13

10 Write these rates in simplest form.
  a 150 km in 10 hours
  b 3000 revolutions in $1\frac{1}{2}$ minutes
  c 15 swimming strokes in $\frac{1}{3}$ of a minute
  d 56 metres in 4 seconds
  e 180 mL in 22.5 hours
  f 207 heart beats in $2\frac{1}{4}$ minutes

The correct ratio of ingredients in a recipe has to be maintained when the amount of product to be made is changed.

11   Hamish rides his bike at an average speed of 22 km/h. How far does he ride in:

  a $2\frac{1}{2}$ hours?   b $\frac{3}{4}$ hours?   c   15 minutes?

Example 14a

12   Determine the best buy in each of the following.

  a   2 kg of washing powder for $11.70 or 3 kg for $16.20

  b   1.5 kg of red delicious apples for $4.80 or 2.2 kg of royal gala
       apples for $7.92

  c   2.4 litres of orange juice for $4.20 or 3 litres of orange juice for
       $5.40

  d   0.7 GB of internet usage for $14 or 1.5 GB for $30.90 with
       different service providers

Example 14b

13   Find the cost of 100 g of each product below then decide which is
     the best buy.

  a   300 g of coffee A at $10.80 or 220 g of coffee B at $8.58.

  b   600 g of pasta A for $7.50 or 250 g of pasta B for $2.35

  c   1.2 kg of cereal A for $4.44 or 825 g of cereal B for $3.30

14   Kirsty manages a restaurant. Each day she buys watermelons and mangoes in the ratio of
     3 : 2. How many watermelons did she buy if, on one day, the total number of watermelons and
     mangoes was 200?

15   If a prize of $6000 was divided among Georgia, Leanne and Maya in the ratio of 5 : 2 : 3, how
     much did each girl get?

16   When a crate of twenty 375 mL soft drink cans is purchased it works out to be $1.68 per litre. If
     a crate of 30 of the same cans is advertised as being a saving of 10 cents per can compared with
     the 20-can crate, calculate how much the 30-can crate costs.

17   The dilution ratio for a particular chemical with
     water is 2 : 3 (chemical to water). If you have 72
     litres of chemical, how much water is needed to
     dilute the chemical?

18   Amy, Belinda, Candice and Diane invested money in
     the ratio of 2 : 3 : 1 : 4 in a publishing company. If
     the profit was shared according to their investment,
     and Amy's profit was $2400, find the profit each
     investor made.

Concentrations of substances in water or
solvents are ratios.

19   Julie is looking through the supermarket catalogue for her favourite cookies and cream ice
     cream. She can buy 2 L of triple chocolate ice cream for $6.30 while the cookies and cream ice
     cream is usually $5.40 for 1.2 L. What saving does there need to be on the price of the 1.2 L
     container of cookies and cream ice cream for it to be of equal value to the 2 L triple chocolate
     container?

20 The ratio of the side lengths of one square to another is 1 : 2. Find the ratio of the areas of the two squares.

21 A quadrilateral (with angle sum 360°) has interior angles in the ratio 1 : 2 : 3 : 4. Find the size of each angle.

22 2.5 kg of cereal A costs $4.80 and 1.5 kg of cereal B costs $2.95. Write down at least two different methods to find which cereal is a better buy.

23 If $a : b$ is in simplest form, state whether the following are true or false.
  a a and b must both be odd.
  b a and b must both be prime.
  c At least one of a or b is odd.
  d The HCF of a and b is 1.

24 A ratio is $a : b$ with $a < b$ and a and b are positive integers. Write an expression for:
  a the total number of parts
  b the fraction of the smaller quantity out of the total
  c the fraction of the larger quantity out of the total.

Enrichment: Mixing drinks

25 Four jugs of cordial have a cordial to water ratio as shown and a given total volume.

Jug	Cordial to water ratio	Total volume
1	1 : 5	600 mL
2	2 : 7	900 mL
3	3 : 5	400 mL
4	2 : 9	330 mL

  a How much cordial is in:
    i Jug 1?   **ii** Jug 2?
  b How much water is in:
    i Jug 3?   **ii** Jug 4?
  c If Jug 1 and 2 were mixed together to give 1500 mL of drink:
    i how much cordial is in the drink?
    ii find the ratio of cordial to water in the drink.
  d Find the ratio of cordial to water if the following jugs are mixed.
    i Jug 1 and 3   **ii** Jug 2 and 3
    iii Jug 2 and 4   **iv** Jug 3 and 4
  e Which combination of two jugs gives the strongest cordial to water ratio?

1.6 Percentages and money

We use percentages for many different things in our daily lives. Some examples are loan rates, the interest given on term deposits and discounts on goods.

We know from our previous studies that a percentage is a fraction that has a denominator of 100. 'Per cent' comes from the Latin word *per centum* and means 'out of 100'.

Let's start: Which is the largest piece?

Four people receive the following portions of a cake:

*   Milly   25.5%
*   Tom $\frac{1}{4}$
*   Adam   0.26
*   Mai   The left over

a   Which person gets the most cake and why?

b   How much cake does Mai get? What is her portion written as a percentage, decimal and fraction?

Key ideas

*   To change a decimal or a fraction into a **percentage**, *multiply* by 100%.
*   To change a percentage into a fraction or decimal, *divide* by 100%.

$$x\% = \frac{x\%}{100\%} = \frac{x}{100}$$

*   A percentage of a number can be found using multiplication.
    For example: 25% of $26 = 0.25 \times \$26$
    $= \$6.50$

*   To find an original amount, use the **unitary method** or use division.
    For example: if 3% of an amount is $36:
    *   Using the unitary method: 1% of the amount is $36 \div 3 = \$12$
        $\therefore$ 100% of the amount is $12 \times 100 = \$1200$
    *   Using division: 3% of the amount is $36
        $0.03 \times \text{amount} = \$36$
        $\text{amount} = \$36 \div 0.03$
        $= \$1200$

Example 15 Converting between percentages, decimals and fractions

a   Write 0.45 as a percentage.

b   Write 25% as a decimal.

c   Write $3\frac{1}{4}\%$ as a fraction.

SOLUTION	EXPLANATION
a $0.45 = 0.45 \times 100\% = 45\%$	Multiply by 100%. This moves the decimal point 2 places to the right.
b $25\% = 25\% \div 100\% = 0.25$	Divide by 100%. This moves the decimal point 2 places to the left.
c $3\frac{1}{4}\% = 3\frac{1}{4}\% \div 100\%$ $= \frac{13}{4} \times \frac{1}{100}$ $= \frac{13}{400}$	Divide by 100%. Write the mixed number as an improper fraction and multiply by the reciprocal of 100 (i.e. $\frac{1}{100}$).

Example 16 Writing a quantity as a percentage

Write 50c out of $2.50 as a percentage.

SOLUTION	EXPLANATION
50c out of $2.50 = $\dfrac{\overset{1}{50}}{\underset{5}{250}} \times 100\%$ $= 20\%$	Convert to the same units ($2.50 = 250c) and write as a fraction. Multiply by 100%, cancelling first.

Example 17 Finding a percentage of a quantity

Find 15% of $35.

SOLUTION	EXPLANATION
15% of $35 = $\dfrac{\overset{3}{15}}{\underset{20}{100}} \times \$35$ $= \$5.25$	Write the percentage as a fraction out of 100 and multiply by $35. Note: 'of' means to 'multiply'.

Example 18 Finding the original amount

Determine the original amount if 5% of the amount is $45.

SOLUTION

Method 1: Unitary

5% of the amount = $45

1% of the amount = $9

100% of the amount = $900

So the original amount is $900

Method 2: Division

5% of amount = $45

0.05 × amount = $45

amount = $45 ÷ 0.05

= $900

EXPLANATION

To use the unitary method, find the value of 1 part or 1% then multiply by 100 to find 100%.

Write 5% as a decimal then divide both sides by this number to find the original amount.

Exercise 1F

1 Divide these percentages by 100% to write them as fractions. For example, $9\% = \dfrac{9}{100}$. Simplify where possible.

$\quad$ **a** 3% $\qquad\qquad$ **b** 11% $\qquad\qquad$ **c** 35% $\qquad\qquad$ **d** 8%

2 Divide these percentages by 100% to write them as decimals. For example, $9\% = 0.09$.

$\quad$ **a** 4% $\qquad\qquad$ **b** 23% $\qquad\qquad$ **c** 86% $\qquad\qquad$ **d** 46.3%

3 Write these simple decimals and fractions as percentages.

$\quad$ **a** 0.5 $\qquad\qquad$ **b** 0.6 $\qquad\qquad$ **c** 0.25 $\qquad\qquad$ **d** 0.9

$\quad$ **e** $\dfrac{3}{4}$ $\qquad\qquad$ **f** $\dfrac{1}{2}$ $\qquad\qquad$ **g** $\dfrac{1}{5}$ $\qquad\qquad$ **h** $\dfrac{1}{8}$

Example 15a

4 Write each of the following as a percentage.

$\quad$ **a** 0.34 $\qquad\qquad$ **b** 0.4 $\qquad\qquad$ **c** 0.06 $\qquad\qquad$ **d** 0.7

$\quad$ **e** 1 $\qquad\qquad\;$ **f** 1.32 $\qquad\qquad$ **g** 1.09 $\qquad\qquad$ **h** 3.1

Example 15b

5 Write each of the following as decimals.

$\quad$ **a** 67% $\qquad\qquad$ **b** 30% $\qquad\qquad$ **c** 250% $\qquad\qquad$ **d** 8%

$\quad$ **e** $4\dfrac{3}{4}\%$ $\qquad\quad\;$ **f** $10\dfrac{5}{8}\%$ $\qquad\quad$ **g** $30\dfrac{2}{5}\%$ $\qquad\quad$ **h** $44\dfrac{1}{4}\%$

Example 15c

6 Write each part of Question **5** as a simplified fraction.

7 Copy and complete this table. Use the simplest form for fractions.

Percentage	Fraction	Decimal
10%		
	$\frac{1}{2}$	
5%		
		0.25
		0.2
	$\frac{1}{8}$	
1%		
	$\frac{1}{9}$	
		$0.\dot{2}$

Percentage	Fraction	Decimal
	$\frac{3}{4}$	
15%		
		0.9
37.5%		
$33\frac{1}{3}\%$	$\frac{1}{3}$	
$66\frac{2}{3}\%$		
		0.625
	$\frac{1}{6}$	

Example 16

8 Convert each of the following to a percentage.
   a $3 out of $12
   b $6 out of $18
   c $0.40 out of $2.50
   d $44 out of $22
   e $140 out of $5
   f 45c out of $1.80

Example 17

9 Find:
   a 10% of $360
   b 50% of $420
   c 75% of 64 kg
   d 12.5% of 240 km
   e 37.5% of 40 apples
   f 87.5% of 400 m
   g $33\frac{1}{3}\%$ of 750 people
   h $66\frac{2}{3}\%$ of 300 cars
   i $8\frac{3}{4}\%$ of $560

Example 18

10 Determine the original amount if:
   a 10% of the amount is $12
   b 6% of the amount is $42
   c 3% of the amount is $9
   d 40% of the amount is $2.80
   e 90% of the amount is $0.18
   f 35% of the amount is $140

11 Determine the value of x in the following if:
   a 10% of x is $54
   b 15% of x is $90
   c 25% of x is $127
   d 18% of x is $225
   e 105% of x is $126
   f 110% of x is $44

12 Bad weather stopped a cricket game for 35 minutes of a scheduled $3\frac{1}{2}$ hour match. What percentage of the scheduled time was lost?

13 Joe lost 4 kg and now weighs 60 kg. What percentage of his original weight did he lose?

14 About 80% of the mass of the human body is water. If Clare is 60 kg, how many kilograms of water make up her body weight?

15 In a class of 25 students, 40% have been to England. How many students have not been to England?

16 20% of the cross country runners in a school team weigh between 60 and 70 kg. If 4% of the school of 1125 students are in the cross country team, how many students in the team weigh between 60 and 70 kg?

17 One week Grace spent 16% of her weekly wage on a new bookshelf that cost $184. What is her weekly wage?

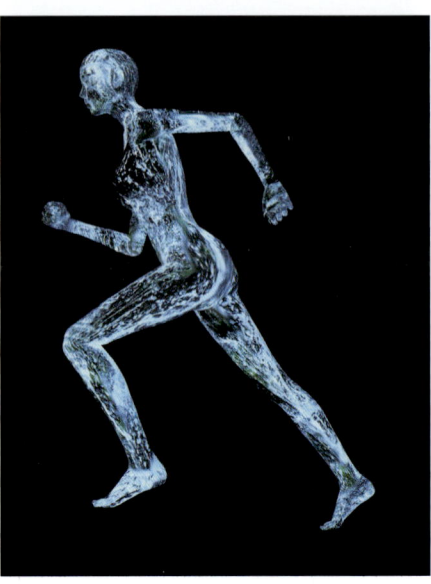

18 Consider the equation $P\%$ of $a = b$ (like 20% of 40 = 8 or 150% of 22 = 33).
  a For what value of P is $P\%$ of $a = b$?   **b** For what values of P is $P\%$ of $a < b$?
  c For what values of P is $P\%$ of $a > b$?

19 What can be said about the numbers x and y if:
  a 10% of $x = 20\%$ of y?   **b** 10% of $x = 50\%$ of y?
  c 5% of $x = 3\%$ of y?   **d** 14% of $x = 5\%$ of y?

Enrichment: More than 100%

20 a Find 120% of 60.   **b** Determine the value of x if 165% of $x = 1.5$.
  c Write 2.80 as a percentage.   **d** Write 325% as a fraction.
  e $2000 in a bank account increases to $5000 over a period of time. By how much has the amount increased as a percentage?

1.7 Percentage increase and decrease

Percentages are often used to describe by how much a quantity has increased or decreased. The price of a car in the new year might be increased by 5%. On a $70 000 car, this equates to a $3500 increase. The price of a shirt might be marked down by 30% and if the shirt originally cost $60, this provides an $18 discount. It is important to note that the increase or decrease is calculated on the original amount.

Let's start: The quicker method

Two students, Nicky and Mila, consider the question: $250 is increased by 15%. What is the final amount?

Nicky puts his solution on the board with two steps.

Step 1. 15% of $250 = 0.15 × $250
$$= \$37.50$$

Step 2. Final amount = $250 + $37.50
$$= \$287.50$$

Mila says that the same problem can be solved with only one step using the number 1.15.

- Can you explain Mila's method? Write it down.
- What if the question was altered so that $250 is decreased by 15%. How would Nicky's and Mila's methods work in this case?
- Which of the two methods do you prefer and why?

■ To increase an amount by a given percentage, multiply by the sum of 100% and the given percentage.
For example: to increase by 30%, multiply by 100% + 30% = 130% = 1.3

■ To decrease an amount by a given percentage, multiply by 100% minus the given percentage.
For example: to decrease by 25%, multiply by 100% − 25% = 75% = 0.75

■ To find a **percentage change** use

$$\text{Percentage change} = \frac{\text{change}}{\text{original amount}} \times 100\%$$

Key ideas

Example 19 Increasing by a percentage

Increase $70 by 15%.

SOLUTION	EXPLANATION
100% + 15% = 115% = 1.15	First add 15% to 100%
$70 × 1.15 = $80.50	Multiply by 1.15 to give $70 plus the increase in one step.

Example 20 Decreasing by a percentage

Decrease $5.20 by 40%.

SOLUTION	EXPLANATION
$100\% - 40\% = 60\%$ $\qquad = 0.6$ $\$5.20 \times 0.6 = \$3.12$	First subtract the 40% from 100% to find the percentage remaining. Multiply by $60\% = 0.6$ to get the result.

Example 21 Finding a percentage change

a The price of a mobile phone increased from $250 to $280. Find the percentage increase.
b The population of a town decreases from 3220 to 2985. Find the percentage decrease and round to one decimal place.

SOLUTION	EXPLANATION
a Increase $= \$280 - \$250$ $\qquad\quad = \$30$ Percentage increase $= \dfrac{30}{250} \times \dfrac{100}{1}\%$ $\qquad\qquad\qquad\quad = 12\%$	First find the actual increase. Divide the increase by the original amount and multiply by 100%.
b Decrease $= 3220 - 2985$ $\qquad\quad = 235$ Percentage decrease $= \dfrac{235}{3220} \times \dfrac{100}{1}\%$ $\qquad\qquad\qquad\quad = 7.3\%$	First find the actual decrease. Divide the decrease by the original population. Round as indicated.

Example 22 Finding the original amount

After rain, the volume of water in a tank increased by 24% to 2200 L. How much water was in the tank before it rained? Round to the nearest litre.

SOLUTION	EXPLANATION
$100\% + 24\% = 124\%$ $\qquad\qquad\quad = 1.24$ Original volume $\times 1.24 = 2200$ $\therefore$ original volume $= 2200 \div 1.24$ $\qquad\qquad\qquad\qquad = 1774$ litres	Write the total percentage as a decimal. The original volume is increased by 24% to give 2200 litres. Divide to find the original volume.

Understanding

Exercise 1G

1 Write the missing number.
  a To increase a number by 40% multiply by _____
  b To increase a number by 26% multiply by _____
  c To increase a number by _____ multiply by 1.6
  d To increase a number by _____ multiply by 1.21
  e To decrease a number by 20% multiply by _____
  f To decrease a number by 73% multiply by _____
  g To decrease a number by _____ multiply by 0.94
  h To decrease a number by _____ multiply by 0.31

2 The price of a watch increases from $120 to $150.
  a What is the price increase?
  b Write this increase as a percentage of the original price.

3 A person's weight decreases from 108 kg to 96 kg.
  a What is the weight decrease?
  b Write this decrease as a percentage of the original weight. Round to one decimal place.

Fluency

Example 19

4 Increase the given amounts by the percentage given in the brackets.
  a $50 (5%)   **b** 35 min (8%)   **c** 250 mL (50%)   **d** 1.6 m (15%)
  e 24.5 kg (12%)   **f** 25 watts (44%)   **g** $13 000 (4.5%)   **h** $1200 (10.2%)

Example 20

5 Decrease the given amounts by the percentage given in the brackets.
  a 24 cm (20%)   **b** 35 cm (30%)   **c** 42 kg (7%)   **d** 55 mins (12%)
  e $90 (12.8%)   **f** 220 mL (8%)   **g** 25°C (28%)   **h** $420 (4.2%)

Example 21a

6 The length of a bike sprint race is increased from 800 m to 1200 m. Find the percentage increase.

7 From the age of 10 to 17, Nick's height increased from 125 cm to 180 cm. Find the percentage increase.

Example 21b

8 The temperature at night decreased from 25°C to 18°C. Find the percentage decrease.

9 Brett, a rising sprint star, lowered his 100 m time from 13 seconds flat to 12.48 seconds. Find the percentage decrease.

10 Find the percentage change in these situations rounding to one decimal place in each case.

  a 22 g increases to 27 g

  b 86°C increases to 109°C

  c 136 km decreases to 94 km

  d $85.90 decreases to $52.90

Example 22

11 After a price increase of 20% the cost of entry to a museum rose to $25.80. Find the original price.

12 Average attendance at a sporting match rose by 8% in the past year to 32 473. Find the average in the previous year to the nearest whole number.

13 A car when resold had decreased in value by 38% to $9235. What was the original price of the car to the nearest dollar?

14 After the redrawing of boundaries, land for a council electorate had decreased by 14.5% to 165 420 hectares. What was the original size of the electorate to the nearest hectare?

15 The total price of an item including GST (at 10%) is $120. How much GST is paid to the nearest cent?

16 A consultant charges a school a fee of $300 per hour including GST (at 10%). The school hires the consultant for 2 hours but can claim back the GST from the government. Find the net cost of the consultant for the school to the nearest cent.

17 An investor starts with $1000.

  a After a bad day the initial investment is reduced by 10%. Find the balance at the end of the day.

  b The next day is better and the balance is increased by 10%. Find the balance at the end of the second day.

  c The initial amount decreased by 10% on the first day and increased by 10% on the second day. Explain why the balance on the second day didn't return to $1000.

18 During a sale in a bookstore all travel guides are reduced from $30 by 20%. What percentage increase is required to take the price back to $30?

19 The cost of an item is reduced by 50%. What percentage increase is required to return to its original price?

20 The cost of an item is increased by 75%. What percentage decrease is required to return to its original price? Round to two decimal places.

Enrichment: Repeated increase and decrease

21 If the cost of a pair of shoes was increased three times by 10%, 15% and 8% from an original price of $80, then the final price would be

$$\$80 \times 1.10 \times 1.15 \times 1.08 = \$109.30$$

Use a similar technique to find the final price of these items. Round to the nearest cent.

a Skis starting at $450 and increasing by 20%, 10% and 7%

b A computer starting at $2750 and increasing by 6%, 11% and 4%

c A DVD player starting at $280 and decreasing by 10%, 25% and 20%

d A circular saw starting at $119 and increasing by 18%, 37% and 11%

22 If an amount is increased by the same percentage each time, powers can be used.

For example 50 kg increased by 12% three times would increase to

$$50 \text{ kg} \times 1.12 \times 1.12 \times 1.12$$
$$= 50 \text{ kg} \times (1.12)^3$$
$$= 70.25 \text{ kg (to two decimal places)}$$

Use a similar technique to find the final value in these situations. Round to two decimal places.

a The mass of a rat initially at 60 grams grows at a rate of 10% every month for 3 months.

b The cost of a new lawnmower initially at $80 000 increases by 5% every year for 4 years.

c The value of a house initially at $380 000 decreases by 4% per year for 3 years.

d The length of a pencil initially at 16 cm decreases through being sharpened by 15% every week for 5 weeks.

1.8 Profits and discounts

Percentages are widely used in the world of finance. Profits, losses, commissions, discounts and taxation are often expressed and calculated using percentages.

Examples of percentages used in the media.

Let's start: The best discount

Two adjacent book shops are selling the same book at a discounted price. The recommended retail price for the book is the same for both shops. Each shop has a sign near the book with the given details:

- Shop A. Discounted by 25%
- Shop B. Reduced by 20% then take a further 10% off that.

Which shop offers the bigger discount and is the difference equal to 5% of the retail price?

Key ideas

- **Profit** is the amount of money made on a sale. If the profit is negative we say that a loss has been made.
  - Profit = selling price − cost price
- **Mark-up** is the amount added to the cost price to produce the selling price.
  - Selling price = cost price + mark-up
- The **percentage profit** or loss can be found by dividing the profit or loss by the cost price and multiplying by 100%.

  - $\% \text{ Profit/Loss} = \dfrac{\text{profit/loss}}{\text{cost price}} \times 100\%$

- **Discount** is the amount by which an item is marked down.
  - New price = original price − discount
  - Discount = % discount × original price

Example 23 Determining profit

A manufacturer produces an item for $400 and sells it for $540.

a   Determine the profit made.

b   Express this profit as a percentage of the cost price.

SOLUTION	EXPLANATION
a Profit = $540 − $400 = $140	Profit = selling price − cost price
b % profit = $\dfrac{140}{400} \times 100\%$ = 35%	% profit = $\dfrac{\text{profit}}{\text{cost price}} \times 100\%$

Example 24 Calculating selling price from mark-up

An electrical store marks up all entertainment systems by 30%.
If the cost price of one entertainment system is $8000, what will be its selling price?

SOLUTION	EXPLANATION

Mark-up = 30% of $8000
    = 0.3 × 8000
    = $2400
	Change percentage to a decimal and evaluate.

∴ Selling price = 8000 + 2400 = $10 400	Selling price = cost price + mark-up

Alternate method

Selling price = 130% of cost price
    = 1.3 × 8000
    = $10 400
	Alternatively, since there is a 30% mark-up added to the cost price (100%), it follows that the selling price is 130% of the cost price.

Example 25 Finding the discount amount

Harvey Norman advertises a 15% discount on all equipment as a Christmas special. Find the sale price on a projection system that has a marked price of $18 000.

SOLUTION	EXPLANATION

Discount = 15% of $18 000
    = 0.15 × 18 000
    = $2700
	Change the percentage to a decimal and evaluate.

∴ The new price = 18 000 − 2700 = $15 300	New price is original price minus discount.

Alternate method

New price = 85% of $18 000
    = 0.85 × 18 000
    = $15 300
	Alternatively, discounting by 15% means the new price is 85% i.e. (100 − 15)% of the original price.

Example 26 Calculating sale saving

Toys 'R' Us discounts a toy by 10%, due to a sale. If the sale price was $10.80, what was the original price?

SOLUTION	EXPLANATION
Let $x be the original price. $0.9 \times x = 10.8$ $\qquad x = 10.8 \div 0.9$ $\qquad x = 12$ The original price was $12.	The discount factor $= 100\% - 10\% = 90\% = 0.9$. Thus $10.80 is 90% of the original price. Write an equation representing this and solve. Write the answer in words.

Exercise 1H

1 Write the missing numbers in these tables.

a

Cost price ($)	7	18	24.80		460.95	3250
Selling price ($)	10	15.50	26.20	11.80	395	
Profit/Loss ($)				4.50 profit		1180 loss

b

Cost price ($)		99.95	199.95			18000
Mark up ($)	10			700	16700	
Selling price ($)	40.95	179.95	595.90	1499.95	35499	26995

c

Original price ($)	100	49.95	29.95			2215
New price ($)	72	40.90		176	299.95	
Discount ($)			7.25	23	45.55	178

2 The following percentage discounts are given on the price of various products. State the percentage of the original price that each product is selling for.

a 10%

b 20%

c 15%

d 8%

Percentage discounts in a sale tell us how much the price is reduced by.

Fluency

3 A manufacturer produces and sells items for the prices shown.

  i Determine the profit made.

  ii Express this profit as a percentage of the cost price.

a Cost price $10, selling price $12

b Cost price $20, selling price $25

c Cost price $120, selling price $136.80

d Cost price $1400, selling price $3850

4 Dom runs a pizza business. Last year he took in $88 000 and it cost him $33 000 to run. What is his percentage profit for the year? Round to the nearest cent.

5 It used to take 20 hours to fly to Los Angeles. It now takes 12 hours. What is the percentage decrease in travel time?

6 Rob goes to the races with $600 in his pocket. He leaves at the end of the day with $45. What is his percentage loss?

7 Helen owns a handicrafts store that has a policy of marking up all of its items by 25%. If the cost price of one article is $30, what will be its selling price?

8 Lenny marks up all computers in his store by 12.5%. If a computer cost him $890, what will be the selling price of the computer, to the nearest dollar?

9 A dining room table sells for $448. If its cost price was $350 determine the percentage mark-up on the table.

10 A used-car dealer purchases a vehicle for $13 000 and sells it for $18 500. Determine the percentage mark-up on the vehicle to one decimal place.

11 A store is offering a 15% discount for customers who pay with cash. Rada wants a microwave oven marked at $175. How much will she pay if she is paying with cash?

12 A camera store displays a camera marked at $595 and a lens marked at $380. Sam is offered a discount of 22% if he buys both items. How much will he pay for the camera and lens?

13 A refrigerator is discounted by 25%. If Paula pays $460 for it what was the original price? Round to the nearest cent.

14 Maria put a $50 000 deposit on a house. What is the cost of the house if the deposit is 15% of the total price? Round to the nearest dollar.

15 A store marks up a $550 widescreen television by 30%. During a sale it is discounted by 20%. What is the percentage change in the original price of the television?

16 An armchair was purchased for a cost price of $380 and marked up to a retail price. It was then discounted by 10% to a sale price of $427.50. What is the percentage mark-up from the cost price to the sale price?

17 Pairs of shoes are manufactured for $24. They are sold to a warehouse with a mark-up of 15%. The warehouse sells the shoes to a distributor after charging a holding fee of $10 per pair. The distributor sells them to 'Fine Shoes' for a percentage profit of 12%. The store then marks them up by 30%.
   a Determine the price of a pair of shoes if you buy it from one of the 'Fine Shoes' stores (round to the nearest 5 cents).
   b What is the overall percentage mark-up of a pair of shoes to the nearest whole percent?

18 An item before being sold includes a percentage mark-up as well as a sale discount. Does it make a difference in which order the mark up and discount occur? Explain your answer.

19 Depreciation relates to a reduction in value. A computer depreciates in value by 30% in its first year. If its original value is $3000, find its value after one year.

20 John buys a car for $75 000. The value of the car depreciates at 15% per year. After 1 year the car is worth 85% of its original value, i.e. 85% of $75 000 = 0.85 × 75 000 = $63 750.
   a What is the value of the car, to the nearest cent, after
      i 2 years?   **ii** 5 years?
   b After how many years will the car first be worth less than $15 000?

Enrichment: Deposits and discounts

21 A car company offers a special discount deal. After the cash deposit is paid, the amount that remains to be paid is discounted by a percentage that is one tenth of the deposit percentage.
   For example, a deposit of $8000 on a $40 000 car represents 20% of the cost. The remaining $32 000 will be discounted by 2%.
   Find the amount paid for each car given the following car price and deposit. Round to two decimal places where necessary.
   a Price = $35 000, deposit = $7000   **b** Price = $45 000, deposit = $15 000
   c Price = $28 000, deposit = $3500   **d** Price = $33 400, deposit = $5344
   e Price = $62 500, deposit = $5000   **f** Price = $72 500, deposit = $10 150

1.9 Income and taxation

Most people's income is made up largely of the money they receive from their paid work – their job. Depending on the job, this payment can be made using a number of different methods. Many professional workers will receive an annual fixed *salary* which may be paid monthly or fortnightly. Casual workers, including those working in the retail area or restaurants, may receive a *wage* where they are paid a rate per hour worked – this rate may be higher out of regular working hours such as weekends or public holidays. Many sales people, including some real estate

agents, may receive a weekly fee (a *retainer*) but may also receive a set percentage of the amount of sales they make (a *commission*). From their income, people have to pay living costs such as electricity, rent, groceries and other items. In addition, they have to pay tax to the government, which funds many of the nation's infrastructure projects and welfare. The method in which this tax is paid from their income may also vary.

Let's start: Which job pays better?

Ben and Nick are both looking for part-time jobs and they spot the following advertisements.

Kitchen hand	Office assistant
$9.40 per hour, $14.10 per hour on weekends.	Receive $516 per month for 12 hours work per week.

- Nick chooses to work as the kitchen hand. If in his first week he works 4 hours during the week and 8 hours at the weekend, how much will he earn?
- Ben works as the office assistant. How much does he earn per week if he works 4 weeks in a month? What does his hourly rate turn out to be?
- If Nick continues to work 12 hours in a week, does he earn more than Ben if he only works on week days? How many weekday hours must Nick work to match Ben's pay?
- Out of the 12 hours, what is the minimum number of hours Nick must work at the weekend to earn at least as much as Ben?

- Workers who earn a **wage** (for example, a casual waiter) are paid a fixed rate per hour. Hours outside the normal working hours (public holidays etc.) are paid at a higher rate called **overtime**. This can occur in a couple of common ways:
  - **Time and a half:** pay is 1.5 times the usual hourly rate
  - **Double time:** pay is twice the usual hourly rate
- Workers who earn a **salary** (for example, an engineer) are paid a fixed amount per year, say $95 000. This is often paid monthly or fortnightly.
  - 12 months in a year and approximately 52 weeks in a year = 26 fortnights

Key ideas

- **Commission** is a proportion of the overall sales amount. Salespeople may receive a commission of their sales as well as a set weekly or monthly fee called a **retainer**.
  - Commission = % commission × total sales
- A person's **gross income** is the total income that they earn. The **net income** is what is left after deductions, such as tax, are taken out.
  - Net income = gross income − deductions
- **Taxation** is paid to the government once a person's taxable income passes a set amount. The amount paid depends on the person's taxable income.

Example 27 Comparing wages and salaries

Ken earns an annual salary of $59 735 and works a 38 hour week. His wife Brooke works part time in retail and earns $21.60 per hour.

a Calculate how much Ken earns per week.
b Determine who has the higher hourly rate of pay.
c If Brooke works on average 18 hours per week, what is her yearly income?

SOLUTION	EXPLANATION
a Weekly rate = $59735 ÷ 52 = $1148.75 ∴ Ken earns $1148.75 per week	$59 735 pay in a year. There are approximately 52 weeks in a year.
b Brooke: $21.60/hr Ken: $1148.75 ÷ 38 = $30.23/hr ∴ Ken is paid more per hour.	 Ken works 38 hours in week. Hourly rate = weekly rate ÷ number of hours. Round to the nearest cent. Compare hourly rates.

c In one week: $21.80 × 18
        = $392.40
 Yearly income = $392.4 × 52
       = $20 404.80
	Weekly income = hourly rate × number of hours.
	
	 Multiply by 52 weeks to get yearly income.

Example 28 Calculating overtime

Georgie works some weekends and late nights in addition to normal working hours and has overtime pay arrangements with her employer.

a Calculate how much Georgie earns if she works 16 hours during the week at the normal hourly rate of $18.50 and 6 hours on the weekend at time and a half.
b Georgie's hourly rate is changed. In a week she works 9 hours at the normal rate, 4 hours at time and a half and 5 hours at double time. If she earns $507.50, what is her hourly rate?

SOLUTION	EXPLANATION
a Earnings at normal rate	
$= 16 \times \$18.50$	16 hours at standard rate
$= \$296$	
Earnings at time and half	Time and a half is 1.5 times the standard rate.
$= 6 \times 1.5 \times \$18.50$	
$= \$166.50$	
$\therefore$ total earnings $= \$296 + \$166.50$	Combine earnings.
$\qquad\qquad = \$462.50$	
b Equivalent hours worked in week	Calculate the number of equivalent hours worked.
$= 9 + (4 \times 1.5) + (5 \times 2)$	4 hours at time and half is the same pay as for working
$= 9 + 6 + 10$	6 hours (4×1.5), 5 hours at double time is the same as
$= 25$ hours	working 10 hours (5×2).
Hourly rate $= \$507.50 \div 25$	Divide weekly earnings by the 25 equivalent hours
$\qquad\qquad = \$20.30$	worked.
$\therefore$ earns \$20.30 per hour	

Example 29 Calculating commission

A saleswoman is paid a retainer of \$1500 per month. She also receives a commission of 1.25% on the value of goods she sells. If she sells goods worth \$5600 during the month, calculate her earnings for that month.

SOLUTION	EXPLANATION
Commission $= 1.25\%$ of \$5600	Calculate the commission on sales. Change the
$\qquad\qquad = 0.0125 \times \$5600$	percentage to a decimal and evaluate.
$\qquad\qquad = \$70$	
Earnings $= \$1500 + \$70$	Earnings = retainer + commission
$\qquad\qquad = \$1570$	

Example 30 Calculating tax to find net income

Liam has an annual salary of \$52 800. His payslip each month shows deductions for taxation of \$968.
a Calculate Liam's net income each month.
b What percentage of Liam's monthly pay is being paid to the government by his employer for taxation?
c If the taxation rate for Liam's salary changes to 24% with the first \$6000 now tax free, calculate Liam's net income for the year.

SOLUTION	EXPLANATION
a Monthly pay = $52 800 ÷ 12 = $4400	Calculate gross income per month.
∴ net monthly income = $4400 − $968 = $3432	Net income = gross income − taxation
b % tax = $\dfrac{968}{4400} \times 100\%$ = 22%	Calculate what fraction $968 is of the monthly income $4400. Multiply by 100% to convert to a percentage.
c Salary for tax purposes = $52 800 − $6000 = $46 800	First $6000 is not taxed.

Tax amount = 24% of $46 800
             = 0.24 × $46 800
             = $11 232
	Calculate tax amount on $46 800. Convert percentage to a decimal and evaluate.

∴ net income = $52 800 − $11 232 = $41 568	Net income = gross income − tax amount.

Exercise 1I

1   An employee has an annual salary of $47 424 and works 38 hour weeks. Find the average earnings:
   a   per month   **b**   per week   **c**   per hour

2   A shop assistant is paid $11.40 per hour. Calculate the assistant's earnings from the following hours worked:
   a   7 hours
   b   5.5 hours
   c   4 hours at twice the hourly rate (double time)
   d   6 hours at 1.5 times the hourly rate (time and a half)

3   Find the commission earned on the given sales figures if the percentage commission is 20%.
   a $1000
   b $280
   c $4500
   d $725.50

4   Find the net annual income given the following:
   a   Gross annual income = $56 300, tax paid = $10 134
   b   Gross annual income = $28 700, tax paid = $5453

Understanding

mple 27 **5** **a** Calculate the hourly rate of pay for a 38 hour working week with an annual salary of:

   i $38 532   **ii** $53 352   **iii** $83 980

  b Calculate the yearly income for someone who earns $24.20 per hour and in a week works, on average:

   i 24 hours   **ii** 35 hours   **iii** 16 hours

ple 28a **6** A job has a normal working hours pay rate of $9.20 per hour. Calculate the pay including overtime from the following hours worked:

  a 3 hours and 4 hours at time and a half

  b 4 hours and 6 hours at time and a half

  c 14 hours and 3 hours at double time

  d 20 hours and 5 hours at double time

  e 10 hours and 8 hours at time and a half and 3 hours double time

  f 34 hours and 4 hours at time and a half and 2 hours double time

7 Calculate how many hours at the standard hourly rate the following working hours are equivalent to:

  a 3 hours and 2 hours at double time

  b 6 hours and 8 hours at time and a half

  c 15 hours and 12 hours at time and a half

  d 10 hours time and a half and 5 hours at double time

  e 20 hours and 6 hours at time and a half and 4 hours at double time

  f 32 hours and 4 hours at time and a half and 1 hour at double time

ple 28b **8** Jim, a part-time gardener, earnt $261 in a week. If he worked 12 hours during normal working hours and 4 hours overtime at time and a half, what was his hourly rate of pay?

9 Sally earned $329.40 in a week. If she worked 10 hours during the week and 6 hours on Saturday at time and a half and 4 hours on Sunday at double time, what was her hourly rate of pay?

mple 29 **10** Amy works at Best Bookshop. During one week she sells books valued at $800. If she earns $450 per week plus 5% commission, how much does she earn in this week?

11 Jason works for a caravan company. If he sells $84 000 worth of caravans in a month, and he earns $650 per month plus 4% commission on sales, how much does he earn that month?

Example 30a,b

12 For each of the following find:
    i the annual net income
    ii the percentage of gross income paid as tax. Round to one decimal place where necessary.

  a Gross annual income = $48 241, tax withdrawn = $8206
  b Gross annual income = $67 487, tax withdrawn = $13 581.20
  c Gross monthly income = $4041, tax withdrawn = $606.15
  d Gross monthly income = $3219, tax withdrawn = $714.62

Example 30c

13 Calculate the amount of tax to be paid using the following annual salaries and tax rates if the first $6000 is tax free.

  a salary = $18 200, tax rate = 15%
  b salary = $44 300, tax rate = 21%
  c salary = $57 500, tax rate = 24.5%
  d salary = $84 200, tax rate = 30.4%

14 Arrange the following workers in order of most to least earnt in a week of work.
- Adam has an annual salary of $33 384.
- Bill works for 26 hours at a rate of $22.70 per hour.
- Cate earns $2964 per month. (Assume 52 weeks in a year.)
- Diana does shift work 4 days of the week between 10 pm and 4 am. She earns $19.90 per hour before midnight and $27.50 per hour after midnight.
- Ed works 18 hours at the normal rate of $18.20 per hour, 6 hours at time and a half and 4 hours at double time in a week.

15 Stephen earns an hourly rate of $17.30 for the first 38 hours, time and a half for the next 3 hours and double time for each extra hour above that. Calculate his earnings if he works 44 hours in a week.

16 Jessica works for Woods Real Estate and earns $800 per week plus 0.05% commission. If this week she sold three houses valued at $334 000, $210 000 and $335 500 respectively, how much will she have earned?

17 A door to door salesman sells 10 security systems in one week at $1200 each. For the week, he earns a total of $850 including a retainer of $300 and a commission. Find his percentage commission correct to two decimal places.

18 Mel has a net annual income of $53 246 after 21% of her income is withdrawn for tax purposes. What was her gross income?

19 Karl is saving and wants to earn $90 from a casual job paying $7.50 per hour.
  a How many hours must he work to earn the $90?
  b Karl can also work some hours where he is paid time and a half. He decides to work x hours at the normal rate and y hours at time and a half to earn the $90. If x and y are both positive whole numbers, find the possible combinations for x and y.

20 A car salesman earns 2% commission on sales up to $60 000 and 2.5% on sales above that.
  a Determine the amount earned on sales worth:
    i $46 000   **ii** $72 000
  b Write a rule for the amount, A dollars, earned on sales of x if:
    i $x \le 60\,000$ **ii** $x > 60\,000$

21 Kim has a job selling jewellery. She is about to enter into one of two new payment plans below.
    Plan A: $220 per week plus 5% of sales   Plan B: 9% of sales and no set weekly retainer
  a What value of sales gives the same return from each plan?
  b Explain how you would choose between Plan A and Plan B.

Enrichment: Taxation systems

22 Many countries use a progressive taxation system where the percentage of tax paid is increased for higher incomes. An example is shown in this table.

Income	Tax rate	Tax payable
$0–$10 000	0%	$0
$10 001–$30 000	20%	$0 + 20% of each dollar over $10 000
$30 001–$100 000	30%	$4000 + 30% of (income − $30 000)
$100 001–	40%	$25 000 + 40% of (income − $100 000)

  a Using the above example, find the tax payable on the following incomes.
    i $20 000   **ii** $55 000   **iii** $125 000

  b Copy and complete the details in this progressive tax system.

Income	Tax rate	Tax payable
$0–$15 000	0%	$0
$15 001–$40 000	15%	$0 + 15% of each dollar over $15 000
$40 001–$90 000	25%	_ _ _ _ _ _ _ _ _ _ _ _ _ _ _ _ _ _
$90 001–	33%	_ _ _ _ _ _ _ _ _ _ _ _ _ _ _ _ _ _

  c A different system on 'Taxation Island' looks like this.
    Find the tax payable on an income of:

Income	Tax rate	Tax payable
$0–$20 000	10%	10% of total income
$20 001–$80 000	30%	30% of total income
$80 001–	50%	50% of total income

    i $20 000   **ii** $21 000
    iii $80 000   **iv** $80 001

  d By referring to your answers in part **c**, describe the problems associated with the taxation system on Taxation Island.

1.10 Simple interest

When paying back the amount borrowed from a bank or other financial institution, the borrower pays interest to the lender. It's like rent paid on the money borrowed. A financial institution might be the lender, giving you a loan, or a borrower, when you invest your savings with them (effectively when you lend them your money). In either case, interest is calculated as a percentage of the amount borrowed. With simple interest, the percentage is calculated on the amount originally borrowed or invested and is paid at agreed times, such as once a year.

Let's start: Developing the rule

$5000 is invested in a bank and 5% simple interest is paid every year. In the table at right, the amount of interest paid is shown for Year 1, the amount of accumulated total interest is shown for Years 1 and 2.

- Complete the table, writing an expression in the last cell for the accumulated total interest after t years.
- Now write a rule using P for the initial amount, t for the number of years and r for the interest rate to find the total interest earned, I.

Year	Interest paid that year	Accumulated total interest
0	$0	$0
1	$\dfrac{5}{100} \times \$5000 = \$250$	$1 \times \$250 = \$250$
2		$2 \times \$250 = \$500$
3		
4		
t		

- To compute **simple interest**, we apply the formula:

  $$I = P \times \frac{r}{100} \times t \text{ or } I = \frac{Prt}{100} \text{ where}$$

  - I is the amount of **simple interest** (in $)
  - P is the **principal** amount; the money borrowed or loaned (in $)
  - $r\%$ is the rate per unit time; usually **per annum** (p.a.) which means per year
  - t is the period of **time**, expressed in the stated units, usually years.
- When using simple interest, the principal amount is constant and remains unchanged from one period to the next.
- The total amount (A) equals the principal plus interest

  $$A = P + I$$

Example 31 Using the simple interest formula

Calculate the simple interest earned if the principal is $1000, the rate is 5% p.a. and the time is 3 years.

SOLUTION	EXPLANATION
$P = 1000, r = 5, t = 3$	List the information given.
$I = P \times \dfrac{r}{100} \times t$	Write the formula and substitute the given values.
$\quad = 1000 \times 0.05 \times 3$	$\dfrac{5}{100} = 0.05$
$\quad = 150$	
Interest $= \$150$	Answer the question.

Example 32 Calculating the final balance

Allan and Rachel plan to invest some money for their child Kaylan. They invest $4000 for 30 months in a bank that pays 4.5% p.a. Calculate the simple interest and the amount available at the end of the 30 months.

SOLUTION	EXPLANATION
$P = 4000, r = 4.5, \ t = \dfrac{30}{12} = 2.5$	t is written in years since interest rate is per annum.
$I = P \times \dfrac{r}{100} \times t$	Write the formula, substitute and evaluate.
$\quad = 4000 \times 0.045 \times 2.5$	
$\quad = 450$	
Interest $= \$450$	
Total amount $= \$4000 + \$450 = \$4450$	Total amount = principal + interest

Example 33 Determining the investment period

Remy invests \$2500 at 8% p.a. simple interest, for a period of time, to produce \$50 interest. For how long did she invest the money?

SOLUTION	EXPLANATION
$I = 50,\ P = 2500,\ r = 8$	List the information.
$I = P \times \dfrac{r}{100} \times t$	Write the formula, substitute the known information and simplify.
$50 = 2500 \times 0.08 \times t$	
$50 = 200t$	Solve the remaining equation for t.
$t = \dfrac{50}{200}$	
$ = 0.25$	
Time $= 0.25$ years	Convert decimal time to months where appropriate.
$ = 0.25 \times 12$ months	
$ = 3$ months	

Exercise 1J

Understanding

1 \$12 000 is invested at 6% p.a. for 42 months.
  a What is the principal amount?
  b What is the interest rate?
  c What is the time period in years?
  d How much interest is earned each year?
  e How much interest is earned after 2 years?
  f How much interest is earned after 42 months?

Example 31

2 Use the rule $I = P \times \dfrac{r}{100} \times t$ to find the simple interest earnt in these financial situations.
  a Principal \$10 000, rate 10% p.a., time 3 years
  b Principal \$6000, rate 12% p.a., time 5 years
  c Principal \$5200, rate 4% p.a., time 24 months
  d Principal \$3500, rate 6% p.a., time 18 months

Fluency

Example 32

3 Wally invests \$15 000 at a rate of 6% p.a. for 3 years. Calculate the simple interest and the amount available at the end of 3 years.

4 Annie invests \$22 000 at a rate of 4% p.a. for 27 months. Calculate the simple interest and the amount available at the end of 27 months.

5 A finance company charges 14% p.a. simple interest. If Lyn borrows \$2000 to be repaid over 2 years, calculate her total repayment.

6 Zac invests $3500 at 8% p.a. simple interest, for a period of time, to produce $210 interest. For how long did he invest the money?

7 If $4500 earns $120 simple interest at a flat rate of 2% p.a. calculate the duration of the investment.

8 Calculate the principal amount which earns $500 simple interest over 3 years at a rate of 8% p.a. Round to the nearest cent.

9 Wendy wins $5000 during a chess tournament. She wishes to invest her winnings, and has the two choices given below. Which one gives her the greater total at the end of the time?
Choice 1: 8.5% p.a. simple interest for 4 years
Choice 2: 8% p.a. simple interest for 54 months

10 Charlotte borrows $9000 to buy a second-hand car. The loan must be repaid over 5 years at 12% p.a. simple interest. Calculate:
a the total amount to be repaid
b the monthly repayment amount if the repayments are spread equally over the 5 years

11 If $5000 earns $6000 simple interest in 12 years, find the interest rate.

12 An investor invests $P and wants to double this amount of money.
a How much interest must be earned to double this initial amount?
b What simple interest rate is required to double the initial amount in 8 years?
c If the simple interest rate is 5% p.a.:
i how many years will it take to double the investment?
ii how many years will it take to triple the investment amount?
iii how do the investment periods in parts **i** and **ii** compare?

13 To find the total amount $T including simple interest, the rule is $T = P(1 + \dfrac{rt}{100})$.
a Use this rule to find the total amount after 10 years if $30 000 is invested at 7% p.a.
b Use the rule to find the time that it takes for an investment to grow from $18 000 to $22 320 invested at 6% p.a. simple interest.

14 Rearrange the rule $I = P \times \dfrac{r}{100} \times t$ to find a rule for:
a P in terms of I, r and t **b** t in terms of I, P and r **c** r in terms of I, P and t

Enrichment: Property investing

15 Many investors use interest only loans to buy shares or property. This is where the principal stays constant and only the interest is paid back each month.

Sasha buys an investment property for $300 000 and borrows the full amount at 7% p.a. simple interest. She rents out the property at $1500 per month and it costs $3000 per year in rates and other costs to keep the property.

a Find the amount of interest Sasha needs to pay back every month.

b Find Sasha's yearly income from rent.

c By considering the other costs in keeping the property, what will Sasha's overall loss be in a year.

d Sasha hopes that the property's value will increase enough to cover any loss she is making. By what percentage of the original price will the property need to increase in value per year?

Using a CAS calculator 1.10 : Number and interest problems

The activity is on the companion website in the form of a printable PDF.

1.11 Compound interest

When interest is added onto an investment total before the next amount of interest is calculated, we say that the interest is compounded. Interest on a $1000 investment at 8% p.a. gives $80 in the first year and if compounded, the interest calculated in the second year is 8% of $1080. This is repeated until the end of the investment period. Other forms of growth and decay work in a similar manner.

In compound interest, the balance grows faster as time passes.

Let's start: Power play

$10 000 is invested at 5% compounded annually. Complete this table showing the interest paid and the balance (original investment plus interest) at the end of each year.

- What patterns can you see developing in the table?
- How can you use the *power* button on your calculator to help find the balance at the end of each year?
- How would you find the balance at the end of 10 years without creating a large table of values?

Year	Interest paid that year	Balance
1	$0.05 \times \$10\,000 = \$\_\_\_\_$	$\$10\,000 \times 1.05 = \$_____$
2	$0.05 \times \$\_\_\_\_\_ = \$\_\_\_\_$	$\$10\,000 \times 1.05 \times 1.05$ $= \$10\,000 \times 1.05^2$ $= \$_____$
3	_____	_____ $= \$10\,000 \times 1.05^{\_\_}$ $= \$_____$

Key ideas

- A repeated product can be written and calculated using a power.
  - For example: $1.06 \times 1.06 \times 1.06 \times 1.06 = (1.06)^4$.
    $$0.85 \times 0.85 \times 0.85 = (0.85)^3.$$
- **Compound interest** is interest which is added to the investment amount before the next amount of interest is calculated.
  - For example: $5000 invested at 6% compounded annually for 3 years gives $5000 \times 1.06 \times 1.06 \times 1.06 = 5000 \times (1.06)^3$.
  - 6% compounded annually can be written as 6% p.a.
  - p.a. means per annum or per year.
  - The initial investment or loan is called the principal.
  - The total interest earned = Final amount − principal.

Example 34 Calculating a balance using compound interest

Find the total value of the investment if $8000 is invested at 5% compounded annually for 4 years.

SOLUTION	EXPLANATION
$100\% + 5\% = 105\%$ $\qquad\qquad = 1.05$ Investment total $= \$8000 \times (1.05)^4$ $\qquad\qquad\qquad\quad = \$9724.05$	Add 5% to 100% to find the multiplying factor. Multiplying by $(1.05)^4$ is the same as multiplying by $1.05 \times 1.05 \times 1.05 \times 1.05$.

Example 35 Finding the initial amount

After 6 years a loan grows to $62 150. If the interest was compounded annually at a rate of 9%, find the size of the initial loan to the nearest dollar.

SOLUTION	EXPLANATION
$100\% + 9\% = 109\%$ $\qquad\qquad = 1.09$ Initial amount $\times (1.09)^6 = \$62\,150$ $\qquad$ Initial amount $= \$62\,150 \div (1.09)^6$ $\qquad\qquad\qquad\qquad = \$37\,058$	Add 9% to 100% to find the multiplying factor. Write the equation including the final total. Divide by $(1.09)^6$ to find the initial amount and round as required.

Exercise 1K

 1 $2000 is invested at 10% compounded annually for 3 years.

- **a** Find the interest earned in the first year.
- **b** Find the total balance at the end of the first year.
- **c** Find the interest earned in the second year.
- **d** Find the total balance at the end of the second year.
- **e** Find the interest earned in the third year.
- **f** Find the total balance at the end of the third year.

 2 Find the value of the following correct to two decimal places.

- **a** $2500 \times 1.03 \times 1.03 \times 1.03$
- **b** $420 \times 1.22 \times 1.22 \times 1.22 \times 1.22$
- **c** $2500 \times (1.03)^3$
- **d** $420 \times (1.22)^4$

 3 Fill in the missing numbers to describe each situation.

- **a** $4000 is invested at 20% compounded annually for 3 years.
  $$\$4000 \times (\underline{\qquad})^3$$
- **b** $15 000 is invested at 7% compounded annually for 6 years.
  $$\$\underline{\qquad} \times (1.07)^{\overline{}}$$
- **c** $825 is invested at 11% compounded annually for 4 years.
  $$\$825 \times (\underline{\qquad})^{\overline{}}$$

Understanding

4 Find the total balance of these investments with the given interest rates and time period.
Assume interest is compounded annually in each case. Round to the nearest cent.
   a $4000, 5%, 10 years   **b** $6500, 8%, 6 years
   c $25 000, 11%, 36 months **d** $4000, 7%, 60 months

 5 Barry borrows $200 000 from a bank for 5 years and does not pay any money back until the
end of the period. The compound interest rate is 8% p.a. How much does he need to pay back at
the end of the 5 years? Round to the nearest cent.

 6 Find the total percentage increase in the value of these amounts, compounded annually at the
given rates. Round to one decimal place.
   a $1000, 4% p.a., 5 years   **b** $20 000, 6% p.a., 3 years
   c $125 000, 9% p.a., 10 years **d** $500 000, 7.5% p.a., 4 years

 7 After 5 years a loan grows to $45 200. If the interest was compounded annually at a rate of
6% p.a., find the size of the initial loan to the nearest dollar.

 8 Find the initial investment amount to the nearest dollar given these final balances, annual
interest rates and time periods. Assume interest is compounded annually in each case.
   a $26 500, 4%, 3 years.   **b** $42 000, 6%, 4 years
   c $35 500, 3.5%, 6 years   **d** $28 200, 4.7%, 2 years

Problem-solving

 9 Average house prices in Hobart are expected to grow by 8% per year for the next 5 years. What is the expected average value of a house in Hobart in 5 years time, to the nearest dollar, if it is currently valued at $370 000?

The future value of any asset that grows by the same percentage every year (which can happen with a house) can also be calculated with the compound interest formula.

10 The population of a country town is expected to fall by 15% per year for the next 8 years due to the downsizing of the iron ore mine. If the population is currently 22 540 people, what is the expected population in 8 years time? Round to the nearest whole number.

 11 It is proposed that the mass of a piece of limestone lying out in the weather has decreased by
4.5% per year for the last 15 years. Its current mass is 3.28 kg. Find its approximate mass
15 years ago. Round to two decimal places.

12 Charlene wants to invest $10 000 long enough for it to grow to at least $20 000. The compound interest rate is 6% p.a. How many whole number of years does she need to invest the money for so that it grows to her $20 000 target?

13 A forgetful person lets a personal loan balance grow from $800 to $1440 with a compound interest rate of 12.5% p.a. Approximately how many years did the person forget about the loan?

14 $400 is invested for 5 years under the following conditions.

    i   Simple interest at 7% p.a.   **ii**   Compound interest at 7% p.a.

  a Find the percentage increase in the total value of the investment using condition **i**.

  b Find the percentage increase in the total value of the investment using condition **ii**. Round to two decimal places.

  c Explain why the total for condition **i** is less than the total for condition **ii**.

15 Find the total percentage increase in these compound interest situations to two decimal places.

  a 5% p.a. for 3 years   **b** 12% p.a. for 2 years   **c** 4.4% p.a. for 5 years

  d 7.2% p.a. for 9 years   **e** r% for t years

Enrichment: Comparing simple and compound interest

16 $16 000 is invested for 5 years at 8% compounded annually.

  a Find the total interest earned over the 5 years to the nearest cent.

  b Find the simple interest rate that would deliver the same overall interest at the end of the 5 years. Round to two decimal places.

17 $100 000 is invested for 10 years at 5.5% compounded annually.

  a Find the total percentage increase in the investment to two decimal places.

  b Find the simple interest rate that would deliver the same overall interest at the end of the 10 years. Round to two decimal places.

18 Find the simple interest rate which is equivalent to these annual compound interest rates for the given periods. Round to two decimal places.

  a 5% p.a. for 4 years   **b** 10.5% p.a. for 12 years

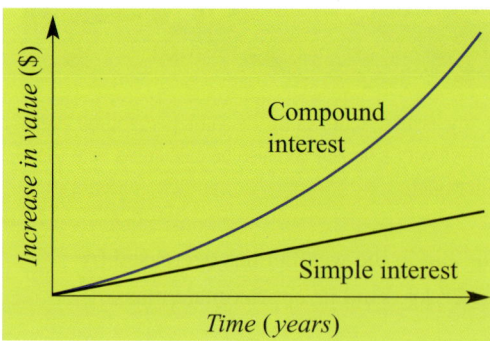

This graph shows the effect of the same rate of compound and simple interest on the increase in value of an investment or loan, compared over time. Simple interest is calculated only on the principal, so yields a balance that increases by the same amount every year, forming a straight-line graph. After the first year, compound interest is calculated on the principal and what has been added by the previous years' interest, so the balance increases by a greater amount each year. This forms an exponential graph.

Compounding investments

Banks offer many types of investments paying compound interest. Recall that for compound interest you gain interest on the money you have invested over a given time period. This increases your investment amount and therefore the amount of interest you gain in the next period.

Calculating yearly interest

Mary invests $1000 at 6% per annum. This means Mary earns 6% of the principal every year in interest. That is, after 1 year the interest earned is

$$6\% \text{ of } \$1000 = \frac{6}{100} \times 1000 = \$60$$

Mary now has $1060 after one year.

a The interest earned is added to the principal at the end of the year, and the total becomes the principal for the second year.
  i Assuming the same rate of interest how much interest will she earn at the end of the second year?
  ii Calculate the interest earned for the third year?
  iii What total amount will Mary have at the end of the third year?
  iv How much interest will her money earn altogether over the 3 years?

b Write down a rule that calculates the total value of Mary's investment after t years. Use an initial investment amount of $1000 and an annual interest rate of 6% p.a.

c Use your rule from part **b** to calculate:
  i the value of Mary's investment after 5 years
  ii the value of Mary's investment after 10 years
  iii the time it takes for Mary's investment to grow to $1500
  iv the time it takes for Mary's investment to grow to $2000.

Using a spreadsheet

This spreadsheet will calculate the compound interest for you if you place the principal in cell B3 and the rate in cell D3.

In Mary's case put 1000 in B3 and $\frac{6}{100}$ in D3.

	A	B	C	D
1	COMPOUND	INTEREST	SIMULATOR	
2				
3	PRINCIPAL	...	RATE OF PERIOD	...
4				
5	PERIOD	OPENING BALANCE	INTEREST EARNED	NEW BALANCE
6	1	=B3	=B6*D3	=B6 + C6
7	2	=D6	=B7*D3	=B7 + C7
8	3	=D7	=B8*D3	=B8 + C8
9	4	=D8	=B9*D3	=B9 + C9

a Copy the spreadsheet shown using 'fill down' at cells B7, C6 and D6.

b Determine how much money Mary would have after 4 years.

Investigating compound interest

a What will be Mary's balance after 10 years? Extend your spreadsheet to find out.

b Draw a graph of Investment value versus time as shown. Plot points using the results from your spreadsheet and join them with a smooth curve. Discuss the shape of the curve.

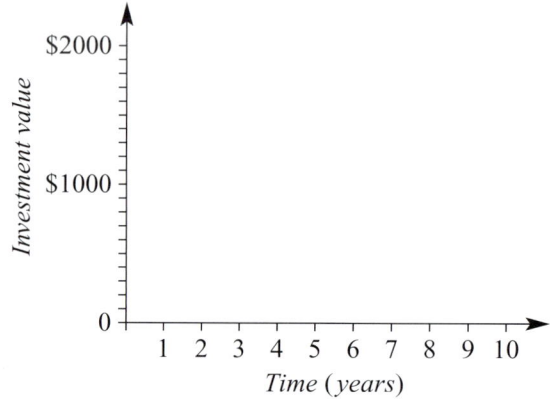

c How long does it take for Mary's investment to grow to $2000? Show on your spreadsheet.

d Now try altering the interest rate.
   i What would Mary's investment grow to in 10 years if the interest rate was 10%?
   ii What would Mary's investment grow to in 10 years if the interest rate was 12%?

e What interest rate makes Mary's investment grow to $2000 in 8 years? Use trial and error to get an answer correct to two decimal places. Record your investigation results using a table.

f Investigate how changing the principal changes the overall investment amount. Record your investigations in a table, showing the principal amounts and investment balance for a given interest rate and period.

1   By only using the four operations $+$, $-$, $\times$ and $\div$ as well as brackets and square root ($\sqrt{}$) the number 4 can be used exactly 4 times to give the answer 9 in the following way $4 \times \sqrt{4} + 4 \div 4$. Use the number 4 exactly 4 times (and no other numbers) and any of the operations (as many times as you like) to give the answer 0 or 1 or 2 or 3 or ..... or 10.

2   What is the value of n if n is the largest of 5 consecutive numbers that multiply to 95 040?

3   Evaluate.

a $\dfrac{1}{1 + \dfrac{1}{1 + \dfrac{1}{3}}}$

b $\dfrac{2}{1 + \dfrac{2}{1 + \dfrac{2}{5}}}$

4   A jug has 1 litre of 10% strength cordial. How much pure cordial needs to be added to make the strength 20%? (The answer is not 100 mL.)

5   An old table in a furniture store is marked down by 10% from its previous price on five separate occasions. What is the total percentage reduction in price correct to two decimal places?

6   What simple interest rate is equivalent to a compound interest rate of 6% p.a. over 10 years correct to two decimal places?

7   Brendon has a rectangular paved area in his yard.

a   If he increases both the length and width by 20%, what is the percentage increase in area?
b   If the length and width were increased by the same percentage and the area increases by 21%, what is the percentage increase of the length and width?

8   A rectangular sandpit is shown on a map which has a scale of 1 : 100. On the map the sandpit has an area of 20 cm². What is its actual area?

9   Arrange the numbers 1 to 15 in a row so that each adjacent pair of numbers sum to a square number.

Chapter summary

Review of numbers

$2 + (-3) = -1$ For 8 and 12
$-4 - (-2) = -2$ HCF is 4
$15 \div (-5) = -3$ LCM is 24
$-7 \times (-3) = 21$
$(-2)^2 = 4$ $\sqrt{36} = 6$
$4^3 = 64$ $\sqrt[3]{27} = 3$

Operations with fractions

$$1\frac{5}{6} - \frac{7}{12} = \frac{11}{6} - \frac{7}{12}$$
$$= \frac{22}{12} - \frac{7}{12}$$
$$= \frac{15}{12}$$
$$= 1\frac{1}{4}$$
$$1\frac{1}{2} \div \frac{7}{2} = \frac{3}{2_1} \times \frac{2^1}{7}$$
$$= \frac{3}{7}$$

Rounding

1.284 to 1 d.p. is 1.3
2 sig. fig. is 1.3
472.543 to 1 d.p. is 472.5
1 sig. fig. is 500

Rates, ratios and best buy

Rate: 180 km per 3 hrs = 60 km/h
Ratio: $\frac{3}{7} : \frac{1}{2} = \frac{6}{14} : \frac{7}{14} = 6 : 7$
$200 divided into 7 : 3
10 parts is $200
1 part is $20
3 parts is $60
7 parts is $140
Best buy: 3 kg of carrots for $6.45
         5 kg for $10.20
3 kg bag : $6.45 \div 3 = \$2.15/kg$
5 kg bag : $10.20 \div 5 = \$2.04/kg$
    $\therefore$ 5 kg is best buy

Reviewing number and financial mathematics

Rational numbers (fractions)

$1\frac{3}{8} = \frac{11}{8} = 1.375$
mixed   improper   terminating
number   fraction   decimal

$\frac{1}{6} = 0.166... = 0.1\dot{6}$
proper   recurring
fraction   decimal

$\frac{2}{3}$ and $\frac{4}{6}$ are equivalent fractions

Irrational numbers cannot be expressed as a fraction

Compound interest

$3000 at 5% for 3 years
Amount $= \$3000 \times (1.05)^3$
         $= \$3472.88$

Simple interest

$I = P \times \dfrac{r}{100} \times t = \$2000 \times \dfrac{5}{100} \times 4$
         $= \$400$

Percentages

$\frac{3}{4} = \frac{3}{4} \times 100\% = 75\%$
$25\frac{1}{2}\% = 25.5 \div 100\% = 0.255$
20% of 60 $= 0.2 \times 60 = 12$
5% of amount $= 32$
   $\therefore$ amount $= 32 \div 0.05$
         $= 640$

Applications of percentages

Percentage profit/loss
$= \dfrac{\text{Profit/loss}}{\text{Cost price}} \times 100\%$
Mark-up and discount
Commission/tax

Percentage increase and decrease

Increase	Decrease
20 by 6%	20 by 5%
$20 \times 1.06 = 21.2$	$20 \times 0.95 = 19$

Percentage change $= \dfrac{\text{change}}{\text{original}} \times 100\%$

Income and tax

Employees can be paid:
wage: hourly rate with overtime at time and a half = 1.5
salary: annual amount
commission: % of sales

net income =
gross income − tax

Multiple-choice questions

1 $\frac{2}{7}$ written as a decimal is:

   A 0.29   B 0.286   C 0.28$\dot{5}$ D $0.\overline{285714}$ E 0.28571$\dot{4}$

2 3.0456 written to three significant figures is:

   A 3.04   B 3.05   C 3.045   D 3.046   E 3.45

3 2.25 written as a fraction in simplest form is:

   A $2\frac{1}{2}$ B $\frac{5}{4}$ C $\frac{9}{4}$ D $9\frac{1}{4}$ E $\frac{225}{100}$

4 $1\frac{1}{2} - \frac{5}{6}$ is equal to:

   A $\frac{2}{3}$ B $\frac{5}{6}$ C $-\frac{1}{2}$ D $\frac{2}{6}$ E $\frac{1}{2}$

5 $\frac{2}{7} \times \frac{3}{4}$ is equivalent to:

   A $\frac{8}{11}$ B $\frac{3}{7}$ C $\frac{5}{11}$ D $\frac{8}{12}$ E $\frac{3}{14}$

6 $\frac{3}{4} \div \frac{5}{6}$ is equivalent to:

   A $\frac{5}{8}$ B 1   C 21   D $\frac{4}{5}$ E $\frac{9}{10}$

7 Simplifying the ratio 50 cm : 4 m gives:

   A 50 : 4   B 8 : 1   C 25 : 2   D 1 : 8   E 5 : 40

8 28% as a fraction in its simplest form is:

   A 0.28   B $\frac{28}{100}$ C $\frac{0.28}{100}$ D $\frac{2.8}{100}$ E $\frac{7}{25}$

9 15% of $1600 is equal to:

   A 24   B 150   C $240   D $24   E 240

10 Jane is paid a wage of $7.80 per hour. If she works 12 hours at this rate during a week plus 4 hours on a public holiday in the week where she gets paid at time and half, her earnings in the week are:

   A $140.40   B $124.80   C $109.20   D $156   E $62.40

11 Simon earns a weekly retainer of $370 and 12% commission of any sales he makes. If he makes $2700 worth of sales in a particular week, he will earn:

   A $595   B $652   C $694   D $738.40   E $649.60

12 $1200 is increased by 10% for two years with compound interest. The total balance at the end of the two years is:

   A $252   B $1452   C $1450   D $240   E $1440

Short-answer questions

1 Evaluate the following.

  a $-4 \times (2 - (-3)) + 4$ **b** $-3 - 4 \times (-2) + (-3)$ **c** $(-8 \div 8 - (-1)) \times (-2)$

  d $\sqrt{25} \times \sqrt[3]{8}$ **e** $(-2)^2 - 3^3$ **f** $\sqrt[3]{1000} - (-3)^2$

2 Round these numbers to three significant figures.

  a 21.483 **b** 29 130 **c** 0.15271 **d** 0.002414

3 Estimate the answer by firstly rounding each number to one significant figure.

  a $294 - 112$ **b** 21.48×2.94 **c** $1.032 \div 0.493$

4 Write these fractions as decimals.

  a $2\frac{1}{8}$ **b** $\frac{5}{6}$ **c** $\frac{13}{7}$

5 Write these decimals as fractions.

  a 0.75 **b** 1.6 **c** 2.55

6 Simplify the following.

  a $\frac{5}{6} - \frac{1}{3}$ **b** $1\frac{1}{2} + \frac{2}{3}$ **c** $\frac{13}{8} - \frac{4}{3}$ **d** $3\frac{1}{2} \times \frac{4}{7}$ **e** $5 \div \frac{4}{3}$ **f** $3\frac{3}{4} \div 1\frac{2}{5}$

7 Simplify these ratios.

  a $30 : 12$ **b** $1.6 : 0.9$ **c** $7\frac{1}{2} : 1\frac{2}{5}$

8 Divide 80 into the given ratio.

  a $5 : 3$ **b** $5 : 11$ **c** $1 : 2 : 5$

 9 Dry dog food can be bought from store A for $18 for 8 kg or from store B for $14.19 for 5.5 kg.

  a Determine the cost per kilogram at each store and state which is the best buy.

  b Determine to the nearest whole number how many grams of each brand you get per dollar.

10 Copy and complete the table (right).

 11 Find:

  a 25% of $310 **b** 110% of 1.5

 12 Determine the original amount if:

  a 20% of the amount is 30

  b 72% of the amount is 18

 13 a Increase 45 by 60%.

  b Decrease 1.8 by 35%.

  c Find the percentage change if $150 is reduced by $30.

 14 The mass of a cat increased by 12% to 14 kg over a 12 month period. What was its previous mass?

Decimal	Fraction	Percentage
0.6		
	$\frac{1}{3}$	
		$3\frac{1}{4}\%$
	$\frac{3}{4}$	
1.2		
		200%

15 Determine the discount given on a $15 000 car if it is discounted by 12%.

16 The cost price of an article is $150. If it is sold for $175:
   a determine the profit made
   b express the profit as a percentage of the cost price.

17 Determine the hourly rate of pay for each of the following cases:
   a a person with an annual salary of $36 062 working a 38 hour week
   b a person who earns $429 working 18 hours at the hourly rate and 8 hours at time and a half.

18 Jo's monthly income is $5270 however 20% of this is paid straight to the government in taxes. What is Jo's net yearly income?

19 Find the simple interest earned on $1500 at 7% p.a. for 5 years.

20 Rob invests $10 000 at 8% p.a. simple interest to produce $3600. How long was the money invested for?

21 Find the total value of an investment if $50 000 is invested at 4% compounded annually for 6 years. Round to the nearest cent.

22 After 8 years a loan grows to $75 210. If the interest was compounded annually at a rate of 8.5%, find the size of the initial loan to the nearest dollar.

Extended-response questions

1 Pauline buys a debutante dress at cost price from her friend Tila. Pauline paid $420 for the dress which is normally marked up by 55%.
   a How much did she save?
   b What is the normal selling price of the dress?
   c If Tila gets a commission of 15%:
      i how much commission did she get?
      ii how much commission did Tila lose by selling the dress at cost price rather than the normal selling price?

2 Matilda has two bank accounts with the given details.
   A. Investment. Principal $25 000, interest rate 6.5% compounded annually
   B. Loan. 11.5% compounded annually
   a Find Matilda's investment account balance after:
      i 1 year
      ii 10 years (to the nearest cent)
   b Find the total percentage increase in Matilda's investment account after 10 years correct to two decimal places.
   c After 3 years Matilda's loan account has increased to $114 250. Find the initial loan amount to the nearest dollar.
   d Matilda reduces her $114 250 loan by $30 000. What is this reduction as a percentage to two decimal places?
   e For Matilda's investment loan, what simple interest rate is equivalent to 5 years of the compounded interest rate of 6.5%? Round to one decimal place.

Chapter 2

Linear and simultaneous equations

What you will learn

On a collision course

Australian curriculum

NUMBER AND ALGEBRA
Patterns and algebra

Apply the distributive law to the expansion of algebraic expressions, including binomials, and collect like terms where appropriate

Linear equations with two variables, such as $2x + 3y = 12$, have an infinite number of solutions. If we plot them on a number plane we get a line. Each point on the line represents a possible solution.

These equations can model many different situations or systems in real life. For instance the two variables might be *total cost* and *quantity* of an item, or the *distance* of an object from its starting point over *time*, when it moves at uniform speed in a straight line.

Although there is no single solution to such a *distance-time* equation for one object, there is only one solution that satisfies both equations for two objects moving at constant speed in the same plane (provided they are moving are not on parallel tracks). In this situation the two equations are called simultaneous. The one solution that satisfies the simultaneous equations can be found using algebra, and this solution represents the position and time at which they meet or collide.

Solving simultaneous equations can be applied to problems such as working out when and where one ship will intercept another, but navigation is only one of many areas where this aspect of algebra has applications.

Pre-test

1 Write algebraic expressions for:
   a 3 more than x **b** the product of a and b
   c 2 lots of y less 3   **d** the sum of x and 2 divided by 3

2 Evaluate the following if $a = 3$ and $b = -2$.
   a $2a - 5$ **b** $ab + 4$ **c** $\dfrac{9}{a} - b$ **d** $2a(b + 1)$

3 Simplify by collecting like terms.
   a $2x + 5x - 4x$ **b** $7y + xy - y$ **c** $-4x - (-4x)$
   d $3x + 12y - 3x + 5y$ **e** $3a - 4a^2 + 7a + 5a^2$ **f** $3xy - 4y + 2yx - 3y$

4 Simplify the following.
   a $3 \times 2a$ **b** $7x \times (-3y)$ **c** $\dfrac{8b}{2}$ **d** $\dfrac{9mn}{6n}$

5 Describe and calculate in two different ways how the area of rectangle $ABCD$ can be found.

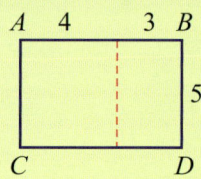

6 Expand the following.
   a $2(x + 3)$ **b** $3(a - 5)$ **c** $4x(3 - 2y)$ **d** $-3(2b - 1)$

7 Which of the following equations is $x = 4$ a solution to?
   a $2x + 3 = 9$ **b** $\dfrac{x}{2} + 3 = 5$ **c** $\dfrac{2x + 1}{3} = 3$ **d** $5 - 2x = -1$

8 Find the value of a that makes the following true.
   a $a + 4 = 13$ **b** $a - 3 = 7$ **c** $2a + 1 = 9$ **d** $\dfrac{a - 1}{4} = 5$

9 State if each of the following are true or false.
   a $5 > 3$ **b** $6 < 2$ **c** $4 \leq 4$
   d $-1 < 5$ **e** $-7 > -2$ **f** $-3 < -1$

10 Find the value of y in each of the following for the given value of x.
   a $y = 2x - 3, x = 5$ **b** $y = -3x + 7, x = 2$
   c $2x + y = 7, x = -1$ **d** $x - 2y = 3, x = 15$

11 Which inequality describes this number line?

   A $x > 3$ **B** $x \geq 3$ **C** $x < 3$
   D $x \leq 3$ **E** $3 \leq x < 4$

12 Which inequality describes this number line?

   A $x \leq -2$ **B** $x > -1$ **C** $x \geq -1$
   D $x < -1$ **E** $x \leq -1$

2.1 Algebraic expressions

Algebra is central to the study of mathematics and is commonly used to solve problems in a vast array of theoretical and practical problems. Algebra involves the representation and manipulation of unknown or varying quantities in a mathematical context. Variables (or pronumerals) are used to represent these unknown quantities.

Let's start: Remembering the vocabulary

State the parts of the expression $5x - 2xy + (4a)^2 - 2$ which match these words.

- variable (or pronumeral)
- term
- coefficient
- constant term
- squared term

Variables representing unknown quantities are used in a wide range of jobs and occupations.

Key ideas

- In algebra, letters are used to represent numbers. These letters are called **variables** or **pronumerals**.
- An **expression** is a combination of numbers and variables connected by the four operations +, −, × and ÷. Brackets can also be used.
  For example: $5x^2 + 4y - 1$ and $3(x + 2) - \dfrac{y}{5}$
- A **term** is a combination of numbers and variables connected with only multiplication and division. Terms are separated with the operations + and −.
  For example: $5x + 7y$ is a two term expression
- **Coefficients** are the numbers being multiplied by pronumerals.
  For example: the 3 in $3x$ and $\dfrac{1}{2}$ in $\dfrac{x^2}{2}$ are coefficients
- **Constant terms** consist of a number only.
  For example: -2 in $x^2 + 4x - 2$ (The sign must be included.)
- Expressions can be **evaluated** by substituting a number for a pronumeral.
  For example: if $a = -2$ then $a + 6 = -2 + 6 = 4$
- Order of operations should be followed when evaluating expressions:
  1 Brackets
  2 Powers
  3 Multiplication and division
  4 Addition and subtraction

Example 1 Writing algebraic expressions for word problems

Write an algebraic expression for the following:
a   the number of tickets needed for 3 boys and r girls
b   the cost of P pies at $3 each
c   the number of grams of peanuts for one child if 300 g of peanuts is shared equally among
    C children.

SOLUTION	EXPLANATION
a $3 + r$	3 tickets plus the number of girls
b $3P$	3 multiplied by the number of pies
c $\dfrac{300}{C}$	300 g divided into C parts

Example 2 Converting words to expressions

Write an algebraic expression for the following:
a   five less than x b   three more than twice x
c   the sum of a and b is divided by 4   d   the square of the sum of x and y

SOLUTION	EXPLANATION
a $x - 5$	5 subtracted from x
b $2x + 3$	Twice x plus 3
c $\dfrac{a + b}{4}$	The sum of a and b is done first $(a + b)$ and the result divided by 4
d $(x + y)^2$	The sum of x and y is done first and then the result is squared

Example 3 Substituting values into expressions

Evaluate these expressions if $a = 5$, $b = -2$ and $c = 3$.
a $7a - 2(a - c)$ b $b^2 - ac$

SOLUTION	EXPLANATION
a $\begin{aligned} 7a - 2(a - c) &= 7 \times 5 - 2(5 - 3) \\ &= 35 - 2 \times 2 \\ &= 35 - 4 \\ &= 31 \end{aligned}$	Substitute the values for a and c. When using order of operations, evaluate brackets before moving to multiplication and division then addition and subtraction.
b $\begin{aligned} b^2 - ac &= (-2)^2 - 5 \times 3 \\ &= 4 - 15 \\ &= -11 \end{aligned}$	Evaluate powers before the other operations. $(-2)^2 = -2 \times (-2) = 4$.

Exercise 2A

1 State the number of terms in these expressions.

   a $5x + 2y$ **b** $1 + 2a^2$ **c** $b^2 + ca - 1$ **d** $\dfrac{x^2}{2}$

2 Match an item in the left column with an item in the right column.

   A Product   **a** Division

   B Sum   **b** Subtraction

   C Difference   **c** Multiplication

   D Quotient   **d** Addition

   E x^2 **e** the reciprocal of a

   F $\dfrac{1}{a}$ **f** the square of x

3 State the coefficient in these terms.

   a $5xy$ **b** $-2a^2$ **c** $\dfrac{x}{3}$ **d** $\dfrac{-2a}{5}$

Example 1 **4** Write an algebraic expression for the following.

   a The number of tickets required for:

     i 4 boys and r girls   **ii** t boys and 2 girls

     iii b boys and g girls   **iv** x boys, y girls and z adults

   b The cost of:

     i P pies at \$6 each   **ii** 10 pies at \$$n$ each

     iii D drinks at \$2 each   **iv** P pies at \$5 and D drinks at \$2

   c The number of grams of lollies for one child if 500 g of lollies is shared equally among C children.

Example 2 **5** Write an algebraic expression for each of the following.

   a The sum of 2 and x **b** The sum of ab and y

   c 5 less than x **d** The product of x and 3

   e The difference between $3x$ and $2y$ **f** Three times the value of p

   g Four more than twice x **h** The sum of x and y is divided by 5

   i 10 less than the product of 4 and x **j** The square of the sum of m and n

   k The sum of the squares of m and n **l** The square root of the sum of x and y

   m The sum of a and its reciprocal   **n** The cube of the square root of x

Example 3 **6** Evaluate these expressions if $a = 4$, $b = -3$ and $c = 7$.

   a $b - ac$ **b** $bc - a$ **c** $a^2 - c^2$ **d** $b^2 - ac$

   e $\dfrac{a+b}{2}$ **f** $\dfrac{b^2+c}{a}$ **g** $\dfrac{1}{c} \times (a - b)$ **h** $a^3 - bc$

7 Evaluate these expressions if $x = -2$, $y = -\dfrac{1}{2}$ and $z = \dfrac{1}{6}$.

   a $xy + z$ **b** $y^2 + x^2$ **c** xyz **d** $\dfrac{xz+1}{y}$

8   A rectangular garden bed is 12 m long and 5 m wide.
   a   Find the area of the garden bed.
   b   The length is increased by x cm and the width is decreased by y cm. Find the new length
          and width of the garden.
   c   Write an expression for the area of the new garden bed.

9   The expression for the area of a trapezium is $\frac{1}{2}(a + b)h$ where a and b are the lengths of the two
       parallel sides and h is the distance between the two parallel sides.
   a   Find the area of the trapezium with $a = 5$, $b = 7$ and $h = 3$.
   b   A trapezium has $h = 4$ and area 12. If a and b are whole numbers, what possible values can
          the variable a have?

10   The cost of 10 identical puzzles is $\$P$.
   a   Write an expression for the cost of one puzzle.
   b   Write an expression for the cost of n puzzles.

11   For each of these shapes, write an expression for:
       i   the perimeter   **ii**   the area
   a   **b**   **c**

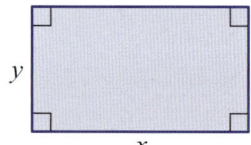
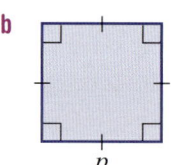
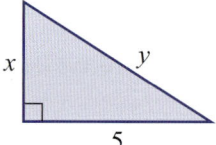

12   Decide if the following statements refer to the same or different expressions. If they are
        different, write an expression for each statement.
   a   **A**   Twice the sum of x and y
          B   The sum of $2x$ and y
   b   **A**   The difference between half of x and half of y
          B   Half of the difference between x and y

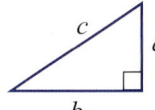

Reasoning

13 For a right-angled triangle with hypotenuse c and shorter sides a and b,
Pythagoras' theorem states that $c^2 = a^2 + b^2$.

   a Which of these two descriptions also describes Pythagoras' theorem?

      A The square of the hypotenuse is equal to the square of the sum of the
two shorter sides.

      B The square of the hypotenuse is equal to the sum of the squares of the two shorter sides.

   b For the incorrect description, write an equation to match.

Enrichment: The sum of the first n positive integers

14 The rule for the sum of the first n positive integers is given by:

    The product of n and one more than n all divided by 2.

   a Write an expression for the above description.

   b Test the expression to find these sums

      i $1 + 2 + 3 + 4$ $(n = 4)$

      ii $1 + 2 + 3 + ... + 10$ $(n = 10)$

   c Another way to describe the same expression is:

      The sum of half of the square of n and half of n.

    Write the expression for this description.

   d Check that your expressions in parts **a** and **c** are equivalent (the same) by testing $n = 4$ and
$n = 10$.

   e $\frac{1}{2}(n^2 + n)$ is also equivalent to the above two expressions. Write this expression in words.

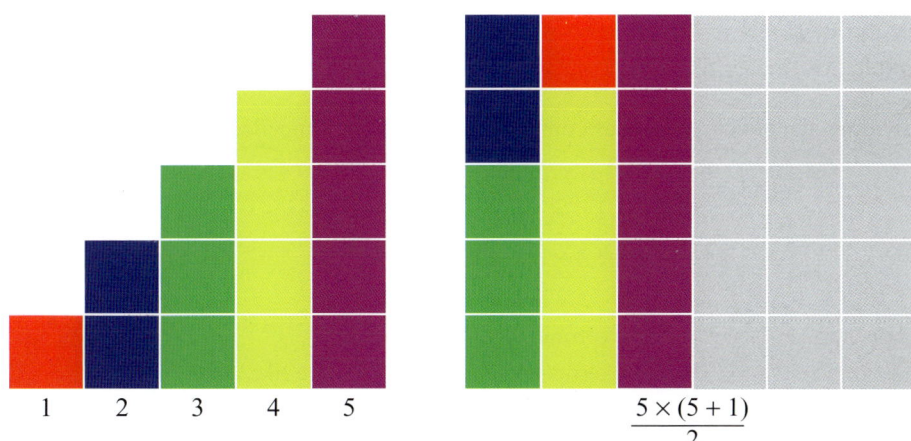

A diagram representing the sum of the first five positive integers arranged according to the expression
in question 14.

2.2 Simplifying algebraic expressions

Just as $2 + 2 + 2 + 2 = 4 \times 2$, so $x + x + x + x = 4 \times x$ or $4x$.
We say that the expression $x + x + x + x$ is simplified to $4x$.
Similarly, $3x + 5x = 8x$ and $8x - 3x = 5x$.
All these expressions have like terms and can be simplified
to an expression with a smaller number of terms.
A single term such as $2 \times 5 \times x \div 10$ can also be simplified
using multiplication and division, so

$$2 \times 5 \times x \div 10 = \frac{10x}{10} = x.$$

Let's start: Are they equivalent?

All these expressions can be separated into two groups.
Group them so that the expressions in each group
are equivalent.

$$2x \qquad 2x - y \qquad 4x - x - x \qquad 10x - y - 8x$$

$$\frac{24x}{12} \qquad y + x - y + x \qquad 2 \times x - 1 \times y \qquad -y + 2x$$

$$0 + \frac{1}{2} \times 4x \qquad \frac{x}{\left(\frac{1}{2}\right)} + 0y \qquad \frac{6x^2}{3x} \qquad -1 \times y + \frac{x^2}{\frac{1}{2}x}$$

- The symbols for multiplication ($\times$) and division ($\div$) are usually not shown in simplified
  algebraic terms.
  For example: $5 \times a \times b = 5ab$ and $-7 \times x \div y^2 = -\dfrac{7x}{y^2}$

- When dividing algebraic expressions common factors can be cancelled.
  For example: $\dfrac{7x}{14} = \dfrac{x}{2}$, $\quad \dfrac{a^2b}{a} = \dfrac{\overset{1}{\cancel{a}} \times a \times b}{\underset{1}{\cancel{a}}} = ab$

  $\dfrac{7xy}{14y} = \dfrac{x}{2}$ $\quad$ and $\quad$ $\dfrac{15a^2b}{10a} = \dfrac{3 \times \cancel{5} \times a \times \cancel{a} \times b}{2 \times \cancel{5} \times \cancel{a}} = \dfrac{3ab}{2}$

- **Like terms** have the same variable (pronumeral) factors.
  - For example: $5x$ and $7x$ are like terms and $3a^2b$ and $-2a^2b$ are like terms
  - Since $a \times b = b \times a$ then ab and ba are also like terms
- The pronumeral part of a term is often written in alphabetical order.
- Like terms can be collected (added and subtracted) to form a single term.
  For example: $5ab + 8ab = 13ab$
  $\qquad\qquad\quad 4x^2y - 2yx^2 = 2x^2y$
- **Unlike terms** do not have the same pronumeral factors.
  For example: $5x$, x^2, xy and $\dfrac{4xyz}{5}$ are all unlike terms.

Example 4 Multiplying algebraic terms

Simplify the following.

a $3 \times 2b$

b $-2a \times 3ab$

SOLUTION	EXPLANATION
a $3 \times 2b = 3 \times 2 \times b$ $\quad\quad\quad = 6b$	Multiply the coefficients.
b $-2a \times 3ab = -2 \times 3 \times a \times a \times b$ $\quad\quad\quad\quad\quad = -6a^2b$	Multiply the coefficients and simplify.

Example 5 Dividing algebraic terms

Simplify the following.

a $\dfrac{6ab}{18b}$

b $12a^2b \div 3ab$

SOLUTION	EXPLANATION
a $\dfrac{^1 6a b^{\,1}}{_3 18\, b_{\,1}} = \dfrac{a}{3}$	Deal with numerals and promumerals separately, cancelling where possible.
b $12a^2b \div 3ab = \dfrac{^4 12\, a^{2\,1} b^{\,1}}{_1 3\, a_{\,1} b_{\,1}}$ $\quad\quad\quad\quad\quad = 4a$	Write as a fraction first. Cancel where possible, recall $a^2 = a \times a$.

Example 6 Collecting like terms

Simplify the following by collecting like terms.

a $3x + 4 - 2x$

b $3x + 2y + 4x + 7y$

c $8ab^2 - 9ab - ab^2 + 3ba$

SOLUTION	EXPLANATION
a $3x + 4 - 2x = 3x - 2x + 4$ $\quad\quad\quad\quad = x + 4$	Collect like terms ($3x$ and $-2x$). The sign belongs to the term that follows. Combine their coefficients $3 - 2 = 1$.
b $3x + 2y + 4x + 7y = 3x + 4x + 2y + 7y$ $\quad\quad\quad\quad\quad\quad\quad = 7x + 9y$	Collect like terms and combine their coefficients.
c $8ab^2 - 9ab - ab^2 + 3ba$ $= 8ab^2 - ab^2 - 9ab + 3ab$ $= 7ab^2 - 6ab$	Collect like terms. Remember $ab = ba$ and $ab^2 = 1ab^2$. $8 - 1 = 7$ and $-9 + 3 = -6$

Exercise 2B

1 Write the missing word/expression.
  a Like terms have the same _____ factors.
  b $3x + 2x$ simplifies to _____.
  c $3a^2b$ and $2a$ are _____ terms.

2 Simplify these fractions.
  a $\dfrac{4}{6}$ **b** $\dfrac{20}{8}$ **c** $\dfrac{30}{10}$ **d** $\dfrac{8}{40}$

  e $\dfrac{-4}{14}$ **f** $\dfrac{-5}{100}$ **g** $\dfrac{-22}{106}$ **h** $\dfrac{-408}{24}$

3 Decide if the following pairs of terms are like terms.
  a $4ab$ and $3ab$ **b** $2x$ and $7xy$ **c** 5 and $4m$
  d $3t$ and $-6tw$ **e** $7yz$ and yz **f** $2mn$ and $9nm$
  g $5a$ and a **h** $3x^2y$ and $7xy^2$ **i** $4ab^2$ and $-3b^2a$

Example 4a

4 Simplify the following.
  a $5 \times 2m$ **b** $2 \times 6b$ **c** $3 \times 5p$ **d** $3x \times 2y$
  e $3p \times 6r$ **f** $4m \times 4n$ **g** $-2x \times 7y$ **h** $5m \times (-3n)$
  i $-4c \times 3d$ **j** $2a \times 3b \times 5$ **k** $-4r \times 3 \times 2s$ **l** $5j \times (-4) \times 2k$

Example 4b

5 Simplify the following.
  a $4n \times 6n$ **b** $-3q \times q$ **c** $5s \times 2s$
  d $7a \times 3ab$ **e** $5mn \times (-3n)$ **f** $-3gh \times (-6h)$
  g $3xy \times 4xy$ **h** $-4ab \times (-2ab)$ **i** $-2mn \times 3mn$

Example 5a

6 Simplify the following by cancelling.
  a $\dfrac{8b}{2}$ **b** $\dfrac{-2a}{6}$ **c** $\dfrac{4ab}{6}$ **d** $\dfrac{3mn}{6n}$ **e** $\dfrac{-5xy}{20y}$
  f $\dfrac{10st}{6t}$ **g** $\dfrac{u^2v}{u}$ **h** $\dfrac{5r^2s^2}{8rs}$ **i** $\dfrac{5ab^2}{9b}$ **j** $\dfrac{7y}{y^2}$

Example 5b

7 Simplify the following by first writing in fraction form.
  a $2x \div 5$ **b** $-4 \div (-3a)$ **c** $11mn \div 3$
  d $12ab \div 2$ **e** $-10 \div (2gh)$ **f** $8x \div x$
  g $-3xy \div (yx)$ **h** $7mn \div (3m)$ **i** $-27pq \div (6p)$
  j $24ab^2 \div (8ab)$ **k** $25x^2y \div (-5xy)$ **l** $9m^2n \div (18mn)$

8 Simplify the following.
  a $x \times 4 \div y$ **b** $5 \times p \div 2$ **c** $6 \times (-a) \times b$
  d $a \times (-3) \div (2b)$ **e** $-7 \div (5m) \times n$ **f** $5s \div (2t) \times 4$
  g $6 \times 4mn \div (3m)$ **h** $8x \times 3y \div (8x)$ **i** $3ab \times 12bc \div (9abc)$
  j $4x \times 3xy \div (2x)$ **k** $10m \times 4mn \div (8mn)$ **l** $3pq \times pq \div p$

Fluency

Example 6a 9 Simplify the following by collecting like terms.

a $3a + 7a$ b $4n + 3n$ c $12y - 4y$

d $5x + 2x + 4x$ e $6ab - 2ab - ba$ f $7mn + 2mn - 2mn$

g $4y - 3y + 8$ h $7x + 5 - 4x$ i $6xy + xy + 4y$

j $5ab + 3 + 7ba$ k $2 - 5m - m$ l $4 - 2x + x$

Example 6b 10 Simplify the following by collecting like terms.

a $2a + 4b + 3a + 5b$ b $4x + 3y + 2x + 2y$

c $6t + 5 - 2t + 1$ d $5x + 1 + 6x + 3$

e $xy + 8x + 4xy - 4x$ f $3mn - 4 + 4nm - 5$

g $4ab + 2a + ab - 3a$ h $3st - 8ts + 2st + 3ts$

Example 6c 11 Simplify the following by collecting like terms.

a $5xy^2 - 4xy^2$ b $3a^2b + 4ba^2$

c $8m^2n - 6nm^2 + m^2n$ d $7p^2q^2 - 2p^2q^2 - 4p^2q^2$

e $2x^2y - 4xy^2 + 5yx^2$ f $10rs^2 + 3rs^2 - 6r^2s$

g $x^2 - 7x - 3x^2$ h $a^2b - 4ab^2 + 3a^2b + b^2a$

i $10pq^2 - 2qp - 3pq^2 - 6pq$ j $12m^2n^2 - 2mn^2 - 4m^2n^2 + mn^2$

Problem-solving

12 A farmer has x pigs and y chickens.

a Write an expression for the total number of heads.

b Write an expression for the total number of legs.

13 A rectangle's length is three times its width x metres. Write an expression for:

a the rectangle's perimeter

b the rectangle's area.

14 A right-angled triangle has side lengths $5x$ cm, $12x$ cm and $13x$ cm. Write an expression for:

a the triangle's perimeter

b the triangle's area.

15 The average (mean) mark on a test for 20 students is x. Another student who scores 75 in the test is added to the list. Write an expression for the new average (mean).

16 Decide if the following are always true for all real numbers.

a $a \times b = b \times a$

b $a \div b = b \div a$

c $a + b = b + a$

d $a - b = b - a$

e $a^2 b = b^2 a$

f $1 \div \dfrac{1}{a} = a$

17 The diagram shows the route taken by a salesperson who travels from A to D via B and C.

a If the salesperson then returns directly to A, write an expression (in simplest form) for the total distance travelled.

b If $y = x + 1$, write an expression for the total distance the salesperson travels in terms of x only. Simplify your expression.

c When $y = x + 1$, how much would the distance have been reduced by (in terms of x) if the salesperson had travelled directly from A to D and straight back to A?

Enrichment: Higher powers

18 For this question, note this example:

$$\frac{\cancel{2}a^3}{\cancel{4}a} = \frac{\cancel{2}_1 \times a \times a \times \cancel{a}_1}{{}^2\cancel{4} \times \cancel{a}_1} = \frac{a^2}{2}$$

Simplify these expressions with higher powers.

a $\dfrac{a^4}{a}$

b $\dfrac{3b^3}{9b}$

c $\dfrac{4ab^3}{12ab}$

d $\dfrac{6a^4 b^2}{16a^3 b}$

e $-\dfrac{2a^5}{3a^2}$

f $-\dfrac{8a^5}{20a^7}$

g $\dfrac{4a^3}{10a^8}$

h $\dfrac{3a^3 b}{12ab^4}$

i $\dfrac{15a^4 b^2}{5ab}$

j $\dfrac{28a^3 b^5}{7a^4 b^2}$

k $\dfrac{2a^5 b^2}{6a^2 b^3}$

l $-\dfrac{5a^3 b^7}{10a^2 b^{10}}$

2.3 Expanding algebraic expressions

A mental technique to find the product of 5 and 23 might be to find 5×20 and add 5×3 to give 115. This technique uses the distributive law over addition.

$$\text{So } 5 \times 23 = 5 \times (20 + 3)$$
$$= 5 \times 20 + 5 \times 3$$

Since variables (pronumerals) represent numbers, the same law applies for algebraic expressions.

➡ Let's start: Rectangular distributions

This diagram shows two joined rectangles with the given dimensions.

- Find two different ways to write expressions for the combined area of the two rectangles.
- Compare your two expressions. Are they equivalent?

This diagram shows a rectangle of length x reduced by a length of 3.

- Find two different ways to write expressions for the remaining area (shaded).
- Compare your two expressions. Are they equivalent?

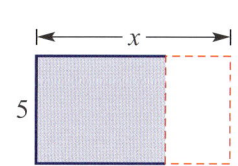

Examples of the distributive law can often be found in everyday tasks.

■ The **distributive law** is used to expand and remove brackets.
- A term on the outside of the brackets is multiplied by each term inside the brackets.

$$a(b + c) = ab + ac \quad \text{or} \quad a(b - c) = ab - ac$$
$$-a(b + c) = -ab - ac \quad \text{or} \quad -a(b - c) = -ab + ac$$

- If the number in front of the bracket is negative, the sign of each of the terms inside the brackets will change when expanded.

For example: $-2(x - 3) = -2x + 6$ since $-2 \times x = -2x$ and $-2 \times (-3) = 6$

Example 7 Expanding simple expressions with brackets

Expand the following.

a $3(x + 4)$ **b** $5(x - 11)$ **c** $-2(x - 5)$

SOLUTION   **EXPLANATION**

a $3(x + 4) = 3x + 12$ $3 \times x = 3x$ and $3 \times 4 = 12$

b $5(x - 11) = 5x - 55$ $5 \times x = 5x$ and $5 \times (-11) = -55$

c $-2(x - 5) = -2x + 10$ $-2 \times x = -2x$ and $-2 \times (-5) = +10$

Example 8 Expanding brackets and simplifying

Expand the following.

a $4(x + 3y)$

b $-2x(4x - 3)$

SOLUTION

a $4(x + 3y) = 4 \times x + 4 \times 3y$
$\qquad\qquad = 4x + 12y$

b $-2x(4x - 3) = -2x \times 4x + -2x \times (-3)$
$\qquad\qquad\quad = -8x^2 + 6x$

EXPLANATION

Multiply each term inside the brackets by 4.
$4 \times x = 4x$ and $4 \times 3 \times y = 12y$.

Each term inside the brackets is multiplied by $-2x$.
$-2 \times 4 = -8$ and $x \times x = x^2$ and $-2 \times (-3) = 6$

Example 9 Simplifying by removing brackets

Expand the following and collect like terms.

a $2 - 3(x - 4)$

b $3(x + 2y) - (3x + y)$

SOLUTION

a $2 - 3(x - 4) = 2 - (3x - 12)$
$\qquad\qquad\quad = 2 - 3x + 12$
$\qquad\qquad\quad = 14 - 3x$

b $3(x + 2y) - (3x + y)$
$= 3x + 6y - 3x - y$
$= 3x - 3x + 6y - y$
$= 5y$

EXPLANATION

$3(x - 4) = 3x - 12$.
$-(3x - 12) = -1(3x - 12)$, so multiplying by negative 1 changes the sign of each term inside the brackets.

$-(3x + y) = -1(3x + y) = -3x - y$.
Collect like terms and simplify.

Exercise 2C

1 This diagram shows two joined rectangles with the given dimensions.

   a Write an expression for the area of:

      i the larger rectangle (x by 5)   **ii** the smaller rectangle (2 by 5)

   b Use your answers from part **a** to find the combined area of both rectangles.

   c Write an expression for the total side length of the side involving x.

   d Use your answer from part **c** to find the combined area of both rectangles.

   e Complete this statement: $5(x + 2) = $ _____ + _____

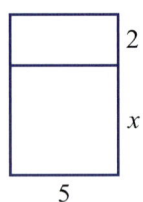

Understanding

2 **a** Substitute the value $x = 5$ into these expressions.

    i $-2(x + 3)$ **ii** $-2x + 6$

  b Do your answers from part **a** suggest that $-2(x + 3) = -2x + 6$? When expanded what should $-2(x + 3)$ equal?

  c Substitute the value $x = 10$ into these expressions.

    i $-3(x - 1)$ **ii** $-3x - 3$

  d Do your answers from part **c** suggest that $-3(x - 1) = -3x - 3$? When expanded what should $-3(x - 1)$ equal?

ple 7a,b **3** Expand the following.

  a $2(x + 3)$ **b** $5(x + 12)$ **c** $2(x - 7)$ **d** $7(x - 9)$

  e $3(2 + x)$ **f** $7(3 - x)$ **g** $4(7 - x)$ **h** $2(x - 6)$

mple 7c **4** Expand the following.

  a $-3(x + 2)$ **b** $-2(x + 11)$ **c** $-5(x - 3)$ **d** $-6(x - 6)$

  e $-4(2 - x)$ **f** $-13(5 + x)$ **g** $-20(9 + x)$ **h** $-300(1 - x)$

ample 8 **5** Expand the following.

  a $2(a + b)$ **b** $5(a - 2)$ **c** $3(m - 4)$ **d** $-8(2x + 5)$

  e $-3(4x + 5)$ **f** $-4x(x - 2y)$ **g** $-9t(2y - 3)$ **h** $a(3a + 4)$

  i $d(2d - 5)$ **j** $-2b(3b - 5)$ **k** $2x(4x + 1)$ **l** $5y(1 - 3y)$

mple 9a **6** Expand the following and collect like terms.

  a $3 + 2(x + 4)$ **b** $4 + 6(x - 3)$ **c** $2 + 5(3x - 1)$ **d** $5 + (3x - 4)$

  e $3 + 4(x - 2)$ **f** $7 + 2(x - 3)$ **g** $2 - 3(x + 2)$ **h** $1 - 5(x + 4)$

  i $5 - (x - 6)$ **j** $9 - (x - 3)$ **k** $5 - (3 + 2x)$ **l** $4 - (3x - 2)$

mple 9b **7** Expand the following and collect like terms.

  a $2(x + 3) + 3(x + 2)$ **b** $2(x - 3) + 2(x - 1)$ **c** $3(2x + 1) + 5(x - 1)$

  d $4(3x + 2) + 5(x - 3)$ **e** $-3(2x + 1) + (2x - 3)$ **f** $-2(x + 2) + 3(x - 1)$

  g $2(4x - 3) - 2(3x - 1)$ **h** $-3(4x + 3) - 5(3x - 1)$ **i** $-(x + 3) - 3(x + 5)$

  j $-2(2x - 4) - 3(3x + 5)$ **k** $3(3x - 1) - 2(2 - x)$ **l** $-4(5 - x) - (2x - 5)$

8 A rectangle's length is 4 more than its width, x. Find an expanded expression for its area.

9 Find the area of these basic shapes in expanded form.

a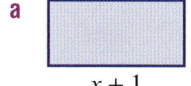

b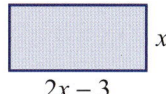

c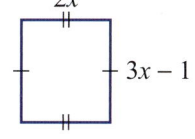

d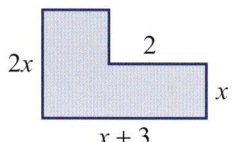

e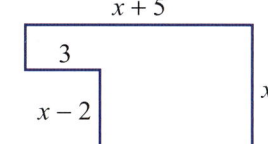

f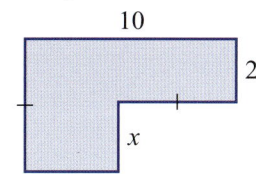

10 Gary gets a bonus $20 for every computer he sells over and above his quota of 10 per week. If he sells n computers in a week and $n > 10$, write an expression for Gary's bonus in that week (in expanded form).

11 Jill pays tax at 20c in the dollar for every dollar earned over $10 000. If Jill earns x and $x > 10 000$, write an expression for Jill's tax in expanded form.

12 Identify the errors in these expressions then write out the correct expansion.

    a $2(x + 6) = 2x + 6$ **b** $x(x - 4) = 2x - 4x$

    c $-3(x + 4) = -3x + 12$ **d** $-7(x - 7) = -7x - 49$

    e $5 - 2(x - 7) = 5 - 2x - 14$ **f** $4(x - 2) - 3(x + 2) = 4x - 8 - 3x + 6$

                  $= -9 - 2x$ $= x - 2$

13 In Year 7 and 8 we explored how to use the distributive law to find products mentally.

    For example: $7 \times 104 = 7 \times (100 + 4)$ and $4 \times 298 = 4 \times (300 - 2)$

                      $= 7 \times 100 + 7 \times 4$ $= 4 \times 300 - 4 \times 2$

                      $= 728$ $= 1192$

    Use the distributive law to evaluate these products mentally.

    a 6×52 **b** 9×102 **c** 5×91 **d** 4×326

    e 3×99 **f** 7×395 **g** 9×990 **h** 6×879

Enrichment: Pronumerals and taxes

14 A progressive income tax system increases the tax rate for higher incomes. Here is an example.

Income	Tax
0 – $20 000	$0
$20 001 – $50 000	$0 + 20% of income above $20 000
$50 001 – $100 000	a + 30% of income above $50 000
$100 000 –	b + 50% of income above $100 000

    a Find the values of a and b in the above table.

    b Find the tax payable for these incomes.

        i $35 000   **ii** $72 000   **iii** $160 000

    c Find an expression for the tax payable for an income of x if:

        i $0 \le x \le 20 000$

        ii $20 000 < x \le 50 000$

        iii $50 000 < x \le 100 000$

        iv $x > 100 000$

    d Check that you have fully expanded and simplified your expressions for part **c**. Add steps if required.

    e Use your expressions from parts **c** and **d** to check your answers to part **b** by choosing a particular income amount and checking against the table above.

2.4 Solving linear equations

A mathematical statement containing an equals sign, a left-hand side and a right-hand side is called an equation. $5 = 10 \div 2$, $3x = 9$, $x^2 + 1 = 10$ and $\dfrac{1}{x} = \dfrac{x}{5}$ are examples of equations. Linear equations can be written in the form $ax + b = c$ where the power of x is 1. $4x - 1 = 6$, $3 = 2(x + 1)$ and $\dfrac{5x}{3} = \dfrac{2x + 1}{4}$ are all linear equations. Equations are solved by finding the value of the variable (or pronumeral) that makes the equation true. This can be done by inspection for very simple linear equations (for example, if $3x = 15$ then $x = 5$ since $3 \times 5 = 15$). More complex linear equations can be solved through a series of steps where each step produces an equivalent equation.

Let's start: Why are they equivalent?

The following list of equations can be categorised into two groups. The equations in each group should be equivalent.

$$5x = 20 \qquad 2x - 1 = -3 \qquad x = 4 \qquad 1 - x = -3$$

$$7x = -7 \qquad 3 - 5x = -17 \qquad \dfrac{8x}{5} - \dfrac{3x}{5} = -1 \qquad x = -1$$

- Discuss how you divided the equations into the two groups.
- How can you check to see if the equations in each group are equivalent?

Key Ideas

- **Equivalent equations** are created by:
  - adding a number to or subtracting a number from both sides of the equation
  - multiplying or dividing both sides of the equation by the same number (not including 0).
- Solve a linear equation by creating equivalent equations using inverse operations (backtracking).
- The solution to an equation can be checked by substituting the solution into the original equation and checking that both sides are equal.

Example 10 Solving simple linear equations

Solve each of the following equations.

a $\quad 2x + 3 = 4$
b $\quad \dfrac{x}{4} - 3 = 7$
c $\quad 5 - 2x = 12$

d $\quad \dfrac{2x}{3} + 5 = 7$
e $\quad \dfrac{2x + 4}{9} = 2$

SOLUTION   **EXPLANATION**

a $\quad 2x + 3 = 4$

$\qquad 2x = 1$
$\qquad x = \dfrac{1}{2}$

Subtract 3 from both sides.
Divide both sides by 2.

Check: $2 \times (\dfrac{1}{2}) + 3 = 4$

Check the answer by substituting $x = \dfrac{1}{2}$ into the original equation.

b $\dfrac{x}{4} - 3 = 7$

$\qquad \dfrac{x}{4} = 10$ 　　　　　　　　Add 3 to both sides.

$\qquad x = 40$ 　　　　　　　　Multiply both sides by 4.

Check: $\dfrac{(40)}{4} - 3 = 10 - 3 = 7$ 　　Check the answer by substituting $x = 40$ into $\dfrac{x}{4} - 3$.
Since this equals 7, $x = 40$ is the solution.

c $5 - 2x = 12$

$\qquad -2x = 7$ 　　　　　　　　Subtract 5 from both sides.

$\qquad x = \dfrac{-7}{2}$ 　　　　　　　Divide both sides by -2.

Check: $5 - 2 \times \left(\dfrac{-7}{2} \right) = 5 + 7 = 12$ 　Check the answer.

d $\dfrac{2x}{3} + 5 = 7$

$\qquad \dfrac{2x}{3} = 2$ 　　　　　　　Subtract 5 from both sides first then multiply both sides by 3.

$\qquad 2x = 6$

$\qquad x = 3$ 　　　　　　　　Divide both sides by 2 and check the answer.

Check: $\dfrac{2 \times (3)}{3} + 5 = 2 + 5 = 7$

e $\dfrac{2x + 4}{9} = 2$

$\qquad 2x + 4 = 18$ 　　　　　　　Multiply both sides by 9 first to eliminate the fraction.

$\qquad 2x = 14$ 　　　　　　　　Solve the remaining equation by subtracting 4 from both sides and then dividing both sides by 2.

$\qquad x = 7$

Check: $\dfrac{2 \times (7) + 4}{9} = \dfrac{18}{9} = 2$ 　Check the answer.

Exercise 2D

1 Write down the value of x that is the solution to these equations. No written working is required.

　a $3x = 9$ 　　　**b** $\dfrac{x}{4} = 10$ 　　　**c** $x + 7 = 12$ 　　　**d** $x - 7 = -1$

2 Use a 'guess and check' (trial and error) method to solve these equations. No written working is required.

　a $2x + 1 = 7$ 　　**b** $11x - 1 = 21$ 　　**c** $4 - x = 2$ 　　**d** $\dfrac{x}{3} + 1 = 5$

　e $2 + \dfrac{x}{3} = 6$ 　**f** $3x - 1 = -16$ 　**g** $\dfrac{x + 1}{7} = 1$ 　**h** $\dfrac{3x + 2}{5} = 1$

3 Which of the following equations are equivalent to $3x = 12$?

　a $3x + 1 = 13$ 　**b** $3x - 1 = 12$ 　**c** $12x = 12$ 　　**d** $-3x = -12$

　e $\dfrac{3x}{4} = 3$ 　　**f** $x = 4$ 　　　**g** $\dfrac{3x}{5} = 10$ 　**h** $3x - x = 12 - x$

Understanding

10a **4** Solve each of the following equations. Check your answers.

a $2x + 5 = 9$ b $5a + 6 = 11$ c $3m - 4 = 8$

d $2x - 4 = -6$ e $2n + 13 = 7$ f $2x + 5 = -7$

g $2b + 15 = 7$ h $3y - 2 = -13$ i $3a + 2 = 7$

j $4b + 7 = 25$ k $24x - 2 = 10$ l $6x - 5 = 3$

m $7y - 3 = -8$ n $2a + \dfrac{1}{2} = \dfrac{1}{4}$ o $5n - \dfrac{1}{4} = -1$

10b **5** Solve each of the following equations.

a $\dfrac{x}{4} + 3 = 5$ b $\dfrac{x}{2} + 4 = 5$ c $\dfrac{b}{3} + 5 = 9$ d $\dfrac{t}{2} + 5 = 2$

e $\dfrac{a}{3} + 4 = 2$ f $\dfrac{y}{5} - 4 = 2$ g $\dfrac{x}{3} - 7 = -12$ h $\dfrac{s}{2} - 3 = -7$

i $\dfrac{x}{4} - 5 = -2$ j $\dfrac{m}{4} - 2 = 3$ k $1 - \dfrac{y}{5} = 2$ l $2 - \dfrac{x}{5} = 4$

10c **6** Solve each of the following equations.

a $12 - 2x = 18$ b $2 - 7x = 9$ c $15 - 5x = 5$ d $3 - 2x = -13$

e $2 - 5x = 9$ f $4 - 7x = 23$ g $5 - 8x = 2$ h $-3 - 4x = -10$

10d **7** Solve these equations.

a $\dfrac{2b}{3} = 6$ b $\dfrac{3x}{2} = 9$ c $\dfrac{4x}{3} = -9$ d $\dfrac{2x}{5} = -3$

e $\dfrac{3x}{4} = \dfrac{1}{2}$ f $\dfrac{5n}{4} = -\dfrac{1}{5}$ g $\dfrac{2x}{3} - 1 = 7$ h $\dfrac{3x}{4} - 2 = 7$

i $3 + \dfrac{2x}{3} = -3$ j $5 + \dfrac{3d}{2} = -7$ k $11 - \dfrac{3f}{2} = 2$ l $3 - \dfrac{4z}{3} = 5$

10e **8** Solve each of the following equations. Check your answers.

a $\dfrac{x + 1}{3} = 4$ b $\dfrac{x + 4}{2} = 5$ c $\dfrac{4 + y}{3} = -2$ d $\dfrac{6 + b}{2} = -3$

e $\dfrac{1 - a}{2} = 3$ f $\dfrac{5 - x}{3} = 2$ g $\dfrac{3m - 1}{5} = 4$ h $\dfrac{2x + 2}{3} = 4$

i $\dfrac{7x - 3}{3} = 9$ j $\dfrac{3b - 6}{2} = 5$ k $\dfrac{4 - 2y}{6} = 3$ l $\dfrac{9 - 5t}{3} = -2$

9 For each of the following, write an equation and solve it to find the unknown value. Use x as the unknown value.

a If 8 is added to a certain number, the result is 34.

b Seven less than a certain number is 21.

c I think of a number, double it and add 4. The result is 10.

d I think of a number, halve it and subtract 4. The result is 10.

e Four less than three times a number is 20.

f A number is multiplied by 7 and the product is divided by 3. The final result is 8.

g Five Easter eggs are added to my initial collection of Easter eggs. I share them between myself and 2 friends and each person gets exactly four. How many were there initially?

h My weekly pay is increased by $200 per week. Half of my pay now goes to pay the rent and $100 to buy groceries. If this leaves me with $450, what was my original weekly pay?

10 Describe the error made in each of these incorrect solutions.

a $2x - 1 = 4$
$x - 1 = 2$
$x = 3$

b $\dfrac{5x + 2}{3} = 7$
$\dfrac{5x}{3} = 5$
$5x = 15$
$x = 3$

c $5 - x = 12$
$x = 7$

d $\dfrac{x}{3} - 4 = 2$
$x - 4 = 6$
$x = 10$

11 An equation like $2(x + 3) = 8$ can be solved without expanding the brackets. The first step is to divide both sides by 2.

a Use this approach to solve these equations.

   i $3(x - 1) = 12$ **ii** $4(x + 2) = -4$ **iii** $7(5x + 1) = 14$

   iv $5(1 - x) = -10$ **v** $-2(3x + 1) = 3$ **vi** $-5(1 - 4x) = 1$

b By considering your solutions to the equations in part **a**, when do you think this method is most appropriate?

Enrichment: Changing the subject

12 Make a the subject of each of the following equations.

a $a - b = c$ **b** $2a + b = c$ **c** $c - ab = 2d$ **d** $b = \dfrac{a}{c} - d$

e $\dfrac{ab}{c} = -d$ **f** $\dfrac{2a}{b} = \dfrac{1}{c}$ **g** $\dfrac{2ab}{c} - 3 = -d$ **h** $b - \dfrac{ac}{2d} = 3$

i $\dfrac{a + b}{c} = d$ **j** $\dfrac{b - a}{c} = -d$ **k** $\dfrac{ad - 6c}{2b} = e$ **l** $\dfrac{d - 4ac}{e} = 3f$

2.5 Equations with brackets and variables on both sides

More complex linear equations may have variables on both sides of the equation and/or brackets. Examples are $3x = 5x - 1$ or $4(x + 2) = 5x$. Brackets can be removed by expanding and equations with variables on both sides can be solved by collecting like terms using addition and subtraction.

Let's start: Steps in the wrong order

The steps to solve $3(2 - x) = -2(2x - 1)$ are listed here in the incorrect order.

$$3(2 - x) = -2(2x - 1)$$
$$x = -4$$
$$6 + x = 2$$
$$6 - 3x = -4x + 2$$

- Arrange them in the correct order working from top to bottom.
- By considering all the steps in the correct order, explain what has happened in each step.

Solving problems in algebra (like many other procedures and puzzles) requires steps to be done in the right order.

Key ideas

- Equations with brackets can be solved by firstly expanding the brackets.
  For example: $3(x + 1) = 2$ becomes $3x + 3 = 2$.
- If an equation has variables on both sides, collect to one side by adding or subtracting one of the terms.
  For example: $3x + 4 = 2x - 3$ becomes $x + 4 = -3$ by subtracting $2x$ from both sides.

Example 11 Solving equations with brackets and variables on both sides

Solve each of the following equations.

a $2(3x - 4) = 11$ **b** $2(x + 3) - 4x = 8$

c $5x - 2 = 3x - 4$ **d** $3(2x + 4) = 8(x + 1)$

SOLUTION

a $2(3x - 4) = 11$
$$6x - 8 = 11$$
$$6x = 19$$
$$x = \frac{19}{6} \text{ or } 3\frac{1}{6}$$

EXPLANATION

Expand the brackets,
$2(3x - 4) = 2 \times 3x + 2 \times (-4)$.
Add 8 to both sides then divide both sides by 6,
leaving your answer in fraction form.

b $2(x + 3) - 4x = 8$

$\qquad$ $2x + 6 - 4x = 8$ $\qquad$ Expand the brackets and collect any like terms,

$\qquad$ $-2x + 6 = 8$ $\qquad$ i.e. $2x - 4x = -2x$.

$\qquad$ $-2x = 2$ $\qquad$ Subtract 6 from both sides.

$\qquad$ $x = -1$ $\qquad$ Divide by -2.

c $5x - 2 = 3x - 4$

$\qquad$ $2x - 2 = -4$ $\qquad$ Collect x terms on one side by subtracting $3x$ from

$\qquad$ $2x = -2$ $\qquad$ both sides.

$\qquad$ $x = -1$ $\qquad$ Add 2 to both sides and then divide both sides by 2.

d $3(2x + 4) = 8(x + 1)$

$\qquad$ $6x + 12 = 8x + 8$ $\qquad$ Expand the brackets on each side.

$\qquad$ $12 = 2x + 8$ $\qquad$ Subtract $6x$ from both sides, alternatively subtract $8x$

$\qquad$ $4 = 2x$ $\qquad$ to end up with $-2x + 12 = 8$. (Subtracting $6x$ keeps

$\qquad$ $2 = x$ $\qquad$ the x-coefficient positive.)

$\qquad$ $\therefore \quad x = 2$ $\qquad$ Solve the equation and make x the subject.

Exercise 2E

Understanding

1 Expand these expressions and simplify.

$\quad$ **a** $3(x - 4) + x$ $\qquad$ **b** $2(1 - x) + 2x$ $\qquad$ **c** $3(x - 1) + 2(x - 3)$

$\quad$ **d** $5(1 - 2x) - 2 + x$ $\qquad$ **e** $2 - 3(3 - x)$ $\qquad$ **f** $7(2 - x) - 5(x - 2)$

2 Show the next step only for the given equations and instructions.

$\quad$ **a** $2(x + 3) = 5$ $\qquad\qquad$ (expand the brackets)

$\quad$ **b** $5 + 2(x - 1) = 7$ $\qquad\quad$ (expand the brackets)

$\quad$ **c** $3x + 1 = x - 6$ $\qquad\qquad$ (subtract x from both sides)

$\quad$ **d** $4x - 3 = 2x + 1$ $\qquad\quad$ (subtract $2x$ from both sides)

Fluency

Example 11a $\quad$ **3** Solve each of the following equations by first expanding the brackets.

$\quad$ **a** $2(x + 3) = 11$ $\qquad$ **b** $5(a + 3) = 8$ $\qquad$ **c** $3(m + 4) = 31$

$\quad$ **d** $5(y - 7) = -12$ $\qquad$ **e** $4(p - 5) = -35$ $\qquad$ **f** $2(k - 5) = 9$

$\quad$ **g** $4(5 - b) = 18$ $\qquad$ **h** $2(1 - m) = 13$ $\qquad$ **i** $5(3 - x) = 19$

$\quad$ **j** $7(2a + 1) = 8$ $\qquad$ **k** $4(3x - 2) = 30$ $\qquad$ **l** $3(3n - 2) = 0$

$\quad$ **m** $5(3 - 2x) = 6$ $\qquad$ **n** $6(1 - 2y) = -8$ $\qquad$ **o** $4(3 - 2a) = 13$

Example 11b $\quad$ **4** Expand and simplify then solve each of the following equations.

$\quad$ **a** $(x + 4) + 2x = 7$ $\qquad\qquad$ **b** $2(x - 3) - 3x = 4$

$\quad$ **c** $4(x - 1) + x - 1 = 0$ $\qquad\quad$ **d** $3(2x + 3) - 1 - 4x = 4$

$\quad$ **e** $3(x - 4) + 2(x + 1) = 15$ $\qquad$ **f** $2(x + 1) - 3(x - 2) = 8$

$\quad$ **g** $6(x + 3) + 2x = 26$ $\qquad\quad$ **h** $3(x + 2) + 5x = 46$

$\quad$ **i** $3(2x - 3) + x = 12$ $\qquad\quad$ **j** $4(3x + 1) + 3x = 19$

Example 11c **5** Solve each of the following equations.

a $5b = 4b + 1$ b $8a = 7a - 4$ c $4t = 10 - t$

d $3m - 8 = 2m$ e $5x - 3 = 4x + 5$ f $9a + 3 = 8a + 6$

g $12x - 3 = 10x + 5$ h $3y + 6 = 2 - y$ i $5m - 4 = 1 - 6m$

Example 11d **6** Solve each of the following equations.

a $5(x - 2) = 2x - 13$ b $3(a + 1) = a + 10$

c $3(y + 4) = y - 6$ d $2(x + 5) = x - 4$

e $5b - 4 = 6(b + 2)$ f $2(4m - 5) = 4m + 2$

g $3(2a - 3) = 5(a + 2)$ h $4(x - 3) = 3(3x + 1)$

i $3(x - 2) = 5(x + 4)$ j $3(n - 2) = 4(n + 5)$

k $2(a + 5) = -2(2a + 3)$ l $-4(x + 2) = 3(2x + 1)$

7 Using x for the unknown number, write down an equation then solve it to find the number.

a The product of 2 and 3 more than a number is 7.

b The product of 3 and 4 less than a number is -4.

c When 2 less than 3 lots of a number is doubled the result is 5.

d When 5 more than 2 lots of a number is tripled the result is 10.

e 2 more than 3 lots of a number is equivalent to 8 lots of the number.

f 2 more than 3 times the number is equivalent to 1 less than 5 times the number.

g 1 less than a doubled number is equivalent to 5 more than 3 lots of the number.

8 Since Tara started work her original hourly wage has been tripled, then decreased by $6. It is now to be doubled so that she gets $18 an hour. What was her original hourly wage?

9 At the start of lunch Jimmy and Jake each brought out a new bag of x marbles to play with their friends. By the end of lunch they were surprised to see they still had the same number as each other even though overall Jimmy had gained 5 marbles and Jake had ended up with the double of 3 less than his original amount. How many marbles were originally in the bags?

10   Consider the equation $3(x - 2) = 9$.
   a   Solve the equation by firstly dividing both sides by 3.
   b   Solve the equation by firstly expanding the brackets.
   c   Which of the above two methods is preferable and why?

11   Consider the equation $3(x - 2) = 7$.
   a   Solve the equation by firstly dividing both sides by 3.
   b   Solve the equation by firstly expanding the brackets.
   c   Which of the above two methods is preferable and why?

12   Consider the equation $3x + 1 = 5x - 7$.
   a   Solve the equation by firstly subtracting $3x$ from both sides.
   b   Solve the equation by firstly subtracting $5x$ from both sides.
   c   Which method above do you prefer and why? Describe the differences.

Enrichment: Literal solutions with factorisation

13   Literal equations contain a variable (such as x) and other variables (or pronumerals) such as a, b and c. To solve such an equation for x, factorisation can be used as shown here.

$$ax = bx + c$$
$$ax - bx = c \qquad \text{Subtract } bx \text{ from both sides}$$
$$x(a - b) = c \qquad \text{Factorise by taking out } x$$
$$x = \frac{c}{a - b} \qquad \text{Divide both sides by } (a - b)$$

Solve each of the following for x in terms of the other pronumerals by using factorisation.

   a $ax = bx + d$
   b $ax + 1 = bx + 3$
   c $5ax = bx + c$
   d $3ax + 1 = 4bx - 5$
   e $ax - bc = xb - ac$
   f $a(x - b) = x - b$
   g $ax - bx - c = d + bd$
   h $a(x + b) = b(x - c) - x$

Using a CAS calculator 2.5: Solving equations

This activity is on the companion website in the form of a printable PDF.

2.6 Solving word problems

Many types of problems can be solved by writing and solving linear equations. Often problems are expressed only in words. Reading and understanding the problem, defining a variable and writing an equation become important steps in solving the problem.

Let's start: Too much television?

Three friends, Rick, Kate and Sue compare how much television they watch in a week at home. Kate watches 3 times the amount of television of Rick and Sue watches 4 hours less television than Kate. In total they watch 45 hours of television. Find the number of hours of television watched by Rick.

- Let x hours be the number of hours of television watched by Rick.
- Write expressions for the number of hours of television watched by Kate and by Sue.
- Write an equation to represent the information above.
- Solve the equation.
- Answer the question in the original problem.

- To solve a **word problem** using algebra:
  - Read the problem and find out what the question is asking for.
  - Define a variable and write a statement such as: 'Let x be the number of ......' The variable is often what you have been asked to find.
  - Write an equation using your defined variable.
  - Solve the equation.
  - Answer the question in words.

Example 12 Turning a word problem into an equation

Five less than a certain number is 9 less than three times the number. Write an equation and solve it to find the number.

SOLUTION	EXPLANATION
Let x be the number.	Define the unknown as a pronumeral.
$x - 5 = 3x - 9$	5 less than x is $x - 5$ and this equals 9 less than three
$-5 = 2x - 9$	times x, i.e. $3x - 9$.
$4 = 2x$	Subtract x from both sides and solve the equation.
$x = 2$	
The number is 2.	Write the answer in words.

Example 13 Solving word problems

Simon and Mike made 254 runs between them in a cricket match. If Mike made 68 more runs than Simon, how many runs did each of them make?

SOLUTION	EXPLANATION
Let the number of runs for Simon be r.	Define the unknown value as a pronumeral.
Number of runs Mike made is $r + 68$.	Write all other unknown values in terms of r.
$r + (r + 68) = 254$ $$2r + 68 = 254$$ $$2r = 186$$ $$r = 93$$	Write an equation: number of runs for Simon + number of runs for Mike = 254 Subtract 68 from both sides and then divide both sides by 2.
Simon made 93 runs and Mike made $93 + 68 = 161$ runs.	Express the answer in words.

Exercise 2F

Example 12 **1** For each of the following examples, make x the unknown number and write an equation.

    a Three less than a certain number is 9 less than four times the number.

    b Seven is added to a number and the result is then multiplied by 3. The result is 9.

    c I think of a number, take away 9, then multiply the result by 4. This gives an answer of 12.

    d A number when doubled results in a number that is 5 more than the number itself.

    e Eight less than a certain number is 2 more than three times the number.

Understanding

Example 13 **2** Leonie and Emma scored 28 goals between them in a netball match. Leonie scored 8 more goals than Emma.

    a Define a variable for the number of goals scored by Emma.

    b Write the number of goals scored by Leonie in terms of the variable in part **a**.

    c Write an equation in terms of your variable to represent the problem.

    d Solve the equation in part **c** to find the unknown value.

    e How many goals did each of them score?

Fluency

3 A rectangle is four times as long as it is wide and its perimeter is 560 cm.
   a Define a variable for the unknown width.
   b Write an expression for the length in terms of your variable in part **a**.
   c Write an equation involving your variable to represent the problem.
   d Solve the equation in part **c**.
   e What is the length and width of the rectangle?

4 Toby rented a car for a total cost of $290. If the rental company charged $40 per day, plus a hiring fee of $50, for how many days did Toby rent the car?

5 Andrew walked a certain distance, and then ran twice as far as he walked. He then caught a bus for the last 2 km. If he travelled a total of 32 km, find how far Andrew walked and ran.

6 A prize of $1000 is divided between Adele and Benita so that Adele receives $280 more than Benita. How much did each person receive?

7 Kate is three times as old as her son. If Kate is 30 years older than her son, what are their ages?

8 A train station is between the towns Antville and Bugville. The station is four times as far from Bugville as it is from Antville. If the distance from Antville to Bugville is 95 km, how far is it from Antville to the station?

9 Andrew, Brenda and Cammi all work part-time at a supermarket. Cammi earns $20 more than Andrew and Brenda earns $30 less than twice Andrew's wage. If their total combined wage is $400, find how much each of these workers earns.

10 Macy bought a total of 12 fiction and non-fiction books. The fiction books cost $12 each and the non-fiction books cost $25 each. If she paid $248 altogether, how many of each kind of book did she purchase?

11 If I multiply my age in six years' time by three, the resulting age is my mother's age now. If my mother is currently 48 years old, how old am I?

12 Twelve years ago Eric's father was seven times as old as Eric was. If Eric's father is now 54 years old, how old is Eric now?

13 In a yacht race the second leg was half the length of the first leg, the third leg was two-thirds of the length of the second leg, and the last leg was twice the length of the second leg. If the total distance was 153 km, find the length of each leg.

14 The Ace Bicycle Shop charges a flat fee of $4, plus $1 per hour, for the hire of a bicycle. The Best Bicycle Shop charges a flat fee of $8, plus 50 cents per hour. Connie and her friends hire three bicycles from Ace, and David and his brother hire two bicycles from Best. After how many hours will their hire costs be the same?

15 Car A left Melbourne for Adelaide at 11.00 am and travelled at an average speed of 70 km per hour.
Car B left Melbourne for Adelaide at 1.00 pm on the same day and travelled at an average speed of 90 km per hour. At what time will Car B catch Car A?

16 Two paddocks in the shapes shown below are to be fenced with wire. If the same total amount of wire is used for each paddock, what are the dimensions of each paddock in metres?

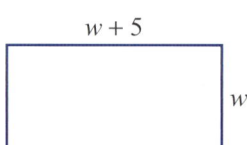

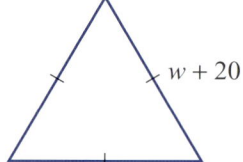

17 Consecutive integers can be represented algebraically as x, $x + 1$, $x + 2$ etc.
  a Find three consecutive numbers that add to 84.
  b **i** Write three consecutive even numbers starting with x.
     ii Find three consecutive even numbers that add to 18.
  c **i** Write three consecutive odd numbers starting with x.
     ii Find three consecutive odd numbers that add to 51.
  d **i** Write three consecutive multiples of 3 starting with x.
     ii Find three consecutive multiples of 3 that add to 81.

18 Tedco produces a teddy bear which sells for $24. Each teddy bear costs the company $8 to manufacture and there is an initial start-up cost of $7200.
  a Write a rule for the total cost, T, of producing x teddy bears.
  b If the cost of a particular production run was $9600, how many teddy bears were manufactured in that run?
  c If x teddy bears are sold, write a rule for the revenue, R, received by the company.
  d How many teddy bears were sold if the revenue was $8400?
  e If they want to make an annual profit of $54 000, how many teddy bears do they need to sell?

Enrichment: Worded challenges

19 An art curator was investigating the price trends of two art works which had the same initial value.

The first painting, 'Green poles', doubled in value in the first year then lost $8000 in the second year. In the third year its value was three-quarters of the previous year.

The second painting, 'Orchids', added $10 000 to its value in the first year then the second year its value was only a third of the previous year. In the third year its value improved to double that of the previous year.

If the value of the paintings was the same in the third year write an equation and solve it to find the initial value of each painting.

20 Julia drove to her holiday destination over a period of five days. On the first day she travels a certain distance, on the second day she travels half that distance, on the third day a third of that distance, on the fourth day one-quarter of the distance and on the fifth day one-fifth of the distance. If her destination was 1000 km away write an equation and solve it to find how far she travelled on the first day to the nearest kilometre.

21 Anna King is x years old. Her brother Henry is two-thirds of her age and her sister Chloe is three times Henry's age. The twins who live next door are 5 years older than Anna. If the sum of the ages of the King children is equal to the sum of the ages of the twins, find the ages of all the children.

2.7 Inequalities

An inequality (or inequation) is a mathematical statement which uses a $<$, $\leq$, $>$ or $\geq$ sign. Some examples of inequalities include:

$$2 < 6, \quad 5 \geq -1, \quad 3x + 1 \leq 7 \quad \text{and} \quad 2x + \frac{1}{3} > \frac{x}{4}.$$

Inequalities can represent an infinite set of numbers. For example, the inequality $2x < 6$ means that $x < 3$ and this is the infinite set of all real numbers less than 3.

Let's start: Infinite solutions

Greg, Kevin and Greta think that they all have a correct solution to the equation

$$4x - 1 \geq x + 6$$

Greg says $x = 4$ is a solution.

Kevin says $x = 10$ is a solution.

Greta says $x = 100$ is a solution.

- Use substitution to show that they are all correct.
- Can you find the smallest whole number which is a solution to the inequality?
- Can you find the smallest number (including fractions) which satisfies the inequality? What method leads you to your answer?

Key ideas

- **Inequalities** can be illustrated using a number line because a line represents an infinite number of points.
  - Use an **open circle** when showing $>$ (greater than) or $<$ (less than).

    For example: $x > 1$

    $x < 1$

  - Use a **closed circle** when showing $\geq$ (greater than or equal to) or $\leq$ (less than or equal to).

    For example: $x \geq 1$

    $x \leq 1$

- A set may have both an upper and lower bound.

  For example: $-2 < x \leq 3$

  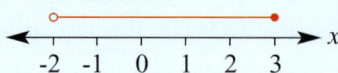

- Linear inequalities can be solved in a similar way to linear equations.
  - If, however, we multiply or divide both sides of an inequality by a negative number, the inequality sign is reversed.

    For example: $5 < 8$ but $-5 > -8$ so if $-x > 1$ then $x < -1$.
  - If we swap the sides of an inequality, then the inequality sign is reversed.

    For example: $3 < 7$ but $7 > 3$ so if $2 > x$ then $x < 2$.

Example 14 Representing inequalities on a number line

Show each of the following examples on a number line:

a x is less than 6 $(x < 6)$

b x is greater than or equal to 2 $(x \geq 2)$

c x is greater than -2 but less than or equal to 3 $(-2 < x \leq 3)$.

SOLUTION

EXPLANATION

a

An open circle is used to indicate that 6 is not included.

b

A closed circle is used to indicate that 2 is included.

c

An open circle is used to indicate that -2 is not included and a closed circle is used to indicate that 3 is included.

Example 15 Solving inequalities

Find the solution set for each of the following inequalities.

a $x - 3 < 7$ b $5 - 2x > 3$ c $\dfrac{d}{4} - 3 \geq -11$ d $2a + 7 \leq 6a + 3$

SOLUTION

EXPLANATION

a $x - 3 < 7$

$\quad x < 10$

Add 3 to both sides

b $5 - 2x > 3$

$\quad -2x > -2$

$\quad\quad x < 1$

Subtract 5 from both sides.

Divide both sides by -2, and reverse the inequality sign.

c $\dfrac{d}{4} - 3 \geq -11$

$\quad \dfrac{d}{4} \geq -8$

$\quad d \geq -32$

Add 3 to both sides.

Multiply both sides by 4; the inequality sign does not change.

d $2a + 7 \leq 6a + 3$

$\quad 7 \leq 4a + 3$

$\quad 4 \leq 4a$

$\quad 1 \leq a$

$\quad a \geq 1$

Gather pronumerals on one side by subtracting $2a$ from both sides.

Subtract 3 from both sides and then divide both sides by 4.

Place the variable a on the left and reverse the inequality.

Exercise 2G

1 Insert the symbol < or > to make each statement true.

   a 3 __ 2   **b** -1 __ 4   **c** -7 __ -3   **d** 5 __ -50

Example 14   **2** Show each of the following inequalities on a number line.

   a $x > 2$ **b** $x \geq 1$ **c** $x \leq 4$ **d** $x < -2$

   e $x \geq -1$ **f** $x < -8$ **g** $-1 < x < 1$ **h** $-2 \leq x \leq 2$

   i $0 \leq x \leq 3$ **j** $2 \leq x \leq 5$ **k** $-3 < x \leq 4$ **l** $-6 \leq x < -2$

Example 15a   **3** Find the solution set for each of the following inequalities.

   a $x + 5 < 8$ **b** $b - 2 > 3$ **c** $y - 8 > -2$ **d** $-12 + m < -7$

   e $5x \geq 15$ **f** $4t > -20$ **g** $\dfrac{x}{3} \geq 4$ **h** $y + 10 \geq 0$

   i $3m - 7 < 11$ **j** $4a + 6 \geq 12$ **k** $7x - 5 < 2$ **l** $2x - 7 > 9$

Example 15b   **4** Find the solution set for each of the following inequalities.

   a $4 - 3x > -8$ **b** $2 - 4n \geq 6$ **c** $4 - 5x \leq 1$

   d $7 - a \leq 3$ **e** $5 - x \leq 11$ **f** $7 - x \leq -3$

   g $-2x - 3 > 9$ **h** $-4t + 2 \geq 10$ **i** $-6m - 14 < 15$

Example 15c   **5** Find the solution set for each of the following inequalities.

   a $\dfrac{x}{2} - 5 \leq 3$ **b** $3 - \dfrac{x}{9} \geq 4$ **c** $\dfrac{2x}{5} \leq 8$

   d $\dfrac{2x + 6}{7} < 4$ **e** $\dfrac{3x - 4}{2} > -6$ **f** $\dfrac{1 - 7x}{5} \leq 3$

6 Solve each of the following inequalities.

   a $4(x + 2) < 12$ **b** $-3(a + 5) > 9$ **c** $5(3 - x) \geq 25$

   d $2(3 - x) > 1$ **e** $5(y + 2) < -6$ **f** $-7(1 - x) < -11$

Example 15d   **7** Find the solution set for each of the following inequalities.

   a $2x + 9 \leq 6x - 1$ **b** $6t + 2 > t - 1$ **c** $7y + 4 \leq 7 - y$

   d $3a - 2 < 4 - 2a$ **e** $1 - 3m \geq 7 - 4m$ **f** $7 - 5b > -4 - 3b$

8 Wendy is x years old and Jay is 6 years younger. The sum of their ages is less than 30. Write an inequality involving x and solve it. What can you say about Wendy's age?

9 The perimeter of a particular rectangle needs to be less than 50 cm. If the length of the rectangle is 12 cm and the width is w cm, write an inequality involving w and solve it. What width does the rectangle need to be?

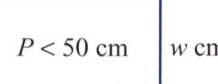

$P < 50$ cm w cm

12 cm

10 How many integers satisfy both of the given equations?

   a $2x + 1 \leq 5$ and $5 - 2x \leq 5$ **b** $7 - 3x > 10$ and $5x + 13 > -5$

   c $\dfrac{x + 1}{3} \geq -2$ and $2 - \dfrac{x}{3} > 3$ **d** $\dfrac{5x + 1}{6} < 2$ and $\dfrac{x}{3} < 2x - 7$

11 The width of a rectangular area is 10 m and its height is $(2x - 4)$ m. If the area is less than 80 m^2, what are the possible whole number values for x?

12 Two car rental companies have the following payment plans:
Carz: $90 per week and 15c per kilometre
Renta: $110 per week and 10c per kilometre
What is the maximum whole number of kilometres that can be travelled in one week with Carz if it is to cost less than it would with Renta?

13 a Consider the inequality $2 > x$.
  i List 5 values of x between -1 and 2 which make the inequality true.
  ii What must be true about all the values of x if the inequality is true?
 b Consider the inequality $-x < 5$.
  i List 5 values of x which make the inequality true.
  ii What must be true about all the values of x if the inequality is true.
 c Complete these statements.
  i If $a > x$ then x __ __
  ii If $-x < a$ then x __ __

14 Consider the equation $9 - 2x > 3$.
 a Solve the equation by firstly adding $2x$ to both sides then solve for x.
 b Solve the equation by firstly subtracting 9 from both sides.
 c What did you have to remember to do in part **b** to ensure that the answer is the same as in part **a**?

15 Combine all your knowledge from this chapter so far to solve these inequalities.
 a $\dfrac{2(x+1)}{3} > x + 5$
 b $2x + 3 \geq \dfrac{x-6}{3}$
 c $\dfrac{2-3x}{2} < 2x - 1$
 d $\dfrac{4(2x-1)}{3} \leq x + 3$
 e $1 - x > \dfrac{7(2-3x)}{4}$
 f $2(3 - 2x) \leq 4x$

Enrichment: Literal inequalities

16 Given a, b, c and d are positive numbers (such that $1 < a < b$), solve each of the following for x.
 a $ax - b > -c$
 b $b - x \leq a$
 c $\dfrac{x}{a} - b \leq c$
 d $\dfrac{bx}{c} \leq a$
 e $\dfrac{ax+b}{c} < d$
 f $\dfrac{b-2x}{c} \leq d$
 g $a(x + b) < c$
 h $\dfrac{ax-b}{c} > -d$
 i $a(b - x) > c$
 j $ax + b \leq x - c$
 k $ax + b > bx - 1$
 l $b - ax \leq c - bx$

Using formulas

A formula (or rule) is an equation that relates two or more variables. You can find the value of one of the variables if you are given the value of all other unknowns. Some common formulas contain squares, square roots, cubes and cube roots. The following are some examples of formulas.

- $A = \pi r^2$ is the formula for finding the area, A, of a circle given its radius, r.

- $F = \dfrac{9}{5}C + 32$ is the formula for converting degrees Celsius, C, to degrees Fahrenheit, F.

- $d = vt$ is the formula for finding the distance, d, given the velocity, v, and time, t.

A, F and d are said to be the subjects of the formulas given above.

→ Let's start: Common formulas

As a class group, try to list at least 10 formulas that you know.
- Write down the formulas and describe what each variable represents.
- Which variable is the subject of each formula?

Key ideas

- The **subject** of a **formula** is a variable that usually sits on its own on the left-hand side. For example, the C in $C = 2\pi r$ is the subject of the formula.
- A variable in a formula can be evaluated by substituting numbers for all other variables.
- A formula can be **transposed** (rearranged) to make another variable the subject.

  $C = 2\pi r$ can be transposed to give $r = \dfrac{C}{2\pi}$

- Note that $\sqrt{a^2} = a$ if $a \geq 0$ and $\sqrt{a^2 + b^2} \neq a + b$.

Example 16 Substituting values into formulas

Substitute the given values into the formula to evaluate the subject.

a $\quad S = \dfrac{a}{1 - r}$, when $a = 3$ and $r = 0.4$ $\qquad$ b $\quad E = \dfrac{1}{2}mv^2$, when $m = 4$ and $v = 5$

SOLUTION $\qquad\qquad\qquad\qquad\qquad\qquad\qquad$ **EXPLANATION**

a $\quad S = \dfrac{a}{1 - r}$

$\quad S = \dfrac{3}{1 - 0.4}$ $\qquad\qquad\qquad\qquad$ Substitute $a = 3$ and $r = 0.4$ and evaluate.

$\quad\ \ = \dfrac{3}{0.6}$

$\quad\ \ = 5$

b $\quad E = \dfrac{1}{2}mv^2$

$\quad E = \dfrac{1}{2} \times 4 \times 5^2$ $\qquad\qquad\qquad$ Substitute $m = 4$ and $v = 5$ and evaluate.

$\quad\ \ = \dfrac{1}{2} \times 4 \times 25$

$\quad\ \ = 50$

Example 17 Finding the unknown value in a formula

The area of a trapezium is given by $A = \dfrac{1}{2}(a + b)h$. Substitute $A = 12$, $a = 5$ and $h = 4$ then find the value of b.

SOLUTION

$A = \dfrac{1}{2}(a + b)h$

$12 = \dfrac{1}{2} \times (5 + b) \times 4$

$12 = 2(5 + b)$

$6 = 5 + b$

$b = 1$

EXPLANATION

Write the formula and substitute the given values of A, a and h. Then solve for b in the usual way.

Example 18 Transposing formulas

Transpose each of the following to make b the subject.

a $c = a(x + b)$

b $c = \sqrt{a^2 + b^2}$ $\quad (b > 0)$

SOLUTION

a $\qquad c = a(x + b)$

$\qquad \dfrac{c}{a} = x + b$

$\dfrac{c}{a} - x = b$

$\qquad b = \dfrac{c}{a} - x \quad \left(or\ b = \dfrac{c - ax}{a} \right)$

b $\qquad c = \sqrt{a^2 + b^2}$

$\qquad c^2 = a^2 + b^2$

$c^2 - a^2 = b^2$

$\qquad b^2 = c^2 - a^2$

$\qquad b = \sqrt{c^2 - a^2}$

EXPLANATION

Divide both sides by a.

Subtract x from both sides.

Make b the subject on the left side.

Square both sides to remove the square root.
Subtract a^2 from both sides.
Make b^2 the subject.
Take the square root of both sides, $b = \sqrt{c^2 - a^2}$ if b is positive.

Exercise 2H

1 State the letter which is the subject of these formulas.

a $A = \dfrac{1}{2}bh$

b $D = b^2 - 4ac$

c $M = \dfrac{a + b}{2}$

d $A = \pi r^2$

Understanding

Example 16 **2** Substitute the given values into each of the following formulas to evaluate the subject. Round to two decimal places where appropriate.

a $A = bh$, when $b = 3$ and $h = 7$

b $F = ma$, when $m = 4$ and $a = 6$

c $m = \dfrac{a+b}{4}$, when $a = 14$ and $b = -6$

d $t = \dfrac{d}{v}$, when $d = 18$ and $v = 3$

e $A = \pi r^2$, when $\pi = 3.14$ and $r = 12$

f $V = \dfrac{4}{3}\pi r^3$, when $\pi = 3.14$ and $r = 2$

g $c = \sqrt{a^2 + b^2}$, when $a = 12$ and $b = 22$

h $Q = \sqrt{2gh}$, when $g = 9.8$ and $h = 11.4$

i $I = \dfrac{MR^2}{2}$, when $M = 12.2$ and $R = 6.4$

j $x = ut + \dfrac{1}{2}at^2$ when $u = 0$, $t = 4$ and $a = 10$

Example 17 **3** Substitute the given values into each of the following formulas then solve the equations to determine the value of the unknown pronumeral each time. Round to two decimal places where appropriate.

a $m = \dfrac{F}{a}$, when $m = 12$ and $a = 3$

b $A = lw$, when $A = 30$ and $l = 6$

c $A = \dfrac{1}{2}(a + b)h$, when $A = 64$, $b = 12$ and $h = 4$

d $C = 2\pi r$, when $C = 26$ and $\pi = 3.14$

e $S = 2\pi r^2$, when $S = 72$ and $\pi = 3.14$

f $v^2 = u^2 + 2as$, when $v = 22$, $u = 6$ and $a = 12$

g $m = \sqrt{\dfrac{x}{y}}$, when $m = 8$ and $x = 4$

Example 18 **4** Transpose each of the following formulas to make the pronumeral shown in brackets the subject.

a $A = 2\pi rh$ (r)

b $I = \dfrac{Prt}{100}$ (r)

c $p = m(x + n)$ (n)

d $d = \dfrac{a+bx}{c}$ (x)

e $V = \pi r^2 h$ $(r > 0)$ (r)

f $P = \dfrac{v^2}{R}$ $(v > 0)$ (v)

g $S = 2\pi rh + 2\pi r^2$ (h)

h $A = (p + q)^2$ (p)

i $T = 2\pi\sqrt{\dfrac{l}{g}}$ (g)

j $\sqrt{A} + B = 4C$ (A)

5 The formula $s = \dfrac{d}{t}$ gives the speed s km/h of a car which has travelled a distance of d km in t hours.

a Find the speed of a car which has travelled 400 km in 4.5 hours. Round to two decimal places.

b i Transpose the formula $s = \dfrac{d}{t}$ to make d the subject.

   ii Find the distance covered if a car travels at 75 km/h for 3.8 hours.

6 The formula $F = \dfrac{9}{5}C + 32$ converts degrees Celsius, C, to degrees Fahrenheit, F.

   a Find what each of the following temperatures is in degrees Fahrenheit.

     i 100°C   **ii** 38°C

   b Transpose the formula to make C the subject.

   c Calculate what each of the following temperatures is in degrees Celsius. Round to one decimal place where necessary.

     i 14°F   **ii** 98°F

7 The velocity, v m/s, of an object is described by the rule $v = u + at$, where u is the initial velocity in m/s, a is the acceleration in m/s^2 and t is the time in seconds.

   a Find the velocity after 3 seconds if the initial velocity is 5 m/s and the acceleration is 10 m/s^2.

   b Find the time taken for a body to reach a velocity of 20 m/s if its acceleration is 4 m/s^2 and its initial velocity is 12 m/s.

8 The volume of water (V litres) in a tank is given by $V = 4000 - 0.1t$ where t is the time in seconds after a tap is turned on.

   a Over time, does the water volume increase or decrease according to the formula?

   b Find the volume after 2 minutes.

   c Find the time it takes for the volume to reach 1500 litres. Round to the nearest minute.

   d How long, to the nearest minute, does it take to completely empty the tank?

9 Write a formula for the following situations. Make the first listed variable the subject.

   a $D given c cents.   **b** d cm given e metres.

   c The discounted price $D which is 30% off the marked price $M.

   d The value of an investment $V which is 15% more than the initial amount $P.

   e The cost $C of hiring a car at $50 upfront plus $18 per hour for t hours.

   f The distance d km remaining in a 42 km marathon after t hours if the running speed is 14 km/h.

   g The cost $C of a bottle of soft drink if b bottles cost $c.

10 Write a formula for the value of a in these diagrams.

   a

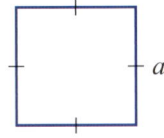

Perimeter P

   b

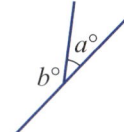

   c

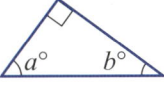

   d

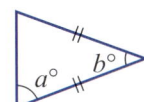

   e

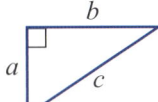

   f

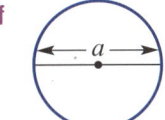

Area = A

Enrichment: Basketball formulas

11 The formula $T = 3x + 2y + f$ can be used to calculate the total number of points made in a basketball game where:

   x = number of three-point goals y = number of two-point goals
   f = number of free throws made T = total number of points

   a Find the total number of points for a game where 12 three-point goals, 15 two-point goals and 7 free throws were made.

   b Find the number of three-point goals made if the total number of points was 36 with 5 two-point goals made and 5 free throws made.

   c The formula $V = \left(p + \dfrac{3r}{2} + 2a + \dfrac{3s}{2} + 2b \right) - \dfrac{1.5t + 2f + m - o}{g}$ can be used to calculate the value, V, of a basketball player where:

   p = points earned r = number of rebounds
   a = number of assists s = number of steals
   b = number of blocks t = number of turnovers
   f = number of personal fouls m = number of missed shots
   o = number of offensive rebounds g = number of games played

   Calculate the value of a player with 350 points earned, 2 rebounds, 14 assists, 25 steals, 32 blocks, 28 turnovers, 14 personal fouls, 24 missed shots, 32 offensive rebounds and 10 games.

2.9 Simultaneous equations: substitution

A linear equation with one unknown has one unique solution. For example, $x = 2$ is the only value of x that makes the equation $2x + 3 = 7$ true.

The linear equation $2x + 3y = 12$ has two unknowns and it has an infinite number of solutions. Each solution is a pair of x and y values that makes the equation true, for example $x = 0$ and $y = 4$ or $x = 3$ and $y = 2$ or $x = 4\frac{1}{2}$ and $y = 1$.

However, if we are told that $2x + 3y = 12$ and also that $y = 2x - 1$, we can find a single solution that satisfies both equations. Equations like this are called simultaneous linear equations, because we can find a pair of x and y values that satisfy both equations at the same time (simultaneously).

A share trader examining computer models of financial data, which can involve finding values that satisfy two equations simultaneously.

Let's start: Multiple solutions

There is more than one pair of numbers x and y which satisfy the equation $x - 2y = 5$.

- Write down at least 5 pairs (x, y) which make the equation true.

A second equation is $y = x - 8$.

- Do any of your pairs that make the first equation true, also make the second equation true? If not, can you find the special pair of numbers that satisfies both equations simultaneously?

Key ideas

- An algebraic method called **substitution** can be used to solve **simultaneous equations**. It is used when at least one of the equations has a single variable as the subject. For example, y is the subject in the equation $y = 3x + 1$.
- To solve simultaneous equations using substitution:
  1 Substitute one equation into the other.
  2 Solve for the remaining variable.
  3 Substitute to find the value of the second variable.

$$2x + 3y = 8 \text{ and } y = x + 1$$
$$2x + 3(x + 1) = 8$$
$$2x + 3x + 3 = 8$$
$$5x + 3 = 8$$
$$5x = 5$$
$$x = 1$$
$$\therefore y = 1 + 1 = 2$$

Example 19 Solving using substitution

Solve each of the following pairs of simultaneous equations by using substitution.

a $x + y = 10$ b $4x - y = 6$ c $3x + 2y = 19$
    $y = 4x$ $y = 2x - 4$ $y = 2x - 8$

SOLUTION	EXPLANATION

a $x + y = 10$ (1)
    $y = 4x$ (2)
 	
    $x + (4x) = 10$
        $5x = 10$
        $x = 2$
From (2) $y = 4x$
            $= 4 \times 2$
            $= 8$
Check: $2 + 8 = 10$ and $8 = 4 \times 2$
	Number the equations for reference.
	
	Substitute $y = 4x$ into (1).
	Combine like terms and solve for x.
	
	Substitute $x = 2$ into (2) to find the value of y.
	
	Check answer by substituting $x = 2$ and $y = 8$ into (1) and (2).

b $4x - y = 6$ (1)
        $y = 2x - 4$ (2)
    $4x - (2x - 4) = 6$
    $4x - 2x + 4 = 6$
        $2x + 4 = 6$
        $2x = 2$
        $x = 1$
From (2) $y = 2x - 4$
            $= 2 \times 1 - 4$
            $= -2$
Check: $4 + 2 = 6$ and $-2 = 2 \times 1 - 4$
	Substitute $y = 2x - 4$ into (1) using brackets.
	Use the distributive law and solve for x.
	
	Substitute $x = 1$ into (2) to find the value of y.
	
	Check: substitute $x = 1$ and $y = -2$ into (1) and (2).

c $3x + 2y = 19$ (1)
        $y = 2x - 8$ (2)
    $3x + 2(2x - 8) = 19$
    $3x + 4x - 16 = 19$
        $7x - 16 = 19$
        $7x = 35$
        $x = 5$
From (2) $y = 2x - 8$
            $= 2 \times 5 - 8$
            $= 2$
Check: $3 \times 5 + 2 \times 2 = 19$ and $2 = 2 \times 5 - 8$
	Substitute $y = 2x - 8$ into (1).
	Use the distributive law and solve for x.
	
	Substitute $x = 5$ into (2) to find the value of y.
	
	Check: substitute $x = 5$ and $y = 2$ into (1) and (2).

Exercise 2I

Understanding

1 Find the value of x or y by substituting the known value.

a $y = 2x - 3$ $(x = 4)$ **b** $x = 5 - 2y$ $(y = 4)$ **c** $2x + 4y = 8$ $(y = -3)$

2 Choose the correct option.

a When substituting $y = 2x - 1$ into $3x + 2y = 5$ the second equation becomes

A $3x + 2(2x - 1) = 5$ **B** $3(2x - 1) + 2y = 5$ **C** $3x + 2y = 2x - 1$

b When substituting $x = 1 - 3y$ into $5x - y = 6$ the second equation becomes

A $1 - 3x - y = 6$ **B** $5(1 - 3y) = 6$ **C** $5(1 - 3y) - y = 6$

3 Check whether $x = -2$ and $y = 2$ is a solution to each of the following pairs of simultaneous equations.

a $x + y = 0$ and $x - y = -4$ **b** $x - 2y = -6$ and $2x + y = 0$

c $3x + 4y = -2$ and $x = -3y - 4$ **d** $2x + y = -2$ and $x = 4y - 10$

Fluency

Example 19a

4 Solve each of the following pairs of simultaneous equations by using substitution.

a $x + y = 3$
   $y = 2x$

b $x + y = 6$
   $x = 5y$

c $x + 5y = 8$
   $y - 3x$

d $x - 5y = 3$
   $x = 2y$

e $3x + 2y = 18$
   $y = 3x$

f $x + 2y = 15$
   $y = -3x$

Example 19b

5 Solve each of the following pairs of simultaneous equations by using substitution.

a $x + y = 12$
   $y = x + 6$

b $2x + y = 1$
   $y = x + 4$

c $5x + y = 5$
   $y = 1 - x$

d $3x - y = 7$
   $y = x + 5$

e $3x - y = 9$
   $y = x - 1$

f $x + 2y = 6$
   $x = 9 - y$

g $y - x = 14$
   $x = 4y - 2$

h $3x + y = 4$
   $y = 2 - 4x$

i $4x - y = 12$
   $y = 8 - 6x$

Example 19c

6 Solve each of the following pairs of simultaneous equations by using substitution.

a $3x + 2y = 8$
   $y = 4x - 7$

b $2x + 3y = 11$
   $y = 2x + 1$

c $4x + y = 4$
   $x = 2y - 8$

d $2x + 5y = -4$
   $y = x - 5$

e $2x - 3y = 5$
   $x = 5 - y$

f $3x + 2y = 5$
   $y = 3 - x$

Problem-solving

7 The sum of two numbers is 48 and the larger number is 14 more than the smaller number. Write two equations and solve them to find the two numbers.

8 The combined mass of two trucks is 29 tonnes. The heavier truck is 1 tonne less than twice the mass of the smaller truck. Write two equations and solve them to find the mass of each truck.

9 The perimeter of a rectangle is 11 cm and the length is 3 cm more than half the width. Find the dimensions of the rectangle.

10 One of the common errors when applying the method of substitution is made in this working. Find the error and describe how to avoid it.

Solve $y = 3x - 1$ and $x - y = 7$.

$x - 3x - 1 = 7$ substituting $y = 3x - 1$ into $x - y = 7$

$-2x - 1 = 7$

$-2x = 8$

$x = -4$

11 If both equations have the same variable as the subject, substitution is still possible.

For example, solve $y = 3x - 1 \ldots (1)$ and $y = 2 - x \ldots (2)$

Substitute (1) into (2)

$3x - 1 = 2 - x$

$4x = 3$

$x = \dfrac{3}{4}$ and $y = \dfrac{5}{4}$

Use this method to solve these simultaneous equations.

a $y = 4x + 1$
      $y = 3 - 2x$

b $y = 3 - 4x$
      $y = 2x + 8$

c $y = \dfrac{1}{2}x + 4$
      $y = \dfrac{x + 1}{3}$

Enrichment: Literally challenging

12 Use substitution to solve each of the following pairs of simultaneous equations for x and y in terms of a and b.

a $ax + y = b$
      $y = bx$

b $ax + by = b$
      $x = by$

c $x + y = a$
      $x = y - b$

d $ax - by = a$
      $y = x - a$

e $ax - y = a$
      $y = bx + a$

f $ax - by = 2a$
      $x = y - b$

Using a CAS calculator 2.9: Solving simultaneous equations

This activity is on the companion website in the form of a printable PDF.

2.10 Simultaneous equations: elimination

Another method used to solve simultaneous linear equations is called elimination. This involves the addition or subtraction of the two equations to eliminate one of the variables. We can then solve for the remaining variable and substitute to find the value of the second variable.

Let's start: To add or subtract?

To use the method of elimination you need to decide if using addition or using subtraction will eliminate one of the variables.

Decide if the terms in these pairs should be added or subtracted to give the result of 0.

- $3x$ and $3x$
- $2y$ and $-2y$
- $-x$ and x
- $-7y$ and $-7y$

Describe under what circumstances addition or subtraction should be used to eliminate a pair of terms.

Key ideas

- **Elimination** involves the addition or subtraction of two equations to remove one variable.
- Elimination is often used when both equations are of the form $ax + by = d$ or $ax + by + c = 0$.
- Add equations to eliminate terms of opposite sign:

$$\begin{array}{r} 3x - y = 4 \\ + \quad 5x + y = 4 \\ \hline 8x \quad\quad = 8 \end{array}$$

- Subtract equations to eliminate terms of the same sign:

$$\begin{array}{r} 2x + 3y = 6 \\ - \quad 2x - 5y = 7 \\ \hline 8y = -1 \end{array}$$

- If terms cannot be eliminated just by using addition or subtraction, first multiply one or both equations to form a matching pair

  For example:

  1 $\begin{array}{l} 3x - 2y = 1 \\ 2x + y = 3 \end{array}$ $\rightarrow$ $\begin{array}{l} 3x - 2y = 1 \\ 4x + 2y = 6 \end{array}$ (Multiply both sides by 2)

  matching pair

  2 $\begin{array}{l} 7x - 2y = 3 \\ 4x - 5y = -6 \end{array}$ $\rightarrow$ $\begin{array}{l} 28x - 8y = 12 \\ 28x - 35y = -42 \end{array}$ (Multiply both sides by 4) (Multiply both sides by 7)

Example 20 Solving simultaneous equations using elimination

Solve the following pairs of simultaneous equations by using elimination.

a $\begin{array}{l} x - 2y = 1 \\ -x + 5y = 2 \end{array}$

b $\begin{array}{l} 3x - 2y = 5 \\ 5x - 2y = 11 \end{array}$

c $\begin{array}{l} 5x + 2y = -7 \\ x + 7y = 25 \end{array}$

d $\begin{array}{l} 4x + 3y = 18 \\ 3x - 2y = 5 \end{array}$

SOLUTION	EXPLANATION

a $x - 2y = 1$ (1)

$-x + 5y = 2$ (2)

$(1) + (2)$ $3y = 3$

$y = 1$

Add the two equations to eliminate x since $x + (-x) = 0$. Then solve for y.

From (1) $x - 2y = 1$

$x - 2 \times (1) = 1$

$x - 2 = 1$

$x = 3$

Substitute $y = 1$ into equation (1) to find x.
Substitute $x = 3$ and $y = 1$ into the original equations to check.

b $3x - 2y = 5$ (1)

$5x - 2y = 11$ (2)

$(2) - (1)$ $2x = 6$

$x = 3$

From (1) $3x - 2y = 5$

$3 \times (3) - 2y = 5$

$-2y = -4$

$y = 2$

Subtract the two equations to eliminate y since they are the same sign, i.e. $-2y - (-2y) = -2y + 2y = 0$.
Alternatively, could do $(1) - (2)$ but $(2) - (1)$ avoids negative coefficients.
Solve for x.
Substitute $x = 3$ into equation (1) to find y.
Substitute $x = 3$ and $y = 2$ into the original equations to check.

c $5x + 2y = -7$ (1)

$x + 7y = 25$ (2)

$5 \times (2)$ $5x + 35y = 125$ (3)

$5x + 2y = -7$ (1)

$(3) - (1)$ $33y = 132$

$y = 4$

From (2) $x + 7y = 25$

$x + 7 \times (4) = 25$

$x + 28 = 25$

$x = -3$

There are different numbers of x and y in each equation so multiply equation (2) by 5 to make the coefficient of x equal in size to (1).

Subtract the equations to eliminate x.

Substitute $y = 4$ in equation (2) to find x.
Substitute $x = -3$ and $y = 4$ into the original equations to check.

d $4x + 3y = 18$ (1)

$3x - 2y = 5$ (2)

$2 \times (1)$ $8x + 6y = 36$ (3)

$3 \times (2)$ $9x - 6y = 15$ (4)

$(3) + (4)$ $17x = 51$

$x = 3$

From (1) $4x + 3y = 18$

$4 \times (3) + 3y = 18$

$12 + 3y = 18$

$3y = 6$

$y = 2$

Multiply equation (1) by 2 and equation (2) by 3 to make the coefficients of y equal in size but opposite in sign.
Add the equations to eliminate y.

Substitute $x = 3$ into equation (1) to find y.

Substitute $x = 3$ and $y = 2$ into the original equations to check.

Exercise 2J

1 Insert a '+' or '−' sign inside each statement to make them true.

a $3x \_\_ 3x = 0$ **b** $-2y \_\_ 2y = 0$ **c** $11y \_\_ (-11y) = 0$ **d** $-4x \_\_ (-4x) = 0$

2 a Decide if addition or subtraction should be chosen to eliminate the variable x in these simultaneous equations.

  i $x + 2y = 3$ **ii** $-2x - y = -9$ **iii** $y - x = 0$

     $x - 5y = -4$ $2x + 3y = 11$ $3y - x = 8$

b Decide if addition or subtraction will eliminate the variable y in these simultaneous equations.

  i $4x - y = 6$ **ii** $7x - 2y = 5$ **iii** $10y + x = 14$

     $x + y = 4$ $-3x - 2y = -5$ $-10y - 3x = -24$

3 Solve these simultaneous equations by firstly adding the equations.

a $x + 2y = 3$ **b** $x - 4y = 2$ **c** $-2x + y = 1$
   $-x + 3y = 2$ $-x + 6y = 2$ $2x - 3y = -7$

d $3x - y = 2$ **e** $2x - 3y = -2$ **f** $4x + 3y = 5$
   $2x + y = 3$ $-5x + 3y = -4$ $-4x - 5y = -3$

4 Solve these simultaneous equations by firstly subtracting the equations.

a $3x + y = 10$ **b** $2x + 7y = 9$ **c** $2x + 3y = 14$
   $x + y = 6$ $2x + 5y = 11$ $2x - y = -10$

5 Solve these simultaneous equations by firstly subtracting the equations.

a $5x - y = -2$ **b** $-5x + 3y = -1$ **c** $9x - 2y = 3$
   $3x - y = 4$ $-5x + 4y = 2$ $-3x - 2y = -9$

6 Solve the following pairs of simultaneous linear equations by using elimination.

a $4x + y = -8$ **b** $2x - y = 3$ **c** $-x + 4y = 2$
   $3x - 2y = -17$ $5x + 2y = 12$ $3x - 8y = -2$

d $3x + 2y = 0$ **e** $4x + 3y = 13$ **f** $3x - 4y = -1$
   $4x + y = -5$ $x + 2y = -3$ $6x - 5y = 10$

g $-4x - 3y = -5$ **h** $3x - 4y = -1$ **i** $5x - 4y = 7$
   $7x - y = 40$ $-5x - 2y = 19$ $-3x - 2y = 9$

7 Solve the following pairs of simultaneous linear equations by using elimination.

a $3x + 2y = -1$ **b** $7x + 2y = 8$ **c** $6x - 5y = -8$
   $4x + 3y = -3$ $3x - 5y = 21$ $-5x + 2y = -2$

d $2x - 3y = 3$ **e** $7x + 2y = 1$ **f** $5x + 7y = 1$
   $3x - 2y = 7$ $4x + 3y = 8$ $3x + 5y = -1$

g $5x + 3y = 16$ **h** $3x - 7y = 8$ **i** $2x - 3y = 1$
   $4x + 5y = 5$ $4x - 3y = -2$ $3x + 2y = 8$

j $2x - 7y = 11$ **k** $3x + 5y = 36$ **l** $2x - 4y = 6$
   $5x + 4y = -37$ $7x + 2y = -3$ $5x + 3y = -11$

8 The sum of two numbers is 30 and their difference is 12.
Write two equations and find the numbers.

9 Two supplementary angles differ by 24°. Write two equations and find the two angles.

10 The perimeter of a rectangular city block is 800 metres and the difference between the length
and width is 123 metres. What are the dimensions of the city block?

11 A teacher collects a total of 17 mobile phones and iPods before a group of students heads off on
a bushwalk. From a second group of students, 40 phones and iPods are collected. The second
group had twice the number of phones and 3 times the number of iPods than the first group.
How many phones and iPods did the first group have?

12 Consider the pair of simultaneous equations

$$2x + y = 5 \;\ldots (1)$$
$$5x + y = 11 \ldots (2)$$

a Solve the equations by firstly subtracting equation (2) from equation (1) i.e. (1) – (2)

b Now solve the equations by firstly subtracting equation (1) from equation (2) i.e. (2) – (1)

c Which method **a** or **b** is preferable and why?

13 To solve any of the pairs of simultaneous equations in this section using the method of substitution, what would need to be done first before the substitution is made?

   Try these using substitution.

a $x + y = 5$
   $2x - y = 7$

b $3x - y = -2$
   $x + 4y = -5$

14 Find the solution to these pairs of simultaneous equations. What do you notice?

a $2x + 3y = 3$ and $2x + 3y = 1$

b $7x - 14y = 2$ and $y = \dfrac{1}{2}x + 1$

Enrichment: Literal elimination

15 Use elimination to solve the following pairs of simultaneous equations to find the value of x and y in terms of the other pronumerals.

a $x + y = a$
   $x - y = b$

b $ax + y = 0$
   $ax - y = b$

c $x - by = a$
   $-x - by = 2a$

d $2ax + y = b$
   $x + y = b$

e $bx + 5ay = 2b$
   $bx + 2ay = b$

f $ax + 3y = 14$
   $ax - y = -10$

g $2ax + y = b$
   $3ax - 2y = b$

h $2ax - y = b$
   $3ax + 2y = b$

i $-x + ay = b$
   $3x - ay = -b$

j $ax + 2y = c$
   $2ax + y = -c$

k $ax - 4y = 1$
   $x - by = 1$

l $ax + by = a$
   $x + y = 1$

m $ax + by = c$
   $-ax + y = d$

n $ax - by = a$
   $-x + y = 2$

o $ax + by = b$
   $3x - y = 2$

p $ax - by = b$
   $cx - y = 2$

q $ax + by = c$
   $dx - by = f$

r $ax + by = c$
   $dx + by = f$

2.11 Applications of simultaneous equations

Many problems can be described mathematically using a pair of simultaneous linear equations from which a solution can be obtained algebraically.

Let's start: The tyre store

In one particular week a total of 83 cars and motorcycles check into a garage to have their tyres changed. All the motorcycles change 2 tyres each and all the cars change 4 tyres each. The total number of tyres sold in the week is 284.

If you have to find the number of motorcycles and the number of cars that have their tyres changed in the week:

- What two variables should you define?
- What two equations can you write?
- Which method (substitution or elimination) would you use to solve the equations?
- What is the solution to the simultaneous equations?
- How would you answer the question in words?

Key ideas

- To solve worded problems with simultaneous equations:
  - Define two variables by writing down what they represent.

    For example: Let C be the cost of ...

    Let x be the number of ...
  - Write a pair of simultaneous equations from the given information using your two variables.
  - Solve the equations simultaneously using substitution or elimination.
  - Check the solution by substituting into the original equations.
  - Express the answer in words.

Example 21 Solving word problems with simultaneous equations

Andrea bought two containers of ice cream and three bottles of maple syrup for a total of $22. At the same shop, Bettina bought one container of ice cream and two bottles of maple syrup for $13. How much does each container of ice cream and each bottle of maple syrup cost?

SOLUTION	EXPLANATION
Let: x be the cost of a container of ice cream	Define the unknowns. Ask yourself what you are
y be the cost of a bottle of maple syrup	being asked to find.
$2x + 3y = 22$ (1)	2 containers of ice cream and 3 bottles of maple
$x + 2y = 13$ (2)	syrup for a total of \$22
	1 container of ice cream and 2 bottles of maple
	syrup for \$13.
	Choose the method of elimination to solve.
$2 \times (2)$ $2x + 4y = 26$ (3)	Multiply (2) by 2 to obtain a matching pair.
$2x + 3y = 22$ (1)	Subtract equation (1) from (3).
$(3) - (1)$ $y = 4$	
From (2) $x + 2y = 13$	
$x + 2 \times (4) = 13$	Substitute $y = 4$ into (2).
$x + 8 = 13$	Solve for x.
$x = 5$	Substitute $y = 4$ and $x = 5$ into original equations to
	check.
The cost of one container of ice cream is \$5 and	Answer the question in a sentence.
the cost of one bottle of maple syrup is \$4.	

Exercise 2K

1 The sum of two numbers is 42 and their difference is 6. Find the two numbers x and y by completing the following steps.

    a Write a pair of simultaneous equations relating x and y.

    b Solve the pair of equations using substitution or elimination.

    c Write your answer in words.

2 The length l cm of a rectangle is 5 cm longer than its width w cm. If the perimeter is 84 cm, find the dimensions of the rectangle by completing the following steps.

    a Write a pair of simultaneous equations relating l and w.

    b Solve the pair of equations using substitution or elimination.

    c Write your answer in words.

3 A rectangular block of land has a perimeter of 120 metres and the length l m of the block is three times the width w m. Find the dimensions of the block of land by completing the following steps.

    a Write a pair of simultaneous equations relating l and w.

    b Solve the pair of equations using substitution or elimination.

    c Write your answer in words.

Understanding

Example 21 **4** Mal bought 3 bottles of milk and 4 bags of chips for a total of $17. At the same shop, Barbara bought 1 bottle of milk and 5 bags of chips for $13. Find how much each bottle of milk and each bag of chips cost by completing the following steps.

    a Define two variables to represent the problem.
    b Write a pair of simultaneous equations relating the two variables.
    c Solve the pair of equations using substitution or elimination.
    d Write your answer in words.

5 Leonie bought seven lip glosses and two eye shadows for a total of $69 and Chrissie bought four lip glosses and three eye shadows for a total of $45. Find how much each lip gloss and each eye shadow costs by completing the following steps.

    a Define two variables to represent the problem.
    b Write a pair of simultaneous equations relating the two variables.
    c Solve the pair of equations using substitution or elimination.
    d Write your answer in words.

6 Steve bought five cricket balls and fourteen tennis balls for $130. Ben bought eight cricket balls and nine tennis balls for $141. Find the cost of a cricket ball and the cost of a tennis ball.

7 At a birthday party for 20 people each person could order a hot dog or chips. If there were four times as many hot dogs as chips calculate how many hot dogs and how many chips were bought.

8 The entry fee for a fun run is $10 for adults and $3 for children. A total of $3360 was collected from the 420 competitors. Find the number of adults running and the number of children running.

9 Mila plants 820 hectares of potatoes and corn. To maximise his profit he plants 140 hectares more of potatoes than of corn. How many hectares of each does he plant?

10 Carrie has 27 coins in her purse. All the coins are 5 cent or 20 cent coins. If the total value of the coins is $3.75, how many of each type does she have?

11 Michael is 30 years older than his daughter. In five years' time Michael will be 4 times as old as his daughter. How old is Michael now?

12 Jenny has twice as much money as Kristy. If I give Kristy $250, she will have three times as much as Jenny. How much did each of them have originally?

13 At a particular cinema the cost of an adult movie ticket is $15 and the cost of a child's ticket is $10. The seating capacity of the cinema is 240. For one movie session all seats are sold and $3200 is collected from the sale of tickets. How many adult and how many children's tickets were sold?

Solve simulatenous equations to find the number of tickets sold to children and the number sold to adults.

14 Wilfred and Wendy have a long distance bike race. Wilfred rides at 20 km/h and has a 2 hour head start. Wendy travels at 28 km/h. How long does it take for Wendy to catch up to Wilfred? Use distance = speed × time.

15 Andrew travelled a distance of 39 km by jogging for 4 hours and cycling for 3 hours. He could have travelled the same distance by jogging for 7 hours and cycling for 2 hours. Find the speed at which he was jogging and the speed at which he was cycling.

16 Malcolm's mother is 27 years older than he is and their ages are both two digit numbers. If Malcolm swaps the digits in his age he gets his mother's age.
   a How old is Malcolm if the sum of the digits in his age is 5?
   b What is the relationship between the digits in Malcolm's age if the sum of the digits is unknown.
   c If the sum of the digits in Malcolm's two-digit age is unknown, how many possible ages could he be? What are these ages?

Enrichment: Digit swap

17 The digits of a two digit number sum to 10. If the digits swap places the number is 36 more than the original number. What is the original number? Can you show an algebraic solution?

18 The difference between the two digits of a two digit number is 2. If the digits swap places the number is 18 less than the original number. What is the original number? Can you show an algebraic solution?

Fire danger

In many countries fire indices have been developed to help predict the likelihood of fire occurring. One of the simplest fire-danger rating systems devised is the Swedish Angstrom Index. This index only considers the relationship between relative humidity, temperature and the likelihood of fire danger.

The index, I, is given by: $I = \dfrac{H}{20} + \dfrac{27 - T}{10}$

where H is the percentage of relative humidity and T is the temperature in degrees Celsius. The table below shows the likelihood of a fire occurring for different index values.

Index	Likelihood of fire occurring
$I > 4.0$	Unlikely
$2.5 < I < 4.0$	Medium
$2.0 < I < 2.5$	High
$I < 2.0$	Very likely

Constant humidity

a If the humidity is 35% ($H = 35$), how hot would it have to be for the occurrence of fire to be

  i very likely?   **ii** unlikely?

  Discuss your findings with regard to the range of summer temperatures for your capital city or nearest town.

b Repeat part **a** for a humidity of 40%.

c Describe how the 5% change in humidity affects the temperature at which fires become

  i very likely   **ii** unlikely

Constant temperature

a If the temperature was 30°C, investigate what humidity would make fire occurrence

  i very likely   **ii** unlikely

b Repeat part **a** for a temperature of 40°C.

c Determine how the ten-degree change in temperature affects the relative humidity at which fire occurrence becomes

  i very likely   **ii** unlikely

Reflection

Is this fire index more sensitive to temperature or to humidity? Explain your answer.

Investigate

Use the internet to investigate fire indices used in Australia. You can type in key words, such as Australia, fire danger and fire index.

Families of equations

If a set of equations has something in common then it may be possible to solve all the equations in the family at once using literal equations. Literal equations use pronumerals in place of numbers.

Family of linear equations

a Solve these linear equations for x.

    i $2x + 3 = 5$ **ii** $2x + 1 = 5$ **iii** $2x - 1 = 5$

b Now solve the literal equation $2x + a = 5$ for x. Your answer will be in terms of a.

c For part **a i**, the value of a is 3. Substitute $a = 3$ into your rule for x in part **b** to check the result.

Literal equations

a Solve these literal equations for x in terms of the other pronumerals.

    i $ax + b = 10$ **ii** $\dfrac{x - a}{b} = c$ **iii** $\dfrac{ax}{b} + c = d$

b Use your results from part **a** to solve these equations.

    i $-3x + 2 = 10$ **ii** $\dfrac{x - 5}{7} = -4$ **iii** $\dfrac{-3x}{4} + 1 = 2$

Factorising to solve for x

To solve for x in an equation like $ax + 1 = bx + 2$ you can use factorisation as shown here.

$$ax + 1 = bx + 2$$
$$ax - bx = 2 - 1$$
$$x(a - b) = 1$$
$$x = \frac{1}{a - b}$$

a Use the above idea to solve these literal equations.

    i $ax + 5 = 1 - bx$ **ii** $a(x + 2) = b(x - 1)$

    iii $\dfrac{ax}{2} + bx = 1$ **iv** $\dfrac{b(x - 1)}{a} = x - 2$

b Solve these literal simultaneous equations for x and y.

    i $ax + y = 1$ **ii** $y = ax + b$

       $bx - y = -11$ $2x + y = 2b$

    iii $ax + by = c$ **iv** $ax + by = 1$

        $x - y = 0$ $bx + ay = 1$

c Check your solutions to parts **a** and **b** above by choosing an equation or a pair of simultaneous equations and solving in the normal way. Choose your equations so that they belong to the family described by the literal equation.

1 In a magic square, all the rows, columns and main diagonals add to the same total. The total for this magic square is 15. Find the value of x then complete the magic square.

$2x-2$	$3x$	$\dfrac{x+1}{2}$
x		

2 A group of office workers had some prize money to distribute amongst themselves. When all but one took \$9 each, the last person only received \$5. When they all took \$8 each there was \$12 left over. How much had they won?

3 The sides of an equilateral triangle have lengths $3y - x$, $5x + 3$ and $2 + 2y$. Find the length of the sides.

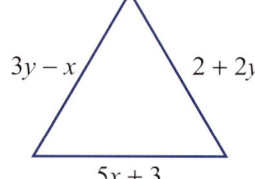

4 a If $a > b > 0$ and $c < 0$, insert an inequality sign to make a true statement.

   i $a + c$ ___ $b + c$

   ii ac ___ bc

   iii $a - b$ ___ 0

   iv $\dfrac{1}{a}$ ___ $\dfrac{1}{b}$

  b Place a, b, c and d in order from smallest to largest given

$$a > b$$
$$a + b = c + d$$
$$b - a > c - d$$

5 Find the values of x, y and z if

$$x - 3y + 2z = 17$$
$$x - y + z = 8$$
$$y + z = 3$$

6 Solve these equations for x.

  a $\dfrac{1}{x} + \dfrac{1}{a} = \dfrac{1}{b}$

  b $\dfrac{1}{2x} + \dfrac{1}{3x} = \dfrac{1}{4}$

  c $\dfrac{x-1}{3} - \dfrac{x+1}{4} = x$

  d $\dfrac{2x-3}{4} - \dfrac{1-x}{5} = \dfrac{x+1}{2}$

Chapter summary

Substitution

The process of replacing a pronumeral with a given value
e.g. if $x = 3$, $2x + 4 = 2 \times 3 + 4$
$= 6 + 4$
$= 10$
e.g. if $x = 2$, $y = -4$, $xy = 2 \times (-4)$
$= -8$

Expanding brackets

e.g. $2(x + 3) = 2 \times x + 2 \times 3$
$= 2x + 6$
$-3(4 - 2x) = -12 + 6x$

Expressions

e.g. $\boxed{2x} \, \ominus \, 3y + 5$

term   constant
coefficient

e.g. 2 more than 3 lots of m
is $3m + 2$

Addition/subtraction

Only like terms can be combined under addition or subtraction.
Like terms, e.g. $3a$ and $7a$
$2ab$ and $5ab$
not $4a$ and $7ab$
e.g. $3x + 2y - x + 4y + 7$
$= 3x - x + 2y + 4y + 7$
$= 2x + 6y + 7$

Solving linear equations

Finding the value that makes an equation true
e.g. $2x + 5 = 9$
$2x = 4$ (subtract 5)
$x = 2$ (divide by 2)
e.g. $5(x - 1) = 2x + 7$
$5x - 5 = 2x + 7$ (expand)
$3x - 5 = 7$ (subtract $2x$)
$3x = 12$ (add 5)
$x = 4$ (divide by 3)

Linear and simultaneous equations

Inequalities

These can be represented using $>, <, \geq, \leq$ rather than $=$.
e.g. $x > 2$

2 not included

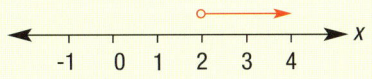

$$\begin{array}{ccccccc} & & & & \circ\!\!\rightarrow & & \\ \hline -1 & 0 & 1 & 2 & 3 & 4 & \end{array} \; x$$

Solving inequalities uses the same steps as solving equations except when multiplying or dividing by a negative number. In this case, the inequality sign must be reversed.
e.g. $4 - 2x < 10$ (-4)
$-2x < 6$ $(\div -2)$
$x > -3$ reverse sign

Solving word problems

1 Define variable(s)
2 Set up equation(s)
3 Solve equation(s)
4 Check each answer and write in words

Formulas

Some common formulas
e.g. $A = \pi r^2$, $C = 2\pi r$
An unknown value can be found by substituting values for the other variables.
A formula can be transposed to make a different variable the subject.
e.g. make r the subject in $A = \pi r^2$
$A = \pi r^2$
$\dfrac{A}{\pi} = r^2$
$\sqrt{\dfrac{A}{\pi}} = r$
$\therefore r = \sqrt{\dfrac{A}{\pi}}$ where $r > 0$

Simultaneous equations

Use substitution or elimination to find the solution that satisfies 2 equations.

Substitution
e.g. $2x + y = 12$ (1)
$y = x + 3$ (2)
In (1) replace y with (2)
$2x + (x + 3) = 12$
$3x + 3 = 12$
$x = 3$
Sub. $x = 3$ to find y
In (2) $y = 3 + 3 = 6$

Elimination
Ensure both equations have a matching pair.
Add 2 equations if matching pair has different sign; subtract if same sign.

e.g. $x + 2y = 2$ (1)
$2x + 3y = 5$ (2)
$(1) \times 2$ $2x + 4y = 4$ (3)
$(3) - (2)$ $y = -1$
In (1) $x + 2(-1) = 2$
$x - 2 = 2$
$\therefore x = 4$

Multiple-choice questions

1 The algebraic expression that represents 2 less than 3 lots of n is

    A $3(n-2)$ **B** $2-3n$ **C** $3n-2$ **D** $3+n-2$ **E** n

2 The simplified form of $6ab + 14a \div 2 - 2ab$ is:

    A $8ab$ **B** $8ab + 7a$ **C** $ab + 7a$ **D** $4ab + 7a$ **E** $4ab + \dfrac{7a}{2}$

3 The solution to $\dfrac{x}{3} - 1 = 4$ is:

    A $x = 13$ **B** $x = 7$ **C** $x = 9$ **D** $x = 15$ **E** $x = \dfrac{5}{3}$

4 The result when a number is tripled and increased by 21 is 96. The original number is:

    A 22   **B** 32   **C** 25   **D** 30   **E** 27

5 The solution to the equation $3(x - 1) = 5x + 7$ is:

    A $x = -4$ **B** $x = -5$ **C** $x = 5$ **D** $x = 3$ **E** $x = 1$

6 $\$x$ is raised from a sausage sizzle. Once the \$50 running cost is taken out, the money is shared equally amongst three charities so that they each get \$120. An equation to represent this is:

    A $\dfrac{x - 50}{3} = 120$ **B** $\dfrac{x}{3} - 50 = 120$ **C** $\dfrac{x}{50} = 360$

    D $\dfrac{x}{3} = 310$ **E** $3x + 50 = 120$

 7 If $A = 2\pi rh$ with $A = 310$ and $r = 4$ then the value of h is closest to:

    A 12.3   **B** 121.7   **C** 24.7   **D** 38.8   **E** 10.4

8 The formula $d = \sqrt{\dfrac{a}{b}}$ transposed to make a the subject is:

    A $a = \sqrt{bd}$ **B** $a = d\sqrt{b}$ **C** $a = \dfrac{d^2}{b^2}$ **D** $a = \sqrt{\dfrac{d}{b}}$ **E** $a = bd^2$

9 The inequality representing the x values on the number line below is:

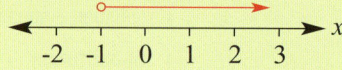

    A $x < -1$ **B** $x > -1$ **C** $x \le -1$ **D** $x \ge -1$ **E** $-1 < x < 3$

10 The solution to the inequality $1 - 2x > 9$ is:

    A $x < -4$ **B** $x < 4$ **C** $x < -5$ **D** $x > -4$ **E** $x > 5$

11 The solution to the simultaneous equations $x + 2y = 16$ and $y = x - 4$ is:

    A $x = 4, y = 0$ **B** $x = 8, y = 4$ **C** $x = 6, y = 2$
    D $x = 12, y = 8$ **E** $x = 5, y = 1$

12 The solution to the simultaneous equations $2x + y = 2$ and $2x + 3y = 10$ is:

    A $x = 0, y = 2$ **B** $x = 2, y = 2$ **C** $x = 2, y = -2$
    D $x = -1, y = 4$ **E** $x = -2, y = 6$

Short-answer questions

1 Write algebraic expressions to represent the following.

   a The product of m and 7   **b** Twice the sum of x and y

   c The cost of 3 movie tickets at m dollars each   **d** n divided by 4 less 3

2 Evaluate the following if $x = 2$, $y = -1$ and $z = 5$.

   a $yz - x$ **b** $\dfrac{2z - 4y}{x}$ **c** $\dfrac{2z^2}{x} + y$ **d** $x(y + z)$

3 Simplify.

   a $2m \times 4n$ **b** $\dfrac{4x^2 y}{12x}$ **c** $3ab \times 4b \div 2a$

   d $4 - 5b + 2b$ **e** $3mn + 2m - 1 - nm$ **f** $4p + 3q - 2p + q$

4 Expand and simplify the following.

   a $2(x + 7)$ **b** $-3(2x + 5)$ **c** $2x(3x - 4)$

   d $-2a(5 - 4a)$ **e** $5 - 4(x - 2)$ **f** $4(3x - 1) - 3(2 - 5x)$

5 Solve the following linear equations for x.

   a $5x + 6 = 51$ **b** $\dfrac{x + 2}{4} = 7$ **c** $\dfrac{2x}{5} - 3 = 3$ **d** $\dfrac{2x - 5}{3} = -1$

   e $7x - 4 = 10$ **f** $3 - 2x = 21$ **g** $1 - \dfrac{4x}{5} = 9$ **h** $2 - 7x = -3$

6 Write an equation to represent each of the following and then solve it for the pronumeral.

   a A number n is doubled and increased by 3 to give 21.

   b A number of lollies l is decreased by 5 and then shared equally among 3 friends so that they each get 7.

   c 5 less than the result of Toni's age x divided by 4 is 0.

7 Solve the following linear equations.

   a $2(x + 4) = 18$ **b** $3(2x - 3) = 2$ **c** $8x = 2x + 24$

   d $5(2x + 4) = 7x + 5$ **e** $3 - 4x = 7x - 8$ **f** $1 - 2(2 - x) = 5(x - 3)$

8 Nick makes an initial bid of $\$x$ in an auction for a signed cricket bat. By the end of the auction he has paid \$550, \$30 more than twice his initial bid. Set up and solve an equation to determine Nick's initial bid.

9 Represent each of the following on a number line.

   a $x > 1$ **b** $x \leq 7$ **c** $x \geq -4$

   d $x < -2$ **e** $2 < x \leq 8$ **f** $-1 < x < 3$

10 Solve the following inequalities.

   a $x + 8 < 20$ **b** $2m - 4 > -6$ **c** $3 - 2y \leq 15$

   d $\dfrac{7 - 2x}{3} > -9$ **e** $3a + 9 < 7(a - 1)$ **f** $-4x + 2 \leq 5x - 16$

11 A car salesman earns \$800 per month plus a 10% commission on the amount of sales for the month. If he is aiming to earn a minimum of \$3200 a month, what is the possible sales amount that will enable this?

12 Find the value of the unknown in each of the following formulas.

   a $E = \sqrt{PR}$ when $P = 90$ and $R = 40$

   b $v = u + at$ when $v = 20$, $u = 10$, $t = 2$

   c $V = \dfrac{1}{3}Ah$ when $V = 20$, $A = 6$

13 Rearrange the following formulas to make the variable in brackets the subject.

   a $v^2 = u^2 + 2ax$ (x) **b** $A = \dfrac{1}{2}r^2\theta$ (θ)

   c $P = RI^2, I > 0$ (I) **d** $S = \dfrac{n}{2}(a + l)$ (a)

14 Solve the following simultaneous equations using an appropriate method.

   a $x + 2y = 12$ **b** $2x + 3y = -6$ **c** $7x - 2y = 6$

       $x = 4y$ $y = x - 1$ $y = 2x + 3$

   d $x + y = 15$ **e** $3x + 2y = -19$ **f** $3x - 5y = 7$

       $x - y = 7$ $4x - y = -7$ $5x + 2y = 22$

15 Billy went to the Show and spent \$78 on a combined total of 9 items including rides and showbags. If each showbag cost \$12 and each ride cost \$7, how many of each did Billy buy?

How many rides did Billy buy?

Extended-response questions

1 The area of a trapezium is given by $A = \frac{1}{2}(a + b)h$. A new backyard deck in the shape of the trapezium shown is being designed.

Currently the dimensions are set such that $a = 12$ m and $h = 10$ m.

a What range of b values is required for an area of at most 110 m²?

b Rearrange the area formula to make b the subject.

c Use your answer to part **b** to find the length b m required to give an area of 100 m².

d Rearrange the area formula to make h the subject.

e If b is set as 8 m, what does the width of the deck (h m) need to be reduced to for an area of 80 m²?

2 Members of the Hayes and Thompson families attend the local Regatta by the Bay.

a The entry fee for an adult is $18 and the entry fee for a student is $8. The father and son from the Thompson family notice that after paying the entry fees and after 5 rides for the son and 3 for the adult, they have each spent the same amount. If the cost of a ride is the same for an adult and a student, write an equation and solve it to determine the cost of a ride.

b For lunch each family purchases some buckets of hot chips and some drinks.

The Hayes family buys 2 drinks and 1 bucket of chips for $11 and the Thompson family buys 3 drinks and 2 buckets of chips for $19. To determine how much each bucket of chips and each drink costs, complete the following:

   i Define two variables to represent the problem.

   ii Set up two equations relating the variables.

   iii Solve your equations in part **b ii** simultaneously.

   iv What is the cost of a bucket of chips and the cost of a drink?

Chapter 3

Pythagoras' theorem and trigonometry

What you will learn

Satellites

Satellite navigation systems work by determining where you are and calculating how far it is to where you want to go. Distances are worked out using the mathematics of trigonometry. The position of the satellite, your position and your destination are three points which form a triangle. This triangle can be divided into two right-angled triangles and, using two known angles and one side length, the distance between where you are and your destination can be found using sine, cosine and tangent functions. Similar techniques are used to navigate the seas, study the stars and map our planet, Earth.

1 Calculate each of the following.

a 3^2 b 20^2 c $2^2 + 4^2$ d $50^2 - 40^2$

2 Use a calculator to calculate each of the following correct to two decimal places.

a $\sqrt{35}$ b $\sqrt{236}$ c $\sqrt{23.6}$ d $\sqrt{65.4}$

3 Given that x is a positive number, find its value in each of the following equations.

a $x^2 = 4$ b $x^2 = 16$ c $x^2 = 3^2 + 4^2$ d $x^2 = 12^2 + 5^2$

4 Given that x is a positive number, solve each equation to find its value.

a $x^2 + 16 = 25$ b $x^2 + 9 = 25$ c $49 = x^2 + 24$ d $100 = x^2 + 36$

5 Round off each number correct to four decimal places.

a 0.45678 b 0.34569 c 0.04562 d 0.27997

6 Round off each number correct to two decimal places.

a 4.234 b 5.678 c 76.895 d 23.899

7 Solve each of the following equations to find the value of x.

a $3x = 6$ b $4x = 12$ c $5x = 60$ d $8x = 48$

e $\dfrac{x}{3} = 4$ f $\dfrac{x}{5} = 6$ g $\dfrac{x}{7} = 4$ h $\dfrac{x}{13} = 14$

i $\dfrac{4x}{3} = 12$ j $\dfrac{6x}{5} = 3$ k $\dfrac{2x}{3} = 8$ l $\dfrac{3x}{4} = 6$

8 Solve each of the following equations to find the value of x correct to two decimal places.

a $\dfrac{x}{3.2} = 4.7$ b $\dfrac{x}{2.1} = 7.43$ c $\dfrac{x}{0.3456} = 4$ d $\dfrac{x}{1.235} = 5.1$

9 Solve each of the following equations to find the value of x correct to one decimal place.

a $\dfrac{3}{x} = 5$ b $\dfrac{4}{x} = 7$ c $\dfrac{32}{x} = 15$ d $\dfrac{14}{x} = 27$

e $\dfrac{3.8}{x} = 6.9$ f $\dfrac{17}{x} = 8.4$ g $\dfrac{29.34}{x} = 3.24$ h $\dfrac{2.456}{x} = 0.345$

10 Find the value of x in these diagrams.

a

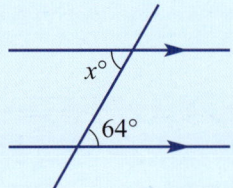

b

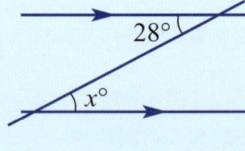

c

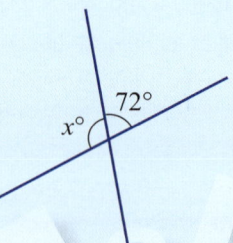

d

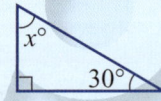

e

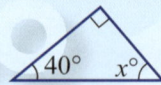

f

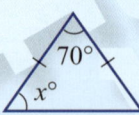

3.1 Pythagoras' theorem

Pythagoras was born on the Greek island of Samos in the 6th century BCE. He received a privileged education and travelled to Egypt and Persia where he developed his ideas in mathematics and philosophy. He settled in Crotone Italy where he founded a school. His many students and followers were called the Pythagoreans and under the guidance of Pythagoras, lived a very structured life with strict rules. They aimed to be pure, self-sufficient and wise, where men and women were treated equally and all property was considered communal. They strove to perfect their physical and mental form and made many advances in their understanding of the world through mathematics.

The Pythagoreans discovered the famous theorem, which is named after Pythagoras, and the existence of irrational numbers such as $\sqrt{2}$, which cannot be written down as a fraction or terminating decimal. Such numbers cannot be measured exactly with a ruler with fractional

The Pythagorean brotherhood in ancient Greece

parts and were thought to be unnatural. The Pythagoreans called these numbers 'unutterable' numbers and it is believed that any member of the brotherhood who mentioned these numbers in public would be put to death.

Let's start: Matching the areas of squares

Look at this right-angled triangle and the squares drawn on each side. Each square is divided into smaller sections.

- Can you see how the parts of the two smaller squares would fit into the larger square?
- What is the area of each square if the side lengths of the right-angled triangle are a, b and c as marked?
- What do the answers to the above two questions suggest about the relationship between a, b and c?

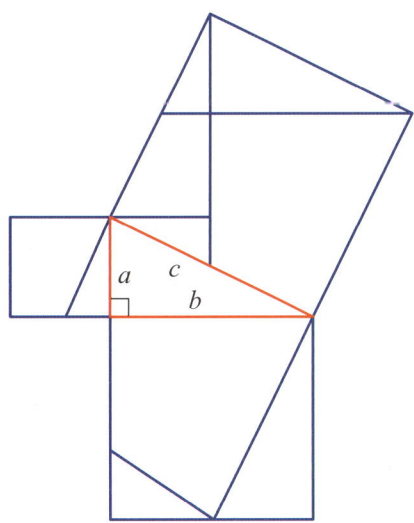

- The longest side opposite the right angle in a right-angled triangle is called the **hypotenuse**.
- The **theorem of Pythagoras** says that the square of the length of the hypotenuse is equal to the sum of the squares of the lengths of the other two sides.
  For the triangle shown, it is:

  $$c^2 = a^2 + b^2$$

  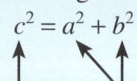

  square of the   squares of the
  hypotenuse   two shorter sides

  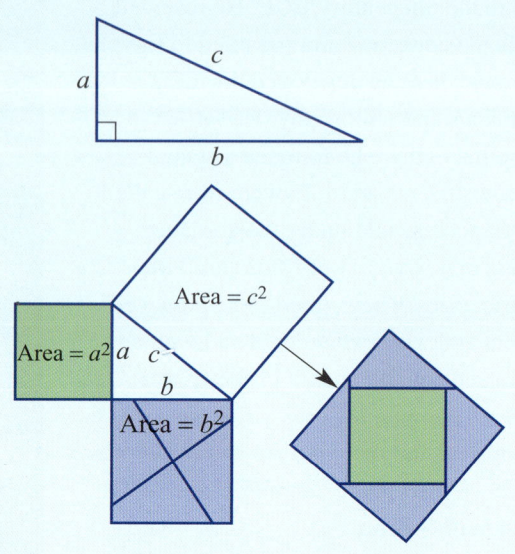

  - The theorem can be illustrated in a diagram like the one on the right. The sum of the areas of the two smaller squares ($a^2 + b^2$) is the same as the area of the largest square (c^2).
- Lengths can be expressed with **exact values** using **surds**. $\sqrt{2}$, $\sqrt{28}$ and $2\sqrt{3}$ are examples of surds.
  - When expressed as a decimal, a surd is an infinite non-recurring decimal with no pattern, for example, $\sqrt{2} = 1.4142135623\ldots$

Example 1 Finding the length of the hypotenuse

Find the length of the hypotenuse in these right-angled triangles. Round to two decimal places in part **b**.

a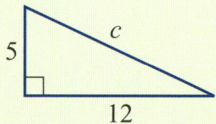

b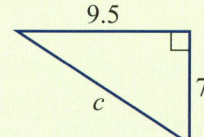

SOLUTION

a $c^2 = a^2 + b^2$
$\quad = 5^2 + 12^2$
$\quad = 169$
$\therefore\ c = \sqrt{169}$
$\quad = 13$

b $c^2 = a^2 + b^2$
$\quad = 7^2 + 9.5^2$
$\quad = 139.25$
$\therefore\ c = \sqrt{139.25}$
$\quad = 11.80$

EXPLANATION

Write the rule and substitute the lengths of the two shorter sides.

If $c^2 = 169$ then $c = \sqrt{169} = 13$.

The order for a and b does not matter since $7^2 + 9.5^2 = 9.5^2 + 7^2$.

Round as required.

Example 2 Finding the length of the hypotenuse using exact values

Find the length of the hypotenuse in this right-angled triangle, leaving your answer as an exact value.

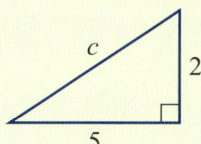

SOLUTION

$$c^2 = a^2 + b^2$$
$$= 5^2 + 2^2$$
$$= 29$$
$$\therefore \quad c = \sqrt{29}$$

EXPLANATION

Apply Pythagoras' theorem to find the value of c.

Express the answer exactly using a surd.

Exercise 3A

Understanding

1 State the value of the hypotenuse (c) in these right-angled triangles.

a
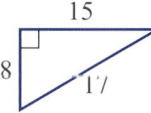

b
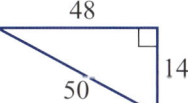

c
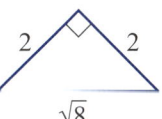

2 Write down Pythagoras' theorem using the given pronumerals for these right-angled triangles. For example: $z^2 = x^2 + y^2$.

a
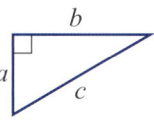

b
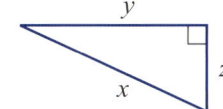

c
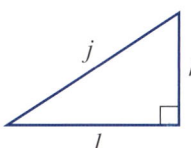

3 Evaluate the following, rounding to two decimal places in parts **g** and **h**.

a 9^2 b 3.2^2 c $3^2 + 2^2$ d $9^2 + 5^2$

e $\sqrt{36}$ f $\sqrt{64 + 36}$ g $\sqrt{24}$ h $\sqrt{3^2 + 2^2}$

Fluency

Example 1a

4 Find the length of the hypotenuse in each of the following right-angled triangles.

a
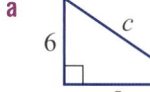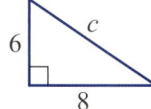

b
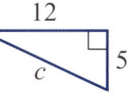

c
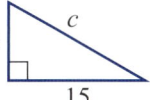

d
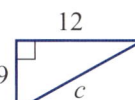

e
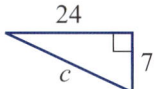

f
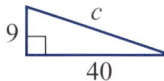

g
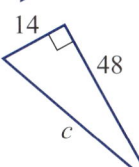

h
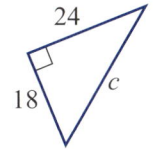

i
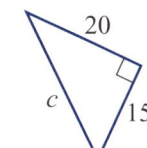

Example 1b

5 Find the length of the hypotenuse in each of these right-angled triangles, correct to two decimal places.

a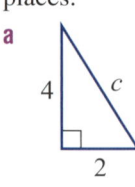

b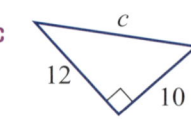

c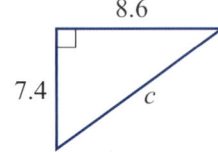

d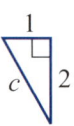

e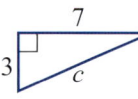

f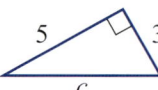

Example 2 **6** Find the length of the hypotenuse in these triangles, leaving your answer as an exact value.

a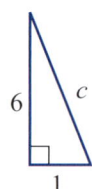

b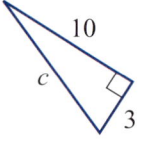

c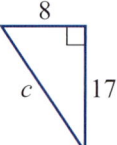

d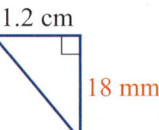

e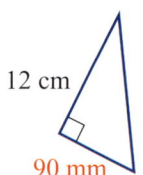

f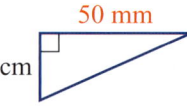

7 Find the length of the hypotenuse in each of these right-angled triangles, rounding to two decimal places where necessary. Convert to the units indicated in red.

a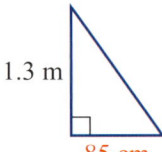

b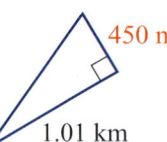

c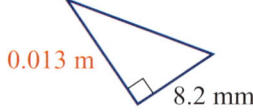

d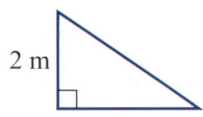

e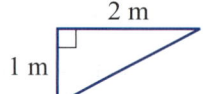

f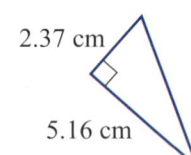

8 For each of these triangles, first calculate the length of the hypotenuse then find the perimeter, correct to two decimal places.

a

b

c

d

0.072 m

0.038 m

e

5 mm

f

3.2 cm

9 Find the perimeter of this triangle. (*Hint:* You will need to find *AB* and *BC* first.)

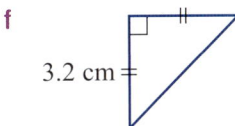

B

12

A

9   5

C

10 Find the length of the diagonal steel brace required to support a wall of length 3.5 m and height 2.6 m. Give your answer correct to one decimal place.

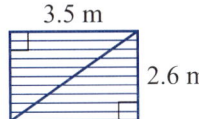

3.5 m

2.6 m

11 A helicopter hovers at a height of 150 m above the ground and is a horizontal distance of 200 m from a beacon on the ground. Find the direct distance of the helicopter from the beacon.

12 A miniature rocket blasts off at an angle of 45° and, after a few seconds, reaches a height of 350 m above the ground. At this point it has also covered a horizontal distance of 350 m. How far has the rocket travelled to the nearest metre?

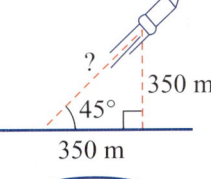

?

45°

350 m

350 m

13 Find the length of the longest rod that will fit inside a cylinder of height 2.1 m and with circular end surface of 1.2 m diameter. Give your answer correct to one decimal place.

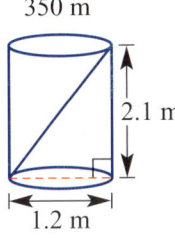

2.1 m

1.2 m

14 For the shape on the right, find the value of:
  a *x*
  b *y* (as a fraction)

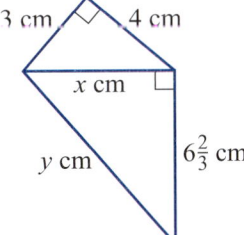

3 cm   4 cm

x cm

y cm

$6\frac{2}{3}$ cm

15 One way to check whether a four-sided figure is a rectangle is to ensure that both its diagonals are the same length. What should the length of the diagonals be if a rectangle has side lengths 3 m and 5 m? Answer to two decimal places.

16 We know that if the triangle has a right angle, then $c^2 = a^2 + b^2$. The converse of this is that if $c^2 = a^2 + b^2$ then the triangle must have a right angle. Test if $c^2 = a^2 + b^2$ to see if these triangles must have a right angle. They may not be drawn to scale.

a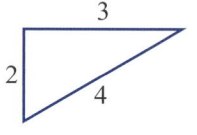

b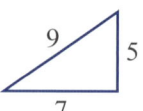

c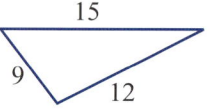

d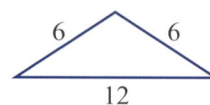

e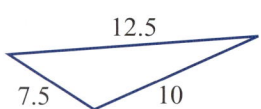

f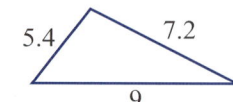

17 Triangle ABC is a right-angled isosceles triangle, and BD is perpendicular to AC. If $DC = 4$ cm and $BD = 4$ cm:

a find the length of BC correct to two decimal places

b state the length of AB and hence AC correct to two decimal places

c use Pythagoras' theorem and $\triangle ABC$ to check that the length of AC is twice the length of DC.

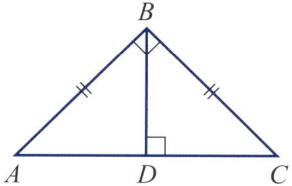

Enrichment: Kennels and kites

18 A dog kennel has the dimensions shown in the diagram on the right. Give your answers to each of the following correct to two decimal places.

a What is the width of the kennel?

b What is the total height, h m, of the kennel?

c If the sloping height of the roof was to be reduced from 55 cm to 50 cm, what difference would this make to the total height of the kennel? (Assume that the width is the same as in part **a**.)

d What is the length of the sloping height of the roof of a new kennel if it is to have a total height of 1.2 m? (The height of the kennel without the roof is still 1 m and its width is unchanged.)

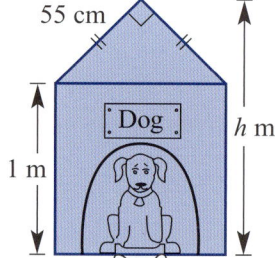

19 The frame of a kite is constructed with six pieces of timber dowel. The four pieces around the outer edge are two 30 cm pieces and two 50 cm pieces. The top end of the kite is to form a right angle. Find the length of each of the diagonal pieces required to complete the construction. Answer to two decimal places.

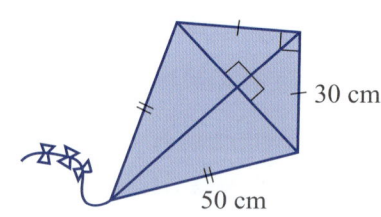

3.2 Finding the shorter sides

Throughout history, mathematicians have utilised known theorems to explore new ideas, discover new theorems and solve a wider range of problems. Similarly, Pythagoras knew that his right-angled triangle theorem could be manipulated so that the length of one of the shorter sides of a triangle can be found if the length of the other two sides are known.

We know that the sum $7 = 3 + 4$ can be written as a difference $3 = 7 - 4$. Likewise, if $c^2 = a^2 + b^2$ then $a^2 = c^2 - b^2$ or $b^2 = c^2 - a^2$.

Applying this to a right-angled triangle means that we can now find the length of one of the shorter sides if the other two sides are known.

Let's start: True or false

Below are some mathematical statements relating to a right-angled triangle with hypotenuse c and the two shorter sides a and b.

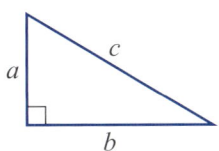

If we know the length of the crane jib and the horizontal distance it extends, Pythagoras' theorem enables us to calculate its vertical height.

Some of these mathematical statements are true and some are false. Can you sort them into true and false groups?

$a^2 + b^2 = c^2$ $a = \sqrt{c^2 - b^2}$ $c^2 - a^2 = b^2$ $a^2 - c^2 = b^2$

$c = \sqrt{a^2 + b^2}$ $b = \sqrt{a^2 - c^2}$ $c = \sqrt{a^2 - b^2}$ $c^2 - b^2 = a^2$

■ When finding the length of a side:
   • Substitute known values into Pythagoras' rule.
   • Solve this equation to find the unknown value.
   For example:
   • If $a^2 + 16 = 30$ then subtract 16 from both sides.
   • If $a^2 = 14$ then take the square root of both sides.
   • $a = \sqrt{14}$ is an **exact** answer (a surd).
   • $a = 3.74$ is a rounded decimal answer.

$c^2 = a^2 + b^2$
$25^2 = a^2 + 15^2$
$625 = a^2 + 225$
$400 = a^2$
$a = 20$

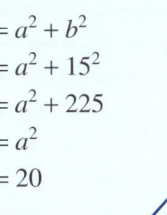
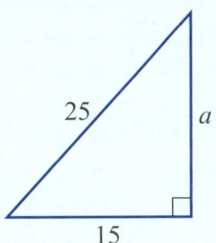

Key ideas

Example 3 Finding a shorter side

In each of the following, find the value of the pronumeral. Round your answer in part **b** to two decimal places and give an exact answer to part **c**.

a 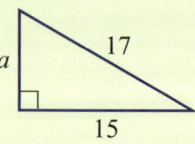   **b** 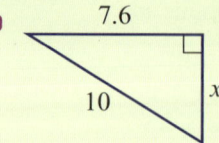   **c**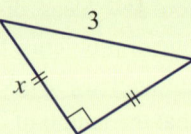

SOLUTION

a $a^2 + 15^2 = 17^2$

$a^2 + 225 = 289$

$a^2 = 64$

$\therefore a = \sqrt{64}$

$a = 8$

b $x^2 + 7.6^2 = 10^2$

$x^2 + 57.76 = 100$

$x^2 = 42.24$

$\therefore x = \sqrt{42.24}$

$x = 6.50$

c $x^2 + x^2 = 3^2$

$2x^2 = 9$

$x^2 = \dfrac{9}{2}$

$\therefore x = \sqrt{\dfrac{9}{2}}$

EXPLANATION

Write the rule and substitute the known sides.

Square 15 and 17.

Subtract 225 from both sides.

Take the square root of both sides.

Write the rule.

Subtract 57.76 from both sides.

Take the square root of both sides.

Round to two decimal places.

Two sides are of length x.

Add like terms.

Divide both sides by 2.

Take the square root of both sides. To express as an exact answer, do not round.

Exercise 3B

1 Find the value of a or b in these equations. (Both a and b are positive numbers.)

a $a = \sqrt{196}$

b $a = \sqrt{121}$

c $a^2 = 144$

d $a^2 = 400$

e $b^2 + 9 = 25$

f $b^2 + 49 = 625$

g $36 + b^2 = 100$

h $15^2 + b^2 = 17^2$

2 If $a^2 + 64 = 100$, decide if the following are true or false.

a $a^2 = 100 - 64$

b $64 = 100 + a^2$

c $100 = \sqrt{a^2 + 64}$

d $a = \sqrt{100 - 64}$

e $a = 6$

f $a = 10$

Understanding

mple 3a **3** In each of the following find the value of the pronumeral.

a
 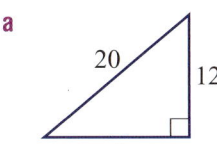

b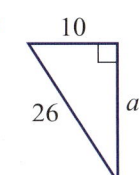

c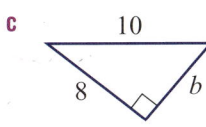

d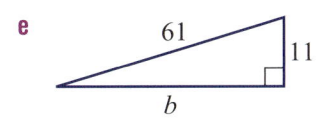

e

f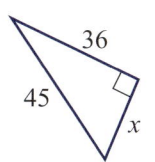

mple 3b **4** In each of the following, find the value of the pronumeral. Express your answers correct to two decimal places.

a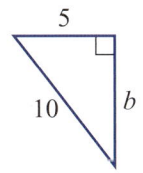

b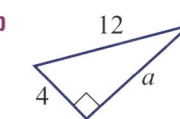

c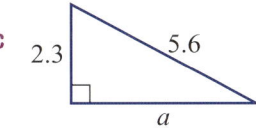

d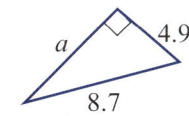

e

f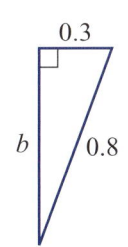

5 Find the length of the unknown side of each of these triangles, correct to two decimal places where necessary. Convert to the units shown in red.

a

b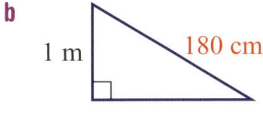

c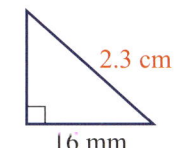

d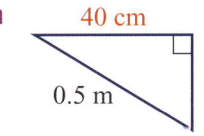

e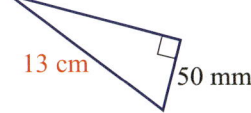

f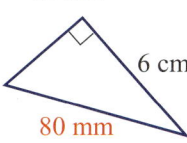

mple 3c **6** In each of the following, find the value of x as an exact answer.

a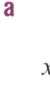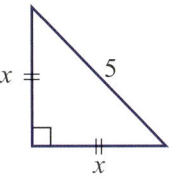

b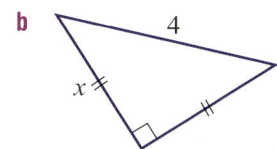

c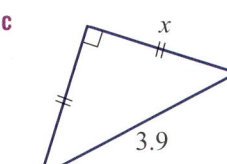

7 For each of the following diagrams, find the value of x. Give an exact answer each time.

a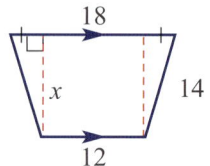

b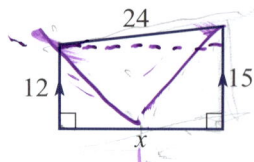

c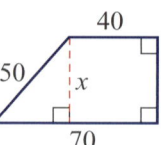

 8 A 32 m communication tower is supported by 35 m cables stretching from the top of the tower to a position at ground level. Find the distance from the base of the tower to the point where the cable reaches the ground, correct to one decimal place.

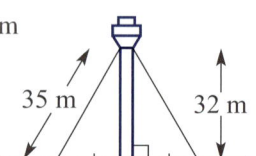

 9 The base of a ladder leaning against a wall is 1.5 m from the base of the wall. If the ladder is 5.5 m long, find how high the top of the ladder is above the ground, correct to one decimal place.

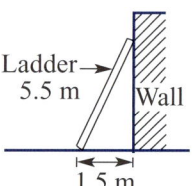

 10 If a television has a screen size of 63 cm it means that the diagonal length of the screen is 63 cm. If the vertical height of a 63 cm screen is 39 cm, find how wide the screen is to the nearest centimetre.

11 A 1.3 m vertical fence post is supported by a 2.27 m bar, as shown in the diagram on the right. Find the distance (d metres) from the base of the post to where the support enters the ground. Give your answer correct to two decimal places.

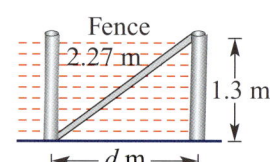

12 For these questions note that $(2x)^2 = 4x^2$ and $(3x)^2 = 9x^2$.
In each of the following find the value of x as an exact answer.

a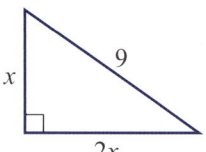

b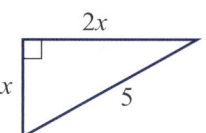

c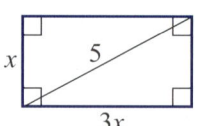

13 A right-angled triangle has a hypotenuse measuring 5 m. Find the lengths of the other sides if their lengths are in the given ratio. Give an exact answer. *Hint:* You can draw a triangle like this for part **a**.

a 1 to 3   **b** 2 to 3   **c** 5 to 7

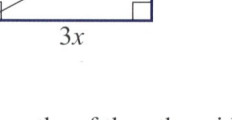

Enrichment: The power of exact values

14 Consider this diagram and the unknown length x.

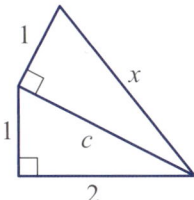

a Explain what needs to be found first before x can be calculated.
b Now try calculating the value x as an exact value.
c Was it necessary to calculate the value of c or was c^2 enough?
d What problems might be encountered if the value of c was calculated and rounded off before the value of x is found?

15 In the diagram below, $OD = 3$ and $AB = BC = CD = 1$.

a Using exact values find the length of:
  i OC
  ii OB
  iii OA

b Round your answer in part **a iii** to one decimal place and use that length to recalculate the lengths of OB, OC and OD (correct to two decimal places) starting with $\triangle OAB$.

c Explain the difference between the given length $OD = 3$ and your answer for OD in part **b**.

d Investigate how changing the side length AB affects your answers to parts **a** to **c** above.

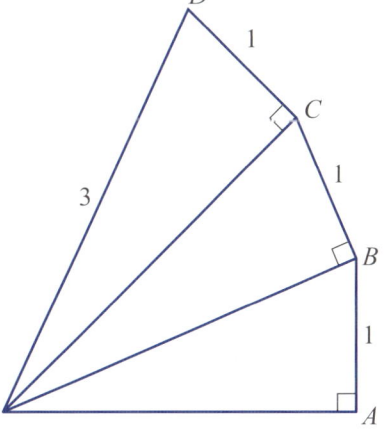

Pythagoras' theorem can be used to ensure that the corners of land plots and building foundations are right angles.

Initially it may not be obvious that Pythagoras' theorem can be used to help solve a particular problem. With further investigation, however, it may be possible to identify and draw in a right-angled triangle which can help solve the problem. As long as two sides of the right-angled triangle are known, the length of the third side can be found.

The length of each cable on the Anzac Bridge, Sydney can be calculated using Pythagoras' theorem.

Let's start: The biggest square

Imagine trying to cut the largest square from a circle of a certain size and calculating the side length of the square. Drawing a simple diagram as shown does not initially reveal a right-angled triangle.

- If the circle has a diameter of 2 cm, can you find a good position to draw the diameter that also helps to form a right-angled triangle?
- Can you determine the side length of the largest square?
- What percentage of the area of a circle does the largest square occupy?

Key ideas

When applying Pythagoras' theorem:
- Identify and draw right-angled triangles which may help to solve the problem.
- Label the sides with their lengths or with a letter (pronumeral) if the length is unknown.
- Use Pythagoras' theorem to solve for the unknown.
- Solve the problem by making any further calculations and answering in words.

Example 4 **Applying Pythagoras' theorem**

Two skyscrapers are located 25 m apart and a cable links the tops of the two buildings. Find the length of the cable if the buildings are 50 m and 80 m in height. Give your answer correct to two decimal places.

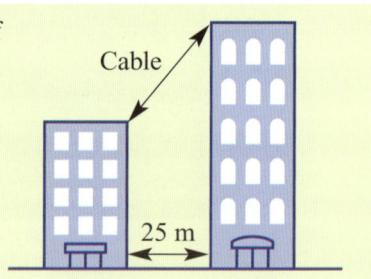

SOLUTION	EXPLANATION
Let x m be the length of the cable.	Draw a right-angled triangle and label the measurements and pronumerals.

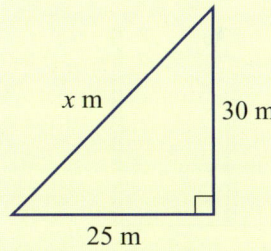

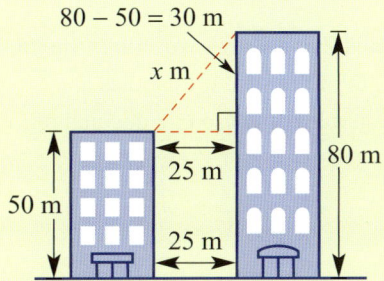

$80 - 50 = 30$ m

$c^2 = a^2 + b^2$	Set up an equation using Pythagoras' theorem and solve for x.
$x^2 = 25^2 + 30^2$	
$x^2 = 625 + 900$	
$\quad = 1525$	
$\therefore x = \sqrt{1525}$	
$\quad = 39.05$	
$\therefore$ The cable is 39.05 m long.	Answer the question in words.

Exercise 3C

1 Match each problem (**a**, **b** or **c**) with both a diagram (**A**, **B** or **C**) and its solution (**I**, **II**, **III**).

a Two trees stand 20 m apart and they are 32 m and 47 m tall. What is the distance between the tops of the two trees?

A

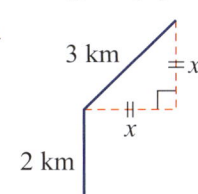

3 km, 2 km, x

I The kite is flying at a height of 30.59 m.

b A man walks due north for 2 km then north-east for 3 km. How far north is he from his starting point?

B

x m, 35 m, 17 m

II The distance between the top of the two trees is 25 m.

c A kite is flying with a kite string of length 35 m. Its horizontal distance from its anchor point is 17 m. How high is the kite flying?

C

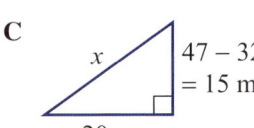

x, $47 - 32 = 15$ m, 20 m

III The man has walked a total of $2 + 2.12 = 4.12$ km north from his starting point.

Understanding

Example 4

2 Two skyscrapers are located 25 m apart and a cable of length 62.3 m links the tops of the two buildings. If the taller building is 200 metres tall, what is the height of the shorter building? Give your answer correct to one decimal place.

3 Two poles are located 2 m apart. A wire links the tops of the two poles. Find the length of the wire if the poles are 2.8 m and 5 m in height. Give your answer correct to one decimal place.

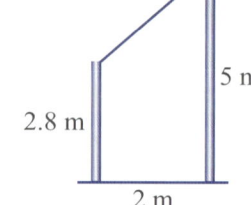

4 A garage is to be built with a skillion roof (a roof with a single slope). The measurements are given in the diagram. Calculate the pitch line length, to the nearest millimetre. Allow 500 mm for each of the eaves.

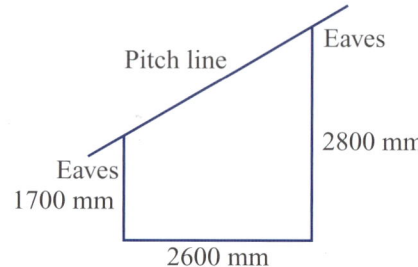

5 Two bushwalkers are standing on different mountain sides. According to their maps, one of them is at a height of 2120 m and the other is at a height of 1650 m. If the horizontal distance between them is 950 m, find the direct distance between the two bushwalkers. Give your answer correct to the nearest metre.

6 Find the direct distance between the points A and B in each of the following, correct to one decimal place.

a

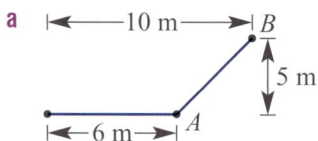

b

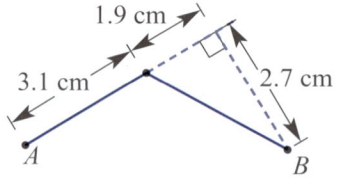

c

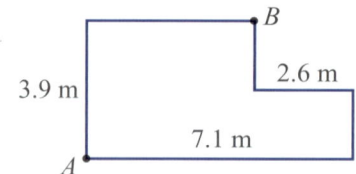

d

7 A 100 m radio mast is supported by six cables in two sets of three cables. They are anchored to the ground at an equal distance from the mast. The top set of three cables is attached at a point 20 m below the top of the mast. Each cable in the lower set of three cables is 60 m long and is attached at a height of 30 m above the ground. If all the cables have to be replaced, find the total length of cable required. Give your answer correct to two decimal places.

8 In a particular circle of radius 2 cm, AB is a diameter and C is a point on the circumference. Angle ACB is a right angle. The chord AC is 1 cm in length.

  a Draw the triangle ABC as described, and mark in all the important information.

  b Find the length of BC correct to one decimal place.

9 A suspension bridge is built with two vertical pylons and two straight beams of equal length that are positioned to extend from the top of the pylons to meet at a point C above the centre of the bridge, as shown in the diagram on the right.

  a Calculate the vertical height of the point C above the tops of the pylons.

  b Calculate the distance between the pylons, that is, the length of the span of the bridge correct to one decimal place.

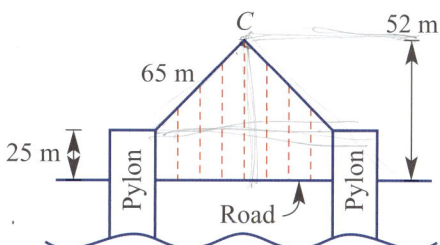

10 Two circles of radius 10 cm and 15 cm respectively are placed inside a square. Find the perimeter of the square to the nearest centimetre. *Hint:* first find the diagonal length of the square using the diagram on the right.

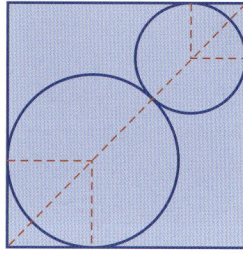

11 It is possible to find the length of the shorter sides of a right isosceles triangle if only the hypotenuse length is known.

  a Find the exact value of x in this right isosceles triangle.

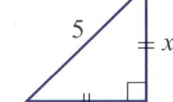

  b Now find the exact value of a in this diagram.

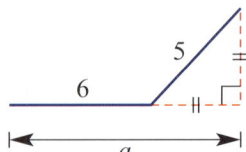

  c Finally, use your results from above to find the length of AB in this diagram correct to one decimal place.

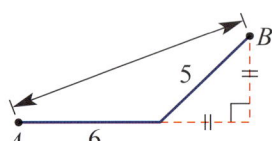

12 Use the method outlined in Question **11** for this problem.

    In an army navigation exercise, a group of soldiers hiked due south from base camp for 2.5 km to a water hole. From there, they turned 45° to the left, to head south-east for 1.6 km to a resting point. When the soldiers were at the resting point, how far (correct to one decimal place):

  a east were they from the water hole?

  b south were they from the water hole?

  c were they in a straight line from base camp?

Enrichment: Folding paper

13 A square piece of paper, $ABCD$, of side length 20 cm is folded to form a right-angled triangle ABC. The paper is folded a second time to form a right-angled triangle ABE as shown in the diagram below.

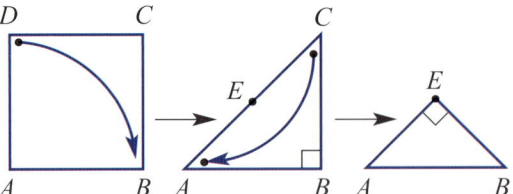

  a Find the length of AC correct to two decimal places.

  b Find the perimeter of each of the following, correct to one decimal place where necessary:

    i square $ABCD$ **ii** triangle ABC **iii** triangle ABE

  c Use Pythagoras' theorem and your answer for part **a** to confirm that $AE = BE$ in triangle ABE.

  d Investigate how changing the initial side length changes the answers to the above.

3.4 Pythagoras in three dimensions

If you cut a solid to form a cross-section a two-dimensional shape is revealed. From that cross-section it may be possible to identify a right-angled triangle that can be used to find unknown lengths. These lengths can then tell us information about the three-dimensional solid.

You can visualise right-angled triangles in all sorts of different solids.

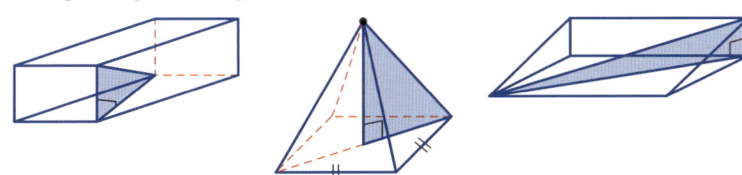

The glass pyramid at the Palais du Louvre, Paris, is made up of a total of 70 triangular and 603 rhombus-shaped glass segments together forming many right-angled triangles.

Let's start: How many triangles in a pyramid?

Here is a drawing of a square-based pyramid. By drawing lines from any vertex to the centre of the base and another point, how many different right-angled triangles can you visualise and draw? The triangles could be inside or on the outside surface of the pyramid.

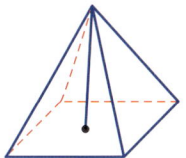

- Right-angled triangles can be identified in many three-dimensional solids.
- It is important to try to draw any identified right-angled triangle using a separate diagram.

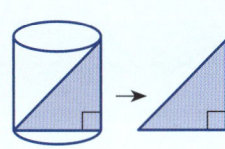

Example 5 Using Pythagoras in 3D

The length of the diagonal on the base of a rectangular prism is 5.3 m and the rectangular prism's height is 3.9 m. Find the distance from one corner of the rectangular prism to the opposite corner. Give your answer correct to two decimal places.

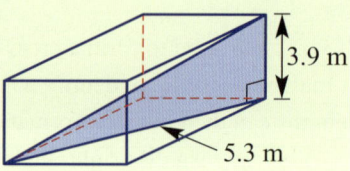

SOLUTION

Let d m be the distance required.

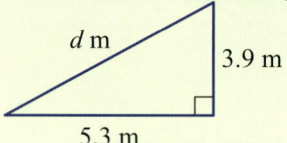

$$d^2 = 3.9^2 + 5.3^2$$
$$= 43.3$$
$$\therefore d = 6.58$$

The distance from one corner of the rectangular prism to the opposite corner is approximately 6.58 m.

EXPLANATION

Draw a right-angled triangle and label all the measurements and pronumerals.

Use Pythagoras' theorem.
Round to two decimal places.

Write your answer in words.

Exercise 3D

1 Decide if the following shaded regions form right-angled triangles.

a
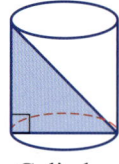
Cylinder

b
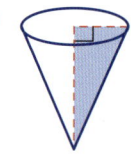
Cone

c
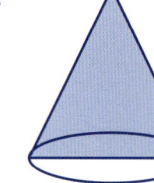
Cone

d
Cube

e
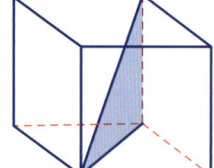
Cube

f
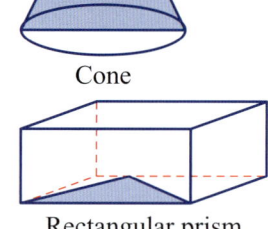
Rectangular prism

g
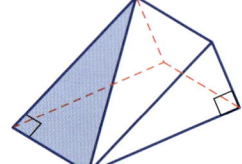
Triangular prism

h

Tetrahedron regular triangular-based pyramid

i
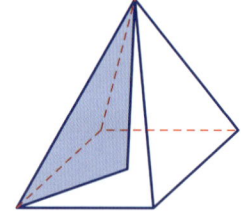
Right square-based pyramid (apex above centre of base)

ample 5 **2** Find the distance, d units, from one corner to the opposite corner in each of the following rectangular prisms. Give your answers correct to two decimal places.

a

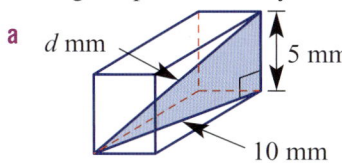

d mm

5 mm

10 mm

b

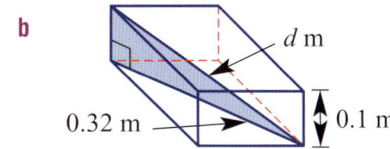

d m

0.32 m

0.1 m

c

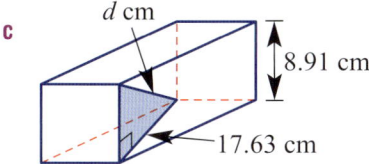

d cm

8.91 cm

17.63 cm

3 Find the slant height, s units, of each of the following cones. Give your answers correct to one decimal place.

a

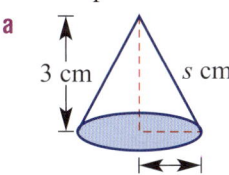

3 cm

s cm

2 cm

b

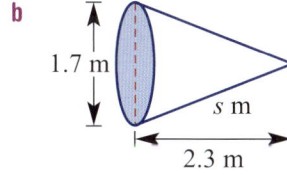

1.7 m

s m

2.3 m

c

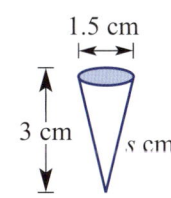

1.5 cm

3 cm

s cm

4 Find the length to the nearest millimetre of the longest rod that will fit inside a cylinder of the following dimensions.

a Diameter 10 cm and height 15 cm

b Radius 2.8 mm and height 4.2 mm

c Diameter 0.034 m and height 0.015 m

Rod

5 The cube in the diagram on the right has 1 cm sides.

a Find the length of AC as an exact value.

b Hence, find the length of AD correct to one decimal place.

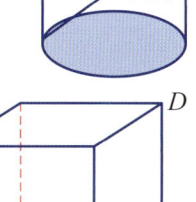

D

C

A B

6 For the shape shown:

a Find the length of AC as an exact value.

b Hence, find the length of AD correct to one decimal place.

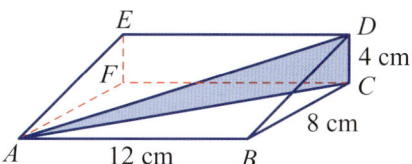

E D

F C

4 cm

8 cm

A 12 cm B

7 A miner makes claim to a circular piece of land with a radius of 40 m from a given point, and is entitled to dig to a depth of 25 m. If the miner can dig tunnels at any angle, find the length of the longest straight tunnel that he can dig, to the nearest metre.

8 A bowl is in the shape of a hemisphere (half sphere) with radius 10 cm. The surface of the water in the container has a radius of 7 cm. How deep is the water? Give your answer to one decimal place.

9 A cube of side length l sits inside a sphere of radius r so that the vertices of the cube sit on the sphere. Find the ratio $r : l$.

10 There are different ways to approach finding the height of a pyramid depending on what information is given. For each of the following square-based pyramids, find:

    i the exact length (using a surd) of the diagonal on the base

    ii the height of the pyramid correct to two decimal places

a

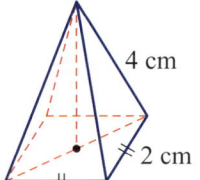

b

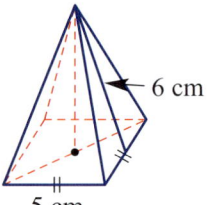

11 For this rectangular prism answer these questions.

    a Find the exact length AB.

    b Find AB correct to two decimal places.

    c Find the length AC using your result from part **a** and then round to two decimal places.

    d Find the length AC using your result from part **b** and then round to two decimal places.

    e How can you explain the difference between your results from parts **c** and **d** above?

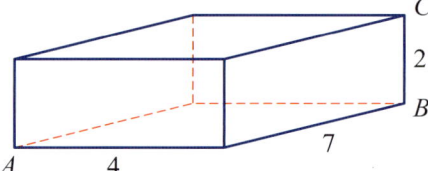

Enrichment: Spider crawl

12 A spider crawls from one corner, A, of the ceiling of a room to the opposite corner, G, on the floor. The room is a rectangular prism with dimensions as given in the diagram on the right.

    a Find how far (correct to two decimal places) the spider crawled if it crawls from A to G via:

        i B **ii** C

        iii D  **iv** F

    b Investigate other paths to determine the shortest distance that the spider could crawl in order to travel from point A to point G.

3.5 Trigonometric ratios

The branch of mathematics called trigonometry deals with the relationship between the side lengths and angles in triangles. Trigonometry dates back to the ancient Egyptian and Babylonian civilisations where a basic form of trigonometry was used in the building of pyramids and in the study of astronomy. The first table of values including chord and arc lengths on a circle for a given angle was created by Hipparchus in the 2nd century BCE in Greece. These tables of values helped to calculate the position of the planets. About three centuries later, Claudius Ptolemy advanced the study of trigonometry writing 13 books called the *Almagest*. Ptolemy also developed tables of values linking the sides and angles of a triangle and produced many theorems which use the sine, cosine and tangent functions.

A basic form of trigonometry was used in the building of pyramids in Ancient Egypt.

Let's start: Constancy of sine, cosine and tangent

In geometry we would say that similar triangles have the same shape but are of different size. Here are three similar right-angled triangles. The angle θ (theta) is the same for all three triangles.

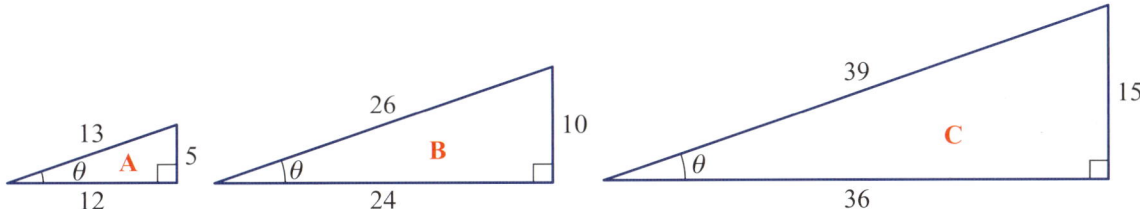

We will now calculate three special ratios: sine, cosine and tangent for the angle θ in the above triangles. We use the sides labelled Hypotenuse (H), Opposite (O) and Adjacent (A) as shown at right.

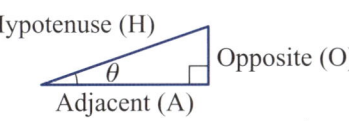

- Complete this table simplifying all fractions.
- What do you notice about the value of:

  a $\sin \theta \left(\dfrac{O}{H} \right)$ for all three triangles?

  b $\cos \theta \left(\dfrac{A}{H} \right)$ for all three triangles?

  c $\tan \theta \left(\dfrac{O}{A} \right)$ for all three triangles?

Triangle	$\dfrac{O}{H}$ (sin θ)	$\dfrac{A}{H}$ (cos θ)	$\dfrac{O}{A}$ (tan θ)
A	$\dfrac{5}{13}$		
B		$\dfrac{24}{26} = \dfrac{12}{13}$	
C			$\dfrac{15}{36} = \dfrac{5}{12}$

- Why are the three ratios (sin θ, cos θ and tan θ) the same for all three triangles? Discuss.

Key ideas

- For a right-angled triangle with a given angle θ, the three ratios **sine (sin)**, **cosine (cos)** and **tangent (tan)** are given by:

  - sine of angle θ (or sin θ) $= \dfrac{\text{length of the opposite side}}{\text{length of the hypotenuse}}$

  - cosine of angle θ (or cos θ) $= \dfrac{\text{length of the adjacent side}}{\text{length of the hypotenuse}}$

  - tangent of angle θ (or tan θ) $= \dfrac{\text{length of the opposite side}}{\text{length of the adjacent}}$

- For any right-angled triangle with the same angles, these ratios are always the same.
- The word **SOHCAHTOA** is useful when trying to remember the three ratios.

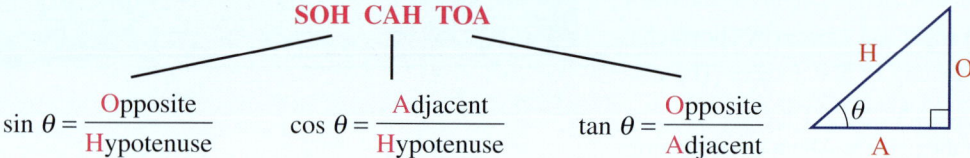

SOH   CAH   TOA

$\sin \theta = \dfrac{\text{Opposite}}{\text{Hypotenuse}}$ $\cos \theta = \dfrac{\text{Adjacent}}{\text{Hypotenuse}}$ $\tan \theta = \dfrac{\text{Opposite}}{\text{Adjacent}}$

Example 6 Labelling the sides of triangles

Copy this triangle and label the sides as opposite to θ (O), adjacent to θ (A) or hypotenuse (H).

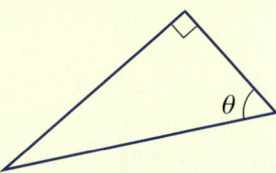

SOLUTION

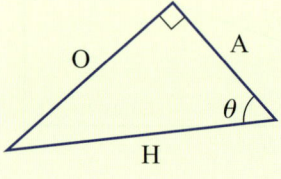

EXPLANATION

Draw the triangle and label the side opposite the right angle as hypotenuse (H), the side opposite the angle θ as opposite (O) and the remaining side next to the angle θ as adjacent (A).

Example 7 Writing trigonometric ratios

Write a trigonometric ratio (in fraction form) for each of the following triangles.

a
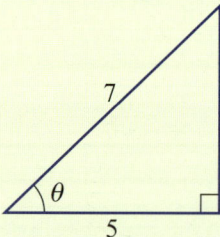

b
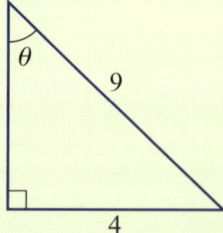

c
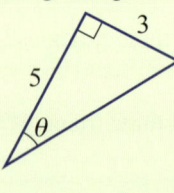

SOLUTION	EXPLANATION

a $\cos \theta = \dfrac{A}{H} = \dfrac{5}{7}$

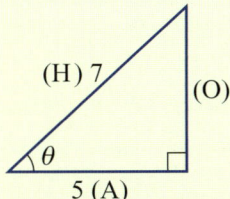

Side length 7 is the longest side so it is the hypotenuse (H). Side length 5 is adjacent to angle θ so it is the adjacent (A).

b $\sin \theta = \dfrac{O}{H} = \dfrac{4}{9}$

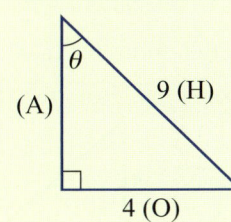

Side length 9 is the longest side so it is the hypotenuse (H). Side length 4 is opposite angle θ so it is the opposite (O).

c $\tan \theta = \dfrac{O}{A} = \dfrac{3}{5}$

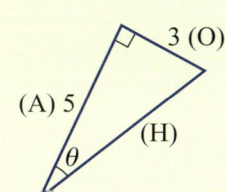

Side length 5 is the adjacent side to angle θ so it is the adjacent (A). Side length 3 is opposite angle θ so it is the opposite (O).

Exercise 3E

1 Write the missing word in these sentences.

a H stands for the word _____.

b O stands for the word _____.

c A stands for the word _____.

d $\sin \theta = $ _____ $\div$ Hypotenuse.

e $\cos \theta = $ Adjacent $\div$ _____.

f $\tan \theta = $ Opposite $\div$ _____.

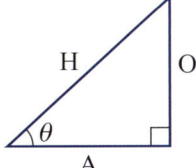

Understanding

ample 6 **2** Copy each of these triangles and label the sides as opposite to θ (O), adjacent to θ (A) or hypotenuse (H).

a
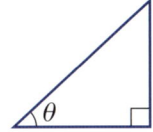

b
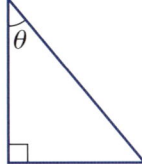

c
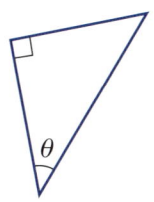

d
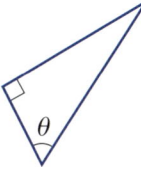

e
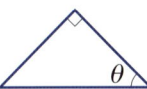

f
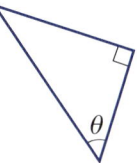

g
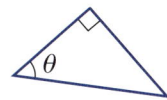

h
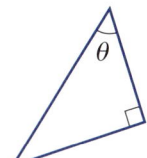

3 For the triangle shown, state the length of the side which corresponds to:

a the hypotenuse

b the side opposite angle θ

c the side opposite angle α

d the side adjacent to angle θ

e the side adjacent to angle α.

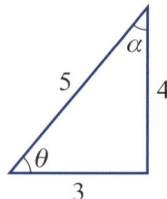

Example 7

4 Write a trigonometric ratio (in fraction form) for each of the following triangles and simplify where possible.

a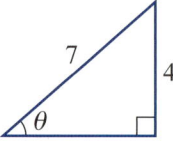

b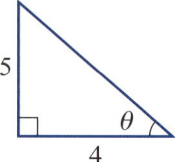

c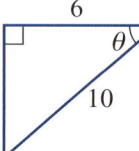

d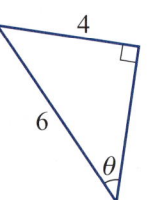

e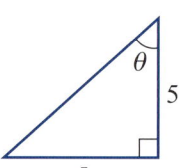

f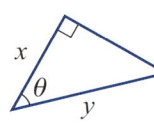

g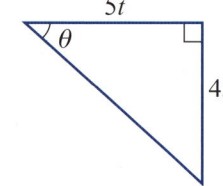

h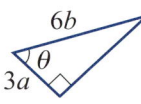

i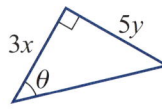

5 Here are two similar triangles A and B.

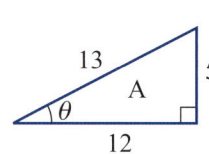
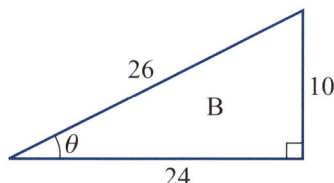

a i Write the ratio $\sin \theta$ (as a fraction) for triangle A.

ii Write the ratio $\sin \theta$ (as a fraction) for triangle B.

iii What do you notice about your two answers from parts **a i** and **a ii** above?

b i Write the ratio $\cos \theta$ (as a fraction) for triangle A.

ii Write the ratio $\cos \theta$ (as a fraction) for triangle B.

iii What do you notice about your two answers from parts **b i** and **b ii** above?

c i Write the ratio $\tan \theta$ (as a fraction) for triangle A.

ii Write the ratio $\tan \theta$ (as a fraction) for triangle B.

iii What do you notice about your two answers from parts **c i** and **c ii** above?

6 For each of these triangles, write a ratio (in simplified fraction form) for sin θ, cos θ and tan θ.

a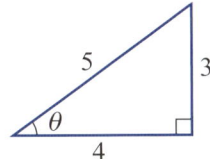

b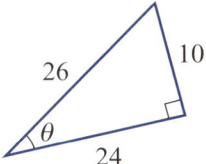

c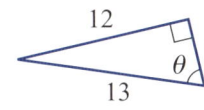

7 For the triangle shown on the right, write a ratio (in fraction form) for:

a sin θ **b** sin α **c** cos θ

d tan α **e** cos α **f** tan θ

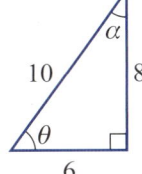

8 A vertical flag pole casts a shadow 20 m long. If the pole is 15 m high, find the ratio for tan θ.

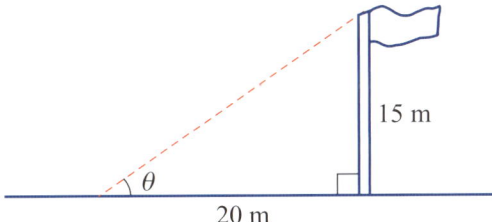

We can use trigonometry to calculate the angle of the shadow that the pole casts.

9 The facade of a roman temple has the given measurements. Write down the ratio for:

a sin θ

b cos θ

c tan θ

The Pantheon, a Roman temple that was built in 126 CE.

10 For each of the following:
   i   Use Pythagoras' theorem to find the unknown side.
   ii Find the ratios for sin θ, cos θ and tan θ.

   a 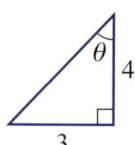   **b** 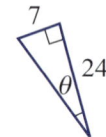   **c** 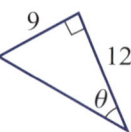   **d**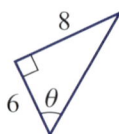

11 a Draw a right-angled triangle and mark one of the angles as θ. Mark in the length of the opposite side as 15 units and the length of the hypotenuse as 17 units.
   b Using Pythagoras' theorem, find the length of the adjacent side.
   c Determine the ratios for sin θ, cos θ and tan θ.

12 This triangle has angles 90°, 60° and 30° and side lengths 1, 2 and $\sqrt{3}$.
   a Write a ratio for:
      i   sin 30°   **ii** cos 30°   **iii** tan 30°
      iv sin 60°   **v**   cos 60°   **vi** tan 60°
   b What do you notice about the following pairs of ratios?
      i   cos 30° and sin 60°   **ii** sin 30° and cos 60°

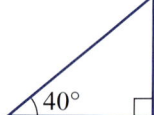

13 a Measure all the side lengths of this triangle to the nearest millimetre.
   b Use your measurements from part **a** to find an approximate ratio for:
      i   cos 40°   **ii** sin 40°   **iii** tan 40°
      iv sin 50°   **v**   tan 50°   **vi** cos 50°
   c Do you notice anything about the trigonometric ratios for 40° and 50°?

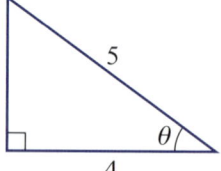

14 Decide if it is possible to draw a right-angled triangle with the given properties. Explain.
   a tan $\theta = 1$ **b** sin $\theta = 1$ **c** cos $\theta = 0$ **d** sin $\theta > 1$ or cos $\theta > 1$

Enrichment: Pythagorean extensions

15 a Given that θ is acute and cos $\theta = \dfrac{4}{5}$, find sin θ and tan θ.
      Hint: Use Pythagoras' theorem.
   b For each of the following, draw a right-angled triangle then use it to find the other two trigonometric ratios.
      i   sin $\theta = \dfrac{1}{2}$ **ii** cos $\theta = \dfrac{1}{2}$ **iii** tan $\theta = 1$
   c Use your results from part **a** to calculate $(\cos \theta)^2 + (\sin \theta)^2$. What do you notice?
   d Evaluate $(\cos \theta)^2 + (\sin \theta)^2$ for other combinations of cos θ and sin θ. Research and describe what you have found.

3.6 Finding side lengths

For similar triangles we know that the ratio of corresponding sides is always the same. This implies that the three trigonometric ratios for similar right-angled triangles are also constant if the internal angles are equal. Since ancient times, mathematicians have attempted to tabulate these ratios for varying angles. Here are the ratios for some angles in a right-angled triangle, correct to three decimal places.

Angle (θ)	sin θ	cos θ	tan θ
0°	0	1	0
15°	0.259	0.966	0.268
30°	0.5	0.866	0.577
45°	0.707	0.707	1
60°	0.866	0.5	1.732
75°	0.966	0.259	3.732
90°	1	0	undefined

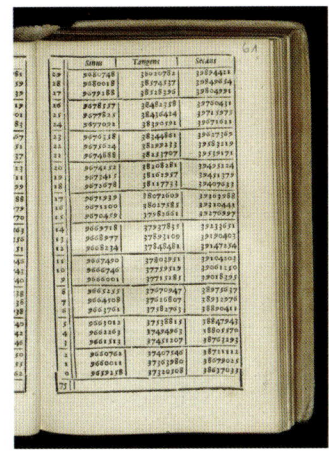

Trigonometric tables in a 400-year old European book.

In modern times these values can be evaluated using calculators to a high degree of accuracy and can be used to help solve problems involving triangles with unknown side lengths.

Let's start: Calculator start up

All scientific or CAS calculators can produce accurate values of sin θ, cos θ and tan θ.

- Ensure that your calculator is in degree mode.
- Check the values in the above table to ensure that you are using the calculator correctly.
- Use trial and error to find (to the nearest degree) an angle θ which satisfies these conditions:
    - sin $\theta = 0.454$ - cos $\theta = 0.588$ - tan $\theta = 9.514$

- If θ is in degrees, the ratios for sin θ, cos θ and tan θ can accurately be found using a calculator in **degree mode**.
- If the angles and one side length of a right-angle triangle are known then the other side lengths can be found using the sin θ, cos θ or tan θ ratios.

Key ideas

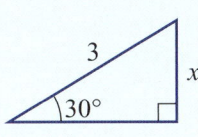

$\sin 30° = \dfrac{x}{3}$

$\therefore x = 3 \times \sin 30°$

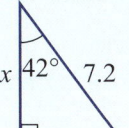

$\cos 42° = \dfrac{x}{7.2}$

$\therefore x = 7.2 \times \cos 42°$

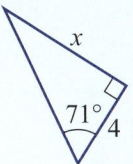

$\tan 71° = \dfrac{x}{4}$

$\therefore x = 4 \times \tan 71°$

Example 8 Using a calculator

Use a calculator to evaluate the following, correct to two decimal places.

a sin 50° **b** cos 16° **c** tan 77°

SOLUTION	EXPLANATION
a sin 50° = 0.77	sin 50° = 0.766044... the 3rd decimal place is greater than 4 so round up.
b cos 16° = 0.96	cos 16° = 0.961261... the 3rd decimal place is less than 5 so round down.
c tan 77° = 4.33	tan 77° = 4.331475... the 3rd decimal place is less than 5 so round down.

Example 9 Solving for x in the numerator of a trigonometric ratio

Find the value of x in the equation $\cos 20° = \dfrac{x}{3}$, correct to two decimal places.

SOLUTION	EXPLANATION
$\cos 20° = \dfrac{x}{3}$ $x = 3 \times \cos 20°$ $\quad = 2.82$	Multiply both sides of the equation by 3 and round as required.

Example 10 Finding side lengths

For each triangle, find the value of x correct to two decimal places.

a
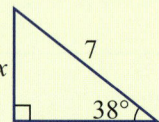

b
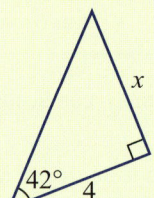

c
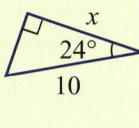

SOLUTION	EXPLANATION
a $\sin 38° = \dfrac{O}{A}$ $\sin 38° = \dfrac{x}{7}$ $\quad\quad x = 7 \sin 38°$ $\quad\quad\quad = 4.31$	Since the opposite side (O) and the hypotenuse (H) are involved, the $\sin \theta$ ratio must be used. 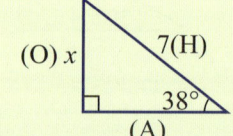 Multiply both sides by 7 and evaluate using a calculator.

b $\tan 42° = \dfrac{O}{A}$

Since the opposite side (O) and the adjacent side (A) are involved, the tan θ ratio must be used.

$\tan 42° = \dfrac{x}{4}$

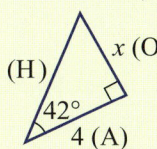

$x = 4 \tan 42°$

$= 3.60$

Multiply both side by 4 and evaluate.

c $\cos 24° = \dfrac{A}{H}$

Since the adjacent side (A) and the hypotenuse (H) are involved, the cos θ ratio must be used.

$\cos 24° = \dfrac{x}{10}$

$x = 10 \cos 24°$

$= 9.14$

Multiply both sides by 10.

Exercise 3F

Understanding

1 For the marked angle θ, decide if x represents the length of the opposite (O), adjacent (A) or hypotenuse (H) side.

a   **b**   **c**

2 Decide if you would use $\sin \theta = \dfrac{O}{H}$, $\cos \theta = \dfrac{A}{H}$ or $\tan \theta = \dfrac{O}{A}$ to help find the value of x in these triangles.

Do not find the value of x, just state which ratio would be used.

a 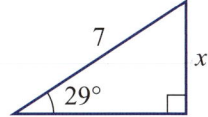   **b** 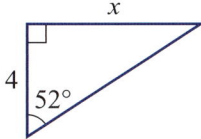   **c**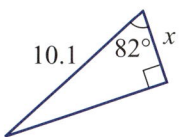

Example 8

3 Use a calculator to evaluate the following correct to two decimal places.

a $\sin 20°$ **b** $\cos 37°$ **c** $\tan 64°$ **d** $\sin 47°$

e $\cos 84°$ **f** $\tan 14.1°$ **g** $\sin 27.4°$ **h** $\cos 76.2°$

Example 9

4 In each of the following, find the value of x correct to two decimal places.

a $\sin 50° = \dfrac{x}{4}$

b $\tan 81° = \dfrac{x}{3}$

c $\cos 33° = \dfrac{x}{6}$

d $\cos 75° = \dfrac{x}{3.5}$

e $\sin 24° = \dfrac{x}{4.2}$

f $\tan 42° = \dfrac{x}{10}$

g $\dfrac{x}{7.1} = \tan 18.4°$

h $\dfrac{x}{5.3} = \sin 64.7°$

i $\dfrac{x}{12.6} = \cos 52.9°$

Example 10

5 For the triangles given below, find the value of x correct to two decimal places.

a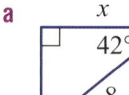

b

c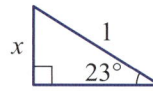

d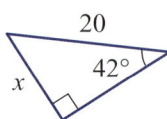

e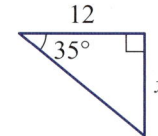

f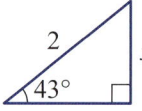

g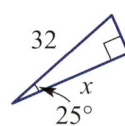

h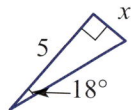

i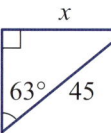

j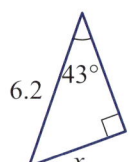

k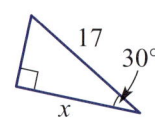

l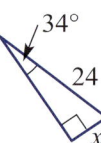

m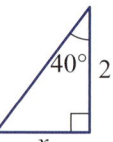

n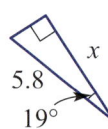

o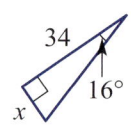

p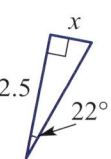

6 Amy walks 5.4 m up a ramp which is inclined at 12° to the horizontal. How high (correct to two decimal places) is she above her starting point?

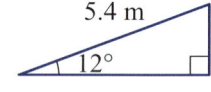

7 Kane wanted to measure the width of a river. He placed two markers, A and B, 72 m apart along the bank. C is a point directly opposite marker B. Kane measured angle CAB to be 32°. Find the width of the river correct to two decimal places.

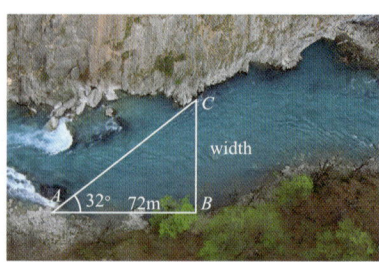

8 One end of a 12.2 m rope is tied to a boat. The other end is tied to an anchor, which is holding the boat steady in the water. If the anchor is making an angle of 34° with the vertical, how deep is the water? Give your answer correct to two decimal places.

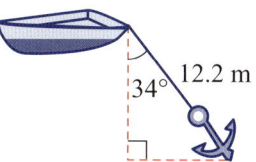

9 Find the length *AB* in these diagrams. Round to two decimal places where necessary.

a

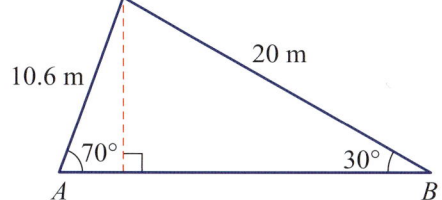

b

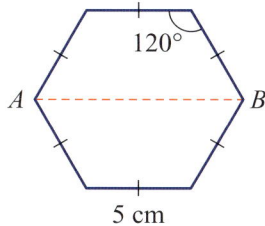

10 For this right-angled triangle:

  a Find the angle ∠*C*.

  b Calculate the value of *x* correct to three decimal places using the sine ratio.

  c Calculate the value of *x* correct to three decimal places but instead use the cosine ratio.

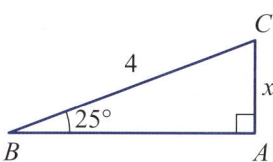

11 Complementary angles sum to 90°.

  a Find the complementary angles to these angles.

    i 10°   **ii** 28°   **iii** 54°   **iv** 81°

  b Evaluate:

    i sin 10° and cos 80°   **ii** sin 28° and cos 62°

    iii cos 54° and sin 36°   **iv** cos 81° and sin 9°

  c What do you notice in part **b**?

  d Complete the following.

    i sin 20° = cos _____   **ii** sin 59° = cos _____

    iii cos 36° = sin _____   **iv** cos 73° = sin _____

Enrichment: Exact values

12 $\sqrt{2}$, $\sqrt{3}$ and $\dfrac{1}{\sqrt{2}}$ are examples of exact values.

  a For the triangle shown (right), use Pythagoras' theorem to find the exact length *BC*.

  b Use your result from part **a** to write down the exact values of:

    i sin 45°   **ii** cos 45°   **iii** tan 45°

  c For this triangle (right) use Pythagoras' theorem to find the exact length *BC*.

  d Use your result from part **c** to write down the exact values of:

    i sin 30°   **ii** cos 30°   **iii** tan 30°

    iv sin 60°   **v** cos 60°   **vi** tan 60°

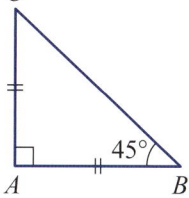

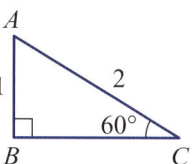

3.7 Solving for the denominator

So far we have constructed trigonometric ratios using a pronumeral which has always appeared in the numerator.

$$\text{For example: } \frac{x}{5} = \sin 40°$$

This makes it easy to solve for x where both sides of the equation can be multiplied by 5.

If, however, the pronumeral appears in the denominator there are a number of algebraic steps that can be taken to find the solution.

Let's start: Solution steps

Three students attempt to solve $\sin 40° = \dfrac{5}{x}$ for x.

Nick says $x = 5 \times \sin 40°$

Sharee says $x = \dfrac{5}{\sin 40°}$

Dori says $x = \dfrac{1}{5} \times \sin 40°$

- Which student has the correct solution?
- Can you show the algebraic steps that support the correct answer?

Key ideas

- If the unknown value of a trigonometric ratio is in the **denominator**, you need to rearrange the equation to make the pronumeral the subject.

  For example, for the triangle shown, $\qquad \cos 30° = \dfrac{5}{x}$

  Multiplying both sides by x $\qquad x \times \cos 30° = 5$

  Dividing both sides by $\cos 30°$ $\qquad x = \dfrac{5}{\cos 30°}$

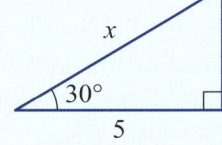

Example 11 Solving for x in the denominator

Solve for x in the equation $\cos 35° = \dfrac{2}{x}$, correct to two decimal places.

SOLUTION

$$\cos 35° = \frac{2}{x}$$

$$x \cos 35° = 2$$

$$x = \frac{2}{\cos 35°}$$

$$= 2.44$$

EXPLANATION

Multiply both sides of the equation by x.
Divide both sides of the equation by $\cos 35°$.

Evaluate and round off to two decimal places.

Example 12 Finding side lengths

Find the values of the pronumerals correct to two decimal places.

a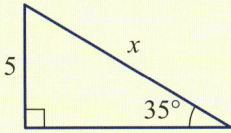

b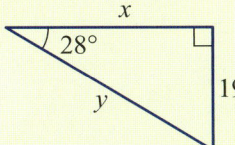

SOLUTION

EXPLANATION

a $\sin 35° = \dfrac{O}{H}$

$\sin 35° = \dfrac{5}{x}$

$x \sin 35° = 5$

$\qquad x = \dfrac{5}{\sin 35°}$

$\qquad\quad = 8.72$

Since the opposite side (O) is given and we require the hypotenuse (H), use sin θ.

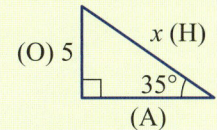

Multiply both sides of the equation by x then divide both sides of the equation by sin 35°.
Evaluate on a calculator and round off to two decimal places.

b $\tan 28° = \dfrac{O}{A}$

$\tan 28° = \dfrac{19}{x}$

$x \tan 28° = 19$

$\qquad x = \dfrac{19}{\tan 28°}$

$\qquad\quad = 35.73$

$y^2 = x^2 + 19^2$

$\quad = 1637.63$

$y = \sqrt{1637.63}$

$\therefore y = 40.47$

Since the opposite side (O) is given and the adjacent (A) is required, use tan θ.

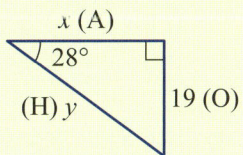

Multiply both sides of the equation by x.

Divide both sides of the equation by tan 28° and round answer to two decimal places.

Find y by using Pythagoras' theorem and substitute the exact value of x, i.e. $\dfrac{19}{\tan 28°}$

Alternatively, y can be found by using sin θ.

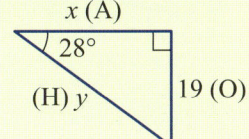

Exercise 3G

1   Solve these simple equations for x.

a $\dfrac{4}{x} = 2$

b $\dfrac{20}{x} = 4$

c $\dfrac{15}{x} = 5$

d $25 = \dfrac{100}{x}$

e $5 = \dfrac{35}{x}$

f $\dfrac{10}{x} = 2.5$

g $\dfrac{2.5}{x} = 5$

h $12 = \dfrac{2.4}{x}$

Example 11 2 For each of the following equations, find the value of x correct to two decimal places.

a $\cos 43° = \dfrac{3}{x}$

b $\sin 36° = \dfrac{4}{x}$

c $\tan 9° = \dfrac{6}{x}$

d $\tan 64° = \dfrac{2}{x}$

e $\cos 67° = \dfrac{5}{x}$

f $\sin 12° = \dfrac{3}{x}$

g $\sin 38.3° = \dfrac{5.9}{x}$

h $\dfrac{45}{x} = \tan 21.4°$

i $\dfrac{18.7}{x} = \cos 32°$

Example 12a 3 Find the value of x correct to two decimal places using the sine, cosine or tangent ratios.

a

b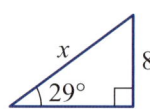

c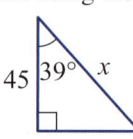

d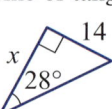

e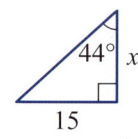

f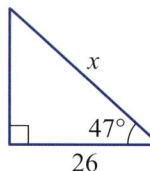

g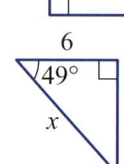

h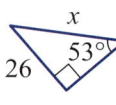

i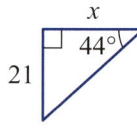

j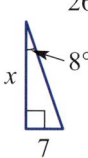

k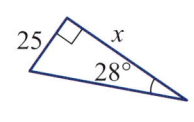

l (shown in k image)

Example 12b 4 Find the value of each pronumeral correct to one decimal place.

a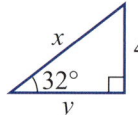

b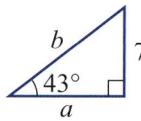

c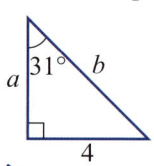

d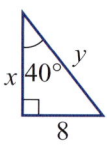

e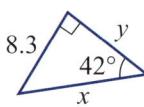

f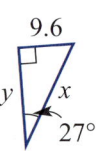

g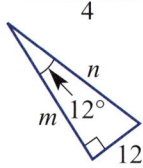

h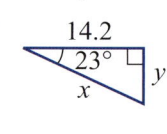

5 A kite is flying at a height of 27 m above the anchor point. If the string is inclined at 42° to the horizontal, find the length of the string correct to the nearest metre.

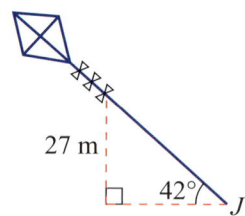

6 A paraglider flying at a height of 800 m descends at an angle of 12° to the horizontal. How far (to the nearest metre) has it travelled in descending to the ground?

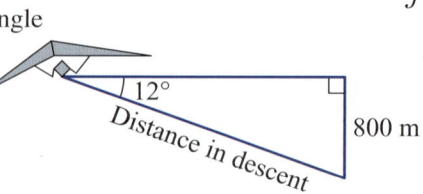

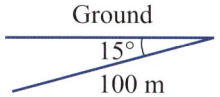

7 A 100 m mine shaft is dug at an angle of 15° to the horizontal. How far (to the nearest metre):

a below ground level is the end of the shaft?

b is the end of the shaft horizontally from the opening?

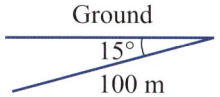

8 Find the perimeter of these triangles correct to one decimal place.

a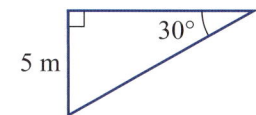

b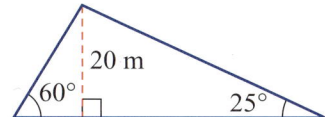

9 In calculating the value of x for this triangle, correct to two decimal places, two students come up with these answers.

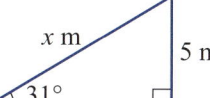

A $x = \dfrac{5}{\sin 31°} = \dfrac{5}{0.52} = 9.62$ **B** $x = \dfrac{5}{\sin 31°} = 9.71$

a Which of the above two answers is more correct and why?

b What advice would you give to the student whose answer is not accurate?

c Find the difference in the answers if the different methods (A and B) are used to calculate the value of x correct to two decimal places in these triangles.

i

ii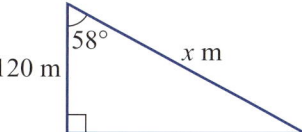

Enrichment: Linking tan θ to sin θ and cos θ

10 a For this triangle find, correct to three decimal places:

   i AB ii BC

b Calculate these ratios to two decimal places.

   i $\sin 20°$ ii $\cos 20°$ iii $\tan 20°$

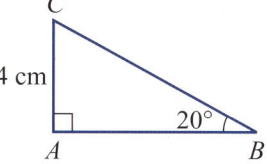

c Evaluate $\dfrac{\sin 20°}{\cos 20°}$ using your results from part **b**. What do you notice?

d For this triangle with side lengths a, b and c, find an expression for:

   i $\sin \theta$ ii $\cos \theta$ iii $\tan \theta$ iv $\dfrac{\sin \theta}{\cos \theta}$

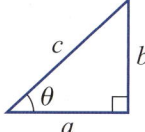

e Simplify your expression for part **d iv**. What do you notice?

Using a CAS calculator 3.7: Trigonometry

This activity is on the companion website in the form of a printable PDF.

3.8 Finding an angle

Logically, if you can use trigonometry to find a side length of a right-angled triangle given one angle and one side, you should be able to find an angle if you are given two sides.

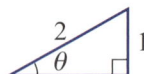

We know that $\sin 30° = \dfrac{1}{2}$ so if we were to determine θ if $\sin \theta = \dfrac{1}{2}$, the answer would be $\theta = 30°$.

We write this as $\theta = \sin^{-1}\left(\dfrac{1}{2}\right) = 30°$ and we say that the inverse sine of $\dfrac{1}{2}$ is $30°$.

Calculators can be used to help solve problems using inverse sine ($\sin^{-1}$), inverse cosine ($\cos^{-1}$) and inverse tangent ($\tan^{-1}$). For angles in degrees, ensure your calculator is in degree mode.

Let's start: Trial and error can be slow

We know that for this triangle, $\sin \theta = \dfrac{1}{3}$.

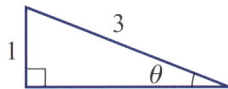

- Guess the angle θ.
- For your guess use a calculator to see if
  $\sin \theta = \dfrac{1}{3} = 0.333\ldots$
- Update your guess and use your calculator to check once again.
- Repeat this trial-and-error process until you think you have the angle θ correct to three decimal places.
- Now evaluate $\sin^{-1}\left(\dfrac{1}{3}\right)$ and check your guess.

- **Inverse sine** ($\sin^{-1}$), **inverse cosine** ($\cos^{-1}$) and **inverse tangent** ($\tan^{-1}$) can be used to find angles in right-angled triangles.

  - $\sin \theta = \dfrac{a}{c}$ means $\theta = \sin^{-1}\left(\dfrac{a}{c}\right)$

  - $\cos \theta = \dfrac{b}{c}$ means $\theta = \cos^{-1}\left(\dfrac{b}{c}\right)$

  - $\tan \theta = \dfrac{a}{b}$ means $\theta = \tan^{-1}\left(\dfrac{a}{b}\right)$

- Note that $\sin^{-1} x$ does *not* mean $\dfrac{1}{\sin x}$.

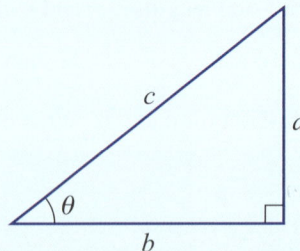

Example 13 Using inverse trigonometric ratios

Find the value of θ to the level of accuracy indicated.

a $\sin \theta = 0.3907$ (nearest degree)

b $\tan \theta = \dfrac{1}{2}$ (one decimal place)

SOLUTION

a $\sin \theta = 0.3907$

$\theta = \sin^{-1}(0.3907)$

$= 23°$

b $\tan \theta = \dfrac{1}{2}$

$\theta = \tan^{-1}\left(\dfrac{1}{2}\right)$

$= 26.6°$

EXPLANATION

Use the $\sin^{-1}$ key on your calculator.
Round off to the nearest whole number.

Use the $\tan^{-1}$ key on your calculator and round the
answer to one decimal place.

Example 14 Finding an angle

Find the value of θ to the nearest degree.

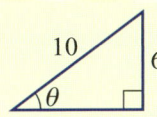

SOLUTION

$\sin \theta = \dfrac{O}{H}$

$= \dfrac{6}{10}$

$\theta = \sin^{-1}\left(\dfrac{6}{10}\right)$

$= 37°$

EXPLANATION

Since the opposite side (O) and
the hypotenuse (H) are given,
use $\sin \theta$.

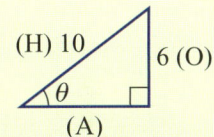

Use the $\sin^{-1}$ key on your calculator and round as
required.

Exercise 3H

1 Use a calculator to evaluate the following rounding to two decimal places.

    a $\sin^{-1}(0.2)$ **b** $\sin^{-1}(0.9)$ **c** $\cos^{-1}(0.75)$

    d $\cos^{-1}(0.43)$ **e** $\tan^{-1}(0.5)$ **f** $\tan^{-1}(2.5)$

2 Write the missing number.

    a If $\sin 30° = \dfrac{1}{2}$ then $30° = \sin^{-1}(\underline{})$.   **b** If $\cos 50° = 0.64$ then $\underline{} = \cos^{-1}(0.64)$.

    c If $\tan 45° = 1$ then $\underline{} = \tan^{-1}(\underline{})$.

Understanding

3 Evaluate each of the following to the nearest degree.

a $\sin^{-1}(0.7324)$ **b** $\cos^{-1}(0.9763)$ **c** $\tan^{-1}(0.3321)$

d $\tan^{-1}(1.235)$ **e** $\sin^{-1}(0.4126)$ **f** $\cos^{-1}(0.7462)$

g $\cos^{-1}(0.1971)$ **h** $\sin^{-1}(0.2247)$ **i** $\tan^{-1}(0.0541)$

4 Which trigonometric ratio should be used to solve for θ?

a 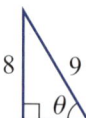   **b** 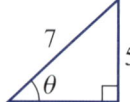   **c** 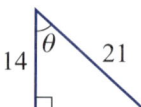   **d**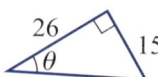

Example 13a

5 Find the value of θ to the nearest degree.

a $\sin\theta = 0.5$ **b** $\cos\theta = 0.5$ **c** $\tan\theta = 1$

d $\cos\theta = 0.8660$ **e** $\sin\theta = 0.7071$ **f** $\tan\theta = 0.5774$

g $\sin\theta = 1$ **h** $\tan\theta = 1.192$ **i** $\cos\theta = 0$

j $\cos\theta = 0.5736$ **k** $\cos\theta = 1$ **l** $\sin\theta = 0.9397$

Example 13b

6 Find the angle θ correct to two decimal places.

a $\sin\theta = \dfrac{4}{7}$ **b** $\sin\theta = \dfrac{1}{3}$ **c** $\sin\theta = \dfrac{9}{10}$

d $\cos\theta = \dfrac{1}{4}$ **e** $\cos\theta = \dfrac{4}{5}$ **f** $\cos\theta = \dfrac{7}{9}$

g $\tan\theta = \dfrac{3}{5}$ **h** $\tan\theta = \dfrac{8}{5}$ **i** $\tan\theta = 12$

Example 14

7 Find the value of θ to the nearest degree.

a 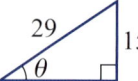   **b** 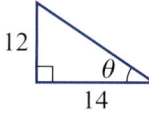   **c** ...   **d**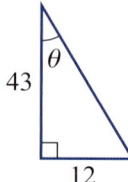

e 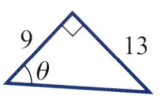   **f** 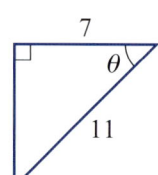   **g** 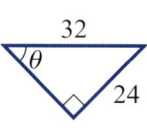   **h**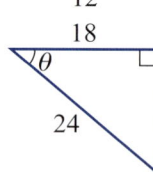

8 A road rises at a grade of 3 in 10. Find the angle (to the nearest degree) the road makes with the horizontal.

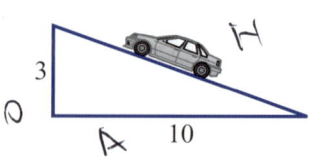

9 When a 2.8 m long seesaw is at its maximum height it is 1.1 m off the ground. What angle (correct to two decimal places) does the seesaw make with the ground?

10 Adam, who is 1.8 m tall, holds up a plank of wood 4.2 m long. Find the angle that the plank makes with the ground, correct to one decimal place.

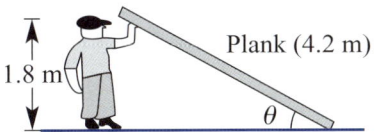
Plank (4.2 m)
1.8 m
θ

11 A children's slide has a length of 5.8 m. The vertical ladder is 2.6 m above the ground. Find the angle the slide makes with the ground, correct to one decimal place.

12 Find the value of θ in these diagrams, correct to one decimal place.

a
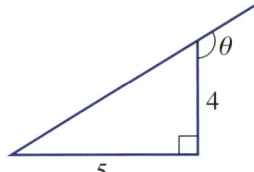
θ
4
5

b
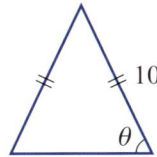
10
6
θ

c
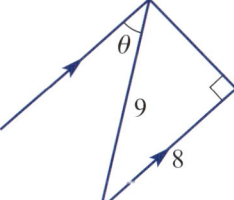
θ
9
8

13 Find all the angles to the nearest degree in right-angled triangles with these side lengths.

a 3, 4, 5   b 5, 12, 13   c 7, 24, 25

14 For what value of θ is $\sin \theta = \cos \theta$?

15 If M is the midpoint of AB, decide if $\angle ACM$ is exactly half of angle $\angle ACB$. Investigate and explain.

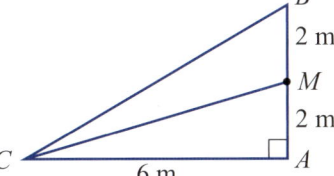
B
2 m
M
2 m
C
6 m
A

Enrichment: Viewing angle

16 Old Joe has trouble with his eyesight but every Sunday goes to view his favourite painting at the gallery. His eye level is at the same level as the base of the painting and the painting is 1 metre tall.

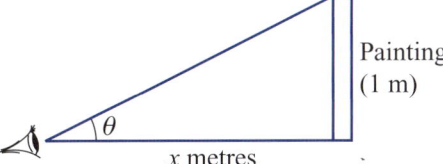
Painting (1 m)
θ
x metres

Answer the following to the nearest degree for angles and to two decimal places for lengths.

a If $x = 3$, find the viewing angle θ.   b If $x = 2$, find the viewing angle θ.

c If Joe can stand no closer than 1 metre to the painting, what is Joe's largest viewing angle?

d When the viewing angle is 10°, Joe has trouble seeing the painting. How far is he from the painting at this viewing angle?

e What would be the largest viewing angle if Joe could go as close as he would like to the painting?

3.9 Applying trigonometry

In many situations, angles are measured up or down from the horizontal. These are called angles of elevation and depression. Combined with the mathematics of trigonometry, these angles can be used to solve problems, provided right-angled triangles can be identified. The line of sight to a helicopter 100 m above the ground, for example, creates an angle of elevation inside a right-angled triangle.

Let's start: Illustrate the situation

For the situation below, draw a detailed diagram showing these features:
- an angle of elevation
- an angle of depression
- any given lengths
- a right-angled triangle that will help to solve the problem

A cat and a bird eye each other from their respective positions. The bird is 20 m up a tree and the cat is on the ground 30 m from the base of the tree. Find the angle their line of sight makes with the horizontal.

Compare your diagram with others in your class. Is there more than one triangle that could be drawn and used to solve the problem?

- To solve application problems involving trigonometry:
  - Draw a diagram and label the key information.
  - Identify and draw the appropriate right angled triangles separately.
  - Solve using trigonometry to find the missing measurements.
  - Express your answer in words.
- The **angle of elevation** or **depression** of a point, Q, from another point, P, is given by the angle the line PQ makes with the horizontal.

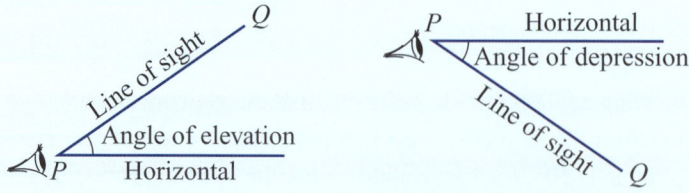

- Angles of elevation or depression are always measured from the horizontal.

Example 15 Using angles of elevation

The angle of elevation of the top of a tower from a point on the ground 30 m away from the base of the tower is 28°. Find the height of the tower to the nearest metre.

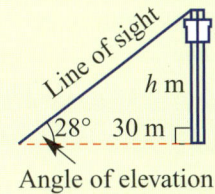

Angle of elevation

SOLUTION

Let the height of the tower be h m.

$$\tan 28° = \frac{O}{A}$$

$$= \frac{h}{30}$$

$$h = 30 \tan 28°$$

$$= 16$$

The height is 16 m.

EXPLANATION

Since the opposite side (O) is required and the adjacent (A) is given, use $\tan \theta$.

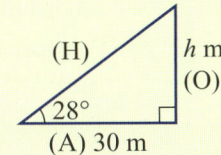

Multiply both sides by 30 and evaluate, rounding to the nearest metre.

Write the answer in words.

Example 16 Finding an angle of depression

From the top of a vertical cliff Andrea spots a boat out at sea. If the top of the cliff is 42 m above sea level and the boat is 90 m away from the base of the cliff, find Andrea's angle of depression to the boat to the nearest degree.

SOLUTION

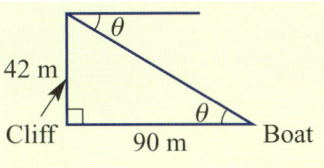

$$\tan \theta = \frac{O}{A}$$

$$= \frac{42}{90}$$

$$\theta = \tan^{-1}\left(\frac{42}{90}\right)$$

$$\theta = 25°$$

The angle of depression is 25°.

EXPLANATION

Draw a diagram and label all the given measurements. Use alternate angles in parallel lines to mark θ inside the triangle.

Since the opposite (O) and adjacent sides (A) are given, use $\tan \theta$.

Use the $\tan^{-1}$ key on your calculator and round off to the nearest degree.

Express the answer in words.

Example 17 Applying trigonometry

A plane flying at an altitude of 1500 m starts to climb at an angle of 15° to the horizontal when the pilot sees a mountain peak 2120 m high, 2400 m away from him horizontally. Will the pilot clear the mountain?

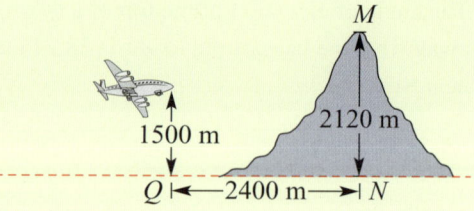

SOLUTION

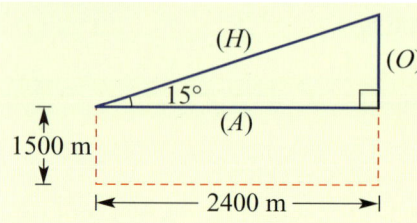

$$\tan 15° = \frac{x}{2400}$$
$$x = 2400 \tan 15°$$
$$= 643$$

Since $x > 620$ m the plane will clear the mountain peak.

EXPLANATION

Draw a diagram, identifying and labelling the right-angled triangle to help solve the problem.

The plane will clear the mountain if the opposite (O) is greater than

$(2120 - 1500)$ m = 620 m

Set up the trigonometric ratio using tan.

Multiply by 2400 and evaluate.

Answer the question in words.

Exercise 3I

1 Find the values of the pronumerals in this diagram.

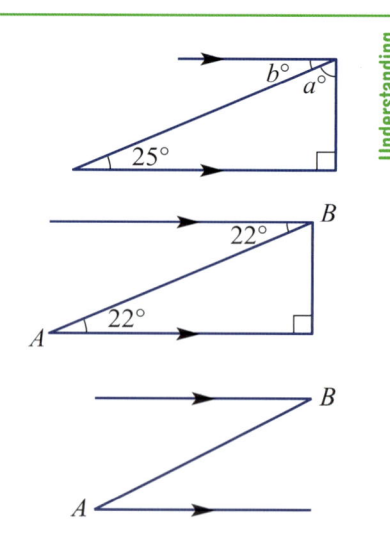

2 For this diagram:

a What is the angle of elevation of B from A?

b What is the angle of depression of A from B?

3 Draw this diagram and complete these tasks.

a Mark in the following:

i the angle of elevation (θ) of B from A.

ii the angle of depression (α) of A from B.

b Is $\theta = \alpha$ in your diagram? Why?

Fluency

mple 15 **4** The angle of elevation of the top of a tower from a point on the ground 40 m from the base of the tower is 36°. Find the height of the tower to the nearest metre.

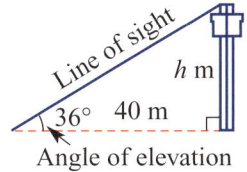

Line of sight

h m

36° 40 m

Angle of elevation

5 The angle of elevation of the top of a castle wall from a point on the ground 25 m from the base of the castle wall is 32°. Find the height of the castle wall to the nearest metre.

6 From a point on the ground, Emma measures the angle of elevation of an 80 m tower to be 27°. Find how far Emma is from the base of the tower, correct to the nearest metre.

7 From a pedestrian overpass, Chris spots a landmark at an angle of depression of 32°. How far away (to the nearest metre) is the landmark from the base of the 24 m high overpass?

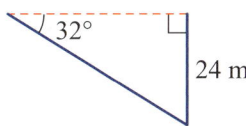

32°

24 m

8 From a lookout tower, David spots a bushfire at an angle of depression of 25°. If the lookout tower is 42 m high, how far away (to the nearest metre) is the bushfire from the base of the tower?

mple 16 **9** From the top of a vertical cliff, Josh spots a swimmer out at sea. If the top of the cliff is 38 m above sea level and the swimmer is 50 m away from the base of the cliff, find the angle of depression from Josh to the swimmer, to the nearest degree.

10 From a ship, a person is spotted floating in the sea 200 m away. If the viewing position on the ship is 20 m above sea level, find the angle of depression from the ship to person in the sea. Give your answer to the nearest degree.

11 A power line is stretched from a pole to the top of a house. The house is 4.1 m high and the power pole is 6.2 m high. The horizontal distance between the house and the power pole is 12 m. Find the angle of elevation of the top of the power pole from the top of the house, to the nearest degree.

Problem-solving

mple 17 **12** A plane flying at 1850 m starts to climb at an angle of 18° to the horizontal when the pilot sees a mountain peak 2450 m high, 2600 m away from him in a horizontal direction. Will the pilot clear the mountain?

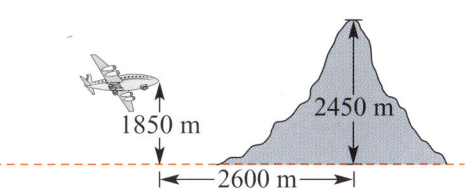

1850 m

2450 m

2600 m

13 A road has a steady gradient of 1 in 10.
   a What angle does the road make with the horizontal? Give your answer to the nearest degree.
   b A car starts from the bottom of the inclined road and drives 2 km along the road. How high vertically has the car climbed? Use your rounded answer from part **a** and give your answer correct to the nearest metre.

14 A house is to be built using the design shown on the right. The eaves are 600 mm and the house is 7200 mm wide, excluding the eaves. Calculate the length (to the nearest mm) of a sloping edge of the roof, which is pitched at 25° to the horizontal.

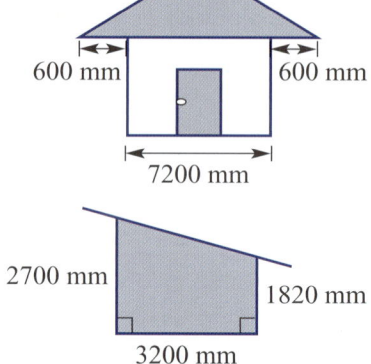

600 mm   600 mm

7200 mm

15 A garage is to be built with measurements as shown in the diagram on the right. Calculate the sloping length and pitch (angle) of the roof if the eaves extend 500 mm on each side. Give your answers correct to the nearest unit.

2700 mm   1820 mm

3200 mm

16 The chains on a swing are 3.2 m long and the seat is 0.5 m off the ground when it is in the vertical position. When the swing is pulled as far back as possible, the chains make an angle of 40° with the vertical. How high off the ground, to the nearest cm, is the seat when it is at this extreme position?

17 A person views a vertical monument x metres away as shown.

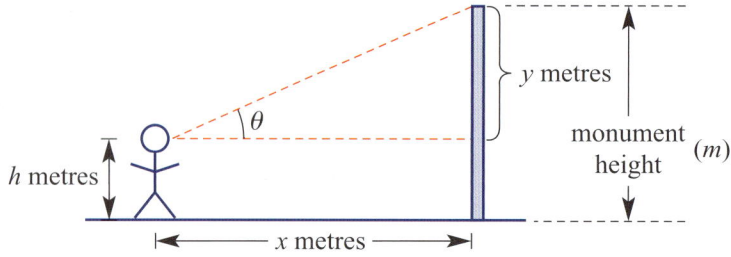

h metres θ y metres

monument height (m)

x metres

   a If $h = 1.5$, $x = 20$ and $\theta = 15°$ find the height of the monument to two decimal places.
   b If $h = 1.5$, $x = 20$ and $y = 10$ find θ correct to one decimal place.
   c Let the height of the monument be m. Write expressions for the following:
      i m using (in terms of) y and h.
      ii y using x and θ.
      iii m using (in terms of) x, θ and h.

18 Find an expression for the area of this triangle using a and θ.

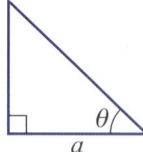

θ

a

Enrichment: Plane trigonometry

19 An aeroplane takes off and climbs at an angle of 20° to the horizontal, at 190 km/h along its flight path for 15 minutes.

a Find:
   i   the distance the aeroplane travels in 15 minutes
   ii the height the aeroplane reaches after 15 minutes correct to two decimal places

b If the angle at which the plane climbs is twice the original angle but its speed is halved, will it reach a greater height after 15 minutes? Explain.

c If the plane's speed is doubled and its climbing angle is halved, will the plane reach a greater height after 15 minutes? Explain.

20 The residents of Skeville live 12 km from an airport. They maintain that any plane flying lower than 4 km disturbs their peace. Each Sunday they have an outdoor concert from 12.00 noon till 2.00 pm.

a Will a plane taking off from the airport at an angle of 15° over Skeville disturb the residents?

b When the plane in part **a** is directly above Skeville, how far (to the nearest m) has it flown?

c If the plane leaves the airport at 11.50 am on Sunday and travels at an average speed of 180 km/h, will it disturb the start of the concert?

d Investigate what average speed the plane can travel at so that it does not disturb the concert. Assume it leaves at 11:50 am.

21 Peter observes a plane flying directly overhead at a height of 820 m. Twenty seconds later, the angle of elevation of the plane from Peter is 32°. Assume the plane flies horizontally.

a How far (to the nearest metre) did the plane fly in 20 seconds?

b What is the plane's speed in km/h correct to two decimal places?

3.10 Bearings

Bearings are used to indicate direction and therefore are commonly used to navigate the sea or air in ships or planes. Bushwalkers use bearings with a compass to help follow a map and navigate a forest. The most common type of bearing is the True bearing measured clockwise from north.

A compass can determine direction using Earth's magnetic field.

Let's start: Opposite directions

Marg at point *A* and Jim at point *B* start walking toward each other. Marg knows that she has to face 50° south of due east.

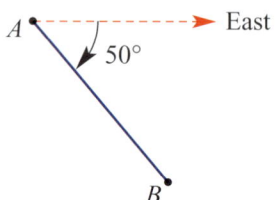

- Measured clockwise from north, can you help Marg determine her True compass bearing that she should walk on?
- Can you find what bearing Jim should walk on?
- Draw a detailed diagram which supports your answers above.

Key ideas

- A **True bearing** is an angle measured clockwise from north.
  - It is written using three digits, for example 008°T, 032°T or 144°T.

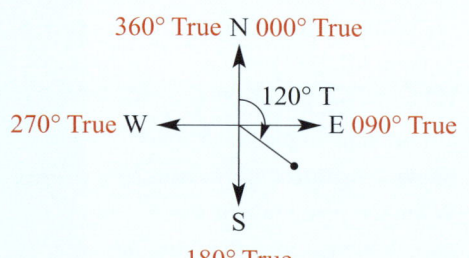

- To describe the true bearing of an object positioned at *A* from an object positioned at *O*, we need to start at *O*, face north then turn clockwise through the required angle to face the object at *A*.

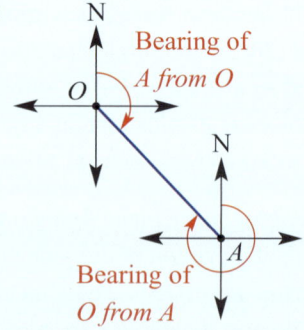

- When solving problems with bearings, draw a diagram including four point compass directions (N, E, S, W) at each point.

Example 18 Stating true bearings

For the diagram shown give:

a the true bearing of A from O

b the true bearing of O from A

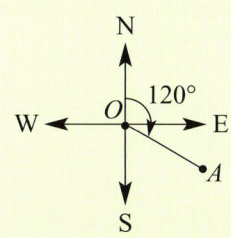

SOLUTION

a The bearing of A from O is $120°$ T.

b

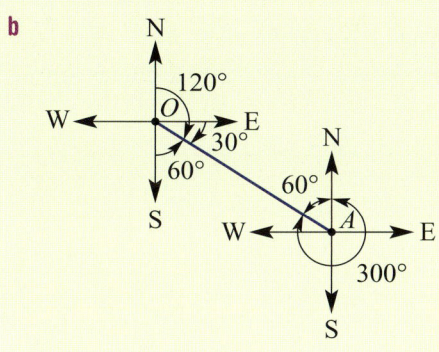

The bearing of O from A is:

$(360 - 60)°$ T $= 300°$ T

EXPLANATION

Start at O, face north and turn clockwise until you are facing A.

Start at A, face north and turn clockwise until you are facing O. Mark in a compass at A and use alternate angles in parallel lines to mark $60°$ angle.

True bearing is then $60°$ short of $360°$.

Example 19 Using bearings with trigonometry

A bushwalker walks 3 km on a true bearing of $060°$ from point A to point B.

Find how far east (correct to one decimal place) point B is from point A.

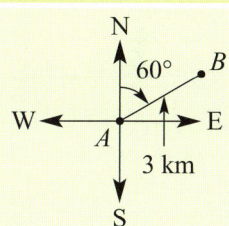

SOLUTION

Let the distance travelled towards the east be d km.

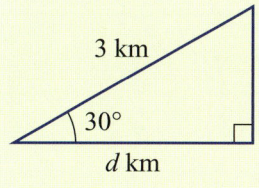

$\cos 30° = \dfrac{d}{3}$

$d = 3 \times \cos 30°$

$= 2.6$

∴ The distance east is 2.6 km.

EXPLANATION

Define the distance required and draw and label the right-angled triangle.

Since the adjacent (A) is required and the hypotenuse (H) is given, use $\cos \theta$.

Multiply both sides of the equation by 3 and evaluate rounding off to one decimal place.

Express the answer in words.

Example 20 Calculating a bearing

A fishing boat starts from point O and sails 75 km on a bearing of 160°
to point B.

a How far east (to the nearest kilometre) of its starting point is
the boat?

b What is the bearing of O from B?

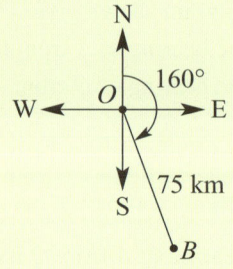

SOLUTION

EXPLANATION

a Let the distance travelled towards the
east be d km.

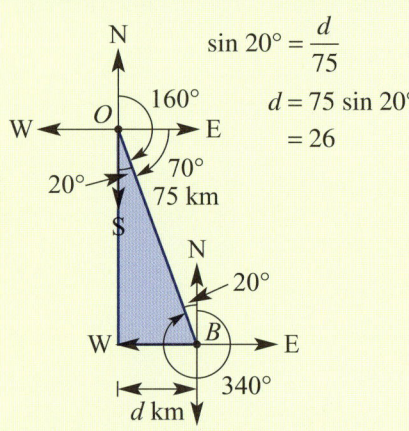

$$\sin 20° = \frac{d}{75}$$
$$d = 75 \sin 20°$$
$$= 26$$

Draw a diagram and label all the given measurements.
Mark in a compass at B and use alternate angles to
label extra angles.

Set up a trigonometric ratio using sine and solve for d.

Alternate angle = 20°

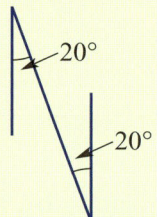

The boat has travelled 26 km to the east
of its starting point.

Write the answer in words.

b The bearing of O from B is
$(360° - 20°)T = 340°\ T$

Start at B, face north then turn clockwise to face O.

Exercise 3J

1 Give the true bearings for these common directions.

    a North (N)   **b** North-east (NE)

    c East (E)   **d** South-east (SE)

    e South (S)   **f** South-west (SW)

    g West (W)   **h** North-west (NW)

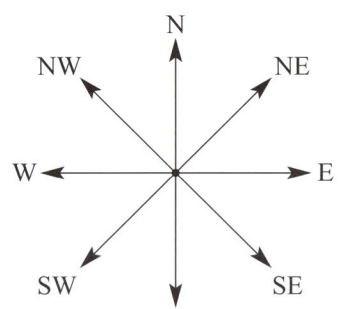

Understanding

2 Write down the true bearings shown in these diagrams. Use three digits, for example, 045°T.

a
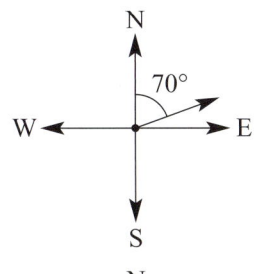

b
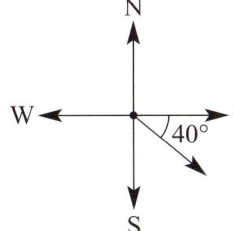

c
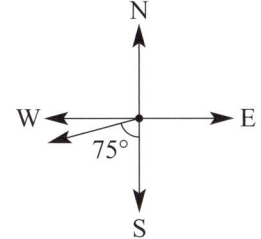

d
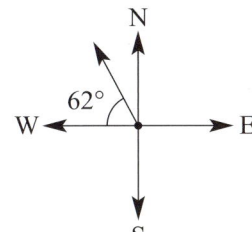

Example 18

3 For each diagram shown, write:

    i the true bearing of *A* from *O*   **ii** the true bearing of *O* from *A*.

a
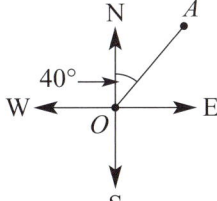

b
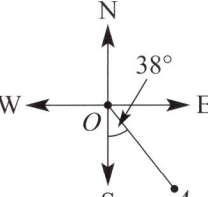

c
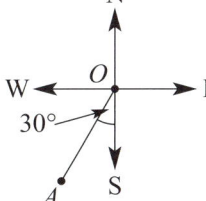

d
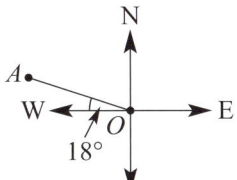

e
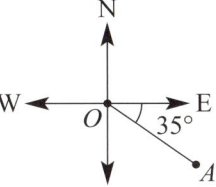

f
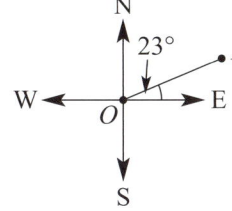

g
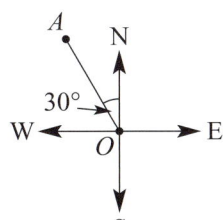

h
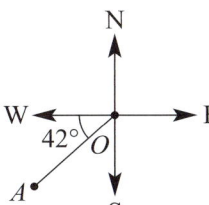

i
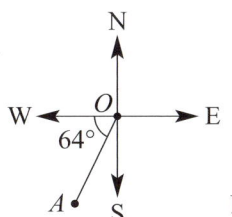

Example 19

4 A bushwalker walks 4 km on a true bearing of 055° from point *A* to point *B*. Find how far east point *B* is from point *A*, correct to two decimal places.

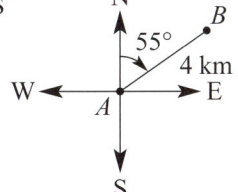

5 A speed boat travels 80 km on a true bearing of 048°. Find how far east of its starting point the speed boat is, correct to two decimal places.

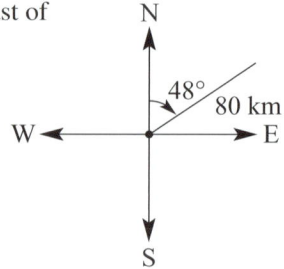

6 After walking due east, then turning and walking due south, a hiker is 4 km 148° T from her starting point. Find how far she walked in a southerly direction, correct to one decimal place.

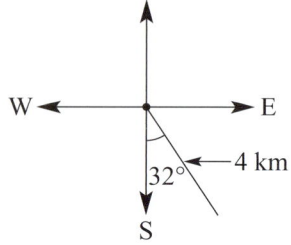

7 A four-wheel drive vehicle travels for 32 km on a true bearing of 200°. How far west (to the nearest km) of its starting point is it?

Example 20

8 A fishing boat starts from point O and sails 60 km on a true bearing of 140° to point B.
  a How far east of its starting point is the boat, to the nearest kilometre?
  b What is the bearing of O from B?

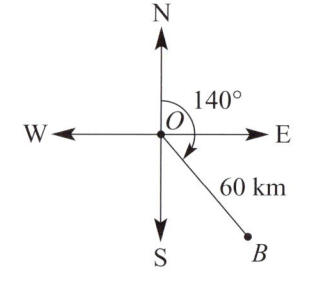

9 Two towns, A and B, are 12 km apart. The true bearing of B from A is 250°.
  a How far west of A is B, correct to one decimal place?
  b Find the bearing of A from B.

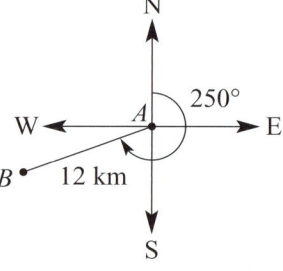

10 A helicopter flies on a bearing of 140° for 210 km then flies due east for 175 km. How far east (to the nearest kilometre) has the helicopter travelled from its starting point?

11 Christopher walks 5 km south then walks on a true bearing of 036° until he is due east of his starting point. How far is he from his starting point, to one decimal place?

12 Two cyclists leave from the same starting point. One cyclist travels due west while the other travels on a bearing of 202°. After travelling for 18 km, the second cyclist is due south of the first cyclist. How far (to the nearest metre) has the first cyclist travelled?

13 A true bearing is $a°$. Write an expression for the true bearing of the opposite direction of $a°$ if

   a a is between 0 and 180   **b** a is between 180 and 360

14 A hiker walks on a triangular pathway starting at point A, walking to point B then C, then A again as shown.

   a Find the bearing from B to A.

   b Find the bearing from B to C.

   c Find the bearing from C to B.

   d If the initial bearing was instead $133°$ and $\angle ABC$ is still $75°$, find the bearing from B to C.

   e If $\angle ABC$ was $42°$, with the initial bearing of $140°$, find the bearing from B to C.

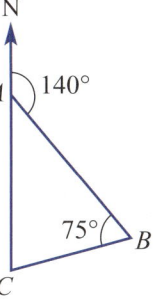

Enrichment: Speed trigonometry

15 A plane flies on a bearing of $168°$ for two hours at an average speed of 310 km/h. How far (to the nearest kilometre):

   a has the plane travelled?

   b south of its starting point is the plane?

   c east of its starting point is the plane?

16 A pilot intends to fly directly to Anderly, which is 240 km due north of his starting point. The trip usually takes 50 minutes. Due to a storm, the pilot changes course and flies to Boxleigh on a true bearing of $320°$ for 150 km, at an average speed of 180 km/h.

   a Find (to the nearest kilometre) how far:

      i north the plane has travelled from its starting point

      ii west the plane has travelled from its starting point

   b How many kilometres is the plane off-course?

   c From Boxleigh the pilot flies directly to Anderly at 240 km/h.

      i Compared to the usual route, how many extra kilometres has the pilot travelled in reaching Anderly?

      ii Compared to the usual trip, how many extra minutes did the trip to Anderly take?

Illustrating Pythagoras

It is possible to use a computer geometry package ('Cabri Geometry' or 'Geometers Sketchpad') to build this construction, which will illustrate Pythagoras' theorem.

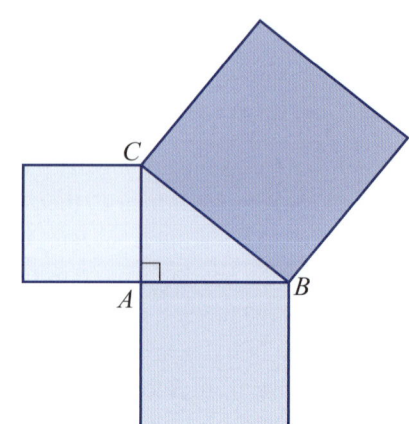

Construct

a Start by constructing the line segment AB.

b Construct the right-angled triangle ABC by using the 'Perpendicular Line' tool.

c Construct a square on each side of the triangle. Circles may help to ensure your construction is exact.

Calculate

a Measure the areas of the squares representing AB^2, AC^2 and BC^2.

b Calculate the sum of the areas of the two smaller squares by using the 'Calculate' tool.

c **i** Drag point A or point B and observe the changes in the areas of the squares.

   ii Investigate how the areas of the squares change as you drag point A or point B. Explain how this illustrates Pythagoras' theorem.

Constructing triangles to solve problems

Illustrations for some problems may not initially look as if they include right-angled triangles. A common mathematical problem solving technique is to construct right-angled triangles so that trigonometry can be used.

Car gap

Two cars are observed in the same lane from an overpass bridge 10 m above the road. The angles of depression to the cars are $20°$ and $35°$.

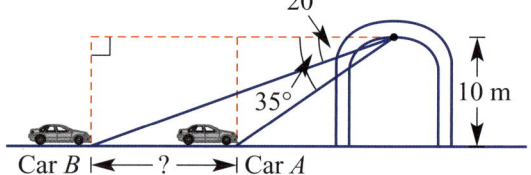

a Find the horizontal distance from car A to the overpass. Show your diagrams and working.

b Find the horizontal distance from car B to the overpass.

c Find the distance between the fronts of the two cars.

Cinema screen

A 5 m vertical cinema screen sits 3 m above the floor of the hall and Wally sits 20 m back from the screen. His eye level is 1 m above the floor.

a Find the angle of elevation from Wally's eye level to the base of the screen. Illustrate your method using a diagram.

b Find the angle of elevation as in part **a** but from his eye level to the top of the screen.

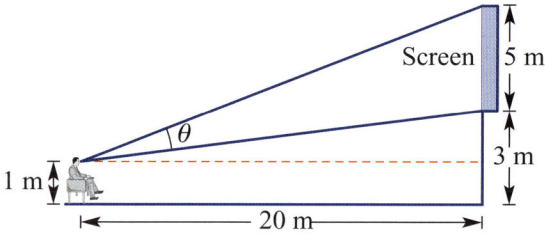

c Use your results from parts **a** and **b** to find Wally's viewing angle θ.

Problem solving without all the help

Solve these similar types of problems. You will need to draw
detailed diagrams and split the problem into parts. Refer to the above
two problems if you need help.

a An observer is 50 m horizontally from a hot air balloon. The
angle of elevation to the top of the balloon is 60° and to the
bottom of the balloon's basket is 40°. Find the total height of the
balloon (to the nearest metre) from the base of the basket to the
top of the balloon.

b A ship (at *A*) is 24 km due east of a lighthouse (*L*). The captain
takes bearings from two landmarks, *M* and *Q*, which are due north
and due south of the lighthouse respectively. The bearings of *M* and
Q from the ship are 322° and 244° respectively. How far apart are
the two landmarks?

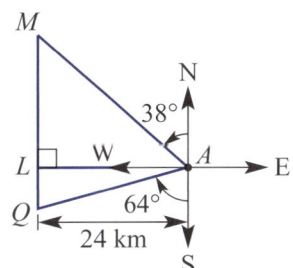

c From the top of a 90 m cliff the angles of depression of
two boats in the water, both directly east of the light
house, are 25° and 38° respectively. What is the
distance between the two boats to the nearest metre?

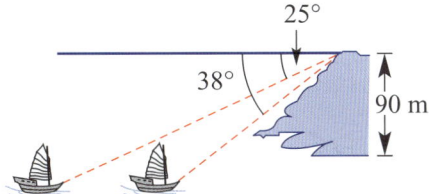

d A person on a boat 200 m out to sea views a 40 m high
castle wall on top of a 32 m high cliff. Find the viewing
angle between the base and top of the castle wall from
the person on the boat.

Design your own problem

Design a problem similar to the ones above that involve a combination of triangles.

a Clearly write the problem.

b See if a friend can understand and solve your problem.

c Show a complete solution including all diagrams.

Challenges

1   A right-angled isosceles triangle has area of 4 square units. Determine the exact perimeter of the triangle.

2   Find the area of this triangle using trigonometry.
    Hint: Insert a line showing the height of the triangle.

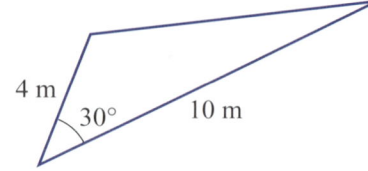

3   A rectangle $ABCD$ has sides $AB = CD = 34$ cm. E is a point on CD such that $CE = 9$ cm and $ED = 25$ cm. AE is perpendicular to EB. What is the length of BC?

4   Find the bearing from B to C in this diagram.

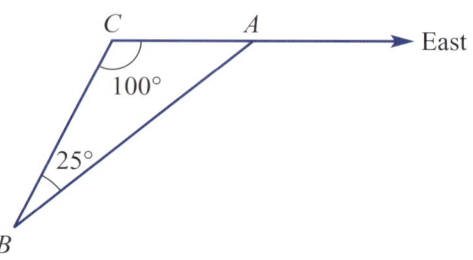

5   Which is a better fit? A square peg in a round hole or a round peg in a square hole. Use area calculations and percentages to investigate.

6   Boat A is 20 km from port on a bearing of 025° and boat B is 25 km from port on a bearing of 070°. Boat B is in distress. What bearing should boat A travel on to reach boat B?

7   For positive integers m and n such that $n < m$, the Pythagorean triples (like 3, 4, 5) can be generated using $a = m^2 - n^2$ and $b = 2mn$, where a and b are the two shorter sides of the right-angled triangle.
    a   Using the above formulas and Pythagoras' theorem to calculate the third side, generate the Pythagorean triples for:
        i $m = 2, n = 1$ ii $m = 3, n = 2$
    b   Using the expressions for a and b and Pythagoras' theorem, find a rule for c (the hypotenuse) in terms of n and m.

Finding the hypotenuse

$c^2 = 2^2 + 1^2$
$\quad = 5$
$c = \sqrt{5}$
$\quad = 2.24$ (to 2 decimal places)

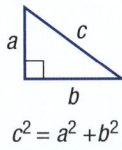

Shorter sides

$a^2 + 5^2 = 7^2$
$a^2 = 7^2 - 5^2$
$\quad = 24$
$\therefore\ a = \sqrt{24}$

Applications

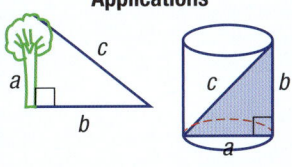

Pythagoras' theorem

$c^2 = a^2 + b^2$

SOHCAHTOA

$\sin\theta = \dfrac{O}{H} = \dfrac{4}{5}$

$\cos\theta = \dfrac{A}{H} = \dfrac{3}{5}$

$\tan\theta = \dfrac{O}{A} = \dfrac{4}{3}$

$5\ (H)$ θ $3\ (A)$
$4\ (O)$

Pythagoras' theorem and trigonometry

Bearings

True bearings are measured clockwise from North.

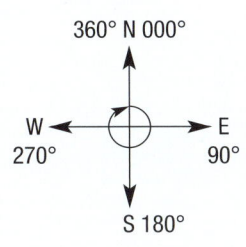

B is $150°$ T from A

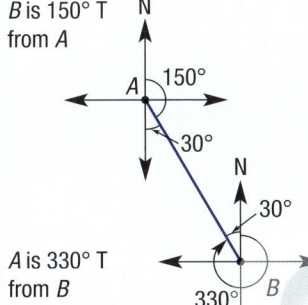

A is $330°$ T from B

Finding side lengths

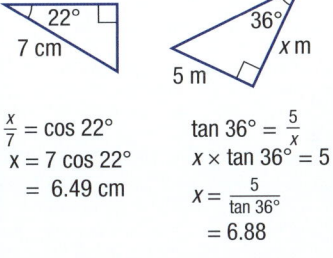

$\dfrac{x}{7} = \cos 22°$
$x = 7\cos 22°$
$\quad = 6.49$ cm

$\tan 36° = \dfrac{5}{x}$
$x \times \tan 36° = 5$
$x = \dfrac{5}{\tan 36°}$
$\quad = 6.88$

Elevation and depression

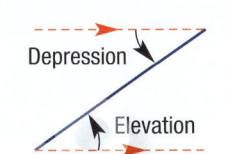

Depression

Elevation

Finding angles

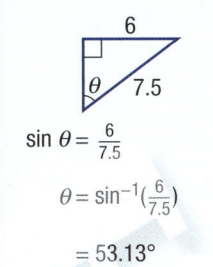

$\sin\theta = \dfrac{6}{7.5}$

$\theta = \sin^{-1}\!\left(\dfrac{6}{7.5}\right)$

$\quad = 53.13°$

Multiple-choice questions

1 For the right-angled triangle shown, the length of the hypotenuse is given by:

A $c^2 = 5^2 + 12^2$

B $c^2 = 5^2 - 12^2$

C $c^2 = 12^2 - 5^2$

D $c^2 = 5^2 \times 12^2$

E $(5 + 12)^2$

2 For the right-angled triangle shown, the value of b is given by:

A $\sqrt{0.7^2 + 0.4^2}$

B $\sqrt{0.7^2 - 0.4^2}$

C $\sqrt{0.4^2 - 0.7^2}$

D $\sqrt{0.7^2 \times 0.4^2}$

E $\sqrt{(0.7 - 0.4^2)^2}$

3 For the right-angled triangle shown:

A $x^2 = \dfrac{49}{2}$

B $7x^2 = 2$

C $x^2 = \dfrac{7}{2}$

D $x^2 + 7^2 = x^2$

E $x^2 = \dfrac{2}{7}$

4 For the triangle shown:

A $\sin\theta = \dfrac{a}{b}$

B $\sin\theta = \dfrac{c}{a}$

C $\sin\theta = \dfrac{a}{c}$

D $\sin\theta = \dfrac{b}{c}$

E $\sin\theta = \dfrac{c}{b}$

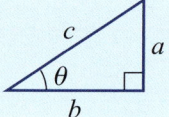

5 The value of $\cos 46°$ correct to four decimal places is:

A 0.7193

B 0.6947

C 0.594

D 0.6532

E 1.0355

6 In the diagram the value of x, correct to two decimal places, is:

A 40

B 13.61

C 4.70

D 9.89

E 6.47

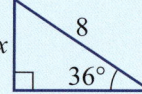

7 The length of x in the triangle is given by:

A $8 \sin 46°$

B $8 \cos 46°$

C $\dfrac{8}{\cos 46°}$

D $\dfrac{8}{\sin 46°}$

E $\dfrac{\cos 46°}{8}$

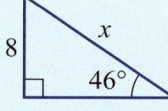

8 The true bearing of A from O is $130°$. The true bearing of O from A is:

A 050°

B 220°

C 310°

D 280°

E 170°

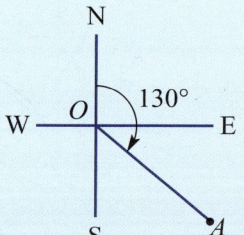

9 A ladder is inclined at an angle of 28° to the horizontal. If the ladder reaches 8.9 m up the wall, the length of the ladder correct to the nearest metre is:

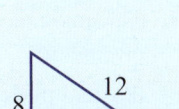

  A 19 m   **B** 4 m   **C** 2 m

  D 10 m   **E** 24 m

10 The value of θ in the diagram, correct to two decimal places, is:

  A 0.73°   **B** 41.81°   **C** 48.19°

  D 33.69°   **E** 4.181°

Short-answer questions

1 Find the unknown length in these triangles. Give an exact answer.

a 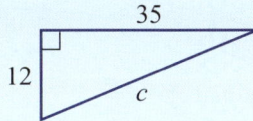   **b** 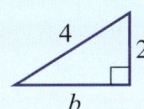   **c**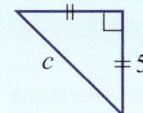

2 A steel support beam of length 6.5 m is connected to a wall at a height of 4.7 m from the ground. Find the distance (to the nearest cm) between the base of the building and the point where the beam is joined to the ground.

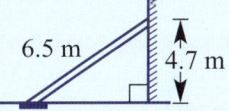

3 For this double triangle find:

  a AC

  b CD (correct to two decimal places)

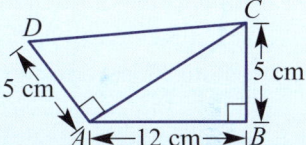

4 Two different cafés on opposite sides of an atrium in a shopping centre are respectively 10 m and 15 m above the ground floor. If the cafés are linked by a 20 m escalator, find the horizontal distance (to the nearest m) across the atrium, between the two cafés.

5 Find the values of the pronumerals in the three-dimensional objects shown below, correct to two decimal places.

a 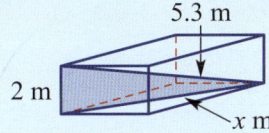   **b**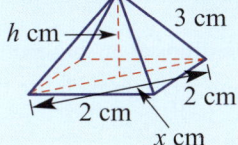

6 Find the value of each of the following, correct to two decimal places.

  a sin 40°   **b** tan 66°   **c** cos 44°

7 Find the value of each pronumeral, correct to two decimal places.

a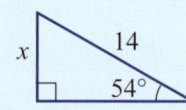

b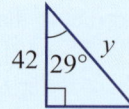

c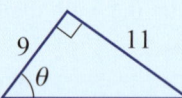

8 The angle of elevation of the top of a lighthouse from a point on the ground 40 m from its base is 35°. Find the height of the lighthouse to two decimal places.

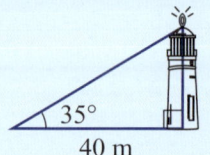

9 A train travels up a slope, making an angle of 7° with the horizontal. When the train is at a height of 3 m above its starting point, find the distance it has travelled up the slope, to the nearest metre.

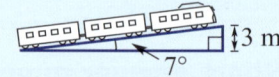

10 A yacht sails 80 km on a true bearing of 048°.

a How far east of its starting point is the yacht, correct to two decimal places?

b How far north of its starting point is the yacht, correct to two decimal places?

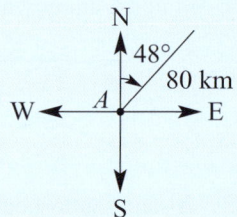

11 From a point on the ground, Geoff measures the angle of elevation of a 120 m tower to be 34°. How far from the base of the tower is Geoff, correct to two decimal places?

12 A ship leaves Coffs Harbour and sails 320 km east. It then changes direction and sails 240 km due north to its destination. What will the ship's bearing be from Coffs Harbour when it reaches its destination, correct to two decimal places?

13 From the roof of a skyscraper, Aisha spots a car at an angle of depression of 51° from the roof of the skyscraper. If the skyscraper is 78 m high how far away is the car from the base of the skyscraper, correct to one decimal place?

14 Penny wants to measure the width of a river. She places two markers, A and B, 10 m apart along one bank. C is a point directly opposite marker B. Penny measures angle BAC to be 28°. Find the width of the river to one decimal place.

15 An aeroplane takes off and climbs at an angle of 15° to the horizontal, at 210 km/h along its flight path for 15 minutes. Find:

a the distance the aeroplane travels

b the height the aeroplane reaches, correct to two decimal places.

Extended-response questions

1 An extension ladder is initially placed so that it reaches 2 metres up a wall. The foot of the ladder is 80 centimetres from the base of the wall.

   a Find the length of the ladder, to the nearest centimetre, in its original position.

   b Without moving the foot of the ladder it is extended so that it reaches one metre further up the wall. How far (to the nearest centimetre) has the ladder been extended?

   c The ladder is placed so that its foot is now 20 cm closer to the base of the wall.

      i How far up the wall can the ladder length found in part **b** reach? Round to two decimal places.

      ii Is this further than the distance in part **a**?

2 From the top of a 100 m cliff Skevi sees a boat out at sea at an angle of depression of 12°.

   a Draw a diagram for this situation.

   b Find how far out to sea the boat is to the nearest metre.

   c A swimmer is 2 km away from the base of the cliff and in line with the boat. What is the angle of depression to the swimmer to the nearest degree?

   d How far away is the boat from the swimmer, to the nearest metre?

3 A pilot takes off from Amber Island and flies for 150 km at 040° true to Barter Island where she unloads her first cargo. She intends to fly to Dream Island but a bad thunderstorm between Barter and Dream islands forces her to fly off-course for 60 km to Crater Atoll on a bearing of 060° true. She then turns on a bearing of 140° true and flies for 100 km until she reaches Dream Island where she unloads her second cargo. She then takes off and flies 180 km on a bearing of 55° true to Emerald Island.

   a How many extra kilometres did she fly trying to avoid the storm? Round to the nearest km.

   b From Emerald Island she flies directly back to Amber Island. How many kilometres did she travel on her return trip? Round to the nearest km.

Chapter 4

Linear relations

What you will learn

Computer-generated imagery (CGI)

Australian curriculum

NUMBER AND ALGEBRA

Real numbers

Solve problems involving direct proportion

Explore the relationship between graphs and equations corresponding to simple rate problems

Linear and non-linear relationships

Find the distance between two points located on a Cartesian plane using a range of strategies, including graphing software

Find the midpoint and gradient of a line segment (interval) on the Cartesian plane using a range of strategies, including graphing software

Sketch linear graphs using the coordinates of two points

Movies and computer games include many scenes and characters that are generated by computer, such as Woody in *Toy Story* or Nemo in *Finding Nemo*. Another classic example is the character Gollum in *The Lord of the Rings* film trilogy, one of the first and most successful CGI characters to interact with live actors in a movie blockbuster. CGI characters are added after filming the other real-life characters. The fundamentals of CGI and computer graphics are more generally based on computer programming, including linear algebra, which is the focus of this chapter. Straight lines described by linear relations can form polygons and with the use of linear algebra can be transformed to create moving three-dimensional images in a two-dimensional plane.

1 Find the value of y in each of the following when $x = 0$.

   a $y = 2x + 3$ **b** $y = 3x - 4$ **c** $x + 2y = 8$ **d** $3x - 4y = 12$

2 Given $y = 3x - 2$, find the value of y when

   a $x = 1$ **b** $x = 3$ **c** $x = -1$ **d** $x = -2$

3 Solve the following equations for x.

   a $0 = x - 4$ **b** $0 = 3x + 6$ **c** $0 = 2x - 8$

   d $0 = \dfrac{1}{2}x + 2$ **e** $3x = 15$ **f** $\dfrac{1}{3}x = 2$

4 Plot and label the following points on a Cartesian plane (x-y axes).

   a $(3, 1)$ **b** $(-2, 4)$ **c** $(0, 0)$ **d** $(5, -3)$

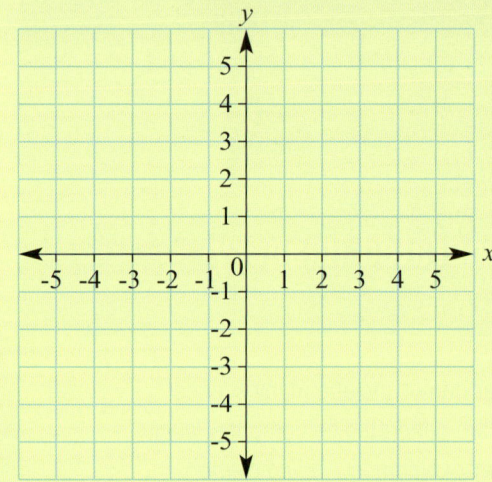

5 Determine the average (mean) of the following pairs of numbers.

   a $4, 10$ **b** $2, 11$ **c** $-1, 7$ **d** $-3, -7$

6 Find the vertical distance between the following pairs of points.

   a $(3, 2)$ and $(3, 7)$ **b** $(-1, 1)$ and $(-1, -3)$ **c** $(2, 3)$ and $(2, -2)$ **d** $(1, -4)$ and $(1, -1)$

7 Find the horizontal distance between the following pairs of points.

   a $(1, 3)$ and $(5, 3)$ **b** $(-1, 2)$ and $(4, 2)$ **c** $(-2, -3)$ and $(5, -3)$ **d** $(-4, 1)$ and $(-1, 1)$

8 Rewrite each of the following in the form $y = mx + c$ by making y the subject.

   a $y - 2x = 5$ **b** $3x + y = 2$ **c** $-4x + 2y = 6$ **d** $3x - \dfrac{1}{2}y = 4$

9 If $x = 2$ and $y = 1$, decide if the following equations are true.

   a $y = 2x + 1$ **b** $y = 3x - 5$ **c** $y = -2x + 5$ **d** $5x - 2y = 6$

10 Determine the value of c in each of the following given:

   a $y = 3x + c$ is true when $x = 2$ and $y = 8$

   b $y = -2x + c$ is true when $x = -1$ and $y = -3$

   c $y = 5x + c$ is true when $x = 1$ and $y = 2$

   d $y = \dfrac{1}{2}x + c$ is true when $x = -4$ and $y = 7$

4.1 Introduction to linear relations

If two variables are related in some way we can use mathematical rules to more precisely describe this relationship. The most simple kind of mathematical relationship is one that can be illustrated with a straight line graph. These are called linear relations. The volume of petrol in your car at a service bowser, for example, might initially be 10 L then be increasing by 1.2 L per second after that. This is an example of a linear relationship between *volume* and *time* because the volume is increasing at a constant rate of 1.2 L/sec.

Let's start: Is it linear?

Here are three rules linking x and y.

1    $y_1 = \dfrac{2}{x} + 1$

2    $y_2 = x^2 - 1$

3    $y_3 = 3x - 4$

First complete this simple table and graph.

x	1	2	3
y_1			
y_2			
y_3			

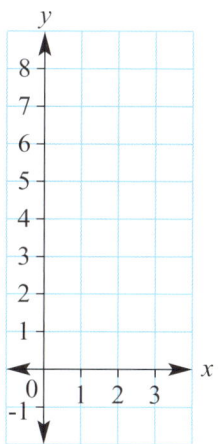

- Which of the three rules do you think is linear?
- How do the table and graph help you decide it's linear?

Key ideas

- **Coordinate geometry** provides a link between geometry and algebra.
- The **Cartesian plane** (or number plane) consists of two axes which divide the number plane into four **quadrants**.
  - The horizontal x-axis and vertical y-axis intersect at the **origin** $(0, 0)$ at right angles.
  - A point is precisely positioned on a Cartesian plane using the **coordinate pair** (x, y) where x describes the horizontal position and y describes the vertical position of the point from the origin.
- A **linear relation** is a set of ordered pairs (x, y) that when graphed give a straight line.
- Linear relations have rules that may be of the form:
  - $y = mx + c$ (or $y = mx + b$) For example, $y = 2x + 1$
  - $ax + by = d$ or $ax + by + c = 0$ For example, $2x - 3y = 4$ or $2x - 3y - 4 = 0$
- The **x-** and **y-intercepts** are the points where a line cuts the axes.

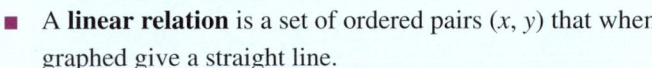

y-intercept

x	-2	-1	0	1	2	3
y	8	6	4	2	0	-2

x-intercept

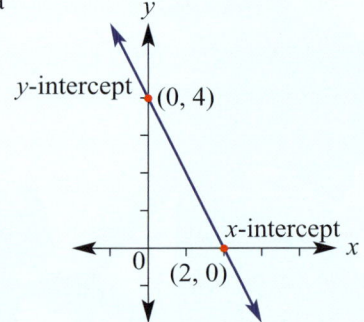

Example 1 Plotting points to graph straight lines

Using $-3 \leq x \leq 3$, construct a table of values and plot a graph for these linear relations.

a $y = x + 2$ **b** $y = -2x + 2$

SOLUTION

a

x	-3	-2	-1	0	1	2	3
y	-1	0	1	2	3	4	5

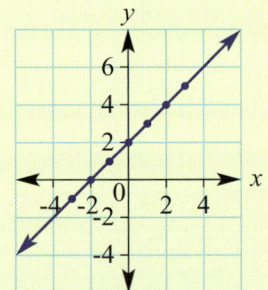

EXPLANATION

Use $-3 \leq x \leq 3$ as instructed and substitute each value of x into the rule $y = x + 2$.

The coordinates of the points are read from the table, i.e. $(-3, -1)$, $(-2, 0)$, etc.

Plot each point and join to form a straight line.
Extend the line to show it continues in either direction.

b

x	-3	-2	-1	0	1	2	3
y	8	6	4	2	0	-2	-4

Use $-3 \leq x \leq 3$ as instructed and substitute each value of x into the rule $y = -2x + 2$.

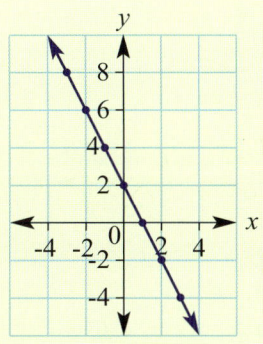

Plot each point and join to form a straight line.
Extend the line beyond the plotted points.

Example 2 Reading off the *x*-intercept and *y*-intercept

Read off the coordinates of the *x*-intercept and *y*-intercept from this table and graph.

a

x	-2	-1	0	1	2	3
y	5	4	3	2	1	0

b

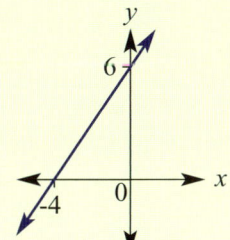

SOLUTION

a The *x*-intercept coordinates are (3, 0).
The *y*-intercept coordinates are (0, 3).

b The *x*-intercept coordinates are (-4, 0).
The *y*-intercept coordinates are (0, 6).

EXPLANATION

The *x*-intercept is the point where $y = 0$ (on the *x*-axis).
The *y*-intercept is the point where $x = 0$ (on the *y*-axis).

The *x*-intercept is the point where $y = 0$ (on the *x*-axis).
The *y*-intercept is the point where $x = 0$ (on the *y*-axis).

Example 3 Rearranging linear equations

Rearrange these linear equations into the form shown in the brackets.

a $4x + 2y = 10$ ($y = mx + b$)   **b** $y = 4x - 7$ ($ax + by = d$)

SOLUTION

a $4x + 2y = 10$
   $2y = -4x + 10$
   $y = -2x + 5$

b $y = 4x - 7$
   $y - 4x = -7$

EXPLANATION

Solve for y
Subtract $4x$ from both sides.
Divide both sides by 2.

Subtract $4x$ from both sides.

Exercise 4A

1 Refer to the Cartesian plane shown.

   a Give the coordinates of all the points *A–L*.

   b Which points lie on:

     i the *x*-axis

     ii the *y*-axis.

   c Which points lie inside the:

     i 2nd quadrant

     ii 4th quadrant.

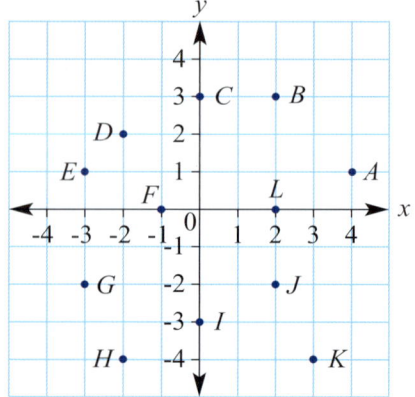

2 For the rule $y = 3x - 4$, find the value of y for these x values.

   a $x = 2$ **b** $x = 1$ **c** $x = 0$ **d** $x = -1$

3 For the rule $y = -2x + 1$, find the value of y for these x values.

   a $x = 0$ **b** $x = 3$ **c** $x = -1$ **d** $x = -10$

Example 1   **4** Using $-3 \le x \le 3$, construct a table of values and plot a graph for these linear relations.

   a $y = x - 1$ **b** $y = x + 3$ **c** $y = -2x - 1$

   d $y = 2x - 3$ **e** $y = -x + 4$ **f** $y = -3x$

Example 2   **5** Read off the coordinates of the *x*- and *y*-intercepts from these tables and graphs.

a

x	-3	-2	-1	0	1	2	3
y	4	3	2	1	0	1	2

b

x	-3	-2	-1	0	1	2	3
y	-1	0	1	2	3	4	5

c

x	-1	0	1	2	3	4
y	10	8	6	4	2	0

d

x	-5	-4	-3	-2	-1	0
y	0	2	4	6	8	10

e

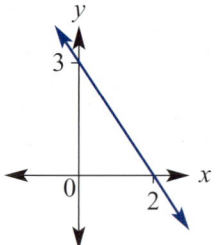

f

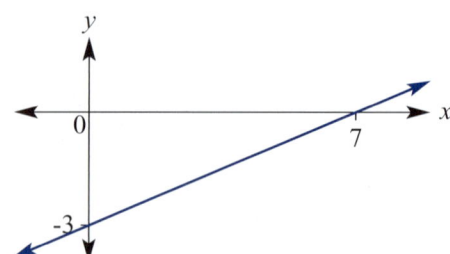

g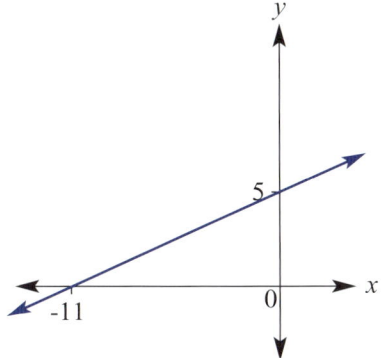

h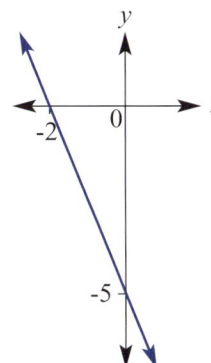

ample 3 **6** Rearrange these linear equations into the form shown in the brackets.

  a $2x + y = 3$ ($y = mx + b$)
  b $-3x + y = -1$ ($y = mx + b$)
  c $6x + 2y = 4$ ($y = mx + b$)
  d $-3x + 3y = 6$ ($y = mx + b$)
  e $y = 2x - 1$ ($ax + by = d$)
  f $y = -3x + 4$ ($ax + by = d$)
  g $3y - x - 1$ ($ax + by = d$)
  h $7y - 2 = 2x$ ($ax + by = d$)

7 Find a rule in the form $y = mx + c$ (e.g. $y = 2x - 1$) which matches these tables of values.

a

x	0	1	2	3	4
y	2	3	4	5	6

b

x	-1	0	1	2	3
y	-2	0	2	4	6

c

x	-2	-1	0	1	2	3
y	-3	-1	1	3	5	7

d

x	-3	-2	-1	0	1	2
y	5	4	3	2	1	0

8 Rearrange these equations into the form $y = mx + c$.

  a $2x + 3y = 6$ **b** $3x + 4y = -3$
  c $x - y = 4$ **d** $2x - y = -7$
  e $x - 3y = 1$ **f** $4x - 7y = 10$

The slope of this mountain railway could be expressed in the form $y = mx + c$

9 Match these rules A, B, C and D to the graphs a, b, c and d.

A $y = 2x + 1$

B $y = -x - 1$

C $y = -2x + 3$

D $x + y = 2$

a

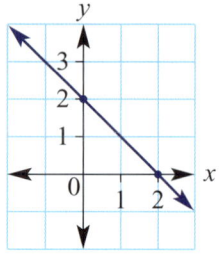

b

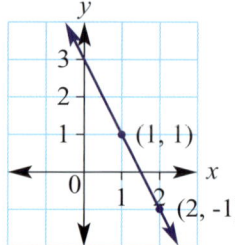

c

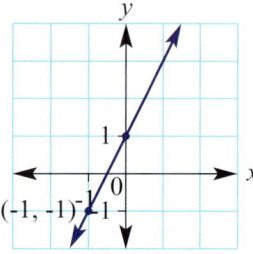

d

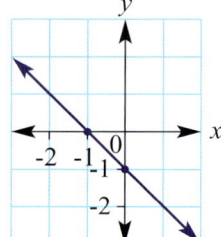

---

10 Decide if the following equations are true or false.

a $\dfrac{2x + 4}{2} = x + 4$

b $\dfrac{3x - 6}{3} = x - 2$

c $\dfrac{1}{2}(x - 1) = \dfrac{1}{2}x - \dfrac{1}{2}$

d $\dfrac{2}{3}(x - 6) = \dfrac{2}{3}x - 12$

11 Give reasons why the x-intercept on these graphs has coordinates $(\dfrac{3}{2}, 0)$.

a

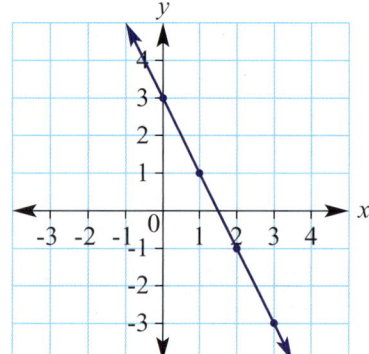

b

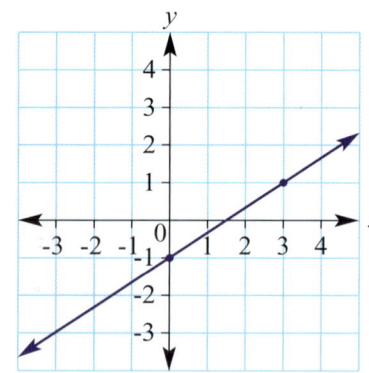

12 Decide if the following rules are equivalent.

a $y = 1 - x$ and $y = -x + 1$

b $y = 1 - 3x$ and $y = 3x - 1$

c $y = -2x + 1$ and $y = -1 - 2x$

d $y = -3x + 1$ and $y = 1 - 3x$

Enrichment: Tough rule finding

13 Find the linear rule linking x and y in these tables.

a

x	-1	0	1	2	3
y	5	7	9	11	13

b

x	-2	-1	0	1	2
y	22	21	20	19	18

c

x	0	2	4	6	8
y	-10	-16	-22	-28	-34

d

x	-5	-4	-3	-2	-1
y	29	24	19	14	9

e

x	1	3	5	7	9
y	1	2	3	4	5

f

x	-14	-13	-12	-11	-10
y	$5\frac{1}{2}$	5	$4\frac{1}{2}$	4	$3\frac{1}{2}$

The lines in this structure can be modelled by linear relations.

4.2 Graphing straight lines with intercepts

When linear rules are graphed, all the points lie in a straight line, so it is therefore possible to graph a straight line using only two points. Two critical points that help draw these graphs are the x-intercept and y-intercept introduced in the previous section.

Let's start: Two key points

Consider the relation $y = \dfrac{1}{2}x + 1$ and complete this table and graph.

x	-4	-3	-2	-1	0	1	2
y							

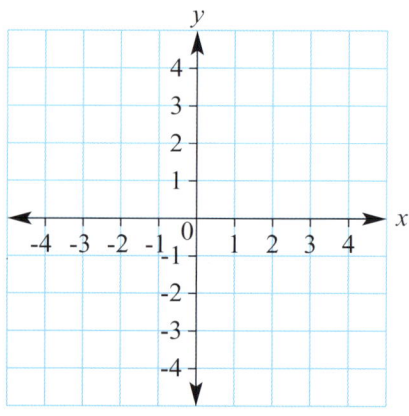

- What are the coordinates of the point where the line crosses the y-axis? That is, state the coordinates of the y-intercept.
- What are the coordinates of the point where the line crosses the x-axis? That is, state the coordinates of the x-intercept.
- Discuss how you might find the coordinates of the x- and y-intercepts without drawing a table and plotting points. Explain your method.

Key ideas

- The **y-intercept** is the point on the y-axis, i.e. the point where $x = 0$.
  - Substitute $x = 0$ to find the y-intercept.
- The **x-intercept** is the point on the x-axis, i.e. the point where $y = 0$.
  - Substitute $y = 0$ to find the x-intercept.

Example: $2x + 3y = 6$

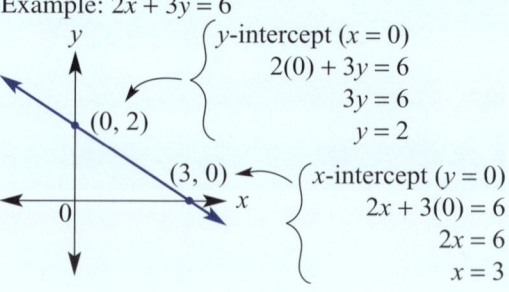

y-intercept ($x = 0$)
$$2(0) + 3y = 6$$
$$3y = 6$$
$$y = 2$$

x-intercept ($y = 0$)
$$2x + 3(0) = 6$$
$$2x = 6$$
$$x = 3$$

Example 4 Sketching with intercepts

Sketch the graph of the following, showing the x- and y-intercepts.

a $2x + 3y = 6$ **b** $y = 2x - 6$

SOLUTION	EXPLANATION
a y-intercept (let $x = 0$):	Only two points are required to generate a straight line.
$2x + 3y = 6$	For the y-intercept, substitute $x = 0$ into the rule and
$2(0) + 3y = 6$	solve for y by dividing each side by 3.
$3y = 6$	
$y = 2$	
$\therefore$ the y-intercept is 2	State the y-intercept. The coordinates are $(0, 2)$.
x-intercept (let $y = 0$):	Similarly to find the x-intercept, substitute $y = 0$ into
$2x + 3(0) = 6$	the rule and solve for x.
$2x = 6$	
$x = 3$	
$\therefore$ the x-intercept is 3	State the x-intercept. The coordinates are $(3, 0)$.
	Mark and label the intercepts on the axes and sketch
	the graph by joining the two intercepts.

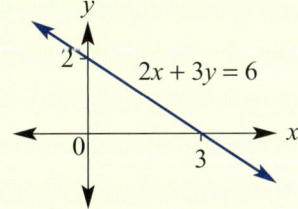

b y-intercept (let $x = 0$):	Substitute $x = 0$ for the y-intercept.
$y = 2x - 6$	Simplify to find the y-coordinate.
$y = 2(0) - 6$	
$y = -6$	
$\therefore$ the y-intercept is -6	The coordinates are $(0, -6)$.
x-intercept (let $y = 0$):	Substitute $y = 0$ for the x-intercept. Solve the remaining
$0 = 2x - 6$	equation for x by adding 6 to both sides and then
$6 = 2x$	dividing both sides by 2.
$x = 3$	
$\therefore$ the x-intercept is 3	The coordinates are $(3, 0)$.
	Mark in the two intercepts and join to sketch the graph.

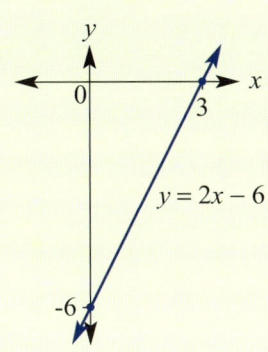

Exercise 4B

1 For each of the given rules, complete a table like the one shown and plot points to draw a graph. Clearly label the coordinates of the x- and y-intercepts.

x	-3	-2	-1	0	1	2	3
y							

a $y = x + 2$ **b** $y = \frac{1}{2}x - 1$ **c** $y = 3x$ **d** $y = -x + 3$

2 a Find the value of y in these equations.

    i $2y = 6$ **ii** $y = 3 \times 0 + 4$ **iii** $y = -2 \times 0 - 3$

    iv $y = \frac{1}{2} \times 0 - 1$ **v** $-2y = 12$ **vi** $-6y = -24$

b Find the value of x in these equations.

    i $3x = 18$ **ii** $-4x = -40$ **iii** $0 = 2x - 2$

    iv $3x - 6 = 0$ **v** $\frac{1}{2}x = 3$ **vi** $\frac{1}{3}x = -1$

3 For these equations find the y-intercept by letting $x = 0$.

    a $x + y = 4$ **b** $x - y = 5$ **c** $2x + 3y = 9$ **d** $y = 2x - 4$

4 For these equations find the x-intercept by letting $y = 0$.

    a $x + 2y = 5$ **b** $2x - y = -4$ **c** $4x - 3y = 12$ **d** $y = 3x - 6$

Example 4a

5 Sketch the graph of the following relations, by finding the x- and y-intercepts.

    a $x + y = 2$ **b** $x + y = 5$ **c** $x - y = 3$

    d $x - y = -2$ **e** $2x + y = 4$ **f** $3x - y = 9$

    g $4x - 2y = 8$ **h** $3x + 2y = 6$ **i** $3x - 2y = 6$

    j $y - 3x = 12$ **k** $-5y + 2x = -10$ **l** $-x + 7y = 21$

Example 4b

6 Sketch the graph of the following relations, showing the x- and y-intercepts.

    a $y = 3x + 3$ **b** $y = 2x + 2$ **c** $y = x - 5$

    d $y = -x - 6$ **e** $y = -2x - 2$ **f** $y = -3x - 6$

    g $y = -2x + 4$ **h** $y = 2x - 3$ **i** $y = -x + 1$

7 Sketch the graph of each of the following mixed linear relations.

    a $x + 2y = 8$ **b** $3x - 5y = 15$ **c** $3x + 4y = 12$

    d $y = 3x - 6$ **e** $3y - 4x = 12$ **f** $5y - x = 10$

    g $2x - y - 4 = 0$ **h** $2x - y + 5 = 0$ **i** $x - 4y + 2 = 0$

8 The distance d metres of a vehicle from an observation point after t seconds is given by the rule $d = 8 - 2t$.

    a Find the distance from the observation point initially (at $t = 0$).

    b Find after what time t the distance d is equal to 0 (substitute $d = 0$).

    c Sketch a graph of d versus t between the d and t intercepts.

Problem-solving

9 The height h, in metres, of a lift above ground after t seconds is given by $h = 100 - 8t$.
   a How high is the lift initially (at $t = 0$)?
   b How long does it take for the lift to reach the ground ($h = 0$)?

10 Find the x- and y-axis intercepts of the graphs with the given rules. Write answers using fractions.
   a $3x - 2y = 5$
   b $x + 5y = -7$
   c $y - 2x = -13$
   d $y = -2x - 1$
   e $2y = x - 3$
   f $-7y = 1 - 3x$

Using a linear graph, we can model the time it takes a lift to reach the ground.

Reasoning

11 Use your algebra and fraction skills to help sketch graphs for these relations by finding x- and y-intercepts.
   a $\dfrac{x}{2} + \dfrac{y}{3} = 1$
   b $y = \dfrac{8 - x}{4}$
   c $\dfrac{y}{2} = \dfrac{2 - 4x}{8}$

12 Explain why the graph of the equation $ax + by = 0$ must pass through the origin for any values of the constants a and b.

13 Write down the rule for the graph with these axes intercepts. Write the rule in the form $ax + by = d$.
   a $(0, 4)$ and $(4, 0)$
   b $(0, 2)$ and $(2, 0)$
   c $(0, -3)$ and $(3, 0)$
   d $(0, 1)$ and $(-1, 0)$
   e $(0, k)$ and $(k, 0)$
   f $(0, -k)$ and $(-k, 0)$

Enrichment: Intercept families

14 Find the x- and y-intercepts in terms of the constants a, b and c for these relations.
   a $ax + by = c$
   b $y = \dfrac{a}{b}x + c$
   c $\dfrac{ax - by}{c} = 1$
   d $ay - bx = c$
   e $ay = bx + c$
   f $a(x + y) = bc$

Using a CAS calculator 4.2: Sketching straight lines

This activity is on the companion website in the form of a printable PDF.

4.3 Lines with one intercept

Lines with one intercept include vertical lines, horizontal lines and other lines that pass through the origin.

Let's start: What rule satisfies all points?

Here is one vertical and one horizontal line.

- For the vertical line shown, write down the coordinates of all the points shown as dots.
- What is always true for each coordinate pair?
- What simple equation describes every point on the line?
- For the horizontal line shown write down the coordinates of all the points shown as dots.
- What is always true for each coordinate pair?
- What simple equation describes every point on the line?
- Where do the two lines intersect?

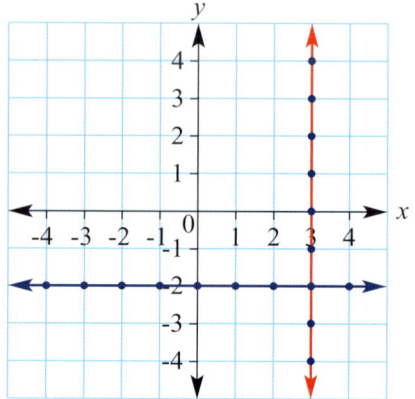

Key ideas

- Vertical line: $x = b$
  - Parallel to the y-axis
  - Equation of the form $x = b$, where b is a constant
  - x-intercept coordinates are $(b, 0)$

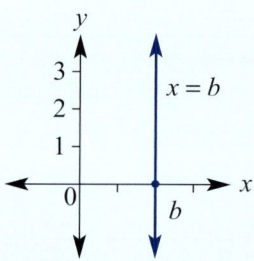

- Horizontal line: $y = c$
  - Parallel to the x-axis
  - Equation of the form $y = c$, where c is a constant
  - y-intercept coordinates are $(0, c)$

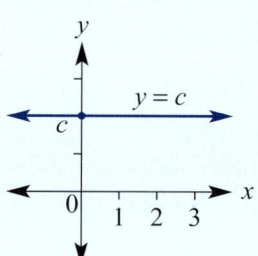

- Lines through the origin $(0, 0)$: $y = mx$
  - y-intercept is $(0, 0)$
  - x-intercept is $(0, 0)$
  - Substitute $x = 1$ or any other value of x to find a second point

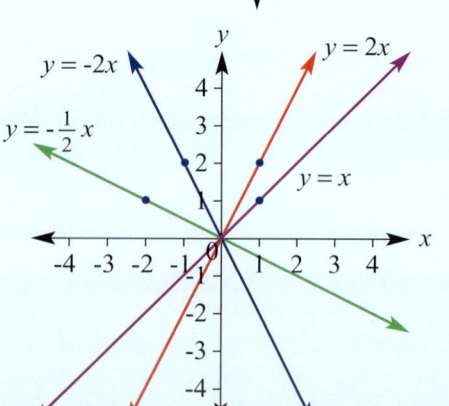

Example 5 Graphing vertical and horizontal lines

Sketch the graph of the following vertical and horizontal lines.

a $y = 3$ **b** $x = -4$

SOLUTION	EXPLANATION

a

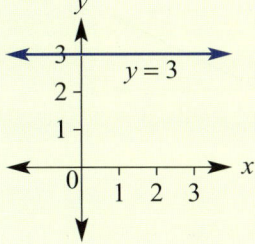

y-intercept is 3.

Sketch a horizontal line through all points where $y = 3$.

b

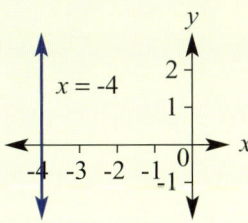

x-intercept is -4.

Sketch a vertical line through all points where $x = -4$.

Example 6 Sketching lines which pass through the origin

Sketch the graph of $y = 3x$.

SOLUTION	EXPLANATION

The x- and y-intercept is at $(0, 0)$.

Another point (let $x = 1$):

$$y = 3 \times 1$$
$$y = 3$$

Another point is at $(1, 3)$.

The equation is of the form $y = mx$.

Since two points are required to generate the straight line, find another point by substituting $x = 1$.

Other x values could also be shown.

Plot and label both points and sketch the graph by joining the points in a straight line.

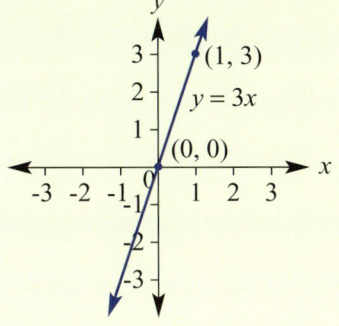

Exercise 4C

1 Write the coordinates of the *x*-intercept for these graphs.

a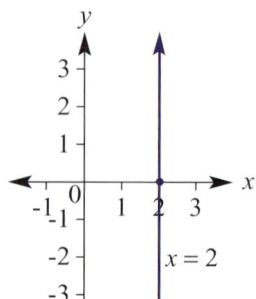

b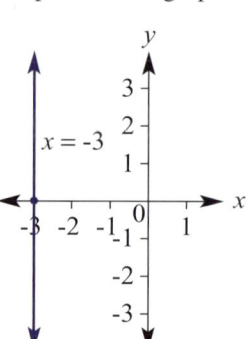

c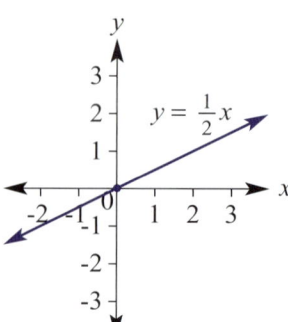

2 Write the coordinates of the *y*-intercept for these graphs.

a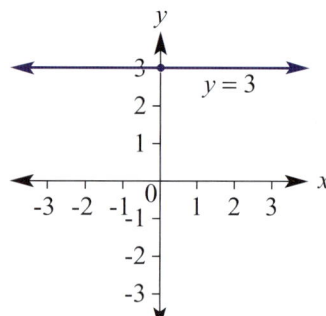

b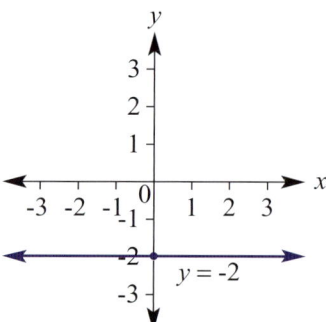

c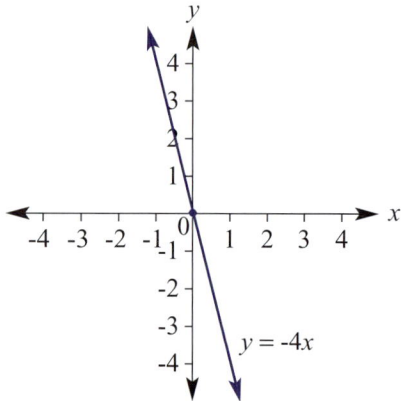

d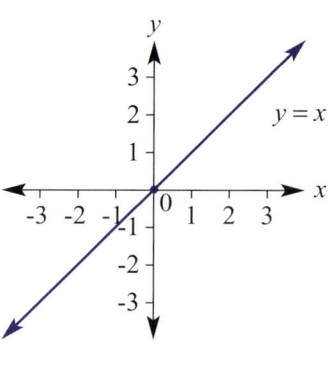

3 Find the value of *y* if *x* = 1 using these rules.

a $y = 5x$

b $y = \frac{1}{3}x$

c $y = -4x$

d $y = -0.1x$

Sample 5 **4** Sketch the graph of the following vertical and horizontal lines.

a $x = 2$	**b** $x = 5$	**c** $y = 4$	**d** $y = 1$
e $x = -3$	**f** $x = -2$	**g** $y = -1$	**h** $y = -3$

Sample 6 **5** Sketch the graph of the following linear relations which pass through the origin.

a $y = 2x$	**b** $y = 5x$	**c** $y = 4x$	**d** $y = x$
e $y = -4x$	**f** $y = -3x$	**g** $y = -2x$	**h** $y = -x$

6 Sketch the graphs of these special lines all on the same set of axes and label with their equations.

a $x = -2$	**b** $y = -3$	**c** $y = 2$	**d** $x = 4$
e $y = 3x$	**f** $y = -\dfrac{1}{2}x$	**g** $y = -1.5x$	**h** $x = 0.5$
i $x = 0$	**j** $y = 0$	**k** $y = 2x$	**l** $y = 1.5x$

7 What is the equation of each of the following graphs?

a
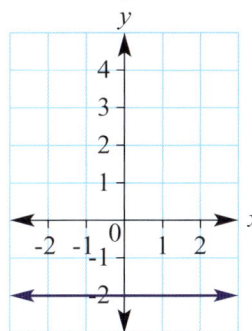

b
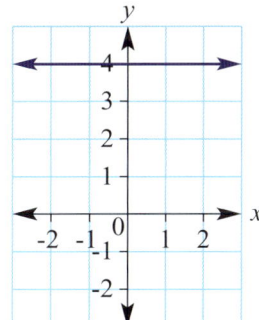

c
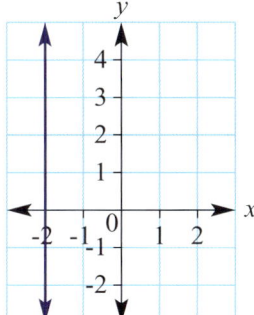

d
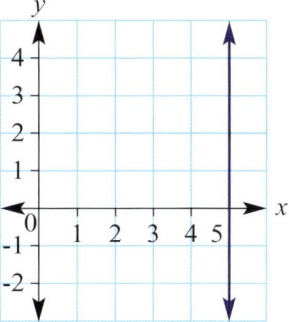

e
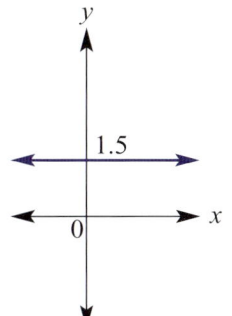

f
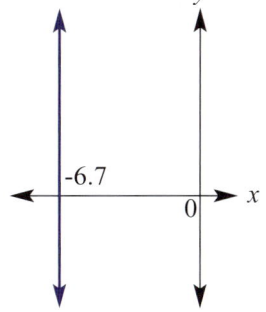

8   Find the equation of the straight line which is:
  a   parallel to the *x*-axis and passes through the point (1, 3)
  b   parallel to the *y*-axis and passes through the point (5, 4)
  c   parallel to the *y*-axis and passes through the point (-2, 4)
  d   parallel to the *x*-axis and passes through the point (0, 0).

9   If in a picture, the surface of the sea is represented by the *x*-axis, state the equation of the following paths.
  a   A plane flies horizontally at 250 m above sea level. One unit is 1 metre.
  b   A submarine travels horizontally 45 m below sea level. One unit is 1 metre.

10   The graph of these pairs of equations intersect at a point. Find the coordinates of the point.
  a $x = 1, y = 2$ **b** $x = -3, y = 5$ **c** $x = 0, y = -4$
  d $x = 4, y = 0$ **e** $y = -6x, x = 0$ **f** $y = 3x, x = 1$
  g $y = -9x, x = 3$ **h** $y = 8x, y = 40$ **i** $y = 5x, y = 15$

11   Find the area of the rectangle contained within the following four lines.
  a $x = 1, x = -2, y = -3, y = 2$ **b** $x = 0, x = 17, y = -5, y = -1$

12   The lines $x = -1$, $x = 3$ and $y = -2$ form three sides of a rectangle. Find the possible equation of the fourth line if:
  a   the area of the rectangle is:
    i   12 square units   **ii**   8 square units   **iii**   22 square units
  b   the perimeter of the rectangle is:
    i   14 units   **ii**   26 units   **iii**   31 units

13 The rules of the following graphs are of the form $y = mx$. Use the points marked with a dot to find m and hence state the equation.

a

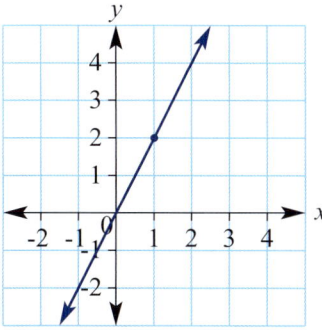

b

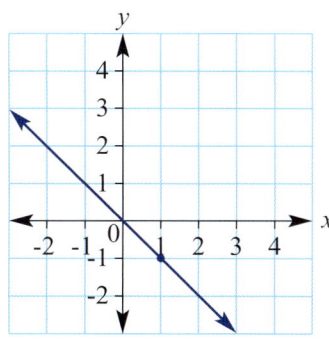

c

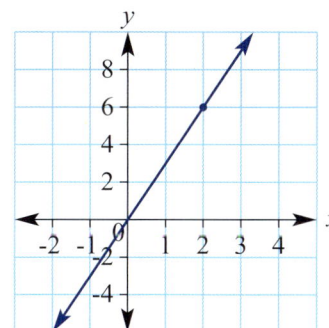

d

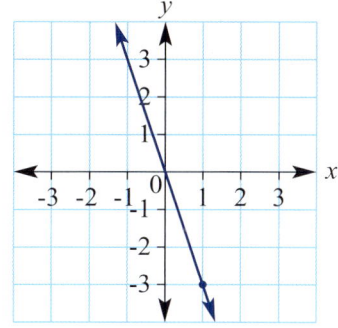

14 Find the equation of the line which passes through the origin and the given point.
  a $(1, 3)$ **b** $(1, 4)$ **c** $(1, -5)$ **d** $(1, -2)$

15 Sketch the graph of each of the following by first making y or x the subject.

  a $y - 8 = 0$ **b** $x + 5 = 0$ **c** $x + \dfrac{1}{2} = 0$ **d** $y - 0.6 = 0$

  e $y + 3x = 0$ **f** $y - 5x = 0$ **g** $2y - 8x = 0$ **h** $5y + 7x = 0$

Enrichment: Trisection

16 A vertical line, horizontal line and another line that passes through the origin all intersect at $(-1, -5)$. What are the equations of the three lines?

17 If $y = c$, $x = b$ and $y = mx$ all intersect at one point:
  a state the coordinates of the intersection point
  b find m in terms of c and b.

18 The area of a triangle formed by $x = 4$, $y = -2$ and $y = mx$ is 16 square units. Find the value of m given $m > 0$.

4.4 Gradient

The gradient of a line is a measure of its slope. It is a number which describes the steepness of a line and is calculated by considering how far a line rises or falls between two points within a given horizontal distance. The horizontal distance between two points is called the *run* and the vertical distance is called the *rise*.

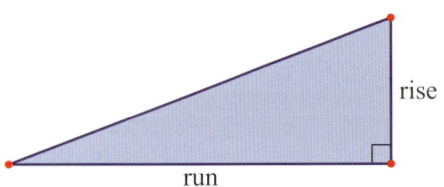

Gradients are used to describe the steepness of this rollercoaster track.

Let's start: Which line is the steepest?

The three lines here connect the points
A, B, C, D, E, F, G and H.

- Calculate the rise and run (working from left to right) and also the fraction $\frac{\text{rise}}{\text{run}}$ for these segments.

  i AB **ii** BC **iii** BD
  iv EF **v** GH

- What do you notice about the fractions ($\frac{\text{rise}}{\text{run}}$) for parts **i**, **ii** and **iii**?
- How does the $\frac{\text{rise}}{\text{run}}$ for EF compare with the $\frac{\text{rise}}{\text{run}}$ for parts **i**, **ii** and **iii**? Which of the two lines is the steepest?
- Your $\frac{\text{rise}}{\text{run}}$ for GH should be negative. Why is this the case?
- Discuss whether or not GH is steeper than AD.

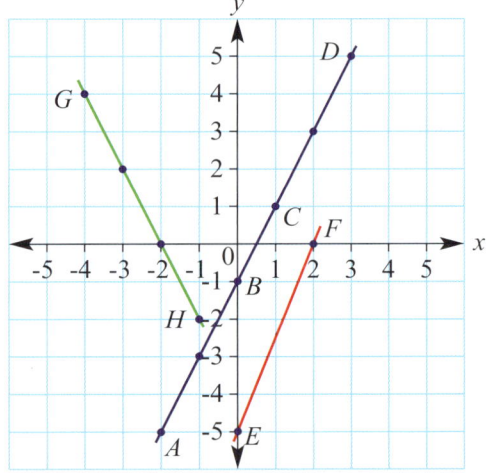

Use computer software (dynamic geometry) to produce a set of axes and grid.
- Construct a line segment with endpoints on the grid. Show the coordinates of the endpoints.
- Calculate the rise (vertical distance between the endpoints) and the run (horizontal distance between the endpoints).
- Calculate the gradient as the *rise* divided by the *run*.
- Now drag the endpoints and explore the effect on the gradient.
- Can you drag the endpoints but retain the same gradient value? Explain why this is possible.
- Can you drag the endpoints so that the gradient is zero or undefined? Describe how this can be achieved.

- **Gradient** $(m) = \dfrac{\text{rise}}{\text{run}}$

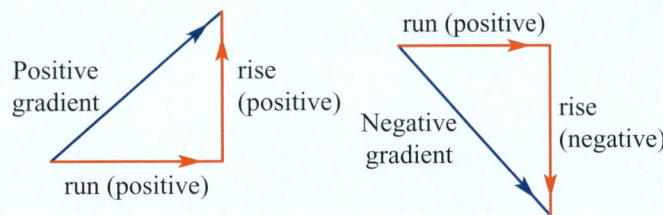

- We work from left to right, so the run is always positive.
- The gradient can be positive, negative, zero or undefined.
- A vertical line has an undefined gradient.

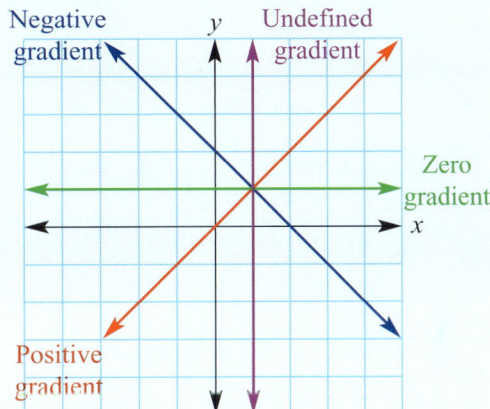

Example 7 Finding the gradient of a line

For each graph, state whether the gradient is positive, negative, zero or undefined, then find the gradient where possible.

a

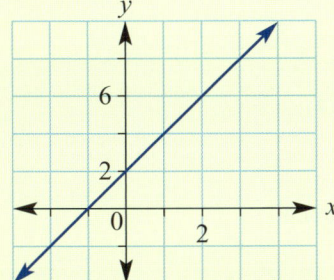

b

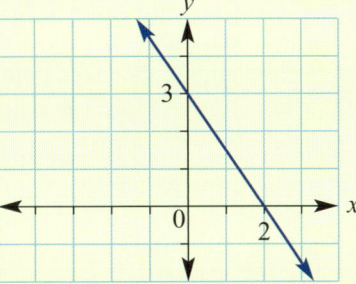

c

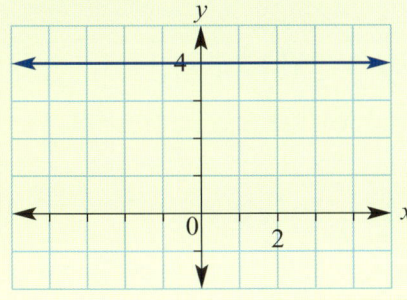

d

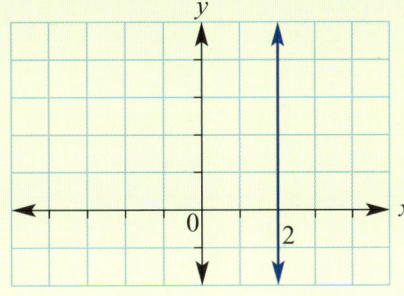

SOLUTION

EXPLANATION

a The gradient is positive.

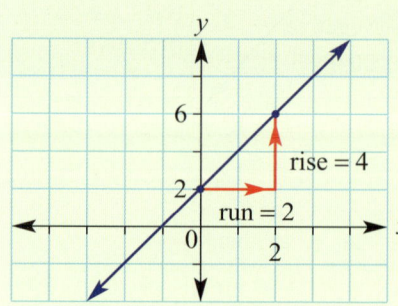

Gradient = $\dfrac{\text{rise}}{\text{run}}$

$= \dfrac{4}{2}$

$= 2$

By inspection, the gradient will be positive since the graph rises from left to right. Select any two points and create a right-angled triangle to determine the rise and run.

Substitute rise = 4 and run = 2.

b The gradient is negative.

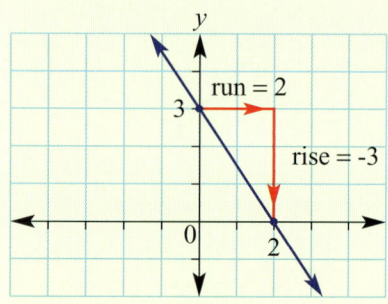

Gradient = $\dfrac{\text{rise}}{\text{run}}$

$= \dfrac{-3}{2}$

$= -\dfrac{3}{2}$

By inspection, the gradient will be negative since y values decrease from left to right.

Rise = -3 and run = 2.

c The gradient is 0.

d The gradient is undefined.

The line is horizontal.

The line is vertical.

Example 8 Finding the gradient between two points

Find the gradient (m) of the line joining the given points.

a $A(3, 4)$ and $B(5, 6)$

b $A(-3, 6)$ and $B(1, -3)$

SOLUTION

EXPLANATION

a $m = \dfrac{\text{rise}}{\text{run}}$

$= \dfrac{6-4}{5-3}$

$= \dfrac{2}{2}$

$= 1$

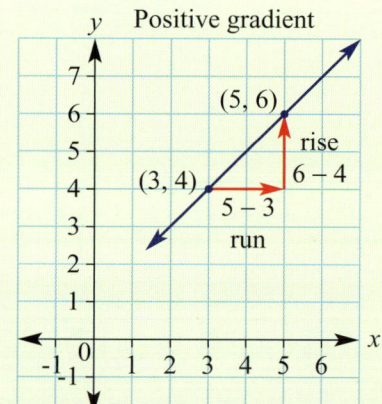

b $m = \dfrac{\text{rise}}{\text{run}}$

$= \dfrac{-9}{4}$ or $-\dfrac{9}{4}$ or -2.25

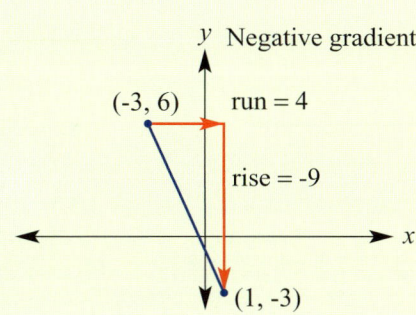

Exercise 4D

Understanding

1 Calculate the gradient using $\dfrac{\text{rise}}{\text{run}}$ for these lines. Remember to give a negative answer if the line is sloping downward from left to right.

a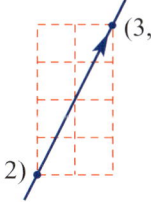

b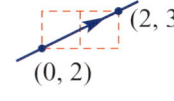

c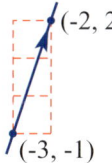

d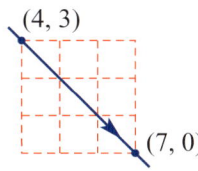

e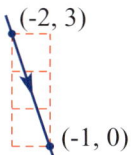

f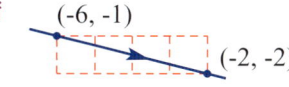

2 Use the words: positive, negative, zero or undefined to complete each sentence.

    a The gradient of a horizontal line is _____.

    b The gradient of the line joining (0, 3) with (5, 0) is _____.

    c The gradient of the line joining (-6, 0) with (1, 1) is _____.

    d The gradient of a vertical line is _____.

Fluency

  3 For each graph state whether the gradient is positive, negative, zero or undefined, then find the gradient where possible.

a

b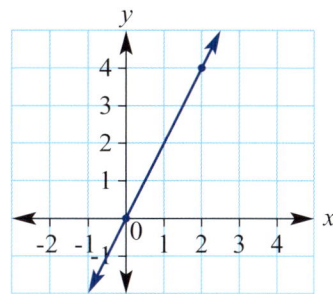

c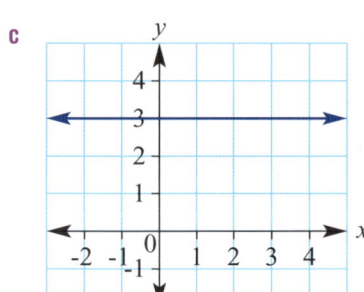

d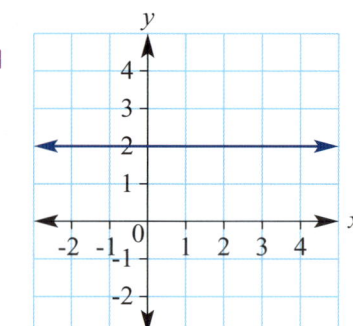

e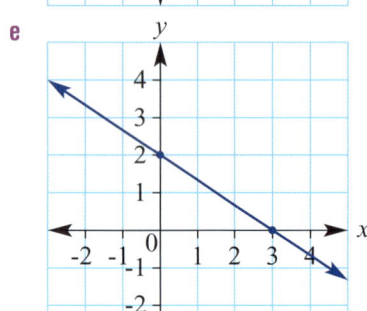

f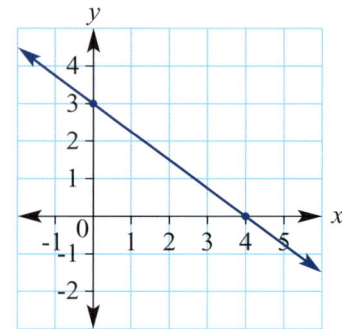

g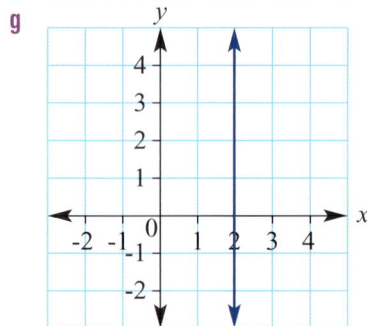

h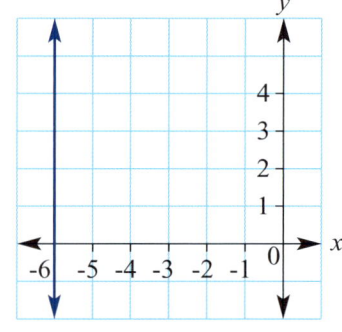

i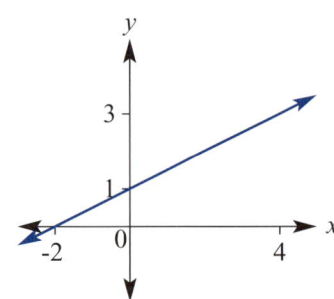

j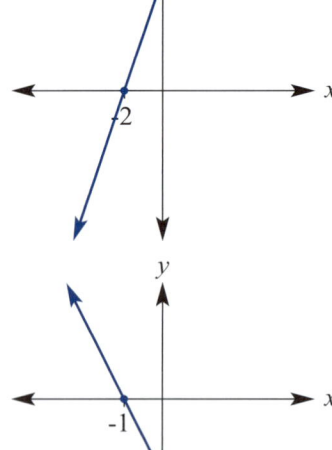

k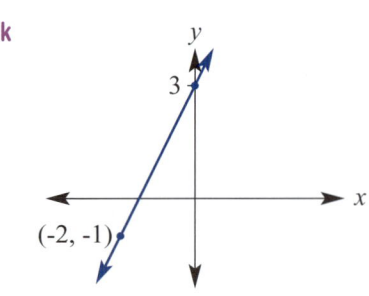

l

Example 8

4 Find the gradient of the lines joining the following pairs of points.

a $A(2, 3)$ and $B(3, 5)$

b $C(-2, 6)$ and $D(0, 8)$

c $E(-4, 1)$ and $F(4, -1)$

d $G(2, 1)$ and $H(5, 5)$

e $A(1, 5)$ and $B(2, 7)$

f $C(-2, 4)$ and $D(1, -2)$

g $E(-3, 4)$ and $F(2, -1)$

h $G(-1, 5)$ and $H(1, 6)$

i $A(-2, 1)$ and $B(-4, -2)$

j $C(3, -4)$ and $D(1, 1)$

k $E(3, 2)$ and $F(0, 1)$

l $G(-1, 1)$ and $H(-3, -4)$

5 Find the gradient of each line A–F on this graph and grid.

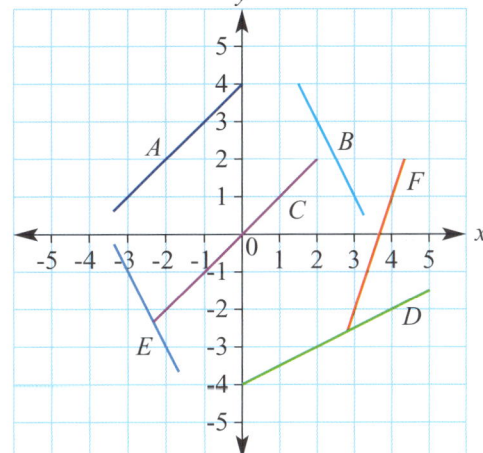

6 Find the gradient corresponding to the following slopes.

a   A road falls 10 m for every 200 horizontal metres.

b   A cliff rises 35 metres for every 2 metres horizontally.

c   A plane descends 2 km for every 10 horizontal kilometre.

d   A submarine ascends 150 m for every 20 horizontal metres.

Gradients can be used to find the measure of slope of these cliff faces.

7 Find the missing number.

a   The gradient joining the points $(0, 2)$ and $(1, ?)$ is 4.

b   The gradient joining the points $(?, 5)$ and $(1, 9)$ is 2.

c   The gradient joining the points $(-3, ?)$ and $(0, 1)$ is -1.

d   The gradient joining the points $(-4, -2)$ and $(?, -12)$ is -4.

8 A train climbs a slope with gradient 0.05. How far horizontally has the train travelled after rising 15 metres?

9 Complete this table showing the gradient, *x*-intercept and *y*-intercept for straight lines.

	A	B	C	D	E	F
Gradient	3	-1	$\frac{1}{2}$	$-\frac{2}{3}$	0.4	-1.25
x-intercept	(-3, 0)			(6, 0)	(1, 0)	
y-intercept		(0, -4)	$\left(0, \frac{1}{2}\right)$			(0, 3)

10 Give reasons why a line with gradient $\frac{7}{11}$ is steeper than a line with gradient $\frac{3}{5}$.

11 The two points *A* and *B* shown here have coordinates (x_1, y_1) and (x_2, y_2).
   a Write a rule for the run using x_1 and x_2.
   b Write a rule for the rise using y_1 and y_2.
   c Write a rule for the gradient *m* using x_1, x_2, y_1 and y_2.
   d Use your rule to find the gradient between these pairs of points.
      i (1, 1) and (3, 4)
      ii (0, 2) and (4, 7)
      iii (-1, 2) and (2, -3)
      iv (-4, -6) and (-1, -2)
   e Does your rule work for points which include negative coordinates? Explain why.

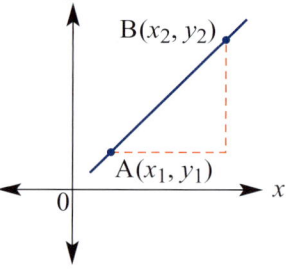

Enrichment: Where does it hit?

12 The line here has gradient $\frac{-2}{3}$ which means that it falls 2 units for every 3 across. The *y*-intercept is (0, 3).

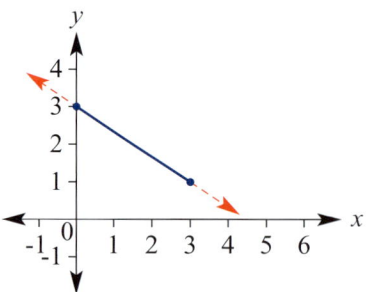

   a Use the gradient to find the *y*-coordinate on the line where:
      i $x = 6$
      ii $x = 9$
   b What will be the coordinates of the *x*-intercept?
   c What would be the *x*-intercept if the gradient was changed to:
      i $\frac{-1}{2}$
      ii $\frac{-5}{4}$
      iii $\frac{-7}{3}$
      iv $\frac{-2}{5}$

4.5 Gradient and direct proportion

The connection between gradient, rate problems and direct proportion can be illustrated through the use of linear rules and graphs. If two variables are directly related then the rate of change of one variable with respect to the other is constant. This implies that the rule linking the two variables is linear and can be represented as a straight line graph passing through the origin. The amount of water squirting from a hose, for example, is directly proportional to the time since it was turned on. The gradient of the graph of *water volume* versus *time* will equal the rate at which water is squirting from the hose.

The volume of water squirting from a hose is directly proportional to the time.

Let's start: Average speed

Over 5 hours, Sandy travels 420 km.

- What is Sandy's average speed for the trip?
- Is speed a rate? Discuss.
- Draw a graph of distance versus time, assuming a constant speed.
- Where does your graph intersect the axes and why?
- Find the gradient of your graph. What do you notice?
- Find a rule linking distance (*d*) and time (*t*).

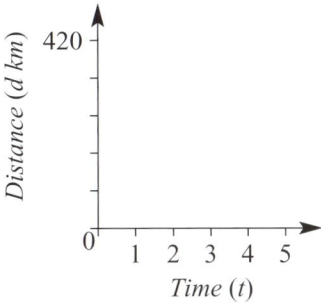

- If two variables are **directly proportional**:
  - The rate of change of one variable with respect to the other is constant.
  - The graph is a straight line passing through the origin.
  - The rule is of the form $y = mx$.
  - The gradient (*m*) of the graph equals the rate of change of *y* with respect to *x*.

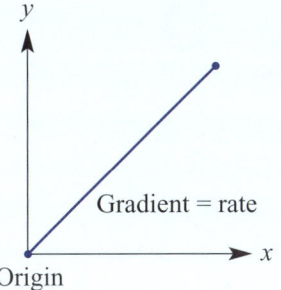

Gradient = rate

Origin

Key-ideas

Example 9 Exploring direct proportion

Water is poured into an empty tank. It takes 3 hours to fill the tank with 6000 litres.
a What is the rate at which water is poured into the tank?
b Draw a graph of volume (V litres) vs time (t hours) using $0 \le t \le 3$.
c Find:
    i the gradient of your graph
    ii the rule for V
d Use your rule to find:
    i the volume after 1.5 hours
    ii the time to fill 5000 litres

SOLUTION

EXPLANATION

a 6000 L in 3 hours = 2000 L/hour

6000 L per 3 hours = 2000 L per 1 hour

b

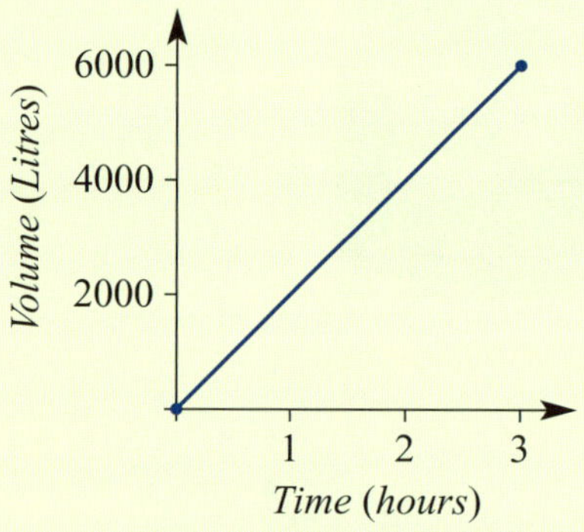

Plot the two end points (0, 0) and (3, 6000) then join with a straight line.

c **i** gradient $= \dfrac{6000}{3} = 2000$

The gradient is the same as the rate.

    ii $V = 2000t$

2000 L are filled for each hour.

d **i** $V = 2000t$
      $= 2000 \times 1.5$
      $= 3000$ litres

Substitute $t = 1.5$ into your rule.

    ii $V = 2000t$
    $5000 = 2000t$
    $2.5 = t$
$\therefore$ it takes $2\dfrac{1}{2}$ hours

Substitute $V = 5000$ into the rule and solve for t.

Exercise 4E

1 This graph shows how far a bike travels over 4 hours.

   a State how far the bike has travelled after:

      i 1 hour

      ii 2 hours

      iii 3 hours.

   b Write down the speed of the bike (rate of change of distance over time).

   c Find the gradient of the graph.

   d What do you notice about your answers from parts **b** and **c**.

2 The rule linking the height of a plant over time is given by $h = 5t$ where h is in millimetres and t is in days.

   a Find the height of the plant after 3 days.

   b Find the time for the plant to reach:

      i 30 mm   **ii** 10 cm

   c Complete this table.

t	0	1	2	3	4
h					

   d Complete this graph.

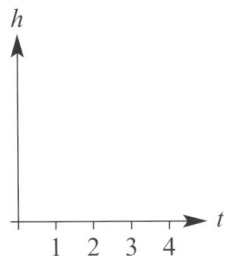

   e Find the gradient of the graph.

Example 9   **3** A 300 litre fish tank takes 3 hours to fill from a hose.

   a What is the rate at which water is poured into the tank?

   b Draw a graph of volume (V litres) vs time (t hours) using $0 \leq t \leq 3$.

   c Find:

      i the gradient of your graph

      ii the rule for V.

   d Use your rule to find:

      i the volume after 1.5 hours

      ii the time to fill 2000 litres.

4 A solar powered car travels 100 km in 4 hours.

  a What is the rate of change of distance over time (i.e. speed)?

  b Draw a graph of distance (d km) vs time (t hours) using $0 \leq t \leq 4$.

  c Find:

  i the gradient of your graph

  ii the rule for d.

  d Use your rule to find:

  i the distance after 2.5 hours

  ii the time to travel 40 km.

5 Write down a rule linking the given variables.

  a I travel 600 km in 12 hours. Use d for distance and t for time.

  b A calf grows 12 cm in 6 months. Use g for growth height and t for time.

  c The cost of petrol is \$100 for 80 litres. Use C for cost and n for the number of litres.

  d The profit is \$10 000 for 500 tonnes. Use P for profit and t for the number of tonnes.

6 Use the gradient to find the rate of change of distance over time (speed) for these graphs. Use the units given on each graph.

  a
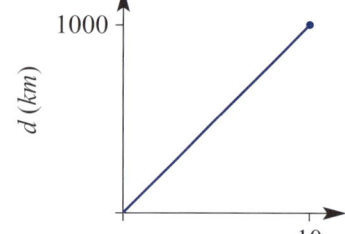

  b
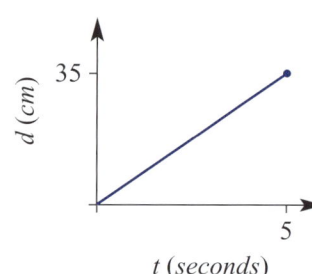

  c
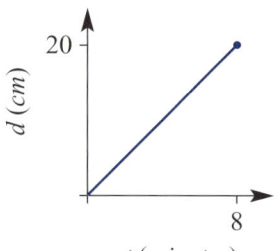

  d
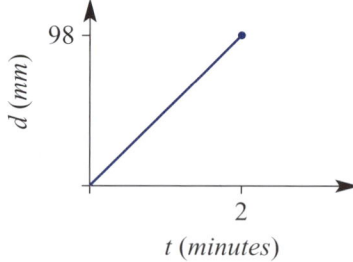

7 A car's trip computer says that the fuel economy for a trip is 8.5 L per 100 km.

  a How many litres would be used for 120 km?

  b How many litres would be used for 850 km?

  c How many kilometres could be travelled if the car's petrol tank capacity was 68 L?

8 Who is travelling the fastest?
- Mick runs 120 m in 20 seconds.
- Sally rides 700 m in 1 minute.
- Udhav jogs 2000 m in 5 minutes.

9 Which animal is travelling the slowest?
- A leopard runs 200 m in 15 seconds.
- A jaguar runs 2.5 km in 3 minutes.
- A panther runs 60 km in 1.2 hours.

10 An investment fund starts at $0 and grows at a rate of $100 per month. Another fund starts at $4000 and reduces by $720 per year. After how long will the funds have the same amount of money?

By using direct proportion, we can determine the slowest wild cat.

Problem-solving

Reasoning

11 The circumference of a circle (given by $C = 2\pi r$) is directly proportional to its radius.
  a Find the circumference for a circle with the given radius. Give an exact answer like 6π.
    i $r = 0$ **ii** $r = 2$ **iii** $r = 6$
  b Draw a graph of C against r for $0 \le r \le 6$. Use exact values for C.
  c Find the gradient of your graph. What do you notice?

12 Is the area of a circle directly proportional to its radius? Give reasons.

13 The base length of a triangle is 4 cm but its height h cm is variable.
  a Write a rule for the area of this triangle.
  b What is the rate at which the area changes with respect to height h?

14 Over a given time interval (say 5 hours), is an object's speed directly proportional to the distance travelled? Give a rule for speed (s) in terms of distance (d).

Enrichment: Rate challenge

15 Hose A can fill a bucket in 2 minutes and hose B can fill the same bucket in 3 minutes. How long would it take to fill the bucket if both hoses were used at the same time?

16 A river is flowing downstream at rate of 2 km/h. Murray can swim at a rate of 3 km/h. Murray jumps in and swims downstream for a certain distance then turns around and swims upstream back to the start. In total it takes 30 minutes. How far did Murray swim downstream?

4.6 Gradient–intercept form

Shown here is the graph of the rule $y = 2x - 1$. It shows a gradient of 2 and a y-intercept of -1. The fact that these two numbers correspond to numbers in the rule is no coincidence. This is why rules written in this form are called gradient–intercept form. Other examples of rules in this form include:

$$y = -5x + 2, \quad y = \frac{1}{2}x - 0.5 \quad \text{and} \quad y = \frac{x}{5} + 20.$$

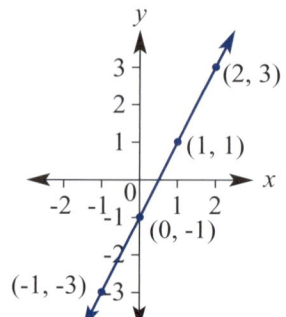

Let's start: Family traits

The graph of a linear relation can be sketched easily if you know the gradient and the y-intercept. If one of these is kept constant, we create a family of graphs.

Different y-intercepts and same gradient

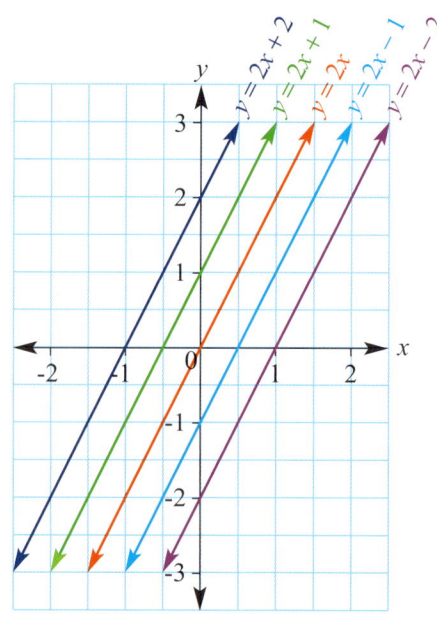

Different gradients and same y-intercept

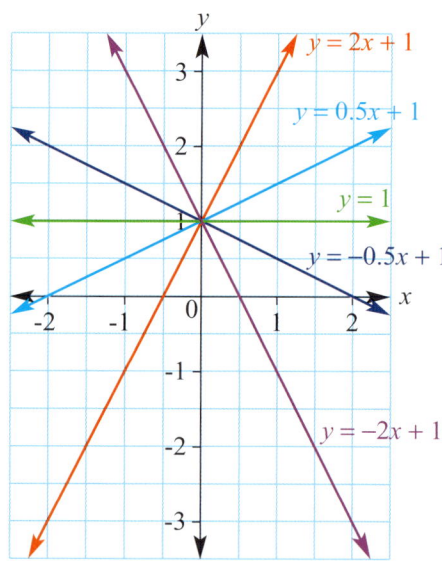

- For the first family, discuss the relationship between the y-intercept and the given rule for each graph.
- For the second family, discuss the relationship between the gradient and the given rule for each graph.

Key ideas

m = gradient y-intercept = c

- $y = mx + c$ (or $y = mx + b$ depending on preference) is the **gradient–intercept form** of a straight line equation.
- If the y-intercept is zero, the equation becomes $y = mx$ and these graphs will therefore pass through the origin.

■ To sketch a graph using the **gradient–intercept method**, locate the y-intercept and use the gradient to find a second point.

For example, if $m = \dfrac{2}{5}$, move 5 across and 2 up.

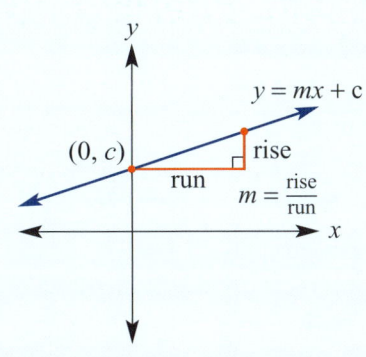

Example 10 Stating the gradient and y-intercept

State the gradient and the y-intercept for the graphs of the following relations.

a $y = 2x + 1$ b $y = -3x$

SOLUTION	EXPLANATION
a $y = 2x + 1$ The gradient $= 2$ y-intercept $= 1$	The rule is given in gradient intercept form. The gradient is the coefficient of x. The constant term is the y-intercept.
b $y = -3x$ The gradient $= -3$ y-intercept $= 0$	The gradient is the coefficient of x including the negative sign. The constant term is not present so the y-intercept $= 0$

Example 11 Sketching linear graphs using the gradient and y-intercept

Find the value of the gradient and y-intercept for these relations and sketch their graphs.

a $y = 2x - 1$ b $x + 2y = 6$

SOLUTION	EXPLANATION
a $y = 2x - 1$ y intercept $= -1$ gradient $= 2 = \dfrac{2}{1}$ 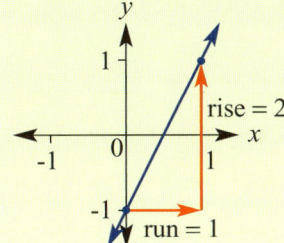	The rule is in gradient–intercept form so we can read off the gradient and the y-intercept. Label the y-intercept at $(0, -1)$. For every 1 across, move 2 up. From $(0, -1)$ this gives a second point at $(1, 1)$. Mark and join the points to form a line.

b $x + 2y = 6$

$2y = -x + 6$

$y = \dfrac{-x + 6}{2}$

$= -\dfrac{1}{2}x + 3$

Make y the subject by subtracting x from both sides and then dividing both sides by 2. Rewrite in the form $y = mx + c$ to read off the gradient and y-intercept.

so y-intercept is 3

$m = -\dfrac{1}{2} = \dfrac{-1}{2}$

Link the negative sign to the rise (-1) so the run is positive (+2).

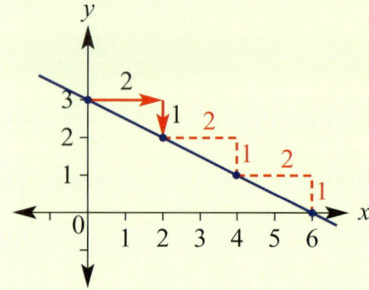

Mark the y-intercept (0, 3) then from this point move 2 right and 1 down to give a second point at (2, 2).

Note that the x-intercept will be 6. If the gradient is $\dfrac{-1}{2}$ then a run of 6 gives a fall of 3.

Example 12 Deciding if a point is on a line

Decide if the point (-2, 4) is on the line with the given rules.

a $y = 2x + 10$

b $y = -x + 2$

SOLUTION

EXPLANATION

a $y = 2x + 10$

Substitute $x = -2$

$y = 2(-2) + 10$

$= 6$

∴ the point (-2, 4) is not on the line

Find the value of y on the graph of the rule for $x = -2$.

The y value is not 4 so (-2, 4) is not on the line.

b $y = -x + 2$

Substitute $x = -2$

$y = -(-2) + 2$

$= 4$

∴ the point (-2, 4) is on the line.

By substituting $x = -2$ into the rule for the line, y is 4.

So (-2, 4) is on the line.

Exercise 4F

1 Write a rule (in gradient–intercept form) for a straight line with the given properties.

a gradient = 2, y-intercept = 5   b gradient = 3, y-intercept = -1

c gradient = -2, y-intercept = 3   d gradient = -1, y-intercept = -2

e gradient = $\dfrac{-1}{2}$, y-intercept = -10   f gradient = $\dfrac{-2}{3}$, y-intercept = $\dfrac{5}{2}$

2 Substitute $x = -3$ to find the value of y for these rules.

a $y = x + 4$ b $y = x - 2$ c $y = 2x + 1$

d $y = 3x - 2$ e $y = -2x + 3$ f $y = -x - 1$

3 Rearrange to make y the subject

a $y - x = 7$ b $x + y = 3$ c $2y - 4x = 10$

Example 10

4 State the gradient and y-intercept for the graphs of the following relations.

a $y = 3x - 4$ b $y = -5x - 2$ c $y = -2x + 3$ d $y = \dfrac{1}{3}x + 4$

e $y = -4x$ f $y = 2x$ g $y = 2.3x$ h $y = -0.7x$

Example 11a

5 Find the gradient and y-intercept for these relations and sketch their graphs.

a $y = x - 2$ b $y = 2x - 1$ c $y = \dfrac{1}{2}x + 1$ d $y = \dfrac{-1}{2}x + 2$

e $y = -3x + 3$ f $y = \dfrac{3}{2}x + 1$ g $y = \dfrac{-4}{3}x$ h $y = \dfrac{5}{3}x - \dfrac{1}{3}$

Example 11b

6 Find the gradient and y-intercept for these relations and sketch their graphs. Rearrange each equation first.

a $x + y = 4$ b $x - y = 6$ c $x + 2y = 6$

d $x - 2y = 8$ e $2x - 3y = 6$ f $4x + 3y = 12$

g $x - 3y = -4$ h $2x + 3y = 6$ i $3x - 4y = 12$

j $x + 4y = 0$ k $x - 5y = 0$ l $x - 2y = 0$

Example 12

7 Decide if the point $(1, 2)$ is on the line with the given rule.

a $y = x + 1$ b $y = 2x - 1$ c $y = -x + 3$

d $y = -2x + 4$ e $y = -x + 5$ f $y = \dfrac{-1}{2}x + \dfrac{1}{2}$

8 Decide if the point $(-3, 4)$ is on the line with the given rule.

a $y = 2x + 8$ b $y = x + 7$ c $y = -x - 1$

d $y = \dfrac{1}{3}x + 6$ e $y = \dfrac{-1}{3}x + 3$ f $y = \dfrac{5}{6}x + \dfrac{11}{2}$

9 Match the following equations to the straight lines shown.

i $y = 3$ **ii** $y = -2x - 1$ **iii** $y = -2x - 4$

iv $y = x + 3$ **v** $x = 2$ **vi** $y = x + 2$

a

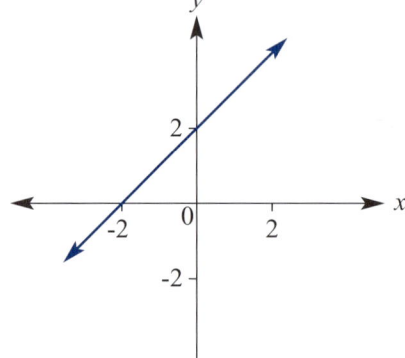

b

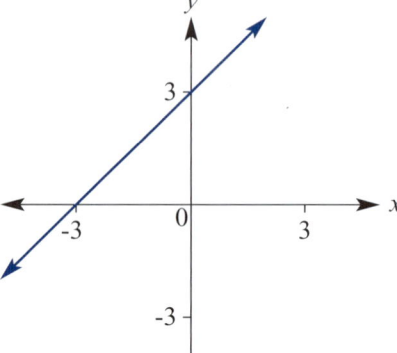

c

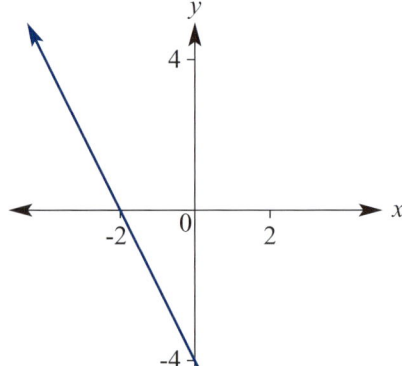

d

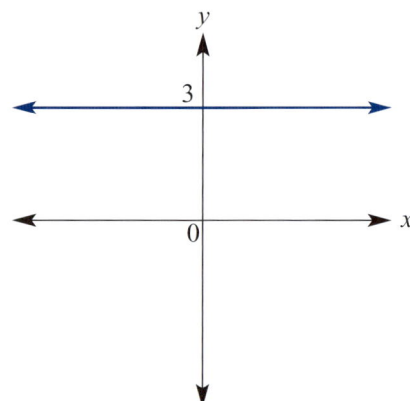

e

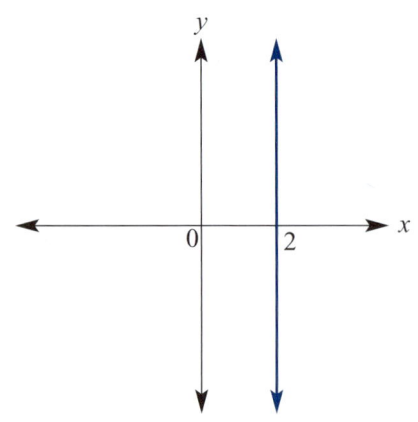

f

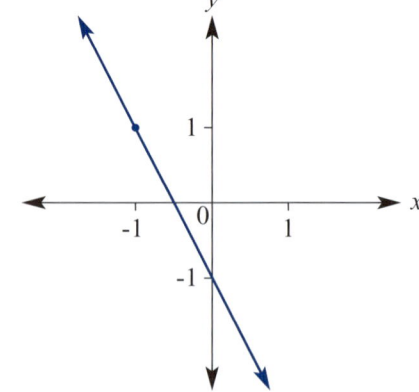

Problem-solving

10 Sketch the graph of each of the following linear relations, by finding the gradient and y-intercept.

  a $5x - 2y = 10$ **b** $y = 6$ **c** $x + y = 0$ **d** $y = 5 - x$

  e $y = \dfrac{x}{2} - 1$ **f** $4y - 3x = 0$ **g** $4x + y - 8 = 0$ **h** $2x + 3y - 6 = 0$

11 Decide if the following points are on the line with rule $3x - y = 7$.

  a $(1, -2)$ **b** $(-1, 4)$ **c** $(5, 8)$ **d** $(-2, -10)$

12 Which of these linear relations have a gradient of 2 and y-intercept of -3?

  a $y = 2(x - 3)$ **b** $y = 3 - 2x$ **c** $y = \dfrac{3 - 2x}{-1}$ **d** $y = 2(x - 1.5)$

  e $y = \dfrac{2x - 6}{2}$ **f** $y = \dfrac{4x - 6}{2}$ **g** $2y = 4x - 3$ **h** $-2y = 6 - 4x$

Reasoning

13 Jeremy says that the graph of the rule $y = 2(x + 1)$ has gradient 2 and y-intercept 1.

  a Explain his error.

  b What can be done to the rule to help show the y-intercept?

14 A horizontal line has gradient 0 and y-intercept at $(0, k)$. Using gradient intercept form, write the rule for the line.

15 Write the rule $ax + by = d$ in gradient–intercept form. Then state the gradient m and the y-intercept.

Enrichment: The missing y-intercept

16 This graph shows two points $(-1, 3)$ and $(1, 4)$ with a gradient of $\dfrac{1}{2}$. By considering the gradient, the y-intercept can be calculated to be 3.5 (or $\dfrac{7}{2}$) so $y = \dfrac{1}{2}x + \dfrac{7}{2}$.

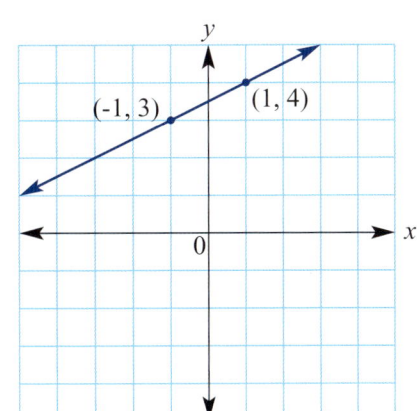

Use this approach to find the rule of the line passing through these points.

  a $(-1, 1)$ and $(1, 5)$ **b** $(-2, 4)$ and $(2, 0)$

  c $(-1, -1)$ and $(2, 4)$ **d** $(-3, 1)$ and $(2, -1)$

4.7 Finding the equation of a line

Using gradient–intercept form, the rule (or equation) of a line can be found by calculating the value of the gradient and the y-intercept. Given a graph, the gradient can be calculated using two points. If the y-intercept is known then the value of the constant in the rule is obvious, but if not, another point can be used to help find its value.

Let's start: But we don't know the y-intercept!

A line with the rule $y = mx + c$ passes through two points (-1, 3) and (1, -2).

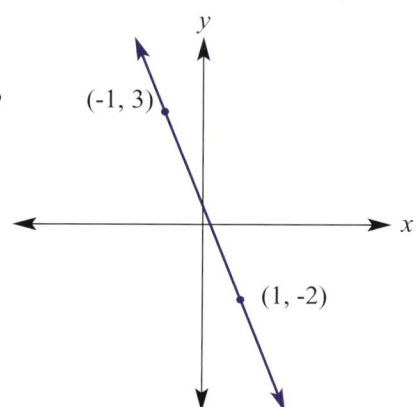

- Using the information given is it possible to find the value of m? If so, calculate its value.
- The y-intercept is not given on the graph. Discuss what information could be used to find the value of the constant c in the rule. Is there more than one way you can find the y-intercept?
- Write the rule for the line.

- To find the equation of a line in gradient–intercept form $y = mx + c$, you need to find:
  - the value of the gradient (m) using $m = \dfrac{\text{rise}}{\text{run}}$
  - the value of the constant (c), by observing the y-intercept or by substituting another point.

Example 13 Finding the equation of a line given the y-intercept and another point

Determine the equation of the straight line shown here.

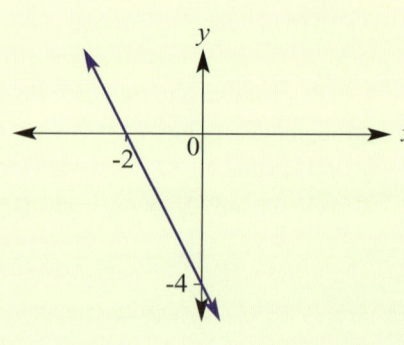

SOLUTION	EXPLANATION
$m = \dfrac{\text{rise}}{\text{run}}$	run = 2 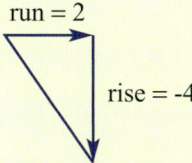
$= \dfrac{-4}{2}$	rise = -4
$= -2$	
y-intercept = -4.	The y-intercept is -4.
$\therefore\ y = -2x - 4$	Write down the general straight line equation and substitute $m = -2$ and the y-intercept.

Example 14 Finding the equation of a line given the gradient and a point

Find the equation of the line which has a gradient m of $\dfrac{1}{3}$ and passes through the point (9, 2).

SOLUTION	EXPLANATION
$y = mx + c$	Substitute $m = \dfrac{1}{3}$ into $y = mx + c$.
$y = \dfrac{1}{3}x + c$	
$2 = \dfrac{1}{3}(9) + c$	Since (9, 2) is on the line, it must satisfy the equation $y = \dfrac{1}{3}x + c$, hence substitute the point (9, 2) where $x = 9$
$2 = 3 + c$	and $y = 2$ to find c. Simplify and solve for c.
$-1 = c$	
$\therefore\ y = \dfrac{1}{3}x - 1$	Write the equation in the form $y = mx + c$.

Exercise 4G

1 Substitute the given values of m and c into $y = mx + c$ to write the rule.

  a $m = 2,\ c = 5$ **b** $m = 4,\ c = -1$

  c $m = -2,\ c = 5$ **d** $m = -1,\ c = \dfrac{-1}{2}$

2 Substitute the point into the given rule and solve to find the value of c. For example, using (3, 4), substitute $x = 3$ and $y = 4$ into the rule.

  a   (3, 4), $y = x + c$ **b**   (1, 5), $y = 2x + c$

  c   (-2, 3), $y = 3x + c$ **d**   (-1, 6), $y = 4x + c$

  e   (3, -1), $y = -2x + c$ **f**   (-2, 4), $y = -x + c$

Understanding

Example 13   **3**   Determine the equation of the following straight lines.

a

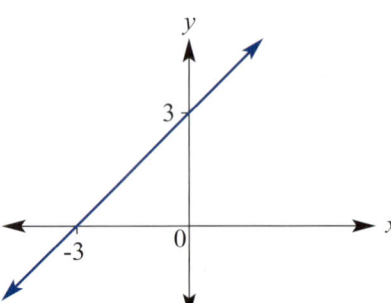

b

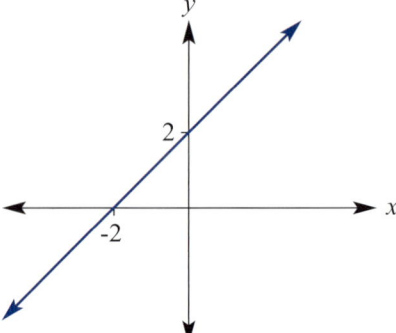

c

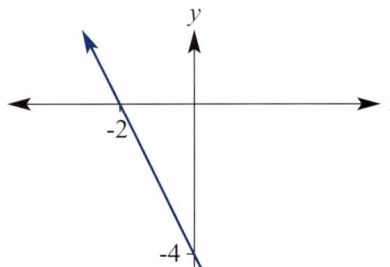

d

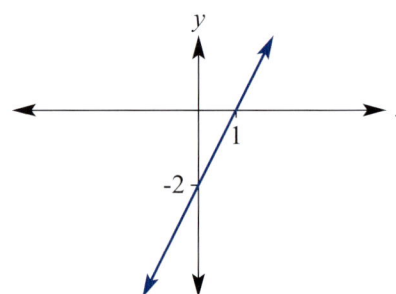

e

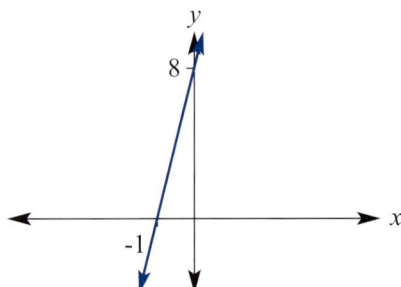

f

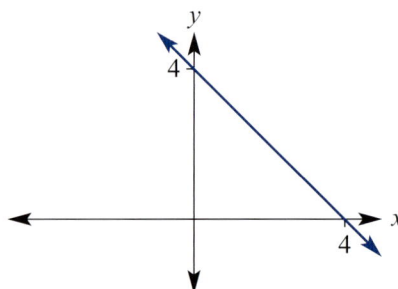

4   Find the equation of these straight lines which have fractional gradients.

a

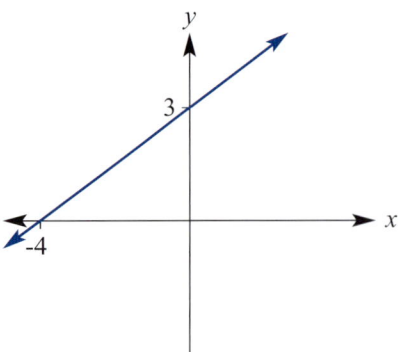

b

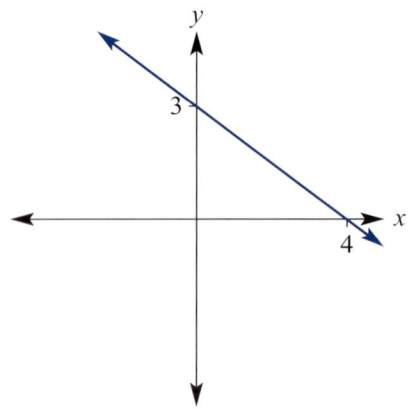

c

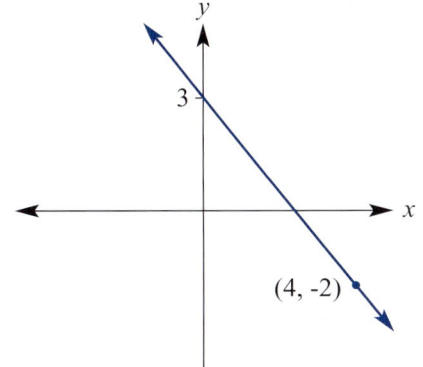

d

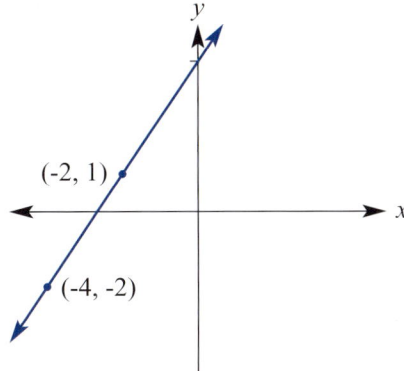

e

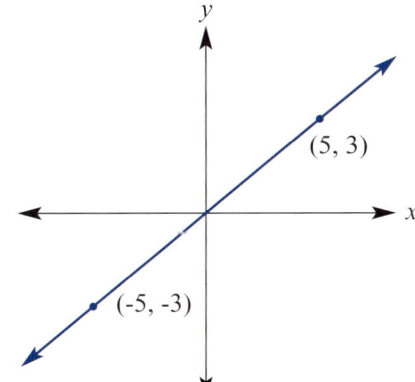

f

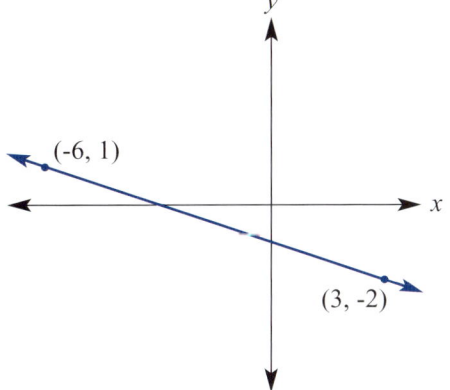

5 Find the equation of the line which:

a has a gradient of 3 and passes through the point $(1, 8)$

b has a gradient of -2 and passes through the point $(2, -5)$

c has a gradient of -3 and passes through the point $(2, 2)$

d has a gradient of 1 and passes through the point $(1, -2)$

e has a gradient of -3 and passes through the point $(-1, 6)$

f has a gradient of 5 and passes through the point $(2, 9)$

g has a gradient of -1 and passes through the point $(4, 4)$

h has a gradient of -3 and passes through the point $(3, -3)$

i has a gradient of -2 and passes through the point $(-1, 4)$

j has a gradient of -4 and passes through the point $(-2, -1)$.

mple 14

6 For the line connecting the following pairs of points:

  i find the gradient **ii** find the equation

a $(2, 6)$ and $(4, 10)$ **b** $(-3, 6)$ and $(5, -2)$

c $(1, 7)$ and $(3, -1)$ **d** $(-4, -8)$ and $(1, -3)$

7 A line has gradient -2 and y-intercept 5. Find its x-intercept.

8 A line passes through the points (-1, -2) and (3, 3). Find its x- and y-intercepts.

9 Water is leaking from a tank. The volume of water in the tank after 1 hour is 100 L and after 5 hours the volume is 20 L. Assuming the relationship is linear, find a rule and then state the initial volume of water in the tank.

10 The coordinates (0, 0) mark the take-off point for a rocket constructed as part of a science class. The positive x direction from (0, 0) is considered to be East.

  a Find the equation of the rocket's path if it rises at a rate of 5 m vertically for every 1 m in an easterly direction.

  b A second rocket is fired 2 m vertically above from where the first rocket was launched. It rises at a rate of 13 m for every 2 m in an easterly direction. Find the equation describing its path.

Problem-solving

11 A line has equation $y = mx - 2$. Find the value of m if the line passes through:

  a (2, 0)   **b** (1, 6)   **c** (-1, 4)   **d** (-2, -7)

12 A line with rule $y = 2x + c$ passes through (1, 5) and (2, 7).

  a Find the value of c using the point (1, 5).

  b Find the value of c using the point (2, 7).

  c Does it matter which point you use? Explain.

13 A line passes through the origin and the point (a, b). Write its equation in terms of a and b.

Reasoning

Enrichment: The general rule

14 To find the equation of a line between two points (x_1, y_1) and (x_2, y_2) some people prefer to use the rule:

$$y - y_1 = m(x - x_1) \text{ where } m = \frac{y_2 - y_1}{x_2 - x_1}.$$

Use this rule to find the equation of the line passing through these pairs of points. Write your answer in the form $y = mx + c$.

  a (1, 2) and (3, 6)   **b** (0, 4) and (2, 0)

  c (-1, 3) and (1, 7)   **d** (-4, 8) and (2, -1)

  e (-3, -2) and (4, 3)   **f** (-2, 5) and (1, -8)

4.8 Midpoint and length of a line segment

A line segment (or line interval) has a defined length and therefore must have a midpoint. Both the midpoint and length can be found by using the coordinates of the endpoints.

Let's start: Choosing a method

This graph shows a line segment between the points at (-2, -1) and (2, 3).

- What is the horizontal distance between the two points?
- What is the vertical distance between the two points?
- What is the *x*-coordinate of the point halfway along the line segment?
- What is the *y*-coordinate of the point halfway along the line segment?
- Discuss and explain a method for finding the midpoint of a line segment.
- Discuss and explain a method for finding the length of a line segment.

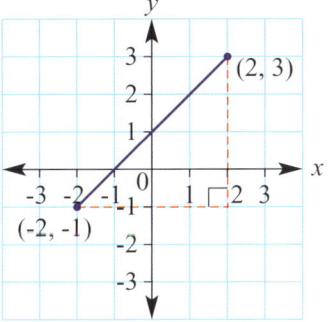

Using graphing software or dynamic geometry software, produce a line segment like the one shown above. Label the coordinates of the endpoints and the midpoint. Also find the length of the line segment. Now drag one or both of the endpoints to a new position.

- Describe how the coordinates of the midpoint relate to the coordinates of the endpoints. Is this true for all positions of the endpoints that you choose?
- Now use your software to calculate the vertical distance and the horizontal distance between the two endpoints. Then square these lengths. Describe these squared lengths compared to the square of the length of the line segment. Is this true for all positions of the endpoints that you choose?

- The **midpoint** (*M*) of a line segment is the halfway point between the two endpoints.
  - The *x*-coordinate is the average (mean) of the *x*-coordinates of the two endpoints.
  - The *y*-coordinate is the average (mean) of the *y*-coordinates of the two end points.
  - $M = \left(\dfrac{x_1 + x_2}{2}, \dfrac{y_1 + y_2}{2} \right)$

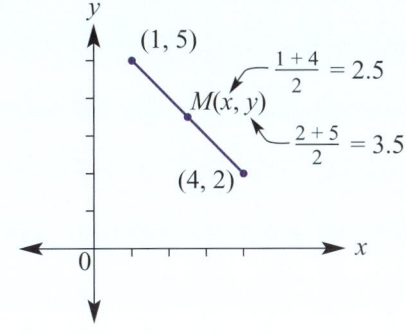

Key ideas

- The **length of a line segment** (or line interval) is found using Pythagoras' theorem.
  - The line segment is the hypotenuse (longest side) of a right-angled triangle.
  - Find the horizontal distance by subtracting the lower x-coordinate from the upper x-coordinate.
  - Find the vertical distance by subtracting the lower y-coordinate from the upper y-coordinate.

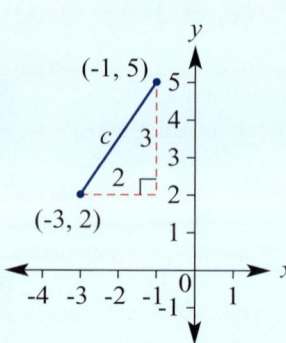

horizontal distance $= -1 - (-3)$
$$= 2$$
vertical distance $= 5 - 2$
$$= 3$$
$$c^2 = 2^2 + 3^2$$
$$= 13$$
$$\therefore c = \sqrt{13}$$

Example 15 Finding a midpoint

Find the midpoint $M(x, y)$ of the line segment joining these pairs of points.

a (1, 0) and (4, 4)

b (-3, -2) and (5, 3)

SOLUTION

a $x = \dfrac{1+4}{2} = 2.5$

$y = \dfrac{0+4}{2} = 2$

$\therefore M = (2.5, 2)$

b $x = \dfrac{-3+5}{2} = 1$

$y = \dfrac{-2+3}{2} = 0.5$

$\therefore M = (1, 0.5)$

EXPLANATION

Find the average (mean) of the x-coordinates and y-coordinates for both points.

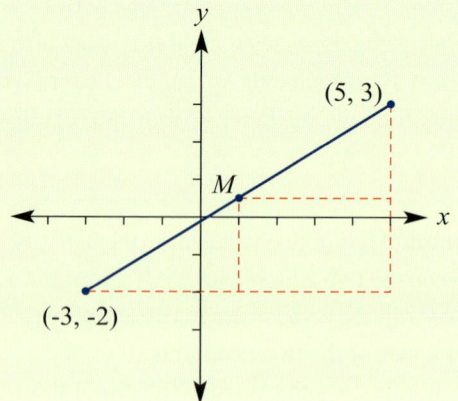

Example 16 Finding the length of a segment

Find the length of the segment joining (-1, 2) and (4, -1), correct to two decimal places.

SOLUTION

Horizontal length $= 4 - (-1)$
$$= 5$$
Vertical length $= 2 - (-1)$
$$= 3$$
$$c^2 = 5^2 + 3^2$$
$$= 34$$
$$\therefore c = \sqrt{34}$$
$$\therefore \text{length} = 5.83$$

EXPLANATION

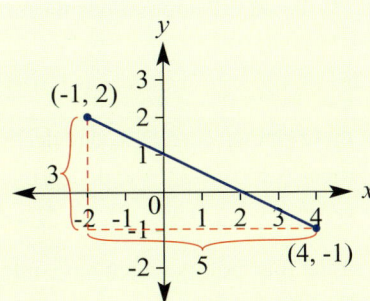

Apply Pythagoras' theorem $c^2 = a^2 + b^2$.

Exercise 4H

Understanding

1 Find the number which is halfway between these pairs of numbers.
  a 1, 7   b 5, 11   c -2, 4   d -6, 0

2 Find the average (mean) of these pairs of numbers.
  a 4, 7   b 0, 5   c -3, 0   d -4, -1

3 Evaluate c in the following correct to two decimal places.
  a $c^2 = 1^2 + 2^2$ b $c^2 = 5^2 + 7^2$ c $c^2 = 10^2 + 2^2$

Fluency

Example 15

4 Find the midpoint $M(x, y)$ of the segment joining these pairs of points.
  a (0, 0) and (6, 6)   b (0, 0) and (4, 4)
  c (0, 2) and (2, 8)   d (3, 0) and (5, 2)
  e (-2, 0) and (0, 6)   f (-4, -2) and (2, 0)
  g (1, 3) and (2, 0)   h (-1, 5) and (6, -1)
  i (-3, 7) and (4, -1)   j (-2, -4) and (-1, -1)
  k (-7, -16) and (1, -1)   l (-4, -3) and (5, -2)

Example 16

5 Find the length of the segment joining these pairs of points correct to two decimal places.
  a (1, 1) and (2, 6)   b (1, 2) and (3, 4)   c (0, 2) and (5, 0)
  d (-2, 0) and (0, -4)   e (-1, 3) and (2, 1)   f (-2, -2) and (0, 0)
  g (-1, 7) and (3, -1)   h (-4, -1) and (2, 3)   i (-3, -4) and (3, -1)

6 Find the missing coordinates in this table if M is the midpoint of points A and B.

A	B	M
(4, 2)		(6, 1)
	(0, -1)	(-3, 2)
	(4, 4)	(-1, 6.5)

7 A circle has centre (2, 1). Find the coordinates of the endpoint of a diameter if the other endpoint has these coordinates.

   a (7, 1)   **b** (3, 6)   **c** (-4, -0.5)

8 Find the perimeter of these shapes correct to one decimal place.

   a A triangle with vertices (-2, 0), (-2, 5) and (1, 3).

   b A trapezium with vertices (-6, -2), (1, -2), (0, 4) and (-5, 4).

9 Find the coordinates of the four points which have integer coordinates and are a distance of $\sqrt{5}$ from the point (1, 2). Hint: $5 = 1^2 + 2^2$.

10 A line segment has two endpoints (x_1, y_1) and (x_2, y_2) and a midpoint $M(x, y)$.

   a Write a rule for x, the x-coordinate of the midpoint.

   b Write a rule for y, the y-coordinate of the midpoint.

   c Test your rule to find the coordinates of M if $x_1 = -3$, $y_1 = 2$, $x_2 = 5$ and $y_2 = -3$.

11 A line segment has two end points (x_1, y_1) and (x_2, y_2). Assume $x_2 > x_1$ and $y_2 > y_1$.

   a Write a rule for:

      i the horizontal distance between the endpoints

      ii the vertical distance between the endpoints

      iii the length of the segment

   b Use your rule to show that the length of the segment joining (-2, 3) with (1, -3) is $\sqrt{45}$.

Enrichment: Division by ratio

12 Looking from left to right, this line segment shows the point $P(-1, 0)$ which divides the segment in the ratio 1 : 2.

   a What fraction of the horizontal distance between the endpoints is P from A?

   b What fraction of the vertical distance between the endpoints is P from A?

   c Find the coordinates of point P on the segment AB if it divides the segment in these ratios.

      i 2 : 1   **ii** 1 : 5

      iii 5 : 1

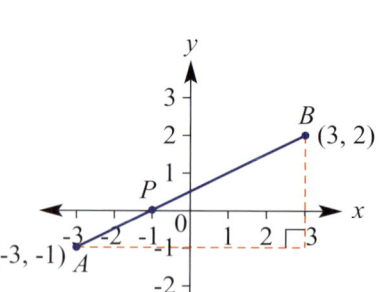

   d Find the coordinates of point P which divides the segments with the given endpoints in the ratio 2 : 3.

      i $A(-3, -1)$ and $B(2, 4)$ **ii** $A(-4, 9)$ and $B(1, -1)$

      iii $A(-2, -3)$ and $B(4, 0)$ **iv** $A(-6, -1)$ and $B(3, 8)$

4.9 Perpendicular and parallel lines

Perpendicular and parallel lines are commonplace in mathematics and in the world around us. Using parallel lines in buildings, for example, ensures that beams or posts point in the same direction. Perpendicular beams help to construct rectangular shapes, which are central in the building of modern structures.

Perpendicular and parallel lines are central to construction.

Let's start: How are they related?

This graph shows a pair of parallel lines and a line perpendicular to the other two. Find the equation of all three lines.

- What do you notice about the equation for the pair of parallel lines?
- What do you notice about the gradient of the line that is perpendicular to the other two lines?
- Write down the equations of three other lines that are parallel to $y = -2x$.
- Write down the equations of three other lines that are perpendicular to $y = -2x$.

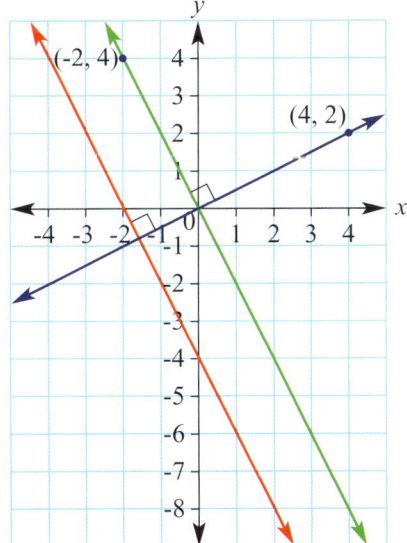

- If two lines are **parallel** then they have the same gradient.
- If two **perpendicular** lines (at right angles) have gradients m_1 and m_2 then

$$m_1 \times m_2 = -1 \text{ or } m_2 = \frac{-1}{m_1}$$

  - The **negative reciprocal** of m_1 gives m_2

    For example: If $m_1 = 4$ then $m_2 = \frac{-1}{4}$

    If $m_1 = \frac{-2}{3}$ then $m_2 = \frac{-1}{\left(\frac{-2}{3}\right)} = -1 \times \frac{-3}{2} = \frac{3}{2}$

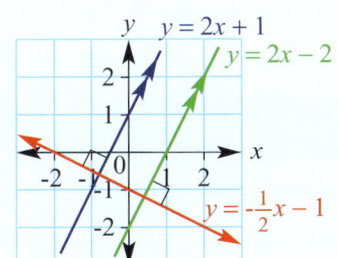

Example 17 Finding the equation of a parallel line

Find the equation of a line which is parallel to $y = 3x - 1$ and passes through $(0, 4)$.

SOLUTION	EXPLANATION
$y = mx + c$	Since it's parallel to $y = 3x - 1$, the gradient is the same
$m = 3$	so $m = 3$.
$c = 4$	The y-intercept is given in the question so $c = 4$.
$\therefore y = 3x + 4$	

Example 18 Finding the equation of a perpendicular line

Find the equation of a line which is perpendicular to the line $y = 2x - 3$ and passes through $(0, -1)$.

SOLUTION	EXPLANATION
$y = mx + c$	Since it is perpendicular to $y = 2x - 3$,
$m = -\dfrac{1}{2}$	$m_2 = \dfrac{-1}{m_1} = -\dfrac{1}{2}$.
$c = -1$	The y-intercept is given.
$y = -\dfrac{1}{2}x - 1$	

Exercise 4I

1 Decide if the pairs of lines with these equations are parallel (have the same gradient).

a $y = 3x - 1$ and $y = 3x + 4$ b $y = 2x - 1$ and $y = 2x - 3$

c $y = 7x - 2$ and $y = 2x - 7$ d $y = x + 4$ and $y = x - 3$

e $y = \dfrac{1}{2}x - 1$ and $y = -\dfrac{1}{2}x + 2$ f $y = -\dfrac{3}{4}x + 4$ and $y = -\dfrac{3}{4}x - 6$

2 Two perpendicular lines with gradients m_1 and m_2 are such that $m_2 = -\dfrac{1}{m_1}$. Find m_2 for the given values of m_1.

a $m_1 = 5$ b $m_1 = 10$

c $m_1 = -3$ d $m_1 = -6$

3 Decide if the pairs of lines with these equations are perpendicular.

a $y = 4x - 2$ and $y = -\dfrac{1}{4}x + 3$ b $y = 2x - 3$ and $y = \dfrac{1}{2}x + 4$

c $y = -\dfrac{1}{2}x + 6$ and $y = -\dfrac{1}{2}x - 2$ d $y = -\dfrac{1}{5}x + 1$ and $y = 5x + 2$

Understanding

mple 17

4 Find the equation of the line which is:

  a parallel to the line with equation $y = 2x + 3$ and passes through $(0, 1)$

  b parallel to the line with equation $y = 4x + 2$ and passes through $(0, 8)$

  c parallel to the line with equation $y = -x + 3$ and passes through $(0, 5)$

  d parallel to the line with equation $y = -2x - 3$ and passes through $(0, -7)$

  e parallel to the line with equation $y = \dfrac{2}{3}x + 6$ and passes through $(0, -5)$

  f parallel to the line with equation $y = -\dfrac{4}{5}x - 3$ and passes through $(0, \dfrac{1}{2})$.

mple 18

5 Find the equation of the line which is:

  a perpendicular to the line with equation $y = 3x - 2$ and passes through $(0, 3)$

  b perpendicular to the line with equation $y = 5x - 4$ and passes through $(0, 7)$

  c perpendicular to the line with equation $y = -2x + 3$ and passes through $(0, -4)$

  d perpendicular to the line with equation $y = -x + 7$ and passes through $(0, 4)$

  e perpendicular to the line with equation $y = -7x + 2$ and passes through $(0, \dfrac{-1}{2})$

  f perpendicular to the line with equation $y = x - \dfrac{3}{2}$ and passes through $(0, \dfrac{5}{4})$.

6 a Write the equation of the line parallel to $y = 4$ which passes through:

  i $(0, 1)$ **ii** $(0, -3)$

  iii $(1, 6)$ **iv** $(-3, -2)$.

  b Write the equation of the line parallel to $x = -2$ which passes through:

  i $(3, 0)$ **ii** $(-4, 0)$

  iii $(1, 5)$ **iv** $(-3, -3)$.

  c Write the equation of the line perpendicular to $y = -3$ which passes through:

  i $(2, 0)$ **ii** $(-1, 0)$

  iii $(0, 0)$ **iv** $(3, 5)$.

  d Write the equation of the line perpendicular to $x = 6$ which passes through:

  i $(0, 7)$ **ii** $\left(0, \dfrac{-1}{2}\right)$ **iii** $(1, 3)$ **iv** $\left(-2, \dfrac{1}{2}\right)$.

7 Find the equation of the line which is:

  a parallel to the line with equation $y = -3x - 7$ and passes through $(3, 0)$; remember to substitute the point $(3, 0)$ to find the value of the y-intercept

  b parallel to the line with equation $y = \dfrac{1}{2}x + 2$ and passes through $(1, 3)$

  c perpendicular to the line with equation $y = 5x - 4$ and passes through $(1, 6)$

  d perpendicular to the line with equation $y = -x - \dfrac{1}{2}$ and passes through $(-2, 3)$.

8 A right-angled isosceles triangle has vertices at (0, 3), (3, 0) and (-3, 0). Find the equation of each of the three sides.

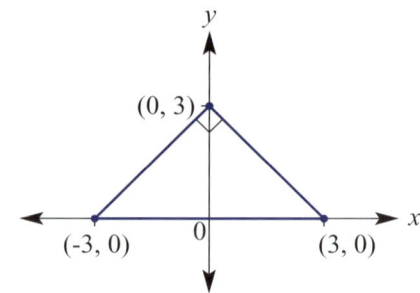

9 A parallelogram has two side lengths of 5 units. Three of its sides have equations $y = 0$, $y = 2$, $y = 2x$. Find the equation of the fourth side.

10 a Using $m_2 = \dfrac{-1}{m_1}$, find the gradient of a line perpendicular to the line with the given gradient.

　i $m_1 = \dfrac{2}{3}$　　**ii** $m_1 = \dfrac{1}{5}$　　**iii** $m_1 = \dfrac{-1}{7}$　　**iv** $m_1 = \dfrac{-3}{11}$

b If $m_1 = \dfrac{a}{b}$, find m_2 given $m_1 \times m_2 = -1$.

11 a Find the gradient of a line that is parallel to:
　i $2x + 4y = 9$　　**ii** $3x - y = 8$
b Find the gradient of a line which is perpendicular to
　i $5x + 5y = 2$　　**ii** $7x - y = -1$

Enrichment: Perpendicular bisectors

12 If a line segment AB is cut by another line PQ at right angles at the midpoint (M) of AB then PQ is called the perpendicular bisector.

By firstly finding the midpoint of AB, find the equation of the perpendicular bisector of the segment connecting these points.

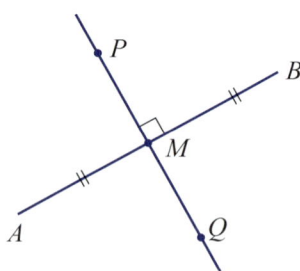

a $A(1, 1)$, $B(3, 5)$
b $A(0, 6)$, $B(4, 0)$
c $A(-2, 3)$, $B(6, -1)$
d $A(-6, -1)$, $B(0, 2)$
e $A(-1, 3)$, $B(2, -4)$
f $A(-6, -5)$, $B(4, 7)$

4.10 Linear modelling

If a relationship between two variables is linear, the graph will be a straight line and the equation linking the two variables can be written in gradient–intercept form. The process of describing and using such line graphs and rules for the relationship between two variables is called linear modelling. A test car, for example, increasing its speed from 100 km/h to 200 km/h in 10 seconds with constant acceleration could be modelled by the rule $S = 10t + 100$. This rule could then be used to calculate the speed at different times in the test run.

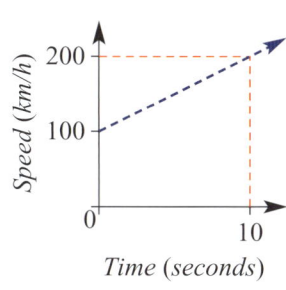

Let's start: The test car

The above graph describes the speed of a racing car over a 10 second period.

- Explain why the rule is $S = 10t + 100$.
- Why might negative values of t not be considered for the graph?
- How could you accurately calculate the speed after 6.5 seconds?
- If the car continued to accelerate at the same rate, how could you accurately predict the car's speed after 13.2 seconds?

- Many situations can often be **modelled** by using a linear rule or graph. The key elements of linear modelling include:
  - Finding the rule linking the two variables
  - Sketching a graph
  - Using the graph or rule to predict or estimate the value of one variable given the other
  - Finding the rate of change of one variable with respect to the other variable. This is equivalent to finding the gradient.

Key ideas

Example 19 Applying linear relations

The deal offered by Netshare, an internet provider, to its new customers is a fixed charge of $20 per month plus $5 per hour of use.

a Write a rule for the total monthly cost, C, of using Netshare for t hours per month.

b Sketch the graph of C versus t using $0 \le t \le 10$.

c What is the total cost in a month when Netshare is used for 4 hours?

d If the monthly cost was $50, for how many hours was Netshare used during the month?

SOLUTION

a $C = 20 + 5t$

b C-intercept is 20
At $t = 10$, $C = 20 + 5(10) = 70$
$\therefore$ end point is $(10, 70)$

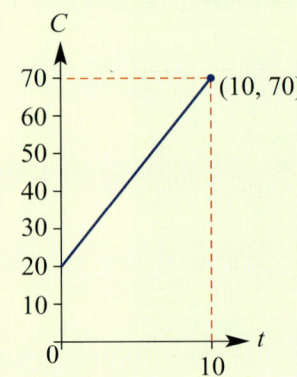

c $C = 20 + 5t$
$\quad = 20 + 5(4)$
$\quad = 40$
The cost is $40

d $C = 20 + 5t$
$\quad 50 = 20 + 5t$
$\quad 30 = 5t$
$\quad\ t = 6$
Netshare was used for 6 hours.

EXPLANATION

A fixed amount of $20 plus $5 for each hour.

Let $t = 0$ to find the C-intercept.
Letting $t = 10$ gives $C = 70$ and this gives the other endpoint.

Sketch the graph using the points $(0, 20)$ and $(10, 70)$.

Substitute $t = 4$ into the rule.

Answer the question using the correct units.

Write the rule and substitute $C = 50$. Solve the resulting equation for t by subtracting 20 from both sides then dividing both sides by 5.

Answer the question in words.

Exercise 4J

1 A person gets paid $50 plus $20 per hour. Decide which rule describes the relationship between the pay $P and number of hours n.

A $P = 50 + n$ **B** $P = 50 + 20n$ **C** $P = 50n + 20$ **D** $P = 20 + 50$

Understanding

2 The amount of money in a bank account is $1000 and is increasing by $100 per month.

   a Find the amount of money in the account after:

      i 2 months   **ii** 5 months   **iii** 12 months

   b Write a rule for the amount of money A dollars after n months.

3 If $d = 5t - 4$, find:

   a d if $t = 10$ **b** d if $t = 1.5$ **c** t if $d = 6$ **d** t if $d = 11$

 4 A sales representative earns $400 a week plus $20 for each sale she makes.

   a Write a rule which gives the total weekly wage, W, if the sales representative makes x sales.

   b Draw a graph of W versus x using $0 \leq x \leq 40$.

   c How much does the sales representative earn if, in a particular week, she makes 12 sales?

   d If, in a particular week, the sales representative earns $1000, how many sales did she make?

5 A plumber charges a $40 fee up-front and $50 for each hour he works.

   a Find a linear equation for the total charge, C, for n hours of work.

   b What will a 4 hour job cost?

   c If the plumber works on a job for two days and averages 6 hours per day, what will the total cost be?

6 A catering company charges $500 for the hire of a marquee, plus $25 per guest.

   a Write a rule for the cost, C, of hiring a marquee and catering for n guests.

   b Draw a graph of C versus n for $0 \leq n \leq 100$.

   c How much would a party catering for 40 guests cost?

   d If a party cost $2250, how many guests were catered for?

7 The cost, C, of recording a music CD is $300, plus $120 per hour of studio time.

   a Write a rule for the cost, C, of recording a CD requiring t hours of studio time.

   b Draw a graph of C versus t for $0 \leq t \leq 10$.

   c How much does a recording requiring 6 hours of studio time cost?

   d If a recording cost $660 to make, for how long was the studio used?

8 A petrol tank holds 66 litres of fuel. If it contains 12 litres of petrol initially and the petrol pump fills it at 3 litres every 10 seconds, find:

  a a linear equation for the amount of fuel (F litres) in the tank after t minutes

  b how long it will take to fill the tank

  c how long it will take to put 45 litres into the petrol tank

9 A tank is initially full with 4000 L of water and water is being used at a rate of 20 L per minute.

  a Write a rule for the volume, V litres, of water after t minutes.

  b Calculate the volume after 1.5 hours.

  c How long will it take for the tank to be emptied?

  d How long will it take for the tank to have only 500 L?

10 A spa pool contains 1500 litres of water. It is draining at the rate of 50 litres per minute.

  a Draw a graph of the volume of water, V litres, remaining after t minutes.

  b Write a rule for the volume of water at time t minutes.

  c What does the gradient represent?

  d What is the volume of water remaining after 5 minutes?

  e After how many minutes is the pool half empty?

11 The rule for distance travelled d km over a given time t hours for a moving vehicle is given by $d = 50 + 80t$.

  a What is the speed of the vehicle?

  b If the speed was actually 70 km per hour, how would this change the rule? Give the new rule.

12 The altitude, h metres, of a helicopter t seconds after it begins its descent is given by $h = 350 - 20t$.

  a At what rate is the helicopter altitude decreasing?

  b At what rate is the helicopter altitude increasing?

  c What is the helicopter's initial height?

  d How long will it take for the helicopter to reach the ground?

  e If instead the rule was $h = 350 + 20t$, describe what the helicopter would be doing.

Enrichment: Sausages and cars

13 Joanne organised a sausage sizzle to raise money for her science club. The hire of the barbecue cost Joanne $20, and the sausages cost 40c each.

   a **i** Write a rule for the total cost, $C, if Joanne buys and cooks n sausages.

       ii If the total cost was $84, how many sausages did Joanne buy?

   b **i** If Joanne sells each sausage for $1.20, write a rule to find her profit, $P, after buying and selling n sausages.

       ii How many sausages must she sell to start making a profit?

      iii If Joanne's profit was $76, how many sausages did she buy and sell?

14 The directors of a car manufacturing company believe that, in order to make a new component, they would need to spend $6700 on set-up costs, and each component would cost $10 to make. They make x components.

   a Write a rule for the total cost, $C, of producing x components.

   b Find the cost of producing 200 components.

   c How many components could be produced for $13 000?

   d Find the cost of producing 500 components.

   e If each component is able to be sold for $20, how many must they sell to make a profit?

   f Write a rule for the profit, $P, in terms of x.

   g Write a rule for the profit, $T, per component in terms of x.

   h Find x, the number of components, if the profit per component is to be $5.

Linear modelling is used in manufacturing and service industries to calculate cost and profit for different rates of production

4.11 Graphical solutions to simultaneous equations

To find a point that satisfies more than one equation involves finding the solution to simultaneous equations. An algebraic approach was considered in Chapter 2. Graphically this involves finding an intersection point.

This road intersection in Perth is an example of an intersection of two linear features.

Let's start: Accuracy counts

Two graphs have the rules $y = x$ and $y = 2 - 4x$.
Accurately sketch the graphs of both rules on a large set of axes like the one shown.

- State the x value of the point at the intersection of your two graphs.
- State the y value of the point at the intersection of your two graphs.
- Discuss how you could use the rules to check if your point is correct.
- If your point does not satisfy both rules, check the accuracy of your graphs and try again.

Key ideas

- When we consider two or more equations at the same time, they are called **simultaneous equations**.
- To determine the **point of intersection** of two lines we can use an accurate graph and determine its coordinates (x, y). Two situations can arise.
  - The two graphs intersect at one point only and there is one solution (x, y).
  - The point of intersection is simultaneously on both lines and is the **solution** to the simultaneous equations.

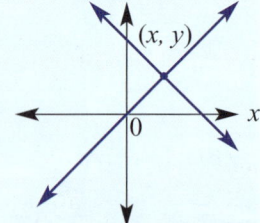

  - The two lines are parallel and there is no intersection.

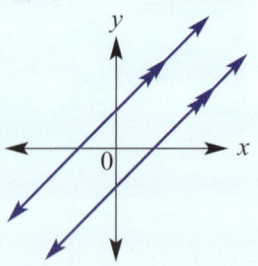

Example 20 Checking an intersection point

Decide if the given point is at the intersection of the two lines with the given equations.

a $y = 2x + 3$ and $y = -x$ with point $(-1, 1)$

b $y = -2x$ and $3x + 2y = 4$ with point $(2, -4)$

SOLUTION

a Substitute $x = -1$

$y = 2x + 3$

$= 2 \times (-1) + 3$

$= 1$

So $(-1, 1)$ satisfies $y = 2x + 3$

$y = -x$

$= -(-1)$

$= 1$

So $(-1, 1)$ satisfies $y = -x$.

∴ $(-1, 1)$ is the intersection point.

b Substitute $x = 2$.

$y = -2x$

$= -2 \times (2)$

$= -4$

So $(2, -4)$ satisfies $y = -2x$.

$3x + 2y = 4$

$3(2) + 2(-4) = 4$

$6 + (-8) = 4$

$-2 = 4$ (false)

So $(2, -4)$ is not on the line.

∴ $(2, -4)$ is not the intersection point.

EXPLANATION

Substitute $x = -1$ into $y = 2x + 3$ to see if $y = 1$. If so, then $(-1, 1)$ is on the line.

Repeat for $y = -x$.

If $(-1, 1)$ is on both lines then it must be the intersection point.

Substitute $x = 2$ into $y = -2x$ to see if $y = -4$.

If so, then $(2, -4)$ is on the line.

Substitute $x = 2$ and $y = -4$ to see if $3x + 2y = 4$ is true.

Clearly, the equation is not satisfied.

Since the point is not on both lines, it cannot be the intersection point.

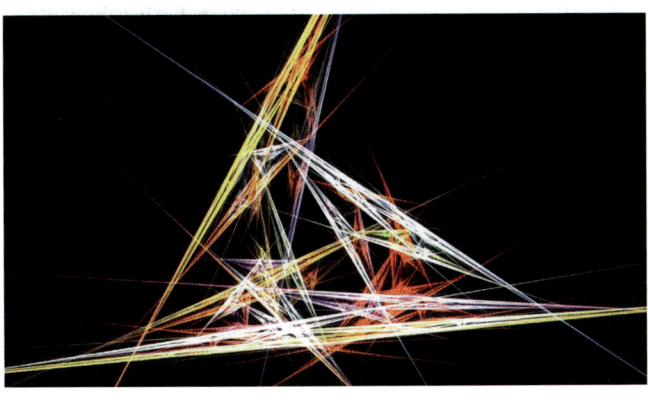

The calculation of intersection points of lines has many applications in science and technology.

Example 21 Solving simultaneous equations graphically

Solve the simultaneous equations $y = 2x - 2$ and $x + y = 4$ graphically.

SOLUTION	EXPLANATION
$y = 2x - 2$ y-intercept (let $x = 0$): $y = 2 \times (0) - 2$ $y = -2$ x-intercept (let $y = 0$): $0 = 2x - 2$ $2 = 2x$ $x = 1$	Sketch each linear graph by first finding the y-intercept (substitute $x = 0$) and the x-intercept (substitute $y = 0$ and solve the resulting equation.)
$x + y = 4$ y-intercept (let $x = 0$): $0 + y = 4$ $y = 4$ x-intercept (let $y = 0$): $x + 0 = 4$ $x = 4$	Repeat the process for the second equation.

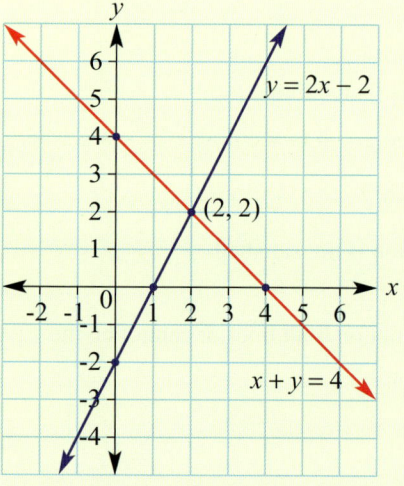

	Sketch both graphs on the same set of axes by marking in intercepts and joining in a straight line. Ensure that the axes are scaled accurately. Locate the intersection point and read off the coordinates. The point (2, 2) simultaneously belongs to both lines.

The intersection point is (2, 2).

Exercise 4K

1 Give the coordinates of the point of intersection for these pairs of lines.

a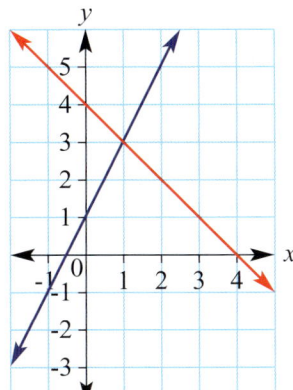

b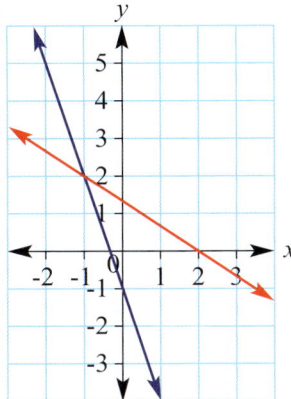

c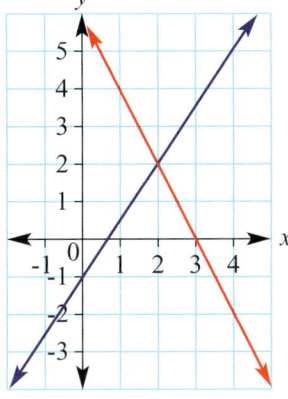

2 Decide if the point (1, 3) satisfies these equations. Hint: substitute (1, 3) into each equation to see if the equation is true.

a $y = 2x + 1$

b $y = -x + 5$

c $y - -2x - 1$

d $y = 4x - 1$

3 Consider the two lines with the rules $y = 5x$ and $y = 3x + 2$ and the point (1, 5).

a Substitute (1, 5) into $y = 5x$. Does (1, 5) sit on the line with equation $y = 5x$?

b Substitute (1, 5) into $y = 3x + 2$. Does (1, 5) sit on the line with equation $y = 3x + 2$?

c Is (1, 5) the intersection point of the lines with the given equations?

Example 20

4 Decide if the given point is at the intersection of the two lines with the given equations.

a $y = x + 2$ and $y = 3x$ with point (1, 3).

b $y = 3x - 4$ and $y = 2x - 2$ with point (2, 2).

c $y = -x + 3$ and $y = -x$ with point (2, 1).

d $y = -4x + 1$ and $y = -x - 1$ with point (1, -3).

e $x + 2y = 6$ and $3x - 4y = -2$ with point (2, 2).

f $x - y = 10$ and $2x + y = 8$ with point (6, -4).

g $2x + y = 0$ and $y = 3x + 4$ with point (-1, 2).

h $x - 3y = 13$ and $y = -x - 1$ with point (4, -3).

Example 21

5 Solve these pairs of simultaneous equations graphically by finding the coordinates of the intersection point.

a $2x + y = 6$
$x + y = 4$

b $3x - y = 7$
$y = 2x - 4$

c $y = x - 6$
$y = -2x$

d $y = 2x - 4$
$x + y = 5$

e $2x - y = 3$
$3x + y = 7$

f $y = 2x + 1$
$y = 3x - 2$

g $x + y = 3$
$3x + 2y = 7$

h $y = x + 2$
$y = 3x - 2$

i $y = x - 3$
$y = 2x - 7$

j $y = 3$
$x + y = 2$

k $y = 2x - 3$
$x = -1$

l $y = 4x - 1$
$y = 3$

Problem-solving

6 A company manufactures electrical components. The cost, $C (including rent, materials and labour), is given by the rule $C = n + 3000$, and its revenue, $R, is given by the rule $R = 5n$, where n is the number of components produced.

   a Sketch the graphs of C and R on the same set of axes and determine the point of intersection.

   b State the number of components n where the costs $C are equal to the revenue $R.

7 Dvdcom and Associates manufacture DVDs. Its costs, $C, are given by the rule $C = 4n + 2400$, and its revenue, $R, is given by the rule $R = 6n$, where n is the number of DVDs produced. Sketch the graphs of C and R on the same set of axes and determine the number of DVDs to be produced if the costs are equal to the revenue.

8 Two asteroids are 1000 km apart and are heading straight for each other. One asteroid is travelling at 59 km per second and the other at 41 km per second. How long does it take for them to collide?

Reasoning

9 Explain why the graphs of the rules $y = 3x - 7$ and $y = 3x + 4$ have no intersection point.

10 For the following families of graphs, determine their points of intersection (if any).

   a $y = x$, $y = 2x$, $y = 3x$ **b** $y = x$, $y = -2x$, $y = 3x$

   c $y = x + 1$, $y = x + 2$, $y = x + 3$ **d** $y = -x + 1$, $y = -x + 2$, $y = -x + 3$

   e $y = 2x + 1$, $y = 3x + 1$, $y = 4x + 1$ **f** $y = 2x + 3$, $y = 3x + 3$, $y = 4x + 3$

11 a If two lines have the equations $y = 3x + 1$ and $y = 2x + c$, find the value of c if the intersection point is at $x = 1$.

   b If two lines have the equations $y = mx - 4$ and $y = -2x - 3$, find the value of m if the intersection point is at $x = -1$.

Enrichment: Intersecting to find triangular areas

12 The three lines with equations $y = 0$, $y = x + 2$ and $y = -2x + 5$ are illustrated here.

   a State the coordinates of the intersection point of $y = x + 2$ and $y = -2x + 5$.

   b Use $A = \dfrac{1}{2}bh$ to find the area of the enclosed triangle ABC.

13 Use the method outlined in Question **12** to find the area enclosed by these sets of three lines.

   a $y = 0$, $y = x + 3$ and $y = -2x + 9$ **b** $y = 0$, $y = \dfrac{1}{2}x + 1$ and $y = -x + 10$

   c $y = 2$, $x - y = 5$ and $x + y = 1$ **d** $y = -5$, $2x + y = 3$ and $y = x$

   e $x = -3$, $y = -3x$ and $x - 2y = -7$

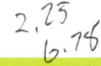

Using a CAS calculator 4.11: Finding intersection points

This activity is on the companion website in the form of a printable PDF.

Coming and going

The distance between two towns, Palton and Verton, is 100 km. Two cyclists travel in opposite directions between the towns, starting their journeys at the same time. Cyclist A travels from Palton to Verton at a speed of 20 km/h while cyclist B travels from Verton to Palton at a speed of 25 km/h.

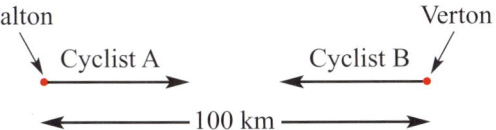

Measuring distance from Palton

a Using d_A km as the distance cyclist A is from Palton after t hours explain why the rule connecting d_A and t is $d_A = 20t$

b Using d_B km as the distance cyclist B is from Palton after t hours explain why the rule connecting d_B and t is $d_B = 100 - 25t$.

Technology – spreadsheet (alternatively use a graphics or CAS calculator – see parts e and f below)

c Instructions:
  • Enter the time in hours into column A starting at 0 hours.
  • Enter the formulae for the distances d_A and d_B into columns B and C.
  • Use the **Fill down** function to fill in the columns. Fill down until the distances show that both cyclists have completed their journey.

	A	B	C
1	0	=20*A1	=100−25*A1
2	=A1+1		
3			

d **i** Determine how long it takes for cyclist A to reach Verton.
  ii Determine how long it takes for cyclist B to reach Palton.
  iii After which hour are the cyclists the closest?

Alternative technology – graphics or CAS calculator

e Instructions:
  • Enter or define the formulae for the distances d_A and d_B.
  • Go to the table and scroll down to view the distance for each cyclist at hourly intervals. You may need to change the settings so that t increases by 1 each time.

f **i** Determine how long it takes for cyclist A to reach Verton.
  ii Determine how long it takes for cyclist B to reach Palton.
  iii After which hour are the cyclists the closest?

Investigating the intersection

a Change the time increment to a smaller unit for your chosen technology.
  - Spreadsheet: Try 0.5 hours using '=A1 + 0.5' or 0.1 hours using '= A1 + 0.1' in column A.
  - Graphics or CAS calculator: Try changing the t increment to 0.5 or 0.1.

b Fill or scroll down to ensure that the distances show that both cyclists have completed their journey.

c Determine the time at which the cyclists are the closest.

d Continue altering the time increment until you are satisfied that you have found the time of intersection of the cyclists correct to one decimal place.

e **Extension** Complete part **d** above but find an answer correct to three decimal places.

The graph

a Sketch a graph of d_A and d_B on the same set of axes. Scale your axes carefully to ensure that the full journey for both cyclists is represented.

b Determine the intersection point as accurately as possible on your graph and hence estimate the time when the cyclists meet.

c Use technology (graphing calculator) to confirm the point of intersection and hence determine the time at which the cyclists meet correct to three decimal places.

Algebra and proof

a At the point of intersection it could be said that $d_A = d_B$.
  This means that $20t = 100 - 25t$.
  Solve this equation for t.

b Find the exact distance from Palton at the point where the cyclists meet.

Reflection

Write a paragraph describing the journey of the two cyclists. Comment on the following:
- the speeds of the cyclists
- their meeting point
- the difference in computer and algebraic approaches in finding the time of the intersection point.

1 Matches are arranged by a student such that the first three diagrams in the pattern are:

How many matches are in the 50th diagram of the pattern?

2 Two cars travel towards each other on a 400 km stretch of road. One car travels at 90 km/h and the other at 70 km/h. How long does it take before they pass each other?

3 The points (-1, 4), (4, 6), (2, 7) and (-3, 5) are the vertices of a parallelogram. Find the midpoints of its diagonals. What do you notice?

4 The first three shapes in a pattern made with matchsticks are

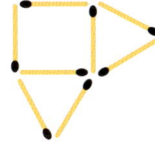 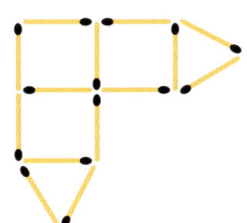 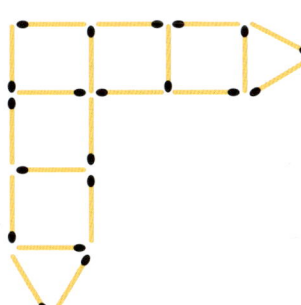

How many matchsticks make up the 100th shape?

5 Prove that the triangle with vertices at the points $A(-1, 3)$, $B(0, -1)$ and $C(3, 2)$ is isosceles.

6 Find the perimeter (to the nearest whole number) and area of the triangle enclosed by the lines with equations $x = -4$, $y = x$ and $y = -2x - 3$.

7 $ABCD$ is a parallelogram. A, B and C have coordinates (5, 8), (2, 5) and (3, 4) respectively. Find the coordinates of D.

8 A tank with 520 L of water begins to leak at a rate of 2 L per day. At the same time, a second tank is being filled at a rate of 1 L per hour starting at 0 L. How long does it take for the tanks to have the same volume?

9 Bill takes 3 days to paint a house, Rory takes 4 days to paint a house and Lucy takes 5 days to paint a house. How long would it take to paint a house (to the nearest hour) if all three of them worked together?

Chapter summary

Direct proportion

If two variables are directly proportional, their rule is of the form $y = mx$. The gradient of the graph represents the rate of change of y with respect to x, e.g. for a car travelling at 60 km/h for t hours, distance $= 60t$.

Graphical solutions of simultaneous equations

Graph each line and read off point of intersection.

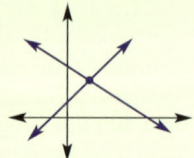

Parallel lines have no intersection point

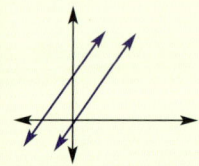

Linear modelling

Define variables to represent the problem and write a rule relating the two variables. The rate of change of one variable with respect to the other is the gradient.

Finding the equation of a line

Gradient–intercept form ($y = mx +$
Require gradient and y-intercept or any other point to substitute e.g. line with gradient 3 passes through point (2, 1)
$\therefore\ y = 3x + c$
substitute $1 = 3(2) + c$
$\therefore\ c = 1 - 6 = -5$
$y = 3x - 5$

Gradient

This measures the slope of a line

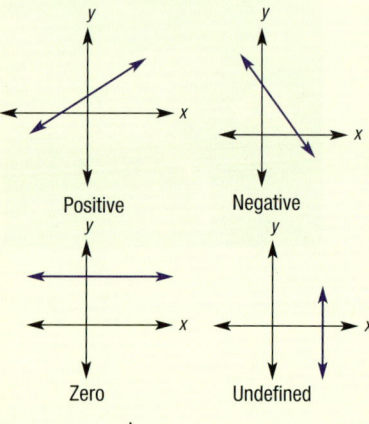

Positive   Negative

Zero   Undefined

Gradient $m = \dfrac{\text{rise}}{\text{run}}$

e.g. $m = \dfrac{4}{2} = 2$

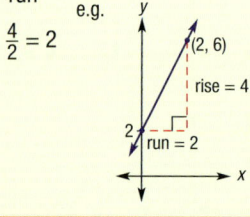

Straight line

$$y = mx + c$$
gradient y-intercept

In the form $ax + by = d$, rearrange to $y = mx + c$ form to read off gradient and y-intercept

Midpoint and length of line segment

Midpoint is halfway between segment endpoints, e.g. midpoints of segment joining (-1, 2) and (3, 6)
$$M = \left(\frac{x_1 + x_2}{2},\ \frac{y_1 + y_2}{2}\right)$$
$x = \dfrac{-1 + 3}{2} = 1$
$y = \dfrac{2 + 6}{2} = 4$, i.e. (1, 4)

Length of segment

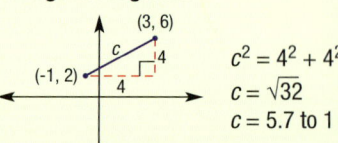

$c^2 = 4^2 + 4^2$
$c = \sqrt{32}$
$c = 5.7$ to 1 d.

Linear relations

A linear relation is made up of points (x, y) that form a straight line when plotted

Parallel and perpendicular lines

Parallel lines have the same gradient
e.g. $y = 2x + 3$, $y = 2x - 1$ and $y = 2x$
Perpendicular lines are at right angles
Their gradients m_1 and m_2 are such that $m_1 m_2 = -1$, i.e. $m_2 = -\dfrac{1}{m_1}$
A line perpendicular to $y = 2x + 3$ has gradient $-\dfrac{1}{2}$.

Special lines

Horizontal line $y = c$
e.g. $y = 3$

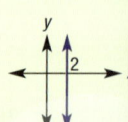

Vertical line $x = b$
e.g. $x = 2$

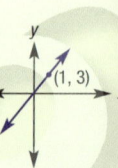

$y = mx$ passes through the origin, substitute $x = 1$ to find another point e.g. $y = 3x$

Linear graphs

Sketch with two points. Often we find the x-intercept ($y = 0$) and y-intercept ($x = 0$)
e.g. $y = 2x - 4$
y-int: $x = 0$, $y = 2(0) - 4$
$\qquad = -4$
x-int: $y = 0$, $0 = 2x - 4$
$\qquad 2x = 4$
$\qquad x = 2$

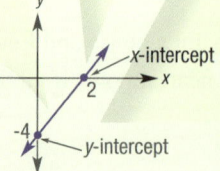

Multiple-choice questions

1 The *x*- and *y*-intercepts of the graph of $2x + 4y = 12$ are respectively:

  A (4, 0), (0, 2)   **B** (0, 3), (0, 2)

  C (6, 0), (0, 3)   **D** (2, 0), (0, 12)

  E (0, 8), (6, 0)

2 The graph of $y = 3x - 6$ is represented by:

  A

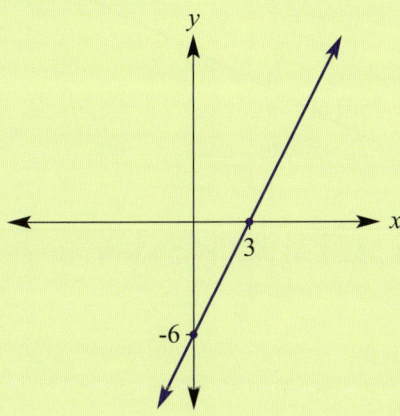

  B

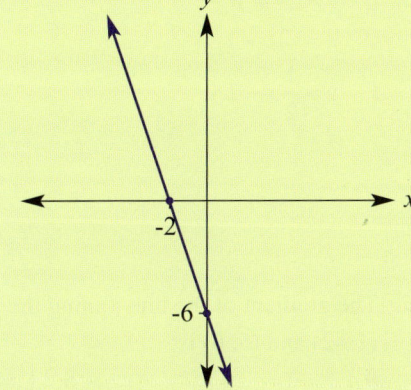

  C

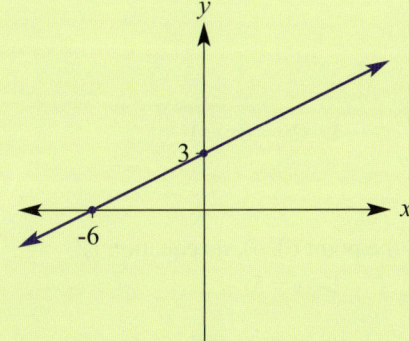

  D

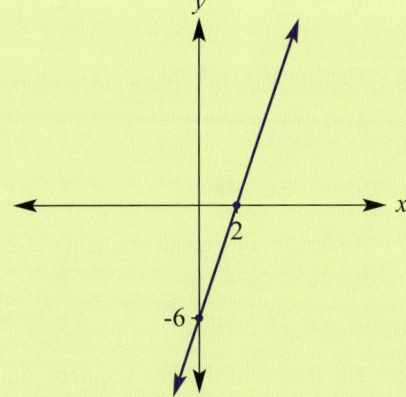

  E

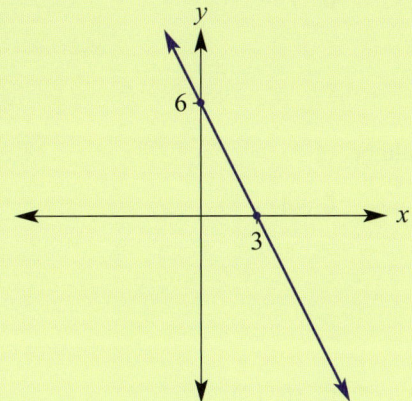

3 The point that is not on the straight line $y = -2x + 3$ is:

A $(1, 1)$ **B** $(0, 3)$ **C** $(2, 0)$

D $(-2, 7)$ **E** $(3, -3)$

4 The equation of the graph shown is:

A $y = x + 1$

B $y = \dfrac{1}{2}x + 4$

C $y = 2x + 1$

D $y = -2x - 1$

E $y = \dfrac{1}{2}x + 2$

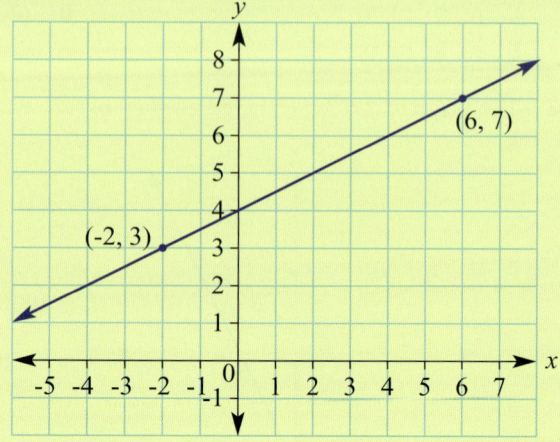

5 The gradient of the line joining the points
$(1, -2)$ and $(5, 6)$ is:

A 2 **B** 1 **C** 3

D -1 **E** $\dfrac{1}{3}$

6 The linear graph that *does not* have a gradient of 3 is:

A $y = 3x + 7$ **B** $\dfrac{y}{3} = x + 2$ **C** $2y - 6x = 1$

D $y - 3x = 4$ **E** $3x + y = -1$

7 A straight line has a gradient of -2 and passes through the point $(0, 5)$, its equation is:

A $2y = -2x + 10$ **B** $y = -2x + 5$ **C** $y = 5x - 2$

D $y - 2x = 5$ **E** $y = -2(x - 5)$

8 The length of the line segment joining the points $A(1, 2)$ and $B(4, 6)$ is:

A 5 **B** $\dfrac{4}{3}$ **C** 7

D $\sqrt{5}$ **E** $\sqrt{2}$

9 The gradient of a line perpendicular to $y = 4x - 7$ would be:

A $\dfrac{1}{4}$ **B** 4 **C** -4

D $\dfrac{-1}{4}$ **E** -7

10 The point of intersection of $y = 2x$ and $y = 6 - x$ is:

A $(6, 2)$ **B** $(-1, -2)$ **C** $(6, 12)$

D $(2, 4)$ **E** $(3, 6)$

Short-answer questions

1 Read off the *x*- and *y*-intercepts from the table and graph.

a

x	-2	-1	0	1	2
y	0	2	4	6	8

b

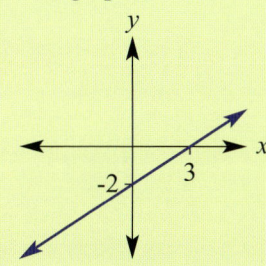

2 Sketch the following linear graphs labelling *x*- and *y*-intercepts.

  a $y = 2x - 4$ **b** $y = 3x + 9$ **c** $y = -2x + 5$ **d** $y = -x + 4$

  e $2x + 4y = 8$ **f** $4x - 2y = 10$ **g** $2x - y = 7$ **h** $-3x + 6y = 12$

3 Holly leaves her beach house by car and drives back to her home. Her distance *d* kilometres from her home after *t* hours is given by $d = 175 - 70t$.

  a How far is her beach house from her home?

  b How long does it take to reach her home?

  c Sketch a graph of her journey between the beach house and her home.

4 Sketch the following lines.

  a $y = 3$ **b** $y = -2$ **c** $x = -4$ **d** $x = 5$ **e** $y = 3x$ **f** $y = -2x$

5 By first plotting the given points, find the gradient of the line passing through the points.

  a (3, 1) and (5, 5)   **b** (2, 5) and (4, 3)   **c** (1, 6) and (3, 1)

  d (-1, 2) and (2, 6)   **e** (-3, -2) and (1, 6)   **f** (-2, 6) and (1, -4)

6 An inflatable backyard swimming pool is being filled with water by a hose. It takes 4 hours to fill 8000 L.

  a What is the rate at which water is poured into the pool?

  b Draw a graph of volume (*V* litres) vs time (*t* hours) for $0 \le t \le 4$.

  c By finding the gradient of your graph, give the rule for *V* in terms of *t*.

  d Use your rule to find the time to fill 5000 L.

7 For each of the following linear relations, state the value of the gradient and the *y*-intercept and then sketch using the gradient–intercept method.

  a $y = 2x + 3$ **b** $y = -3x + 7$ **c** $2x + 3y = 9$ **d** $2y - 3x - 8 = 0$

8 Give the equation of the straight line that:

  a has gradient 3 and passes through the point (0, 2)

  b has gradient -2 and passes through the point (3, 0)

  c has gradient $\dfrac{4}{3}$ and passes through the point (6, 3).

9 Find the equations of the linear graphs below.

a

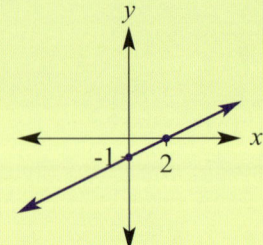

b

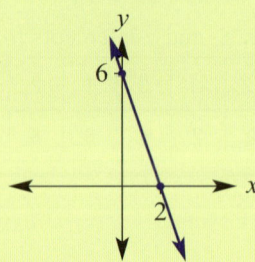

c

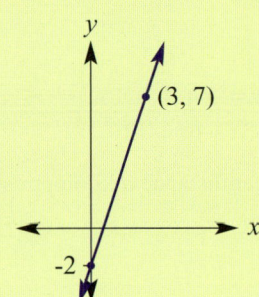

d

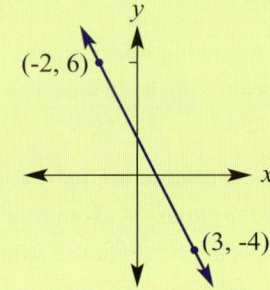

10 Determine the linear equation that is:

a parallel to the line $y = 2x - 1$ and passes through the point $(0, 4)$

b parallel to the line $y = -x + 4$ and passes through the point $(0, -3)$

c perpendicular to the line $y = 2x + 3$ and passes through the point $(0, -1)$

d perpendicular to the line $y = -\dfrac{1}{3}x - 2$ and passes through the point $(0, 4)$

e parallel to the line $y = 3x - 2$ and passes through the point $(1, 4)$

f parallel to the line $3x + 2y = 10$ and passes through the point $(-2, 7)$.

11 For the line segment joining the following pairs of points, find

    i the midpoint   **ii** the length (to two decimal places where applicable)

a $(2, 4)$ and $(6, 8)$ **b** $(5, 2)$ and $(10, 7)$

c $(-2, 1)$ and $(2, 7)$ **d** $(-5, 7)$ and $(-1, -2)$

12 Find the missing coordinate n if:

a the line joining $(-1, 3)$ and $(2, n)$ has gradient 2

b the line segment joining $(-2, 2)$ and $(4, n)$ has length 10, $n > 0$

c the midpoint of the segment joining $(n, 1)$ and $(1, -3)$ is $(3.5, -1)$.

13 Determine if the point $(2, 5)$ is the intersection point of the graphs of the following pairs of equations.

a $y = 4x - 3$ and $y = -2x + 6$ **b** $3x - 2y = -4$ and $2x + y = 9$

14 Find the point of intersection of the following straight lines.

a $y = 2x - 4$ and $y = 6 - 3x$ **b** $2x + 3y = 8$ and $y = -x + 2$

Extended-response questions

1   Joe requires an electrician to come to his house to do some work. He is trying to choose between two electricians he has been recommended.

   a   The first electrician's cost C is given by $C = 80 + 40n$ where n is the number of hours the job takes.

       i   State the hourly rate this electrician charges and his initial fee for coming to the house.

       ii   Sketch a graph of C vs n for $0 \leq n \leq 8$.

       iii   What is the cost of a job that takes 2.5 hours?

       iv   If the job costs $280, how many hours did it take?

   b   The second electrician charges a call out fee of $65 to visit the house and then $45 per hour thereafter.

       i   Give the equation for the cost C of a job that takes n hours.

       ii   Sketch the graph of part **b i** for $0 \leq n \leq 8$ on the same axes as the graph in part **a**.

   c   Determine the point of intersection of the two graphs.

   d   After how many hours does the first electrician become the cheaper option?

2   Abby has set up a small business making clay vases. She is trying to determine the selling price of these vases to ensure that she makes a weekly profit.

   Abby has determined that the cost of producing 7 vases in a week was $146 and the cost of producing 12 vases in a week was $186.

   a   Find a linear rule relating the production cost $C to the number of vases produced, v.

   b   Use your rule to state:

       i   the initial cost of materials each week

       ii   the ongoing cost of production per vase

   At a selling price of $12 per vase Abby determines her weekly profit to be given by $P = 4v - 90$.

   c   How many vases must she sell in order to make a profit?

Chapter 5 Measurement

What you will learn

The Millau Viaduct

Australian curriculum

MEASUREMENT AND GEOMETRY

Using units of measurement

Calculate the areas of composite shapes

Calculate the surface area and volume of cylinders and solve related problems

Solve problems involving the surface area and volume of right prisms

The Millau Viaduct in France opened in 2005 and is the tallest bridge structure in the world. Some of the measurements for the construction of the bridge include:

- maximum pylon height 343 m above ground
- length 2.46 km
- concrete volume 80 000 m^3
- steel cables 1500 tonnes
- road/deck area 70 000 m^2

Many of these measurements are calculated by considering the simple and basic shapes that make up the bridge's structure. These include circles (cross-section for the main piers) and trapeziums (cross-section for the bridge deck). Lengths, areas and volumes were measured using metric units like kilometres (km) for length, square metres (m^2) for area and cubic metres (m^3) for volume. You can imagine how important accurate measurements are to the planning, financing and building of such a bridge structure.

Pre-test

1 Calculate the following.

   a 2.3×10 **b** 0.048×1000 **c** $270 \div 100$

   d $52\,134 \div 10\,000$ **e** $0.0005 \times 100\,000$ **f** $72\,160 \div 1000$

2 For these basic shapes find:

   i   the number of squares inside the shape (area)

   ii the distance around the outside of the shape (perimeter)

   a 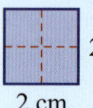 2 cm   **b** 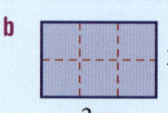 2 m   **c** 8 cm 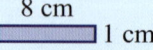 1 cm

        2 cm   3 m

3 **a** Name this solid.

   b What is the name of the shape (shaded) on top of the solid?

4 Estimate the area (number of squares) in these shapes.

   a    **b**   **c**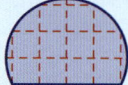

5 Count the number of cubes in these solids to find the volume.

   a 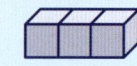   **b**    **c**

6 Convert the following to the units shown in the brackets.

   a 3 cm (mm)   **b** 20 m (cm)   **c** 1.6 km (m)   **d** 23 mm (cm)

   e 3167 m (km)   **f** 72 cm (m)   **g** 20 000 mm (m) **h** 0.03 km (cm)

7 Find the area of these basic shapes.

   a 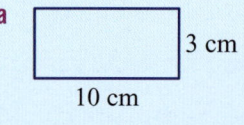 3 cm   **b** 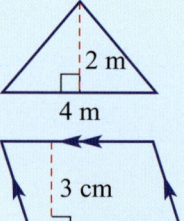   **c** 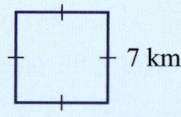 7 km

      10 cm   2 m / 4 m

   d 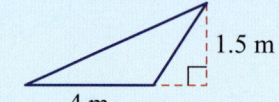 1.5 m   **e** 3 cm / 8 cm   **f** 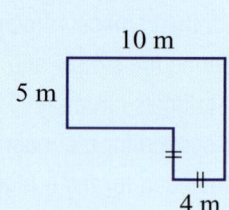 10 m / 5 m / 4 m

      4 m

8 Find the circumference ($C = 2\pi r$) and area ($A = \pi r^2$) of this circle, rounding to two decimal places.

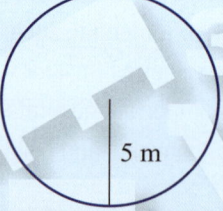

5 m

5.1 Length

Length is at the foundation of measurement from which the concepts of perimeter, circumference, area and volume are developed. From the use of the royal cubit (distance from tip of middle finger to the elbow) used by the ancient Egyptians to the calculation of pi (π) by modern computers, units of length have helped to create the world in which we live.

Units of length are essential in measuring distance area and volume.

Let's start: Not enough information?

All the angles at each vertex in this shape are 90° and the two given lengths are 10 cm and 13 cm.

- The simple question is: Is there enough information to find the perimeter of the shape?
- If there is enough information, find the perimeter and discuss your method. If not then say what information needs to be provided.

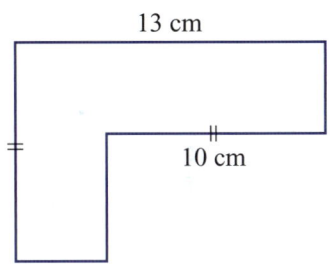

- To convert between **metric units** of length multiply or divide by the appropriate power of 10.

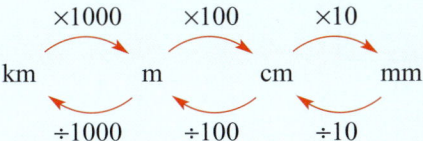

- **Perimeter** is the distance around a closed shape.
  - Sides with the same markings are of equal length

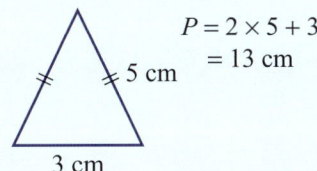

$P = 2 \times 5 + 3$
$= 13$ cm

Example 1 Finding perimeters of simple shapes

Find the perimeter of each of the following shapes.

a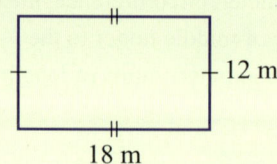

b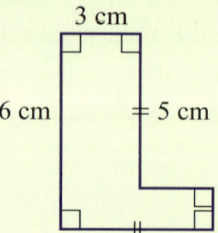

SOLUTION

a Perimeter $= 2 \times 12 + 2 \times 18$
$= 24 + 36$
$= 60$ m

b Perimeter $= (2 \times 5) + 6 + 3 + 2 + 1$
$= 22$ cm

EXPLANATION

Two lengths of 12 m and two lengths of 18 m.

Missing sides are:
5 cm − 3 cm = 2 cm
6 cm − 5 cm = 1 cm

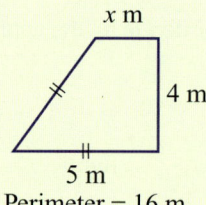

Example 2 Finding missing sides given a perimeter

Find the unknown side length in this shape with the given perimeter.

x m

4 m

5 m

Perimeter = 16 m

SOLUTION

$2 \times 5 + 4 + x = 16$
$14 + x = 16$
$x = 2$
∴ missing length = 2 m

EXPLANATION

Add all the lengths and set equal to the given perimeter.
Solve for the unknown.

Understanding

Exercise 5A

1 Convert the following length measurements into the units given in the brackets.
  a 5 cm (mm)   **b** 2.8 m (cm)   **c** 521 mm (cm)
  d 83.7 cm (m)   **e** 4.6 km (m)   **f** 2170 m (km)

2 A steel beam is 8.25 m long and 22.5 mm wide. Write down the length and the width of the beam in centimetres.

3 Write down the values of the pronumerals in these shapes.
  a 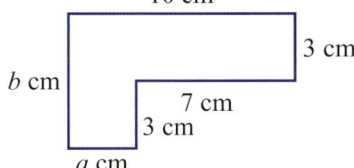   **b** 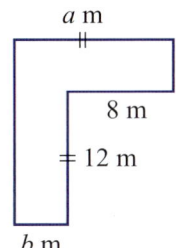   **c**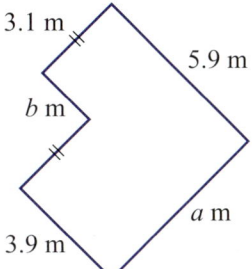

mple 1a **4** Find the perimeter of each of the following shapes.
  a 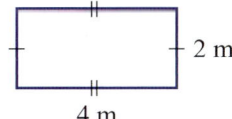   **b** 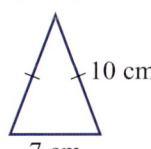   **c**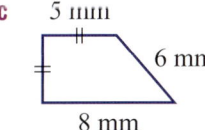

  d 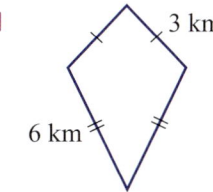   **e** 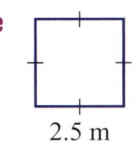   **f**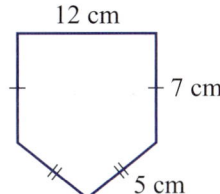

Fluency

mple 1b **5** Find the perimeter of each of the following composite shapes.
  a 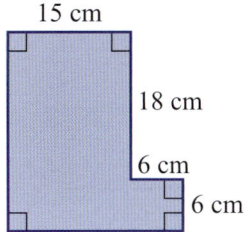   **b** 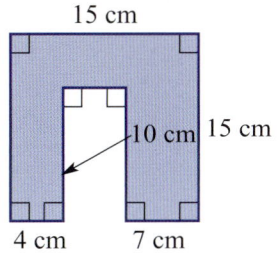   **c**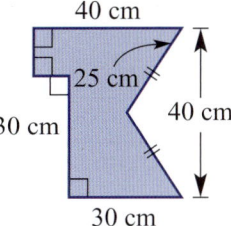

  d 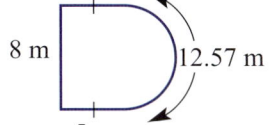   **e** 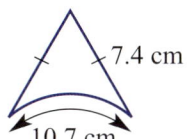   **f**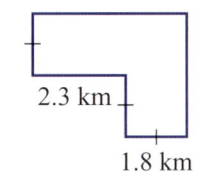

6 Find the perimeter of each of these shapes. You will need to convert the measurements to the same units. Give your answers in the units given in red.

a
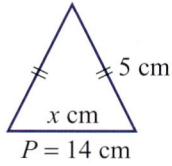
9 mm
1.8 cm

b
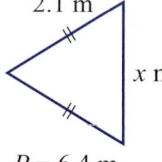
950 m
400 m
1.315 km

c
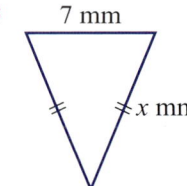
0.43 m
201 mm
39 cm

7 Convert the following measurements into the units given in the brackets.

a 8 m (mm) **b** 110 000 mm (m) **c** 0.00001 km (cm)
d 0.02 m (mm) **e** 28 400 cm (km) **f** 62 743 000 mm (km)

Example 2

8 Find the unknown side length in these shapes with the given perimeters.

a
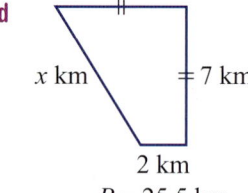
5 cm
x cm
$P = 14$ cm

b
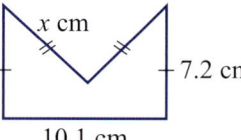
2.1 m
x m
$P = 6.4$ m

c
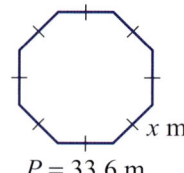
7 mm
x mm
$P = 35$ mm

d
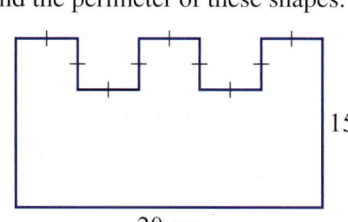
x km
7 km
2 km
$P = 25.5$ km

e
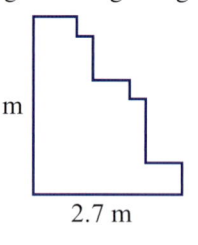
x cm
7.2 cm
10.1 cm
$P = 36.5$ cm

f
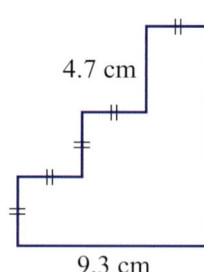
x m
$P = 33.6$ m

9 A lion enclosure is made up of five straight fence sections. Three sections are 20 m in length and the other two sections are 15.5 m and 32.5 m. Find the perimeter of the enclosure.

10 Find the perimeter of these shapes. Assume all angles are right angles.

a
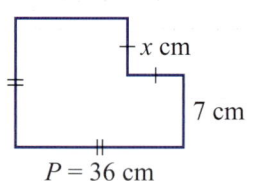
15 cm
20 cm

b
4.1 m
2.7 m

c
4.7 cm
9.3 cm

11 Find the value of x in these shapes with the given perimeter.

a
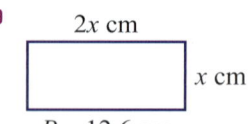
x cm
7 cm
$P = 36$ cm

b
$2x$ cm
x cm
$P = 12.6$ cm

c
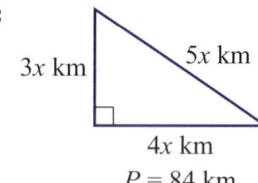
3x km
5x km
4x km
$P = 84$ km

12 A photo 12 cm wide and 20 cm long is surrounded with a picture frame 3 cm wide. Find the outside perimeter of the framed picture.

13 Give the rule for the perimeter of these shapes using the given pronumerals, e.g. $P = 3a + 2b$.

a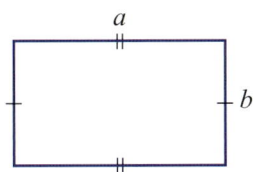

b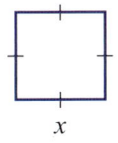

c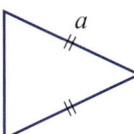

d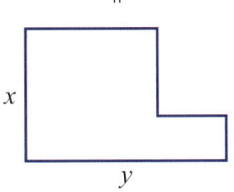

e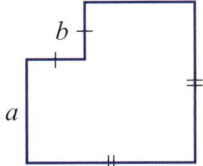

f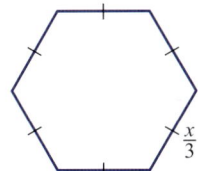

14 Explain why you do not need any more information to find the perimeter of this shape assuming all angles are right angles.

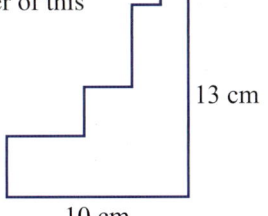

13 cm

10 cm

15 A piece of string 1 m long is divided into the given ratios. Find the length of each part.
   a $1 : 3$ **b** $2 : 3$ **c** $5 : 3$ **d** $1 : 2 : 3 : 4$

Enrichment: Picture framing

16 A square picture of side length 20 cm is surrounded by a frame of width x cm.
   a Find the perimeter of the framed picture if:
      i $x = 2$ **ii** $x = 3$ **iii** $x = 5$
   b Write a rule for the perimeter P of the framed picture in terms of x.
   c Use your rule to find the perimeter if:
      i $x = 3.7$ **ii** $x = 7.05$
   d Use your rule to find the value of x if:
      i the perimeter is 90 cm   **ii** the perimeter is 102 cm
   e Is there a value of x for which the perimeter is 75 cm? Explain.

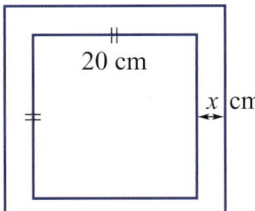

20 cm

x cm

5.2 Circumference and perimeter of a sector

A portion of a circle enclosed by two radii and an arc is called a sector. The perimeter of a sector is made up of three components: two radii of the same length and the circular arc. Given an angle θ it is possible to find the length of the arc using the rule for the circumference of a circle $C = 2\pi r$ or $C = \pi d$.

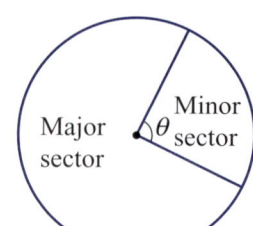

Let's start: Perimeter of a sector

A sector is formed by dividing a circle with two radius cuts. The angle between the two radii determines the size of the sector. The perimeter will therefore depend on both the radius length and the angle between them.

- Complete this table to see if you can determine a rule for the perimeter of a sector. Remember that the circumference C of a circle is given by $C = 2\pi r$ where r is the radius length.

Shape	Fraction of full circle	Working
	$\dfrac{90}{360} = \dfrac{1}{4}$	$P = 2 \times 3 + \dfrac{1}{4} \times 2\pi \times 3 \approx 10.71$
	$\dfrac{270}{360} = \underline{}$	$P =$
	$\underline{} = \underline{}$	$P =$
	$\underline{} = \underline{}$	$P =$
	$\underline{}$	$P =$

■ **Circumference** of a circle $C = 2\pi r$ or $C = \pi d$.

• Use $\dfrac{22}{7}$ or 3.14 to approximate π or use technology for more precise calculations.

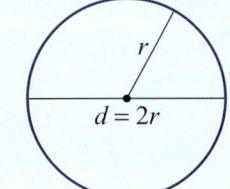

■ A **sector** is a portion of a circle enclosed by two radii and an arc. Special sectors include:

• a half circle is called a **semicircle**

• a quarter circle is called a **quadrant**.

■ The perimeter of a sector is given by $P = 2r + \dfrac{\theta}{360} \times 2\pi r$.

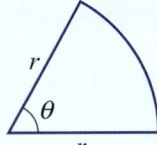

■ The symbol for pi (π) can be used to write an answer exactly.
For example, $C = 2\pi r$
$$= 2\pi \times 3$$
$$= 6\pi$$

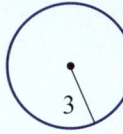

Example 3 Finding the circumference of a circle and perimeter of a sector

Find the circumference of this circle and perimeter of this sector correct to two decimal places.

a
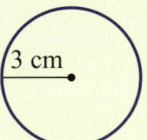

b
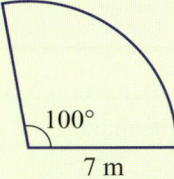

SOLUTION

EXPLANATION

a $C = 2\pi r$

$\quad = 2 \times \pi \times 3$

$\quad = 6\pi$

$\quad = 18.85$ cm

Use the formula $C = 2\pi r$ or $C = \pi d$ and substitute $r = 3$ (or $d = 6$).

6π would be the exact answer and 18.85 is the rounded answer.

b $P = 2r + \dfrac{\theta}{360} \times 2\pi r$

$\quad = 2 \times 7 + \dfrac{100}{360} \times 2 \times \pi \times 7$

$\quad = 14 + \dfrac{35\pi}{9}$

$\quad = 26.22$ m

Write the formula.

The fraction of the circle is $\dfrac{100}{360}$ (or $\dfrac{5}{18}$).

$14 + \dfrac{35\pi}{9}$ is the exact answer.

Example 4 Using exact values

Give the exact circumference/perimeter of these shapes.

a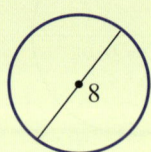

b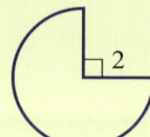

SOLUTION

EXPLANATION

a $C = 2\pi r$

    $= 2 \times \pi \times 4$

    $= 8\pi$

$r = 8 \div 2 = 4$.

Alternatively, use $C = \pi d$ with $d = 8$.

Write the answer exactly in terms of π.

b $P = 2 \times r + \dfrac{\theta}{360} \times 2\pi r$

    $= 2 \times 2 + \dfrac{270}{360} \times 2\pi \times 2$

    $= 4 + \dfrac{3}{4} \times 4\pi$

    $= 4 + 3\pi$

The angle inside the sector is $270°$ so the fraction

is $\dfrac{270}{360} = \dfrac{3}{4}$.

$4 + 3\pi$ cannot be simplified further.

Exercise 5B

Understanding

1   **a**   What is the radius of a circle if its diameter is 5.6 cm?

    b   What is the diameter of a circle if its radius is 48 mm?

2   Simplify these numbers to give an exact answer. Do not evaluate with a calculator or round off. The first one is done for you.

   a $2 \times 3 \times \pi = 6\pi$ **b** $6 \times 2\pi$ **c** $7 \times 2.5 \times \pi$

   d $3 + \dfrac{1}{2} \times 4\pi$ **e** $2 \times 6 + \dfrac{1}{4} \times 12\pi$ **f** $2 \times 5 + \dfrac{2}{5} \times 2 \times \pi \times 5$

   g $2 \times 4 + \dfrac{90}{360} \times 2 \times \pi \times 4$ **h** $3 + \dfrac{270}{360} \times \pi$ **i** $7 + \dfrac{30}{360} \times \pi$

3   Determine the fraction of a circle shown in these sectors. Write the fraction in simplest form.

   a   **b**    **c**    **d**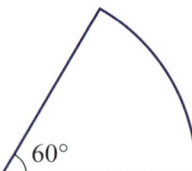

e 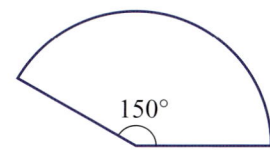 150°

f 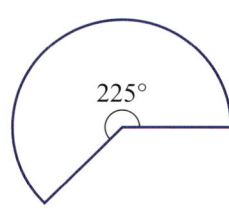 225°

mple 3a

4 Find the circumference of these circles correct to two decimal places. Use a calculator for the value of π.

a 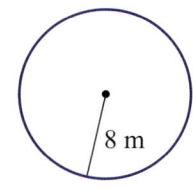 8 m

b 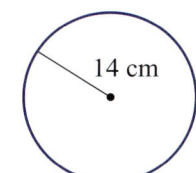 14 cm

c 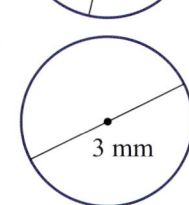 3 mm

d 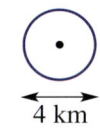 4 km

mple 3b

5 Find the perimeter of these sectors correct to two decimal places.

a 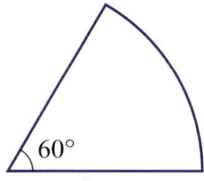 60° 3 cm

b 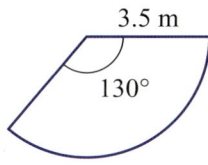 3.5 m 130°

c 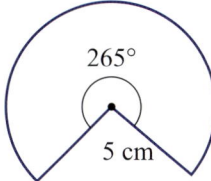 265° 5 cm

d (Quadrant)  2.8 cm

e (Semicircle) 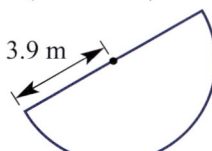 3.9 m

f 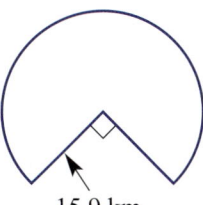 15.9 km

6 Find the circumference of these circles without a calculator using the given approximation of π.

a 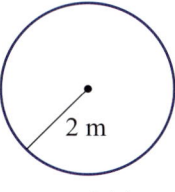 2 m $\pi = 3.14$

b 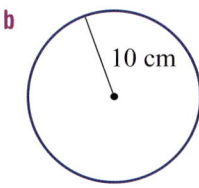 10 cm $\pi = 3.14$

c 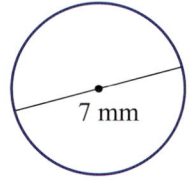 7 mm $\pi = \dfrac{22}{7}$

d 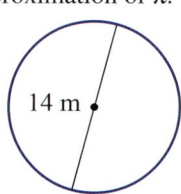 14 m $\pi = \dfrac{22}{7}$

Example 4a **7** Give the exact circumference of these circles.

a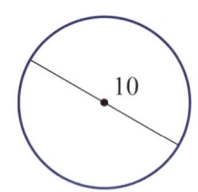

b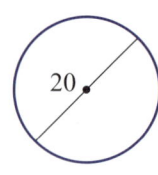

c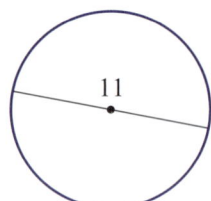

d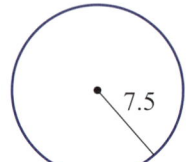

e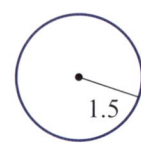

f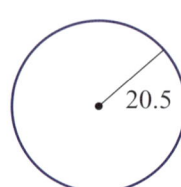

Example 4b **8** Give the exact perimeter of these sectors.

a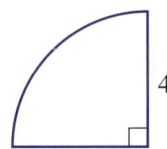

b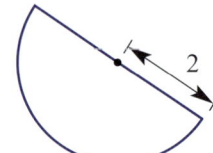

c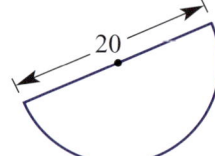

d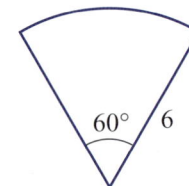

e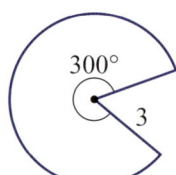

f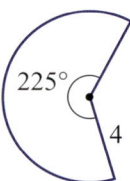

 9 Find the distance around the outside of a circular pool of radius 4.5 m, correct to two decimal places.

 10 Find the length of string required to surround the circular trunk of a tree that has a diameter of 1.3 m, correct to one decimal place.

 11 The end of a cylinder has a radius of 5 cm. Find the circumference of the end of the cylinder, correct to two decimal places.

 12 A wheel of radius 30 cm is rolled in a straight line.
   a Find the circumference of the wheel correct to two decimal places.
   b How far, correct to two decimal places, has the wheel rolled after completing:
      i 2 rotations?   **ii** 10.5 rotations?
   c Can you find how many rotations would be required to cover at least 1 km in length? Round to the nearest whole number.

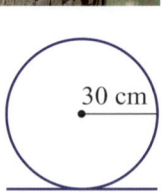

30 cm

13 Give exact answers for the perimeter of these shapes. Express answers using fractions.

a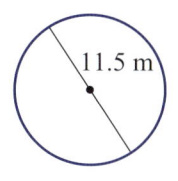
11.5 m

b
1.2 cm

c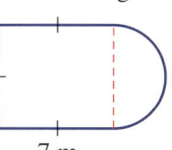
7 m

d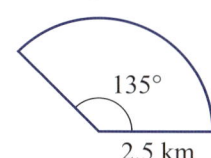
135°
2.5 km

e 20 mm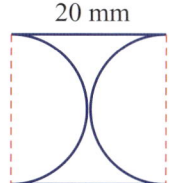

f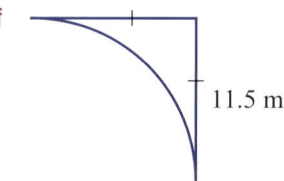
11.5 m

14 We know that the rule for the circumference of a circle is $C = 2\pi r$.

  a Find a rule for r in terms of C.

  b Find the radius of a circle to one decimal place if its circumference is:

   i   10 cm   **ii**   25 m

  c Give the rule for the diameter of a circle in terms of its circumference C.

  d After 1000 rotations a wheel has travelled 2.12 km. Find its diameter to the nearest centimetre.

Enrichment: The ferris wheel

15 A large ferris wheel has a radius of 21 m. Round to two decimal places for these questions.

  a Find the distance a person will travel on one rotation of the wheel.

  b A ride includes 6 rotations of the wheel. What distance is travelled in one ride?

  c How many rotations would be required to ride a distance of:

   i   500 m   **ii**   2 km?

  d A ferris wheel has a sign which reads, 'One ride of 10 rotations will cover 2 km'. What must be the diameter of the wheel?

We can find the distance travelled from one rotation by calculating its circumference.

5.3 Area

The number of square centimetres in this rectangle is 6; therefore the area is 6 cm².

A quicker way to find the number of squares is to note that there are two rows of three squares and hence the area is $2 \times 3 = 6$ cm². This leads to the formula $A = l \times w$ for the area of a rectangle.

For many common shapes, such as the parallelogram and trapezium, the rules for their area can be developed through consideration of simple rectangles and triangles. Shapes that involve circles or sectors rely on calculations involving pi (π).

Let's start: Formula for the area of a sector

We know that the area of a circle with radius r is given by the rule $A = \pi r^2$.

Complete this table of values to develop the rule for the area of a sector.

How many tiles cover this area?

Shape	Fraction of full circle	Working and answers
	1	$A = \pi \times 2^2 \approx 12.57$
	$\dfrac{180}{360} = \underline{\quad}$	$A = \dfrac{1}{2} \times \underline{\quad}$
	$\underline{\quad} = \underline{\quad}$	$A =$
	$\underline{\quad} = \underline{\quad}$	$A =$
	$\underline{\qquad}$	$A =$

Key ideas

■ Conversion of area units

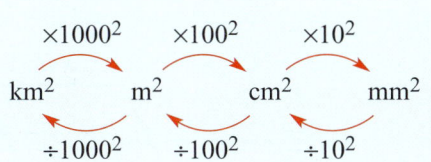

$$10^2 = 10 \times 10 = 100$$
$$100^2 = 100 \times 100 = 10\,000$$
$$1000^2 = 1000 \times 1000 = 1\,000\,000$$

■ The area of a two-dimensional shape is a measure of the space enclosed within its boundaries.

Square

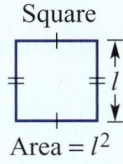

Area $= l^2$

Rectangle

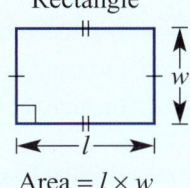

Area $= l \times w$

Triangle

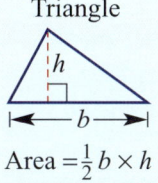

Area $= \frac{1}{2}b \times h$

Parallelogram

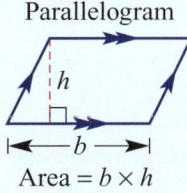

Area $= b \times h$

Trapezium

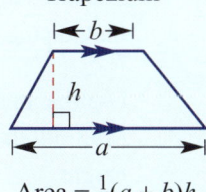

Area $= \frac{1}{2}(a + b)h$

Rhombus

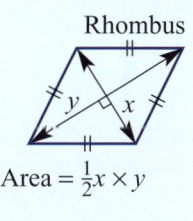

Area $= \frac{1}{2}x \times y$

Kite

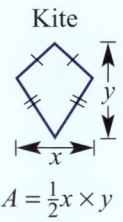

$A = \frac{1}{2}x \times y$

Circle

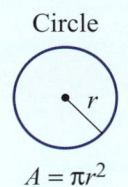

$A = \pi r^2$

Sector

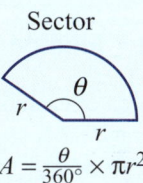

$A = \frac{\theta}{360°} \times \pi r^2$

Example 5 Converting units of area

Convert the following area measurements into the units given in the brackets.
a 859 mm² (cm²)   **b** 2.37 m² (cm²)

SOLUTION

a $859 \text{ mm}^2 = 859 \div 10^2 \text{ cm}^2$
$= 8.59 \text{ cm}^2$

b $2.37 \text{ m}^2 = 2.37 \times 100^2 \text{ cm}^2$
$= 23\,700 \text{ cm}^2$

EXPLANATION

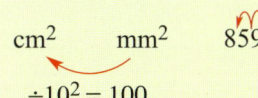

Example 6 Finding areas of rectangles, triangles and parallelograms

Find the area of each of the following plane figures.

a
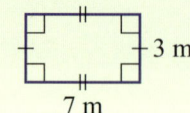
3 m
7 m

b
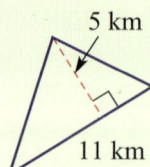
5 km
11 km

c
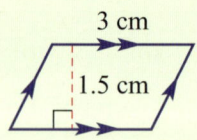
3 cm
1.5 cm

SOLUTION

a Area $= l \times w$
   $= 7 \times 3$
   $= 21 \text{ m}^2$

b Area $= \dfrac{1}{2} \times b \times h$

   $= \dfrac{1}{2} \times 11 \times 5$

   $= 27.5 \text{ km}^2$

c Area $= b \times h$
   $= 3 \times 1.5$
   $= 4.5 \text{ cm}^2$

EXPLANATION

Use the area formula for a rectangle. Substitute $l = 7$ and $w = 3$.
Include the correct units.

Use the area formula for a triangle.

Substitute $b = 11$ and $h = 5$.
Include the correct units.

Use the area formula for a parallelogram.
Multiply the base length by the perpendicular height.

Example 7 Finding areas of rhombuses and trapeziums

Find the area of each of the following plane figures.

a
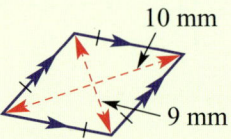
10 mm
9 mm

b
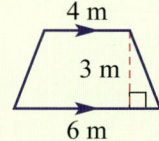
4 m
3 m
6 m

SOLUTION

a Area $= \dfrac{1}{2} \times x \times y$

   $= \dfrac{1}{2} \times 10 \times 9$

   $= 45 \text{ mm}^2$

b Area $= \dfrac{1}{2}(a + b) \times h$

   $= \dfrac{1}{2}(4 + 6) \times 3$

   $= 15 \text{ m}^2$

EXPLANATION

Use the area formula for a rhombus.
Substitute $x = 10$ and $y = 9$.

Include the correct units.

Use the area formula for a trapezium.

Substitute $a = 4$, $b = 6$ and $h = 3$.

Include the correct units.

Example 8 Finding areas of circles and sectors

Find the area of this circle and sector correct to two decimal places.

a

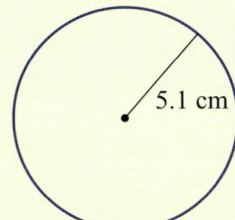

5.1 cm

b

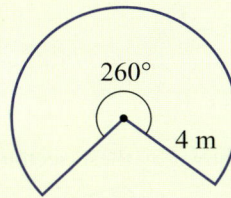

260°

4 m

SOLUTION

a $A = \pi r^2$
 $= \pi \times (5.1)^2$
 $= 81.71 \text{ cm}^2$

b $A = \dfrac{\theta}{360} \times \pi r^2$

 $= \dfrac{260}{360} \times \pi \times 4^2$

 $= \dfrac{13}{18} \times \pi \times 16$

 $= 36.30 \text{ m}^2$

EXPLANATION

Write the rule and substitute $r = 5.1$.
81.7128 rounds to 81.71 since the third decimal place is 2.

The fraction of the full circle is $\dfrac{260}{360} = \dfrac{13}{18}$,
so multiply this by πr^2 to get the sector area.

Exercise 5C

1 Count the number of squares to find the area of these shapes. Each square in each shape represents one square unit.

a

b

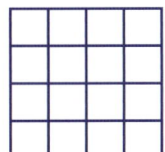

c

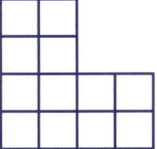

d

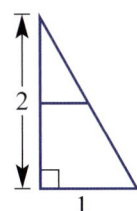

2

1

e

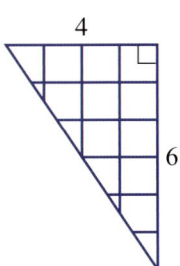

4

6

f

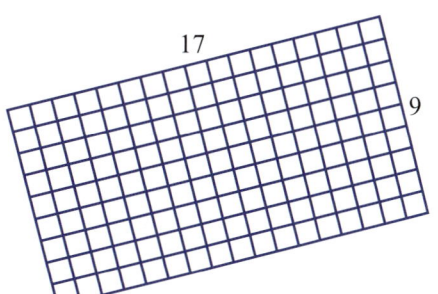

17

9

Understanding

2 Name the shape that has the given area formula.

  a $A = lw$ **b** $A = \pi r^2$ **c** $A = \dfrac{1}{2}xy$ (2 shapes)

  d $A = \dfrac{\theta}{360} \times \pi r^2$ **e** $A = \dfrac{1}{2}bh$ **f** $A = \dfrac{1}{2}(a + b)h$

  g $A = bh$ **h** $A = l^2$ **i** $A = \dfrac{1}{2}\pi r^2$

3 What fraction of a full circle is shown by these sectors? Simplify your fraction.

  a 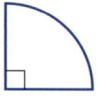   **b** 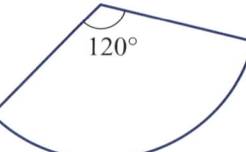   **c**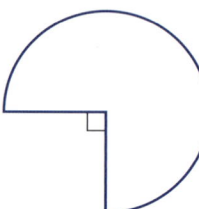

  d 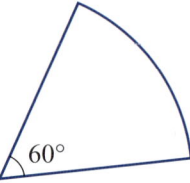   **e** 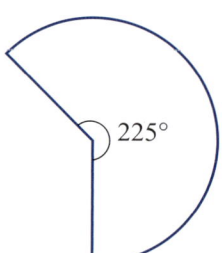   **f**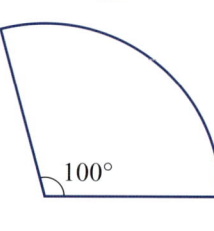

Example 5   **4** Convert the following area measurements into the units given in the brackets.

  a 2 cm² (mm²)   **b** 500 mm² (cm²)   **c** 2.1 m² (cm²)

  d 210 000 cm² (m²)   **e** 0.001 km² (m²)   **f** 3 200 000 m² (km²)

Example 6   **5** Find the area of each of the following plane figures.

  a 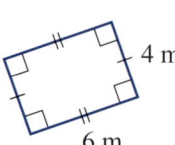   **b** 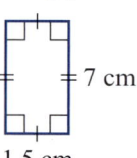   **c**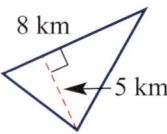

  d 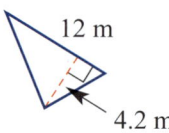   **e** 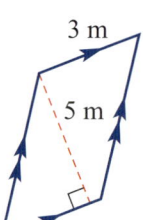   **f**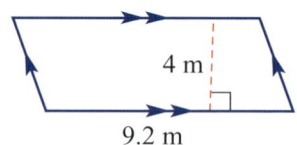

ample 7

6 Find the area of each of the following plane figures.

a

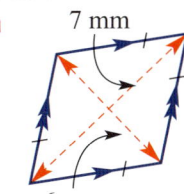

7 mm

6 mm

b

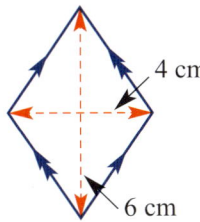

4 cm

6 cm

c

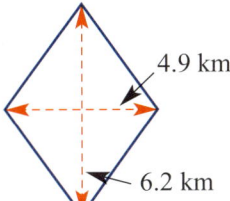

7 cm

2 cm

10 cm

d

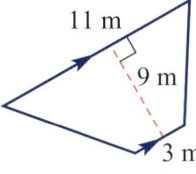

11 m

9 m

3 m

e

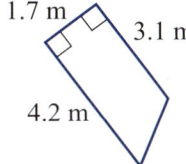

1.7 m

3.1 m

4.2 m

f

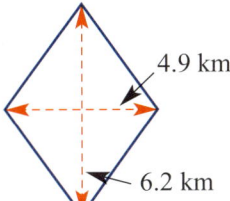

4.9 km

6.2 km

7 Find the area of each of the following mixed-plane figures.

a

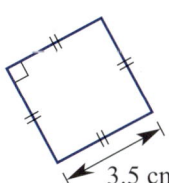

3.5 cm

b

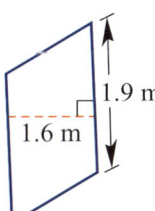

1.9 m

1.6 m

c

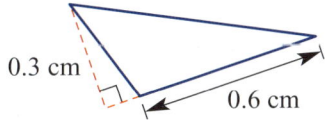

0.3 cm

0.6 cm

d

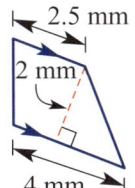

2.5 mm

2 mm

4 mm

e

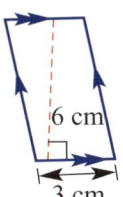

6 cm

3 cm

f

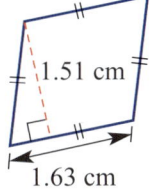

1.51 cm

1.63 cm

nple 8a

8 Find the area of these circles using the given value for pi (π). Round to two decimal places.

a $\pi = 3.14$

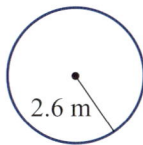

2.6 m

b $\pi = \dfrac{22}{7}$

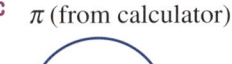

8.3 km

c π (from calculator)

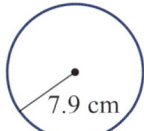

7.9 cm

Example 8b   **9**   Find the area of these sectors rounding to two decimal places.

a   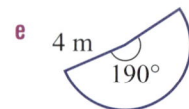 3 m

b   10 cm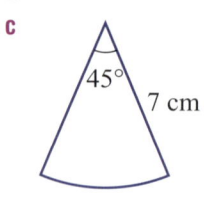

c   45° 7 cm

d   6 m

e   4 m 190°

f   147° 7 m

10   Convert the following measurements into the units given in the brackets.

   a 1.5 km^2 (cm^2) **b** 0.000005 m^2 (mm^2) **c** $75\,000 \text{ mm}^2$ (m^2)

11   A valuer tells you that your piece of land has an area of one-half a square kilometre (0.5 km^2).
How many square metres (m^2) do you own?

12   A rectangular park covers an area of $175\,000 \text{ m}^2$. Give
the area of the park in km^2.

   13   An old picture frame that was once square now leans
to one side to form a rhombus. If the distances between
pairs of opposite corners are 85 cm and 1.2 m, find the
area enclosed within the frame in m^2.

   14   A pizza shop is considering increasing the diameter of its family pizza tray from 32 cm to
34 cm. Find the percentage increase in area, correct to two decimal places, from the 32 cm tray
to the 34 cm tray.

15   A tennis court area is illuminated by 4 corner lights. The
illumination of the sector area close to each light is considered
to be good (G) while the remaining area is considered to be lit
satisfactorily (S).

   What percentage of the area is considered 'good'? Round to
the nearest percent.

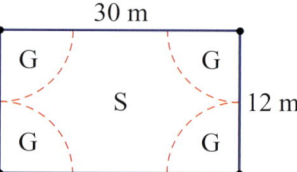

30 m

G   G

S   12 m

G   G

16 The rule for the area of a circle is given by $A = \pi r^2$.

   a Rearrange this rule to find a rule for r in terms of A.

   b Find the radius of a circle with the given areas. Round to one decimal place.

     i 5 cm^2 **ii** 6.9 m^2 **iii** 20 km^2

17 A sector has a radius of 3 m.

   a Find the angle θ, correct to the nearest degree, if its area is:

     i 5 m^2 **ii** 25 m^2

   b Explain why the area of the sector could not be 30 m^2.

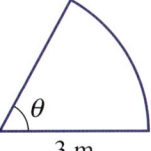

3 m

Enrichment: Windows

18 Six square windows of side length 2 m are to be placed into a 12 m wide by 8.5 m high wall as shown. The windows are to be positioned so that the vertical spacing between the windows and the wall edges are equal. Similarly, the horizontal spacings are also equal.

2 m

2 m

8.5 m

12 m

   a **i** Find the horizontal distance between the windows.

     ii Find the vertical distance between the windows.

   b Find the area of the wall not including the window spaces.

   c If the wall included 3 rows of 4 windows (instead of 2 rows of 3) investigate if it would be possible to space all the windows so that the horizontal and vertical spacings are uniform (although not necessarily equal to each other).

19 A rectangular window is wiped by a wiper blade forming the given sector shape.

What percentage area is cleaned by the wiper blade? Round to one decimal place.

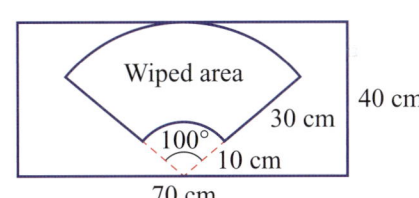

Wiped area

40 cm

30 cm

100°

10 cm

70 cm

Using a CAS calculator 5.3: Measurement formulas

This activity is on the companion website in the form of a printable PDF.

5.4 Composite shapes

Composite shapes can be thought of as a combination of more simplistic shapes such as triangles and rectangles. Finding perimeters and areas of such shapes is a matter of identifying the more basic shapes they consist of and combining any calculations in an organised fashion.

The area of glass in this window can be calculated using the area of trapeziums, triangles and rectangles.

Let's start: Incorrect layout

Three students write their solution to finding the area of this shape on the board.

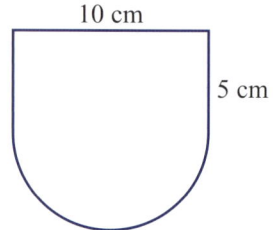

Chris	Matt	Moira
$A = l \times w$ $= 50 + \frac{1}{2}\pi r^2$ $= \frac{1}{2}\pi \times 5^2$ $= 39.27 + 50$ $= 89.27 \text{ cm}^2$	$A = \frac{1}{2}\pi \times 5^2$ $= 39.27 + 10 \times 5$ $= 89.27 \text{ cm}^2$	$A = l \times w + \frac{1}{2}\pi r^2$ $= 10 \times 5 + \frac{1}{2}\pi \times 5^2$ $= 89.27 \text{ cm}^2$

- All three students have the correct answer but only one student receives full marks. Who is it?
- Explain what is wrong with the layout of the other two solutions.

Key ideas

- **Composite shapes** are made up of more than one basic shape.
- Addition and/or subtraction can be used to find areas and perimeters of composite shapes.
- The layout of the relevant mathematical working needs to make sense so that the reader of your work understands each step.

Example 9 Finding perimeters and areas of composite shapes

Find the perimeter and area of this composite shape, rounding answers to two decimal places.

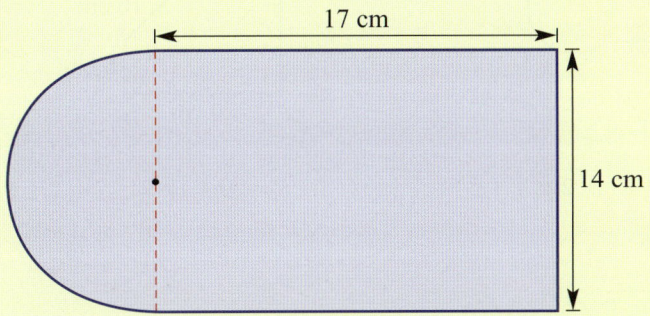

SOLUTION	EXPLANATION
$P = 2 \times l + w + \dfrac{1}{2} \times 2\pi r$	3 straight sides ⊐ + semicircle arc ⊂
$\quad = 2 \times 17 + 14 + \dfrac{1}{2} \times 2\pi \times 7$	Substitute $l = 17$, $w = 14$ and $r = 7$.
$\quad = 34 + 14 + \pi \times 7$	Simplify.
$\quad = 69.99 \text{ cm}$	Calculate and round to two decimal places.
$A = l \times w + \dfrac{1}{2}\pi r^2$	Area of rectangle ▭ + area of semicircle ◖
$\quad = 17 \times 14 + \dfrac{1}{2} \times \pi \times 7^2$	Substitute $l = 17$, $w = 14$ and $r = 7$.
$\quad = 238 + \dfrac{1}{2} \times \pi \times 49$	Simplify.
$\quad = 314.97 \text{ cm}^2$	Calculate and round to two decimal places.

Exercise 5D

1 Name the two different shapes that make up these composite shapes, e.g. square and semicircle.

a    b 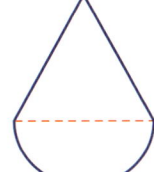   c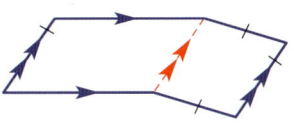

2 Copy and complete the working to find the perimeter and area of these composite shapes. Round to one decimal place.

a

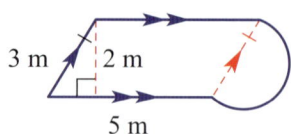

b

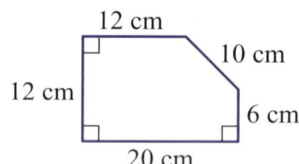

$P = 2 \times \underline{\quad} + 3 + \dfrac{1}{2} \times 2\pi r$

$= \underline{\quad} + 3 + \underline{\quad}$

$= \underline{\qquad\qquad}$

$= \underline{\quad}$ m

$A = bh + \dfrac{1}{2} \underline{\quad}$

$= 5 \times \underline{\quad} + \dfrac{1}{2} \times \underline{\quad}$

$= \underline{\quad} + \underline{\quad}$

$= \underline{\quad}$ m^2

$P = 20 + 12 + \underline{\quad} + \underline{\quad} + \underline{\quad}$

$= \underline{\quad}$ cm

$A = lw - \dfrac{1}{2}bh$

$= 12 \times \underline{\quad} - \dfrac{1}{2} \times 8 \times \underline{\quad}$

$= \underline{\quad} - \underline{\quad}$

$= \underline{\quad}$ cm^2

Example 9

3 Find the perimeter and the area of each of these simple composite shapes, rounding answers to two decimal places where necessary.

a

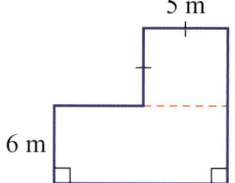

b

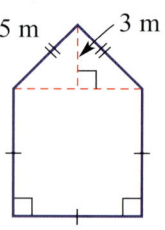

c

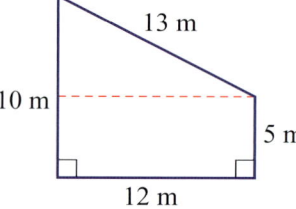

d

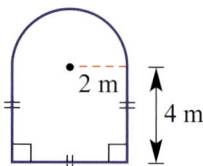

e

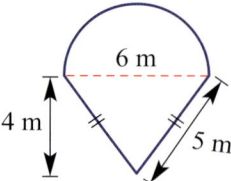

f

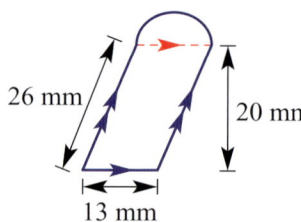

4 Find the area of each of the following composite shapes.

a

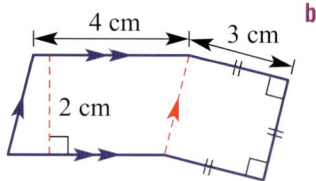

b

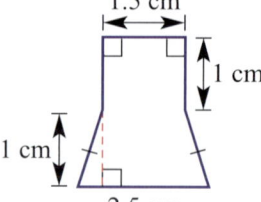

c

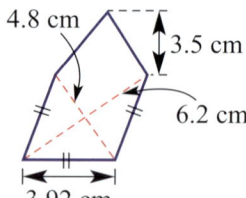

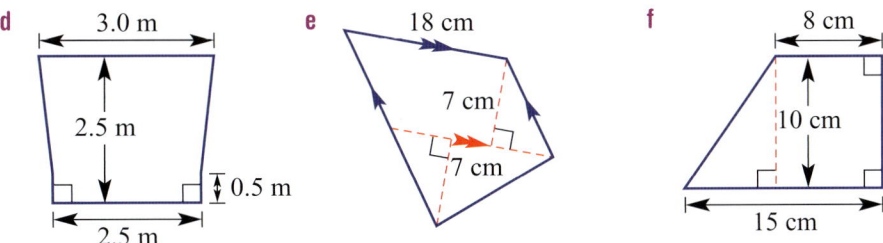

d 3.0 m 2.5 m 2.5 m 0.5 m

e 18 cm 7 cm 7 cm

f 8 cm 10 cm 15 cm

5 Find the area of each of these composite shapes. Hint: Use subtraction.

a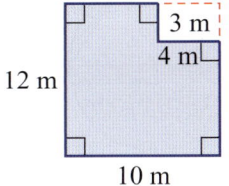
3 m
4 m
12 m
10 m

b
6 cm
11 cm

c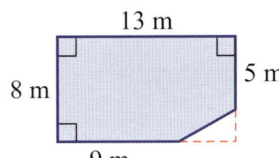
13 m
8 m
5 m
9 m

d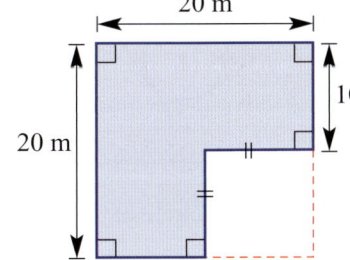
20 m
10 m
20 m

e
5 cm
4 cm
2 cm

f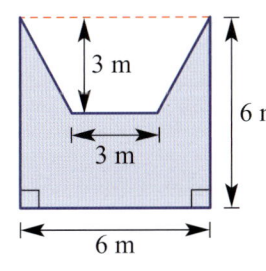
3 m
3 m
6 m
6 m

6 Find the perimeter and the area of each of the following composite shapes correct to two decimal places where necessary.

a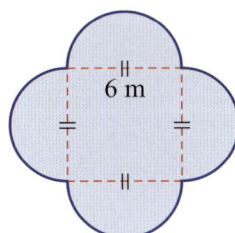
6 m

b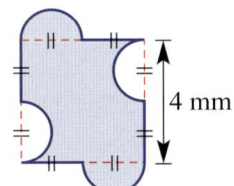
4 mm

c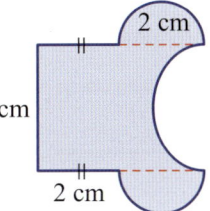
2 cm
3 cm
2 cm

d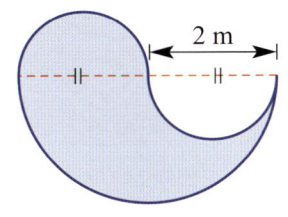
2 m

e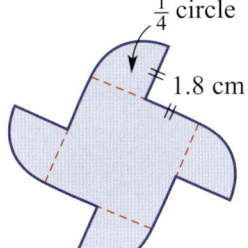
$\frac{1}{4}$ circle
1.8 cm

f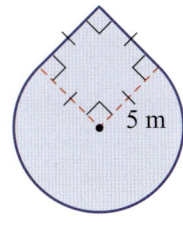
5 m

7 Find the area of the shaded region of each of the following shapes by subtracting the area of the clear shape from the total area. Round to one decimal place where necessary.

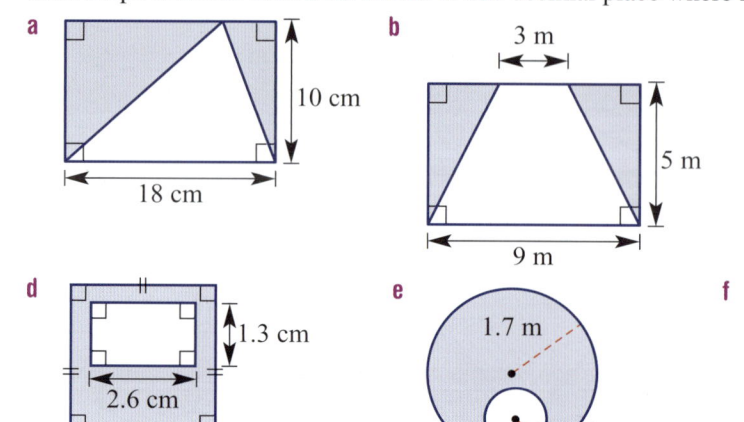

a

10 cm

18 cm

b

3 m

5 m

9 m

c

3 m

6 m

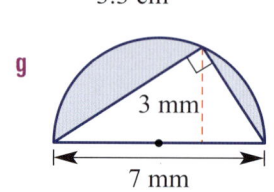

d

1.3 cm

2.6 cm

3.3 cm

e

1.7 m

0.6 m

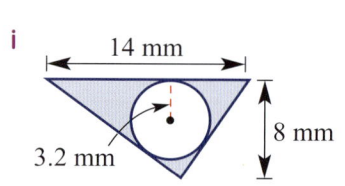

f

15 cm   10 cm

9.01 cm

g

3 mm

7 mm

h

4 cm

3 cm

i

14 mm

8 mm

3.2 mm

8 An area of lawn is made up of a rectangle measuring 10 m by 15 m and a semicircle of radius 5 m. Find the total area of lawn correct to two decimal places.

9 Twenty circular pieces of pastry, each of diameter 4 cm, are cut from a rectangular layer of pastry 20 cm long and 16 cm wide. What is the area, correct to two decimal places, of pastry remaining after the twenty pieces are removed?

10 These shapes include sectors. Find their area to one decimal place.

a

18 cm

24 cm

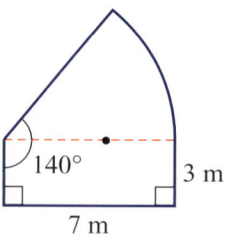

b

140°   3 m

7 m

c

11 m

11 A new car manufacturer is designing a logo. It is in the shape of a diamond inside a rectangle. The diamond is to have a horizontal width of 3 cm and an area equal to one-sixth of the area of the rectangle. Find the required height of the diamond.

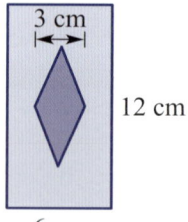

3 cm

12 cm

6 cm

12 Using exact values (e.g. $10 + 4\pi$), find the area of the shapes given in Question **6** above.

 13 A circle of radius 10 cm has a hole cut out of its centre to form a ring. Find the radius of the hole if the remaining area is 50% of the original area. Round to one decimal place.

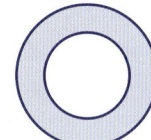

 14 Use Pythagoras' theorem (illustrated in this diagram) to help explain why these composite shapes include incorrect information.

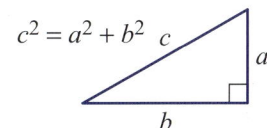
$$c^2 = a^2 + b^2$$

a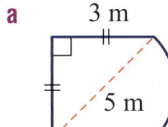

b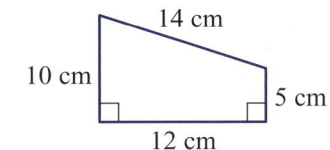

c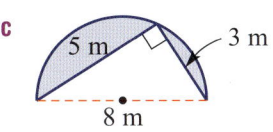

Enrichment: Construction cut-outs

 15 The front of a grandfather clock consists of a timber board with dimensions as shown. A circle of radius 20 cm is cut from the board to form the clock face. Find the remaining area of the timber board correct to one decimal place.

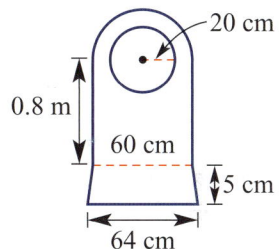

 16 The number 10 is cut from a rectangular piece of paper. The dimensions of the design are shown below.

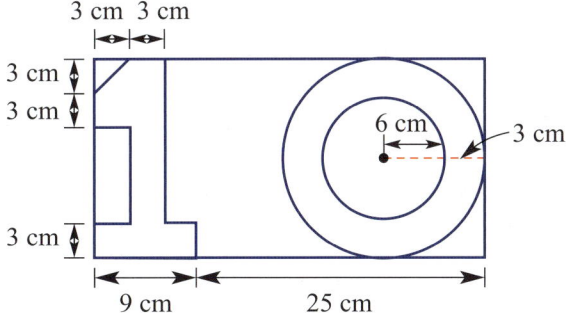

a Find the length and width of the rectangular piece of paper shown.

b Find the sum of the areas of the two cut-out digits, 1 and 0, correct to one decimal place.

c Find the area of paper remaining after the digits have been removed (include the centre of the '0' in your answer) and round to one decimal place.

5.5 Surface area of prisms and pyramids

Three-dimensional objects or solids have outside surfaces which together form the total surface area. Nets are very helpful for determining the number and shape of the surfaces of a three-dimensional object.

For this section we will deal with right prisms and pyramids. A right prism has a uniform cross-section with two identical ends and the remaining sides are rectangles. A right pyramid has its apex sitting above the centre of its base.

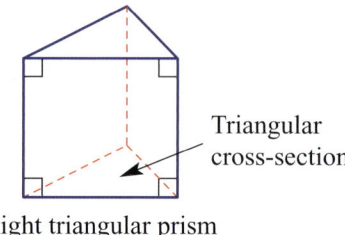

Triangular cross-section

Right triangular prism

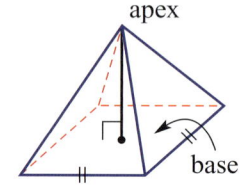

apex

base

Right square-based pyramid

Let's start: Drawing prisms and pyramids

Prisms are named by the shape of their cross-section and pyramids by the shape of their base.

- Try to draw as many different right prisms and pyramids as you can.
- Describe the different kinds of shapes that make up the surface of your solids.
- Which solids are the most difficult to draw and why?

Key ideas

- The **total surface area** (TSA) of a solid is the sum of the areas of all the surfaces.
- A **net** is a two-dimensional illustration of all the surfaces of a solid.
- A right **prism** is a solid with a uniform cross-section and remaining sides are rectangles.
  - They are named by the shape of their cross-section.
- The nets for a **rectangular prism** (**cuboid**) and square-based **pyramid** are shown here.

Solid	Net	TSA
Rectangular prism		$TSA = 2(lw) + 2(lh) + 2(hw)$
Square-based pyramid		$TSA = b^2 + 4\left(\dfrac{1}{2}bh\right)$ $= b^2 + 2bh$

Example 10 Finding a total surface area

Find the total surface area of each of the following solid objects.

a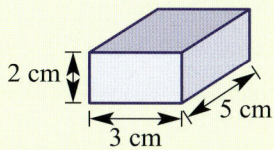

b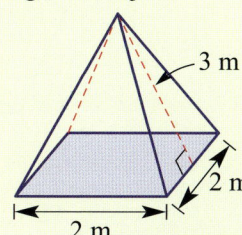

SOLUTION

a $\text{TSA} = 2 \times (5 \times 3) + 2 \times (5 \times 2) + 2 \times (2 \times 3)$

$= 30 + 20 + 12$

$= 62 \text{ cm}^2$

b $\text{TSA} = 2 \times 2 + 4 \times \dfrac{1}{2} \times 2 \times 3$

$= 4 + 12$

$= 16 \text{ m}^2$

EXPLANATION

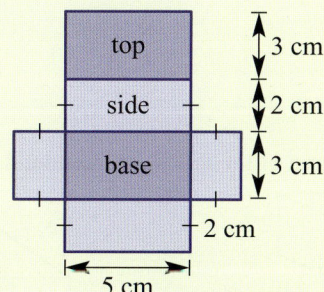

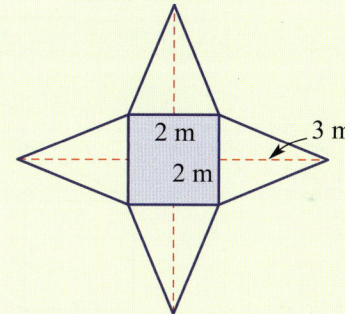

Exercise 5E

1   Draw a suitable net for these prisms and pyramids and name each solid.

a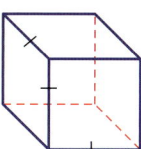

b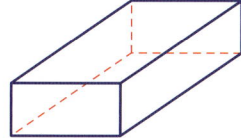

c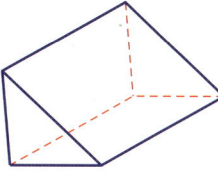

d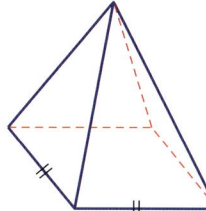

e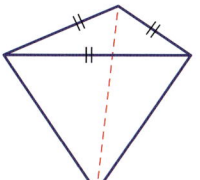

f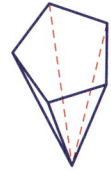

2 Copy and complete the working to find the surface area of these solids.

a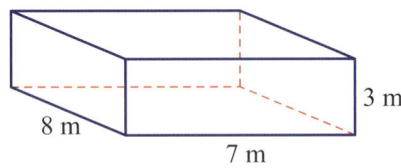

b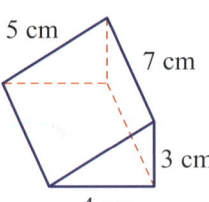

$\text{TSA} = 2 \times 8 \times 7 + 2 \times 8 \times \underline{} + 2 \times \underline{} \times \underline{}$

$\phantom{\text{TSA}} = \underline{} + \underline{} + \underline{}$

$\phantom{\text{TSA}} = \underline{} \text{ m}^2$

$\text{TSA} = 2 \times \dfrac{1}{2} \times 4 \times \underline{} + 5 \times 7 + 4 \times \underline{} + \underline{} \times \underline{}$

$\phantom{\text{TSA}} = \underline{} + \underline{} + \underline{} + \underline{}$

$\phantom{\text{TSA}} = \underline{} \text{ cm}^2$

3 Find the surface area of the following rectangular prisms. Draw a net of the solid to help you.

a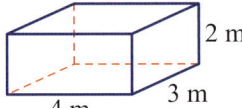

b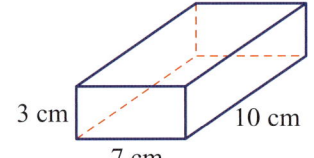

c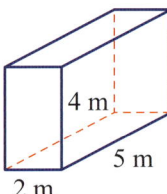

d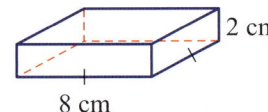

e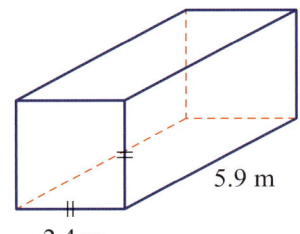

f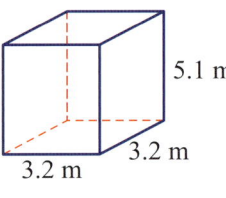

4 Find the surface area of each of these pyramids. Draw a net of the solid to help you.

a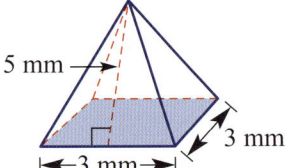

b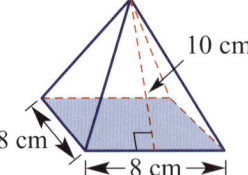

c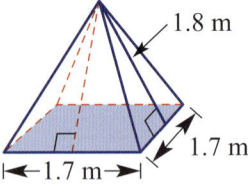

5 Find the surface area of each of the following solid objects.

a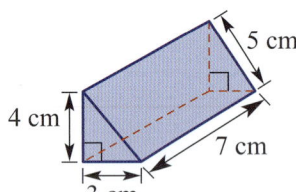

b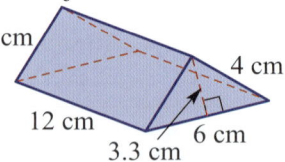

c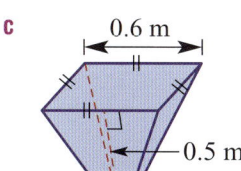
0.6 m
0.5 m

d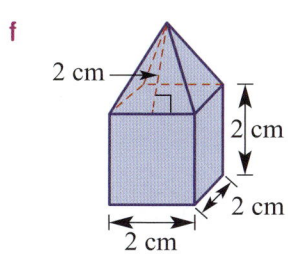
6.2 cm   3.5 cm
4 cm

e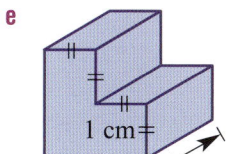
1 cm
2 cm
2 cm

f
2 cm
2 cm
2 cm
2 cm

6   Find the total surface area of a cube of side length 1 metre.

7   A rectangular box is to be covered in material. How much is required to cover the entire box if it has the dimensions 1.3 m, 1.5 m and 1.9 m?

8   Two wooden boxes, both with dimensions 80 cm, 1 m and 25 cm, are placed on the ground, one on top of the other as shown. The entire outside surface is then painted. Find the area of the painted surface.

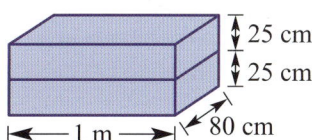
25 cm
25 cm
1 m   80 cm

9   The four walls and roof of a barn (shown) are to be painted.
    a   Find the surface area of the barn, not including the floor.
    b   If 1 litre of paint covers 10 m², find how many litres are required to complete the job.

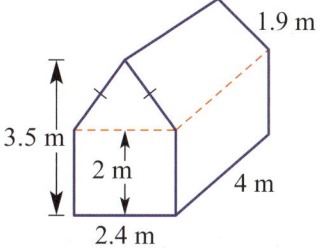
1.9 m
3.5 m
2 m
4 m
2.4 m

10 An open top rectangular box 20 cm wide, 25 cm long and 10 cm high is made from wood 1 cm thick. Find the surface area:
    a   outside the box (do not include the top edge)
    b   inside the box (do not include the top edge)

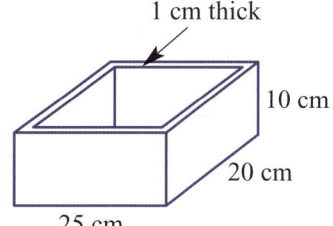
1 cm thick
10 cm
20 cm
25 cm

11 Draw the stack of 1 cm cube blocks that gives the minimum outside surface area and state this surface area if there are
    a   2 blocks   b   4 blocks   c   8 blocks

12 Cubes of side length one unit are stacked as shown.

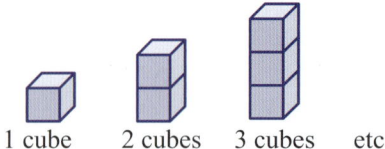

1 cube   2 cubes   3 cubes   etc.

a Complete this table.

Number of cubes (n)	1	2	3	4	5	6	7	8	9
Surface area (S)									

b Can you find the rule for the surface area (S) for n cubes stacked in this way? Write down the rule for S in terms of n.

c Investigate other ways of stacking cubes and look for rules for surface area in terms of n, the number of cubes.

Enrichment: Pythagoras required

13 For prisms and pyramids involving triangles, Pythagoras' theorem ($c^2 = a^2 + b^2$) can be used. Apply the theorem to help find the surface area of these solids. Round to one decimal place.

a
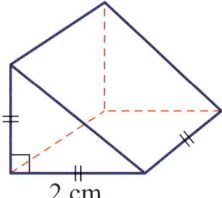
2 cm

b
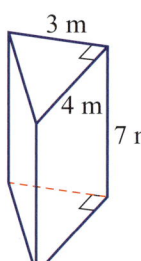
3 m
4 m
7 m

c
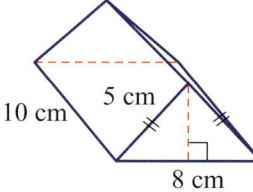
10 cm   5 cm
8 cm

d
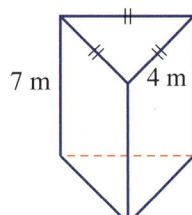
7 m   4 m

e
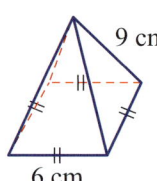
9 cm
6 cm

f
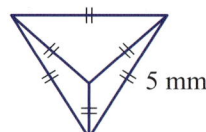
5 mm

5.6 Surface area of a cylinder

The net of a cylinder includes two circles and one rectangle. The length of the rectangle is equal to the circumference of the circle.

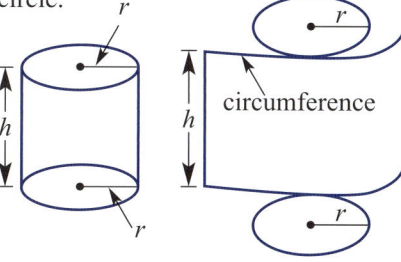
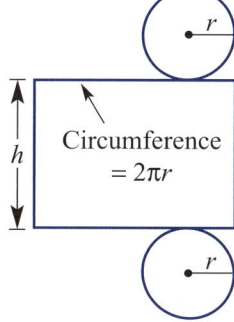

These pipes are hollow cylinders, like the rolled-up paper sheets.

→ Let's start: Curved area

- Roll a piece of paper to form the curved surface of a cylinder.
- Do not stick the ends together so you can allow the paper to return to a flat surface.
- What shape is the paper when lying flat on a table?
- When curved to form the cylinder, what do the sides of the rectangle represent on the cylinder? How does this help to find the surface area of a cylinder?

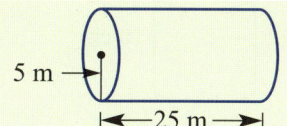

■ Surface area of a **cylinder** = 2 circles + 1 rectangle
$$= 2 \times \pi r^2 + 2\pi r \times h$$
$$\therefore \text{TSA} = 2\pi r^2 + 2\pi r h$$

2 circular ends   curved area

or TSA $= 2\pi r(r + h)$

Key ideas

Example 11 Finding the surface area of a cylinder

Find the surface area of this cylinder, rounding to two decimal places.

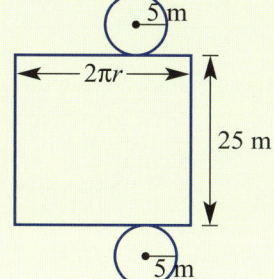

5 m

⊢—25 m—⊣

SOLUTION

TSA $= 2\pi r^2 + 2\pi r h$
$= 2 \times \pi \times 5^2 + 2\pi \times 5 \times 25$
$= 50 \times \pi + 250 \times \pi$
$= 50\pi + 250\pi$
$= 300\pi$
$= 942.48 \text{ m}^2$

EXPLANATION

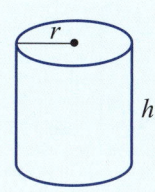

Example 12 Finding surface areas of cylindrical portions

Find the surface area of this half-cylinder, rounding to two decimal places.

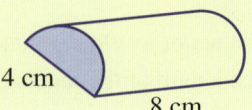
4 cm
8 cm

SOLUTION

$$\text{TSA} = 2\left(\frac{1}{2}\pi r^2\right) + \frac{1}{2}(2\pi r) \times 8 + 4 \times 8$$

$$= 2 \times \frac{1}{2}\pi \times 2^2 + \frac{1}{2} \times 2 \times \pi \times 2 \times 8 + 32$$

$$= 20\pi + 32$$

$$= 94.83 \text{ cm}^2$$

EXPLANATION

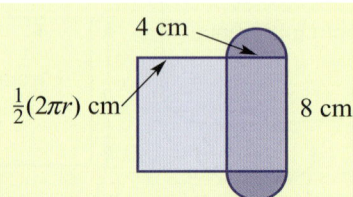
4 cm
$\frac{1}{2}(2\pi r)$ cm
8 cm

Exercise 5F

Understanding

1 Draw a net suited to these cylinders. Label the sides using the given measurements.

a $C = 26$

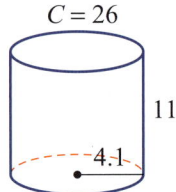
11
4.1

b $C = 31.4$

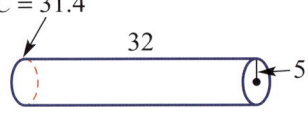
32
5

2 The curved surface of these cylinders is allowed to flatten out to form a rectangle. What would be the length and width of this rectangle? Round to two decimal places where necessary.

a $C = 22$ cm

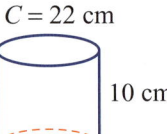
10 cm

b

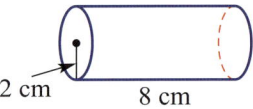
2 cm
8 cm

c

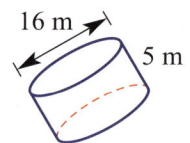
16 m
5 m

Fluency

Example 11

3 Find the surface area of these cylinders, rounding to two decimal places. Use a net to help.

a   1 m

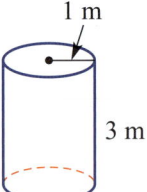
3 m

b

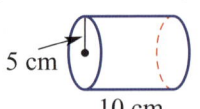
5 cm
10 cm

c   2 m

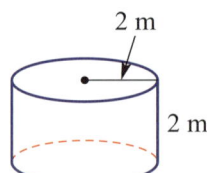
2 m

4 Find the surface area of these cylinders, rounding to one decimal place. Remember that the radius of a circle is half the diameter.

a
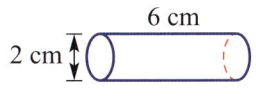
6 cm
2 cm

b
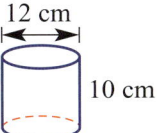
12 cm
10 cm

c
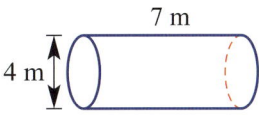
7 m
4 m

5 Find the surface area of a cylindrical plastic container of height 18 cm and with a circle of radius 3 cm at each end, correct to two decimal places.

6 Find the area of the curved surface only for these cylinders, correct to two decimal places.

a
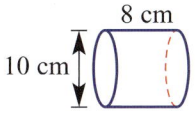
8 cm
10 cm

b
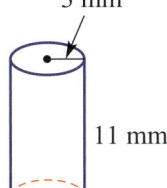
3 mm
11 mm

c
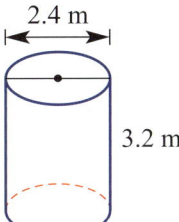
2.4 m
3.2 m

Example 12

7 Find the surface area of these solids, rounding to two decimal places.

a
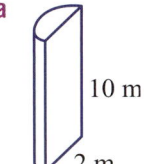
10 m
2 m

b
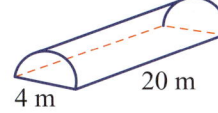
20 m
4 m

c
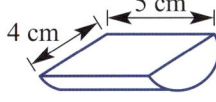
5 cm
4 cm

d
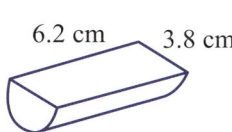
6.2 cm   3.8 cm

e
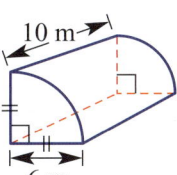
10 m
6 m

f
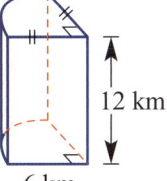
12 km
6 km

g
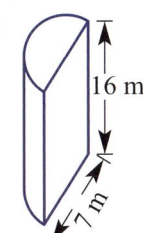
16 m
7 m

h
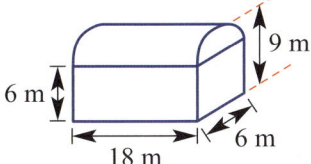
9 m
6 m
18 m
6 m

i
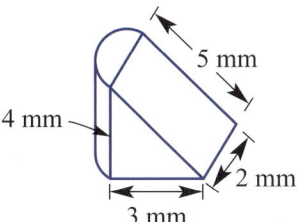
5 mm
4 mm
2 mm
3 mm

8 A water trough is in the shape of a half-cylinder. Its semicircular ends have diameter 40 cm and the trough length is 1 m. Find the outside surface area in cm² of the curved surface plus the two semicircular ends, correct to two decimal places.

9 A log with diameter 60 cm is 3 m in length. Its hollow centre is 20 cm in diameter. Find the surface area of the log in cm², including the ends and the inside, correct to one decimal place.

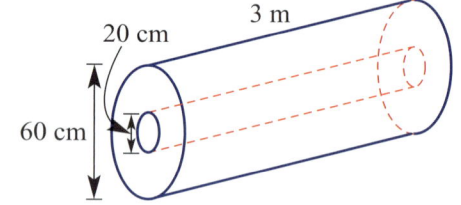

10 A cylindrical roller is used to press crushed rock in preparation for a tennis court. The rectangular tennis court area is 30 m long and 15 m wide. The roller has a width of 1 m and diameter 60 cm.

a Find the surface area of the curved part of the roller in cm² correct to three decimal places.

b Find the area, in m² to two decimal places, of crushed rock that can be pressed after:

i 1 revolution **ii** 20 revolutions

c Find the minimum number of complete revolutions required to press the entire tennis court area.

Problem-solving

---

11 It is more precise to give exact values for calculations involving π, e.g. 24π. Give the exact answers to the surface area of the cylinders in Question **3**.

12 A cylinder cut in half gives half the volume but not half the surface area. Explain why.

Reasoning

Enrichment: Solid sectors

13 The sector area rule $A = \dfrac{\theta}{360} \times \pi r^2$ can be applied to find the surface areas of solids which have ends that are sectors. Find the exact surface area of these solids.

a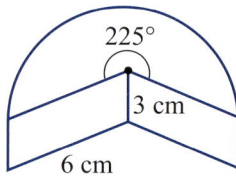

b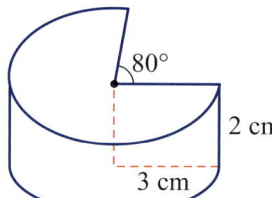

c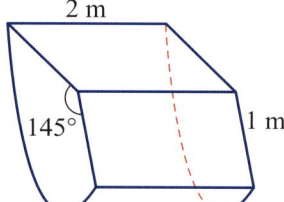

5.7 Volume

Volume is the number of cubic units contained within a three-dimensional object.

To find the volume we can count 24 cubic centimetres (24 cm^3) *or* multiply $3 \times 4 \times 2 = 24$ cm^3.

We can see that the area of the base ($3 \times 4 = 12$ cm^2) also gives the volume of the base layer 1 cm high. The number of layers equals the height, hence, multiplying the area of the base by the height will give the volume.

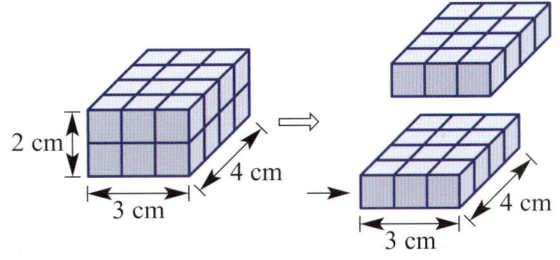

This idea can be applied to all right prisms provided a uniform cross-section can be identified. In such solids, the height length used to calculate the volume is the length of the edge running perpendicular to the base or cross-section.

Let's start: Cubic units

Consider this 1 cm cube divided into cubic millimetres.

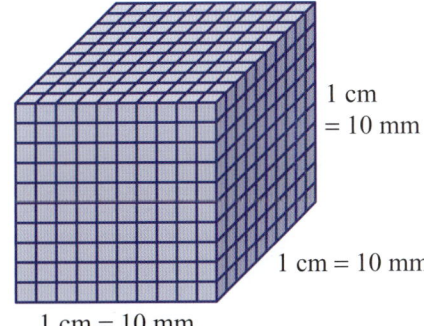

1 cm = 10 mm
1 cm = 10 mm
1 cm = 10 mm

- How many cubic mm sit on one edge of the 1 cm cube?
- How many cubic mm sit on one layer of the 1 cm cube?
- How many cubic mm are there in total in the 1 cm cube?
- Complete this statement 1 cm^3 = _____ mm^3
- Explain how you can find how many:
  - cm^3 in 1 m^3 • m^3 in 1 km^3

- Common metric units for **volume** include **cubic kilometres** (km^3), **cubic metres** (m^3), **cubic centimetres** (cm^3) and **cubic millimetres** (mm^3).

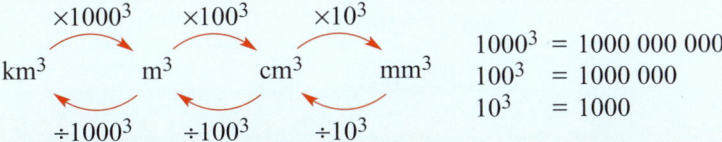

$$1000^3 = 1\,000\,000\,000$$
$$100^3 = 1\,000\,000$$
$$10^3 = 1000$$

- For **capacity** common units include:
  - **Megalitres** (ML)   1 ML = 1000 kL   • **Litres** (L)   1 L = 1000 mL
  - **Kilolitres** (kL)   1 kL = 1000 L   • **Millilitres** (mL)

  Also 1 cm^3 = 1 mL so 1 L = 1000 cm^3 and 1 m^3 = 1000 L
- Volume of solids with a uniform **cross-section** is equal to area of cross-section (A) × height (h).
  $$V = A \times h$$

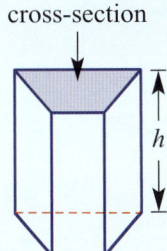

cross-section

h

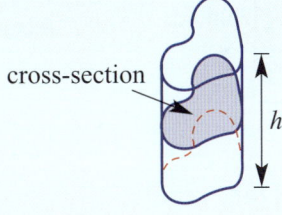

cross-section

h

- The 'height' is the length of the edge that runs perpendicular to the cross-section.

Some common formulas for volume include:

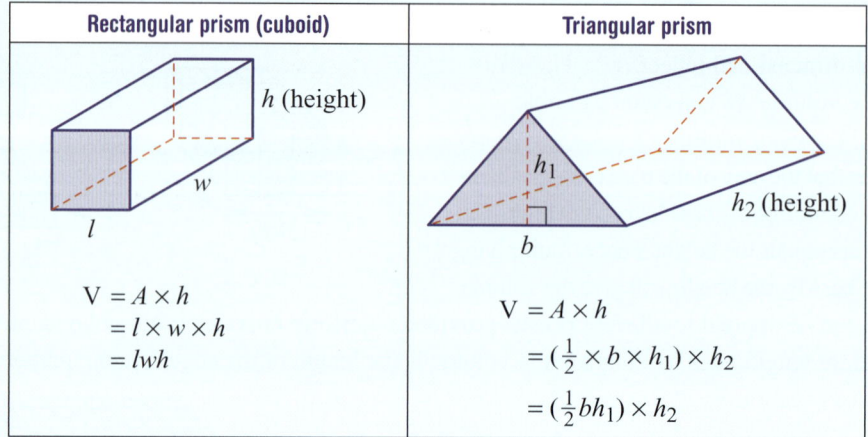

Rectangular prism (cuboid)	Triangular prism

h (height)
w
l

$V = A \times h$
$\quad = l \times w \times h$
$\quad = lwh$

h_1
h_2 (height)
b

$V = A \times h$
$\quad = (\frac{1}{2} \times b \times h_1) \times h_2$
$\quad = (\frac{1}{2}bh_1) \times h_2$

Example 13 Converting units of volume

Convert the following volume measurements into the units given in the brackets.

a 2.5 m^3 (cm^3)
b 458 mm^3 (cm^3)

SOLUTION

EXPLANATION

a $2.5 \text{ m}^3 = 2.5 \times 100^3 \text{ cm}^3$
$\quad = 2\,500\,000 \text{ cm}^3$

$\times 100^3 = 1\,000\,000$

$\text{m}^3 \qquad \text{cm}^3 \qquad 2.500000$

b $458 \text{ mm}^3 = 458 \div 10^3 \text{ cm}^3$
$\quad = 0.458 \text{ cm}^3$

$\text{cm}^3 \qquad \text{mm}^3$

$\div 10^3 = 1000 \qquad 458.$

Example 14 Finding volumes of prisms and other solids

Find the volume of each of these three-dimensional objects.

a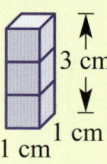
3 cm
1 cm
1 cm

b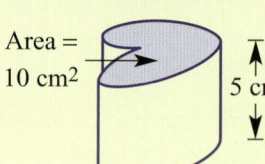
Area = 10 cm²
5 cm

c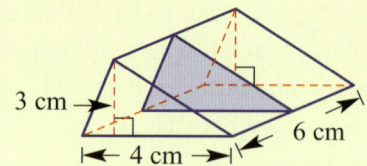
3 cm
4 cm
6 cm

SOLUTION

EXPLANATION

a Volume $= l \times w \times h$
$\quad = 1 \times 1 \times 3$
$\quad = 3 \text{ cm}^3$

The solid is a rectangular prism.
Length = 1 cm, width = 1 cm and height = 3 cm

b Volume = area of cross-section × height   Substitute cross-sectional area = 10 and height = 5.

$= 10 \times 5$

$= 50 \text{ cm}^3$

c Volume = area of cross-section × height   The cross-section is a triangle.

$= \left(\dfrac{1}{2} \times b \times h_1 \right) \times h_2$

$= \dfrac{1}{2}(4 \times 3) \times 6$

$= 36 \text{ cm}^3$

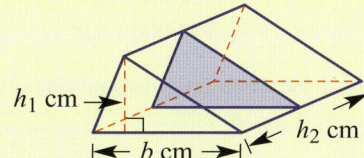

h_1 cm h_2 cm b cm

Exercise 5G

1 Draw the cross-sectional shape for these prisms and state the 'height' (perpendicular to the cross-section).

a
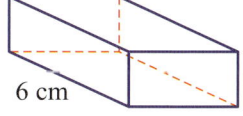
6 cm

b
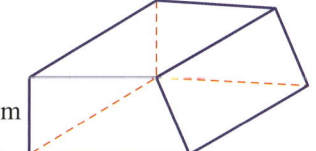
10 cm

c
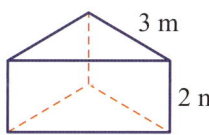
3 m
2 m

d
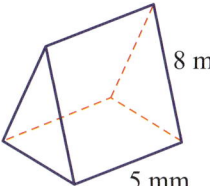
8 mm
5 mm

e
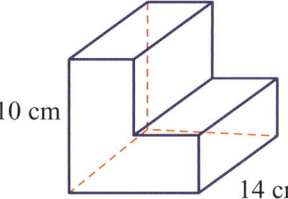
10 cm
8 cm   14 cm

f
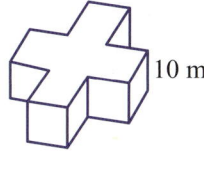
10 m

2 What is the name given to the shape of the shaded cross-section of each of the following solids?

a
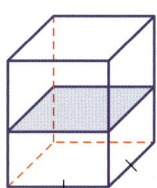

b
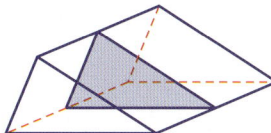

c
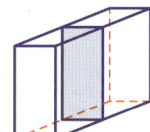

d
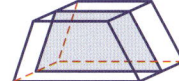

e
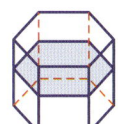

f
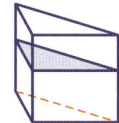

Example 13   **3**   Convert the following volume measurements into the units given in the brackets.

       a 3 cm^3 (mm^3)   **b** 2000 mm^3 (cm^3)   **c** 8.7 m^3 (cm^3)

       d 5900 cm^3 (m^3)   **e** 0.00001 km^3 (m^3)   **f** $21\,700 \text{ m}^3$ (km^3)

       g   3 L (mL)   **h**   0.2 kL (L)   **i**   3500 mL (L)

       j   0.021 L (mL)   **k**   37 000 L (kL)   **l**   42 900 kL (ML)

Example 14a   **4**   Find the volume of these three-dimensional rectangular prisms.

       a 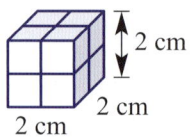 **b** 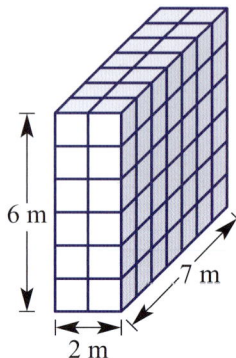 **c**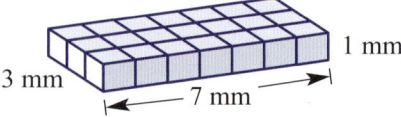

Example 14b   **5**   Find the volume of each of these three-dimensional objects. The cross-sectional area has been given.

       a   Area = 2 cm^2 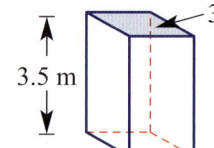 **b** 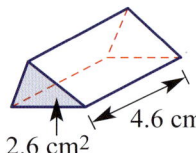 **c**

       d 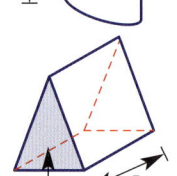 **e** 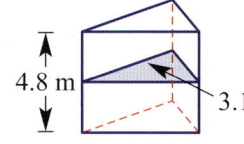 **f**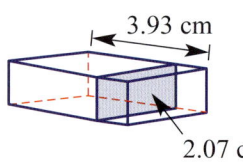

       g 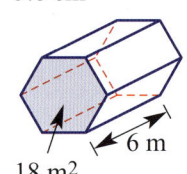 **h** 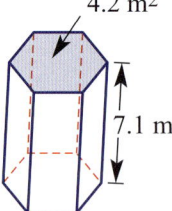 **i**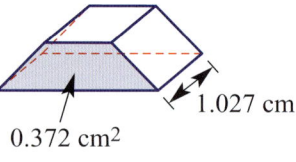

Example 14c   **6**   Find the volume of these prisms.

       a 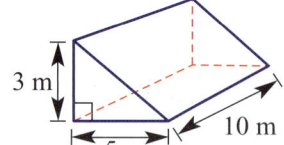 **b** 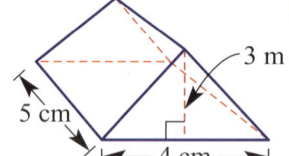 **c**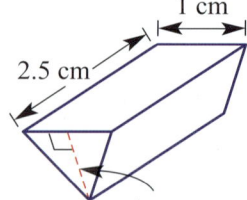

7 Find the volume of each of these rectangular prisms (cuboids).

a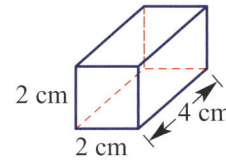
2 cm
2 cm
4 cm

b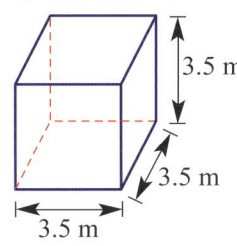
3.5 m
3.5 m
3.5 m

c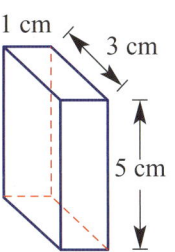
1 cm
3 cm
5 cm

8 Find the volume of these solids converting your answer to litres.

a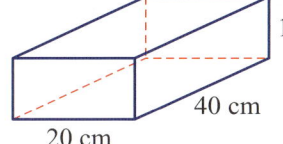
10 cm
40 cm
20 cm

b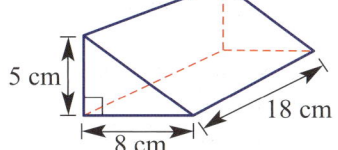
5 cm
8 cm
18 cm

c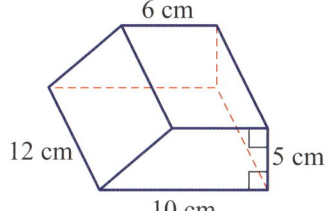
6 cm
12 cm
10 cm
5 cm

9 A brick is 10 cm wide, 20 cm long and 8 cm high. How much space would five of these bricks occupy?

10 How much air space is contained inside a rectangular cardboard box that has the dimensions 85 cm by 62 cm by 36 cm. Answer using cubic metres (m^3) correct to two decimal places.

11 25 L of water is poured into a rectangular fish tank which is 50 cm long, 20 cm wide and 20 cm high. Will it overflow?

12 Find the volume of each of the following solids, rounding to one decimal place where necessary.

a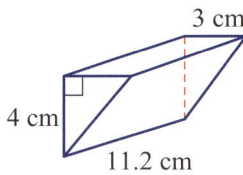
3 cm
4 cm
11.2 cm

b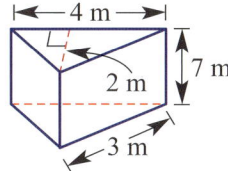
4 m
2 m
7 m
3 m

c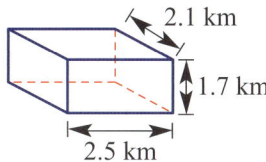
2.1 km
1.7 km
2.5 km

d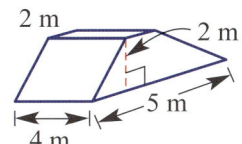
2 m
2 m
5 m
4 m

e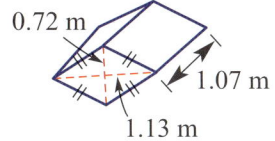
0.72 m
1.07 m
1.13 m

f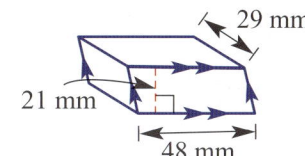
29 mm
21 mm
48 mm

13 Use units for capacity to find the volume of these solids in litres.

a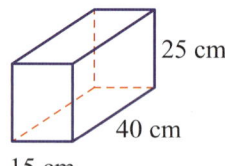

b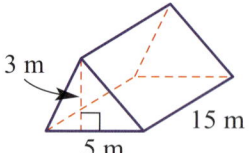

c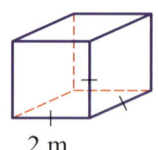

14 The given diagram is a sketch of a new 25 m swimming pool to be installed in a school sports complex.

a Find the area of one side of the pool (shaded).

b Find the volume of the pool in litres.

15 a What single number do you multiply by to convert from:

  i L to cm^3?

  ii L to m^3?

  iii mL to mm^3?

b What single number do you divide by to convert from:

  i mm^3 to L?

  ii m^3 to ML?

  iii cm^3 to kL?

16 Write rules for the volume of these solids using the given pronumerals.

a A rectangular prism with length = width = x and height h.

b A cube with side length s.

c A rectangular prism with a square base (with side length t) and height 6 times the side length of the base.

Enrichment: Volume of a pyramid

17 Earlier we looked at finding the total surface area of a right pyramid like the one shown here.

Imagine the pyramid sitting inside a prism with the same base.

a Make an educated guess as to what fraction of the prism's volume is the pyramid's volume.

b Use the internet to find the actual answer to part **a**.

c Draw some pyramids and find their volume using the results from part **b**.

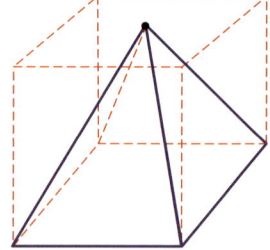

5.8 Volume of a cylinder

Technically, a cylinder is not a right prism because its sides are not rectangles. It does, however, have a uniform cross-section (a circle) and so a cylinder's volume can be calculated in a similar way to that of a right prism. Cylindrical objects are commonly used to store gases and liquids and so working out the volume of a cylinder is an important measurement calculation.

The volume of liquid in this tanker can be calculated using the volume formula for a cylinder.

Let's start: Writing the rule

Previously we used the formula $V = A \times h$ to find the volume of solids with a uniform cross-section.

- Discuss any similarities between the two given solids.
- How can the rule $V = A \times h$ be developed further to find the rule for the volume of a cylinder?

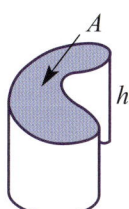 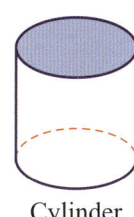

Cylinder

- The volume of a cylinder is given by
  $V = \pi r^2 \times h$ or $V = \pi r^2 h$
  - r is the radius of the circular ends
  - h is the length or distance between the circular ends

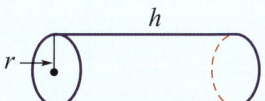

Key ideas

Example 15 Finding the volume of a cylinder

Find the volume of these cylinders correct to two decimal places.

a
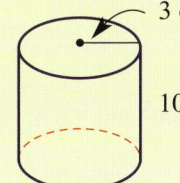
3 cm
10 cm

b
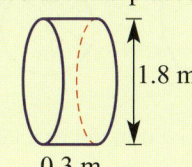
1.8 m
0.3 m

SOLUTION

a $V = \pi r^2 h$
  $= \pi \times (3)^2 \times 10$
  $= 90\pi$
  $= 282.74 \text{ cm}^3$

b $V = \pi r^2 h$
  $= \pi \times (0.9)^2 \times 0.3$
  $= 0.76 \text{ m}^3$

EXPLANATION

Substitute $r = 3$ and $h = 10$ into the rule.
$90\pi \text{ cm}^3$ would be the exact answer.

The diameter is 1.8 m so $r = 0.9$.

Example 16 Finding the capacity of a cylinder

Find the capacity in litres of a cylinder with radius 30 cm and height 90 cm. Round to the nearest litre.

SOLUTION	EXPLANATION
$V = \pi r^2 h$	
$\quad = \pi \times (30)^2 \times 90$	Substitute $r = 30$ and $h = 90$.
$\quad = 254469 \text{ cm}^3$	There are 1000 cm³ in 1 L so divide by 1000 to
$\quad = 254 \text{ L}$	convert to litres.

Exercise 5H

Understanding

1 State the radius and the height of these cylinders.

a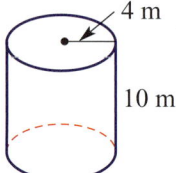
4 m
10 m

b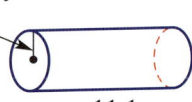
2.6 cm
11.1 cm

c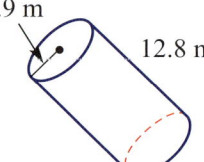
2.9 m
12.8 m

d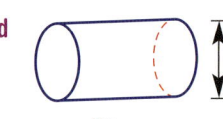
18 m
23 m

e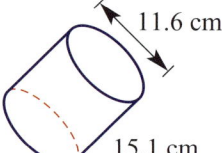
11.6 cm
15.1 cm

f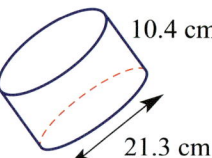
10.4 cm
21.3 cm

2 Find the area of these circles correct to two decimal places.

a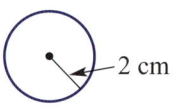
2 cm

b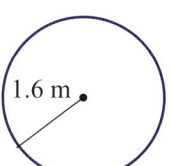
1.6 m

c
10 cm

d
1.8 km

3 Convert the following into the units given in the brackets. Remember, 1 L = 1000 cm³ and
1 m³ = 1000 L.

a 2000 cm³ (L) **b** 4.3 cm³ (mL) **c** 3.7 L (cm³)
d 1 m³ (L) **e** 38 000 L (m³) **f** 0.0002 m³ (mL)

Example 15

4 Find the volume of these cylinders correct to two decimal places.

a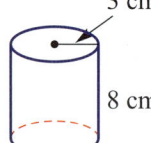
3 cm
8 cm

b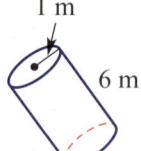
1 m
6 m

c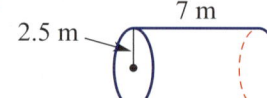
7 m
2.5 m

Fluency

d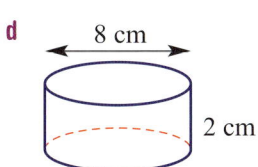
8 cm
2 cm

e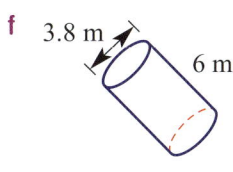
3 m
1.2 m

f 3.8 m
6 m

mple 16

5 Find the capacity in litres of these cylinders. Round to the nearest litre. Remember
1 L = 1000 cm^3 and 1 m^3 = 1000 L.

a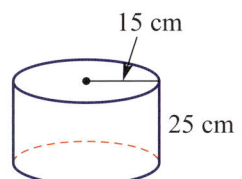
15 cm
25 cm

b
40 cm 100 cm

c 50 cm
10 cm

d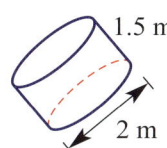
1.5 m
2 m

e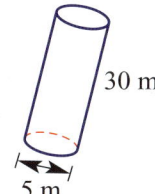
30 m
5 m

f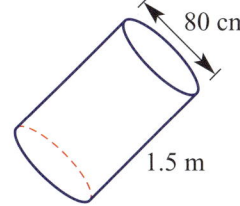
80 cm
1.5 m

6 A cylindrical water tank has a radius of 2 m and a height of 2 m.
  a Find its capacity in m^3 rounded to three decimal places.
  b Find its capacity in L rounded to the nearest litre.

7 How many litres of gas can a tanker carry if its tank is cylindrical with a 2 m diameter and is
12 m in length? Round to the nearest litre.

8 Which has a bigger volume and what is the difference in volume to two decimal places? A cube
with side length 1 m or a cylinder with radius 1 m and height 0.5 m.

9 Find the volume of these cylindrical portions correct to two decimal places.

a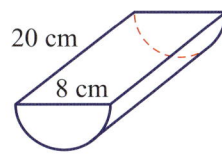
20 cm
8 cm

b
1.2 m
1.8 m

c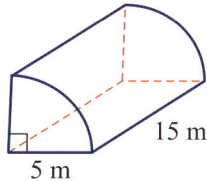
15 m
5 m

d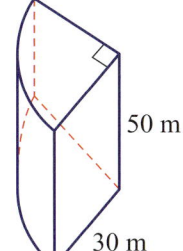
50 m
30 m

e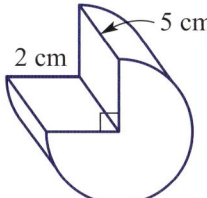
5 cm
2 cm

f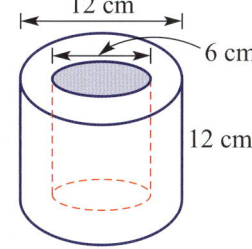
12 cm
6 cm
12 cm

10 The rule for the volume of a cylinder is $V = \pi r^2 h$. Show how you could use this rule to find, correct to three decimal places:

a h if $V = 20$ and $r = 3$.

b r if $V = 100$ and $h = 5$.

11 Using exact values (e.g. 20π) find the volume of these solids.

a 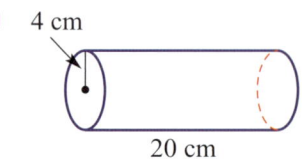 8 m · 10 m

b 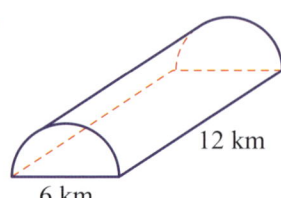 4 cm · 20 cm

c 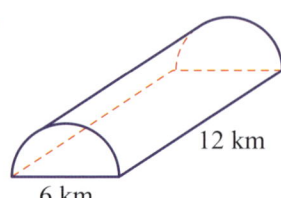 12 km · 6 km

d 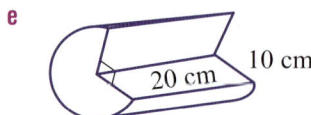 3 cm · 1 cm

e 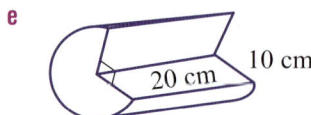 20 cm · 10 cm

f 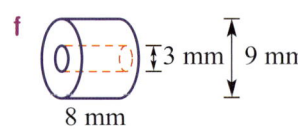 3 mm · 9 mm · 8 mm

12 Draw a cylinder with its circumference equal to its height. Try to draw it to scale.

Enrichment: Solid sectors

13 You will recall that the area of a sector is given by $A = \dfrac{\theta}{360} \times \pi r^2$.

Use this fact to help find the volume of these solids correct to two decimal places.

a 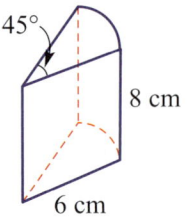 45° · 8 cm · 6 cm

b 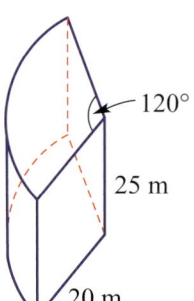 120° · 25 m · 20 m

c 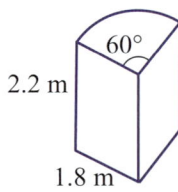 60° · 2.2 m · 1.8 m

d 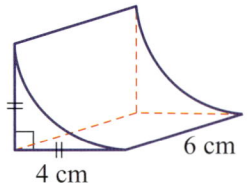 4 cm · 6 cm

e 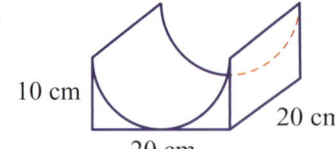 10 cm · 20 cm · 20 cm

f 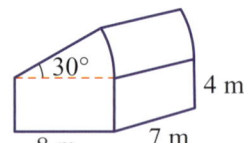 30° · 4 m · 8 m · 7 m

Capacity and depth

Finding capacity

Find the capacity in litres of these containers (i.e. find the total volume of fluid they can hold).

a
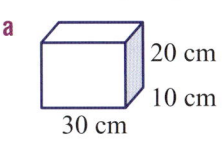
20 cm
10 cm
30 cm

b
30 cm
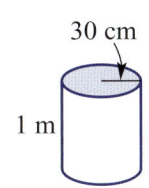
1 m

> Remember: 1 millilitre (mL) of fluid occupies 1 cm^3 of space therefore 1 litre (L) occupies 1000 cm^3 as there are 1000 mL in 1 litre.

Designing containers

Design a container with the given shape which has a 10 litre capacity. You will need to state the dimensions – length, width, height, radius etc. and calculate its capacity.

a   rectangular prism

b   cylinder

Finding depth

The depth of water in a prism can be found if the base (cross-sectional) area and volume of water are given.

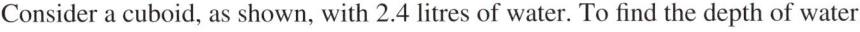
10 cm
20 cm
depth
(d)
20 cm

Consider a cuboid, as shown, with 2.4 litres of water. To find the depth of water:

- Convert the volume to cm^3: 2.4 L $= 2.4 \times 1000$
$$= 2400 \text{ cm}^3$$

- Find the depth: Volume = area of base $\times d$
$$2400 = 20 \times 20 \times d$$
$$2400 = 400 \times d$$
$$\therefore d = 6$$
$$\therefore \text{depth is 6 cm}$$

Use the above method to find the depth of water in these prisms.

a
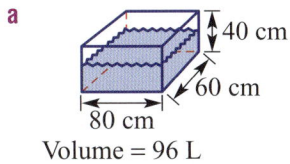
40 cm
60 cm
80 cm
Volume = 96 L

b
20 cm
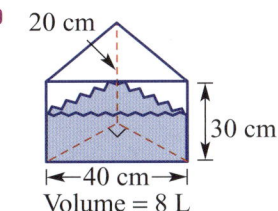
30 cm
40 cm
Volume = 8 L

c
60 cm
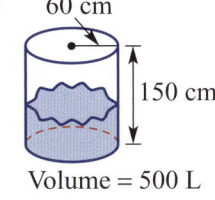
150 cm
Volume = 500 L

Volumes of odd-shaped objects

Some solids may be peculiar in shape and their volume may be difficult to measure.

a   A rare piece of rock is placed into a cylindrical jug of water and the water depth rises from 10 cm to 11 cm. The radius of the jug is 5 cm.

    i   Find the area of the circular base of the cylinder.

    ii   Find the volume of water in the jug before the rock is placed in the jug.

    iii   Find the volume of water in the jug including the rock.

    iv   Hence find the volume of the rock.

b   Use the procedure outlined in part **a i–iv** above to find the volume of an object of your choice. Explain and show your working and compare your results with other students in your class if they are measuring the volume of the same object.

Challenges

1   A 100 m² factory flat roof feeds all the water collected to a rainwater tank. If there is 1 mm of rainfall, how many litres of water go into the tank?

2   What is the relationship between the shaded and non-shaded regions in this circular diagram?

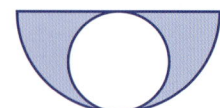

3   A goat is tethered to the centre of one side of a shed with a 10 m length of rope. What area of grass can the goat graze?

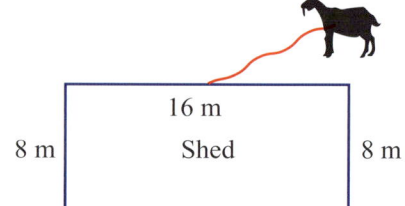

4   A rain gauge is in the shape of a triangular prism with dimensions as shown. What is the depth of water when it is half full?

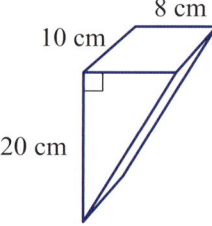

5   A rectangular fish tank has base area 0.3 m² and height 30 cm and is filled with 80 L of water. Ten large fish with volume 50 cm³ each are placed into the tank. By how much does the water rise?

6   If it takes 4 people 8 days to knit 2 rugs, how many days will it take for 1 person to knit 1 rug?

7   Find the rule for the volume of a cylinder in terms of r only if the height is equal to its circumference.

8   The surface area of a cylinder is 2π square units. Find a rule for h in terms of r.

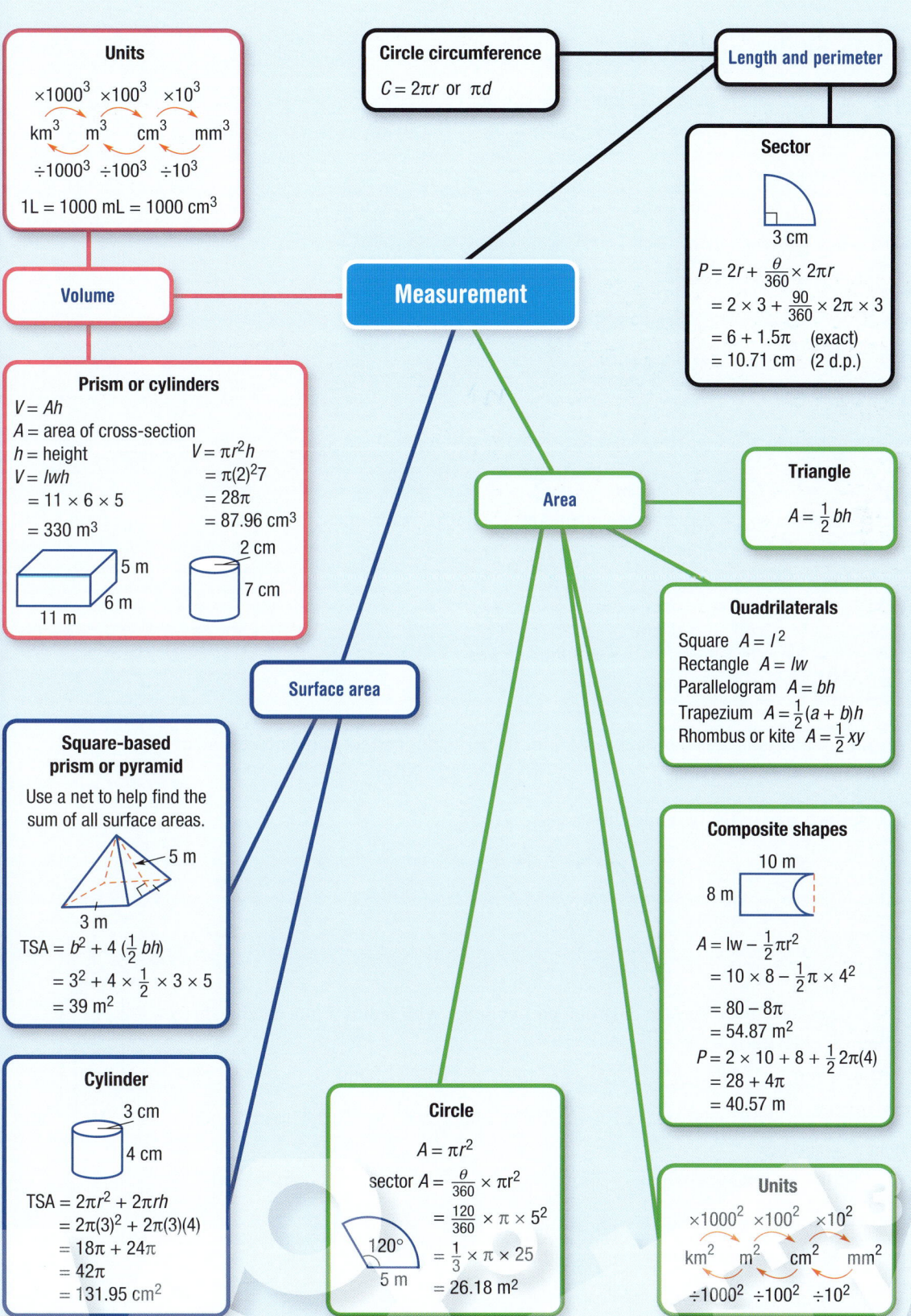

Chapter summary

Units

$\times 1000^3 \quad \times 100^3 \quad \times 10^3$

$km^3 \quad m^3 \quad cm^3 \quad mm^3$

$\div 1000^3 \quad \div 100^3 \quad \div 10^3$

$1L = 1000 \text{ mL} = 1000 \text{ cm}^3$

Circle circumference

$C = 2\pi r$ or πd

Length and perimeter

Sector

3 cm

$P = 2r + \dfrac{\theta}{360} \times 2\pi r$

$= 2 \times 3 + \dfrac{90}{360} \times 2\pi \times 3$

$= 6 + 1.5\pi \quad (\text{exact})$

$= 10.71 \text{ cm} \quad (2 \text{ d.p.})$

Measurement

Volume

Prism or cylinders

$V = Ah$
A = area of cross-section
h = height
$V = lwh \qquad\qquad V = \pi r^2 h$
$= 11 \times 6 \times 5 \qquad = \pi(2)^2 7$
$= 330 \text{ m}^3 \qquad\quad = 28\pi$
$\qquad\qquad\qquad = 87.96 \text{ cm}^3$

5 m
6 m
11 m

2 cm
7 cm

Area

Triangle

$A = \dfrac{1}{2}bh$

Quadrilaterals

Square $A = l^2$
Rectangle $A = lw$
Parallelogram $A = bh$
Trapezium $A = \dfrac{1}{2}(a + b)h$
Rhombus or kite $A = \dfrac{1}{2}xy$

Surface area

Square-based prism or pyramid

Use a net to help find the sum of all surface areas.

5 m
3 m

$\text{TSA} = b^2 + 4\left(\dfrac{1}{2}bh\right)$
$= 3^2 + 4 \times \dfrac{1}{2} \times 3 \times 5$
$= 39 \text{ m}^2$

Composite shapes

10 m
8 m

$A = lw - \dfrac{1}{2}\pi r^2$
$= 10 \times 8 - \dfrac{1}{2}\pi \times 4^2$
$= 80 - 8\pi$
$= 54.87 \text{ m}^2$
$P = 2 \times 10 + 8 + \dfrac{1}{2}2\pi(4)$
$= 28 + 4\pi$
$= 40.57 \text{ m}$

Cylinder

3 cm
4 cm

$\text{TSA} = 2\pi r^2 + 2\pi rh$
$= 2\pi(3)^2 + 2\pi(3)(4)$
$= 18\pi + 24\pi$
$= 42\pi$
$= 131.95 \text{ cm}^2$

Circle

$A = \pi r^2$

sector $A = \dfrac{\theta}{360} \times \pi r^2$
$= \dfrac{120}{360} \times \pi \times 5^2$
$= \dfrac{1}{3} \times \pi \times 25$
$= 26.18 \text{ m}^2$

120°
5 m

Units

$\times 1000^2 \quad \times 100^2 \quad \times 10^2$

$km^2 \quad m^2 \quad cm^2 \quad mm^2$

$\div 1000^2 \quad \div 100^2 \quad \div 10^2$

Multiple-choice questions

1 If the area of a square field is 25 km^2, its perimeter is:

    A 10 km   **B** 20 km   **C** 5 km   **D** 50 km   **E** 25 km

2 2.7 m^2 is the same as:

    A 270 cm^2 **B** 0.0027 km^2 **C** 27 000 cm^2 **D** 2700 mm^2 **E** 27 cm^2

3 The perimeter of this shape is:

    A 21 cm

    B 14 cm

    C 24 cm

    D 20 cm

    E 22 cm

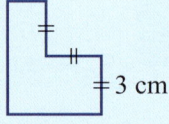

4 A parallelogram has area 10 m^2 and base 5 m. Its perpendicular height is:

    A 50 m   **B** 2 m   **C** 50 m^2 **D** 2 m^2 **E** 0.5 m

5 This composite shape could be considered as a rectangle with an area in the shape of a trapezium removed. The shape's area is:

    A 16 km^2

    B 12 km^2

    C 20 km^2

    D 24 km^2

    E 6 km^2

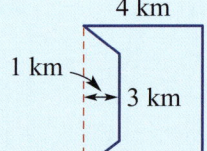

6 A semicircular goal area has diameter 20 m. Its perimeter correct to the nearest metre is:

    A 41 m   **B** 36 m   **C** 83 m   **D** 51 m   **E** 52 m

7 The surface area of the pyramid shown is:

    A 185 cm^2

    B 105 cm^2

    C 65 cm^2

    D 100 cm^2

    E 125 cm^2

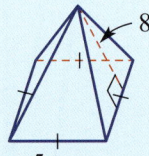

8 The area of the curved surface only of a half-cylinder with radius 5 mm and height 12 mm is closest to:

    A 942.5 mm^2 **B** 94.2 mm^2 **C** 377 mm^2 **D** 471.2 mm^2 **E** 188.5 mm^2

9 A prism's cross-sectional area is 100 m^2. If its volume is 6500 m^3, the prism's total height would be:

    A 0.65 m   **B** 650 000 m   **C** 65 m   **D** 6.5 m   **E** 650 m

10 The exact volume of a cylinder with radius 3 cm and height 10 cm is:

    A 60π cm^2 **B** 80π cm   **C** 45π cm^3 **D** 30π cm^3 **E** 90π cm^3

Short-answer questions

1 Convert the following measurements into the units given in brackets.

  a 3.8 m (cm) **b** 1.27 km (m) **c** 273 mm^2 (cm^2)

  d 5.2 m^2 (cm^2) **e** 0.01 m^3 (cm^3) **f** 53 100 mm^3 (cm^3)

  g 3100 mL (L) **h** 0.043 L (mL) **i** 2.83 kL (L)

2 Find the perimeter of each of the following shapes.

  a 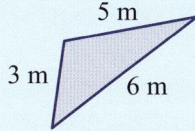 **b** 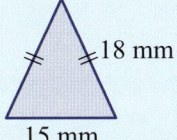 **c**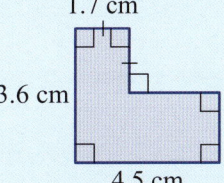

3 Find the area of each of the following plane figures.

  a 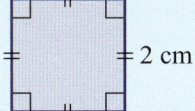 **b** 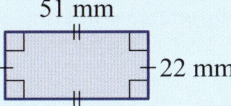 **c**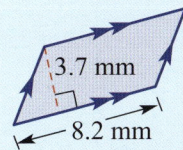

  d 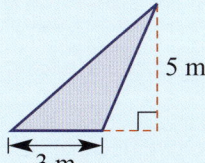 **e** 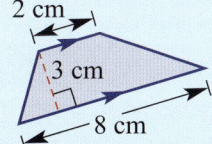 **f**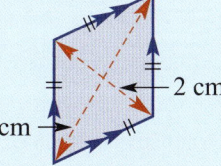

4 Inside a rectangular lawn area of length 10.5 m and width 3.8 m, a new garden bed is to be constructed. The garden bed is to be the shape of a triangle with base 2 m and height 2.5 m. With the aid of a diagram, find:

  a the area of the garden bed

  b the area of the lawn remaining around the garden bed.

5 Find the area and circumference/perimeter of each of the following shapes correct to two decimal places.

  a 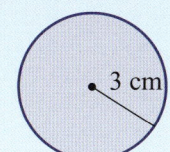 **b** 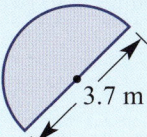 **c**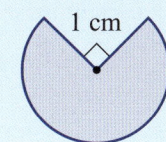

6 Find the perimeter and area of these sectors. Round to two decimal places.

a

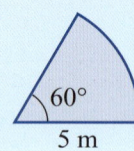

60°
5 m

b

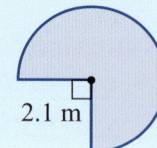

2.1 m

c

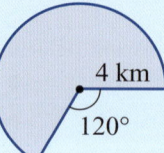

4 km
120°

7 Find the perimeter and area of each of the following composite shapes correct to two decimal places.

a

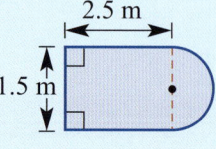

2.5 m
1.5 m

b

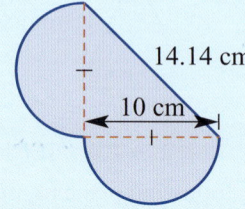

14.14 cm
10 cm

8 Find the total surface area of each of the following solid objects.

a

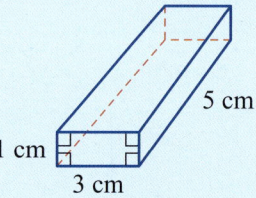

5 cm
1 cm
3 cm

b

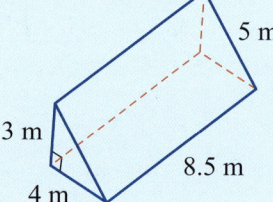

5 m
3 m
4 m
8.5 m

9 Find the total surface area of each of the following solid objects correct to two decimal places.

a

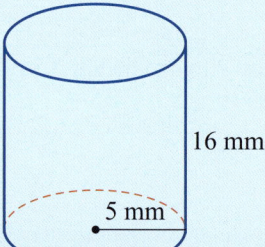

16 mm
5 mm

b

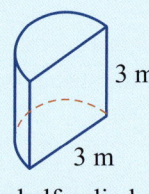

3 m
3 m
half-cylinder

10 Find the volume of each of these solid objects, rounding to two decimal places where necessary.

a

Area = 5 cm²

6 cm

b

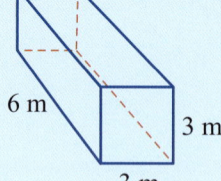

6 m
3 m
3 m

c

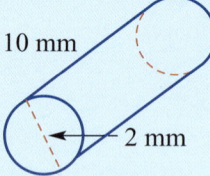

10 mm
2 mm

Extended-response questions

1 An office receives five new desks with a bench shape made up of a rectangle and quarter-circle as shown.

The edge of the bench is lined with a rubber strip at a cost of $2.50 per metre.

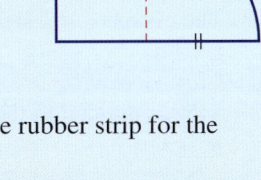

80 cm

1 m

a Find the length of the rubber edging strip in centimetres for one desk correct to two decimal places.

b By converting your answer in part **a** to metres, find the total cost of the rubber strip for the five desks. Round to the nearest dollar.

The manufacturer claims that the desk top area space is more than 1.5 m^2.

c Find the area of the desk top in cm^2 correct to two decimal places.

d Convert your answer to m^2 and determine whether or not the manufacturer's claim is correct.

2 Circular steel railing of diameter 6 cm is to be used to fence the side of a bridge. The railing is hollow and the radius of the hollow circular space is 2 cm.

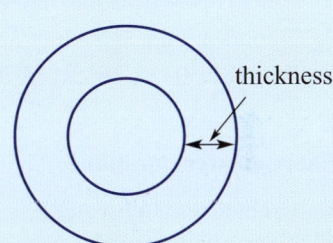

thickness

a By adding the given information to this diagram of the cross-section of the railing, determine the thickness of the steel.

b Determine, correct to two decimal places, the area of steel in the cross-section.

Eight lengths of railing at 10 m each are required for the bridge.

c Using your result from part **b**, find the volume of steel required for the bridge in cm^3.

d Convert your answer in part **c** to m^3.

The curved outside surface of the steel railings is to be painted to help protect the steel from the weather.

e Find the outer circumference of the cross-section of the railing correct to two decimal places.

f Find the total surface area in m^2 of the eight lengths of railing that are to be painted. Round to the nearest m^2.

The cost of the railing paint is $80 per m^2.

g Using your answer from part **f**, find the cost of painting the bridge rails to the nearest dollar.

Reviewing number and financial mathematics

Multiple-choice questions

1 $-3 + (4 + (-10)) \times (-2)$ is equal to:

   A 21   **B** 9   **C** 18   **D** -15   **E** -6

2 The estimate of $221.7 \div 43.4 - 0.0492$ using one significant figure rounding is:

   A 4.9   **B** 5.06   **C** 5.5   **D** 5   **E** 4.95

3 $450 is divided in the ratio 4 : 5. The value of the smaller portion is:

   A $210   **B** $250   **C** $90   **D** $200   **E** $220

4 A book that costs $27 is discounted by 15%. The new price is:

   A $20.25   **B** $31.05   **C** $4.05   **D** $22.95   **E** $25.20

5 Anna is paid a normal rate of $12.10 per hour. If in a week she works 6 hours at the normal rate, 2 hours at time and a half and 3 hours at double time, how much does she earn?

   A $181.50   **B** $145.20   **C** $193.60   **D** $175.45   **E** $163.35

Short-answer questions

1 Evaluate the following.

   a $\dfrac{3}{7} + \dfrac{1}{4}$ **b** $2\dfrac{1}{3} - 1\dfrac{5}{9}$ **c** $\dfrac{9}{10} \times \dfrac{5}{12}$ **d** $3\dfrac{3}{4} \div 2\dfrac{1}{12}$

2 Convert each of the following to a percentage.

   a 0.6   **b** $\dfrac{5}{16}$ **c** 2 kg out of 20 kg   **d** 75c out of $3

3 Write these rates and ratios in simplest form.

   a Prize money is shared between two people in the ratio 60 : 36.

   b Jodie travels 165 km in three hours.

   c 3 mL of rain falls in $1\dfrac{1}{4}$ hours.

4 Jeff earns a weekly retainer of $400 plus 6% of the sales he makes. If he sells $8200 worth of goods, how much will he earn for the week?

Extended-response question

Husband and wife Jim and Jill are trialling new banking arrangements.

   a Jill plans to trial a simple interest plan. Before investing her money she increases the amount in her account by 20% to $21 000.

     i What was the original amount in her account?

     ii She invests the $21 000 for 4 years at an interest rate of 3% p.a. How much does she have in her account at the end of the four years?

     iii She continues with this same plan and after a certain number of years has obtained $5670 interest. How many years has she had the money invested for?

     iv What percentage increase does this interest represent on her initial investment?

b Jim is investing his $21 000 in an account that compounds annually at 3% p.a. How much does he have after 4 years to the nearest cent?

c i Who had the most money after 4 years and by how much? Round to the nearest dollar.

  ii Who will have the most money after 10 years and by how much? Round to the nearest dollar.

Linear and simultaneous equations

Multiple-choice questions

1 The simplified form of to $5ab + 6a \div 2 + a \times 2b - a$ is:

  A $10ab$ **B** $10ab + 3a$ **C** $13ab - a$ **D** $5ab + 3a + 2b$ **E** $7ab + 2a$

2 The expanded form of $-2(3m - 4)$ is:

  A $-6m + 8$ **B** $-6m + 4$ **C** $-6m - 8$ **D** $-5m - 6$ **E** $5m + 8$

3 The solution to $\dfrac{d}{4} - 7 = 2$ is:

  A $d = -20$ **B** $d = 15$ **C** $d = 36$ **D** $d = 1$ **E** $d = 30$

4 The solution to $1 - 3x < 10$ represented on a number line is:

  A 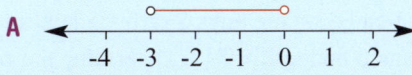   **B**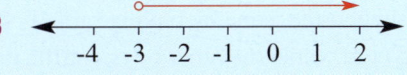

  C 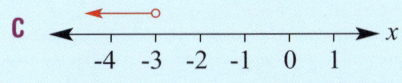   **D**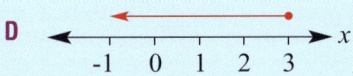

  E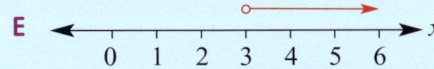

5 The formula $m = \sqrt{\dfrac{b-1}{a}}$ with b as the subject is:

  A $b = a\sqrt{m} + 1$ **B** $b = \dfrac{m^2}{a} + 1$ **C** $b = a^2 m^2 + 1$

  D $b = am^2 + 1$ **E** $b = m^2\sqrt{a} + 1$

Short-answer questions

1 Solve the following equations and inequalities.

  a $3x + 7 = 25$ **b** $\dfrac{2x - 1}{4} > 2$

  c $4(2m + 3) = 15$ **d** $-3(2y + 4) - 2y = -4$

  e $3(a + 1) \le 4 - 8a$ **f** $3(2x - 1) = -2(4x + 3)$

2 Noah receives m dollars pocket money per week. His younger brother Jake gets half of three dollars less than Noah's amount. If Jake receives $6:

  a write an equation to represent the problem

  b solve the equation in part **a** to determine how much Noah receives each week.

3 The formula $S = \dfrac{n}{2}(a + l)$ gives the sum S of a sequence of n numbers with first term a and last term l.

   a Find the sum of the sequence of 10 terms 2, 5, 8, ..., 29.

   b Rearrange the formula to make l the subject.

   c If a sequence of 8 terms has a sum of 88 and a first term equal to 4, use your answer to part **b** to find the last term of this sequence.

4 Solve the following equations simultaneously.

   a $x + 4y = 18$ **b** $7x - 2y = 3$ **c** $2x + 3y = 4$ **d** $3x + 4y = 7$

       $x = 2y$ $y = 2x - 3$ $x + y = 3$ $5x + 2y = -7$

Extended-response question

a Chris referees junior basketball games on a Sunday. He is paid $20 plus $12 per game he referees. He is trying to earn more than $74 one Sunday. Let x be the number of games he referees.

   i Write an inequality to represent the problem.

   ii Solve the inequality to find the minimum number of games he must referee.

b Two parents support the game by buying raffle tickets and badges. One buys 5 raffle tickets and 2 badges for $11.50 while the other buys 4 raffle tickets and 3 badges for $12. Determine the cost of a raffle ticket and the cost of a badge by:

   i defining two variables

   ii setting up two equations to represent the problem

   iii solving your equations simultaneously.

Pythagoras' theorem and trigonometry

Multiple-choice questions

1 The exact value of x in the triangle shown is:

   A 3.9   **B** $\sqrt{113}$ **C** $\sqrt{57}$ **D** $\sqrt{15}$ **E** 2.7

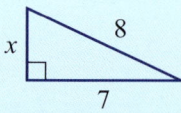

2 The correct expression for the triangle shown is:

   A $x = \dfrac{6}{\sin 42°}$ **B** $x = 6\tan 42°$ **C** $x = 6\sin 42°$

   D $x = \dfrac{6}{\cos 42°}$ **E** $x = \dfrac{\sin 42°}{6}$

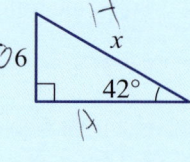

3 The correct expression for the angle θ is:

   A $\theta = \tan^{-1}\left(\dfrac{x}{z}\right)$ **B** $\theta = \sin^{-1}\left(\dfrac{x}{z}\right)$ **C** $\theta = \tan^{-1}\left(\dfrac{y}{x}\right)$

   D $\theta = \cos^{-1}\left(\dfrac{z}{x}\right)$ **E** $\theta = \cos^{-1}\left(\dfrac{x}{y}\right)$

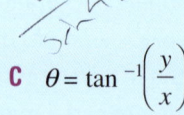
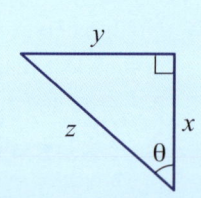

4   A 5-metre plank of wood is leaning up against a side of a building as
    shown. If the wood touches the ground 3 m from the base of the building,
    the angle the wood makes with the building is closest to:
    A 36.9°   **B** 59°   **C** 53.1°   **D** 31°   **E** 41.4°

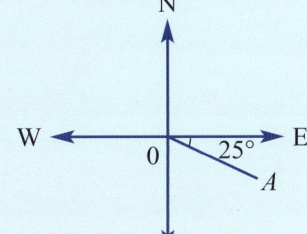

5   The true bearing of A from O is:
    A 025°   **B** 125°   **C** 155°
    D 065°   **E** 115°

Short-answer questions

1   Find the value of each pronumeral, correct to one decimal place.
    a 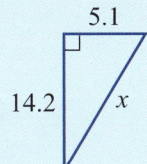   **b** 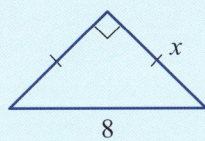   **c** 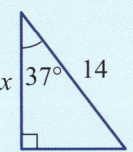   **d**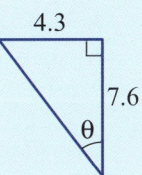

2   Find the value of the pronumerals. Round to one decimal place where necessary.
    a 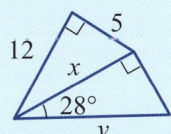   **b**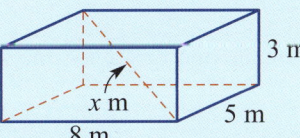

3   A wire is to be connected from the edge of the top of a 28 m high building to the edge of the top
    of a 16 m high building. The buildings are 15 m apart.
    a What length of wire, to the nearest centimetre, is required?
    b What is the angle of depression from the top of the taller building to the top of the smaller
       building? Round to one decimal place.

4   A yacht sails 18 km from its start location on a bearing of 295°T.
    a How far east or west is it from its start location? Answer correct to one decimal place.
    b On what true bearing would it need to sail to return directly to its start location?

Extended-response question

A skateboard ramp is constructed as shown.

a Calculate the distance d metres up the ramp correct to
   two decimal places.

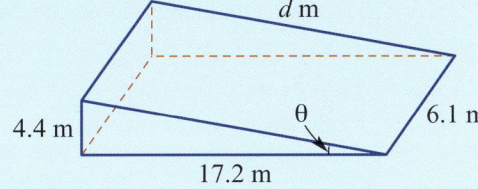

b What is the angle of inclination (θ) between the ramp and
   the ground correct to one decimal place?

c i If the skateboarder rides from one corner of the ramp diagonally to the other corner, what
       distance would be travelled? Round to one decimal place.
   ii If the skateboarder travels at an average speed of 10 km/h, how many seconds does it take to
       ride diagonally across the ramp? Answer correct to one decimal place.

Linear relations

Multiple-choice questions

1   The x- and y-intercepts respectively for the graph shown are:

   A   (-2, 4) and (4, -2)

   B   (0, 4) and (-2, 0)

   C   (-2, 0) and (0, 4)

   D   (4, 0) and (0, -2)

   E   (2, 0) and (0, -4)

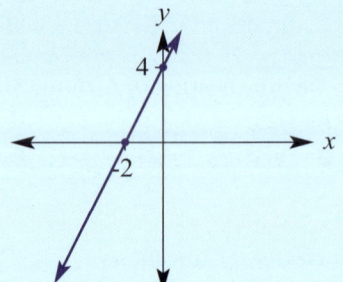

2   The graph shown has equation:

   A $y = 3x$

   B $y = 3$

   C $y = x + 3$

   D $x = 3$

   E $x + y = 3$

3   If the point (-1, 3) is on the line $y = 2x + c$, the value of c is:

   A   1

   B   5

   C   -7

   D   -5

   E   -1

4   The line passing through the points (-3, -1) and (1, y) has gradient 2. The value of y is:

   A   3

   B   5

   C   7

   D   1

   E   4

5   The midpoint and length to one decimal place of the line segment joining the points (-2, 1) and (4, 6) are:

   A   (1, 3.5) and 7.8

   B   (3, 5) and 5.4

   C   (3, 3.5) and 6.1

   D   (1, 3.5) and 3.3

   E   (3, 3.5) and 3.6

Short-answer questions

1 Sketch the following linear graphs labelling x- and y-intercepts.

   a $y = 2x - 6$ b $3x + 4y = 24$ c $y = 4x$

2 Find the gradient of each of the following.

   a The line passing through the points (-1, 2) and (2, 4)

   b The line passing through the points (-2, 5) and (1, -4)

   c The line with equation $y = -2x + 5$

   d The line with equation $-4x + 3y = 9$

3 Give the equation of the following lines in gradient–intercept form.

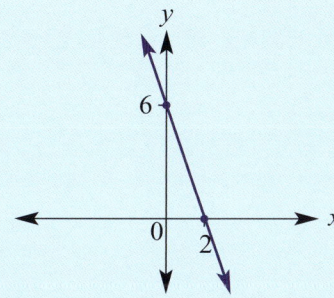

   a The line with the given graph

   b The line with gradient 3 and passing through the point (2, 5)

   c The line parallel to the line with equation $y = 2x - 1$ that passes through the origin

   d The line perpendicular to the line with equation $y = 3x + 4$ that passes through the point (0, 2)

4 Solve the simultaneous equations $y = 2x - 4$ and $x + y = 5$ graphically by finding the coordinates of the point of intersection.

Extended-response question

Doug works as a labourer. He is digging a trench and has 180 kg of soil to remove. He has taken 3 hours to remove 36 kg.

a What is the rate at which he is removing the soil?

b If he maintains this rate, write a rule for the amount of soil, S (kg), remaining after t hours.

c Draw a graph of your rule.

d How long will it take to remove all of the soil?

e Doug is paid $40 for the job plus $25 per hour worked.

   i Write a rule for his pay P dollars for working h hours.

   ii How much will he be paid to remove all the soil?

Measurement

Multiple-choice questions

1 The perimeter and area of the figure shown are:

   A   20.2 m, 22.42 m²
   B   24.8 m, 22.42 m²
   C   24.8 m, 25.15 m²
   D   20.2 m, 25.15 m²
   E   21.6 m, 24.63 m²

2 The exact perimeter in centimetres of this sector is:

   A   127.2

   B $\dfrac{81\pi}{2} + 27$

   C $12\pi + 27$

   D   45.8

   E $6\pi + 27$

3 420 cm² is equivalent to:

   A   4.2 m²
   B   0.42 m²
   C   42 000 m²
   D   0.042 m²
   E   0.0042 m²

4 This square pyramid has a total surface area of:

   A   525 m²
   B   300 m²
   C   750 m²
   D   450 m²
   E   825 m²

5 The volume of the cylinder shown is closest to:

   A   703.7 cm³   B   351.9 cm³   C   2814.9 cm³
   D   452.4 cm³   E   1105.8 cm³

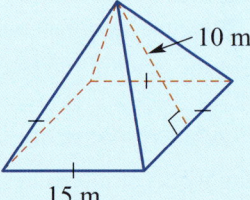

Short-answer questions

1 Find the area of each of the figures below. Round to two decimal places where necessary.

   a   b

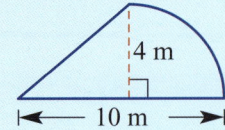   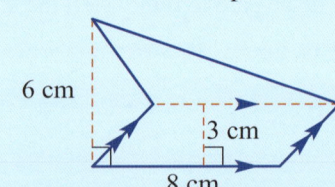

2   A tin of varnish for the timber (shaded) on the deck shown covers 6.2 square metres. How many tins will be required to completely varnish the deck?

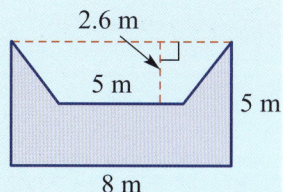

3   Find the total surface area of these solid objects. Round to two decimal places where necessary.

a

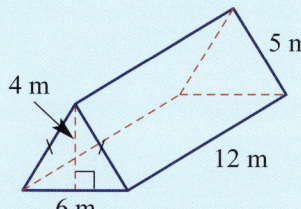

b

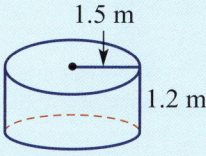

4   Find the value of the pronumeral for the given volume.

a

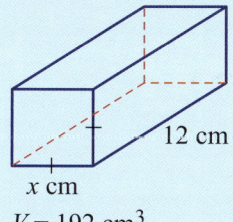

b

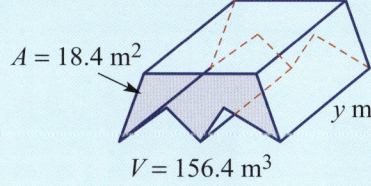

Extended-response question

A barn in the shape of a rectangular prism with a semicylindrical roof and with the dimensions shown is used to store hay.

a   The roof and the two long side walls of the barn are to be painted. Calculate the surface area to be painted correct to two decimal places.

b   A paint roller has a width of 20 cm and a radius of 3 cm.
  i   Find the area of the curved surface of the paint roller in m². Round to four decimal places.
  ii   Hence, state the area that the roller will cover in 100 revolutions.

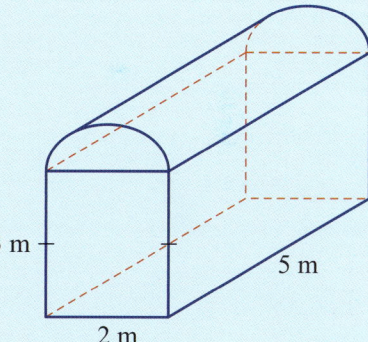

c   Find the minimum number of revolutions required to paint the area of the barn in part **a** with one coat.

d   Find the volume of the barn correct to two decimal places.

e   A rectangular bail of hay has dimensions 1 m by 40 cm by 40 cm. If there are 115 bails of hay in the barn, what volume of air space remains? Answer to two decimal places.

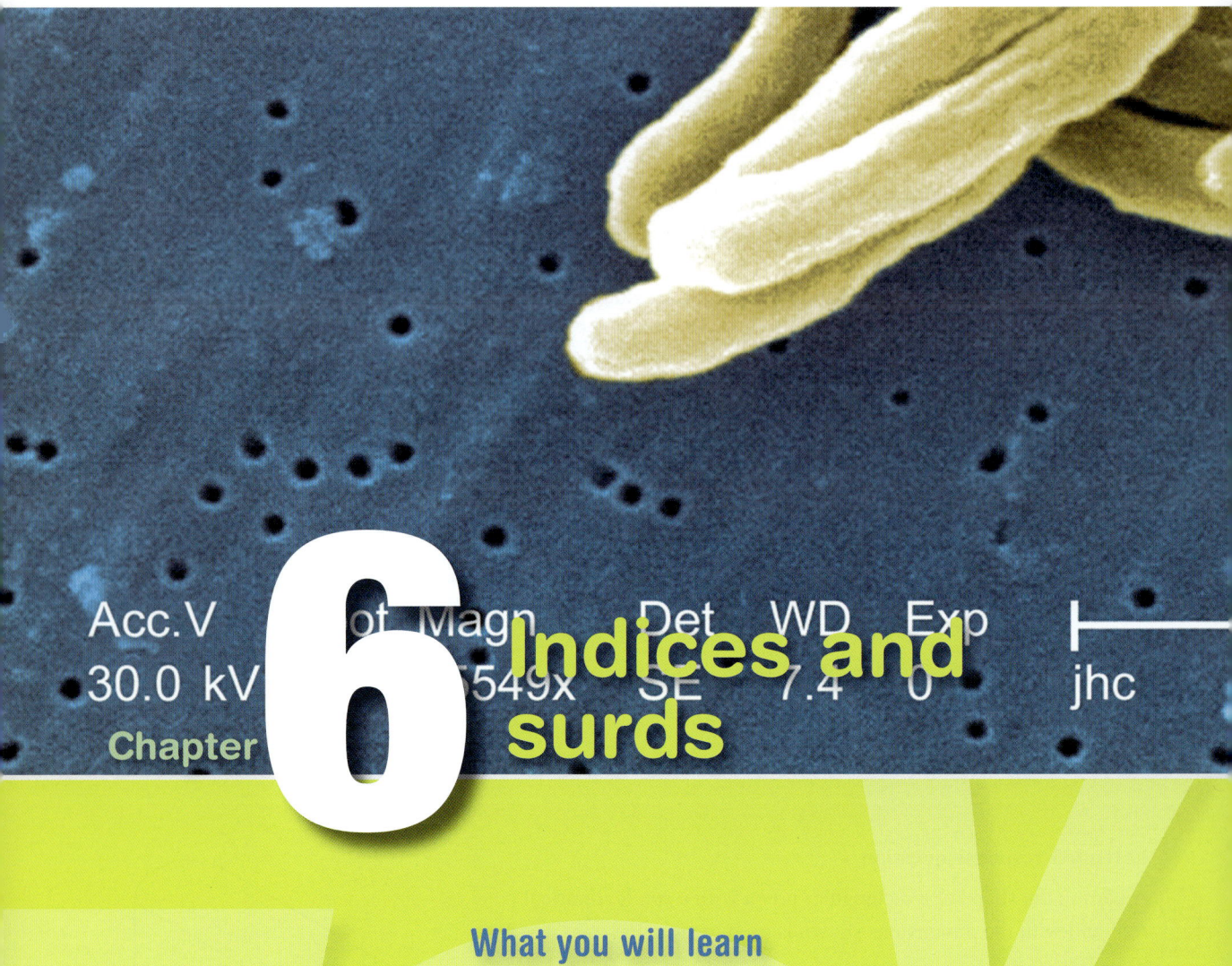

Acc.V
30.0 kV
Chapter

6 Indices and surds

ot Magn   Det   WD   Exp
5549x   SE   7.4   0   jhc

What you will learn

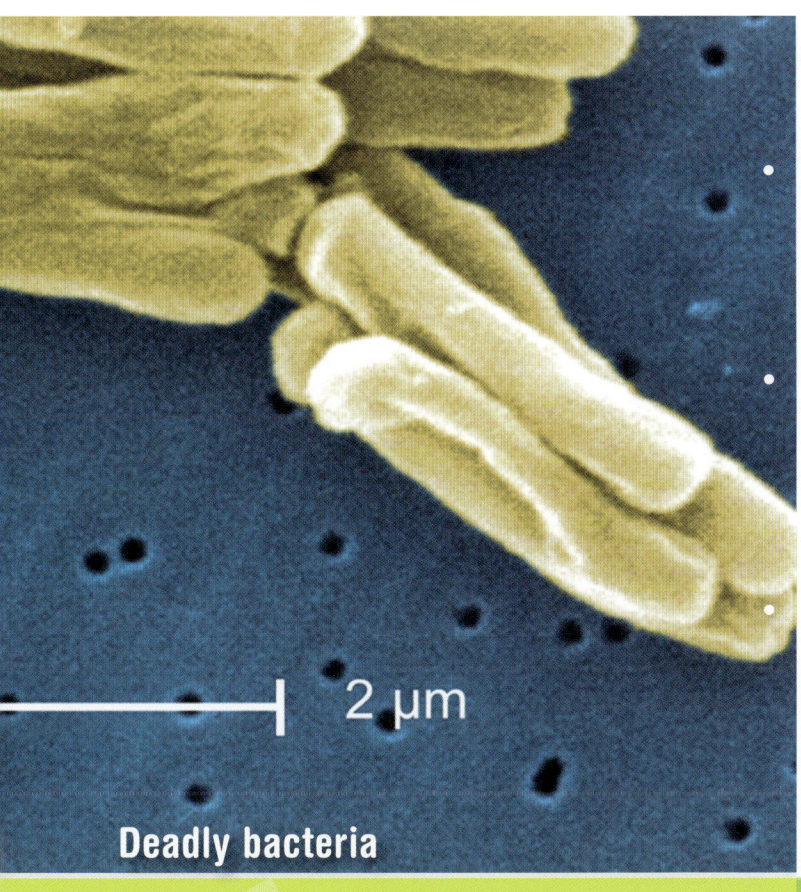

2 μm

Deadly bacteria

Australian curriculum

NUMBER AND ALGEBRA
Real numbers

Apply index laws to numerical expressions with integer indices

Express numbers in scientific notation

Patterns and algebra

Extend and apply the index laws to variables, using positive integral indices and the zero index

MEASUREMENT AND GEOMETRY
Using units of measurement

Investigate very small and very large time scales and intervals

Mycobacterium tuberculosis is a deadly bacteria that cause the disease tuberculosis. In 1900, tuberculosis was one of the most common causes of death in developed countries and is still one of the most common causes of death today. In the developing world about 1.5 million deaths are caused by tuberculosis every year.

Bacteria, such as tuberculosis, reproduce rapidly under favourable conditions. The bacteria cells undergo binary fission where each cell divides in two within a given period of time. So after n divisions the number of cells N is given by $N = 2^n$ where n is the index in the rule. Such rules involving indices help to model population growth of bacteria and other forms of growth and decay.

1 Evaluate:

   a 5^2 **b** 10^2 **c** 2^4 **d** 3^3 **e** $(-3)^2$

2 **a** List the factors of 24.

   b List the factors of 45.

   c List the prime factors of 24.

   d List the prime factors of 45.

3 Write each of the following in index form (as a power).

   a $a \times b \times b$ **b** $5b \times 5b \times 5a$

   c $3x \times 3x$ **d** $2 \times a \times c \times 3 \times c \times c$

4 Write each of the following as 2 raised to a single power.

   a $2^2 \times 2$ **b** $2^4 \times 2^2$ **c** $2^3 \times 2^2$

5 Simplify the following by removing brackets.

   a $(3^2)^2$ **b** $(xy)^2$ **c** $(2a)^2$ **d** $\left(\dfrac{3}{4}\right)^2$

6 Evaluate:

   a $\dfrac{1}{4^2}$ **b** $\dfrac{1}{2^3}$ **c** $\dfrac{1}{6^3}$ **d** $\dfrac{1}{\left(\dfrac{9}{4}\right)}$

7 Round the following to two decimal places.

   a 3.732   **b** 24.6174   **c** 18.3654   **d** 4.3971

8 State the number of significant figures in each of the following.

   a 23.102   **b** 30.05   **c** 0.0012   **d** 49 500

9 Complete the following.

   a $3.8 \times 10 = $ _____   **b** $2.31 \times 1000 = $ _____

   c $17.2 \div 100 = $ _____   **d** $0.18 \div 100 = $ _____

   e $3827 \div $ ____ $ = 3.827$ **f** $6.49 \times $ ____ $ = 64\,900$

10 Complete the following.

   a $15^2 = 225$ so $\sqrt{225} = $ _____   **b** $4^3 = 64$ so $\sqrt[3]{64} = $ _____

   c $\sqrt[3]{125} = 5$ so $5^3 = $ _____   **d** $\sqrt[5]{32} = 2$ so $2^5 = $ _____

11 Simplify by collecting like terms.

   a $3a + 7a - 4b$ **b** $5a - 2a + 3$

   c $2ab + 8a - ab$ **d** $3a^2b + 2ab^2 - 4a^2b$

6.1 Index notation

When a product includes the repeated multiplication of the same factor, indices can be used to produce a more concise expression. For example, $5 \times 5 \times 5$ can be written as 5^3 and $x \times x \times x \times x \times x$ can be written as x^5. The expression 5^3 is a power and we can say '5 to the power of 3'. The 5 is called the base and the 3 is the index, exponent or power. Numbers written with indices are common in mathematics and can be applied to many types of problems. The mass of a 100 kg limestone block, for example, might decrease by 2 per cent per year for 20 years. The mass after 20 years could be calculated by multiplying 100 by 0.98, 20 times. This is written as $100 \times (0.98)^{20}$.

Index notation is a convenient way for expressing large numbers or for carrying out calculations such as how much mass is lost over time from ancient stone monuments.

Let's start: Who has the most?

A person offers you one of two prizes.
- Which offer would you take?
- Try to calculate the final amount for prize B.
- How might you use indices to help calculate the value of prize B?
- How can a calculator help to find the amount for prize B using the power button ⌃?

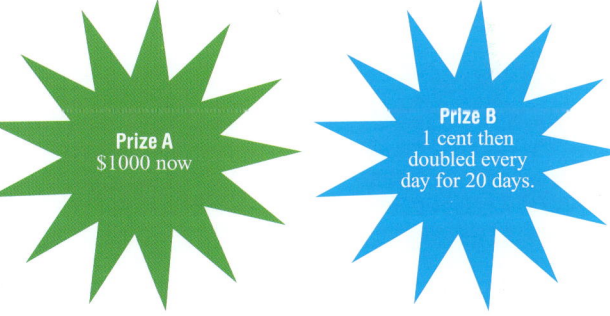

Prize A
$1000 now

Prize B
1 cent then doubled every day for 20 days.

Key ideas

- **Indices** (plural of **index**) can be used to represent a product of the same factor.
- The **base** is the factor in the product.
- The index (**exponent** or **power**) is the number of times the factor (base number) is repeated.
- **Prime factorisation** involves writing a number as a product of its prime factors.
- Note that $a^1 = a$.
  For example: $5^1 = 5$

Expanded form   Index form

$$\underbrace{2 \times 2 \times 2 \times 2 \times 2}_{} = \underset{\text{base}\ \ \text{index}}{2^5} = \underset{\text{basic numeral}}{32}$$

$$\underbrace{x \times x \times x \times x}_{} = \underset{\text{base}\quad\text{index}}{x^4}$$

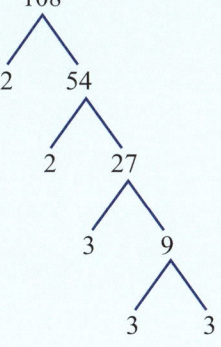

$$108 = 2 \times 2 \times 3 \times 3 \times 3$$
$$= \underline{2^2 \times 3^3}$$
prime factor form

Example 1 Writing in expanded form

Write in expanded form:

a a^3 b $(xy)^4$ c $2a^3b^2$

SOLUTION

a $a^3 = a \times a \times a$

b $(xy)^4 = xy \times xy \times xy \times xy$

c $2a^3b^2 = 2 \times a \times a \times a \times b \times b$

EXPLANATION

Factor a is repeated three times.

Factor xy is repeated four times.

Factor a is repeated three times and factor b is repeated twice. Factor 2 only appears once.

Example 2 Expanding and evaluating

Write each of the following in expanded form and then evaluate.

a 5^3 b $(-2)^5$ c $\left(\dfrac{2}{5}\right)^3$

SOLUTION

a $5^3 = 5 \times 5 \times 5$
$= 125$

b $(-2)^5 = (-2) \times (-2) \times (-2) \times (-2) \times (-2)$
$= -32$

c $\left(\dfrac{2}{5}\right)^3 = \dfrac{2}{5} \times \dfrac{2}{5} \times \dfrac{2}{5}$
$= \dfrac{8}{125}$

EXPLANATION

Write in expanded form with 5 repeated three times and evaluate.

Write in expanded form with -2 repeated five times and evaluate.

Write in expanded form.
Evaluate by multiplying numerators and denominators.

Example 3 Writing in index form

Write each of the following in index form.

a $6 \times x \times x \times x \times x \times x$ b $\dfrac{3}{7} \times \dfrac{3}{7} \times \dfrac{4}{5} \times \dfrac{4}{5} \times \dfrac{4}{5}$ c $8 \times a \times a \times 8 \times b \times b \times a \times b$

SOLUTION

a $6 \times x \times x \times x \times x \times x = 6x^4$

b $\dfrac{3}{7} \times \dfrac{3}{7} \times \dfrac{4}{5} \times \dfrac{4}{5} \times \dfrac{4}{5} = \left(\dfrac{3}{7}\right)^2 \times \left(\dfrac{4}{5}\right)^3$

c $8 \times a \times a \times 8 \times b \times b \times a \times b$
$= 8 \times 8 \times a \times a \times a \times b \times b \times b$
$= 8^2 a^3 b^3$

EXPLANATION

Factor x is repeated 4 times, 6 only once.

There are two groups of $\left(\dfrac{3}{7}\right)$ and three groups of $\left(\dfrac{4}{5}\right)$.

Group the numerals and like pronumerals and write in index form.

Example 4 Finding the prime factor form

Express 48 as a product of prime factors in index form.

SOLUTION

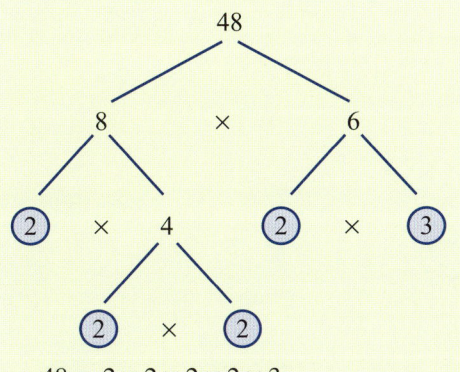

$\therefore 48 = 2 \times 2 \times 2 \times 2 \times 3$

$\quad = 2^4 \times 3$

EXPLANATION

Choose a pair of factors of 48, for example 8 and 6.

Choose a pair of factors of 8, i.e. 2 and 4.

Choose a pair of factors of 6, i.e. 2 and 3.

Continue this process until the factors are all prime numbers.

Write the prime factors of 48.

Express in index notation.

Exercise 6A

1 Evaluate:

a 5^2 **b** 2^3 **c** 3^3 **d** $(-4)^2$

2 Write the number or variable that is the base in these expressions.

a 3^7 **b** 6^4 **c** $(1.2)^5$ **d** $(-7)^3$

e $\left(\dfrac{2}{3}\right)^4$ **f** y^{10} **g** w^6 **h** t^2

3 Write the number that is the index in these expressions.

a 4^3 **b** 10^8 **c** $(-3)^7$ **d** $\left(\dfrac{1}{2}\right)^4$

e x^{11} **f** $(xy)^{13}$ **g** $\left(\dfrac{x}{2}\right)^9$ **h** $(1.3x)^2$

4 Write the prime factors of these numbers.

a 6 **b** 15 **c** 30 **d** 77

Example 1

5 Write each of the following in expanded form.

a a^4 **b** b^3 **c** x^3 **d** $(xp)^6$

e $(5a)^4$ **f** $(3y)^3$ **g** $4x^2y^5$ **h** $(pq)^2$

i $-3s^3t^2$ **j** $6x^3y^5$ **k** $5(yz)^6$ **l** $4(ab)^3$

Example 2 6 Write each of the following in expanded form and then evaluate.

a 6^2 b 2^4 c 3^5 d 12^1

e $(-2)^3$ f $(-1)^7$ g $(-3)^4$ h $(-5)^2$

i $\left(\dfrac{2}{3}\right)^3$ j $\left(\dfrac{3}{4}\right)^2$ k $\left(\dfrac{1}{6}\right)^3$ l $\left(\dfrac{5}{2}\right)^2$

m $\left(\dfrac{2}{-3}\right)^3$ n $\left(\dfrac{-3}{4}\right)^4$ o $\left(\dfrac{-1}{4}\right)^2$ p $\left(\dfrac{5}{-2}\right)^5$

Example 3a 7 Write each of the following in index form.

a $3 \times 3 \times 3$ b $8 \times 8 \times 8 \times 8 \times 8 \times 8$

c $y \times y$ d $3 \times x \times x \times x$

e $4 \times c \times c \times c \times c \times c$ f $5 \times 5 \times 5 \times d \times d$

g $x \times x \times y \times y \times y$ h $7 \times b \times 7 \times b \times 7$

Example 3b 8 Write each of the following in index form.

a $\dfrac{2}{3} \times \dfrac{2}{3} \times \dfrac{2}{3} \times \dfrac{2}{3}$ b $\dfrac{3}{5} \times \dfrac{3}{5} \times \dfrac{3}{5} \times \dfrac{3}{5} \times \dfrac{3}{5}$ c $\dfrac{4}{7} \times \dfrac{4}{7} \times \dfrac{1}{5} \times \dfrac{1}{5} \times \dfrac{1}{5} \times \dfrac{1}{5}$ d $\dfrac{7x}{9} \times \dfrac{7x}{9} \times \dfrac{y}{4} \times \dfrac{y}{4} \times \dfrac{y}{4}$

Example 3c 9 Write each of the following in index form.

a $3 \times x \times y \times x \times 3 \times x \times 3 \times y$ b $3x \times 2y \times 3x \times 2y$

c $4d \times 2e \times 4d \times 2e$ d $6by(6by)(6y)$

e $3pq(3pq)(3pq)(3pq)$ f $7mn \times 7mn \times mn \times 7$

Example 4 10 Express each of the following as a product of prime factors in index form.

a 10   b 8   c 144

d 512   e 216   f 500

11 If $a = 3$, $b = 2$ and $c = -3$, evaluate these expressions.

a $(ab)^2$ b $(bc)^3$ c $\left(\dfrac{a}{c}\right)^4$ d $\left(\dfrac{b}{c}\right)^3$

e $(abc)^1$ f $c^2 + ab$ g ab^2c h c^2ab^3

12 Find the missing number.

a $3^? = 81$ b $2^? = 256$ c $?^3 = 125$ d $?^5 = 32$

e $?^3 = -64$ f $?^7 = -128$ g $?^3 = \dfrac{1}{8}$ h $\left(\dfrac{2}{3}\right)^? = \dfrac{16}{81}$

13 Bacteria cells split in 2 every 5 minutes. New cells also continue splitting in the same way. Use a table to help.

a How long will it take for 1 cell to divide into:

i 4 cells   ii 16 cells

iii 64 cells?

b A single cell is set aside to divide for two hours. How many cells will there be after this time?

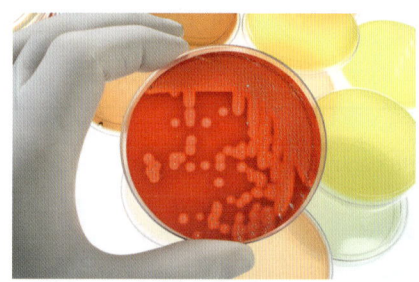

Problem-solving

14 A share broker says he can triple your money every year, so you invest $1000 with him.

   a How much should your investment be worth in 5 years?

   b How many years should you invest for if you were hoping for a total of at least $100 000? Give a whole number of years.

15 A fat cat that was initially 12 kg reduces its weight by 10% each month. How long does it take for the cat to be at least 6 kg lighter than its original weight? Give your answer as a whole number of months.

Reasoning

16 a Evaluate the following.

   i 3^2 **ii** $(-3)^2$ **iii** $-(3)^2$ **iv** $-(-3)^2$

   b Explain why the answers to parts **i** and **ii** are positive.

   c Explain why the answers to parts **iii** and **iv** are negative.

17 a Evaluate the following.

   i 2^3 **ii** $(-2)^3$ **iii** $-(2)^3$ **iv** $-(-2)^3$

   b Explain why the answers to parts **i** and **iv** are positive.

   c Explain why the answers to parts **ii** and **iii** are negative.

18 It is often easier to evaluate a decimal raised to a power by firstly converting the decimal to a fraction as shown, right.

Use this idea to evaluate these as a fraction.

   a $(0.5)^3$ **b** $(0.25)^2$ **c** $(0.2)^3$

   d $(0.5)^6$ **e** $(0.7)^2$ **f** $(1.5)^4$

   g $(2.6)^2$ **h** $(11.3)^2$ **i** $(3.4)^2$

$$(0.5)^4 = \left(\frac{1}{2}\right)^4$$
$$= \frac{1}{2} \times \frac{1}{2} \times \frac{1}{2} \times \frac{1}{2}$$
$$= \frac{1}{16}$$

Enrichment: LCM and HCF from prime factorisation

19 Last year you may have used prime factorisation to find the LCM (Lowest Common Multiple) and the HCF (Highest Common Factor) of two numbers. Here are the definitions.

• The LCM of two numbers in their prime factor form is the product of all the different primes raised to their highest power.

• The HCF of two numbers in their prime factor form is the product of all the common primes raised to their smallest power.

For example: $12 = 2^2 \times 3$ and $30 = 2 \times 3 \times 5$

The prime factors 2 and 3 are common.

$\therefore$ LCM $= 2^2 \times 3 \times 5$ $\therefore$ HCF $= 2 \times 3$

$\quad\quad\quad = 60$ $\quad\quad\quad\quad = 6$

Find the LCM and HCF of these pairs of numbers by firstly writing them in prime factor form.

   a 4, 6   **b** 42, 28   **c** 24, 36   **d** 10, 15

   e 40, 90   **f** 100, 30   **g** 196, 126   **h** 2178, 1188

6.2 Index laws 1 and 2

An index law (or identity) is an equation that is true for all possible values of the variables in that equation. When multiplying or dividing numbers with the same base, index laws can be used to simplify the expression.

Consider $a^m \times a^n$:

Using expanded form: $a^m \times a^n = \underbrace{\overbrace{a \times a \times a \times \ldots \times a}^{m \text{ factors of } a} \times \overbrace{a \times a \times \ldots \times a}^{n \text{ factors of } a}}_{m + n \text{ factors of } a}$

$$= a^{m + n}$$

So the total number of factors of a is $m + n$.

Also

$$a^m \div a^n = \frac{\overbrace{a \times a \times \ldots \times \cancel{a} \times \cancel{a} \times \cancel{a} \times \cancel{a}}^{m \text{ factors of } a}}{\underbrace{\cancel{a} \times \ldots \times \cancel{a} \times \cancel{a}}_{n \text{ factors of } a}}$$

$$= a^{m - n}$$

So the total number of factors of a is $m - n$.

→ Let's start: Discovering laws 1 and 2

Consider the two expressions $2^3 \times 2^5$ and $6^8 \div 6^6$.
Complete this working.

$2^3 \times 2^5 = 2 \times \square \times \square \times 2 \times \square \times \square \times \square \times \square$

$\quad = 2^{\square}$

$6^8 \div 6^6 = \dfrac{6 \times \square \times \square \times \square \times \square \times \square \times \square \times \square}{6 \times \square \times \square \times \square \times \square \times \square}$

$\quad = \dfrac{6 \times 6}{1}$

$\quad = 6^{\square}$

Index laws have applications in calculations involving very large (or very small) numbers

- What do you notice about the given expression and the answer in each case? Can you express this as a rule or law in words?

- Repeat the type of working given above and test your laws on these expressions.
  a $3^2 \times 3^7$ **b** $4^{11} \div 4^8$

Example 5 Using laws 1 and 2 with numbers

Simplify, giving your answer in index form.

a $3^6 \times 3^4$

b $7^9 \div 7^5$

SOLUTION

a $3^6 \times 3^4 = 3^{10}$

b $7^9 \div 7^5 = 7^4$

EXPLANATION

$a^m \times a^n = a^{m+n}$ (add the powers)

$a^m \div a^n = a^{m-n}$ (subtract the powers)

Example 6 Using index law 1

Simplify each of the following using the first index law.

a $x^4 \times x^5$

b $x^3y^4 \times x^2y$

c $3m^4 \times 2m^5$

SOLUTION

a $x^4 \times x^5 = x^{4+5}$

$= x^9$

b $x^3y^4 \times x^2y = x^{3+2}y^{4+1}$

$= x^5y^5$

c $3m^4 \times 2m^5 = 3 \times 2 \times m^{4+5}$

$= 6m^9$

EXPLANATION

Use law 1 to add the indices.

Use law 1 to add the indices corresponding to each different base. Recall $y = y^1$.

Multiply the numbers then use law 1 to add the indices of the base m.

Example 7 Using index law 2

Simplify each of the following using the second index law.

a $x^{10} \div x^2$

b $\dfrac{8a^6b^3}{12a^2b^2}$

SOLUTION

a $x^{10} \div x^2 = x^{10-2}$

$= x^8$

b $\dfrac{8a^6b^3}{12a^2b^2} = \dfrac{^2\cancel{8}a^{6-2}b^{3-2}}{^3\cancel{12}}$

$= \dfrac{2a^4b}{3}$

EXPLANATION

Use law 2 to subtract the indices.

Cancel the numbers using the highest common factor (4) and use law 2 to subtract the indices for each different base.

Example 8 Combining index laws 1 and 2

Simplify each of the following using the first two index laws.

a $x^2 \times x^3 \div x^4$

b $\dfrac{2a^3b \times 8a^2b^3}{4a^4b^2}$

SOLUTION	EXPLANATION
a $x^2 \times x^3 \div x^4 = x^5 \div x^4$ $\qquad\qquad\qquad\quad = x$	Use law 1 to add the indices for $x^2 \times x^3$. Use law 2 to subtract the indices for $x^5 \div x^4$.
b $\dfrac{2a^3b \times 8a^2b^3}{4a^4b^2} = \dfrac{16a^5b^4}{4a^4b^2}$ $\qquad\qquad\qquad = 4ab^2$	Multiply the numbers and use law 1 to add the indices for each different base in the numerator. Use law 2 to subtract the indices of each different base and cancel the numbers.

Exercise 6B

Understanding (side tab)

1 Write the missing words.

   a Index law 1 states that if you _____ two terms with the same _____ you _____ the powers.

   b Index law 2 states that if you _____ two terms with the same _____ you _____ the powers.

2 Copy and complete to give an answer in index form. Use cancelling in parts **c** and **d**.

   a $3^2 \times 3^4 = 3 \times \square \times 3 \times \square \times \square \times \square$

              $= 3^{\square}$

   b $6^4 \times 6^3 = 6 \times \square \times \square \times \square \times 6 \times \square \times \square$

              $= 6^{\square}$

   c $5^5 \div 5^3 = \dfrac{5 \times \square \times \square \times \square \times \square}{5 \times \square \times \square}$

              $= 5^{\square}$

   d $9^4 \div 9^2 = \dfrac{9 \times \square \times \square \times \square}{9 \times \square}$

              $= 9^{\square}$

3 Decide if these statements are true or false.

   a $5 \times 5 \times 5 \times 5 = 5^4$ **b** $2^6 \times 2^2 = 2^{6+2}$

   c $7^2 \times 7^4 = 7^{4-2}$ **d** $8^4 \div 8^2 = 8^{4+2}$

   e $a \times a^2 = a^3$ **f** $a^5 \times a^2 = a^{5-2}$

   g $x^7 \div x = x^7$ **h** $b^4 \div b = b^3$

ample 5 4 Simplify, giving your answers in index form.

a $2^4 \times 2^3$ b $5^6 \times 5^3$ c $7^2 \times 7^4$ d $8^9 \times 8$

e $3^4 \times 3^4$ f $6^5 \times 6^9$ g $3^7 \div 3^4$ h $6^8 \div 6^3$

i $5^4 \div 5$ j $10^6 \div 10^5$ k $9^9 \div 9^6$ l $(-2)^5 \div (-2)^3$

ample 6 5 Simplify each of the following using the first index law.

a $x^4 \times x^3$ b $a^6 \times a^3$ c $t^5 \times t^3$ d $y \times y^4$

e $d^2 \times d$ f $y^2 \times y \times y^4$ g $b \times b^5 \times b^2$ h $q^6 \times q^3 \times q^2$

i $x^3y^3 \times x^4y^2$ j $x^7y^3 \times x^2y$ k $5x^3y^5 \times xy^4$ l $xy^4z \times 4xy$

m $3m^3 \times 5m^2$ n $4e^4f^2 \times 2e^2f^2$ o $5c^4d \times 4c^3d$ p $9yz^2 \times 2yz^5$

ample 7 6 Simplify each of the following using the second index law.

a $a^6 \div a^4$ b $x^5 \div x^2$ c $\dfrac{q^{12}}{q^2}$ d $\dfrac{d^7}{d^6}$

e $\dfrac{8b^{10}}{4b^5}$ f $\dfrac{12d^{10}}{36d^5}$ g $\dfrac{4a^{14}}{2a^7}$ h $\dfrac{18y^{15}}{9y^7}$

i $9m^3 \div m^2$ j $14x^4 \div x$ k $5y^4 \div y^2$ l $6a^6 \div a^5$

m $\dfrac{3m^7}{12m^2}$ n $\dfrac{5w^2}{25w}$ o $\dfrac{4a^4}{20a^3}$ p $\dfrac{7x^5}{63x}$

q $\dfrac{16x^8y^6}{12x^2y^3}$ r $\dfrac{6s^6t^3}{14s^5t}$ s $\dfrac{8m^5n^4}{6m^4n^3}$ t $-\dfrac{5x^2y}{xy}$

ample 8 7 Simplify each of the following using the first two index laws.

a $b^5 \times b^2 \div b$ b $y^5 \times y^4 \div y^3$ c $c^4 \div c \times c^4$ d $x^4 \times x^2 \div x^5$

e $\dfrac{t^4 \times t^3}{t^6}$ f $\dfrac{p^2 \times p^7}{p^3}$ g $\dfrac{d^5 \times d^3}{d^2}$ h $\dfrac{x^9 \times x^2}{x}$

i $\dfrac{3x^3y^4 \times 8xy}{6x^2y^2}$ j $\dfrac{9b^4}{2g^3} \times \dfrac{4g^4}{3b^2}$

k $\dfrac{24m^7n^5}{5m^3n} \times \dfrac{5m^2n^4}{8mn^2}$ l $\dfrac{p^4q^3}{p^2q} \times \dfrac{p^6q^4}{p^3q^2}$

8 Simplify each of the following.

a $\dfrac{m^4}{n^2} \times \dfrac{m}{n^3}$ b $\dfrac{x}{y} \times \dfrac{x^3}{y}$ c $\dfrac{a^4}{b^3} \times \dfrac{b^6}{a}$

d $\dfrac{12a}{3c^3} \times \dfrac{6a^4}{4c^4}$ e $\dfrac{3f^2 \times 8f^7}{4f^3}$ f $\dfrac{4x^2b \times 9x^3b^2}{3xb}$

g $\dfrac{8k^4m^5}{5km^3} \times \dfrac{15km}{4k}$ h $\dfrac{12x^7y^3}{5x^4y} \times \dfrac{25x^2y^3}{8xy^4}$ i $-\dfrac{9m^5n^2 \times 4mn^3}{12mn \times m^4n^2} \times \dfrac{m^3n^2}{2m^2n}$

9 Write the missing number.

a $2^7 \times 2^{\square} = 2^{19}$ b $6^{\square} \times 6^3 = 6^{11}$ c $11^6 \div 11^{\square} = 11^3$

d $19^{\square} \div 19^2 = 19$ e $x^6 \times x^{\square} = x^7$ f $a^{\square} \times a^2 = a^{20}$

g $b^{13} \div b^{\square} = b$ h $y^{\square} \div y^9 = y^2$ i $\square \times x^2 \times 3x^4 = 12x^6$

j $15y^4 \div \square\, y^3 = y$ k $\square\, a^9 \div 4a = \dfrac{a^8}{2}$ l $13b^6 \div \square\, b^5 = \dfrac{b}{3}$

10 Evaluate without using a calculator.

a $7^7 \div 7^5$ b $10^6 \div 10^5$ c $13^{11} \div 13^9$ d $2^{20} \div 2^{17}$

e $101^5 \div 101^4$ f $200^{30} \div 200^{28}$ g $7 \times 31^{16} \div 31^{15}$ h $3 \times 50^{200} \div 50^{198}$

11 If m and n are positive integers, how many combinations of m and n satisfy the following?

a $a^m \times a^n = a^8$ b $a^m \times a^n = a^{15}$

12 The given answers are incorrect. Give the correct answer and explain the error made.

a $a^4 \times a = a^4$ b $x^7 \div x = x^7$ c $3a^5 \div 6a^3 = 2a^2$

d $5x^7 \div 10x^3 = \dfrac{1}{2x^4}$ e $2x^7 \times 3x^4 = 5x^{11}$ f $a^5 \div a^2 \times a = a^5 \div a^3 = a^2$

13 Given that $a = 2x$, $b = 4x^2$ and $c = 5x^3$, find expressions for:

a $2a$ b $3b$ c $2c$ d $-2a$

e abc f $\dfrac{c}{b}$ g $\dfrac{ab}{c}$ h $\dfrac{-2bc}{a}$

14 Simplify these expressions using the given variables.

a $2^x \times 2^y$ b $5^a \times 5^b$ c $t^x \times t^y$

d $3^x \div 3^y$ e $10^p \div 10^y$ f $t^x \div t^y$

g $2^p \times 2^q \div 2^r$ h $10^p \div 10^q \div 10^r$ i $2^a \times 2^{a+b} \times 2^{3a-b}$

j $a^{x-2}b^x \times a^{2x}b^3$ k $a^x b^y \times a^y b^x$ l $a^x b^y \div a^y b^x$

m $w^{x+2}b^x \div w^{2x} \times b^3$ n $\dfrac{a^x \times 3a^y}{3a^2}$ o $\dfrac{4p^a \times 5q^b}{20q^5}$

p $\dfrac{10k^x m^y}{8km^3} \div \dfrac{5k^x m^{2x}}{16k}$

Enrichment: Equal to ab

15 Show working to prove that these expressions simplify to ab.

a $\dfrac{5a^2 b^7}{9a^3 b} \times \dfrac{9a^4 b^2}{5a^2 b^7}$ b $\dfrac{3a^5 bc^3}{6a^4 c} \times \dfrac{4b^3}{2abc} \times \dfrac{2a^3 b^2 c}{2a^2 b^4 c^2}$

c $\dfrac{3a^4 b^5}{a^5 b^2} \div \dfrac{6b^3}{2a^2 b}$ d $\dfrac{2a}{3a^2 b^3} \times \dfrac{9a^4 b^7}{ab^5} \div \dfrac{6a}{b^2}$

16 Make up your own expressions which simplify to ab. Test them on a friend.

6.3 Index law 3 and the zero power

Sometimes we find expressions already written in index form are raised to another power, such as $(2^3)^4$ or $(a^2)^5$.

Consider $(a^m)^n$.

Using expanded form $(a^m)^n = \overbrace{a^m \times a^m \times \ldots \times a^m}^{n \text{ factors of } a^m}$

$$= \underbrace{\overbrace{a \times a \times \ldots \times a}^{m \text{ factors of } a} \times \overbrace{a \times a \times \ldots \times a}^{m \text{ factors of } a} \times \ldots \times \overbrace{a \times a \times \ldots \times a}^{m \text{ factors of } a}}_{m \times n \text{ factors of } a}$$

$$= a^{m \times n}$$

So the total number of factors of a is $m \times n$.

We also know that $a^m \div a^m = \dfrac{\cancel{a} \times \cancel{a} \times \cancel{a} \times \ldots \times \cancel{a}}{\cancel{a} \times \cancel{a} \times \cancel{a} \times \ldots \times \cancel{a}}$

$$= \frac{1}{1}$$

$$= 1$$

But using index law number 2: $a^m \div a^m = a^{m-m}$

$$= a^0$$

This implies that $a^0 = 1$.

Any number raised to the power of zero is one

→ Let's start: Discovering law 3 and the zero power

Use the expanded form of 5^3 to simplify $(5^3)^2$ as shown.

$$(5^3)^2 = 5 \times \square \times \square \times 5 \times \square \times \square$$
$$= 5^{\square}$$

- Repeat these steps to also simplify $(3^2)^4$ and $(x^4)^2$.
- What do you notice about the given expression and answer in each case? Can you express this as a law or rule in words?

Now complete this table.

Index form	3^5	3^4	3^3	3^2	3^1	3^0
Basic Numeral	243	81				

- What pattern do you notice in the basic numerals?
- What conclusion do you come to regarding 3^0?

Example 9 Using index law 3

Apply index law 3 to simplify each of the following.

a $(x^5)^4$ b $3(y^5)^2$

SOLUTION   **EXPLANATION**

a $(x^5)^4 = x^{5 \times 4}$ Retain x as the base and multiply the indices.
$= x^{20}$

b $3(y^5)^2 = 3y^{5 \times 2}$ Retain y and multiply the indices.
$= 3y^{10}$

Example 10 Using the zero power

Apply the zero power rule to evaluate each of the following.

a $(-3)^0$ b $-(5x)^0$ c $2y^0 - (3y)^0$

SOLUTION   **EXPLANATION**

a $(-3)^0 = 1$ Any number raised to the power of 0 is 1.

b $-(5x)^0 = -1$ Everything in the brackets is to the power of 0 so $(5x)^0$ is 1.

c $2y^0 - (3y)^0 = 2 \times 1 - 1$ $2y^0$ has no brackets so the power applies to the y
$= 2 - 1$ only so $2y^0 = 2 \times y^0 = 2 \times 1$ while $(3y)^0 = 1$.
$= 1$

Example 11 Combining index laws

Simplify each of the following by applying the various index laws.

a $(x^2)^3 \times (x^3)^5$ b $\dfrac{(m^3)^4}{m^7}$ c $\dfrac{4x^2 \times 3x^3}{6x^5}$

SOLUTION   **EXPLANATION**

a $(x^2)^3 \times (x^3)^5 = x^6 \times x^{15}$ Use index law 3 to remove brackets first by multiplying
$= x^{21}$ indices. Then use index law 1 to add indices.

b $\dfrac{(m^3)^4}{m^7} = \dfrac{m^{12}}{m^7}$ Remove brackets by multiplying indices then
simplify using index law 2.
$= m^5$

c $\dfrac{4x^2 \times 3x^3}{6x^5} = \dfrac{12x^5}{6x^5}$ Simplify the numerator first by multiplying
numbers and adding indices of base x.
$= 2x^0$ Then cancel and subtract indices.
$= 2 \times 1$ The zero power says $x^0 = 1$.
$= 2$

Exercise 6C

1 Write the missing words or numbers in these sentences.

   a When raising a term or numbers in index form to another power, _____ the indices.

   b Any number (except 0) raised to the power 0 is equal to ___.

2 Write the missing numbers in these tables.

   a

Index form	2^6	2^5	2^4	2^3	2^2	2^1	2^0
Basic numeral	64	32					

   b

Index form	4^5	4^4	4^3	4^2	4^1	4^0
Basic numeral	1024	256				

3 Copy and complete this working.

   a $(4^2)^3 = 4 \times \square \times 4 \times \square \times 4 \times \square$

       $= 4^{\square}$

   b $(12^3)^3 = \left(12 \times \square \times \square\right) \times \left(12 \times \square \times \square\right) \times \left(12 \times \square \times \square\right)$

       $= 12^{\square}$

   c $(x^4)^2 = \left(x \times \square \times \square \times \square\right) \times \left(x \times \square \times \square \times \square\right)$

       $= x^{\square}$

   d $(a^2)^5 = \left(a \times \square\right) \times \left(a \times \square\right) \times \left(a \times \square\right) \times \left(a \times \square\right) \times \left(a \times \square\right)$

       $= a^{\square}$

Example 9   **4** Apply index law 3 to simplify each of the following. Leave your answers in index form.

   a $(y^6)^2$ **b** $(m^3)^6$ **c** $(x^2)^5$ **d** $(b^3)^4$

   e $(3^2)^3$ **f** $(4^3)^5$ **g** $(3^5)^6$ **h** $(7^5)^2$

   i $5(m^8)^2$ **j** $4(q^7)^4$ **k** $-3(c^2)^5$ **l** $2(j^4)^6$

Example 10   **5** Evaluate each of the following.

   a 5^0 **b** 9^0 **c** $(-6)^0$ **d** $(-3)^0$

   e $-(4^0)$ **f** $\left(\dfrac{3}{4}\right)^0$ **g** $\left(-\dfrac{1}{7}\right)^0$ **h** $(4y)^0$

   i $5m^0$ **j** $-3p^0$ **k** $6x^0 - 2x^0$ **l** $-5n^0 - (8n)^0$

   m $(3x^4)^0$ **n** $1^0 + 2^0 + 3^0$ **o** $(1 + 2 + 3)^0$ **p** $100^0 - a^0$

Example 11a   **6** Simplify each of the following by combining various index laws.

   a $4 \times (4^3)^2$ **b** $(3^4)^2 \times 3$ **c** $x \times (x^0)^5$

   d $y^5 \times (y^2)^4$ **e** $b^5 \times (b^3)^3$ **f** $(a^2)^3 \times a^4$

   g $(d^3)^4 \times (d^2)^6$ **h** $(y^2)^6 \times (y)^4$ **i** $z^4 \times (z^3)^2 \times (z^5)^3$

   j $a^3 f \times (a^4)^2 \times (f^4)^3$ **k** $x^2 y \times (x^3)^4 \times (y^2)^2$ **l** $(s^2)^3 \times 5(r^0)^3 \times r s^2$

Example 11b **7** Simplify each of the following.

a $7^8 \div (7^3)^2$ b $(4^2)^3 \div 4^5$ c $(3^6)^3 \div (3^5)^2$

d $(m^3)^6 \div (m^2)^9$ e $(y^5)^3 \div (y^6)^2$ f $(h^{11})^2 \div (h^5)^4$

g $\dfrac{(b^2)^5}{b^4}$ h $\dfrac{(x^4)^3}{x^7}$ i $\dfrac{(y^3)^3}{y^3}$

Example 11c **8** Simplify each of the following using various index laws.

a $\dfrac{3x^4 \times 6x^3}{9x^{12}}$ b $\dfrac{5x^5 \times 4x^2}{2x^{10}}$ c $\dfrac{24(x^4)^4}{8(x^4)^2}$

d $\dfrac{4(d^4)^3 \times (e^4)^2}{8(d^2)^5 \times e^7}$ e $\dfrac{6(m^3)^2(n^5)^3}{15(m^5)^0(n^2)^7}$ f $\dfrac{2(a^3)^4(b^2)^6}{16(a)^0(b^6)^2}$

9 There are 100 rabbits on Mt Burrow at the start of the year 2000. The rule for the number of rabbits N after t years (from the start of the year 2000) is $N = 100 \times 2^t$.

a Find the number of rabbits at:
  i $t = 2$ ii $t = 6$ iii $t = 0$
b Find the number of rabbits at the beginning of:
  i 2003 ii 2007 iii 2010
c How many years will it take for the population to first rise to more than 500 000? Give a whole number of years.

10 If m and n are positive integers, in how many ways can $(a^m)^n = a^{16}$?

11 Evaluate these without using a calculator.

a $(2^4)^8 \div 2^{30}$ b $(10^3)^7 \div 10^{18}$ c $(x^4)^9 \div x^{36}$

d $((-1)^{11})^2 \times ((-1)^2)^{11}$ e $-2((-2)^3)^3 \div (-2)^8$ f $\dfrac{(a^2)^3}{(b^4)^7} \times \dfrac{(b^7)^4}{(a^3)^2}$

Problem-solving

12 Explain the error made in the following problems then give the correct answer.

   a $(a^4)^5 = a^9$ **b** $3(x^3)^2 = 9x^6$ **c** $(2x)^0 = 2$

13 a Simplify these by firstly working with the inner brackets. Leave your answer in index form.

   i $(2^3)^4)^2$ **ii** $(((-2)^2)^5)^3$ **iii** $((x^6)^2)^7$ **iv** $(((a^2)^4)^3)^2$

   b Simplify these expressions.

   i $((2^a)^b)^c$ **ii** $((a^m)^n)^p$ **iii** $(x^{2y})^{3z}$

14 a Show that $\dfrac{5a^2b}{2ab^2} \div \dfrac{10a^4b^7}{4a^3b^8}$ is equal to 1.

   b Make up your own expression like the one above where the answer is equal to 1. Test it on a friend.

Enrichment: Changing the base

15 The base of a number in index form can be changed using index law number 3.

For example: $8^2 = (2^3)^2$
$$= 2^6$$

Change the base numbers and simplify the following using the smallest possible base integer.

   a 8^4 **b** 32^3 **c** 9^3

   d 81^5 **e** 25^5 **f** 243^{10}

   g 256^9 **h** 2401^{20} **i** $100\,000^{10}$

A research scientist in a microbiology laboratory would use indices to express the numbers of microbes being studied

6.4 Index laws 4 and 5

It is common to find expressions such as $(2x)^3$ and $\left(\dfrac{x}{3}\right)^4$ in mathematical problems. These differ from most of the expressions in previous sections as they contain more than one single number or variable, connected by multiplication or division, raised to a power. These expressions can also be simplified using two index laws which effectively remove the brackets.

Consider $(a \times b)^m$:

$$\text{Using expanded form: } (a \times b)^m = \overbrace{ab \times ab \times ab \times \ldots \times ab}^{m \text{ factors of } ab}$$

$$= \overbrace{a \times a \times \ldots \times a}^{m \text{ factors of } a} \times \overbrace{b \times b \times \ldots \times b}^{m \text{ factors of } b}$$

$$= a^m \times b^m$$

So this becomes a product of m factors of a and m factors of b.

Also,
$$\left(\frac{a}{b}\right)^m = \overbrace{\frac{a}{b} \times \frac{a}{b} \times \frac{a}{b} \times \ldots \times \frac{a}{b}}^{m \text{ factors of } \frac{a}{b}}$$

$$= \frac{\overbrace{a \times a \times a \times \ldots \times a}^{m \text{ factors of } a}}{\underbrace{b \times b \times b \times \ldots \times b}_{m \text{ factors of } b}}$$

$$= \frac{a^m}{b^m}$$

 So to remove the brackets we can raise each of a and b to the power m.

Let's start: Discovering laws 4 and 5

Use the expanded form of $(2x)^3$ and $\left(\dfrac{x}{3}\right)^4$ to help simplify the expressions.

$(2x)^3 = 2x \times \square \times \square$

$\qquad = 2 \times 2 \times 2 \times \square \times \square \times \square$

$\qquad = 2^{\square} \times \square^{\square}$

$\left(\dfrac{x}{3}\right)^4 = \dfrac{x}{3} \times \square \times \square \times \square$

$\qquad = \dfrac{x \times \square \times \square \times \square}{3 \times \square \times \square \times \square}$

$\qquad = \dfrac{\square^{\square}}{\square^{\square}}$

- Repeat these steps to also simplify these expressions $(3y)^4$ and $\left(\dfrac{x}{2}\right)^5$.

- What do you notice about the given expressions and the answer in each case? Can you express this as a rule or law in words?

- **Index law 4:** $(a \times b)^m = (ab)^m = a^m b^m$
  - When multiplying two or more numbers raised to the power of m, raise each number in the brackets to the power of m. For example: $(2x)^2 = 2^2 x^2 = 4x^2$.
- **Index law 5:** $\left(\dfrac{a}{b}\right)^m = \dfrac{a^m}{b^m}$ and $b \neq 0$
  - When dividing two numbers raised to the power of m, raise each number in the brackets to the power of m. For example: $\left(\dfrac{y}{3}\right)^3 = \dfrac{y^3}{3^3} = \dfrac{y^3}{27}$.

Example 12 Using index law 4

Expand each of the following using the fourth index law.

a $(5b)^3$ b $(-2x^3 y)^4$ c $4(c^2 d^3)^5$

SOLUTION	EXPLANATION
a $(5b)^3 = 5^3 b^3$ $\quad = 125b^3$	Raise each numeral and pronumeral in the brackets to the power of 3. Evaluate $5^3 = 5 \times 5 \times 5$.
b $(-2x^3 y)^4 = (-2)^4 (x^3)^4 y^4$ $\quad = 16x^{12} y^4$	Raise each value in the brackets to the power of 4. Evaluate $(-2)^4$ and simplify using law 3.
c $4(c^2 d^3)^5 = 4(c^2)^5 (d^3)^5$ $\quad = 4c^{10} d^{15}$	Raise each value in the brackets to the power of 5. Note that the coefficient (4) is not raised to the power of 5. Simplify using index laws.

Example 13 Using index law 5

Apply the fifth index law to the following.

a $\left(\dfrac{6}{b}\right)^3$ b $\left(\dfrac{-2a^2}{3bc^3}\right)^4$ c $\left(\dfrac{x^2 y^3}{c}\right)^3 \times \left(\dfrac{xc}{y}\right)^4$

SOLUTION	EXPLANATION
a $\left(\dfrac{6}{b}\right)^3 = \dfrac{6^3}{b^3}$ $\quad = \dfrac{216}{b^3}$	Raise each value in the brackets to the power of 3 and evaluate 6^3.
b $\left(\dfrac{-2a^2}{3bc^3}\right)^4 = \dfrac{(-2)^4 a^8}{3^4 b^4 c^{12}}$ $\quad = \dfrac{16a^8}{81 b^4 c^{12}}$	Raise each value in the brackets to the power of 4. Evaluate $(-2)^4$ and 3^4.

c $\left(\dfrac{x^2 y^3}{c}\right)^3 \times \left(\dfrac{xc}{y}\right)^4 = \dfrac{x^6 y^9}{c^3} \times \dfrac{x^4 c^4}{y^4}$

$= \dfrac{x^{10} y^9 c^4}{c^3 y^4}$

$= x^{10} y^5 c$

Raise each value in the brackets to the power.
Multiply the numerators using law 1 then divide using law 2.

Exercise 6D

Understanding

1 Copy and complete index laws 4 and 5.

a $(a \times b)^m = a^m \times \boxed{}$

b $\left(\dfrac{a}{b}\right)^m = \dfrac{a^m}{\boxed{}}$

2 Copy and complete this working.

a $(5a)^3 = 5a \times \boxed{} \times \boxed{}$
$= 5 \times 5 \times 5 \times a \times \boxed{} \times \boxed{}$
$= 5^3 \times \boxed{}$

b $(ab)^4 = ab \times \boxed{} \times \boxed{} \times \boxed{}$
$= a \times \boxed{} \times \boxed{} \times \boxed{} \times b \times \boxed{} \times \boxed{} \times \boxed{}$
$= a^4 \times \boxed{}$

c $\left(\dfrac{x}{6}\right)^3 = \dfrac{x}{6} \times \boxed{} \times \boxed{}$
$= \dfrac{x \times \boxed{} \times \boxed{}}{6 \times \boxed{} \times \boxed{}}$
$= \dfrac{x^3}{\boxed{}}$

d $\left(\dfrac{a}{b}\right)^5 = \dfrac{a}{b} \times \boxed{} \times \boxed{} \times \boxed{} \times \boxed{}$
$= \dfrac{a \times \boxed{} \times \boxed{} \times \boxed{} \times \boxed{}}{b \times \boxed{} \times \boxed{} \times \boxed{} \times \boxed{}}$
$= \dfrac{a^5}{\boxed{}}$

Fluency

Example 12

3 Expand each of the following using the fourth index law.

a $(2x)^3$ b $(5y)^2$ c $(4a^2)^3$ d $(-3r)^2$

e $-(3b)^4$ f $-(7r)^3$ g $(-2h^2)^4$ h $(5c^2 d^3)^4$

i $(2x^3 y^2)^5$ j $9(p^2 q^4)^3$ k $2(x^3 y)^2$ l $(8t^2 u^9 v^4)^0$

m $(-3w^3 y)^3$ n $-4(p^4 qr)^2$ o $(-5s^7 t)^2$ p $-(-2x^4 yz^3)^3$

Example 13a,b

4 Apply the fifth index law to expand the following.

a $\left(\dfrac{p}{q}\right)^3$ b $\left(\dfrac{x}{y}\right)^4$ c $\left(\dfrac{4}{y}\right)^3$ d $\left(\dfrac{5}{p^2}\right)^4$

e $\left(\dfrac{2}{r^3}\right)^2$ f $\left(\dfrac{s^3}{7}\right)^2$ g $\left(\dfrac{2m}{n}\right)^5$ h $\left(\dfrac{2a^2}{3}\right)^3$

i $\left(\dfrac{3n^3}{2m^4}\right)^3$ j $\left(\dfrac{-2r}{n}\right)^4$ k $\left(\dfrac{-3f}{2^3 g^5}\right)^2$ l $\left(\dfrac{5w^4 y}{2x^3}\right)^2$

m $\left(\dfrac{-3x}{2y^3 g^5}\right)^2$ n $\left(\dfrac{3km^3}{4n^7}\right)^3$ o $-\left(\dfrac{-5w^4 y}{2zx^3}\right)^2$ p $\left(-\dfrac{3x^2 y^3}{2a^5 b^3}\right)^2$

5 Simplify each of the following by applying the various index laws.

a $a(3b)^2$

b $a(3b^2)^3$

c $-3(2a^3b^4)^2a^2$

d $2(3x^2y^3)^3$

e $(-4b^2c^5d)^3$

f $a(2a)^3$

g $a(3a^2)^2$

h $5a^3(-2a^4b)^3$

i $-5(-2m^3pt^2)^5$

j $-(-7d^2f^4g)^2$

k $-2(-2^3x^4yz^3)^3$

l $-4a^2b^3(-2a^3b^2)^2$

ple 13c

6 Simplify each of the following.

a $((x^2)^3)^4$

b $((2x^3)^2)^4$

c $(a^3b^2)^3 \times (a^4b)^2$

d $(a^2b)^3 \times (ab^2)^4$

e $\dfrac{(2m^3n)^3}{m^4}$

f $\dfrac{3(2^2c^4d^5)^3}{(2cd^2)^4}$

g $\left(\dfrac{-3x^2y^0}{5a^5b^3}\right)^3$

h $\dfrac{-3(2^4a^4b^3)^3}{(-2^3a^2b)^4}$

i $\dfrac{-5(3^5m^3n^2)^2}{(-3^3m^2n)^3}$

j $\left(\dfrac{a^3b}{c}\right)^3 \times \left(\dfrac{ac^4}{b}\right)^2$

k $\left(\dfrac{x^2z}{y}\right)^4 \times \left(\dfrac{xy^2}{z}\right)^3$

l $\left(\dfrac{r^3s}{t}\right)^2 \div \left(\dfrac{s}{rt^4}\right)^3$

7 The rule for the number of seeds germinating in a glass house over a two-week period is given by $N = \left(\dfrac{t}{2}\right)^3$ where N is the number of germinating seeds and t is the number of days.

a Find the number of germinating seeds after:

i 4 days

ii 10 days

b Use index law 5 to rewrite the rule without brackets.

c Use your rule in part **b** to find the number of seeds germinating after:

i 6 days

ii 4 days

d Find the number of days required to germinate:

i 64 seeds

ii 1 seed

8 Find the value of a that makes these equations true, given $a > 0$.

a $\left(\dfrac{a}{3}\right)^2 = \dfrac{4}{9}$

b $\left(\dfrac{a}{2}\right)^4 = 16$

c $(5a)^3 = 1000$

d $(2a)^4 = 256$

e $\left(\dfrac{2a}{3}\right)^2 = \dfrac{4}{9}$

f $\left(\dfrac{6a}{7}\right)^3 = 1728$

9 Rather than evaluating $\dfrac{2^4}{4^4}$ as $\dfrac{16}{256} = \dfrac{1}{16}$, it is easier to evaluate $\dfrac{2^4}{4^4}$ in the following way (below).

a Explain why this method is helpful.

b Use this idea to evaluate these without the use of a calculator.

    i $\dfrac{6^3}{3^3}$ **ii** $\dfrac{10^4}{5^4}$

    iii $\dfrac{4^4}{12^4}$ **iv** $\dfrac{3^3}{30^3}$

$$\dfrac{2^4}{4^4} = \left(\dfrac{2}{4}\right)^4$$
$$= \left(\dfrac{1}{2}\right)^4$$
$$= \dfrac{1^4}{2^4}$$
$$= \dfrac{1}{16}$$

10 Decide if the following are true or false. Give reasons.

a $(-2x)^2 = -(2x)^2$

b $(-3x)^3 = -(3x)^3$

c $\left(\dfrac{-5}{x}\right)^5 = -\left(\dfrac{5}{x}\right)^5$

d $\left(\dfrac{-4}{x}\right)^4 = -\left(\dfrac{4}{x}\right)^4$

Enrichment: False laws

11 Consider the equation $(a + b)^2 = a^2 + b^2$.

a Using $a = 2$ and $b = 3$, evaluate $(a + b)^2$.

b Using $a = 2$ and $b = 3$, evaluate $a^2 + b^2$.

c Would you say that the equation is true for all values of a and b?

d Now decide if $(a - b)^2 = a^2 - b^2$ for all values of a and b. Give an example to support your answer.

e Decide if these equations are true or false for all values of a and b.

    i $(-ab)^2 = a^2b^2$ **ii** $-(ab)^2 = a^2b^2$

    iii $\left(\dfrac{-a}{b}\right)^3 = \dfrac{-a^3}{b^3}$ **iv** $\left(\dfrac{-a}{b}\right)^4 = \dfrac{-a^4}{b^4}$

6.5 Negative indices

We know that $2^3 = 8$ and $2^0 = 1$ but what about 2^{-1} or 2^{-6}? Such numbers written in index form using negative indices also have meaning in mathematics.

Consider $a^2 \div a^5$.

Method 1: Using law 2

$$\frac{a^2}{a^5} = a^{2-5}$$
$$= a^{-3} \text{ (from index law 2)}$$

Method 2: By cancelling

$$\frac{a^2}{a^5} = \frac{\overset{1}{\cancel{a}} \times \overset{1}{\cancel{a}}}{a \times a \times a \times \underset{1}{\cancel{a}} \times \underset{1}{\cancel{a}}}$$
$$= \frac{1}{a^3}$$

$$\therefore a^{-3} = \frac{1}{a^3}$$

Also, using index law 1 we can write:
$$a^m \times a^{-m} = a^{m + (-m)}$$
$$= a^0$$
$$= 1$$

So dividing by a^m we have $a^{-m} = \dfrac{1}{a^m}$ or dividing by a^{-m} we have $a^m = \dfrac{1}{a^{-m}}$.

Let's start: Continuing the pattern

Explore the use of negative indices by completing this table.

Index form	2^4	2^3	2^2	2^1	2^0	2^{-1}	2^{-2}	2^{-3}
Whole number or fraction	16	8					$\dfrac{1}{4} = \dfrac{1}{2^2}$	

$\div 2$ $\div 2$ $\div 2$

- What do you notice about the numbers with negative indices in the top row in comparison to the fractions in the second row?
- Can you describe this connection formally in words?
- What might be another way of writing 2^{-7} or 5^{-4}?

Key ideas

- $a^{-m} = \dfrac{1}{a^m}$ and $a^m = \dfrac{1}{a^{-m}}$

  a raised to the power $-m$ is equal to the reciprocal of a raised to the power m. ($a \neq 0$)

Example 14 Writing expressions using positive indices

Express each of the following with positive indices only.

a x^{-2} **b** $3a^{-2}b^4$

SOLUTION

a $x^{-2} = \dfrac{1}{x^2}$

b $3a^{-2}b^4 = \dfrac{3}{1} \times \dfrac{1}{a^2} \times \dfrac{b^4}{1}$

$= \dfrac{3b^4}{a^2}$

EXPLANATION

$a^{-m} = \dfrac{1}{a^m}$.

Rewrite a^{-2} using a positive power and multiply numerators and denominators.

Example 15 Using $\dfrac{1}{a^{-m}} = a^m$

Express each of the following using positive indices only.

a $\dfrac{1}{c^{-2}}$ **b** $\dfrac{x^{-3}}{y^{-5}}$ **c** $\dfrac{5}{x^3 y^{-4}}$

SOLUTION

a $\dfrac{1}{c^{-2}} = c^2$

b $\dfrac{x^{-3}}{y^{-5}} = x^{-3} \times \dfrac{1}{y^{-5}}$

$= \dfrac{1}{x^3} \times \dfrac{y^5}{1}$

$= \dfrac{y^5}{x^3}$

c $\dfrac{5}{x^3 y^{-4}} = \dfrac{5y^4}{x^3}$

EXPLANATION

$\dfrac{1}{a^{-m}} = a^m$.

Express x^{-3} and $\dfrac{1}{y^{-5}}$ with positive indices using

$a^{-m} = \dfrac{1}{a^m}$ and $\dfrac{1}{a^{-m}} = a^m$.

Express $\dfrac{1}{y^{-4}}$ as a positive power.

Example 16 Evaluating without a calculator

Express using positive powers only, then evaluate without using a calculator.

a 3^{-4} **b** $\dfrac{-5}{3^{-2}}$ **c** $\left(\dfrac{2}{3}\right)^{-4}$

SOLUTION	EXPLANATION
a $3^{-4} = \dfrac{1}{3^4}$ $= \dfrac{1}{81}$	Express 3^{-4} as a positive power and evaluate 3^4.
b $\dfrac{-5}{3^{-2}} = -5 \times \dfrac{1}{3^{-2}}$ $= -5 \times 3^2$ $= -5 \times 9$ $= -45$	Express $\dfrac{1}{3^{-2}}$ as a positive power and simplify.
c $\left(\dfrac{2}{3}\right)^{-4} = \dfrac{2^{-4}}{3^{-4}}$ $= 2^{-4} \times \dfrac{1}{3^{-4}}$ $= \dfrac{1}{2^4} \times 3^4$ $= \dfrac{3^4}{2^4}$ $= \dfrac{81}{16}$	Apply the power to each numeral in the brackets using index law 5. Express 2^{-4} and $\dfrac{1}{3^{-4}}$ with positive indices and evaluate.

Exercise 6E

Understanding

1 Write the following using positive indices. For example: $\dfrac{1}{8} = \dfrac{1}{2^3}$.

a $\dfrac{1}{4}$ **b** $\dfrac{1}{9}$ **c** $\dfrac{1}{125}$ **d** $\dfrac{1}{27}$

2 Complete the tables with the missing numbers.

a

Index form	3^4	3^3	3^2	3^1	3^0	3^{-1}	3^{-2}	3^{-3}
Whole number or fraction	81	27					$\dfrac{1}{9} = \dfrac{1}{3^2}$	

$\div 3 \qquad \div 3 \qquad\qquad\qquad \div 3$

b

Index form	10^4	10^3	10^2	10^1	10^0	10^{-1}	10^{-2}	10^{-3}
Whole number or fraction	10 000							$\dfrac{1}{1000} = \dfrac{1}{10^3}$

$\div 10 \qquad\qquad\qquad\qquad\qquad \div 10$

Example 14 **3** Express each of the following with positive indices only.

a x^{-1} b a^{-4} c b^{-6} d 5^{-2}

e 4^{-3} f 9^{-1} g $5x^{-2}$ h $4y^{-3}$

i $3m^{-5}$ j $p^7 q^{-2}$ k mn^{-4} l $x^4 y^{-4}$

m $2a^{-3}b^{-1}$ n $7r^{-2}s^{-3}$ o $5^{-1}u^{-8}v^2$ p $9^{-1}m^{-3}n^{-5}$

Example 15a **4** Express each of the following using positive indices only.

a $\dfrac{1}{y^{-1}}$ b $\dfrac{1}{b^{-2}}$ c $\dfrac{1}{m^{-5}}$ d $\dfrac{1}{x^{-4}}$

e $\dfrac{7}{q^{-1}}$ f $\dfrac{3}{t^{-2}}$ g $\dfrac{5}{h^{-4}}$ h $\dfrac{4}{p^{-4}}$

i $\dfrac{a}{b^{-2}}$ j $\dfrac{e}{d^{-1}}$ k $\dfrac{2n^2}{m^{-3}}$ l $\dfrac{y^5}{3x^{-2}}$

m $\dfrac{-3}{7y^{-4}}$ n $\dfrac{-2}{b^{-8}}$ o $\dfrac{-3g}{4h^{-3}}$ p $\dfrac{(-3u)^2}{5t^{-2}}$

Example 15b **5** Express each of the following using positive indices only.

a $\dfrac{a^{-3}}{b^{-3}}$ b $\dfrac{x^{-2}}{y^{-5}}$ c $\dfrac{g^{-2}}{h^{-3}}$ d $\dfrac{m^{-1}}{n^{-1}}$

e $\dfrac{5^{-1}}{7^{-3}}$ f $\dfrac{3^{-2}}{4^{-3}}$ g $\dfrac{5^{-2}}{6^{-1}}$ h $\dfrac{4^{-3}}{8^{-2}}$

Example 15c **6** Express each of the following using positive indices only.

a $\dfrac{7}{x^{-4}y^3}$ b $\dfrac{1}{u^{-3}v^2}$ c $\dfrac{a^{-3}5^{-1}}{y^{-3}}$ d $\dfrac{2a^{-4}}{b^{-5}c^2}$

e $\dfrac{5a^2c^{-4}}{6b^{-2}d}$ f $\dfrac{5^{-1}h^3k^{-2}}{4^{-1}m^{-2}p}$ g $\dfrac{4t^{-1}u^{-2}}{3^{-1}v^2w^{-6}}$ h $\dfrac{4^{-1}x^2y^{-5}}{4m^{-1}n^{-4}}$

Example 16 **7** Evaluate without the use of a calculator. Hint: write expressions using positive indices.

a 5^{-1} b 3^{-2} c $(-4)^{-2}$ d -5^{-2}

e 4×10^{-2} f -5×10^{-3} g -3×2^{-2} h $8 \times (2^2)^{-2}$

i $6^4 \times 6^{-6}$ j $8^{-7} \times (8^2)^3$ k $(5^2)^{-1} \times (2^{-2})^{-1}$ l $(3^{-2})^2 \times (7^{-1})^{-1}$

m $\dfrac{1}{8^{-1}}$ n $\dfrac{1}{10^{-2}}$ o $\dfrac{-2}{5^{-3}}$ p $\dfrac{2}{2^{-3}}$

q $\dfrac{-5}{2^{-1}}$ r $\dfrac{2^3}{2^{-3}}$ s $\left(\dfrac{3}{8}\right)^{-2}$ t $\left(\dfrac{-4}{3}\right)^{-3}$

u $\dfrac{(-5)^2}{2^{-2}}$ v $\dfrac{(3^{-2})^3}{3^{-5}}$ w $\dfrac{(-2^{-3})^{-3}}{(2^{-2})^{-4}}$ x $\left(\dfrac{2^{-4}}{7^{-2}}\right)^{-1} \times \left(\dfrac{7^{-1}}{2^{-1}}\right)^{-4}$

8 The mass of a small insect is 2^{-9} kg. How many grams is this? Round to two decimal places.

9 Find the value of x in these equations.

a $2^x = \dfrac{1}{16}$ **b** $5^x = \dfrac{1}{625}$ **c** $(-3)^x = \dfrac{1}{81}$

d $(0.5)^x = 2$ **e** $(0.2)^x = 25$ **f** $3(2^{2x}) = 0.75$

10 Describe the error made in these problems then give the correct answer.

a $2x^{-2} = \dfrac{1}{2x^2}$ **b** $\dfrac{5}{a^4} = \dfrac{a^{-4}}{5}$ **c** $\dfrac{2}{(3b)^{-2}} = \dfrac{2b^2}{9}$

11 Consider the number $\left(\dfrac{2}{3}\right)^{-1}$.

a Complete this working: $\left(\dfrac{2}{3}\right)^{-1} = \dfrac{1}{\left(\dfrac{2}{3}\right)}$

$$= 1 \div \boxed{}$$

$$= 1 \times \boxed{}$$

$$= \dfrac{3}{2}$$

b Show similar working as in part **a** to simplify these.

i $\left(\dfrac{5}{4}\right)^{-1}$ **ii** $\left(\dfrac{2}{7}\right)^{-1}$ **iii** $\left(\dfrac{x}{3}\right)^{-1}$ **iv** $\left(\dfrac{a}{b}\right)^{-1}$

c What conclusion can you come to regarding the simplification of fractions raised to the power -1?

d Simplify these fractions.

i $\left(\dfrac{2}{3}\right)^{-2}$ **ii** $\left(\dfrac{4}{5}\right)^{-2}$ **iii** $\left(\dfrac{1}{2}\right)^{-5}$ **iv** $\left(\dfrac{7}{3}\right)^{-3}$

Enrichment: Exponential equations

12 To find x in $2^x = 32$ you could use trial and error; however, the following approach is more useful.

$$2^x = 32$$
$$2^x = 2^5 \qquad \text{(express 32 using a matching base)}$$
$$\therefore x = 5$$

Use this idea to solve for x in these equations.

a $2^x = 16$ **b** $3^x = 81$ **c** $5^x = 25$ **d** $\left(\dfrac{1}{2}\right)^x = \dfrac{1}{8}$

e $\left(\dfrac{1}{7}\right)^x = \dfrac{1}{49}$ **f** $\left(\dfrac{2}{3}\right)^x = \dfrac{16}{81}$ **g** $4^{2x} = 64$ **h** $3^{x+1} = 243$

i $2^{3x-1} = 64$

6.6 Scientific notation

It is common in the practical world to be working with very large or very small numbers. For example, the number of cubic metres of concrete used to build the Hoover Dam in the United States was 3 400 000 m^3 and the mass of a molecule of water is 0.000000000000000000000299 grams. Such numbers can be written more efficiently using powers of 10 with positive or negative indices. This is called scientific notation or standard form. The number is written using a number between 1 inclusive and 10 and this is multiplied by a power of 10. Such notation is also used to state very large and very small time intervals.

At the time of construction, the Hoover Dam was the largest concrete structure in the world.

Let's start: Building scientific notation

Use the information given to complete the table.

Decimal form	Working	Scientific notation
2 350 000	$2.35 \times 1\,000\,000$	2.35×10^6
502 170		
314 060 000		
0.000298	$2.98 \div 10\,000 = \dfrac{2.98}{10^4}$	2.98×10^{-4}
0.000004621		
0.003082		

- Discuss how each number using scientific notation is formed.
- When are positive indices used and when are negative indices used?
- Where does the decimal point appear to be placed when using scientific notation?

- Numbers written in **scientific notation** are expressed in the form $a \times 10^m$ where $1 \leq a < 10$ and m is an integer.
- Large numbers will use positive powers of 10.
  For example: 38 million years = 38 000 000 years
  $$= 3.8 \times 10^7 \text{ years}$$
- Small numbers will use negative powers of 10.
  For example: 417 nanoseconds = 0.000000417 seconds
  $$= 4.17 \times 10^{-7} \text{ seconds}$$
- To write numbers using scientific notation, place the decimal point after the first non-zero digit then multiply by a power of 10.
- Examples of units where very large or small numbers may be used:
  - 2178 km = 2 178 000 m = 2.178×10^6 metres
  - 4517 centuries = 451 700 years = 4.517×10^5 years
  - 12 million years = 12 000 000 years = 12×10^6 or 1.2×10^7 years
  - 2320 tonnes = 2320×10^3 kg = 2.32×10^6 kg
  - 27 microns (millionth of a metre) = 0.000027 m = 27×10^{-6} or 2.7×10^{-5} metres
  - 109 milliseconds (thousandths of a second) = 0.109 seconds = 109×10^{-3} or 1.09×10^{-1} seconds
  - 3.8 microseconds (millionth of a second) = 0.0000038 = 3.8×10^{-6} seconds
  - 54 nanoseconds (billionth of a second) = 0.000000054 = 54×10^{-9} or 5.4×10^{-8} seconds

The big bang theory deals with measurements from microscopically small to astronomically large, all expressed conveniently in scientific notation

Example 17 Writing numbers using scientific notation

Write the following in scientific notation.
a   4 500 000
b   0.0000004

SOLUTION

EXPLANATION

a $4\,500\,000 = 4.5 \times 10^6$

Place the decimal point after the first non-zero digit (4) then multiply by 10^6 since decimal place has been moved 6 places to the left.

b $0.0000004 = 4.0 \times 10^{-7}$

The first non-zero digit is 4. Multiply by 10^{-7} since decimal place has been moved 7 places to the right.

Example 18 Writing numbers in decimal form

Express each of the following in decimal form.

a 9.34×10^5

b 4.71×10^{-5}

SOLUTION

EXPLANATION

a $9.34 \times 10^5 = 934\,000$

Move the decimal point 5 places to the right.

b $4.71 \times 10^{-5} = 0.0000471$

Move the decimal point 5 places to the left and insert zeros where necessary.

Exercise 6F

Understanding

1 Which of the numbers 1000, 10 000 or 100 000 completes each equation?

a $6.2 \times \underline{\hspace{1cm}} = 62\,000$

b $9.41 \times \underline{\hspace{1cm}} = 9410$

c $1.03 \times \underline{\hspace{1cm}} = 103\,000$

d $3.2 \div \underline{\hspace{1cm}} = 0.0032$

e $5.16 \div \underline{\hspace{1cm}} = 0.0000516$

f $1.09 \div \underline{\hspace{1cm}} = 0.000109$

2 Write the following as powers of 10.

a 100 000

b 100

c 1 000 000 000

3 If these numbers were written using scientific notation, would positive or negative indices be used?

a 2000

b 0.0004

c 19 300

d 0.00101431

Fluency

Example 17a

4 Write the following in scientific notation.

a 40 000

b 2 300 000 000 000

c 16 000 000 000

d -7 200 000

e -3500

f -8 800 000

g 52 hundreds

h 3 million

i 21 thousands

Example 17b

5 Write the following in scientific notation.

a 0.000003

b 0.0004

c -0.00876

d 0.00000000073

e -0.00003

f 0.000000000125

g -0.00000000809

h 0.000000024

i 0.0000345

6 Write each of the following numbers in scientific notation.

a 6000

b 720 000

c 324.5

d 7869.03

e 8459.12

f 0.2

g 0.000328

h 0.00987

i -0.00001

j -460 100 000

k 17 467

l -128

Example 18a

7 Express each of the following in decimal form.

a 5.7×10^4

b 3.6×10^6

c 4.3×10^8

d 3.21×10^7

e 4.23×10^5

f 9.04×10^{10}

g 1.97×10^8

h 7.09×10^2

i 6.357×10^5

Example 18b

8 Express each of the following in decimal form.

a 1.2×10^{-4}	**b** 4.6×10^{-6}	**c** 8×10^{-10}
d 3.52×10^{-5}	**e** 3.678×10^{-1}	**f** 1.23×10^{-7}
g 9×10^{-5}	**h** 5×10^{-2}	**i** 4×10^{-1}

9 Express each of the following approximate numbers using scientific notation.

a The mass of Earth is
6 000 000 000 000 000 000 000 000 kg.

b The diameter of Earth is 40 000 000 m.

c The diameter of a gold atom is 0.0000000001 m.

d The radius of Earth's orbit around the Sun is
150 000 000 km.

e The universal constant of gravitation is
0.0000000000667 Nm^2/kg^2.

f The half-life of polonium-214 is 0.00015 seconds.

g Uranium-238 has a half-life of 4 500 000 000 years.

Image of gold atoms formed by a very powerful electron microscope.

10 Express each of the following in decimal form.

a Neptune is approximately 4.6×10^9 km from Earth.

b A population of bacteria contained 8×10^{12} organisms.

c The Moon is approximately 3.84×10^5 km from Earth.

d A fifty-cent coin is approximately 3.8×10^{-3} m thick.

e The diameter of the nucleus of an atom is approximately 1×10^{-14} m.

f The population of a city is 7.2×10^5.

Earth is about 3.84×10^5 km from the Moon.

11 Write the following using scientific notation in the units given in the brackets.

Recall: 1 second = 1000 milliseconds

1 millisecond = 1000 microseconds

1 microsecond = 1000 nanoseconds

a 3 million years (months)
b 0.03 million years (months)
c 492 milliseconds (seconds)
d 0.38 milliseconds (seconds)
e 2.1 microseconds (seconds)
f 0.052 microseconds (seconds)
g 4 nanoseconds (seconds)
h 139.2 nanoseconds (seconds)
i 39.5 centuries (years)
j 438 decades (years)
k 430 tonnes (kg)
l 0.5 kg (grams)
m 2.3 hours (milliseconds)
n 5 minutes (nanoseconds)

12 When Sydney was planning for the 2000 Olympic Games, the Olympic Organising Committee made the following predictions:

- The cost of staging the games would be A\$1.7 billion ($\$1.7 \times 10^9$) (excluding infrastructure). In fact, \$140 million extra was spent on staging the games.
- The cost of constructing or upgrading infrastructure would be \$807 million.

Give each of the following answers in scientific notation.

a The actual total cost of staging the Olympic Games.

b The total cost of staging the games and constructing or upgrading the infrastructure.

Sydney Olympic Stadium

13 Two planets are 2.8×10^8 km and 1.9×10^9 km from their closest sun. What is the difference between these two distances in scientific notation?

14 Two particles weigh 2.43×10^{-2} g and 3.04×10^{-3} g. Find the difference in their weight in scientific notation.

15 The number 47×10^4 is not written using scientific notation since 47 is not a number between 1 and 10. The following shows how to convert to scientific notation.
$$47 \times 10^4 = 4.7 \times 10 \times 10^4$$
$$= 4.7 \times 10^5$$

Write these numbers using scientific notation.

a 32×10^3 b 41×10^5 c 317×10^2 d 5714×10^2
e 0.13×10^5 f 0.092×10^3 g 0.003×10^8 h 0.00046×10^9
i 61×10^{-3} j 424×10^{-2} k 1013×10^{-6} l $490\,000 \times 10^{-1}$
m 0.02×10^{-3} n 0.0004×10^{-2} o 0.00372×10^{-1} p 0.04001×10^{-6}

16 Use index law 3: $(a^m)^n = a^{m \times n}$ and index law 5: $(a \times b)^m = a^m \times b^m$ to simplify these numbers. Then write your answer in scientific notation where necessary.

a $(2 \times 10^2)^3$ b $(3 \times 10^4)^2$ c $(2.5 \times 10^{-2})^2$ d $(1.5 \times 10^{-3})^3$
e $(2 \times 10^{-3})^{-3}$ f $(5 \times 10^{-4})^{-2}$ g $\left(\dfrac{1}{3} \times 10^2\right)^{-2}$ h $\left(\dfrac{2}{5} \times 10^{-4}\right)^{-1}$

Enrichment: Scientific notation with index laws

17 Use index laws to simplify these and write using scientific notation.

a $(3 \times 10^2) \times (2 \times 10^4)$ b $(4 \times 10^4) \times (2 \times 10^7)$
c $(8 \times 10^6) \div (4 \times 10^2)$ d $(9 \times 10^{20}) \div (3 \times 10^{11})$
e $(7 \times 10^2) \times (8 \times 10^2)$ f $(1.5 \times 10^3) \times (8 \times 10^4)$
g $(6 \times 10^4) \div (0.5 \times 10^2)$ h $(1.8 \times 10^6) \div (0.2 \times 10^3)$
i $(3 \times 10^{-4}) \times (3 \times 10^{-5})$ j $(15 \times 10^{-2}) \div (2 \times 10^6)$
k $(4.5 \times 10^{-3}) \div (3 \times 10^2)$ l $(8.8 \times 10^{-1}) \div (8.8 \times 10^{-1})$

18 Determine, using index laws, how long it takes for light to travel from the Sun to Earth in seconds given that Earth is 1.5×10^8 km from the Sun and the speed of light is 3×10^5 km/s.

19 Using index laws and the fact that the speed of light is equal to 3×10^5 km/s, determine:

a how far light travels in one nanosecond (1×10^{-9} seconds). Answer in scientific notation in km then convert your answer to cm.

b how long light takes to travel 300 kilometres. Answer in seconds.

6.7 Scientific notation using significant figures

The number of digits used to record measurements depends on how accurately the measurements can be recorded. The volume of Earth, for example, has been calculated as $1\,083\,210\,000\,000$ km^3. This shows six significant figures and could be written using scientific notation as 1.08321×10^{12}. A more accurate calculation may include more non-zero digits in the last seven places.

The mass of a single oxygen molecule is known to be $0.000000000000000000000000053$ g. This shows two significant figures and is written using scientific notation as 5.3×10^{-26}. On many calculators you will notice that very large or very small numbers are automatically converted to scientific notation using a certain number of significant figures. Numbers can also be entered into a calculator using scientific notation.

The accuracy of a measurement of the volume of Earth depends in part on the number of significant figures.

Let's start: Significant discussions

Begin a discussion regarding scientific figures by referring to these questions.

- Why is the volume of Earth given as $1\,083\,210\,000\,000$ km^3 written using seven zeros at the end of the number? Wouldn't the exact mass of Earth include some other digits in these places?
- Why is the mass of an oxygen molecule given as 5.3×10^{-26} written using only two digits to the left of the power of 10? Wouldn't the exact mass of a water molecule include more decimal places?

key ideas

- **Significant figures** are counted from left to right starting at the first non-zero digit. Zeros with no non-zero digit on their right are not counted. For example:
  - $38\,041\,000$ has five significant figures
  - 0.0016 has two significant figures
  - 3.21×10^4 has three significant figures.
- When using scientific notation the first significant figure sits to the left of the decimal point.
- Calculators can be used to work with scientific notation.
  - $\boxed{E}$ or $\boxed{EE}$ or $\boxed{EXP}$ are common key names on calculators.
  - Pressing 2.37 $\boxed{EE}$ 5 gives 2.37×10^5.
  - 2.37E5 means 2.37×10^5.

Example 19 Stating the number of significant figures

State the number of significant figures given in these numbers.

a 451 000   **b** 0.005012   **c** 3.2×10^7

SOLUTION   **EXPLANATION**

a 3 significant figures   Do not count the group of zeros to the right.

b 4 significant figures   Start counting at the first non-zero digit.

c 2 significant figures   With scientific notation the first significant figure is to the left of the decimal point.

Example 20 Writing numbers in scientific notation using significant figures

Write these numbers using scientific notation and three significant figures.

a 2 183 000   **b** 0.0019482

SOLUTION   **EXPLANATION**

a $2\ 183\ 000 = 2.18 \times 10^6$ Put the decimal point after the first non-zero digit. The decimal point has moved 6 places so multiply by 10^6. Round the third significant figure down since the following digit is less than 5.

b $0.0019482 = 1.95 \times 10^{-3}$ Move the decimal point 3 places to the right and multiply by 10^{-3}. Round the third significant figure up to 5 since the following digit is greater than 4.

Example 21 Using a calculator with scientific notation

Use a calculator to evaluate each of the following, leaving your answers in scientific notation correct to four significant figures.

a $3.67 \times 10^5 \times 23.6 \times 10^4$ **b** $7.6 \times 10^{-3} + \sqrt{2.4 \times 10^{-2}}$

SOLUTION   **EXPLANATION**

a $3.67 \times 10^5 \times 23.6 \times 10^4$
$= 8.661 \times 10^{10}$

Graphics or CAS calculator

Use a calculator with the key sequence shown. Write in scientific notation with four significant figures.

$\boxed{3}\boxed{.}\boxed{6}\boxed{7}\boxed{\text{EE}}\boxed{5}\boxed{\times}\boxed{2}\boxed{3}\boxed{.}\boxed{6}\boxed{\text{EE}}\boxed{4}\boxed{\text{ENTER}}$

b $7.6 \times 10^{-3} + \sqrt{2.4 \times 10^{-2}}$
$= 0.1625$
$= 1.625 \times 10^{-1}$

Use a calculator with the key sequence shown. Write in scientific notation with a number between 1 and 10.

Graphics or CAS calculator

$\boxed{7}\boxed{.}\boxed{6}\boxed{\text{EE}}\boxed{(\text{-})}\boxed{3}\boxed{+}\boxed{\sqrt{\ }}\boxed{2}\boxed{.}\boxed{4}\boxed{\text{EE}}\boxed{(\text{-})}\boxed{2}\boxed{)}\boxed{\text{ENTER}}$

Exercise 6G

1 Complete the tables, rounding each number to the given number of significant figures.

a 57 263

Significant figures	Rounded number
4	
3	57 300
2	
1	

b 4 170 162

Significant figures	Rounded number
5	
4	
3	4 170 000
2	
1	

c 0.0036612

Significant figures	Rounded number
4	
3	
2	
1	0.004

d 24.8706

Significant figures	Rounded number
5	
4	
3	
2	25
1	

2 Decide if the following numbers are written using scientific notation with three significant figures. (Yes or no).

a 4.21×10^4
b 32×10^{-3}
c 1800×10^6
d 0.04×10^2
e 1.89×10^{-10}
f 9.04×10^{-6}
g 5.56×10^{-14}
h 0.213×10^2
i 26.1×10^{-2}

Example 19

3 State the number of significant figures given in these numbers.

a 27 200
b 1007
c 301 010
d 190
e 0.0183
f 0.20
g 0.706
h 0.00109
i 4.21×10^3
j 2.905×10^{-2}
k 1.07×10^{-6}
l 5.90×10^5

Example 20

4 Write these numbers using scientific notation and three significant figures.

a 242 300
b 171 325
c 2829
d 3247000
e 0.00034276
f 0.006859
g 0.01463
h 0.001031
i 23.41
j 326.042
k 19.618
l 0.172046

5 Write each number using scientific notation rounding to the number of significant figures given in the brackets.

a 47 760 (3)
b 21 610 (2)
c 4 833 160 (4)
d 37.16 (2)
e 99.502 (3)
f 0.014427 (4)
g 0.00201 (1)
h 0.08516 (1)
i 0.0001010 (1)

Fluency

6 Use a calculator to evaluate each of the following, leaving your answers in scientific notation correct to four significant figures.

a 4^{-6}

b 78^{-3}

c $(-7.3 \times 10^{-4})^{-5}$

d $\dfrac{3.185}{7 \times 10^4}$

e $2.13 \times 10^4 \times 9 \times 10^7$

f $5.671 \times 10^2 \times 3.518 \times 10^5$

g $9.419 \times 10^5 \times 4.08 \times 10^{-4}$

h $2.85 \times 10^{-9} \times 6 \times 10^{-3}$

i $12\,345^2$

j 87.14^8

k $\dfrac{1.8 \times 10^{26}}{4.5 \times 10^{22}}$

l $\dfrac{-4.7 \times 10^{-2} \times 6.18 \times 10^7}{3.2 \times 10^6}$

7 Use a calculator to evaluate each of the following, leaving your answers in scientific notation correct to five significant figures.

a $\sqrt{8756}$

b $\sqrt{634 \times 7.56 \times 10^7}$

c $8.6 \times 10^5 + \sqrt{2.8 \times 10^{-2}}$

d $-8.9 \times 10^{-4} + \sqrt{7.6 \times 10^{-3}}$

e $\dfrac{5.12 \times 10^{21} - 5.23 \times 10^{20}}{2 \times 10^6}$

f $\dfrac{8.942 \times 10^{47} - 6.713 \times 10^{44}}{2.5 \times 10^{19}}$

g $\dfrac{2 \times 10^7 + 3 \times 10^8}{5}$

h $\dfrac{4 \times 10^8 + 7 \times 10^9}{6}$

i $\dfrac{6.8 \times 10^{-8} + 7.5 \times 10^{27}}{4.1 \times 10^{27}}$

j $\dfrac{2.84 \times 10^{-6} - 2.71 \times 10^{-9}}{5.14 \times 10^{-6} + 7 \times 10^{-8}}$

Problem-solving

8 The mass of Earth is approximately 6 000 000 000 000 000 000 000 000 kg. Given that the mass of the Sun is 330 000 times the mass of Earth, find the mass of the Sun. Express your answer in scientific notation correct to three significant figures.

9 The diameter of Earth is approximately 12 756 000 m. If the Sun's diameter is 109 times that of Earth, compute its diameter in kilometres. Express your answer in scientific notation correct to three significant figures.

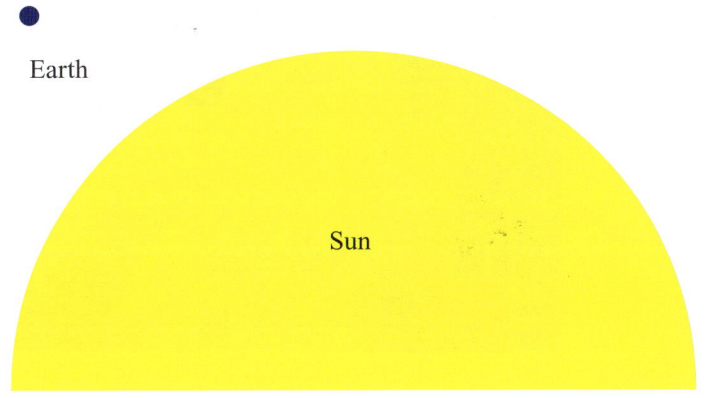

Earth

Sun

The size of the Sun and Earth compared (distance of Earth to Sun is not to scale).

10 Using the formula for the volume of a sphere, $V = \dfrac{4\pi r^3}{3}$, and, assuming Earth to be spherical, calculate the volume of Earth in km^3. Use the data given in Question **9**. Express your answer in scientific notation correct to three significant figures.

11 Write these numbers from largest to smallest.
2.41×10^6, 24.2×10^5, 0.239×10^7, 2421×10^3, 0.02×10^8

12 The following output is common on a number of different calculators and computers. Write down the number that you think they represent.

a 4.26E6   **b** 9.1E-3   **c** 5.04EXP11
d 1.931EXP-1   **e** 2.1^{06} **f** 6.14^{-11}

13 Anton writes down $352\,000 \times 250\,000 = 8.8^{10}$. Explain his error.

14 a Round these numbers to three significant figures. Retain the use of scientific notation.

   i 2.302×10^2 **ii** 4.9045×10^{-2} **iii** 3.996×10^6

  b What do you notice about the digit which is the third significant figure?

  c Why do you think that it might be important to a scientist to show a significant figure at the end of a number which is a zero?

Enrichment: Combining bacteria

15 A flask of type A bacteria contains 5.4×10^{12} cells and a flask of type B bacteria contains 4.6×10^8 cells. The two types of bacteria are combined in the same flask.

  a How many bacterial cells are there in the flask?

  b If type A bacterial cells double every 8 hours and type B bacterial cells triple every 8 hours how many cells are in the flask after:

    i one day?

    ii a week?

    iii 30 days?

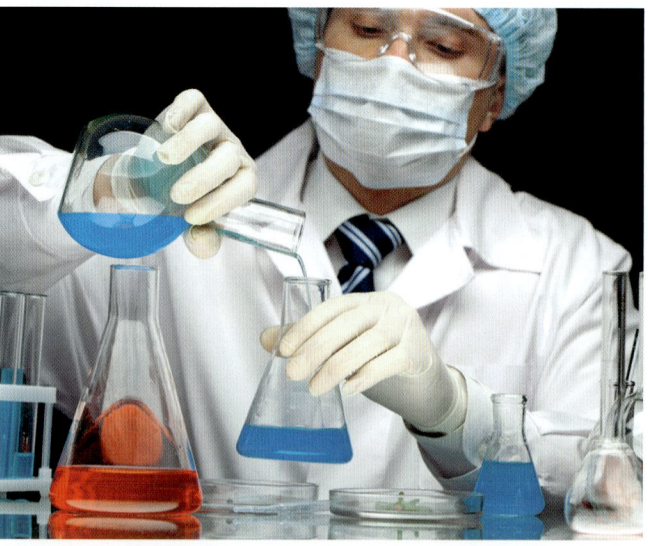

Express your answers in scientific notation correct to three significant figures.

6.8 Fractional indices and surds

So far we have considered indices including positive and negative integers and zero. Numbers can also be expressed using fractional indices. Two examples are $9^{\frac{1}{2}}$ and $5^{\frac{1}{3}}$.

Using index law 1: $9^{\frac{1}{2}} \times 9^{\frac{1}{2}} = 9^{\frac{1}{2}+\frac{1}{2}} = 9^1 = 9$

Since $\sqrt{9} \times \sqrt{9} = 9$ and $9^{\frac{1}{2}} \times 9^{\frac{1}{2}} = 9$ then $9^{\frac{1}{2}} = \sqrt{9}$.

Similarly, $5^{\frac{1}{3}} \times 5^{\frac{1}{3}} \times 5^{\frac{1}{3}} = 5^{\frac{1}{3}+\frac{1}{3}+\frac{1}{3}} = 5^1 = 5$

Since $\sqrt[3]{5} \times \sqrt[3]{5} \times \sqrt[3]{5} = 5$ and $5^{\frac{1}{3}} \times 5^{\frac{1}{3}} \times 5^{\frac{1}{3}} = 5$ then $5^{\frac{1}{3}} = \sqrt[3]{5}$.

This shows that numbers with fractional powers can be written using root signs. In the example above, $9^{\frac{1}{2}}$ is the square root of 9 ($\sqrt{9}$) and $5^{\frac{1}{3}}$ is the cubed root of $5\left(\sqrt[3]{5}\right)$.

You will have noticed that $9^{\frac{1}{2}} = \sqrt{9} = 3 = \frac{3}{1}$ and so $9^{\frac{1}{2}}$ is a rational number (a fraction) but $5^{\frac{1}{3}} = \sqrt[3]{5}$ does not appear to be able to be expressed as a fraction. In fact, $\sqrt[3]{5}$ is irrational and cannot be expressed as a fraction and is called a surd. As a decimal $\sqrt[3]{5} = 1.70997594668...$, which is an infinite non-recurring decimal with no repeated pattern. This is a characteristic of all surds.

Let's start: A surd or not?

Surds are numbers with a root sign that cannot be expressed as a fraction. As a decimal they are infinite and non-recurring (with no pattern).

Use a calculator to help complete this table then decide if you think the numbers are surds.

Index form	With root sign	Decimal	Surd (Yes or No)
$2^{\frac{1}{2}}$	$\sqrt{2}$		
$4^{\frac{1}{2}}$	$\sqrt{4}$		
$11^{\frac{1}{2}}$			
$36^{\frac{1}{2}}$			
$1\frac{1}{9}^{\frac{1}{2}}$			
$(0.1)^{\frac{1}{2}}$			
$3^{\frac{1}{3}}$	$\sqrt[3]{3}$		
$8^{\frac{1}{3}}$	$\sqrt[3]{8}$		
$15^{\frac{1}{3}}$			
$\left(\frac{1}{27}\right)^{\frac{1}{3}}$			
$5^{\frac{1}{4}}$			
$64^{\frac{1}{6}}$			

■ Numbers written with **fractional indices** can also be written using a root sign.

- $a^{\frac{1}{m}} = \sqrt[m]{a}$
- $\sqrt[2]{a}$ is written $\sqrt{a}$

  For example: $3^{\frac{1}{2}} = \sqrt{3}$, $7^{\frac{1}{3}} = \sqrt[3]{7}$, $2^{\frac{1}{5}} = \sqrt[5]{2}$

■ **Surds** are irrational numbers written with a root sign.
- Irrational numbers cannot be expressed as a fraction.
- The decimal expansion is infinite and non-recurring with no pattern.

$\sqrt{2} = 1.41421356237\ldots$
$\sqrt[3]{10} = 2.15443469003\ldots$
$3^{1/2} = 1.73205080757\ldots$

Example 22 Writing numbers using a root sign

Write these numbers using a root sign.

a $6^{\frac{1}{2}}$

b $2^{\frac{1}{5}}$

SOLUTION

a $6^{\frac{1}{2}} = \sqrt{6}$

b $2^{\frac{1}{5}} = \sqrt[5]{2}$

EXPLANATION

$a^{\frac{1}{m}} = \sqrt[m]{a}$ so $6^{\frac{1}{2}} = \sqrt[2]{6}$ (or $\sqrt{6}$) the square root of 6.

$\sqrt[5]{2}$ is called the 5th root of 2.

Example 23 Evaluating numbers with fractional indices

Evaluate:

a $144^{\frac{1}{2}}$

b $27^{\frac{1}{3}}$

SOLUTION

a $144^{\frac{1}{2}} = \sqrt{144}$
$= 12$

b $27^{\frac{1}{3}} = \sqrt[3]{27}$
$= 3$

EXPLANATION

$a^{\frac{1}{m}} = \sqrt[m]{a}$ where $m = 2$ and the square root of $144 = 12$ since $12^2 = 144$.

The cubed root of 27 is 3 since $3^3 = 3 \times 3 \times 3 = 27$

Example 24 Using index laws

Use index laws to simplify these expressions.

a $a^{\frac{1}{2}} \times a^{\frac{3}{2}}$

b $\dfrac{x^{\frac{1}{2}}}{x^{\frac{1}{3}}}$

c $(y^2)^{\frac{1}{4}}$

SOLUTION	EXPLANATION
a $a^{\frac{1}{2}} \times a^{\frac{3}{2}} = a^{\frac{1}{2}+\frac{3}{2}}$ $= a^{\frac{4}{2}}$ $= a^2$	When multiplying indices with the same base add the powers.
b $\dfrac{x^{\frac{1}{2}}}{x^{\frac{1}{3}}} = x^{\frac{1}{2}-\frac{1}{3}}$ $= x^{\frac{1}{6}}$	When dividing indices with the same base, subtract the powers. $\dfrac{1}{2} - \dfrac{1}{3} = \dfrac{3}{6} - \dfrac{2}{6} = \dfrac{1}{6}$.
c $(y^2)^{\frac{1}{4}} = y^{2 \times \frac{1}{4}}$ $= y^{\frac{1}{2}}$	When raising a power to a power, multiply the indices. $\dfrac{2}{4} = \dfrac{1}{2}$

Exercise 6H

1 Evaluate these numbers.

Understanding

  a 2^2 and $\sqrt{4}$ **b** 2^3 and $\sqrt[3]{8}$ **c** 3^2 and $\sqrt{9}$

  d 3^3 and $\sqrt[3]{27}$ **e** 4^2 and $\sqrt{16}$ **f** 4^3 and $\sqrt[3]{64}$

2 State whether or not the following are true or false.

  a Rational numbers are fractions.   **b** A surd is a rational number.

  c A surd in decimal form will be infinite and non recurring (with no pattern).

  d $\sqrt{3} = 3^{\frac{1}{2}}$ **e** $\sqrt{8} = 8^{\frac{1}{3}}$ **f** $5^{\frac{1}{3}} = \sqrt{5}$ **g** $10^{\frac{1}{6}} = \sqrt[10]{6}$

3 Use a calculator to evaluate these surds and round to four decimal places.

  a $7^{\frac{1}{2}}$ (or $\sqrt{7}$)   **b** $13^{\frac{1}{2}}$ (or $\sqrt{13}$)   **c** $83^{\frac{1}{2}}$ (or $\sqrt{83}$)

Fluency

Example 22

4 Write these numbers using a root sign.

  a $3^{\frac{1}{2}}$ **b** $7^{\frac{1}{2}}$ **c** $5^{\frac{1}{3}}$ **d** $12^{\frac{1}{3}}$

  e $31^{\frac{1}{5}}$ **f** $18^{\frac{1}{7}}$ **g** $9^{\frac{1}{9}}$ **h** $3^{\frac{1}{8}}$

5 Write these numbers in index form.

  a $\sqrt{8}$ **b** $\sqrt{19}$ **c** $\sqrt[3]{10}$ **d** $\sqrt[3]{31}$

  e $\sqrt[4]{5}$ **f** $\sqrt[5]{9}$ **g** $\sqrt[8]{11}$ **h** $\sqrt[11]{20}$

Example 23   **6**   Without a calculator, evaluate these numbers with fractional indices.

a $25^{\frac{1}{2}}$ b $49^{\frac{1}{2}}$ c $81^{\frac{1}{2}}$ d $169^{\frac{1}{2}}$

e $8^{\frac{1}{3}}$ f $64^{\frac{1}{3}}$ g $125^{\frac{1}{3}}$ h $1000^{\frac{1}{3}}$

i $16^{\frac{1}{4}}$ j $81^{\frac{1}{4}}$ k $625^{\frac{1}{4}}$ l $32^{\frac{1}{5}}$

Example 24   **7**   Use index laws to simplify these expressions. Leave your answer in index form.

a $a^{\frac{1}{2}} \times a^{\frac{1}{2}}$ b $a^{\frac{1}{3}} \times a^{\frac{1}{3}}$ c $a^{\frac{2}{3}} \times a^{\frac{4}{3}}$ d $a^{2} \times a^{\frac{1}{2}}$

e $\dfrac{x^{\frac{2}{3}}}{x^{\frac{1}{3}}}$ f $\dfrac{x^{\frac{3}{2}}}{x^{\frac{1}{2}}}$ g $\dfrac{x^{\frac{7}{6}}}{x^{\frac{2}{6}}}$ h $\dfrac{x^{\frac{4}{3}}}{x^{\frac{1}{3}}}$

i $(y^{2})^{\frac{1}{2}}$ j $(y^{3})^{\frac{2}{3}}$ k $(y^{\frac{1}{2}})^{3}$ l $(x^{\frac{1}{2}})^{\frac{1}{2}}$

m $(x^{\frac{2}{3}})^{4}$ n $(a^{\frac{2}{5}})^{\frac{1}{3}}$ o $(a^{\frac{3}{4}})^{\frac{1}{2}}$ p $(n^{\frac{2}{5}})^{\frac{10}{3}}$

8   Use index laws to simplify these expressions.

a $a \times a^{\frac{1}{3}}$ b $a^{\frac{1}{2}} \times a^{\frac{1}{5}}$ c $a^{\frac{2}{3}} \times a^{\frac{3}{7}}$ d $a^{5} \div a^{\frac{7}{3}}$ e $b^{\frac{2}{3}} \div b^{\frac{1}{2}}$ f $x^{\frac{4}{5}} \div x^{\frac{2}{3}}$

9   Evaluate the following without a calculator. Hint: first rewrite each question using positive indices.

a $4^{-\frac{1}{2}}$ b $8^{-\frac{1}{3}}$ c $32^{-\frac{1}{5}}$ d $81^{-\frac{1}{4}}$

e $25^{-\frac{1}{2}}$ f $27^{-\frac{1}{3}}$ g $1000^{-\frac{1}{3}}$ h $256^{-\frac{1}{4}}$

10   Note that $8^{\frac{2}{3}} = (8^{\frac{1}{3}})^{2}$ using index law 3

$$= (\sqrt[3]{8})^{2} \qquad\qquad \text{since } 8^{\frac{1}{3}} = \sqrt[3]{8}$$
$$= 2^{2} \qquad\qquad\qquad \sqrt[3]{8} = 2 \text{ since } 2^{3} = 8$$
$$= 4$$

Use the approach shown in the example above to evaluate these numbers.

a $27^{\frac{2}{3}}$ b $64^{\frac{2}{3}}$ c $9^{\frac{3}{2}}$ d $25^{\frac{3}{2}}$ e $16^{\frac{5}{4}}$ f $4^{\frac{5}{2}}$ g $81^{\frac{3}{2}}$ h $125^{\frac{5}{3}}$

11   Find the length of the hypotenuse (c) in these right angled triangles. Use Pythagoras' theorem ($c^{2} = a^{2} + b^{2}$) and write your answer as a surd.

a   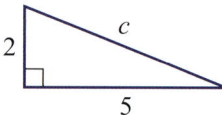   b   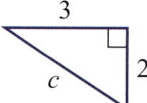   c 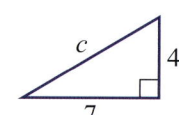

d   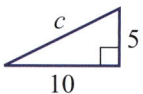   e   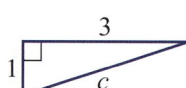   f 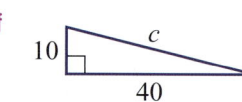

12 Show working to prove that the answers to all these questions simplify to 1. Remember $a^0 = 1$.

a $a^{\frac{1}{2}} \times a^{-\frac{1}{2}}$

b $a^{\frac{2}{3}} \times a^{-\frac{2}{3}}$

c $a^{\frac{4}{7}} \times a^{-\frac{4}{7}}$

d $a^{\frac{5}{6}} \div a^{\frac{5}{6}}$

e $\left(a^{\frac{1}{2}}\right)^{\frac{1}{2}} \div a^{\frac{1}{4}}$

f $a^2 \div (a^3)^{\frac{2}{3}}$

13 A student tries to evaluate $9^{\frac{1}{2}}$ on a calculator and types 9^1/2 and gets 4.5. But you know that $9^{\frac{1}{2}} = \sqrt{9} = 3$. What has the student done wrong? (Note: ^ on some calculators is x^y.)

14 a Evaluate the following.

    i $\sqrt{3^2}$ **ii** $\sqrt{5^2}$ **iii** $\sqrt{10^2}$

  b Simplify $\sqrt{a^2}$.

  c Use fractional indices to show that $\sqrt{a^2} = a$ if $a \geq 0$.

  d Evaluate the following.

    i $(\sqrt{4})^2$ **ii** $(\sqrt{9})^2$ **iii** $(\sqrt{36})^2$

  e Simplify $(\sqrt{a})^2$.

  f Use fractional indices to show that $(\sqrt{a})^2 = a$. Assume $a \geq 0$.

  g Simplify:

    i $\sqrt[3]{a^3}$ **ii** $\sqrt[5]{a^5}$ **iii** $(\sqrt[3]{a})^3$ **iv** $(\sqrt[6]{a})^6$

Enrichment: Fractions raised to fractions

15 Note, for example, that $\left(\frac{4}{9}\right)^{\frac{1}{2}} = \sqrt{\frac{4}{9}} = \frac{2}{3}$ since $\frac{2}{3} \times \frac{2}{3} = \frac{4}{9}$. Now evaluate the following.

a $\left(\frac{16}{25}\right)^{\frac{1}{2}}$ **b** $\left(\frac{9}{49}\right)^{\frac{1}{2}}$ **c** $\left(\frac{4}{81}\right)^{\frac{1}{2}}$ **d** $\left(\frac{8}{27}\right)^{\frac{1}{3}}$

e $\left(\frac{64}{125}\right)^{\frac{1}{3}}$ **f** $\left(\frac{16}{81}\right)^{\frac{1}{4}}$ **g** $\left(\frac{256}{625}\right)^{\frac{1}{4}}$ **h** $\left(\frac{1000}{343}\right)^{\frac{1}{3}}$

16 Note that $\left(\frac{4}{9}\right)^{-\frac{1}{2}} = \frac{1}{\left(\frac{4}{9}\right)^{\frac{1}{2}}} = \frac{1}{\sqrt{\frac{4}{9}}} = \frac{1}{\left(\frac{2}{3}\right)} = \frac{3}{2}$. Now evaluate the following.

a $\left(\frac{9}{4}\right)^{-\frac{1}{2}}$ **b** $\left(\frac{49}{144}\right)^{-\frac{1}{2}}$ **c** $\left(\frac{8}{125}\right)^{-\frac{1}{3}}$ **d** $\left(\frac{1296}{625}\right)^{-\frac{1}{4}}$

6.9 Simple operations with surds

Since surds, such as $\sqrt{2}$ and $\sqrt{7}$, are numbers, they can be added, subtracted, multiplied or divided. Expressions with surds can also be simplified but this depends on the surds themselves and the types of operations that sit between them.

$\sqrt{2} + \sqrt{3}$ cannot be simplified since $\sqrt{2}$ and $\sqrt{3}$ are not 'like' surds. This is like trying to simplify $x + y$. However, $\sqrt{2} + 5\sqrt{2}$ simplifies to $6\sqrt{2}$ and this is like simplifying $x + 5x = 6x$. Subtraction of surds is treated in the same manner.

Products and quotients involving surds can also be simplified as in these examples:

$$\sqrt{11} \times \sqrt{2} = \sqrt{22} \quad \text{and} \quad \sqrt{30} \div \sqrt{3} = \sqrt{10}$$

→ Let's start: Rules for multiplication and division

Use a calculator to find a decimal approximation for each of the expressions in these pairs.

- $\sqrt{2} \times \sqrt{3}$ and $\sqrt{6}$

- $\sqrt{10} \times \sqrt{5}$ and $\sqrt{50}$

What does this suggest about the simplification of $\sqrt{a} \times \sqrt{b}$?

Repeat the above exploration for these.

- $\sqrt{6} \div \sqrt{2}$ and $\sqrt{\dfrac{6}{2}}$

- $\sqrt{80} \div \sqrt{8}$ and $\sqrt{\dfrac{80}{8}}$

What does this suggest about the simplification of $\sqrt{a} \div \sqrt{b}$?

Key ideas

- **Surds** can be simplified using addition or subtraction if they are **'like' surds**.
  - $2\sqrt{3} + 3\sqrt{3} = 5\sqrt{3}$
  - $11\sqrt{7} - 2\sqrt{7} = 9\sqrt{7}$
  - $\sqrt{3} + \sqrt{5}$ cannot be simplified.

- $(\sqrt{a})^2 = a$

- $\sqrt{a} \times \sqrt{b} = \sqrt{ab}$

  For example: $\sqrt{5} \times \sqrt{3} = \sqrt{5 \times 3} = \sqrt{15}$

- $\sqrt{a} \div \sqrt{b} = \sqrt{\dfrac{a}{b}}$

  For example: $\sqrt{10} \div \sqrt{5} = \sqrt{\dfrac{10}{5}} = \sqrt{2}$

Example 25 Adding and subtracting surds

Simplify:

a $2\sqrt{5}+6\sqrt{5}$

b $\sqrt{3}-5\sqrt{3}$

SOLUTION	EXPLANATION
a $2\sqrt{5}+6\sqrt{5}=8\sqrt{5}$	This is like simplifying $2x+6x=8x$. $2\sqrt{5}$ and $6\sqrt{5}$ contain like surds.
b $\sqrt{3}-5\sqrt{3}=-4\sqrt{3}$	This is similar to $x-5x=-4x$ in algebra.

Example 26 Multiplying and dividing surds

Simplify:

a $\sqrt{3}\times\sqrt{10}$

b $\sqrt{24}\div\sqrt{8}$

SOLUTION	EXPLANATION
a $\sqrt{3}\times\sqrt{10}=\sqrt{3\times10}$ $=\sqrt{30}$	Use $\sqrt{a}\times\sqrt{b}=\sqrt{ab}$
b $\sqrt{24}\div\sqrt{8}=\sqrt{\dfrac{24}{8}}$ $=\sqrt{3}$	Use $\sqrt{a}\div\sqrt{b}=\sqrt{\dfrac{a}{b}}$

Exercise 6I

1 Decide if the following pairs of numbers contain 'like' surds.

a $3\sqrt{2}$, $4\sqrt{2}$ **b** $5\sqrt{3}$, $2\sqrt{3}$ **c** $4\sqrt{2}$, $5\sqrt{7}$ **d** $\sqrt{3}$, $2\sqrt{5}$

e $6\sqrt{6}$, $3\sqrt{3}$ **f** $\sqrt{8}$, $3\sqrt{8}$ **g** $19\sqrt{2}$, $-\sqrt{2}$ **h** $-3\sqrt{6}$, $3\sqrt{5}$

2 **a** Use a calculator to find a decimal approximation for both $\sqrt{5}\times\sqrt{2}$ and $\sqrt{10}$. What do you notice?

b Use a calculator to find a decimal approximation for both $\sqrt{7}\times\sqrt{3}$ and $\sqrt{21}$. What do you notice?

c Use a calculator to find a decimal approximation for both $\sqrt{15}\div\sqrt{5}$ and $\sqrt{3}$. What do you notice?

d Use a calculator to find a decimal approximation for both $\sqrt{60}\div\sqrt{10}$ and $\sqrt{6}$. What do you notice?

Understanding

Example 25   **3**   Simplify by collecting like surds.

    a $3\sqrt{7} + 5\sqrt{7}$ **b** $2\sqrt{11} + 6\sqrt{11}$ **c** $\sqrt{5} + 8\sqrt{5}$

    d $3\sqrt{6} + \sqrt{6}$ **e** $3\sqrt{3} + 2\sqrt{5} + 4\sqrt{3}$ **f** $5\sqrt{7} + 3\sqrt{5} + 4\sqrt{7}$

    g $3\sqrt{5} - 8\sqrt{5}$ **h** $6\sqrt{7} - 10\sqrt{7}$ **i** $3\sqrt{7} - 2\sqrt{7} + 4\sqrt{7}$

    j $5\sqrt{14} + \sqrt{14} - 7\sqrt{14}$ **k** $3\sqrt{2} - \sqrt{5} + 4\sqrt{2}$ **l** $6\sqrt{3} + 2\sqrt{7} - 3\sqrt{3}$

Example 26   **4**   Simplify:

    a $\sqrt{5} \times \sqrt{6}$ **b** $\sqrt{3} \times \sqrt{7}$ **c** $\sqrt{10} \times \sqrt{7}$

    d $\sqrt{8} \times \sqrt{2}$ **e** $\sqrt{12} \times \sqrt{3}$ **f** $\sqrt{2} \times \sqrt{11}$

    g $\sqrt{3} \times \sqrt{3}$ **h** $\sqrt{12} \times \sqrt{12}$ **i** $\sqrt{36} \div \sqrt{12}$

    j $\sqrt{20} \div \sqrt{2}$ **k** $\sqrt{42} \div \sqrt{6}$ **l** $\sqrt{60} \div \sqrt{20}$

    m $\sqrt{45} \div \sqrt{5}$ **n** $\sqrt{32} \div \sqrt{2}$ **o** $\sqrt{49} \div \sqrt{7}$

5   Simplify:

    a $2 - \sqrt{3} + 6 - 2\sqrt{3}$ **b** $\sqrt{2} - \sqrt{3} + 5\sqrt{2}$ **c** $7\sqrt{5} - \sqrt{2} + 1 + \sqrt{2}$

    d $\dfrac{\sqrt{2}}{3} + \dfrac{\sqrt{2}}{2}$ **e** $\dfrac{\sqrt{7}}{2} + \dfrac{\sqrt{7}}{5}$ **f** $\dfrac{2\sqrt{6}}{7} - \dfrac{\sqrt{6}}{2}$

    g $\sqrt{10} - \dfrac{\sqrt{10}}{3}$ **h** $5 - \dfrac{2\sqrt{3}}{3} + \sqrt{3}$ **i** $\dfrac{2\sqrt{8}}{7} - \dfrac{5\sqrt{8}}{8}$

6   Note, for example, that $2\sqrt{3} \times 5\sqrt{2} = 2 \times 5 \times \sqrt{3} \times \sqrt{2}$

$$= 10\sqrt{6}$$

   Now simplify the following.

    a $5\sqrt{2} \times 3\sqrt{3}$ **b** $3\sqrt{7} \times 2\sqrt{3}$

    c $4\sqrt{5} \times 2\sqrt{6}$ **d** $2\sqrt{6} \times 5\sqrt{3}$

    e $10\sqrt{6} \div 5\sqrt{2}$ **f** $18\sqrt{12} \div 6\sqrt{2}$

    g $20\sqrt{28} \div 5\sqrt{2}$ **h** $6\sqrt{14} \div 12\sqrt{7}$

7   Expand and simplify.

    a $2\sqrt{3}(3\sqrt{5} + 1)$ **b** $\sqrt{5}(\sqrt{2} + \sqrt{3})$

    c $5\sqrt{6}(\sqrt{2} + 3\sqrt{5})$ **d** $7\sqrt{10}(2\sqrt{3} - \sqrt{10})$

    e $\sqrt{13}(\sqrt{13} - 2\sqrt{3})$ **f** $\sqrt{5}(\sqrt{7} - 2\sqrt{5})$

8 Using $\sqrt{ab} = \sqrt{a} \times \sqrt{b}$, the surd $\sqrt{18}$ can be simplified as shown.

$$\begin{aligned}\sqrt{18} &= \sqrt{9 \times 2} \\ &= \sqrt{9} \times \sqrt{2} \\ &= 3\sqrt{2}\end{aligned}$$

This simplification is possible because 18 has a factor that is a perfect square (9). Use this technique to simplify these surds.

a $\sqrt{8}$ b $\sqrt{12}$ c $\sqrt{27}$ d $\sqrt{45}$

e $\sqrt{75}$ f $\sqrt{200}$ g $\sqrt{60}$ h $\sqrt{72}$

9 Building on the idea discussed in Question **8**, expressions like $\sqrt{8} - \sqrt{2}$ can be simplified as shown:

$$\begin{aligned}\sqrt{8} - \sqrt{2} &= \sqrt{4 \times 2} - \sqrt{2} \\ &= 2\sqrt{2} - \sqrt{2} \\ &= \sqrt{2}\end{aligned}$$

Now simplify these expressions.

a $\sqrt{8} + 3\sqrt{2}$ b $3\sqrt{2} - \sqrt{8}$ c $\sqrt{18} + \sqrt{2}$ d $5\sqrt{3} - 2\sqrt{12}$

e $4\sqrt{8} - 2\sqrt{2}$ f $\sqrt{27} + 2\sqrt{3}$ g $3\sqrt{45} - 7\sqrt{5}$ h $6\sqrt{12} - 8\sqrt{3}$

Enrichment: Binomial products

10 Simplify the following by using the rule $(a + b)(c + d) = ac + ad + bc + bd$.

a $(\sqrt{2} + \sqrt{3})(\sqrt{2} + \sqrt{5})$ b $(\sqrt{3} - \sqrt{5})(\sqrt{3} + \sqrt{2})$

c $(2\sqrt{5} - 1)(3\sqrt{2} + 4)$ d $(1 - 3\sqrt{7})(2 + 3\sqrt{2})$

e $(2 - \sqrt{3})(2 + \sqrt{3})$ f $(\sqrt{5} - 1)(\sqrt{5} + 1)$

g $(3\sqrt{2} + \sqrt{3})(3\sqrt{2} - \sqrt{3})$ h $(8\sqrt{2} + \sqrt{5})(8\sqrt{2} - \sqrt{5})$

i $(1 + \sqrt{2})^2$ j $(\sqrt{6} - 3)^2$

k $(2\sqrt{3} - 1)^2$ l $(\sqrt{2} + 2\sqrt{5})^2$

Cell growth

Many cellular organisms reproduce by a process of subdivision. A single cell, for example, may divide into two every hour as shown at right. After another hour, the single starting cell has become four:

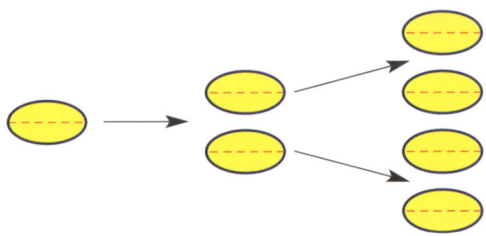

A cell dividing in two

Dividing into two

A single cell divides into two every hour.

a How many cells will there be after the following number of hours? Explain how you obtained your answers.

   i 1   **ii** 2   **iii** 5

b Complete the table showing the number of cells after n hours.

n hours	0	1	2	3	4	5	6
Number of cells, N	1	2	4				
N in index form	2^0	2^1	2^2				

c Write a rule for the number of cells N after n hours.

d Use your rule from part **c** to find the number of cells after:

   i 8 hours   **ii** 12 hours   **iii** 2 days

e Find how long it takes for a single cell to divide into a total of:

   i 128 cells   **ii** 1024 cells   **iii** 65 536 cells

Dividing into three or more

a Complete a table similar to the table in the previous section for a cell that divides into 3 every hour.

b Write a rule for N in terms of n if a cell divides into 3 every hour. Then use the rule to find the number of cells after:

   i 2 hours   **ii** 4 hours   **iii** 8 hours

c Write a rule for N in terms of n if a single cell divides into the following number of cells every hour.

   i 4   **ii** 5   **iii** 10

Cell cycle times

a If a single cell divides into two every 20 minutes investigate how many cells there will be after 4 hours.

b If a single cell divides into three every 10 minutes investigate how many cells there will be after 2 hours.

c Use the internet to research the cell cycle time and the types of division for at least two different types of cells. Describe the cells and explain the reproductive process.

Constructing surds

Since surds are not fractions it is difficult to precisely measure a length representing a surd. Pythagoras' theorem can however be used to construct lengths which represent surds.

Using Pythagoras' theorem

Use Pythagoras' theorem to find the hypotenuse (c) in these triangles.

a 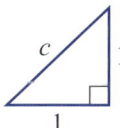 **b** 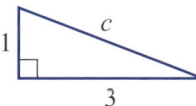 **c**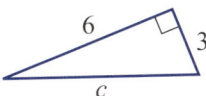

Constructing surds

Show how you can use a single triangle to construct a hypotenuse with the following length. The lengths of the shorter sides have to be whole numbers.

a $\sqrt{5}$ **b** $\sqrt{13}$ **c** $\sqrt{26}$

Combined triangles

The diagram below shows how you can construct the surd $\sqrt{3}$.

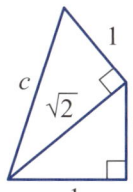

$$c^2 = 1^2 + (\sqrt{2})^2$$
$$= 1 + 2$$
$$= 3$$
$$c = \sqrt{3}$$

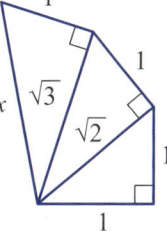

a Copy this diagram (right) to find the value of x.

b Show how you can add other triangles to construct a line segment with the following lengths.

   i $\sqrt{5}$ **ii** $\sqrt{6}$ **iii** $\sqrt{7}$

c Using compasses, draw exact right-angles and transfer exact lengths to a number line. Mark these exact lengths on a number line.

   i $\sqrt{2}$ **ii** $\sqrt{3}$ **iii** $-\sqrt{5}$ **iv** $-\sqrt{7}$

1 Determine the last digit of each of the following without using a calculator.

   a 2^{222} **b** 3^{300} **c** 6^{87}

2 Determine the smallest value of n such that:

   a $24n$ is a square number

   b $750n$ is a square number.

3 Simplify $\left(\dfrac{32}{243}\right)^{-\frac{2}{5}}$ without a calculator.

4 If $2^x = t$, express the following in terms of t:

   a 2^{2x+1} **b** 2^{1-x}

5 A single cell divides in two every 5 minutes and each new cell continues to divide every 5 minutes. How long does it take for the cell population to reach at least 1 million?

6 Find the value of x if $3^{3x-1} = \dfrac{1}{27}$.

7 **a** Write the following in index form

     i $\sqrt{2\sqrt{2}}$ **ii** $\sqrt{2\sqrt{2\sqrt{2}}}$ **iii** $\sqrt{2\sqrt{2\sqrt{2\sqrt{2}}}}$

   b What value do your answers to part **a** appear to be approaching?

8 Determine the highest power of 2 that divides exactly into $2\,000\,000$.

9 Simplify these surds.

   a $5\sqrt{8} - \sqrt{18}$ **b** $\dfrac{1}{\sqrt{2}} + \sqrt{2}$ **c** $(\sqrt{2} + 3\sqrt{5})^2 - (\sqrt{2} - 3\sqrt{5})^2$

10 Prove that:

   a $\dfrac{1}{\sqrt{2}} = \dfrac{\sqrt{2}}{2}$ **b** $\dfrac{3}{\sqrt{3}} = \sqrt{3}$ **c** $\dfrac{1}{\sqrt{2}-1} = \sqrt{2}+1$

11 Solve for x. There are two solutions for each.

   a $2^{2x} - 3 \times 2^x + 2 = 0$ **b** $3^{2x} - 12 \times 3^x + 27 = 0$

Index laws 4 and 5

Law 4: $(ab)^m = a^m b^m$

e.g. $(3x^2)^3 = 3^3 (x^2)^3$
$= 27x^6$

Law 5: $\left(\dfrac{a}{b}\right)^m = \dfrac{a^m}{b^m}$

e.g. $\left(\dfrac{x}{2}\right)^4 = \dfrac{x^4}{2^4}$
$= \dfrac{x^4}{16}$

Zero power

$a^0 = 1$

Any number (except 0) to the power 0 equals 1.

e.g. $3x^0 = 3 \times 1$
$= 3$
$(3x)^0 = 1$

Index law 3

Law 3: $(a^m)^n = a^{mn}$

To expand brackets, multiply indices.

e.g. $(x^2)^5 = x^{2 \times 5}$
$= x^{10}$

Negative indices

$a^{-m} = \dfrac{1}{a^m}$

e.g. $2x^{-3} = \dfrac{2}{1} \times \dfrac{1}{x^3}$
$= \dfrac{2}{x^3}$

$\dfrac{1}{a^{-m}} = a^m$

e.g. $\dfrac{1}{(2x)^{-2}} = (2x)^2$
$= 4x^2$

Index form

$a^m \leftarrow$ index
base

e.g. $2^3 = 2 \times 2 \times 2$
$3^4 = 3 \times 3 \times 3 \times 3$
$a \times b \times a \times b \times b = a^2 b^3$

Index laws 1 and 2

Law 1: $a^m \times a^n = a^{m+n}$

When multiplying terms with the same base, add indices.

e.g. $x^3 \times x^5 = x^{3+5}$
$= x^8$

Law 2: $a^m \div a^n = a^{m-n}$

When dividing terms with the same base, subtract indices.

e.g. $\dfrac{x^7}{x^4} = x^{7-4}$
$= x^3$

Scientific notation

In scientific notation, very large or very small numbers are written in the form $a \times 10^m$ where $1 \leq a < 10$

Large numbers will use positive powers of 10.

e.g. 2 350 000 kg $= 2.35 \times 10^6$ kg

Small numbers will use negative powers of 10.

e.g. 16 nanoseconds
$= 0.000000016\,\text{s}$
$= 1.6 \times 10^{-8}$ seconds

Indices and surds

Fractional indices

$a^{\frac{1}{n}} = \sqrt[n]{a}$

e.g. $a^{\frac{1}{2}} = \sqrt{a}$

$a^{\frac{1}{3}} = \sqrt[3]{a}$

e.g. $25^{\frac{1}{2}} = \sqrt{25} = 5$
since $5^2 = 25$

$8^{\frac{1}{3}} = \sqrt[3]{8} = 2$
since $2^3 = 8$

Operations with surds

'Like' surds can be added or subtracted.
$3\sqrt{7}$ and $5\sqrt{7}$ are 'like surds'

e.g. $3\sqrt{7} + 4\sqrt{2} + 5\sqrt{7} = 8\sqrt{7} + 4\sqrt{2}$

$\sqrt{a} \times \sqrt{b} = \sqrt{ab}$

e.g. $\sqrt{3} \times \sqrt{7} = \sqrt{3 \times 7} = \sqrt{21}$

$\dfrac{\sqrt{a}}{\sqrt{b}} = \sqrt{\dfrac{a}{b}}$

e.g. $\dfrac{\sqrt{20}}{\sqrt{5}} = \sqrt{\dfrac{20}{5}}$
$= \sqrt{4} = 2$

Surds

A surd is a number written with a root sign which has a decimal expansion that is infinite and non-recurring with no pattern.

e.g. $\sqrt{2} = 1.41421356\ldots$

Multiple-choice questions

1 $3x^7 \times 4x^4$ is equivalent to:

A $12x^7$ **B** $12x^{28}$ **C** $7x^{11}$ **D** $12x^{11}$ **E** $7x^3$

2 $3(2y^2)^0$ simplifies to:

A 6 **B** 3 **C** $6y^2$ **D** $3y$ **E** 12

3 $(2x^2)^3$ expands to:

A $2x^5$ **B** $2x^6$ **C** $6x^6$ **D** $8x^5$ **E** $8x^6$

4 $2x^3 y \times \dfrac{x^5 y^2}{4x^2 y}$ simplifies to:

A $\dfrac{x^6 y^2}{2}$ **B** $2x^8 y$ **C** $2x^6 y^2$ **D** $\dfrac{x^4 y^2}{2}$ **E** $8x^6 y$

5 $\left(\dfrac{-x^2 y}{3z^4}\right)^3$ is equal to:

A $\dfrac{x^6 y^3}{3z^{12}}$ **B** $\dfrac{-x^5 y^4}{9z^7}$ **C** $\dfrac{-x^6 y^3}{27z^{12}}$ **D** $\dfrac{-x^2 y^3}{3z^{12}}$ **E** $\dfrac{x^6 y^3}{9z^{12}}$

6 $2x^{-3} y^4$ expressed with positive indices is:

A $\dfrac{y^4}{2x^3}$ **B** $\dfrac{2y^4}{x^3}$ **C** $-2x^3 y^4$ **D** $\dfrac{2}{x^3 y^4}$ **E** $\dfrac{y^4}{8x^3}$

7 $\dfrac{3}{(2x)^{-2}}$ is equivalent to:

A $\dfrac{-3}{(2x)^2}$ **B** $6x^2$ **C** $\dfrac{3x^2}{2}$ **D** $12x^2$ **E** $\dfrac{-3x^2}{4}$

8 The weight of a cargo crate is 2.32×10^4 kg. In expanded form this weight in kilograms is:

A $2\,320\,000$ **B** 232 **C** $23\,200$ **D** 0.000232 **E** 2320

9 0.00032761 in scientific notation rounded to three significant figures is:

A 328×10^{-5} **B** 3.27×10^{-4} **C** 3.28×10^4 **D** 3.30×10^4 **E** 3.28×10^{-4}

10 $36^{\frac{1}{2}}$ is equal to:

A 18 **B** 6 **C** 1296 **D** 9 **E** 81

11 The simplified form of $2\sqrt{7} - 3 + 4\sqrt{7}$ is:

A $-2\sqrt{7} - 3$ **B** $3\sqrt{7}$ **C** $6\sqrt{7} - 3$ **D** $\sqrt{7}$ **E** $8\sqrt{7} - 3$

12 $\sqrt{3} \times \sqrt{7}$ is equivalent to:

A $\sqrt{21}$ **B** $\sqrt{10}$ **C** $2\sqrt{10}$ **D** $10\sqrt{21}$ **E** $21\sqrt{10}$

Short-answer questions

1 Express each of the following in index form.

   a $3 \times 3 \times 3 \times 3$ b $2 \times x \times x \times x \times x \times y \times y$

   c $3 \times a \times a \times a \times \dfrac{b}{a} \times b$ d $\dfrac{3}{5} \times \dfrac{3}{5} \times \dfrac{3}{5} \times \dfrac{1}{7} \times \dfrac{1}{7}$

2 Write the following as a product of prime factors in index form.

   a 45 b 300

3 Simplify using index laws 1 and 2.

   a $x^3 \times x^7$ b $2a^3b \times 6a^2b^5c$ c $3m^2n \times 8m^5n^3 \times \dfrac{1}{2}m^{-3}$

   d $a^{12} \div a^3$ e $x^5y^3 \div x^2y$ f $\dfrac{5a^6b^3}{10a^8b}$

4 Simplify:

   a $(m^2)^3$ b $(3a^4)^2$ c $(-2a^2b)^5$

   d $3a^0b$ e $2(3m)^0$ f $\left(\dfrac{a^2}{3}\right)^3$

5 Express each of the following with positive indices.

   a x^{-3} b $4t^{-3}$ c $(3t)^{-2}$

   d $\dfrac{2}{3}x^2y^{-3}$ e $5\left(\dfrac{x^2}{y^{-1}}\right)^{-3}$ f $\dfrac{5}{m^{-3}}$

6 Fully simplify each of the following.

   a $\dfrac{5x^8y^{-12}}{x^{10}} \times \dfrac{(x^2y^5)^2}{10}$ b $\left(\dfrac{(3x)^0}{3x^0y^2}\right)^4 \times \dfrac{9y^{10}}{x^{-3}}$ c $\dfrac{(4m^2n^3)^2}{2m^5n^4} \div \dfrac{mn^5}{(m^3n^2)^3}$

7 Arrange the following numbers in ascending order:
   2.35, 0.007×10^2, 0.0012, 3.22×10^{-1}, 0.4, 35.4×10^{-3}.

8 Write the following numbers in scientific notation in decimal form.

   a 3.24×10^2 b 1.725×10^5 c 2.753×10^{-1} d 1.49×10^{-3}

9 Write each of the following values in scientific notation using three significant figures.

   a The population of Australia during 2010 was projected to be 22 475 056

   b The area of the USA is 9 629 091 km^2

   c The time taken for light to travel 1 metre (in a vacuum) is 0.00000000333564 seconds

   d The wavelength of ultraviolet light from a fluorescent lamp is 0.000000294 m.

10 Write each of the following values using scientific notation in the units given in brackets.

   a 25 years (hours)   **b** 12 milliseconds (seconds)

   c 432 nanoseconds (seconds)   **d** 5 tonnes (grams)

11 Use a calculator to evaluate the following, giving your answer in scientific notation correct to two significant figures.

   a $m_s \times m_e$ where m_s (mass of Sun) $= 1.989 \times 10^{30}$ kg and m_e (mass of Earth) $= 5.98 \times 10^{24}$ kg.

   b The speed, v, in m/s of an object of mass $m = 2 \times 10^{-3}$ kg and kinetic energy

$$E = 1.88 \times 10^{-12} \text{ joules where } v = \sqrt{\frac{2E}{m}}.$$

12 Evaluate without using a calculator.

   a $\sqrt[4]{16}$ **b** $\sqrt[3]{125}$ **c** $49^{\frac{1}{2}}$

   d $81^{\frac{1}{4}}$ **e** $27^{-\frac{1}{3}}$ **f** $121^{-\frac{1}{2}}$

13 Simplify the following expressing all answers in positive index form.

   a $\sqrt[3]{s^6}$ **b** $\sqrt{81t^3}$ **c** $3x^{\frac{1}{2}} \times 5x^2$

   d $(3m^{\frac{1}{2}}n^2)^2 \times m^{-\frac{1}{4}}$ **e** $\dfrac{t}{2\sqrt{t}}$ **f** $\dfrac{4}{a^{\frac{1}{3}}} \times \dfrac{(a^{\frac{1}{2}})^4}{a}$

14 Simplify the following operations with surds.

   a $8\sqrt{7} - \sqrt{7} + 2$ **b** $2\sqrt{3} + 5\sqrt{2} - \sqrt{3} + 4\sqrt{2}$ **c** $\sqrt{8} \times \sqrt{8}$

   d $\sqrt{5} \times \sqrt{3}$ **e** $2\sqrt{7} \times \sqrt{2}$ **f** $3\sqrt{2} \times 5\sqrt{11}$

   g $\sqrt{42} \div \sqrt{7}$ **h** $2\sqrt{75} \div \sqrt{3}$ **i** $\sqrt{50} \div (2\sqrt{10})$

Extended-response questions

1 Simplify each of the following using a combination of index laws.

   a $\dfrac{(4x^2y)^3 \times x^2y}{12(xy^2)^2}$ **b** $\dfrac{2a^3b^4}{(5a^3)^2} \times \dfrac{20a}{3b^{-4}}$

   c $\dfrac{(5m^4n^{-3})^2}{m^{-1}n^2} \div \dfrac{5(m^{-1}n)^{-2}}{mn^{-4}}$ **d** $\dfrac{(8x^4)^{\frac{1}{3}}}{2(y^3)^0} \times \dfrac{(3x^{\frac{1}{3}})^2}{3(x^2)^{\frac{1}{2}}}$

2 The law of gravitational force is given by $F = \dfrac{Gm_1m_2}{d^2}$ where F is the magnitude of the gravitational force (in newtons, N) between two objects of mass m_1 and m_2 (in kilograms) a distance d (metres) apart. G is the universal gravitational constant which is approximately 6.67×10^{-11} Nm²kg⁻².

a If two objects of masses 2 kg and 4 kg are 3 m apart, calculate the gravitational force F between them. Answer in scientific notation correct to three significant figures.

b The average distance between Earth and the Sun is approximately 149 597 870 700 m.

  i Write this distance in scientific notation with three significant figures.

  ii Hence, if the mass of Earth is approximately 5.98×10^{24} kg and the mass of the Sun is approximately 1.99×10^{30}, calculate the gravitational force between them in scientific notation to three significant figures.

c The universal gravitational constant, G, is constant throughout the universe. However, acceleration due to gravity (a, units ms⁻²) varies according to where you are in the solar system. Using the formula $a = \dfrac{Gm}{r^2}$ and the following table, workout and compare the acceleration due to gravity on Earth and on Mars. Answer to three significant figures.

Planet	Mass, m	Radius, r
Earth	5.98×10^{24} kg	6.375×10^6 m
Mars	6.42×10^{23} kg	3.37×10^6 m

© James Gurney 2006

Chapter **7** Geometry

What you will learn

Penrose stairs

Penrose stairs are an example of an impossible object. They are a two-dimensional illusion which appears to show a three-dimensional, never-ending staircase. Such an illusion was featured in the 2010 movie *Inception*. The Penrose stairs are a variation of the Penrose Triangle which shows three right angles, which have been joined in an impossible way to add up to 270 degrees.

The Dutch artist MC Escher (1898–1972) became famous for his fascinating drawings based on such impossible objects. His work has a strong geometrical component and a number of his works such as 'The Waterfall' were based on the Penrose Triangle. They can easily be found on the internet.

As you look at each part of the waterfall you cannot find any errors but when you view it as a whole you see the problem of water travelling up a flat plane yet the water is falling and spinning in the wheel. The towers appear to be the same height yet one is three stories and the other only two.

Escher has drawn a building which is impossible as it displays a different reality if looked at from above or below. You need to look at his work more than once to see the illusion. The two-dimensional representations are impossible to construct in three-dimensional space.

To draw his designs, Escher needed a clear understanding of the properties of both two- and three-dimensional geometrical shapes.

1 Name the following types of angles.

a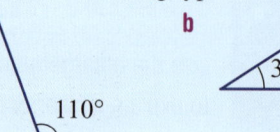

b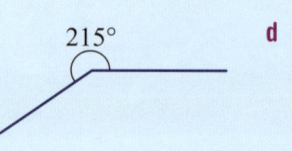

c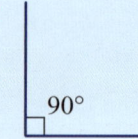

d

2 Identify the following triangles as equilateral, isosceles, scalene or right angled.

a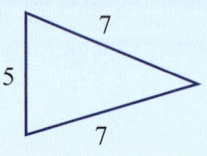

b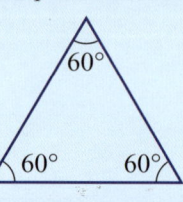

c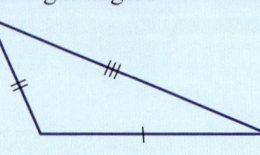

d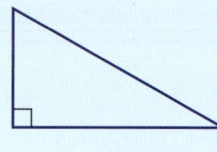

e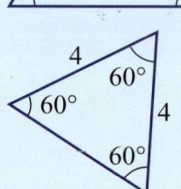

f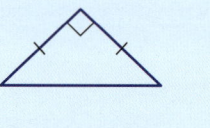

3 Find any missing angles in these triangles.

a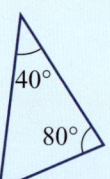

b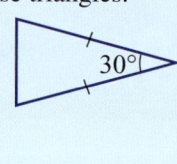

c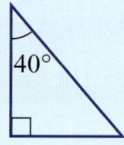

4 Solve the following equations.

a $x + 35 = 90$

b $x + 80 = 180$

c $x + 20 + 50 = 180$

d $2x + 90 = 180$

e $x + 2x + 240 = 360$

f $5x = 540$

5 Find the value of the pronumerals in each of the following.

a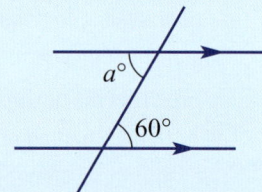

b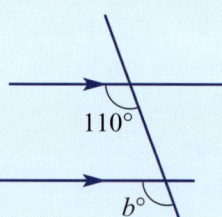

c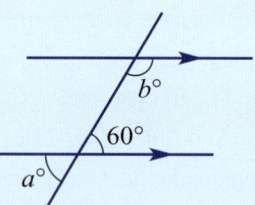

6 Name the following shapes.

a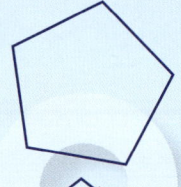

b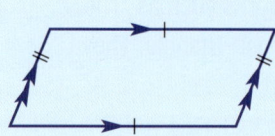

c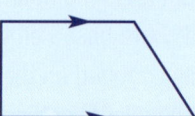

d

e

f

7.1 Angles and triangles

Geometry is all around us. The properties of the shape of a window, doorway or roofline, depend on their geometry. When lines meet, angles are formed and it is these angles which help define the shape of an object. Fundamental to geometry are the angles formed at a point and the three angles in a triangle. Lines meeting at a point and triangles have special properties and will be revised in this section.

Let's start: Impossible triangles

Triangles are classified either by their side lengths or by their angles.

- First, write the list of three triangles which are classified by their side lengths and the three triangles that are classified by their angles.
- Now try to draw a triangle for each of these descriptions. Then decide which are possible and which are impossible.
  - Acute scalene triangle
  - Obtuse isosceles triangle
  - Right equilateral triangle
  - Obtuse scalene triangle
  - Right isosceles triangle
  - Acute equilateral triangle

Modern architecture using geometric shapes: the spire of the Arts Centre, Melbourne

---

Key ideas

- When two **rays**, **lines** or **line segments** meet at a point, an **angle** is formed.
  - This angle is named $\angle A$ or $\angle BAC$ or $\angle CAB$
- Angle types
  - **Acute** between 0° and 90°
  - **Obtuse** between 90° and 180°
  - **Reflex** between 180° and 360°
  - **Right** 90°
  - **Straight** 180°
  - **Revolution** 360°

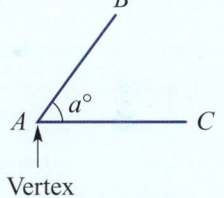

Vertex

- Angles at a point
  - **Complementary** (sum to 90°)
  - **Supplementary** (sum to 180°)
  - **Revolution** (sum to 360°)
  - **Vertically opposite** (are equal)

60°
$a°$
$a + 60 = 90$

$a°$
41°
$a + 41 = 180$

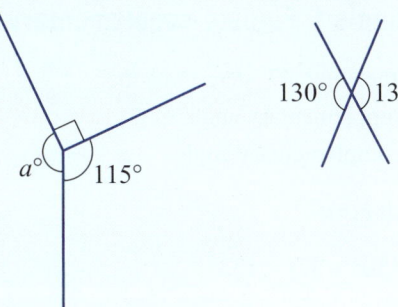

$a°$ 115°
$a + 90 + 115 = 360$

130° 130°

Key ideas

■ Types of triangles

	Right angled (includes a 90° angle)	Obtuse angled (one angle > 90°)
Acute angled (all angles < 90°)		
Scalene (all sides and angles are different sizes)	Scalene	Scalene
Equilateral (all angles 60° and all sides equal) Isosceles (two angles equal and two sides equal)	45° Isosceles 45°	Isosceles

- The sum of the angles in a triangle is 180°.

$$a + b + c = 180$$

with $b°$, $a°$, $c°$ labelled.

■ An **exterior angle** is formed by extending one side of a shape.
- **Exterior angle theorem of a triangle**. The exterior angle of a triangle is equal to the sum of the two opposite interior angles.

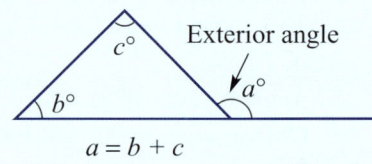

$$a = b + c$$

with Exterior angle $a°$, and interior angles $b°$, $c°$ labelled.

Example 1 Finding supplementary and complementary angles

For the angle 47° determine the:
a supplementary angle
b complementary angle

SOLUTION	**EXPLANATION**
a $180° - 47° = 133°$	Supplementary angles sum to 180°.
b $90° - 47° = 43°$	Complementary angles sum to 90°.

Example 2 Finding unknown angles in triangles

Name the types of triangles shown here and determine the values of the pronumerals.

a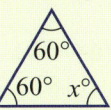

b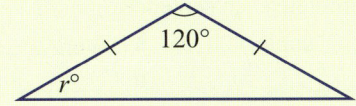

c

SOLUTION	EXPLANATION
a Equilateral triangle $x = 60$	All sides are equal, therefore all angles are equal.
b Obtuse isosceles triangle $2r + 120 = 180$ $2r = 60$ $r = 30$	One angle is more than 90° and two sides are equal. Angles in a triangle add to 180°. Subtract 120° from both sides and then divide both sides by 2.
c Acute scalene triangle $s + 50 + 60 = 180$ $s + 110 = 180$ $s = 70$	All angles are less than 90° and all sides are of different length. Angles in a triangle add to 180°. Simplify and solve for s.

Example 3 Finding exterior angles

Find the value of each pronumeral. Give reasons for your answers.

a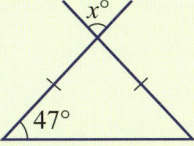

b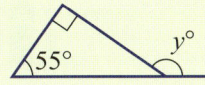

SOLUTION

a $x + 47 + 47 = 180$ (Angle sum)
  $x + 94 = 180$
  $x = 86$

b Let a be the unknown angle.
  $a + 90 + 55 = 180$ (Angle sum)
  $a = 35$
  $y + 35 = 180$
  $y = 145$

Alternative method:
$y = 90 + 55$
  $= 145$

EXPLANATION

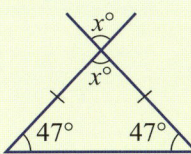

Note the isosceles triangle and vertically opposite angles.
Angles in a triangle add to 180° and vertically opposite angles are equal. Simplify and solve for x.

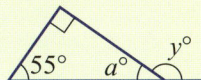

Angles in a triangle sum to 180°.

Angles in a straight line are supplementary (sum to 180°).

Alternatively, use the exterior angle theorem which says that the exterior angle is equal to the sum of the two opposite interior angles.

Exercise 7A

1 Choose a word or number to complete each sentence.

    a A 90° angle is called a _____ angle.
    b A _____ angle is called a straight angle.
    c A 360° angle is called a _____.
    d _____ angles are between 90° and 180°.
    e _____ angles are between 0° and 90°.
    f Reflex angles are between _____ and 360°.
    g Complementary angles sum to _____.
    h _____ angles sum to 180°.
    i The three angles in a triangle sum to _____.
    j Vertically opposite angles are _____.

2 What type of triangle has:

    a a pair of equal length sides
    b one obtuse angle
    c all angles 60°
    d one pair of equal angles
    e all angles acute
    f all sides of different length
    g one right angle?

3 For each diagram:

    i name the angle shown (e.g. ∠ABC)
    ii state the type of angle given
    iii estimate the size of the angle
    iv measure the angle using a protractor.

a

b

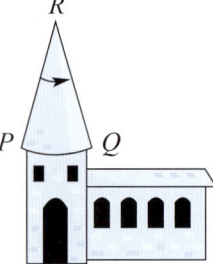

c

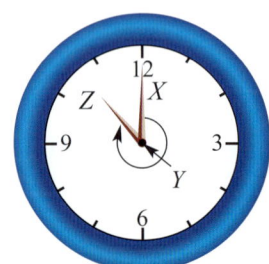

d

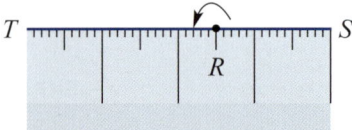

e

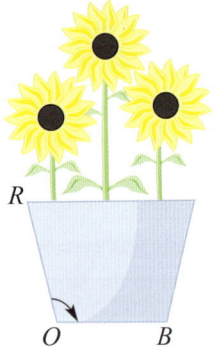

f

4 Estimate the size of each of the following angles and use your protractor to determine an accurate measurement.

a
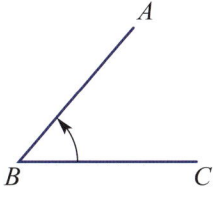

b
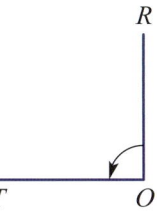

c
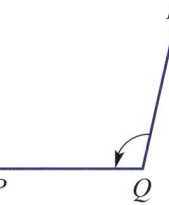

d
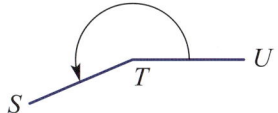

e
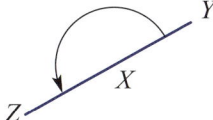

f
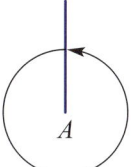

Example 1

5 For each of the following angles determine:

  i the supplementary angle

  ii the complementary angle

  a $55°$ **b** $31°$ **c** $74°$ **d** $10°$ **e** $89°$

  f $22°$ **g** $38°$ **h** $65°$ **i** $47°$ **j** $77°$

6 State whether each of the following pairs of angles is supplementary (S), complementary (C) or neither (N).

  a $30°, 60°$ **b** $45°, 135°$ **c** $100°, 90°$ **d** $50°, 40°$

  e $70°, 110°$ **f** $14°, 66°$ **g** $137°, 43°$ **h** $24°, 56°$

7 Find the value of a in these diagrams.

a
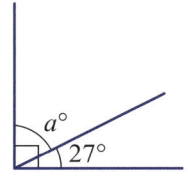

b
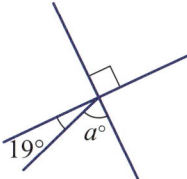

c
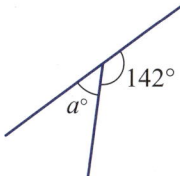

d
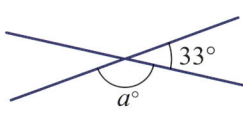

e
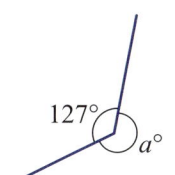

f
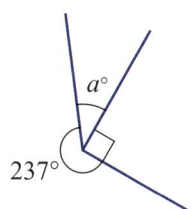

Example 2 **8** Name the types of triangles shown here and determine the values of the pronumerals.

a
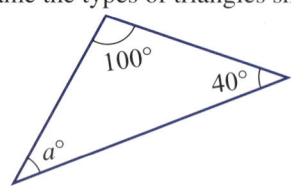
100°
40°
$a°$

b
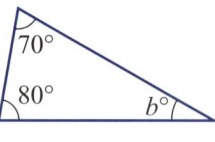
70°
80°
$b°$

c
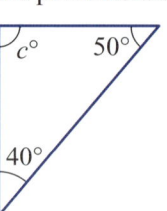
$c°$
50°
40°

d
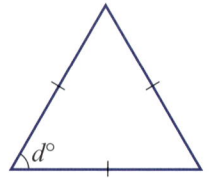
$d°$

e
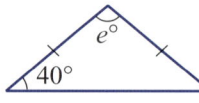
$e°$
40°

f
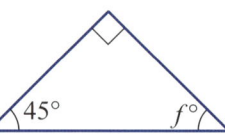
45°
$f°$

g
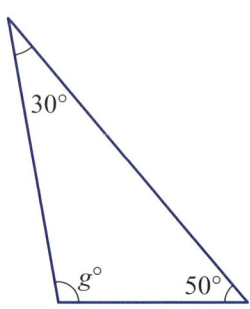
30°
$g°$
50°

h
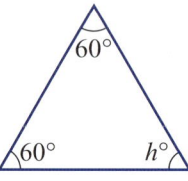
60°
60°
$h°$

i
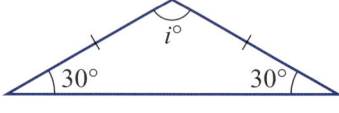
$i°$
30°
30°

j
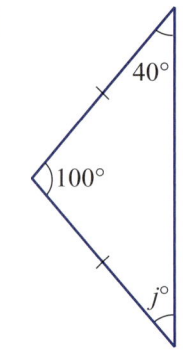
40°
100°
$j°$

k
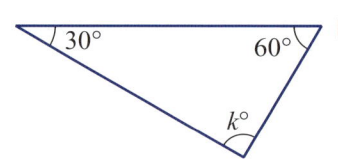
30°
60°
$k°$

l
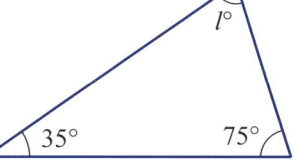
$l°$
35°
75°

Example 3 **9** Find the value of each pronumeral.

a
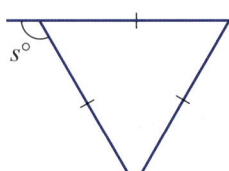
$s°$

b
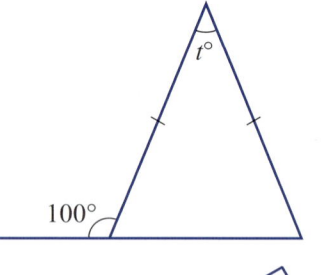
$t°$
100°

c
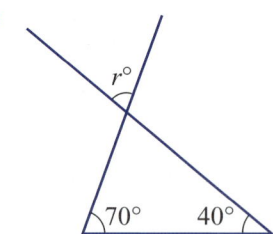
$r°$
70°   40°

d
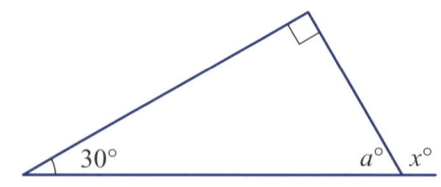
30°
$a°$ $x°$

Fluency

e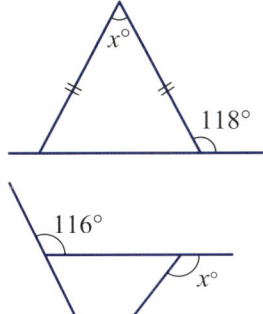

f

Problem-solving

10 Calculate how many degrees the minute hand of a clock rotates in:

a 1 hour **b** $\frac{1}{4}$ of an hour **c** 10 minutes **d** 15 minutes

e 72 minutes **f** 1 minute **g** 2 hours **h** 1 day

11 Find the value of x in these diagrams.

a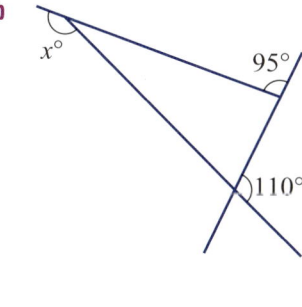

b

c

12 Find the acute angle between the hour and minute hands at these times. Remember to consider how the hour hand moves between each whole number.

a 3:00 pm **b** 5:00 am **c** 6:30 pm
d 11:30 pm **e** 3:45 am **f** 1:20 am
g 4:55 am **h** 2:42 am **i** 9:27 am

Reasoning

13 A tangent to a circle is 90° to its radius.
Explain why $x = 330$ in this diagram.

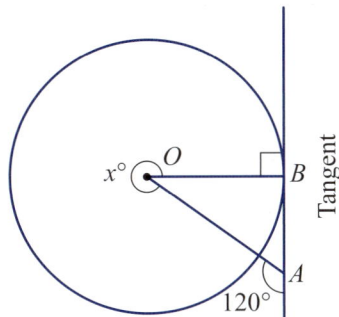

14 Explain why $\angle OAB$ is $32°$ in this circle if O is the centre of the circle.

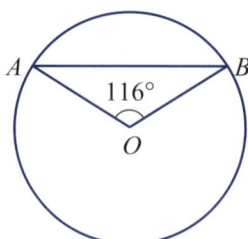

15 In this diagram, $\angle XYZ$ is an exterior angle. *Do not* use the exterior angle theorem in the following.

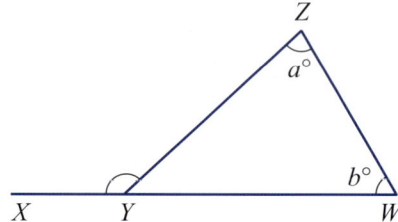

   a If $a = 85$ and $b = 75$, find $\angle XYZ$.
   b If $a = 105$ and $b = 60$, find $\angle XYZ$.
   c Now using the pronumerals a and b, prove that $\angle XYZ = a° + b°$.

16 Prove that the three exterior angles of a triangle sum to $360°$. Use the fact that the three interior angles sum to $180°$.

Enrichment: Algebra in geometry

17 Write an equation for each diagram and solve it to find x.

   a

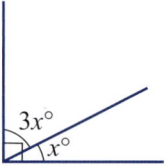

   b

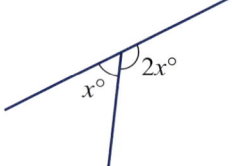

   c

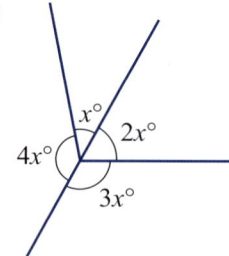

   d

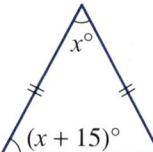

   e

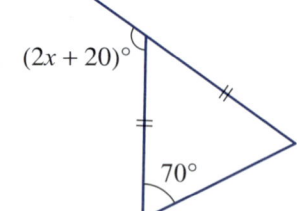

   f

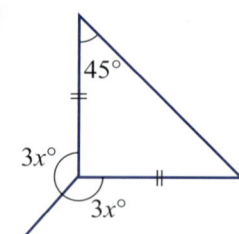

7.2 Parallel lines

A line crossing two or more other lines (called a transversal) creates a number of special pairs of angles. If the transversal cuts two parallel lines then these special pairs of angles will be either equal or supplementary.

Double lines on straight roads are parallel.

→ Let's start: Are they parallel?

Here are three diagrams including a transversal crossing two other lines.

1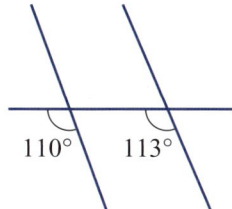
110° 113°

2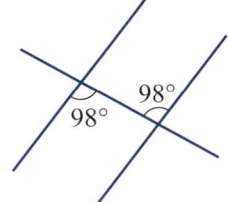
98° 98°

3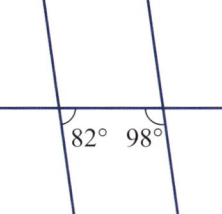
82° 98°

- Decide if each diagram contains a pair of parallel lines. Give reasons for your answer.
- What words do you remember regarding the name given to each pair of angles shown in the diagrams?

■ A **transversal** is a line crossing two or more other lines.

	Non-parallel lines	Parallel lines
Corresponding angles • If lines are parallel corresponding angles are equal		
Alternate angles • If lines are parallel alternate angles are equal		
Cointerior angles • If lines are parallel cointerior angles are supplementary		$a°$ $b°$ $a + b = 180$

Key ideas

- If a line *AB* is parallel to a line *CD* we write *AB* ∥ *CD*.
- A parallel line can be added to diagrams to help find other angles.

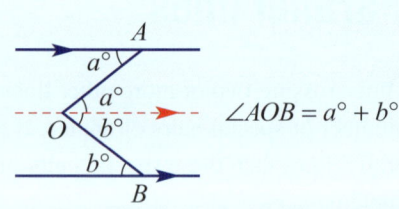

$$\angle AOB = a° + b°$$

Example 4 Deciding if lines are parallel

Decide if each diagram contains a pair of parallel lines. Give a reason.

a
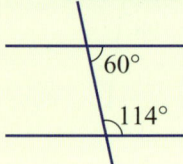

b
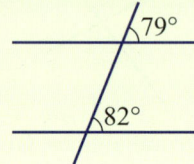

c
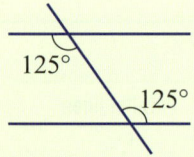

SOLUTION	**EXPLANATION**
a No. The two cointerior angles are not supplementary.	$60° + 114° = 174° \neq 180°$
b No. The two corresponding angles are not equal.	$79° \neq 82°$
c Yes. The two alternate angles are equal.	If alternate angles are equal then the lines are parallel.

Example 5 Finding angles in parallel lines

Find the value of each of the pronumerals. Give reasons for your answers.

a
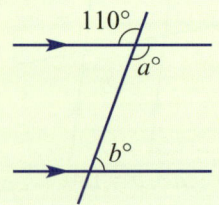

b
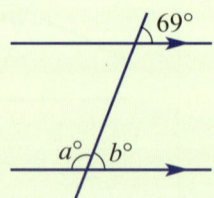

SOLUTION   **EXPLANATION**

a $a = 110$ (vertically opposite angles)

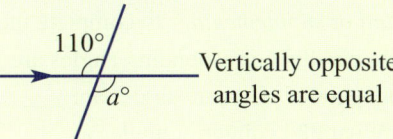

Vertically opposite
angles are equal

$b + 110 = 180$
$b = 70$ (cointerior angles in parallel lines)

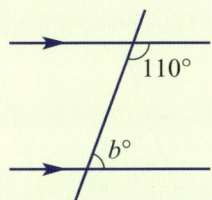

Cointerior angles
add to 180° in
parallel lines

b $b = 69$ (corresponding angles in parallel
lines)

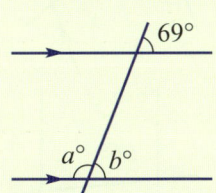

Corresponding
angles are equal
in parallel lines

$a + 69 = 180$
$a = 111$ (supplementary angles)

Supplementary angles add to 180° so $a + b = 180$.

Example 6 Adding a third parallel line

Add a third parallel line to help find $\angle ABC$ in this diagram.

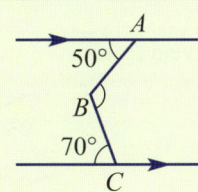

SOLUTION   **EXPLANATION**

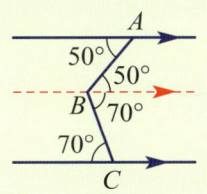

Add a third parallel line through B to create two pairs
of equal alternate angles.

$\angle ABC = 50° + 70°$
        $= 120°$

Add 50° and 70° to give the size of $\angle ABC$.

Exercise 7B

1 Use the word *equal* or *supplementary* to complete these sentences.

  a If two lines are parallel corresponding angles are _____.

  b If two lines are parallel alternate angles are _____.

  c If two lines are parallel cointerior angles are _____.

2 Find the values of the pronumerals. Give reasons for your answers.

a
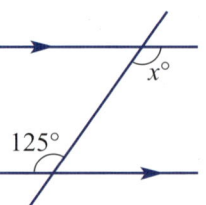
125°, x°

b
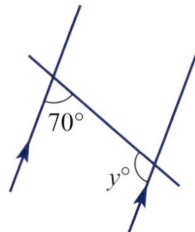
70°, y°

c
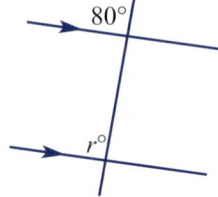
80°, r°

d
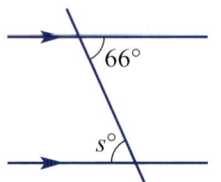
66°, s°

e
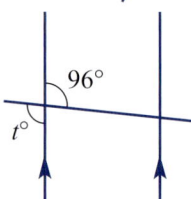
96°, t°

f
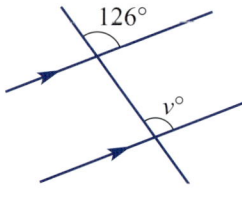
126°, v°

g
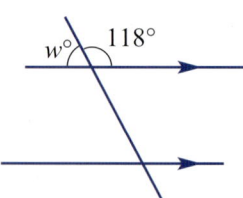
w°, 118°

h
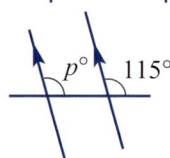
p°, 115°

i
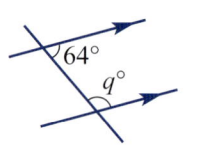
64°, q°

Example 4

3 Decide if each diagram contains a pair of parallel lines. Give a reason.

a
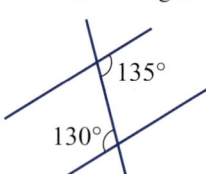
135°, 130°

b
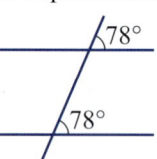
78°, 78°

c
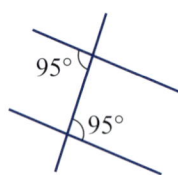
95°, 95°

d
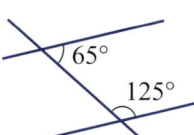
65°, 125°

e
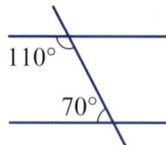
110°, 70°

f
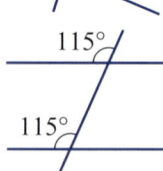
115°, 115°

g
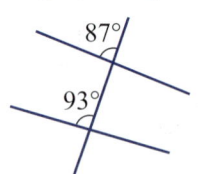
87°, 93°

h
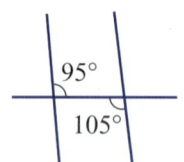
95°, 105°

i
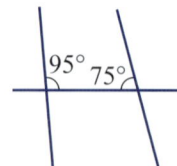
95°, 75°

4 Find the value of each pronumeral. Give reasons for your answers.

ample 5

a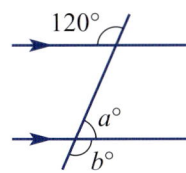

b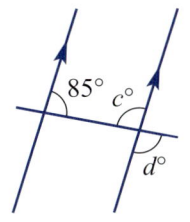

c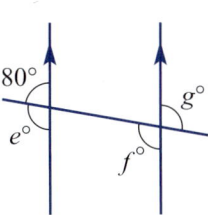

d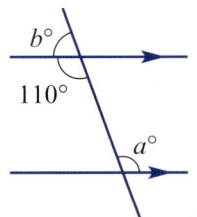

e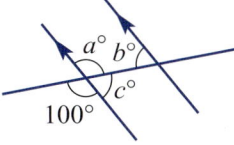

f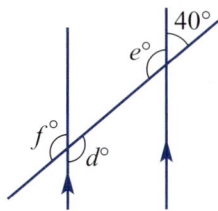

Problem-solving

5 Find the value of each pronumeral.

a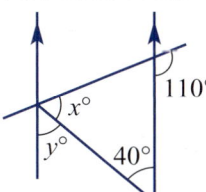

b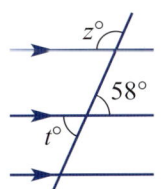

c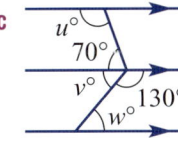

d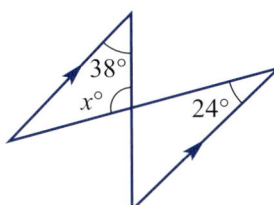

e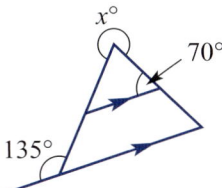

f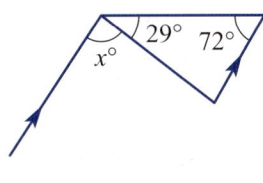

ample 6

6 Add a third parallel line to help find $\angle ABC$ in these diagrams.

a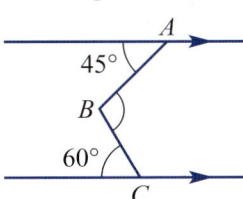

b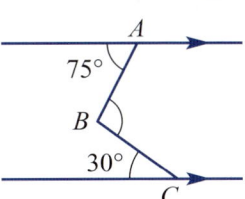

c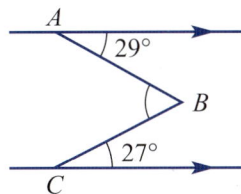

d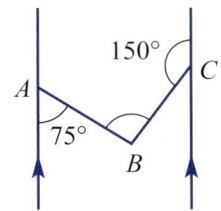

e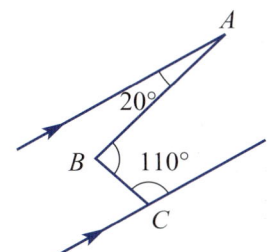

f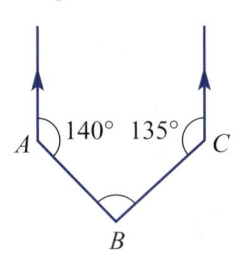

7 Find the value of x.

a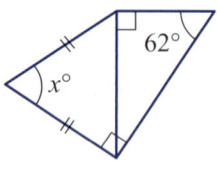

b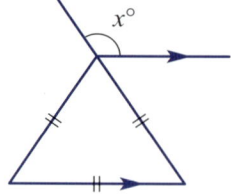

c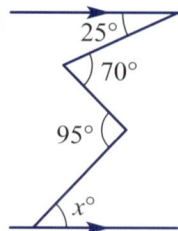

8 Write an expression (for example, $180° - a°$) for $\angle ABC$ in these diagrams.

a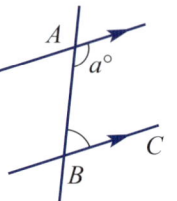

b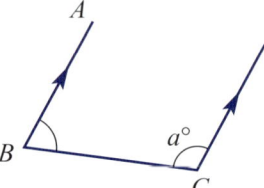

c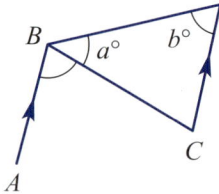

d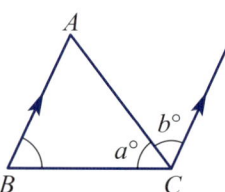

e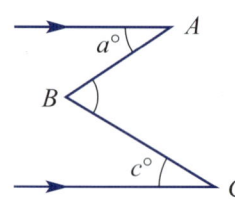

f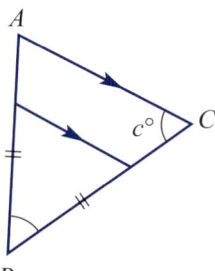

9 Give reasons why $AB \parallel DC$ (AB is parallel to DC) in this diagram.

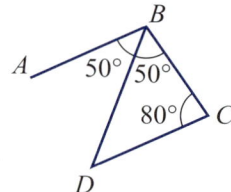

10 This diagram includes a triangle and a pair of parallel lines.
  a Using the parallel lines explain why $a + b + c = 180$.
  b Explain why $\angle ACB = c°$.
  c Explain why this diagram helps to prove that the angle sum of a triangle is $180°$.

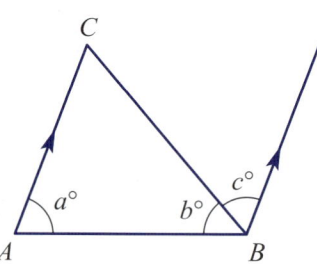

Enrichment: Proof in geometry

11 Here is a written proof showing that $\angle ABC = a° - b°$.

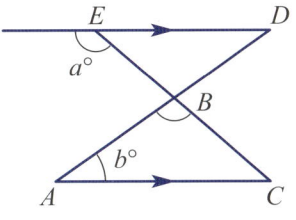

$\angle BED = 180° - a°$	(Supplementary angles)
$\angle BCA = 180° - a°$	(Alternate angles and $ED \parallel AC$)
$\angle ABC = 180° - b° - (180 - a)°$	(Angle sum of a triangle)
$= 180° - b° - 180° + a°$	
$= -b° + a°$	
$= a° - b°$	

Write proofs similar to the above for each of the following.

a $\angle ABC = a° - c°$

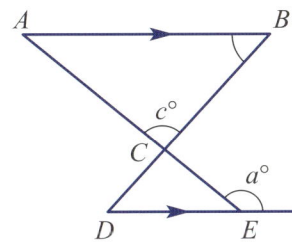

b $\angle ABC = a° + b°$

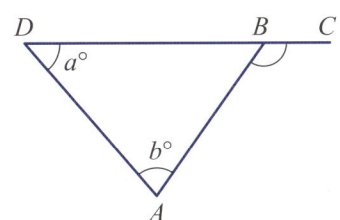

c $\angle ABC = a° + b°$

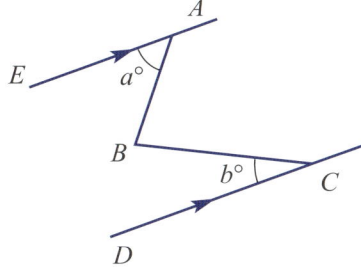

d $\angle ABC = 180° + b° - a°$

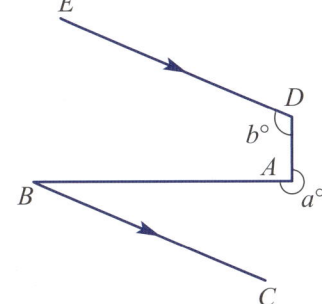

7.3 Quadrilaterals and other polygons

Closed two-dimensional shapes with straight sides are called polygons and are classified by their number of sides. Quadrilaterals have four sides and are classified further by their special properties.

Mosaics are made of numerous polygons.

→ Let's start: Draw that shape

Use your knowledge of polygons to draw each of the following shapes. Mark any features, including parallel sides and sides of equal length.

- convex quadrilateral
- non-convex pentagon
- regular hexagon
- square, rectangle, rhombus and parallelogram
- kite and trapezium

Compare the properties of each shape to ensure you have indicated each property on your drawings.

Key ideas

- **Convex polygons** have all interior angles less than 180°. A **non-convex polygon** has at least one interior angle greater than 180°.

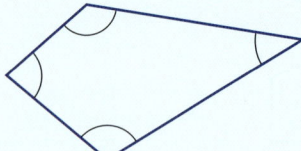

Convex quadrilateral

Non-convex hexagon

- **The sum of the interior angles**, S, in a polygon with n sides is given by $S = 180(n - 2)$

Polygon	Number of sides	Angle sum
Triangle	3	180°
Quadrilateral	4	360°
Pentagon	5	540°
Hexagon	6	720°
Heptagon	7	900°
Octagon	8	1080°
Nonagon	9	1260°
Decagon	10	1440°
Undecagon	11	1620°
Dodecagon	12	1800°
n-gon	n	$180(n - 2)°$

- **Regular polygons** have equal length sides and equal interior angles.

■ **Parallelograms** are **quadrilaterals** with two pairs of parallel sides. They include:

• Parallelogram

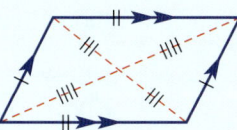

• Rhombus

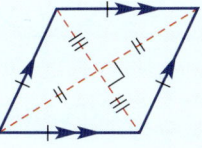

• Rectangle

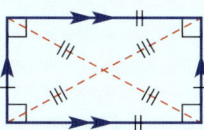

• Square

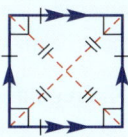

■ The kite and trapezium are also special quadrilaterals.

• Kite 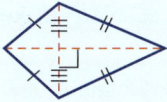   • Trapezium

Example 7 Finding angles in quadrilaterals

Find the value of the pronumeral in each of these quadrilaterals.

a 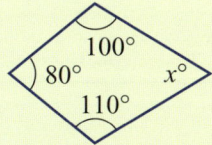   b 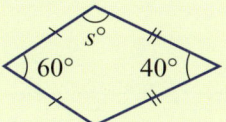   c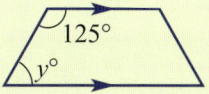

SOLUTION

a $x + 80 + 100 + 110 = 360$
$\qquad x + 290 = 360$
$\qquad\qquad x = 70$

b $2s + 60 + 40 = 360$
$\qquad 2s + 100 = 360$
$\qquad\qquad 2s = 260$
$\qquad\qquad s = 130$

c $y + 125 = 180$
$\qquad y = 55$

EXPLANATION

The angles in a quadrilateral add to 360°.
Simplify and solve for x.

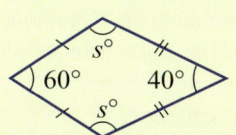

The angles in a quadrilateral add to 360° and the opposite angles ($s°$) are equal in a kite.

Simplify and solve for s.
Cointerior angles inside parallel lines are supplementary.

Example 8 Finding angles in polygons

For each polygon find the angle sum using $S = 180(n - 2)$ then find the value of a.

a
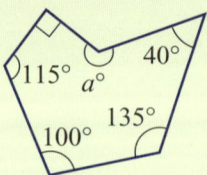

b
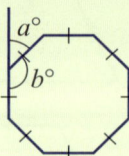

SOLUTION

EXPLANATION

a $n = 6$ and $S = 180(n - 2)$

$\qquad = 180(6 - 2)$

$\qquad = 720$

$a + 90 + 115 + 100 + 135 + 40 = 720$

$\qquad\qquad\qquad a + 480 = 720$

$\qquad\qquad\qquad\qquad a = 240$

The shape is a hexagon with 6 sides so $n = 6$.

The sum of all angles is 720°. Simplify and solve for a.

b $n = 8$ and $S = 180(n - 2)$

$\qquad = 180(8 - 2)$

$\qquad = 1080$

$\qquad 8b = 1080$

$\qquad b = 135$

$a + 135 = 180$

$\qquad a = 45$

The regular octagon has 8 sides so use $n = 8$.

Each interior angle is equal so $8b°$ makes up the angle sum.

$a°$ is an exterior angle and $a°$ and $b°$ are supplementary.

Exercise 7C

Understanding

1 How many sides do these polygons have?

    a pentagon   **b** heptagon

    c quadrilateral   **d** undecagon

    e nonagon   **f** dodecagon

2 Use $S = 180(n - 2)$ to find the angle sum S of these polygons.

    a hexagon   **b** octagon

    c undecagon

3 Write the word to complete these sentences.

    a A parallelogram has two pairs of _____ sides.

    b The diagonals in a rhombus intersect at _____ angles.

    c A _____ has one pair of parallel sides.

    d The diagonals in a rectangle are _____ in length.

4 Name each of these shapes as convex or non convex.

a
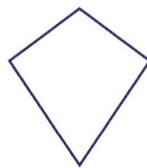

b

c
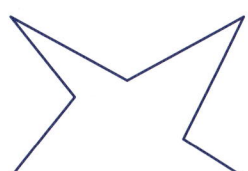

nple 7a **5** Find the values of the pronumerals.

a
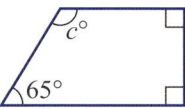

b
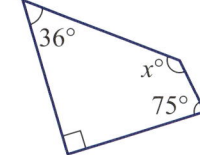

c
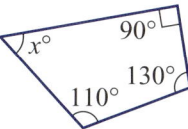

d
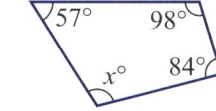

e
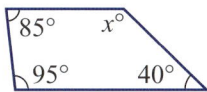

f
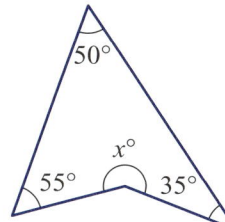

le 7b,c **6** Find the value of the pronumerals.

a
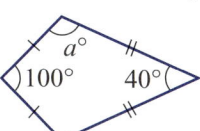

b
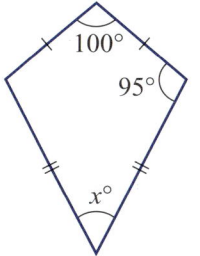

c
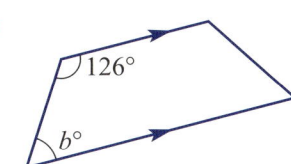

d
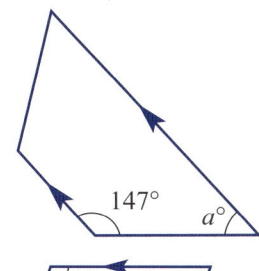

e

f
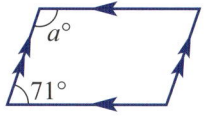

Example 8

7 For each polygon find the angle sum using $S = 180(n - 2)$ then find the value of a.

a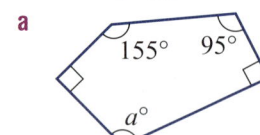

b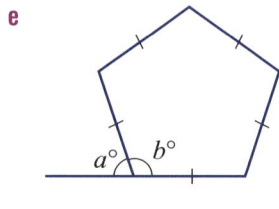

c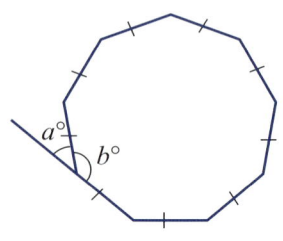

d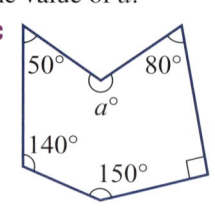

e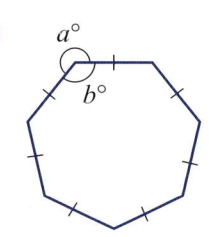

f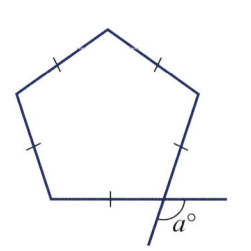

g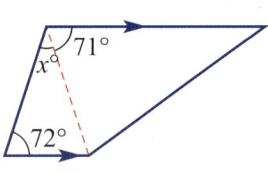

h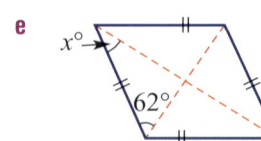

i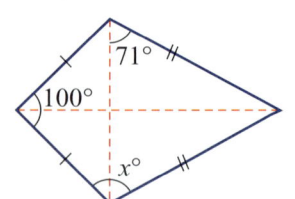

8 List all the quadrilaterals which have these properties.
   a 2 pairs of equal length sides
   b All interior angles 90°
   c Diagonals of equal length
   d Diagonals intersecting at right angles

9 Calculate the number of sides if a polygon has the given angle sum. Suggestion: Use the rule $S = 180(n - 2)$.
   a 2520°
   b 4140°
   c 18000°

10 Find the value of x in these diagrams.

   a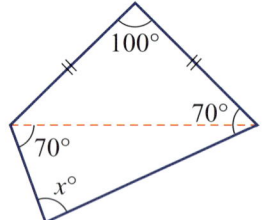

   b

   c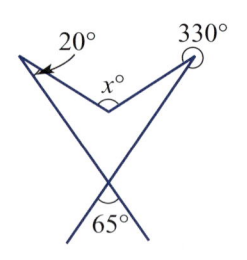

   d

   e

   f

11 Explain why a rectangle, square and rhombus are all parallelograms.

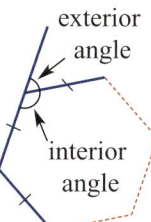

exterior
angle

interior
angle

12 For a regular polygon with n sides:
   a write the rule for the sum of interior angles (S)
   b write the rule for the size of each interior angle (I)
   c write the rule for the size of each exterior angle (E)
   d use your rule from part **c** to find the size of the exterior angle of a regular decagon.

13 Recall that a non-convex polygon has at least one reflex interior angle.
   a What is the maximum number of interior reflex angles possible for these polygons?
      i quadrilateral   **ii** pentagon   **iii** octagon
   b Write an expression for the maximum number of interior reflex angles for a polygon with n sides.

Enrichment: Angle sum proof

14 Note that if you follow the path around this pentagon starting and finishing at point A (provided you finish by pointing in the same direction as you started) you will have turned a total of $360°$.

Complete this proof of the angle sum of a pentagon ($540°$).

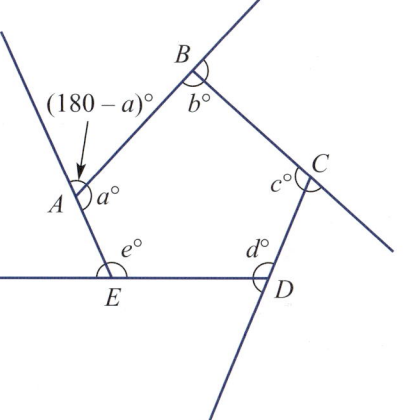

B
$b°$
$(180 - a)°$
$c°$ C
A $a°$
$e°$ $d°$
E D

$(180 - a) + (180 - b) + (\quad) + (\quad) + (\quad) = \underline{\quad}$
    (Sum of exterior angles is $\underline{\quad}$)
$180 + 180 + \underline{\ } + \underline{\ } + \underline{\ } - (a + b + \underline{\ } + \underline{\ } + \underline{\ }) = 360$
        $\underline{\quad} - (\quad\quad\quad) = 360$
            $(\quad\quad\quad) = \underline{\ }$

Now complete a similar proof for the angle sum of these polygons.
a Hexagon   **b** Heptagon
Extension. Try to complete a similar proof for a polygon with n sides.

7.4 Congruent triangles

When two shapes have the same shape and size we say they are congruent. Matching sides will be the same length and matching angles will be the same size. The area of congruent shapes will also be equal. However, not every property of a pair of shapes needs to be known in order to determine their congruence. This is highlighted in the study of congruent triangles where four tests can be used to establish congruence.

The Petronas Twin Towers in Kuala Lumpur look congruent.

Let's start: Constructing congruent triangles

To complete this task you will need a ruler, pencil and protractor. (For accurate constructions you may wish to use compasses.) Divide these constructions up equally amongst the members of the class. Each group is to construct their triangle with the given properties.

1 Triangle ABC with $AB = 8$ cm, $AC = 5$ cm and $BC = 4$ cm
2 Triangle DEF with $DE = 7$ cm, $DF = 6$ cm and $\angle EDF = 40°$
3 Triangle GHI with $GH = 6$ cm, $\angle IGH = 50°$ and $\angle IHG = 50°$
4 Triangle JKL with $\angle JKL = 90°$, $JL = 5$ cm and $KL = 4$ cm

- Now compare all triangles with the vertices ABC. What do you notice? What does this say about two triangles that have three pairs of equal side lengths?
- Compare all triangles with the vertices DEF. What do you notice? What does this say about two triangles that have two pairs of equal side lengths and the included angles equal?
- Compare all triangles with the vertices GHI. What do you notice? What does this say about two triangles that have two equal corresponding angles and one corresponding equal length side?
- Compare all triangles with the vertices JKL. What do you notice? What does this say about two triangles that have one right angle, the hypotenuse and one other corresponding equal length side?

Key ideas

- **Congruent figures** have the same shape and size.
  - If two figures are congruent, one of them can be transformed by using rotation, reflection and/or translation to match the other figure exactly.

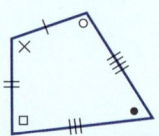 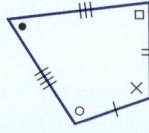

- If triangle ABC ($\triangle ABC$) is congruent to triangle DEF ($\triangle DEF$) we write $\triangle ABC \equiv \triangle DEF$. This is called a **congruence statement**.

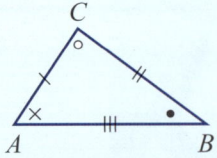 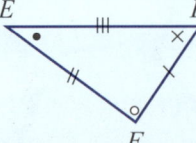

Corresponding sides	Corresponding angles
$AB = DE$	$\angle A = \angle D$
$BC = EF$	$\angle B = \angle E$
$AC = DF$	$\angle C = \angle F$

- **Corresponding** sides are opposite equal corresponding angles.

Key ideas

■ **Tests for triangle congruence.**

- Side, Side, Side (SSS)

  Three pairs of corresponding sides are equal.

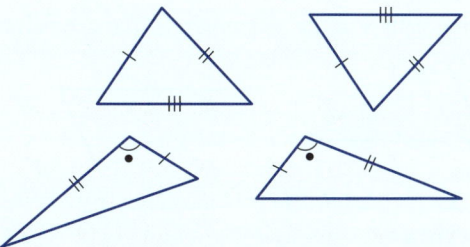

- Side, Angle, Side (SAS)

  Two pairs of corresponding sides and the included angle are equal.

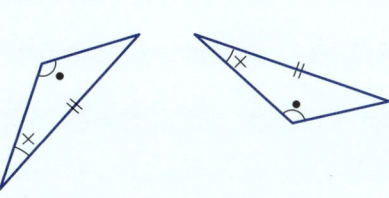

- Angle, Angle, Side (AAS)

  Two angles and any pair of corresponding sides are equal.

- Right angle, Hypotenuse, Side (RHS)

  A right angle, the hypotenuse and one other pair of corresponding sides are equal.

Example 9 Choosing a congruence test

Which congruence test (SSS, SAS, AAS or RHS) would be used to show that these pairs of triangles are congruent?

a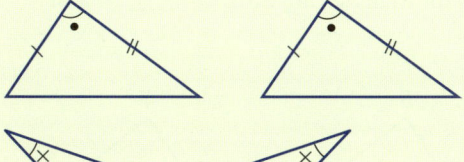

b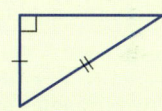

c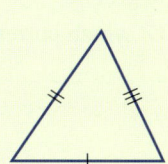

d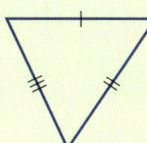

SOLUTION	EXPLANATION
a SAS	Two pairs of corresponding sides and the included angle are equal.
b RHS	A right angle, hypotenuse and one pair of corresponding sides are equal.
c AAS	Two angles and a pair of corresponding sides are equal.
d SSS	Three pairs of corresponding sides are equal.

Example 10 Finding missing side lengths and angles using congruence

Find the values of the pronumerals in these pairs of congruent triangles.

a
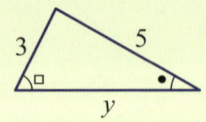
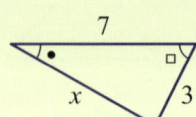

b
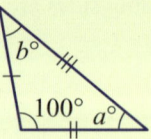
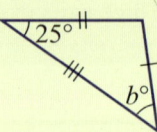

SOLUTION

a $x = 5$

$y = 7$

b $a = 25$

$b = 180 - 100 - 25$
$\quad = 55$

EXPLANATION

The side of length x and the side of length 5 are in corresponding positions (opposite the □).
The longest side on both triangles must be equal.

The angle marked $a°$ corresponds to the 25° angle in the other triangle.
The sum of three angles in a triangle is 180°.

Exercise 7D

1 Copy and complete the sentences below.
  a Congruent figures are exactly the same shape and _____.
  b If triangle ABC is congruent to triangle STU then we write $\triangle ABC \equiv$ _____.
  c The abbreviated names of the four congruence tests for triangles are SSS, ____, ____ and
   _____.

2 These two triangles are congruent.
  a Name the side on $\triangle XYZ$ which corresponds to (matches):
    i AB
    ii AC
    iii BC
  b Name the angle in $\triangle ABC$ which corresponds to (matches):
    i $\angle X$
    ii $\angle Y$
    iii $\angle Z$

3 Write a congruence statement (e.g. $\triangle ABC \equiv \triangle DEF$) if:
  a triangle ABC is congruent to triangle FGH
  b triangle DEF is congruent to triangle STU
  c triangle AMP is congruent to triangle CBD
  d triangle BMW is congruent to triangle SLK.

Understanding

ample 9 | **4** Which congruence test (SSS, SAS, AAS or RHS) would be used to show that these pairs of triangles are congruent?

a 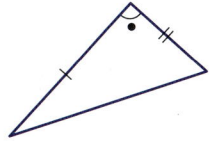   **b**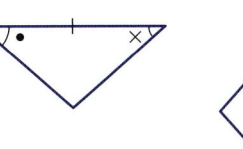

c 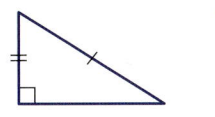   **d**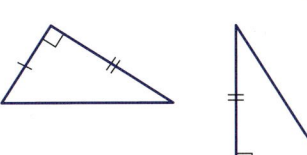

e 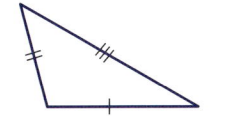   **f**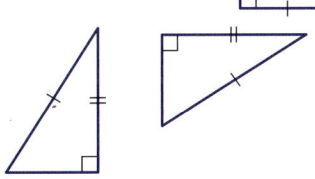

g 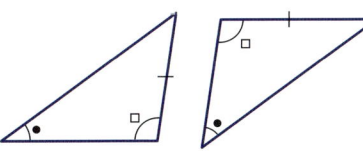   **h**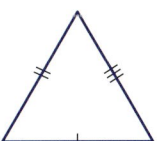

ample 10 | **5** Find the values of the pronumerals in these pairs of congruent triangles.

a 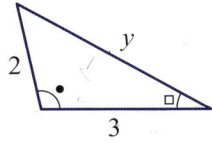   **b**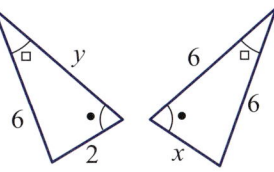

c 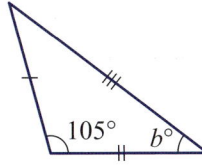   **d**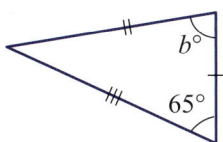

e 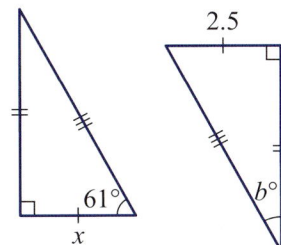   **f**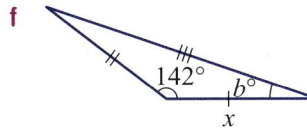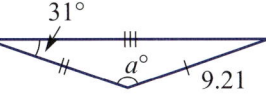

g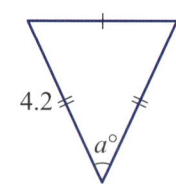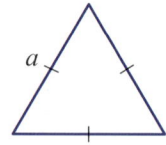

h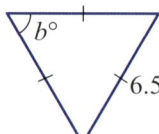

6 For each set of three triangles choose the two which are congruent. Give a reason (SSS, SAS, AAS or RHS) and write a congruence statement (e.g. $\triangle ABC \equiv \triangle FGH$).

a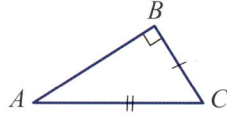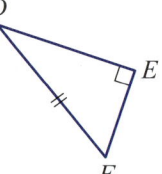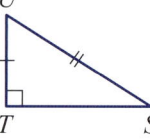

b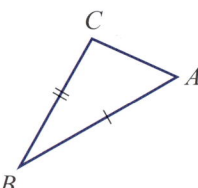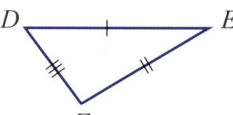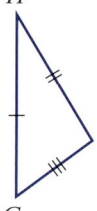

c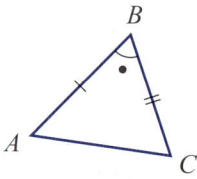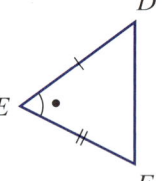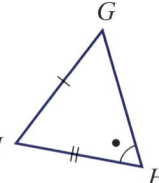

d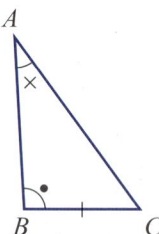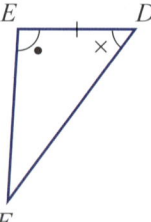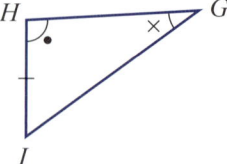

7 Identify all pairs of congruent triangles from those below. Angles with the same mark are equal.

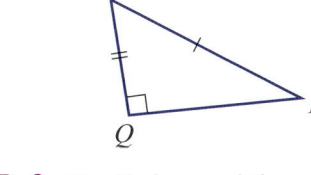
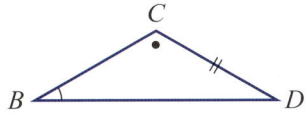
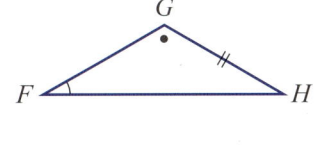

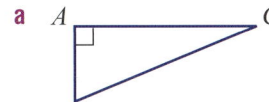
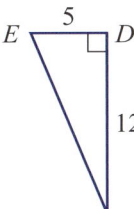

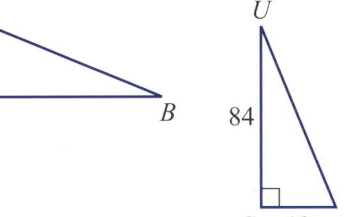

8 Use Pythagoras' theorem to help find the length *BC* in these pairs of congruent triangles.

a

b

9 Are all triangles with three pairs of equal corresponding angles congruent? Explain why or why not.

10 Consider this diagram including two triangles.

   a Explain why there are two pairs of equal matching angles.

   b Give the reason (SSS, SAS, AAS or RHS) why there are two congruent triangles.

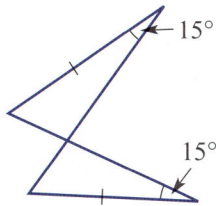

11 *ABCD* is a parallelogram.

    a   Give the reason why $\triangle ABC \equiv \triangle CDA$.

    b   What does this say about $\angle B$ and $\angle D$?

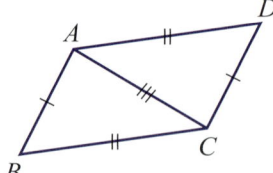

12 Consider this diagram.

    a   Explain why there are two pairs of corresponding sides of equal length for the two triangles.

    b   Give the reason (SSS, SAS, AAS or RHS) why there are two congruent triangles.

    c   Write a congruence statement.

    d   Explain why *AC* is perpendicular (90°) to *DB*.

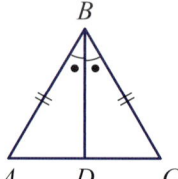

Reasoning

Enrichment: Why not ASS?

13 Angle, Side, Side (ASS) is not a test for congruence of triangles. Complete these tasks to see why.

    a   Draw two line segments *AB* and *EF* both 5 cm long.

    b   Draw two rays *AG* and *EH* so that both $\angle A$ and $\angle E$ are 40°.

    c   Now place a point *C* on ray *AG* so that *BC* = 4 cm.

    d   Place a point *I* on ray *EH* so that *FI* is 4 cm but place it in a different position so that $\triangle ABC$ is not congruent to $\triangle EFI$.

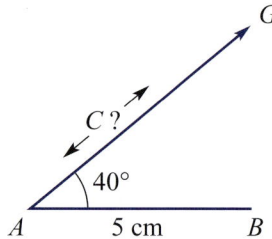 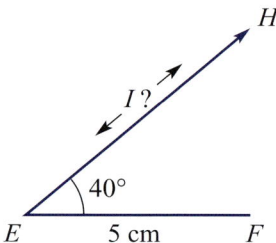

    e   Show how you could use compasses to find the two different places you could put the points *C* or *I* so that *BC* and *FI* are 4 cm.

7.5 Using congruence in proof

A mathematical proof is a sequence of correct statements that leads to a result. It should not contain any big 'leaps' and should provide reasons at each step. The proof that two triangles are congruent should list all the corresponding pairs of sides and angles. Showing that two triangles are congruent can then lead to the proof of other geometrical results.

→ Let's start: Complete the proof

Help complete the proof that $\triangle ABC \equiv \triangle EDC$ for this diagram. Give the missing reasons and congruent triangle in the final statement.

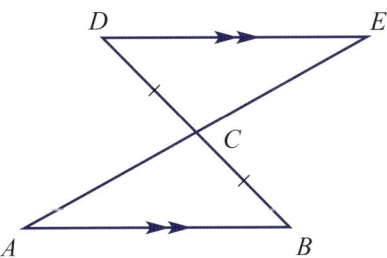

$\angle DCE = \angle BCA$ (_____)
$\angle ABC = \angle EDC$ (_____)
$\quad BC = DC$ (given equal sides)
$\therefore \triangle ABC \equiv$ _____ (AAS)

A mathematical proof is like a puzzle in which each step of the solution needs a reason for being correct.

■ Prove that two triangles are congruent by listing all the corresponding equal angles and sides.
  • Give reasons at each step.
  • Conclude by writing a congruence statement and the abbreviated reason
    (SSS, SAS, AAS or RHS).
  • Vertex labels are usually written in matching order.
■ Other geometrical results can be proved by using the properties of congruent triangles.

Key ideas

Example 11 Proving that two triangles are congruent

Prove that $\triangle ABC \equiv \triangle ADC$

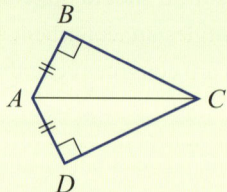

SOLUTION

$\angle B = \angle D = 90°$ (given equal angles)

AC is common

$AB = AD$ (given equal sides)

$\therefore \triangle ABC \equiv \triangle ADC$ (RHS)

EXPLANATION

Both triangles have a right angle.

AC is common to both triangles (hypotenuse).

AB and AD are marked as equal.

Write the congruence statement and the abbreviated reason. Write the vertex labels in matching order.

Example 12 Proving geometrical results using congruence

a Prove that $\triangle ABC \equiv \triangle EDC$

b Hence prove that $AB \parallel DE$ (AB is parallel to DE)

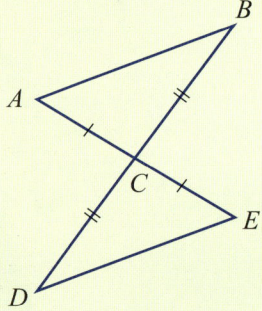

SOLUTION

a $AC = EC$ (given equal sides)

     $BC = DC$ (given equal sides)

  $\angle ACB = \angle ECD$ (vertically opposite angles)

   $\therefore \triangle ABC \equiv \triangle EDC$ (SAS)

b $\angle BAC = \angle DEC$ (matching angles in congruent triangles)

    $\therefore AB \parallel DE$ (Alternate angles are equal)

EXPLANATION

List the given pairs of equal length sides and the vertically opposite angles. The included angle is between the given sides.

All matching angles are equal.

If alternate angles are equal then AB and DE must be parallel.

Exercise 7E

Understanding

1 Name the line segment which is common to both triangles in each diagram.

a
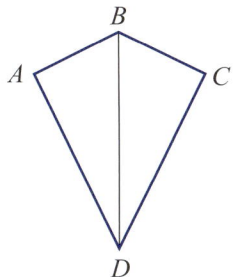

b
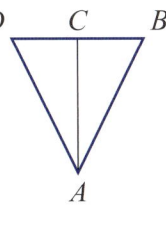

c
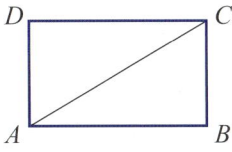

2 Why is $\triangle OAB$ an isosceles triangle in this circle? O is the centre of the circle.

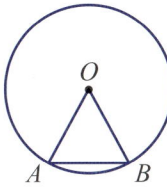

3 For this diagram name the angle which is:

a vertically opposite to $\angle ACB$

b alternate to $\angle CDE$

c alternate to $\angle BAC$.

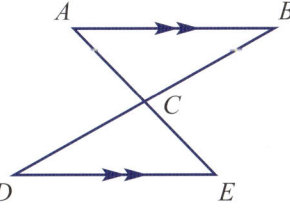

4 For this isosceles triangle, CM is common to $\triangle AMC$ and $\triangle BMC$.

a Which congruence test would be used to prove that $\triangle AMC \equiv \triangle BMC$?

b Which angle in $\triangle BMC$ corresponds to $\angle AMC$ in $\triangle AMC$?

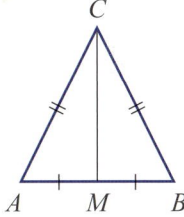

Fluency

Example 11

5 Prove that each pair of triangles is congruent. List your reasons and give the abbreviated congruence test.

a
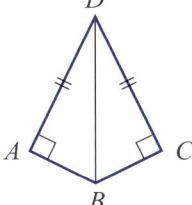

b
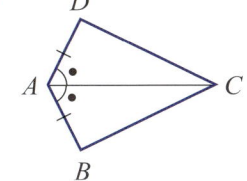

c
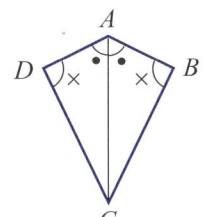

d

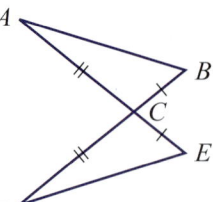

e

f

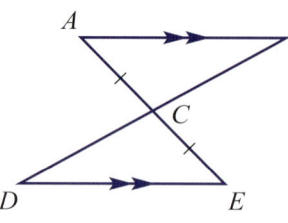

g

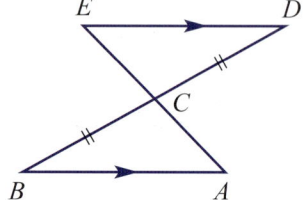

h

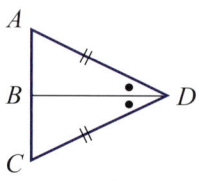

i

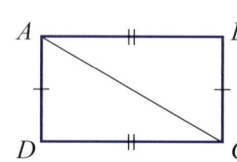

j

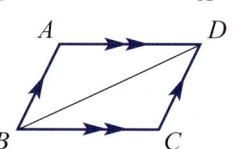

k

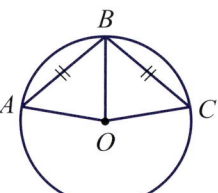

l

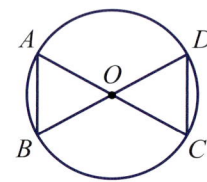

Example 12

6 **a** Prove $\triangle ABC \equiv \triangle EDC$.

b Hence, prove $AB \parallel DE$.

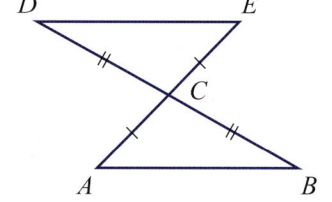

7 **a** Prove $\triangle ABE \equiv \triangle CBD$.

b Hence, prove $AE \parallel CD$.

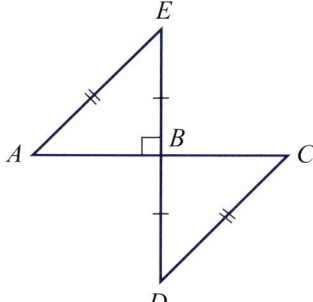

8 **a** Prove $\triangle ABD \equiv \triangle CDB$.

b Hence, prove $AD \parallel BC$.

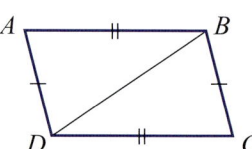

9 **a** Prove that $\triangle AOB \equiv \triangle DOC$. ($O$ is the centre of the circle)

b Hence, prove that $AB \parallel CD$.

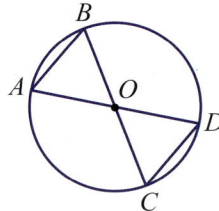

10 a Prove that $\triangle ABD \equiv \triangle CBD$.
  b Hence, prove that AC is perpendicular to BD. ($AC \perp BD$)

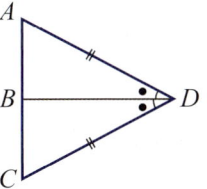

11 a Prove that $\triangle ABD \equiv \triangle CBD$.
  b Hence, prove that $\triangle ACD$ is isosceles.

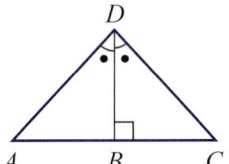

12 Use congruence to explain why OC is perpendicular to AB in this diagram.

13 Use congruence to explain why $AD = BC$ and $AB = DC$ in this parallelogram.

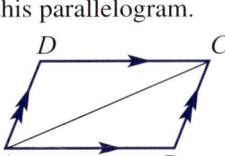

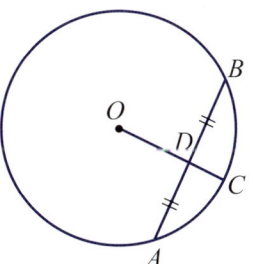

14 Use $\triangle ABE$ and $\triangle CDE$ to explain why $AE = CE$ and $BE = DE$ in this parallelogram.

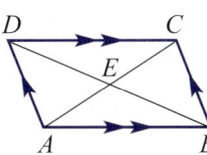

15 Use congruence to show that the diagonals of a rectangle are equal in length.

Enrichment: **Extended proofs**

16 $ABCD$ is a rhombus. Prove that AC bisects BD at $90°$. Show all steps.
  a Prove that $\triangle ABE \equiv \triangle CDE$.
  b Hence prove that AC bisects BD at $90°$.

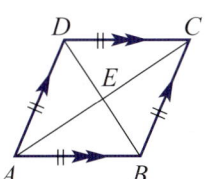

17 Use congruence to prove that the three angles in an equilateral triangle (given three equal side lengths) are all $60°$.

7.6 Enlargement and similar figures

Similar figures have the same shape but not necessarily the same size. If two figures are similar then one of them can be enlarged or reduced so that it is identical (congruent) to the other. If a figure is enlarged by a scale factor greater than 1 the image will be larger than the original. If the scale factor is between 0 and 1, the image will be smaller.

Photographic images that are reduced or enlarged to any given size are similar figures.

Let's start: Enlarging a kite

After drawing a kite design, Mandy cuts out a larger shape to make the actual kite. The actual kite shape is to be similar to the design drawing. The 10 cm length on the drawing matches a 25 cm length on the kite.

- How should the interior angles compare between the drawing and the actual kite?
- By how much has the drawing been enlarged i.e. what is the scale factor? Explain your method to calculate the scale factor.
- What length on the kite matches the 15 cm length on the drawing?

Drawing

10 cm

15 cm

- **Enlargement** is a transformation which involves the increase or decrease in size of an object.
  - The 'shape' of the object is unchanged.
  - Enlargement uses a **centre of enlargement** and an **enlargement factor** or **scale factor**.

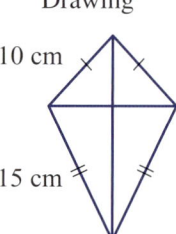

Centre of enlargement

Image

Scale factor
$$\frac{OA'}{OA} = \frac{OB'}{OB} = \frac{OC'}{OC}$$

- Two figures are **similar** if one can be enlarged to be congruent to the other.
  - Corresponding angles are equal.
  - Pairs of corresponding sides are in the same proportion or ratio.

- The **scale factor** = $\dfrac{\text{image length}}{\text{original length}}$

■ The symbols ||| and ~ are used to describe similarity.
- For example, $ABCD \; ||| \; EFGH$ or $ABCD \sim EFGH$
- The letters are usually written down in matching order.

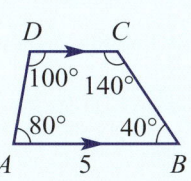 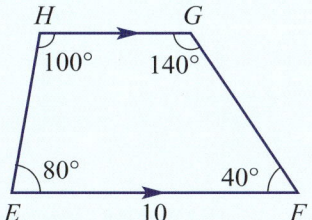

- Scale factor $= \dfrac{EF}{AB} = \dfrac{10}{5} = 2$

Example 13 Enlarging figures

Copy the given diagram using plenty of space and use the given centre of enlargement (O) and these scale factors to enlarge $\triangle ABC$.

a Scale factor $\dfrac{1}{2}$

b Scale factor 3

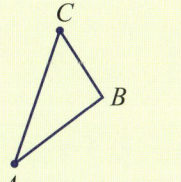

SOLUTION

EXPLANATION

a

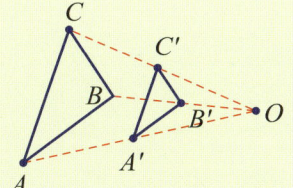

Connect dashed lines between O and the vertices A, B and C.

Since the scale factor is $\dfrac{1}{2}$, place A' so that OA' is half of OA.

Repeat for B' and C'. Join vertices A', B' and C'.

b

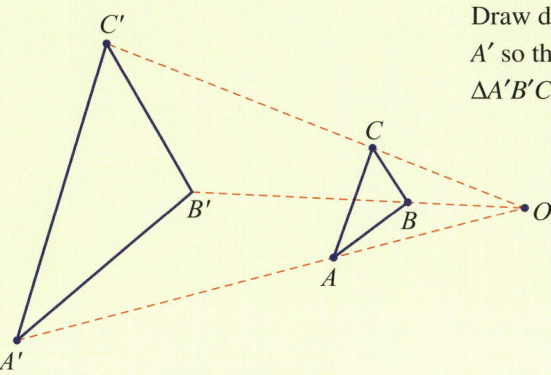

Draw dashed lines from O through A, B and C. Place A' so that $OA' = 3OA$. Repeat for B' and C' and form $\triangle A'B'C'$.

Example 14 Using the scale factor

These figures are similar.

a   Find a scale factor.

b   Find the value of x.

c   Find the value of y.

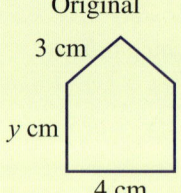

Original

3 cm

y cm

4 cm

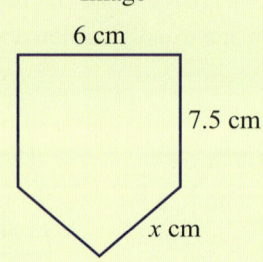

Image

6 cm

7.5 cm

x cm

SOLUTION

a   Scale factor $= \dfrac{6}{4} = 1.5$.

b $x = 3 \times 1.5$
    $= 4.5$

c $y = 7.5 \div 1.5$
    $= 5$

EXPLANATION

Choose two corresponding sides and use

$$\text{scale factor} = \frac{\text{image length}}{\text{original length}}$$

Multiply the side lengths on the original by the scale factor to get the length of the corresponding side on the image.

Divide the side lengths on the image by the scale factor to get the length of the corresponding side on the original.

Exercise 7F

1   The two figures below are similar.

   a   Name the angle in the larger figure which corresponds to $\angle A$.

   b   Name the angle in the smaller figure which corresponds to $\angle I$.

   c   Name the side in the larger figure which corresponds to BC.

   d   Name the side in the smaller figure which corresponds to FJ.

   e   Use FG and AB to find the scale factor.

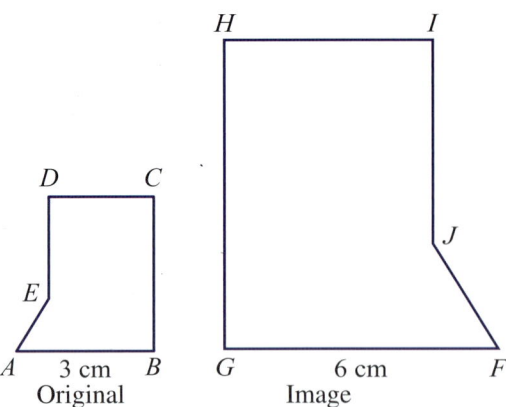

Original

Image

Understanding

2 This diagram shows △ABC enlarged to give the image △A'B'C'.
  a Measure the lengths OA and OA'. What do you notice?
  b Measure the lengths OB and OB'. What do you notice?
  c Measure the lengths OC and OC'. What do you notice?
  d What is the scale factor?
  e Is A'B' twice the length of AB? Measure to check.

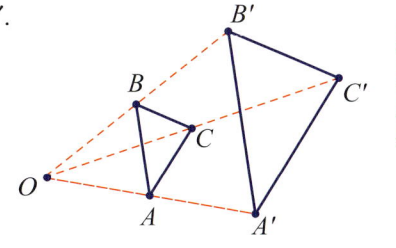

3 This diagram shows rectangle ABCD enlarged (in this case reduced) to rectangle A'B'C'D'.
  a Measure the lengths OA and OA'. What do you notice?
  b Measure the lengths OD and OD'. What do you notice?
  c What is the scale factor?
  d Compare the lengths AD and A'D'. Is A'D' one quarter of the length of AD?

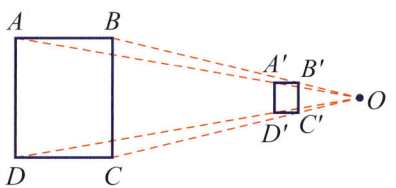

4 A square is enlarged by a scale factor of 4.   Original   Image
  a Are the internal angles the same for both the original and the image?
  b If the side length of the original square was 2 cm, what would be the side length of the image square?
  c If the side length of the image square was 100 m, what would be the side length of the original square?

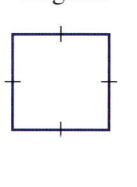
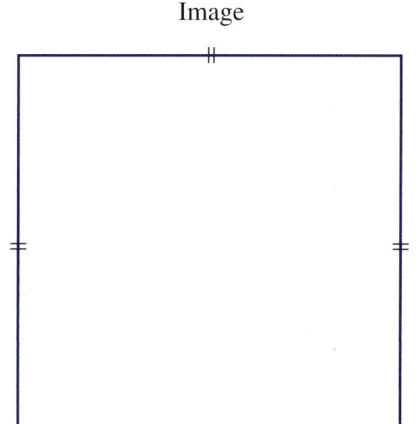

Example 13

5 Copy the given diagram leaving plenty of space around it and use the given centre of enlargement (O) and given scale factors to enlarge △ABC.

  a Scale factor $\frac{1}{3}$ **b** Scale factor 2

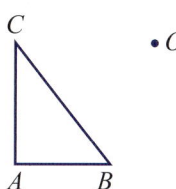

6 This diagram includes a square with centre O and vertices ABCD.
  a Copy the diagram leaving plenty of space around it.
  b Enlarge square ABCD by these scale factors and draw the image. Use O as the centre of enlargement.
    i $\frac{1}{2}$ **ii** 1.5

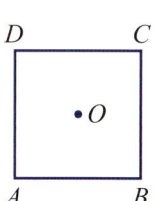

Example 14

7 Each of the pairs of figures shown here are similar. For each pair:

   i Find a scale factor.   **ii** Find the value of x.   **iii** Find the value of y.

a 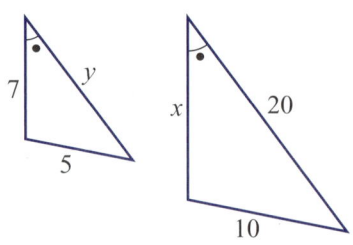   **b**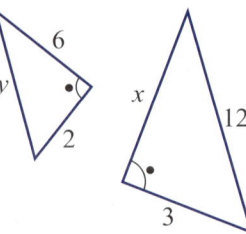

c 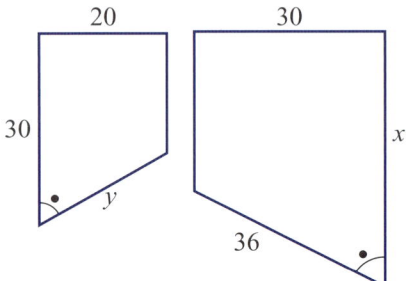   **d**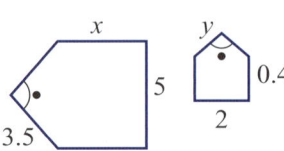

e 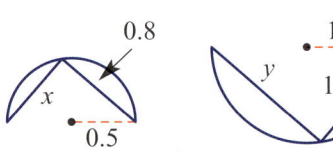   **f**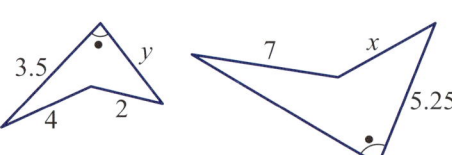

8 These diagrams show a shape and its image after enlargement. For each part, find:

   i the scale factor   **ii** the coordinates (x, y) of the centre of enlargement.

a 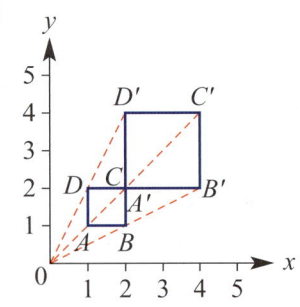   **b**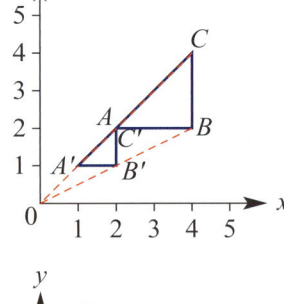

c 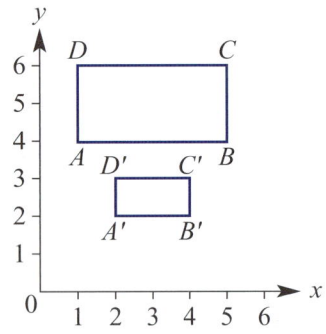   **d**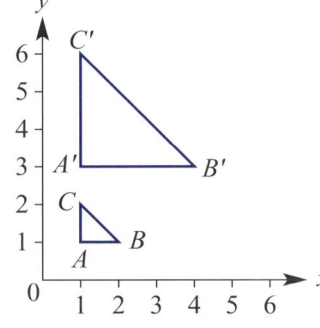

9 A person 1.8 m tall stands in front of a light which sits on the floor.

The person casts a shadow on the wall behind them.

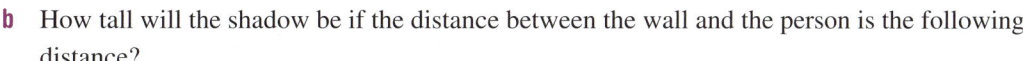

a How tall will the shadow be if the distance between the wall and the light is:

   i 4 m

   ii 10 m

   iii 3 m?

b How tall will the shadow be if the distance between the wall and the person is the following distance?

   i 4 m   **ii** 5 m

c Find the distance from the wall to the person if the shadow is the following height.

   i 5.4 m   **ii** 7.2 m

10 This truck is 12.7 m long.

a Measure the length of the truck in the photo.

b Measure the height of the truck in the photo.

c Estimate the actual height of the truck.

11 A figure is enlarged by a scale factor of a where $a > 0$.

a For what values of a will the image be larger than the original figure?

b For what values of a will the image be smaller than the original figure?

c For what value of a will the image be congruent to the original figure?

12 Explain why:
   a any two squares are similar
   b any two equilateral triangles are similar
   c any two rectangles are not necessarily similar
   d any two isosceles triangles are not necessarily similar.

13 An object is enlarged by a factor of k. What scale factor should be used to reverse this enlargement?

14 A map has a scale ratio of 1 : 50 000.
   a What length on the ground is represented by 2 cm on the map?
   b What length on the map is represented by 12 km on the ground?

Enrichment: The Sierpinslki triangle

15 The Sierpinski triangle shown is a mathematically generated pattern.

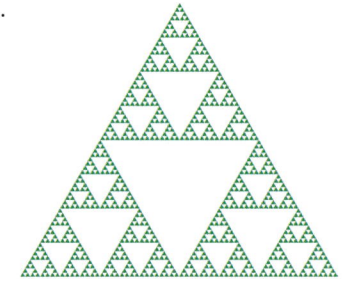

It is created by repeatedly enlarging triangles by a factor of $\frac{1}{2}$.
The steps are:

1 Start with an equilateral triangle as in figure 1.

2 Enlarge the triangle by a factor $\frac{1}{2}$.

3 Arrange three copies of the image as in figure 2.

4 Continue repeating steps 2 and 3 with each triangle.

   a Make a large copy of figures 1 to 3 then draw the next two figures in the pattern.

   b If the original triangle (figure 1) had side length l, find the side length of the smallest triangle in:
      i figure 2
      ii figure 3
      iii figure 8 (assuming figure 8 is the 8th diagram in the pattern)

   c What fraction of the area is shaded in:
      i figure 2?   **ii** figure 3?
      iii figure 6 (assuming figure 6 is the 6th diagram in the pattern)?

   d The Sierpinski triangle is one where the process of enlargement and copying is continued forever. What is the area of a Sierpinski triangle?

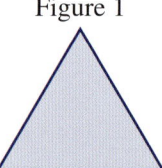

Figure 1

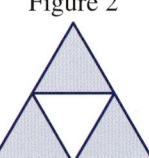

Figure 2

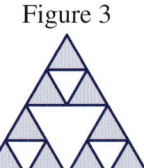

Figure 3

7.7 Similar triangles

Many geometric problems can be solved by using similar triangles. Shadows, for example, can be used to determine the height of a tall mast where the shadows form the base of two similar triangles. To solve such problems firstly involves the identification of two triangles and an explanation as to why they are similar. As with congruence of triangles there is a set of minimum conditions to establish similarity in triangles.

Similar triangles can be used to calculate distances in the natural world.

Let's start: Are they similar?

Each point below describes two triangles. Accurately draw each pair and decide if they are similar (same shape but of different size).

- $\triangle ABC$ with $AB = 2$ cm, $AC = 3$ cm and $BC = 4$ cm
  $\triangle DEF$ with $DE = 4$ cm, $DF = 6$ cm and $EF = 8$ cm

- $\triangle ABC$ with $AB = 3$ cm, $AC = 4$ cm and $\angle A = 40°$
  $\triangle DEF$ with $DE = 6$ cm, $DF = 8$ cm and $\angle D = 50°$

- $\triangle ABC$ with $\angle A = 30°$ and $\angle B = 70°$
  $\triangle DEF$ with $\angle D = 30°$ and $\angle F = 80°$

- $\triangle ABC$ with $\angle A = 90°$, $AB = 3$ cm and $BC = 5$ cm
  $\triangle DEF$ with $\angle D = 90°$, $DE = 6$ cm and $EF = 9$ cm

Which pairs are similar and why? For the pairs that are not similar, what measurements could be changed so that they are similar?

- Two triangles are **similar** if:
  - corresponding angles are equal
  - corresponding sides are in proportion (the same ratio)
- The **similarity statement** for two similar triangles $\triangle ABC$ and $\triangle DEF$ is:
  - $\triangle ABC \,|||\, \triangle DEF$ or
  - $\triangle ABC \sim \triangle DEF$

  Letters are usually written in matching order so AB corresponds to DE etc.

Key ideas

■ **Tests for similar triangles**. (Not to be confused with the congruence tests for triangles).

• Side, Side, Side (SSS)

All three pairs of corresponding sides are in the same ratio.

$$\frac{12}{6} = \frac{8}{4} = \frac{14}{7}$$

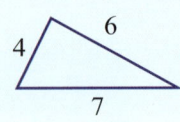
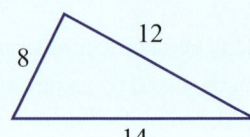

• Side, Angle, Side (SAS)

Two pairs of corresponding sides are in the same ratio and the included angle is equal.

$$\frac{22}{11} = \frac{10}{5}$$

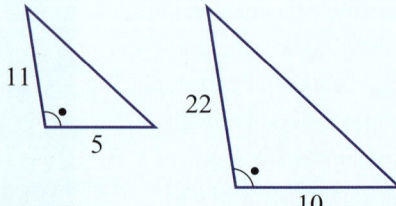

• Angle, Angle, Angle (AAA or AA)

All three corresponding angles are equal. (If there are two equal pairs then the third pair must be equal.)

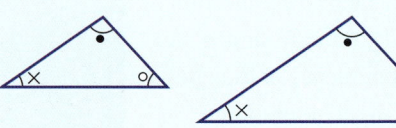

• Right angle, Hypotenuse, Side (RHS)

The hypotenuses of right-angled triangles and another corresponding pair of sides are in the same ratio.

$$\frac{15}{5} = \frac{6}{2}$$

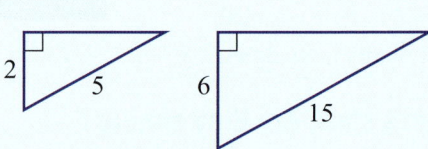

Example 15 Choosing a similarity test for triangles

Choose the similarity test which proves that these pairs of triangles are similar.

a

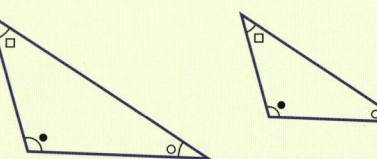

b

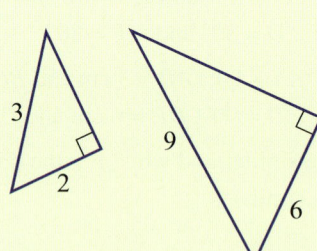

c

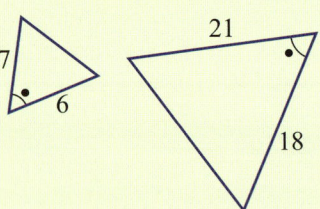

d

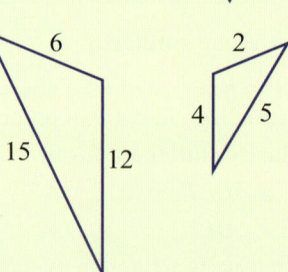

SOLUTION	EXPLANATION
a AAA	Three pairs of angles are equal.
b RHS	Both are right-angled triangles and the hypotenuses and another pair of sides are in the same ratio $\left(\dfrac{9}{3} = \dfrac{6}{2}\right)$.
c SAS	Two pairs of corresponding sides are in the same ratio $\left(\dfrac{21}{7} = \dfrac{18}{6}\right)$ and the included angles are equal.
d SSS	Three pairs of corresponding sides are in the same ratio $\left(\dfrac{15}{5} = \dfrac{12}{4} = \dfrac{6}{2}\right)$.

Example 16 Finding a missing length using similarity

For this pair of triangles:

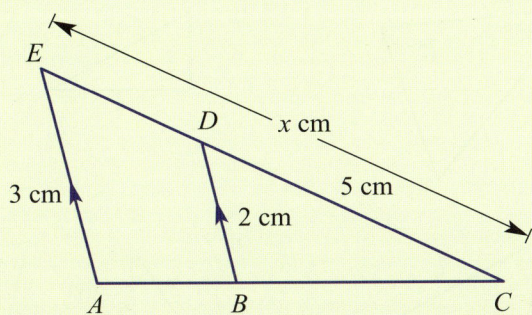

a Give a reason (SSS, SAS, AAA or RHS) why the two triangles are similar.
b Find the value of x.

SOLUTION	EXPLANATION
a AAA or just AA.	$\angle EAC = \angle DBC$ since AE is parallel to BD and $\angle C$ is common to both triangles. (Also $\angle AEC = \angle BDC$ since AE is parallel to BC).
b Scale factor $= \dfrac{3}{2} = 1.5$.	$\dfrac{AE}{BD} = \dfrac{3}{2}$.
$\therefore x = 5 \times 1.5$	Multiply CD by the scale factor to find the length of the corresponding length CE.
$\quad = 7.5$	

Exercise 7G

1 These two triangles are similar.

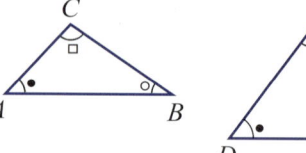
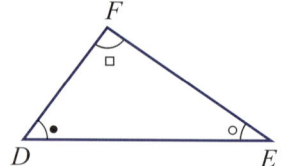

   a Which vertex on ΔDEF corresponds
   to (matches) vertex B on ΔABC?

   b Which vertex on ΔABC corresponds
   to (matches) vertex F on ΔDEF?

   c Which side on ΔDEF corresponds to (matches) side AC on ΔABC?

   d Which side on ΔABC corresponds to (matches) side EF on ΔDEF?

   e Which angle on ΔABC corresponds to (matches) $\angle D$ on ΔDEF?

   f Which angle on ΔDEF corresponds to (matches) $\angle B$ on ΔABC?

2 What is the scale factor on this pair of similar
triangles which enlarges ΔABC to ΔDEF?

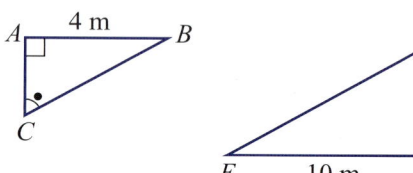

3 Copy and complete the following sentences.

   a The abbreviated tests for similar triangles are
   SSS, _____, _____ and _____.

   b Similar figures have the same _____ but are not necessarily the same _____.

Example 15   **4** Choose the similarity test which proves that these pairs of triangles are similar.

   a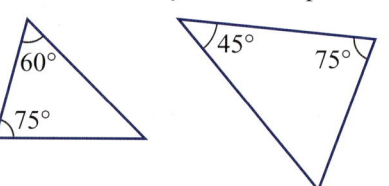

   b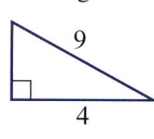

   c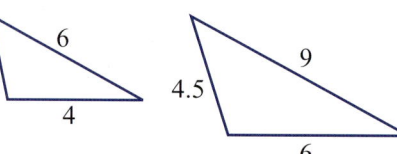

   d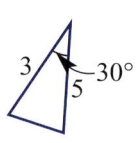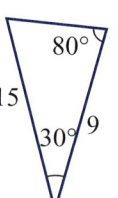

   e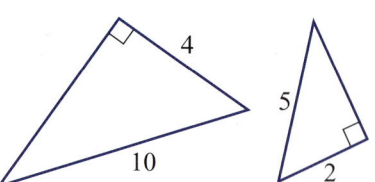

   f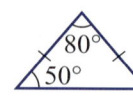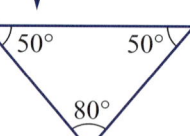

   g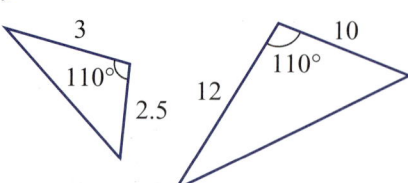

   h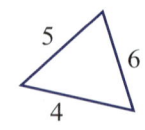

5 Write similarity statements for these pairs of similar triangles. Write letters in matching order.

a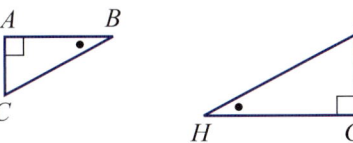

b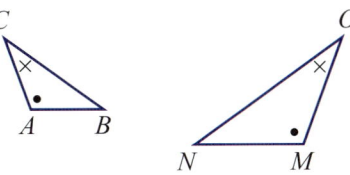

c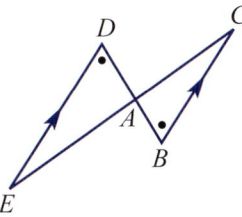

d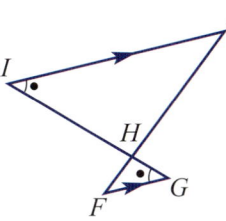

e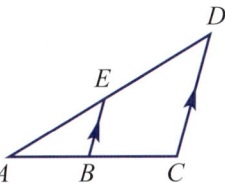

f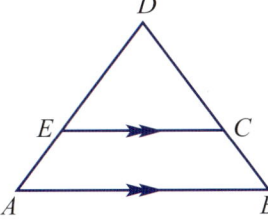

Example 16

6 For this pair of triangles:
   a give a reason (SSS, SAS, AAA or RHS) why the two triangles are similar
   b find the value of x.

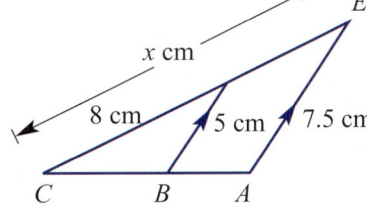

7 For this pair of triangles:
   a give a reason (SSS, SAS, AAA or RHS) why the two triangles are similar
   b find the value of x.

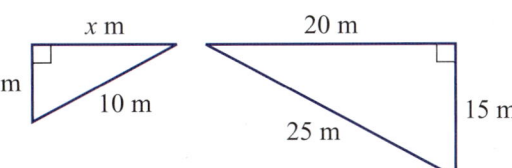

8 Each given pair of triangles is similar.
   For each pair find:
   i the enlargement factor (scale factor) which enlarges the smaller triangle to the larger triangle
   ii the value of x.

a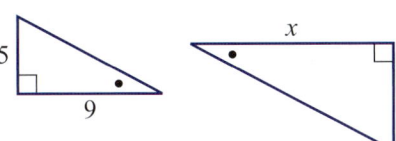

b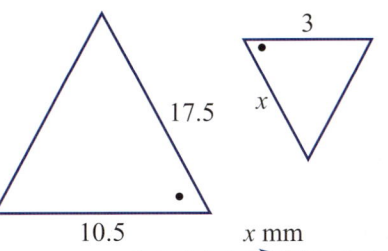

9 For this pair of triangles:
   a give a reason (SSS, SAS, AAA or RHS) why the two triangles are similar
   b find the value of x.

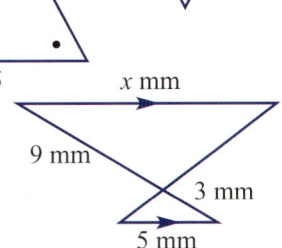

10 For each pair of similar triangles:

   i give a reason (SSS, SAS, AAA or RHS) why the two triangles are similar

   ii find the value of x.

a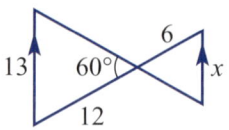

b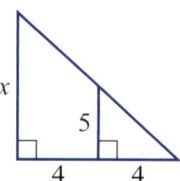

c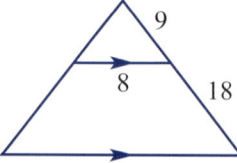

11 Find the value of x in these triangles.

a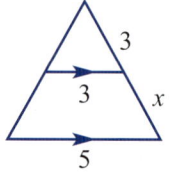

b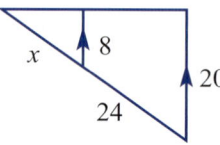

c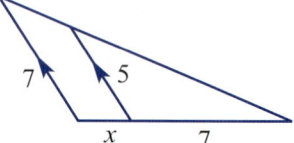

12 Name the triangle which is not similar to the other two in each group of three triangles.

a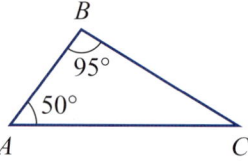

b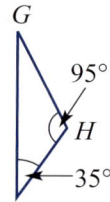

c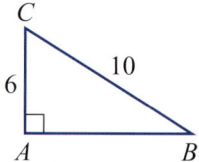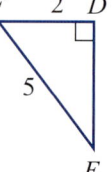

d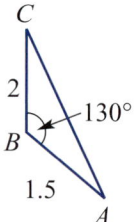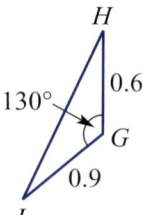

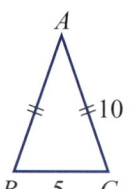 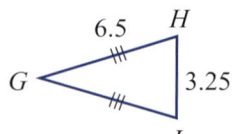

13 Give reasons why these two triangles are similar.

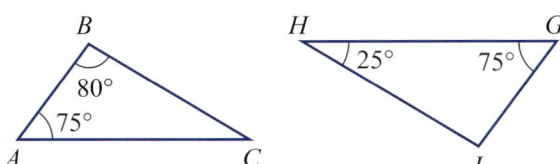

14 Give reasons why the two triangles in these diagrams are not similar.

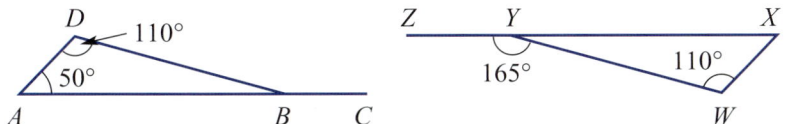

15 When two intersecting transversals join parallel lines, two triangles are formed. Explain why these two triangles are similar.

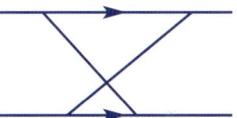

16 The four tests for similarity closely resemble the tests for congruence. Which similarity test closely matches the AAS congruence test? Explain the difference.

Enrichment: Area ratio

17 Consider these three similar triangles (not drawn to scale).

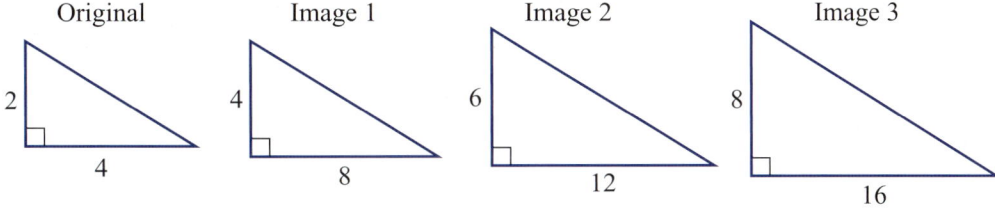

a Complete this table.

Triangle	Original	Image 1	Image 2	Image 3
Length scale factor	1	2		
Area				
Area scale factor	1			

b What do you notice about the area scale factor compared to the length scale factor?
c What would be the area scale factor if the length scale factor is n?
d What would be the area scale factor if the length scale factor is:
  i 10?   **ii** 20?   **iii** 100?

e What would be the area scale factor if the length scale factor is $\dfrac{1}{2}$?

7.8 Proving and applying similar triangles

Similar triangles can be used in many mathematical and practical problems. If two triangles are proved to be similar then the properties of similar triangles can be used to find missing lengths or unknown angles. Finding the approximate height of a tall object, or the width of a projected image, for example, can be found using similar triangles.

Let's start: How far is the rock?

Ali is at the beach and decides to estimate how far an exposed rock is from seashore. He places four pegs in the sand as shown and measures the distance between them.

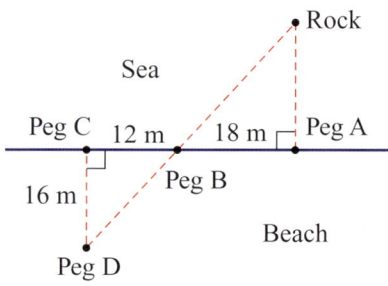

- Why do you think Ali has placed the four pegs in the way that is shown in the diagram?
- Why are the two triangles similar? Which test (SSS, SAS, AAA or RHS) could be used and why?
- How would Ali use the similar triangles to find the distance from the beach at peg A to the rock?

The height of even the tallest building in the world, the Burj Khalifa in Dubai, can be verified using similar triangles.

Key ideas

■ To prove triangles are similar, list any pairs of corresponding equal angles or pairs of sides in a given ratio.
  • Give reasons at each step.
  • Write a similarity statement, for example, $\triangle ABC \;|||\; \triangle DEF$ or $\triangle ABC \sim \triangle DEF$
  • Write the triangle similarity test in abbreviated form (SSS, SAS, AAA, RHS).
■ To apply similarity in practical problems:
  • Prove two triangles are similar.
  • Find a scale factor.
  • Find the value of any unknowns.

Example 17 Proving two triangles are similar

Prove that each pair of triangles is similar.

a

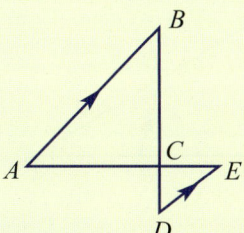

b

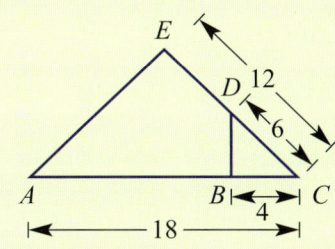

SOLUTION

a $\angle BAC = \angle DEC$ (Alternate angles
    and $DE \parallel AB$)

$\angle ABC = \angle EDC$ (Alternate angles
    and $DE \parallel AB$)

$\angle ACB = \angle ECD$ (Vertically opposite
    angles)

$\therefore \triangle ABC \mathbin{|||} \triangle EDC$ (AAA)

b $\dfrac{AC}{DC} = \dfrac{18}{6} = 3$

$\angle ACE = \angle DCB$ (common)

$\dfrac{EC}{BC} = \dfrac{12}{4} = 3$

$\therefore \triangle ACE \mathbin{|||} \triangle DCB$ (SAS)

EXPLANATION

Parallel lines cut by a
transversal will create a pair
of equal alternate angles.
Vertically opposite angles
are also equal. Write the
similarity statement and
the abbreviated reason.

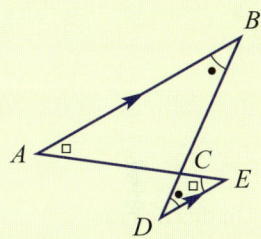

Note that there is a common angle and two pairs of
corresponding sides. Find the scale factor for both pairs
of sides to see if they are equal. Complete the proof
with a similarity statement.

Example 18 Applying similarity

Chris' shadow is 1.2 m long while a 1 m vertical stick has a
shadow 0.8 m long.

a Give a reason why the two triangles are similar.

b Determine Chris' height.

SOLUTION

a All angles are the same.

b   Scale factor $= \dfrac{1.2}{0.8} = 1.5$

$\therefore$ Chris' height $= 1 \times 1.5$

$= 1.5$ m

EXPLANATION

The sun's rays will pass over Chris and the stick and hit
the ground at approximately the same angle.

First find the scale factor.

Multiply the height of the stick by the scale factor to
find Chris' height.

Exercise 7H

1 In this diagram, name the angle which is common to both △ACE and △BCD.

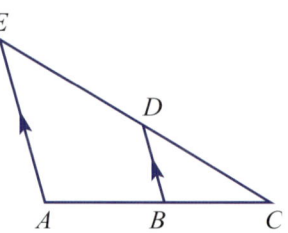

2 In this diagram:
   a name the pair of vertically opposite angles
   b name the two pairs of equal alternate angles.

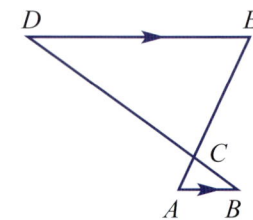

3 In this diagram:
   a name the common angle for the two triangles
   b which side corresponds to side
      i DC?   ii AE?

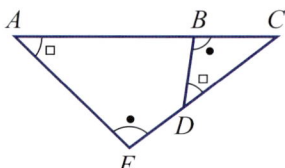

Example 17a

4 Prove that each pair of triangles is similar.

a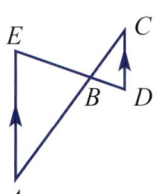

b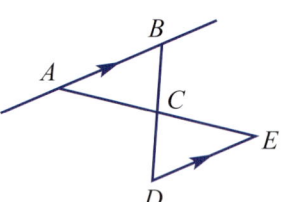

c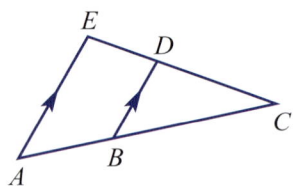

d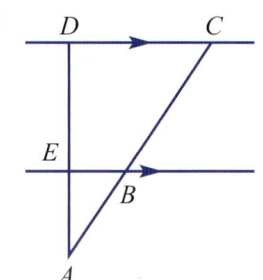

e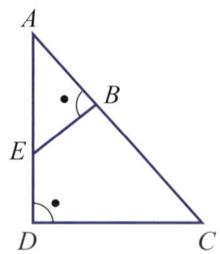

f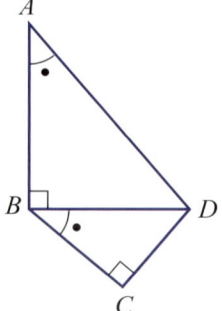

ple 17b **5** Prove that each pair of triangles is similar.

a

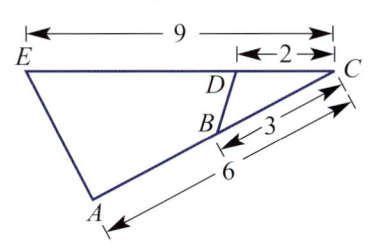

b

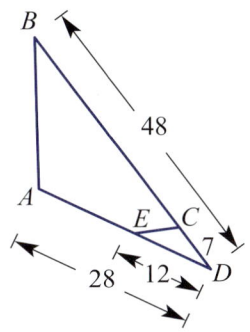

c

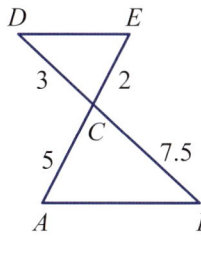

ple 18 **6** A tree's shadow is 20 m long while a 2 m vertical stick has a shadow 1 m long.

    a Give a reason why the two triangles contained within the objects and their shadows are similar.

    b Find the height of the tree.

7 Two cables support a steel pole at the same angle as shown. The two cables are 4 m and 10 m in length while the shorter cable reaches 3 m up the pole.

    a Give a reason why the two triangles are similar.

    b Find the height of the pole.

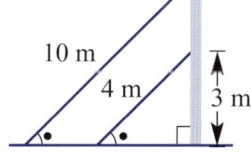

8 John stands 6 m from a lamp post and casts a 2 m shadow. The shadow from the pole and from John end at the same place. Determine the height of the lamp post if John is 1.5 m tall.

9 Joanne wishes to determine the width of the river shown without crossing it. She places four pegs as shown. Calculate the river's width.

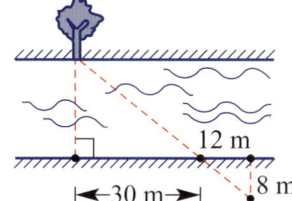

10 A deep chasm has a large rock (R) sitting on its side as shown. Find the width of the chasm.

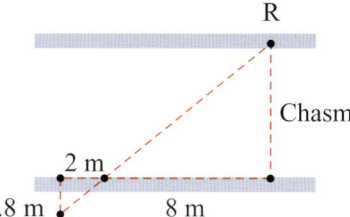

11 Find the length *AB* in this diagram if the two triangles are similar.

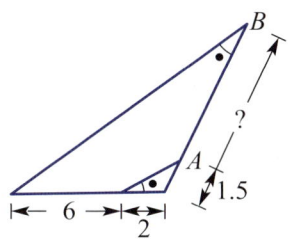

12 In this diagram $\triangle ADC$ is isosceles.

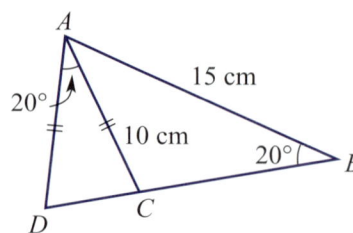

   a There are two triangles which are similar. Identify them and complete a proof. You may need to find another angle first.

   b Find the lengths DC and CB expressing your answers as fractions.

13 In this diagram AC is perpendicular to BD and $\triangle ABD$ is right angled.

   a Prove that $\triangle ABD$ is similar to:

     i $\triangle CBA$ **ii** $\triangle CAD$

   b Find the lengths:

     i BD **ii** AC **iii** AB

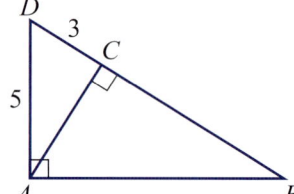

Enrichment: Extended proofs

14 a Prove $AE = 4AC$.

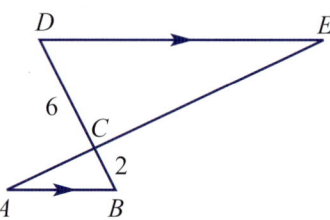

   b Prove $BC = \dfrac{1}{2}CE$.

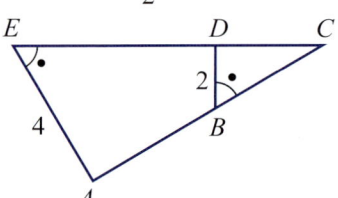

   c Prove $CE = \dfrac{7}{5}CD$.

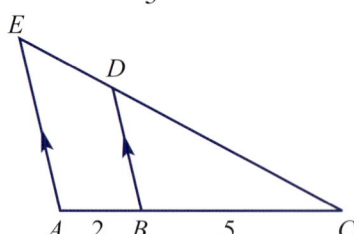

   d Prove $AB = 3BC$.

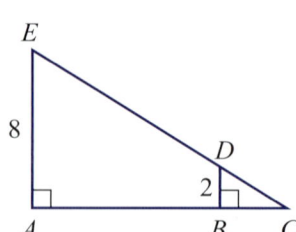

Technology

Use a computer dynamic geometry package like 'Geometers Sketchpad' or 'Cabri Geometry' to construct the shapes in each of the following questions.

The circumcentre of a triangle

The point at which all perpendicular bisectors of the sides of a triangle meet is called the circumcentre.

a Draw any triangle.

b Label the vertices A, B and C.

c Draw a perpendicular bisector for each side.

d Label the intersection point of the bisectors O.

e Using O as the centre, construct a circle that touches the vertices of the triangle.

f Drag any of the vertices and describe what happens to your construction.

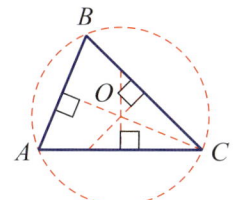

The incentre of a triangle

The point at which all angle bisectors of a triangle meet is called the incentre.

a Draw any triangle.

b Label the vertices A, B and C.

c Draw the three angle bisectors, through the vertices.

d Label the intersection point of the bisectors O.

e Using O as your centre, construct a circle that touches the sides of the triangle.

f Drag any of the vertices and describe what happens to your construction.

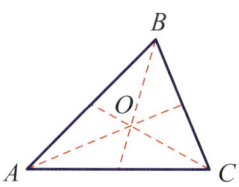

The centroid of a triangle

The point of intersection of the three medians of a triangle is called the centroid. It can also be called the centre of gravity.

a Draw a triangle and label the vertices A, B and C.

b Find the midpoint of each line and draw a line segment from each midpoint to its opposite vertex.

c Label the intersection point of these lines O. This is the centroid of the triangle.

d Show your teacher the final construction and print it. Cut out the triangle and place a sharp pencil under the centroid. The triangle should balance perfectly.

The equilateral triangle: the special triangle

a Construct an equilateral triangle. Determine its incentre, circumcentre and centroid.

b What do you notice?

The tethered goat

A goat is tied to a post by a rope. The area over which the goat can graze will vary in shape depending on where the post is placed or the length of the rope.

Fixed distance from a fence

Assume the post is 3 m from the centre of a high fence 8 m long.

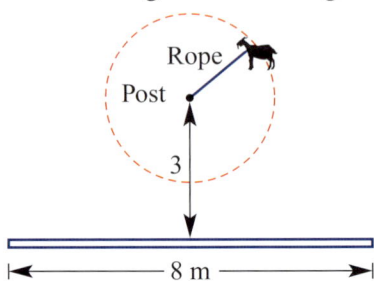

If the rope is quite short as shown in the diagram the area the goat can graze in is circular in shape. For longer lengths of the rope, the shape of the accessible area is different.

a   On a sheet of paper draw a scale diagram of the location of the post and fence shown above.
b   On your scale diagram use a compass (or a string and drawing pins) to help you trace out the shape of the area accessible to the goat if the length of the rope is:

   i   2 m   **ii**   3 m   **iii**   4 m   **iv**   5 m
   v   6 m   **vi**   9 m   **vii**   11 m   **viii**   13 m

Be careful! Think about what will happen when the goat reaches either end of the fence.

Fixed length of rope

For the following situations the goat is tied to a post on the fence by a 3 m length of rope. Draw a scale diagram of each one and determine the shape of the accessible area.

a
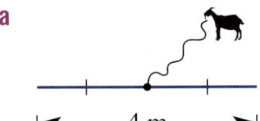

b
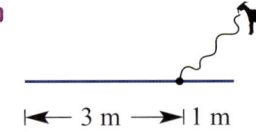

c
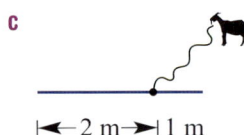

Shed problem

In this diagram the goat is tied to a post of a shed, which is 2 m long and 1 m wide by a 3 m length of rope.

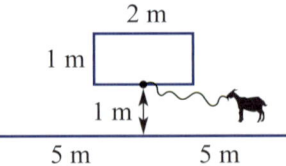

a   Draw a scale diagram and determine the shape of the accessible area.
b   Investigate other situations where the goat is tied to other positions on the shed. Clearly show your diagrams and post position.

1 Use 12 match sticks to make 6 equilateral triangles.

2 How many acute angles are there in this diagram (right)?

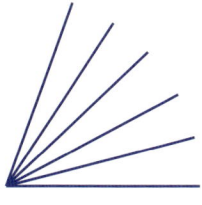

3 Find the value of a.

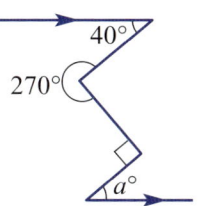

4 Explore (using dynamic geometry) where the points A, B and C should be on the sides of ΔDEF so that the perimeter of ΔABC is a minimum.

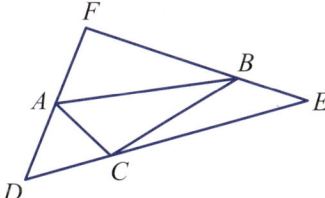

5 How many triangles are there in this diagram (right)?

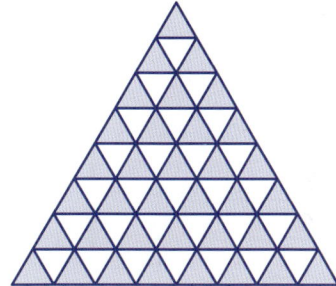

6 A circle is divided using chords (one chord is shown here). What is the maximum number of regions that can be formed if the circle is divided with 4 chords?

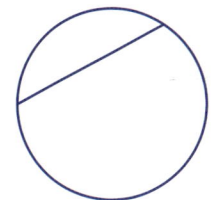

7 Two poles are 30 m and 40 m high. Cables connect the top of each vertical pole to the base of the other pole. How high is the intersection point of the cables above the ground?

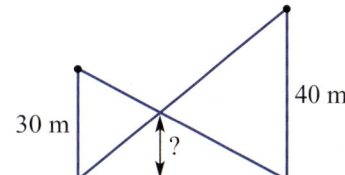

Chapter summary

Angles

Acute $0° < \theta < 90°$
Right $90°$
Obtuse $90° < \theta < 180°$
Straight $180°$
Reflex $180° < \theta < 360°$
Revolution $360°$
Complementary angles sum to $90°$
Supplementary angles sum to $180°$

Parallel lines

If the lines are parallel:

corresponding angles
are equal

Alternate angles
are equal

Vertically opposite
angles are equal

Cointerior angles
are supplementary
$a + b = 180$

Quadrilaterals

Four-sided figures – sum of the
interior angles is $360°$

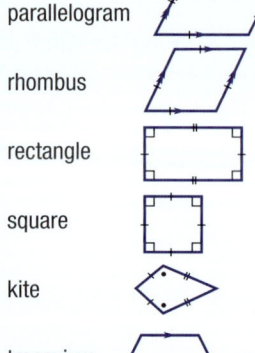

parallelogram

rhombus

rectangle

square

kite

trapezium

Congruent triangles

These are identical in shape and size.
They may need to be rotated or
reflected. We write $\triangle ABC \equiv \triangle DEF$

congruent to

Tests for congruence:
(SSS) – three pairs of corresponding
sides equal
(SAS) – two pairs of corresponding
sides and included angle are equal
(AAS) – two angles and any pair of
corresponding sides are equal
(RHS) – a right angle, hypotenuse and
one other pair of corresponding sides
are equal

Polygons

The sum of the interior angles
in a polygon with n sides is
$S = 180(n - 2)$. Regular polygons
have all sides and angles equal.

Geometry

Triangles

Sum of angles is $180°$.
Exterior angle equals sum of
two opposite interior angles

$$a = b + c$$
exterior angle

Types:
Acute angled – all angles $< 90°$
Obtuse angled – 1 angle $> 90°$
Right angled – 1 angle $90°$
Equilateral – all angles $60°$ – all
sides are equal
Isosceles – 2 angles and 2 sides
are equal
Scalene – all sides and angles
are different sizes

Proving congruence/similarity

List corresponding pairs of equal
angles and pairs of sides that are
equal/in same ratio. Give reasons for
each pair. Write a congruence/
similarity statement giving the
abbreviated reason.
e.g.
AC (common)
$BC = DC$ (given)
$\angle ACD = \angle ACB = 90°$
(given)
$\therefore \triangle ACD \equiv \triangle ACB$ (SAS)

Similar figures

These are the same shape but
different size.
Two figures are similar if one can
be enlarged to be congruent to
the other.
Enlargement uses a scale factor.

Scale factor = $\dfrac{\text{image length}}{\text{original length}}$

Similar triangles

Similar triangles have corresponding angles equal and
corresponding sides are in the same ratio.
We say $\triangle ABC ||| \triangle DEF$ or $\triangle ABC \sim \triangle DEF$
similar to

Tests for similar triangles:
(SSS) – three pairs of corresponding sides in the same ratio
(SAS) – two pairs of corresponding sides in the same ratio
and included angle equal
(AAA or AA) – all three pairs of corresponding angles are
equal; two pairs is enough to prove this
(RHS) – the hypotenuses of right-angled triangles and another
pair of corresponding sides are in the same ratio

Applying similar triangles

In practical problems, look to identify and prove pairs of
similar triangles. Find a scale factor and use this to find the
value of any unknowns, e.g. shadow cast by a tree is 10.5 m
while a person 1.7 m tall has a 1.5 m shadow. How tall is the
tree?
Similar (AAA)
Scale factor = $\dfrac{10.5}{1.5} = 7$
$\therefore h = 1.7 \times 7$
$= 11.9$ m
Tree is 11.9 m tall.

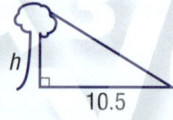
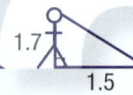

Multiple-choice questions

1 The angle that is supplementary to an angle of 55° is:

A 35° **B** 55° **C** 95°

D 125° **E** 305°

2 What is the value of x if AB is parallel to CD?

A 110 **B** 70

C 20 **D** 130

E 120

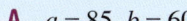

3 If two angles in a triangle are complementary then the third angle is:

A acute **B** a right angle

C obtuse **D** reflex

E supplementary

4 The values of x and y in the diagram are:

A $x = 35, y = 85$

B $x = 45, y = 45$

C $x = 50, y = 60$

D $x = 55, y = 65$

E $x = 65, y = 55$

5 The sum of the interior angles in a hexagon is:

A 1078° **B** 360° **C** 720°

D 900° **E** 540°

6 The quadrilateral with all sides equal, two pairs of opposite parallel sides and no right angles is:

A a kite **B** a trapezium **C** a parallelogram

D a rhombus **E** a square

7 The values of a and b in the diagram are:

A $a = 85, b = 60$

B $a = 75, b = 80$

C $a = 80, b = 55$

D $a = 70, b = 55$

E $a = 75, b = 50$

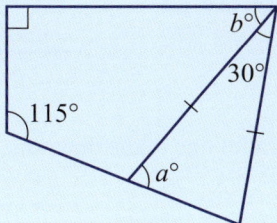

8 The abbreviated reason for congruence in the two triangles shown is:

A AA

B SAS

C SSS

D AAS

E RHS

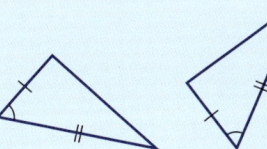

9 The scale factor in the two similar figures that enlarges the original figure to its image is:

A $\frac{2}{3}$

B 2

C 1.2

D 1.5

E 0.5

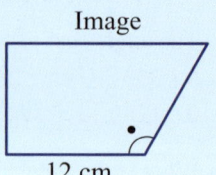

10 The value of x in the diagram is:

A 6   B 9

C 10   D 8

E 7.5

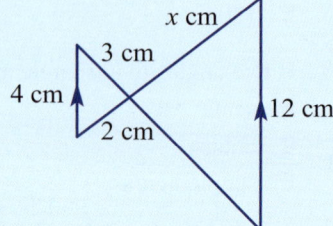

Short-answer questions

1 Name the following triangles and find the value of the pronumerals.

a

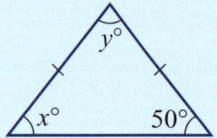

b

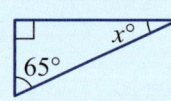

c

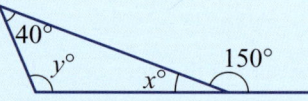

2 Find the value of each pronumeral in the diagrams. Give reasons for your answers.

a

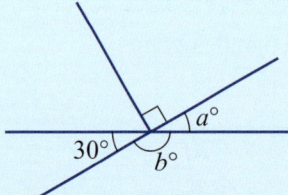

b

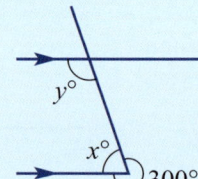

c

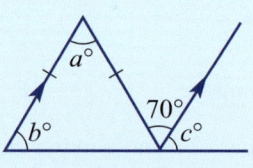

3 By adding a third parallel line to the diagram, find $\angle ABC$.

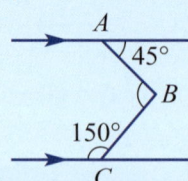

4 Find the value of each pronumeral in the following polygons.

a
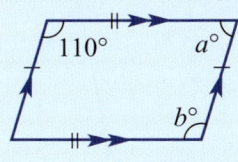
110°   a°
b°

b
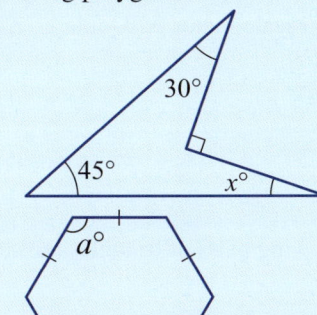
30°
45°
x°

c
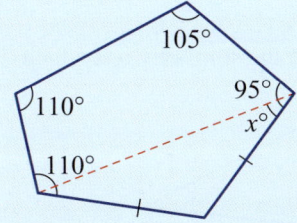
105°
110°   95°
x°
110°

d
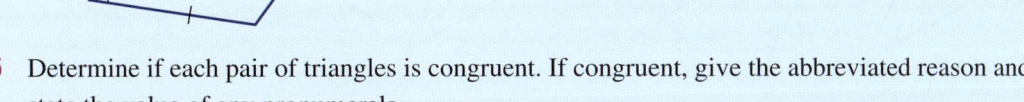
a°

5 Determine if each pair of triangles is congruent. If congruent, give the abbreviated reason and state the value of any pronumerals.

a
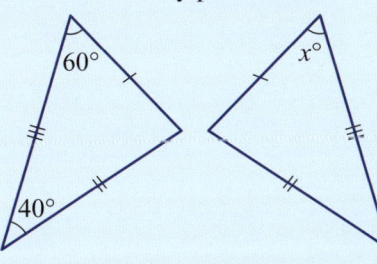
60°
40°
x°

b
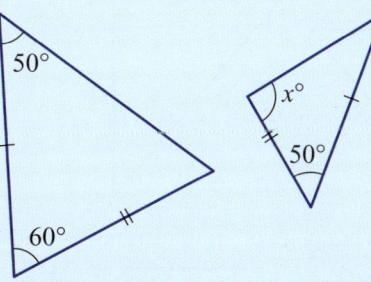
50°
60°
x°
50°

c
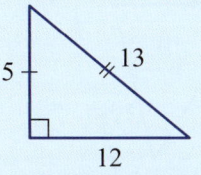
5   13
12   x

d
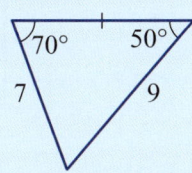
70°   50°
7   9
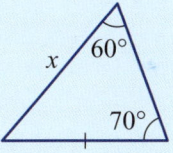
x   60°
70°

6 a Prove that $\triangle ADB \equiv \triangle ADC$. List your reasons and give the abbreviated congruence test.

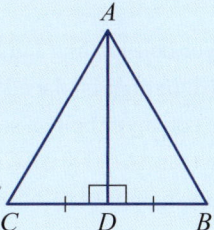
A
C   D   B

b i Prove that $\triangle ACB \equiv \triangle ECD$. List your reason and give the abbreviated congruence test.
   ii Hence, prove that $AB \parallel DE$.

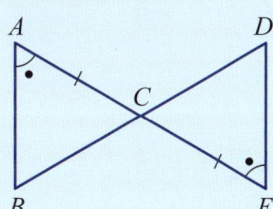
A   D
C
B   E

7 Copy the given diagram using plenty of space. Using the centre of enlargement (*O*) and a scale factor of 3, enlarge △*ABC*.

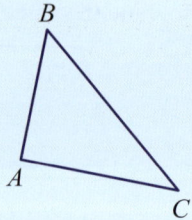

8 Determine if the following pairs of triangles are similar, and state the similarity test which proves this.

a
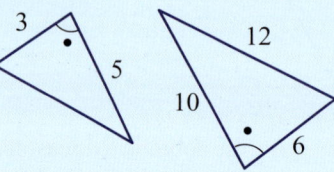

b
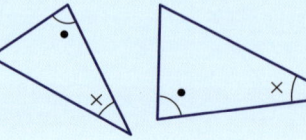

c
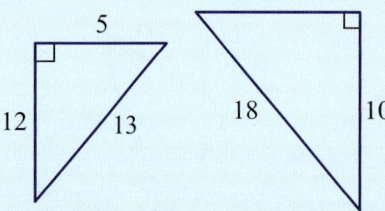

9 For the following pairs of similar triangles find the value of *x*.

a
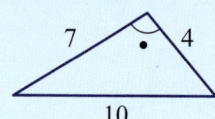

b
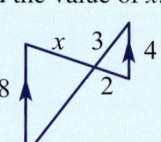

c
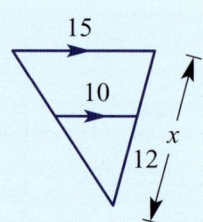

10 A conveyor belt loading luggage onto a plane is 12.5 m long. A vertical support 1.6 m high is placed under the conveyor belt such that it is 4 m along the conveyor belt as shown.

a Prove that △*BCD* ||| △*ACE*.

b Find the height (*AE*) of the luggage door above the ground.

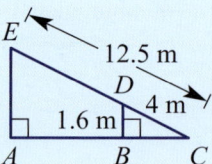

Extended-response questions

1   Complete the following.

a   Prove that $DE \parallel CF$.

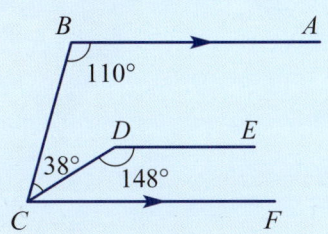

b   Show, with reasons, that $a = 20$.

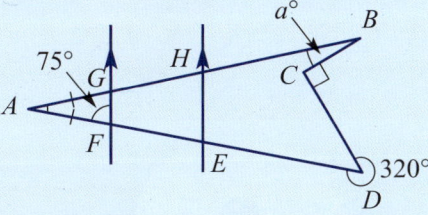

c   Use congruence to prove that $AC = BD$ in the diagram, given $AB = CD$ and $\angle ABC = \angle DCB$.

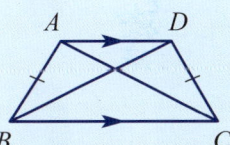

2   A buoy (E) is floating in the sea at some unknown distance from the beach as shown. The points A, B, C and D are measured and marked out on the beach as shown.

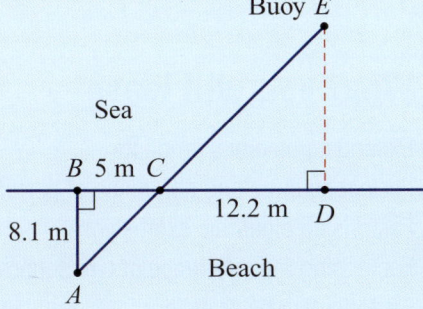

a   Name the angle which is vertically opposite to $\angle ACB$.

b   Explain, with reasons, why $\triangle ABC \parallel\mid\mid \triangle EDC$.

c   Find the distance from the buoy to the beach (ED) to one decimal place

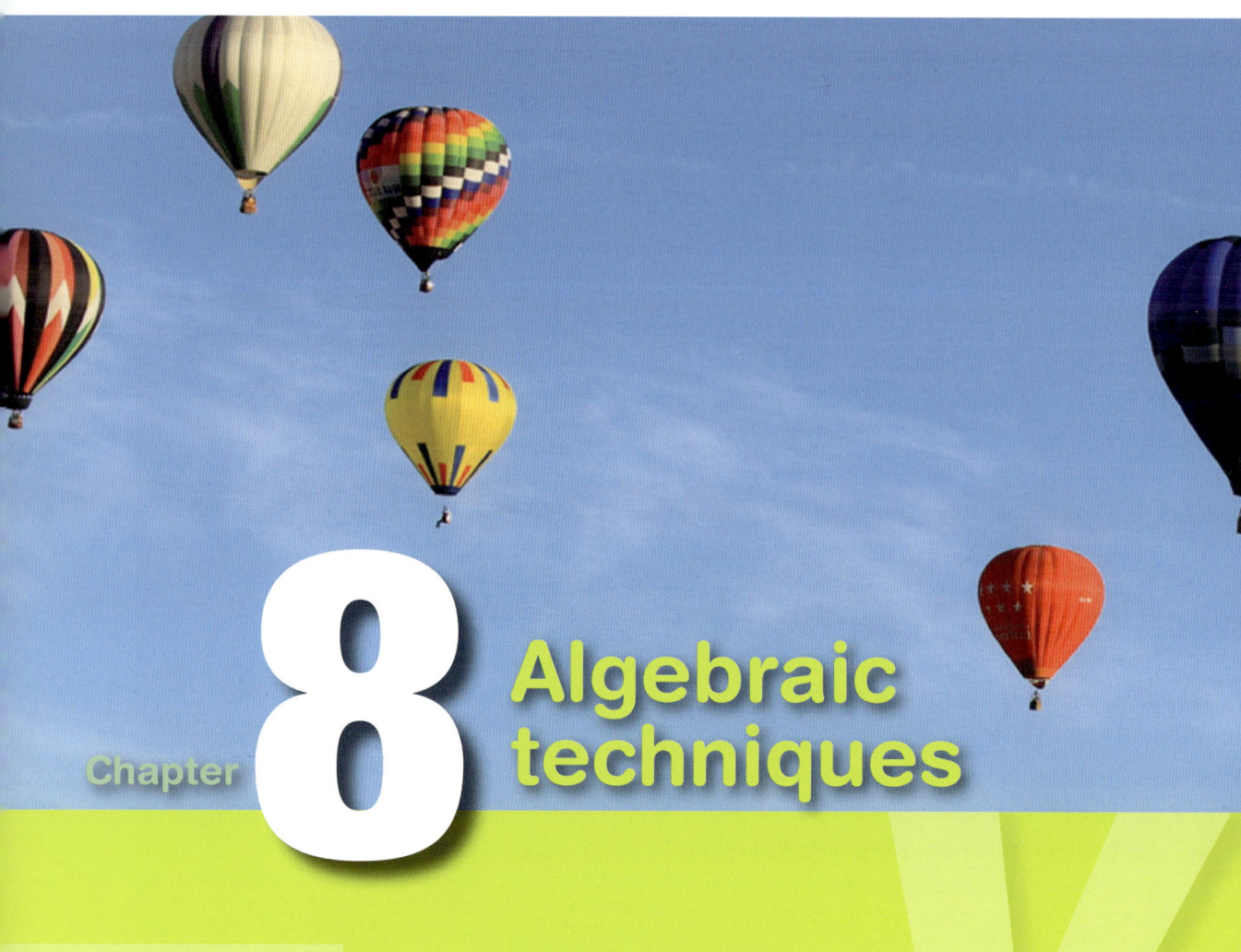

Chapter 8

Algebraic techniques

What you will learn

Free falling

Australian curriculum

NUMBER AND ALGEBRA

Patterns and algebra

Apply the distributive law to the expansion of algebraic expressions, including binomials, and collect like terms where appropriate

The distance (x) of an object from the top of a building after it has been dropped (where air resistance is negligible) can be found using the formula $x = ut + \frac{1}{2}at^2$ where u is the initial velocity of the object, t the time since the object has been dropped and a the acceleration due to gravity, which is approximately equal to -9.8 m/s^2. When an object is dropped it has an initial velocity of 0 m/s, so the distance the object has fallen becomes $x = -4.9t^2$. Using algebra, the distance from the building after t seconds can be found or the time taken to reach ground level could be calculated. If the object is instead dropped from a hot air balloon ascending at 10 m/s, the object first travels in an upward direction. Its distance (x metres) above or below the height of the balloon from when the object is dropped can be found using $x = 10t - 4.9t^2$. Knowing the time taken for the object to reach the ground, we could again use algebra to find factors, such as the height of the balloon, the greatest height reached by the object and the time taken for the object to return to the height it was released from.

1 Expand the following.

   a $2(x + 3)$ **b** $3(a - 5)$ **c** $4x(3 - 2y)$ **d** $-3(2b - 1)$

2 Evaluate.

   a 9^2 **b** 4^2 **c** 1^2

   d $(2x)^2$ if $x = 4$ **e** $(5a)^2$ if $a = -1$ **f** b if $b^2 = 49$ and $b > 0$

   g y if $y^2 = 9$ and $y > 0$ **h** m if $m^2 = 36$ and $m < 0$

3 Write down the highest common factor of:

   a 4 and 6   **b** 12 and 18   **c** $2x$ and $4x$

   d $3xy$ and $9y$ **e** $10x$ and $15x^2$ **f** $3a^2b$ and $4ab^2$

4 Factorise by taking out the highest common factor.

   a $2a + 6$ **b** $3x + 12y$ **c** $5x^2 - 15x$ **d** $4m - 6mn$

5 List the pairs of whole numbers that multiply to each of the following.

   a 6   **b** 12   **c** -10   **d** -27

6 Simplify:

   a $\dfrac{2}{7} + \dfrac{2}{3}$ **b** $\dfrac{7}{9} - \dfrac{1}{6}$

   c $\dfrac{3}{8} \times \dfrac{2}{9}$ **d** $\dfrac{5}{8} \div \dfrac{5}{12}$

7 Expand and simplify.

   a $3(x - 1) + 5$ **b** $4(1 - x) + 5x$

   c $-2(5 + x) - x$ **d** $4(2x + 1) - 3(x + 2)$

8 Solve each of the following equations.

   a $2x - 3 = 9$ **b** $\dfrac{x+1}{3} = 4$ **c** $2(x - 1) = 3(1 - 2x)$

9 Write two expressions for the area of these rectangles, one with brackets and one without.

   a 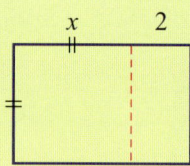   **b**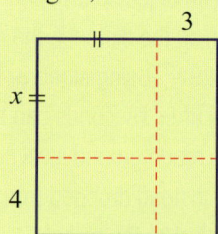

8.1 Expanding binomial products

A binomial is an expression with two terms such as $x + 5$ or $x^2 + 3$. You will recall from Chapter 2 that we looked at the product of a single term with a binomial expression, e.g. $2(x - 3)$ or $x(3x - 1)$. The product of two binomial expressions can also be expanded using the distributive law. This involves multiplying every term in one expression by every term in the other expression.

Expanding the product of two binomial expressions can be applied to problems involving the expansion of rectangular areas such as a farmer's paddock.

Let's start: Rectangular expansions

If $(x + 1)$ and $(x + 2)$ are the side lengths of a rectangle as shown, the total area can be found as an expression in two different ways.

- Write an expression for the total area of the rectangle using length $= (x + 2)$ and width $= (x + 1)$.
- Now find the area of each of the four parts of the rectangle and combine to give an expression for the total area.
- Compare your two expressions above and complete this equation:
$$(x + 2)(\underline{}) = x^2 + \underline{} + \underline{}.$$
- Can you explain a method for expanding the left-hand side to give the right-hand side?

- Expanding **binomial products** uses the **distributive law**.
$$(a + b)(c + d) = a(c + d) + b(c + d)$$
$$= ac + ad + bc + bd$$

- Diagrammatically $(a + b)(c + d) = ac + ad + bc + bd$

  For example: $(x + 1)(x + 5) = x^2 + 5x + x + 5$
  $$= x^2 + 6x + 5$$

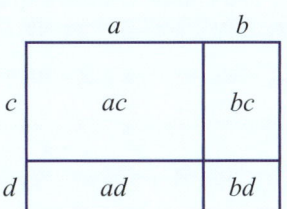

Example 1 Expanding binomial products

Expand the following.

a $(x + 3)(x + 5)$

b $(x - 4)(x + 7)$

c $(2x - 1)(x - 6)$

d $(5x - 2)(3x + 7)$

SOLUTION

EXPLANATION

a $(x + 3)(x + 5) = x^2 + 5x + 3x + 15$

$= x^2 + 8x + 15$

Use the distributive law to expand the brackets and then collect the like terms $5x$ and $3x$.

b $(x - 4)(x + 7) = x^2 + 7x - 4x - 28$

$= x^2 + 3x - 28$

After expanding to get the four terms, collect the like terms $7x$ and $-4x$.

c $(2x - 1)(x - 6) = 2x^2 - 12x - x + 6$

$= 2x^2 - 13x + 6$

Remember $2x \times x = 2x^2$ and $-1 \times (-6) = 6$.

d $(5x - 2)(3x + 7) = 15x^2 + 35x - 6x - 14$

$= 15x^2 + 29x - 14$

Recall $5x \times 3x = 5 \times 3 \times x \times x = 15x^2$.

Exercise 8A

1 The given diagram shows the area $(x + 2)(x + 3)$.

a Write down an expression for the area of each of the four regions inside the rectangle.

b Copy and complete $(x + 2)(x + 3) = \underline{} + 3x + \underline{} + 6$

$= \underline{} + 5x + \underline{}$

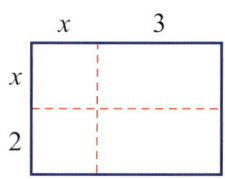

2 The given diagram shows the area $(2x + 3)(x + 1)$.

a Write down an expression for the area of each of the four regions inside the rectangle.

b Copy and complete $(2x + 3)(\underline{}) = 2x^2 + \underline{} + 3x + \underline{}$

$= \underline{} + \underline{} + \underline{}$

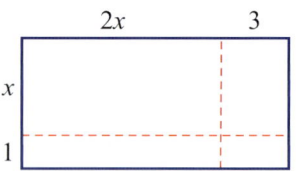

3 Copy and complete these expansions

a $(x + 1)(x + 5) = \underline{} + 5x + \underline{} + 5$

$= \underline{} + 6x + \underline{}$

b $(x - 3)(x + 2) = \underline{} + \underline{} - 3x - \underline{}$

$= \underline{} - x - \underline{}$

c $(3x - 2)(7x + 2) = \underline{} + 6x - \underline{} - \underline{}$

$= \underline{} - \underline{} + \underline{}$

d $(4x - 1)(3x - 4) = \underline{} - \underline{} - 3x + \underline{}$

$= \underline{} - 19x + \underline{}$

Understanding

mple 1a   **4**   Expand the following.

    a $(x + 2)(x + 5)$ **b** $(b + 3)(b + 4)$ **c** $(t + 8)(t + 7)$

    d $(p + 6)(p + 6)$ **e** $(x + 9)(x + 6)$ **f** $(d + 15)(d + 4)$

    g $(a + 1)(a + 7)$ **h** $(y + 10)(y + 2)$ **i** $(m + 4)(m + 12)$

e 1b,c,d   **5**   Expand the following.

    a $(x + 3)(x - 4)$ **b** $(x + 5)(x - 2)$ **c** $(x + 4)(x - 8)$

    d $(x - 6)(x + 2)$ **e** $(x - 1)(x + 10)$ **f** $(x - 7)(x + 9)$

    g $(x - 2)(x + 7)$ **h** $(x - 1)(x - 2)$ **i** $(x - 4)(x - 5)$

    j $(4x + 3)(2x + 5)$ **k** $(3x + 2)(2x + 1)$ **l** $(3x + 1)(5x + 4)$

    m $(2x - 3)(3x + 5)$ **n** $(8x - 3)(3x + 4)$ **o** $(3x - 2)(2x + 1)$

    p $(5x + 2)(2x - 7)$ **q** $(2x + 3)(3x - 2)$ **r** $(4x + 1)(4x - 5)$

    s $(3x - 2)(6x - 5)$ **t** $(5x - 2)(3x - 1)$ **u** $(7x - 3)(3x - 4)$

6   Expand these binomial products.

    a $(a + b)(a + c)$ **b** $(a - b)(a + c)$ **c** $(b - a)(a + c)$

    d $(x - y)(y - z)$ **e** $(y - x)(z - y)$ **f** $(1 - x)(1 + y)$

    g $(2x + y)(x - 2y)$ **h** $(2a + b)(a - b)$ **i** $(3x - y)(2x + y)$

    j $(2a - b)(3a + 2)$ **k** $(4x - 3y)(3x - 4y)$ **l** $(xy - yz)(z + 3x)$

7   A room in a house with dimensions 4 m by 5 m is to be extended. Both the length and width are to be increased by x m.

    a Find an expanded expression for the area of the new room.

    b If $x = 3$:

        i find the area of the new room

        ii by how much has the area increased?

8 A picture frame 5 cm wide has a length which is twice the width x cm.

   a Find an expression for the total area of the frame and picture.

   b Find an expression in expanded form for the area of the picture only.

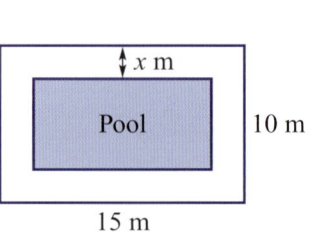

9 The outside edge of a path around a rectangular swimming pool is 15 m long and 10 m wide. The path is x metres wide.

   a Find an expression for the area of the pool in expanded form.

   b Find the area of the pool if $x = 2$.

10 Write the missing terms in these expansions.

   a $(x + 2)(x + \underline{\ \ }) = x^2 + 5x + 6$

   b $(x + \underline{\ \ })(x + 5) = x^2 + 7x + 10$

   c $(x + 1)(x + \underline{\ \ }) = x^2 + 7x + \underline{\ \ }$

   d $(x + \underline{\ \ })(x + 9) = x^2 + 11x + \underline{\ \ }$

   e $(x + 3)(x - \underline{\ \ }) = x^2 + x - \underline{\ \ }$

   f $(x - 5)(x + \underline{\ \ }) = x^2 - 2x - \underline{\ \ }$

   g $(x + 1)(\underline{\ \ } + 3) = 2x^2 + \underline{\ \ } + \underline{\ \ }$

   h $(\underline{\ \ } - 4)(3x - 1) = 9x^2 - \underline{\ \ } + \underline{\ \ }$

   i $(x + 2)(\underline{\ \ } + \underline{\ \ }) = 7x^2 + \underline{\ \ } + 6$

   j $(\underline{\ \ } - \underline{\ \ })(2x - 1) = 6x^2 - \underline{\ \ } + 4$

11 Consider the binomial product $(x + a)(x + b)$. Find the possible integer values of a and b if:

   a $(x + a)(x + b) = x^2 + 5x + 6$

   b $(x + a)(x + b) = x^2 - 5x + 6$

   c $(x + a)(x + b) = x^2 + x - 6$

   d $(x + a)(x + b) = x^2 - x - 6$

Enrichment: Trinomial expansions

12 Using the distributive law $(a + b)(c + d + e) = ac + ad + ae + bc + bd + be$.

Use this knowledge to expand and simplify these products. Note: $x \times x^2 = x^3$.

   a $(x + 1)(x^2 + x + 1)$

   b $(x - 2)(x^2 - x + 3)$

   c $(2x - 1)(2x^2 - x + 4)$

   d $(x^2 - x + 1)(x + 3)$

   e $(5x^2 - x + 2)(2x - 3)$

   f $(2x^2 - x + 7)(4x - 7)$

   g $(x + a)(x^2 - ax + a)$

   h $(x - a)(x^2 - ax - a^2)$

   i $(x + a)(x^2 - ax + a^2)$

   j $(x - a)(x^2 + ax + a^2)$

13 Now try to expand $(x + 1)(x + 2)(x + 3)$.

8.2 Perfect squares and difference of perfect squares

There are two special types of binomial products that involve perfect squares. $2^2 = 4$, $15^2 = 225$, x^2 and $(a + b)^2$ are all examples of perfect squares. To expand $(a + b)^2$ we multiply $(a + b)$ by $(a + b)$ and use the distributive law:

$$(a + b)^2 = (a + b)(a + b)$$
$$= a^2 + ab + ba + b^2$$
$$= a^2 + 2ab + b^2$$

A similar result is obtained for the square of $(a - b)$:

$$(a - b)^2 = (a - b)(a - b)$$
$$= a^2 - ab - ba + b^2$$
$$= a^2 - 2ab + b^2$$

Another type of expansion involves the case that deals with the product of the sum and difference of the same two terms. The result is the difference of two perfect squares:

Binomial products can be used to calculate the most efficient way to cut the shapes required for a fabrication out of a metal sheet.

$$(a + b)(a - b) = a^2 - ab + ba - b^2$$
$$= a^2 - b^2 \text{ (since } ab = ba \text{ the two middle terms cancel each other out.)}$$

→ Let's start: Seeing the pattern

Using $(a + b)(c + d) = ac + ad + bc + bd$, expand and simplify the binomial products in the two sets below.

Set A

$$(x + 1)(x + 1) = x^2 + x + x + 1$$
$$=$$
$$(x + 3)(x + 3) =$$
$$=$$
$$(x - 5)(x - 5) =$$
$$=$$

Set B

$$(x + 1)(x - 1) = x^2 - x + x - 1$$
$$=$$
$$(x - 3)(x + 3) =$$
$$=$$
$$(x - 5)(x + 5) =$$
$$=$$

- Describe what patterns you see in both sets of expansions above.
- Generalise your observations by completing the following expansions.

  A $(a + b)(a + b) = a^2 + \underline{} + \underline{} + \underline{}$
  $$= a^2 + \underline{} + \underline{}$$
  $$(a - b)(a - b) =$$
  $$=$$

  B $(a + b)(a - b) = a^2 - \underline{} + \underline{} - \underline{}$
  $$=$$

- $3^2 = 9$, a^2, $(2y)^2$, $(x - 1)^2$ and $(3 - 2y)^2$ are all examples of **perfect squares**.
- Expanding perfect squares

  - $(a + b)^2 = (a + b)(a + b)$

    $\qquad\qquad = a^2 + ab + ba + b^2$

    $\qquad\qquad = a^2 + 2ab + b^2$

  - $(a - b)^2 = (a - b)(a - b)$

    $\qquad\qquad = a^2 - ab - ba + b^2$

    $\qquad\qquad = a^2 - 2ab + b^2$

- **Difference of perfect squares** (DOPS)

  - $(a + b)(a - b) = a^2 - ab + ba - b^2$

    $\qquad\qquad\quad = a^2 - b^2$

  - $(a - b)(a + b)$ also expands to $a^2 - b^2$

  - The result is a difference of two perfect squares.

The logical skills of algebra have applications in computer programming.

Example 2 Expanding perfect squares

Expand each of the following.

a $(x - 2)^2$ **b** $(2x + 3)^2$

SOLUTION	EXPLANATION
a $(x - 2)^2 = (x - 2)(x - 2)$	Write in expanded form.
$\qquad\qquad = x^2 - 2x - 2x + 4$	Use the distributive law.
$\qquad\qquad = x^2 - 4x + 4$	Collect like terms.
Alternative solution:	
$(x - 2)^2 = x^2 - 2 \times x \times 2 + 2^2$	Expand using $(a - b)^2 = a^2 - 2ab + b^2$ where $a = x$
$\qquad\quad = x^2 - 4x + 4$	and $b = 2$.
b $(2x + 3)^2 = (2x + 3)(2x + 3)$	Write in expanded form.
$\qquad\qquad = 4x^2 + 6x + 6x + 9$	Use the distributive law.
$\qquad\qquad = 4x^2 + 12x + 9$	Collect like terms.
Alternative solution:	
$(2x + 3)^2 = (2x)^2 + 2 \times 2x \times 3 + 3^2$	Expand using $(a + b)^2 = a^2 + 2ab + b^2$ where $a = 2x$ and
$\qquad\qquad = 4x^2 + 12x + 9$	$b = 3$. Recall $(2x)^2 = 2x \times 2x = 4x^2$.

Example 3 Forming a difference of perfect squares

Expand and simplify the following.

a $(x + 2)(x - 2)$

b $(3x - 2y)(3x + 2y)$

SOLUTION

EXPLANATION

a $(x + 2)(x - 2) = x^2 - 2x + 2x - 4$

$= x^2 - 4$

Expand using the distributive law.

$-2x + 2x = 0$.

Alternate solution:

$(x + 2)(x - 2) = (x)^2 - (2)^2$

$= x^2 - 4$

$(a + b)(a - b) = a^2 - b^2$. Here $a = x$ and $b = 2$.

b $(3x - 2y)(3x + 2y) = 9x^2 + 6xy - 6xy - 4y^2$

$= 9x^2 - 4y^2$

Expand using the distributive law.

$6xy - 6xy = 0$.

Alternate solution:

$(3x - 2y)(3x + 2y) = (3x)^2 - (2y)^2$

$= 9x^2 - 4y^2$

$(a + b)(a - b) = a^2 - b^2$ with $a = 3x$ and $b = 2y$ here.

Exercise 8B

1 Complete these expansions.

a $(x + 3)(x + 3) = x^2 + 3x + \underline{} + \underline{}$

$= \underline{}$

b $(x + 5)(x + 5) = x^2 + 5x + \underline{} + \underline{}$

$= \underline{}$

c $(x - 2)(x - 2) = x^2 - 2x - \underline{} + \underline{}$

$= \underline{}$

d $(x - 7)(x - 7) = x^2 - 7x - \underline{} + \underline{}$

$= \underline{}$

2 **a** Substitute the given value of b into $x^2 + 2bx + b^2$ and simplify.

  i $b = 3$ **ii** $b = 11$ **iii** $b = 15$

b Substitute the given value of b into $x^2 - 2bx + b^2$ and simplify.

  i $b = 2$ **ii** $b = 9$ **iii** $b = 30$

3 Complete these expansions.

a $(x + 4)(x - 4) = x^2 - 4x + \underline{} - \underline{}$

$= \underline{}$

b $(x - 10)(x + 10) = x^2 + 10x - \underline{} - \underline{}$

$= \underline{}$

c $(2x - 1)(2x + 1) = 4x^2 + \underline{} - \underline{} - \underline{}$

$= \underline{}$

d $(3x + 4)(3x - 4) = 9x^2 - \underline{} + \underline{} - \underline{}$

$= \underline{}$

4 Expand each of the following perfect squares.

a $(x + 1)^2$ **b** $(x + 3)^2$ **c** $(x + 2)^2$ **d** $(x + 5)^2$

e $(x + 4)^2$ **f** $(x + 9)^2$ **g** $(x + 7)^2$ **h** $(x + 10)^2$

i $(x - 2)^2$ **j** $(x - 6)^2$ **k** $(x - 1)^2$ **l** $(x - 3)^2$

m $(x - 9)^2$ **n** $(x - 7)^2$ **o** $(x - 4)^2$ **p** $(x - 12)^2$

Understanding

Fluency

mple 2a

Example 2b

5 Expand each of the following perfect squares.

   a $(2x+1)^2$ **b** $(2x+5)^2$ **c** $(3x+2)^2$

   d $(3x+1)^2$ **e** $(5x+2)^2$ **f** $(4x+3)^2$

   g $(7+2x)^2$ **h** $(5+3x)^2$ **i** $(2x-3)^2$

   j $(3x-1)^2$ **k** $(4x-5)^2$ **l** $(2x-9)^2$

   m $(3x+5y)^2$ **n** $(2x+4y)^2$ **o** $(7x+3y)^2$

   p $(6x+5y)^2$ **q** $(4x-9y)^2$ **r** $(2x-7y)^2$

   s $(3x-10y)^2$ **t** $(4x-6y)^2$ **u** $(9x-2y)^2$

6 Expand each of the following perfect squares.

   a $(3-x)^2$ **b** $(5-x)^2$ **c** $(1-x)^2$

   d $(6-x)^2$ **e** $(11-x)^2$ **f** $(4-x)^2$

   g $(7-x)^2$ **h** $(12-x)^2$ **i** $(8-2x)^2$

   j $(2-3x)^2$ **k** $(9-2x)^2$ **l** $(10-4x)^2$

Example 3a

7 Expand and simplify the following to form a difference of perfect squares.

   a $(x+1)(x-1)$ **b** $(x+3)(x-3)$ **c** $(x+8)(x-8)$

   d $(x+4)(x-4)$ **e** $(x+12)(x-12)$ **f** $(x+11)(x-11)$

   g $(x-9)(x+9)$ **h** $(x-5)(x+5)$ **i** $(x-6)(x+6)$

   j $(5-x)(5+x)$ **k** $(2-x)(2+x)$ **l** $(7-x)(7+x)$

Example 3b

8 Expand and simplify the following.

   a $(3x-2)(3x+2)$ **b** $(5x-4)(5x+4)$ **c** $(4x-3)(4x+3)$

   d $(7x-3y)(7x+3y)$ **e** $(9x-5y)(9x+5y)$ **f** $(11x-y)(11x+y)$

   g $(8x+2y)(8x-2y)$ **h** $(10x-9y)(10x+9y)$ **i** $(7x-5y)(7x+5y)$

   j $(6x-11y)(6x+11y)$ **k** $(8x-3y)(8x+3y)$ **l** $(9x-4y)(9x+4y)$

9 Lara is x years old and her two best friends are $(x-2)$ and $(x+2)$ years old.

   a Write an expression for:

      i the square of Lara's age

      ii the product of the ages of Lara's best friends

   b Are the answers from parts **a i** and **ii** equal? If not, by how much do they differ?

10 A square piece of tin of side length 20 cm has four
squares of side length x cm removed from each corner.
The sides are folded up to form a tray. The centre square
forms the tray base.

   a Write an expression for the side length of the base of
the tray.

   b Write an expression for the area of the base of the
tray. Expand your answer.

   c Find the area of the tray base if $x=3$.

   d Find the volume of the tray if $x=3$.

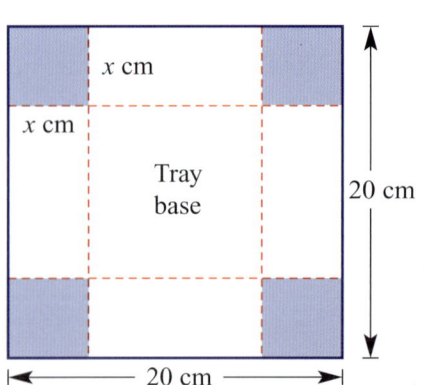

11 Four tennis courts are arranged as shown with a square storage area in the centre. Each court area has the same dimensions $a \times b$.

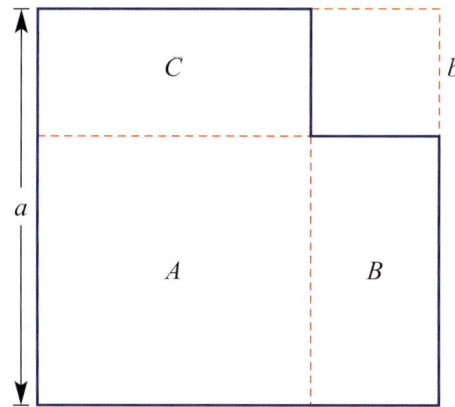

  a Write an expression for the side length of the total area.
  b Write an expression for the area of the total area.
  c Write an expression for the side length of the inside storage area.
  d Write an expression for the area of the inside storage area.
  e Subtract your answer to part **d** from your answer to part **b** to find the area of the four courts.
  f Find the area of one court. Does your answer confirm that your answer to part **e** is correct?

12 A square of side length x has one side reduced by 1 unit and the other increased by 1 unit.
  a Find an expanded expression for the area of the resulting rectangle.
  b Is the area of the original square the same as the area of the resulting rectangle? Explain why/why not?

13 A square of side length b is removed from a square of side length a.

  a Using subtraction write down an expression for the remaining area.
  b Write expressions for the area of the regions:
    i A **ii** B **iii** C
  c Add all the expressions from part **b** to see if you get your answer from part **a**.

Enrichment: Extended expansions

14 Expand and simplify these expressions.
  a $(x + 2)^2 - 4$
  b $(2x - 1)^2 - 4x^2$
  c $(x + 3)(x - 3) + 6x$
  d $1 - (x + 1)^2$
  e $x^2 - (x + 1)(x - 1)$
  f $(x + 1)^2 - (x - 1)^2$
  g $(3x - 2)(3x + 2) - (3x + 2)^2$
  h $(5x - 1)^2 - (5x + 1)(5x - 1)$
  i $(x + y)^2 - (x - y)^2 + (x + y)(x - y)$
  j $(2x - 3)^2 + (2x + 3)^2$
  k $(2 - x)^2 - (2 + x)^2$
  l $(3 - x)^2 + (x - 3)^2$
  m $2(3x - 4)^2 - (3x - 4)(3x + 4)$
  n $2(x + y)^2 - (x - y)^2$

8.3 Factorising algebraic expressions

The process of factorisation is a key step in the simplification of many algebraic expressions and in the solution of equations. It is the reverse process of expansion and involves writing an expression as a product of its factors.

Factorising is a key mathematical skill required in many diverse occupations, such as in business, science, technology and engineering.

Let's start: Which factorised form?

The product $x(4x + 8)$ when expanded gives $4x^2 + 8x$.

- Write down three other products that when expanded give $4x^2 + 8x$. (Do not use fractions.)
- Which of your products uses the highest common factor of $4x^2$ and $8x$? What is this highest common factor?

Key ideas

- When **factorising** expressions with common factors, take out the highest common factor (HCF). The HCF could be:
  - a number
    For example: $2x + 10 = 2(x + 5)$
  - a variable
    For example: $x^2 + 5x = x(x + 5)$
  - the product of numbers and variables
    For example: $2x^2 + 10x = 2x(x + 5)$
- A factorised expression can be checked by using expansion.

  For example: $2x(x + 5) = 2x^2 + 10x$.

Example 4 Finding the HCF

Determine the HCF of the following.

a $6a$ and $8ab$ **b** $3x^2$ and $6xy$

SOLUTION	EXPLANATION
a HCF of $6a$ and $8ab$ is $2a$	HCF of 6 and 8 is 2. HCF of a and ab is a.
b HCF of $3x^2$ and $6xy$ is $3x$	HCF of 3 and 6 is 3. HCF of x^2 and xy is x.

Example 5 Factorising expressions

Factorise the following.

a $40 - 16b$

b $-8x^2 - 12x$

SOLUTION

a $40 - 16b = 8(5 - 2b)$

b $-8x^2 - 12x = -4x(2x + 3)$

EXPLANATION

The HCF of 40 and $16b$ is 8. Place 8 in front of brackets and divide each term by 8.

The HCF of the terms is $-4x$, including the common negative. Place the factor in front of brackets and divide each term by $-4x$.

Example 6 Taking out a binomial factor

Factorise the following.

a $3(x + y) + x(x + y)$

b $(7 - 2x) - x(7 - 2x)$

SOLUTION

a $3(x + y) + x(x + y)$
   $= (x + y)(3 + x)$

b $(7 - 2x) - x(7 - 2x)$
   $= 1(7 - 2x) - x(7 - 2x)$
   $= (7 - 2x)(1 - x)$

EXPLANATION

HCF $= (x + y)$. The second pair of brackets contains what remains when $3(x + y)$ and $x(x + y)$ are divided by $(x + y)$.

Insert 1 in front of the first bracket.
HCF $= (7 - 2x)$. The second bracket must contain the initial 1 after dividing $(7 - 2x)$ and $x(7 - 2x)$ by $(7 - 2x)$.

Exercise 8C

1   Write down the highest common factor (HCF) of these pairs of numbers.
   a   8, 12   b   10, 20   c   5, 60   d   24, 30
   e   3, 5   f   100, 75   g   16, 24   h   36, 72

2   Write down the missing factor.
   a $5 \times \underline{\quad} = 5x$
   b $7 \times \underline{\quad} = 7x$
   c $2a \times \underline{\quad} = 2a^2$
   d $5a \times \underline{\quad} = 10a^2$
   e $\underline{\quad} \times 3y = -6y^2$
   f $\underline{\quad} \times 12x = -36x^2$
   g $-3 \times \underline{\quad} = 6x$
   h $-2x \times \underline{\quad} = 20x^2$
   i $\underline{\quad} \times 7xy = -14x^2y$

3   a   Write down the missing factor in each part.
      i $\underline{\quad} (x^2 + 2x) = 6x^2 + 12x$
      ii $\underline{\quad} (2x + 4) = 6x^2 + 12x$
      iii $\underline{\quad} (x + 2) = 6x^2 + 12x$
   b   Which equation above uses the HCF of $6x^2$ and $12x$?
   c   By looking at the terms left in the brackets, how do you know you have taken out the HCF?

Understanding

Example 4 **4** Determine the HCF of the following.

  a $6x$ and $14xy$ **b** $12a$ and $18a$ **c** $10m$ and 4 **d** $12y$ and 8

  e $15t$ and $6s$ **f** 15 and p **g** $9x$ and $24xy$ **h** $6n$ and $21mn$

  i $10y$ and $2y$ **j** $8x^2$ and $14x$ **k** $4x^2y$ and $18xy$ **l** $5ab^2$ and $15a^2b$

Example 5a **5** Factorise the following.

  a $7x + 7$ **b** $3x + 3$ **c** $4x - 4$ **d** $5x - 5$

  e $4 + 8y$ **f** $10 + 5a$ **g** $3 - 9b$ **h** $6 - 2x$

  i $12a + 3b$ **j** $6m + 6n$ **k** $10x - 8y$ **l** $4a - 20b$

  m $x^2 + 2x$ **n** $a^2 - 4a$ **o** $y^2 - 7y$ **p** $x - x^2$

  q $3p^2 + 3p$ **r** $8x - 8x^2$ **s** $4b^2 + 12b$ **t** $6y - 10y^2$

  u $12a - 15a^2$ **v** $9m + 18m^2$ **w** $16xy - 48x^2$ **x** $7ab - 28ab^2$

Example 5b **6** Factorise the following by factorising out the negative sign.

  a $-8x - 4$ **b** $-4x - 2$ **c** $-10x - 5y$ **d** $-7a - 14b$

  e $-9x - 12$ **f** $-6y - 8$ **g** $-10x - 15y$ **h** $-4m - 20n$

  i $-3x^2 - 18x$ **j** $-8x^2 - 12x$ **k** $-16y^2 - 6y$ **l** $-5a^2 - 10a$

  m $-6x - 20x^2$ **n** $-6p - 15p^2$ **o** $-16b - 8b^2$ **p** $-9x - 27x^2$

Example 6 **7** Factorise the following which involve a binomial common factor.

  a $4(x + 3) + x(x + 3)$ **b** $3(x + 1) + x(x + 1)$ **c** $7(m - 3) + m(m - 3)$

  d $x(x - 7) + 2(x - 7)$ **e** $8(a + 4) - a(a + 4)$ **f** $5(x + 1) - x(x + 1)$

  g $y(y + 3) - 2(y + 3)$ **h** $a(x + 2) - x(x + 2)$ **i** $t(2t + 5) + 3(2t + 5)$

  j $m(5m - 2) + 4(5m - 2)$ **k** $y(4y - 1) - (4y - 1)$ **l** $(7 - 3x) + x(7 - 3x)$

8 Factorise these mixed expressions.

  a $6a + 30$ **b** $5x - 15$ **c** $8b + 18$

  d $x^2 - 4x$ **e** $y^2 + 9y$ **f** $a^2 - 3a$

  g $x^2y - 4xy + xy^2$ **h** $6ab - 10a^2b + 8ab^2$ **i** $m(m + 5) + 2(m + 5)$

  j $x(x + 3) - 2(x + 3)$ **k** $b(b - 2) + (b - 2)$ **l** $x(2x + 1) - (2x + 1)$

  m $y(3 - 2y) - 5(3 - 2y)$ **n** $(x + 4)^2 + 5(x + 4)$ **o** $(y + 1)^2 - 4(y + 1)$

9 Write down the perimeter of these shapes in factorised form.

  a

  b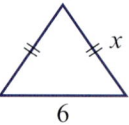

  c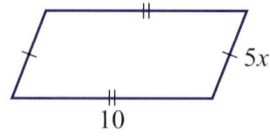

  d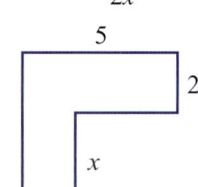

  e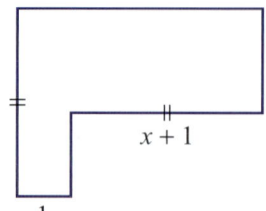

  f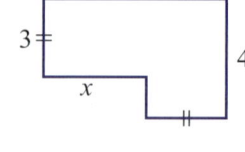

10 The expression for the area of a rectangle is $(4x^2 + 8x)$. Find an expression for its width if the length is $(x + 2)$.

11 The height, in metres, of a ball thrown in the air is given by $5t - t^2$ where t is the time in seconds.

  a Write an expression for the ball's height in factorised form.
  b Find the ball's height at these times:
     i $t = 0$ ii $t = 2$ iii $t = 4$
  c How long does it take for the ball's height to return to 0 metres? Use trial and error if required.

12 $7 \times 9 + 7 \times 3$ can be evaluated by firstly factorising to $7(9 + 3)$. This gives $7 \times 12 = 84$. Use a similar technique to evaluate the following.

  a $9 \times 2 + 9 \times 5$ b $6 \times 3 + 6 \times 9$ c $-2 \times 4 - 2 \times 6$
  d $-5 \times 8 - 5 \times 6$ e $23 \times 5 - 23 \times 2$ f $63 \times 11 - 63 \times 8$

13 Common factors can also be removed from expressions with more than two terms.
   For example: $2x^2 + 6x + 10xy = 2x(x + 3 + 5y)$
   Factorise these expressions by taking out the HCF.

  a $3a^2 + 9a + 12$ b $5z^2 - 10z + zy$ c $x^2 - 2xy + x^2y$
  d $4by - 2b + 6b^2$ e $-12xy - 8yz - 20xyz$ f $3ab + 4ab^2 + 6a^2b$

14 Sometimes we can choose to factor out a negative or a positive HCF. Both factorisations are correct. For example:

$$-13x + 26 = -13(x - 2) \quad \text{(HCF is -13)}$$
$$\text{OR} \quad -13x + 26 = 13(-x + 2) \quad \text{(HCF is 13)}$$
$$= 13(2 - x)$$

   Factorise in two different ways by first factoring out a negative and then a positive HCF.

  a $-4x + 12$ b $-3x + 9$ c $-8n + 8$ d $-3b + 3$
  e $-5m + 5m^2$ f $-7x + 7x^2$ g $-5x + 5x^2$ h $-4y + 22y^2$
  i $-8n + 12n^2$ j $-8y + 20$ k $-15mn + 10$ l $-15x + 45$

Enrichment: Factoring out a negative

15 Using the fact that $a - b = -(b - a)$ you can factorise $x(x - 2) - 5(2 - x)$ by following these steps.

$$x(x - 2) - 5(2 - x) = x(x - 2) + 5(x - 2)$$
$$= (x - 2)(x + 5)$$

   Use this idea to factorise these expressions.

  a $x(x - 4) + 3(4 - x)$ b $x(x - 5) - 2(5 - x)$ c $x(x - 3) - 3(3 - x)$
  d $3x(x - 4) + 5(4 - x)$ e $3(2x - 5) + x(5 - 2x)$ f $2x(x - 2) + (2 - x)$
  g $-4(3 - x) - x(x - 3)$ h $x(x - 5) + (10 - 2x)$ i $x(x - 3) + (6 - 2x)$

8.4 Factorising the difference of two squares

Recall that a difference of two perfect squares is formed when expanding the product of the sum and difference of two terms. For example, $(x + 2)(x - 2) = x^2 - 4$. Reversing this process means that a difference of two perfect squares can be factorised into two binomial expressions of the form $(a + b)$ and $(a - b)$.

Let's start: Expanding to understand factorising

Complete the steps in these expansions then write the conclusion.

- $(x + 3)(x - 3) = x^2 - 3x + \underline{} - \underline{}$

  $\qquad\qquad\quad = x^2 - \underline{}$

  $\therefore\ x^2 - 9 = (\ \underline{} + \underline{}\ )(\ \underline{} - \underline{}\ )$

- $(2x - 5)(2x + 5) = 4x^2 + 10x - \underline{} - \underline{}$

  $\qquad\qquad\qquad = \underline{} - \underline{}$

  $\therefore\ 4x^2 - \underline{} = (\ \underline{} + \underline{}\ )(\ \underline{} - \underline{}\ )$

- $(a + b)(a - b) = a^2 - ab + \underline{} - \underline{}$

  $\qquad\qquad\quad = \underline{} - \underline{}$

  $\therefore\ a^2 - \underline{} = (\ \underline{} + \underline{}\ )(\ \underline{} - \underline{}\ )$

- Factorising the difference of perfect squares (DOPS) uses the rule $a^2 - b^2 = (a + b)(a - b)$.
  - $x^2 - 16 = x^2 - 4^2 = (x + 4)(x - 4)$
  - $9x^2 - 100 = (3x)^2 - 10^2 = (3x + 10)(3x - 10)$
  - $25 - 4y^2 = 5^2 - (2y)^2 = (5 + 2y)(5 - 2y)$
- First take out common factors where possible.
  - $2x^2 - 18 = 2(x^2 - 9) = 2(x + 3)(x - 3)$

Example 7 Factorising DOPS

Factorise each of the following.

a $\quad x^2 - 4$

b $\quad 9a^2 - 25$

c $\quad 81x^2 - y^2$

d $\quad 2b^2 - 32$

e $\quad (x + 1)^2 - 4$

SOLUTION

EXPLANATION

a $\quad x^2 - 4 = x^2 - 2^2$

$\qquad\quad = (x + 2)(x - 2)$

Write as a DOPS (4 is the same as 2^2).

Write in factorised form $a^2 - b^2 = (a + b)(a - b)$. Here $a = x$ and $b = 2$.

b $\quad 9a^2 - 25 = (3a)^2 - 5^2$

$\qquad\qquad = (3a + 5)(3a - 5)$

Write as a DOPS. $9a^2$ is the same as $(3a)^2$. Write in factorised form.

c $\quad 81x^2 - y^2 = (9x)^2 - y^2$

$\qquad\qquad = (9x + y)(9x - y)$

$81x^2 = (9x)^2$

d $2b^2 - 32 = 2(b^2 - 16)$ First, factor out the common factor of 2.
$\qquad\qquad = 2(b^2 - 4^2)$ Write as a DOPS and then factorise.
$\qquad\qquad = 2(b + 4)(b - 4)$

e $(x + 1)^2 - 4 = (x + 1)^2 - 2^2$ Write as a DOPS. In $a^2 - b^2$ here, a is the expression
$\qquad\qquad = (x + 1 + 2)(x + 1 - 2)$ $x + 1$ and $b = 2$.
$\qquad\qquad = (x + 3)(x - 1)$ Write in factorised form and simplify.

Exercise 8D

Understanding

1   Expand these binomial products to form a difference of perfect squares.
  a $(x + 2)(x - 2)$ **b** $(x - 7)(x + 7)$ **c** $(2x - 1)(2x + 1)$
  d $(x + y)(x - y)$ **e** $(3x - y)(3x + y)$ **f** $(a + b)(a - b)$

2   Write the missing term. Assume it is a positive number.
  a $(\underline{\ \ })^2 = 9$ **b** $(\underline{\ \ })^2 = 121$ **c** $(\underline{\ \ })^2 = 81$ **d** $(\underline{\ \ })^2 = 400$
  e $(\underline{\ \ })^2 = 4x^2$ **f** $(\underline{\ \ })^2 = 9a^2$ **g** $(\underline{\ \ })^2 = 25b^2$ **h** $(\underline{\ \ })^2 = 49y^2$

3   Complete these factorisations.
  a $x^2 - 16 = x^2 - 4^2$ **b** $x^2 - 144 = x^2 - (\underline{\ \ })^2$
  $\qquad\qquad = (x + 4)(\underline{\ \ } - \underline{\ \ })$ $\qquad\qquad = (\underline{\ \ } + 12)(x - \underline{\ \ })$
  c $16x^2 - 1 = (\underline{\ \ })^2 - (\underline{\ \ })^2$ **d** $9a^2 - 4b^2 = (\underline{\ \ })^2 - (\underline{\ \ })^2$
  $\qquad\qquad = (4x + \underline{\ \ })(\underline{\ \ } - 1)$ $\qquad\qquad = (3a + \underline{\ \ })(\underline{\ \ } - 2b)$

Fluency

Example 7a

4   Factorise each of the following.
  a $x^2 - 9$ **b** $y^2 - 25$ **c** $y^2 - 1$ **d** $x^2 - 64$
  e $x^2 - 16$ **f** $b^2 - 49$ **g** $a^2 - 81$ **h** $x^2 - y^2$
  i $a^2 - b^2$ **j** $16 - a^2$ **k** $25 - x^2$ **l** $1 - b^2$
  m $36 - y^2$ **n** $121 - b^2$ **o** $x^2 - 400$ **p** $900 - y^2$

Example 7b,c

5   Factorise each of the following.
  a $4x^2 - 25$ **b** $9x^2 - 49$ **c** $25b^2 - 4$ **d** $4m^2 - 121$
  e $100y^2 - 9$ **f** $81a^2 - 4$ **g** $1 - 4x^2$ **h** $25 - 64b^2$
  i $16 - 9y^2$ **j** $36x^2 - y^2$ **k** $4x^2 - 25y^2$ **l** $64a^2 - 49b^2$
  m $4p^2 - 25q^2$ **n** $81m^2 - 4n^2$ **o** $25a^2 - 49b^2$ **p** $100a^2 - 9b^2$

Example 7d

6   Factorise each of the following by first taking out the common factor.
  a $3x^2 - 108$ **b** $10a^2 - 10$ **c** $6x^2 - 24$
  d $4y^2 - 64$ **e** $98 - 2x^2$ **f** $32 - 8m^2$
  g $5x^2y^2 - 5$ **h** $3 - 3x^2y^2$ **i** $63 - 7a^2b^2$

Example 7e

7   Factorise each of the following.
  a $(x + 5)^2 - 9$ **b** $(x + 3)^2 - 4$ **c** $(x + 10)^2 - 16$
  d $(x - 3)^2 - 25$ **e** $(x - 7)^2 - 1$ **f** $(x - 3)^2 - 36$
  g $49 - (x + 3)^2$ **h** $4 - (x + 2)^2$ **i** $81 - (x + 8)^2$

8 The height above ground (in metres) of an object thrown off the top of a building is given by $36 - 4t^2$ where t is in seconds.

 a Factorise the expression for the height of the object by firstly taking out the common factor.

 b Find the height of the object:

  i initially ($t = 0$)

  ii at 2 seconds ($t = 2$).

 c How long does it take for the object to hit the ground? Use trial and error if you wish.

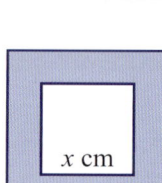

9 This 'multisize' square picture frame has side length 30 cm and can hold a square picture with any side length less than 26 cm.

 a If the side length of the picture is x cm, write an expression for:

  i the area of the picture

  ii the area of the frame (in factorised form)

 b Use your result from part **a ii** to find the area of the frame if:

  i $x = 20$ **ii** the area of the picture is 225 cm²

x cm   30 cm

10 Initially it may not appear that an expression such as $-4 + 9x^2$ is a difference of perfect squares. However, swapping the position of the two terms makes $-4 + 9x^2 = 9x^2 - 4$, which can be factorised to $(3x + 2)(3x - 2)$. Use this idea to factorise these difference of perfect squares.

 a $-9 + x^2$ **b** $-121 + 16x^2$ **c** $-25a^2 + 4$ **d** $-y^2 + x^2$

 e $-25a^2 + 4b^2$ **f** $-36a^2b^2 + c^2$ **g** $-16x^2 + y^2z^2$ **h** $-900a^2 + b^2$

11 Olivia factorises $16x^2 - 4$ to get $(4x + 2)(4x - 2)$ but the answer says $4(2x + 1)(2x - 1)$.

 a What should Olivia do to get from her answer to the actual answer?

 b What should Olivia have done initially to avoid this issue?

12 Find and explain the error in this working and correct it.

$$9 - (x - 1)^2 = (3 + x - 1)(3 - x - 1)$$
$$= (2 + x)(2 - x)$$

Enrichment: Factorising with fractions and powers of 4

13 Some expressions with fractions or powers of 4 can be factorised in a similar way. Factorise these.

 a $x^2 - \dfrac{1}{4}$ **b** $x^2 - \dfrac{4}{25}$ **c** $25x^2 - \dfrac{9}{16}$ **d** $\dfrac{x^2}{9} - 1$

 e $\dfrac{a^2}{4} - \dfrac{b^2}{9}$ **f** $\dfrac{5x^2}{9} - \dfrac{5}{4}$ **g** $\dfrac{7a^2}{25} - \dfrac{28b^2}{9}$ **h** $\dfrac{a^2}{8} - \dfrac{b^2}{18}$

 i $x^4 - y^4$ **j** $2a^4 - 2b^4$ **k** $21a^4 - 21b^4$ **l** $\dfrac{x^4}{3} - \dfrac{y^4}{3}$

8.5 Factorisation by grouping

When an expression contains four terms, such as $x^2 + 2x - ax - 2a$, it may be possible to factorise it into a product of two binomial terms like $(x - a)(x + 2)$. In such situations the method of grouping is often used.

Let's start: Two methods – same result

The four-term expression $x^2 - ax - a + x$ is written on the board.

Tommy chooses to rearrange the terms to give $x^2 - ax + x - a$ then factorises by grouping.

Factorising by grouping is a bit like arranging scattered objects into some sort of order.

Sharon chooses to rearrange the terms to give $x^2 + x - ax - a$ then also factorises by grouping.

Tommy
$x^2 - ax + x - a = x(x - a) + 1(\underline{\quad})$
$= (x - a)(\underline{\quad})$

Sharon
$x^2 + x - ax - a = x(\underline{\quad}) - a(\underline{\quad})$
$= (x + 1)(\underline{\quad})$

- Complete Tommy's and Sharon's factorisation working.
- Discuss the differences in the methods. Is there any difference in their answers?
- Whose method do you prefer?

Example 8 Factorising by grouping

Use the method of grouping to factorise these expressions.

a $x^2 + 2x + ax + 2a$ **b** $xa + 3a - 5x - 15$

SOLUTION

EXPLANATION

a $x^2 + 2x + ax + 2a = (x^2 + 2x) + (ax + 2a)$
$= x(x + 2) + a(x + 2)$
$= (x + 2)(x + a)$

Group the first and second pair of terms.
Factorise each group.
Take the common factor $(x + 2)$ out of both groups.

b $xa + 3a - 5x - 15 = (xa + 3a) + (-5x - 15)$
$= a(x + 3) - 5(x + 3)$
$= (x + 3)(a - 5)$

Group the first and second pair of terms.
Factorise each group.
Take the common factor $(x + 3)$ out of both groups.

Example 9 Rearranging an expression to factorise by grouping

Factorise $2xa - 9 - 18a + x$ using grouping.

SOLUTION

$$2xa - 9 - 18a + x = 2xa + x - 18a - 9$$
$$= x(2a + 1) - 9(2a + 1)$$
$$= (2a + 1)(x - 9)$$

Alternatively:
$$2xa - 9 - 18a + x = 2xa - 18a + x - 9$$
$$= 2a(x - 9) + 1(x - 9)$$
$$= (x - 9)(2a + 1)$$

EXPLANATION

Rearrange so that each group has a common factor. Factorise each group then take out $(2a + 1)$.

Alternatively, group so that both terms with the pronumeral a are together. Then factorise.

Exercise 8E

Understanding

1 Expand each expression.

a $2(x - 1)$ **b** $3(a + 4)$ **c** $-5(1 - a)$
d $-2(3 - x)$ **e** $a(a + 5)$ **f** $b(2 - b)$
g $x(x - 4)$ **h** $y(4 - y)$ **i** $x(a + 1) + 2(a + 1)$
j $a(x - 3) + 5(x - 3)$ **k** $b(x - 2) - 3(x - 2)$ **l** $c(1 - x) - 4(1 - x)$

2 Copy and then fill in the missing information.

a $2(x + 1) + a(x + 1) = (x + 1)(\_\_\_)$ **b** $3(x + 3) - a(x + 3) = (x + 3)(\_\_\_)$
c $5(x + 5) - a(x + 5) = (x + 5)(\_\_\_)$ **d** $a(x + 7) + 4(x + 7) = (a + 4)(\_\_\_)$
e $a(x - 3) + (x - 3) = (x - 3)(\_\_\_)$ **f** $a(x + 4) - (x + 4) = (x + 4)(\_\_\_)$
g $(x - 3) - a(x - 3) = (x - 3)(\_\_\_)$ **h** $(4 - x) + 2a(4 - x) = (4 - x)(\_\_\_)$

3 Take out the common binomial term to factorise each expression.

a $x(x - 3) - 2(x - 3)$ **b** $x(x + 4) + 3(x + 4)$ **c** $x(x - 7) + 4(x - 7)$
d $3(2x + 1) - x(2x + 1)$ **e** $4(3x - 2) - x(3x - 2)$ **f** $2x(2x + 3) - 3(2x + 3)$
g $3x(5 - x) + 2(5 - x)$ **h** $2(x + 1) - 3x(x + 1)$ **i** $x(x - 2) + (x - 2)$

Fluency

Example 8

4 Use the method of grouping to factorise these expressions.

a $x^2 + 3x + ax + 3a$ **b** $x^2 + 4x + cx + 4c$ **c** $x^2 + 7x + bx + 7b$
d $x^2 - 6x + xb - 6b$ **e** $x^2 - 4x + 2xa - 8a$ **f** $x^2 - 3x + 2xb - 6b$
g $x^2 + 2x - 3xc - 6c$ **h** $x^2 + 3x - 2xa - 6a$ **i** $x^2 + 4x - 2xb - 8b$
j $x^2 - 2x - xa + 2a$ **k** $x^2 - 3x - 3xc + 9c$ **l** $x^2 - 5x - 3xa + 15a$

5 Use the method of grouping to factorise these expressions.

a $3ab + 5bc + 3ad + 5cd$ **b** $4ab - 7ac + 4bd - 7cd$ **c** $2xy - 8xz + 3wy - 12wz$
d $5rs - 10r + st - 2t$ **e** $4x^2 + 12xy - 3x - 9y$ **f** $2ab - a^2 - 2bc + ac$

Fluency

6 Factorise these expressions. Remember to use a factor of 1 where necessary, for example,
$x^2 - ax + x - a = x(x - a) + 1(x - a)$.

a $\quad x^2 - bx + x - b$ b $\quad x^2 - cx + x - c$ c $\quad x^2 + bx + x + b$

d $\quad x^2 + cx - x - c$ e $\quad x^2 + ax - x - a$ f $\quad x^2 - bx - x + b$

Problem-solving

 7 Factorise these expressions by first rearranging the terms.

a $\quad 3b + 4a + ab + 12$ b $\quad 5x + 2y + xy + 10$ c $\quad 2ax - 3 - x + 6a$

d $\quad 3x - 8y - 6xy + 4$ e $\quad 11x - 5a - 55 + ax$ f $\quad 12y + 2x - 8xy - 3$

g $\quad 6m - n + 3mn - 2$ h $\quad 15p - 8r - 5pr + 24$ i $\quad 16x - 3y - 8xy + 6$

8 What expanded expression factorises to the following?

a $\quad (x - a)(x + 4)$ b $\quad (x - c)(x - d)$ c $\quad (x + y)(2 - z)$ d $\quad (x - 1)(a + b)$

e $\quad (3x - b)(c - b)$ f $\quad (2x - y)(y + z)$ g $\quad (3a + b)(2b + 5c)$ h $\quad (m - 2x)(3y + z)$

9 Note that $x^2 + 5x + 6 = x^2 + 2x + 3x + 6$ which can be factorised by grouping. Use a similar
method to factorise the following.

a $\quad x^2 + 7x + 10$ b $\quad x^2 + 8x + 15$ c $\quad x^2 + 10x + 24$

d $\quad x^2 - x - 6$ e $\quad x^2 + 4x - 12$ f $\quad x^2 - 11x + 18$

Reasoning

10 $xa - 21 + 7a - 3x$ could be rearranged in two different ways before factorising.

         Method 1   Method 2

$xa + 7a - 3x - 21 = a(x + 7) - 3(\underline{\quad\quad})$ $xa - 3x + 7a - 21 = x(a - 3) + 7(\underline{\quad\quad})$

$\qquad\qquad\qquad = \underline{\quad\quad\quad\quad}$ $= \underline{\quad\quad\quad\quad}$

a Copy and complete both methods for the above expression.

b Use different arrangements of the four terms to complete the factorisation of the following
in two ways. Show working using both methods.

    i $\quad xb - 6 - 3b + 2x$ ii $\quad xy - 8 + 2y - 4x$ iii $\quad 4m^2 - 15n + 6m - 10mn$

    iv $\quad 2m + 3n - mn - 6$ v $\quad 4a - 6b^2 + 3b - 8ab$ vi $\quad 3ab - 4c - b + 12ac$

11 Make up at least three of your own four-term expressions that factorise to a binomial product.
Describe the method that you used to make up each four-term expression.

Enrichment: Grouping with more than four terms

12 Factorise by grouping.

a $\quad 2(a - 3) - x(a - 3) - c(a - 3)$ b $\quad b(2a + 1) + 5(2a + 1) - a(2a + 1)$

c $\quad x(a + 1) - 4(a + 1) - ba - b$ d $\quad 3(a - b) - b(a - b) - 2a^2 + 2ab$

e $\quad c(1 - a) - x + ax + 2 - 2a$ f $\quad a(x - 2) + 2bx - 4b - x + 2$

g $\quad a^2 - 3ac - 2ab + 6bc + 3abc - 9bc^2$ h $\quad 3x - 6xy - 5z + 10yz + y - 2y^2$

i $\quad 8z - 4y + 3x^2 + xy - 12x - 2xz$ j $\quad -ab - 4cx + 3aby + 2abx + 2c - 6cy$

 ## Using a CAS calculator 8.5: Expanding and factorising

This activity is on the companion website in the form of a printable PDF.

Factorising quadratic trinomials

An expression that takes the form $x^2 + bx + c$, where b and c are constants, is an example of a monic quadratic trinomial which has the coefficient of x^2 equal to 1. To factorise a quadratic expression, we need to use the distributive law in reverse. Consider the following:

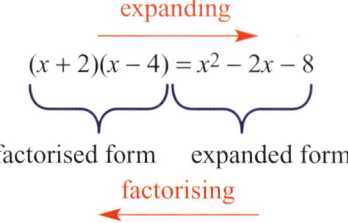

$$(x + 2)(x - 4) = x^2 - 2x - 8$$

factorised form   expanded form

If we examine the diagram above we can see how each term of the product is formed.

Product of x and x is x^2

$$(x + 2)(x - 4) = x^2 - 2x - 8$$

Product of 2 and -4 is -8
($2 \times$ -4 = -8, the constant term)

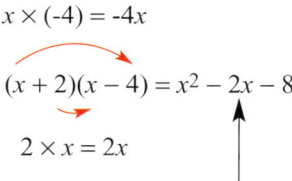

$x \times (-4) = -4x$

$$(x + 2)(x - 4) = x^2 - 2x - 8$$

$2 \times x = 2x$

Add -4x and 2x to give the middle term, -2x
(-4 + 2 = -2, the coefficient of x)

→ ## Let's start: So many choices

Mia says that since $-2 \times 3 = -6$ then $x^2 + 5x - 6$ must equal $(x - 2)(x + 3)$.

- Expand $(x - 2)(x + 3)$ to see if Mia is correct.
- What other pairs of numbers multiply to give -6?
- Which pair of numbers should Mia choose to correctly factorise $x^2 + 5x - 6$?
- What advice can you give Mia when trying to factorise these types of trinomials?

Key ideas

- To factorise a **quadratic trinomial** of the form $x^2 + bx + c$, find two numbers which:
  - multiply to give c and
  - add to give b.

For example,
$x^2 - 3x - 10 = (x - 5)(x + 2)$
choose -5 and +2 since
- $-5 \times 2 = -10$
- $-5 + 2 = -3$

Example 10 Factorising quadratic trinomials

Factorise each of the following quadratic expressions.

a $x^2 + 7x + 10$ **b** $x^2 + 2x - 8$ **c** $x^2 - 7x + 10$

SOLUTION

a $x^2 + 7x + 10 = (x + 5)(x + 2)$

b $x^2 + 2x - 8 = (x + 4)(x - 2)$

c $x^2 - 7x + 10 = (x - 2)(x - 5)$

EXPLANATION

Factors of 10 include: (10, 1) and (5, 2).
The pair that adds to 7 is (5, 2).

Factors of -8 are (-8, 1) or (8, -1) or
(4, -2) or (-4, 2) and 4 + (-2) = 2
so choose (4, -2).

Factors of 10 are: (10, 1) or (-10, -1) or (5, 2)
or (-5, -2).
To add to a negative (-7), both factors must then be
negative: -5 + (-2) = -7 so choose (-5, -2).

Example 11 Factorising with a common factor

Factorise the quadratic expression $2x^2 - 2x - 12$.

SOLUTION

$2x^2 - 2x - 12 = 2(x^2 - x - 6)$
$ = 2(x - 3)(x + 2)$

EXPLANATION

First take out common factor of 2.
Factors of -6 are: (-6, 1) or (6, -1) or (-3, 2) or (3, -2).
-3 + 2 = -1 so choose (-3, 2).

Exercise 8F

1 Expand these binomial products.

a $(x + 1)(x + 3)$ **b** $(x + 2)(x + 7)$ **c** $(x - 3)(x + 11)$

d $(x - 5)(x + 6)$ **e** $(x + 12)(x - 5)$ **f** $(x + 13)(x - 4)$

g $(x - 2)(x - 6)$ **h** $(x - 20)(x - 11)$ **i** $(x - 9)(x - 1)$

2 Decide what two numbers multiply to give the first number and add to give the second number.

a 6, 5   **b** 10, 7   **c** 12, 13

d 20, 9   **e** -5, 4   **f** -7, -6

g -15, 2   **h** -30, -1   **i** 6, -5

j 18, -11   **k** 40, -13   **l** 100, -52

Understanding

Example 10a 3 Factorise each of the following quadratic expressions.

a $x^2 + 3x + 2$ b $x^2 + 4x + 3$ c $x^2 + 7x + 6$

d $x^2 + 10x + 9$ e $x^2 + 8x + 7$ f $x^2 + 15x + 14$

g $x^2 + 6x + 8$ h $x^2 + 7x + 12$ i $x^2 + 10x + 16$

j $x^2 + 8x + 15$ k $x^2 + 9x + 20$ l $x^2 + 11x + 24$

Example 10b 4 Factorise each of the following quadratic expressions.

a $x^2 + 3x - 4$ b $x^2 + x - 2$ c $x^2 + 4x - 5$

d $x^2 + 5x - 14$ e $x^2 + 2x - 15$ f $x^2 + 8x - 20$

g $x^2 + 3x - 18$ h $x^2 + 7x - 18$ i $x^2 + x - 12$

Example 10c 5 Factorise each of the following quadratic expressions.

a $x^2 - 6x + 5$ b $x^2 - 2x + 1$ c $x^2 - 5x + 4$

d $x^2 - 9x + 8$ e $x^2 - 4x + 4$ f $x^2 - 8x + 12$

g $x^2 - 11x + 18$ h $x^2 - 10x + 21$ i $x^2 - 5x + 6$

6 Factorise each of the following quadratic expressions.

a $x^2 - 7x - 8$ b $x^2 - 3x - 4$ c $x^2 - 5x - 6$

d $x^2 - 6x - 16$ e $x^2 - 2x - 24$ f $x^2 - 2x - 15$

g $x^2 - x - 12$ h $x^2 - 11x - 12$ i $x^2 - 4x - 12$

Example 11 7 Factorise each of the following quadratic expressions by first taking out a common factor.

a $2x^2 + 10x + 8$ b $2x^2 + 22x + 20$ c $3x^2 + 18x + 24$

d $2x^2 + 14x - 60$ e $2x^2 - 14x - 36$ f $4x^2 - 8x + 4$

g $2x^2 + 2x - 12$ h $6x^2 - 30x - 36$ i $5x^2 - 30x + 40$

j $3x^2 - 33x + 90$ k $2x^2 - 6x - 20$ l $3x^2 - 3x - 36$

8 Find the missing term in these trinomials if they are to factorise using integers. For example: the missing term in $x^2 + ? + 10$ could be $7x$ because $x^2 + 7x + 10$ factorises to $(x + 5)(x + 2)$ and 5 and 2 are integers. There may be more than one answer in each case.

a $x^2 + ? + 5$ b $x^2 - ? + 9$ c $x^2 - ? - 12$ d $x^2 + ? - 12$

e $x^2 + ? + 18$ f $x^2 - ? + 18$ g $x^2 - ? - 16$ h $x^2 + ? - 25$

9 A backyard, rectangular in area, has a length 2 metres more than its width (x metres). Inside the rectangle are three square paved areas each of area 5 m² as shown. The remaining area is lawn.

a Find an expression for:

     i the total backyard area

     ii the area of lawn in expanded form

     iii the area of lawn in factorised form.

b Find the area of lawn if:

     i $x = 10$

     ii $x = 7$

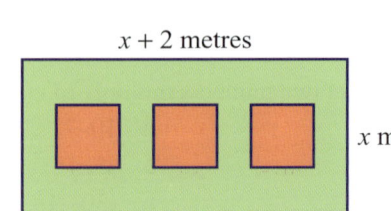

$x + 2$ metres

x metres

10 The expression $x^2 - 6x + 9$ factorises to $(x-3)(x-3) = (x-3)^2$, which is a perfect square.
Factorise these perfect squares.

a $x^2 + 8x + 16$ b $x^2 + 10x + 25$ c $x^2 + 30x + 225$

d $x^2 - 2x + 1$ e $x^2 - 14x + 49$ f $x^2 - 26x + 169$

g $2x^2 + 4x + 2$ h $5x^2 - 30x + 45$ i $-3x^2 + 36x - 108$

11 Sometimes it is not possible to factorise quadratic trinomials using integers. Decide which of
the following cannot be factorised using integers.

a $x^2 - x - 56$ b $x^2 + 5x - 4$ c $x^2 + 7x - 6$

d $x^2 + 3x - 108$ e $x^2 + 3x - 1$ f $x^2 + 12x - 53$

Enrichment: Completing the square

12 It is useful to be able to write a simple quadratic trinomial in the form $(x + b)^2 + c$. This
involves adding (and subtracting) a special number to form the first perfect square. This
procedure is called completing the square. Here is an example.

$$\left(-\frac{6}{2}\right)^2 = 9$$

$$x^2 - 6x - 8 = x^2 - 6x + 9 - 9 - 8$$
$$= (x-3)(x-3) - 17$$
$$= (x-3)^2 - 17$$

Complete the square for these trinomials.

a $x^2 - 2x - 8$ b $x^2 + 4x - 1$ c $x^2 + 10x + 3$

d $x^2 - 16x - 3$ e $x^2 + 18x + 7$ f $x^2 - 32x - 11$

8.7 Factorising trinomials of the form $ax^2 + bx + c$

So far we have factorised quadratic trinomials where the coefficient of x^2 is 1, such as $x^2 - 3x - 40$. These are called monic trinomials. We will now consider non-monic trinomials where the coefficient of x is not equal to 1 and is also not a common factor to all three terms, such as in $6x^2 + x - 15$.

Let's start: How the grouping method works

Consider the trinomial $2x^2 + 9x + 10$.

- First write $2x^2 + 9x + 10 = 2x^2 + 4x + 5x + 10$ then factorise by grouping.
- Note that $9x$ was split to give $4x + 5x$ and the product of $2x^2$ and $10 = 20x^2$. Describe the link between the pair of numbers $\{4, 5\}$ and the pair of numbers $\{2, 10\}$.
- Why was $9x$ split to give $4x + 5x$ and not, say, $3x + 6x$?
- Describe how the $13x$ should be split in $2x^2 + 13x + 15$ so it can be factorised by grouping.
- Now try your method for $2x^2 - 7x - 15$.

Key ideas

- To factorise a trinomial of the form $ax^2 + bx + c$ by grouping, find two numbers which sum to give b and multiply to give $a \times c$.

  For example:

  $5x^2 + 13x - 6$

  $= 5x^2 + 15x - 2x - 6$ $a \times c = 5 \times (-6) = -30$ so the two numbers

  $= 5x(x + 3) - 2(x + 3)$ are 15 and -2 since $15 + (-2) = 13$ and

  $= (x + 3)(5x - 2)$ $15 \times (-2) = -30$.

- Mentally check your factors by expanding your answer

  $$(x + 3)(5x - 2)$$

  $15x - 2x = 13x$

Example 12 Factorising trinomials of the form $ax^2 + bx + c$

Factorise $2x^2 + 7x + 3$.

SOLUTION

$2x^2 + 7x + 3 = 2x^2 + x + 6x + 3$

$ = x(2x + 1) + 3(2x + 1)$

$ = (2x + 1)(x + 3)$

EXPLANATION

$a \times c = 2 \times 3 = 6$ then ask what factors of this number (6) add to 7. The answer is 1 and 6, so split $7x = x + 6x$. Then factorise by grouping.

Example 13 Factorising trinomials with negative numbers

Factorise the quadratic trinomials.

a $10x^2 + 9x - 9$ b $6x^2 - 17x + 12$

SOLUTION

EXPLANATION

a $10x^2 + 9x - 9 = 10x^2 + 15x - 6x - 9$
$= 5x(2x + 3) - 3(2x + 3)$
$= (2x + 3)(5x - 3)$

$10 \times (-9) = -90$ so ask what factors of -90 add to give 9. Choose 15 and -6. Then complete the factorisation by grouping.

b $6x^2 - 17x + 12 = 6x^2 - 9x - 8x + 12$
$= 3x(2x - 3) - 4(2x - 3)$
$= (2x - 3)(3x - 4)$

$6 \times 12 = 72$ so ask what factors of 72 add to give -17. Choose -9 and -8.
Complete a mental check.
$$(2x - 3)(3x - 4)$$
$-9x$
$-8x$ $-9x - 8x = -17x$

Exercise 8G

Understanding

1 List the two numbers which satisfy each part.
   a Multiply to give 6 and add to give 5
   b Multiply to give 12 and add to give 8
   c Multiply to give -10 and add to give 3
   d Multiply to give -24 and add to give 5
   e Multiply to give 18 and add to give -9
   f Multiply to give 35 and add to give -12
   g Multiply to give -30 and add to give -7
   h Multiply to give -28 and add to give -3

2 Copy and complete.
   a $2x^2 + 7x + 5 = 2x^2 + 2x + \underline{\quad} + 5$
      $= 2x(\underline{\quad}) + 5(\underline{\quad})$
      $= (\underline{\quad})(\underline{\quad})$

   b $3x^2 + 8x + 4 = 3x^2 + 6x + \underline{\quad} + 4$
      $= 3x(\underline{\quad}) + 2(\underline{\quad})$
      $= (\underline{\quad})(\underline{\quad})$

   c $2x^2 - 7x + 6 = 2x^2 - 3x - \underline{\quad} + 6$
      $= x(\underline{\quad}) - 2(\underline{\quad})$
      $= (\underline{\quad})(\underline{\quad})$

   d $5x^2 + 9x - 2 = 5x^2 + 10x - \underline{\quad} - 2$
      $= 5x(\underline{\quad}) - 1(\underline{\quad})$
      $= (\underline{\quad})(\underline{\quad})$

   e $4x^2 + 11x + 6 = 4x^2 + \underline{\quad} + 3x + 6$
      $= \underline{\quad}(x + 2) + 3(\underline{\quad})$
      $= (\underline{\quad})(\underline{\quad})$

   f $6x^2 - 7x - 3 = 6x^2 - 9x + \underline{\quad} - 3$
      $= \underline{\quad}(\underline{\quad}) + 1(\underline{\quad})$
      $= (\underline{\quad})(\underline{\quad})$

Fluency

Example 12

3 Factorise these quadratic trinomials.
   a $2x^2 + 9x + 4$
   b $3x^2 + 7x + 2$
   c $2x^2 + 7x + 6$
   d $3x^2 + 8x + 4$
   e $5x^2 + 12x + 4$
   f $2x^2 + 11x + 12$
   g $6x^2 + 13x + 5$
   h $4x^2 + 5x + 1$
   i $8x^2 + 14x + 5$

Example 13

4 Factorise these quadratic trinomials.
   a $3x^2 + 2x - 5$
   b $5x^2 + 6x - 8$
   c $8x^2 + 10x - 3$
   d $6x^2 - 13x - 8$
   e $10x^2 - 3x - 4$
   f $5x^2 - 11x - 12$
   g $4x^2 - 16x + 15$
   h $2x^2 - 15x + 18$
   i $6x^2 - 19x + 10$
   j $12x^2 - 13x - 4$
   k $4x^2 - 12x + 9$
   l $7x^2 + 18x - 9$
   m $9x^2 + 44x - 5$
   n $3x^2 - 14x + 16$
   o $4x^2 - 4x - 15$

5 Factorise these quadratic trinomials.

a $10x^2 + 27x + 11$ b $15x^2 + 14x - 8$ c $20x^2 - 36x + 9$

d $18x^2 - x - 5$ e $25x^2 + 5x - 12$ f $32x^2 - 12x - 5$

g $27x^2 + 6x - 8$ h $33x^2 + 41x + 10$ i $54x^2 - 39x - 5$

j $12x^2 - 32x + 21$ k $75x^2 - 43x + 6$ l $90x^2 + 33x - 8$

6 Factorise by firstly taking out a common factor.

a $30x^2 - 14x - 4$ b $12x^2 + 18x - 30$ c $27x^2 - 54x + 15$

d $21x^2 - 77x + 42$ e $36x^2 + 36x - 40$ f $50x^2 - 35x - 60$

7 Factorise these trinomials.

a $-2x^2 + 7x - 6$ b $-5x^2 - 3x + 8$ c $-6x^2 + 13x + 8$

d $18 - 9x - 5x^2$ e $16x - 4x^2 - 15$ f $14x - 8x^2 - 5$

8 When splitting the $3x$ in $2x^2 + 3x - 20$, you could write:

   A $2x^2 + 8x - 5x - 20$ or   **B** $2x^2 - 5x + 8x - 20$

a Complete the factorisation using **A**.   b Complete the factorisation using **B**.

c Does the order matter when you split the $3x$?

d Factorise these trinomials twice each. Factorise once by grouping then repeat but reverse the order of the two middle terms in the first line of working.

   i $3x^2 + 5x - 12$ ii $5x^2 - 3x - 14$ iii $6x^2 + 5x - 4$

9 Make up five non-monic trinomials with the coefficient of x^2 not equal to 1 which factorise using the above method. Explain your method in finding these trinomials.

Enrichment: The cross method

10 The cross method is another way to factorise trinomials of the form $ax^2 + bx + c$. It involves finding factors of ax^2 and factors of c then choosing pairs of these factors that add to bx.

For example: Factorise $6x^2 - x - 15$.

Factors of $6x^2$ include $(x, 6x)$ and $(2x, 3x)$.

Factors of -15 include $(15, -1)$, $(-15, 1)$, $(5, -3)$ and $(-5, 3)$.

We arrange a chosen pair of factors vertically then cross-multiply and add to get $-1x$.

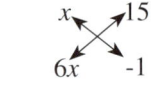   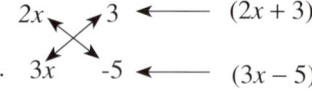

$x \times (-1) + 6x \times 15$ $x \times (-3) + 6x \times 5$ $2x \times (-5) + 3x \times 3$

$= 89x \neq -1x$ $= 27x \neq -1x$ $= -1x$

You will need to continue until a particular combination works. The third cross-product gives a sum of $-1x$ so choose the factors $(2x + 3)$ and $(3x - 5)$ so:

$$6x^2 - x - 15 = (2x + 3)(3x - 5)$$

Try this method on the trinomials from Questions **4** and **5**.

8.8 Simplifying algebraic fractions: multiplication and division

With a numerical fraction such as $\dfrac{6}{9}$, the highest common factor of 6 and 9 is 3, which can be cancelled $\dfrac{6}{9} = \dfrac{{}^{1}\cancel{3} \times 2}{{}_{1}\cancel{3} \times 3} = \dfrac{2}{3}$. For algebraic fractions the process is the same. If expressions are in a factorised form, common factors can be easily identified and cancelled.

Let's start: Correct cancelling

Consider this cancelling attempt:

$$\frac{5x + \cancel{10}^{1}}{\cancel{20}_{2}} = \frac{5x + 1}{2}$$

- Substitute $x = 6$ into the left-hand side to evaluate $\dfrac{5x + 10}{20}$.

- Substitute $x = 6$ into the right-hand side to evaluate $\dfrac{5x + 1}{2}$.

- What do you notice about the two answers to the above? How can you explain this?
- Decide how you might correctly cancel the expression on the left-hand side. Show your steps and check by substituting a value for x.

- Simplify **algebraic fractions** by factorising and cancelling common factors.

Incorrect	*Correct*
$\dfrac{2x + \cancel{4}^{2}}{\cancel{2}^{1}} = 2x + 2$	$\dfrac{2x + 4}{2} = \dfrac{{}^{1}\cancel{2}(x + 2)}{\cancel{2}^{1}}$
	$= x + 2$

- To multiply algebraic fractions:
  - factorise expressions where possible
  - cancel if possible
  - multiply the numerators and denominators together.
- To divide algebraic fractions:
  - multiply by the reciprocal of the fraction following the division sign
  - the reciprocal of $\dfrac{a}{b}$ is $\dfrac{b}{a}$
  - follow the rules for multiplication.

Example 14 Simplifying algebraic fractions

Simplify the following by cancelling.

a $\dfrac{3(x+2)(x-4)}{6(x-4)}$ b $\dfrac{20-5x}{8-2x}$ c $\dfrac{x^2-x-20}{x-5}$

SOLUTION   **EXPLANATION**

a $\dfrac{{}^{1}\cancel{3}(x+2)\cancel{(x-4)}^{1}}{{}^{2}\cancel{6}\cancel{(x-4)}^{1}} = \dfrac{x+2}{2}$

Cancel the common factors $(x-4)$ and 3.

b $\dfrac{20-5x}{8-2x} = \dfrac{5\cancel{(4-x)}^{1}}{2\cancel{(4-x)}^{1}}$

       $= \dfrac{5}{2}$

Factorise the numerator and denominator then cancel common factor of $(4-x)$.

c $\dfrac{x^2-x-20}{x-5} = \dfrac{{}^{1}\cancel{(x-5)}(x+4)}{\cancel{(x-5)}_{1}}$

       $= x+4$

Factorise the quadratic trinomial in the numerator then cancel the common factor.

Example 15 Multiplying and dividing algebraic fractions

Simplify the following.

a $\dfrac{3(x-1)}{(x+2)} \times \dfrac{4(x+2)}{9(x-1)(x-7)}$ b $\dfrac{(x-3)(x+4)}{x(x+7)} \div \dfrac{3(x+4)}{x+7}$ c $\dfrac{x^2-4}{25} \times \dfrac{5x+5}{x^2-x-2}$

SOLUTION   **EXPLANATION**

a $\dfrac{{}^{1}\cancel{3}\cancel{(x-1)}^{1}}{\cancel{(x+2)}_{1}} \times \dfrac{4\cancel{(x+2)}^{1}}{{}_{3}\cancel{9}\cancel{(x-1)}_{1}(x-7)}$

     $= \dfrac{1 \times 4}{1 \times 3(x-7)}$

     $= \dfrac{4}{3(x-7)}$

First cancel any factors in the numerator with a common factor in the denominators. Then multiply the numerators and denominators.

b $\dfrac{(x-3)(x+4)}{x(x+7)} \div \dfrac{3(x+4)}{x+7}$

$= \dfrac{(x-3)\cancel{(x+4)}^{1}}{x\cancel{(x+7)}_{1}} \times \dfrac{\cancel{x+7}^{1}}{3\cancel{(x+4)}^{1}}$

$= \dfrac{x-3}{3x}$

Multiply by the reciprocal of the fraction after division sign.
Cancel common factors and multiply remaining numerators and denominators.

c $\dfrac{x^2-4}{25} \times \dfrac{5x+5}{x^2-x-2}$

First factorise all the algebraic expressions. Note that x^2-4 is a difference of perfect squares. Then cancel as normal.

$$= \dfrac{{}^{1}\cancel{(x-2)}\,(x+2)}{25^{\,5}} \times \dfrac{\cancel{5}^{\,1}\,\cancel{(x+1)}^{\,1}}{{}_{1}\cancel{(x-2)}\,\cancel{(x+1)}_{\,1}}$$

$$= \dfrac{x+2}{5}$$

Exercise 8H

Understanding

1 Simplify these fractions by cancelling.

a $\dfrac{5}{15}$
b $\dfrac{24}{16}$
c $\dfrac{5x}{10}$
d $\dfrac{42x}{12}$

e $\dfrac{24}{8x}$
f $\dfrac{9}{18x}$
g $\dfrac{3(x+1)}{6}$
h $\dfrac{22(x-4)}{11}$

2 Factorise these by taking out common factors.

a $3x+6$
b $20-40x$
c x^2-7x
d $6x^2+24x$

3 Copy and complete.

a $\dfrac{2x-4}{8} = \dfrac{2(\quad)}{8}$

$= \dfrac{\quad}{4}$

b $\dfrac{12-18x}{2x-3x^2} = \dfrac{6(\quad)}{x(\quad)}$

$= \dfrac{6}{x}$

c $\dfrac{x-1}{x+3} \div \dfrac{2(x-1)}{(x+3)(x+2)} = \dfrac{x-1}{x+3} \times \underline{\qquad}$

$= \dfrac{x+2}{2}$

Fluency

Example 14a

4 Simplify the following by cancelling.

a $\dfrac{3(x+2)}{4(x+2)}$
b $\dfrac{x(x-3)}{3x(x-3)}$
c $\dfrac{20(x+7)}{5(x+7)}$

d $\dfrac{(x+5)(x-5)}{(x+5)}$
e $\dfrac{6(x-1)(x+3)}{9(x+3)}$
f $\dfrac{8(x-2)}{4(x-2)(x+4)}$

Example 14b

5 Simplify the following by factorising and then cancelling.

a $\dfrac{5x-5}{5}$
b $\dfrac{4x-12}{10}$
c $\dfrac{2x-4}{3x-6}$
d $\dfrac{12-4x}{6-2x}$

e $\dfrac{x^2-3x}{x}$
f $\dfrac{4x^2+10x}{5x}$
g $\dfrac{3x+3y}{2x+2y}$
h $\dfrac{4x-8y}{3x-6y}$

Example 14c   **6**   Simplify by firstly factorising.

a $\dfrac{x^2 - x - 6}{x - 3}$ b $\dfrac{x^2 + 8x + 16}{x + 4}$

c $\dfrac{x^2 - 7x + 12}{x - 4}$ d $\dfrac{x - 2}{x^2 + x - 6}$

e $\dfrac{x + 7}{x^2 + 5x - 14}$ f $\dfrac{x - 9}{x^2 - 19x + 90}$

Example 15a   **7**   Simplify the following by cancelling.

a $\dfrac{2x(x - 4)}{4(x + 1)} \times \dfrac{(x + 1)}{x}$ b $\dfrac{(x + 2)(x - 3)}{x - 5} \times \dfrac{x - 5}{x + 2}$

c $\dfrac{x - 3}{x + 2} \times \dfrac{3(x + 4)(x + 2)}{x + 4}$ d $\dfrac{2(x + 3)(x + 4)}{(x + 1)(x - 5)} \times \dfrac{(x + 1)}{4(x + 3)}$

Example 15b   **8**   Simplify the following by cancelling.

a $\dfrac{x(x + 1)}{x + 3} \div \dfrac{x + 1}{x + 3}$ b $\dfrac{x + 3}{x + 2} \div \dfrac{x + 3}{2(x - 2)}$

c $\dfrac{x - 4}{(x + 3)(x + 1)} \div \dfrac{x - 4}{4(x + 3)}$ d $\dfrac{4x}{x + 2} \div \dfrac{8x}{x - 2}$

e $\dfrac{3(4x - 9)(x + 2)}{2(x + 6)} \div \dfrac{9(x + 4)(4x - 9)}{4(x + 2)(x + 6)}$ f $\dfrac{5(2x - 3)}{(x + 7)} \div \dfrac{(x + 2)(2x - 3)}{x + 7}$

9   Simplify the following. These expressions involve difference of perfect squares.

a $\dfrac{x^2 - 100}{x + 10}$ b $\dfrac{x^2 - 49}{x + 7}$

c $\dfrac{x^2 - 25}{x + 5}$ d $\dfrac{2(x - 20)}{x^2 - 400}$

e $\dfrac{5(x - 6)}{x^2 - 36}$ f $\dfrac{3x + 27}{x^2 - 81}$

Example 15c   **10**   These expressions involve a combination of trinomials, difference of perfect squares and simple common factors. Simplify by firstly factorising where possible.

a $\dfrac{x^2 + 5x + 6}{x + 5} \div \dfrac{x + 3}{x^2 - 25}$ b $\dfrac{x^2 + 6x + 8}{x^2 - 9} \div \dfrac{x + 4}{x - 3}$

c $\dfrac{x^2 + x - 12}{x^2 + 8x + 16} \times \dfrac{x^2 - 16}{x^2 - 8x + 16}$ d $\dfrac{x^2 + 12x + 35}{x^2 - 25} \times \dfrac{x^2 - 10x + 25}{x^2 + 9x + 14}$

e $\dfrac{9x^2 - 3x}{6x - 45x^2}$ f $\dfrac{x^2 - 4x}{3x - x^2}$

g $\dfrac{3x^2 - 21x + 36}{2x^2 - 32} \times \dfrac{2x + 10}{6x - 18}$ h $\dfrac{2x^2 - 18x + 40}{x^2 - x - 12} \times \dfrac{3x + 15}{4x^2 - 100}$

11 The expression $\dfrac{5-2x}{2x-5}$ can be written in the form $\dfrac{-1(-5+2x)}{2x-5} = \dfrac{-1(2x-5)}{2x-5}$, which can be cancelled to -1.

Use this idea to simplify these algebraic fractions.

a $\dfrac{7-3x}{3x-7}$ **b** $\dfrac{4x-1}{1-4x}$ **c** $\dfrac{8x+16}{-2-x}$

d $\dfrac{x+3}{-9-3x}$ **e** $\dfrac{5-3x}{18x-30}$ **f** $\dfrac{x^2-9}{3-x}$

12 Just like $\dfrac{a^2}{2a}$ can be cancelled to $\dfrac{a}{2}$, $\dfrac{(a+5)^2}{2(a+5)}$ cancels to $\dfrac{a+5}{2}$. Use this idea to cancel these fractions.

a $\dfrac{(a+1)^2}{(a+1)}$ **b** $\dfrac{5(a-3)^2}{(a-3)}$ **c** $\dfrac{7(x+7)^2}{14(x+7)}$

d $\dfrac{3(x-1)(x+2)^2}{18(x-1)(x+2)}$ **e** $\dfrac{x^2+6x+9}{2x+6}$ **f** $\dfrac{11x-22}{x^2-4x+4}$

Enrichment: All in together

13 Use your knowledge of factorisation and the ideas in Questions **11** and **12** above to simplify these algebraic fractions.

a $\dfrac{2x^2-2x-24}{16-4x}$ **b** $\dfrac{x^2-14x+49}{21-3x}$

c $\dfrac{x-16x+64}{64-x^2}$ **d** $\dfrac{4-x^2}{x^2+x-6} \times \dfrac{2x+6}{x+4x+4}$

e $\dfrac{2x^2-18}{x^2-6x+9} \times \dfrac{6-2x}{x^2+6x+9}$ **f** $\dfrac{x^2-2x+1}{4-4x} \div \dfrac{1-x^2}{3x^2+6x+3}$

g $\dfrac{4x^2-9}{x^2-5x} \div \dfrac{6-4x}{15-3x}$ **h** $\dfrac{x^2-4x+4}{8-4x} \times \dfrac{-2}{4-x^2}$

i $\dfrac{(x+2)^2-4}{(1-x)^2} \times \dfrac{x^2-2x+1}{3x+12}$ **j** $\dfrac{2(x-3)^2-50}{x^2-11x+24} \div \dfrac{x^2-4}{3-x}$

8.9 Simplifying algebraic fractions: addition and subtraction

The process required for adding or subtracting algebraic fractions is similar to that used for fractions without variables.

To simplify $\frac{2}{3} + \frac{4}{5}$, for example, you would find the lowest common multiple of the denominators (15) then express each fraction with this denominator. Adding the numerators completes the task.

Let's start: Compare the working

Here is the working for the simplification of the sum of a pair of numerical fractions and the sum of a pair of algebraic fractions.

$$\frac{2}{5} + \frac{3}{4} = \frac{8}{20} + \frac{15}{20}$$
$$= \frac{23}{20}$$

$$\frac{2x}{5} + \frac{3x}{4} = \frac{8x}{20} + \frac{15x}{20}$$
$$= \frac{23x}{20}$$

Although algebraic fractions, seem abstract, performing operations on them and simplifying them is essential to many calculations in real-life mathematical problems.

- What type of steps were taken to simplify the algebraic fractions that are the same as for the numerical fractions?
- Write down the steps required to add (or subtract) algebraic fractions.

■ To add or subtract algebraic fractions:
- determine the lowest common denominator (LCD)
- express each fraction using the LCD
- add or subtract the numerators.

Example 16 Adding and subtracting with a numeral in the denominator

Simplify:

a $\dfrac{x}{4} - \dfrac{2x}{5}$ b $\dfrac{7x}{3} + \dfrac{x}{6}$ c $\dfrac{x+3}{2} + \dfrac{x-2}{5}$

SOLUTION   **EXPLANATION**

a $\dfrac{x}{4} - \dfrac{2x}{5} = \dfrac{5x}{20} - \dfrac{8x}{20}$

$\qquad = -\dfrac{3x}{20}$

Determine the LCD of 4 and 5, i.e. 20. Express each fraction as an equivalent fraction with a denominator of 20. $2x \times 4 = 8x$. Then subtract numerators.

b $\dfrac{7x}{3} + \dfrac{x}{6} = \dfrac{14x}{6} + \dfrac{x}{6}$

$\qquad = \dfrac{15x}{6}$

$\qquad = \dfrac{5x}{2}$

Note the LCD of 3 and 6 is 6 not $3 \times 6 = 18$.

$\dfrac{15}{6} = \dfrac{5}{2}$

c $\quad \dfrac{x+3}{2} + \dfrac{x-2}{5} = \dfrac{5(x+3)}{10} + \dfrac{2(x-2)}{10}$

$\qquad\qquad = \dfrac{5x+15+2x-4}{10}$

$\qquad\qquad = \dfrac{7x+11}{10}$

The LCD of 2 and 5 is 10, write as equivalent fractions with denominator 10.
Expand the brackets and simplify the numerator by adding and collecting like terms.

Example 17 Adding and subtracting with algebraic terms in the denominator

Simplify:

a $\quad \dfrac{2}{x} - \dfrac{5}{2x}$

b $\quad \dfrac{2}{x} + \dfrac{3}{x^2}$

SOLUTION

a $\quad \dfrac{2}{x} - \dfrac{5}{2x} = \dfrac{4}{2x} - \dfrac{5}{2x}$

$\qquad\qquad = -\dfrac{1}{2x}$

b $\quad \dfrac{2}{x} + \dfrac{3}{x^2} = \dfrac{2x}{x^2} + \dfrac{3}{x^2}$

$\qquad\qquad = \dfrac{2x+3}{x^2}$

EXPLANATION

The LCD of x and $2x$ is $2x$, so rewrite the first fraction so its denominator is also $2x$.

The LCD of x and x^2 is x^2 so change the first fraction so its denominator is also x^2, then add numerators.

Exercise 8I

1 Find the lowest common multiple of these pairs of numbers.

a (6, 8)   b (3, 5)   c (11, 13)   d (12, 18)

2 Write equivalent fractions by stating the missing expression.

a $\quad \dfrac{2x}{5} = \dfrac{\square}{10}$

b $\quad \dfrac{7x}{3} = \dfrac{\square}{9}$

c $\quad \dfrac{x+1}{4} = \dfrac{\square(x+1)}{12}$

d $\quad \dfrac{3x+5}{11} = \dfrac{\square(3x+5)}{22}$

e $\quad \dfrac{4}{x} = \dfrac{\square}{2x}$

f $\quad \dfrac{30}{x+1} = \dfrac{\square}{3(x+1)}$

3 Copy and complete these simplifications.

a $\quad \dfrac{x}{4} + \dfrac{2x}{3} = \dfrac{\square}{12} + \dfrac{\square}{12} = \dfrac{\square}{12}$

b $\quad \dfrac{5x}{7} - \dfrac{2x}{5} = \dfrac{\square}{35} - \dfrac{\square}{35} = \dfrac{\square}{35}$

c $\quad \dfrac{x+1}{2} + \dfrac{2x+3}{4} = \dfrac{\square(x+1)}{4} + \dfrac{2x+3}{4} = \dfrac{(\boxed{}+2x+3)}{4} = \dfrac{\boxed{}}{4}$

4 Write down the LCD for these pairs of fractions.

a $\dfrac{x}{3}, \dfrac{2x}{5}$ b $\dfrac{3x}{7}, \dfrac{x}{2}$ c $\dfrac{-5x}{4}, \dfrac{x}{8}$ d $\dfrac{2x}{3}, \dfrac{-5x}{6}$ e $\dfrac{7x}{10}, \dfrac{-3x}{5}$

Example 16a,b

5 Simplify:

a $\dfrac{x}{7} + \dfrac{x}{2}$ b $\dfrac{x}{3} + \dfrac{x}{15}$ c $\dfrac{x}{4} - \dfrac{x}{8}$ d $\dfrac{x}{9} + \dfrac{x}{5}$

e $\dfrac{y}{7} - \dfrac{y}{8}$ f $\dfrac{a}{2} + \dfrac{a}{11}$ g $\dfrac{b}{3} - \dfrac{b}{9}$ h $\dfrac{m}{3} - \dfrac{m}{6}$

i $\dfrac{m}{6} + \dfrac{3m}{4}$ j $\dfrac{a}{4} + \dfrac{2a}{7}$ k $\dfrac{2x}{5} + \dfrac{x}{10}$ l $\dfrac{p}{9} - \dfrac{3p}{7}$

m $\dfrac{b}{2} - \dfrac{7b}{9}$ n $\dfrac{9y}{8} + \dfrac{2y}{5}$ o $\dfrac{4x}{7} - \dfrac{x}{5}$ p $\dfrac{3x}{4} - \dfrac{x}{3}$

Example 16c

6 Simplify:

a $\dfrac{x+1}{2} + \dfrac{x+3}{5}$ b $\dfrac{x+3}{3} + \dfrac{x-4}{4}$ c $\dfrac{a-2}{7} + \dfrac{a-5}{8}$

d $\dfrac{y+4}{5} + \dfrac{y-3}{6}$ e $\dfrac{m-4}{8} + \dfrac{m+6}{5}$ f $\dfrac{x-2}{12} + \dfrac{x-3}{8}$

g $\dfrac{2b-3}{6} + \dfrac{b+2}{8}$ h $\dfrac{3x+8}{6} + \dfrac{2x-4}{3}$ i $\dfrac{2y-5}{7} + \dfrac{3y+2}{14}$

j $\dfrac{2t-1}{8} + \dfrac{t-2}{16}$ k $\dfrac{4-x}{3} + \dfrac{2-x}{7}$ l $\dfrac{2m-1}{4} + \dfrac{m-3}{6}$

Example 17a

7 Simplify:

a $\dfrac{3}{x} + \dfrac{5}{2x}$ b $\dfrac{7}{3x} - \dfrac{2}{x}$ c $\dfrac{7}{4x} - \dfrac{5}{2x}$ d $\dfrac{4}{3x} + \dfrac{2}{9x}$

e $\dfrac{3}{4x} - \dfrac{2}{5x}$ f $\dfrac{2}{3x} + \dfrac{1}{5x}$ g $\dfrac{-3}{4x} - \dfrac{7}{x}$ h $\dfrac{-5}{3x} - \dfrac{3}{4x}$

Example 17b

8 Simplify:

a $\dfrac{3}{x} + \dfrac{2}{x^2}$ b $\dfrac{5}{x^2} + \dfrac{4}{x}$ c $\dfrac{7}{x} + \dfrac{3}{x^2}$ d $\dfrac{4}{x} - \dfrac{5}{x^2}$

e $\dfrac{3}{x^2} - \dfrac{8}{x}$ f $-\dfrac{4}{x^2} + \dfrac{1}{x}$ g $\dfrac{3}{x} - \dfrac{7}{2x^2}$ h $-\dfrac{2}{3x} + \dfrac{3}{x^2}$

9 Simplify these mixed algebraic fractions.

a $\dfrac{2}{x} + \dfrac{x}{4}$ b $\dfrac{-5}{x} + \dfrac{x}{2}$ c $\dfrac{-2}{x} - \dfrac{4x}{3}$ d $\dfrac{3}{2x} - \dfrac{5x}{4}$

e $\dfrac{3x}{4} - \dfrac{5}{6x}$ f $\dfrac{1}{3x} - \dfrac{x}{9}$ g $-\dfrac{2}{5x} + \dfrac{3x}{2}$ h $-\dfrac{5}{4x} - \dfrac{3x}{10}$

10 Find the missing algebraic fraction. The fraction should be in simplest form.

a $\dfrac{x}{2} + \dfrac{\square}{\square} = \dfrac{5x}{6}$

b $\dfrac{\square}{\square} + \dfrac{x}{4} = \dfrac{3x}{8}$

c $\dfrac{2x}{5} + \dfrac{\square}{\square} = \dfrac{9x}{10}$

d $\dfrac{2x}{3} - \dfrac{\square}{\square} = \dfrac{7x}{15}$

e $\dfrac{\square}{\square} - \dfrac{x}{3} = \dfrac{5x}{9}$

f $\dfrac{2x}{3} - \dfrac{\square}{\square} = \dfrac{5x}{12}$

11 Find and describe the error in each set of working. Then give the correct answer.

a $\dfrac{4x}{5} - \dfrac{x}{3} = \dfrac{3x}{2}$

b $\dfrac{x+1}{5} + \dfrac{x}{2} = \dfrac{2x+1}{10} + \dfrac{5x}{10}$

$$= \dfrac{7x+1}{10}$$

c $\dfrac{5x}{3} + \dfrac{x-1}{2} = \dfrac{10x}{6} + \dfrac{3x-1}{6}$

$$= \dfrac{13x-1}{6}$$

d $\dfrac{2}{x} - \dfrac{3}{x^2} = \dfrac{2}{x^2} - \dfrac{3}{x^2}$

$$= \dfrac{-1}{x^2}$$

12 A student thinks that the LCD to use when simplifying $\dfrac{x+1}{2} + \dfrac{2x-1}{4}$ is 8.

 a Complete the simplification using a common denominator of 8.

 b Now complete the simplification using the actual LCD of 4.

 c How does your working for parts **a** and **b** compare? Which method is preferable and why?

Enrichment: More than two fractions!

13 Simplify by finding the LCD.

a $\dfrac{2x}{5} - \dfrac{3x}{2} - \dfrac{x}{3}$

b $\dfrac{x}{4} - \dfrac{2x}{3} + \dfrac{5x}{6}$

c $\dfrac{5x}{8} - \dfrac{5x}{6} + \dfrac{3x}{4}$

d $\dfrac{x+1}{4} + \dfrac{2x-1}{3} - \dfrac{x}{5}$

e $\dfrac{2x-1}{3} - \dfrac{2x}{7} + \dfrac{x-3}{6}$

f $\dfrac{1-2x}{5} - \dfrac{3x}{8} + \dfrac{3x+1}{2}$

g $\dfrac{2}{3x} + \dfrac{5}{x} - \dfrac{1}{x}$

h $-\dfrac{1}{2x} + \dfrac{2}{x} - \dfrac{4}{3x}$

i $-\dfrac{4}{5x} - \dfrac{1}{2x} + \dfrac{3}{4x}$

j $\dfrac{4}{x^2} + \dfrac{3}{2x} - \dfrac{5}{3x}$

k $\dfrac{5}{x} - \dfrac{3}{2x^2} - \dfrac{5}{7x}$

l $\dfrac{2}{x^2} - \dfrac{4}{9x} - \dfrac{5}{3x^2}$

m $\dfrac{2}{x} + \dfrac{x}{5} - \dfrac{x}{3}$

n $\dfrac{3x}{2} - \dfrac{1}{2x} + \dfrac{x}{3}$

o $-\dfrac{4x}{9} + \dfrac{2}{5x} + \dfrac{2x}{5}$

8.10 Further simplification of algebraic fractions

More complex addition and subtraction of algebraic fractions involves expressions like:

$$\frac{2x-1}{3} - \frac{x+4}{4} \text{ and } \frac{2}{x-3} - \frac{5}{(x-3)^2}.$$

In such examples, care needs to be taken at each step in the working to avoid common errors.

Let's start: Three critical errors

The following simplification of algebraic fractions has three critical errors. Can you find them?

$$\frac{2x+1}{3} - \frac{x+2}{2} = \frac{2x+1}{6} - \frac{3(x+2)}{6}$$

$$= \frac{2x+1-3x+6}{6}$$

$$= \frac{x+7}{6}$$

The correct answer is $\frac{x-4}{6}$.

Fix the solution to produce the correct answer.

- When combining algebraic fractions which involve subtraction signs, recall that:
  - the product of two numbers of opposite sign is a negative number
  - the product of two negative numbers is a positive number.

  For example: $\dfrac{2(x-1)}{6} - \dfrac{3(x+2)}{6} = \dfrac{2x-2-3x-6}{6}$

  and $\dfrac{5(1-x)}{8} - \dfrac{2(x-1)}{8} = \dfrac{5-5x-2x+2}{8}$

- A common denominator can be a product of two binomial terms.

  For example: $\dfrac{2}{x+3} + \dfrac{3}{x-1} = \dfrac{2(x-1)}{(x+3)(x-1)} + \dfrac{3(x+3)}{(x+3)(x-1)}$

Example 18 Simplifying with more complex numerators

Simplify:

a $\dfrac{x-1}{3} - \dfrac{x+4}{5}$

b $\dfrac{2x-3}{6} - \dfrac{3-x}{5}$

SOLUTION

a
$$\dfrac{x-1}{3} - \dfrac{x+4}{5} = \dfrac{5(x-1)}{15} - \dfrac{3(x+4)}{15}$$
$$= \dfrac{5x-5-3x-12}{15}$$
$$= \dfrac{2x-17}{15}$$

b
$$\dfrac{2x-3}{6} - \dfrac{3-x}{5} = \dfrac{5(2x-3)}{30} - \dfrac{6(3-x)}{30}$$
$$= \dfrac{10x-15-18+6x}{30}$$
$$= \dfrac{16x-33}{30}$$

EXPLANATION

The LCD of 3 and 5 is 15. Insert brackets around each numerator.

Note: $-3(x+4) = -3x - 12$ not $-3x + 12$.

Determine the LCD and express as equivalent fractions. Insert brackets.

Expand the brackets, recall $-6 \times -x = 6x$ and then simplify the numerator.

Example 19 Simplifying with more complex denominators

Simplify:

a $\dfrac{4}{x+1} + \dfrac{3}{x-2}$

b $\dfrac{3}{(x-1)^2} - \dfrac{2}{x-1}$

SOLUTION

a
$$\dfrac{4}{x+1} + \dfrac{3}{x-2} = \dfrac{4(x-2)}{(x+1)(x-2)} + \dfrac{3(x+1)}{(x+1)(x-2)}$$
$$= \dfrac{4x-8+3x+3}{(x+1)(x-2)}$$
$$= \dfrac{7x-5}{(x+1)(x-2)}$$

b
$$\dfrac{3}{(x-1)^2} - \dfrac{2}{x-1} = \dfrac{3}{(x-1)^2} - \dfrac{2(x-1)}{(x-1)^2}$$
$$= \dfrac{3-2x+2}{(x-1)^2}$$
$$= \dfrac{5-2x}{(x-1)^2}$$

EXPLANATION

The lowest common multiple of $(x + 1)$ and $(x - 2)$ is $(x + 1)(x - 2)$. Rewrite each fraction with this denominator then add numerators.

Just like the LCD of 3^2 and 3 is 3^2, the LCD of $(x - 1)^2$ and $x - 1$ is $(x - 1)^2$.

Remember that $-2(x - 1) = -2x + 2$.

Exercise 8J

1 Expand the following.

a $-2(x+3)$ **b** $-5(x+1)$ **c** $-7(2+3x)$

d $-3(x-1)$ **e** $-10(3-2x)$ **f** $-16(1-4x)$

2 Write the LCD for these pairs of fractions.

a $\dfrac{1}{3}, \dfrac{5}{9}$ **b** $\dfrac{3}{16}, \dfrac{1}{8}$ **c** $\dfrac{3}{x}, \dfrac{5}{x^2}$ **d** $-\dfrac{5}{2x}, \dfrac{3}{2}$

e $\dfrac{3}{x-1}, \dfrac{2}{x+1}$ **f** $\dfrac{7}{x-2}, \dfrac{3}{x+3}$ **g** $\dfrac{4}{2x-1}, \dfrac{-1}{x-4}$ **h** $\dfrac{5}{(x+1)^2}, \dfrac{4}{x+1}$

Example 18a

3 Simplify:

a $\dfrac{x+3}{4} - \dfrac{x+2}{3}$ **b** $\dfrac{x-1}{3} - \dfrac{x+3}{5}$ **c** $\dfrac{x-4}{3} - \dfrac{x+1}{6}$

d $\dfrac{3-x}{5} - \dfrac{x+4}{2}$ **e** $\dfrac{5x-1}{4} - \dfrac{2+x}{8}$ **f** $\dfrac{3x+2}{14} - \dfrac{x+4}{4}$

g $\dfrac{1+3x}{4} - \dfrac{2x+3}{6}$ **h** $\dfrac{2-x}{5} - \dfrac{3x+1}{3}$ **i** $\dfrac{2x-3}{6} - \dfrac{4+x}{15}$

Example 18b

4 Simplify:

a $\dfrac{x+5}{3} - \dfrac{x-1}{2}$ **b** $\dfrac{x-4}{5} - \dfrac{x-6}{7}$ **c** $\dfrac{3x-7}{4} - \dfrac{x-1}{2}$

d $\dfrac{5x-9}{7} - \dfrac{2-x}{3}$ **e** $\dfrac{3x+2}{4} - \dfrac{5-x}{10}$ **f** $\dfrac{9-4x}{6} - \dfrac{2-x}{8}$

g $\dfrac{4x+3}{3} - \dfrac{5-2x}{9}$ **h** $\dfrac{2x-1}{4} - \dfrac{1-3x}{14}$ **i** $\dfrac{3x-2}{8} - \dfrac{4x-3}{7}$

Example 19a

5 Simplify:

a $\dfrac{3}{x-1} + \dfrac{4}{x+1}$ **b** $\dfrac{5}{x+4} + \dfrac{2}{x-3}$ **c** $\dfrac{3}{x-2} + \dfrac{4}{x+3}$

d $\dfrac{3}{x-4} + \dfrac{2}{x+7}$ **e** $\dfrac{7}{x+2} - \dfrac{3}{x+3}$ **f** $\dfrac{3}{x+4} - \dfrac{2}{x-6}$

g $\dfrac{-1}{x+5} + \dfrac{2}{x+1}$ **h** $\dfrac{-2}{x-3} - \dfrac{4}{x-2}$ **i** $\dfrac{3}{x-5} - \dfrac{5}{x-6}$

Example 19b

6 Simplify:

a $\dfrac{4}{(x+1)^2} - \dfrac{3}{x+1}$ **b** $\dfrac{2}{(x+3)^2} - \dfrac{4}{x+3}$ **c** $\dfrac{3}{x-2} + \dfrac{4}{(x-2)^2}$

d $\dfrac{-2}{x-5} + \dfrac{8}{(x-5)^2}$ **e** $\dfrac{-1}{x-6} + \dfrac{3}{(x-6)^2}$ **f** $\dfrac{2}{(x-4)^2} - \dfrac{3}{x-4}$

g $\dfrac{5}{(2x+1)^2} + \dfrac{2}{2x+1}$ **h** $\dfrac{9}{(3x+2)^2} - \dfrac{4}{3x+2}$ **i** $\dfrac{4}{(1-4x)^2} - \dfrac{5}{1-4x}$

7 Simplify:

a $\dfrac{3x}{(x-1)^2} + \dfrac{2}{x-1}$

b $\dfrac{3x+2}{3x} + \dfrac{7}{12}$

c $\dfrac{2x-1}{4} + \dfrac{2-3x}{10x}$

d $\dfrac{2x}{x-5} - \dfrac{x}{x+1}$

e $\dfrac{3}{4-x} - \dfrac{2x}{x-1}$

f $\dfrac{5x+1}{(x-3)^2} + \dfrac{x}{x-3}$

g $\dfrac{3x-7}{(x-2)^2} - \dfrac{5}{x-2}$

h $\dfrac{-7x}{2x+1} + \dfrac{3x}{x+2}$

i $\dfrac{x}{x+1} - \dfrac{5x+1}{(x+1)^2}$

8 One of the most common errors made when subtracting algebraic fractions is hidden in this working shown on the right:

$\dfrac{7x}{2} - \dfrac{x-2}{5} = \dfrac{35x}{10} - \dfrac{2(x-2)}{10}$

$= \dfrac{35x - 2x - 4}{10}$

$= \dfrac{33x - 4}{10}$

a What is the error and in which step is it made?

b By correcting the error how does the answer change?

9 Simplify:

a $\dfrac{1}{(x+3)(x+4)} + \dfrac{2}{(x+4)(x+5)}$

b $\dfrac{3}{(x+1)(x+2)} - \dfrac{5}{(x+1)(x+4)}$

c $\dfrac{4}{(x-1)(x-3)} - \dfrac{6}{(x-1)(2-x)}$

d $\dfrac{5x}{(x+1)(x-5)} - \dfrac{2}{x-5}$

e $\dfrac{3}{x-4} + \dfrac{8x}{(x-4)(3-2x)}$

f $\dfrac{3x}{(x+4)(2x-1)} - \dfrac{x}{(x+4)(3x+2)}$

10 Use the fact that $a - b = -1(b - a)$ to help simplify these.

a $\dfrac{3}{1-x} - \dfrac{2}{x-1}$

b $\dfrac{4x}{5-x} + \dfrac{3}{x-5}$

c $\dfrac{2}{7x-3} - \dfrac{7}{3-7x}$

d $\dfrac{1}{4-3x} + \dfrac{2x}{3x-4}$

e $\dfrac{-3x}{5-3x} - \dfrac{5}{3x-5}$

f $\dfrac{4}{x-6} + \dfrac{4}{6-x}$

Enrichment: Factorise first

11 Factorising a denominator before further simplification is a useful step. Simplify these by firstly factorising the denominators if possible.

a $\dfrac{3}{x+2} + \dfrac{5}{2x+4}$

b $\dfrac{7}{3x-3} - \dfrac{2}{x-1}$

c $\dfrac{3}{8x-4} - \dfrac{5}{1-2x}$

d $\dfrac{4}{x^2-9} - \dfrac{3}{x+3}$

e $\dfrac{5}{2x+4} + \dfrac{2}{x^2-4}$

f $\dfrac{10}{3x-4} - \dfrac{7}{9x^2-16}$

g $\dfrac{7}{x^2+7x+12} + \dfrac{2}{x^2-2x-15}$

h $\dfrac{3}{(x+1)^2-4} - \dfrac{2}{x^2+6x+9}$

i $\dfrac{3}{x^2-7x+10} - \dfrac{2}{10-5x}$

j $\dfrac{1}{x^2+x} - \dfrac{1}{x^2-x}$

8.11 Equations with algebraic fractions

For equations with more than one fraction it is often best to try to simplify the equation by dealing with all the denominators at once. This involves finding and multiplying both sides by the lowest common denominator.

Let's start: Why use the LCD?

For this equation follow each instruction

$$\frac{x+1}{3}+\frac{x}{4}=1$$

- Multiply every term in the equation by 3. What effect does this have on the fractions on the left hand side?
- Starting with the original equation, multiply every term in the equation by 4. What effect does this have on the fractions on the left hand side?
- Starting with the original equation, multiply every term in the equation by 12 and simplify.

Which instruction above does the best job in simplifying the algebraic fractions? Why?

■ For equations with more than one fraction multiply both sides by the **lowest common denominator (LCD)**.
- Multiply every term on both sides, not just the fractions.
- Simplify the fractions and solve the equation using the methods learnt earlier.

Example 20 Solving equations involving algebraic fractions

Solve each of the following equations.

a $\dfrac{2x}{3}+\dfrac{x}{2}=7$

b $\dfrac{x-2}{5}-\dfrac{x-1}{3}=1$

c $\dfrac{5}{2x}-\dfrac{4}{3x}=2$

d $\dfrac{3}{x+1}=\dfrac{2}{x+4}$

SOLUTION

EXPLANATION

a
$$\frac{2x}{3}+\frac{x}{2}=7$$

$$\frac{2x}{\cancel{3}_1}\times\cancel{6}^2+\frac{x}{\cancel{2}_1}\times\cancel{6}^3=7\times6$$

Multiply each term by the LCD (LCD of 3 and 2 is 6) and cancel.

$$4x+3x=42$$
$$7x=42$$
$$x=6$$

Simplify and solve for x.

b

$$\frac{x-2}{5} - \frac{x-1}{3} = 1$$

$$\frac{\overset{3}{\cancel{15}}(x-2)}{\cancel{5}_1} - \frac{\overset{5}{\cancel{15}}(x-1)}{\cancel{3}_1} = 15 \times 1$$

$$3(x-2) - 5(x-1) = 15$$

$$3x - 6 - 5x + 5 = 15$$

$$-2x - 1 = 15$$

$$-2x = 16$$

$$x = -8$$

Multiply each term on both sides by 15 (LCD of 3 and 5 is 15) and cancel.

Expand the brackets and simplify by combining like terms.

Note: $-5(x-1) = -5x + 5$ not $-5x - 5$.

c

$$\frac{5}{2x} - \frac{4}{3x} = 2$$

$$\frac{5}{\cancel{2x}_1} \times \cancel{6x}^{3} - \frac{4}{\cancel{3x}_1} \times \cancel{6x}^{2} = 2 \times 6x$$

$$15 - 8 = 12x$$

$$7 = 12x$$

$$\frac{7}{12} = x$$

$$x = \frac{7}{12}$$

LCD of $2x$ and $3x$ is $6x$.

Multiply each term by $6x$. Cancel and simplify.

Solve for x leaving the answer in fraction form.

d

$$\frac{3}{x+1} = \frac{2}{x+4}$$

$$\frac{3\,\cancel{(x+1)}(x+4)}{\cancel{x+1}} = \frac{2(x+1)\cancel{(x+4)}}{\cancel{x+4}}$$

$$3(x+4) = 2(x+1)$$

$$3x + 12 = 2x + 2$$

$$x + 12 = 2$$

$$x = -10$$

Multiply each term by the common denominator $(x+1)(x+4)$.

Expand the brackets.

Subtract $2x$ from both sides to gather x terms on one side then subtract 12 from both sides.

or

$$\frac{3}{x+1} = \frac{2}{x+4}$$

$$3(x+4) = 2(x+1)$$

$$3x + 12 = 2x + 2$$

$$x + 12 = 2$$

$$x = -10$$

Since each side is a single fraction you can 'cross-multiply': $\dfrac{3}{x+1} \;\bowtie\; \dfrac{2}{x+4}$

This gives the same result as above.

Exercise 8K

1 Write down the lowest common denominator of all the fractions in these equations.

a $\dfrac{x}{3} - \dfrac{2x}{5} = 1$ **b** $\dfrac{x}{2} - \dfrac{3x}{4} = 3$ **c** $\dfrac{x+1}{3} - \dfrac{x}{6} = 5$

d $\dfrac{2x-1}{7} + \dfrac{5x+2}{4} = 6$ **e** $\dfrac{x}{3} + \dfrac{x}{2} = \dfrac{1}{5}$ **f** $\dfrac{x-1}{4} - \dfrac{3x}{8} = \dfrac{1}{8}$

Understanding

2   Simplify the fractions by cancelling.

a $\dfrac{12x}{3}$

b $\dfrac{21x}{7}$

c $\dfrac{4(x+3)}{2}$

d $\dfrac{5(2x+5)}{5}$

e $\dfrac{15x}{5x}$

f $\dfrac{-7(x+1)(x+2)}{7(x+1)}$

g $\dfrac{36(x-7)(x-1)}{9(x-7)}$

h $\dfrac{18(3-2x)(1-x)}{9(3-2x)}$

i $\dfrac{-8(2-3x)(2x-1)}{-8(2-3x)}$

Example 20a   3   Solve each of the following equations.

a $\dfrac{x}{2}+\dfrac{x}{5}=7$

b $\dfrac{x}{2}+\dfrac{x}{3}=10$

c $\dfrac{y}{3}+\dfrac{y}{4}=14$

d $\dfrac{x}{2}-\dfrac{3x}{5}=-1$

e $\dfrac{5m}{3}-\dfrac{m}{2}=1$

f $\dfrac{3a}{5}-\dfrac{a}{3}=2$

g $\dfrac{3x}{4}-\dfrac{5x}{2}=14$

h $\dfrac{8a}{3}-\dfrac{2a}{5}=34$

i $\dfrac{7b}{2}+\dfrac{b}{4}=15$

Example 20b   4   Solve each of the following equations.

a $\dfrac{x-1}{2}+\dfrac{x+2}{3}=11$

b $\dfrac{b+3}{2}+\dfrac{b-4}{3}=1$

c $\dfrac{n+2}{3}+\dfrac{n-2}{2}=1$

d $\dfrac{a+1}{5}-\dfrac{a+1}{6}=2$

e $\dfrac{x+5}{2}-\dfrac{x-1}{4}=3$

f $\dfrac{x+3}{2}-\dfrac{x+1}{3}=2$

g $\dfrac{m+4}{3}-\dfrac{m-4}{4}=3$

h $\dfrac{2a-8}{2}+\dfrac{a+7}{6}=1$

i $\dfrac{2y-1}{4}-\dfrac{y-2}{6}=-1$

5   Solve each of the following equations.

a $\dfrac{x+1}{2}=\dfrac{x}{3}$

b $\dfrac{x-2}{3}=\dfrac{x}{2}$

c $\dfrac{n+3}{4}=\dfrac{n-1}{2}$

d $\dfrac{a+2}{3}=\dfrac{a+1}{2}$

e $\dfrac{3+y}{2}=\dfrac{2-y}{3}$

f $\dfrac{2m+4}{4}=\dfrac{m+6}{3}$

Example 20c   6   Solve each of the following equations.

a $\dfrac{3}{4x}-\dfrac{1}{2x}=4$

b $\dfrac{2}{3x}-\dfrac{1}{2x}=2$

c $\dfrac{4}{2m}-\dfrac{2}{5m}=3$

d $\dfrac{1}{2x}-\dfrac{1}{4x}=9$

e $\dfrac{1}{2b}+\dfrac{1}{b}=2$

f $\dfrac{1}{2y}+\dfrac{1}{3y}=4$

g $\dfrac{1}{3x}+\dfrac{1}{2x}=2$

h $\dfrac{2}{3x}-\dfrac{1}{x}=2$

i $\dfrac{7}{2a}-\dfrac{2}{3a}=1$

Example 20d   7   Solve each of the following equations.

a $\dfrac{3}{x+1}=\dfrac{1}{x+2}$

b $\dfrac{2}{x+3}=\dfrac{3}{x+2}$

c $\dfrac{2}{x+5}=\dfrac{3}{x-2}$

d $\dfrac{1}{x-3}=\dfrac{1}{2x+1}$

e $\dfrac{2}{x-1}=\dfrac{1}{2x+1}$

f $\dfrac{1}{x-2}=\dfrac{2}{3x+2}$

8 Half of a number (x) plus one-third of twice the same number is equal to 4.

   a Write an equation describing the situation.

   b Solve the equation to find the number.

9 Use your combined knowledge of all the methods learnt earlier to solve these equations with algebraic fractions.

  a $\dfrac{2x+3}{1-x}=4$ **b** $\dfrac{5x+2}{x+2}=3$ **c** $\dfrac{3x-2}{x-1}=2$

  d $\dfrac{2x}{3}+\dfrac{x-1}{4}=2x-1$ **e** $\dfrac{3}{x^2}-\dfrac{2}{x}=\dfrac{5}{x}$ **f** $\dfrac{1-3x}{x^2}+\dfrac{3}{2x}=\dfrac{4}{x}$

  g $\dfrac{x-1}{2}+\dfrac{3x-2}{4}=\dfrac{2x}{3}$ **h** $\dfrac{4x+1}{3}-\dfrac{x-3}{6}=\dfrac{x+5}{6}$ **i** $\dfrac{1}{x+2}-\dfrac{2}{x-3}=\dfrac{5}{(x+2)(x-3)}$

10 Molly and Billy each have the same number of computer games (x computer games each). Hazel takes one-third of Molly's computer games and a quarter of Billy's computer games to give her a total of 77 computer games.

   a Write an equation describing the total number of computer games for Hazel.

   b Solve the equation to find how many computer games Molly and Billy each had.

11 A common error when solving equations with algebraic fractions is made in this working. Find the error and explain how to avoid it.

$$\frac{3x-1}{4}+2x=\frac{x}{3} \qquad (\text{LCD}=12)$$

$$\frac{12(3x-1)}{4}+2x=\frac{12x}{3}$$

$$3(3x-1)+2x=4x$$

$$9x-3+2x=4x$$

$$7x=3$$

$$x=\frac{3}{7}$$

12 Another common error is made in this working. Find and explain how to avoid this error.

$$\frac{x}{2} - \frac{2x-1}{3} = 1 \qquad (\text{LCD} = 6)$$

$$\frac{6x}{2} - \frac{6(2x-1)}{3} = 6$$

$$3x - 2(2x - 1) = 6$$

$$3x - 4x - 2 = 6$$

$$-x = 8$$

$$x = -8$$

13 A similar technique to that used in Questions **11** and **12** can be used to solve equations with decimals. Here is an example.

$$0.8x - 1.2 = 2.5$$

$$8x - 12 = 25 \quad \text{Multiply both sides by 10 to remove all decimals.}$$

$$8x = 37$$

$$x = \frac{37}{8}$$

Solve these decimal equations using the same idea. For parts **d–f** you will need to multiply by 100.

a $0.4x + 1.4 = 3.2$ **b** $0.3x - 1.3 = 0.4$ **c** $0.5 - 0.2x = 0.2$

d $1.31x - 1.8 = 2.13$ **e** $0.24x + 0.1 = 3.7$ **f** $2 - 3.25x = 8.5$

Enrichment: Literal equations

14 Solve each of the following equations for x in terms of the other pronumerals.
Hint: You may need to use factorisation.

a $\dfrac{x}{a} - \dfrac{x}{2a} = b$ **b** $\dfrac{ax}{b} - \dfrac{cx}{2} = d$ **c** $\dfrac{x-a}{b} = \dfrac{x}{c}$

d $\dfrac{x+a}{b} = \dfrac{d+e}{c}$ **e** $\dfrac{ax+b}{4} = \dfrac{x+c}{3}$ **f** $\dfrac{x+a}{3b} + \dfrac{x-a}{2b} = 1$

g $\dfrac{2a-b}{a} + \dfrac{a}{x} = a$ **h** $\dfrac{1}{a} - \dfrac{1}{x} = \dfrac{1}{c}$ **i** $\dfrac{a}{x} = \dfrac{b}{c}$

j $\dfrac{a}{x} + b = \dfrac{c}{x}$ **k** $\dfrac{ax-b}{x-b} = c$ **l** $\dfrac{cx+b}{x+a} = d$

m $\dfrac{2a+x}{a} = b$ **n** $\dfrac{1}{x-a} = \dfrac{1}{ax+b}$ **o** $\dfrac{a}{b} - \dfrac{a}{a+x} = 1$

Expanding quadratics using area

Consider the expansion of the quadratic $(x + 3)(x + 6)$. This can be represented by finding the area of the diagram shown.

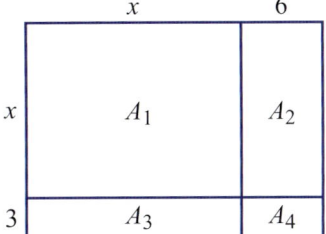

Total area $= A_1 + A_2 + A_3 + A_4$
$= x^2 + 6x + 3x + 18$

Therefore:

$(x + 3)(x + 6) = x^2 + 9x + 18$

Expanding with positive signs

a Draw a diagram and calculate the area to determine the expansion of the following quadratics.

i $(x + 4)(x + 5)$ **ii** $(x + 7)(x + 8)$

iii $(x + 3)^2$ **iv** $(x + 5)^2$

b Using the same technique establish the rule for expanding $(a + b)^2$.

Expanding with negative signs

Consider the expansion of $(x - 4)(x - 7)$.

Area required $=$ total area $- (A_2 + A_3 + A_4)$
$= x^2 - [(A_2 + A_4) + (A_3 + A_4) - A_4]$
$= x^2 - (7x + 4x - 28)$
$= x^2 - 11x + 28$

Therefore:

$(x - 4)(x - 7) = x^2 - 11x + 28$

a Draw a diagram and calculate the area to determine the expansion of the following quadratics.

i $(x - 3)(x - 5)$

ii $(x - 6)(x - 4)$

iii $(x - 4)^2$

iv $(x - 2)^2$

This area is counted twice when we add $7x + 4x$.

b Using the same technique establish the rule for expanding $(a - b)^2$.

Difference of perfect squares

Using a diagram to represent $(a - b)(a + b)$, determine the appropriate area and establish a rule for the expansion of $(a - b)(a + b)$.

Numerical applications of perfect squares

The expansion and factorisation of perfect squares and difference of perfect squares can be applied to the mental calculation of some numerical problems.

Evaluating a perfect square

The perfect square 32^2 can be evaluated using $(a + b)^2 = a^2 + 2ab + b^2$.
$$32^2 = (30 + 2)^2 \quad \text{(Let } a = 30, b = 2)$$
$$= 30^2 + 2(30)(2) + 2^2$$
$$= 900 + 120 + 4$$
$$= 1024$$

a Use the same technique to evaluate these perfect squares.

i	22^2	**ii**	21^2	**iii**	33^2	**iv**	51^2
v	1.2^2	**vi**	3.2^2	**vii**	6.1^2	**viii**	9.01^2

Similarly, the perfect square 29^2 can be evaluated using $(a - b)^2 = a^2 - 2ab + b^2$.
$$29^2 = (30 - 1)^2 \quad \text{(Let } a = 30, b = 1)$$
$$= 30^2 - 2(30)(1) + 1^2$$
$$= 900 - 60 + 1$$
$$= 841$$

b Use the same technique to evaluate these perfect squares.

i	19^2	**ii**	39^2	**iii**	98^2	**iv**	87^2
v	1.9^2	**vi**	4.7^2	**vii**	8.8^2	**viii**	3.96^2

Evaluating the difference of perfect squares

The difference of perfect squares $14^2 - 9^2$ can be evaluated using $a^2 - b^2 = (a + b)(a - b)$.
$$14^2 - 9^2 = (14 + 9)(14 - 9) \quad \text{(Let } a = 14, b = 9)$$
$$= 23 \times 5$$
$$= 115$$

a Use the same technique to evaluate these difference of perfect squares.

i	$13^2 - 8^2$	**ii**	$25^2 - 23^2$	**iii**	$42^2 - 41^2$	**iv**	$85^2 - 83^2$
v	$1.4^2 - 1.3^2$	**vi**	$4.9^2 - 4.7^2$	**vii**	$1001^2 - 1000^2$	**viii**	$2.01^2 - 1.99^2$

The expansion $(a + b)(a - b) = a^2 - b^2$ can also be used to evaluate some products. Here is an example:
$$31 \times 29 = (30 + 1)(30 - 1) \text{ (Let } a = 30, b = 1)$$
$$= 30^2 - 1^2$$
$$= 900 - 1$$
$$= 899$$

b Use the same technique to evaluate these products.

i	21×19	**ii**	32×28	**iii**	63×57	**iv**	105×95
v	2.1×1.9	**vi**	7.4×6.6	**vii**	520×480	**viii**	915×885

1 **a** The difference between the squares of two consecutive numbers is 97. What are the two numbers?

b The difference between the squares of two consecutive odd numbers is 136. What are the two numbers?

c The difference between the squares of two consecutive multiples of 3 is 81. What are the two numbers?

2 **a** If $x^2 + y^2 = 6$ and $(x + y)^2 = 36$, find the value of xy?

b If $x + y = 10$ and $xy = 2$, find the value of $\dfrac{1}{x} + \dfrac{1}{y}$?

3 Find the values of the different digits a, b, c and d if the four digit number $abcd \times 4 = dcba$.

4 **a** Find the quadratic rule that relates the width n to the number of matches in the pattern below.

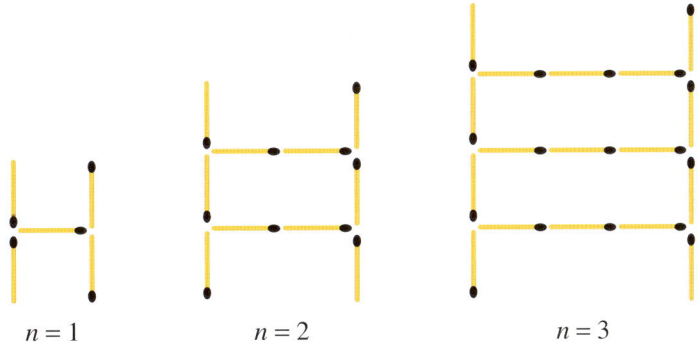

$n = 1$ $n = 2$ $n = 3$

b Draw a possible pattern for these rules.

   i $n^2 + 3$

   ii $n(n - 1)$

5 Factorise $n^2 - 1$ and use the factorised form to explain why when n is prime and greater than 3, $n^2 - 1$ is:

i divisible by 4

ii divisible by 3

iii thus divisible by 12.

6 Prove that this expression is equal to 1.

$$\frac{2x^2 - 8}{5x^2 - 5} \div \frac{x - 2}{5x - 5} \div \frac{2x^2 - 10x - 28}{x^2 - 6x - 7}$$

7 Prove that $4x^2 - 4x + 1 \geq 0$ for all x.

8 In a race over 4 km Ryan ran at a constant speed. Sophie, however, ran the first 2 km at a speed 1 km/h more than Ryan and ran the second 2 km at a speed 1 km/h less than Ryan. Who won the race?

Monic quadratic trinomials

These are of the form:
$x^2 + bx + c$
Require two numbers that multiply to c and add to b
e.g. $x^2 - 7x - 18 = (x - 9)(x + 2)$
since $-9 \times 2 = -18$
and $-9 + 2 = -7$

DOPS

$a^2 - b^2 = (a - b)(a + b)$
e.g. $x^2 - 16 = x^2 - 4^2$
$= (x - 4)(x + 4)$
e.g. $4x^2 - 9 = (2x)^2 - 3^2$
$= (2x - 3)(2x + 3)$

Expansion

The process of removing brackets

e.g. $2(x + 5) = 2x + 10$

$(x + 3)(2x - 4) = x(2x - 4) + 3(2x - 4)$
$= 2x^2 - 4x + 6x - 12$
$= 2x^2 + 2x - 12$

Special cases

DOPS (difference of perfect squares)
$(a - b)(a + b) = a^2 - b^2$
e.g. $(x - 5)(x + 5) = x^2 + 5x - 5x - 25$
$= x^2 - 25$

Perfect squares
$(a + b)^2 = a^2 + 2ab + b^2$
$(a - b)^2 = a^2 - 2ab + b^2$
e.g. $(2x + 3)^2 = (2x + 3)(2x + 3)$
$= 4x^2 + 6x + 6x + 9$
$= 4x^2 + 12x + 9$

Factorisation

The reverse process of expansion. Always remove the highest common factor first.

e.g. $2ab + 8b$ HCF = $2b$
$= 2b(a + 4)$
e.g. $3(x + 2) + y(x + 2)$ HCF = $x + 2$
$= (x + 2)(3 + y)$

Algebra

Add/subtract

Must find lowest common denominator (LCD) before applying operation

e.g. $\dfrac{2}{3x} + \dfrac{3}{x + 1}$

$= \dfrac{2(x + 1)}{3x(x + 1)} + \dfrac{3x \times 3}{3x(x + 1)}$

$= \dfrac{2(x + 1) + 9x}{3x(x + 1)}$

$= \dfrac{2x + 2 + 9x}{3x(x + 1)}$

$= \dfrac{11x + 2}{3x(x + 1)}$

Algebraic fractions

These involve algebraic expressions in the numerator and/or denominator

e.g. $\dfrac{2x}{x - 7}, \dfrac{3}{5x}, \dfrac{7}{(x - 1)^2}$

By grouping

If there are four terms, we may be able to group into two binomial terms
e.g. $2ax + 4a - 3bx - 6b$
$= 2a(x + 2) - 3b(x + 2)$
$= (x + 2)(2a - 3b)$
Note: $3a(x - 4) + x - 4$
$= 3a(x - 4) + 1(x - 4)$
$= (x - 4)(3a + 1)$

Multiply/divide

To divide, multiply by the reciprocal. Factorise all expressions, cancel and then multiply.

e.g. $\dfrac{3}{x^2 - 9} \div \dfrac{15}{2x + 6}$

$= \dfrac{3^{\,1}}{(x - 3)(x + 3)_1} \times \dfrac{2(x + 3)^{\,1}}{15^{\,5}}$

$= \dfrac{2}{5(x - 3)}$

Trinomials of the form $ax^2 + bx + c$

Can be factorised using grouping also
e.g. $3x^2 + 7x - 6$, $3 \times (-6) = -18$
$= 3x^2 + 9x - 2x - 6$, $9 + (-2) = 7$
$= 3x(x + 3) - 2(x + 3)$
$= (x + 3)(3x - 2)$

Solving equations with algebraic fractions

Find lowest common denominator (LCD) and multiply every term by the LCD.
e.g. LCD of $2x$ and $3x$ is $6x$
     LCD of $(x - 1)$ and $(x + 3)$
     is $(x - 1)(x + 3)$
     LCD of $2x$ and x^2 is $2x^2$

Multiple-choice questions

1 $(2x - 1)(x + 5)$ in expanded and simplified form is:

  A $2x^2 + 9x - 5$ **B** $x^2 + 11x - 5$ **C** $4x^2 - 5$

  D $3x^2 - 2x + 5$ **E** $2x^2 + 4x - 5$

2 $(3a + 2b)^2$ is equivalent to:

  A $9a^2 + 6ab + 4b^2$ **B** $9a^2 + 4b^2$ **C** $3a^2 + 6ab + 2b^2$

  D $3a^2 + 12ab + 2b^2$ **E** $9a^2 + 12ab + 4b^2$

3 $16x^2 - 49$ in factorised form is:

  A $(4x - 7)^2$ **B** $(16x - 49)(16x + 49)$ **C** $(2x - 7)(8x + 7)$

  D $(4x - 7)(4x + 7)$ **E** $4(4x^2 - 49)$

4 The factorised form of $b^2 + 3b - 2b - 6$ is:

  A $(b - 3)(b + 2)$ **B** $b - 2(b + 3)^2$ **C** $(b + 3)(b - 2)$

  D $b - 2(b + 3)$ **E** $b(b + 3) - 2$

5 If $(x - 2)$ is a factor of $x^2 + 5x - 14$ the other factor is:

  A x **B** $x + 7$ **C** $x - 7$ **D** $x - 16$ **E** $x + 5$

6 The factorised form of $3x^2 + 10x - 8$ is:

  A $(3x + 1)(x - 8)$

  B $(x - 4)(3x + 2)$

  C $(3x + 2)(x + 5)$

  D $(3x - 2)(x + 4)$

  E $(x + 1)(3x - 8)$

7 The simplified form of $\dfrac{3x + 6}{x^2 + 6x + 5} \times \dfrac{x + 5}{x + 2}$ is:

  A $\dfrac{3}{x + 1}$ **B** $\dfrac{15}{2x^2 + 5}$ **C** $x + 3$ **D** $\dfrac{5}{x + 2}$ **E** $3(x + 5)$

8 $\dfrac{x + 2}{5} + \dfrac{2x - 1}{3}$ written as a single fraction is:

  A $\dfrac{11x + 1}{15}$ **B** $\dfrac{11x + 9}{8}$ **C** $\dfrac{3x + 1}{8}$ **D** $\dfrac{11x + 7}{15}$ **E** $\dfrac{13x + 1}{15}$

9 The LCD of $\dfrac{3x + 1}{2x}$ and $\dfrac{4}{x + 1}$ is:

  A $8x$ **B** $2x(x + 1)$ **C** $(x + 1)(3x + 1)$

  D $8x(3x + 1)$ **E** $x(x + 1)$

10 The solution to $\dfrac{3}{1 - x} = \dfrac{4}{2x + 3}$ is:

  A $x = -\dfrac{1}{2}$ **B** $x = -\dfrac{9}{11}$ **C** $x = \dfrac{1}{7}$ **D** $x = 2$ **E** $x = -\dfrac{4}{5}$

Short-answer questions

1 Expand the following binomial products.

    a $(x-3)(x+4)$ **b** $(x-7)(x-2)$

    c $(2x-3)(3x+2)$ **d** $3(x-1)(3x+4)$

2 Expand the following.

    a $(x+3)^2$ **b** $(x-4)^2$ **c** $(3x-2)^2$

    d $(x-5)(x+5)$ **e** $(7-x)(7+x)$ **f** $(11x-4)(11x+4)$

3 Write the following in fully factorised form by removing the highest common factor.

    a $4a+12b$ **b** $6x-9x^2$ **c** $-5x^2y-10xy$

    d $3(x-7)+x(x-7)$ **e** $x(2x+1)-(2x+1)$ **f** $(x-2)^2-4(x-2)$

4 Factorise the following DOPS.

    a x^2-100 **b** $3x^2-48$ **c** $25x^2-y^2$

    d $49-9x^2$ **e** $(x-3)^2-81$ **f** $1-x^2$

5 Factorise the following by grouping.

    a $x^2-3x+2xy-6y$

    b $4ax+10x-2a-5$

    c $3x-8b+2bx-12$

6 Factorise the following trinomials.

    a $x^2+8x+15$ **b** $x^2-3x-18$ **c** x^2-7x+6 **d** $3x^2+15x-42$

    e $2x^2+16x+32$ **f** $5x^2+17x+6$ **g** $4x^2-4x-3$ **h** $6x^2-17x+12$

7 Simplify the following.

    a $\dfrac{3x+12}{3}$ **b** $\dfrac{2x-16}{3x-24}$ **c** $\dfrac{x^2-9}{5(x+3)}$

8 Simplify the following algebraic fractions by first factorising and cancelling where possible.

    a $\dfrac{3}{2x}\times\dfrac{x}{6}$ **b** $\dfrac{x(x-4)}{8(x+1)}\times\dfrac{4(x+1)}{x}$ **c** $\dfrac{(x^2+3x)}{3x+6}\times\dfrac{x+2}{x+3}$

    d $\dfrac{2x}{5x+20}\div\dfrac{x}{x+4}$ **e** $\dfrac{x^2+5x+6}{x+3}\div\dfrac{x^2-4}{4x-8}$ **f** $\dfrac{4x^2-9}{10x^2}\div\dfrac{10x-15}{x}$

9 Simplify the following by first finding the lowest common denominator.

    a $\dfrac{x}{4}+\dfrac{2x}{3}$ **b** $\dfrac{x-1}{6}-\dfrac{x+3}{8}$ **c** $\dfrac{3}{4x}+\dfrac{1}{2x}$

    d $\dfrac{7}{x}-\dfrac{2}{x^2}$ **e** $\dfrac{3}{x+1}+\dfrac{5}{x+2}$ **f** $\dfrac{7}{(x-4)^2}-\dfrac{2}{x-4}$

10 Solve the following equations involving fractions.

    a $\dfrac{x}{4}+\dfrac{2x}{5}=13$ **b** $\dfrac{4}{x}-\dfrac{2}{3x}=20$

    c $\dfrac{x+3}{2}+\dfrac{x-4}{3}=6$ **d** $\dfrac{4}{1-x}=\dfrac{5}{x+4}$

Extended-response questions

1   A pig pen for a small farm is being redesigned. It is originally a square of side length x m.

   a   In the planning the length is initially kept as x m and the width altered such that the area of the pen is $(x^2 + 3x)$ square metres. What is the new width?

   b   Instead, it is determined that the original length will be increased by 1 metre and the original width will be decreased by 1 metre.

      i   What effect does this have on the perimeter of the pig pen compared with the original size?

      ii   Determine an expression for the new area of the pig pen in expanded form. How does this compare to the original area?

   c   The final set of dimensions requires an extra 8 m of fencing to go around the pen compared with the original pen. If the length of the pen has been increased by 7 m, then the width of the pen must decrease. Find:

      i   what change has been made to the width of the pen

      ii   the new area enclosed by the pen

      iii   what happens when $x = 3$.

2   The security tower for a palace is on a small square piece of land 20 m by 20 m with a moat of width x metres the whole way around it as shown.

   a   State the area of the piece of land.

   b   i   Give expressions for the length and the width of the combined moat and land.

      ii   Find an expression, in expanded form, for the entire area occupied by the moat and the land.

   c   If the tower occupies an area of $(x + 10)^2$ m^2, what fraction of the total area in part **b ii** is this?

   d   Use your answers to parts **a** and **b** to give an expression for the area occupied by the moat alone, in factorised form.

   e   Use trial and error to find the value of x such that the area of the moat alone is 500 m^2.

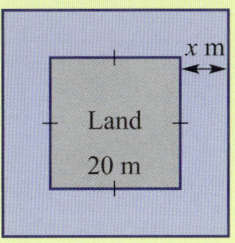

Chapter 9 Probability and statistics

What you will learn

Are lotteries worth it?

The probability of winning first division in a lottery such as Tattslotto (also known as Saturday Lotto and Gold Lotto), based on the choice of six numbers chosen from 45, is 1 in 8 145 060. This means that you would expect to win first division once in every eight million, one hundred and forty-five thousand and sixty attempts. This is calculated by counting the number of possible ways of winning as well as the total number of ways that six numbers can be drawn from 45. If you played 1 game per week every week of the year, you would expect to win once every 1562 centuries. Many thousands of people take this chance every week. Looking at the statistics, adults in Australia gamble an average of about $1000 per year trying their luck in various national and state lotteries and other games of chance.

Pre-test

1 Write the following as decimals.

   a $\dfrac{1}{10}$ b $\dfrac{2}{8}$ c 30%   d 85%   e 23.7%

2 Express in simplest form.

   a $\dfrac{4}{8}$ b $\dfrac{7}{21}$ c $\dfrac{20}{30}$ d $\dfrac{100}{100}$ e $\dfrac{0}{4}$

   f $\dfrac{12}{144}$ g $\dfrac{36}{72}$ h $\dfrac{36}{58}$ i $\dfrac{72}{108}$ j $\dfrac{2}{7}$

3 A six-sided die is tossed.

   a List the possible outcomes.

   b How many of the outcomes are:

      i even   ii less than 3   iii less than or equal to 3

      iv at least 2   v not a 6   vi not odd

4 One number is selected from the group of the first 10 integers {1, 2, …, 10}. How many of the numbers are:

   a odd   b less than 8   c greater than or equal to 5

   d no more than 7   e prime   f not prime

5 Several cards were randomly selected from a pack of playing cards. The suit of each card was noted, the card was replaced and the pack was shuffled. The frequency of each suit is shown in the column graph.

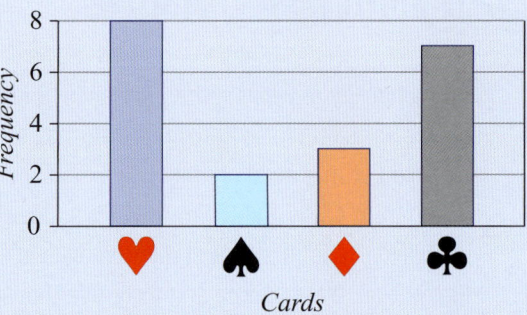

   a How many times was a heart selected?

   b How many times was a card selected in total?

   c In what fraction of the trials was a diamond selected?

6 Consider this simple data set: 1, 2, 3, 5, 5, 7, 8, 10, 13.

   a Find the mean.

   b Find the median (the middle value).

   c Find the mode (most common value).

   d Find the range (difference between highest and lowest value).

   e Find the probability of randomly selecting:

      i a 5

      ii a number which is not 5

      iii a number which is no more than 5

9.1 Probability review

The mathematics associated with describing chance is called probability. We can precisely calculate the chance of some events occurring like rolling a sum of 12 from two dice or flipping 3 heads if a coin is tossed 5 times. To do this we need to know how many outcomes there are in total and how many of the outcomes are favourable (i.e. which match the result we are interested in). The number of favourable outcomes in comparison to the total number of outcomes will determine how likely it is that the favourable event will occur.

Using probability we can find the likelihood of rolling a particular total score with two dice.

Let's start: Choose an event

As a class group, write down and discuss at least three events which have the following chance of occurring.

- impossible chance
- very low chance
- medium to low chance
- even (50–50) chance
- medium to high chance
- very high chance
- certain chance

Key ideas

- A **random experiment** results in a list of **outcomes** which occur without interference.
- The **sample space** is the list of all possible outcomes of an experiment.
- An **event** is a collection of outcomes resulting from an experiment.
  For example, rolling a die is a random experiment with six possible outcomes: 1, 2, 3, 4, 5 and 6. The event 'rolling a number greater than 4' includes the outcomes 5 and 6.
- The probability of an event where all outcomes are **equally likely** is given by:

$$\text{Pr(Event)} = \frac{\text{Number of outcomes where event occurs}}{\text{Total number of outcomes}}$$

- Probabilities are numbers between 0 and 1 and can be written as a decimal, fraction or percentage. For example: 0.55 or $\frac{11}{20}$ or 55%

- For all events, $0 \leq \text{Pr(Event)} \leq 1$.

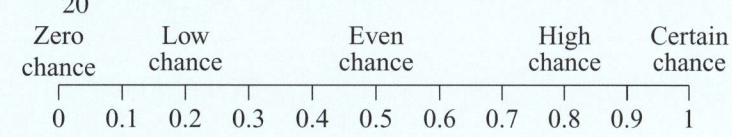

- The **complement** of an event A is the event where A does not occur.

$$\text{Pr(not A)} = 1 - \text{Pr(A)}$$

Example 1 Finding probabilities of events

This spinner has five equally divided sections.

a   List the sample space using the given numbers.
b   Find Pr(3).
c   Find Pr(not a 3).
d   Find Pr(a 3 or a 7).
e   Find Pr(a number which is at least a 3).

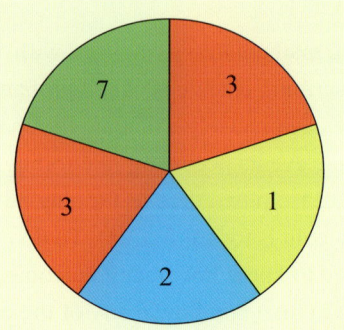

SOLUTION

a   {1, 2, 3, 3, 7}

b $Pr(3) = \dfrac{2}{5}$ or 0.4

c   Pr (not a 3) = 1 − Pr(3)

$\qquad = 1 - \dfrac{2}{5}$ or 1 − 0.6

$\qquad = \dfrac{3}{5}$ or 0.4

d $Pr(\text{a 3 or a 7}) = \dfrac{2}{5} + \dfrac{1}{5}$

$\qquad\qquad\qquad = \dfrac{3}{5}$

e $Pr(\text{at least a 3}) = \dfrac{3}{5}$

EXPLANATION

Use set brackets and list all the possible outcomes in any order.

$Pr(3) = \dfrac{\text{number of sections labelled 3}}{\text{number of equal sections}}$

'Not a 3' is the complementary event of obtaining a 3.

Alternatively, count the number of sectors which are not 3.

There are two 3s and one 7 in the five sections.

Three of the sections have the numbers 3 or 7 which are 3 or more.

Example 2 Choosing letters from a word

A letter is randomly chosen from the word PROBABILITY. Find the following probabilities.

a   Pr(L)
b   Pr(not L)
c   Pr(vowel)
d   Pr(consonant)
e   Pr(vowel or a B)
f   Pr(vowel or consonant)

SOLUTION

a $Pr(L) = \dfrac{1}{11}$

EXPLANATION

One of the 11 letters is an L.

b $Pr(\text{not } L) = 1 - \dfrac{1}{11}$

$\qquad = \dfrac{10}{11}$

The event 'not L' is the complement of the event selecting an L. Complementary events sum to 1.

c $Pr(\text{vowel}) = \dfrac{4}{11}$

There are 4 vowels: O, A and two letter Is.

d $Pr(\text{consonant}) = 1 - \dfrac{4}{11}$

$\qquad\qquad = \dfrac{7}{11}$

The events 'vowel' and 'consonant' are complementary.

e $Pr(\text{vowel or a B}) = \dfrac{6}{11}$

There are 4 vowels and 2 letter Bs.

f $Pr(\text{vowel or consonant}) = 1$

This event includes all possible outcomes.

Exercise 9A

Understanding

1 Jim believes that there is a 1 in 4 chance that the flower on his prized rose will bloom tomorrow.
  a Write the chance '1 in 4' as:
    i a fraction **ii** a decimal **iii** a percentage
  b Draw a number line from 0 to 1 and mark the level of chance described by Jim.

2 Copy and complete this table.

	Percentage	Decimal	Fraction	Number line
a	50%	0.5	$\dfrac{1}{2}$	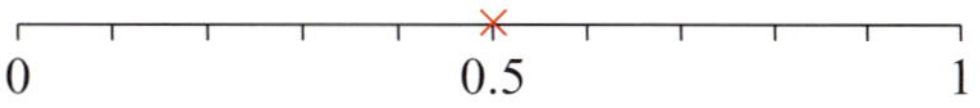 0 —— 0.5 (×) —— 1
b	25%			
c			$\dfrac{3}{4}$	
d				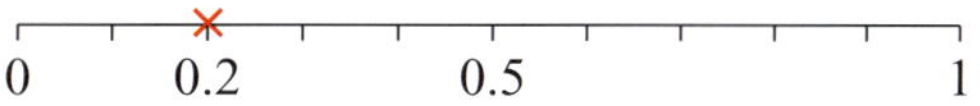 0 — 0.2 (×) — 0.5 —— 1
e		0.6		
f			$\dfrac{17}{20}$	

3 Ten people make the following guesses of the chance that they will get a salary bonus this year.

$0.7, \dfrac{2}{5}, 0.9, \dfrac{1}{3}, 2 \text{ in } 3, \dfrac{3}{7}, 1 \text{ in } 4, 0.28, \dfrac{2}{9}, 0.15$

Can you order their chances from lowest to highest? (*Hint:* change each into a decimal.)

Example 1

4 The spinners below have equally divided sections. Complete the following for each spinner.

    i List the sample space using the given numbers.   **ii** Find Pr(2).

    iii Find Pr(not a 2).   **iv** Find Pr(a 2 or a 3).

    v Find Pr(a number which is at least a 2).

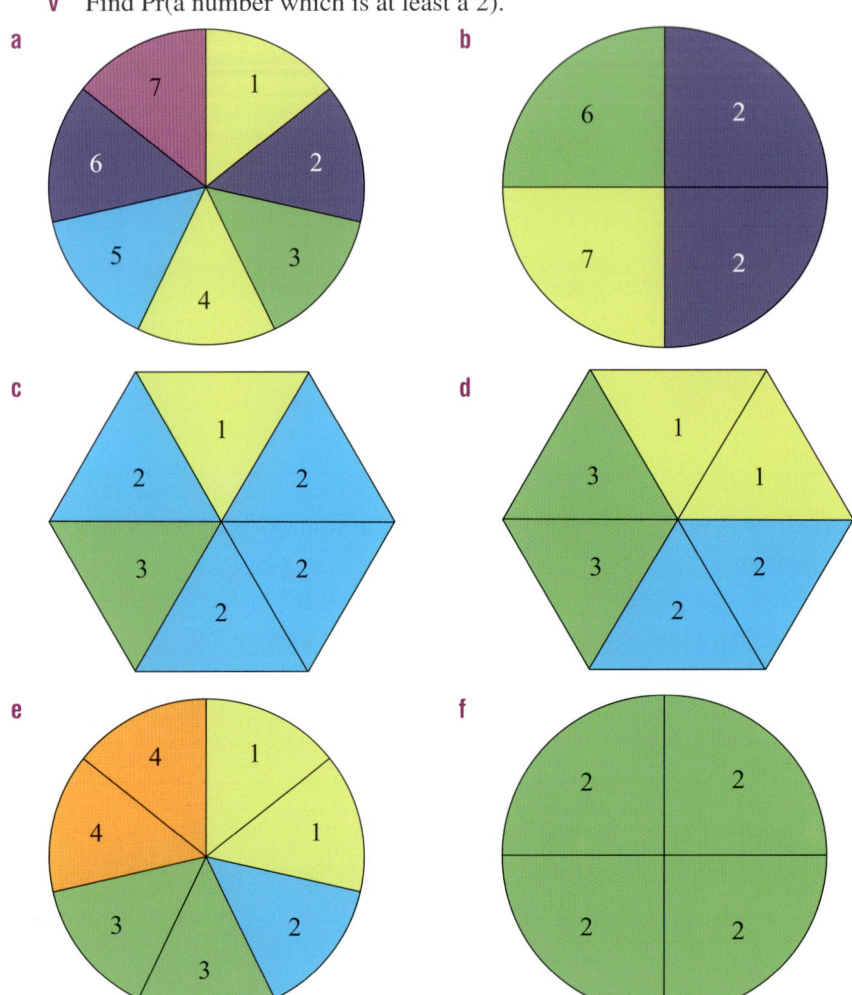

a   **b**

c   **d**

e   **f**

5 Find the probability of obtaining a blue ball if a ball is selected at random from a box which contains:

    a 4 blue balls and 4 red balls

    b 3 blue balls and 5 red balls

    c 1 blue ball, 3 red balls and 2 white balls

    d 8 blue balls, 15 black balls and 9 green balls

    e 15 blue balls only

    f 5 yellow balls and 2 green balls.

6 Find the probability of *not* selecting a blue ball if a ball is selected at random from a box containing the balls described in Question **5** parts **a** to **f** above.

7 If a swimming pool has eight lanes and each of eight swimmers has an equal chance of being placed in lane 1, find the probability that a particular swimmer:

a will swim in lane 1

b will not swim in lane 1.

8 A letter is chosen at random from the word ALPHABET. Find the following probabilities.

a Pr(L)   **b** Pr(A)

c Pr(A or L)   **d** Pr(vowel)

e Pr(consonant)   **f** Pr(vowel or consonant)

g Pr(Z)   **h** Pr(A or Z)

i Pr(not an A)   **j** Pr(letter from the first half of the alphabet)

9 The school captain is to be chosen at random from four candidates. Two are girls (Hayley and Alisa) and two are boys (Rocco and Stuart).

a List the sample space.

b Find the probability that the school captain will be:

    i Hayley   **ii** male   **iii** neither Stuart nor Alisa

10 From a pack of 52 playing cards a card is drawn at random. The pack includes 13 black spades, 13 black clubs, 13 red hearts and 13 red diamonds. This includes four of each of ace, king, queen, jack, 2, 3, 4, 5, 6, 7, 8, 9 and 10. Find the probability that the card will be:

a the queen of diamonds   **b** an ace

c a red king   **d** a red card

e a jack or a queen   **f** any card except a 2

g any card except a jack or a black queen

h not a black ace.

11 A six-sided die is tossed and the upper-most face is observed and recorded. Find the following probabilities.

a Pr(6)   **b** Pr(3)   **c** Pr(not a 3)

d Pr(1 or 2)   **e** Pr(a number less than 5)   **f** Pr(even number or odd number)

g Pr(square number)   **h** Pr(not a prime number)   **i** Pr(a number greater than 1)

12 A letter is chosen at random from the word PROBABILITY. Find the probability that the letter will be:

a a B   **b** not a B   **c** a vowel

d not a vowel   **e** a consonant

f a letter belonging to one of the first five letters in the alphabet

g a letter from the word RABBIT   **h** a letter that is not in the word RABBIT.

13 Amanda selects a letter from the word SOLO and writes $Pr(S) = \frac{1}{3}$. Explain her error.

14 A six-sided die is rolled. Which of the following events have a probability equal to $\frac{1}{3}$?

   a more than 4   **b** at least 4

   c less than or equal to 3   **d** no more than 2

   e at most 4   **f** less than 3

15 A number is selected from the set $\{1, 2, 3, \ldots , 25\}$. Find the probability that the number chosen is:

   a a multiple of 2   **b** a factor of 24   **c** a square number

   d a prime number   **e** divisible by 3   **f** divisible by 3 or 2

   g divisible by 3 and 2   **h** divisible by 2 or 3 or 7   **i** divisible by 13 and 7.

Enrichment: Faulty CD player

16 A compact disc (CD) contains eight tracks. The time
length for each track is as shown in the table on the right.

    The CD is placed in a faulty CD player which begins
playing randomly at an unknown place somewhere on the
CD, not necessarily at the beginning of a track.

   a Find the total number of minutes of music available
on the CD.

   b Find the probability that the CD player will begin
playing somewhere on track 1.

   c Find the probability that the CD player will begin
somewhere on:

Track	Time (minutes)
1	3
2	4
3	4
4	5
5	4
6	3
7	4
8	4

    i track 2   **ii** track 3   **iii** a track that is 4 minutes long

    iv track 4   **v** track 7 or 8   **vi** a track that is not 4 minutes long.

9.2 Venn diagrams and two-way tables

When the results of an experiment involve overlapping categories it can be very helpful to organise the information into a Venn diagram or two-way table. Probabilities can easily be calculated from these types of diagrams.

Let's start: Mac or PC

Twenty people were surveyed to find out whether or not they owned a Mac or PC computer at home. The survey revealed that 8 people owned a Mac and 15 people owned a PC. All people surveyed owned at least one type of computer.

- Do you think some people owned both a Mac and PC? Discuss.
- Use these diagrams to help organise the number of people who own Macs and PCs.

Venn diagram

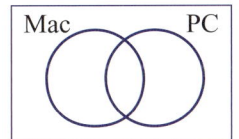

Two-way table

	Mac	No Mac	Total
PC			
No PC			
Total			

- Use your diagrams to describe the proportion (fraction) of people owning Macs and/or PCs for all the different areas in the diagrams.

Survey data such as computer ownership can be helpfully displayed in Venn diagrams and two-way tables.

■ A **Venn diagram** and a **two-way table** help to organise outcomes into different categories. This example shows the type of computers owned by 100 people.

Venn diagram

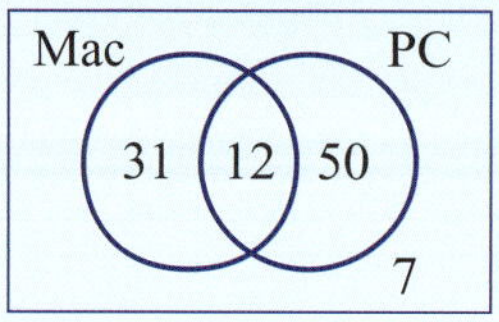

Two-way table

	Mac	**No Mac**	**Total**
PC	12	50	62
No PC	31	7	38
Total	43	57	100

These diagrams show, for example:

- 12 people own both a Mac and a PC
- 62 people own a PC
- 57 people do not own a Mac

- $\Pr(\text{Mac}) = \dfrac{43}{100}$

- $\Pr(\text{only Mac}) = \dfrac{31}{100}$

- $\Pr(\text{Mac or PC}) = \dfrac{93}{100}$

- $\Pr(\text{Mac and PC}) = \dfrac{12}{100} = \dfrac{3}{25}$

Example 3 Using a Venn diagram

A survey of 30 people found that 21 like AFL and 12 like soccer. Also 7 people like both AFL and soccer and 4 like neither AFL nor soccer.

a   Construct a Venn diagram for the survey results.
b   How many people:
   i   like AFL or soccer   ii   do not like soccer   iii   like only AFL?
c   If one of the 30 people was randomly selected, find:
   i   Pr(like AFL and soccer)
   ii   Pr(like neither AFL nor soccer)
   iii   Pr(like only soccer)

SOLUTION

a

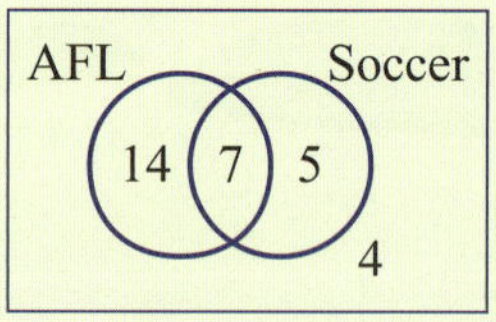

EXPLANATION

Place the appropriate number in each category ensuring that:

- the total that like AFL is 21
- the total that like soccer is 12

b i 26

The total number of people that like AFL, soccer or both is $14 + 7 + 5 = 26$.

   ii $30 - 12 = 18$

12 like soccer so 18 do not.

   iii 14

21 like AFL but 7 of these also like soccer.

c i Pr(like AFL and soccer)

7 out of 30 people like AFL and soccer.

   $= \dfrac{7}{30}$

   ii Pr(like neither AFL nor soccer)

The 4 people who like neither AFL nor soccer sit outside both categories.

   $= \dfrac{4}{30}$

   $= \dfrac{2}{15}$

   iii Pr(like soccer only)

5 people like soccer but not AFL.

   $= \dfrac{5}{30}$

   $= \dfrac{1}{6}$

Example 4 Using a two-way table

At a car yard, 24 cars are tested for fuel economy. Eighteen of the cars run on petrol, 8 cars run on gas and 3 cars can run on both petrol and gas.

a Illustrate the situation using a two-way table.

b How many of the cars:
   i do not run on gas?   **ii** run on neither petrol nor gas?

c Find the probability that a randomly selected car:
   i runs on gas   **ii** runs on only gas   **iii** runs on gas or petrol

SOLUTION

EXPLANATION

a

	Gas	Not gas	Total
Petrol	3	15	18
Not petrol	5	1	6
Total	8	16	24

Set up a table as shown and enter the numbers (in black) from the given information.

Fill in the remaining numbers (in red) ensuring that each column and row adds to the correct total.

b i 16

ii 1

The total at the base of the 'Not gas' column is 16.

The number at the intersection of the 'Not gas' column and the 'Not petrol' row is 1.

c i $\Pr(\text{gas}) = \dfrac{8}{24}$

$= \dfrac{1}{3}$

8 cars in total run on gas out of the 24 cars.

ii $\Pr(\text{only gas}) = \dfrac{5}{24}$

Of the 8 cars that run on gas, 5 of them do not also run on petrol.

iii $\Pr(\text{gas or petrol}) = \dfrac{15+5+3}{24}$

$= \dfrac{23}{24}$

Of the 24 cars, some run on petrol only (15), some run on gas only (5) and some run on gas and petrol (3).

Exercise 9B

Understanding

1 This Venn diagram shows the number of people who enjoy riding and running.

a How many people in total are represented by this Venn diagram?

b How many people enjoy:
   i   only riding
   ii riding (in total)
   iii only running
   iv running (in total)
   v   both riding and running
   vi neither riding nor running
   vii riding or running?

c How many people do not enjoy:
   i   riding
   ii running?

2 Match the diagrams A, B, C or D with the given description.
   a S
   b S only
   c S and T
   d S or T

A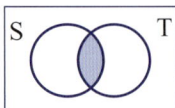

B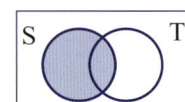

C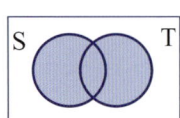

D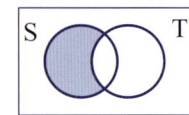

3 Fill in the missing numbers in these two-way tables.

a

	A	not A	Total
B	7	8	
not B		1	
Total	10		

b

	A	not A	Total
B	2		7
not B		4	
Total			20

ample 3 **4** In a class of 30 students, 22 carried a phone and 9 carried an iPod. Three carried both a phone and an iPod and 2 students carried neither.

    a Represent the information using a Venn diagram.

    b How many people:

       i carried a phone or an iPod (includes carrying both)

       ii do not carry an iPod

       iii carry only an iPod

    c If one of the 30 people were selected at random, find the following probabilities.

       i Pr(carry a phone and an iPod)

       ii Pr(carry neither a phone nor an iPod)

       iii Pr(carry only a phone)

5 For each simple Venn diagram, find the following probabilities. You will need to calculate the total number in the sample first.

    i Pr(A)   **ii** Pr(A only)   **iii** Pr(not B)

    iv Pr(A and B)   **v** Pr(A or B)   **vi** Pr(neither A nor B)

a
```
 A         B
  ( 5 (1) 7 )
          2
```

b
```
 A            B
  ( 12 (3) 19 )
            1
```

ample 4 **6** From 50 desserts served at a restaurant one evening, 25 were served with ice cream, 21 were served with cream and 5 were served with both cream and ice cream.

    a Illustrate the situation using a two-way table.

    b How many of the desserts:

       i did not have cream

       ii had neither cream nor ice cream?

    c Find the probability that a chosen dessert:

       i had cream

       ii had only cream

       iii had cream or ice cream.

7 Find the following probabilities using each of the given tables. First fill in the missing numbers.

    i Pr(A)   **ii** Pr(not A)   **iii** Pr(A and B)

    iv Pr(A or B)   **v** Pr(B only)   **vi** Pr(neither A nor B)

a

	A	not A	Total
B	3	1	
not B	2		4
Total			

b

	A	not A	Total
B		4	15
not B	6		
Total			26

8 For each two-way table, fill in the missing numbers then transfer the information to a Venn diagram.

a

	A	not A	Total
B	2		8
not B			
Total		7	12

b

	A	not A	Total
B		4	
not B	9		13
Total	12		

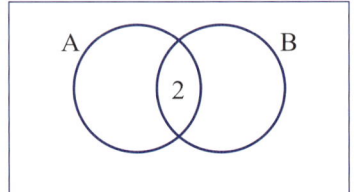

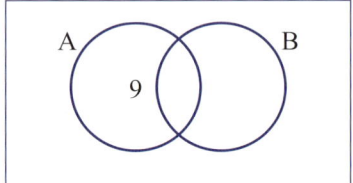

9 In a group of 10 people, 6 rented their house, 4 rented a car and 3 did not rent either a car or their house.
   a Draw a Venn diagram.
   b How many people rented both a car and their house?
   c Find the probability that one of them rented only a car.

10 One hundred citizens were surveyed regarding their use of water for their garden. 23 said that they use rain water, 48 said that they used tap water and 41 said that they did not water at all.
   a Represent this information in a two-way table.
   b How many people used both rain and tap water?
   c What is the probability that one of the people uses only tap water?
   d What is the probability that one of the people uses tap water or rain water?

11 All members of a ski club enjoy either skiing and/or snowboarding. Seven enjoy only snowboarding, 16 enjoy skiing and 4 enjoy both snowboarding and skiing. How many people are in the ski club?

12 Of a group of 30 cats, 24 eat tinned or dry food, 10 like dry food and 5 like both tinned and dry food. Find the probability that a selected cat likes only tinned food.

13 Complete the two-way table and transfer to a Venn diagram using the pronumerals w, x, y and z.

	A	not A	Total
B	x	y	
not B	z	w	
Total			

→

14 The total number of people in a survey is T. The number of males in the survey is x and the number of doctors is y. The number of doctors that are males is z. Write algebraic expressions for the following using any of the variables x, y, z and T.

a The number who are neither male nor a doctor.

b The number who are not males.

c The number who are not doctors.

d The number who are male but not a doctor.

e The number who are a doctor but not male.

f The number who are female and a doctor.

g The number who are female or a doctor.

15 Explain what is wrong with this two-way table. Try to complete it to find out.

	A	not A	Total
B		12	
not B			7
Total	11		19

16 How many numbers need to be given in a two-way table so that all numbers in the table can be calculated?

Enrichment: Finding a rule for A and B

17 Two overlapping events, A and B, include 20 elements with 0 elements in the 'neither A nor B' region.

a Draw a Venn diagram for the following situations.

  i the number in A is 12 and the number in B is 10.

  ii the number in A is 15 and the number in B is 11.

  iii the number in A is 18 and the number in B is 6.

b If the total number in A or B is now 100 (not 20), complete a Venn diagram for the following situations.

  i the number in A is 50 and the number in B is 60.

  ii the number in A is 38 and the number in B is 81.

  iii the number in A is 83 and the number in B is 94.

c Now describe a method that finds the number in the common area for A and B. Your method should work for all the above examples.

9.3 Using set notation

Using symbols to describe different sets of objects can make the writing of mathematics more efficient and easier to read. For example, *the probability that a randomly chosen person likes both apples and bananas could be written* Pr(A ∩ B) provided the events A and B are clearly defined.

→ Let's start: English language meaning to mathematical meaning

Two events called A and B are illustrated in this Venn diagram. Use your understanding of the English language meaning of the given words to match with one of the mathematical terms and a number from the Venn diagram. They are in jumbled order.

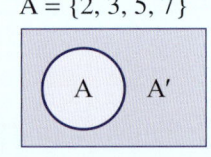

English		Mathematical		Number in Venn diagram	
a	not A	A	A union B	i	1
b	A or B	B	sample space	ii	7
c	A and B	C	complement of A	iii	13
d	anyone	D	A intersection B	iv	17

- The **sample space** (list of all possible outcomes) is sometimes called the universal set and is given the symbol S, Ω, U or ξ.

  For example, $\Omega = \{1, 2, 3, 4, 5, 6, 7, 8, 9, 10\}$

- A is a particular **subset** (⊂) of the sample space if all the elements in A are contained in the sample space. For example, A is the set of prime numbers less than or equal to 10 which is a subset of all the integers less than 10.

  $A = \{2, 3, 5, 7\}$

  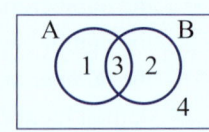

- A′ is the complement of A and contains the elements not in A.

  $A' = \{1, 4, 6, 8, 9, 10\}$

- $5 \in A$ means that 5 is **an element of** A.
- ∅ is the **null** or **empty** set and contains no elements. ∴ ∅ = { }
- $n(A)$ is the **cardinal number** of A and means the number of elements in A. $n(A) = 4$

  A Venn diagram can be used to illustrate how different subsets in the sample space are grouped.

  For example: A = {2, 3, 5, 7}
  B = {1, 3, 5, 7, 9}

- A ∩ B means A **and** B which means the **intersection** of A and B and includes the elements in common with both sets. ∴ A ∩ B = {3, 5, 7}
- A ∪ B means A **or** B which means the **union** of A and B and includes the elements in either A or B or both. ∴ A ∪ B = {1, 2, 3, 5, 7, 9}
- A **only** is the elements in A but not in B. ∴ A only = {2}

Example 5 Using set notation

A number is chosen from the set of positive integers between 1 and 8 inclusive. A is the set of odd numbers between 1 and 8 inclusive and B is the set of prime numbers between 1 and 8 inclusive.

a List the sets: **i** the sample space   **ii** A   **iii** B

b Draw a Venn diagram.

c List the sets: **i** $A \cap B$ **ii** $A \cup B$ **iii** A' **iv** B only

d Find: **i** $n(A)$ **ii** $Pr(A)$ **iii** $n(A \cap B)$ **iv** $Pr(A \cap B)$

SOLUTION

EXPLANATION

a **i** $\{1, 2, 3, 4, 5, 6, 7, 8\}$

List all the numbers, using set brackets.

    ii $A = \{1, 3, 5, 7\}$

A includes all the odd numbers.

    iii $B = \{2, 3, 5, 7\}$

B includes all the prime numbers. 1 is not prime.

b

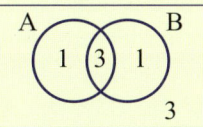

Place each cardinal number into the appropriate region, i.e. there are 3 numbers common to sets A and B so 3 is placed in the overlapping region.

c **i** $A \cap B = \{3, 5, 7\}$

$\{3, 5, 7\}$ are common to both A and B.

    ii $A \cup B = \{1, 2, 3, 5, 7\}$

$\{1, 2, 3, 5, 7\}$ are in either A or B or both.

    iii $A' = \{2, 4, 6, 8\}$

A' means the elements not in A.

    iv B only $= \{2\}$

B only means the elements in B but not in A.

d **i** $n(A) = 4$

$n(A)$ is the cardinal number of A. There are four elements in A.

    ii $Pr(A) = \dfrac{4}{8} = \dfrac{1}{2}$

$Pr(A)$ means the chance that the element will belong to A. There are 4 numbers in A compared with 8 in the sample space.

    iii $n(A \cap B) = 3$

There are three elements in $A \cap B$.

    iv $Pr(A \cap B) = \dfrac{3}{8}$

Three out of eight elements are in $A \cap B$.

Exercise 9C

1 Match each of the terms in the first list with the symbols in the second list.

    a complement   **A** $\cap$

    b union   **B** $n(A)$

    c element of   **C** A'

    d intersection   **D** $\cup$

    e empty or null set   **E** $\in$

    f number of elements   **F** $\varnothing$

Understanding

2 Choose a diagram that matches each of these sets.

   a $A \cup B$ **b** A' **c** $A \cap B$ **d** B only

A

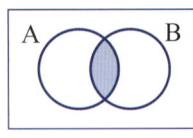

B

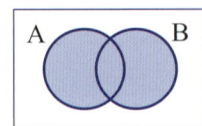

C

D

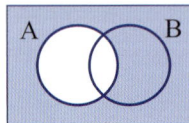

3 Using the given two-way table, find the following.

   a $n(A \cap B)$

   b $n(B)$

   c $n(A)$

   d $n(A')$

	A	A'	Total
B	2	8	10
B'	5	1	6
Total	7	9	16

Example 5

4 A number is chosen from the set of positive integers between 1 and 10 inclusive. If A is the set of odd numbers between 1 and 10 inclusive and B is the set of prime numbers between 1 and 10 inclusive:

   a list the sets:

     i the sample space   **ii** A   **iii** B

   b draw a Venn diagram.

   c list the sets:

     i $A \cap B$ **ii** $A \cup B$ **iii** A' **iv** B only

   d find:

     i $n(A)$ **ii** $Pr(A)$ **iii** $n(A \cap B)$ **iv** $Pr(A \cap B)$

5 A number is chosen from the set of positive integers between 1 and 20 inclusive. If A is the set of multiples of 3 less than 20 and B is the set of factors of 15:

   a draw a Venn diagram.

   b list the sets:

     i $A \cap B$ **ii** $A \cup B$ **iii** A' **iv** B only

   c find:

     i $n(B)$ **ii** $Pr(B)$ **iii** $n(A \cap B)$

     iv $Pr(A \cap B)$ **v** $n(A \cup B)$ **vi** $Pr(A \cup B)$

6 Consider the sample space $\{1, 2, 3, 4, 5, 6\}$ and the sets A = $\{1, 4, 7\}$ and B = $\{2, 3, 5\}$.

   a State whether the following are true (T) or false (F).

     i $A \subset$ the sample space   **ii** $B \subset$ the sample space

     iii $3 \in A$ **iv** $5 \in B$

     v $n(B) = 3$ **vi** $n(B') = 2$

     vii $A \cap B = \varnothing$ **viii** $A \cup B = \varnothing$

   b Find the following probabilities.

     i $Pr(B)$ **ii** $Pr(B')$ **iii** $Pr(A \cap B)$

7 For each diagram, find the following probabilities.

   i Pr(A∩B)   **ii** Pr(A∪B)   **iii** Pr(A′)

a

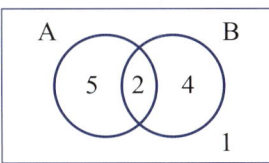

b

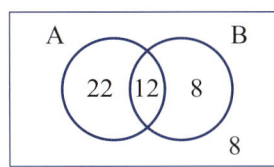

c

	A	A′	Total
B	5	2	
B′			
Total	9		15

d

	A	A′	Total
B		8	13
B′	4		
Total		12	

8 Four students have the names FRED, RON, RACHEL and HELEN while the sets A, B and C are defined by:

   A = {students with a name including the letter R}

   B = {students with a name including the letter E}

   C = {students with a name including the letter Z}

a List the sets:

   i A   **ii** B

   iii C   **iv** A ∩ B

b If a student is chosen at random from the group, find these probabilities.

   i Pr(A)   **ii** Pr(A′)

   iii Pr(C)   **iv** Pr(C′)

   v Pr(A ∩ B)   **vi** Pr(A ∪ B)

9 Consider all the letters of the alphabet. Let A = {the set of vowels} and B = {letters of the word MATHEMATICS}. Find:

   a n(sample space)   **b** n(A)

   c n(A ∩ B)   **d** n(B′)

   e Pr(A)   **f** Pr(A′)

   g Pr(A ∩ B)   **h** Pr(A∪B)

10 From 50 people all of which have at least a cat or a dog, let A be the set of all pet owners who have a dog and B be the set of all pet owners who have a cat. If n(A) = 32 and n(B) = 29, find the following.

   a n(A ∩ B)   **b** n(A only)

   c Pr(A ∪ B)   **d** Pr(A′)

How many people have both a dog and a cat?

11 From Question **10**, A is the set of dog owners and B is the set of cat owners. Write a brief description of the following groups of people.
   a $A \cap B$ **b** $A \cup B$
   c B' **d** B only

12 **a** Is $n(A) + n(B)$ ever equal to $n(A \cup B)$? If so, show an example using a Venn diagram.
    b Is $n(A) + n(B)$ ever less than $n(A \cup B)$? Explain.

13 The region A only could be thought of as the intersection of A and the complement of B so A only $= A \cap B'$. Use set notation to describe the region 'B only'.

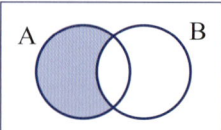

14 The four inner regions of a two-way table can be described using intersections. The A only region is described by $n(A \cap B')$. Describe the other three regions using intersections.

	A	A′	Total
B			$n(B)$
B′	$n(A \cap B')$		$n(B')$
Total	$n(A)$	$n(A')$	$n(\text{sample space})$

15 Research what it means if we say that two events A and B are **mutually exclusive**. Give a brief description.

Enrichment: How are A′ ∩ B′ and (A ∪ B)′ related?

16 Consider the set of integers $\{1, 2, 3, \ldots, 20\}$. Let A = {prime numbers less than 20} and B = {factors of 12}.
   a List:
      i A   **ii** B   **iii** $A \cap B$
      iv $A \cup B$ **v** $A' \cap B$ **vi** $A \cap B'$
      vii $A' \cup B$ **viii** $A \cup B'$ **ix** $A' \cup B'$
   b Find the following probabilities.
      i $\Pr(A \cup B)$ **ii** $\Pr(A \cap B)$ **iii** $\Pr(A' \cap B)$ **iv** $\Pr(A' \cap B')$
      v $\Pr(A \cup B')$ **vi** $\Pr((A \cap B)')$ **vii** $\Pr(A' \cup B')$ **viii** $\Pr((A \cup B)')$
   c Draw Venn diagrams to shade the regions $A' \cap B'$ and $(A \cup B)'$. What do you notice?

9.4 Multiple events using tables

When an experiment consists of two multiple events like tossing two dice or selecting two people from a group, we can use a table to systematically list the sample space.

Let's start: Is it a 1 in 3 chance?

Billy tosses two coins on the kitchen table at home and asks what the chance is of getting two tails.

- Dad says that there are 3 outcomes: two heads, two tails or one of each, so there is a 1 in 3 chance.
- Mum says that with coins, all outcomes have a 1 in 2 chance of occurring.
- Billy's sister Betty says that there are 4 outcomes so it's a 1 in 4 chance.

Can you explain who is correct and why?

Tossing one coin gives a 1 in 2 chance of heads or tails, but what are the chances of getting two tails with two coins?

■ **Multiple events** consist of more than one component. They are also called **compound events** or **multi-stage experiments**.
■ A table is often used to list the sample space for multiple events with two components.
■ When listing outcomes it is important to be consistent with the order for each outcome. For example: the outcome (heads, tails) is different from the outcome (tails, heads).
■ Some experiments are conducted **without replacement** which means some outcomes that may be possible **with replacement** are not possible.
  For example: Two letters are chosen from the word CAT.

Key ideas

With replacement

		1st		
		C	A	T
	C	(C, C)	(A, C)	(T, C)
2nd	A	(C, A)	(A, A)	(T, A)
	T	(C, T)	(A, T)	(T, T)

9 outcomes

Without replacement

		1st		
		C	A	T
	C	×	(A, C)	(T, C)
2nd	A	(C, A)	×	(T, A)
	T	(C, T)	(A, T)	×

6 outcomes

Example 6 Finding the sample space for events with replacement

Two coins are tossed.

a Draw a table to list the sample space.   **b** Find the probability of obtaining (H, T).

c Find Pr(1 head).

SOLUTION

EXPLANATION

a

		Toss 1	
		H	T
Toss 2	H	(H, H)	(T, H)
	T	(H, T)	(T, T)

Sample space = {(H, H), (H, T), (T, H), (T, T)}

Represent the results of each coin toss.

The table shows four possible outcomes.

b $\Pr(H, T) = \dfrac{1}{4}$

One of the four outcomes is (H, T).

c $\Pr(1 \text{ head}) = \dfrac{2}{4} = \dfrac{1}{2}$

Two outcomes have one head: (H, T), (T, H).

Example 7 Finding the sample space for events without replacement

Two letters are chosen from the word TREE without replacement.

a List the outcomes in a table.

b Find the probability that the two letters chosen are both E.

c Find the probability that at least one of the letters is an E.

SOLUTION

EXPLANATION

a

		1st			
		T	R	E	E
	T	×	(R, T)	(E, T)	(E, T)
2nd	R	(T, R)	×	(E, R)	(E, R)
	E	(T, E)	(R, E)	×	(E, E)
	E	(T, E)	(R, E)	(E, E)	×

List all the outcomes maintaining a consistent order. Note that the same letter cannot be chosen twice. Both Es need to be listed so that each outcome in the sample space is equally likely.

b $\Pr(E, E) = \dfrac{2}{12}$

$= \dfrac{1}{6}$

Since there are 2 Es in the word TREE it is still possible to obtain the outcome (E, E) in two ways.

c $\Pr(\text{at least one E}) = \dfrac{10}{12}$

$= \dfrac{5}{6}$

10 of the 12 outcomes contain at least one E.

Exercise 9D

1 Fill in these tables to show all the outcomes then count the total number of outcomes. Parts **a** and **b** are *with replacement* and parts **c** and **d** are *without replacement*.

a

		1st		
		1	2	3
	1	(1, 1)	(2, 1)	
2nd	2			
	3			

b

		Die					
		1	2	3	4	5	6
Coin	H	(1, H)					
	T			(3, T)			

c

		1st		
		A	B	C
	A	×	(B, A)	(C, A)
2nd	B		×	
	C			×

d

		1st		
		•	○	○
	•	×	(○, •)	
2nd	○		×	(○, ○)
	○			×

2 These two tables list the outcomes for the selection of two letters from the word MAT.

Table A

	M	A	T
M	(M, M)	(A, M)	(T, M)
A	(M, A)	(A, A)	(T, A)
T	(M, T)	(A, T)	(T, T)

Table B

	M	A	T
M	×	(A, M)	(T, M)
A	(M, A)	×	(T, A)
T	(M, T)	(A, T)	×

a Which table shows selection where replacement is allowed (with replacement)?

b Which table shows selection where replacement is not allowed (without replacement)?

c What is the probability of choosing the outcome (T, M) from:
  i Table A
  ii Table B?

d How many outcomes include the letter A using:
  i Table A   **ii** Table B?

3 Two dot circles are selected, one from each of the sets A and B where A = {•, ○} and B = {•, ○, ○}.

a Copy and complete this table, showing all the possible outcomes.

b State the total number of outcomes.

c Find the probability that the outcome will:
  i be (•, ○)
  ii contain one black dot
  iii contain two of the same dots.

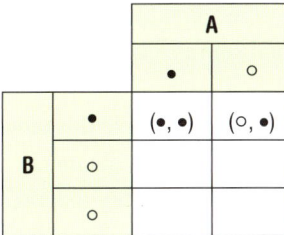

Example 6 **4** Two four-sided dice (numbered 1, 2, 3, 4) are tossed.

a Complete a table like the one shown and list the sample space.

b Find the probability of obtaining (2, 3).

c Find Pr(double). A double is an outcome with two of the same number.

		1st			
		1	2	3	4
2nd	1	(1, 1)	(2, 1)		
	2				
	3				
	4				

5 A six-sided die is tossed twice.

a Complete a table like the one shown.

b What is the total number of outcomes?

c Find the probability that the outcome is:

i (1, 1)

ii a double

iii (3, 1), (2, 2) or (1, 3)

iv any outcome containing a 1 or a 6.

		1st					
		1	2	3	4	5	6
2nd	1	(1, 1)	(2, 1)				
	2						
	3						
	4						
	5						
	6						

Example 7 **6** Two letters are chosen from the word DOG *without replacement*.

a Complete the given table.

b Find the probability of obtaining the (G, D) outcome.

c Find the probability of obtaining an outcome with an O in it.

		1st		
		D	O	G
2nd	D	×	(O, D)	(G, D)
	O		×	
	G			×

7 Two digits are selected *without replacement* from the set {1, 2, 3, 4}.

a Draw a table to show the sample space. Remember doubles like (1, 1), (2, 2) etc. are not allowed.

b Find: i Pr(1, 2) ii Pr(4, 3)

c Find the probability that:

i both numbers will be at least 3

ii the outcome will contain a 1 or a 4

iii the outcome will contain a 1 and a 4

iv the outcome will not contain a 3.

8 The total sum is recorded from tossing two four-sided dice.

a Copy and complete this table, showing all possible totals that can be obtained.

b Find the probability that the total sum is:

i 2

ii 2 or 3

iii less than or equal to 4

iv more than 6 v at most 6

		Toss 1			
		1	2	3	4
Toss 2	1	2	3		
	2				
	3				
	4				

9 Jill guesses the answers to two multiple-choice questions with options A, B, C, D or E.

Problem-solving

		Guess 1				
		A	**B**	**C**	**D**	**E**
Guess 2	**A**	(A, A)	(B, A)			
	B					
	C					
	D					
	E					

  a Copy and complete this table, showing all possible guesses that can be obtained.

  b Find the probability that she will guess:

  i (D, A)

  ii the same letter

  iii different letters.

  c Find the probability that Jill will get:

  i exactly one of her answers correct

  ii both of her answers correct.

10 Many board games involve the tossing of two six-sided dice.

  a Use a table to help find the probability that the sum of the two dice is:

  i 12   **ii** 2 or 3

  iii 11 or 12   **iv** less than or equal to 7

  v less than 7   **vi** at least 10

  vii at most 4   **viii** 1

  b Which total sum has the highest probability and what is the probability of tossing that sum?

Reasoning

11 Two letters are chosen from the word MATHEMATICIAN.

  a How many outcomes sit in the sample space if selections are made:

  i with replacement?   **ii** without replacement?

  b How many of the outcomes contain the same letter if selection is made:

  i with replacement?   **ii** without replacement?

12 Two letters are chosen from the word WOOD without replacement. Is it possible to obtain the outcome (O, O)? Explain why.

13 In a bag are five counters each of a different colour: green (G), yellow (Y), red (R), blue (B) and purple (P).

   a If one counter is drawn from the bag, replaced and then a second is selected, find the probability that a green counter then a blue counter is selected. That is, find Pr(G, B).

   b If the first counter selected is not replaced before the second is selected, find the probability that a green counter then a blue counter is selected.

14 A six-sided die and a ten-sided die have been tossed simultaneously. What total sum(s) has the highest probability?

15 A spinner numbered 1 to 50 is spun twice. Find the probability that the total from the two spins is:

   a 100   **b** 51   **c** 99   **d** 52   **e** 55

Enrichment: Two cards from the deck

16 Two cards are dealt to you from a pack of playing cards which includes four of each of {2, 3, 4, 5, 6, 7, 8, 9, 10, J, Q, K, A}. You keep both cards.

   a Does this situation involve with replacement or without replacement?

   b How many outcomes would there be in your sample space (all possible selections of two cards)?

   c What is the probability of receiving an ace of diamonds and an ace of hearts?

   d Find the probability of obtaining two cards which:

      i are both twos

      ii are both hearts.

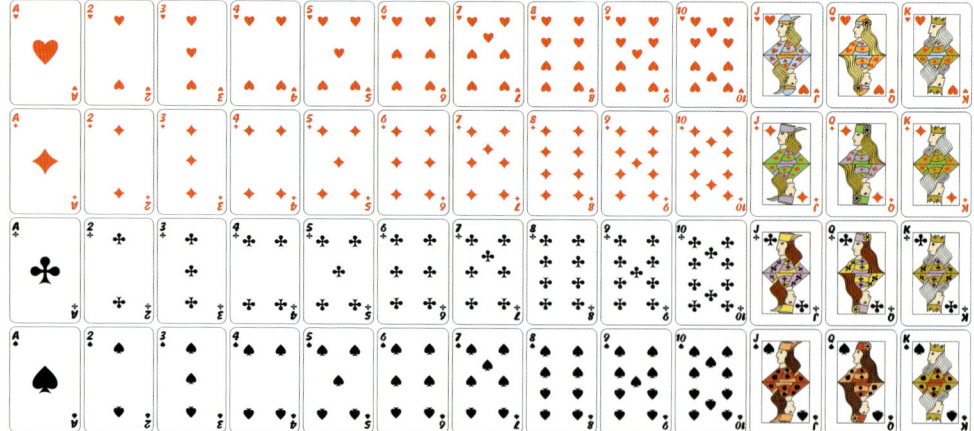

9.5 Tree diagrams

When multistage experiments consist of two or more components, a tree diagram can be used to list the sample space. While tables are often used for two-step experiments, a tree diagram can be extended for experiments with any number of steps.

Let's start: What's the difference?

You are offered a choice of two pieces of fruit from a banana, an apple and an orange. You choose two at random. This tree diagram shows selection with replacement.

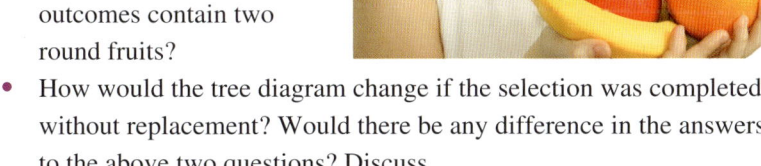

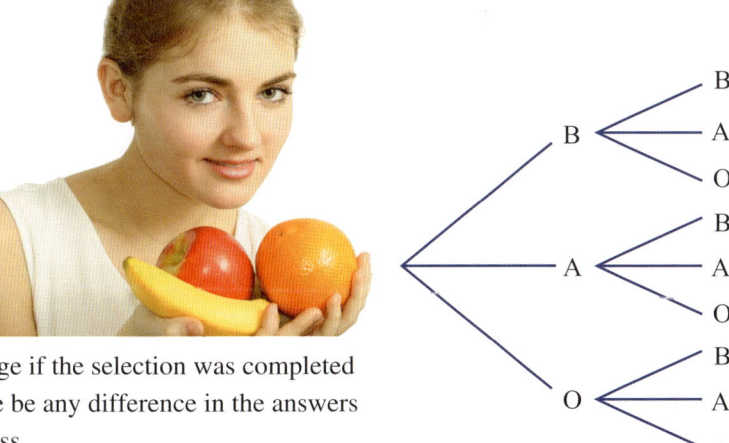

- How many outcomes will there be?
- How many of the outcomes contain two round fruits?
- How would the tree diagram change if the selection was completed without replacement? Would there be any difference in the answers to the above two questions? Discuss.

- **Tree diagrams** are used to list the sample space for multistage experiments with two or more steps.
  - The outcomes for each stage of the experiment are listed vertically and each stage is connected with branches.

    For example:

    Tossing a coin 3 times (with replacement)   Outcomes

    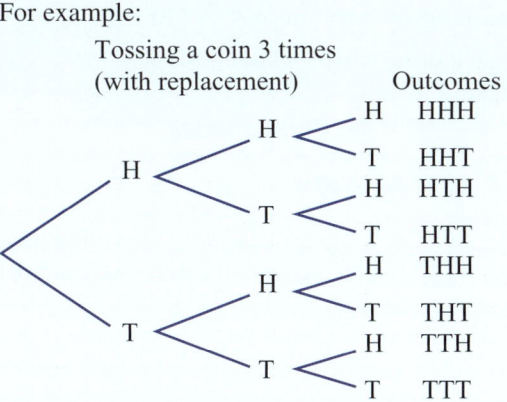

    Selecting 2 letters from {A, B, C} without replacement   Outcomes

    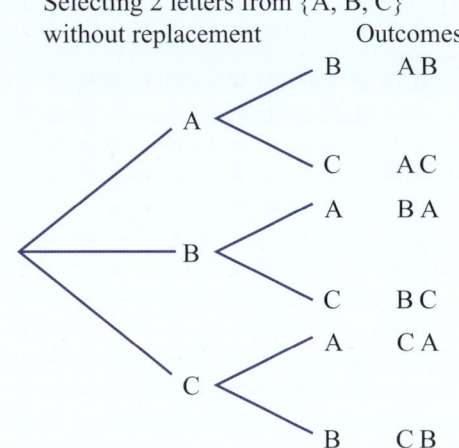

    In these examples, each set of branches produce outcomes which are all equally likely.

Key ideas

Example 8 Constructing a tree diagram

An experiment involves tossing two coins.
a Complete a tree diagram to show all possible outcomes.
b What is the total number of outcomes?
c Find the probability of tossing:
    i two tails   **ii** one tail   **iii** at least one head

SOLUTION

a

Toss 1	Toss 2	Outcomes

```
            H ─── HH
      H ──<
            T ─── HT

            H ─── TH
      T ──<
            T ─── TT
```

b The total number of outcomes = 4

c **i** $\Pr(TT) = \dfrac{1}{4}$

    ii $\Pr(1 \text{ tail}) = \dfrac{2}{4} = \dfrac{1}{2}$

    iii $\Pr(\geq 1 \text{ head}) = \dfrac{3}{4}$

EXPLANATION

Tree diagram shows two coin tosses one after the other resulting in $2 \times 2 = 4$ outcomes.

There are four possibilities in the outcomes column.

One out of the four outcomes is TT.
Two outcomes have one tail:
{HT, TH}
Three outcomes have at least one head:
{HH, HT, TH}

Example 9 Constructing a tree diagram without replacement

Two people are selected without replacement from a group of three: Annabel (A), Brodie (B) and Chris (C).
a List all the possible combinations for the selection using a tree diagram.
b Find the probability that the selection will contain:
    i Annabel and Brodie   **ii** Chris   **iii** Chris or Brodie

SOLUTION

a

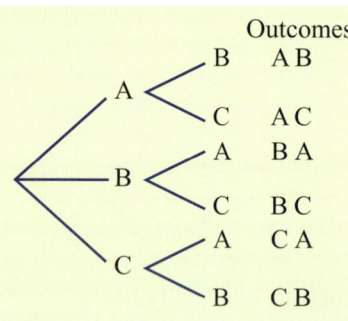

EXPLANATION

On the first choice there are three options (A, B or C) but on the second choice there are only two remaining.

b i $\text{Pr(Annabel and Brodie)} = \dfrac{2}{6}$

$= \dfrac{1}{3}$

2 of the 6 outcomes contain Annabel and Brodie (A, B) and (B, A).

ii $\text{Pr(Chris)} = \dfrac{4}{6}$

$= \dfrac{2}{3}$

4 out of the 6 outcomes contain Chris.

iii $\text{Pr(Chris or Brodie)} = \dfrac{6}{6}$

$= 1$

All of the outcomes contain at least one of Chris or Brodie.

Exercise 9E

Understanding

1 Find the total number of outcomes from these experiments *with replacement*. First, complete each tree diagram.

a Tossing a coin 3 times

b Selecting 2 letters from the word TO

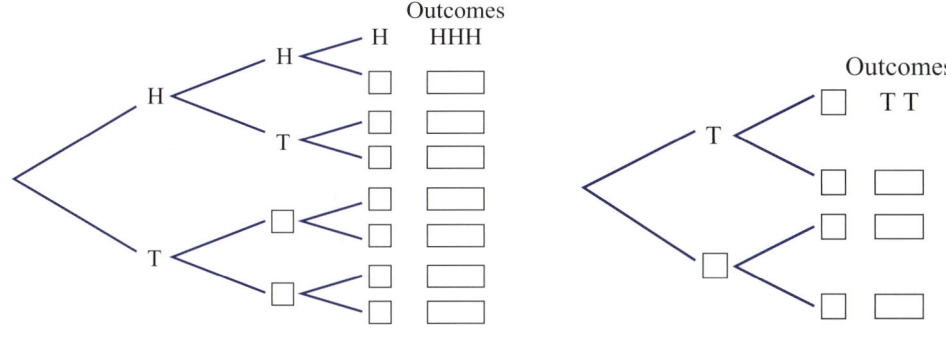

2 By first completing each tree diagram, find the total number of outcomes from these experiments *without replacement*.

a Selecting two letters from the word TWO

b Selecting two people from a group of three (A, B and C).

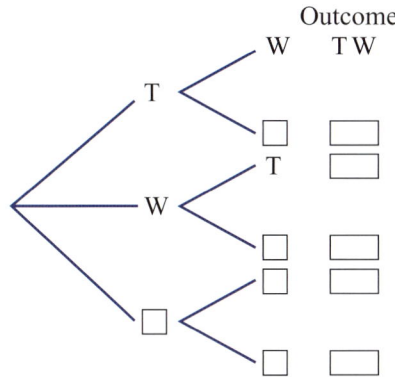

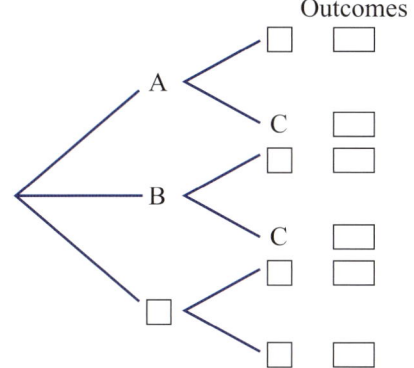

Example 8   **3**   A coin is tossed twice.

    a   Complete this tree diagram to show all the possible outcomes.

    b   What is the total number of outcomes?

    c   Find the probability of obtaining:

       i   two heads   **ii**   one head

       iii   at least one head   **iv**   at least one tail.

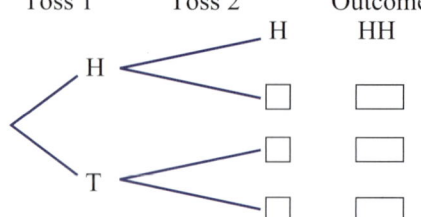

4   A spinner with three numbers, 1, 2 and 3, is spun twice.

    a   List the set of possible outcomes, using a tree diagram.

    b   What is the total number of possible outcomes?

    c   Find the probability of spinning:

       i   two 3s   **ii**   at least one 3   **iii**   no more than one 2   **iv**   two odd numbers.

Example 9   **5**   Two people are selected without replacement from a group of three: Donna (D), Elle (E) and Fernando (F).

    a   List all the possible combinations for the selection using a tree diagram.

    b   Find the probability that the selection will contain:

       i   Donna and Elle   **ii**   Fernando   **iii**   Fernando or Elle.

6   A drawer contains 2 red socks (R), 1 blue sock (B) and 1 yellow sock (Y) and two socks are selected at random without replacement.

    a   Complete this tree diagram.

    b   Find the probability of obtaining:

       i   a red sock and a blue sock

       ii   two red socks

       iii   any pair of socks of the same colour

       iv   any pair of socks of different colour.

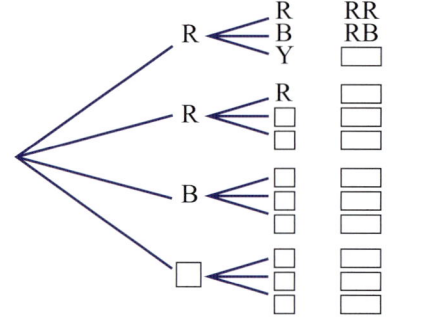

7   A student who has not studied for a multiple-choice test decides to guess the answers for every question. There are three questions, and three choices of answer (A, B and C) for each question. If only one of the possible choices (A, B or C) is correct for each question, find the probability that the student guesses:

    a   1 correct answer   **b**   2 correct answers   **c**   3 correct answers   **d**   0 correct answers

8   A discount supermarket shelf contains a large number of tomato tins and peach tins with no labels. There are an equal number of tins all mixed together on the same shelf. You select four tins in a hurry. Use a tree diagram to help find the probability of selecting the correct number of tins of tomatoes and/or peaches for each of these recipe requirements.

    a   You need four tins of tomatoes for a stew.

    b   You need four tins of peaches for a peach crumble.

    c   You need at least three tins of tomatoes for a bolognaise.

    d   You need at least two tins of peaches for a fruit salad.

    e   You need at least one tin of tomatoes for a vegetable soup.

9 Michael needs to deliver parcels to three places (A, B and C in order) in the city. This diagram shows the different ways that he can travel.

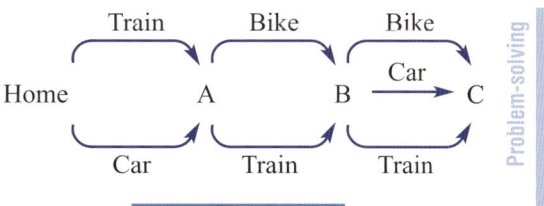

a Draw a tree diagram showing all the possible combinations of transportation.

b What is the total number of possible outcomes?

c Find the probability that Michael will use:

   i the train all three times

   ii the train twice

   iii his bike once

   iv different transport each time

   v a car at least once.

10 If a coin is tossed four times, use a tree diagram to find the probability that you receive:

  a 0 tails   **b** 1 tail   **c** 2 tails   **d** 3 tails   **e** 4 tails

11 **a** A coin is tossed 5 times. How many outcomes will there be?

  b A coin is tossed n times. Write a rule for the number of outcomes in the sample space.

12 Use a tree diagram to investigate the probability of selecting two counters from a bag of 3 black and 2 white counters if the selection is drawn

  a with replacement   **b** without replacement

  Is there any difference?

Enrichment: Selecting matching clothes

13 A man randomly selects a tie from his collection of one green and two red ties, a shirt from a collection of one red and two white, and either a red or black hat. Use a tree diagram to help find the probability that the man selects a tie, shirt and hat according to the following descriptions:

  a a red tie, red shirt and black hat

  b all three items red

  c one item red

  d two items red

  e at least two items red

  f green hat

  g green tie and a black hat

  h green tie or a black hat

  i not a red item

  j red tie or white shirt or black hat

Experimental probability

In some situations it may not be possible to list all the outcomes in the sample space and find theoretical probabilities. If this is the case then an experiment, survey or simulation can be conducted to find experimental probabilities. Provided the experiment includes a sufficient number of trials, these probabilities can be used to estimate the chance of particular events. Experimental probability is frequently used in science experiments and for research in medicine and economics.

Let's start: Newspaper theories

A tabloid newspaper reports that of 10 people interviewed in the street 5 had a dose of the flu. At a similar time a medical student tested 100 people and found that 21 had the flu.

- What is the experimental probability of having the flu, according to the newspaper's survey?
- What is the experimental probability of having the flu, according to the medical student's results?
- Which of the two sets of results would be most reliable and why? Discuss the reasons.
- Using the results from the medical student, how many people would you expect to have the flu in a group of 1000 and why?

- **Experimental probability** is calculated using the results of an experiment or survey.

$$\text{Experimental probability} = \frac{\text{number of times the outcome occurs}}{\text{total number of trials in the experiment}}$$

- The **long-run proportion** is the experimental probability for a sufficiently large number of trials.
- The **expected number of occurrences** = probability × number of trials

Example 10 Finding the experimental probability

A box contains an unknown number of coloured balls and a ball is drawn from the box and then replaced. The procedure is repeated 100 times and the colour of the ball drawn is recorded each time. Twenty-five red balls were recorded.

a Find the experimental probability for the number of red balls.

b Find the expected number of red balls if the box contained 500 balls in total.

SOLUTION	EXPLANATION
a $\text{Pr(red balls)} = \dfrac{25}{100}$ $\quad\quad\quad\quad\quad = 0.25$	$\text{Pr(red balls)} = \dfrac{\text{number of red balls drawn}}{\text{total number of balls drawn}}$ There are 25 red balls and 100 balls in total.
b Expected number of red balls in 500 $\quad = 0.25 \times 500$ $\quad = 125$	Expected number of occurrences $= \text{probability} \times \text{number of trials}$

Exercise 9F

Understanding

1 This table shows the results of three different surveys of how many people in Perth use public transport (PT).

Survey	Number who use PT	Survey size	Experimental probability
A	2	10	$\dfrac{2}{10} = 0.2$
B	5	20	_____
C	30	100	_____

   a What are the two missing numbers in the experimental probability list?

   b Which survey should be used to estimate the probability that a person uses public transport and why?

2 The experimental probability of Jess hitting a bullseye on a dartboard is 0.05 (or $\dfrac{5}{100}$). How many bullseyes would you expect Jess to get if he threw the following number of darts?

   a 100 darts   **b** 200 darts   **c** 1000 darts   **d** 80 darts

3 The results of tossing a drawing pin and observing how many times the pin lands with the spike pointing up are shown in the table. Results are recorded at different stages of the experiment.

Using probability, we can predict the chance of a dart hitting the bullseye.

Number of throws	Frequency (spike up)	Experimental probability
1	1	1.00
5	2	0.40
10	5	0.50
20	9	0.45
50	18	0.36
100	41	0.41

Which experimental probability would you choose to best represent the probability that the pin will land spike up? Why?

Example 10   **4**   A bag contains an unknown number of counters, and a counter is selected from the bag and then replaced. The procedure is repeated 100 times and the colour of the counter is recorded each time. Sixty of the counters drawn were blue.

   a   Find the experimental probability for the number of blue counters.

   b   Find the expected number of blue counters if the bag contained:

   i   100 counters   **ii**   200 counters   **iii**   600 counters

5   In an experiment involving 200 people chosen at random, 175 people said that they owned a home computer.

   a   Calculate the experimental probability of choosing a person who owns a home computer.

   b   Find the expected number of people who own a home computer from the following group sizes:

   i   400 people   **ii**   5000 people   **iii**   40 people

6   By calculating the experimental probability, estimate the chance that each of the following events will occur.

   a   Nat will walk to work today, given that she walked to work five times in the last 75 working days.

   b   Mike will win the next game of cards if, in the last 80 games, he has won 32.

   c   Brett will hit the bullseye on the dartboard with his next attempt if, in the last 120 attempts, he was successful 22 times.

7   A six-sided die is rolled 120 times. How many times would you expect the following events to occur?

   a   6   **b**   1 or 2   **c**   a number less than 4

   d   a number which is at least 5

8   The colour of cars along a highway was noted over a short period of time and summarised in this frequency table.

Colour	White	Silver	Blue	Green
Frequency	7	4	5	4

   a   How many cars had their colour recorded?

   b   Find the experimental probability that a car's colour is:

   i   blue   **ii**   white

   c   If the colour of 100 cars was recorded, find the expected number of:

   i   blue cars

   ii   green cars

   iii   blue or green cars.

9 The letters from a three-letter word are written separately onto cards. A card is chosen at random and replaced and this is repeated 100 times. The results are shown in the table.

Letter	E	S
Frequency	64	36

    a Find the experimental probability of obtaining an E.

    b Based on these results what is the three-letter word likely to be?

10 A spinner is divided into three regions not necessarily of equal size. The regions are numbered 1, 2 and 3 and the spinner is spun 50 times. The table shows the results.

Number	1	2	3
Frequency	26	11	13

    a Find the experimental probability of obtaining:

      i a 1   **ii** at least a 2   **iii** a 1 or a 3

    b Based on these results, how many 3s would you expect if the spinner is spun 300 times?

    c In fact, the spinner is divided up using simple and common fractions. Give a likely example describing how the regions might be divided.

11 Phil tossed a fair six-sided die 10 times and receives 9 sixes.

    a Find the experimental probability of rolling a six.

    b Is it likely that Phil will receive the same number of sixes if he tossed the die 10 more times? Explain.

12 Do you think that a coin is fair or biased given the following experimental results? Give reasons.

    a 47 tails out of 100 tosses

    b 23 heads out of 24 tosses

    c 1 tail out of 1 toss

13 One hundred darts are randomly thrown at the given dartboards. No darts miss the dartboard entirely. How many darts do you expect to hit the blue shaded region? Give reasons.

    a   **b**

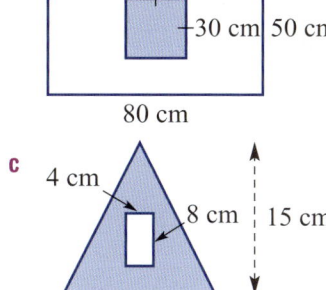

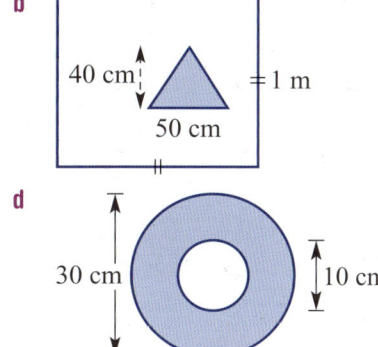

14 Decide if the following statements are true.

  a The experimental probability is always equal to the theoretical probability.

  b The experimental probability can be greater than the theoretical probability.

  c If the experimental probability is zero then the theoretical probability is zero.

  d If the theoretical probability is zero then the experimental probability is zero.

Enrichment: More than a guessing game

15 A bag of 10 counters includes counters with four different colours. The results from drawing and replacing one counter at a time for 80 trials are shown in this table.

Use the given information to find out how many counters of each colour were likely to be in the bag.

Colour	Total
Blue	26
Red	17
Green	29
Yellow	8

16 A box of 12 chocolates all of which are the same size and shape include five different centres. The results from selecting and replacing one chocolate at a time for 60 trials are shown in this table.

Use the given information to find out how many chocolates of each type were likely to be in the box.

Centre	Total
Strawberry	11
Caramel	14
Coconut	9
Nut	19
Mint	7

9.7 Summarising data: measures of centre

The discipline of statistics involves collecting and summarising data. It also involves drawing conclusions and making predictions, which is why many of the decisions we make today are based on statistical analysis. The type and amount of product stocked on supermarket shelves, for example, is determined by the sales statistics and other measures such as average cost and price range.

Let's start: Game purchase

Arathi purchases 7 computer games at a sale. 3 games cost $20 each, 2 games cost $30, 1 game costs $50 and the last game cost $200.

- Recall and discuss the meaning of the words mean, median and mode.
- Can you work out the mean, median or mode for the cost of Arathi's games?
- Which of the mean, median or mode gives the best 'average' for the cost of Arathi's games?
- Why is the mean greater than the median in this case?

- **Mean ($\bar{x}$)**
  If there are n values, $x_1, x_2, x_3, \ldots x_n$, then the mean is calculated as follows:

  $$\bar{x} = \frac{\text{sum of all the values}}{\text{number of scores}}$$

  $$= \frac{x_1 + x_2 + x_3 + \ldots + x_n}{n}$$

- **Median**
  The median is the middle value if the data is placed in order.
  - If there are two middle values, the median is calculated as the mean of these two values.

Odd data set	Even data set
1 3 5 ⑤ 6 7 10	13 17 17 20 21 27 27 28
median	20.5
	median

- **Mode**
  The mode is the most common value.
  - There can be more than one mode.
  - If there are two modes, we say that the data set is **bimodal**.
- An **outlier** is a score that is much larger or smaller than the rest of the data.

Example 11 Finding measures of centre

For the given data sets, find the following.

i the mean ii the median iii the mode

a 5 2 4 10 6 1 2 9 6

b 17 13 26 15 9 10

SOLUTION | **EXPLANATION**

a i Mean $= \dfrac{5+2+4+10+6+1+2+9+6}{9}$

$= 5$

Find the sum of all the numbers and divide by the number of values.

ii 1 2 2 4 ⑤ 6 6 9 10

Median $= 5$

First, order the data.
The median is the middle value.

iii Mode $= 2$ and 6

The data set is bimodal since there are two numbers with the highest frequency.

b i Mean $= \dfrac{17+13+26+15+9+10}{6}$

$= 15$

The sum is 90 and there are 6 values.

ii 9 10 13 15 17 26

14

Median $= \dfrac{13+15}{2}$

$= 14$

First, order the data.
Since there are two values in the middle find the mean of them.

iii No mode

None of the values are repeated so there is no mode.

Example 12 Finding a data value for a required mean

The hours a shop assistant spends cleaning the store in eight successive weeks are:
8, 9, 12, 10, 10, 8, 5, 10.

a Calculate the mean for this set of data.

b Determine the score that needs to be added to this data to make the mean equal to 10.

SOLUTION | **EXPLANATION**

a Mean $= \dfrac{8+9+12+10+10+8+5+10}{8}$

$= 9$

Sum of the 8 data values is 72.

b Let a be the new score.

Require $\dfrac{72+a}{8+1}=10$

$\dfrac{72+a}{9}=10$

$72+a=90$

$a=18$

The new score would need to be 18.

$72+a$ is the total of the new data and $8+1$ is the new total number of scores. Set this equal to the required mean of 10.
Solve for a.

Write the answer.

Exercise 9G

mple 11

Understanding

1 Write the missing word.
   a The mode is the most _____ value.   **b** The median is the _____ value.
   c To calculate the _____, you add up all the values and divide by the number of values.

2 Find the mean, median and mode for these simple ordered data sets.
   a 1 2 2 2 4 4 6
   b 1 4 8 8 9 10 10 10 12
   c 1 5 7 7 8 10 11
   d 3 3 6 8 10 12
   e 7 11 14 18 20 20
   f 2 2 2 4 10 10 12 14

Fluency

3 For the given data sets, find:
   i the mean   **ii** the median   **iii** the mode
   a 7 2 3 8 5 9 8
   b 6 13 5 4 16 10 3 5 10
   c 12 9 2 5 8 7 2 3
   d 10 17 5 16 4 14
   e 3.5 2.1 4.0 8.3 2.1
   f 0.7 3 2.9 10.4 6 7.2 1.3 8.5
   g 6 0 -3 8 2 -3 9 5
   h 3 -7 2 3 -2 -3 4

4 These data sets include an outlier. Write down the outlier then calculate the mean and the median. Include the outlier in your calculations.
   a 5 7 7 8 12 33
   b 1.3 1.1 1.0 1.7 1.5 1.6 -1.1 1.5
   c -58 -60 -59 -4 -64

5 Decide if the following data sets are bimodal.
   a 2 7 9 5 6 2 8 7 4
   b 1 6 2 3 3 1 5 4 1 9
   c 10 15 12 11 18 13 9 16 17
   d 23 25 26 23 19 24 28 26 27

Problem-solving

6 In three races Paula recorded the times 25.1 seconds, 24.8 seconds and 24.1 seconds.
   a What is the mean time of the races? Round to two decimal places.
   b Find the median time.

Example 12   **7**   A netball player scored the following number of goals in her 10 most recent games:

15 14 16 14 15 12 16 17 16 15

a   What is her mean score?

b   What number of goals does she need to score in the next game for the mean of her scores to be 16?

8   Stevie obtained the following scores on her first five Maths tests:

92 89 94 82 93

a   What is her mean test score?

b   If there is one more test left to complete, and she wants to achieve an average of at least 85, what is the lowest score Stevie can obtain for her final test?

9   Seven numbers have a mean of 8. Six of the numbers are 9, 7, 6, 4, 11 and 10. Find the seventh number.

10   Write down a set of 5 numbers which has the following values:

a   a mean of 5, median of 6 and mode of 7

b   a mean of 5, median of 4 and mode of 8

c   a mean of 4, median of 4 and mode of 4

d   a mean of 4.5, median of 3 and mode of 2.5

e   a mean of 1, median of 0 and mode of 5

f   a mean of 1, median of $1\frac{1}{4}$ and mode of $1\frac{1}{4}$.

11   This data contains six houses prices in Darwin.

$324 000 $289 000 $431 000 $295 000 $385 000 $1 700 000

a   Which price would be considered the outlier?

b   If the outlier was removed from the data set, by how much would the median change? (First work out the median for each case.)

c   If the outlier was removed from the data set, by how much would the mean change, to the nearest dollar? (First work out the mean for each case.)

12 Explain why outliers significantly affect the mean but not the median.

13 This dot plot shows the frequency of households with 0, 1, 2 or 3 pets.

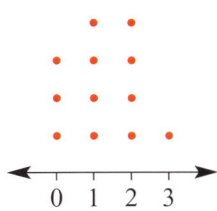

  a How many households were surveyed?

  b Find the mean number of pets correct to one decimal place.

  c Find the median number of pets.

  d Find the mode.

  e Another household with 7 pets is added to the list. Does this change the median? Explain.

14 This simple data set contains nine numbers.

  1 2 2 2 2 2 3 4 5

  a Find the median.

  b How many numbers greater than 5 need to be added to the list to change the median? (Give the least number.)

  c How many numbers less than 1 need to be added to the list to change the median? (Give the least number.)

Enrichment: Formula to get an A

15 A school awards grades in Mathematics each semester according to this table.

Ryan has scored the following results for four topics this semester and has one topic to go.

75 68 85 79

Average score	Grade
90–100	A+
80–	A
70–	B+
60–	B
50–	C+
0–	C

  a What is Ryan's mean score so far? Round to one decimal place.

  b What grade will Ryan get for the semester if his fifth score is:

    i 50   **ii** 68   **iii** 94?

  c Find the maximum average score Ryan can receive for the semester. Is it possible for him to get an A+?

  d Find the least score that Ryan needs in his fifth topic for him to receive an average of:

    i B+   **ii** A

  e Write a rule for the mean score M for the semester if Ryan receives a mark of m in the fifth topic.

  f Write a rule for the mark m in the fifth topic if he wants an average of M for the semester.

Using a CAS calculator 9.7: Finding measures of centre

The activity is on the companion website in the form of a printable PDF.

9.8 Stem-and-leaf plots

Stem-and-leaf plots (or stem plots) are commonly used to display a single data set or two related data sets. They help to show how the data is distributed like a histogram but retain all the individual data elements so no detail is lost. The median and mode can be easily read from a stem-and-leaf plot because all the data sits in order.

For this data below, digits representing the stem give the tens and digits representing the leaves give the units.

Let's start: Ships vs Chops

At a school, Ms Ships' class and Mr Chops' class sit the same exam. The scores are displayed using this back-to-back stem-and-leaf plot. Discuss the following.

- Which class had the most students?
- What were the lowest and highest scores from each class?
- What were the median scores from each class?
- Which class could be described as symmetrical and which as skewed?
- Which class had the better results?

Ms Ships' class		Mr Chops' class
3 1	5	0 1 1 3 5 7
8 8 7 5	6	2 3 5 5 7 9 9
6 4 4 2 1	7	8 9 9
7 4 3	8	0 3
6	9	1

7 | 8 means 78

- A **stem-and-leaf plot** uses a stem number and leaf number to represent data.
  - The data is shown in two parts: a stem and a leaf.
  - The 'key' tells you how the plot is to be read.
  - The graph is similar to a histogram on its side or a bar graph with class intervals but there is no loss of detail of the original data.

Ordered stem-and-leaf plot

Stem	Leaf
1	2 6
2	2 3 4 7
3	1 2 4 7 8 9
4	2 3 4 5 8
5	7 9

2 | 4 represents 24 people

A key is added to show the place value of the stems and leaves.

- **Back-to-back stem-and-leaf plots** can be used to compare two sets of data. The stem is drawn in the middle with the leaves on either side.

Scores for the last 30 football games

Winning scores		Losing scores
	7	4 5 8 8 9
1	8	0 0 3 3 6 7
7 5	9	1 2 3 6
8 4 4 1	10	3 9
9 5 0	11	1
3 1	12	

81 lowest winning score

Skewed

Symmetrical

111 highest losing score

10 | 9 represents 109

- **Symmetrical data** will produce a graph which is symmetrical about the centre.
- **Skewed data** will produce a graph which includes data bunched to one side of the centre.

Example 13 Constructing and using a stem-and-leaf plot

For this set of data:

0.3 2.5 4.1 3.7 2.0 3.3 4.8 3.3 4.6 0.1 4.1 7.5 1.4 2.4
5.7 2.3 3.4 3.0 2.3 4.1 6.3 1.0 5.8 4.4 0.1 6.8 5.2 1.0

a Organise the data into an ordered stem-and-leaf plot.

b Find the median.

c Find the mode.

d Describe the data as symmetrical or skewed.

SOLUTION

EXPLANATION

a

Stem	Leaf
0	1 1 3
1	0 0 4
2	0 3 3 4 5
3	0 3 3 4 7
4	1 1 1 4 6 8
5	2 7 8
6	3 8
7	5

3 | 4 means 3.4

The minimum is 0.1 and the maximum is 7.5 so stems range from 0 to 7.

Place leaves in order from smallest to largest. Since some numbers appear more than once, e.g. 0.1, their leaf (1) appears the same number of times.

b Median $= \dfrac{3.3 + 3.4}{2}$

  $= 3.35$

There are 28 data values. The median is the average of the two middle values (the 14th and 15th values).

c Mode is 4.1.

The most common value is 4.1.

d Data is approximately symmetrical.

The distribution of numbers is approximately symmetrical about the stem containing the median.

Statisticians work in many fields, particularly business, finance, health, government, science and technology.

Example 14 Constructing back-to-back stem-and-leaf plots

A shop owner has two jeans shops. The daily sales in each shop over a 16-day period are monitored and recorded as follows.

Shop A

   3   12   12   13   14   14   15   15   21   22   24   24   24   26   27   28

Shop B

   4   6   6   7   7   8   9   9   10   12   13   14   14   16   17   27

a Draw a back-to-back stem-and-leaf plot with an interval of 10.

b Compare and comment on differences between the sales made by the two shops.

SOLUTION

a

Shop A		Shop B
3	0	4 6 6 7 7 8 9 9
5 5 4 4 3 2 2	1	0 2 3 4 4 6 7
8 7 6 4 4 4 2 1	2	7

1 | 3 means 13

b Shop A has the highest number of daily sales. Its sales are generally between 12 and 28, with one day of very low sales of 3. Shop B sales are generally between 4 and 17 with only one high sale day of 27.

EXPLANATION

The data for each shop is already ordered. Stems are in intervals of 10. Record leaf digits for Shop A on the left and Shop B on the right.

Look at both sides of the plot for the similarities and differences.

Exercise 9H

1 This stem-and-leaf plot shows the number of minutes Alexis spoke on her phone for a number of calls.

Stem	Leaf
0	8
1	5 9
2	1 1 3 7
3	4 5

2 | 1 means 21 minutes

a How many calls are represented by the stem and leaf plot?

b What is the length of the:

   i   shortest phone call?

   ii   longest phone call?

c What is the mode (the most common call time)?

d What is the median call time (middle value)?

Understanding

2 This back-to-back stem-and-leaf plot shows the thickness of tyre tread on a selection of cars from the city and country.

   a How many car tyres were tested altogether?

   b What was the smallest tyre tread thickness in:

   i the city? **ii** the country?

   c What was the largest tyre tread thickness in:

   i the city? **ii** the country?

   d Find the median tyre tread thickness for tyres in:

   i the city **ii** the country

   e Is the distribution of tread thickness for city cars more symmetrical or skewed?

   f Is the distribution of tread thickness for country cars more symmetrical or skewed?

City		Country
8 7 3 1 0 0 0	0	6 8 8 9
8 6 3 1 0	1	0 4 5 5 6 9
1	2	3 4 4

1 | 3 means 13 mm

mple 13

3 For each of the following data sets:

   i organise the data into an ordered stem-and-leaf plot

   ii find the median **iii** find the mode

   iv describe the data as symmetrical or skewed

   a 41 33 28 24 19 32 54 35 26 28 19 23 32 26 28

   b 31 33 23 35 15 23 48 50 35 42 45 15 21 45
   51 31 34 23 42 50 26 30 45 37 39

   c 34.5 34.9 33.7 34.5 35.8 33.8 34.3 35.2 37.0 34.7
   35.2 34.4 35.5 36.5 36.1 33.3 35.4 32.0 36.3 34.8

   d 167 159 159 193 161 164 167 157 158 175 177 185
   177 202 185 187 159 189 167 159 173 198 200

4 The number of vacant rooms in a motel each week over a 20-week period is shown below.

   12 8 11 10 21 12 6 11 12 16 14 22 5 15 20 6 17 8 14 9

   a Draw a stem-and-leaf plot of this data.

   b In how many weeks were there fewer than 12 vacant rooms?

   c Find the median number of vacant rooms.

mple 14

5 For each of the following sets of data:

   i Draw a back-to-back stem-and-leaf plot.

   ii Compare and comment on the difference between the two data sets.

   a Set A: 46 32 40 43 45 47 53 54 40 54 33 48 39 43
   Set B: 48 49 31 40 43 47 48 41 49 51 44 46 53 44

   b Set A: 1 43 24 26 48 50 2 2 36 11 16 37 41 3 36
   6 8 9 10 17 22 10 11 17 29 30 35 4 23 23
   Set B: 9 18 19 19 20 21 23 24 27 28 31 37 37 38 39 39 39
   40 41 41 43 44 44 45 47 50 50 51 53 53 54 54 55 56

   c Set A: 0.7 0.8 1.4 8.8 9.1 2.6 3.2 0.3 1.7 1.9 2.5 4.1 4.3 3.3 3.4
   3.6 3.9 3.9 4.7 1.6 0.4 5.3 5.7 2.1 2.3 1.9 5.2 6.1 6.2 8.3
   Set B: 0.1 0.9 0.6 1.3 0.9 0.1 0.3 2.5 0.6 3.4 4.8 5.2 8.8 4.7 5.3
   2.6 1.5 1.8 3.9 1.9 0.1 0.2 1.2 3.3 2.1 4.3 5.7 6.1 6.2 8.3

6 **a** Draw back-to-back stem-and-leaf plots for the final scores of St. Kilda and Collingwood in the 24 games given here.

St. Kilda:	126	68	78	90	87	118
	88	125	111	117	82	82
	80	66	84	138	109	113
	122	80	94	83	106	68
Collingwood:	104	80	127	88	103	95
	78	118	89	82	103	115
	98	77	119	91	71	70
	63	89	103	97	72	68

b In what percentage of games did each team score more than 100 points?

c Comment on the distribution of the scores for each team.

7 The data below gives the maximum temperature each day for a three-week period in spring.

18 18 15 17 19 17 21
20 15 17 15 18 19 19
20 22 19 17 19 15 17

Use a stem-and-leaf plot to determine the following:

a how many days the temperature was higher than 18°C

b the median temperature

c the difference in the minimum and maximum temperatures.

8 This stem-and-leaf plot shows the time taken, in seconds, by Helena to run 100 m in her last 25 races.

a Find Helena's median time.

b What is the difference between the slowest and fastest time?

c If in her 26th race her time was 14.8 seconds and this was added to the stem-and-leaf plot, would her median time change? If so, by how much?

Stem	Leaf
14	9
15	4 5 6 6 7 7 7 8 9
16	0 0 1 1 2 2 3 4 4 5 5 5 7 7
17	2

14 | 9 represents 14.9 seconds

9 Two brands of batteries were tested to determine their lifetime in hours. The data below shows the lifetime of 20 batteries of each brand.

Brand A: 7.3 8.2 8.4 8.5 8.7 8.8 8.9 9.0 9.1 9.2
9.3 9.4 9.4 9.5 9.5 9.6 9.7 9.8 9.9 9.9

Brand B: 7.2 7.3 7.4 7.5 7.6 7.8 7.9 7.9 8.0 8.1
8.3 9.0 9.1 9.2 9.3 9.4 9.5 9.6 9.8 9.8

a Draw a back-to-back stem-and-leaf plot for this data.

b How many batteries from each brand lasted more than 9 hours?

c Compare the two sets of data and comment on any similarities or differences.

10 This ordered stem-and-leaf plot has some unknown digits.

   a What is the value of c?

   b What is the smallest number in the data set?

   c What values could the following pronumerals take?

      i a **ii** b

0	2 3 8
1	1 5 a 8
c	0 b 6 6 2
3	2 5 9

3 | 5 means 0.35

11 The back-to-back stem-and-leaf plot below shows the birth weight in kilograms of babies born to mothers who do or don't smoke.

Birth weight of babies

Smoking mothers		Non-smoking mothers
4 3 2 2	2	4
9 9 8 7 6 6 5 5	2*	8 9
4 3 2 1 1 1 0 0 0	3	0 0 1 2 2 3
6 5 5	3*	5 5 5 6 6 7 7 8
1	4	
	4*	5 5 6

2 | 4 means 2.4
2* | 5 means 2.5

Do babies born to mothers who smoke weigh more or less than those born to mothers who don't smoke?

   a What percentage of babies born to smoking mothers have a birth weight of less than 3 kg?

   b What percentage of babies born to non-smoking mothers have a birth weight of less than 3 kg?

   c Compare and comment on the differences between the birth weights of babies born to mothers who smoke and those born to mothers who don't smoke.

12 Explain why in a symmetrical distribution the mean is close to the median.

13 Find the median if all the data in each back-to-back stem-and-leaf plot was combined.

a

	5	3	8 9
9 7 7 1	4	0 2 2 3 6 8
8 6 5 2 2	5	3 3 7 9
7 4 0	6	1 4

4 | 2 means 42

b

	3	16	0 3 3 6 7 9
9 6 6 1	17	0 1 1 4 8 8
8 7 5 5 4 0	18	2 2 6 7
2	19	0 1

16 | 3 means 16.3

Enrichment: How skewed?

14 Skewness can be positive or negative. If the tail of the distribution is pointing up in a stem-and-leaf plot (towards the smaller numbers) then we say the data is negatively skewed. If the tail is pointing in the reverse direction then the data is positively skewed.

1	3
2	1 4
3	0 2 7
4	1 1 3 8 9 9
5	0 4 4 5 7

Negatively skewed data

3 | 2 means 32

   a Find the mean (correct to two decimal places) and the median for the above data.

   b Which of the mean or median is higher for the given data? Can you explain why?

   c Which of the mean or median would be higher for a set of positively skewed data? Why?

   d What type of distribution would lead to the median and mean being quite close?

9.9 Grouped data

For some data, especially large sets, it makes sense to group the data and then record the frequency for each group to produce a frequency table. For numerical data, a graph generated from a frequency table gives a histogram. Like a stem-and-leaf plot, a histogram shows how the data is distributed across the full range of values. A histogram, for example, is used to display the level of exposure of the pixels in an image in digital photography. It uses many narrow columns to show how the luminance values are distributed across the scale from black to white.

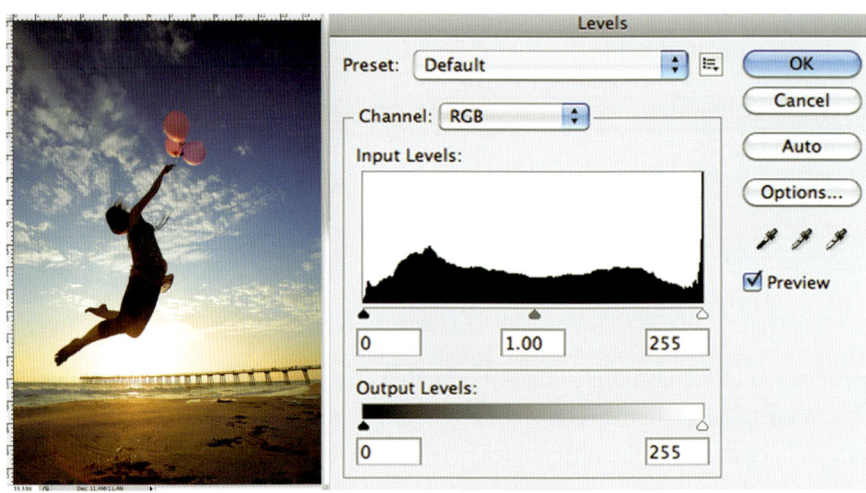

A luminance value histogram used in digital photography software

Let's start: Baggage check

This histogram shows the distribution of the weight of a number of bags checked at the airport.

- How many bags had a weight in the range 10–15 kg?
- How many bags were checked in total?
- Is it possible to determine the exact mean, median or mode of the weight of the bags by looking at the histogram? Discuss.
- Describe the distribution of checked bag weights for the given graph.

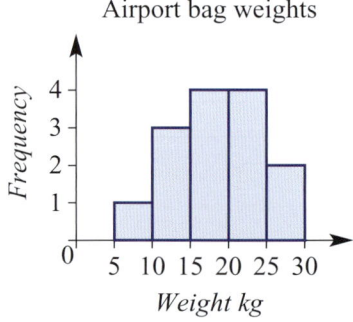

Key ideas

- A **frequency table** shows the number of values within a set of categories or **class intervals**.
- Grouped numerical data can be illustrated using a **histogram**.
  - The height of a column corresponds to the frequency of values in that class interval.
  - There are usually no gaps between columns.
  - The scales are evenly spread with each bar spreading across the boundaries of the class interval.
  - A **percentage frequency histogram** shows the frequencies as percentages of the total.

- Like a stem-and-leaf plot, a histogram can show if the data is **skewed** or **symmetrical**.

Frequency table

Class interval	Frequency	Percentage frequency
60–	3	12
65–	4	16
70–	6	24
75–	8	32
80–85	4	16
Total	25	100

- 70– includes numbers from 70 to less than 75.

Frequency histogram

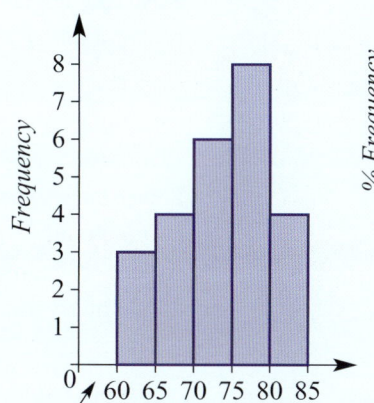

This gap may be used when our intervals do not start at zero.

Percentage frequency histogram

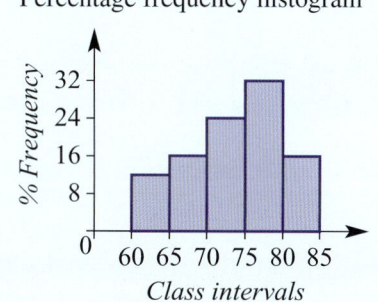

Example 15 Constructing frequency tables and histograms

The data below shows the number of hamburgers sold each hour by a 24-hour fast-food store during a 50-hour period.

1	10	18	14	20	11	19	10	17	21
5	16	7	15	21	15	10	22	11	18
12	12	3	12	8	12	6	5	14	14
14	4	9	15	17	19	6	24	16	17
14	11	17	18	19	19	19	18	18	20

a Set up and complete a grouped frequency table, using class intervals 0–, 5–, 10–, etc. Include a percentage frequency column.

b Construct a frequency histogram.

c How many hours did the fast-food store sell:

  i fewer than 10 hamburgers?   **ii** at least 15 hamburgers?

SOLUTION

a

Class interval	Frequency	Percentage frequency
0–	3	6
5–	7	14
10–	15	30
15–	19	38
20–24	6	12
Total	50	100

EXPLANATION

Create class intervals of 5 from 0 up to 25, since 24 is the maximum number. Record the number of data values in each interval in the frequency column. Convert to a percentage by dividing by the total (50) and multiplying by 100.

b

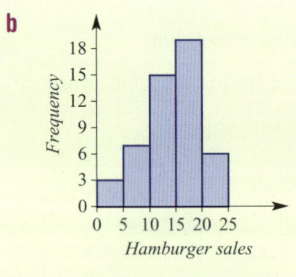

Hamburger sales

Create a frequency histogram with frequency on the vertical axis and the class intervals on the horizontal axis. The height of the column shows the frequency of that interval.

c i $3 + 7 = 10$ hours

ii $19 + 6 = 25$ hours

Fewer than 10 hamburgers covers the 0–4 and 5–9 intervals.
At least 15 hamburgers covers the 15–19 and 20–24 intervals.

Exercise 9I

1 This frequency histogram shows in how many years the number of international visitors to South Australia is within a given range for the decade from 2000 to 2009.

a How many years in the decade were there less than 330 000 international visitors?

b Which range of visitor numbers had the highest frequency?

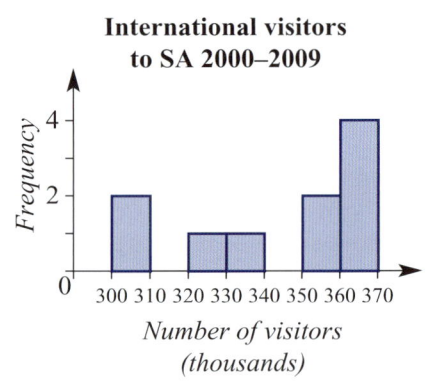

International visitors to SA 2000–2009

Number of visitors (thousands)

2 Write down the missing numbers in these frequency tables, i.e. find the values of the pronumerals.

a

Class interval	Frequency	Percentage frequency
0–4	1	10
5–9	3	c
10–14	4	d
a–19	b	e
Total	10	f

b

Class interval	Frequency	Percentage frequency
40–	20	20
a–	28	b
60–	12	c
70–	d	40
Total	100	e

3 This frequency histogram shows in how many books the number of pages is within a given interval for some text books selected from a school library.

a How many textbooks had between 100 and 200 pages?

b How many textbooks were selected from the library?

c What percentage of textbooks had between:

   i 200 and 300 pages?

   ii 200 and 400 pages?

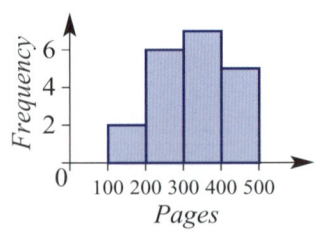

Pages

Understanding

Example 15   **4**   The data below shows the number of ice creams sold from an ice cream van over a 50-day period.

0	5	0	35	14	15	18	21	21	36	45	2	8
2	2	3	17	3	7	28	35	7	21	3	46	47
1	1	3	9	35	22	7	18	36	3	9	2	
11	37	37	45	11	12	14	17	22	1	2	2	

a   Set up and complete a grouped frequency table using class intervals 0–, 10–, 20–, etc. Include a percentage frequency column.

b   Construct a frequency histogram.

c   How many days did the ice cream van sell:
  i   fewer than 20 ice creams?
  ii   at least 30 ice creams?

d   What percentage of days were 20 or more ice creams sold?

5   The data below shows the mark out of 100 on the Science exam for 60 Year 9 students.

50	67	68	89	82	81	50	50	89	52	60	82	52	60	87	89	71	73	75	83
86	50	52	71	80	95	87	87	87	74	60	60	61	63	63	65	82	86	96	88
50	94	87	64	64	72	71	72	88	86	89	69	71	80	89	92	89	89	60	83

a   Set up and complete a grouped frequency table, using class intervals 50–, 60–, 70–, etc.
Include a percentage frequency column rounding to two decimal places where necessary.

b   Construct a frequency histogram.

c   i   How many marks were less than 70 out of 100?
  ii   What percentage of marks were at least 80 out of 100?

6   The number of goals kicked by a country footballer in each of his last 30 football matches is given below.

| 8 | 9 | 3 | 6 | 12 | 14 | 8 | 3 | 4 | 5 | 2 | 5 | 6 | 4 | 13 |
| 8 | 9 | 12 | 11 | 7 | 12 | 14 | 10 | 9 | 8 | 12 | 10 | 11 | 4 | 5 |

a   Organise the data into a grouped frequency table using a class interval width of 3 starting at 0.

b   Draw a frequency histogram for the data.

c   In how many games did the player kick fewer than six goals?

d   In how many games did he kick more than 11 goals?

7   Which one of these histograms illustrates a symmetrical data set and which one shows a skewed data set?

a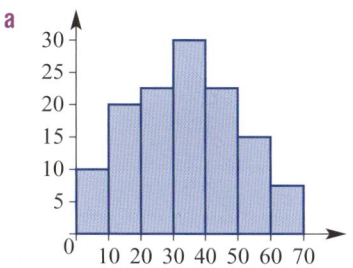

b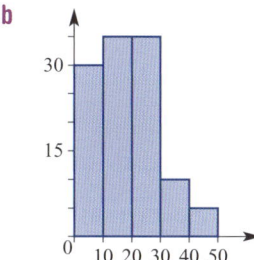

8 Find the unknown numbers (pronumerals) in these frequency tables.

a

Class interval	Frequency	Percentage frequency
10–	a	15
15–	11	b
20–	7	c
25–	d	10
30–34	e	f
Total	40	g

b

Class interval	Frequency	Percentage frequency
0–	a	2
3–	9	b
6–	c	16
9–	12	d
12–	e	f
Total	50	g

9 This percentage frequency histogram shows the heights of office towers in a city.

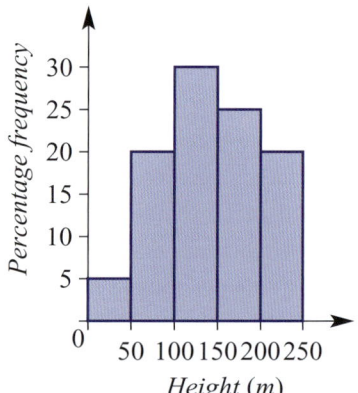

a What percentage of office towers have the following heights?
  i between 50 m and 100 m
  ii less than 150 m
  iii no more than 200 m
  iv at least 100 m
  v between 100 m and 150 m or greater than 200 m

b If the city had 100 office towers, how many have a height of:
  i between 100 m and 150 m?
  ii at least 150 m?

c If the city had 40 office towers, how many have a height of:
  i between 0 m and 50 m?
  ii no more than 150 m?

10 The data below shows the length of overseas phone calls (in minutes) made by a particular household over a six-week period.

1.5	1	1.5	1	4.8	4	4	10.1	9.5	1	3
8	5.9	6	6.4	7	3.5	3.1	3.6	3	4.2	4.3
4	12.5	10.2	10.3	4.5	4.5	3.4	3.5	3.5	5	3.5
3.6	4.5	4.5	12	11	12	14	14	12	13	10.8
12.1	2.4	3.8	4.2	5.6	10.8	11.2	9.3	9.2	8.7	8.5

What percentage of phone calls were more than 3 minutes in length? Answer to one decimal place.

11 Explain why you cannot work out the exact value for the mean, median and mode for a set of data presented in a histogram.

12 What can you work out from a frequency histogram that you cannot work out from a percentage frequency histogram? Completing Question **9** will provide a clue.

13 Two students show different histograms for the same set of data.

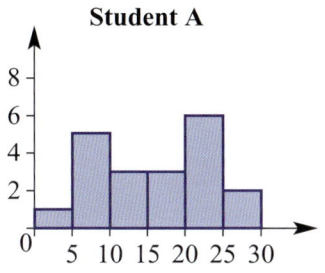

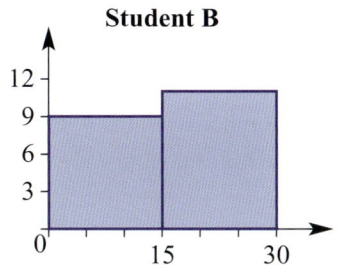

   a Which histogram is more useful in helping to analyse the data?

   b What would you advise student B to do differently when constructing the histogram?

Enrichment: The distribution of weekly wages

14 The data below shows the weekly wages of 50 people in dollars.

400	500	552	455	420	424	325	204	860	894	464	379	563	230
940	384	370	356	345	380	720	540	654	678	628	656	670	725
740	750	730	766	760	700	700	768	608	576	890	920	874	860
450	674	725	612	605	600	548	670

   a What is the minimum weekly wage and the maximum weekly wage?

   b i Organise the data into about 10 class intervals.

      ii Draw a frequency histogram for the data.

   c i Organise the data into about five class intervals.

      ii Draw a frequency histogram for the data.

   d Discuss the shapes of the two graphs. Which graph represents the data better and why?

Using a CAS calculator 9.9: Graphing grouped data

The activity is on the companion website in the form of a printable PDF.

9.10 Measures of spread

The mean, median and mode are three numbers which help define the centre of a data set; however, it is also important to describe the spread. Two teams of swimmers from different countries, for example, might have similar mean race times but the spread of race times for each team could be very different.

→ Let's start: Swim times

Two Olympic swimming teams are competing in the 4 × 100 m relay. The 100 m personal best times for the four members of each team are:

Team A 48.3 s, 48.5 s, 48.9 s, 49.2 s

Team B 47.4 s, 48.2 s, 49.0 s, 51.2 s

• Find the mean for each team.
• Which team's times are more spread out?
• What does the difference in the range of values for each team tell you about the spread?

- The **range** is the difference between the highest and lowest values.
  - Range = highest value – lowest value
- If a set of numerical data is placed in order, from smallest to largest, then:
  - the middle number of the lower half is called the **lower quartile** (Q_1)
  - the middle number of the data is called the median (Q_2)
  - the middle number of the upper half is called the **upper quartile** (Q_3)
  - the difference between the upper quartile and lower quartile is called the **interquartile range** (IQR).

  $$IQR = Q_3 - Q_1$$

  - if there is an odd number of values, remove the middle value (the median) before calculating Q_1 and Q_3.
- An **outlier** is a value that is not in the vicinity of the rest of the data.

Example 16 Finding the range and quartiles for an odd number of data values

The following data values are the results for a school Mathematics test.

67 96 62 85 73 56 79 19 76 23 68 89 81

a List the data in order, from smallest to largest.

b Find the range.

c Find:

  i the median (Q_2)   ii the lower quartile (Q_1)

  iii the upper quartile (Q_3)   iv the interquartile range (IQR)

SOLUTION   **EXPLANATION**

a 19 23 56 62 67 68 (73) 76 79 81 85 89 96   Order the data.
$\underbrace{}_{Q_1}$ $\underbrace{}_{Q_2}$ $\underbrace{}_{Q_3}$

b Range = 96 − 19   Range = highest value − lowest value.
$= 77$

c **i** $Q_2 = 73$ The middle number is 73.

   ii $Q_1 = \dfrac{56+62}{2} = 59$ Q_1 (the middle value of the lower half) is
halfway between 56 and 62. Exclude the
number 73 before finding Q_1 and Q_3

  iii $Q_3 = \dfrac{81+85}{2} = 83$ Q_3 (the middle value of the upper half) is
halfway between 81 and 85.

  iv IQR = 83 − 59 = 24   IQR is the difference between Q_1 and Q_3.

Example 17 Finding quartiles for an even number of data values

Here is a set of measurements, collected by measuring the lengths, in metres, of 10 long-jump attempts.
6.7   9.2   8.3   5.1   7.9   8.4   9.0   8.2   8.8   7.1
a   List the data in order, from smallest to largest.
b   Find the range.
c   Find:
   i   the median (Q_2)   **ii**   the lower quartile (Q_1)
  iii   the upper quartile (Q_3)   **iv**   the interquartile range (IQR)
d   Interpret the IQR.

SOLUTION   **EXPLANATION**

a   5.1 6.7 7.1 7.9 8.2 8.3 8.4 8.8 9.0 9.2   Order the data to locate Q_1, Q_2 and Q_3.
$\underbrace{}_{Q_1}\ \ \underbrace{8.2\ 8.3}_{Q_2}\ \ \underbrace{}_{Q_3}$

b   Range = 9.2 − 5.1   Range = highest value − lowest value.
$= 4.1$

c **i** $Q_2 = \dfrac{8.2+8.3}{2}$ Q_2 is halfway between 8.2 and 8.3.

$= 8.25\text{ m}$

   ii $Q_1 = 7.1$ m   The middle value of the lower half is 7.1.
  iii $Q_3 = 8.8$ m   The middle value of the upper half is 8.8.
  iv IQR = 8.8 − 7.1   IQR is the difference between Q_1 and Q_3.
$= 1.7$ m

d   The middle 50% of jumps differed by less   The IQR is the range of the middle 50% of the
than 1.7 m.   data.

Exercise 9J

1 This ordered data set shows the number of hours of sleep 11 people had the night before.

3   5   5   6   7   7   7   8   8   8   9

a Find the range (the difference between the highest and lowest values).

b Find the median (Q_2, the middle number).

c Remove the middle number then find:

    i the lower quartile (Q_1, the middle of the lower half)

    ii the upper quartile (Q_3, the middle of the upper half).

d Find the interquartile range (IQR, the difference between the upper quartile and lower quartile).

2 This ordered data set shows the number of fish Daniel caught in the 12 weekends that he went fishing during the year.

1   2   3   3   4   4   6   7   7   9   11   13

a Find the range (the difference between the highest and lowest values).

b Find the median (Q_2, the middle number).

c Split the data in half then find:

    i the lower quartile (Q_1, the middle of the lower half)

    ii the upper quartile (Q_3, the middle of the upper half).

d Find the interquartile range (IQR, the difference between the upper quartile and lower quartile).

Example 16

3 For each of the following sets of data:

    i list the set of data in order, from smallest to largest   **ii** find the range

    iii find the median (Q_2)   **iv** find the lower quartile (Q_1)

    v find the upper quartile (Q_3)   **vi** find the interquartile range (IQR).

    a 5   7   3   6   2   1   9   7   11   9   0   8   5

    b 38   36   21   18   27   41   29   35   37   30   30   21   26

    c 180   316   197   176   346   219   183   253   228

    d 256   163   28   520   854   23   367   64   43   787   12   343   76   3   28

    e 1.8   1.9   1.3   1.2   2.1   1.2   0.9   1.7   0.8

    f 10   35   0.1   2.3   23   12   0.02

mple 17 **4** The running time, in minutes, of 16 movies at the cinema were as follows:

123   110   98   120   102   132   112   140   120   139   42   96   152   115   119   128

   a Find the range.

   b Find:

      i   the median (Q_2)   **ii**   the lower quartile (Q_1)

      iii the upper quartile (Q_3)   **iv** the interquartile range (IQR).

   c Interpret the IQR.

5 The following set of data represents the sale price, in thousands of dollars, of 14 vintage cars.

89   46 76 41 12 52 76

97 547 59 67 76 78 30

   a For the 14 vintage cars, find:

      i   the lowest price paid

      ii   the highest price paid

     iii the median price

      iv the lower quartile of the data

      v   the upper quartile of the data

      vi the IQR.

   b Interpret the IQR for the price of the vintage cars.

   c If the price of the most expensive vintage car increased, what effect would this have on Q_1, Q_2 and Q_3? What effect would it have on the mean price?

6 Find the interquartile range for the data in these stem-and-leaf plots.

a

Stem	Leaf
3	4 8 9
4	1 4 8 8
5	0 3 6 9
6	2 6

5 | 2 means 52

b

Stem	Leaf
17	5 8
18	0 4 6 7
19	1 1 2 9 9
20	4 4 7 8
21	2 6 8

21 | 3 means 21.3

7 Over a period of 30 days, Lara records how many fairies she sees in the garden each day. The data is organised into this frequency table.

Number of fairies each day	0	1	2	3	4	5
Frequency	7	4	8	4	6	1

   a Find the median number of fairies seen in the 30 days.

   b Find the interquartile range.

   c If Lara changes her mind about the day she saw 5 fairies and now says that she saw 10 fairies, would this change the IQR? Explain.

8 Two data sets have the same range. Does this mean they have the same lowest and highest values? Explain.

9 A second-hand car yard has more than 10 cars listed for sale. One expensive car is priced at $600 000 while the remaining cars are all priced near $40 000. Later the salesperson realises that there was an error in the price for the expensive car – there was one too many zeros printed onto the price.

    a Does the change in price for the expensive car change the value of the range? Give reasons.

    b Does the change in price for the expensive car change the value of the median? Give reasons.

    c Does the change in price for the expensive car change the value of the IQR? Give reasons.

10 **a** Is it possible for the range to equal the IQR? If so, give an example.

    b Is it possible for the IQR to equal zero? If so, give an example.

Enrichment: How many lollies in the jar?

11 The following two sets of data represent the number of jelly beans found in 10 jars purchased from two different confectionery stores, A and B.

Shop A: 25 26 24 24 28 26 27 25 26 28
Shop B: 22 26 21 24 29 19 25 27 31 22

    a Find Q_1, Q_2 and Q_3 for:

       i shop A   **ii** shop B

    b The top 25% of the data is above which value for shop A?

    c The lowest 25% of the data is below which value for shop B?

    d Find the interquartile range (IQR) for the number of jelly beans in 10 jars from:

       i shop A   **ii** shop B

    e By looking at the given sets of data, why should you expect there to be a significant difference between the IQR of shop A and the IQR of shop B?

    f Which shop offers greater consistency in the number of jelly beans in each jar it sells?

9.11 Box plots

A box plot is a commonly used graph for a data set showing the maximum and minimum values, the median and the upper and lower quartiles. Box plots are often used to show how a data set is distributed and how two sets compare. Box plots are used, for example, to compare a school's examination performance against the performance of all schools in a state.

Let's start: School performance

These two box plots show the performance of two schools on their English exams.

Box High School

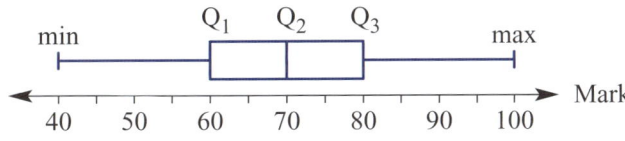

Plot Secondary College

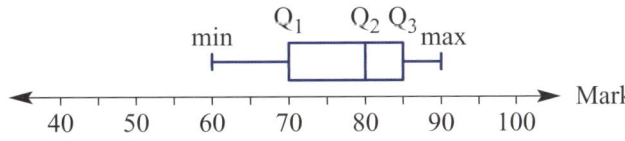

- Which school produced the highest mark?
- Which school produced the highest median (Q_2)?
- Which school produced the highest IQR?
- Which school produced the highest range?
- Describe the performance of Box High School against Plot Secondary College. Which school has better overall results and why?

■ A **box plot** (also called a box-and-whisker plot) is a graph which shows:
  - maximum and minimum values
  - median
  - lower and upper quartiles.
■ A quarter of the data is spread across each of the four sections of the graph

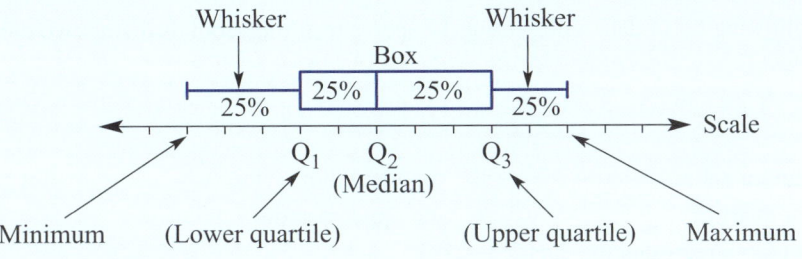

Key ideas

Example 18 Interpreting a box plot

This box plot summarises the price of all the books in a book shop.

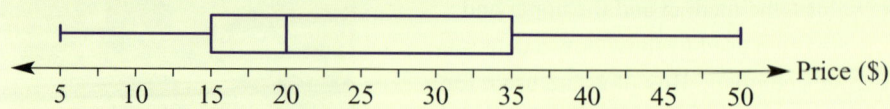

a State the minimum and maximum book prices.
b Find the range of the book prices.
c State the median book price.
d Find the interquartile range.
e Fifty percent of the books are priced below what amount?
f Twenty-five percent of the books are priced above what amount?
g If there were 1000 books in the store, how many would be priced below $15?

SOLUTION

a Minimum book price = $5
  Maximum book price = $50

b Range = $50 − $5
       = $45

c Median book price = $20

d Interquartile range = $35 − $15
                     = $20

e $20

f $35

g $0.25 \times 1000 = 250$
  250 books would be below $15

EXPLANATION

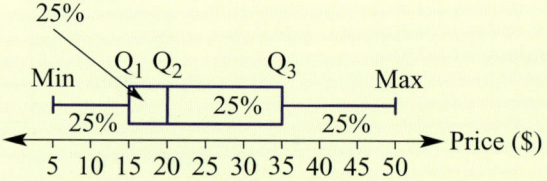

Range = maximum price − minimum price

The median is Q_2.

Interquartile range = $Q_3 − Q_1$

50% of books are below Q_2.

The top 25% of books are above Q_3.

25% of books are priced below $15.

Example 19 Constructing a box plot

Consider the following set of data representing 11 scores resulting from throwing two dice and adding their scores.

7 10 7 12 8 9 6 6 5 4 8

a Find:
  i   the minimum value
  ii the maximum value
  iii the median
  iv the lower quartile
  v   the upper quartile
b Draw a box plot to represent the data.

SOLUTION

EXPLANATION

a

    Q_1 Q_2 Q_3

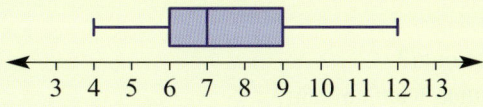

  4 5 6 6 7 7 8 8 9 10 12

  i Min. value = 4   **ii** Max. value = 12

  iii $Q_2 = 7$ **iv** $Q_1 = 6$

  v $Q_3 = 9$

b Box plot: Throwing two dice

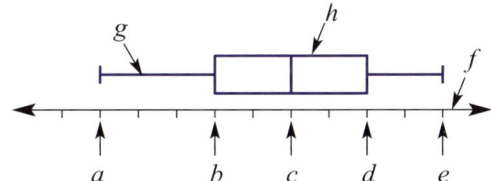

Order the data.

Determine the minimum and maximum value.

The median is the middle value.

Remove the middle value then locate the lower quartile and upper quartile.

Draw a scaled horizontal axis.

Place the box plot above the axis marking in the five key statistics from part **a**.

Exercise 9K

1 Write down the names of all the features labelled *a* to *h* on this box plot.

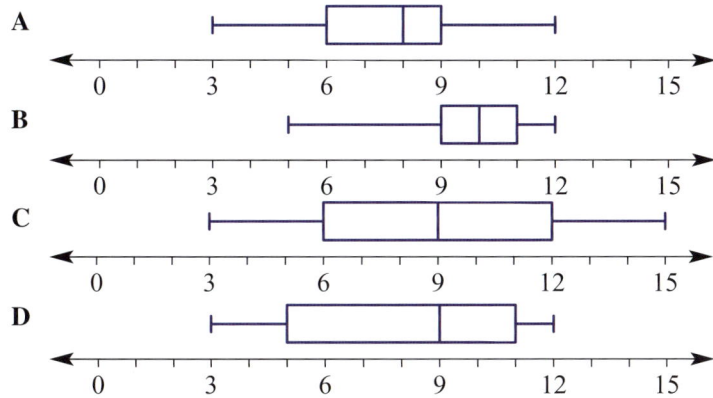

2 Write the missing words.

  a To find the range, you subtract the _____ from the _____.

  b To find the interquartile range, you subtract the _____ from the _____.

3 Choose the correct box plot for a data set which has all these measures:

- minimum = 3
- maximum = 12
- median = 9
- lower quartile = 5
- upper quartile = 11

A

B

C

D

Example 18 4 This box plot summarises the length of babies born in a particular week in a hospital.

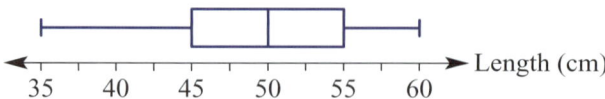

Length (cm)

a State the minimum and maximum baby lengths.
b Find the range of the length of the babies.
c State the median baby length.
d Find the interquartile range.
e Fifty percent of the baby lengths are below what amount?
f Twenty-five percent of the babies are born longer than what amount?
g If there were 80 babies born in the week, how many would be expected to be less than 45 cm in length?

5 This box plot summarises the number of rabbits spotted per day in a paddock over a 100-day period.

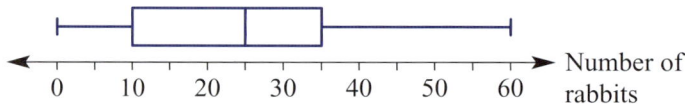

Number of rabbits

a State the minimum and maximum number of rabbits spotted.
b Find the range of the number of rabbits spotted.
c State the median number of rabbits spotted.
d Find the interquartile range.
e Seventy-five percent of the days the number of rabbits spotted is below what amount?
f Fifty percent of the days the number of rabbits spotted is more than what amount?
g How many days was the number of spotted rabbits less than 10?

Example 19 6 For each of the sets of data below:
i   state the minimum value
ii   state the maximum value
iii find the median (Q_2)
iv   find the lower quartile (Q_1)
v   find the upper quartile (Q_3)
vi   draw a box plot to represent the data.
  a 2 2 3 3 4 6 7 7 7 8 8 8 8 9 11 11 13 13 13
  b 43 21 65 45 34 42 40 28 56 50 10 43 70 37 61 54 88 19
  c 435 353 643 244 674 364 249 933 523 255 734
  d 0.5 0.7 0.1 0.2 0.9 0.5 1.0 0.6 0.3 0.4 0.8 1.1 1.2 0.8 1.3 0.4 0.5

7 The following set of data describes the number of cars parked in a street on 18 given days.

14   26   39   46   13   30   5   46   37   26   39   8   8   9   17   48   29   27

  a Represent the data as a box plot.

  b On what percentage of days were the number of cars parked on the street between:

    i 5 and 48?   **ii** 13 and 39?

    iii 5 and 39?   **iv** 39 and 48?

8 The weight of a sample of adult leopards from Africa and Asia are summarised in these box plots.

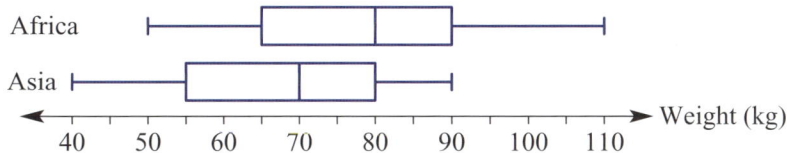

  a Which leopard population sample has the highest minimum weight?

  b What is the difference between the ranges for both population samples?

  c Is the IQR the same for both leopard samples? If so, what is it?

  d What percentage of leopards have a weight less than 80 kg for:

    i African leopards

    ii Asian leopards?

  e A leopard has a weight of 90 kg. Is it likely to be an Asian or African leopard?

9 The time that it takes for a sample of computers to start up is summarised in these box plots.

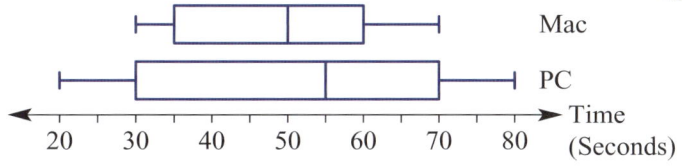

  a What type of computer has the lowest median?

  b What percentage of Mac computers loaded in less than 1 minute?

  c What percentage of PC computers took longer than 55 seconds to load?

  d What do you notice about the range for Mac computers and the IQR for PC computers? What does this mean?

10 The number of points per game for two
basketball players over a season is summarised in these
box plots.

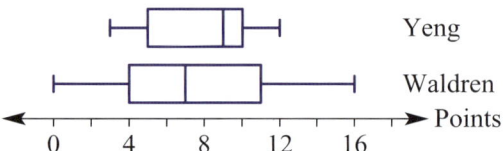

Box plots can be used to compare the
performance of each basketballer.

   a   Which player has the highest maximum?

   b   Which player has the highest median?

   c   Which player has the smallest IQR?

   d   Which player is a more consistent basketball scorer?
Give reasons.

   e   Which player most likely scored the greatest number
of points? Give reasons.

11 Give an example of a small data set which has the
following.

   a   maximum = upper quartile   **b**   median = lower quartile

12 Does the median always sit exactly in the middle of a box on a box plot? Explain.

13 Could the mean of a data set be greater than Q_3? Explain.

Enrichment: Outliers and battery life

14 Outliers on box plots are shown as a separate point.

                                                          Outlier

The life in months of a particular kind of battery used in a special type of high-powered
calculator is shown in this data set.

3   3   3   4   4   5   6   6   6   7   8   8   9   17

   a   Use all the values to calculate Q_1, Q_2 and Q_3 for the data set.

   b   Do any of the values appear to be outliers?

   c   Not including the outlier, what is the next highest value?

   d   Draw a box plot for the data using a cross (×) to show the outlier.

   e   Can you give a logical reason for the outlier?

Using a CAS calculator 9.11: Finding measures of spread and drawing box plots

The activity is on the companion website in the form of a printable PDF.

How many in the bag?

For this activity you will need:

- a bag or large pocket
- different-coloured counters
- paper and pen

Five counters

a Form pairs then without watching, have a third person (e.g. a teacher) place five counters of two different colours into the bag or pocket. An example of five counters could be two red, three blue but at this point in the activity you will not know this.

b Without looking, one person selects a counter from the bag while the other person records its colour. Replace the counter in the bag.

c Repeat part **b** for a total of 100 trials. Record the results in a table similar to this one.

Colour	Tally	Frequency
Red	⦀ ⦀⦀ ⦀⦀⦀ …	…
Blue	⦀⦀⦀ ⦀⦀⦀ ⦀⦀ …	…
Total	100	100

d Find the experimental probability for each colour, for example if 42 red counters were recorded then the experimental probability $= \dfrac{42}{100} = 0.42$.

e Use these experimental probabilities to help estimate how many of each colour of counter are in the bag. For example: 0.42 is close to $0.4 = \dfrac{2}{5}$, therefore guess two red and three blue.

Use this table to help.

Colour	Frequency	Experimental probability	Closest multiple of 0.2, e.g. 0.2, 0.4, …	Guess of how many counters of this colour
Total	100	1	1	5

f Now take the counters out of the bag to see if your estimate is correct.

More colours and counters

a Repeat the steps above but this time use three colours and 8 counters.

b Repeat the steps above but this time use four colours and 12 counters.

How do Australians get to work?

The collection of data is an important part of statistics. There are a number of ways that data may be collected. Some methods are: a **census** which includes the whole population, a **survey** which includes only a sample of the population, a **controlled experiment** where cause and effect is recorded, and an **observational study** where data is recorded without a controlled experiment.

If a survey is to be used as the method of data collection, it is important that it is well designed. If the data is to be representative of the *population*, the selection of the *sample* that is surveyed must be thought through carefully.

Sampling

Different methods are used to generate a random sample (a subset of the population) to survey.

Write down some of the problems with the following selection processes for selecting a sample from a population for the given topic.

a   A morning survey of the people on a train about their current employment.
b   A survey of the people on the electoral roll about their favourite music.
c   A phone poll of every 10th person in the phone book about their mobile phone plan.
d   A survey of people in a shopping centre on their yearly income.
e   A survey of the people in your year level on Australia's most popular television shows.
f   A call for volunteers in a newspaper advertisement for a medical trial.
g   A phone poll on a television news program about capital punishment.

Census data

The major collection of data about the population of Australia occurs in the national census. In the census, a person in each household completes a range of questions about the people staying in their house that night. Census data can be accessed via the Australian Bureau of Statistics (ABS) website.

a   Access the census data and list four topics of interest that contain data on the site.
b   Find the data on 'Method of Travel to Work' for 2006 (the last census before 2011).
c   Use the data to calculate the proportion of people in each category. Show your results using a table and a graph.
d   Design a survey to collect the same information as that recorded in the census information in part **b**. Include at least three questions. Use this to survey a class on their parents' method of travel to work.
e   Work out the proportion of people in each category for your data in part **d**. Show your results using a table and a graph.
f   Compare your answers in parts **c** and **e** for each category. Comment on any similarities or differences. What can you say about the quality of your sample based on these results? Discuss some of the limitations of your sample and how it could be improved.

1 A fair coin is tossed 5 times.
a How many outcomes are there?
b Find the probability of obtaining at least 4 tails.
c Find the probability of obtaining at least 1 tail.

2 Three cards, A, B and C, are randomly arranged in a row.
a Find the probability that the cards will be arranged in the order A B C from left to right.
b Find the probability that the B card will take the right-hand position.

3 Four students, Rick, Belinda, Katie and Chris are the final candidates for the selection of school captain and vice-captain. Two of the four students will be chosen at random to fill the positions.
a Find the probability that Rick will be chosen for:
i captain
ii captain or vice-captain.
b Find the probability that Rick and Belinda will be chosen for the two positions.
c Find the probability that Rick will be chosen for captain and Belinda will be chosen for vice-captain.
d Find the probability that the two positions will be filled by two boys or two girls.

4 State what would happen to the mean, median and range of a data set in these situations.
a Five is added to each value in the data set.
b Each value in the data set is doubled.
c Each value in the data set is doubled and then decreased by 1.

5 Three pieces of fruit have an average weight of m grams. After another piece of fruit is added, the average weight doubles. Find the weight of the extra piece of fruit in terms of m.

6 **a** Five different data values have a range and median equal to 7. If two of the values are 3 and 5, what are the possible combinations of values?
b Four data values have a range of 10, a mode of 2 and a median of 5. What are the four values?

7 Five integer scores out of 10 are all greater than 0. If the median is x and the mode is one more than the median and the mean is one less than the median, find all the possible sets of values if $x < 7$.

Chapter summary

Multiple events

These can be represented by tables or tree diagrams. They involve more than one component and can occur with or without replacement.
e.g. a bag contains 2 blue counters and 1 green, 2 are selected at random.
(I) Table with replacement.

		pick 1		
		b	b	g
	b	(b, b)	(b, b)	(g, b)
pick 2	b	(b, b)	(b, b)	(g, b)
	g	(b, g)	(b, g)	(g, g)

Sample space of 9 outcomes

$Pr(2 \text{ of same colour}) = \frac{5}{9}$

(II) Tree without replacement

Pick 1   Pick 2

$$\left.\begin{array}{l} b \begin{cases} b \quad bb \\ g \quad bg \end{cases} \\ b \begin{cases} b \quad bb \\ g \quad bg \end{cases} \\ g \begin{cases} b \quad gb \\ b \quad gb \end{cases} \end{array}\right\} \begin{array}{l} 6 \\ \text{outcomes} \end{array}$$

$Pr(2 \text{ of same colour}) = \frac{2}{6} = \frac{1}{3}$

Set notation

Within a sample space are a number of subsets.
A' = not A

A ∪ B means A or B; the union of A and B
A ∩ B means A and B; the intersection of A and B
A only is the elements in A but not in B

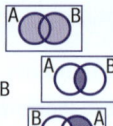

$n(A)$ is the number of elements in A
Ø is the empty or null set
e.g. A = {1, 2, 3, 4, 5}   B = {2, 4, 6, 8}
A ∪ B = {1, 2, 3, 4, 5, 6, 8}
A ∩ B = {2, 4} $n(B) = 4$
B only = {6, 8}
3 ∈ A means 3 is an element of A

Venn diagrams and two-way tables

These organise data from two or more categories

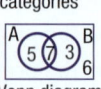

	A	A'	
B	7	3	10
B'	5	6	11
	12	9	21

Venn diagram

i.e. 6 in neither category, 7 in both categories

$Pr(A) = \frac{12}{21} = \frac{4}{7}$

$Pr(B \text{ only}) = \frac{3}{21} = \frac{1}{7}$

Probability review

The sample space is the list of all possible outcomes of an experiment. For all possible outcomes:
Pr(event) =
$$\frac{\text{number of outcomes where event occurs}}{\text{total number of outcomes}}$$
e.g. roll a normal six-sided die
$Pr(>4) = \frac{2}{6} = \frac{1}{3}$
$0 \leq Pr(\text{event}) \leq 1$
$Pr(\text{not A}) = 1 - Pr(A)$

Probability and statistics

Experimental probability

This is calculated from results of experiment or survey.
Experimental probability $= \frac{\text{number of times event occurs}}{\text{total number of trials}}$
Expected number = probability × number of occurrences of trials

---

Stem-and-leaf plots

These display all the data values using a stem and a leaf. An ordered back-to-back stem-and-leaf plot.

skewed

Leaf	Stem	Leaf
9 8 7 2	1	0 3
7 4 3 3	2	2 2 4
5 2 1	3	3 6 7 8
7	4	4 5 9
0	5	0

symmetrical

3 | 5 means 35
← key

Grouped data

Data values can be grouped into class intervals, e.g. 0–4, 5–9, etc. and recorded in a frequency table.
The frequency or percentage frequency of each interval can be recorded in a histogram.
e.g.

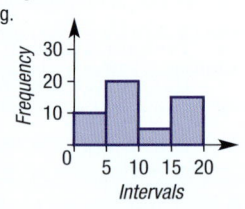

Summarising data: Measures of centre

Mode is the most common value (there can be more than one). Two modes means data is bimodal.
Mean = average
$= \frac{\text{sum of all values}}{\text{number of values}}$
Median is the middle value of data that is ordered.

odd data set   even data set

2 4 ⑦ 10 12   2 4 6 10 15 18
    median   ⎣8⎦
                          median

An outlier is a value that is not in the vicinity of the rest of the data.

Measures of spread

Range = maximum value − minimum value
Interquartile = upper quartile − lower quartile
range (IQR) (Q_3) (Q_1)
IQR is the range of the middle 50% of data.
e.g. Finding Q_1 and Q_3. First, locate median (Q_2) then find middle values of upper and lower half.

1 2 ⑤ 6 7 | 9 10 ⑫ 12 15

e.g. Q_1 $Q_2 = 8$ Q_3

For odd number of values exclude median from each half.

Box plots

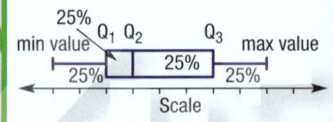

25% of data is in each of the four sections.

Multiple-choice questions

1 A letter is randomly chosen from the word XYLOPHONE. The probability that it is an O is:

A $\frac{1}{8}$ **B** $\frac{2}{9}$ **C** $\frac{1}{4}$ **D** $\frac{1}{9}$ **E** $\frac{1}{3}$

2 The values of x and y in the two-way table are:

A $x = 12, y = 8$ **B** $x = 12, y = 11$
C $x = 16, y = 4$ **D** $x = 10, y = 1$
E $x = 14, y = 6$

	A	A′	Total
B		5	9
B′	8	y	
Total	x		25

3 Which shaded region represents $A \cup B$?

A 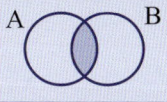 **B**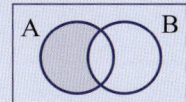

C  **D**  **E**

4 A bag contains 2 green balls and 1 red ball. Two balls are randomly selected *without replacement*. The probability of selecting one of each colour is:

A $\frac{1}{2}$ **B** $\frac{2}{3}$ **C** $\frac{5}{6}$ **D** $\frac{1}{3}$ **E** $\frac{3}{4}$

5 From rolling a biased die, a class finds an experimental probability of 0.3 of rolling a 5. From 500 rolls of the die, the expected number of 5s would be:

A 300 **B** 167 **C** 180 **D** 150 **E** 210

6 The median of the data in this stem-and-leaf plot is:

A 74 **B** 71 **C** 86
D 65 **E** 70

Stem	Leaf
5	3 5 8
6	1 4 7
7	0 2 4 7 9
8	2 6 6

7 | 4 means 74

7 If Jacob achieved scores of 12, 9, 7 and 12 on his last four language vocabulary tests, what score must he get on the fifth test to have a mean of 11?

A 16 **B** 14 **C** 11 **D** 13 **E** 15

8 This frequency histogram shows the times of finishers in a fun run. The percentage of competitors that finished in better than 40 minutes was:

A 55% **B** 85% **C** 50%
D 62.5% **E** 60%

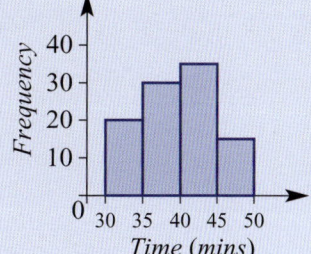

9 The interquartile range of the set of ordered data below is:

1.1   2.3   2.4   2.8   3.1   3.4   3.6   3.8   3.8   4.1   4.5   4.7   4.9

A 2–5   **B** 1.7   **C** 3.8   **D** 1.3   **E** 2.1

10 Choose the *incorrect* statement about the box plot below.

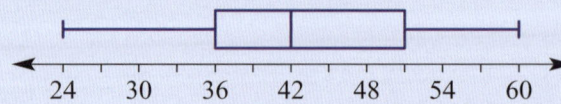

A The range is 36.   **B** Fifty percent of values are between 36 and 51.

C The median is 42.   **D** Twenty-five percent of values are below 36.

E The interquartile range is 20.

Short-answer questions

1 Determine the probability of each of the following.

  a Rolling more than 2 on a normal six-sided die

  b Selecting a vowel from the word **EDUCATION**

  c Selecting a pink or white jelly bean from a packet containing 4 pink, 2 white and 4 black jelly beans

2 From a survey of 50 people, 30 have the newspaper delivered, 25 read it online, 10 do both and 5 do neither.

  a Construct a Venn diagram for the survey results.

  b How many people only read the newspaper online?

  c If one of the 50 people were randomly selected, find:

  i Pr(have paper delivered and read it online)

  ii Pr(don't have it delivered)

  iii Pr(only read it online).

3 **a** Copy and complete this two-way table.

	A	A′	Total
B		16	
B′	8		20
Total	17		

  b Convert the information into a Venn diagram as shown.

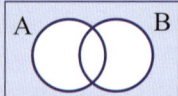

  c Find the following probabilities.

  i Pr(B′)   **ii** Pr(A ∩ B)

  iii n(A only)   **iv** n(A ∪ B)

4 A spinner with equal areas of red, green and blue is spun and a four-sided die numbered 1 to 4 is rolled.

		Die			
		1	2	3	4
Spinner	**red**	(red, 1)	(red, 2)		
	green				
	blue				

  a Complete a table like the one shown and state the number of outcomes in the sample space.

  b Find the probability that:

    i the outcome is red and an even number

    ii the outcome is blue or green and a 4

    iii the outcome does not involve blue.

5 Libby randomly selects two coins from her pocket *without replacement*. Her pocket contains a $1 coin, and two 10-cent coins.

  a List all the possible combinations using a tree diagram.

  b If a chocolate bar costs $1.10, find the probability that she can hand over the two coins to pay for it.

6 A quality controller records the frequency of the types of chocolates from a sample of 120 off its production line.

Centre	Soft	Hard	Nut
Frequency	50	22	48

  a What is the experimental probability of randomly selecting a nut centre?

  b In a box of 24 chocolates, how many would be expected to have a non-soft centre?

7 Claudia records the number of emails she receives each weekday for two weeks as follows.

        30   31   33   23   29   31   21   15   24   23

Find:

  a the mean   **b** the median

  c the mode.

8 Two mobile phone salespeople are both aiming for a promotion to be the new assistant store manager. The best salesperson over a 15-week period will achieve the promotion. The number of mobile phones they sold each week is recorded below.

Employee 1: 21 34 40 38 46 36 23 51 35 25 39 19 35 53 45

Employee 2: 37 32 29 41 24 17 28 20 37 48 42 38 17 40 45

  a Draw an ordered back-to-back stem-and-leaf plot for the data.

  b For each employee, find:

    i the median number of sales

    ii the mean number of sales.

  c By comparing the two sets of data, state, with reasons who you think should get the promotion.

  d Describe each employee's data as approximately symmetrical or skewed.

9 The data below represents the finish times, in minutes, of 25 competitors in a local car rally race.

134 147 162 164 145 159 151 143 136 155 163 157 168
171 152 128 144 161 158 136 178 152 167 154 161

a Record the above data in a frequency table in class intervals of 10 minutes. Include a percentage frequency column.

b Construct a frequency histogram.

c Determine:

i the number of competitors that finished in less than 140 minutes

ii the percentage of competitors that finished between 130 and 160 minutes.

10 Scott scores the following runs in each of his innings across the course of a cricket season:

20 5 34 42 10 3 29 55 25 37 51 12 34 22

a Find the range.

b Construct a box plot to represent the data by first finding the quartiles.

c From the box plot, 25% of his innings were above what number of runs?

Extended-response questions

1 The local Sunday market has a number of fundraising activities.

a For $1 you can spin a spinner numbered 1–5 twice. If you spin two even numbers you receive $2 (your dollar back plus an extra dollar), if you spin two odd numbers you get your dollar back and otherwise you lose your dollar.

	First spin				
Second spin	1	2	3	4	5
1	(1, 1)	(2, 1)			
2					
3					
4					
5					

i Complete the table shown to list the sample space.

ii What is the probability of losing your dollar?

iii What is the probability of making a dollar profit?

iv In 50 attempts, how many times would you expect to lose your dollar?

v If you start with $100 and have 100 attempts, how much money would you expect to end up with?

b Forty-five people were surveyed as they walked through the market as to whether they bought a sausage and/or a drink from the sausage sizzle. Twenty-five people bought a sausage, 30 people bought a drink, with 15 buying both. Let S be the set of people who bought a sausage and D the set of people who bought a drink.

   i Construct a Venn diagram to represent this information.

   ii How many people bought neither a drink nor a sausage?

   iii How many people bought a sausage only?

   iv If a person was randomly selected from the 45, what is the probability they bought a drink but not a sausage?

   v Find $\Pr(S')$.

   vi Find $\Pr(S' \cup D)$ and state what this probability represents.

2 The data below represents the data collected over a month of 30 consecutive days of the delay time (in minutes) of the flight departure of the same evening flight of two rival airlines.

Airline A

  2 11 6 14 18   1   7   4 12 14   9   2 13   4 19
13 17 3 52 24 19 12 14   0   7 13 18   1 23   8

Airline B

  6 12   9 22   2 15 10 5 10 19   5 12   7 11 18
21 15 10   4 10   7 18 1 18   8 25   4 22 19 26

a Does the data for airline A appear to have any outliers (numbers not near the majority of data elements)?

b By removing any outliers listed in part **a**, find the following for airline A:

   i median (Q_2)

   ii lower quartile (Q_1)

   iii upper quartile (Q_3).

c Hence, complete a box plot of the delay times for airline A.

d Airline A reports that half its flights for that month had a delay time of less than 10 minutes. Is this claim correct? Explain.

e On the same axis as in part **c**, construct a box plot for airline B's delay times.

f By finding the range and interquartile range of the two airlines' data, comment on the spread of the delay times for each company.

g Use the previous question parts to explain which airline you would choose based on their delay times and why.

Chapter 10

Introduction to quadratic equations and graphs

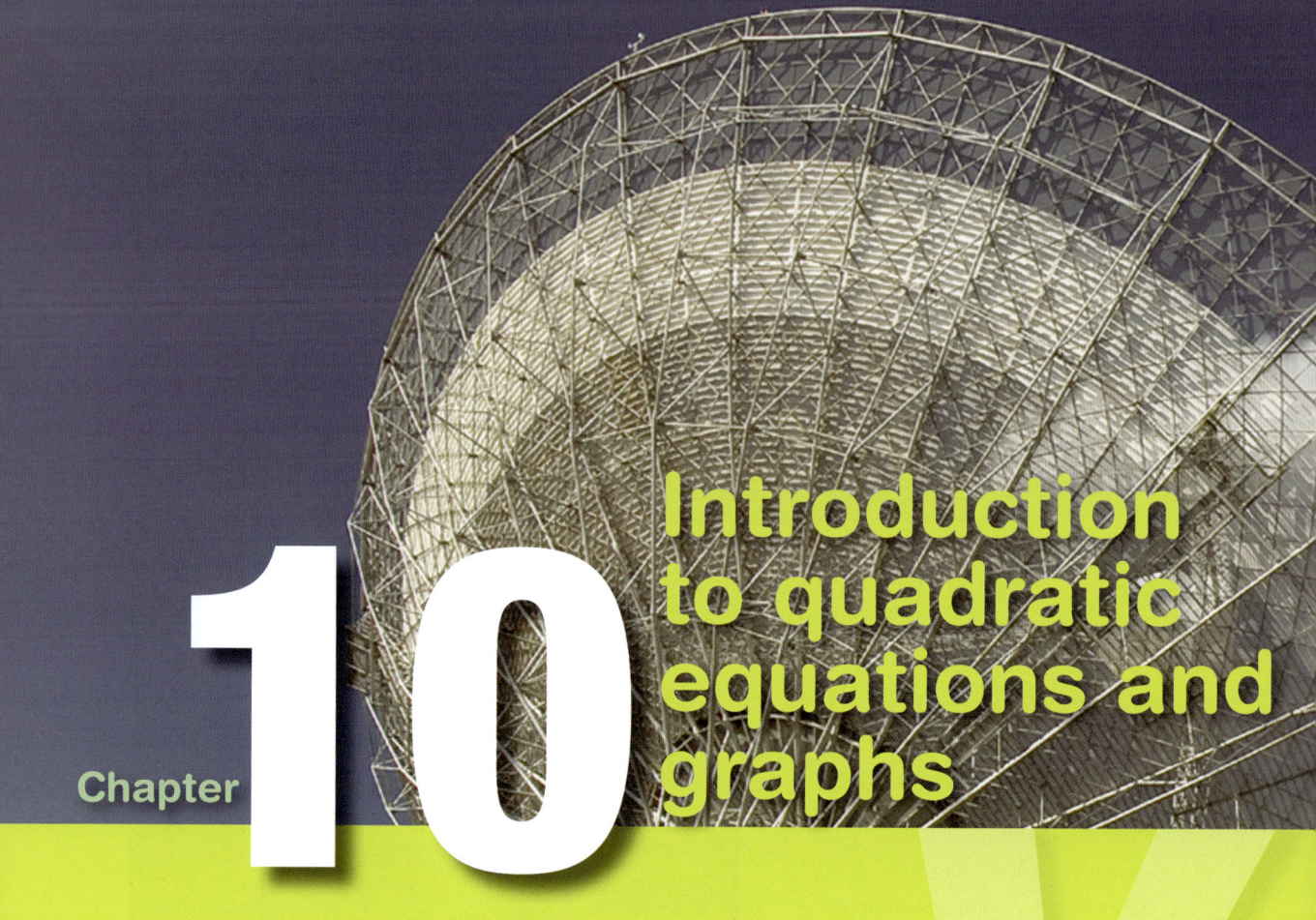

What you will learn

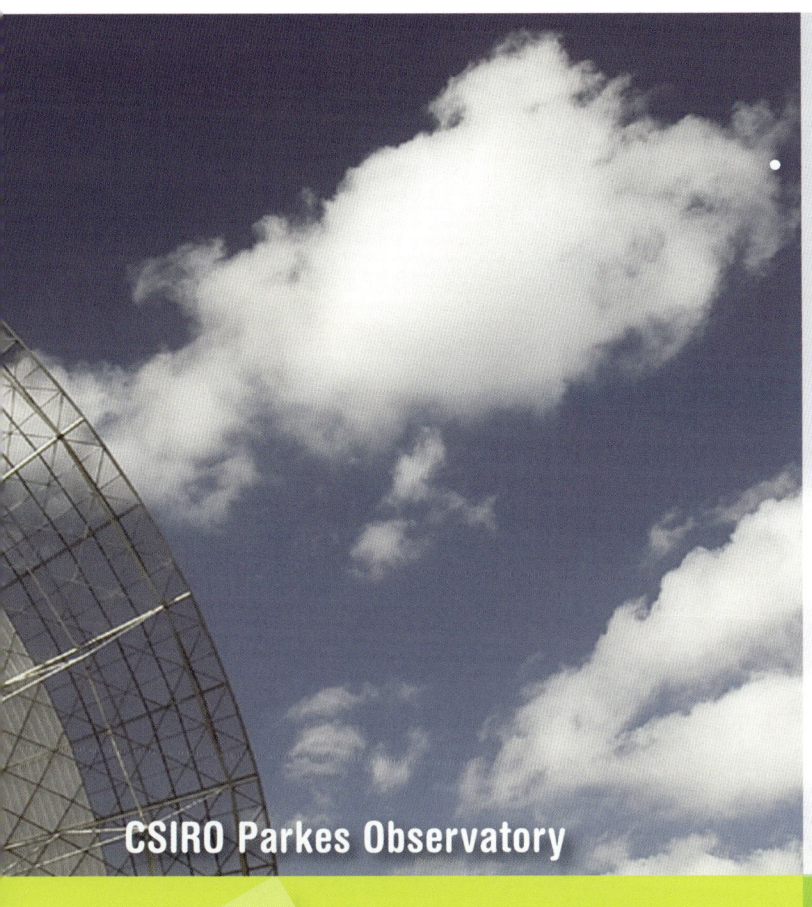

Australian curriculum

NUMBER AND ALGEBRA
Linear and non-linear relationships

Sketch simple non-linear relations with and without the use of digital technologies

CSIRO Parkes Observatory

The CSIRO Parkes Observatory in New South Wales is home to the Parkes Radio Telescope which is famous for providing the first pictures to the world of the Apollo 11 moonwalk in 1969. The telescope's gigantic dish has a diameter of 64 metres and receives radio and microwave signals from outer space.

The shape of the dish is parabolic meaning that its curvature can be described by a quadratic equation. The parabolic shape guarantees that all the radio and microwave signals bounce off the dish surface and are reflected to the receiver, which sits at a special point (called the focus) above the dish.

The Parkes Radio Telescope is still in use today as part of the Australia Telescope National Facility.

1 Evaluate the following by substituting each of the four values of x into each expression.

    i $x = 0$ **ii** $x = 2$ **iii** $x = -1$ **iv** $x = -3$

    a x^2 **b** $2x^2 - 3x$ **c** $-x^2 + 3$ **d** $x^2 + 2x - 1$

2 Does $x = 1$ satisfy the following equations? Substitute to find out.

    a $x^2 - 4x + 3 = 0$ **b** $x^2 - 2x = 0$ **c** $1 - x^2 = 0$

3 Solve the following for x.

    a $2x = 0$ **b** $x - 3 = 0$ **c** $x + 5 = 0$

    d $2x + 6 = 0$ **e** $3x - 12 = 0$ **f** $3x - 4 = 0$

4 Rearrange the following to produce 0 on the right-hand side.

    a $a^2 = 2a$ **b** $a^2 = 3a - 1$

5 State the highest common factor of the following pairs of terms.

    a $4x$ and $2xy$ **b** x^2 and $2x$ **c** $3x$ and $9x^2$

    d $2x^2$ and $4x$ **e** $4x^2$ and 36 **f** $5x^2$ and 20

6 Factorise the following difference of perfect squares.

    a $x^2 - 9$ **b** $x^2 - 25$ **c** $x^2 - 64$ **d** $x^2 - 16$

7 Factorise the following quadratic trinomials.

    a $x^2 + 8x + 12$ **b** $x^2 + 5x + 4$ **c** $x^2 - 3x - 28$ **d** $x^2 - 9x + 20$

8 Expand these expressions.

    a $2(x - 3)$ **b** $x(2 - x)$ **c** $(x + 1)(x - 2)$ **d** $(x - 3)(x - 4)$

9 Write expanded expressions for the areas of the following rectangles.

    a 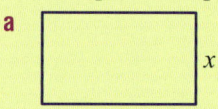   **b**    **c**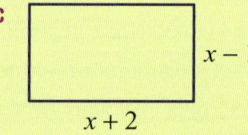

10 Find the x- and y-intercepts of the straight lines with the given rules.

    a $y = 2x - 4$ **b** $3x + 6y = 12$

11 Give the x-coordinate of the point halfway between the following pairs of points.

    a $(0, 0)$ and $(10, 0)$ **b** $(2, 0)$ and $(4, 0)$

    c $(-1, 0)$ and $(3, 0)$ **d** $(3, 0)$ and $(8, 0)$

10.1 Quadratic equations

Quadratic equations are commonplace in theoretical and practical applications of mathematics. They are used to solve problems in geometry and measurement as well as in number theory and physics. The path that a projectile takes while flying through the air, for example, can be analysed using quadratic equations.

A quadratic equation can be written in the form $ax^2 + bx + c = 0$ where a, b and c are constants and $a \neq 0$. Examples include $x^2 - 2x + 1 = 0$, $5x^2 - 3 = 0$ and $-0.2x^2 + 4x = 0$. Unlike a linear equation which has a single solution, quadratic equations can have zero, one or two solutions. For example: $x = 2$ and $x = -1$ are solutions to the quadratic equation $x^2 - x - 2 = 0$ since $2^2 - 2 - 2 = 0$ and $(-1)^2 - (-1) - 2 = 0$. One method for finding the solutions to quadratic equations involves the use of the Null Factor Law where each factor of a factorised quadratic expression is equated to zero.

The trajectory of this arrow can be modelled using quadratic equations.

Let's start: Exploring the Null Factor Law

$x = 1$ is not a solution to the quadratic equation $x^2 - x - 12 = 0$ since $1^2 - 1 - 12 \neq 0$.

- Use trial and error to find at least one of the two numbers which are solutions to $x^2 - x - 12 = 0$.
- Rewrite the equation in factorised form.

$$x^2 - x - 12 = 0 \text{ becomes } (\quad)(\quad) = 0$$

- Now repeat the first task above to find solutions to the equation using the factorised form.
- Was the factorised form easier to work with? Discuss.

Key ideas

- A **quadratic equation** can be written in the form $ax^2 + bx + c = 0$
  - This is called **standard form**.
  - a, b and c are constants and $a \neq 0$.
- The **Null Factor Law** states that if the product of two numbers is zero then either or both of the two numbers is zero.
  - If $a \times b = 0$ then $a = 0$ or $b = 0$.
  - If $(x + 1)(x - 3) = 0$ then $x + 1 = 0$ (so $x = -1$) or $x - 3 = 0$ (so $x = 3$).
  - $x + 1$ and $x - 3$ are the linear factors of $(x + 1)(x - 3)$ (which equals $x^2 - 2x - 3$).

Example 1 Writing in standard form

Write these quadratic equations in standard form.

a $x^2 = 2x + 7$

b $2(x^2 - 3x) = 5$

SOLUTION

EXPLANATION

a $x^2 = 2x + 7$
  $x^2 - 2x - 7 = 0$

We require the form $ax^2 + bx + c = 0$. Subtract $2x$ and 7 from both sides to move all terms to the left-hand side.

b $2(x^2 - 3x) = 5$
  $2x^2 - 6x = 5$
  $2x^2 - 6x - 5 = 0$

First expand brackets then subtract 5 from both sides.

Example 2 Testing for a solution

Substitute the given x value into the equation and say whether or not it is a solution.

a $x^2 + x - 6 = 0$ $(x = 2)$

b $2x^2 + 5x - 3 = 0$ $(x = -4)$

SOLUTION

EXPLANATION

a $x^2 + x - 6 = 2^2 + 2 - 6$
     $= 6 - 6$
     $= 0$
  $\therefore x = 2$ is a solution

Substitute $x = 2$ into the equation to see if the left-hand side equals zero.

$x = 2$ satisfies the equation so $x = 2$ is a solution.

b $2x^2 + 5x - 3 = 2(-4)^2 + 5(-4) - 3$
     $= 2 \times 16 + (-20) - 3$
     $= 32 - 20 - 3$
     $= 9$
  $\therefore x = -4$ is not a solution

Substitute $x = -4$. Recall that $(-4)^2 = 16$ and $5 \times (-4) = -20$.

The equation is not satisfied so $x = -4$ is not a solution.

Example 3 Using the Null Factor Law

Use the Null Factor Law to solve these equations.

a $x(x + 2) = 0$

b $(x - 1)(x + 5) = 0$

c $(2x - 1)(5x + 3) = 0$

SOLUTION

EXPLANATION

a $x(x + 2) = 0$
  $x = 0$ or $x + 2 = 0$
  $x = 0$ or $x = -2$

The factors are x and $(x + 2)$. Solve each linear factor equal to zero.

b $(x - 1)(x + 5) = 0$
  $x - 1 = 0$ or $x + 5 = 0$
  $x = 1$ or $x = -5$

Solve each factor $(x - 1)$ and $(x + 5)$ equal to zero.

c $(2x - 1)(5x + 3) = 0$

$2x - 1 = 0$ or $5x + 3 = 0$

$2x = 1$ or $5x = -3$

$x = \dfrac{1}{2}$ or $x = -\dfrac{3}{5}$

The two factors are $(2x - 1)$ and $(5x + 3)$. Each one results in a two-step linear equation.

Exercise 10A

Understanding

1 Evaluate these quadratic expressions by substituting the given x value.

a $x^2 + 3\ (x = 3)$ **b** $x^2 - 5\ (x = 1)$ **c** $x^2 + x\ (x = 2)$

d $x^2 + 2x\ (x = -1)$ **e** $x^2 - x\ (x = -4)$ **f** $2x^2 - x + 1\ (x = -1)$

g $3x^2 - x + 2\ (x = 5)$ **h** $5x^2 + 2x - 3\ (x = -1)$ **i** $-2x^2 + 2x - 3\ (x = 4)$

2 Decide if the following equations are quadratics.

a $x + 1 = 0$ **b** $1 - 2x = 0$ **c** $x^2 + 3x + 1 = 0$

d $5x^2 - x + 2 = 0$ **e** $x^2 - 1 = 0$ **f** $x^3 + x^2 - 2 = 0$

g $x^5 + 1 - x = 0$ **h** $x^2 = x + 2$ **i** $x + 2 = 4x^2$

3 Solve these linear equations.

a $x - 1 = 0$ **b** $x + 3 = 0$ **c** $x + 11 = 0$

d $2x + 4 = 0$ **e** $3x - 9 = 0$ **f** $5x + 30 = 0$

4 Copy and complete the following working which uses the Null Factor Law.

a $x(x - 5) = 0$

    $x = 0$ or _____ $= 0$

    $x = 0$ or $x =$ ____

b $(2x + 1)(x - 3) = 0$

    _____ $= 0$ or $x - 3 = 0$

    $2x =$ ____ or $x =$ _____

        $x =$ ____

Fluency

Example 1

5 Write these quadratic equations in standard form ($ax^2 + bx + c = 0$).

a $x^2 + 2x = 5$ **b** $x^2 - 5x = -2$ **c** $x^2 = 4x - 1$

d $x^2 = 7x + 2$ **e** $2(x^2 + x) + 1 = 0$ **f** $3(x^2 - x) = -4$

g $4 = -3x^2$ **h** $3x = x^2 - 1$ **i** $5x = 2(-x^2 + 5)$

Example 2

6 Substitute the given x value into the quadratic equation and say whether or not it is a solution.

a $x^2 - 1 = 0\ (x = 1)$ **b** $x^2 - 25 = 0\ (x = 5)$ **c** $x^2 - 4 = 0\ (x = 1)$

d $2x^2 + 1 = 0\ (x = 0)$ **e** $x^2 - 9 = 0\ (x = -3)$ **f** $x^2 + 2x + 1 = 0\ (x = -1)$

g $x^2 - x - 12 = 0\ (x = 5)$ **h** $2x^2 - x + 3 = 0\ (x = -1)$ **i** $5 - 2x + x^2 = 0\ (x = -2)$

7 Substitute $x = -2$ and $x = 5$ into the equation $x^2 - 3x - 10 = 0$. What do you notice?

8 Substitute $x = -3$ and $x = 4$ into the equation $x^2 - x - 12 = 0$. What do you notice?

Example 3a,b

9 Use the Null Factor Law to solve these equations.

a $x(x + 1) = 0$

b $x(x + 5) = 0$

c $x(x - 2) = 0$

d $x(x - 7) = 0$

e $(x + 1)(x - 3) = 0$

f $(x - 4)(x + 2) = 0$

g $(x + 7)(x - 3) = 0$

h $\left(x + \dfrac{1}{2}\right)\left(x - \dfrac{1}{2}\right) = 0$

i $2x(x + 5) = 0$

j $5x\left(x - \dfrac{2}{3}\right) = 0$

k $\dfrac{x}{3}\left(x + \dfrac{2}{3}\right) = 0$

l $\dfrac{2x}{5}(x + 2) = 0$

Example 3c

10 Use the Null Factor Law to solve these equations.

a $(2x - 1)(x + 2) = 0$

b $(x + 2)(3x - 1) = 0$

c $(5x + 2)(x + 4) = 0$

d $(x - 1)(3x - 1) = 0$

e $(x + 5)(7x + 2) = 0$

f $(3x - 2)(5x + 1) = 0$

g $(11x - 7)(2x - 13) = 0$

h $(4x + 9)(2x - 7) = 0$

i $(3x - 4)(7x + 1) = 0$

11 Find the numbers which satisfy the given condition.

a The product of x and a number 3 more than x is zero.

b The product of x and a number 7 less than x is zero.

c The product of a number 1 less than x and a number 4 more than x is zero.

d The product of a number 1 less than twice x and 6 more than x is zero.

e The product of a number 3 more than twice x and 1 less than twice x is zero.

12 Write these equations as quadratics in standard form. Remove any brackets and fractions.

a $5x^2 + x = x^2 - 1$

b $2x = 3x^2 - x$

c $3(x^2 - 1) = 1 + x$

d $2(1 - 3x^2) = x(1 - x)$

e $\dfrac{x}{2} = x^2 - \dfrac{3}{2}$

f $\dfrac{4x}{3} - x^2 = 2(1 - x)$

g $\dfrac{5}{x} + 1 = x$

h $\dfrac{3}{x} + \dfrac{5}{2} = 2x$

13 These quadratic equations have two integer solutions between -5 and 5. Use trial and error to find them.

a $x^2 - x - 2 = 0$

b $x^2 - 4x + 3 = 0$

c $x^2 - 4x = 0$

d $x^2 + 3x = 0$

e $x^2 + 3x - 4 = 0$

f $x^2 - 16 = 0$

14 Consider the quadratic equation $(x + 2)^2 = 0$.

a Write the equation in the form (_____)(_____) = 0.

b Use the Null Factor Law to find the solutions to the equation. What do you notice?

c Now solve these quadratic equations.

 i $(x + 3)^2 = 0$

 ii $(x - 5)^2 = 0$

 iii $(2x - 1)^2 = 0$

 iv $(5x - 7)^2 = 0$

15 Consider the equation $3(x - 1)(x + 2) = 0$.

   a First divide both sides of the equation by 3. Write down the new equation.

   b Solve the equation using the Null Factor Law.

   c Compare the given original equation with the equation found in part **a**. Explain why the solutions are the same.

   d Solve these equations.

      i $7(x + 2)(x - 3) = 0$ **ii** $11x(x + 2) = 0$ **iii** $\dfrac{(x + 1)(x - 3)}{4} = 0$

16 Consider the equation $(x - 3)^2 + 1 = 0$.

   a Substitute these x values to decide if they are solutions to the equation.

      i $x = 3$ **ii** $x = 4$ **iii** $x = 0$ **iv** $x = -2$

   b Do you think the equation will have a solution? Explain why.

Enrichment: Polynomials

17 Polynomials are sums of integer powers of x.

Example	Polynomial Name
2	Constant
$2x + 1$	Linear
$x^2 - 2x + 5$	Quadratic
$x^3 - x^2 + 6x - 1$	Cubic
$7x^4 + x^3 + 2x^2 - x + 4$	Quartic
$4x^5 - x + 1$	Quintic

Name these polynomial equations.

   a $3x - 1 = 0$ **b** $x^2 + 2 = 0$ **c** $x^5 - x^4 + 3 = 0$

   d $5 - 2x + x^3 = 0$ **e** $3x - 2x^4 + x^2 = 0$ **f** $5 - x^5 = x^4 + x$

18 Solve these polynomial equations using the Null Factor Law.

   a $(x + 1)(x - 3)(x + 2) = 0$ **b** $(x - 2)(x - 5)(x + 11) = 0$

   c $(2x - 1)(3x + 2)(5x - 1) = 0$ **d** $(3x + 2)(5x + 4)(7x + 10)(2x - 13) = 0$

A CNC (computer numerically-controlled) milling machine cuts mechanical components out of solid steel. The software may have to solve thousands of polynomials to cut complex shapes.

10.2 Solving $ax^2 + bx = 0$ and $x^2 - d^2 = 0$

When using the Null Factor Law we notice that equations must first be expressed as a product of two factors. Hence, any equation not in this form must first be factorised. Two types of quadratic equations are studied here. The first is of the form $ax^2 + bx = 0$ where x is a common factor and the second is of the form $x^2 - d^2 = 0$ which is a difference of two perfect squares.

Remember 'null' means 'zero'.

Let's start: Which factorisation technique?

These two equations may look similar but they are not the same: $x^2 - 9x = 0$ and $x^2 - 9 = 0$

- Discuss how you could factorise each expression on the left-hand side of the equations.
- How does the factorised form help to solve the equations? What are the solutions? Are the solutions the same for both equations?

Key ideas

■ When solving an equation of the form $ax^2 + bx = 0$, factorise by taking out common factors including x.

$$2x^2 - 8x = 0$$
$$2x(x - 4) = 0$$
$$2x = 0 \text{ or } x - 4 = 0$$
$$x = 0 \text{ or } x = 4$$

■ When solving an equation of the form $a(x^2 - d^2) = 0$, look for common factors and a difference of perfect squares.
  - Recall: $a^2 - b^2 = (a + b)(a - b)$

$$5x^2 - 20 = 0$$
$$5(x^2 - 4) = 0$$
$$5(x + 2)(x - 2) = 0$$
$$x + 2 = 0 \text{ or } x - 2 = 0$$
$$x = \text{-}2 \text{ or } x = 2$$

Example 4 Solving when x is a common factor

Solve each of the following equations.

a $x^2 + 4x = 0$

b $2x^2 = 8x$

SOLUTION

a $x^2 + 4x = 0$
$x(x + 4) = 0$
$x = 0 \text{ or } x + 4 = 0$
$x = 0 \text{ or } x = \text{-}4$

b $2x^2 = 8x$
$2x^2 - 8x = 0$
$2x(x - 4) = 0$
$2x = 0 \text{ or } x - 4 = 0$
$x = 0 \text{ or } x = 4$

EXPLANATION

Factorise by taking out the common factor x.
Using the Null Factor Law, set each factor, x and $(x + 4)$, equal to 0. Solve for x.

Make the right-hand side equal to zero by subtracting $8x$ from both sides.
Factorise by taking out the common factor of $2x$ and apply the Null Factor Law to solve.

Example 5 Solving with a difference of perfect squares

Solve each of these equations.

a $x^2 - 16 = 0$

b $3x^2 - 27 = 0$

SOLUTION

a
$$x^2 - 16 = 0$$
$$(x + 4)(x - 4) = 0$$
$$x + 4 = 0 \text{ or } x - 4 = 0$$
$$x = -4 \text{ or } x = 4$$

b
$$3x^2 - 27 = 0$$
$$3(x^2 - 9) = 0$$
$$3(x + 3)(x - 3) = 0$$
$$x + 3 = 0 \text{ or } x - 3 = 0$$
$$x = -3 \text{ or } x = 3$$

EXPLANATION

Factorise using $a^2 - b^2 = (a + b)(a - b)$ then use the Null Factor Law to find the solutions.

Note that 3 is a common factor. Then factorise the difference of perfect squares.

Exercise 10B

Understanding

1 Write down the highest common factor of these pairs of terms.

a $2x$ and 4
b $5x$ and 10
c $4x$ and 6
d $16x$ and 24
e x^2 and $2x$
f x^2 and $7x$
g $3x^2$ and $6x$
h $9x^2$ and $15x$

2 Factorise these expressions fully by first taking out the highest common factor.

a $2x^2 - 8$
b $4x^2 - 36$
c $3x^2 - 75$
d $12x^2 - 12$
e $x^2 - 3x$
f $x^2 + 7x$
g $2x^2 - 4x$
h $5x^2 - 15x$
i $6x^2 + 4x$
j $9x^2 - 27x$
k $4x - 16x^2$
l $14x - 21x^2$

3 Use the Null Factor Law to write down the solutions to these equations.

a $x(x - 3) = 0$
b $4x(x + 1) = 0$
c $-7x(x + 2) = 0$
d $(x + 1)(x - 1) = 0$
e $(x + 5)(x - 5) = 0$
f $(2x + 1)(2x - 1) = 0$

Fluency

mple 4a **4** Solve each of these equations.

a $x^2 + 3x = 0$
b $x^2 + 7x = 0$
c $x^2 + 4x = 0$
d $x^2 - 5x = 0$
e $x^2 - 8x = 0$
f $x^2 - 2x = 0$
g $x^2 + \dfrac{1}{3}x = 0$
h $x^2 - \dfrac{1}{2}x = 0$

5 Solve these equations by first taking out the highest common factor.

a $2x^2 - 6x = 0$
b $3x^2 - 12x = 0$
c $4x^2 + 20x = 0$
d $6x^2 - 18x = 0$
e $-5x^2 + 15x = 0$
f $-2x^2 - 8x = 0$

mple 4b **6** Solve each of the following equations.

a $x^2 = 3x$
b $5x^2 = 10x$
c $4x^2 = 16x$
d $3x^2 = -9x$
e $2x^2 = -8x$
f $7x^2 = -21x$

Example 5a

7 Solve each of the following equations, noting the difference of perfect squares.

a $x^2 - 9 = 0$ b $x^2 - 16 = 0$ c $x^2 - 25 = 0$

d $x^2 - 144 = 0$ e $x^2 - 81 = 0$ f $x^2 - 400 = 0$

Example 5b

8 Solve each of the following equations by taking out a common factor first.

a $7x^2 - 28 = 0$ b $5x^2 - 45 = 0$ c $2x^2 - 50 = 0$ d $6x^2 - 24 = 0$

e $2x^2 = 8$ f $3x^2 = 12$ g $5x^2 = 80$ h $8x^2 = 72$

9 Rearrange these equations then solve them.

a $4 = x^2$ b $-x^2 + 25 = 0$ c $-x^2 = -100$

d $-3x^2 = 21x$ e $-5x^2 + 35x = 0$ f $1 - x^2 = 0$

g $12x = 18x^2$ h $2x^2 + x = 7x^2 - 2x$ i $9 - 2x^2 = x^2$

10 Remove brackets or fractions to help solve these equations.

a $x - \dfrac{4}{x} = 0$ b $\dfrac{36}{x} - x = 0$ c $\dfrac{3}{x^2} = 3$

d $5(x^2 + 1) = 3x^2 + 7$ e $x(x - 3) = 2x^2 + 4x$ f $3x(5 - x) = x(7 - x)$

11 Write an equation and solve it to find the number.

a The square of the number is 7 times the same number.

b The difference between the square of a number and 64 is zero.

c 3 times the square of a number is equal to -12 times the number.

12 Consider the equation $x^2 + 4 = 0$.

a Explain why it cannot be written in the form $(x + 2)(x - 2) = 0$.

b Are there any solutions to the equation $x^2 + 4 = 0$? Why/Why not?

13 An equation of the form $ax^2 + bx = 0$ will always have two solutions if a and b are not zero.

a Explain why one of the solutions will always be $x = 0$.

b Write the rule for the second solution in terms of a and b.

Enrichment: Tougher DOPS

14 Note for example that $4x^2 - 9 = 0$ factorises to $(2x + 3)(2x - 3) = 0$. Now solve these equations.

a $9x^2 - 16 = 0$ b $25x^2 - 36 = 0$ c $4 - 100x^2 = 0$

d $81 - 25x^2 = 0$ e $64 = 121x^2$ f $-49x^2 = -144$

15 Note for example that $(x - 1)^2 - 4 = 0$ factorises to $((x - 1) + 2)((x - 1) - 2) = 0$, which is equivalent to $(x + 1)(x - 3) = 0$. Now solve these equations.

a $(x - 2)^2 - 9 = 0$ b $(x + 5)^2 - 16 = 0$ c $(2x + 1)^2 - 1 = 0$

d $(5x - 3)^2 - 25 = 0$ e $(4 - x)^2 = 9$ f $(3 - 7x)^2 = 100$

Using a CAS calculator 10.2: Solving quadratic equations

This activity is on the companion website in the form of a printable PDF.

10.3 Solving $x^2 + bx + c = 0$

Earlier in Chapter 8 we learnt to factorise quadratic trinomials with three terms. For example, $x^2 + 5x + 6$ factorises to $(x + 2)(x + 3)$. This means that the Null Factor Law can be used to solve equations of the form $x^2 + bx + c = 0$.

Let's start: Remembering how to factorise quadratic trinomials

First expand these quadratics using the distributive law:

Distributive law

$(a + b)(c + d) = ac + ad + bc + bd$.

- $(x + 1)(x + 2)$
- $(x - 3)(x + 4)$
- $(x - 5)(x - 2)$

Now factorise these expressions.

- $x^2 + 5x + 6$
- $x^2 - x - 12$
- $x^2 - 8x + 7$

Discuss your method for finding the factors of each quadratic above.

■ Solve quadratics of the form $x^2 + bx + c = 0$ by factorising the quadratic trinomial.	$x^2 - 3x - 28 = 0$ and $-7 \times 4 = -28$
	$(x - 7)(x + 4) = 0$ $-7 + 4 = -3$
• Ask 'What factors of c add to give b?'	$x - 7 = 0$ or $x + 4 = 0$
• Then use the Null Factor Law.	$x = 7$ or $x = -4$
• $x^2 + bx + c$ is called a monic quadratic since the coefficient of x^2 is 1.	
■ Perfect squares will give only one solution.	$x^2 - 6x + 9 = 0$
	$(x - 3)(x - 3) = 0$
	$x - 3 = 0$
	$x = 3$

Key ideas

Example 6 Solving equations with quadratic trinomials

Solve these quadratic equations.

a $x^2 + 7x + 12 = 0$ b $x^2 - 2x - 8 = 0$ c $x^2 - 8x + 15 = 0$

SOLUTION

a $x^2 + 7x + 12 = 0$
      $(x + 3)(x + 4) = 0$
      $x + 3 = 0$ or $x + 4 = 0$
        $x = -3$ or $x = -4$

EXPLANATION

Factors of 12 which add to 7 are 3 and 4.
$3 \times 4 = 12$, $3 + 4 = 7$
Use the Null Factor Law to solve the equation.

b $x^2 - 2x - 8 = 0$

$(x - 4)(x + 2) = 0$

$x - 4 = 0$ or $x + 2 = 0$

$x = 4$ or $x = -2$

Factors of -8 which add to -2 are -4 and 2.

$-4 \times 2 = -8$, $-4 + 2 = -2$,

Finish using the Null Factor Law.

c $x^2 - 8x + 15 = 0$

$(x \quad 5)(x \quad 3) = 0$

$x - 5 = 0$ or $x - 3 = 0$

$x = 5$ or $x = 3$

The factors of 15 must add to give -8. $-5 \times (-3) = 15$ and $-5 + (-3) = -8$, so -5 and -3 are the two numbers.

Example 7 Solving with perfect squares and other trinomials

Solve these quadratic equations.

a $x^2 - 8x + 16 = 0$

b $x^2 = x + 6$

SOLUTION

EXPLANATION

a $x^2 - 8x + 16 = 0$

$(x - 4)(x - 4) = 0$

$x - 4 = 0$

$x = 4$

Factors of 16 which add to -8 are -4 and -4.

$(x - 4)(x - 4) = (x - 4)^2$ is a perfect square so there is only one solution.

b $x^2 = x + 6$

$x^2 - x - 6 = 0$

$(x - 3)(x + 2) = 0$

$x - 3 = 0$ or $x + 2 = 0$

$x = 3$ or $x = -2$

First make the right-hand side equal zero by subtracting x and 6 from both sides. This is standard form. Factors of -6 which add to -1 are -3 and 2.

Exercise 10C

1 Decide what two factors of the first number add to give the second number.

a 6, 5   **b** 8, 6   **c** 2, -3   **d** 10, -7

e -2, 1   **f** -5, 4   **g** -12, -1   **h** -12, -4

2 Copy and complete the working to solve each equation.

a $x^2 + 9x + 20 = 0$

$(x + 5)(\_\_\_) = 0$

$x + 5 = 0$ or $\_\_\_ = 0$

$x = \_\_\_$ or $x = \_\_\_$

b $x^2 - 2x - 24 = 0$

$(x - 6)(\_\_\_) = 0$

$x - 6 = 0$ or $\_\_\_ = 0$

$x = \_\_\_$ or $x = \_\_\_$

c $x^2 + 4x - 45 = 0$

$(x + 9)(\_\_\_) = 0$

$x + 9 = 0$ or $\_\_\_ = 0$

$x = \_\_\_$ or $x = \_\_\_$

d $x^2 - 10x + 16 = 0$

$(x - 8)(\_\_\_) = 0$

$x - 8 = 0$ or $\_\_\_ = 0$

$x = \_\_\_$ or $x = \_\_\_$

Understanding

3 Solve these quadratic equations. *(Example 6)*

a $x^2 + 8x + 12 = 0$ b $x^2 + 11x + 24 = 0$ c $x^2 + 7x + 10 = 0$

d $x^2 + 5x - 14 = 0$ e $x^2 + 4x - 12 = 0$ f $x^2 + 7x - 30 = 0$

g $x^2 - 12x + 32 = 0$ h $x^2 - 9x + 18 = 0$ i $x^2 - 10x + 21 = 0$

j $x^2 - 2x - 15 = 0$ k $x^2 - 6x - 16 = 0$ l $x^2 - 4x - 45 = 0$

m $x^2 - 10x + 24 = 0$ n $x^2 - x - 42 = 0$ o $x^2 + 5x - 84 = 0$

p $x^2 + 4x + 3 = 0$ q $x^2 - 6x - 27 = 0$ r $x^2 - 12x + 20 = 0$

4 Solve these quadratic equations which include perfect squares. *(Example 7a)*

a $x^2 + 6x + 9 = 0$ b $x^2 + 4x + 4 = 0$ c $x^2 + 14x + 49 = 0$

d $x^2 + 24x + 144 = 0$ e $x^2 - 10x + 25 = 0$ f $x^2 - 16x + 64 = 0$

g $x^2 - 12x + 36 = 0$ h $x^2 - 18x + 81 = 0$ i $x^2 - 20x + 100 = 0$

5 Solve these quadratic equations by first rearranging to standard form. *(Example 7b)*

a $x^2 = 3x + 10$ b $x^2 = 7x - 10$ c $x^2 = 6x - 9$

d $x^2 = 4 - 3x$ e $14 - 5x = x^2$ f $x^2 + 16 = 8x$

g $x^2 - 12 = -4x$ h $6 - x^2 = 5x$ i $15 = 8x - x^2$

j $16 - 6x = x^2$ k $-6x = x^2 + 8$ l $-x^2 - 7x = -18$

6 Solve these equations by first taking out a common factor.

a $2x^2 - 2x - 12 = 0$ b $3x^2 + 24x + 45 = 0$ c $4x^2 - 24x - 64 = 0$

d $4x^2 - 20x + 24 = 0$ e $2x^2 - 8x + 8 = 0$ f $3x^2 + 6x + 3 = 0$

g $7x^2 - 70x + 175 = 0$ h $2x^2 + 12x = -18$ i $5x^2 = 35 - 30x$

7 Remove brackets, decimals or fractions and write in standard form to help solve these equations.

a $x^2 = 5(x - 1.2)$ b $2x(x - 3) = x^2 - 9$ c $3(x^2 + x - 10) = 2x^2 - 5(x + 2)$

d $x - 2 = \dfrac{35}{x}$ e $2 + \dfrac{1}{x} = -x$ f $\dfrac{x}{4} = 1 - \dfrac{1}{x}$

8 Write down a quadratic equation in standard form which has the following solutions.

a $x = 1$ and $x = 2$ b $x = 3$ and $x = -2$ c $x = -4$ and $x = 1$

d $x = -3$ and $x = 10$ e $x = 5$ only   f $x = -11$ only

9 The temperature in °C inside a room at a scientific base in Antarctica after 10.00 am is given by the expression $t^2 - 9t + 8$ where t is in hours. Find the times in the day when the temperature is $0\,°C$.

10 Consider this equation and solution.

$$x^2 - x - 12 = -6$$
$$(x - 4)(x + 3) = -6$$
$$x - 4 = -6 \text{ or } x + 3 = -6$$
$$x = -2 \text{ or } x = -9$$

a Explain what is wrong with the solution.

b Find the correct solutions to the equation.

11 Explain why $x^2 - 2x + 1 = 0$ only has one solution.

12 Write down a quadratic equation that has these solutions. Write in factorised form.

a $x = a$ only

b $x = a$ and $x = b$

Enrichment: Coefficient of x^2 other than 1

13 Many quadratic equations have a coefficient of x^2 not equal to 1. These are called non-monic quadratics. Factorisation can be trickier but is still possible. You may have covered this in Chapter 8. Here is an example.

$$2x^2 + 5x - 3 = 0 \qquad \text{(factors of -6 that add to give 5 are -1 and 6.)}$$
$$2x^2 - x + 6x - 3 = 0$$
$$x(2x - 1) + 3(2x - 1) = 0$$
$$(2x - 1)(x + 3) = 0 \qquad\qquad (6x - 1x = 5x)$$
$$2x - 1 = 0 \text{ or } x + 3 = 0$$
$$x = \frac{1}{2} \text{ or } x = -3$$

Solve these quadratic equations.

a $5x^2 + 16x + 3 = 0$ **b** $3x^2 + 4x - 4 = 0$ **c** $6x^2 + x - 1 = 0$

d $10x^2 + 5x - 5 = 0$ **e** $2x^2 = 15 - 7x$ **f** $4x^2 = 12x - 9$

g $x = 3x^2 - 14$ **h** $17x = 12 - 5x^2$ **i** $25 = -9x^2 - 30x$

j $17x - 6x^2 = 5$

The trails of the projectiles shot out by this firework can be modelled by quadratic equations.

10.4 Applications of quadratic equations

When using mathematics to solve problems we often arrive at a quadratic equation. In solving the quadratic equation we obtain the solutions to the problem. Setting up the original equation and then interpreting the solution are important parts of the problem-solving process.

Let's start: Solving for the unknown number

The product of a positive number and 6 more than the same number is 16.

- Using x as the unknown number, write an equation describing the given condition.
- Solve your equation for x.
- Are both solutions feasible (allowed)?
- Discuss how this method compares to the method of trial and error.

When using quadratic equations to solve problems, follow these steps.

- Define your variable.
  - Write 'Let x be ... '
- Write an equation describing the situation.
- Solve your equation using the Null Factor Law.
- Check that your solutions are feasible.
  - Some problems may not allow solutions which are negative numbers or fractions.
- Answer the original question in words.

Key ideas

Example 8 Solving area problems

The length of a book is 4 cm more than its width and the area of the face of the book is 320 cm². Find the dimensions of the face of the book.

SOLUTION	EXPLANATION
Let x cm be the width of the book face. Length $= (x + 4)$ cm	Define a variable for width then write the length in terms of the width.
$x(x + 4) = 320$ $x^2 + 4x - 320 = 0$ $(x + 20)(x - 16) = 0$ $x + 20 = 0$ or $x - 16 = 0$ $x = -20$ or $x = 16$	Write an equation to suit the given situation. Expand and subtract 320 from both sides. Solve using the Null Factor Law but note that a width of -20 cm is not feasible.
$\therefore x = 16$ $\therefore$ width $= 16$ cm length $= 20$ cm	Finish by writing the dimensions; width and length as required. Length $= x + 4 = 16 + 4 = 20$ cm

Exercise 10D

1 This rectangle has an area of 8 cm^2 and a length which is 2 cm more than its width.

$(x + 2)$ cm

8 cm^2 | x cm

  a Using length × width = area, write an equation.
  b Solve your equation by expanding and subtracting 8 from both sides. Then use the Null Factor Law.
  c Which of your two solutions is feasible for the width of the rectangle?
  d Write down the dimensions (width and length) of the rectangle.

2 This rectangle has an area of 14 m^2 and a length which is 5 m more than its width.

$(x + 5)$ m

14 m^2 | x m

  a Using length × width = area, write an equation.
  b Solve your equation by expanding and subtracting 14 from both sides. Then use the Null Factor Law.
  c Which of your two solutions is feasible for the width of the rectangle?
  d Write down the dimensions (width and length) of the rectangle.

3 Solve these equations for x by first expanding and producing a zero on the right-hand side.
  a $x(x + 3) = 18$ **b** $x(x - 1) = 20$ **c** $(x - 1)(x + 4) = 6$

4 The product of a number and 2 more than the same number is 48. Write an equation and solve to find the two possible solutions.

5 The product of a number and 7 less than the same number is 60. Write an equation and solve to find the two possible solutions.

6 The product of a number and 13 less than the same number is 30. Write an equation and solve to find the two possible solutions.

Example 8 **7** The length of a rectangular brochure is 5 cm more than its width and the area of the face of the brochure is 36 cm^2. Find the dimensions of the face of the brochure.

8 The length of a small kindergarten play area is 20 metres less than its width and the area is 69 m^2. Find the dimensions of the kindergarten play area.

Problem-solving

9 A square of side length 10 metres has a square of side length x metres removed from one corner.

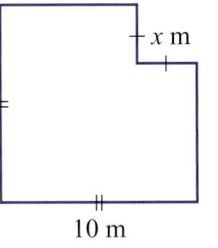

  a Write an expression for the area remaining after the square of side length x metres is removed. Hint: use subtraction.
  b Find the value of x if the area remaining is to be 64 m².

10 m

10 An isosceles triangle has height (h) equal to half its base length. Find the value of h if the area is 25 square units.

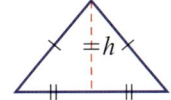

11 A farm shed (3 m by 5 m) is to be extended to form an 'L' shape.

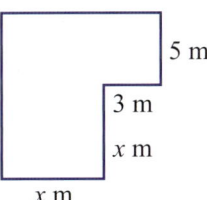

  a Write an expression for the total area of the extended farm shed.
  b Find the value of x if the total area is to be 99 m².

5 m
3 m
x m
x m

12 Use Pythagoras' theorem to find the value of x in these right-angled triangles.

  a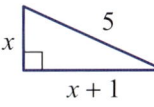

  b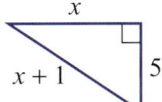

  c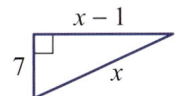

Reasoning

13 The equation for this rectangle is $x^2 + 2x - 48 = 0$ which has solutions $x = -8$ and $x = 6$. Which solution do you ignore and why?

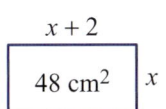

$x + 2$
48 cm² x

14 The product of an integer and one less than the same integer is 6. The equation for this is $x^2 - x - 6 = 0$. How many different solutions are possible and why?

15 This table shows the sum of the first n positive integers.
If $n = 3$ then the sum is $1 + 2 + 3 = 6$.

n	1	2	3	4	5	6
sum	1	3	6			

  a Write the sum for $n = 4$, $n = 5$ and $n = 6$.

  b The expression for the sum is given by $\dfrac{n(n+1)}{2}$. Use this expression to find the sum if:

  i $n = 7$ **ii** $n = 20$

  c Use the expression to find n for these sums. Write an equation and solve it.

  i sum = 45   **ii** sum = 120

16 The number of diagonals in a polygon with n sides is given by $\dfrac{n}{2}(n-3)$. Shown here are the diagonals for a quadrilateral and a pentagon.

n	4	5	6	7
Diagonals	2	5		

a Use the given expression to find the two missing numbers in the table.
b Find the value of n if the number of diagonals is:
  i 20
  ii 54

Enrichment: Picture frames

17 A square picture is to be edged with a border of width x cm.
The inside picture has side length of 20 cm.
  a Write an expression for the total area.
  b Find the width of the frame if the total area is to be 1600 cm².

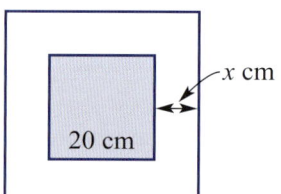

18 A square picture is surrounded by a rectangular frame as shown.
The total area is to be 320 cm². Find the side length of the picture.

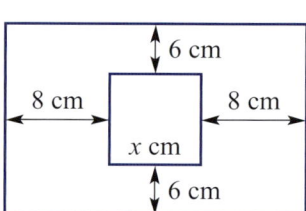

10.5 The parabola

Relations that have rules in which the highest power of x is 2, such as $y = x^2$, $y = 2x^2 - 3$ or $y = 3x^2 + 2x - 4$, are called quadratics and their graphs are called parabolas. Parabolic shapes can be seen in many modern day objects or situations such as the arches of bridges, the paths of projectiles and the surface of reflectors.

Jets of water angled away from the vertical show parabolic trajectories.

Let's start: Finding features

A quadratic is given by the equation $y = x^2 - 2x - 3$. Complete these tasks to discover its graphical features.

- Use the rule to complete this table of values.

x	-2	-1	0	1	2	3	4
y							

- Plot your points on a copy of the axes shown at right and join them to form a smooth curve.
- Describe these features:
  - minimum turning point
  - axis of symmetry
  - coordinates of the y-intercept
  - coordinates of the x-intercepts

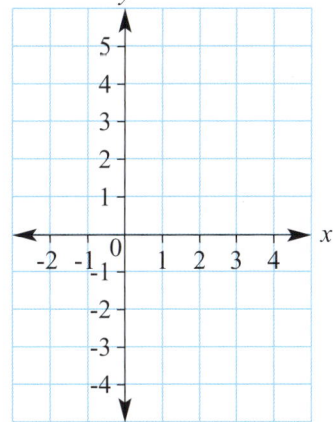

- The graph of a quadratic relation is called a **parabola**. Its basic shape is as shown here.
  - The basic quadratic rule is $y = x^2$.
- The general equation of a quadratic is $y = ax^2 + bx + c$.
- A parabola is symmetrical about a line called the **axis of symmetry** and it has one **turning point** (a vertex), which may be a **maximum** or a **minimum**.

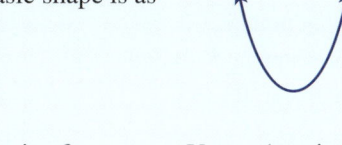

Axis of symmetry

Vertex (maximum turning point

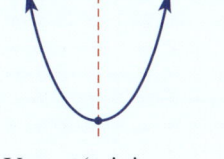

Vertex (minimum turning point

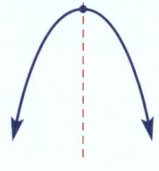

Axis of symmetry

Key ideas

Key ideas

Here is an example of a quadratic graph with equation $y = x^2 - 4x + 3$, showing all the key features.

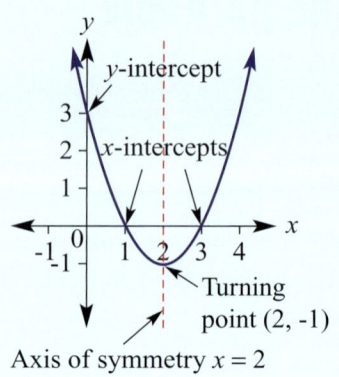

Example 9 Identifying features

For this graph state the:

a equation of the axis of symmetry

b type of turning point

c coordinates of the turning point

d x-intercepts

e y-intercept

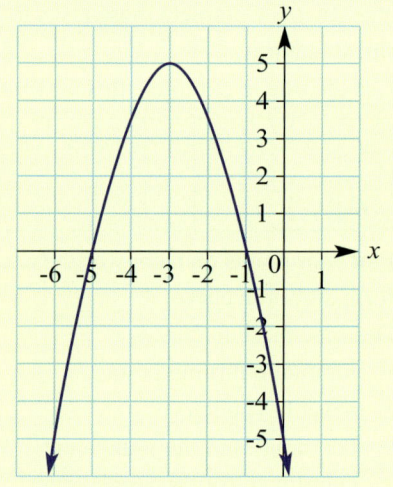

SOLUTION

a $x = -3$

b maximum turning point

c turning point is $(-3, 5)$

d x-intercepts: $(-5, 0)$ and $(-1, 0)$

e y-intercept: $(0, -5)$

EXPLANATION

Graph is symmetrical about the vertical line $x = -3$. Graph has its highest y-coordinate at the turning point, so it is a maximum point.

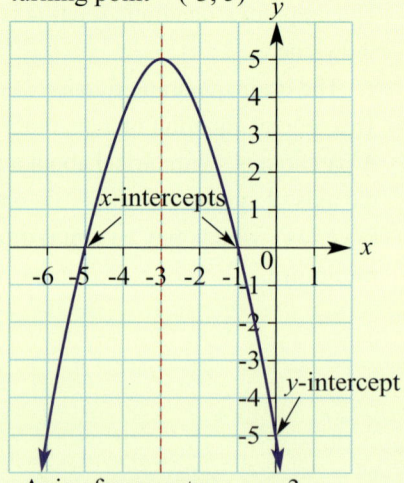

Example 10 Plotting a parabola

Use the quadratic rule $y = x^2 - 4$ to complete these tasks.

x	-3	-2	-1	0	1	2	3
y							

a Complete this table of values.

b Draw a set of axes using a scale that suits the numbers in your table. Then plot the points to form a parabola.

c State these features.

   i   Type of turning point   **ii**   Axis of symmetry

   iii   Coordinates of the turning point   **iv**   Coordinates of the y-intercept

   v   Coordinates of the x-intercepts

SOLUTION

EXPLANATION

a

x	-3	-2	-1	0	1	2	3
y	5	0	-3	-4	-3	0	5

Substitute each x value into the rule to find each y value, e.g. $x = -3$, $y = (-3)^2 - 4 = 9 - 4 = 5$.

b

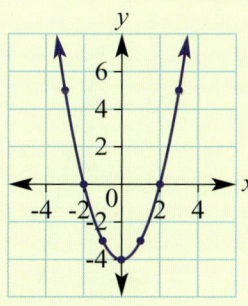

Plot each coordinate pair and join to form a smooth curve.

c   **i**   Minimum

     ii $x = 0$

     iii   (0, -4)

     iv   (0, -4)

     v   (-2, 0) and (2, 0)

The turning point at (0, -4) has the lowest y-coordinate for the entire graph.

The vertical line $x = 0$ divides the graph like a mirror line. The y-intercept is at $x = 0$.

The x-intercepts are at $y = 0$ on the x-axis.

Exercise 10E

1   Choose a word from this list to complete each sentence.

    lowest, parabola, vertex, highest, intercepts, zero

    a   A maximum turning point is the _____ point on the graph.

    b   The graph of a quadratic is called a _____.

    c   The x-_____ are the points where the graph cuts the x-axis.

    d   The axis of symmetry is a vertical line passing through the _____.

    e   A minimum turning point is the _____ point on the graph.

    f   The y-intercept is at x equals _____.

2   Write down the equation of a vertical line (e.g. $x = 2$) that passes through these points.

    a   (3, 0)   **b**   (1, 5)   **c**   (-2, 4)   **d**   (-5, 0)

Understanding

Example 9   **3**   For each of the following graphs, state:

   i   the equation of the axis of symmetry   **ii**   the coordinates of the turning point

   iii   the type of turning point (maximum or minimum)

   iv   the x-intercepts   **v**   the y-intercept

a
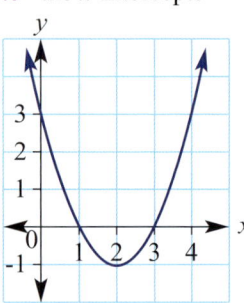

b
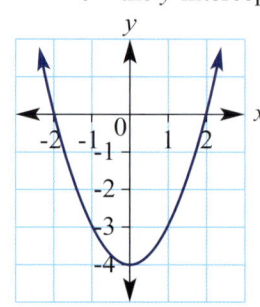

c
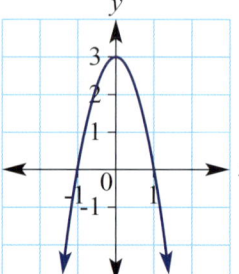

d
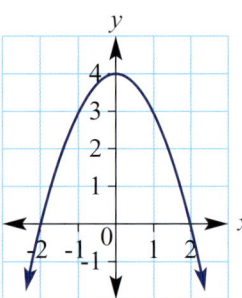

e
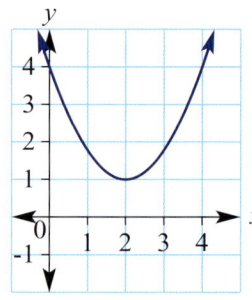

f
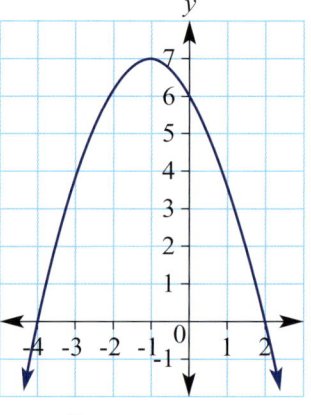

g
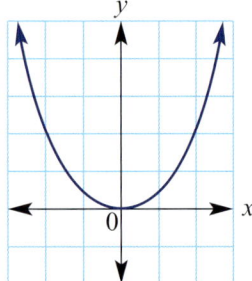

h
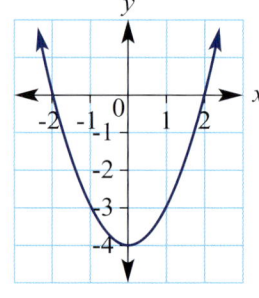

i
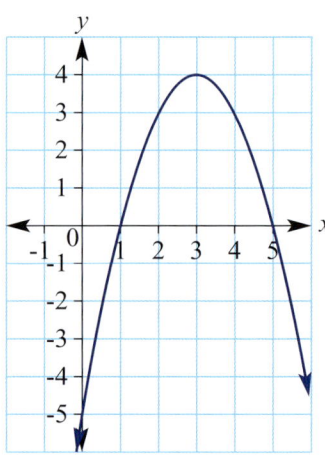

j
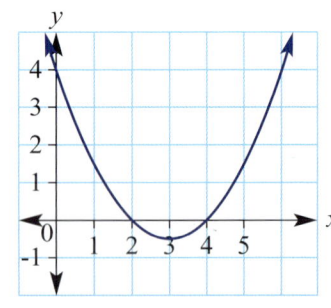

k
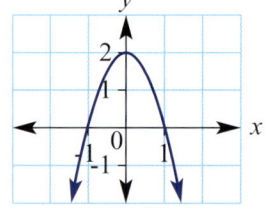

l
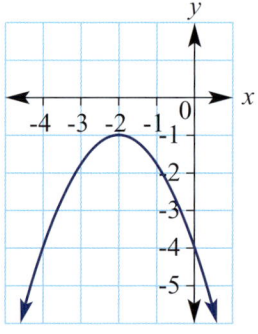

mple 10 **4** Use the quadratic rule $y = x^2 - 1$ to complete these tasks.

   a Complete the table of values.

x	-2	-1	0	1	2
y					

   b Draw a set of axes using a scale that suits the numbers in your table. Then plot the points to form a parabola.

   c State these features.

      i Type of turning point   **ii** Coordinates of the turning point   **iii** Axis of symmetry

      iv Coordinates of the y-intercept   **v** Coordinates of the x-intercepts

5 Use the quadratic rule $y = 9 - x^2$ to complete these tasks.

   a Complete the table of values.

x	-3	-2	-1	0	1	2	3
y							

   b Draw a set of axes using a scale that suits the numbers in your table. Then plot the points to form a parabola.

   c State these features.

      i Type of turning point   **ii** Coordinates of the turning point   **iii** Axis of symmetry

      iv Coordinates of the y-intercept   **v** Coordinates of the x-intercepts

6 Use the quadratic rule $y = x^2 + 2x - 3$ to complete these tasks.

   a Complete the table of values.

x	-4	-3	-2	-1	0	1	2
y							

   b Draw a set of axes using a scale that suits the numbers in your table. Then plot the points to form a parabola.

   c State these features.

      i Type of turning point   **ii** Coordinates of the turning point   **iii** Axis of symmetry

      iv Coordinates of the y-intercept   **v** Coordinates of the x-intercepts

7 Use the quadratic rule $y = -x^2 + x + 2$ to complete these tasks.

Recall that $-x^2 = -1 \times x^2$.

   a Complete the table of values.

x	-2	-1	0	1	2	3
y						

   b Draw a set of axes using a scale that suits the numbers in your table. Then plot the points to form a parabola.

   c State these features.

      i Type of turning point   **ii** Coordinates of the turning point

      iii Axis of symmetry   **iv** Coordinates of the y-intercept

      v Coordinates of the x-intercepts

8 This graph shows the height of a cricket ball, y metres, as a function of time t seconds.

   a **i**   At what times is the ball at a height of 9 m?

      ii Why are there two different times?

   b **i**   At what time is the ball at its greatest height?

      ii What is the greatest height the ball reaches?

      iii After how many seconds does it hit the ground?

9 The graph gives the height, h m, at time t seconds, of a rocket which is fired up in the air.

   a From what height is the rocket launched?

   b What is the approximate maximum height that the rocket reaches?

   c For how long is the rocket in the air?

   d What is the difference in time for when the rocket is going up and when it is going down?

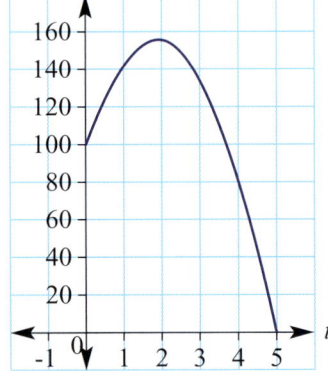

10 A parabola has two x-intercepts at $(-2, 0)$ and $(4, 0)$. The y-coordinate of the turning point is -3.

   a What is the equation of its axis of symmetry?

   b What are the coordinates of the turning point?

11 A parabola has a turning point at $(1, 3)$ and one x-intercept at $(0, 0)$.

   a What is the equation of its axis of symmetry?

   b What are the coordinates of the other x-intercept?

12 Write the rule for these parabolas. Use trial and error to help and check your rule by substituting a known point.

a
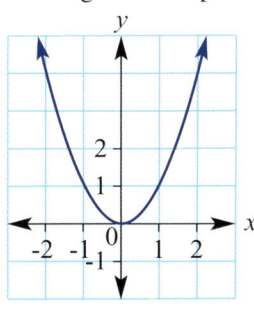

b
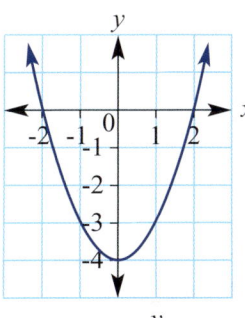

c
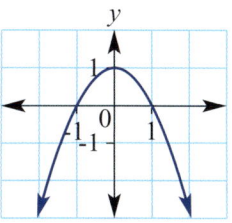

d
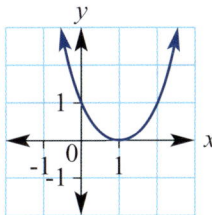

e
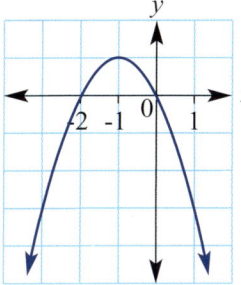

f
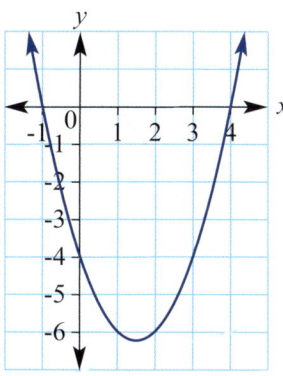

13 Is it possible to draw a parabola with the following properties? If yes, draw an example.
  a Two x-intercepts
  b One x-intercept
  c No x-intercepts
  d No y-intercept

14 a Mal calculates the y value for $x = 2$ using $y = -x^2 + 2x$ and gets $y = 8$. Explain his error.
  b Mai calculates the y value for $x = -3$ using $y = x - x^2$ and gets $y = 6$. Explain her error.

15 This graph shows the parabola for $y = x^2 - 4$.
  a For what values of x is $y = 0$?
  b For what value of x is $y = -4$?
  c How many values of x give a y value which is:
    i greater than -4   **ii** equal to -4   **iii** less than -4?

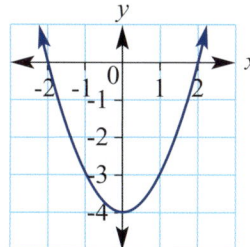

16 This table corresponds to the rule $y = x^2 - 2x$.

x	-1	0	1	2	3	4
y	3	0	-1	0	3	8

  a Use this table to solve these equations
    i $0 = x^2 - 2x$ **ii** $3 = x^2 - 2x$
  b How many solutions would there be to the equation $8 = x^2 - 2x$? Why?
  c How many solutions would there be to the equation $-1 = x^2 - 2x$? Why?
  d How many solutions would there be to the equation $-2 = x^2 - 2x$? Why?

Enrichment: Using software to construct a parabola

17 Follow the steps below to construct a parabola using a **dynamic geometry package**.

Step 1. Show the coordinate axes system by selecting **Show Axes** from the **Draw** toolbox.

Step 2. Construct a line which is parallel to the *x*-axis and passes through a point *F* on the *y*-axis near the point (0, -1).

Step 3. Construct a line segment *AB* on this line as shown in the diagram.

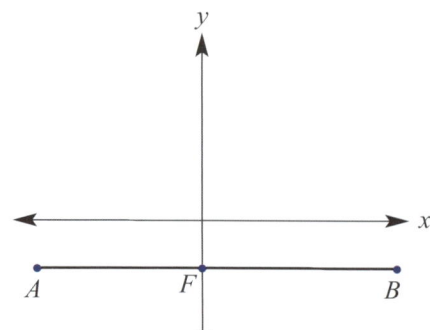

Step 4. Hide the line *AB* and then construct:
- a point *C* on the line segment *AB*
- a point *P* on the *y*-axis near the point (0, 1).

Step 5. Construct a line which passes through the point *C* and is perpendicular to *AB*.

Step 6. Construct the point *D* which is equidistant from point *P* and segment *AB*.
Hint: use the perpendicular bisector of *PC*.

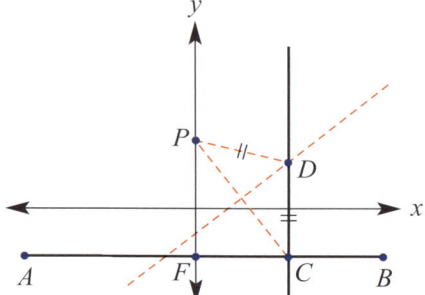

Step 7. Select **Trace** from the **Display** toolbox and click on the point *D*.

Step 8. Animate point *C* and observe what happens.

Step 9. Select **Locus** from the **Construct** toolbox and click at *D* and then at *C*.

Step 10. Drag point *P* and/or segment AB (by dragging *F*). (Clear the trace points by selecting **Refresh** drawing from the **Edit** menu.) What do you notice?

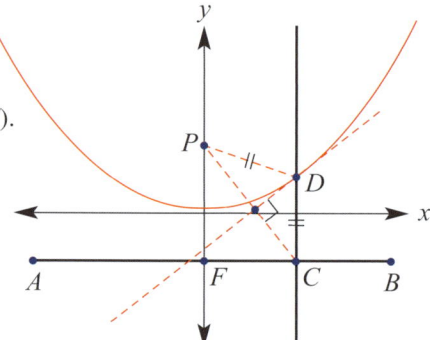

Using a CAS calculator 10.5: Sketching parabolas

This activity is on the companion website in the form of a printable PDF.

10.6 Sketching $y = ax^2$ with dilations and reflections

In geometry we know that shapes can be transformed by applying reflections, rotations, translations and dilations (enlargement). The same types of transformations can also be applied to graphs including parabolas. Altering the value of a in $y = ax^2$ causes both dilations and reflections.

Let's start: What is the effect of *a*?

This table and graph show a number of examples of $y = ax^2$ with varying values of a. They could also be produced using technology.

x	-2	-1	0	1	2
$y = x^2$	4	1	0	1	4
$y = 2x^2$	8	2	0	2	8
$y = \dfrac{1}{2}x^2$	2	$\dfrac{1}{2}$	0	$\dfrac{1}{2}$	2
$y = -x^2$	-4	-1	0	-1	-4

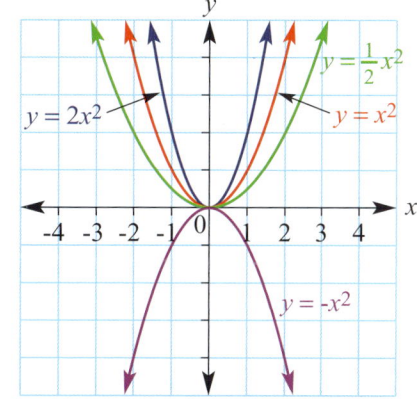

- Discuss how the different values of a affect the y-values in the table.
- Discuss how the different values of a affect the shape of the graph.
- Why does $y = -x^2$ look like a graph of $y = x^2$ reflected in the x-axis?
- How would the graphs of the following rules compare to the graphs shown above?

  a $y = 3x^2$

  b $y = \dfrac{1}{4}x^2$

  c $y = -\dfrac{1}{2}x^2$

■ For $y = ax^2$:

- the vertex (or turning point) is $(0, 0)$
- the axis of symmetry is $x = 0$
- if $a > 0$ the graph is **upright** (or **concave up**) and has a minimum turning point
- if $a < 0$ the graph is **inverted** (or **concave down**) and has a maximum turning point.

- If $a > 1$ or $a < -1$:

  the graph is narrower than either $y = x^2$ or $y = -x^2$. For example: $y = 2x^2$ or $y = -2x^2$

  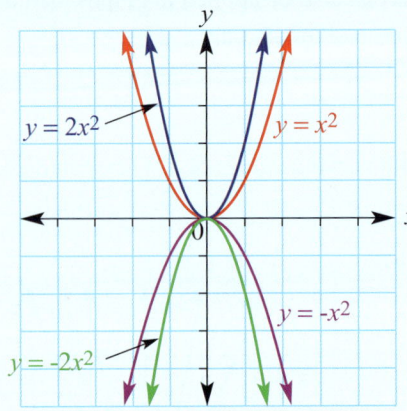

- If $-1 < a < 1$:

  the graph is wider than either $y = x^2$ or $y = -x^2$.

  For example: $y = \dfrac{1}{2}x^2$ or $y = -\dfrac{1}{2}x^2$

  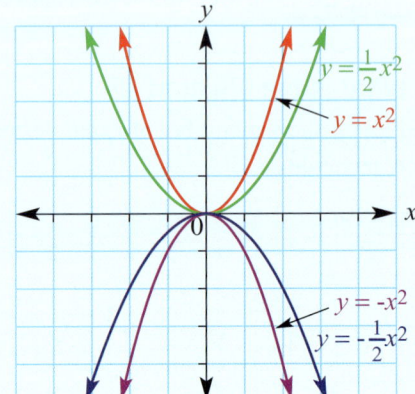

- For $y = 2x^2$ we say that the graph of $y = x^2$ is **dilated** from the x-axis by a factor of 2.
- For $y = -x^2$ we say that the graph of $y = x^2$ is **reflected** in the x-axis.

Example 11 Comparing graphs of $y = ax^2$, $a > 0$

Complete the following for $y = x^2$, $y = 2x^2$ and $y = \dfrac{1}{2}x^2$.

a Draw up and complete a table of values for $-2 \le x \le 2$.

b Plot their graphs on the same set of axes.

c Write down the the equation of the axis of symmetry and the coordinates of the turning point.

d **i** Is the graph of $y = 2x^2$ wider or narrower than $y = x^2$?

   ii Is the graph of $y = \dfrac{1}{2}x^2$ wider or narrower than $y = x^2$?

SOLUTION

a $y = x^2$

x	-2	-1	0	1	2
y	4	1	0	1	4

$y = 2x^2$

x	-2	-1	0	1	2
y	8	2	0	2	8

$y = \dfrac{1}{2}x^2$

x	-2	-1	0	1	2
y	2	$\dfrac{1}{2}$	0	$\dfrac{1}{2}$	2

EXPLANATION

Substitute each x value into $y = x^2$, $y = 2x^2$ and $y = \dfrac{1}{2}x^2$.

e.g. for $y = 2x^2$, if $x = 2$

$$y = 2(2)^2$$
$$= 2(4)$$
$$= 8$$

If $x = -1$, $y = 2(-1)^2$
$$= 2(1)$$
$$= 2$$

b

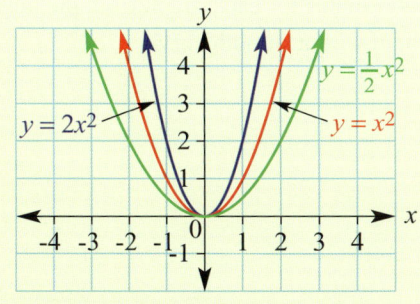

Plot the points for each graph using the coordinates from the tables and join them with a smooth curve.

c axis of symmetry: y-axis ($x = 0$)

turning point: minimum at $(0, 0)$

Look at graphs to see symmetry about the y-axis and a minimum turning point at the origin.

d **i** The graph of $y = 2x^2$ is narrower than the graph of $y = x^2$.

For each value of x, $2x^2$ is twice that of x^2; hence, the graph (y-values) of $2x^2$ rises more quickly.

ii The graph of $y = \frac{1}{2}x^2$ is wider than the graph of $y = x^2$.

For each value of x, $\frac{1}{2}x^2$ is half that of x^2; hence, the graph of $\frac{1}{2}x^2$ rises more slowly.

Example 12 Comparing graphs of $y = ax^2$, $a < 0$

Complete the following for $y = -x^2$, $y = -3x^2$ and $y = -\frac{1}{2}x^2$.

a Draw up and complete a table of values for $-2 \leq x \leq 2$.
b Plot their graphs on the same set of axes.
c Write down the the equation of the axis of symmetry and the coordinates of the turning point.
d **i** Is the graph of $y = -3x^2$ wider or narrower than $y = -x^2$?

   ii Is the graph of $y = -\frac{1}{2}x^2$ wider or narrower than $y = -x^2$?

SOLUTION

a $y = -x^2$

x	-2	-1	0	1	2
y	-4	-1	0	-1	-4

$y = -3x^2$

x	-2	-1	0	1	2
y	-12	-3	0	-3	-12

$y = -\frac{1}{2}x^2$

x	-2	-1	0	1	2
y	-2	$-\frac{1}{2}$	0	$-\frac{1}{2}$	-2

EXPLANATION

Substitute each x-value into $y = -x^2$, $y = -3x^2$ and $y = -\frac{1}{2}x^2$.

e.g. for $y = -3x^2$, if $x = 2$

$$y = -3(2)^2$$
$$= -3(4)$$
$$= -12$$

If $x = -1$, $y = -3(-1)^2$

$$= -3(1)$$
$$= -3$$

b

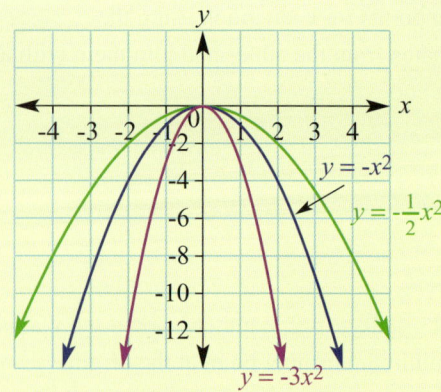

Plot the coordinates for each graph from the tables and join them with a smooth curve.

c axis of symmetry: y-axis ($x = 0$)
turning point: maximum at $(0, 0)$

Graphs are symmetrical about the y-axis with a maximum turning point at the origin.

d **i** The graph of $y = -3x^2$ is narrower than the graph of $y = -x^2$.

For each value of x, $-3x^2$ is three times that of $-x^2$; hence, the graph of $-3x^2$ gets larger in the negative direction more quickly.

ii The graph of $y = -\frac{1}{2}x^2$ is wider than the graph of $y = -x^2$.

For each value of x, $-\frac{1}{2}x^2$ is half that of $-x^2$.

Exercise 10F

1 Shown here are the graphs of $y = x^2$, $y = 3x^2$, $y = \frac{1}{2}x^2$, $y = -x^2$, $y = -3x^2$ and $y = -\frac{1}{2}x^2$.

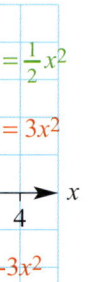

a Write the rules of the three graphs which have a minimum turning point.

b Write the rules of the three graphs which have a maximum turning point.

c What are the coordinates of the turning point for all the graphs?

d What is the equation of the axis of symmetry for all the graphs?

e Write the rule of the graph which is:
   i upright (concave up) and narrower than $y = x^2$
   ii upright (concave up) and wider than $y = x^2$
   iii inverted (concave down) and narrower than $y = -x^2$
   iv inverted (concave down) and wider than $y = -x^2$.

f Write the rule of the graph which is:
   i a reflection of $y = x^2$ in the x-axis   **ii** a reflection of $y = 3x^2$ in the x-axis
   iii a reflection of $y = -\frac{1}{2}x^2$ in the x-axis.

2 Select the word *positive* or *negative* to suit each sentence.

  a The graph of $y = ax^2$ will be upright (concave up) with a minimum turning point if a is ___.

  b The graph of $y = ax^2$ will be inverted (concave down) with a maximum turning point if a is ___.

3 **a** Write the rule of a graph which is a reflection in the x-axis of the graph of the rule $y = x^2$.

  b Write the rule of a graph which is a reflection in the x-axis of the graph of the rule $y = 4x^2$.

  c Write the rule of a graph which is a reflection in the x-axis of the graph of the rule $y = -5x^2$.

  d Write the rule of a graph which is a reflection in the x-axis of the graph of the rule $y = -\dfrac{1}{3}x^2$.

ample 11 **4** Complete the following for $y = x^2$, $y = 3x^2$ and $y = \dfrac{1}{3}x^2$.

  a Draw up and complete a table of values for $-2 \le x \le 2$.

  b Plot their graphs on the same set of axes.

  c Write down the coordinates of the turning point and the equation of the axis of symmetry.

  d **i** Is the graph of $y = 3x^2$ wider or narrower than $y = x^2$?

   ii Is the graph of $y = \dfrac{1}{3}x^2$ wider or narrower than $y = x^2$?

5 For the equations given below, complete these tasks.

  i Draw up and complete a table of values for $-2 \le x \le 2$.

  ii Plot the graphs of the equations on the same set of axes.

  iii Write down the coordinates of the turning point and the equation of the axis of symmetry.

  iv Determine whether the graphs of the equations are each wider or narrower than the graph of $y = x^2$.

  a $y = 4x^2$ **b** $y = 5x^2$ **c** $y = \dfrac{1}{4}x^2$ **d** $y = \dfrac{1}{5}x^2$

mple 12 **6** For the equations given below, complete these tasks.

  i Draw up and complete a table of values for $-2 \le x \le 2$.

  ii Plot the graphs of the equations on the same set of axes.

  iii List the key features for each graph, such as the axis of symmetry, turning point, x-intercept and y-intercept.

  iv Determine whether the graphs of the equations are each wider or narrower than the graph of $y = -x^2$.

  a $y = -2x^2$ **b** $y = -3x^2$ **c** $y = -\dfrac{1}{2}x^2$ **d** $y = -\dfrac{1}{3}x^2$

7 Here are eight quadratics of the form $y = ax^2$.

  A $y = 6x^2$ **B** $y = -7x^2$ **C** $y = 4x^2$ **D** $y = \dfrac{1}{9}x^2$

  E $y = \dfrac{x^2}{7}$ **F** $y = 0.3x^2$ **G** $y = -4.8x^2$ **H** $y = -0.5x^2$

  a Which rule would give a graph which is upright (concave up) and the narrowest?

  b Which rule would give a graph which is inverted (concave down) and the widest?

8 Match each of the following parabolas with the appropriate equation from the list below. Do a mental check by substituting the coordinates of a known point.

i $y = 3x^2$ ii $y = -x^2$ iii $y = 5x^2$

iv $y = \dfrac{1}{2}x^2$ v $y = -5x^2$ vi $y = 2x^2$

a
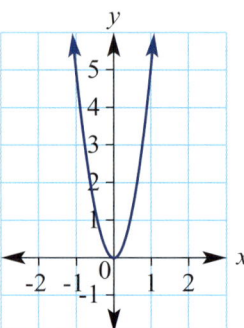

b
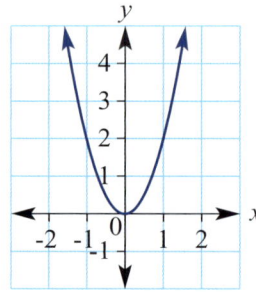

c
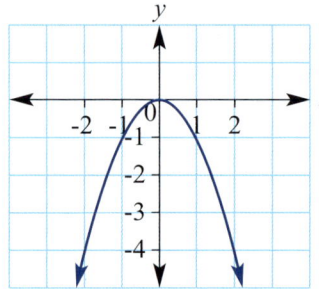

d
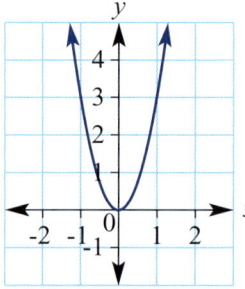

e
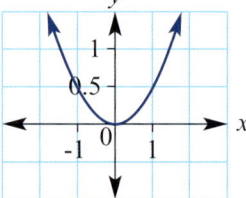

f
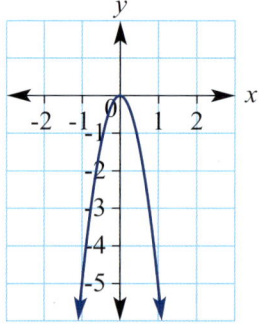

9 The graph of $y = -2x^2$ can be obtained from $y = x^2$ by conducting these transformations:

* reflecting in the x-axis
* dilating by a factor of 2 from the x-axis

In the same way as above, describe the two transformations which take:

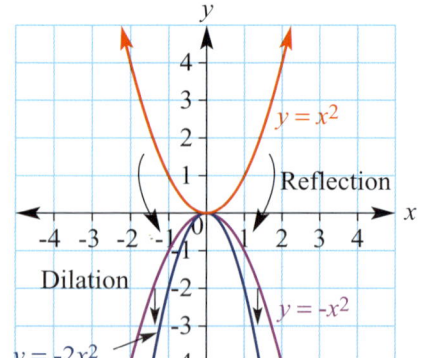

a $y = x^2$ to $y = -3x^2$ b $y = x^2$ to $y = -6x^2$

c $y = x^2$ to $y = -\dfrac{1}{2}x^2$ d $y = -x^2$ to $y = 2x^2$

e $y = -x^2$ to $y = 3x^2$ f $y = -x^2$ to $y = \dfrac{1}{3}x^2$

10 Write the rule for the graph after each set of transformations.

a The graph of $y = x^2$ is reflected in the x-axis then dilated by a factor of 4 from the x-axis.

b The graph of $y = -x^2$ is reflected in the x-axis then dilated by a factor of $\frac{1}{3}$ from the x-axis.

c The graph of $y = 2x^2$ is reflected in the x-axis then dilated by a factor of 2 from the x-axis.

d The graph of $y = \frac{1}{3}x^2$ is reflected in the x-axis then dilated by a factor of 4 from the x-axis.

11 The graph of $y = ax^2$ is reflected in the x-axis and dilated from the x-axis by a given factor. Does it matter which transformation is completed first? Explain.

12 The graph of the rule $y = ax^2$ is reflected in the y-axis. What is the new rule of the graph?

Reasoning

Enrichment: Substitute to find the rule

13 If a rule is of the form $y = ax^2$ and it passes through a point, say $(1, 4)$, we can substitute this point to find the value of a.

So $y = ax^2$

$\quad 4 = a \times 1^2$

$\therefore a = 4$ and $y = 4x^2$

Use this method to determine the equation of a quadratic relation if it has an equation of the form $y = ax^2$ and passes through:

a $(1, 5)$ **b** $(1, 7)$ **c** $(-1, 1)$ **d** $(-2, 7)$

e $(-5, 4)$ **f** $(3, 26)$ **g** $(4, 80)$ **h** $(-1, -52)$

14 This photo shows the parabolic cables of the Golden Gate Bridge. The rule of the form $y = ax^2$ describes the shape of the parabolic cables. If the cable is centred at $(0, 0)$ and the top of the right pylon has the coordinates $(492, 67)$, find a possible equation that describes this shape. The numbers given are in metres.

10.7 Translations of $y = x^2$

Added to reflection and dilation is a third type of transformation called translation. This involves a shift of every point on the graph horizontally and/or vertically. Unlike reflections and dilations, a translation alters the coordinates of the turning point. The shape of the curve is unchanged but a horizontal shift changes the equation of the axis of symmetry.

Let's start: Which way: left, right, up or down?

This table and graph shows the quadratics $y = x^2$, $y = (x - 2)^2$, $y = (x + 1)^2$, $y = x^2 - 4$ and $y = x^2 + 2$. The table could also be produced using technology.

x	-3	-2	-1	0	1	2	3
$y = x^2$	9	4	1	0	1	4	9
$y = (x - 2)^2$	25	16	9	4	1	0	1
$y = (x + 1)^2$	4	1	0	1	4	9	16
$y = x^2 - 4$	5	0	-3	-4	-3	0	5
$y = x^2 + 2$	11	6	3	2	3	6	11

- Discuss what effect the different numbers in the rules had on the y values in the table.
- Also discuss what effect the numbers in the rules have on each graph. How are the coordinates of the turning point changed?
- What conclusions could you draw on the effect of h in the rule $y = (x - h)^2$?
- What conclusions could you draw on the effect of k in the rule $y = x^2 + k$?
- What if the rule was $y = -x^2 + 2$ or $y = -(x + 1)^2$? Describe how the graphs would look.

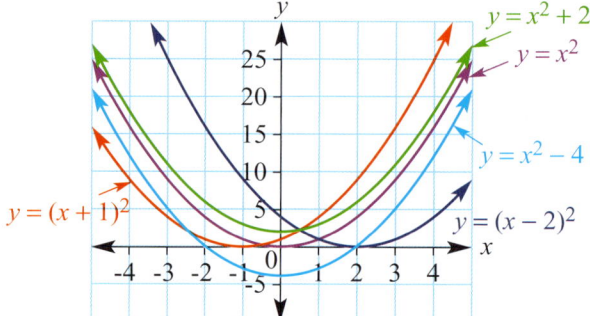

- A **translation** of a graph involves a shift of every point horizontally and/or vertically.
- Vertical translations: $y = x^2 + k$
  - If $k > 0$, the graph is translated k units up (red curve).
  - If $k < 0$, the graph is translated k units down (green curve).

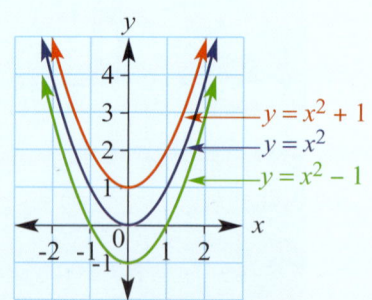

  - The turning point is $(0, k)$ for all curves.
  - The axis of symmetry is the line $x = 0$ for all curves.
  - The y-intercept is the point $(0, k)$ for all curves.

■ Horizontal translations: $y = (x - h)^2$

- If $h > 0$, the graph is translated h units to the right.

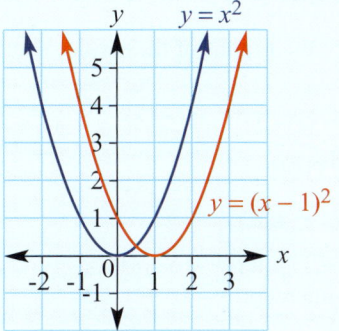

- If $h < 0$, the graph is translated h units to the left.

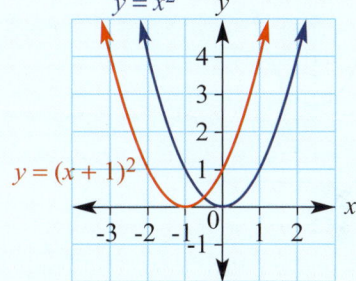

- The turning point is $(h, 0)$ in both cases.
- The axis of symmetry is the line $x = h$ in both cases.
- The y-intercept is the point $(0, h^2)$ in both cases.

■ The **turning point form** of a quadratic is given by:

$$y = a(x - h)^2 + k$$

$a > 0$ upright (concave up) graph $\cup$

$a < 0$ graph inverted (concave down) $\cap$

Translates the graph up or down
$k > 0 \uparrow$ $k < 0 \downarrow$

Translates the graph left or right:
$h > 0 \longrightarrow$
$h < 0 \longleftarrow$

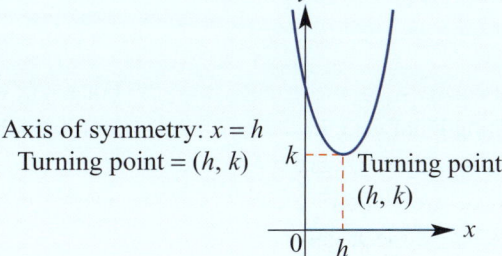

Axis of symmetry: $x = h$
Turning point $= (h, k)$

■ To sketch a graph of a quadratic equation in turning point form, follow these steps.

- Draw and label a set of axes.
- Identify important points including the turning point and y-intercept.
- Sketch the curve connecting the key points and making the curve symmetrical.

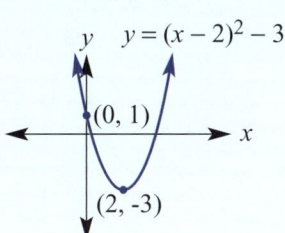

Example 13 Sketching with horizontal and vertical translations

Sketch the graphs of these rules showing the coordinates of the turning point and the y-intercept.

a $y = x^2 + 2$ **b** $y = -x^2 - 1$

c $y = (x - 3)^2$ **d** $y = -(x + 2)^2$

SOLUTION

EXPLANATION

a $y = x^2 + 2$

Turning point is $(0, 2)$

y-intercept: $y = 0^2 + 2 = 2$

For $y = x^2 + k$, $k = 2$ so the graph of $y = x^2$ is translated 2 units up.

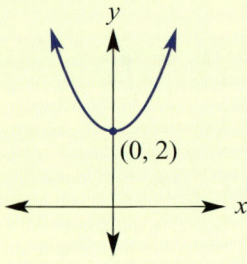

The point $(0, 0)$ shifts to $(0, 2)$.

b $y = -x^2 - 1$

Turning point is $(0, -1)$

y-intercept: $y = -0^2 - 1 = -1$

The graph of $y = -x^2$ is a reflection of the graph of $y = x^2$ in the x-axis.

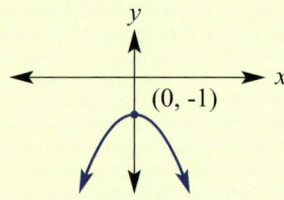

For $y = -x^2 + k$, $k = -1$ so the graph of $y = -x^2$ is translated down 1 unit.

c $y = (x - 3)^2$

Turning point is $(3, 0)$

y-intercept: $y = (0 - 3)^2$

$\qquad\qquad = (-3)^2$

$\qquad\qquad = 9$

For $y = (x - h)^2$, $h = 3$ so the graph of $y = x^2$ is translated 3 units to the right.

The y-intercept is found by substituting $x = 0$ into the rule.

d $y = -(x + 2)^2$

Turning point is (-2, 0)

y-intercept: $y = -(0 + 2)^2$

$= -2^2$

$= -4$

For $y = -(x - h)^2$, $h = -2$ since $-(x - (-2))^2 = -(x + 2)^2$. So the graph of $y = -x^2$ is translated 2 units to the left. The y-intercept is found by substituting $x = 0$.

The negative sign in front means the graph is inverted.

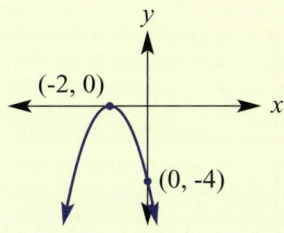

Example 14 Sketching with combined translations

Sketch these graphs on the same set of axes showing the coordinates of each turning point and each y-intercept.

a $y = (x - 2)^2 - 1$

b $y = -(x + 3)^2 + 2$

SOLUTION

a $y = (x - 2)^2 - 1$

Turning point is (2, -1)

y-intercept: $y = (0 - 2)^2 - 1$

$= 4 - 1$

$= 3$

b $y = -(x + 3)^2 + 2$

Turning point is (-3, 2)

y-intercept: $y = -(0 + 3)^2 + 2$

$= -9 + 2$

$= -7$

EXPLANATION

For $y = (x - h)^2 + k$, $h = 2$ and $k = -1$ so the graph of $y = x^2$ is shifted 2 to the right and 1 down. Substitute $x = 0$ for the y-intercept.

For $y = -(x - h)^2 + k$, $h = -3$ and $k = 2$ so the graph of $y = x^2$ is shifted 3 to the left and 2 up.

First, position the coordinates of the turning point and y-intercept then join to form each curve.

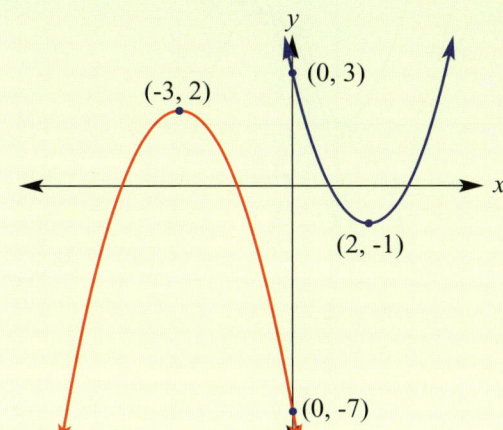

Exercise 10G

1 This diagram shows the graphs of $y = x^2$, $y = -x^2$, $y = (x + 2)^2$ and $y = -(x - 3)^2$.

   a State the turning point of the graph of:

   i $y = (x + 2)^2$ ii $y = -(x - 3)^2$

   b State the y-intercept for the graph of:

   i $y = (x + 2)^2$ ii $y = -(x - 3)^2$

   c Compared to the graph of $y = x^2$, which way has the graph of $y = (x + 2)^2$ been translated (left or right)?

   d Compared to the graph of $y = -x^2$ which way has the graph of $y = -(x - 3)^2$ been translated (left or right)?

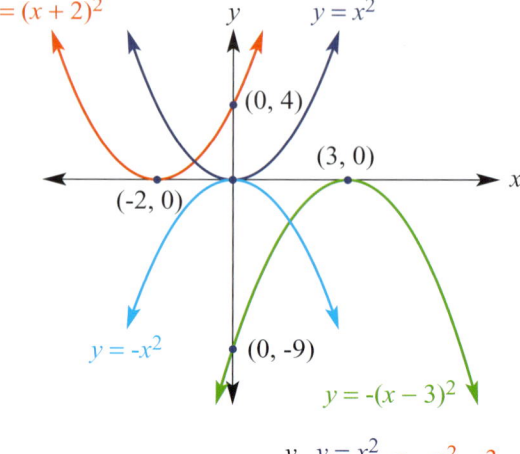

2 This diagram shows the graphs of $y = x^2$, $y = -x^2$ $y = x^2 - 3$ and $y = -x^2 + 2$.

   a State the turning point of the graph of:

   i $y = x^2 - 3$ ii $y = -x^2 + 2$

   b State the y-intercept for the graph of:

   i $y = x^2 - 3$ ii $y = -x^2 + 2$

   c Compared to the graph of $y = x^2$, which way has the graph of $y = x^2 - 3$ been translated (up or down)?

   d Compared to the graph of $y = -x^2$, which way has the graph of $y = -x^2 + 2$ been translated (up or down)?

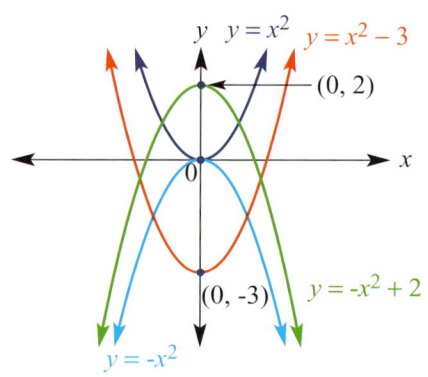

3 This diagram shows the graphs of $y = x^2$, $y = -x^2$, $y = -(x - 2)^2 + 3$ and $y = (x + 1)^2 - 1$.

   a State the turning point of the graph of:

   i $y = -(x - 2)^2 + 3$ ii $y = (x + 1)^2 - 1$

   b State the y-intercept for the graph of:

   i $y = -(x - 2)^2 + 3$ ii $y = (x + 1)^2 - 1$

   c State the missing words and numbers.

   i Compared to the graph of $y = x^2$, the graph of $y = (x + 1)^2 - 1$ has to be translated _____ unit to the _____ and _____ unit _____.

   ii Compared to the graph of $y = -x^2$, the graph of $y = -(x - 2)^2 + 3$ has to be translated _____ units to the _____ and _____ units _____.

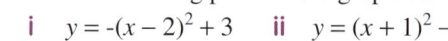

4 Substitute $x = 0$ to find the y-intercept for these rules.

   a $y = x^2 + 3$ b $y = -x^2 - 4$ c $y = -(x - 2)^2$ d $y = (x + 5)^2$

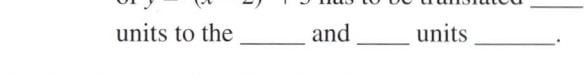

le 12a,b **5** Sketch the graphs of these rules showing the coordinates of the turning point and y-intercept.

   a $y = x^2 + 1$ **b** $y = x^2 + 3$ **c** $y = x^2 - 2$

   d $y = -x^2 + 4$ **e** $y = -x^2 + 1$ **f** $y = -x^2 - 5$

le 12c,d **6** Sketch the graphs of these rules showing the coordinates of the turning point and y-intercept.

   a $y = (x - 2)^2$ **b** $y = (x - 4)^2$ **c** $y = (x + 3)^2$

   d $y = -(x - 3)^2$ **e** $y = -(x + 2)^2$ **f** $y = -(x + 6)^2$

ample 13 **7** Sketch each graph showing the coordinates of the turning point and the y-intercept.

   a $y = (x - 3)^2 + 2$ **b** $y = (x - 1)^2 - 1$ **c** $y = (x + 2)^2 - 3$

   d $y = (x + 1)^2 + 7$ **e** $y = -(x - 2)^2 + 1$ **f** $y = -(x - 5)^2 + 3$

   g $y = -(x + 3)^2 - 4$ **h** $y = -(x + 1)^2 - 5$ **i** $y = -(x - 3)^2 - 6$

8 Match each of the following parabolas with the appropriate equation from the list below.

   i $y = x^2$ **ii** $y = (x + 2)^2$ **iii** $y = x^2 - 4$ **iv** $y = -x^2 - 3$

   v $y = (x - 2)^2$ **vi** $y = x^2 + 4$ **vii** $y = 4 - x^2$ **viii** $y = (x + 3)^2$

   ix $y = (x - 5)^2$ **x** $y = x^2 + 3$ **xi** $y = -(x + 3)^2$ **xii** $y = -x^2 + 3$

a
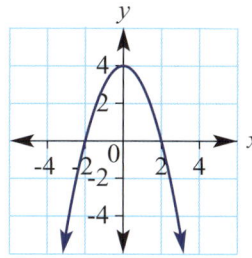

b
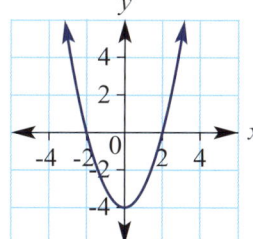

c
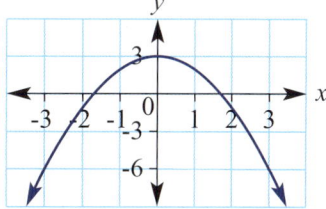

d
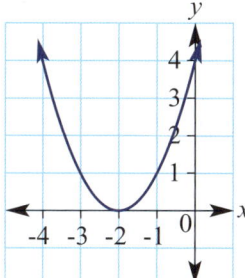

e
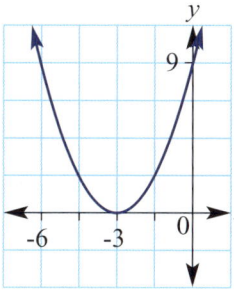

f
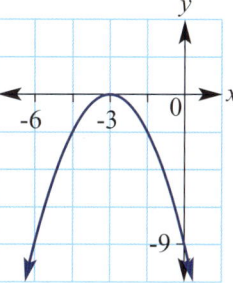

g
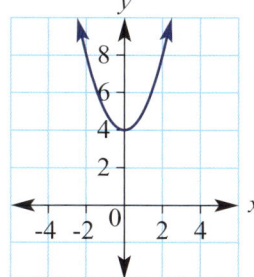

h
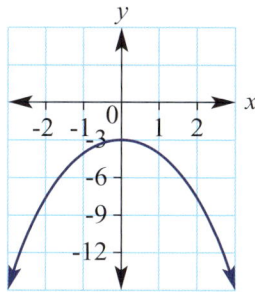

i
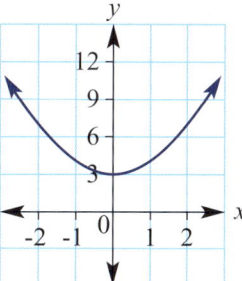

j 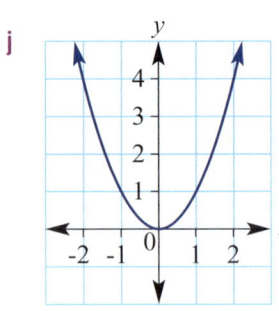 **k** 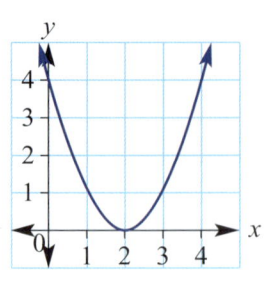 **l**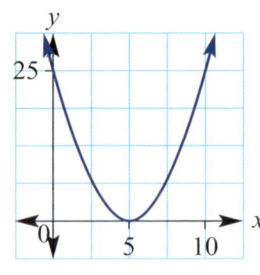

9 Write the rule for each graph in turning point form.

a 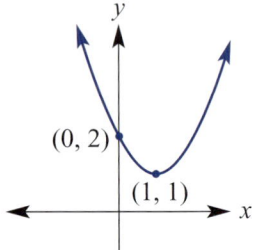 **b** 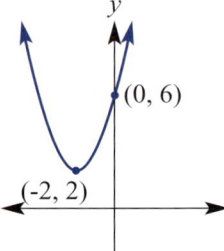 **c**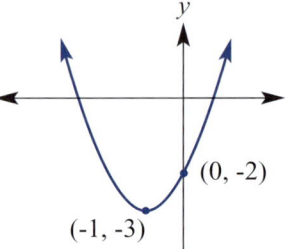

d 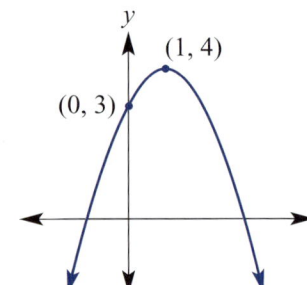 **e** 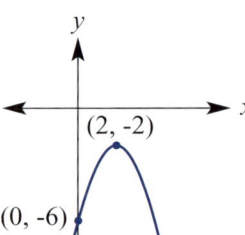 **f**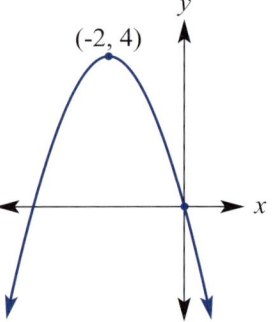

10 A bike track can be modelled approximately by combining two different quadratic equations. The first part of the bike path can be modelled by the equation $y = -(x - 2)^2 + 9$ for $-2 \le x \le 5$. The second part of the bike track can be modelled by the equation $y = (x - 7)^2 - 4$ for $5 \le x \le 10$.

  a Find the turning point of the graph of each quadratic equation.

  b Sketch each graph on the same set of axes. On your sketch of the bike path you need to show the coordinates of the start and finish of the track and where it crosses the x-axis.

11 Written in the form $y = a(x - h)^2 + k$, the rule $y = 4 - (x + 2)^2$ could be rearranged to give $y = -(x + 2)^2 + 4$.

  a Rearrange these rules and write in the form $y = a(x - h)^2 + k$.

  i $y = 3 - (x + 1)^2$ **ii** $y = 4 + (x + 3)^2$ **iii** $y = -3 + (x - 1)^2$

  iv $y = -7 - (x - 5)^2$ **v** $y = -2 - x^2$ **vi** $y = -6 + x^2$

  b Write down the coordinates of the turning point for each of the above quadratics.

12 A quadratic has the rule $y = a(x - h)^2 + k$.

   a What are the coordinates of the turning point?

   b Write an expression for the y-intercept.

13 Investigate and explain how the graph of:

   a $y = (2 - x)^2$ compares to the graph of $y = (x - 2)^2$

   b $y = (1 - x)^2$ compares to the graph of $y = (x - 1)^2$

Enrichment: Finding rules

14 Find the equation of the quadratic relation which is of the form $y = x^2 + c$ and passes through:

   a $(1, 4)$ **b** $(3, 5)$ **c** $(2, 1)$ **d** $(2, -1)$

15 Find the equation of the quadratic relation which is of the form $y = -x^2 + c$ and passes through:

   a $(1, 3)$ **b** $(-1, 3)$ **c** $(3, 15)$ **d** $(-2, 6)$

16 Find the possible equations of each of the following quadratics if their equation is of the form $y = (x - h)^2$ and their graph passes through the point:

   a $(1, 16)$ **b** $(3, 1)$ **c** $(-1, 9)$ **d** $(3, 9)$

17 Find the rule for each of these graphs with the given turning point (TP) and y-intercept.

   a TP $= (1, 1)$, y-int $= 0$ **b** TP $= (-2, 0)$, y-int $= 4$

   c TP $= (3, 0)$, y-int $= -9$ **d** TP $= (-3, 2)$, y-int $= -7$

   e TP $= (-1, 4)$, y-int $= 5$ **f** TP $= (3, -9)$, y-int $= 0$

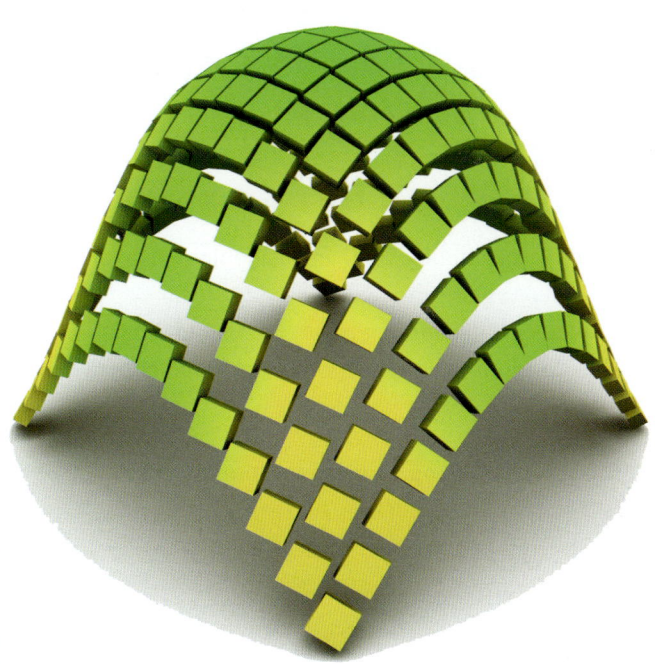

10.8 Sketching parabolas using intercept form

So far we have sketched parabolas using rules of the form $y = a(x - h)^2 + k$ where the coordinates of the turning point can be determined directly from the rule. An alternative method for sketching parabolas uses the factorised form of the quadratic rule and the Null Factor Law to find the x-intercepts. The turning point can be found by considering the axis of symmetry halfway between the two x-intercepts.

Let's start: From x-intercepts to turning point

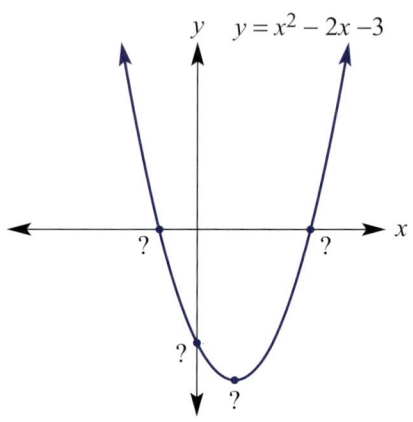

This graph has the rule $y = x^2 - 2x - 3$ but all its important features are not shown.

Find the features by discussing these questions.

- Can the quadratic rule be factorised?
- What is true about the coordinates of both x-intercepts?
- How can the factorised form of the rule help to find the x-intercepts?
- How does the x-coordinate of the turning point relate to the x-intercepts?
- Discuss how the y-coordinate of the turning point can be found.
- Finish by finding the y-intercept.

Key ideas

- All parabolas have one y-intercept and can have two, one or zero x-intercepts.

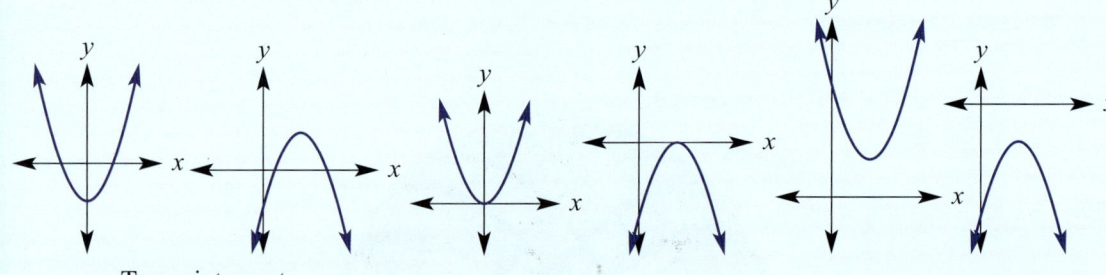

Two x-intercepts   One x-intercept   Zero x-intercepts

- x-intercepts can be found by substituting $y = 0$ and using the Null Factor Law
- If the graph has two x-intercepts, the turning point can be found by:
  - calculating the x-coordinate of the turning point, the midpoint of a and b; that is, $x = \dfrac{a+b}{2}$
  - calculating the y value of the turning point by substituting the x-coordinate into the rule for the quadratic.

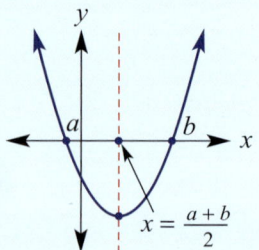

$$y = (x - a)(x - b)$$
$$0 = (x - a)(x - b)$$
$$x - a = 0 \text{ or } x - b = 0$$
$$x = a \text{ or } x = b$$

Example 15 Finding intercepts

For each of the following quadratic relations, find the coordinates of:
   i the x-intercepts   **ii** the y-intercept
a $y = x(x + 1)$
b $y = 2(x + 2)(x - 3)$

SOLUTION

EXPLANATION

a **i** x-intercepts (let $y = 0$):

    $x(x + 1) = 0$

    $x = 0$ or $x + 1 = 0$

    $x = 0$ or $x = -1$

    x-intercepts $(0, 0)$ and $(-1, 0)$

Let $y = 0$ to find the x-intercepts.

Apply the Null Factor Law to set each factor equal to 0 and solve.

Give the coordinates.

 ii y-intercept (let $x = 0$):

    $y = 0(0 + 1)$

    $y = 0$

    y-intercept $(0, 0)$

Let $x = 0$ to find the y-intercept.

b **i** $y = 2(x + 2)(x - 3)$ has two x-intercepts

    x-intercepts (let $y = 0$):

    $2(x + 2)(x - 3) = 0$

    $x + 2 = 0$ or $x - 3 = 0$

      $x = -2$ or $x = 3$

    x-intercepts $(-2, 0)$ and $(3, 0)$

There are two different factors.

Let $y = 0$ to find the x-intercepts. Set each factor equal to 0 and solve.

 ii y-intercept (let $x = 0$):

    $y = 2(2)(-3)$

    $y = -12$

    y-intercept $(0, -12)$

Let $x = 0$ to find the y-intercept.

Example 16 Sketching using intercept form

For the quadratic relation $y = x^2 - 2x$:
a factorise the relation
b find the y-intercept
c find the x-intercepts
d find the axis of symmetry
e find the turning point
f sketch the graph clearly showing all the key features

SOLUTION

EXPLANATION

a $y = x^2 - 2x$

   $= x(x - 2)$

Take out common factor of x.

b y-intercept (let $x = 0$): $y = 0$

Let $x = 0$ to find the y-intercept.

c x-intercepts (let $y = 0$):

   $0 = x(x - 2)$

   $x = 0$ or $x - 2 = 0$

   $x = 0$ or $x = 2$

Let $y = 0$ to find the x-intercepts. Set each factor equal to 0 and solve.

d Axis of symmetry: $x = \dfrac{0+2}{2} = 1$

The axis of symmetry is halfway between the x-intercepts.

e Turning point occurs when $x = 1$.
When $x = 1$, $y = 1^2 - 2(1)$
$\qquad\qquad y = -1$
∴ there is a minimum turning point at $(1, -1)$.

Substitute $x = 1$ into $y = x^2 - 2x$ to find the y-coordinate.
$x = 1$ and $y = -1$
The coefficient of x^2 is positive therefore the basic shape is ∪.

f Graph of $y = x^2 - 2x$

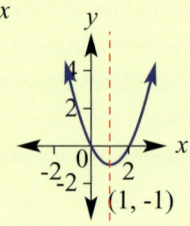

Sketch the graph, labelling the key features found above.

Example 17 Sketching a quadratic trinomial

For quadratic relation $y = x^2 + 2x - 8$:

a factorise the relation
b find the y-intercept
c find the x-intercepts
d find the axis of symmetry
e find the turning point
f sketch the graph clearly showing all the key features.

SOLUTION

a $y = x^2 + 2x - 8$
$\quad = (x + 4)(x - 2)$

b y-intercept (let $x = 0$): $y = -8$

c x-intercepts (let $y = 0$):
$0 = (x + 4)(x - 2)$
$x + 4 = 0$ or $x - 2 = 0$
$x = -4$ or $x = 2$

d Axis of symmetry: $x = \dfrac{-4+2}{2} = -1$

e Turning point occurs when $x = -1$.
When $x = -1$, $y = (-1)^2 + 2(-1) - 8$
$\qquad\qquad\qquad = -9$
∴ there is a minimum turning point at $(-1, -9)$.

f

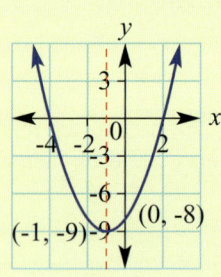

EXPLANATION

Factorise the quadratic trinomial.
$4 \times (-2) = -8$ and $4 + (-2) = 2$.

Let $x = 0$ to find the y-intercept.

Let $y = 0$ to find the x-intercepts.

The axis of symmetry is halfway between the x-intercepts

Substitute $x = -1$ into $y = x^2 + 2x - 8$ to find the y-coordinate.
$x = -1$ and $y = -9$
The coefficient of x^2 is positive therefore the basic shape is ∪

Sketch the graph showing the key features.

Exercise 10H

Understanding

1 Factorise these quadratics.

a $x^2 + 2x$ **b** $x^2 - 3x$ **c** $5x^2 - 10x$ **d** $x^2 - 9$

e $x^2 - 1$ **f** $x^2 - 49$ **g** $x^2 + 3x + 2$ **h** $x^2 + 5x + 6$

i $x^2 - x - 12$ **j** $x^2 - 3x - 28$ **k** $x^2 - 4x + 4$ **l** $x^2 + 10x + 25$

2 For these factorised quadratics, use the Null Factor Law to solve for x then find the x value halfway between.

a $0 = (x - 2)(x + 2)$ **b** $0 = (x - 5)(x + 5)$ **c** $0 = (x + 1)(x + 5)$

d $0 = (x - 6)(x - 10)$ **e** $0 = (x - 1)(x + 3)$ **f** $0 = (x - 3)(x + 5)$

g $0 = (x - 2)(x + 3)$ **h** $0 = (x - 10)(x + 1)$ **i** $0 = (x - 15)(x + 3)$

3 Use substitution to find the y-coordinate of the turning point of these quadratics. The x-coordinate of the turning point is given.

a $y = x^2 - 4, x = 0$ **b** $y = x^2 + 2x, x = -1$ **c** $y = x^2 - 6x, x = 3$

d $y = x^2 + 4x + 3, x = -2$ **e** $y = x^2 + 2x - 8, x = -1$ **f** $y = x^2 - 4x - 5, x = 2$

Fluency

Example 14

4 For each of the following quadratic relations, find the coordinates of:

i the x-intercepts **ii** the y-intercept

a $y = x(x + 7)$ **b** $y = x(x + 3)$ **c** $y = x(x + 4)$

d $y = (x - 4)(x + 2)$ **e** $y = (x + 2)(x - 5)$ **f** $y = (x - 7)(x + 3)$

g $y = 2(x + 3)(x - 1)$ **h** $y = 3(x + 4)(x + 1)$ **i** $y = (2 - x)(3 - x)$

Example 15

5 For each of the following quadratic relations:

i factorise the relation **ii** find the y-intercept

iii find the x-intercepts **iv** find the axis of symmetry

v find the turning point **vi** sketch the graph clearly showing all the key features.

a $y = x^2 - 5x$ **b** $y = x^2 + x$ **c** $y = x^2 - 3x$

d $y = 2x + x^2$ **e** $y = 5x + x^2$ **f** $y = 3x - x^2$

g $y = -x^2 - 8x$ **h** $y = -2x - x^2$ **i** $y = -x^2 + x$

Example 16

6 For each of the following quadratic relations:

i factorise the relation **ii** find the y-intercept

iii find the x-intercepts **iv** find the axis of symmetry

v find the turning point **vi** sketch each graph clearly showing all the key features.

a $y = x^2 - 3x + 2$ **b** $y = x^2 - 4x + 3$ **c** $y = x^2 + 2x - 3$

d $y = x^2 + 4x + 4$ **e** $y = x^2 + 2x + 1$ **f** $y = x^2 + 2x - 8$

7 For each of the following relations, sketch the graph clearly showing the x- and y-intercepts and the turning point.

a $y = x^2 - 1$ **b** $y = 9 - x^2$ **c** $y = x^2 + 5x$

d $y = 2x^2 - 6x$ **e** $y = 4x^2 - 8x$ **f** $y = x^2 - 3x - 4$

g $y = x^2 + x - 12$ **h** $y = x^2 + 2x + 1$ **i** $y = x^2 - 6x + 9$

8 State the missing number in these quadratic graphs.

a

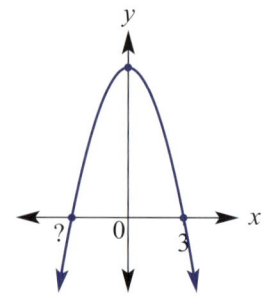

b

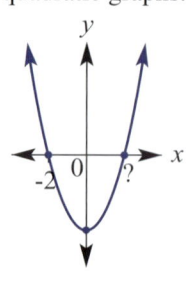

c

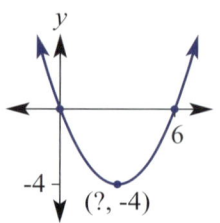

d

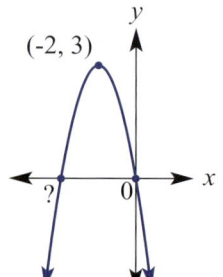

e

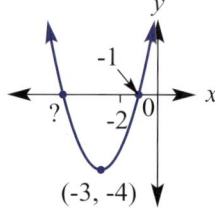

f

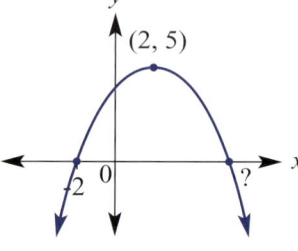

9 A golf ball's path is given by the rule $y = 30x - x^2$, where y is the height in metres above the ground and x is the horizontal distance in metres. Find:

   a how far the ball travels horizontally
   b how high the ball reaches mid flight.

10 A test rocket is fired and follows a path described by $y = 0.1x(200 - x)$. The height is y metres above ground and x is the horizontal distance in metres.

   a How far does the rocket travel horizontally?
   b How high does the rocket reach mid-flight?

11 Explain why the coordinates of the x-intercept and the turning point for $y = (x - 2)^2$ are the same.

12 Write down an expression for the y-intercept for these quadratics.

   a $y = ax^2 + bx + c$ **b** $y = (x - a)(x - b)$

13 $y = x^2 - 2x - 15$ can also be written in the form $y = (x - 1)^2 - 16$.

   a Use the second rule to state the coordinates of the turning point.
   b Use the first rule to find the x-intercepts then the turning point. Check you get the same result.
   c $y = x^2 - 4x - 45$ can be written in the form $y = (x - h)^2 + k$. Find the value of h and k.

Enrichment: Rule finding

14 Find the rule for these graphs using intercept form. The first one is done for you.

a

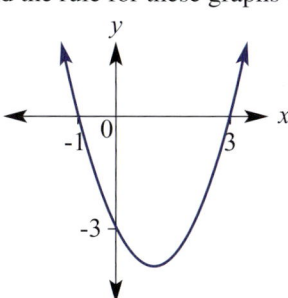

$$y = a(x + 1)(x - 3)$$
Sub (0, -3) $-3 = a(0 + 1)(0 - 3)$
$$-3 = a(1) \times (-3)$$
$$-3 = -3a$$
$$a = 1$$
$$\therefore \ y = (x + 1)(x - 3)$$

b

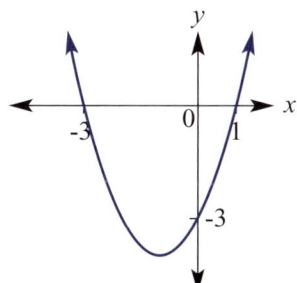

c

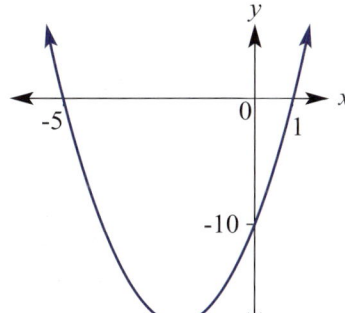

d

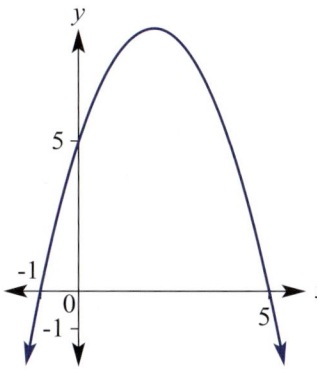

e

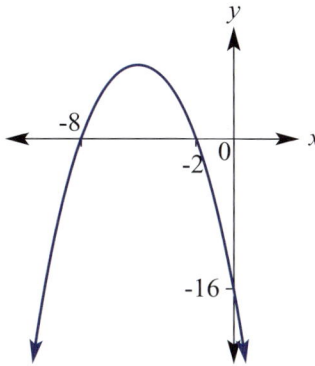

f

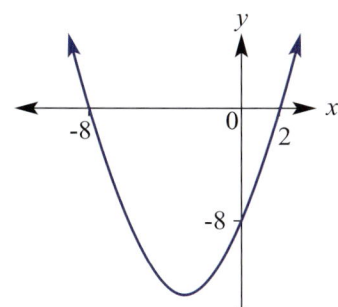

g

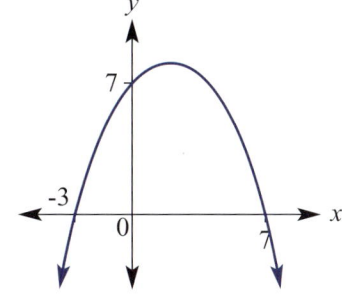

Investigating non-linear relations

The graph of a quadratic relation called a parabola was thoroughly investigated in this chapter. Many other relations also produce graphs which are non-linear. Two examples are the circle and the hyperbola.

Investigating rules and graphs of circles

The general equation of a circle is given by the rule $(x - a)^2 + (y - b)^2 = r^2$ where a, b and r are constants. Examples include: $x^2 + y^2 = 1$, $x^2 + y^2 = 25$, $(x - 1)^2 + (y + 3)^2 = 9$ and $(x + 3)^2 + y^2 = 100$.

Use graphing software to investigate graphs of circles with the rule $x^2 + y^2 = r^2$. (Note: for some software you may have to enter the rule for a circle in two parts: $y = \sqrt{r^2 - x^2}$ and $y = -\sqrt{r^2 - x^2}$).

a Sketch the graph of the relation $x^2 + y^2 = r^2$ if r takes the following values.
   i $r = 1$ **ii** $r = 2$ **iii** $r = 3$ **iv** $r = 7$

b Describe how the value of r relates to the graphs of the circles.

c Sketch by hand, the graphs of these circles.
   i $x^2 + y^2 = 16$ **ii** $x^2 + y^2 = 25$ **iii** $x^2 + y^2 = 10$

d **Extension** Investigate the effect of the values of a and b in the graph of the rule of $(x - a)^2 + (y - b)^2 = r^2$. Write a brief report showing your rules and graphs and describing your conclusions.

Investigating rules and graphs of hyperbolas

The basic form of the rule for a hyperbola is given by $y = \dfrac{a}{x - b} + c$ where a, b and c are constants.

Examples include: $y = \dfrac{1}{x}$, $y = -\dfrac{5}{x}$, $y = \dfrac{3}{x} - 1$ and $y = \dfrac{-2}{x - 3} + 2$.

Use graphing software to investigate graphs of hyperbolas with the rule $y = \dfrac{a}{x - b} + c$.

a Sketch the graph of the relation $y = \dfrac{a}{x}$ if a takes the following values.

   i $a = 1$ **ii** $a = 2$ **iii** $a = -1$ **iv** $a = -2$

b Describe the key features of the graphs including the asymptotes. (Research the meaning of the word *asymptote* if you are unsure.) Also describe how changing the value of a changes the shape of your graph.

c Now investigate how changing the value of c in $y = \dfrac{1}{x} + c$ changes the graph. Show your graphs for your chosen values of c and describe the effect.

d Now investigate how changing the value of b in $y = \dfrac{1}{x - b}$ changes the graph. Show your graphs for your chosen values of b and describe the effect.

Grazing Crown land

Land along the side of rivers is usually owned by the government and is sometimes called Crown land. Farmers can often lease this land to graze their sheep or cattle.

 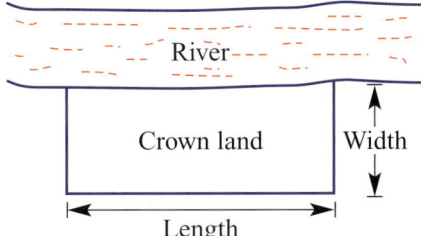

A farmer has a permit to fence off a rectangular area of land alongside the river. She has 400 m of fencing available and does not need to fence along the river.

A given width

a Find the length of the rectangular area if the width is:
   i 50 m   **ii** 120 m   **iii** 180 m

b Find the area of the land if the width is:
   i 50 m   **ii** 120 m   **iii** 180 m

c Which width from part **b** above gave the most area? Explain why the area decreases for small and large values for the width.

The variable width

a Using x metres to represent the width write an expression for the length showing working.

b Write an expression for the area of the land in terms of x.

c Use your area expression from part **b** to find the area of the land if x is the following value.
   i 20   **ii** 80   **iii** 160

The graph

a Using your expression from part **b** above sketch a graph of Area (A) vs x. You should find the following to help complete the graph.
   i y-intercept   **ii** x-intercepts   **iii** axis of symmetry   **iv** turning point

b What value of x gives the maximum area of land for grazing? Explain your choice and give the dimensions of the rectangular area of land.

General observations

a What do you notice about the width and the length when there is a maximum area?

b See if the same is true if the farmer had 600 m of fencing instead. Show your expressions and graph.

c **Extension** Prove your observation to parts **a** and **b** above by finding the x value that gives a maximum area using k metres of fencing. Hint: use $A = x(k - 2x)$.

1 **a** What do you notice about the sum of these numbers?

     i $1 + 3$ **ii** $1 + 3 + 5$

     iii $1 + 3 + 5 + 7$ **iv** $1 + 3 + 5 + 7 + 9$

   b Find the sum of the first 100 odd integers.

2 Solve these equations.

   a $6x^2 = 35 - 11x$ **b** $\dfrac{2}{x^2} = 1 - \dfrac{1}{x}$ **c** $\sqrt{x-1} = \dfrac{2}{x-1}$

3 A projectile's height (in metres) above ground is given by the expression $t(14 - t)$ where time t is in seconds. How long is the projectile above a height of 40 m?

4 Find the quadratic rule that relates the number of balls to the term number (n) in the following pattern.

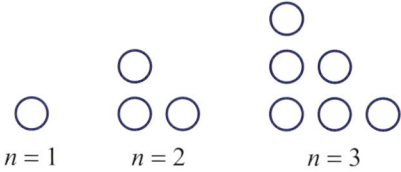

            $n = 1$ $n = 2$ $n = 3$

   If 66 balls are in the pattern, what term number is it?

5 Find the value of x in this diagram.

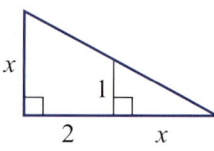

6 **a** A right-angled triangle's shortest side is of length x, the hypotenuse is 9 units longer than the shortest side while the other side is 1 unit longer than the shortest side. Find the side lengths of the triangle.

   b The area of a right-angled triangle is 60 square units and the lengths of the two shorter sides differ by 7 units. Find the length of the hypotenuse.

7 Given $a > 0$, for what values of k does $y = a(x - h)^2 + k$ have:

   a two x-intercepts

   b one x-intercept

   c no x-intercepts?

Turning point form

$y = a(x - h)^2 + k$
turning point (h, k)
e.g. $y = 2(x + 1)^2 + 3$
TP: (-1, 3)
y-int: $x = 0$, $y = 2(0 + 1)^2 + 3$
$\qquad\qquad = 2(1)^2 + 3$
$\qquad\qquad = 5$

Forms

A quadratic is of the form
$y = ax^2 + bx + c$, $a \neq 0$

Translation

$y = x^2 + k$ $\quad k > 0$, graph shifts up k units
$\qquad\qquad\quad k < 0$, graph shifts down k units
$y = (x - h)^2$ $\quad h > 0$, graph shifts h units right
$\qquad\qquad\quad h < 0$, graph shift h units left

e.g.

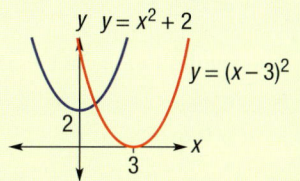

Parabola

Basic form $y = x^2$

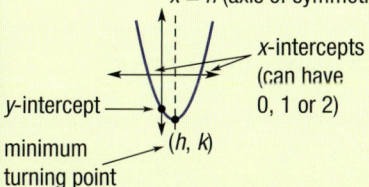

Turning point form
$y = a(x - h)^2 + k$

$x = h$ (axis of symmetry)

x-intercepts
(can have
0, 1 or 2)

y-intercept

minimum
turning point

(h, k)

Introduction to quadratic equations and graphs

Dilation and reflection

$y = ax^2$
$a < 0$, graph is reflected in x-axis

$-1 < a < 1$:
graph is wider than
$y = x^2$ or $y = -x^2$

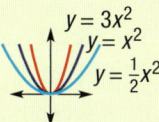
$y = -x^2$

$a > 1$ or $a < -1$:
graph is narrower than
$y = x^2$ or $y = -x^2$
e.g.

$y = 3x^2$
$y = x^2$
$y = \frac{1}{2}x^2$

Sketching $y = ax^2 + bx + c$

Find x- and y-intercepts and turning
point then sketch.
e.g. $y = x^2 - 6x + 5$
y-int: $x = 0$, $y = 0^2 - 6(0) + 5$
$\qquad\qquad = 5$
x-int: $y = 0$, $0 = x^2 - 6x + 5$
$\qquad\qquad 0 = (x - 1)(x - 5)$
$\qquad\quad x - 1 = 0$ or $x - 5 = 0$
$\qquad\qquad x = 1$ or $x = 5$
Turning point: halfway between the
x-intercepts:
$x = \frac{1 + 5}{2} = 3$

substitute $x = 3$ into rule
$y = 3^2 - 6(3) + 5$
$\quad = -4$
(3, -4) minimum
turning point

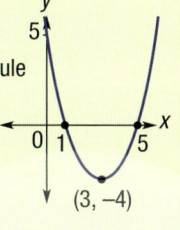

Applications

Define variable.
Set up equation.
Solve using Null Factor Law.
Check answer makes sense.
Answer the question in words.

Solving quadratic equations

Rewrite equation in standard form,
i.e. $ax^2 + bx + c = 0$
Factorise
Apply Null Factor Law:
If $ab = 0$, $a = 0$ or $b = 0$,
solve remaining equation
e.g. $x^2 + 5x = 0$
$\qquad x(x + 5) = 0$
$\qquad x = 0$ or $x + 5 = 0$
$\qquad x = 0$ or $x = -5$
e.g. $x^2 - 12 = 4x$
$\qquad x^2 - 4x - 12 = 0$
$\qquad (x - 6)(x + 2) = 0$
$\qquad x - 6 = 0$ or $x + 2 = 0$
$\qquad x = 6$ or $x = -2$

Multiple-choice questions

1 $(1, 3)$ is a point on which curve?

    A $y = x^2$ **B** $y = (x - 3)^2$ **C** $y = x^2 + 2x - 3$

    D $y = x^2 + 2$ **E** $y = 6 - x^2$

2 The solution(s) to $2x(x - 3) = 0$ is/are

    A $x = -3$ **B** $x = 0$ or $x = 3$ **C** $x = 2$ or $x = 3$

    D $x = 0$ or $x = -3$ **E** $x = 0$

3 The quadratic equation $x^2 = 7x - 12$ in standard form is:

    A $x^2 - 7x - 12 = 0$ **B** $-x^2 + 7x + 12 = 0$ **C** $x^2 - 7x + 12 = 0$

    D $x^2 + 7x - 12 = 0$ **E** $x^2 + 7x + 12 = 0$

4 The solution(s) to $x(x + 2) = 2x + 9$ are:

    A $x = -3$ or $x = 3$ **B** $x = 0$ or $x = -2$ **C** $x = 3$

    D $x = 9$ or $x = -1$ **E** $x = 9$ or $x = 0$

The following applies to Questions **5** and **6**.

The height, h metres, of a toy rocket above ground t seconds after launch is given by $h = 6t - t^2$.

5 The rocket returns to ground level after:

    A 5 seconds   **B** 3 seconds   **C** 12 seconds

    D 6 seconds   **E** 8 seconds

6 The rocket reaches its maximum height after:

    A 6 seconds   **B** 3 seconds   **C** 10 seconds

    D 4 seconds   **E** 9 seconds

7 The turning point of $y = (x - 2)^2 - 4$ is:

    A a maximum at $(2, 4)$ **B** a minimum at $(-2, 4)$ **C** a maximum at $(2, 4)$

    D a minimum at $(-2, -4)$ **E** a minimum at $(2, -4)$

8 The transformation of the graph of $y = x^2$ to $y = x^2 - 2$ is described by:

    A a translation of 2 units to the left   **B** a translation of 2 units to the right

    C a translation of 2 units down   **D** a translation of 2 units up

    E a translation of 2 units right and 2 units down

9 The graph of $y = -(x - 3)^2$ is:

    A 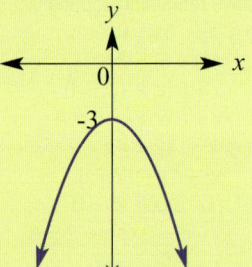   **B** 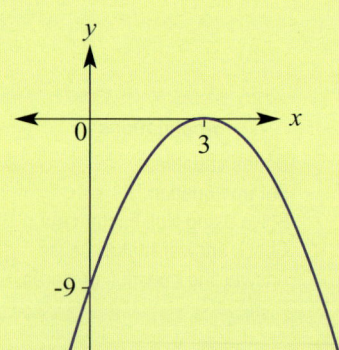   **C**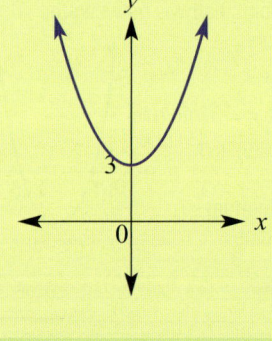

D

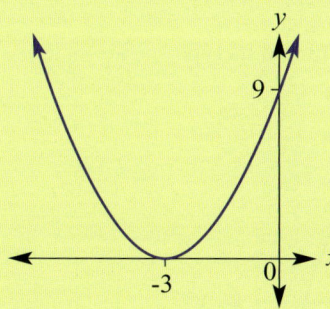

E

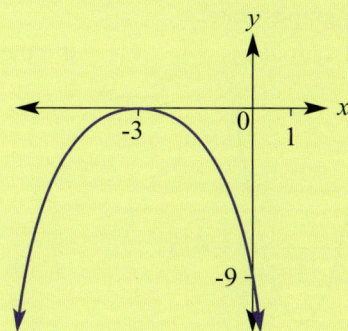

10 Compared to $y = x^2$, the narrowest graph is:

A $y = 5x^2$ **B** $y = 0.2x^2$ **C** $y = 2x^2$ **D** $y = \dfrac{1}{2}x^2$ **E** $y = 3.5x^2$

Short-answer questions

1 Consider the quadratic $y = x^2 - 2x - 3$.

  a Complete this table of values for the equation.

x	-3	-2	-1	0	1	2	3
y							

  b Plot the points in part **a** on a Cartesian plane and join in a smooth curve.

2 Use the Null Factor Law to solve the following equations.

  a $x(x + 2) = 0$ **b** $3x(x - 4) = 0$ **c** $(x + 3)(x - 7) = 0$

  d $(x - 2)(2x + 4) = 0$ **e** $(x + 1)(5x - 2) = 0$ **f** $(2x - 1)(3x - 4) = 0$

3 Solve the following quadratic equations by first factorising.

  a $x^2 + 3x = 0$ **b** $2x^2 - 8x = 0$ **c** $x^2 - 25 = 0$

  d $x^2 - 81 = 0$ **e** $5x^2 - 20 = 0$ **f** $3x^2 - 48 = 0$

  g $x^2 + 10x + 21 = 0$ **h** $x^2 - 3x - 40 = 0$ **i** $x^2 - 8x + 16 = 0$

4 Write the following quadratic equations in standard form and solve for x.

  a $x^2 = 5x$ **b** $3x^2 = 18x$ **c** $x^2 + 12 = -8x$

  d $2x + 15 = x^2$ **e** $x^2 + 15 = 8x$ **f** $4 - x^2 = 3x$

5 Set up and solve a quadratic equation to determine the value of x that gives the specified area of the shapes below.

  a

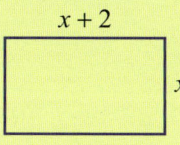

$A = 80$ sq. units

  b

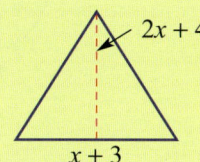

$A = 30$ sq. units

  c

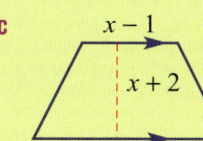

$A = 30$ sq. units

6 For the following graphs state:

    i the axis of symmetry   **ii** the turning point and its type

a

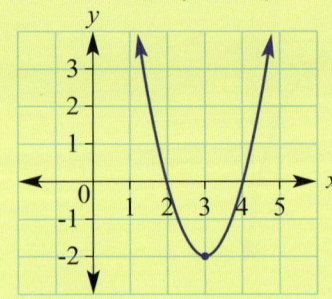

b

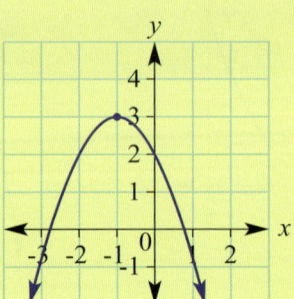

c

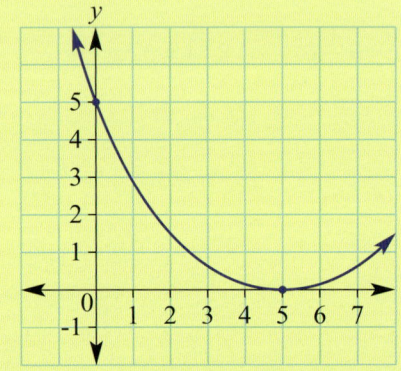

7 Match the following quadratic rules with their graphs.

$y = x^2 - 4$, $y = 2x^2$, $y = (x + 1)^2$, $y = (x - 3)^2$, $y = -x^2 + 2$

a

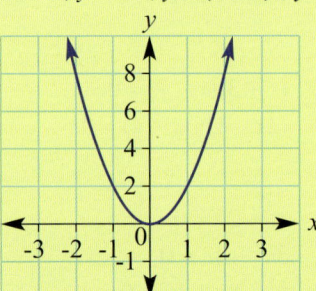

b

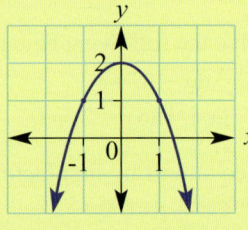

c

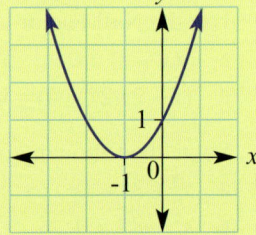

d

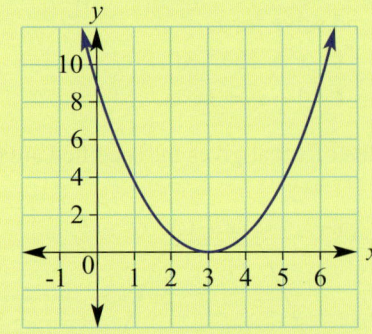

e

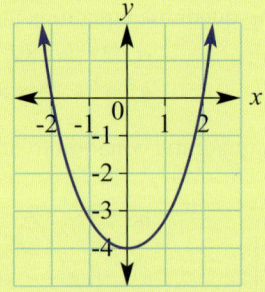

8 Sketch the following graphs labelling the turning point and y-intercept.

  a $y = x^2 + 2$ **b** $y = -x^2 - 5$ **c** $y = (x + 2)^2$

  d $y = -(x - 3)^2$ **e** $y = (x - 1)^2 + 3$ **f** $y = 2(x + 2)^2 - 4$

9 State the transformations that take $y = x^2$ to each of the graphs in Question **8**.

10 Sketch the following graphs labelling the y-intercept, turning point and x-intercepts.

  a $y = x^2 - 8x + 12$ **b** $y = x^2 + 10x + 16$

  c $y = x^2 + 2x - 15$ **d** $y = x^2 + 4x - 5$

Extended-response questions

1 A sail of a yacht is in the shape of a right-angled triangle. It has a base length of $2x$ metres and its height is 5 metres more than half its base.

  a Write an expression for the height of the sail.

  b Give an expression for the area of the sail in expanded form.

  c If the area of the sail is 14 m², find the value of x.

  d Hence, state the dimensions of the sail.

Using quadratic relations, we can find the area of this sail.

2 Connor and Sam are playing in the park with toy rockets they have made. They each launch their rockets at the same time to see whose is better.

  a The path of Sam's rocket is modelled by the equation $h = 12t - 2t^2$ where h is the height of the rocket in metres after t seconds.

   i Find the axis intercepts.

   ii Find the turning point.

   iii Sketch a graph of the height of Sam's rocket over time.

  b The path of Connor's rocket is modelled by the equation $h = -(t - 4)^2 + 16$ where h is the height of the rocket in metres after t seconds.

   i Find the h-intercept.

   ii State the turning point.

   iii Use the answers from parts **b i** and **ii** to state the two t-intercepts.

   iv Sketch a graph of the height of Connor's rocket over time.

  c **i** Whose rocket was in the air longest?

   ii Whose rocket reached the greatest height and by how much?

   iii How high was Sam's rocket when Connor's was at its maximum height?

Indices and surds

Multiple-choice questions

1   $3a^2b^3 \times 4ab^2$ is equivalent to:

   A $12a^2b^6$ B $7a^3b^5$ C $12a^3b^5$ D $12a^4b^5$ E $7a^2b^6$

2   $\left(\dfrac{2x}{5}\right)^3$ is equivalent to:

   A $\dfrac{6x^3}{5}$ B $\dfrac{8x^3}{125}$ C $\dfrac{2x^3}{5}$ D $\dfrac{2x^4}{15}$ E $\dfrac{2x^3}{125}$

3   4^{-2} can be expressed as:

   A $\dfrac{1}{4^{-2}}$ B $\dfrac{1}{8}$ C -16 D $\dfrac{1}{16}$ E -8

4   $3x^{-4}$ written with positive indices is:

   A $-3x^4$ B $\dfrac{1}{3x^4}$ C $-\dfrac{3}{x^4}$ D $\dfrac{1}{3x^{-4}}$ E $\dfrac{3}{x^4}$

5   0.00371 in scientific notation is:

   A 0.371×10^{-3} B 3.7×10^{-2} C 3.71×10^{-3} D 3.71×10^3 E 371×10^3

Short-answer questions

1   Use index laws to simplify the following.

   a $\dfrac{9a^6b^3}{18a^4b^2}$ b $\dfrac{(-3x^4y^2)^2 \times 6xy^2}{27x^6y}$ c $(2x^2)^3 - 3x^0 + (5x)^0$

2   Write each of the following using positive indices and simplify.

   a $\dfrac{5}{m^{-2}}$ b $\dfrac{4a^6b^{-4}}{6a^{-2}b}$ c $3(x^{\frac{1}{2}})^3 y^{-\frac{1}{3}} \times x^{\frac{1}{2}} y^{-\frac{2}{3}}$

3   Convert these numbers to the units given in brackets. Write your answer in scientific notation using three significant figures.

   a 30.71 g (kg)   b 4236 tonnes (kg)

   c 3.4 hours (seconds)   d 235 nanoseconds (seconds)

4   Simplify the following.

   a $144^{\frac{1}{2}}$ b $27^{\frac{1}{3}}$ c $2\sqrt{3} + 3\sqrt{5} - \sqrt{3} + 4\sqrt{5}$ d $\sqrt{35} \div \sqrt{5}$

Extended-response question

The average human body contains about 74 billion cells.

a   Write this number of cells:

   i   in decimal form   ii   in scientific notation

b If the population of a particular city is 2.521×10^6, how many human cells are there in the city? Give your answer in scientific notation correct to three significant figures.

c If the average human weighs 64.5 kilograms, what is the average mass of one cell in grams? Give your answer in scientific notation correct to three significant figures.

Geometry

Multiple-choice questions

1 The supplementary angle to 55° is:

   A 55°   **B** 35°   **C** 125°   **D** 135°   **E** 70°

2 A quadrilateral with all four sides equal and opposite sides parallel is best described by a:

   A parallelogram   **B** rhombus   **C** rectangle

   D trapezium   **E** kite

3 The size of the interior angle in a regular pentagon is:

   A 108°   **B** 120°   **C** 96°   **D** 28°   **E** 115°

4 The test that proves congruence in these two triangles is:

   A SAS   **B** RHS   **C** AAA

   D SSS   **E** AAS

5 What is the scale factor that enlarges shape 1 to shape 2 in these similar figures, and what is the value of x?

   A 2 and $x = 8$ **B** 2.5 and $x = 7.5$

   C 3.33 and $x = 13.33$ **D** 2.5 and $x = 12.5$

   E 2 and $x = 6$

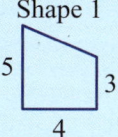
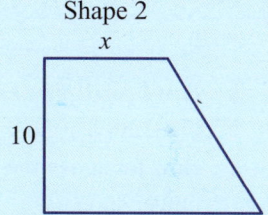

Short-answer questions

1 Find the value of each pronumeral in the following.

a

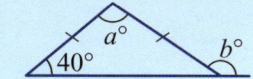

b

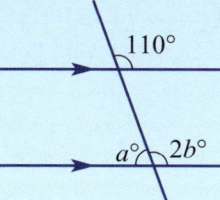

c

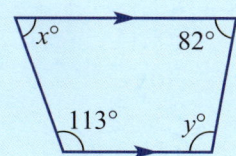

d

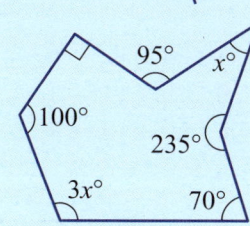

2   Find the value of ∠ABC by adding a third parallel line.

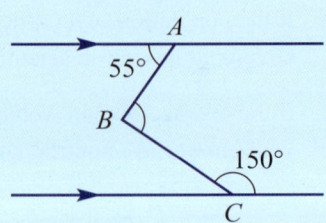

3   Prove $\triangle ABC \equiv \triangle ADC$.

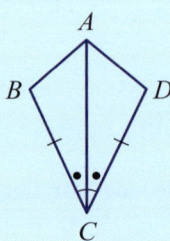

4   For this pair of triangles:
  a   Give a reason (SSS, SAS, AAA or RHS) why the two triangles are similar.
  b   Find the value of x.

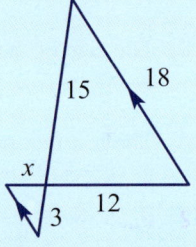

Extended-response question

A vertical wall is being supported by a piece of timber that touches the ground 10 metres from the base of the wall. A vertical metal support 4.5 m high is placed under the timber support 4 m from the wall.

a   Prove $\triangle ABD \,|||\, \triangle ECD$.
b   Find how far the timber reaches up the wall.
c   How far above the ground is the point halfway along the timber support?
d   The vertical metal support is moved so that the timber support is able to reach one metre higher up the wall. If the piece of timber now touches the ground 9.2 m from the wall, find how far the metal support is from the wall. Give your answer correct to one decimal place.

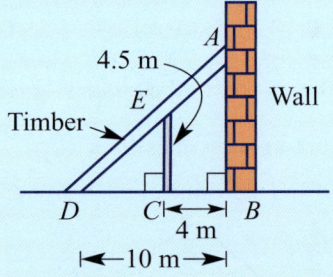

Algebraic techniques
Multiple-choice questions

1   The expanded form of $(x + 4)(3x - 2)$ is:
  A $3x^2 + 12x - 8$ **B** $4x^2 + 14x - 8$ **C** $3x^2 + 12x - 10$
  D $3x^2 - 8$ **E** $3x^2 + 10x - 8$

2 $2(x + 2y) - x(x + 2y)$ factorises to:
  A $2x(x + 2y)$ **B** $(x + 2y)^2(2 - x)$ **C** $(2 + x)(x + 2y)$
  D $(x + 2y)(2 - x)$ **E** $(x + 2y)(2 - x^2 - 2xy)$

3 $x^2 - 2x - 24$ in factorised form is:

A $(x-2)(x+12)$ **B** $(x-6)(x+4)$ **C** $(x-8)(x+3)$
D $(x+6)(x-4)$ **E** $(x-6)(x-4)$

4 $\dfrac{3x+6}{(x-2)(x-4)} \times \dfrac{x^2-4}{(x+2)^2}$ is equivalent to:

A $\dfrac{3}{x-4}$ **B** $\dfrac{3(x-2)}{(x-4)(x+2)}$ **C** $\dfrac{3x-2}{(x+1)^2}$ **D** $\dfrac{3}{(x+2)(x-2)}$ **E** $\dfrac{3x^2}{(x-2)(x+2)}$

5 $\dfrac{7}{(x+1)^2} - \dfrac{4}{x+1}$ simplifies to:

A $\dfrac{3x+1}{(x+1)^2}$ **B** $\dfrac{6-4x}{(x+1)^2}$ **C** $\dfrac{-9}{(x+1)^2}$ **D** $\dfrac{3-4x}{(x+1)^2}$ **E** $\dfrac{11-4x}{(x+1)^2}$

Short-answer questions

1 Find the area of the following shapes in expanded form.

a $x+3$ 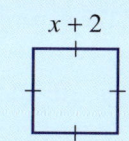 $x-3$ **b** $x+2$ **c** $3x-4$ 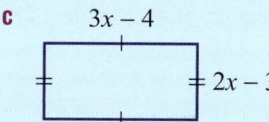 $2x-3$

2 Factorise each of the following fully.

a $8ab + 2a^2b$ **b** $9m^2 - 25$ **c** $3b^2 - 48$
d $(a+7)^2 - 9$ **e** $x^2 + 6x + 9$ **f** $x^2 + 8x - 20$
g $2x^2 - 16x + 30$ **h** $2x^2 - 11x + 12$ **i** $6x^2 + 5x - 4$

3 Factorise the following by grouping.

a $x^2 - 3ax - x + 3a$ **b** $2ax - 10b - 5bx + 4a$

4 a Simplify these algebraic fractions.

    i $\dfrac{3x+24}{2x+16}$ **ii** $\dfrac{12}{x^2-9} \div \dfrac{3}{x-3}$ **iii** $\dfrac{x+3}{2} + \dfrac{3x}{7}$

    iv $\dfrac{2}{x} - \dfrac{5}{3x}$ **v** $\dfrac{7}{x+1} + \dfrac{4}{x-2}$ **vi** $\dfrac{5}{x-5} - \dfrac{3}{x+2}$

b Solve these equations involving algebraic fractions.

    i $\dfrac{5}{2x} + \dfrac{1}{3x} = 2$ **ii** $\dfrac{4}{x-5} = \dfrac{2}{x+3}$

Extended-response question

A room that is 10 metres long and 8 metres wide has a rectangular rug in the middle of it that leaves a border, x metres wide, all the way around it as shown.

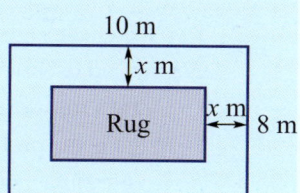

10 m

x m

Rug x m   8 m

a Write expressions for the length and the width of the rug.

b Write an expression for the area of the rug in expanded form.

c What is the area of the rug when $x = 1$?

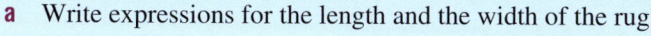

d   Fully factorise your expression in part **b** by first removing the common factor.

e   What happens when $x = 4$?

f   Use trial and error to find the value of x that gives an area of 15 m².

Probability and statistics

Multiple-choice questions

1   The probability of not rolling a number less than three on a normal six-sided die is:

    A $\dfrac{1}{3}$ B 4   C $\dfrac{1}{2}$ D $\dfrac{2}{3}$ E 3

2   From the two-way table, $Pr(A \cap B)$ is:

    A $\dfrac{1}{5}$ B 4   C $\dfrac{9}{20}$ D $\dfrac{1}{4}$ E 16

	A	A′	Total
B		7	
B′	5		
Total		11	20

3   In the selection of 40 marbles, 28 were blue. The experimental probability of the next one selected being blue is:

    A 0.28   B 0.4   C 0.7   D 0.54   E 0.75

4   The median, mean and range of the data set 12 3 1 6 10 1 5 18 11 15 are, respectively:

    A 5.5, 8.2, 1–18   B 8, 8.2, 17   C 5.5, 8, 17   D 8, 8.2, 1–18   E 8, 74.5, 18

5   The interquartile range of the data in the box plot shown is:

    A 10   B 27   C 13   D 30   E 17

Short-answer questions

1   In a survey of 30 people, 18 people drink coffee during the day, 14 people drink tea and 8 people drink both. Let C be the set of people who drink coffee and T the set of people who drink tea.

    a   Construct a Venn diagram for the survey results.

    b   Find:

        i $n(C \cup T)$ ii $n(T')$

    c   If one of the 30 people was randomly selected, find:

        i   Pr(drinks neither coffee nor tea)   ii   Pr(C only)

2   Two ice creams are randomly selected without replacement from a box containing one vanilla (V), two strawberry (S) and one chocolate (C) flavoured ice creams.

    a   Draw a tree diagram to show each of the possible outcomes.

    b   What is the probability of selecting:

        i   a vanilla and a strawberry flavoured ice cream?

        ii   two strawberry flavoured ice creams?

        iii no vanilla flavoured ice cream?

3 The data below shows the number of aces served by a player in each of their grand slam tennis matches for the year.

          15   22   11   17   25   25   12   31   26   18   32   11   25   32   13   10

   a Construct a stem-and-leaf plot for the data.

   b From the stem-and-leaf plot, find the mode and median number of aces.

   c Is the data symmetrical or skewed?

4 The frequency table shows the number of visitors, in intervals of fifty, to a theme park each day in April.

   a Complete the frequency table shown. Round to one decimal place where necessary.

   b Construct a frequency histogram.

   c **i**   How many days were there fewer than 100 visitors?

   ii What percentage of days had between 50 and 200 visitors?

Class interval	Frequency	Percentage frequency
0–	2	
50–	4	
100–	5	
150–	9	
200–		
250–	3	
Total	30	

Extended-response question

A game at the school fair involves randomly selecting a green ball and a red ball each numbered 1, 2 or 3.

a List the outcomes in a table.

b What is the probability of getting an odd and an even number?

c Participants win $1 when they draw each ball showing the same number.

   i   What is the probability of winning $1?

   ii If someone wins six times, how many games are they likely to have played?

d The ages of those playing the game in the first hour are recorded and are shown below.

          12   16   7   24   28   9   11   17   18   18   37   9   40   16   32   42   14

   i   Draw a box plot to represent the data.

   ii Twenty-five percent of the participants are below what age?

   iii If this data is used as a model for the 120 participants throughout the day, how many would be expected to be aged less than 30?

Introduction to quadratic equations and graphs

Multiple-choice questions

1 The solution(s) to $3x(x + 5) = 0$ is/are:

   A $x = -5$ **B** $x = 0, -5$ **C** $x = 3, 5$ **D** $x = 5$ **E** $x = 0, 5$

2 $x^2 = 3x - 2$ is the same as the equation:

   A $x^2 + 3x - 2 = 0$ **B** $x^2 - 3x + 2 = 0$ **C** $x^2 - 3x - 2 = 0$

   D $-x^2 + 3x + 2 = 0$ **E** $x^2 + 3x + 2 = 0$

3 The *incorrect* statement about the graph of $y = 2x^2$ is:

   A the graph is the shape of a parabola   **B** the point $(-2, 8)$ is on the graph

   C its turning point is at $(0, 0)$ **D** it has a minimum turning point

   E the graph is wider than the graph of $y = x^2$

4 The type and coordinates of the turning point of the graph of $y = -(x + 3)^2 + 2$ are:

    A a minimum at (3, 2)   **B** a maximum at (3, 2)   **C** a maximum at (-3, 2)

    D a minimum at (-3, 2)   **E** a minimum at (3, -2)

5 The graph shown has the equation:

    A $y = 4x^2$

    B $y = x^2 + 4$

    C $y = (x + 2)^2$

    D $y = x^2 + 2$

    E $y = (x - 2)^2$

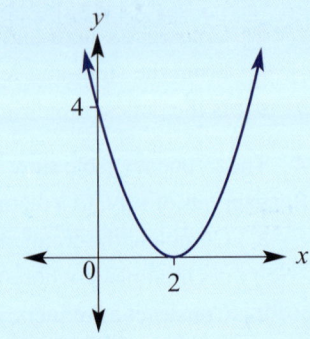

Short-answer questions

1 Solve the following quadratic equations.

    a $(x + 5)(x - 3) = 0$ **b** $(2x - 1)(3x + 5) = 0$ **c** $4x^2 + 8x = 0$

    d $5x^2 - 45 = 0$ **e** $x^2 - 9x + 14 = 0$ **f** $8x = -x^2 - 16$

2 The length of a rectangular swimming pool is x m and its width is 7 m less than its length. If the area occupied by the pool is 120 m^2, solve an appropriate equation to find the dimensions of the pool.

3 Sketch the following graphs showing the y-intercept and turning point and state the transformations that have taken place from the graph of $y = x^2$.

    a $y = x^2 + 3$ **b** $y = -(x + 4)^2$ **c** $y = (x - 2)^2 + 5$

4 Consider the quadratic relation $y = x^2 - 4x - 12$.

    a Find the y-intercept.   **b** Factorise the relation and find the x-intercepts.

    c Find the coordinates of the turning point.   **d** Sketch the graph.

Extended-response question

The flight path of a soccer ball kicked upwards from the ground is given by the equation $y = 120x - 20x^2$ where y is the height of the ball above the ground in centimetres at any time, x seconds.

a Find the x-intercepts to determine when the ball lands on the ground.

b Find the coordinates of the turning point and state:

    i the maximum height reached by the ball

    ii after how many seconds the ball reaches this maximum height.

c At what times was the ball at a height of 160 cm?

d Sketch a graph of the path of the ball until it returns to the ground.

Answers

Chapter 1

Pre-test

1 a 17   **b** 11   **c** 3   **d** 8

   e -4   **f** -1   **g** -6   **h** 2

2 a $2\frac{1}{5}$ **b** 2.2

3 a 9   **b** 5   **c** 16   **d** 8

4 $\frac{7}{9} > \frac{3}{4}$

5 a 2.654, 2.645, 2.564, 2.465

   b 0.654, 0.564, 0.456, 0.0456

6 a 7.99   **b** 10.11   **c** 7.11

7 a 1.4   **b** 0.06   **c** 3.68

   d 16.38   **e** 3.7   **f** 180

8 a 34.5   **b** 374 000   **c** 0.03754   **d** 0.00003754

9 a 15   **b** 12   **c** 10

10 a $\frac{5}{7}$ **b** 1   **c** $\frac{1}{2}$ **d** $\frac{1}{4}$

11 a 13   **b** 60   **c** 8.1

Exercise 1A

1 a 1, 2, 4, 8, 16   **b** 1, 2, 4, 7, 8, 14, 28, 56

   c HCF = 8   **d** 3, 6, 9, 12, 15, 18, 21

   e 5, 10, 15, 20, 25, 30   **f** LCM = 15

   g 2, 3, 5, 7, 11, 13, 17, 19, 23, 29

   h 83, 89, 97, 101, 103, 107, 109

2 a 121   **b** 225   **c** 12   **d** 20

   e 27   **f** 125   **g** 2   **h** 4

3 a -5   **b** -8   **c** -1   **d** 9

   e -1   **f** -16   **g** 15   **h** 9

   i -6   **j** -84   **k** 22   **l** 42

   m -9   **n** -6   **o** 10   **p** 19

4 a 2   **b** 2   **c** 10   **d** 16

   e -9   **f** -3   **g** -4   **h** 10

   i -11   **j** 2   **k** -3   **l** 4

   m -23   **n** 10   **o** 0   **p** 3

   q -9   **r** 7   **s** -1   **t** 4

5 a 28   **b** 24   **c** 187   **d** 30

6 a 4   **b** 5   **c** 1   **d** 23

7 a 4   **b** 23   **c** -3   **d** 2   **e** -2

   f -18   **g** -6   **h** -1   **i** 1

8 a -2   **b** -38   **c** -8   **d** 27

   e 1   **f** 24   **g** 21   **h** 0

9 a $-2 \times [11 + (-2)] = -18$ **b** $[-6 + (-4)] \div 2 = -5$

   c $[2 - 5] \times (-2) = 6$ **d** $-10 \div [3 + (-5)] = 5$

   e $3 - [(-2) + 4] \times 3 = -3$ **f** $[(-2)^2 + 4] \div (-2) = -2^2$

10 4   **11** 252 days

12 a 7 and -2   **b** -5 and 2   **13** 8

14 a i 16   **ii** 16   **b** $a = \pm 4$ **c** $a = 3$

   d the square of a negative number has negative signs occurring in pairs and will create a positive answer

   e -3

   f as the squaring of any number produces a positive answer

   g i -4   **ii** -125   **iii** -9   **iv** -16

   h no   **i** yes

   j Prime numbers have only two factors – itself and one, therefore the only common factor for any pair of prime numbers is 1.

   k again as there are only 2 factors of any prime, the LCM must be the multiple of primes

15 a False   **b** False   **c** True   **d** True   **e** False   **f** True

16 a i $1 + 2 + 3 = 6$

   ii $28 (1 + 2 + 4 + 7 + 14 = 28)$

   iii $1 + 2 + 4 + 8 + 16 + 31 + 62 + 124 + 248 = 496$

   b i

<!-- dot triangle figures labelled 6, 10, 15, 21 -->

     6   10   15   21

   ii 28, 36

   c i 0, 1, 1, 2, 3, 5, 8, 13, 21, 34

   ii -21, 13, -8, 5, -3, 2, -1, 1, 0, 1 … ∴ -21, -8, -3, -1

Exercise 1B

1 a 40   **b** 270   **c** 7.9   **d** 0.04

2 a 32 100   **b** 432   **c** 5.89

   d 0.443   **e** 0.001 97

3 a 60   **b** 57.375   **c** 2.625

4 a 17.96   **b** 11.08   **c** 72.99   **d** 47.86

   e 63.93   **f** 23.81   **g** 804.53   **h** 500.57

   i 821.27   **j** 5810.25   **k** 1005.00   **l** 2650.00

5 a 7   b 73   c 130   d 36 200

6 a 0.333   b 0.286   c 1.182   d 13.793

7 a 2400   b 35 000   c 0.060   d 34

   e 110 000   f 0.0025   g 2.1   h 0.71

8 a 30 000   b 200   c 0.05   d 0.0006

9 a 3600, 3693   b 760, 759.4

   c 4000, 4127.16   d 3000, 3523.78

   e 0, 0.722 16   f 4, 0.716 245

   g 0.12, 0.1186   h 0.02, 0.02254

   i 10, 8.4375   j 1600, 1683.789156

   k 0.08, 0.074957...   l 11, 10.25538...

10 a A: 54.3, B: 53.8, 0.5   b A: 54.28, B: 53.79, 0.49

   c A: 54, B: 54, 0   d A: 50, B: 50, 0

11 a each to 1 significant figure

   b each to 2 significant figures

   c each to the nearest whole number

12 8.33 m   **13** 0.143 tonnes

14 2.14999 is closer to 2.1 correct to 1 decimal place $\therefore$ round down

15 as magnesium in this case would be zero if rounded to two decimal places rather than 2 significant figures

16 a i 50   ii 624   b i 50   c 600

   d The addition is the same as the original but the multiplication is lower $- 20 \times 30 < 24 \times 26$

17 a 0.18181818   b i 8   ii 1   iii 8

   c 0.1428571428571   d i 4   ii 2   iii 8   e Not possible

Exercise 1C

1 a $1\frac{2}{5}$ b $4\frac{1}{3}$ c $4\frac{4}{11}$ d $6\frac{8}{53}$

2 a $\frac{11}{7}$ b $\frac{16}{3}$ c $\frac{19}{2}$ d $\frac{238}{13}$

3 a $\frac{2}{5}$ b $\frac{4}{29}$ c $4\frac{1}{6}$ d $-72\frac{1}{8}$

4 a 9   b 24   c 21   d 35

   e 3   f 7   g 10   h 6

5 a 2.75   b 0.35   c 3.4   d 1.875

   e 2.625   f 3.8   g 2.3125   h 0.218 75

6 a $0.\overline{27}$ b $0.\overline{7}$ c $1.\overline{285714}$ d $0.41\dot{6}$

   e $1.\dot{1}$ f $3.8\dot{3}$ g $7.2\dot{6}$ h $2.\overline{63}$

7 a $\frac{7}{20}$ b $\frac{3}{50}$ c $3\frac{7}{10}$ d $\frac{14}{25}$

   e $1\frac{7}{100}$ f $\frac{3}{40}$ g $3\frac{8}{25}$ h $7\frac{3}{8}$

   i $2\frac{1}{200}$ j $10\frac{11}{250}$ k $6\frac{9}{20}$ l $2\frac{101}{1000}$

8 a $\frac{5}{6}$ b $\frac{13}{20}$ c $\frac{7}{10}$ d $\frac{5}{12}$

   e $\frac{7}{16}$ f $\frac{11}{14}$ g $\frac{19}{30}$ h $\frac{11}{27}$

9 a $\frac{5}{12}, \frac{7}{18}, \frac{3}{8}$ b $\frac{5}{24}, \frac{3}{16}, \frac{1}{6}$ c $\frac{7}{12}, \frac{23}{40}, \frac{8}{15}$

10 a $\frac{9}{20}$ b $\frac{3}{20}$ c $\frac{32}{45}$ d $\frac{23}{75}$

11 a $\frac{11}{6}, \frac{7}{3}$ b $\frac{2}{5}, \frac{2}{15}$ c $\frac{11}{12}, 1$ d $\frac{5}{7}, \frac{11}{14}$

12 Weather forecast

13 a $\frac{3}{5}$ b $\frac{5}{9}$ c $\frac{8}{13}$ d $\frac{23}{31}$

14 a 31, 32   b 36, 37, 38, . . . , 55

   c 4, 5   d 2, 3

   e 43, 44, 45, . . . 55   f 4, 5, 6

15 $\frac{ac+b}{c}$

16 a yes, e.g. $\frac{7}{14} = \frac{1}{2}$ and 7 is prime

   b no as **a** and **b** will have no common factors other than one

   c no as then a factor of 2 can be used to cancel

   d yes e.g. $\frac{5}{7}$

17 a $\frac{8}{9}$ b $1\frac{2}{9}$ c $\frac{81}{99}$ d $3\frac{43}{99}$

   e $9\frac{25}{33}$ f $\frac{44}{333}$ g $2\frac{917}{999}$ h $13\frac{8125}{9999}$

Exercise 1D

1 a 6   b 63   c 65   d 30

   e 4   f 33   g 60   h 87

2 a $\frac{7}{3}$ b $\frac{39}{5}$ c $\frac{41}{4}$ d $\frac{137}{6}$

3 a $\frac{9}{6} + \frac{8}{6} = \frac{17}{6}$ b $\frac{4}{3} - \frac{2}{5} = \frac{20}{15} - \frac{6}{15} = \frac{14}{15}$ c $\frac{5}{3} \times \frac{7}{2} = \frac{35}{6}$

4 a $\frac{3}{5}$ b $\frac{4}{9}$ c $1\frac{2}{7}$ d $\frac{19}{20}$

   e $\frac{19}{21}$ f $1\frac{7}{40}$ g $\frac{7}{10}$ h $\frac{17}{27}$

5 a 5   b $3\frac{2}{5}$ c $5\frac{1}{7}$

   d $6\frac{11}{15}$ e $7\frac{17}{63}$ f $17\frac{13}{16}$

6 a $\frac{2}{5}$ b $\frac{1}{45}$ c $\frac{11}{20}$ d $\frac{1}{10}$

   e $\frac{1}{18}$ f $\frac{1}{8}$ g $\frac{13}{72}$ h $\frac{5}{48}$

7 a $1\frac{1}{2}$ b $\frac{3}{4}$ c $\frac{13}{20}$

   d $\frac{29}{40}$ e $\frac{5}{6}$ f $1\frac{16}{77}$

8 a $\frac{6}{35}$ b $\frac{1}{2}$ c $\frac{1}{12}$ d $\frac{4}{9}$

   e $4\frac{1}{2}$ f $5\frac{1}{3}$ g $7\frac{1}{2}$ h 5

i 15 **j** 26 **k** $\frac{2}{3}$ **l** $\frac{5}{6}$

m $2\frac{1}{4}$ **n** $3\frac{1}{2}$ **o** 6 **p** $1\frac{1}{3}$

9 a $\frac{1}{3}$ **b** $\frac{7}{5}$ **c** 8 **d** $\frac{9}{13}$

10 a $\frac{20}{21}$ **b** $1\frac{1}{8}$ **c** $\frac{45}{56}$ **d** $\frac{27}{28}$

e $1\frac{1}{3}$ **f** $1\frac{1}{2}$ **g** 6 **h** $\frac{7}{8}$

i 18 **j** 9 **k** 16 **l** 64

m $\frac{1}{10}$ **n** $\frac{1}{12}$ **o** $\frac{4}{27}$ **p** $3\frac{1}{3}$

q 4 **r** $\frac{1}{6}$ **s** $1\frac{1}{2}$ **t** $\frac{7}{8}$

11 a $\frac{2}{7}$ **b** $\frac{8}{15}$ **c** 16

d $\frac{66}{85}$ **e** $2\frac{10}{21}$ **f** $\frac{3}{13}$

12 $\frac{7}{8}$ tonnes **13** $5\frac{29}{56}$ tonnes **14** $\frac{5}{12}$ hours (25 min)

15 7 truckloads **16** 3 hours

17 $\frac{5}{6}$, problem is the use of negatives in the method since $\frac{1}{3} < \frac{1}{2}$

18 a $\frac{b}{a}$ **b** $\frac{c}{ac+b}$

19 a 1 **b** $\frac{a^2}{b^2}$ **c** 1 **d** $\frac{c}{a}$ **e** a **f** $\frac{c}{b}$

20 a $\frac{-2}{3}$ **b** $\frac{5}{4}$ **c** $\frac{83}{10}$ **d** 1 **e** $\frac{50}{31}$ **f** $\frac{81}{400}$

g $\frac{329}{144}$ **h** $\frac{969}{100}$ **i** $\frac{583}{144}$ **j** $\frac{5}{11}$

Exercise 1E

1 a 4 **b** 12 **c** 24 **d** 72 **e** 3 **f** 9 **g** 11 **h** 3

2 a 9 **b** $\frac{4}{9}$ **c** $\frac{5}{9}$ **d** 8 **e** 10

3 a i 240 km **ii** 40 km **iii** 520 km

b i 5 h **ii** $4\frac{1}{2}$ h **iii** 15 min

4 a $4 **b** $3 **c** $2.50

5 a 1 : 5 **b** 2 : 5 **c** 3 : 2 **d** 4 : 3

e 9 : 20 **f** 45 : 28 **g** 3 : 14 **h** 22 : 39

i 1 : 3 **j** 1 : 5 **k** 20 : 7 **l** 10 : 3

6 a 1 : 10 **b** 1 : 5 **c** 2 : 3 **d** 7 : 8

e 25 : 4 **f** 1 : 4 **g** 1 : 4 **h** 24 : 5

i 4 : 20 : 5 **j** 4 : 3 : 10 **k** 5 : 72 **l** 3 : 10 : 40

7 a $200, $300 **b** $150, $350

c $250, $250 **d** $175, $325

8 126 g

9 a $10, $20, $40 **b** $14, $49, $7 **c** $40, $25, $5

10 a 15 km/h **b** 2000 rev/min

c 45 strokes/min **d** 14 m/s

e 8 mL/h **f** 92 beats/min

11 a 55 km **b** $16\frac{1}{2}$ km **c** $5\frac{1}{2}$ km

12 a 3 kg deal **b** red delicious **c** 2.4 L **d** 0.7 GB

13 a coffee A: $3.60, coffee B: $3.90. Therefore, coffee A is the best buy.

b pasta A: $1.25, pasta B: $0.94. Therefore, pasta B is the best buy.

c cereal A: $0.37, cereal B: $0.40. Therefore, cereal A is the best buy.

14 120

15 $3000, $1200, $1800 respectively

16 $15.90

17 108 L

18 $3600, $1200, $4800 respectively

19 $1.62

20 1 : 4

21 36°, 72°, 108°, 144°

22 Find cost per kilogram or number of grams per dollar. Cereal A is the best buy.

23 a False **b** False **c** True **d** True

24 a $a+b$ **b** $\frac{a}{a+b}$ **c** $\frac{b}{a+b}$

25 a i 100 mL **ii** 200 mL **b i** 250 mL **ii** 270 mL

c i 300 mL **ii** 1 : 4

d i 1 : 3 **ii** 7 : 19 **iii** 26 : 97 **iv** 21 : 52

e jug 3 and 4

Exercise 1F

1 a $\frac{3}{100}$ **b** $\frac{11}{100}$ **c** $\frac{7}{20}$ **d** $\frac{2}{25}$

2 a 0.04 **b** 0.23 **c** 0.86 **d** 0.463

3 a 50% **b** 60% **c** 25% **d** 90%

e 75% **f** 50% **g** 20% **h** $12\frac{1}{2}$%

4 a 34% **b** 40% **c** 6% **d** 70%

e 100% **f** 132% **g** 109% **h** 310%

5 a 0.67 **b** 0.3 **c** 2.5 **d** 0.08

e 0.0475 **f** 0.10625 **g** 0.304 **h** 0.4425

6 a $\frac{67}{100}$ **b** $\frac{3}{10}$ **c** $2\frac{1}{2}$ **d** $\frac{2}{25}$

e $\frac{19}{400}$ **f** $\frac{17}{160}$ **g** $\frac{38}{125}$ **h** $\frac{177}{400}$

7

Percentage	Fraction	Decimal
10%	$\frac{1}{10}$	0.1
50%	$\frac{1}{2}$	0.5
5%	$\frac{1}{20}$	0.05
25%	$\frac{1}{4}$	0.25
20%	$\frac{1}{5}$	0.2
12.5%	$\frac{1}{8}$	0.125

Percentage	Fraction	Decimal
1%	$\frac{1}{100}$	0.01
11.1%	$\frac{1}{9}$	0.1̇
22.2%	$\frac{2}{9}$	0.2̇
75%	$\frac{3}{4}$	0.75
15%	$\frac{3}{20}$	0.15
90%	$\frac{9}{10}$	0.9
37.5%	$\frac{3}{8}$	0.375
$33\frac{1}{3}$%	$\frac{1}{3}$	0.3̇
$66\frac{2}{3}$%	$\frac{2}{3}$	0.6̇
62.5%	$\frac{5}{8}$	0.625
16.6%	$\frac{1}{6}$	0.16̇

8 a 25% **b** $33\frac{1}{3}$% **c** 16%

  d 200% **e** 2800% **f** 25%

9 a $36 **b** $210 **c** 48 kg

  d 30 km **e** 15 apples **f** 350 m

  g 250 people **h** 200 cars **i** $49

10 a $120 **b** $700 **c** $300

  d $7 **e** $0.20 **f** $400

11 a $540 **b** $600 **c** $508

  d $1250 **e** $120 **f** $40

12 $16\frac{2}{3}$% **13** $6\frac{1}{4}$%

14 48 kg **15** 15 students

16 9 students **17** $1150

18 a $P = 100$ **b** $P > 100$ **c** $P < 100$

19 a $x = 2y$ **b** $x = 5y$ **c** $x = \frac{3}{5}y$ (or $5x = 3y$) **d** $14x = 5y$

20 a 72 **b** $\frac{10}{11}$ **c** 280% **d** $3\frac{1}{4}$ **e** 150%

Exercise 1G

1 a 1.4 **b** 1.26 **c** 60% **d** 21%

  e 0.8 **f** 0.27 **g** 6% **h** 69%

2 a $30 **b** 25% **3 a** 12 kg **b** 11.1%

4 a $52.50 **b** 37.8 min (37 min 48 s)

  c 375 mL **d** 1.84 m **e** 27.44 kg

  f 36 watts **g** $13 585 **h** $1322.40

5 a 19.2 cm **b** 24.5 cm **c** 39.06 kg

  d 48.4 min (49 m 24 s) **e** $78.48

  f 202.4 mL **g** 18°C **h** $402.36

6 50% **7** 44%

8 28% **9** 4%

10 a 22.7% **b** 26.7% **c** 30.9% **d** 38.4 %

11 $21.50 **12** 30 068

---

13 $14 895 **14** 193 474 ha

15 $10.91 **16** $545.45

17 a $900 **b** $990

  c as 10% of 1000 = 100 but 10% of 900 = 90

18 25% **19** 100% **20** 42.86%

21 a $635.58 **b** $3365.08

  c $151.20 **d** $213.54

22 a 79.86 g **b** $ 97 240.50

  c $336 199.68 **d** 7.10 cm

Exercise 1H

1 a $3 profit, $2.50 loss, $1.40 profit, $7.30, $65.95 loss, $2070

  b $30.95, $80, $395.95, $799.95, $18 799, $8995

  c $28, $9.05, $22.70, $199, $345.50, $2037

2 a 90% **b** 80% **c** 85% **d** 92%

3 a i $2 **ii** 20% **b i** $5 **ii** 25%

  c i $16.80 **ii** 14% **d i** $2450 **ii** 175%

4 167.67% **5** 40%

6 92.5% **7** $37.50

8 $1001.25 **9** 28%

10 42.3% **11** $148.75

12 $760.50 **13** $613.33

14 $333 333 **15** increased by 4%

16 25%

17 a $54.75 **b** 128%

18 No, either way it gives the same price.

19 $2100

20 a i $54 187.50 **ii** $33 277.90 **b** 10 years

21 a $34 440 **b** $44 000 **c** $27 693.75

  d $32 951.10 **e** $62 040 **f** $71 627.10

Exercise 1I

1 a $3952 **b** $912 **c** $24

2 a $79.80 **b** $62.70 **c** $91.20 **d** $102.60

3 a $200 **b** $56 **c** $ 900 **d** $145.10

4 a $46 166 **b** $23 247

5 a i $19.50 **ii** $27 **iii** $42.50

  b i $30 201.60 **ii** $44 044 **iii** $20 134.40

6 a $82.80 **b** $119.60 **c** $184

  d $276 **e** $257.60 **f** $404.80

7 a 7 **b** 18 **c** 33 **d** 25 **e** 37 **f** 40

8 $14.50 per hour **9** $12.20 per hour

10 $490 **11** $4010

12 a i $40 035 **ii** 17.0%

  b i $53 905.80 **ii** 20.1%

  c i $41 218.20 **ii** 15%

  d i $30 052.56 **ii** 22.2%

13 a $1830 **b** $8043

  c $12 617.50 **d** $23 772.80

14 Cate, Adam, Ed, Diana, Bill   **15** $839.05

16 $1239.75   **17** 4.58%   **18** $67 400

19 a 12 hours

  b 12 and 0, 9 and 2, 6 and 4, 3 and 6 or 0 and 8

20 a i $920   **ii** $1500

  b i $A = 0.02x$ **ii** $A = 1200 + 0.025(x - 60\,000)$

21 a $5500

  b Choose plan A if you expect that you will sell less than $5500 worth of jewellery in a week or plan B if you expect to sell more than $5500.

22 a i $2000   **ii** $11 500   **iii** $35 000

  b

Income	Rate	Tax payable
$40 001 – $90 000	25%	$3750 + 25% of (income − $40 000)
$90 001 –	33%	$16 250 + 33% of (income − $90 000)

  c i $2000   **ii** $6300   **iii** $24000   **iv** $40 000.50

  d an extra dollar of income can push you into a higher tax bracket where you don't just pay the higher tax rate on the dollar but on your entire income. No incentive to earn more.

Exercise 1J

1 a $12 000   **b** 6% p.a.   **c** 3.5 years

  d $720   **e** $1440   **f** $2520

2 a $3000   **b** $3600   **c** $416   **d** $315

3 $2700, $17 700   **4** $1980, $23 980

5 $2560   **6** 9 months

7 16 months   **8** $2083.33

9 choice 2   **10 a** $14 400   **b** $240

11 10%

12 a $P   **b** 12.5%

  c i 20 years   **ii** 40 years   **iii** double

13 a $51000   **b** 4 years

14 a $P = \dfrac{100I}{rt}$ **b** $t = \dfrac{100I}{Pr}$ **c** $r = \dfrac{100I}{Pt}$

15 a $1750 a month   **b** $18 000

  c $6000   **d** 2%

Exercise 1K

1 a $200   **b** $2200   **c** $220

  d $2420   **e** $242   **f** $2662

2 a 2731.82   **b** 930.44

  c 2731.82   **d** 930.44

3 a $4000 \times (1.2)^3$ **b** $15 000 \times (1.07)^6$

  c $825 \times (1.11)^4$

4 a $6515.58   **b** $10 314.68

  c $34 190.78   **d** $5610.21

5 $293 865.62

6 a 21.7%   **b** 19.1%   **c** 136.7%   **d** 33.5%

7 $33 776

8 a $23 558   **b** $33 268   **c** $28 879   **d** $25 725

9 $543 651   **10** 6142 people   **11** 6.54 kg

12 Trial and error gives 12 years   **13** Trial and error gives 5 years

14 a 35%   **b** 40.26%

  c as it calculates each years interest on the original $400 not the accumulated total that compound interest uses

15 a 15.76%   **b** 25.44%   **c** 24.02%

  d 86.96%   **e** $\left(\left(1+\dfrac{r}{100}\right)^{t}-1\right)\times 100\%$

16 a $7509.25   **b** 9.39% p.a.

17 a 70.81%   **b** 7.08%

18 a 5.39% p.a.   **b** 19.28% p.a.

Challenges

1 Discuss with classmates as more than one answer for each may be possible. Some suggestions are given below (be creative).

$(4 - 4) \times (4 + 4) = 0$ $(4 - 4) + (4 \div 4) = 1$

$4 \div 4 + 4 \div 4 = 2$ $\sqrt{4 \times 4} - (4 \div 4) = 3$

$4 + (4 - 4) \times 4 = 4$ $\sqrt{4 \times 4} + 4 \div 4 = 5$

$(4 + 4 + 4) \div \sqrt{4} = 6$ $4 + 4 - 4 \div 4 = 7$

$\sqrt{4} + \sqrt{4} + \sqrt{4} + \sqrt{4} = 8$ $\sqrt{4} \times \sqrt{4} \times \sqrt{4} + \sqrt{4} = 10$

2 12   **3 a** $\dfrac{4}{7}$ **b** $\dfrac{14}{17}$

4 125 mL   **5** 40.95% reduction

6 7.91% p.a.   **7 a** 44%   **b** 10%

8 200 000 cm² (20 m²)

9 9, 7, 2, 14, 11, 5, 4, 12, 13, 3, 6, 10, 15, 1, 8

Multiple-choice questions

| **1** D | **2** B | **3** C | **4** A | **5** E | **6** E |
| **7** D | **8** E | **9** C | **10** A | **11** C | **12** B |

Short-answer questions

1 a −16   **b** 2   **c** 0

  d 10   **e** -23   **f** 1

2 a 21.5   **b** 29 100   **c** 0.153   **d** 0.002 41

3 a 200   **b** 60   **c** 2

4 a 2.125   **b** 0.83   **c** $1.85\overline{7142}$

5 a $\dfrac{3}{4}$ **b** $1\dfrac{3}{5}$ **c** $2\dfrac{11}{20}$

6 a $\dfrac{1}{2}$ **b** $2\dfrac{1}{6}$ **c** $\dfrac{7}{24}$

  d 2   **e** $3\dfrac{3}{4}$ **f** $2\dfrac{19}{28}$

7 a $5:2$ **b** $16:9$ **c** $75:14$

8 a $50, 30$ **b** $25, 55$ **c** $10, 20, 50$

9 a store A: \$2.25/kg; store B: \$2.58/kg $\therefore$ A is best buy

b store A: 444 g/\$; store B: 388 g/\$

10

Decimal	Fraction	Percentage
0.6	$\frac{3}{5}$	60%
$0.\dot{3}$	$\frac{1}{3}$	$33\frac{1}{3}\%$
0.0325	$\frac{13}{400}$	$3\frac{1}{4}\%$
0.75	$\frac{3}{4}$	75%
1.2	$1\frac{1}{5}$	120%
2	2	200%

11 a \$77.50 **b** 1.65 **12 a** 150 **b** 25

13 a 72 **b** 1.17 **c** 20% **14** 12.5 kg

15 \$1800 **16 a** \$25 **b** $16\frac{2}{3}\%$

17 a \$18.25 **b** \$14.30 **18** \$50 592 **19** \$525

20 $4\frac{1}{2}$ years **21** \$63 265.95 **22** \$39 160

Extended-response questions

1 a \$231 **b** \$651 **c i** \$63 **ii** \$34.65

2 a i \$26 625 **ii** \$46 928.44 **b** 87.71%

c \$82 420 **d** 26.26% **e** 7.4 % p.a.

Chapter 2

Pre-test

1 a $x + 3$ **b** ab **c** $2y - 3$ **d** $\frac{x+2}{3}$

2 a 1 **b** -2 **c** 5 **d** -6

3 a $3x$ **b** $6y + xy$ **c** 0 **d** $17y$

e $10a + a^2$ **f** $5xy - 7y$

4 a $6a$ **b** $-21xy$ **c** $4b$ **d** $\frac{3m}{2}$

5 $4 \times 5 + 3 \times 5 = 35$ or $(4 + 3) \times 5 = 35$

6 a $2x + 6$ **b** $3a - 15$ **c** $12x - 8xy$ **d** $-6b + 3$

7 b, c

8 a 9 **b** 10 **c** 4 **d** 21

9 a T **b** F **c** T **d** T

e F **f** T

10 a $y = 7$ **b** $y = 1$ **c** $y = 9$ **d** $y = 6$

11 A **12** E

Exercise 2A

1 a 2 **b** 2 **c** 3 **d** 1

2 A c B d C b D a E f F e

---

3 a 5 **b** -2 **c** $\frac{1}{3}$ **d** $-\frac{2}{5}$

4 a i $4 + r$ **ii** $t + 2$ **iii** $b + g$ **iv** $x + y + z$

b i $6P$ **ii** $10n$ **iii** $2D$ **iv** $5P + 2D$

c $\frac{500}{C}$

5 a $2 + x$ **b** $ab + y$ **c** $x - 5$ **d** $3x$

e $3x - 2y$ or $2y - 3x$ **f** $3p$ **g** $2x + 4$

h $\frac{x+y}{5}$ **i** $4x - 10$ **j** $(m + n)^2$ **k** $m^2 + n^2$

l $\sqrt{x+y}$ **m** $a + \frac{1}{a}$ **n** $(\sqrt{x})^3$

6 a -31 **b** -25 **c** -33 **d** -19

e $\frac{1}{2}$ **f** 4 **g** 1 **h** 85

7 a $1\frac{1}{6}$ **b** $4\frac{1}{4}$ **c** $\frac{1}{6}$ **d** $-1\frac{1}{3}$

8 a $60 \ m^2$ **b** length $= 12 + x$, width $= 5 - y$

c $A = (12 + x)(5 - y)$

9 a 18 square units **b** 1, 2, 3, 4, 5

10 a $\frac{P}{10}$ **b** $\frac{nP}{10}$

11 a i $P = 2x + 2y$ **ii** $A = xy$ **b i** $P = 4p$ **ii** $A = p^2$

c i $P = x + y + 5$ **ii** $A = \frac{5x}{2}$

12 a $A : 2(x + y)$ $B : 2x + y$, different **b** Same

13 a B **b** $A : c^2 = (a + b)^2$

14 a $\frac{n(n+1)}{2}$ **b i** 10 **ii** 55 **c** $\frac{n^2}{2} + \frac{n}{2}$

d 10, 55 **e** Half the sum of n and the square of n.

Exercise 2B

1 a variable (pronumeral) **b** $5x$ **c** unlike

2 a $\frac{2}{3}$ **b** $\frac{5}{2}$ **c** 3 **d** $\frac{1}{5}$

e $-\frac{2}{7}$ **f** $-\frac{1}{20}$ **g** $-\frac{11}{53}$ **h** -17

3 a like **b** unlike **c** unlike **d** unlike **e** like

f like **g** like **h** unlike **i** like

4 a $10m$ **b** $12b$ **c** $15p$ **d** $6xy$

e $18pr$ **f** $16mn$ **g** $-14xy$ **h** $-15mn$

i $-12cd$ **j** $30ab$ **k** $-24rs$ **l** $-40jk$

5 a $24n^2$ **b** $-3q^2$ **c** $10s^2$ **d** $21a^2b$ **e** $-15mn^2$

f $18gh^2$ **g** $12x^2y^2$ **h** $8a^2b^2$ **i** $-6m^2n^2$

6 a $4b$ **b** $-\frac{a}{3}$ **c** $\frac{2ab}{3}$ **d** $\frac{m}{2}$ **e** $-\frac{x}{4}$

f $\frac{5s}{3}$ **g** uv **h** $\frac{5rs}{8}$ **i** $\frac{5ab}{9}$ **j** $\frac{7}{y}$

7 a $\frac{2x}{5}$ **b** $\frac{4}{3a}$ **c** $\frac{11mn}{3}$ **d** $6ab$

e $-\dfrac{5}{gh}$ f 8 g -3 h $\dfrac{7n}{3}$

i $-\dfrac{9q}{2}$ j $3b$ k $-5x$ l $\dfrac{m}{2}$

8 a $\dfrac{4x}{y}$ b $\dfrac{5p}{2}$ c $-6ab$ d $-\dfrac{3a}{2b}$

e $-\dfrac{7n}{5m}$ f $\dfrac{10s}{t}$ g $8n$ h $3y$

i $4b$ j $6xy$ k $5m$ l $3pq^2$

9 a $10a$ b $7n$ c $8y$ d $11x$

e $3ab$ f $7mn$ g $y+8$ h $3x+5$

i $7xy+4y$ j $12ab+3$ k $2-6m$ l $4-x$

10 a $5a+9b$ b $6x+5y$ c $4t+6$ d $11x+4$

e $5xy+4x$ f $7mn-9$ g $5ab-a$ h 0

11 a xy^2 b $7a^2b$ c $3m^2n$ d p^2q^2

e $7x^2y-4xy^2$ f $13rs^2-6r^2s$ g $-7x-2x^2$

h $4a^2b-3ab^2$ i $7pq^2-8pq$ j $8m^2n^2-mn^2$

12 a $x+y$ b $4x+2y$ 13 a $8x$ b $3x^2$

14 a $30x$ cm   b $30x^2$ cm²   15 $\dfrac{20x+75}{21}$

16 a True b False c True d False   e False   f True

17 a $4x+4y$ b $8x+4$ c $2x-2$

18 a a^3 b $\dfrac{b^2}{3}$ c $\dfrac{b^2}{3}$ d $\dfrac{3ab}{8}$

e $-\dfrac{2a^3}{3}$ f $-\dfrac{2}{5a^2}$ g $\dfrac{2}{5a^5}$ h $\dfrac{a^2}{4b^3}$

i $3a^3b$ j $\dfrac{4b^3}{a}$ k $\dfrac{a^3}{3b}$ l $-\dfrac{a}{2b^3}$

Exercise 2C

1 a i $5x$ ii 10

b $5x+10$ c $x+2$ d $5(x+2)$ e $5x+10$

2 a i -16 ii -4 b No, $-2x-6$

c i -27 ii -33 d No, $-3x+3$

3 a $2x+6$ b $5x+60$ c $2x-14$ d $7x-63$

e $6+3x$ f $21-7x$ g $28-4x$ h $2x-12$

4 a $-3x-6$ b $-2x-22$ c $-5x+15$ d $-6x+36$

e $-8+4x$ f $-65-13x$ g $-180-20x$ h $-300+300x$

5 a $2a+2b$ b $5a-10$ c $3m-12$ d $-16x-40$

e $-12x-15$ f $-4x^2+8xy$ g $-18ty+27t$ h $3a^2+4a$

i $2d^2-5d$ j $-6b^2+10b$ k $8x^2+2x$ l $5y-15y^2$

6 a $2x+11$ b $6x-14$ c $15x-3$ d $1+3x$

e $4x-5$ f $2x+1$ g $-3x-4$ h $-5x-19$

i $11-x$ j $12-x$ k $2-2x$ l $6-3x$

7 a $5x+12$ b $4x-8$ c $11x-2$ d $17x-7$

e $-4x-6$ f $x-7$ g $2x-4$ h $-27x-4$

i $-4x-18$ j $-13x-7$ k $11x-7$ l $2x-15$

8 $A=x^2+4x$

9 a $2x+2$ b $2x^2-3x$ c $6x^2-2x$

d $2x^2+4x$ e x^2+2x+6 f $20+8x-x^2$

10 $20n-200$ 11 $0.2x-2000$

12 a $2x+12$ b x^2-4x c $-3x-12$

d $-7x+49$ e $19-2x$ f $x-14$

13 a $6(50+2)=312$ b $9(100+2)=918$

c $5(90+1)=455$ d $4(300+26)=1304$

e $3(100-1)=297$ f $7(400-5)=2765$

g $9(1000-10)=8910$ h $6(900-21)=5274$

14 a $a=\$6000$, $b=\$21\,000$

b i $\$3000$ ii $\$12\,600$ iii $\$51\,000$

c i 0 ii $0.2x-4000$ iii $0.3x-9000$

iv $0.5x-29\,000$

Exercise 2D

1 a 3 b 40 c 5 d 6

2 a 3 b 2 c 2 d 12

e 12 f -5 g 6 h 1

3 a, d, e, f, h

4 a 2 b 1 c 4 d -1

e -3 f -6 g -4 h $-3\tfrac{2}{3}$

i $1\tfrac{2}{3}$ j $4\tfrac{1}{2}$ k $\tfrac{1}{2}$ l $1\tfrac{1}{3}$

m $-\tfrac{5}{7}$ n $-\tfrac{1}{8}$ o $-\tfrac{3}{20}$

5 a 8 b 2 c 12 d -6

e -6 f 30 g -15 h -8

i 12 j 20 k -5 l -10

6 a -3 b -1 c 2 d 8

e $-1\tfrac{2}{5}$ f $-2\tfrac{5}{7}$ g $\tfrac{3}{8}$ h $1\tfrac{3}{4}$

7 a 9 b 6 c $-6\tfrac{3}{4}$ d $-7\tfrac{1}{2}$

e $\tfrac{2}{3}$ f $-\tfrac{4}{25}$ g 12 h 12

i -9 j -8 k 6 l $-1\tfrac{1}{2}$

8 a 11 b 6 c -10 d -12

e -5 f -1 g 7 h 5

i $4\tfrac{2}{7}$ j $5\tfrac{1}{3}$ k -7 l 3

9 a 26 b 28 c 3 d 28

e 8 f $3\tfrac{3}{7}$ g 7 h $\$900$

10 a should have $+1$ before $\div 2$

b should have $\times 3$ before -2

c need to $\div -1$ as $-x=7$

d should have $+4$ before $\times 3$

11 a i 5 ii -3 iii $\tfrac{1}{5}$ iv 3 v $-\tfrac{5}{6}$ vi $\tfrac{3}{10}$

b When the common factor divides evenly into the RHS

12 a $a = b + c$ **b** $a = \dfrac{c-b}{2}$ **c** $a = \dfrac{c-2d}{b}$ **d** $a = c(b+d)$

e $a = -\dfrac{cd}{b}$ **f** $a = \dfrac{b}{2c}$ **g** $a = \dfrac{c(3-d)}{2b}$ **h** $a = \dfrac{2d(b-3)}{c}$

i $a = cd - b$ **j** $a = b + cd$ **k** $a = \dfrac{2be+6c}{d}$ **l** $a = \dfrac{d-3ef}{4c}$

Exercise 2E

1 a $4x - 12$ **b** 2 **c** $5x - 9$ **d** $3 - 9x$

e $3x - 7$ **f** $24 - 12x$

2 a $2x + 6 = 5$ **b** $5 + 2x - 2 = 7$ **c** $2x + 1 = -6$ **d** $2x - 3 = 1$

3 a $2\frac{1}{2}$ **b** $-1\frac{2}{5}$ **c** $6\frac{1}{3}$ **d** $4\frac{3}{5}$

e $-3\frac{3}{4}$ **f** $9\frac{1}{2}$ **g** $\frac{1}{2}$ **h** $-5\frac{1}{2}$

i $-\frac{4}{5}$ **j** $\frac{1}{14}$ **k** $3\frac{1}{6}$ **l** $\frac{2}{3}$

m $\frac{9}{10}$ **n** $1\frac{1}{6}$ **o** $-\frac{1}{8}$

4 a 1 **b** -10 **c** 1 **d** -2 **e** 5 **f** 0

g 1 **h** 5 **i** 3 **j** 1

5 a 1 **b** -4 **c** 2 **d** 8 **e** 8 **f** 3

g 4 **h** -1 **i** $\frac{5}{11}$

6 a -1 **b** $3\frac{1}{2}$ **c** -9 **d** -14

e -16 **f** 3 **g** 19 **h** -3

i -13 **j** -26 **k** $-2\frac{2}{3}$ **l** $-1\frac{1}{10}$

7 a $\frac{1}{2}$ **b** $2\frac{2}{3}$ **c** $1\frac{1}{2}$ **d** $-\frac{5}{6}$

e $\frac{2}{5}$ **f** $1\frac{1}{2}$ **g** -6

8 \$5/hour   **9** 11 marbles

10 a $x = 5$ **b** $x = 5$

c Dividing both sides by 3 is faster because $9 \div 3$ is a whole number

11 a $x = 4\frac{1}{3}$ **b** $x = 4\frac{1}{3}$

c Expanding the brackets is faster because $7 \div 3$ gives a fraction answer

12 a $x = 4$ **b** $x = 4$

c Method a: don't have to deal with negatives
Final step in method a: divide both sides by a positive number
Final step in method b: divide both sides by a negative number

13 a $x = \dfrac{d}{a-b}$ **b** $x = \dfrac{2}{a-b}$ **c** $x = \dfrac{c}{5a-b}$

d $x = -\dfrac{6}{3a-4b}$ or $\dfrac{6}{4b-3a}$ **e** $x = -c$ **f** $x = b$

g $x = \dfrac{d+bd+c}{a-b}$ **h** $x = -\dfrac{ab+bc}{a-b+1}$ or $\dfrac{ab+bc}{b-a-1}$

Exercise 2F

1 a $x - 3 = 4x - 9$ **b** $3(x+7) = 9$ **c** $4(x-9) = 12$

d $2x = x + 5$ **e** $x - 8 = 3x + 2$

2 a Let e be the number of goals for Emma

b $e + 8$ **c** $e + e + 8 = 28$ **d** $e = 10$

e Emma scored 10 goals, Leonie scored 18 goals

3 a Let w be the width in centimetres   **b** length $= 4w$

c $2w + 2(4w) = 560$ **d** $w = 56$

e length $= 224$ cm, width $= 56$ cm

4 6 days   **5** 10 km, 20 km   **6** \$360, \$640

7 15, 45   **8** 19 km   **9** A \$102.50, B \$175, C \$122.50

10 4 fiction, 8 non-fiction books   **11** I am 10 years old

12 Eric is 18 yrs old now

13 First leg $= 54$ km, Second leg $= 27$km, Third leg $= 18$ km, Fourth leg $= 54$ km

14 2 hours   **15** 8 pm

16 Rectangle $L = 55$ m, $W = 50$ m. Triangle side $= 70$ m

17 a 27, 28, 29

b i $x, x+2, x+4$ **ii** 4, 6, 8

c i $x, x+2, x+4$ **ii** 15, 17, 19

d i $x, x+3, x+6$ **ii** 24, 27, 30

18 a $T = 8x + 7200$ **b** 300   **c** $R = 24x$

d $x = 350$ **e** 3825

19 \$15 200   **20** 438 km   **21** Anna 6; Henry 4; Chloe 12; twins 11

Exercise 2G

1 a $3 > 2$ **b** $-1 < 4$ **c** $-7 < -3$ **d** $5 > -50$

2 a

b

c

d

e

f

g

h

i

j

k

l

3 a $x<3$ **b** $b>5$ **c** $y>6$ **d** $m<5$

   e $x\geq3$ **f** $t>-5$ **g** $x\geq12$ **h** $y\geq-10$

   i $m<6$ **j** $a\geq1\frac{1}{2}$ **k** $x<1$ **l** $x>8$

4 a $x<4$ **b** $n\leq-1$ **c** $x\geq\frac{3}{5}$ **d** $a\geq4$

   e $x\geq-6$ **f** $x\geq10$ **g** $x<-6$ **h** $t\leq-2$

   i $m>-4\frac{5}{6}$

5 a $x\leq16$ **b** $x\leq-9$ **c** $x\leq20$ **d** $x<11$

   e $x>-2\frac{2}{3}$ **f** $x\geq-2$

6 a $x<1$ **b** $a<-8$ **c** $x\leq-2$

   d $x<2\frac{1}{2}$ **e** $y<-3\frac{1}{5}$ **f** $x<-\frac{4}{7}$

7 a $x\geq2\frac{1}{2}$ **b** $t>-\frac{3}{5}$ **c** $y\leq\frac{3}{8}$

   d $a<1\frac{1}{5}$ **e** $m\geq6$ **f** $b<5\frac{1}{2}$

8 less than 18   **9** $w<13$

10 a 3   **b** 2   **c** 4   **d** 0

11 $x=3$ or $x=4$ or $x=5$ **12** 399 km

13 a i -0.9, 0, 0.5, 1, 1.8 etc **ii** numbers must be less than 2

   b i -4, -2, 0, 1, 5 etc   **ii** numbers must be greater than -5

   c i $x<a$ **ii** $x>-a$

14 a $x<3$ **b** $x<3$

   c Reverse inequality sign when dividing by a negative number

15 a $x<-13$ **b** $x\geq-3$ **c** $x>\frac{4}{7}$ **d** $x\leq\frac{13}{5}$

   e $x>\frac{10}{17}$ **f** $x\geq\frac{3}{4}$

16 a $x>\frac{b-c}{a}$ **b** $x\geq b-a$ **c** $x\leq a(b+c)$ **d** $x\leq\frac{ac}{b}$

   e $x<\frac{cd-b}{a}$ **f** $x\geq\frac{b-cd}{2}$ **g** $x<\frac{c}{a}-b$ **h** $x>\frac{b-cd}{a}$

   i $x<b-\frac{c}{a}$ **j** $x\leq\frac{b+c}{1-a}$ **k** $x<\frac{b+1}{b-a}$ **l** $x\leq\frac{c-b}{b-a}$

Exercise 2H

1 a A **b** D **c** M **d** A

2 a 21   **b** 24   **c** 2   **d** 6

   e 452.16   **f** 33.49   **g** 25.06   **h** 14.95

   i 249.86   **j** 80

3 a 36   **b** 5   **c** 20   **d** 4.14

   e 3.39   **f** 18.67   **g** 0.06

4 a $r=\frac{A}{2\pi h}$ **b** $r=\frac{100I}{Pt}$ **c** $n=\frac{p}{m}-x$ **d** $x=\frac{cd-a}{b}$

   e $r=\sqrt{\frac{v}{\pi h}}$ **f** $v=\sqrt{PR}$ **g** $h=\frac{S-2\pi r^2}{2\pi r}$

   h $p=-q\pm\sqrt{A}$ **i** $g=\frac{4\pi^2 l}{T^2}$ **j** $A=(4C-B)^2$

5 a 88.89 km/h   **b i** $d=st$ **ii** 285 km

6 a i 212° F   **ii** 100.4° F   **b** $C=\frac{5}{9}(F-32)$

   c i -10° C   **ii** 36.7° C

7 a 35 m/s   **b** 2 s

8 a decrease   **b** 3988 L

   c 6 hours 57 minutes   **d** 11 hours 7 minutes

9 a $D=\frac{c}{100}$ **b** $d=100e$ **c** $D=0.7\,M$ **d** $V=1.15\,P$

   e $C=50+18t$ **f** $d=42-14t$ **g** $C=\frac{c}{b}$

10 a $a=\frac{P}{4}$ **b** $a=180-b$ **c** $a=90-b$

   d $a=\frac{180-b}{2}$ **e** $a=\sqrt{c^2-b^2}$ **f** $a=\sqrt{\frac{4A}{\pi}}$

11 a 73   **b** 7   **c** 476.3

Exercise 2I

1 a $y=5$ **b** $x=-3$ **c** $x=10$

2 a A   **b** C

3 a yes   **b** no   **c** no   **d** yes

4 a $x=1, y=2$ **b** $x=5, y=1$ **c** $x=\frac{1}{2}, y=\frac{3}{2}$

   d $x=-2, y=-1$ **e** $x=2, y=6$ **f** $x=-3, y=9$

5 a $x=3, y=9$ **b** $x=-1, y=3$ **c** $x=1, y=0$

   d $x=6, y=11$ **e** $x=4, y=3$ **f** $x=12, y=-3$

   g $x=-18, y=-4$ **h** $x=-2, y=10$ **i** $x=2, y=-4$

6 a $x=2, y=1$ **b** $x=1, y=3$ **c** $x=0, y=4$

   d $x=3, y=-2$ **e** $x=4, y=1$ **f** $x=-1, y=4$

7 17, 31

8 10 tonnes, 19 tonnes

9 width $=1\frac{2}{3}$ cm, length $=3\frac{5}{6}$ cm

10 $x-(3x-1)=x-3x+1$, to avoid sign error use brackets when substituting

11 a $x=\frac{1}{3}, y=2\frac{1}{3}$ **b** $x=-\frac{5}{6}, y=6\frac{1}{3}$ **c** $x=-22, y=-7$

12 a $x=\frac{b}{a+b}, y=\frac{b^2}{a+b}$ **b** $x=\frac{b}{a+1}, y=\frac{1}{a+1}$

   c $x=\frac{a-b}{2}, y=\frac{a+b}{2}$ **d** $x=\frac{a-ab}{a-b}, y=\frac{a-ab}{a-b}-a$

   e $x=\frac{2a}{a-b}, y=\frac{2ab}{a-b}+a$ **f** $x=\frac{2a+ab}{a-b}-b, y=\frac{2a+ab}{a-b}$

Exercise 2J

1 a − **b** + **c** + **d** −

2 a i subtraction **ii** addition **iii** subtraction

b i addition **ii** subtraction **iii** addition

3 a $x = 1, y = 1$ **b** $x = 10, y = 2$ **c** $x = 1, y = 3$

d $x = 1, y = 1$ **e** $x = 2, y = 2$ **f** $x = 2, y = -1$

4 a $x = 2, y = 4$ **b** $x = 8, y = -1$ **c** $x = -2, y = 6$

5 a $x = -3, y = -13$ **b** $x = 2, y = 3$ **c** $x = 1, y = 3$

6 a $x = -3, y = 4$ **b** $x = 2, y = 1$ **c** $x = 2, y = 1$

d $x = -2, y = 3$ **e** $x = 7, y = -5$ **f** $x = 5, y = 4$

g $x = 5, y = -5$ **h** $x = -3, y = -2$ **i** $x = -1, y = -3$

7 a $x = 3, y = -5$ **b** $x = 2, y = -3$ **c** $x = 2, y = 4$

d $x = 3, y = 1$ **e** $x = -1, y = 4$ **f** $x = 3, y = -2$

g $x = 5, y = -3$ **h** $x = -2, y = -2$ **i** $x = 2, y = 1$

j $x = -5, y = -3$ **k** $x = -3, y = 9$ **l** $x = -1, y = -2$

8 21 and 9 **9** 102, 78 **10** $L = 261.5$ m, $W = 138.5$ m

11 11 mobile phones, 6 iPods

12 a $x = 2, y = 1$ **b** $x = 2, y = 1$

c method (b) is preferable as it avoids the use of a negative coefficient

13 rearrange one equation to make x or y the subject

a $x = 4, y = 1$ **b** $x = -1, y = -1$

14 a no solution **b** no solution

15 a $x = \dfrac{a+b}{2}, y = \dfrac{a-b}{2}$ **b** $x = \dfrac{b}{2a}, y = -\dfrac{b}{2}$

c $x = \dfrac{-a}{2}, y = \dfrac{3a}{2b}$ **d** $x = 0, y = b$

e $x = \dfrac{1}{3}, y = \dfrac{b}{3a}$ **f** $x = -\dfrac{4}{a}, y = 6$

g $x = \dfrac{3b}{7a}, y = \dfrac{b}{7}$ **h** $x = \dfrac{3b}{7a}, y = -\dfrac{b}{7}$

i $x = 0, y = \dfrac{b}{a}$ **j** $x = -\dfrac{c}{a}, y = c$

k $x = \dfrac{b-4}{ab-4}, y = \dfrac{1-a}{ab-4}$ **l** $x = 1, y = 0$

m $x = \dfrac{c-bd}{a(b+1)}, y = \dfrac{c+d}{b+1}$ **n** $x = \dfrac{a+2b}{a-b}, y = \dfrac{3a}{a-b}$

o $x = \dfrac{3b}{a+3b}, y = \dfrac{3b-2a}{a+3b}$ **p** $x = -\dfrac{b}{a-bc}, y = \dfrac{bc-2a}{a-bc}$

q $x = \dfrac{c+f}{a+d}, y = \dfrac{cd-af}{b(a+d)}$ **r** $x = \dfrac{c-f}{a-d}, y = \dfrac{af-cd}{b(a-d)}$

Exercise 2K

1 a $x + y = 42, x - y = 6$ **b** $x = 18, y = 24$

c One number is 18, the other number is 24

2 a $l = w + 5, 2l + 2w = 84$ **b** $L = 23.5, w = 18.5$

c length = 23.5 cm, width = 18.5 cm

3 a $l = 3w, 2l + 2w = 120$ **b** $L = 45, w = 15$

c length = 45 m, width = 15 m

4 a Let $m be the cost of milk

Let $c be the cost of chips

b $3m + 4c = 17, m + 5c = 13$

c $m = 3, c = 2$

d bottle of milk costs $3 and a bag of chips $2.

5 a Let $g be the cost of lip gloss.

Let $e be the cost of eye shadow.

b $7g + 2e = 69, 4g + 3e = 45$

c $g = 9, e = 3$

d lip gloss $9; eye shadow $3

6 cricket ball $12; tennis ball $5

7 4 chips, 16 hot dogs

8 300 adults, 120 children

9 potatoes 480; corn 340

10 11 five-cent and 16 twenty-cent

11 Michael is 35 years old now.

12 Jenny $100, Kristy $50

13 160 adults and 80 children

14 5 hours

15 jogging 3 km/h, cycling 9 km/h

16 a Malcolm is 14 years old

b The second digit of Malcolm's age is 3 more than the first digit.

c 6: 14, 25, 36, 47, 58 or 69

17 Original number is 37

18 Any two-digit number that has the first digit 2 more than the second (e.g. 42 or 64 etc.)

Challenges

1 $x = 3$

4	9	2
3	5	7
8	1	6

2 $140

3 8

4 a i > **ii** < **iii** > **iv** <

b c, b, a, d

5 $x = 1, y = -2, z = 5$

6 a $x = \dfrac{ab}{a-b}$ **b** $x = \dfrac{10}{3}$ **c** $x = -\dfrac{7}{11}$ **d** $x = \dfrac{29}{4}$

Multiple-choice questions

1 C **2** D **3** D **4** C **5** B **6** A

7 A **8** E **9** B **10** A **11** B **12** D

Short-answer questions

1 a 7m **b** $2(x + y)$ **c** 3m **d** $\dfrac{n}{4} - 3$

2 a -7 **b** 7 **c** 24 **d** 8

3 a $8mn$ **b** $\dfrac{xy}{3}$ **c** $6b^2$ **d** $4 - 3b$

e $2mn + 2m - 1$ **f** $2p + 4q$

4 a $2x + 14$ **b** $-6x - 15$ **c** $6x^2 - 8x$

d $-10a + 8a^2$ **e** $13 - 4x$ **f** $27x - 10$

10 a i 5

ii $\sin \theta = \dfrac{3}{5}$

$\cos \theta = \dfrac{4}{5}$

$\tan \theta = \dfrac{3}{4}$

b i 25

ii $\sin \theta = \dfrac{7}{25}$

$\cos \theta = \dfrac{24}{25}$

$\tan \theta = \dfrac{7}{24}$

c i 15

ii $\sin \theta = \dfrac{9}{15} = \dfrac{3}{5}$

$\cos \theta = \dfrac{12}{15} = \dfrac{4}{5}$

$\tan \theta = \dfrac{9}{12} = \dfrac{3}{4}$

d i 10

ii $\sin \theta = \dfrac{8}{10} = \dfrac{4}{5}$

$\cos \theta = \dfrac{6}{10} = \dfrac{3}{5}$

$\tan \theta = \dfrac{8}{6} = \dfrac{4}{3}$

11 a

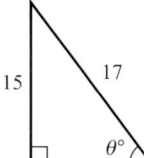

b 8   **c** $\sin \theta = \dfrac{15}{17}$, $\cos \theta = \dfrac{8}{17}$, $\tan \theta = \dfrac{15}{8}$

12 a i $\dfrac{1}{2}$ **ii** $\dfrac{\sqrt{3}}{2}$ **iii** $\dfrac{1}{\sqrt{3}}$

iv $\dfrac{\sqrt{3}}{2}$ **v** $\dfrac{1}{2}$ **vi** $\sqrt{3}$

b i they are equal   **ii** they are equal

13 a answers may vary

b i 0.766   **ii** 0.643   **iii** 0.839

iv 0.766   **v** 1.192   **vi** 0.643

c $\sin 40° = \cos 50°$, $\sin 50° = \cos 40°$, $\tan 50° = \dfrac{1}{\tan 40°}$

$\tan 40° = \dfrac{1}{\tan 50°}$

14 a yes, any isosceles right-angled triangle

b no, as it would require the hypotenuse (the longest side) to equal the opposite

c no, adjacent side can't be zero

d no, as the numerator $<$ denominator for sin and cos as the hypotenuse is the longest side

15 a $\sin \theta = \dfrac{3}{5}$ $\tan \theta = \dfrac{3}{4}$

b i $\cos \theta = \dfrac{\sqrt{3}}{2}$ $\tan \theta = \dfrac{1}{\sqrt{3}}$

ii $\tan \theta = \sqrt{3}$ $\sin \theta = \dfrac{\sqrt{3}}{2}$

iii $\sin \theta = \dfrac{1}{\sqrt{2}}$ $\cos \theta = \dfrac{1}{\sqrt{2}}$

c equals one

d $(\sin \theta)^2 + (\cos \theta)^2 = 1$ (the Pythagorean identity)

Exercise 3F

1 a A   **b** 0   **c** H

2 a sin   **b** tan   **c** cos

3 a 0.34   **b** 0.80   **c** 2.05   **d** 0.73

e 0.10   **f** 0.25   **g** 0.46   **h** 0.24

4 a 3.06   **b** 18.94   **c** 5.03

d 0.91   **e** 1.71   **f** 9.00

g 2.36   **h** 4.79   **i** 7.60

5 a 5.95   **b** 0.39   **c** 13.38   **d** 3.83

e 8.40   **f** 1.36   **g** 29.00   **h** 1.62

i 40.10   **j** 4.23   **k** 14.72   **l** 13.42

m 17.62   **n** 5.48   **o** 9.75   **p** 1.01

6 1.12 m   **7** 44.99 m   **8** 10.11 m

9 a 20.95 m   **b** 10 cm

10 a 65°   **b** 1.69   **c** 1.69

11 a i 80°   **ii** 62°   **iii** 36°   **iv** 9°

b i both 0.173...   **ii** both 0.469...

iii both 0.587...   **iv** both 0.156...

c $\sin \theta° = \cos (90° - \theta°)$

d i 70°   **ii** 31°   **iii** 54°   **iv** 17°

12 a $\sqrt{2}$

b i $\dfrac{1}{\sqrt{2}}$ **ii** $\dfrac{1}{\sqrt{2}}$ **iii** 1   **c** $\sqrt{3}$

d i $\dfrac{1}{2}$ **ii** $\dfrac{\sqrt{3}}{2}$ **iii** $\dfrac{1}{\sqrt{3}}$ **iv** $\dfrac{\sqrt{3}}{2}$ **v** $\dfrac{1}{2}$ **vi** $\sqrt{3}$

Exercise 3G

1 a $x = 2$ **b** $x = 5$ **c** $x = 3$ **d** $x = 4$

e $x = 7$ **f** $x = 4$ **g** $x = 0.5$ **h** $x = 0.2$

2 a 4.10   **b** 6.81   **c** 37.88   **d** 0.98

e 12.80   **f** 14.43   **g** 9.52   **h** 114.83

i 22.05

3 a 13.45   **b** 16.50   **c** 57.90   **d** 26.33

e 15.53   **f** 38.12   **g** 9.15   **h** 32.56

i 21.75   **j** 49.81   **k** 47.02   **l** 28.70

4 a $x = 7.5, y = 6.4$ **b** $a = 7.5, b = 10.3$
c $a = 6.7, b = 7.8$ **d** $x = 9.5, y = 12.4$
e $x = 12.4, y = 9.2$ **f** $x = 21.1, y = 18.8$
g $m = 56.9, n = 58.2$ **h** $x = 15.4, y = 6.0$
5 40 m   **6** 3848 m
7 a 26 m **b** 97 m **8 a** 23.7 m **b** 124.9 m
9 a B as student B did not use an approximation in their working out
b use your calculator and do not round sin 31° during working
c i difference of 0.42 **ii** difference of 0.03
10 a i 10.990 **ii** 11.695 **b i** 0.34 **ii** 0.94 **iii** 0.36
c equal to tan 20° **d i** $\dfrac{b}{c}$ **ii** $\dfrac{a}{c}$ **iii** $\dfrac{b}{a}$ **iv** $\dfrac{b}{a}$
e same as tan θ

Exercise 3H

1 a 11.54 **b** 64.16 **c** 41.41
d 64.53 **e** 26.57 **f** 68.20
2 a $\dfrac{1}{2}$ **b** 50° **c** $45° = \tan^{-1}(1)$
3 a 47° **b** 12° **c** 18° **d** 51°
e 24° **f** 42° **g** 79° **h** 13°
i 3°
4 a sine **b** sine **c** cosine **d** tan
5 a 30° **b** 60° **c** 45° **d** 30°
e 45° **f** 30° **g** 90° **h** 50°
i 90° **j** 55° **k** 0° **l** 70°
6 a 34.85° **b** 19.47° **c** 64.16° **d** 75.52°
e 36.87° **f** 38.94° **g** 30.96° **h** 57.99°
i 85.24°
7 a 43° **b** 31° **c** 41° **d** 16°
e 55° **f** 50° **g** 49° **h** 41°
8 17° **9** 23.13° **10** 25.4° **11** 26.6°
12 a 128.7° **b** 72.5° **c** 27.3°
13 a 90°, 37°, 53° **b** 90°, 23°, 67° **c** 90°, 16°, 74°
14 45° **15** $\angle ACM = 18.4°$ $\angle ACB = 33.7°$, no it is not half
16 a 18° **b** 26° **c** 45° **d** 5.67 m **e** up to 90°

Exercise 3I

1 $a = 65, b = 25$
2 a 22° **b** 22°
3 a i 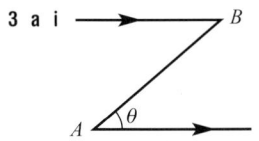 **ii**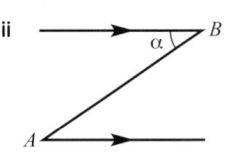

b yes, $\theta = \alpha$, alternate angles are equal on parallel lines
4 29 m **5** 16 m **6** 157 m **7** 38 m
8 90 m **9** 37° **10** 6° **11** 10°
12 yes by 244.8 m **13 a** 6° **b** 209 m
14 4634 mm **15** 15°, 4319 mm **16** 1.25 m

17 a 6.86 m **b** 26.6° **c i** $m = h + y$
ii $y = x \tan \theta$ **iii** $m = h + x \tan\theta$
18 $A = \dfrac{1}{2}a^2 \tan \theta$
19 a i 47.5 km **ii** 16.25 km **b** no, $\sin(2 \times \theta) < 2 \times \sin \theta$
c yes, $\sin\left(\dfrac{1}{2}\theta\right) > \dfrac{1}{2}\sin \theta$
20 a yes **b** 12.42 km
c no, after 10 mins will be above 4 km
d 93 km/h or more
21 a 1312 m **b** 236.16 km/h

Exercise 3J

1 a 0° **b** 045° **c** 090° **d** 135°
e 180° **f** 225° **g** 270° **h** 315°
2 a 070° **b** 130° **c** 255° **d** 332°
3 a i 040°T **ii** 220°T **b i** 142°T **ii** 322°T
c i 210°T **ii** 030°T **d i** 288°T **ii** 108°T
e i 125°T **ii** 305°T **f i** 067°T **ii** 247°T
g i 330°T **ii** 150°T **h i** 228°T **ii** 048°T
i i 206°T **ii** 26°T
4 3.28 km **5** 59.45 km **6** 3.4 km **7** 11 km
8 a 39 km **b** 320°T **9 a** 11.3 km **b** 070°T
10 310 km **11** 3.6 km **12** 6.743 km
13 a $180 + a$ **b** $a - 180$
14 a 320° **b** 245° **c** 065° **d** 238° **e** 278°
15 a 620 km **b** 606 km **c** 129 km
16 a i 115 km **ii** 96 km **b** 158 km
c i 68 km **ii** 39.5 min

Investigation

a 45 m **b** 42.4 km **c** 78 m
d top $\angle = 20°$ bottom $\angle = 9°$ $\therefore$ viewing $\angle = 11°$

Challenges

1 $P = 4 + 2\sqrt{8}$ **2** 10 m² **3** 15 cm **4** 010°
5 round peg square hole **6** 122°
7 a i 3, 4, 5 **ii** 5, 12, 13 **b** $m^2 + n^2$

Multiple-choice questions

1 A **2** B **3** A **4** C **5** B
6 C **7** D **8** C **9** A **10** B

Short-answer questions

1 a 37 **b** $\sqrt{12}$ **c** $\sqrt{50}$
2 4.49 m **3 a** 13 cm **b** 13.93 cm **4** 19 m
5 a 4.91 m **b** $x = 2.83, h = 2.65$
6 a 0.64 **b** 2.25 **c** 0.72

7 a 11.33 **b** 48.02 **c** 50.71
8 28.01 m **9** 25 m **10 a** 59.45 km **b** 53.53 km
11 177.91 m **12** 053.13° **13** 63.2 m **14** 5.3 m
15 a 52.5 km **b** 13.59 km

Extended-response questions

1 a 2.15 m **b** 0.95 m **c i** 3.05 m **ii** yes
2 a

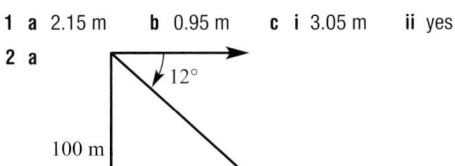

b 470 m **c** 3° **d** 1530 m
3 a 35 km **b** 399 km

Chapter 4

Pre-test

1 a 3 **b** -4 **c** 4 **d** -3
2 a 1 **b** 7 **c** -5 **d** -8
3 a $x = 4$ **b** $x = -2$ **c** $x = 4$
 d $x = -4$ **e** $x = 5$ **f** $x = 6$
4

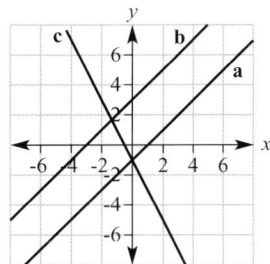

5 a 7 **b** 6.5 **c** 3 **d** -5
6 a 5 **b** 4 **c** 5 **d** 3
7 a 4 **b** 5 **c** 7 **d** 3
8 a $y = 2x + 5$ **b** $y = -3x + 2$
 c $y = 2x + 3$ **d** $y = 6x - 8$
9 a False **b** True **c** True **d** False
10 a 2 **b** -5 **c** -3 **d** 9

Exercise 4A

1 a A (4, 1) **B** (2, 3) **C** (0, 3) **D** (-2, 2)
 E (-3, 1) **F** (-1, 0) **G** (-3, -2) **H** (-2, -4)
 I (0, -3) **J** (2, -2) **K** (3, -4) **L** (2, 0)
 b i F, L **ii** C, I **c i** D, E **ii** J, K
2 a 2 **b** -1 **c** -4 **d** -7
3 a 1 **b** -5 **c** 3 **d** 21

4 a

x	-3	-2	-1	0	1	2	3
y	-4	-3	-2	-1	0	1	2

b

x	-3	-2	-1	0	1	2	3
y	0	1	2	3	4	5	6

c

x	-3	-2	-1	0	1	2	3
y	5	3	1	-1	-3	-5	-7

 a $y = x - 1$ **b** $y = x + 3$ **c** $y = -2x - 1$

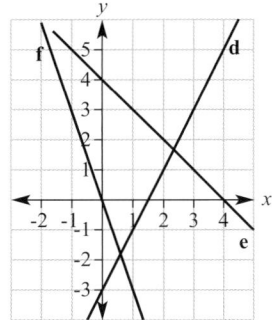

d

x	-3	-2	-1	0	1	2	3
y	-9	-7	-5	-3	-1	1	3

e

x	-3	-2	-1	0	1	2	3
y	7	6	5	4	3	2	1

f

x	-3	-2	-1	0	1	2	3
y	9	6	3	0	-3	-6	-9

 d $y = 2x - 3$ **e** $y = -x + 4$ **f** $y = -3x$

5 a (1, 0) (0, 1) **b** (-2, 0) (0, 2) **c** (4, 0) (0, 8)
 d (-5, 0) (0, 10) **e** (2, 0) (0, 3) **f** (7, 0) (0, -3)
 g (-11, 0) (0, 5) **h** (-2, 0) (0, -5)
6 a $y = -2x + 3$ **b** $y = 3x - 1$ **c** $y = -3x + 2$
 d $y = x + 2$ **e** $2x - y = 1$ **f** $3x + y = 4$
 g $x - 3y = 1$ **h** $2x - 7y = -2$
7 a $y = x + 2$ **b** $y = 2x$ **c** $y = 2x + 1$ **d** $y = -x + 2$
8 a $y = -\dfrac{2}{3}x + 2$ **b** $y = \dfrac{3}{4}x - \dfrac{3}{4}$ **c** $y = x - 4$
 d $y = 2x + 7$ **e** $y = \dfrac{1}{3}x - \dfrac{1}{3}$ **f** $y = \dfrac{4}{7}x - \dfrac{10}{7}$
9 A c, B d, C b, D a
10 a False **b** True **c** True **d** False
11 a For $\dfrac{1}{2}$ across, graph moves 1 down.
 b For $1\dfrac{1}{2}$ across, graph moves 1 up.

12 a yes   **b** no   **c** no   **d** yes

13 a $y = 2x + 7$ **b** $y = -x + 20$ **c** $y = -3x - 10$

    d $y = -5x + 4$ **e** $y = \frac{1}{2}x + \frac{1}{2}$ **f** $y = -\frac{1}{2}x - \frac{3}{2}$

Exercise 4B

1 a $y = x + 2$ **b** $y = \frac{1}{2}x - 1$

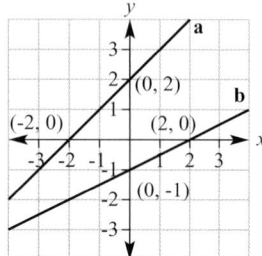

c $y = 3x$ **d** $y = -x + 3$

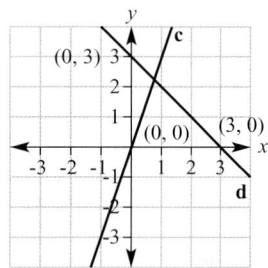

2 a i 3   **ii** 4   **iii** -3   **iv** -1   **v** -6   **vi** 4

   b i 6   **ii** 10   **iii** 1   **iv** 2   **v** 6   **vi** -3

3 a (0, 4)   **b** (0, -5)   **c** (0, 3)   **d** (0, -4)

4 a (5, 0)   **b** (-2, 0)   **c** (3, 0)   **d** (2, 0)

5 a

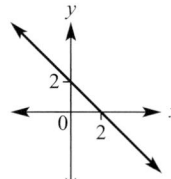

b

c

d

e

f

g

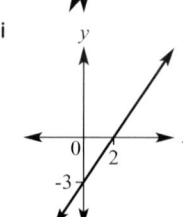

h

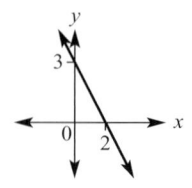

i

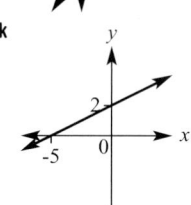

j

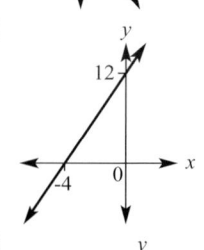

k

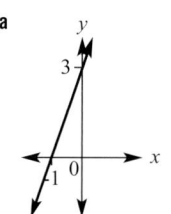

l

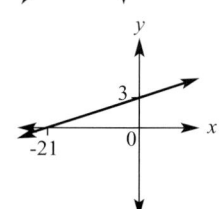

6 a

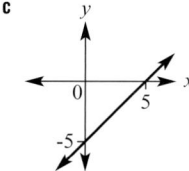

b

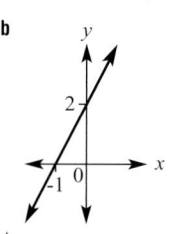

c

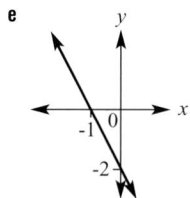

d

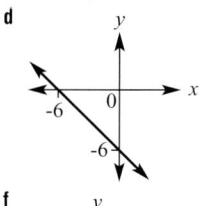

e

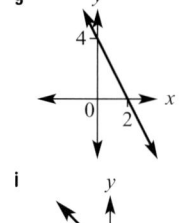

f

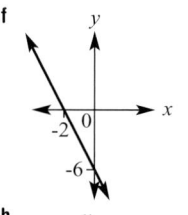

g

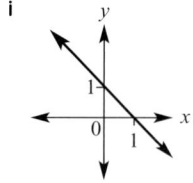

h

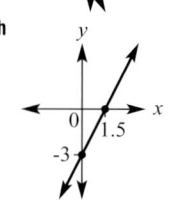

i

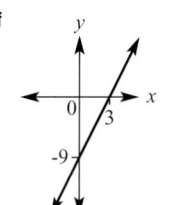

7 a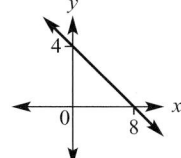

b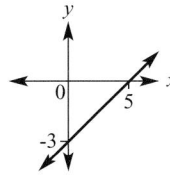

c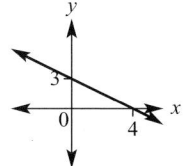

d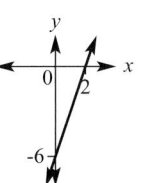

e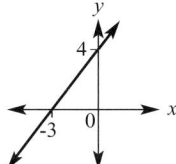

f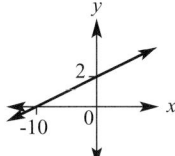

g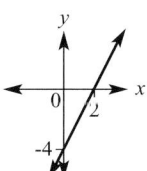

h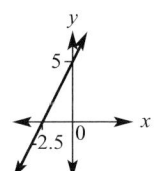

i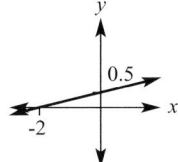

8 a 8 m   **b** 4 seconds   **c**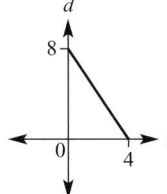

9 a 100 m   **b** 12.5 s

10 a $\left(1\frac{2}{3}, 0\right) \left(0, -2\frac{1}{2}\right)$ **b** $(-7, 0) \left(0, -1\frac{2}{5}\right)$

c $\left(6\frac{1}{2}, 0\right) (0, -13)$ **d** $\left(-\frac{1}{2}, 0\right) (0, -1)$

e $(3, 0) \left(0, -1\frac{1}{2}\right)$ **f** $\left(\frac{1}{3}, 0\right) \left(0, -\frac{1}{7}\right)$

11 a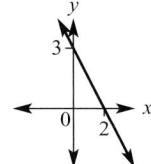

b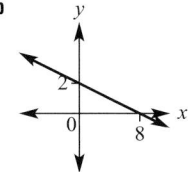

c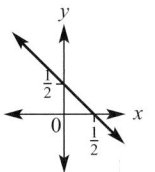

12 (0, 0) is the x- and y- intercept for all values of a and b

13 a $x + y = 4$ **b** $x + y = 2$ **c** $x - y = 3$

d $x - y = -1$ **e** $x + y = k$ **f** $x + y = -k$

14 a $\left(\frac{c}{a}, 0\right), \left(0, \frac{c}{b}\right)$ **b** $\left(-\frac{cb}{a}, 0\right), (0, c)$ **c** $\left(\frac{c}{a}, 0\right), \left(0, -\frac{c}{b}\right)$

d $\left(\frac{-c}{b}, 0\right), \left(0, \frac{c}{a}\right)$ **e** $\left(-\frac{c}{b}, 0\right), \left(0, \frac{c}{a}\right)$ **f** $\left(\frac{bc}{a}, 0\right), \left(0, \frac{bc}{a}\right)$

Exercise 4C

1 a (2, 0)   **b** (-3, 0)   **c** (0, 0)

2 a (0, 3)   **b** (0, -2)   **c** (0, 0)   **d** (0, 0)

3 a 5   **b** $\frac{1}{3}$ **c** -4   **d** -0.1

4 a 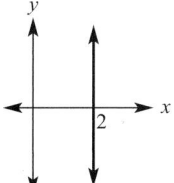   **b**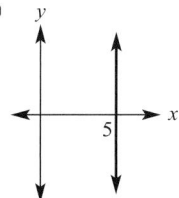

c 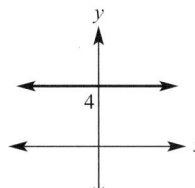   **d**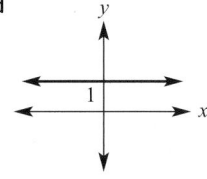

e 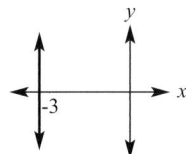   **f**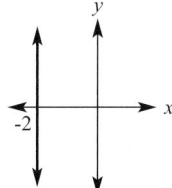

g 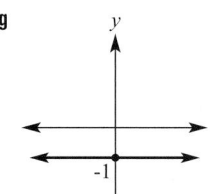   **h**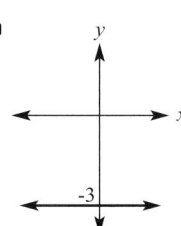

5 a 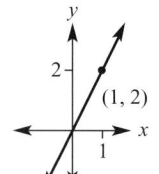   **b**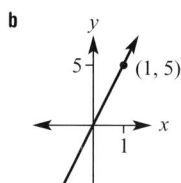

c 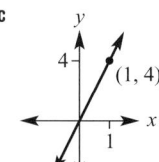   **d**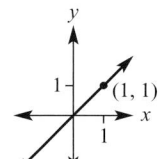

e 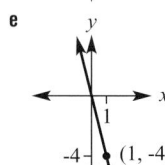   **f**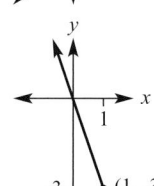

g 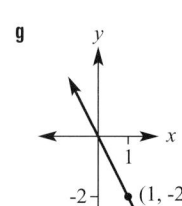   **h**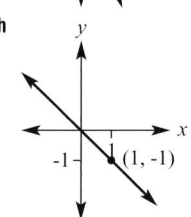

6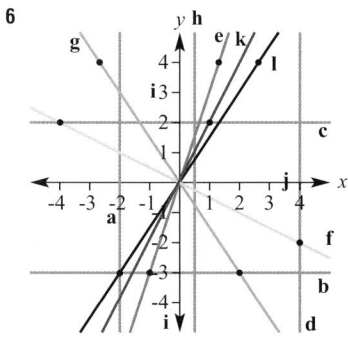

7 a $y = -2$ **b** $y = 4$ **c** $x = -2$
d $x = 5$ **e** $y = 1.5$ **f** $x = -6.7$

8 a $y = 3$ **b** $x = 5$ **c** $x = -2$ **d** $y = 0$

9 a $y = 250$ **b** $y = -45$

10 a $(1, 2)$ **b** $(-3, 5)$ **c** $(0, -4)$
d $(4, 0)$ **e** $(0, 0)$ **f** $(1, 3)$
g $(3, -27)$ **h** $(5, 40)$ **i** $(3, 15)$

11 a $A = 15$ square units   **b** $A = 68$ square units

12 a i $y = 1$ or $y = -5$ **ii** $y = 0$ or $y = -4$

iii $y = 3\frac{1}{2}$ or $y = -7\frac{1}{2}$

b i $y = 1$ or $y = -5$ **ii** $y = 7$ or $y = -11$

iii $y = 9\frac{1}{2}$ or $y = -13\frac{1}{2}$

13 a $y = 2x$ **b** $y = -x$ **c** $y = 3x$ **d** $y = -3x$
14 a $y = 3x$ **b** $y = 4x$ **c** $y = -5x$ **d** $y = -2x$
15 a 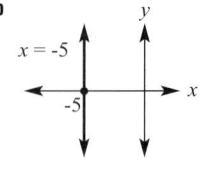   **b**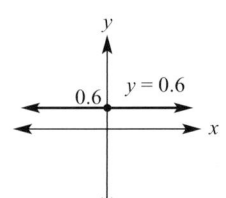

c 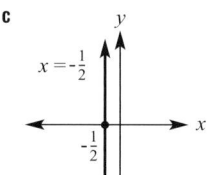   **d**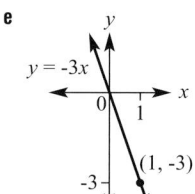

e 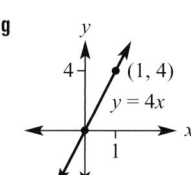   **f**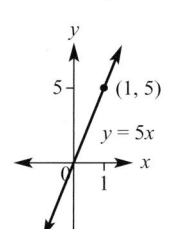

g 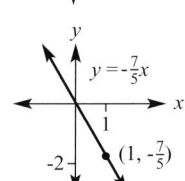   **h**

16 $x = -1$, $y = -5$, $y = 5x$

17 a (b, c) **b** $m = \dfrac{c}{b}$ **18** $m = \dfrac{1}{2}$

Exercise 4D

1 a 2   **b** $\frac{1}{2}$ **c** 3   **d** -1   **e** -3   **f** $-\frac{1}{4}$

2 a zero   **b** negative   **c** positive   **d** undefined

3 a positive, 1   **b** positive, 2   **c** zero   **d** zero

e negative, $-\frac{2}{3}$ **f** negative, $-\frac{3}{4}$ **g** undefined **h** undefined

i positive, $\frac{1}{2}$ **j** positive, 3   **k** positive, 2 **l** negative, -4

4 a 2   **b** 1   **c** $-\frac{1}{4}$ **d** $\frac{4}{3}$ **e** 2   **f** -2

g -1 **h** $\frac{1}{2}$ **i** $\frac{3}{2}$ **j** $-\frac{5}{2}$ **k** $\frac{1}{3}$ **l** $\frac{5}{2}$

5 A 1   **B** -2   **C** 1   **D** $\frac{1}{2}$ **E** -2   **F** 3

6 a $-\frac{1}{20}$ **b** 17.5   **c** $-\frac{1}{5}$ **d** 7.5

7 a 6   **b** -1   **c** 4   **d** $-1\frac{1}{2}$

8 300 m

9 A (0, 9)　　**B** (-4, 0)　　**C** (-1, 0)

　　D (0, 4)　　**E** (0, -0.4)　　**F** (2.4, 0)

10 $\frac{7}{11} = \frac{35}{55}, \frac{3}{5} = \frac{33}{55}$ hence $\frac{7}{11} > \frac{3}{5}$ so $\frac{7}{11}$ is steeper

11 a run = $x_2 - x_1$　　**b** rise = $y_2 - y_1$　　**c** $m = \dfrac{y_2 - y_1}{x_2 - x_1}$

　　d i $m = \dfrac{3}{2}$　　ii $m = \dfrac{5}{4}$　　iii $m = -\dfrac{5}{3}$　　iv $m = \dfrac{4}{3}$

　　e yes, the rise and the run work out regardless

12 a i -1　　ii -3　　**b** (4.5, 0)

　　c i (6, 0)　　ii (2.4, 0)　　iii $\left(1\dfrac{2}{7}, 0\right)$　　iv (7.5, 0)

Exercise 4E

1 a i 10 km　　ii 20 km　　iii 30 km

　　b 10 km/h　　**c** 10　　**d** they are the same

2 a 15 mm　　**b** i 6 days　　ii 20 days

　　c

t	0	1	2	3	4
h	0	5	10	15	20

　　d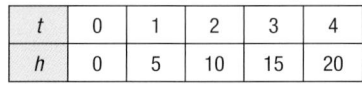

　　e $m = 5$

3 a 100 L/hour

　　b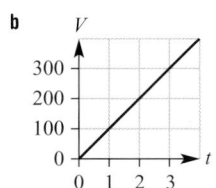

　　c i 100　　ii $V = 100t$　　**d** i $V = 150$ L　　ii $t = 20$ hours

4 a 25 km/h

　　b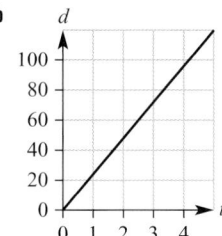

　　c i 25　　ii $d = 25t$　　**d** i 62.5 km　　ii 1.6 hours

5 a $d = 50t$　　**b** $g = 2t$　　**c** $C = 1.25n$　　**d** $P = 20t$

6 a 100 km/h　**b** 7 cm/s　**c** 2.5 cm/minute　d 49 mm/min

7 a 10.2 L　　**b** 72.25 L　**c** 800 km

8　Sally　　**9** Leopard　　**10** 25 months

11 a i 0　　ii 4π　　iii 12π

　　b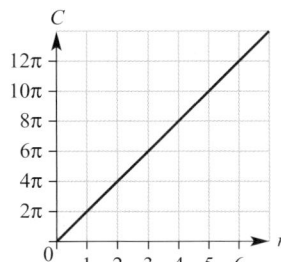

　　c gradient is 2π, the coefficient of r

12 No, $A = \pi r^2$ so area (A) is proportional to square of radius (r^2).

13 a $A = 2h$

　　b 2 cm² increase for each 1 cm increase in height

14 Yes, for any fixed time, e.g. $t = 5$, $s = \dfrac{d}{5}$

15 1.2 mins or 72 seconds　　**16** $\dfrac{5}{12}$ km

Exercise 4F

1 a $y = 2x + 5$　　**b** $y = 3x - 1$　　**c** $y = -2x + 3$

　　d $y = -x - 2$　　**e** $y = -\dfrac{1}{2}x - 10$　　**f** $y = -\dfrac{2}{3}x + \dfrac{5}{2}$

2 a 1　　**b** -5　　**c** -5　　**d** -11　　**e** 9　　**f** 2

3 a $y = x + 7$　　**b** $y = -x + 3$　　**c** $y = 2x + 5$

4 a gradient = 3, y-intercept = -4

　　b gradient = -5, y-intercept = -2

　　c gradient = -2, y-intercept = 3

　　d gradient = $\dfrac{1}{3}$, y-intercept = 4

　　e gradient = -4, y-intercept = 0

　　f gradient = 2, y-intercept = 0

　　g gradient = 2.3, y-intercept = 0

　　h gradient = -0.7, y-intercept = 0

5 a 1, -2,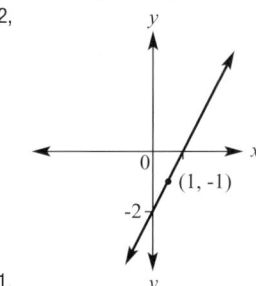

　　b 2, -1,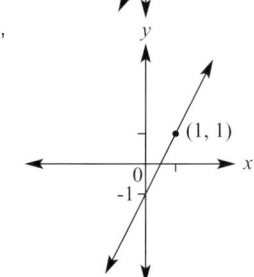

c $\frac{1}{2}$, 1,

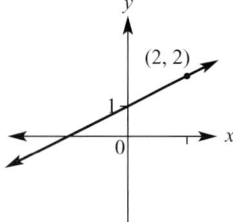

d $-\frac{1}{2}$, 2,

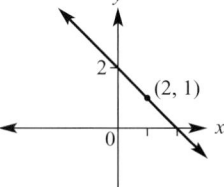

e -3, 3,

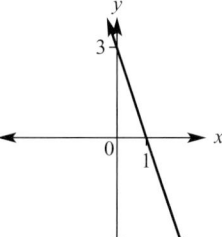

f $\frac{3}{2}$, 1,

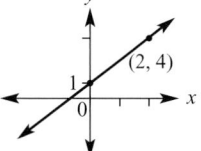

g $-\frac{4}{3}$, 0,

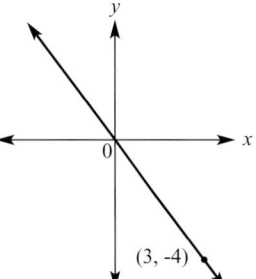

h $\frac{5}{3}$, $-\frac{1}{3}$,

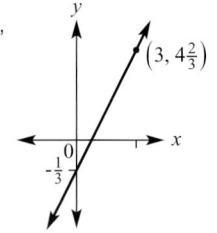

6 a -1, 4,

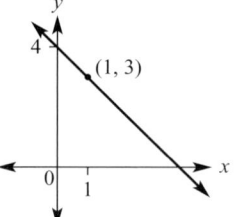

b 1, -6,

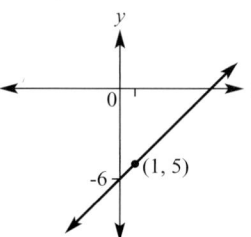

c $-\frac{1}{2}$, 3,

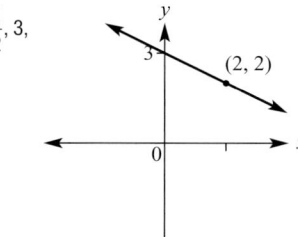

d $\frac{1}{2}$, -4,

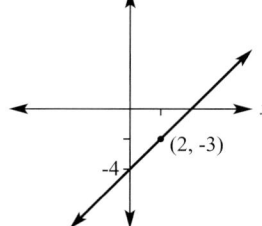

e $\frac{2}{3}$, -2,

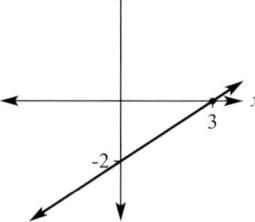

f $-\frac{4}{3}$, 4,

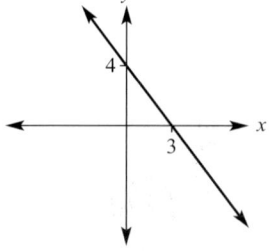

g $\frac{1}{3}, \frac{4}{3},$

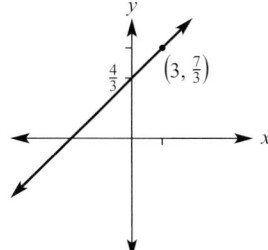

h $-\frac{2}{3}, 2,$

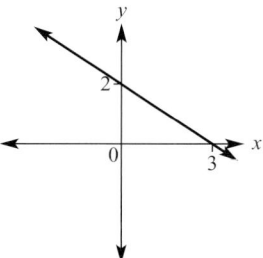

i $\frac{3}{4}, -3,$

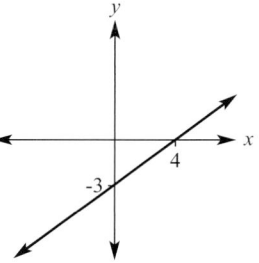

j $-\frac{1}{4}, 0,$

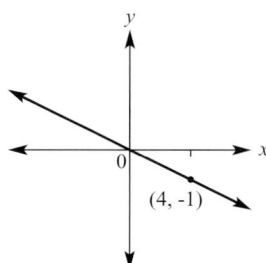

k $\frac{1}{5}, 0,$

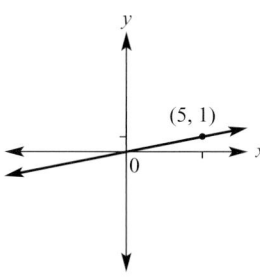

l $\frac{1}{2}, 0,$

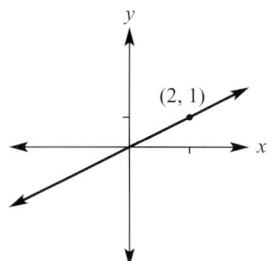

7 a yes **b** no **c** yes **d** yes **e** no **f** no
8 a no **b** yes **c** no **d** no **e** yes **f** no
9 i d **ii** f **iii** c **iv** b **v** e **vi** a
10 a

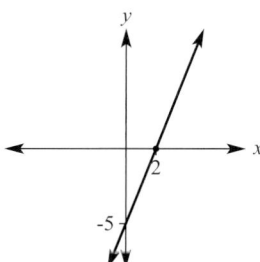

b

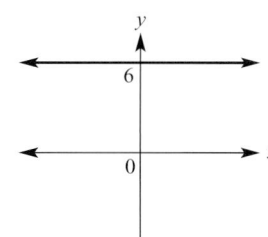

c

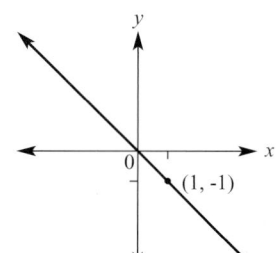

d

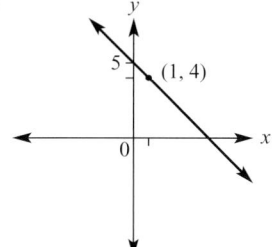

e

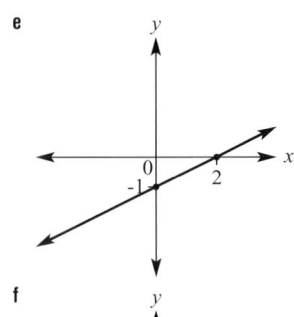

f

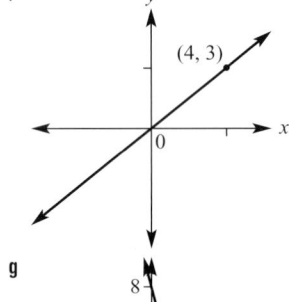

g

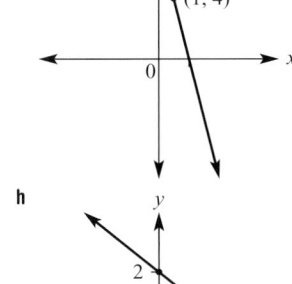

h

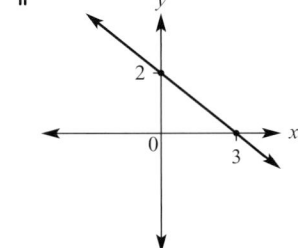

11 a no **b** no **c** yes **d** no

12 c, d, f, h

13 a $y = 2x + 2$, y-intercept is 2 **b** expand brackets and simplify

14 $y = k$ **15** $y = -\dfrac{a}{b}x + \dfrac{d}{b}$, $m = -\dfrac{a}{b}$, $c = \dfrac{d}{b}$

16 a $y = 2x + 3$ **b** $y = -x + 2$ **c** $y = \dfrac{5}{3}x + \dfrac{2}{3}$

 d $y = -\dfrac{2}{5}x - \dfrac{1}{5}$

Exercise 4G

1 a $y = 2x + 5$ **b** $y = 4x - 1$

 c $y = -2x + 5$ **d** $y = -x - \dfrac{1}{2}$

2 a 1 **b** 3 **c** 9 **d** 10 **e** 5 **f** 2

3 a $y = x + 3$ **b** $y = x + 2$ **c** $y = -2x - 4$

 d $y = 2x - 2$ **e** $y = 8x + 8$ **f** $y = -x + 4$

4 a $y = \dfrac{3}{4}x + 3$ **b** $y = -\dfrac{3}{4}x + 3$ **c** $y = -\dfrac{5}{4}x + 3$

 d $y = \dfrac{3}{2}x + 4$ **e** $y = \dfrac{3}{5}x$ **f** $y = -\dfrac{1}{3}x - 1$

5 a $y = 3x + 5$ **b** $y = -2x - 1$ **c** $y = -3x + 8$

 d $y = x - 3$ **e** $y = -3x + 3$ **f** $y = 5x - 1$

 g $y = -x + 8$ **h** $y = -3x + 6$ **i** $y = -2x + 2$

 j $y = -4x - 9$

6 a i 2 **ii** $y = 2x + 2$ **b i** -1 **ii** $y = -x + 3$

 c i -4 **ii** $y = -4x + 11$ **d i** 1 **ii** $y = x - 4$

7 $x = 2\dfrac{1}{2}$ **8** $\left(\dfrac{3}{5}, 0\right), \left(0, -\dfrac{3}{4}\right)$

9 $V = -20t + 120$, $V = 120$ L initially

10 a $y = 5x$ **b** $y = 6.5x + 2$

11 a 1 **b** 8 **c** -6 **d** $\dfrac{5}{2}$

12 a $c = 3$ **b** $c = 3$

 c no, y-intercept is fixed for any given line

13 $y = \dfrac{b}{a}x$

14 a $y = 2x$ **b** $y = -2x + 4$ **c** $y = 2x + 5$

 d $y = -\dfrac{3}{2}x + 2$ **e** $y = \dfrac{5}{7}x + \dfrac{1}{7}$ **f** $y = -\dfrac{13}{3}x - \dfrac{11}{3}$

Exercise 4H

1 a 4 **b** 8 **c** 1 **d** -3

2 a 5.5 **b** 2.5 **c** -1.5 **d** -2.5

3 a 2.24 **b** 8.60 **c** 10.20

4 a (3, 3) **b** (2, 2) **c** (1, 5) **d** (4, 1)

 e (-1, 3) **f** (-1, -1) **g** (1.5, 1.5) **h** (2.5, 2)

 i (0.5, 3) **j** (-1.5, -2.5) **k** (-3, -8.5) **l** (0.5, -2.5)

5 a 5.10 **b** 2.83 **c** 5.39 **d** 4.47

 e 3.61 **f** 2.83 **g** 8.94 **h** 7.21

 i 6.71

6 $B(8, 0)$ $A(-6, 5)$ $A(-6, 9)$

7 a (-3, 1) **b** (1, -4) **c** (8, 2.5)

8 a 12.8 **b** 24.2

9 (0, 0) (0, 4) (2, 0) (2, 4)

10 a $x = \dfrac{x_1 + x_2}{2}$ **b** $y = \dfrac{y_1 + y_2}{2}$ **c** $M(1, -0.5)$

11 a i $x_2 - x_1$ **ii** $y_2 - y_1$ **iii** $\sqrt{(x_2 - x_1)^2 + (y_2 - y_1)^2}$

12 a $\dfrac{1}{3}$ **b** $\dfrac{1}{3}$

 c i (1, 1) **ii** (-2, -0.5) **iii** (2, 1.5)

 d i (-1, 1) **ii** (-2, 5) **iii** (0.4, -1.8) **iv** (-2.4, 2.6)

Exercise 4I

1 a yes **b** yes **c** no

 d yes **e** no **f** yes

2 a $-\dfrac{1}{5}$ **b** $-\dfrac{1}{10}$ **c** $\dfrac{1}{3}$ **d** $\dfrac{1}{6}$

3 a yes   **b** no   **c** no   **d** yes

4 a $y = 2x + 1$ **b** $y = 4x + 8$ **c** $y = -x + 5$

   d $y = -2x - 7$ **e** $y = \frac{2}{3}x - 5$ **f** $y = -\frac{4}{5}x + \frac{1}{2}$

5 a $y = -\frac{1}{3}x + 3$ **b** $y = -\frac{1}{5}x + 7$ **c** $y = \frac{1}{2}x - 4$

   d $y = x + 4$ **e** $y = \frac{1}{7}x - \frac{1}{2}$ **f** $y = -x + \frac{5}{4}$

6 a i $y = 1$ **ii** $y = -3$ **iii** $y = 6$ **iv** $y = -2$
   b i $x = 3$ **ii** $x = -4$ **iii** $x = 1$ **iv** $x = -3$
   c i $x = 2$ **ii** $x = -1$ **iii** $x = 0$ **iv** $x = 3$
   d i $y = 7$ **ii** $y = -\frac{1}{2}$ **iii** $y = 3$ **iv** $y = \frac{1}{2}$

7 a $y = -3x + 9$ **b** $y = \frac{1}{2}x + \frac{5}{2}$

   c $y = -\frac{1}{5}x + 6\frac{1}{5}$ **d** $y = x + 5$

8 $y = 0, y = x + 3, y = -x + 3$ **9** $y = 2x - 10$ or $y = 2x + 10$

10 a i $-\frac{3}{2}$ **ii** -5 **iii** 7 **iv** $\frac{11}{3}$ **b** $-\frac{b}{a}$

11 a i $-\frac{1}{2}$ **ii** 3 **b i** 1 **ii** $-\frac{1}{7}$

12 a $y = -\frac{1}{2}x + 4$ **b** $y = \frac{2}{3}x + 1\frac{2}{3}$ **c** $y = 2x - 3$

   d $y = -2x - 5\frac{1}{2}$ **e** $y = \frac{3}{7}x - \frac{5}{7}$ **f** $y = -\frac{5}{6}x + \frac{1}{6}$

Exercise 4J

1 B

2 a i $1200   **ii** $1500   **iii** $2200   **b** $A = 1000 + 100n$

3 a 46   **b** 3.5   **c** 2   **d** 3

4 a $W = 20x + 400$
   b

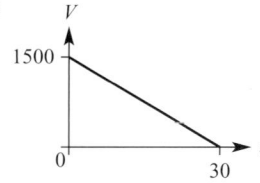

   c $640   **d** 30

5 a $C = 50n + 40$ **b** $240   **c** $640

6 a $C = 25n + 500$
   b

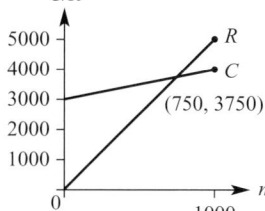

   c $1500   **d** 70

7 a $C = 120t + 300$
   b

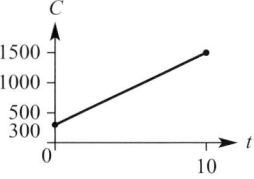

   c $1020   **d** 3 hours

8 a $F = 18t + 12$ **b** 3 minutes   **c** 2.5 minutes

9 a $V = 4000 - 20t$ **b** 2200 L   **c** 175 minutes
   d 2 hours 55 minutes or 175 minutes

10 a

   b $V = 1500 - 50t$
   c the number of litres drained per minute
   d 1250 L   **e** 15 minutes

11 a 80 km/h
   b rate changes i.e. new gradient = 70, $d = 50 + 70t$

12 a 20 m/sec   **b** -20 m/sec   **c** 350 m
   d 17.5 sec   **e** increasing altitude at rate of 20 m/sec

13 a i $C = 0.4n + 20$ **ii** 160
   b i $P = 0.8n - 20$ **ii** 25   **iii** 120

14 a $C = 10x + 6700$ **b** $8700
   c 630   **d** $11 700
   e 670   **f** $P = 10x - 6700$
   g $T = \dfrac{10x - 6700}{x}$ **h** 1340

Exercise 4K

1 a (1, 3)   **b** (-1, 2)   **c** (2, 2)

2 a True   **b** False   **c** False   **d** True

3 a yes   **b** yes   **c** yes

4 a yes   **b** yes   **c** no   **d** no
   e yes   **f** yes   **g** no   **h** no

5 a (2, 2)   **b** (3, 2)   **c** (2, -4)   **d** (3, 2)
   e (2, 1)   **f** (3, 7)   **g** (1, 2)   **h** (2, 4)
   i (4, 1)   **j** (-1, 3)   **k** (-1, -5)   **l** (1, 3)

6 a

   b 750

7 1200 DVDs

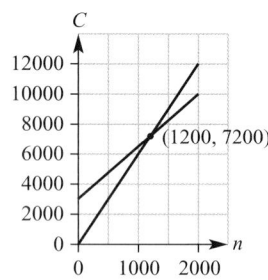

8 10 seconds

9 Parallel lines i.e. same gradient

10 a (0, 0)   **b** (0, 0)

   c no intersection   **d** no intersection

   e (0, 1)   **f** (0, 3)

11 a 2   **b** -3

12 a (1, 3)   **b** $A = 6.75$ units^2

13 a 18.75 units^2 **b** 24 units^2 **c** 16 units^2

   d 27 units^2 **e** 7 units^2

Challenges

1 101   **2** 2.5 hours

3 (0.5, 5.5), diagonals intersect at their midpoint

4 602   **5** length $AB =$ length AC

6 $A = 13.5$ square units, $P = 20$ units

7 (6, 7)   **8** 20 days   **9** 31 hours

Multiple-choice questions

1 C   **2** D   **3** C   **4** B   **5** A   **6** E

7 B   **8** A   **9** D   **10** D

Short-answer questions

1 a (-2, 0), (0, 4)

   b (3, 0), (0, -2)

2 a

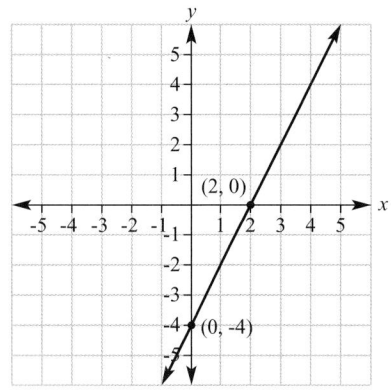

b

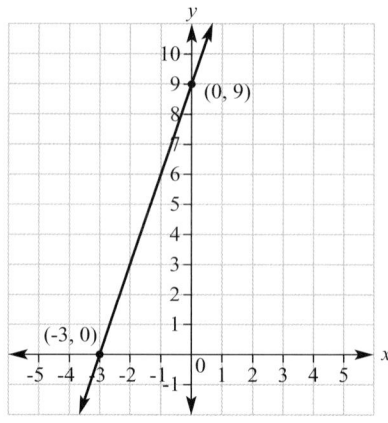

c

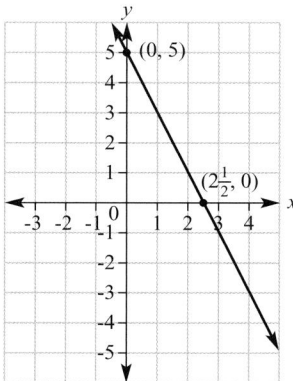

d

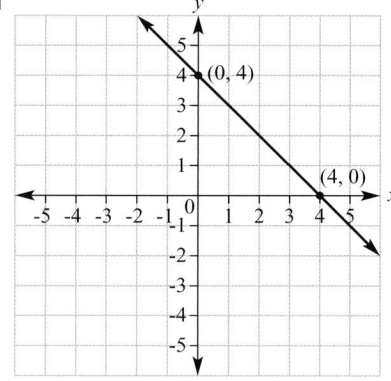

e

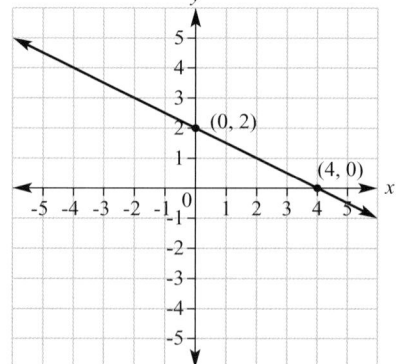

f

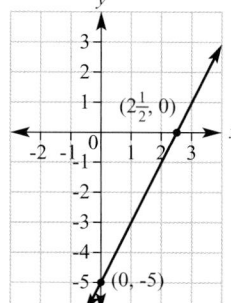

g

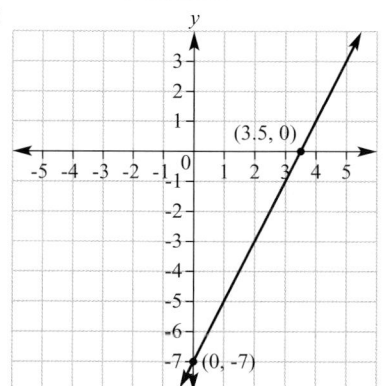

h

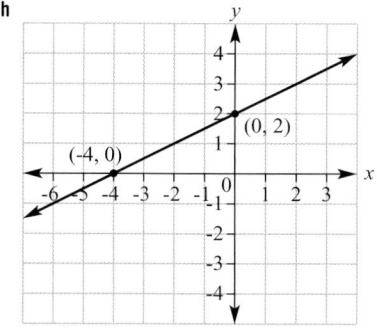

3 a 175 km

b 2.5 hours

c

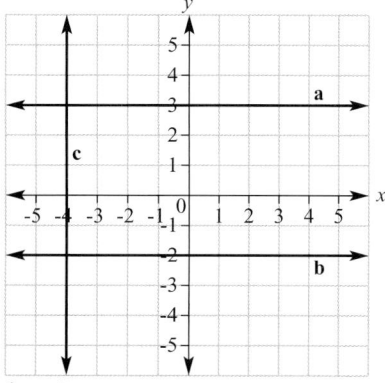

4 a $y = 3$

b $y = -2$

c $x = -4$

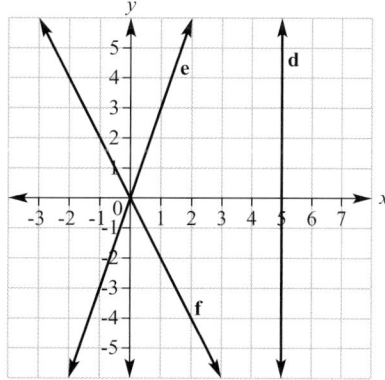

d $x = 5$

e $y = 3x$

f $y = -2x$

5 a 2   **b** -1

c $-\dfrac{5}{2}$ **d** $\dfrac{4}{3}$

e 2   **f** $-\dfrac{10}{3}$

6 a 2000 L/hr

b

c $V = 2000t$

d 2.5 hours

7 a Gradient = 2   *y*-intercept = 3

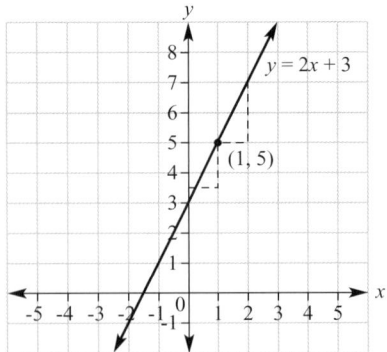

b Gradient = -3   *y*-intercept = 7

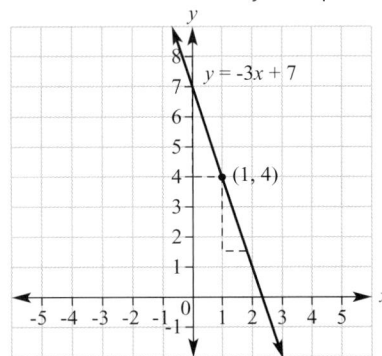

c Gradient = $-\dfrac{2}{3}$ *y*-intercept = 3

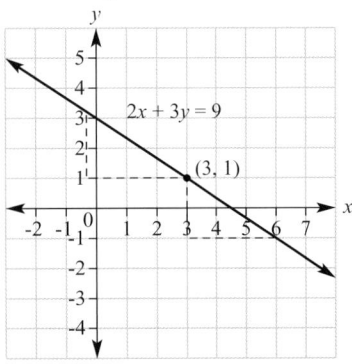

d Gradient = $\dfrac{3}{2}$ *y*-intercept = 4

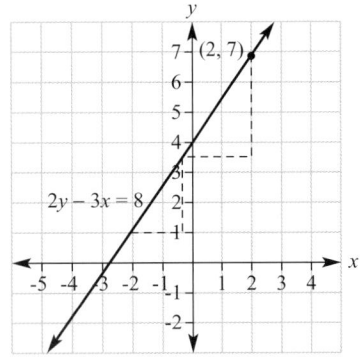

8 a $y = 3x + 2$ **b** $y = -2x + 6$ **c** $y = \dfrac{4}{3}x - 5$

9 a $y = \dfrac{x}{2} - 1$ **b** $y = -3x + 6$ **c** $y = 3x - 2$ **d** $y = -2x + 2$

10 a $y = 2x + 4$ **b** $y = -x - 3$ **c** $y = -\dfrac{1}{2}x - 1$ **d** $y = 3x + 4$

   e $y = 3x + 1$ **f** $3x + 2y = 8$ or $y = -\dfrac{3x}{2} + 4$

11 a $M(4, 6)$, 5.66 **b** $M(7.5, 4.5)$, 7.07
   c $M(0,4)$, 7.21 **d** $M(-3, 2.5)$, 9.85

12 a $n = 9$ **b** $n = 10$ **c** $n = 6$

13 a no **b** yes **14 a** $(2, 0)$ **b** $(-2, 4)$

Extended-response questions

1 a **i** \$40/hr, \$80 **ii**

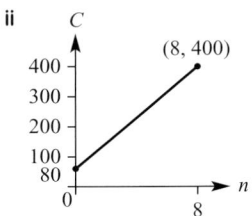

   iii \$180 **iv** 5 hours

b **i** $C = 65 + 45n$

   ii

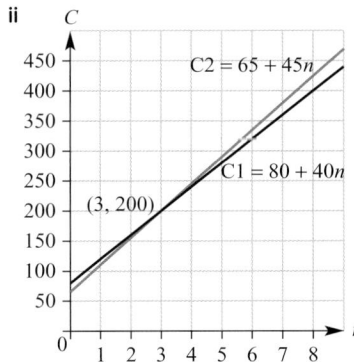

c $(3, 200)$ **d** 3 hours

2 a $C = 8v + 90$ **b** **i** \$90 **ii** \$8 per vase **c** 23 vases

Chapter 5

Pre-test

1 a 23 **b** 48 **c** 2.7
   d 5.2134 **e** 50 **f** 72.16

2 a $A = 4$ cm^2 $P = 8$ cm **b** $A = 6$ m^2, $P = 10$ m
   c $A = 8$ cm^2, $P = 18$ cm

3 a cylinder **b** circle

4 a 7 **b** 4.5 **c** 12

5 a 3 **b** 6 **c** 27

6 a 30 mm **b** 2000 cm **c** 1600 m **d** 2.3 cm
   e 3.167 km **f** 0.72 m **g** 20 m **h** 3000 cm

7 a 30 cm² **b** 4 m² **c** 49 km²
d 3 m² **e** 24 cm² **f** 66 m²

8 $C = 31.42$ m $A = 78.54$ m²

Exercise 5A

1 a 50 mm **b** 280 cm **c** 52.1 cm
d 0.837 m **e** 4600 m **f** 2.17 km

2 825 cm, 2.25 cm

3 a $a = 3, b = 6$ **b** $a = 12, b = 4$ **c** $a = 6.2\ b = 2$

4 a 12 m **b** 27 cm **c** 24 mm
d 18 km **e** 10 m **f** 36 cm

5 a 90 cm **b** 80 cm **c** 170 cm
d 30.57 m **e** 25.5 cm **f** 15.4 km

6 a 9 cm **b** 4015 m **c** 102.1 cm

7 a 8000 mm **b** 110 m **c** 1 cm
d 20 mm **e** 0.284 km **f** 62.743 km

8 a $x = 4$ **b** $x = 2.2$ **c** $x = 14$
d $x = 9.5$ **e** $x = 6$ **f** $x = 4.2$

9 108 m

10 a 86 cm **b** 13.6 m **c** 40.4 cm

11 a $x = 2$ **b** $x = 2.1$ **c** $x = 7$

12 88 cm

13 a $P = 2a + 2b$ **b** $P = 4x$ **c** $P = 2a + b$
d $P = 2x + 2y$ **e** $P = 4(a + b)$ **f** $P = 2x$

14 All vertical sides add to 13 cm and all horizontal sides add to 10 cm

15 a 25 cm, 75 cm **b** 40 cm, 60 cm
c 62.5 cm, 37.5 cm **d** 10 cm, 20 cm, 30 cm, 40 cm

16 a i 96 cm **ii** 104 cm **iii** 120 cm
b $P = 4(20 + 2x)$ ∴ $P = 8x + 80$
c i 109.6 cm **ii** 136.4 cm **d i** $x = 1.25$ **ii** $x = 2.75$
e No, as with no frame the picture has a perimeter of 80 cm

Exercise 5B

1 a 2.8 cm **b** 96 mm

2 a 6π **b** 12π **c** $\dfrac{35\pi}{2}$
d $3 + 2\pi$ **e** $12 + 3\pi$ **f** $10 + 4\pi$
g $8 + 2\pi$ **h** $3 + \dfrac{3\pi}{4}$ **i** $7 + \dfrac{\pi}{12}$

3 a $\dfrac{1}{4}$ **b** $\dfrac{1}{2}$ **c** $\dfrac{3}{4}$ **d** $\dfrac{1}{6}$ **e** $\dfrac{5}{12}$ **f** $\dfrac{5}{8}$

4 a 50.27 m **b** 87.96 cm **c** 9.42 mm **d** 12.57 km

5 a 9.14 cm **b** 14.94 m **c** 33.13 cm
d 10.00 cm **e** 20.05 m **f** 106.73 km

6 a 12.56 m **b** 62.8 cm **c** 22 mm **d** 44 m

7 a 10π **b** 20π **c** 11π
d 15π **e** 3π **f** 41π

8 a $8 + 2\pi$ **b** $4 + 2\pi$ **c** $10\pi + 20$
d $12 + 2\pi$ **e** $5\pi + 6$ **f** $5\pi + 8$

9 28.27 m **10** 4.1 m **11** 31.42 cm

12 a 188.50 cm **b i** 376.99 cm **ii** 1979.20 cm **c** 531

13 a $\dfrac{23\pi}{2}$ m **b** $2.4 + 0.6\pi$ **c** $21 + \dfrac{7\pi}{2}$
d $5 + \dfrac{15\pi}{8}$ **e** $40 + 20\pi$ **f** $23 + \dfrac{23\pi}{4}$

14 a $r = \dfrac{C}{2\pi}$ **b i** 1.6 cm **ii** 4.0 m **c** $d = \dfrac{C}{\pi}$ **d** 67 cm

15 a 131.95 m **b** 791.68 m **c i** 3.79 **ii** 15.16 **d** 63.66 m

Exercise 5C

1 a 6 **b** 16 **c** 12 **d** 1 **e** 12 **f** 153

2 a rectangle **b** circle **c** rhombus/kite
d sector of circle **e** triangle **f** trapezium
g parallelogram **h** square **i** semicircle

3 a $\dfrac{1}{4}$ **b** $\dfrac{1}{3}$ **c** $\dfrac{3}{4}$ **d** $\dfrac{1}{6}$ **e** $\dfrac{5}{8}$ **f** $\dfrac{5}{18}$

4 a 200 mm² **b** 5 cm² **c** 21 000 cm²
d 21 m² **e** 1000 m² **f** 3.2 km²

5 a 24 m² **b** 10.5 cm² **c** 20 km²
d 25.2 m² **e** 15 m² **f** 36.8 m²

6 a 21 mm² **b** 12 cm² **c** 17 cm²
d 63 m² **e** 6.205 m² **f** 15.19 km²

7 a 12.25 cm² **b** 3.04 m² **c** 0.09 cm²
d 6.5 mm² **e** 18 cm² **f** 2.4613 cm²

8 a 21.23 m² **b** 216.51 km² **c** 196.07 cm²

9 a 7.07 m² **b** 157.08 cm² **c** 19.24 cm²
d 84.82 m² **e** 26.53 m² **f** 62.86 m²

10 a 1.5×10^{10} (15 000 000 000) cm² **b** 5 mm² **c** 0.075 m²

11 500 000 m² **12** 0.175 km² **13** 0.51 m²

14 12.89% **15** 31%

16 a $r = \sqrt{\dfrac{A}{\pi}}$ **b i** 1.3 cm **ii** 1.5 m **iii** 2.5 km

17 a i 64° **ii** 318°
b as angle would be greater than 360° which is not possible (28.3 m² is the largest area possible, i.e. full circle)

18 a i 1.5 m **ii** 1.5 m **b** 78 m² **c** yes

19 46.7%

Exercise 5D

1 a semicircle and rectangle **b** triangle and semicircle
c rhombus and parallelogram

2 a $P = 2 \times 5 + 3 + \dfrac{1}{2} \times 2\pi r$ $\qquad A = bh + \dfrac{1}{2}\pi r^2$
$\qquad = 10 + 3 + 1.5\pi$ $\qquad\qquad = 5 \times 2 + \dfrac{1}{2} \times \pi \times 1.5^2$
$\qquad = 13 + 1.5\pi$ $\qquad\qquad = 10 + 1.125\pi$
$\qquad = 17.7$ m $\qquad\qquad = 13.5$ m²

b $P = 20 + 12 + 12 + 10 + 6$ $\qquad A = lw - \dfrac{1}{2}bh$
$\qquad = 60$ cm $\qquad\qquad = 12 \times 20 - \dfrac{1}{2} \times 8 \times 6$
$\qquad\qquad\qquad = 240 - 24$
$\qquad\qquad\qquad = 216$ cm²

3 a 46 m, 97 m² **b** 34 m, 76 m²
c 40 m, 90 m² **d** 18.28 m, 22.28 m²
e 19.42 m, 26.14 m² **f** 85.42 mm, 326.37 mm²

4 a 17 cm^2 **b** 3.5 cm^2 **c** 21.74 cm^2
  d 6.75 m^2 **e** 189 cm^2 **f** 115 cm^2
5 a 108 m^2 **b** 33 cm^2 **c** 98 m^2
  d 300 m^2 **e** 16 cm^2 **f** 22.5 m^2
6 a 37.70 m, 92.55 m^2 **b** 20.57 mm, 16 mm^2
  c 18.00 cm, 11.61 cm^2 **d** 12.57 m, 6.28 m^2
  e 25.71 cm, 23.14 cm^2 **f** 33.56 m, 83.90 m^2
7 a 90 cm^2 **b** 15 m^2 **c** 9 m^2 **d** 7.51 cm^2
  e 7.95 m^2 **f** 180.03 cm^2 **g** 8.74 mm^2 **h** 21.99 cm^2
  i 23.83 mm^2
8 189.27 m^2 **9** 68.67 cm^2
10 a 136.3 cm^2 **b** 42.4 m^2 **c** 345.6 m^2 **11** 8 cm
12 a $36 + 18\pi$ **b** 16 **c** $12 - \dfrac{\pi}{8}$ **d** 2π

  e $12.96 + 3.24\pi$ **f** $25 + \dfrac{75\pi}{4}$
13 7.1 cm
14 a hypotenuse (diameter) would equal 4.24 not 5
  b hypotenuse (sloped edge) should be 13 cm not 14 cm
  c hypotenuse (diameter) should be 5.83 not 8 m
15 5267.1 cm^2
16 a 34 cm, 18 cm **b** 222.4 cm^2 **c** 389.6 cm^2

Exercise 5E

1 a

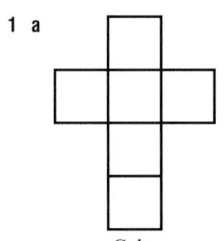

Cube

b

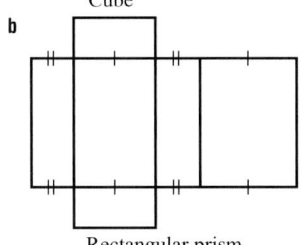

Rectangular prism

c

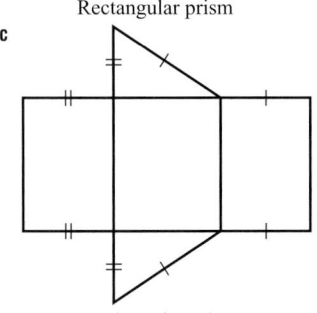

Triangular prism

d

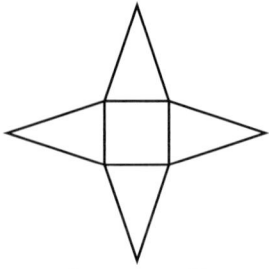

Square pyramid

e

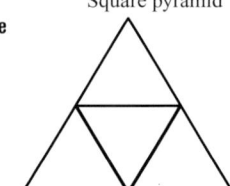

Tetrahedron
(triangular pyramid)

f

Pentagonal pyramid

2 a TSA $= 2 \times 8 \times 7 + 2 \times 8 \times 3 + 2 \times 7 \times 3$
    $= 112 + 48 + 42$
    $= 202$ m^2
  b TSA $= 2 \times \dfrac{1}{2} \times 4 \times 3 + 5 \times 7 + 4 \times 7 + 3 \times 7$
    $= 12 + 35 + 28 + 21$
    $= 96$ cm^2

3 a 52 cm^2 **b** 242 cm^2 **c** 76 m^2
  d 192 cm^2 **e** 68.16 m^2 **f** 85.76 m^2
4 a 39 mm^2 **b** 224 cm^2 **c** 9.01 m^2
5 a 96 cm^2 **b** 199.8 cm^2 **c** 0.96 m^2 **d** 44.2 m^2
  e 22 cm^2 **f** 28 cm^2
6 6 m^2
7 14.54 m^2
8 34 000 cm^2
9 a 44.4 m^2 **b** 4.44 L
10 a 1400 cm^2 **b** 1152 cm^2
11 a 10 cm^2 **b** 16 cm^2

  c 24 cm^2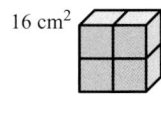

12 a [6, 10, 14, 18, 22, 26, 30, 34, 38] **b** $S = 4n + 2$
13 a 17.7 cm^2 **b** 96 m^2 **c** 204 cm^2
  d 97.9 m^2 **e** 137.8 cm^2 **f** 43.3 mm^2

Exercise 5F

1 a

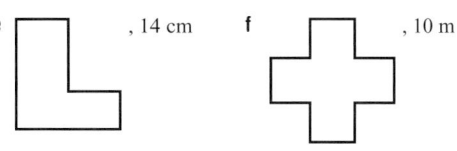

(diagram: two circles of radius 4.1 and a rectangle 26 by 11)

b

(diagram: three circles of radius 5, Radius 5, and a rectangle 31.4 by 32)

2 a 22 cm by 10 cm   **b** 12.57 cm by 8 cm

   c 50.27 m by 5 m

3 a 25.13 m²   **b** 471.24 cm²   **c** 50.27 m²

4 a 44.0 cm²   **b** 603.2 cm²   **c** 113.1 m²

5 395.84 cm²

6 a 251.33 cm²   **b** 207.35 mm²   **c** 24.13 m²

7 a 54.56 m²   **b** 218.23 m²   **c** 63.98 cm²

   d 71.91 cm²   **e** 270.80 m²   **f** 313.65 km²

   g 326.41 m²   **h** 593.92 m²   **i** 43.71 mm²

8 7539.82 cm²   **9** 80 424.8 cm²

10 a 18 849.556 cm² **b i** 1.88 m² **ii** 37.70 m² **c** 239

11 a 8π m²   **b** 150π cm²   **c** 16π m²

12 Half cylinder is more than half surface area as it includes new
rectangular surface.

13 a $\left(\dfrac{135\pi}{2}+36\right)$ cm²   **b** $\left(\dfrac{70\pi}{3}+12\right)$ cm²   **c** $\left(\dfrac{29\pi}{12}+4\right)$ m²

Exercise 5G

1 a 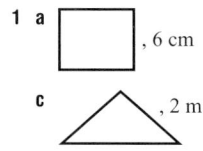 , 6 cm   **b** , 10 cm

   c 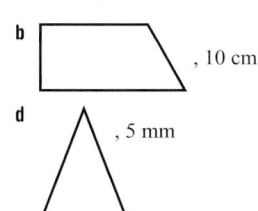 , 2 m   **d** , 5 mm

e *(L-shape)* , 14 cm   **f** *(cross shape)* , 10 m

2 a square   **b** triangle   **c** rectangle

   d trapezium   **e** hexagon   **f** triangle

3 a 3000 mm³ **b** 2 cm³   **c** 8 700 000 cm³

   d 0.0059 m³ **e** 10 000 m³ **f** 0.000 0217 km³

   g 3000 mL **h** 200 L   **i** 3.5 L

   j 21 mL   **k** 37 kL   **l** 42.9 ML

4 a 8 cm³   **b** 84 m³   **c** 21 mm³

5 a 4 cm³   **b** 10.5 m³   **c** 11.96 cm³

   d 29 cm³   **e** 14.88 m³   **f** 8.1351 cm³

   g 108 m³   **h** 29.82 m³   **i** 0.382 044 cm³

6 a 75 m³   **b** 30 cm³   **c** 1.25 cm³

7 a 16 cm³   **b** 42.875 m³ **c** 15 cm³

8 a 8 L   **b** 0.36 L   **c** 0.48 L

9 8000 cm³   **10** 0.19 m³

11 Yes, the tank only holds 20 L

12 a 67.2 cm³   **b** 28 m³   **c** 8.9 km³

   d 28 m³   **e** 0.4 m³   **f** 29232 mm³

13 a 15 L   **b** 112 500 L **c** 8000 L

14 a 55 m²   **b** 825 m³

15 a i 1000   **ii** $\dfrac{1}{1000}$ **iii** 1000

   b i 1000 000 **ii** 1000   **iii** 1000 000 or 1000²

16 a $V = x^2 h$ **b** $V = s^3$ **c** $V = 6t^3$ **17 b** $\dfrac{1}{3}$

Exercise 5H

1 a $r = 4, h = 10$ **b** $r = 2.6, h = 11.1$

   c $r = 2.9, h = 12.8$ **d** $r = 9, h = 23$

   e $r = 5.8, h = 15.1$ **f** $r = 10.65, h = 10.4$

2 a 12.57 cm² **b** 8.04 m²   **c** 78.54 cm² **d** 2.54 km²

3 a 2 L   **b** 4.3 mL   **c** 3700 cm³

   d 1000 L   **e** 38 m³   **f** 200 mL

4 a 226.19 cm³ **b** 18.85 m³   **c** 137.44 m³

   d 100.53 cm³ **e** 8.48 m³   **f** 68.05 m³

5 a 18 L   **b** 503 L   **c** 20 L

   d 4712 L   **e** 589 049 L **f** 754 L

6 a 25.133 m³ **b** 25 133 L

7 37 699 L   **8** Cylinder by 0.57 m³

9 a 502.65 cm³   **b** 1.02 m³   **c** 294.52 m³

   d 35 342.92 m³   **e** 47.12 cm³   **f** 1017.88 cm³

10 a 0.707   **b** 2.523

11 a 160π m³   **b** 320π cm³   **c** 54π km³

   d $\dfrac{3\pi}{4}$ cm³   **e** 1500π cm³   **f** 144π mm³

12 A number of answers. Require $h = 2\pi r$.

13 a 113.10 cm³   **b** 10471.98 m³   **c** 3.73 m³

   d 20.60 cm³   **e** 858.41 cm³   **f** 341.29 m³

Challenges

1 100 L **2** non-shaded is half the shaded area
3 163.4 m^2 **4** $\sqrt{200}$ cm = 14.14 cm **5** $1\frac{1}{6}$ cm
6 16 days **7** $V = 2\pi^2 r^3$ **8** $h = \dfrac{1-r^2}{r}$

Multiple-choice questions

1 B **2** C **3** E **4** B **5** A
6 D **7** B **8** E **9** C **10** E

Short-answer questions

1 a 380 cm **b** 1270 m **c** 2.73 cm^2
d 52 000 cm^2 **e** 10 000 cm^3 **f** 53.1 cm^3
g 3.1 L **h** 43 mL **i** 2830 L
2 a 14 m **b** 51 mm **c** 16.2 cm
3 a 4 cm^2 **b** 1122 mm^2 **c** 30.34 mm^2
d 7.5 m^2 **e** 15 cm^2 **f** 3 cm^2
4 a 2.5 m^2 **b** 37.4 m^2
5 a $A = 28.27$ cm^2, $P = 18.85$ cm **b** $A = 5.38$ m^2, $P = 9.51$ m
c $A = 2.36$ cm^2, $P = 6.71$ cm
6 a $P = 15.24$ m, $A = 13.09$ m^2 **b** $P = 14.10$ m, $A = 10.39$ m^2
c $P = 24.76$ km, $A = 33.51$ km^2
7 a 8.86 m, 4.63 m^2 **b** 45.56 cm, 128.54 cm^2
8 a 46 cm^2 **b** 114 m^2 **9 a** 659.73 mm^2 **b** 30.21 m^2
10 a 30 cm^3 **b** 54 m^3 **c** 31.42 mm^3

Extended-response questions

1 a 517.08 cm **b** $65
c 15853.98 cm^2 **d** 1.58 m^2, claim is correct
2 a 1 cm **b** 15.71 cm^2 **c** 125 680 cm^3 **d** 0.125 68 m^3
e 18.85 cm **f** 15 m^2 **g** $1200

Semester review 1

Reviewing number and financial mathematics
Multiple-choice questions

1 B **2** E **3** D **4** D **5** A

Short-answer questions

1 a $\dfrac{19}{28}$ **b** $\dfrac{7}{9}$ **c** $\dfrac{3}{8}$ **d** $1\dfrac{4}{5}$
2 a 60% **b** 31.25% **c** 10% **d** 25%
3 a 5 : 3 **b** 55 km/h **c** 2.4 mL/h **4** $892

Extended-response question

a i $17 500 **ii** $23 520 **iii** 9 years **iv** 27%
b $23635.69
c i Jim by $116 **ii** Jim by $922

Linear and simultaneous equations
Multiple-choice questions

1 E **2** A **3** C **4** B **5** D

Short-answer questions

1 a $x = 6$ **b** $x > \dfrac{9}{2}$ **c** $m = \dfrac{3}{8}$
d $y = -1$ **e** $a \leq \dfrac{1}{11}$ **f** $x = -\dfrac{3}{14}$
2 a $\dfrac{m-3}{2} = 6$ **b** Noah gets $15 pocket money
3 a 155 **b** $l = \dfrac{2S}{n} - a$ **c** 18
4 a $x = 6, y = 3$ **b** $x = -1, y = -5$
c $x = 5, y = -2$ **d** $x = -3, y = 4$

Extended-response question

a i $12x + 20 > 74$ **ii** 5 games
b i Let $x be the cost of a raffle ticket and $y the cost of a badge.
ii $5x + 2y = 11.5$ and $4x + 3y = 12$
iii A raffle ticket costs $1.50 and a badge costs $2.

Pythagoras' theorem and trigonometry
Multiple-choice questions

1 D **2** A **3** C **4** A **5** E

Short-answer questions

1 a $x = 15.1$ **b** $x = 5.7$ **c** $x = 11.2$ **d** $\theta = 29.5$
2 a $x = 13, y = 14.7$ **b** $x = 9.9$
3 a 19.21 m **b** $38.7°$
4 a 16.3 km west **b** $115°$

Extended-response question

a 17.75 m **b** $14.3°$ **c i** 18.8 m **ii** 6.8 s

Linear relations
Multiple-choice questions

1 C **2** D **3** B **4** C **5** A

Short-answer questions

1 a

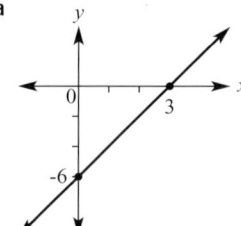

b

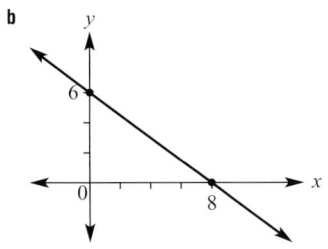

c

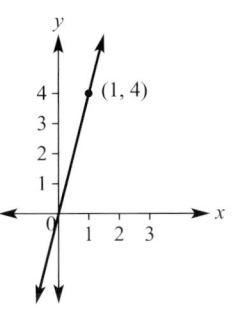

2 a $\dfrac{2}{3}$ **b** -3 **c** -2 **d** $\dfrac{4}{3}$

3 a $y = -3x + 6$ **b** $y = 3x - 1$
  c $y - 2x$ **d** $y = -\dfrac{1}{3}x + 2$

4 $(3, 2)$

Extended-response question

a 12 kg/hr **b** $S = 180 - 12t$

c

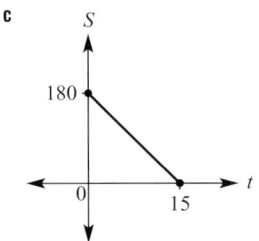

d 15 hours **e i** $P = 40 + 25h$ **ii** $415

Measurement
Multiple-choice questions

1 C **2** E **3** D **4** A **5** A

Short-answer questions

1 a 24.57 m^2 **b** 36 cm^2
2 4 tins
3 a 216 m^2 **b** 25.45 m^2
4 a $x = 4$ **b** $y = 8.5$

Extended-response question

a 45.71 m^2
b i 0.0377 m^2 **ii** 3.77 m^2
c 1213 **d** 37.85 m^3 **e** 19.45 m^3

Chapter 6

Pre-test

1 a 25 **b** 100 **c** 16 **d** 27 **e** 9
2 a 24, 1, 12, 2, 8, 3, 6, 4 **b** 45, 1, 15, 3, 9, 5
  c 2, 3 **d** 3, 5
3 a ab^2 **b** $5^3\,ab^2$ **c** $3^2\,x^2$ **d** $6ac^3$
4 a 2^3 **b** 2^6 **c** 2^5
5 a 3^4 **b** x^2y^2 **c** 2^2a^2 **d** $\dfrac{3^2}{4^2}$
6 a $\dfrac{1}{16}$ **b** $\dfrac{1}{8}$ **c** $\dfrac{1}{216}$ **d** $\dfrac{4}{9}$
7 a 3.73 **b** 24.62 **c** 18.37 **d** 4.40
8 a 5 **b** 4 **c** 2 **d** 3
9 a 38 **b** 2310 **c** 0.172 **d** 0.0018
  e 1000 **f** 10 000
10 a 15 **b** 4 **c** 125 **d** 32
11 a $10a - 4b$ **b** $3a + 3$ **c** $ab + 8a$ **d** $2ab^2 - a^2b$

Exercise 6A

1 a 25 **b** 8 **c** 27 **d** 16
2 a 3 **b** 6 **c** 1.2 **d** -7
  e $\dfrac{2}{3}$ **f** y **g** w **h** t
3 a 3 **b** 8 **c** 7 **d** 4
  e 11 **f** 13 **g** 9 **h** 2
4 a 2, 3 **b** 3, 5 **c** 2, 3, 5 **d** 7, 11
5 a a, a, a, a **b** b, b, b **c** x, x, x
  d $x \times p \times x \times p \times x \times p \times x \times p \times x \times p \times x \times p$
  e $5 \times a \times 5 \times a \times 5 \times a \times 5 \times a$
  f $3 \times y \times 3 \times y \times 3 \times y$
  g $4 \times x \times x \times y \times y \times y \times y \times y$
  h $p \times q \times p \times q$
  i $-3 \times s \times s \times s \times t \times t$
  j $6 \times x \times x \times x \times x \times y \times y \times y \times y$
  k $5 \times y \times z \times y \times z \times y \times z \times y \times z \times y \times z \times y \times z$
  l $4 \times a \times b \times a \times b \times a \times b$
6 a 36 **b** 16 **c** 243 **d** 12
  e -8 **f** -1 **g** 81 **h** 25
  i $\dfrac{8}{27}$ **j** $\dfrac{9}{16}$ **k** $\dfrac{1}{216}$ **l** $\dfrac{25}{4}$
  m $-\dfrac{8}{27}$ **n** $\dfrac{81}{256}$ **o** $\dfrac{1}{16}$ **p** $-\dfrac{3125}{32}$
7 a 3^3 **b** 8^6 **c** y^2 **d** $3x^3$
  e $4c^5$ **f** 5^3d^2 **g** x^2y^3 **h** 7^3b^2
8 a $\left(\dfrac{2}{3}\right)^4$ **b** $\left(\dfrac{3}{5}\right)^5$ **c** $\left(\dfrac{4}{7}\right)^2\left(\dfrac{1}{5}\right)^4$ **d** $\left(\dfrac{7x}{9}\right)^2\left(\dfrac{y}{4}\right)^3$
9 a $3^3x^3y^2$ **b** $(3x)^2(2y)^2$ or $3^22^2x^2y^2$
  c $(4d)^2(2e)^2$ or $4^22^2d^2e^2$ **d** $6^3b^2y^3$
  e $(3pq)^4$ or $3^4p^4q^4$ **f** $(7mn)^3$ or $7^3m^3n^3$

10 a 2×5 **b** 2^3 **c** $2^4 \times 3^2$ **d** 2^9

   e $2^3 \times 3^3$ **f** $2^2 \times 5^3$

11 a 36   **b** -216   **c** 1   **d** $-\dfrac{8}{27}$

   e -18   **f** 15   **g** -36   **h** 216

12 a 4   **b** 8   **c** 5   **d** 2

   e -4   **f** -2   **g** $\dfrac{1}{2}$ **h** 4

13 a i 10 mins   **ii** 20 mins   **iii** 30 mins

   b $2^{24} = 16\,777\,216$ cells

14 a $1000 \times 3^5 = \$243\,000$ **b** 5 years

15 7 months

16 a i 9   **ii** 9   **iii** -9   **iv** -9

   b Same signs give positive when multiplying

   c A positive answer is multiplied by the negative one out the front

17 a i 8   **ii** -8   **iii** -8   **iv** 8

   b i A positive cubed is positive

     ii A negative answer is multiplied by negative

   c ii A negative number cubed will be negative

     iii A positive answer is multiplied by negative one

18 a $\dfrac{1}{8}$ **b** $\dfrac{1}{16}$ **c** $\dfrac{1}{125}$ **d** $\dfrac{1}{64}$ **e** $\dfrac{49}{100}$

   f $\dfrac{81}{16}$ **g** $\dfrac{169}{25}$ **h** $\dfrac{12769}{100}$ **i** $\dfrac{289}{25}$

19 a LCM = 12, HCF = 2   **b** LCM = 84, HCF = 14

   c LCM = 72, HCF = 12   **d** LCM = 30, HCF = 5

   e LCM = 360, HCF = 10   **f** LCM = 300, HCF = 10

   g LCM = 1764, HCF = 14   **h** LCM = 13068, HCF = 198

Exercise 6B

1 a multiply, base, add   **b** divide, base, subtract

2 a $3 \times 3 \times 3 \times 3 \times 3 \times 3 = 3^6$

   b $6 \times 6 \times 6 \times 6 \times 6 \times 6 \times 6 = 6^7$

   c $\dfrac{5 \times 5 \times 5 \times 5 \times 5}{5 \times 5 \times 5} = 5^2$ **d** $\dfrac{9 \times 9 \times 9 \times 9}{9 \times 9} = 9^2$

3 a True   **b** True   **c** False   **d** False

   e True   **f** False   **g** False   **h** True

4 a 2^7 **b** 5^9 **c** 7^6 **d** 8^{10}

   e 3^8 **f** 6^{14} **g** 3^3 **h** 6^5

   i 5^3 **j** 10   **k** 9^3 **l** $(-2)^2$

5 a x^7 **b** a^9 **c** t^8 **d** y^5

   e d^3 **f** y^7 **g** b^8 **h** q^{11}

   i $x^7 y^5$ **j** $x^9 y^4$ **k** $5x^4 y^9$ **l** $4x^2 y^5 z$

   m $15m^5$ **n** $8e^6 f^4$ **o** $20c^7 d^2$ **p** $18y^2 z^7$

6 a a^2 **b** x^3 **c** q^{10} **d** d

   e $2b^5$ **f** $\dfrac{d^5}{3}$ **g** $2a^7$ **h** $2y^8$

   i $9m$ **j** $14x^3$ **k** $5y^2$ **l** $6a$

   m $\dfrac{m^5}{4}$ **n** $\dfrac{w}{5}$ **o** $\dfrac{a}{5}$ **p** $\dfrac{x^4}{9}$

   q $\dfrac{4x^6 y^3}{3}$ **r** $\dfrac{3st^2}{7}$ **s** $\dfrac{4mn}{3}$ **t** $-5x$

7 a b^6 **b** y^6 **c** c^7 **d** x

   e t **f** p^6 **g** d^6 **h** x^{10}

   i $4x^2 y^3$ **j** $6b^2 g$ **k** $3m^5 n^6$ **l** $p^5 q^4$

8 a $\dfrac{m^5}{n^5}$ **b** $\dfrac{x^4}{y^2}$ **c** $a^3 b^3$ **d** $\dfrac{6a^5}{c^7}$ **e** $6f^6$

   f $12x^4 b^2$ **g** $6k^3 m^3$ **h** $\dfrac{15x^4 y}{2}$ **i** $-\dfrac{3m^2 n^3}{2}$

9 a 12   **b** 8   **c** 3   **d** 3

   e 1   **f** 18   **g** 12   **h** 11

   i 4   **j** 15   **k** 2   **l** 39

10 a $7^2 = 49$ **b** 10   **c** $13^2 = 169$ **d** $2^3 = 8$

   e 101   **f** $200^2 = 40\,000$

   g $7 \times 31 = 217$ **h** $3 \times 50^2 = 7500$

11 a 7 ways   **b** 14 ways

12 a a^5, power of one not added

   b x^6, power of one not subtracted

   c $\dfrac{a^2}{2}$, $3 \div 6$ is $\dfrac{1}{2}$ not 2

   d $\dfrac{x^4}{2}$, numerator power is larger hence x^4 in numerator

   e $6x^{11}$, mutiply coefficients not add

   f $= a^3 \times a = a^4$, order of operations done incorrectly

13 a $4x$ **b** $12x^2$ **c** $10x^3$ **d** $-4x$

   e $40x^6$ **f** $\dfrac{5x}{4}$ **g** $\dfrac{8}{5}$ **h** $-20x^4$

14 a 2^{x+y} **b** 5^{a+b} **c** t^{x+y} **d** 3^{x-y}

   e 10^{p-y} **f** t^{x-y} **g** 2^{p+q-r} **h** 10^{p-q-r}

   i 2^{5a} **j** $a^{3x-2} b^{x+3}$ **k** $a^{x+y} b^{x+y}$ **l** $a^{x-y} b^{y-x}$

   m $w^{2-x} b^{x+3}$ **n** a^{x+y-2} **o** $p^a q^{b-5}$ **p** $4m^{y-3-2x}$

Exercise 6C

1 a multiply   **b** 1

2 a 16, 8, 4, 2, 1   **b** 64, 16, 4, 1

3 a $4 \times 4 \times 4 \times 4 \times 4 \times 4 = 4^6$

   b $12 \times 12 \times 12 \times 12 \times 12 \times 12 \times 12 \times 12 \times 12 = 12^9$

   c $x \times x \times x \times x \times x \times x \times x \times x = x^8$

   d $a \times a \times a \times a \times a \times a \times a \times a \times a \times a = a^{10}$

4 a y^{12} **b** m^{18} **c** x^{10} **d** b^{12}

   e 3^6 **f** 4^{15} **g** 3^{30} **h** 7^{10}

   i $5m^{16}$ **j** $4q^{28}$ **k** $-3c^{10}$ **l** $2j^{24}$

5 a 1   **b** 1   **c** 1   **d** 1

   e -1   **f** 1   **g** 1   **h** 1

   i 5   **j** -3   **k** 4   **l** -6

   m 1   **n** 3   **o** 1   **p** 0

6 a 4^7 **b** 3^9 **c** x **d** y^{13}

   e b^{14} **f** a^{10} **g** d^{24} **h** y^{16}

   i z^{25} **j** $a^{11} f^{13}$ **k** $x^{14} y^5$ **l** $5rs^8$

7 a 7^2 **b** 4   **c** 3^8 **d** 1   **e** y^3

   f h^2 **g** b^6 **h** x^5 **i** y^6

8 a $\dfrac{2}{x^5}$ **b** $\dfrac{10}{x^3}$ **c** $3x^8$ **d** $\dfrac{d^2e}{2}$ **e** $\dfrac{2m^6n}{5}$ **f** $\dfrac{a^{12}}{8}$

9 a i 400   **ii** 6400   **iii** 100

   b i 800   **ii** 12 800   **iii** 102 400   **c** 13 years

10 5 ways

11 a 4   **b** 1000   **c** 1   **d** 1   **e** 4   **f** 1

12 a 4×5 not $4 + 5$, a^{20}

   b power of 2 only applies to x^3, $3x^6$

   c power zero applies to whole bracket, 1

13 a i 2^{24} **ii** $(-2)^{30} = 2^{30}$ **iii** x^{84} **iv** a^{48}

   b i 2^{abc} **ii** a^{mnp} **iii** x^{6yz}

15 a 2^{12} **b** 2^{15} **c** 3^6 **d** 3^{20} **e** 5^{10}

   f 3^{50} **g** 2^{72} **h** 7^{80} **i** 10^{50}

Exercise 6D

1 a $a^m \times b^m$ **b** $\dfrac{a^m}{b^m}$

2 a $5a \times 5a \times 5a$

$$= 5 \times 5 \times 5 \times a \times a \times a$$
$$= 5^3 \times a^3$$

   b $ab \times ab \times ab \times ab$

$$= a \times a \times a \times a \times b \times b \times b \times b$$
$$= a^4 \times b^4$$

   c $\dfrac{x}{6} \times \dfrac{x}{6} \times \dfrac{x}{6}$

$$= \dfrac{x \times x \times x}{6 \times 6 \times 6}$$
$$= \dfrac{x^3}{6^3}$$

   d $\dfrac{a}{b} \times \dfrac{a}{b} \times \dfrac{a}{b} \times \dfrac{a}{b} \times \dfrac{a}{b}$

$$= \dfrac{a \times a \times a \times a \times a}{b \times b \times b \times b \times b}$$
$$= \dfrac{a^5}{b^5}$$

3 a $8x^3$ **b** $25y^2$ **c** $64a^6$ **d** $9r^2$

   e $-81b^4$ **f** $-343r^3$ **g** $(-2)^4 h^8 = 16h^8$ **h** $625c^8d^{12}$

   i $32x^{15}y^{10}$ **j** $9p^6q^{12}$ **k** $2x^6y^2$ **l** 1

   m $-27w^9y^3$ **n** $-4p^8q^2r^2$ **o** $25s^{14}t^2$ **p** $8x^{12}y^3z^9$

4 a $\dfrac{p^3}{q^3}$ **b** $\dfrac{x^4}{y^4}$ **c** $\dfrac{64}{y^3}$ **d** $\dfrac{625}{p^8}$

   e $\dfrac{4}{r^6}$ **f** $\dfrac{s^6}{49}$ **g** $\dfrac{32m^5}{n^5}$ **h** $\dfrac{8a^6}{27}$

   i $\dfrac{27n^9}{8m^{12}}$ **j** $\dfrac{16r^4}{n^4}$ **k** $\dfrac{9f^2}{64g^{10}}$ **l** $\dfrac{25w^8y^2}{4x^6}$

   m $\dfrac{9x^2}{4y^6g^{10}}$ **n** $\dfrac{27k^3m^9}{64n^{21}}$ **o** $-\dfrac{25w^8y^2}{4z^2x^6}$ **p** $\dfrac{9x^4y^6}{4a^{10}b^6}$

5 a $9ab^2$ **b** $27ab^6$ **c** $-12a^8b^8$ **d** $54x^6y^9$

   e $-64b^6c^{15}d^3$ **f** $8a^4$ **g** $9a^5$ **h** $-40a^{15}b^3$

   i $160m^{15}p^5t^{10}$ **j** $-49d^4f^8g^2$ **k** $1024x^{12}y^3z^9$ **l** $-16a^8b^7$

6 a x^{24} **b** $256x^{24}$ **c** $a^{17}b^8$ **d** $a^{10}b^{11}$

   e $8m^5n^3$ **f** $12c^8d^7$ **g** $\dfrac{-27x^6}{125a^{15}b^9}$ **h** $-3a^4b^5$

   i $15n$ **j** $a^{11}bc^5$ **k** $x^{11}y^2z$ **l** $\dfrac{r^9t^{10}}{s}$

7 a i 8   **ii** 125   **b** $N = \dfrac{t^3}{8}$

   c i 27   **ii** 8   **d i** 8   **ii** 2

8 a 2   **b** 4   **c** 2

   d 2   **e** 1   **f** 14

9 a By simplifying, there are smaller numbers to raise to powers

   b i 8   **ii** 16   **iii** $\dfrac{1}{81}$ **iv** $\dfrac{1}{1000}$

10 a F, $(-2)^2 = +(2)^2$ **b** T, $(-3)^3 = -(3)^3$

   c T, $(-5)^5 = -(5)^5$ **d** F, $(-4)^4 = +(4)^4$

11 a 25   **b** 13   **c** no

   d no, $(3 - 2)^2 \neq 3^2 - 2^2$

   e i T   **ii** F   **iii** T   **iv** F

Exercise 6E

1 a $\dfrac{1}{2^2}$ **b** $\dfrac{1}{3^2}$ **c** $\dfrac{1}{5^3}$ **d** $\dfrac{1}{3^3}$

2 a

Index form	3^4	3^3	3^2	3^1
Whole number or fraction	81	27	9	3

Index form	3^0	3^{-1}	3^{-2}	3^{-3}
Whole number or fraction	1	$\dfrac{1}{3}$	$\dfrac{1}{9} = \dfrac{1}{3^2}$	$\dfrac{1}{27} = \dfrac{1}{3^3}$

b

Index form	10^4	10^3	10^2	10^1
Whole number or fraction	10000	1000	100	10

Index form	10^0	10^{-1}	10^{-2}	10^{-3}
Whole number or fraction	1	$\dfrac{1}{10}$	$\dfrac{1}{100} = \dfrac{1}{10^2}$	$\dfrac{1}{1000} = \dfrac{1}{10^3}$

3 a $\dfrac{1}{x}$ **b** $\dfrac{1}{a^4}$ **c** $\dfrac{1}{b^6}$ **d** $\dfrac{1}{25}$

   e $\dfrac{1}{64}$ **f** $\dfrac{1}{9}$ **g** $\dfrac{5}{x^2}$ **h** $\dfrac{4}{y^3}$

   i $\dfrac{3}{m^5}$ **j** $\dfrac{p^7}{q^2}$ **k** $\dfrac{m}{n^4}$ **l** $\dfrac{x^4}{y^4}$

   m $\dfrac{2}{a^3b}$ **n** $\dfrac{7}{r^2s^3}$ **o** $\dfrac{v^2}{5u^8}$ **p** $\dfrac{1}{9m^3n^5}$

4 a y **b** b^2 **c** m^5 **d** x^4

   e $7q$ **f** $3t^2$ **g** $5h^4$ **h** $4p^4$

   i ab^2 **j** de **k** $2m^3n^2$ **l** $\dfrac{x^2y^5}{3}$

   m $-\dfrac{3y^4}{7}$ **n** $-2b^8$ **o** $-\dfrac{3gh^3}{4}$ **p** $\dfrac{9u^2t^2}{5}$

5 a $\dfrac{b^3}{a^3}$ **b** $\dfrac{y^5}{x^2}$ **c** $\dfrac{h^3}{g^2}$ **d** $\dfrac{n}{m}$

   e $\dfrac{343}{5}$ **f** $\dfrac{64}{9}$ **g** $\dfrac{6}{25}$ **h** 1

6 a $\dfrac{7x^4}{y^3}$ **b** $\dfrac{u^3}{v^2}$ **c** $\dfrac{y^3}{5a^3}$ **d** $\dfrac{2b^5}{a^4c^2}$

   e $\dfrac{5a^2b^2}{6c^4d}$ **f** $\dfrac{4h^3m^2}{5k^2p}$ **g** $\dfrac{12w^6}{tu^2v^2}$ **h** $\dfrac{mn^4x^2}{16y^5}$

7 a $\dfrac{1}{5}$ **b** $\dfrac{1}{9}$ **c** $\dfrac{1}{16}$ **d** $-\dfrac{1}{25}$

   e $\dfrac{1}{25}$ **f** $-\dfrac{1}{200}$ **g** $-\dfrac{3}{4}$ **h** $\dfrac{1}{2}$

   i $\dfrac{1}{36}$ **j** $\dfrac{1}{8}$ **k** $\dfrac{4}{25}$ **l** $\dfrac{7}{81}$

   m 8   **n** 100   **o** -250   **p** 16

   q -10   **r** 64   **s** $\dfrac{64}{9}$ **t** $-\dfrac{27}{64}$

   u 100   **v** $\dfrac{1}{3}$ **w** -2   **x** 49

8 1.95 g

9 a -4   **b** -4   **c** -4   **d** -1   **e** -2   **f** -1

10 a negative power only applies to x, $\dfrac{2}{x^2}$

   b $5 = 5^1$ has a positive power, $5a^{-4}$

   c $\dfrac{2}{3^{-2}b^{-2}} = 2 \times 3^2 \times b^2 = 18b^2$

11 a $1 \div \dfrac{2}{3} = 1 \times \dfrac{3}{2}$ **b i** $\dfrac{4}{5}$ **ii** $\dfrac{7}{2}$ **iii** $\dfrac{3}{x}$ **iv** $\dfrac{b}{a}$

   c $(\text{fraction})^{-1} = $ reciprocal of fraction

   d i $\dfrac{9}{4}$ **ii** $\dfrac{25}{16}$ **iii** 32   **iv** $\dfrac{27}{343}$

12 a 4   **b** 4   **c** 2   **d** 3   **e** 2

   f 4   **g** $\dfrac{3}{2}$ **h** 4   **i** $\dfrac{7}{3}$

Exercise 6F

1 a 10 000   **b** 1000   **c** 100 000

   d 1000   **e** 100 000   **f** 10 000

2 a 10^5 **b** 10^2 **c** 10^9

3 a positive   **b** negative   **c** positive   **d** negative

4 a 4×10^4 **b** 2.3×10^{12} **c** 1.6×10^{10}

   d -7.2×10^6 **e** -3.5×10^3 **f** -8.8×10^6

   g 5.2×10^3 **h** 3×10^6 **i** 2.1×10^4

5 a 3×10^{-6} **b** 4×10^{-4} **c** -8.76×10^{-3}

   d 7.3×10^{-10} **e** -3×10^{-5} **f** 1.25×10^{-10}

   g -8.09×10^{-9} **h** 2.4×10^{-8} **i** 3.45×10^{-5}

6 a 6×10^3 **b** 7.2×10^5 **c** 3.245×10^2

   d $7.869\,03 \times 10^3$ **e** $8.459\,12 \times 10^3$ **f** 2×10^{-1}

   g 3.28×10^{-4} **h** 9.87×10^{-3} **i** -1×10^{-5}

   j -4.601×10^8 **k** 1.7467×10^4 **l** -1.28×10^2

7 a 57 000   **b** 3 600 000   **c** 430 000 000

   d 32 100 000   **e** 423 000   **f** 90 400 000 000

   g 197 000 000   **h** 709   **i** 635 700

8 a 0.000 12   **b** 0.000 0046   **c** 0.000 000 0008

   d 0.000 0352   **e** 0.3678   **f** 0.000 000 123

   g 0.000 09   **h** 0.05   **i** 0.4

9 a 6×10^{24} **b** 4×10^7 **c** 1×10^{-10}

   d 1.5×10^8 **e** 6.67×10^{-11} **f** 1.5×10^{-4}

   g 4.5×10^9

10 a 4 600 000 000   **b** 8 000 000 000 000   **c** 384 000

   d 0.0038   **e** 0.000 000 000 00001   **f** 720 000

11 a 3.6×10^7 **b** 3.6×10^5 **c** 4.92×10^{-1}

   d 3.8×10^{-4} **e** 2.1×10^{-6} **f** 5.2×10^{-8}

   g 4×10^{-9} **h** 1.392×10^{-7} **i** 3.95×10^3

   j 4.38×10^3 **k** 4.3×10^5 **l** 5×10^2

   m 8.28×10^6 **n** 3×10^{11}

12 a $\$1.84 \times 10^9$ **b** $\$2.647 \times 10^9$

13 1.62×10^9 km   **14** 2.126×10^{-2} g

15 a 3.2×10^4 **b** 4.1×10^6 **c** 3.17×10^4

   d 5.714×10^5 **e** 1.3×10^4 **f** 9.2×10^1

   g 3×10^5 **h** 4.6×10^5 **i** 6.1×10^{-2}

   j 4.24   **k** 1.013×10^{-3} **l** 4.9×10^4

   m 2×10^{-5} **n** 4×10^{-6} **o** 3.72×10^{-4}

   p 4.001×10^{-8}

16 a 8×10^6 **b** 9×10^8 **c** 6.25×10^{-4}

   d 3.375×10^{-9} **e** 1.25×10^8 **f** 4×10^6

   g 9×10^{-4} **h** 2.5×10^4

17 a 6×10^6 **b** 8×10^{11} **c** 2×10^4

   d 3×10^9 **e** 5.6×10^5 **f** 1.2×10^8

   g 1.2×10^3 **h** 9×10^3 **i** 9×10^{-9}

   j 7.5×10^{-8} **k** 1.5×10^{-5} **l** 1

18 $5 \times 10^2 = 500$ seconds

19 a 3×10^{-4} km = 30 cm

   b 1×10^{-3} seconds (one thousandth of a second)
= 0.001 seconds

Exercise 6G

1 a 57 260, 57 300, 57 000, 60 000

   b 4 170 200, 4 170 000, 4 170 000, 4 200 000, 4 000 000

   c 0.003 661, 0.003 66, 0.0037, 0.004

   d 24.871, 24.87, 24.9, 25, 20

2 a yes   **b** no   **c** no   **d** no   **e** yes

   f yes   **g** yes   **h** no   **i** no

3 a 3   **b** 4   **c** 5   **d** 2

   e 3   **f** 1   **g** 3   **h** 3

   i 3   **j** 4   **k** 3   **l** 3

4 a 2.42×10^5 **b** 1.71×10^5 **c** 2.83×10^3

   d 3.25×10^6 **e** 3.43×10^{-4} **f** 6.86×10^{-3}

   g 1.46×10^{-2} **h** 1.03×10^{-3} **i** 2.34×10^1

   j 3.26×10^2 **k** 1.96×10^1 **l** 1.72×10^{-1}

5 a 4.78×10^4 **b** 2.2×10^4 **c** 4.833×10^6

   d 3.7×10^1 **e** 9.95×10^1 **f** 1.443×10^{-2}

   g 2×10^{-3} **h** 9×10^{-2} **i** 1×10^{-4}

6 a 2.441×10^{-4} **b** 2.107×10^{-6} **c** -4.824×10^{15}

   d 4.55×10^{-5} **e** 1.917×10^{12} **f** 1.995×10^8

   g 3.843×10^2 **h** 1.71×10^{-11} **i** 1.524×10^8

   j 3.325×10^{15} **k** 4×10^3 **l** -9.077×10^{-1}

7 a 9.3574×10^1 **b** 2.1893×10^5 **c** 8.6000×10^5

   d 8.6288×10^{-2} **e** 2.2985×10^{15} **f** 3.5741×10^{28}

   g 6.4×10^7 **h** 1.2333×10^9 **i** 1.8293

   j 5.4459×10^{-1}

8 1.98×10^{30} kg

9 1.39×10^6 km

10 1.09×10^{12} km^3

11 $2421 \times 10^3, 24.2 \times 10^5, 2.41 \times 10^6, 0.239 \times 10^7, 0.02 \times 10^8$

12 a 4.26×10^6 **b** 9.1×10^{-3} **c** 5.04×10^{11}

   d 1.931×10^{-1} **e** 2.1×10^6 **f** 6.14×10^{-11}

13 should be 8.8×10^{10}

14 a i 2.30×10^2 **ii** 4.90×10^{-2} **iii** 4.00×10^6

   b It is zero

   c It clarifies the precision of the number

15 a 5.40046×10^{12}

   b i 4.32×10^{13} **ii** 1.61×10^{19} **iii** 4.01×10^{51}

Exercise 6H

1 a $4, 2$ **b** $8, 2$ **c** $9, 3$ **d** $27, 3$

   e $16, 4$ **f** $64, 4$

2 a True   **b** False   **c** True   **d** True

   e False   **f** False   **g** False

3 a 2.6458 **b** 3.6056 **c** 9.1104

4 a $\sqrt{3}$ **b** $\sqrt{7}$ **c** $\sqrt[3]{5}$ **d** $\sqrt[3]{12}$

   e $\sqrt[5]{31}$ **f** $\sqrt[7]{18}$ **g** $\sqrt[9]{9}$ **h** $\sqrt[8]{3}$

5 a $8^{\frac{1}{2}}$ **b** $19^{\frac{1}{2}}$ **c** $10^{\frac{1}{3}}$ **d** $31^{\frac{1}{3}}$

   e $5^{\frac{1}{4}}$ **f** $9^{\frac{1}{5}}$ **g** $11^{\frac{1}{8}}$ **h** $20^{\frac{1}{11}}$

6 a 5 **b** 7 **c** 9 **d** 13

   e 2 **f** 4 **g** 5 **h** 10

   i 2 **j** 3 **k** 5 **l** 2

7 a a **b** $a^{\frac{2}{3}}$ **c** a^2 **d** $a^{\frac{5}{2}}$

   e $x^{\frac{1}{3}}$ **f** x **g** $x^{\frac{5}{6}}$ **h** x

   i y **j** y^2 **k** $y^{\frac{3}{2}}$ **l** $x^{\frac{1}{4}}$

   m $x^{\frac{8}{3}}$ **n** $a^{\frac{2}{15}}$ **o** $a^{\frac{3}{8}}$ **p** $n^{\frac{4}{3}}$

8 a $a^{\frac{4}{3}}$ **b** $a^{\frac{7}{10}}$ **c** $a^{\frac{23}{21}}$ **d** $a^{\frac{8}{3}}$

   e $b^{\frac{1}{6}}$ **f** $x^{\frac{2}{15}}$

9 a $\dfrac{1}{2}$ **b** $\dfrac{1}{2}$ **c** $\dfrac{1}{2}$ **d** $\dfrac{1}{3}$

   e $\dfrac{1}{5}$ **f** $\dfrac{1}{3}$ **g** $\dfrac{1}{10}$ **h** $\dfrac{1}{4}$

10 a 9 **b** 16 **c** 27 **d** 125

   e 32 **f** 32 **g** 729 **h** 3125

11 a $\sqrt{29}$ **b** $\sqrt{13}$ **c** $\sqrt{65}$ **d** $\sqrt{125}$

   e $\sqrt{10}$ **f** $\sqrt{1700}$

12 a $a^{\frac{1}{2}+\left(-\frac{1}{2}\right)} = a^0 = 1$ **b** $a^{\frac{2}{3}+\left(-\frac{2}{3}\right)} = a^0 = 1$

   c $a^{\frac{4}{7}-\frac{4}{7}} = a^0 = 1$ **d** $a^{\frac{5}{6}-\frac{5}{6}} = a^0 = 1$

   e $a^{\frac{1}{4}} \times a^{-\frac{1}{4}} = a^{\frac{1}{4}+\left(-\frac{1}{4}\right)} = a^0 = 1$

   f $a^2 \div a^2 = a^{2-2} = a^0 = 1$

13 Brackets needed for fractional power, $9 \wedge (1/2) = 3$

14 a i 3 **ii** 5 **iii** 10

   b a **c** $(a^2)^{\frac{1}{2}} = a^{2 \times \frac{1}{2}} = a$

   d i 4 **ii** 9 **iii** 36

   e a **f** $(a^{\frac{1}{2}})^2 = a^{\frac{1}{2} \times 2} = a$

   g i a **ii** a **iii** a **iv** a

15 a $\dfrac{4}{5}$ **b** $\dfrac{3}{7}$ **c** $\dfrac{2}{9}$ **d** $\dfrac{2}{3}$

   e $\dfrac{4}{5}$ **f** $\dfrac{2}{3}$ **g** $\dfrac{4}{5}$ **h** $\dfrac{10}{7}$

16 a $\dfrac{2}{3}$ **b** $\dfrac{12}{7}$ **c** $\dfrac{5}{2}$ **d** $\dfrac{5}{6}$

Exercise 6I

1 a like   **b** like   **c** unlike   **d** unlike

   e unlike   **f** like   **g** like   **h** unlike

2 a both $= 3.162$ **b** both $= 4.583$

   c both $= 1.732$ **d** both $= 2.449$

3 a $8\sqrt{7}$ **b** $8\sqrt{11}$ **c** $9\sqrt{5}$ **d** $4\sqrt{6}$

   e $7\sqrt{3}+2\sqrt{5}$ **f** $9\sqrt{7}+3\sqrt{5}$ **g** $-5\sqrt{5}$ **h** $-4\sqrt{7}$

   i $5\sqrt{7}$ **j** $-\sqrt{14}$ **k** $7\sqrt{2}-\sqrt{5}$ **l** $3\sqrt{3}+2\sqrt{7}$

4 a $\sqrt{30}$ **b** $\sqrt{21}$ **c** $\sqrt{70}$ **d** 4

   e 6 **f** $\sqrt{22}$ **g** 3 **h** 12

   i $\sqrt{3}$ **j** $\sqrt{10}$ **k** $\sqrt{7}$ **l** $\sqrt{3}$

   m 3 **n** 4 **o** $\sqrt{7}$

5 a $8-3\sqrt{3}$ **b** $6\sqrt{2}-\sqrt{3}$ **c** $7\sqrt{5}+1$

   d $\dfrac{5\sqrt{2}}{6}$ **e** $\dfrac{7\sqrt{7}}{10}$ **f** $-\dfrac{3\sqrt{6}}{14}$

   g $\dfrac{2\sqrt{10}}{3}$ **h** $5+\dfrac{\sqrt{3}}{3}$ **i** $-\dfrac{19\sqrt{8}}{56}$

6 a $15\sqrt{6}$ b $6\sqrt{21}$ c $8\sqrt{30}$ d $10\sqrt{18}$

   e $2\sqrt{3}$ f $3\sqrt{6}$ g $4\sqrt{14}$ h $\dfrac{\sqrt{2}}{2}$

7 a $6\sqrt{15}+2\sqrt{3}$ b $\sqrt{10}+\sqrt{15}$ c $5\sqrt{12}+15\sqrt{30}$

   d $14\sqrt{30}-70$ e $13-2\sqrt{39}$ f $\sqrt{35}-10$

8 a $2\sqrt{2}$ b $2\sqrt{3}$ c $3\sqrt{3}$ d $3\sqrt{5}$

   e $5\sqrt{3}$ f $10\sqrt{2}$ g $2\sqrt{15}$ h $6\sqrt{2}$

9 a $5\sqrt{2}$ b $\sqrt{2}$ c $4\sqrt{2}$ d $\sqrt{3}$

   e $6\sqrt{2}$ f $5\sqrt{3}$ g $2\sqrt{5}$ h $4\sqrt{3}$

10 a $2+\sqrt{10}+\sqrt{6}+\sqrt{15}$ b $3+\sqrt{6}-\sqrt{15}-\sqrt{10}$

   c $6\sqrt{10}+8\sqrt{5}-3\sqrt{2}-4$ d $2+3\sqrt{2}-6\sqrt{7}-9\sqrt{14}$

   e 1 f 4 g 15 h 123

   i $3+2\sqrt{2}$ j $15-6\sqrt{6}$ k $13-4\sqrt{3}$ l $22+4\sqrt{10}$

Challenges

1 a 4 b 1 c 6

2 a 6 b 30

3 $\dfrac{9}{4}$ 4 a $2t^2$ b $\dfrac{2}{t}$

5 100 minutes   6 $-\dfrac{2}{3}$

7 a i $2^{\frac{3}{4}}$ ii $2^{\frac{7}{8}}$ iii $2^{\frac{15}{16}}$ b 2

8 2^7

9 a $7\sqrt{2}$ b $\dfrac{3}{\sqrt{2}}$ c $12\sqrt{10}$

11 a $x=0$ or 1 b $x=1$ or 2

Multiple-choice questions

1 D 2 B 3 E 4 A 5 C 6 B
7 D 8 C 9 E 10 B 11 C 12 A

Short-answer questions

1 a 3^4 b $2x^3y^2$ c $3a^2b^2$ d $\left(\dfrac{3}{5}\right)^3\times\left(\dfrac{1}{7}\right)^2$

2 a $3^2\times5$ b $2^2\times3\times5^2$

3 a x^{10} b $12a^5b^6c$ c $12m^4n^4$ d a^9

   e x^3y^2 f $\dfrac{b^2}{2a^2}$

4 a m^6 b $9a^8$ c $-32a^{10}b^5$ d $3b$

   e 2 f $\dfrac{a^6}{27}$

5 a $\dfrac{1}{x^3}$ b $\dfrac{4}{t^3}$ c $\dfrac{1}{9t^2}$ d $\dfrac{2x^2}{3y^3}$

   e $\dfrac{5}{x^6y^3}$ f $5m^3$

6 a $\dfrac{x^2}{2y^2}$ b $\dfrac{x^3y^2}{9}$ c $8m^7n^3$

7 0.0012, 35.4×10^{-3}, 3.22×10^{-1}, 0.4, 0.007×10^2, 2.35

8 a 324 b $172\,500$ c 0.2753 d 0.00149

9 a 2.25×10^7 people b 9.63×10^6 km^2

   c 3.34×10^{-9} seconds d 2.94×10^{-7} m

10 a 2.19×10^5 b 1.2×10^{-2}

   c 4.32×10^{-7} d 5×10^6

11 a 1.2×10^{55} b 4.3×10^{-5}

12 a 2 b 5 c 7 d 3 e $\dfrac{1}{3}$ f $\dfrac{1}{11}$

13 a s^2 b $9t^{\frac{3}{2}}$ c $15x^{\frac{5}{2}}$ d $9m^4n^{\frac{3}{4}}$

   e $\dfrac{t^{\frac{1}{2}}}{2}$ f $4a^{\frac{2}{3}}$

14 a $7\sqrt{7}+2$ b $\sqrt{3}+9\sqrt{2}$ c 8 d $\sqrt{15}$

   e $2\sqrt{14}$ f $15\sqrt{22}$ g $\sqrt{6}$ h 10 i $\dfrac{\sqrt{5}}{2}$

Extended-response questions

1 a $\dfrac{16x^6}{3}$ b $\dfrac{8b^8}{15a^2}$ c $\dfrac{5m^8}{n^{10}}$ d $3x$

2 a 5.93×10^{-11} N b i 1.50×10^{11} m ii 3.53×10^{22} N

   c Earth $a=9.81$ ms^{-2}, Mars $a=3.77$ ms^{-2}

   Acceleration due to gravity on Earth is more than $2\dfrac{1}{2}$ times that on Mars

Chapter 7

Pre-test

1 a obtuse b acute c reflex d right

2 a isosceles b equilateral

   c scalene d right-angled

   e equilateral f right-angled, isosceles triangle

3 a $60°$ b $75°$ each c $50°$

4 a $x=55$ b $x=100$ c $x=110$ d $x=45$

   e $x=40$ f $x=108$

5 a $a=60$ b $b=110$ c $a=60, b=120$

6 a pentagon b parallelogram c trapezium

   d rhombus e hexagon f nonagon

Exercise 7A

1 a right b $180°$ c revolution d obtuse

   e acute f $180°$ g $90°$

   h supplementary i $180°$ j equal

2 a isosceles triangle b obtuse angle triangle

   c equilateral triangle d isosceles triangle

   e acute angled triangle f scalene triangle

   g right-angled triangle

3 a i $\angle BAC$ ii obtuse iv $120°$

   b i $\angle PRQ$ ii acute iv $30°$

   c i $\angle XYZ$ ii reflex iv $310°$

d **i** $\angle SRT$ **ii** straight angle   **iv** 180°

e **i** $\angle ROB$ **ii** obtuse   **iv** 103°

f **i** $\angle AOB$ **ii** right   **iv** 90°

4 a 50°   **b** 90°   **c** 101°

   d 202°   **e** 180°   **f** 360°

5 a i 125°   **ii** 35°   **b i** 149°   **ii** 59°

   c i 106°   **ii** 16°   **d i** 170°   **ii** 80°

   e i 91°   **ii** 1°   **f i** 158°   **ii** 68°

   g i 142°   **ii** 52°   **h i** 115°   **ii** 25°

   i i 133°   **ii** 43°   **j i** 103°   **ii** 13°

6 a C   **b** S   **c** N   **d** C

   e S   **f** N   **g** S   **h** N

7 a $a = 63°$ **b** $a = 71°$ **c** $a = 38°$

   d $a = 147°$ **e** $a = 233°$ **f** $a = 33°$

8 a obtuse isosceles, 40°   **b** acute scalene, 30°

   c right-angled scalene, 90°   **d** equilateral, 60°

   e obtuse isosceles, 100°   **f** right-angled isosceles, 45°

   g obtuse scalene, 100°   **h** equilateral, 60°

   i obtuse isosceles, 120°   **j** obtuse isosceles, 40°

   k right-angled scalene, 90°   **l** acute scalene, 70°

9 a $s = 120$ **b** $t = 20$ **c** $r = 70$

   d $a = 60, x = 120$ **e** $a = 100, b = 140$ **f** $c = 115, d = 65$

10 a 360°   **b** 90°   **c** 60°   **d** 90°

   e 432°   **f** 6°   **g** 720°   **h** 8640°

11 a $x = 56$ **b** $x = 155$ **c** $x = 116$

12 a 90°   **b** 150°   **c** 15°

   d 165°   **e** 157.5°   **f** 80°

   g 177.5°   **h** 171°   **i** 121.5°

13 $\angle AOB + \angle ABO = 120°$ (exterior angle of triangle)

         $\angle AOB = 30°$

   (reflex) $x = 330$

14 AO = BO (radii)

   $\triangle AOB$ is isoceles, 2 sides equal, $\angle AOB = 116°$

   $\therefore \angle OAB = 32°$, base angles of isosceles triangle

15 a 160°   **b** 165°

   c $\angle WYZ + a° + b° = 180°$ angle sum of a triangle

       $\angle XYZ + \angle WYZ = 180°$ straight line

       $\therefore \angle XYZ = a° + b°$

16 Let the interior angles of any triangle be a, b and c

   Now $a + b + c = 180°$

   The exterior angles become, $180° - a°$, $180° - b°$,

   $180° - c°$ (straight line)

     Exterior sum $= (180 - a) + (180 - b) + (180 - c)$

               $= 540 - a - b - c$

               $= 540 - (a + b + c)$

               $= 540 - 180$

               $= 360°$

17 a $4x = 90, x = 22.5$ **b** $3x = 180, x = 60$

   c $10x = 360, x = 36$ **d** $2(x + 15) + x = 180, x = 50$

   e $2x + 20 = 140, x = 60$ **f** $6x + 90 = 360, x = 45$

Exercise 7B

1 a equal   **b** equal   **c** supplementary

2 a 125°, alternate angles in ∥ lines

   b 110°, cointerior angles in ∥ lines

   c 80°, corresponding angles in ∥ lines

   d 66°, alternate angles in ∥ lines

   e 96°, vertically opposite

   f 126°, corresponding angles on ∥ lines

   g 62°, supplementary angles

   h 115°, corresponding angles on ∥ lines

   i 116°, cointerior angles on ∥ lines

3 a no, alternate angles are not equal

   b yes, corresponding angles are equal

   c yes, alternate angles are equal

   d no, cointerior angles don't add to 180°

   e yes, cointerior angles add to 180°

   f yes, corresponding angles are equal

   g no, corresponding angles are not equal

   h no, alternate angles are not equal

   i no, cointerior angles do not add to 180°

4 a $a = 60, b = 120$ **b** $c = 95, d = 95$

   c $e = 100, f = 100, g = 100$ **d** $a = 110, b = 70$

   e $a = 100, b = 80, c = 80$

   f $e = 140, f = 140, d = 140$

5 a $x = 70, y = 40$ **b** $t = 58, z = 122$

   c $u = 110, v = 50, w = 50$ **d** $x = 118$

   e $x = 295$ **f** $x = 79$

6 a 105°   **b** 105°   **c** 56°

   d 105°   **e** 90°   **f** 85°

7 a 56   **b** 120   **c** 50

8 a $180° - a°$ **b** $180° - a°$

   c $180° - (a° + b°)$ **d** $180° - (a° + b°)$

   e $a° + c°$ **f** $180° - 2c°$

9 $\angle ABC = 100°$

   $\angle BCD = 80°$

   $\therefore$ AB ∥ DC as cointerior angles are supplementary

   $\angle ABC + \angle BCD = 180°$

10 a cointerior angles on parallel lines add to 180°

   b alternate angles are equal, on parallel lines

   c $\triangle ABC => a + b + c = 180$ and these are the three angles

      of the triangle

11 a $\angle BAE = 180° - a°$ (alternate angles and AB ∥ DE)

      $\angle ABC = 180° - c° - (180 - a)°$ (angle sum of a triangle)

              $= 180° - c° - 180° + a°$

              $= -c° + a°$

              $= a° - c°$

   b $\angle ABD = 180° - (a° + b°)$ (angle sum of triangle $\triangle ABD$)

      $\angle ABC + \angle ABD = 180°$ (straight line)

         $\therefore \angle ABC = a° + b°$

c construct XY through B parallel to AE

$\therefore \angle ABY = a°$ (alternate angles, $AE \parallel XY$)

$\therefore \angle CBY = b°$ (alternate angles, $DC \parallel XY$)

$\therefore \angle ABC = a° + b°$

d Construct XY through A parallel to ED

Now

$\angle XAD = 180° - b°$ (co-interior angles, $ED \parallel XY$)

$\angle DAB = 360° - a°$ (revolution)

$\therefore \angle XAB = 360° - a° - (180° - b°)$

$\qquad = 180° + b° - a°$

$\angle ABC = \angle XAB$ (alternate angles and $XY \parallel BC$)

Exercise 7C

1 a 5   **b** 7   **c** 4   **d** 11   **e** 9   **f** 12

2 a 720°   **b** 1080°   **c** 1620°

3 a parallel   **b** right   **c** trapezium   **d** equal

4 a convex quadrilateral   **b** non-convex hexagon

    c non-convex heptagon

5 a 115   **b** 159   **c** 30

    d 121   **e** 140   **f** 220

6 a 110   **b** 70   **c** 54

    d 33   **e** 63   **f** 109

7 a 110   **b** 150

    c 210   **d** 20

    e $b = 108, a = 72$ **f** $a = 140, b = 40$

    g $b = 120, a = 240$ **h** $b = 120\frac{4}{7}, a = 231\frac{3}{7}$

    i 108

8 a parallelogram, rectangle, kite   **b** rectangle, square

    c square, rectangle   **d** square, rhombus, kite

9 a 16   **b** 25   **c** 102

10 a 255   **b** 80   **c** 115   **d** 37   **e** 28   **f** 111

11 A parallelogram has opposite sides parallel and equal and rectangles, squares and rhombi have these properties (and more) and are therefore all parallelograms.

12 a $S = 180(n - 2)$ **b** $I = \dfrac{180(n-2)}{n}$ **c** $E = \dfrac{360}{n}$ **d** 36°

13 a i one   **ii** two   **iii** five   **b** $(n - 3)$

14 $(180 - a) + (180 - b) + (180 - c) + (180 - d) + (180 - e) = 360$

(sum of exterior angles is 360°)

$\qquad 180 + 180 + 180 + 180 + 180 - (a + b + c + d + e) = 360$

$\qquad\qquad\qquad\qquad\qquad 900 - (a + b + c + d + e) = 360$

$\qquad\qquad\qquad\qquad\qquad\qquad\qquad a + b + c + d + e = 540$

    a $a + b + c + d + e + f = 720$

    b $a + b + c + d + e + f + g = 900$

Exercise 7D

1 a size   **b** $\triangle ABC \equiv \triangle STU$ **c** SAS, RHS, AAS

2 a i XY **ii** XZ **iii** YZ

    b i $\angle A$ **ii** $\angle B$ **iii** $\angle C$

3 a $\triangle ABC \equiv \triangle FGH$ **b** $\triangle DEF \equiv \triangle STU$

    c $\triangle AMP \equiv \triangle CBD$ **d** $\triangle BMW \equiv \triangle SLK$

4 a SAS   **b** AAS   **c** RHS   **d** SAS

    e SSS   **f** RHS   **g** AAS   **h** SSS

5 a $x = 3, y = 5$ **b** $x = 2, y = 6$

    c $a = 105, b = 40$ **d** $a = 65, b = 85$

    e $x = 2.5, b = 29$ **f** $a = 142, x = 9.21 , b = 7$

    g $y = 4.2, a = 28$ **h** $a = 6.5, b = 60$

6 a $\triangle ABC \equiv \triangle STU$, RHS   **b** $\triangle DEF \equiv \triangle GHI$, SSS

    c $\triangle ABC \equiv \triangle DEF$, SAS   **d** $\triangle ABC \equiv \triangle GHI$, AAS

7 $\triangle PBR \equiv \triangle FDE$

   $\triangle LMN \equiv \triangle KIJ$

   $\triangle FGH \equiv \triangle BCD$

   $\triangle MNO \equiv \triangle RQP$

8 a $BC = 13$ **b** $BC = 85$

9 no – they can all be different sizes, one might have all sides 2 cm and another all sides 5 cm.

10 a one given, the other pair are vertically opposite

    b AAS

11 a SSS   **b** equal

12 a one given ($BA = BC$) and side BD is common

    b SAS

    c $\triangle ABD \equiv \triangle CBD$

    d $\angle ADB = \angle CDB$ (corresponding angles in congruent triangles)

       but $\angle ADB + \angle CDB = 180°$ (straight angle)

       $\therefore \angle ADB = \angle CDB = 90°$

       and AC is perpendicular to DB

Exercise 7E

1 a BD **b** AC **c** AC

2 $OA = OB$ radii of circle centre O

3 a $\angle ECD$ **b** $\angle CBA$ **c** $\angle DEC$

4 a SSS   **b** $\angle BMC$

5 a $AD = CD$ (given)

       $\angle DAB = \angle DCB = 90°$ (given)

       DB is common

       $\therefore \triangle ABD \equiv \triangle CBD$ (RHS)

    b AC is common

       $AD = AB$ (given)

       $\angle DAC = \angle BAC$ (given)

       $\therefore \triangle ADC \equiv \triangle ABC$ (SAS)

    c AC is common

       $\angle ADC = \angle ABC$ (given)

       $\angle DAC = \angle BAC$ (given)

       $\triangle ADC \equiv \triangle ABC$ (AAS)

    d AC is common

       $AD = AB$ (given)

       $DC = BC$ (given)

       $\therefore \triangle ADC \equiv \triangle ABC$ (SSS)

e $AC = DC$ (given)

       $BC = EC$ (given)

       $\angle ACB \equiv \angle DCE$ (vertically opposite)

       $\therefore \triangle ABC \equiv \triangle DEC$ (SAS)

f $AC = EC$ (given)

       $\angle CAB = \angle CED$ (alternate angles, $AB \parallel DE$)

       $\angle ACB = \angle ECD$ (vertically opposite)

       $\therefore \triangle ABC \equiv \triangle EDC$ (AAS)

g $DC = BC$ (given)

       $\angle EDC = \angle ABC$ (alternate angles, $DE \parallel AB$)

       $\angle DCE = \angle BCA$ (vertically opposite)

       $\triangle CDE \equiv \triangle CBA$ (AAS)

h BD is common

       $AD = CD$ (given)

       $\angle ADB = \angle CDB$ (given)

       $\triangle ABD \equiv \triangle CBD$ (SAS)

i AC is common

       $AB = CD$ (given)

       $BC = DA$ (given)

       $\therefore \triangle ABC \equiv \triangle CDA$ (SSS)

j BD is common

       $\angle ABD = \angle CDB$ (alternate angles, $AB \parallel CD$)

       $\angle ADB = \angle CBD$ (alternate angles, $AD \parallel CB$)

       $\therefore \triangle ABD \equiv \triangle CDB$ (AAS)

k $OA = OC$ (radii)

       OB is common

       $AB = CB$ given

       $\therefore \triangle AOB \equiv \triangle COB$ (SSS)

l $OA = OD$ and $OB = OC$ (radii)

       $\angle AOB = \angle COD$ (vertically opposite)

       $\triangle AOB \equiv \triangle COD$ (SAS)

6 a $DC = BC$ (given)

       $EC = AC$ (given)

       $\angle DCE = \angle BCA$ (vertically opposite)

       $\therefore \triangle ABC \equiv \triangle EDC$ (SAS)

b $\angle EDC = \angle ABC$ (corresponding angles in congruent triangles)

       $\therefore$ $AB \parallel DE$ (alternate angles are equal)

7 a $AE = CD$ (given)

       $BE = BD$ (given)

       $\angle ABE = \angle CBD$ (vertically opposite with $\angle ABE$ given 90°)

       $\therefore \triangle ABE \equiv \triangle CBD$ (RHS)

b $\angle EAB = \angle DCB$ (corresponding angles in congruent triangles)

       $\therefore$ $AE \parallel CD$ (alternate angles equal)

8 a DB is common

       $AB = CD$ (given)

       $AD = CB$ (given)

       $\therefore \triangle ABD \equiv \triangle CDB$ (SSS)

b $\angle ADB = \angle CBD$ (corresponding angles in congruent triangles)

       $\therefore$ AD $\parallel$ BC (alternate angles equal)

9 a $OB = OC$ (radii)

       $OA = OD$ (radii)

       $\angle AOB = \angle DOC$ (vertically opposite)

       $\therefore \triangle AOB \equiv \triangle DOC$ (SAS)

b $\angle ABO = \angle DCO$ (corresponding angles in congruent triangles)

       $\therefore$ $AB \parallel CD$ (alternate angles equal)

10 a BD is common

       $AD = CD$ (given)

       $\angle ADB = \angle CDB$ (given)

       $\therefore \triangle ABD \equiv \triangle CBD$ (SAS)

b $\angle ABD = \angle CBD$ (corresponding angles in congruent triangles)

       and $\angle ABD + \angle CBD = 180°$ (straight line)

       $\therefore$ $\angle ABD = \angle CBD = 90°$ and AC is perpendicular to BD

11 a DB is common

       $\angle ABD = \angle CBD$ (given 90°)

       $\angle ADB = \angle CDB$ (given)

       $\therefore \triangle ABD \equiv \triangle CBD$ (AAS)

b $AD = CD$ (corresponding side in congruent triangles)

       $\therefore \triangle ACD$ is isosceles (2 equal sides)

12 Consider $\triangle OAD$ and $\triangle OBD$

     OD is common

     $OA = OB$ (radii)

     $AD = BD$ (given)

     $\therefore \triangle OAD \equiv \triangle OBD$ (SSS)

     $\angle ODA = \angle ODB = 90°$ (corresponding angles in congruent triangles are equal and supplementary to a straight line)

     $\therefore$ $OC \perp AB$

13 Consider $\triangle ADC$ and $\triangle CBA$

     AC is common

     $\angle DAC = \angle BCA$ (alternate angles, $AD \parallel BC$)

     $\angle DCA = \angle BAC$ (alternate angles, $DC \parallel AB$)

     $\therefore \triangle ADC \equiv \triangle CBA$ (AAS)

     So $AD = BC$, $AB = DC$ are equal corresponding sides in congruent triangles

14 $AB = DC$ (opposite sides of parallelogram)

     $\angle AEB = \angle CED$ (vertically opposite)

     $\angle BAE = \angle DCE$ (alternate angles $DC \parallel AB$)

     $\therefore \triangle ABE \equiv \triangle CDE$ (AAS)

     So $AE = CE$ and $BE = DE$, corresponding sides in congruent triangles

15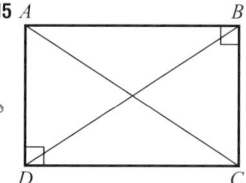

Consider $\triangle ADC$ and $\triangle BCD$

$AD = CB$ and DC is common (opposite sides of a rectangle are equal)

∠ADC = ∠BCD = 90° (angles of a rectangle)

∴△ADC ≡ △BCD (SAS)

So $AC = BD$ (corresponding sides in congruent triangles)

∴The diagonals of a rectangle are equal

16 a Consider △ABE and △CDE

$AB = CD$ (sides of a rhombus)

∠ABE = ∠CDE (alternate angles, $AB \parallel CD$)

∠BAE = ∠DCE (alternate angles, $AB \parallel CD$)

∴ △ABE ≡ △CDE (AAS)

b Consider △DCE and △BCE

CE is common

$DC = BC$ (sides of a rhombus)

$DE = BE$ (corresponding sides in congruent triangles)

∴ △DCE ≡ △BCE (SSS)

∴ $DE = BE$ (corresponding sides in congruent triangles)

∠DEC = ∠BEC (corresponding angles in congruent triangles)

∠DEC + ∠BEC = 180° (straight line)

∴ ∠DEC = ∠BEC = 90°

and $AE = CE$ (corresponding sides in congruent triangles)

∴ AC bisects BD at 90°

17

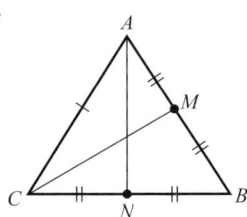

let △ABC be any equilateral triangle $AB = CB = AC$

Step one

Join C to M the midpoint of AB

Prove △CAM ≡ △CBM (SSS)

∴ ∠CAM = ∠CBM (corresponding angles in congruent triangles)

Step two

Join A to N, the midpoint of CB

Prove △ANC ≡ △ANB

∴ ∠ACN = ∠ABN (corresponding angles in congruent triangles)

Now ∠CAB = ∠ABC = ∠ACB

and as ∠CAB + ∠ABC + ∠ACB = 180° (angle sum of △ABC)

∠CAB = ∠ABC = ∠ACB = 60°

Exercise 7F

1 a ∠F   **b** ∠D **c** GH **d** AE **e** 2

2 a double   **b** double   **c** double   **d** 2   **e** yes

3 a OA' is a quarter of OA **b** OD' is a quarter of OD

c $\frac{1}{4}$ **d** yes

4 a yes   **b** 8 cm   **c** 25 m

5 drawings   **a** $A'B'C'$ should have sides $\frac{1}{3}$ that of ABC

b $A'B'C'$ should have sides double that of ABC

6 b i $A'B'C'D'$ should have sides lengths $\frac{1}{2}$ that of $ABCD$

ii $A'B'C'D'$ should have side lengths 1.5 times that of $ABCD$

7 a i 2   **ii** 14   **iii** 10

b i $1\frac{1}{2}$ **ii** 9   **iii** 8

c i $1\frac{1}{2}$ **ii** 45   **iii** 24

d i $\frac{2}{5}$ **ii** 1   **iii** 1.4

e i 2.5   **ii** 0.6   **iii** 2

f i 1.75   **ii** 3.5   **iii** 3

8 a i 2   **ii** (0,0)   **b i** $\frac{1}{2}$ **ii** (0,0)

c i $\frac{1}{2}$ **ii** (3,0)   **d i** 3   **ii** (1,0)

9 a i 3.6 m   **ii** 9 m   **iii** 2.7 m

b i 5.4 m   **ii** 6.3 m   **c i** 4 m   **ii** 6 m

10 a 12.7 cm   **b** 3 cm   **c** 3 m

11 a $a > 1$ **b** $a < 1$ **c** $a = 1$

12 a all angles of any square equal 90°, with only 1 side length

b all angles in any equilateral triangle equal 60° with only 1 side length

c The length and width might be multiplied by different numbers

d 2 isosceles triangles do not have to have the same size equal angles

13 $\frac{1}{k}$ **14 a**   100 000 cm = 1 km   **b** 24 cm

15 b i $\frac{l}{2}$ **ii** $\frac{l}{4}$ **iii** $\frac{l}{128}$ **c i** $\frac{3}{4}$ **ii** $\frac{9}{16}$ **iii** $\frac{243}{1024}$

d zero

Exercise 7G

1 a E **b** C **c** DF **d** BC **e** ∠A **f** ∠E

2 2.5

3 a SAS, AAA, and RHS   **b** shape, size

4 a AAA   **b** RHS   **c** SSS   **d** SAS

e RHS   **f** AAA   **g** SAS   **h** SSS

5 a △ABC ||| △GHI **b** △ABC ||| △MNO

c △ABC ||| △ADE **d** △HFG ||| △HJI

e △ADC ||| △AEB **f** △ABD ||| △ECD

6 a AAA   **b** 12   **7 a** RHS   **b** 8

8 a i $\frac{8}{5}$ **ii** 14.4   **b i** 3.5   **ii** 5

9 a AAA   **b** 15

10 a i AAA   **ii** 6.5   **b i** AAA   **ii** 10

c i AAA   **ii** 24

11 a 2   **b** 16   **c** 2.8

12 a △DEF **b** △DEF **c** △ABC **d** △DEF

13 ∠ACB = 25°, AAA

14 ∠WXY = 55°, not similar as angles not equal

15 2 pairs of equal alternate angles are always formed

16 AAA, in congruency a side length is needed for the triangles to be the same size, in similarity it is not needed.

17 a

Triangle	Original	Image 1	2	3
Length scale factor	1	2	3	4
Area	4	16	36	64
Area scale Factor	1	4	9	16

b Area scale factor = (length scale factor)^2

c n^2 **d i** 100   **ii** 400   **iii** 10 000   **e** $\frac{1}{4}$

Exercise 7H

1 $\angle C$

2 a $\angle ACB$ and $\angle ECD$

b $\angle BAC = \angle DEC$ and $\angle CBA = \angle CDE$

3 a $\angle C$ **b i** AC **ii** DB

4 a $\angle AEB = \angle CDB$ (alternate angles, $EA \parallel DC$)

$\angle EAB = \angle DCB$ (alternate angles, $EA \parallel DC$)

$\angle EBA = \angle DBC$ (vertically opposite)

$\therefore \triangle AEB \parallel\!\parallel\!\parallel \triangle CDB$ (AAA)

b $\angle BAC = \angle DEC$ (alternate angles, $AB \parallel DE$)

$\angle ABC = \angle EDC$ (alternate angles, $AB \parallel DE$)

$\angle ACB = \angle ECD$ (vertically opposite)

$\therefore \triangle ACB \parallel\!\parallel\!\parallel \triangle ECD$ (AAA)

c $\angle C$ is common

$\angle CDB = \angle CEA$ (corresponding angles, $AE \parallel BD$)

$\angle CBD = \angle CAE$ (corresponding angles, $AE \parallel BD$)

$\therefore \triangle CBD \parallel\!\parallel\!\parallel \triangle CAE$ (AAA)

d $\angle A$ is common

$\angle AEB = \angle ADC$ (corresponding angles, $EB \parallel DC$)

$\angle ABE = \angle ACD$ (corresponding angles, $EB \parallel DC$)

$\therefore \triangle AEB \parallel\!\parallel\!\parallel \triangle ADC$ (AAA)

e $\angle A$ is common

$\angle ABE = \angle ADC$ (given)

$\therefore \triangle ABE \parallel\!\parallel\!\parallel \triangle ADC$ (AA)

(note 2 angles is enough – $\angle AEB = \angle ACD$ (angle sum of a triangle))

f $\angle ABD = \angle BCD$ (given 90°)

$\angle BAD = \angle CBD$ (given)

$\therefore \triangle ABD \parallel\!\parallel\!\parallel \triangle BCD$ (AA)

5 a $\angle C$ is common.

$\frac{CA}{CD} = \frac{6}{2} = \frac{3}{1} = 3$

$\frac{CE}{CB} = \frac{9}{3} = 3$

$\therefore \triangle CDB \parallel\!\parallel\!\parallel \triangle CAE$ (SAS)

b $\angle D$ is common

$\frac{AD}{CD} = \frac{28}{7} = 4$

$\frac{DB}{DE} = \frac{48}{12} = 4$

$\therefore \triangle ABD \parallel\!\parallel\!\parallel \triangle CED$ (SAS)

c $\angle DCE = \angle BCA$ (vertically opposite)

$\frac{EC}{AC} = \frac{2}{5}$

$\frac{DC}{BC} = \frac{3}{7.5} = \frac{2}{5}$

$\therefore \triangle DCE \parallel\!\parallel\!\parallel \triangle BCA$ (SAS)

6 a AAA   **b** 40 m   **7 a** AAA   **b** 7.5 m

8 6 m   **9** 20 m   **10** 7.2 m   **11** $\frac{55}{6}$

12 a Firstly, $\angle ADC = \angle ACD = 80°$ (base angles of isosceles $\triangle ADC$)

$\angle ACB = 100°$ (straight angle)

$\angle CAB = 60°$ (angle sum of $\triangle ACB$)

Now $\angle DAB = 80°$

Proof $\angle DAC = \angle DBA$ (given 20°)

$\angle D$ is common

$\angle ACD = \angle BAD$ (both 80°)

$\therefore \triangle ACD \parallel\!\parallel\!\parallel \triangle BAD$ (AAA)

b $DC = \frac{20}{3}$ $CB = \frac{25}{3}$

13 a i $\angle B$ is common

$\angle DAB = \angle ACB$ (given 90°)

$\therefore \triangle ABD \parallel\!\parallel\!\parallel \triangle CBA$ (AAA)

ii $\angle D$ is common

$\angle DCA = \angle DAB$ (given 90°)

$\therefore \triangle ABD \parallel\!\parallel\!\parallel \triangle CAD$ (AAA)

b i $BD = \frac{25}{3}$ **ii** $AC = 4$ **iii** $AB = \frac{20}{3}$

14 a $\angle ACB = \angle ECD$ (vertically opposite)

$\angle CAB = \angle CED$ (alternate angles, DE ∥ BA)

$\therefore \triangle ABC \parallel\!\parallel\!\parallel \triangle EDC$ (AAA)

$\therefore \frac{DC}{BC} = \frac{EC}{AC}$ (ratio of corresponding sides in similar triangles)

$\frac{6}{2} = \frac{EC}{AC}$

$\therefore 3AC = CE$

as $AC + CE = AE$

$AE = 4AC$

b $\angle C$ is common

$\angle DBC = \angle AEC$ (given)

$\therefore \triangle CBD \parallel\!\parallel\!\parallel \triangle CEA$ (AAA)

$\therefore \frac{DB}{AE} = \frac{2}{4} = \frac{BC}{CE}$ (ratio of corresponding sides in similar triangles)

$\therefore 4BC = 2CE$

$BC = \frac{1}{2} CE$

c $\angle C$ is common

$\angle CBD = \angle CAE$ (corresponding angles, BD ∥ AE)

$\therefore \triangle CBD \parallel\!\parallel\!\parallel \triangle CAE$ (AAA)

$\therefore \frac{CB}{CA} = \frac{CD}{CE}$ (ratio of corresponding sides in similar triangles)

$\therefore \frac{5}{7} = \frac{CD}{CE}$

$\therefore 5CE = 7CD$

$CE = \frac{7}{5} CD$

d ∠C is common

∠CBD = ∠CAE (given 90°)

∴△CBD ||| △CAE (AAA)

∴$\dfrac{BD}{AE} = \dfrac{CB}{CA}$ (ratio of corresponding sides in similar triangles)

$\dfrac{2}{8} = \dfrac{CB}{CA}$

$\dfrac{1}{4} = \dfrac{CB}{CB + AB}$

$CB + AB = 4CB$

∴ $AB = 3CB$

Challenges

1

2 15   **3** 40°

4 A, B and C should be placed where the three altitudes of the triangle intersect the three sides.

5 170   **6** 11   **7** $\dfrac{120}{7}$

Multiple-choice questions

1 D   **2** A   **3** B   **4** D   **5** C
6 D   **7** E   **8** B   **9** D   **10** A

Short-answer questions

1 a isosceles, $x = 50$, $y = 80$ **b** right angled, $x = 25$
   c obtuse angled, $x = 30$, $y = 110$

2 a $a = 30$ (vertically opposite) $b = 150$ (straight angle)
   b $x = 60$ (revolution) $y = 120$ (co-interior angles in parallel lines)
   c $a = 70$ (alternate angles and parallel lines)
     $b = 55$ (angle sum of isosceles triangle)
     $c = 55$ (corresponding angles and parallel lines)

3 ∠ABC = 75°

4 a $a = 70$, $b = 110$ **b** $x = 15$ **c** $x = 30$ **d** $a = 120$

5 a SSS, $x = 60$ **b** not congruent
   c RHS, $x = 12$ **d** AAS, $x = 9$

6 a AD is common

∠ADC = ∠ADB (given 90°)

$CD = BD$ (given)

∴△ADC ≡ △ADB (SAS)

   b i $AC = EC$ (given)

∠BAC = ∠DEC (given)

∠ACB = ∠ECD (vertically opposite)

∴ △ACB ≡ △ECD (AAS)

     ii as ∠BAC = ∠DEC (alternate angles are equal)

∴ AB || DE

7 For image △$A'B'C'$, $OA' = 3OA$, $OB' = 3OB$, $OC' = 3OC$

8 a yes, SAS   **b** yes, AAA   **c** not similar

9 a 3.5   **b** 4   **c** 18

10 a ∠C is common

∠DBC = ∠EAC = 90° (given)

∴△BCD ||| △ACE (AAA)

   b 5 m

Extended-response questions

1 a ∠ABC + ∠BCF = 180° (cointerior angles, AB || CF)

∴ ∠BCF = 70°

∴ ∠DCF = 32°

Now ∠EDC + ∠DCF = 32° + 148°

       = 180°

∴ DE || CF as cointerior angles add to 180°

   b ∠CDA = 40° (revolution)

reflex ∠BCD = 270° (revolution)

∠DAB = 30° (angle sum in isosceles triangle)

$BADC$ quadrilateral angle sum 360°

∴ $a = 360 - (30 + 270 + 40)$

     = 20

or other proof.

   c $AB = CD$ (given)

∠ABC = ∠DCB (given)

BC is common

∴△ABC ≡ △DCB (SAS)

∴$AC = BD$ (corresponding sides in congruent triangles)

2 a ∠ECD

   b ∠ABC = ∠EDC (given 90°)

∠ACB = ∠ECD (vertically opposite)

∴ △ABC ||| △EDC (AAA)

   c 19.8 m

Chapter 8

Pre-test

1 a $2x + 6$ **b** $3a - 15$ **c** $12x - 8xy$ **d** $3 - 6b$

2 a 81   **b** 16   **c** 1   **d** 64
   e 25   **f** 7   **g** 3   **h** -6

3 a 2   **b** 6   **c** $2x$ **d** $3y$
   e $5x$ **f** ab

4 a $2(a + 3)$ **b** $3(x + 4y)$ **c** $5x(x - 3)$ **d** $2m(2 - 3n)$

5 a (1, 6), (2, 3), (-1, -6), (-2, -3)
   b (1, 12), (2, 6), (3, 4), (-1, -12), (-2, -6), (-3, -4)
   c (-1, 10), (1, -10), (-2, 5), (2, -5)
   d (-1, 27), (1, -27), (-3, 9), (3, -9)

6 a $\dfrac{20}{21}$ **b** $\dfrac{11}{18}$ **c** $\dfrac{1}{12}$ **d** $1\dfrac{1}{2}$

7 a $3x + 2$ **b** $x + 4$ **c** $-10 - 3x$ **d** $5x - 2$

8 a $x = 6$ **b** $x = 11$ **c** $x = \dfrac{5}{8}$

9 a $x(x + 2), x^2 + 2x$ **b** $(x + 3)(x + 4), x^2 + 7x + 12$

Exercise 8A

1 a $x^2, 2x, 3x, 6$ **b** $x^2 + 3x + 2x + 6 = x^2 + 5x + 6$

2 a $2x^2, 2x, 3x, 3$

   b $(2x + 3)(x + 1) = 2x^2 + 2x + 3x + 3$
                         $= 2x^2 + 5x + 3$

3 a $x^2 + 5x + x + 5 = x^2 + 6x + 5$

   b $x^2 + 2x - 3x - 6 = x^2 - x - 6$

   c $21x^2 + 6x - 14x - 4 = 21x^2 - 8x - 4$

   d $12x^2 - 16x - 3x + 4 = 12x^2 - 19x + 4$

4 a $x^2 + 7x + 10$ **b** $b^2 + 7b + 12$

   c $t^2 + 15t + 56$ **d** $p^2 + 12p + 36$

   e $x^2 + 15x + 54$ **f** $d^2 + 19d + 60$

   g $a^2 + 8a + 7$ **h** $y^2 + 12y + 20$

   i $m^2 + 16m + 48$

5 a $x^2 - x - 12$ **b** $x^2 + 3x - 10$

   c $x^2 - 4x - 32$ **d** $x^2 - 4x - 12$

   e $x^2 + 9x - 10$ **f** $x^2 + 2x - 63$

   g $x^2 + 5x - 14$ **h** $x^2 - 3x + 2$

   i $x^2 - 9x + 20$ **j** $8x^2 + 26x + 15$

   k $6x^2 + 7x + 2$ **l** $15x^2 + 17x + 4$

   m $6x^2 + x - 15$ **n** $24x^2 + 23x - 12$

   o $6x^2 - x - 2$ **p** $10x^2 - 31x + 14$

   q $6x^2 + 5x - 6$ **r** $16x^2 - 16x - 5$

   s $18x^2 - 27x + 10$ **t** $15x^2 - 11x + 2$

   u $21x^2 - 37x + 12$

6 a $a^2 + ac + ab + bc$ **b** $a^2 + ac - ab - bc$

   c $ab + bc - a^2 - ac$ **d** $xy - xz - y^2 + yz$

   e $yz - y^2 - xz + xy$ **f** $1 + y - x - xy$

   g $2x^2 - 3xy - 2y^2$ **h** $2a^2 - ab - b^2$

   i $6x^2 + xy - y^2$ **j** $6a^2 + 4a - 3ab - 2b$

   k $12x^2 - 25xy + 12y^2$ **l** $3x^2y - yz^2 - 2xyz$

7 a $x^2 + 9x + 20$

   b i $56 \, \text{m}^2$ **ii** $36 \, \text{m}^2$

8 a $2x^2$ **b** $2x^2 - 30x + 100$

9 a $150 - 50x + 4x^2$ **b** $66 \, \text{m}^2$

10 a 3   **b** 2   **c** 6, 6   **d** 2, 18

   e 2, 6   **f** 3, 15   **g** $2x, 5x, 3$ **h** $3x, 15x, 4$

   i $7x, 3, 17x$ **j** $3x, 4, 11x$

11 a $a = 3, b = 2$ or $a = 2, b = 3$

   b $a = -3, b = -2$ or $a = -2, b = -3$

   c $a = 3, b = -2$ or $a = -2, b = 3$

   d $a = 2, b = -3$ or $a = -3, b = 2$

12 a $x^3 + 2x^2 + 2x + 1$ **b** $x^3 - 3x^2 + 5x - 6$

   c $4x^3 - 4x^2 + 9x - 4$ **d** $x^3 + 2x^2 - 2x + 3$

   e $10x^3 - 17x^2 + 7x - 6$ **f** $8x^3 - 18x^2 + 35x - 49$

   g $x^3 + ax - a^2x + a^2$ **h** $x^3 - 2ax^2 + a^3$

   i $x^3 + a^3$ **j** $x^3 - a^3$

13 $x^3 + 6x^2 + 11x + 6$

Exercise 8B

1 a $+3x + 9 = x^2 + 6x + 9$ **b** $+5x + 25 = x^2 + 10x + 25$

   c $-2x + 4 = x^2 - 4x + 4$ **d** $-7x + 49 = x^2 - 14x + 49$

2 a i $x^2 + 6x + 9$ **ii** $x^2 + 22x + 121$

    iii $x^2 + 30x + 225$

   b i $x^2 - 4x + 4$ **ii** $x^2 - 18x + 81$

    iii $x^2 - 60x + 900$

3 a $+4x - 16 = x^2 - 16$ **b** $-10x - 100 = x^2 - 100$

   c $+2x - 2x - 1 = 4x^2 - 1$ **d** $-12x + 12x - 16 = 9x^2 - 16$

4 a $x^2 + 2x + 1$ **b** $x^2 + 6x + 9$

   c $x^2 + 4x + 4$ **d** $x^2 + 10x + 25$

   e $x^2 + 8x + 16$ **f** $x^2 + 18x + 81$

   g $x^2 + 14x + 49$ **h** $x^2 + 20x + 100$

   i $x^2 - 4x + 4$ **j** $x^2 - 12x + 36$

   k $x^2 - 2x + 1$ **l** $x^2 - 6x + 9$

   m $x^2 - 18x + 81$ **n** $x^2 - 14x + 49$

   o $x^2 - 8x + 16$ **p** $x^2 - 24x + 144$

5 a $4x^2 + 4x + 1$ **b** $4x^2 + 20x + 25$

   c $9x^2 + 12x + 4$ **d** $9x^2 + 6x + 1$

   e $25x^2 + 20x + 4$ **f** $16x^2 + 24x + 9$

   g $49 + 28x + 4x^2$ **h** $25 + 30x + 9x^2$

   i $4x^2 - 12x + 9$ **j** $9x^2 - 6x + 1$

   k $16x^2 - 40x + 25$ **l** $4x^2 - 36x + 81$

   m $9x^2 + 30xy + 25y^2$ **n** $4x^2 + 16xy + 16y^2$

   o $49x^2 + 42xy + 9y^2$ **p** $36x^2 + 60xy + 25y^2$

   q $16x^2 - 72xy + 81y^2$ **r** $4x^2 - 28xy + 49y^2$

   s $9x^2 - 60xy + 100y^2$ **t** $16x^2 - 48xy + 36y^2$

   u $81x^2 - 36xy + 4y^2$

6 a $9 - 6x + x^2$ **b** $25 - 10x + x^2$

   c $1 - 2x + x^2$ **d** $36 - 12x + x^2$

   e $121 - 22x + x^2$ **f** $16 - 8x + x^2$

   g $49 - 14x + x^2$ **h** $144 - 24x + x^2$

   i $64 - 32x + 4x^2$ **j** $4 - 12x + 9x^2$

   k $81 - 36x + 4x^2$ **l** $100 - 80x + 16x^2$

7 a $x^2 - 1$ **b** $x^2 - 9$ **c** $x^2 - 64$

   d $x^2 - 16$ **e** $x^2 - 144$ **f** $x^2 - 121$

   g $x^2 - 81$ **h** $x^2 - 25$ **i** $x^2 - 36$

   j $25 - x^2$ **k** $4 - x^2$ **l** $49 - x^2$

8 a $9x^2 - 4$ **b** $25x^2 - 16$

   c $16x^2 - 9$ **d** $49x^2 - 9y^2$

   e $81x^2 - 25y^2$ **f** $121x^2 - y^2$

   g $64x^2 - 4y^2$ **h** $100x^2 - 81y^2$

   i $49x^2 - 25y^2$ **j** $36x^2 - 121y^2$

   k $64x^2 - 9y^2$ **l** $81x^2 - 16y^2$

9 a i x^2 **ii** $x^2 - 4$

   b No, they differ by 4

10 a $20 - 2x$

b $(20 - 2x)(20 - 2x) = 400 - 80x + 4x^2$

c 196 cm^2 **d** 588 cm^3

11 a $a + b$ **b** $(a + b)(a + b) = a^2 + 2ab + b^2$

c $a - b$ **d** $(a - b)(a - b) = a^2 - 2ab + b^2$

e $4ab$ **f** ab so yes four courts area is $4ab$

12 a $x^2 - 1$ **b** No, area of rectangle is 1 square unit less

13 a $a^2 - b^2$

b **i** $(a - b)^2 = a^2 - 2ab + b^2$

ii $b(a - b) = ab - b^2$

iii $b(a - b) = ab - b^2$

c yes, $a^2 - 2ab + b^2 + ab - b^2 + ab - b^2 = a^2 - b^2$

14 a $x^2 + 4x$ **b** $-4x + 1$

c $x^2 + 6x - 9$ **d** $-x^2 - 2x$

e 1 **f** $4x$

g $-12x - 8$ **h** $-10x + 2$

i $x^2 + 4xy - y^2$ **j** $8x^2 + 18$

k $-8x$ **l** $2x^2 - 12x + 18$

m $9x^2 - 48x + 48$ **n** $x^2 + 6xy + y^2$

Exercise 8C

1 a 4 **b** 10 **c** 5 **d** 6

e 1 **f** 25 **g** 8 **h** 36

2 a x **b** x **c** a **d** $2a$

e $-2y$ **f** $-3x$ **g** $-2x$ **h** $-10x$

i $-2x$

3 a i 6 **ii** $3x$ **iii** $6x$

b iii

c terms have no common factor

4 a $2x$ **b** $6a$ **c** 2 **d** 4

e 3 **f** 1 **g** $3x$ **h** $3n$

i $2y$ **j** $2x$ **k** $2xy$ **l** $5ab$

5 a $7(x + 1)$ **b** $3(x + 1)$ **c** $4(x - 1)$

d $5(x - 1)$ **e** $4(1 + 2y)$ **f** $5(2 + a)$

g $3(1 - 3b)$ **h** $2(3 - x)$ **i** $3(4a + b)$

j $6(m + n)$ **k** $2(5x - 4y)$ **l** $4(a - 5b)$

m $x(x + 2)$ **n** $a(a - 4)$ **o** $y(y - 7)$

p $x(1 - x)$ **q** $3p(p + 1)$ **r** $8x(1 - x)$

s $4b(b + 3)$ **t** $2y(3 - 5y)$ **u** $3a(4 - 5a)$

v $9m(1 + 2m)$ **w** $16x(y - 3x)$ **x** $7ab(1 - 4b)$

6 a $-4(2x + 1)$ **b** $-2(2x + 1)$ **c** $-5(2x + y)$

d $-7(a + 2b)$ **e** $-3(3x + 4)$ **f** $-2(3y + 4)$

g $-5(2x + 3y)$ **h** $-4(m + 5n)$ **i** $-3x(x + 6)$

j $-4x(2x + 3)$ **k** $-2y(8y + 3)$ **l** $-5a(a + 2)$

m $-2x(3 + 10x)$ **n** $-3p(2 + 5p)$ **o** $-8b(2 + b)$

p $-9x(1 + 3x)$

7 a $(x + 3)(4 + x)$ **b** $(x + 1)(3 + x)$ **c** $(m - 3)(7 + m)$

d $(x - 7)(x + 2)$ **e** $(a + 4)(8 - a)$ **f** $(x + 1)(5 - x)$

g $(y + 3)(y - 2)$ **h** $(x + 2)(a - x)$ **i** $(2t + 5)(t + 3)$

j $(5m - 2)(m + 4)$ **k** $(4y - 1)(y - 1)$ **l** $(7 - 3x)(1 + x)$

8 a $6(a + 5)$ **b** $5(x - 3)$ **c** $2(4b + 9)$

d $x(x - 4)$ **e** $y(y + 9)$ **f** $a(a - 3)$

g $xy(x - 4 + y)$ **h** $2ab(3 - 5a + 4b)$ **i** $(m + 5)(m + 2)$

j $(x + 3)(x - 2)$ **k** $(b - 2)(b + 1)$ **l** $(2x + 1)(x - 1)$

m $(3 - 2y)(y - 5)$ **n** $(x + 4)(x + 9)$ **o** $(y + 1)(y - 3)$

9 a $4(x + 2)$ **b** $2(x + 3)$ **c** $10(x + 2)$

d $2(x + 7)$ **e** $2(2x + 3)$ **f** $2(x + 7)$

10 $4x$

11 a $t(5 - t)$

b i 0 m **ii** 6 m **iii** 4 m

c 5 seconds

12 a 63 **b** 72 **c** -20 **d** -70

e 69 **f** 189

13 a $3(a^2 + 3a + 4)$ **b** $z(5z - 10 + y)$

c $x(x - 2y + xy)$ **d** $2b(2y - 1 + 3b)$

e $-4y(3x + 2z + 5xz)$ **f** $ab(3 + 4b + 6a)$

14 a $-4(x - 3) = 4(3 - x)$ **b** $-3(x - 3) = 3(3 - x)$

c $-8(n - 1) = 8(1 - n)$ **d** $-3(b - 1) = 3(1 - b)$

e $-5m(1 - m) = 5m(m - 1)$ **f** $-7x(1 - x) = 7x(x - 1)$

g $-5x(1 - x) = 5x(x - 1)$ **h** $-2y(2 - 11y) = 2y(11y - 2)$

i $-4n(2 - 3n) = 4n(3n - 2)$ **j** $-4(2y - 5) = 4(5 - 2y)$

k $-5(3mn - 2) = 5(2 - 3mn)$ **l** $-15(x - 3) = 15(3 - x)$

15 a $(x - 4)(x - 3)$ **b** $(x - 5)(x + 2)$

c $(x - 3)(x + 3)$ **d** $(x - 4)(3x - 5)$

e $(2x - 5)(3 - x)$ **f** $(x - 2)(2x - 1)$

g $(x - 3)(4 - x)$ **h** $(x - 5)(x - 2)$

i $(x - 3)(x - 2)$

Exercise 8D

1 a $x^2 - 4$ **b** $x^2 - 49$ **c** $4x^2 - 1$ **d** $x^2 - y^2$

e $9x^2 - y^2$ **f** $a^2 - b^2$

2 a 3 **b** 11 **c** 9 **d** 20

e $2x$ **f** $3a$ **g** $5b$ **h** $7y$

3 a $(x + 4)(x - 4)$ **b** $(x + 12)(x - 12)$

c $(4x + 1)(4x - 1)$ **d** $(3a + 2b)(3a - 2b)$

4 a $(x + 3)(x - 3)$ **b** $(y + 5)(y - 5)$

c $(y + 1)(y - 1)$ **d** $(x + 8)(x - 8)$

e $(x + 4)(x - 4)$ **f** $(b + 7)(b - 7)$

g $(a + 9)(a - 9)$ **h** $(x + y)(x - y)$

i $(a + b)(a - b)$ **j** $(4 + a)(4 - a)$

k $(5 + x)(5 - x)$ **l** $(1 + b)(1 - b)$

m $(6 + y)(6 - y)$ **n** $(11 + b)(11 - b)$

o $(x + 20)(x - 20)$ **p** $(30 + y)(30 - y)$

5 a $(2x + 5)(2x - 5)$ **b** $(3x + 7)(3x - 7)$

c $(5b + 2)(5b - 2)$ **d** $(2m + 11)(2m - 11)$

e $(10y + 3)(10y - 3)$ **f** $(9a + 2)(9a - 2)$

g $(1 + 2x)(1 - 2x)$ **h** $(5 + 8b)(5 - 8b)$

i $(4 + 3y)(4 - 3y)$ **j** $(6x + y)(6x - y)$

k $(2x + 5y)(2x - 5y)$ **l** $(8a + 7b)(8a - 7b)$

m $(2p + 5q)(2p - 5q)$ **n** $(9m + 2n)(9m - 2n)$

o $(5a + 7b)(5a - 7b)$ **p** $(10a + 3b)(10a - 3b)$

6 a $3(x + 6)(x - 6)$ **b** $10(a + 1)(a - 1)$

c $6(x + 2)(x - 2)$ **d** $4(y + 4)(y - 4)$

e $2(7 + x)(7 - x)$ **f** $8(2 + m)(2 - m)$

g $5(xy + 1)(xy - 1)$ **h** $3(1 + xy)(1 - xy)$

i $7(3 + ab)(3 - ab)$

7 a $(x + 8)(x + 2)$ **b** $(x + 5)(x + 1)$ **c** $(x + 14)(x + 6)$

d $(x + 2)(x - 8)$ **e** $(x - 6)(x - 8)$ **f** $(x + 3)(x - 9)$

g $(10 + x)(4 - x)$ **h** $-x(x + 4)$ **i** $(17 + x)(1 - x)$

8 a $4(3 + t)(3 - t)$ **b i** 36 m   **ii** 20 m

c 3 seconds

9 a i x^2 **ii** $(30 + x)(30 - x)$

b i 500 cm^2 **ii** 675 cm^2

10 a $(x + 3)(x - 3)$ **b** $(4x + 11)(4x - 11)$

c $(2 + 5a)(2 - 5a)$ **d** $(x + y)(x - y)$

e $(2b + 5a)(2b - 5a)$ **f** $(c + 6ab)(c - 6ab)$

g $(yz + 4x)(yz - 4x)$ **h** $(b + 30a)(b - 30a)$

11 a Factorise each binomial

$(4x + 2)(4x - 2) = 2(2x + 1)\ 2(2x - 1) = 4(2x + 1)(2x - 1)$

b Take out common factor of 4

12 $9 - (x - 1)^2$

$= (3 + x - 1)(3 - (x - 1))$ insert brackets when subtracting a binomial

$= (2 + x)(3 - x + 1)$ remember $-1 \times -1 = +1$

$= (2 + x)(4 - x)$

13 a $\left(x + \dfrac{1}{2}\right)\left(x - \dfrac{1}{2}\right)$ **b** $\left(x + \dfrac{2}{5}\right)\left(x - \dfrac{2}{5}\right)$

c $\left(5x + \dfrac{3}{4}\right)\left(5x - \dfrac{3}{4}\right)$ **d** $\left(\dfrac{x}{3} + 1\right)\left(\dfrac{x}{3} - 1\right)$

e $\left(\dfrac{a}{2} + \dfrac{b}{3}\right)\left(\dfrac{a}{2} - \dfrac{b}{3}\right)$ **f** $5\left(\dfrac{x}{3} + \dfrac{1}{2}\right)\left(\dfrac{x}{3} - \dfrac{1}{2}\right)$

g $7\left(\dfrac{a}{5} + \dfrac{2b}{3}\right)\left(\dfrac{a}{5} - \dfrac{2b}{3}\right)$ **h** $\dfrac{1}{2}\left(\dfrac{a}{2} + \dfrac{b}{3}\right)\left(\dfrac{a}{2} - \dfrac{b}{3}\right)$

i $(x + y)(x - y)(x^2 + y^2)$ **j** $2(a + b)(a - b)(a^2 + b^2)$

k $21(a + b)(a - b)(a^2 + b^2)$ **l** $\dfrac{1}{3}(x + y)(x - y)(x^2 + y^2)$

Exercise 8E

1 a $2x - 2$ **b** $3a + 12$

c $-5 + 5a$ **d** $-6 + 2x$

e $a^2 + 5a$ **f** $2b - b^2$

g $x^2 - 4x$ **h** $4y - y^2$

i $ax + x + 2a + 2$ **j** $ax - 3a + 5x - 15$

k $bx - 2b - 3x + 6$ **l** $c - cx - 4 + 4x$

2 a $2 + a$ **b** $3 - a$ **c** $5 - a$ **d** $x + 7$

e $a + 1$ **f** $a - 1$ **g** $1 - a$ **h** $1 + 2a$

3 a $(x - 3)(x - 2)$ **b** $(x + 4)(x + 3)$

c $(x - 7)(x + 4)$ **d** $(2x + 1)(3 - x)$

e $(3x - 2)(4 - x)$ **f** $(2x + 3)(2x - 3)$

g $(5 - x)(3x + 2)$ **h** $(x + 1)(2 - 3x)$

i $(x - 2)(x + 1)$

4 a $(x + 3)(x + a)$ **b** $(x + 4)(x + c)$

c $(x + 7)(x + b)$ **d** $(x - 6)(x + b)$

e $(x - 4)(x + 2a)$ **f** $(x - 3)(x + 2b)$

g $(x + 2)(x - 3c)$ **h** $(x + 3)(x - 2a)$

i $(x + 4)(x - 2b)$ **j** $(x - 2)(x - a)$

k $(x - 3)(x - 3c)$ **l** $(x - 5)(x - 3a)$

5 a $(3a + 5c)(b + d)$ **b** $(4b - 7c)(a + d)$

c $(y - 4z)(2x + 3w)$ **d** $(s - 2)(5r + t)$

e $(x + 3y)(4x - 3)$ **f** $(2b - a)(a - c)$

6 a $(x - b)(x + 1)$ **b** $(x - c)(x + 1)$

c $(x + b)(x + 1)$ **d** $(x + c)(x - 1)$

e $(x + a)(x - 1)$ **f** $(x - b)(x - 1)$

7 a $(b + 4)(a + 3)$ **b** $(y + 5)(x + 2)$

c $(x + 3)(2a - 1)$ **d** $(1 - 2y)(3x + 4)$

e $(x - 5)(11 + a)$ **f** $(3 - 2x)(4y - 1)$

g $(n + 2)(3m - 1)$ **h** $(3 - r)(5p + 8)$

i $(2 - y)(8x + 3)$

8 a $x^2 + 4x - ax - 4a$ **b** $x^2 - dx - cx + cd$

c $2x - xz + 2y - yz$ **d** $ax + bx - a - b$

e $3cx - 3bx - bc + b^2$ **f** $2xy + 2xz - y^2 - yz$

g $6ab + 15ac + 2b^2 + 5bc$ **h** $3my + mz - 6xy - 2xz$

9 a $(x + 2)(x + 5)$ **b** $(x + 3)(x + 5)$

c $(x + 4)(x + 6)$ **d** $(x - 3)(x + 2)$

e $(x + 6)(x - 2)$ **f** $(x - 9)(x - 2)$

10 a Method 1: $a(x + 7) - 3(x + 7) = (x + 7)(a - 3)$

Method 2: $x(a - 3) + 7(a - 3) = (a - 3)(x + 7)$

b i $(x - 3)(b + 2)$ **ii** $(x + 2)(y - 4)$

iii $(2m + 3)(2m - 5n)$ **iv** $(2 - n)(m - 3)$

v $(1 - 2b)(4a + 3b)$ **vi** $(3a - 1)(b + 4c)$

12 a $(a - 3)(2 - x - c)$ **b** $(2a + 1)(b + 5 - a)$

c $(a + 1)(x - 4 - b)$ **d** $(a - b)(3 - b - 2a)$

e $(1 - a)(c - x + 2)$ **f** $(x - 2)(a + 2b - 1)$

g $(a - 3c)(a - 2b + 3bc)$ **h** $(1 - 2y)(3x - 5z + y)$

i $(x - 4)(3x + y - 2z)$ **j** $(ab - 2c)(2x + 3y - 1)$

Exercise 8F

1 a $x^2 + 4x + 3$ **b** $x^2 + 9x + 14$ **c** $x^2 + 8x - 33$

d $x^2 + x - 30$ **e** $x^2 + 7x - 60$ **f** $x^2 + 9x - 52$

g $x^2 - 8x + 12$ **h** $x^2 - 31x + 220$ **i** $x^2 - 10x + 9$

2 a 3, 2   **b** 5, 2   **c** 12, 1

d 4, 5   **e** 5, -1   **f** -7, 1

g 5, -3   **h** -6, 5   **i** -3, -2

j -9, -2   **k** -5, -8   **l** -50, -2

3 a $(x + 2)(x + 1)$ **b** $(x + 3)(x + 1)$ **c** $(x + 6)(x + 1)$

d $(x + 9)(x + 1)$ **e** $(x + 7)(x + 1)$ **f** $(x + 14)(x + 1)$

g $(x + 4)(x + 2)$ **h** $(x + 3)(x + 4)$ **i** $(x + 8)(x + 2)$

j $(x + 5)(x + 3)$ **k** $(x + 4)(x + 5)$ **l** $(x + 8)(x + 3)$

4 a $(x+4)(x-1)$ **b** $(x+2)(x-1)$ **c** $(x+5)(x-1)$
 d $(x+7)(x-2)$ **e** $(x+5)(x-3)$ **f** $(x+10)(x-2)$
 g $(x+6)(x-3)$ **h** $(x+9)(x-2)$ **i** $(x+4)(x-3)$
5 a $(x-5)(x-1)$ **b** $(x-1)(x-1)$ **c** $(x-1)(x-4)$
 d $(x-8)(x-1)$ **e** $(x-2)(x-2)$ **f** $(x-6)(x-2)$
 g $(x-9)(x-2)$ **h** $(x-7)(x-3)$ **i** $(x-3)(x-2)$
6 a $(x-8)(x+1)$ **b** $(x-4)(x+1)$ **c** $(x-6)(x+1)$
 d $(x-8)(x+2)$ **e** $(x-6)(x+4)$ **f** $(x-5)(x+3)$
 g $(x-4)(x+3)$ **h** $(x-12)(x+1)$ **i** $(x-6)(x+2)$
7 a $2(x+4)(x+1)$ **b** $2(x+10)(x+1)$ **c** $3(x+2)(x+4)$
 d $2(x+10)(x-3)$ **e** $2(x-9)(x+2)$ **f** $4(x-1)(x-1)$
 g $2(x-2)(x+3)$ **h** $6(x-6)(x+1)$ **i** $5(x-4)(x-2)$
 j $3(x-5)(x-6)$ **k** $2(x-5)(x+2)$ **l** $3(x-4)(x+3)$
8 a $6x$ **b** $6x$ or $10x$ **c** $x, 4x, 11x$
 d $x, 4x, 11x$ **e** $9x, 11x, 19x$ **f** $9x, 11x, 19x$
 g $0x, 6x, 15x$ **h** $0x, 24x$
9 a i $x(x+2)$ **ii** $x^2+2x-15$ **iii** $(x+5)(x-3)$
 b i 105 m^2 **ii** 48 m^2
10 a $(x+4)^2$ **b** $(x+5)^2$ **c** $(x+15)^2$ **d** $(x-1)^2$
 e $(x-7)^2$ **f** $(x-13)^2$ **g** $2(x+1)^2$ **h** $5(x-3)^2$
 i $-3(x-6)^2$
11 b, c, e, f
12 a $(x-1)^2-9$ **b** $(x+2)^2-5$ **c** $(x+5)^2-22$
 d $(x-8)^2-67$ **e** $(x+9)^2-74$ **f** $(x-16)^2-267$

Exercise 8G

1 a 2, 3 **b** 2, 6 **c** 5, -2 **d** 8, -3
 e -6, -3 **f** -5, -7 **g** -10, 3 **h** -7, 4
2 a $= 2x^2+2x+5x+5$
   $= 2x(x+1)+5(x+1)$
   $= (x+1)(2x+5)$
 b $= 3x^2+6x+2x+4$
   $= 3x(x+2)+2(x+2)$
   $= (x+2)(3x+2)$
 c $= 2x^2-3x-4x+6$
   $= x(2x-3)-2(2x-3)$
   $= (2x-3)(x-2)$
 d $= 5x^2+10x-x-2$
   $= 5x(x+2)-1(x+2)$
   $= (x+2)(5x-1)$
 e $= 4x^2+8x+3x+6$
   $= 4x(x+2)+3(x+2)$
   $= (x+2)(4x+3)$
 f $= 6x^2-9x+2x-3$
   $= 3x(2x-3)+1(2x-3)$
   $= (2x-3)(3x+1)$
3 a $(2x+1)(x+4)$ **b** $(3x+1)(x+2)$ **c** $(2x+3)(x+2)$
 d $(3x+2)(x+2)$ **e** $(5x+2)(x+2)$ **f** $(2x+3)(x+4)$
 g $(3x+5)(2x+1)$ **h** $(4x+1)(x+1)$ **i** $(4x+5)(2x+1)$

4 a $(3x+5)(x-1)$ **b** $(5x-4)(x+2)$ **c** $(2x+3)(4x-1)$
 d $(2x+1)(3x-8)$ **e** $(2x+1)(5x-4)$ **f** $(x-3)(5x+4)$
 g $(2x-5)(2x-3)$ **h** $(x-6)(2x-3)$ **i** $(2x-5)(3x-2)$
 j $(3x-4)(4x+1)$ **k** $(2x-3)(2x-3)$ **l** $(x+3)(7x-3)$
 m $(x+5)(9x-1)$ **n** $(x-2)(3x-8)$ **o** $(2x-5)(2x+3)$
5 a $(2x+1)(5x+11)$ **b** $(3x+4)(5x-2)$ **c** $(2x-3)(10x-3)$
 d $(2x+1)(9x-5)$ **e** $(5x-3)(5x+4)$ **f** $(4x+1)(8x-5)$
 g $(3x+2)(9x-4)$ **h** $(3x+1)(11x+10)$ **i** $(6x-5)(9x+1)$
 j $(2x-3)(6x-7)$ **k** $(3x-1)(25x-6)$ **l** $(6x-1)(15x+8)$
6 a $2(3x-2)(5x+1)$ **b** $6(x-1)(2x+5)$ **c** $3(3x-5)(3x-1)$
 d $7(x-3)(3x-2)$ **e** $4(3x-2)(3x+5)$ **f** $5(2x-3)(5x+4)$
7 a $-(x-2)(2x-3)$ **b** $-(x-1)(5x+8)$ **c** $-(2x+1)(3x-8)$
 d $-(x+3)(5x-6)$ **e** $-(2x-5)(2x-3)$ **f** $-(2x-1)(4x-5)$
8 a $(x+4)(2x-5)$
 b $(2x-5)(x+4)$
 c No, you get the same result
 d i $(x+3)(3x-4)$ **ii** $(x-2)(5x+7)$ **iii** $(2x-1)(3x+4)$
10 see answers to Questions **4** and **5**

Exercise 8H

1 a $\dfrac{1}{3}$ **b** $\dfrac{3}{2}$ **c** $\dfrac{x}{2}$ **d** $\dfrac{7x}{2}$
 e $\dfrac{3}{x}$ **f** $\dfrac{1}{2x}$ **g** $\dfrac{x+1}{2}$ **h** $2(x-4)$
2 a $3(x+2)$ **b** $20(1-2x)$ **c** $x(x-7)$ **d** $6x(x+4)$
3 a $\dfrac{2(x-2)}{8}=\dfrac{x-2}{4}$ **b** $\dfrac{6(2-3x)}{x(2-3x)}$ **c** $\dfrac{(x+3)(x+2)}{2(x-1)}$
4 a $\dfrac{3}{4}$ **b** $\dfrac{1}{3}$ **c** 4 **d** $x-5$
 e $\dfrac{2(x-1)}{3}$ **f** $\dfrac{2}{x+4}$
5 a $x-1$ **b** $\dfrac{2(x-3)}{5}$ **c** $\dfrac{2}{3}$ **d** 2
 e $x-3$ **f** $\dfrac{2(2x+5)}{5}$ **g** $\dfrac{3}{2}$ **h** $\dfrac{4}{3}$
6 a $x+2$ **b** $x+4$ **c** $x-3$ **d** $\dfrac{1}{x+3}$
 e $\dfrac{1}{x-2}$ **f** $\dfrac{1}{x-10}$
7 a $\dfrac{x-4}{2}$ **b** $x-3$ **c** $3(x-3)$ **d** $\dfrac{x+4}{2(x-5)}$
8 a x **b** $\dfrac{2(x-2)}{x+2}$ **c** $\dfrac{4}{x+1}$ **d** $\dfrac{x-2}{2(x+2)}$
 e $\dfrac{2(x+2)^2}{3(x+4)}$ **f** $\dfrac{5}{x+2}$
9 a $x-10$ **b** $x-7$ **c** $x-5$ **d** $\dfrac{2}{x+20}$
 e $\dfrac{5}{x+6}$ **f** $\dfrac{3}{x-9}$
10 a $(x+2)(x-5)$ **b** $\dfrac{x+2}{x+3}$

c $\dfrac{x-3}{x-4}$ **d** $\dfrac{x-5}{x+2}$

e $\dfrac{3x-1}{2-15x}$ **f** $\dfrac{x-4}{3-x}=-\dfrac{x-4}{x-3}$

g $\dfrac{x+5}{2(x+4)}$ **h** $\dfrac{3}{2(x+3)}$

11 a -1 **b** -1 **c** -8

d $-\dfrac{1}{3}$ **e** $-\dfrac{1}{6}$ **f** $-(x+3)$

12 a $a+1$ **b** $5(a-3)$ **c** $\dfrac{x+7}{2}$

d $\dfrac{x+2}{6}$ **e** $\dfrac{x+3}{2}$ **f** $\dfrac{11}{x-2}$

13 a $-\dfrac{x+3}{2}$ **b** $-\dfrac{x-7}{3}$ **c** $-\dfrac{x-8}{x+8}$ **d** $-\dfrac{2}{x+2}$

e $-\dfrac{4}{x+3}$ **f** $\dfrac{3(x+1)}{4}$ **g** $\dfrac{3(2x+3)}{2x}$ **h** $-\dfrac{1}{2(x+2)}$

i $\dfrac{x}{3}$ **j** $-\dfrac{2}{x-2}$

Exercise 8I

1 a 24 **b** 15 **c** 143 **d** 36
2 a $4x$ **b** $21x$ **c** 3 **d** 2
e 8 **f** 90

3 a $\dfrac{3x}{12}+\dfrac{8x}{12}=\dfrac{11x}{12}$

b $\dfrac{25x}{35}-\dfrac{14x}{35}=\dfrac{11x}{35}$

c $\dfrac{2(x+1)}{4}+\dfrac{(2x+3)}{4}=\dfrac{2x+2+2x+3}{4}=\dfrac{4x+5}{4}$

4 a 15 **b** 14 **c** 8 **d** 6 **e** 10

5 a $\dfrac{9x}{14}$ **b** $\dfrac{2x}{5}$ **c** $\dfrac{x}{8}$ **d** $\dfrac{14x}{45}$

e $\dfrac{y}{56}$ **f** $\dfrac{13a}{22}$ **g** $\dfrac{2b}{9}$ **h** $\dfrac{m}{6}$

i $\dfrac{11m}{12}$ **j** $\dfrac{15a}{28}$ **k** $\dfrac{x}{2}$ **l** $-\dfrac{20p}{63}$

m $-\dfrac{5b}{18}$ **n** $\dfrac{61y}{40}$ **o** $\dfrac{13x}{35}$ **p** $\dfrac{5x}{12}$

6 a $\dfrac{7x+11}{10}$ **b** $\dfrac{7x}{12}$ **c** $\dfrac{15a-51}{56}$ **d** $\dfrac{11y+9}{30}$

e $\dfrac{13m+28}{40}$ **f** $\dfrac{5x-13}{24}$ **g** $\dfrac{11b-6}{24}$ **h** $\dfrac{7x}{6}$

i $\dfrac{7y-8}{14}$ **j** $\dfrac{5t-4}{16}$ **k** $\dfrac{34-10x}{21}$ **l** $\dfrac{8m-9}{12}$

7 a $\dfrac{11}{2x}$ **b** $\dfrac{1}{3x}$ **c** $-\dfrac{3}{4x}$ **d** $\dfrac{14}{9x}$

e $\dfrac{7}{20x}$ **f** $\dfrac{13}{15x}$ **g** $-\dfrac{31}{4x}$ **h** $-\dfrac{29}{12x}$

8 a $\dfrac{3x+2}{x^2}$ **b** $\dfrac{5+4x}{x^2}$ **c** $\dfrac{7x+3}{x^2}$

d $\dfrac{4x-5}{x^2}$ **e** $\dfrac{3-8x}{x^2}$ **f** $\dfrac{x-4}{x^2}$

g $\dfrac{6x-7}{2x^2}$ **h** $\dfrac{9-2x}{3x^2}$

9 a $\dfrac{8+x^2}{4x}$ **b** $\dfrac{x^2-10}{2x}$ **c** $\dfrac{-6-4x^2}{3x}$

d $\dfrac{6-5x^2}{4x}$ **e** $\dfrac{9x^2-10}{12x}$ **f** $\dfrac{3-x^2}{9x}$

g $\dfrac{15x^2-4}{10x}$ **h** $\dfrac{-25-6x^2}{20x}$

10 a $\dfrac{x}{3}$ **b** $\dfrac{x}{8}$ **c** $\dfrac{x}{2}$ **d** $\dfrac{x}{5}$

e $\dfrac{8x}{9}$ **f** $\dfrac{x}{4}$

11 a didn't make a common denominator, $\dfrac{7x}{15}$

b didn't use brackets: $2(x+1)=2x+2$, $\dfrac{7x+2}{10}$

c didn't use brackets: $3(x-1)=3x-3$, $\dfrac{13x-3}{6}$

d didn't multiply numerator in $\dfrac{2}{x}$ by x as well as denominator,

$\dfrac{2x-3}{x^2}$

12 a $\dfrac{8x+2}{8}=\dfrac{2(4x+1)}{8}=\dfrac{4x+1}{4}$ **b** $\dfrac{4x+1}{4}$

c Using denominator 8 does not give answer in simplified form and requires extra steps. Preferable to use actual LCD

13 a $-\dfrac{43x}{30}$ **b** $\dfrac{5x}{12}$ **c** $\dfrac{13x}{24}$ **d** $\dfrac{43x-5}{60}$

e $\dfrac{23x-35}{42}$ **f** $\dfrac{29x+28}{40}$ **g** $\dfrac{14}{3x}$ **h** $\dfrac{1}{6x}$

i $-\dfrac{11}{20x}$ **j** $\dfrac{24-x}{6x^2}$ **k** $\dfrac{60x-21}{14x^2}$ **l** $\dfrac{3-4x}{9x^2}$

m $\dfrac{30-2x^2}{15x}$ **n** $\dfrac{11x^2-3}{6x}$ **o** $\dfrac{18-2x^2}{45x}$

Exercise 8J

1 a $-2x-6$ **b** $-5x-5$ **c** $-14-21x$
d $-3x+3$ **e** $-30+20x$ **f** $-16+64x$
2 a 9 **b** 16 **c** x^2 **d** $2x$
e $(x-1)(x+1)$ **f** $(x-2)(x+3)$
g $(2x-1)(x-4)$ **h** $(x+1)^2$

3 a $\dfrac{1-x}{12}$ **b** $\dfrac{2x-14}{15}$ **c** $\dfrac{x-9}{6}$

d $\dfrac{-7x-14}{10}$ **e** $\dfrac{9x-4}{8}$ **f** $\dfrac{-x-24}{28}$

g $\dfrac{5x-3}{12}$ **h** $\dfrac{1-18x}{15}$ **i** $\dfrac{8x-23}{30}$

4 a $\dfrac{13-x}{6}$ b $\dfrac{2x+2}{35}$ c $\dfrac{x-5}{4}$

  d $\dfrac{22x-41}{21}$ e $\dfrac{17x}{20}$ f $\dfrac{30-13x}{24}$

  g $\dfrac{14x+4}{9}$ h $\dfrac{20x-9}{28}$ i $\dfrac{10-11x}{56}$

5 a $\dfrac{7x-1}{(x-1)(x+1)}$ b $\dfrac{7x-7}{(x+4)(x-3)}$ c $\dfrac{7x+1}{(x-2)(x+3)}$

  d $\dfrac{5x+13}{(x-4)(x+7)}$ e $\dfrac{4x+15}{(x+2)(x+3)}$ f $\dfrac{x-26}{(x+4)(x-6)}$

  g $\dfrac{x+9}{(x+5)(x+1)}$ h $\dfrac{16-6x}{(x-3)(x-2)}$ i $\dfrac{7-2x}{(x-5)(x-6)}$

6 a $\dfrac{1-3x}{(x+1)^2}$ b $\dfrac{-4x-10}{(x+3)^2}$ c $\dfrac{3x-2}{(x-2)^2}$ d $\dfrac{18-2x}{(x-5)^2}$

  e $\dfrac{9-x}{(x-6)^2}$ f $\dfrac{14-3x}{(x-4)^2}$ g $\dfrac{4x+7}{(2x+1)^2}$ h $\dfrac{1-12x}{(3x+2)^2}$

  i $\dfrac{20x-1}{(1-4x)^2}$

7 a $\dfrac{5x-2}{(x-1)^2}$ b $\dfrac{19x+8}{12x}$ c $\dfrac{10x^2-11x+4}{20x}$

  d $\dfrac{x^2+7x}{(x-5)(x+1)}$ e $\dfrac{2x^2-5x-3}{(4-x)(x-1)}$ f $\dfrac{x^2+2x+1}{(x-3)^2}$

  g $\dfrac{3-2x}{(x-2)^2}$ h $\dfrac{-x^2-11x}{(2x+1)(x+2)}$ i $\dfrac{x^2-4x-1}{(x+1)^2}$

8 a second line $-2 \times (-2) = +4$ not -4 b $\dfrac{33x+4}{10}$

9 a $\dfrac{3x+11}{(x+3)(x+4)(x+5)}$ b $\dfrac{2-2x}{(x+1)(x+2)(x+4)}$

  c $\dfrac{26-10x}{(x-1)(x-3)(2-x)}$ d $\dfrac{3x-2}{(x+1)(x-5)}$

  e $\dfrac{2x+9}{(x-4)(3-2x)}$ f $\dfrac{7x^2+7x}{(x+4)(2x-1)(3x+2)}$

10 a $\dfrac{5}{1-x}$ b $\dfrac{4x-3}{5-x}$ c $\dfrac{9}{7x-3}$

  d $\dfrac{1-2x}{4-3x}$ e 1 f 0

11 a $\dfrac{11}{2(x+2)}$ b $\dfrac{1}{3(x-1)}$

  c $\dfrac{23}{4(2x-1)}$ d $\dfrac{13-3x}{(x+3)(x-3)}$

  e $\dfrac{5x-6}{2(x+2)(x-2)}$ f $\dfrac{30x+33}{(3x-4)(3x+4)}$

  g $\dfrac{9x-27}{(x+3)(x+4)(x-5)}$ h $\dfrac{x+11}{(x-1)(x+3)^2}$

  i $\dfrac{2x+5}{5(x-2)(x-5)}$ j $\dfrac{-2}{x(x-1)(x+1)}$

Exercise 8K

1 a 15 b 4 c 6 d 28 e 30 f 8

2 a $4x$ b $3x$ c $2(x+3)$ d $2x+5$ e 3

  f $-(x+2)$ g $4(x-1)$ h $2(1-x)$ i $2x-1$

3 a 10 b 12 c 24 d 10 e $\dfrac{6}{7}$

  f $7\dfrac{1}{2}$ g -8 h 15 i 4

4 a 13 b 1 c $1\dfrac{3}{5}$ d 59 e 1

  f 5 g 8 h $3\dfrac{2}{7}$ i $-3\dfrac{1}{4}$

5 a -3 b -4 c 5 d 1

  e -1 f 6

6 a $\dfrac{1}{16}$ b $\dfrac{1}{12}$ c $\dfrac{8}{15}$ d $\dfrac{1}{36}$ e $\dfrac{3}{4}$

  f $\dfrac{5}{24}$ g $\dfrac{5}{12}$ h $-\dfrac{1}{6}$ i $2\dfrac{5}{6}$

7 a $-\dfrac{5}{2}$ b -5 c -19 d -4

  e -1 f -6

8 a $\dfrac{x}{2}+\dfrac{2x}{3}=4$ b $x=3\dfrac{3}{7}$

9 a $\dfrac{1}{6}$ b 2 c 0

  d $\dfrac{9}{13}$ e $\dfrac{3}{7}$ f $\dfrac{2}{11}$

  g $1\dfrac{5}{7}$ h 0 i -12

10 a $\dfrac{x}{3}+\dfrac{x}{4}=77$ b 132 games

11 On the second line, not every term has been multiplied by 12. The $2x$ should be $24x$ to give an answer $x=\dfrac{3}{29}$.

12 On third line of working, $-2 \times (-1) = +2$ not -2, giving answer $x=-4$

13 a $4\dfrac{1}{2}$ b $5\dfrac{2}{3}$ c $1\dfrac{1}{2}$

  d 3 e 15 f -2

14 a $x=2ab$ b $x=\dfrac{2bd}{2a-bc}$ c $x=\dfrac{ac}{c-b}$

  d $x=\dfrac{bd+be-ac}{c}$ e $x=\dfrac{4c-3b}{3a-4}$ f $x=\dfrac{6b+a}{5}$

  g $x=-\dfrac{a^2}{2a-b-a^2}$ h $x=\dfrac{ac}{c-a}$ i $x=\dfrac{ac}{b}$

  j $x=\dfrac{c-a}{b}$ k $x=\dfrac{b-bc}{a-c}$ l $x=\dfrac{ad-b}{c-d}$

  m $x=ab-2a$ n $x=\dfrac{a+b}{1-a}$ o $x=\dfrac{2ab-a^2}{a-b}$

Challenges

1 a 48, 49 b 33, 35 c 12, 15

2 a 15 b 5

3 $a=2, b=1, c=7$ and $d=8$

4 a $(n+1)^2+1$ or n^2+2n+2 b a number of answers

5 $(n-1)(n+1)$

  i $n-1$ and $n+1$ are both even, since they are consecutive even numbers one of them is divisible by 4 hence their product is

ii $n-1$, n, $n+1$ are 3 consecutive numbers, one of them must be divisible by 3. Since n is prime it must be $n-1$ or $n+1$ so their product is divisible by 3

iii n^2-1 is divisible by 3 and 4 and since they have no common factor it must also be divisible by $3 \times 4 = 12$.

6 Factorise each expression and cancel.

7 $4x^2-4x+1=(2x-1)^2$ which is always greater than or equal to zero

8 Ryan

Multiple-choice questions

1 A   **2** E   **3** D   **4** C   **5** B

6 D   **7** A   **8** E   **9** B   **10** A

Short-answer questions

1 a x^2+x-12 **b** $x^2-9x+14$
   c $6x^2-5x-6$ **d** $9x^2+3x-12$

2 a x^2+6x+9 **b** $x^2-8x+16$ **c** $9x^2-12x+4$
   d x^2-25 **e** $49-x^2$ **f** $121x^2-16$

3 a $4(a+3b)$ **b** $3x(2-3x)$ **c** $-5xy(x+2)$
   d $(x-7)(x+3)$ **e** $(2x+1)(x-1)$ **f** $(x-2)(x-6)$

4 a $(x+10)(x-10)$ **b** $3(x+4)(x-4)$ **c** $(5x+y)(5x-y)$
   d $(7+3x)(7-3x)$ **e** $(x-12)(x+6)$ **f** $(1-x)(1+x)$

5 a $(x-3)(x+2y)$ **b** $(2a+5)(2x-1)$ **c** $(x-4)(3+2b)$

6 a $(x+3)(x+5)$ **b** $(x-6)(x+3)$ **c** $(x-6)(x-1)$
   d $3(x+7)(x-2)$ **e** $2(x+4)^2$ **f** $(5x+2)(x+3)$
   g $(2x-3)(2x+1)$ **h** $(3x-4)(2x-3)$

7 a $x+4$ **b** $\dfrac{2}{3}$ **c** $\dfrac{x-3}{5}$

8 a $\dfrac{1}{4}$ **b** $\dfrac{x-4}{2}$ **c** $\dfrac{x}{3}$
   d $\dfrac{2}{5}$ **e** 4 **f** $\dfrac{2x+3}{50x}$

9 a $\dfrac{11x}{12}$ **b** $\dfrac{x-13}{24}$ **c** $\dfrac{5}{4x}$
   d $\dfrac{7x-2}{x^2}$ **e** $\dfrac{8x+11}{(x+1)(x+2)}$ **f** $\dfrac{15-2x}{(x-4)^2}$

10 a $x=20$ **b** $x=\dfrac{1}{6}$ **c** $x=7$ **d** $x=-1\dfrac{2}{9}$

Extended-response questions

1 a $(x+3)$ m
   b i No change
     ii (x^2-1) m^2, 1 square metre less in area
   c i width $=(x-3)$ m, decreased by 3 metres
     ii $A=(x+7)(x-3)=(x^2+4x-21)$ m^2
     iii $A=0$ m^2

2 a 400 m^2
   b i $L=W=(20+2x)$ m
     ii $(4x^2+80x+400)$ m^2
   c $\dfrac{1}{4}$ **d** $4x(x+20)$ m^2 **e** $x=5$

Chapter 9

Pre-test

1 a 0.1   **b** 0.25   **c** 0.3   **d** 0.85   **e** 0.237

2 a $\dfrac{1}{2}$ **b** $\dfrac{1}{3}$ **c** $\dfrac{2}{3}$ **d** 1
   e 0   **f** $\dfrac{1}{12}$ **g** $\dfrac{1}{2}$ **h** $\dfrac{18}{29}$
   i $\dfrac{2}{3}$ **j** $\dfrac{2}{7}$

3 a 1, 2, 3, 4, 5 or 6
   b i 3   **ii** 2   **iii** 3   **iv** 5   **v** 5   **vi** 3

4 a 5   **b** 7   **c** 6   **d** 7   **e** 4   **f** 6

5 a 8   **b** 20   **c** $\dfrac{3}{20}$

6 a 6   **b** 5   **c** 5   **d** 12
   e i $\dfrac{2}{9}$ **ii** $\dfrac{7}{9}$ **iii** $\dfrac{5}{9}$

Exercise 9A

1 a i $\dfrac{1}{4}$ **ii** 0.25   **iii** 25%

   b

2

	Percentage	Decimal	Fraction	Number line
a	50%	0.5	$\dfrac{1}{2}$	
b	25%	0.25	$\dfrac{1}{4}$	
c	75%	0.75	$\dfrac{3}{4}$	
d	20%	0.2	$\dfrac{1}{5}$	
e	60%	0.6	$\dfrac{3}{5}$	
f	85%	0.85	$\dfrac{17}{20}$	

3 0.15, $\dfrac{2}{9}$, 1 in 4, 0.28, $\dfrac{1}{3}$, $\dfrac{2}{5}$, $\dfrac{3}{7}$, 2 in 3, 0.7, 0.9

4 a i $\{1, 2, 3, 4, 5, 6, 7\}$ **ii** $\dfrac{1}{7}$ **iii** $\dfrac{6}{7}$
   iv $\dfrac{2}{7}$ **v** $\dfrac{6}{7}$

b i {2, 2, 6, 7} **ii** $\frac{1}{2}$ **iii** $\frac{1}{2}$ **iv** $\frac{1}{2}$ **v** 1

c i {1, 2, 2, 2, 2, 3} **ii** $\frac{2}{3}$ **iii** $\frac{1}{3}$ **iv** $\frac{5}{6}$ **v** $\frac{5}{6}$

d i {1, 1, 2, 2, 3, 3} **ii** $\frac{1}{3}$ **iii** $\frac{2}{3}$ **iv** $\frac{2}{3}$ **v** $\frac{2}{3}$

e i {1, 1, 2, 3, 3, 4, 4} **ii** $\frac{1}{7}$ **iii** $\frac{6}{7}$ **iv** $\frac{3}{7}$ **v** $\frac{5}{7}$

f i {2, 2, 2, 2} **ii** 1 **iii** 0 **iv** 1 **v** 1

5 a $\frac{1}{2}$ **b** $\frac{3}{8}$ **c** $\frac{1}{6}$ **d** $\frac{1}{4}$ **e** 1 **f** 0

6 a $\frac{1}{2}$ **b** $\frac{5}{8}$ **c** $\frac{5}{6}$ **d** $\frac{3}{4}$ **e** 0 **f** 1

7 a $\frac{1}{8}$ **b** $\frac{7}{8}$

8 a $\frac{1}{8}$ **b** $\frac{1}{4}$ **c** $\frac{3}{8}$ **d** $\frac{3}{8}$ **e** $\frac{5}{8}$ **f** 1

g 0 **h** $\frac{1}{4}$ **i** $\frac{3}{4}$ **j** $\frac{3}{4}$

9 a {H, A, R, S} **b i** $\frac{1}{4}$ **ii** $\frac{1}{2}$ **iii** $\frac{1}{2}$

10 a $\frac{1}{52}$ **b** $\frac{1}{13}$ **c** $\frac{1}{26}$ **d** $\frac{1}{2}$

e $\frac{2}{13}$ **f** $\frac{12}{13}$ **g** $\frac{23}{26}$ **h** $\frac{25}{26}$

11 a $\frac{1}{6}$ **b** $\frac{1}{6}$ **c** $\frac{5}{6}$ **d** $\frac{1}{3}$ **e** $\frac{2}{3}$

f 1 **g** $\frac{1}{3}$ **h** $\frac{1}{2}$ **i** $\frac{5}{6}$

12 a $\frac{2}{11}$ **b** $\frac{9}{11}$ **c** $\frac{4}{11}$ **d** $\frac{7}{11}$

e $\frac{7}{11}$ **f** $\frac{3}{11}$ **g** $\frac{7}{11}$ **h** $\frac{4}{11}$

13 The sample space has four elements as the letter O appears twice {S, L, O, O} Amanda has only considered the name of the letter, not the total number of elements in the sample space. Pr (S) = $\frac{1}{4}$

14 a, d, f

15 a $\frac{12}{25}$ **b** $\frac{8}{25}$ **c** $\frac{1}{5}$ **d** $\frac{9}{25}$ **e** $\frac{8}{25}$

f $\frac{16}{25}$ **g** $\frac{4}{25}$ **h** $\frac{17}{25}$ **i** 0

16 a 31 mins **b** $\frac{3}{31}$

c i $\frac{4}{31}$ **ii** $\frac{4}{31}$ **iii** $\frac{20}{31}$ **iv** $\frac{5}{31}$ **v** $\frac{8}{31}$ **vi** $\frac{11}{31}$

Exercise 9B

1 a 26

b i 10 **ii** 14 **iii** 5 **iv** 9

v 4 **vi** 7 **vii** 19

c i 12 **ii** 17

2 a B **b** D **c** A **d** C

3 a

	A	Not A	Total
B	7	8	15
Not B	3	1	4
Total	10	9	19

b

	A	Not A	Total
B	2	5	7
Not B	9	4	13
Total	11	9	20

4 a

b i 28 **ii** 21 **iii** 6

c i $\frac{1}{10}$ **ii** $\frac{1}{15}$ **iii** $\frac{19}{30}$

5 a i $\frac{2}{5}$ **b i** $\frac{3}{7}$

ii $\frac{1}{3}$ **ii** $\frac{12}{35}$

iii $\frac{7}{15}$ **iii** $\frac{13}{35}$

iv $\frac{1}{15}$ **iv** $\frac{3}{35}$

v $\frac{13}{15}$ **v** $\frac{34}{35}$

vi $\frac{2}{15}$ **vi** $\frac{1}{35}$

6 a

	Cream	Not cream	Total
Ice cream	5	20	25
Not ice cream	16	9	25
Total	21	29	50

b i 29 **ii** 9 **c i** $\frac{21}{50}$ **ii** $\frac{8}{25}$ **iii** $\frac{41}{50}$

7 a i $\frac{5}{8}$ **ii** $\frac{3}{8}$ **iii** $\frac{3}{8}$ **iv** $\frac{3}{4}$ **v** $\frac{1}{8}$ **vi** $\frac{1}{4}$

b i $\frac{17}{26}$ **ii** $\frac{9}{26}$ **iii** $\frac{11}{26}$ **iv** $\frac{21}{26}$

v $\frac{2}{13}$ **vi** $\frac{5}{26}$

8 a

	A	Not A	Total
B	2	6	8
Not B	3	1	4
Total	5	7	12

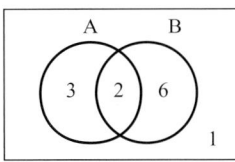

b

	A	Not A	Total
B	3	4	7
Not B	9	4	13
Total	12	8	20

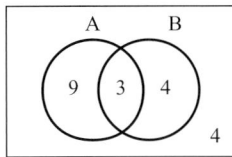

9 a

Car   House

1   3   3

3

b 3   **c** $\dfrac{1}{10}$

10 a

	Rain water	No rain water	Total
Tap water	12	36	48
No tap water	11	41	52
Total	23	77	100

b 12   **c** $\dfrac{9}{25}$ **d** $\dfrac{59}{100}$

11 23   **12** $\dfrac{7}{15}$

13

A   B

z x y

w

14 a $T - x - y + z$ **b** $T - x$
c $T - y$ **d** $x - z$
e $y - z$ **f** $y - z$
g $T - x + z$

15

	A	Not A	Total
B	⓪	12	12
Not B	11	-4	7
Total	11	⑧	19

Filling in table so totals add up requires a negative
number– impossible!

16 4

17 a i

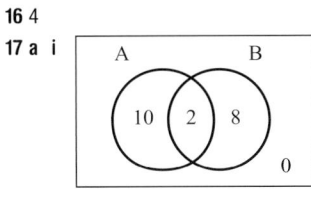

ii

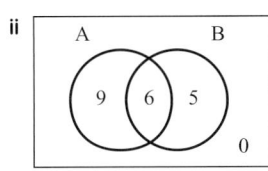

iii

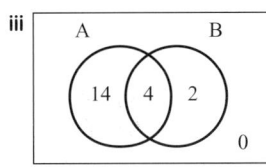

b i

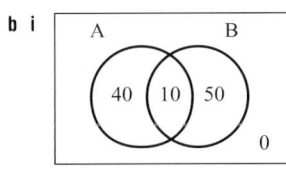

ii

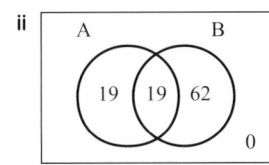

iii

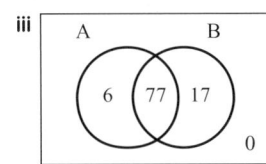

c   overlap = (A + B) − Total

Exercise 9C

1 a C   **b** D   **c** E   **d** A
  e F   **f** B
2 a B   **b** D   **c** A   **d** C
3 a 2   **b** 10   **c** 7   **d** 9
4 a i {1, 2, 3, 4, 5, 6, 7, 8, 9, 10}
  ii {1, 3, 5, 7, 9}
  iii {2, 3, 5, 7}
b

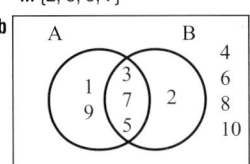

c **i** {3, 5, 7} **ii** {1, 2, 3, 5, 7, 9}
  iii {2, 4, 6, 8, 10} **iv** {2}

d **i** 5 **ii** $\frac{1}{2}$ **iii** 3 **iv** $\frac{3}{10}$

5 a

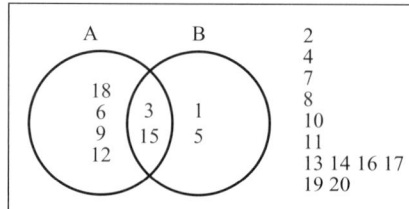

b **i** {3, 15} **ii** {1, 3, 5, 6, 9, 12, 15, 18}
  iii {1, 2, 4, 5, 7, 8, 10, 11, 13, 14, 16, 17, 19, 20}
  iv {1, 5}

c **i** 4 **ii** $\frac{1}{5}$ **iii** 2 **iv** $\frac{1}{10}$ **v** 8 **vi** $\frac{2}{5}$

6 a **i** False **ii** True **iii** False **iv** True
  v True **vi** False **vii** True **viii** False

b **i** $\frac{1}{2}$ **ii** $\frac{1}{2}$ **iii** 0

7 a **i** $\frac{1}{6}$ **ii** $\frac{11}{12}$ **iii** $\frac{5}{12}$

b **i** $\frac{6}{25}$ **ii** $\frac{21}{25}$ **iii** $\frac{8}{25}$

c **i** $\frac{1}{3}$ **ii** $\frac{11}{15}$ **iii** $\frac{2}{5}$

d **i** $\frac{5}{21}$ **ii** $\frac{17}{21}$ **iii** $\frac{4}{7}$

8 a **i** {Fred, Ron, Rachel} **ii** {Fred, Rachel, Helen}
  iii {} **iv** {Fred, Rachel}

b **i** $\frac{3}{4}$ **ii** $\frac{1}{4}$ **iii** 0 **iv** 1
  v $\frac{1}{2}$ **vi** 1

9 a 26 **b** 5 **c** 3 **d** 18
  e $\frac{5}{26}$ **f** $\frac{21}{26}$ **g** $\frac{3}{26}$ **h** $\frac{5}{13}$

10 a 11 **b** 21 **c** 1 **d** $\frac{9}{25}$

11 a own both a dog and a cat
  b own dogs or cats or both
  c does not own a cat
  d owns a cat but no dogs

12 a yes

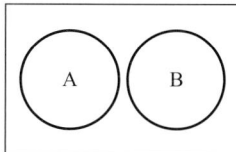

b No as A ∪ B includes only elements from sets A and B
13 B only = B ∩ A'

14

	A	A'	Total
B	$n(A \cap B)$	$n(B \cap A')$	$n(B)$
B'	$n(A \cap B')$	$n(A' \cap B')$	$n(B')$
Total	$n(A)$	$n(A')$	n(sample space)

15 Mutually exclusive events have no common elements,
  i.e. A ∩ B = ∅

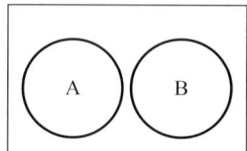

16 a **i** {2, 3, 5, 7, 11, 13, 17, 19}
  ii {1, 2, 3, 4, 6, 12}
  iii {2, 3}
  iv {1, 2, 3, 4, 5, 6, 7, 11, 12, 13, 17, 19}
  v {1, 4, 6, 12}
  vi {5, 7, 11, 13, 17, 19}
  vii {1, 2, 3, 4, 6, 8, 9, 10, 12, 14, 15, 16, 18, 20}
  viii {2, 3, 5, 7, 8, 9, 10, 11, 13, 14, 15, 16, 17, 18, 19, 20}
  ix {1, 4, 5, 6, 7, 8, 9, 10, 11, 12, 13, 14, 15, 16, 17, 18, 19, 20}

b **i** $\frac{3}{5}$ **ii** $\frac{1}{10}$ **iii** $\frac{1}{5}$ **iv** $\frac{2}{5}$
  v $\frac{4}{5}$ **vi** $\frac{9}{10}$ **vii** $\frac{9}{10}$ **viii** $\frac{2}{5}$

c they are equal

Exercise 9D

1 a 9 outcomes

	1	2	3
1	(1, 1)	(2, 1)	(3, 1)
2	(1, 2)	(2, 2)	(3, 2)
3	(1, 3)	(2, 3)	(3, 3)

b 12 outcomes

	1	2	3	4	5	6
H	(1, H)	(2, H)	(3, H)	(4, H)	(5, H)	(6, H)
T	(1, T)	(2, T)	(3, T)	(4, T)	(5, T)	(6, T)

c 6 outcomes

	A	B	C
A	X	(B, A)	(C, A)
B	(A, B)	X	(C, B)
C	(A, C)	(B, C)	X

d 6 outcomes

		1st		
		●	○	○
2nd	●	×	(○, ●)	(○, ●)
	○	(●, ○)	×	(○, ○)
	○	(●, ○)	(○, ○)	×

2 a Table A **b** Table B

c i $\frac{1}{9}$ **ii** $\frac{1}{6}$ **d i** 5 **ii** 4

3 a

		A	
		●	○
B	●	(●, ●)	(○, ●)
	○	(●, ○)	(○, ○)
	○	(●, ○)	(○, ○)

b 6 **c i** $\frac{1}{3}$ **ii** $\frac{1}{2}$ **iii** $\frac{1}{2}$

4 a

	1	2	3	4
1	(1, 1)	(2, 1)	(3, 1)	(4, 1)
2	(1, 2)	(2, 2)	(3, 2)	(4, 2)
3	(1, 3)	(2, 3)	(3, 3)	(4, 3)
4	(1, 4)	(2, 4)	(3, 4)	(4, 4)

Sample space = {(1, 1), (2, 1), … (4, 4)} i.e. all pairs from table.

b $\frac{1}{16}$ **c** $\frac{1}{4}$

5 a

	1	2	3	4	5	6
1	(1, 1)	(2, 1)	(3, 1)	(4, 1)	(5, 1)	(6, 1)
2	(1, 2)	(2, 2)	(3, 2)	(4, 2)	(5, 2)	(6, 2)
3	(1, 3)	(2, 3)	(3, 3)	(4, 3)	(5, 3)	(6, 3)
4	(1, 4)	(2, 4)	(3, 4)	(4, 4)	(5, 4)	(6, 4)
5	(1, 5)	(2, 5)	(3, 5)	(4, 5)	(5, 5)	(6, 5)
6	(1, 6)	(2, 6)	(3, 6)	(4, 6)	(5, 6)	(6, 6)

b 36

c i $\frac{1}{36}$ **ii** $\frac{1}{6}$ **iii** $\frac{1}{12}$ **iv** $\frac{5}{9}$

6 a

	D	O	G
D	X	(O, D)	(G, D)
O	(D, O)	X	(G, O)
G	(D, G)	(O, G)	X

b $\frac{1}{6}$ **c** $\frac{2}{3}$

7 a

		1st			
		1	2	3	4
	1	X	(2, 1)	(3, 1)	(4, 1)
2nd	2	(1, 2)	X	(3, 2)	(4, 2)
	3	(1, 3)	(2, 3)	X	(4, 3)
	4	(1, 4)	(2, 4)	(3, 4)	X

b i $\frac{1}{12}$ **ii** $\frac{1}{12}$

c i $\frac{1}{6}$ **ii** $\frac{5}{6}$ **iii** $\frac{1}{6}$ **iv** $\frac{1}{2}$

8 a

	1	2	3	4
1	2	3	4	5
2	3	4	5	6
3	4	5	6	7
4	5	6	7	8

b i $\frac{1}{16}$ **ii** $\frac{3}{16}$ **iii** $\frac{3}{8}$

iv $\frac{3}{16}$ **v** $\frac{13}{16}$

9 a

	A	B	C	D	E
A	(A, A)	(B, A)	(C, A)	(D, A)	(E, A)
B	(A, B)	(B, B)	(C, B)	(D, B)	(E, B)
C	(A, C)	(B, C)	(C, C)	(D, C)	(E, C)
D	(A, D)	(B, D)	(C, D)	(D, D)	(E, D)
E	(A, E)	(B, E)	(C, E)	(D, E)	(E, E)

b i $\frac{1}{25}$ **ii** $\frac{1}{5}$ **iii** $\frac{4}{5}$ **c i** $\frac{8}{25}$ **ii** $\frac{1}{25}$

10 a i $\frac{1}{36}$ **ii** $\frac{1}{12}$ **iii** $\frac{1}{12}$ **iv** $\frac{7}{12}$

v $\frac{5}{12}$ **vi** $\frac{1}{6}$ **vii** $\frac{1}{6}$ **viii** 0

b 7, $\frac{1}{6}$

11 a i 169 **ii** 156 **b i** 25 **ii** 12

12 yes as if one O is removed another remains to be used.

13 a $\frac{1}{25}$ **b** $\frac{1}{20}$

14 7, 8, 9, 10, 11

15 a $\frac{1}{2500}$ **b** $\frac{1}{50}$ **c** $\frac{1}{1250}$

d $\frac{49}{2500}$ **e** $\frac{23}{1250}$

16 a without replacement

b 2652 **c** $\frac{1}{1326}$ **d i** $\frac{1}{221}$ **ii** $\frac{1}{17}$

Exercise 9E

1 a HHH, HHT, HTH, HTT, THH, THT, TTH, TTT (8 outcomes)

  b TT, TO, OT, OO (4 outcomes)

2 a 6 outcomes   **b** 6 outcomes

3 a HH, HT, TH, TT

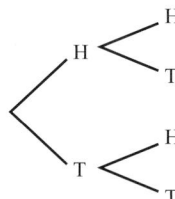

  b 4

  c i $\frac{1}{4}$ **ii** $\frac{1}{2}$ **iii** $\frac{3}{4}$ **iv** $\frac{3}{4}$

4 a

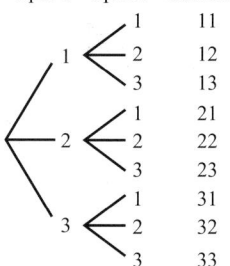

  b 9   **c i** $\frac{1}{9}$

               ii $\frac{5}{9}$

               iii $\frac{8}{9}$

               iv $\frac{4}{9}$

5 a

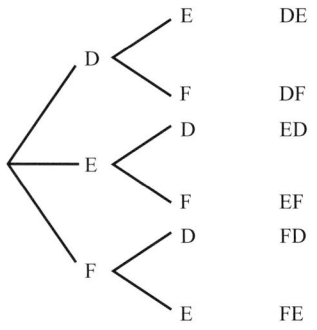

  b i $\frac{1}{3}$ **ii** $\frac{2}{3}$ **iii** 1

6 a

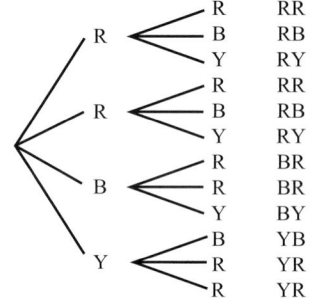

  b i $\frac{1}{3}$ **ii** $\frac{1}{6}$ **iii** $\frac{1}{6}$ **iv** $\frac{5}{6}$

7 a $\frac{4}{9}$ **b** $\frac{2}{9}$ **c** $\frac{1}{27}$ **d** $\frac{8}{27}$

8 a $\frac{1}{16}$ **b** $\frac{1}{16}$ **c** $\frac{5}{16}$ **d** $\frac{11}{16}$ **e** $\frac{15}{16}$

9 a

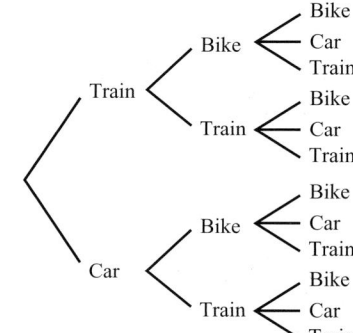

  b 12

  c i $\frac{1}{12}$ **ii** $\frac{1}{3}$ **iii** $\frac{1}{2}$ **iv** $\frac{1}{4}$ **v** $\frac{2}{3}$

10 a $\frac{1}{16}$ **b** $\frac{1}{4}$ **c** $\frac{3}{8}$ **d** $\frac{1}{4}$ **e** $\frac{1}{16}$

11 a 32   **b** 2^n

12 yes, there is a difference; probability of obtaining two of the same colour is lower without replacement

13 a $\frac{1}{9}$ **b** $\frac{1}{9}$ **c** $\frac{7}{18}$ **d** $\frac{7}{18}$ **e** $\frac{1}{2}$

   f 0   **g** $\frac{1}{6}$ **h** $\frac{2}{3}$ **i** $\frac{1}{9}$ **j** $\frac{17}{18}$

Exercise 9F

1 a A: $\frac{5}{20} = 0.25$ B: $\frac{30}{100} = 0.3$

  b C as it is a larger sample size

2 a 5   **b** 10   **c** 50   **d** 4

3 0.41, from the 100 throws as the more times an experiment is carried out the closer the experimental probability becomes to the actual/theoretical probability

4 a 0.6

   b i 60   **ii** 120   **iii** 360

5 a $\dfrac{7}{8}$

   b i 350   **ii** 4375   **iii** 35

6 a $\dfrac{1}{15}$ **b** $\dfrac{2}{5}$ **c** $\dfrac{11}{60}$

7 a 20   **b** 40   **c** 60   **d** 40

8 a 20

   b i $\dfrac{1}{4}$ **ii** $\dfrac{7}{20}$ **c i** 25   **ii** 20   **iii** 45

9 a 0.64   **b** SEE

10 a i 0.52   **ii** 0.48   **iii** 0.78

   b 78

   c $\dfrac{1}{2},\dfrac{1}{4},\dfrac{1}{4}$

11 a $\dfrac{9}{10}$

   b No, as the number of throws increases, the experiment should produce results closer to the theoretical probability ($\dfrac{1}{6}$).

12 a fair, close to 0.5 chance of tails

   b biased, nearly all results are heads

   c can't determine on such a small sample

13 a $\dfrac{\text{Shaded Area}}{\text{Total Area}} = 0.225$ $\therefore 100$ shots ≈ 23

   b $\dfrac{1}{10} \times 100 = 10$

   c $\dfrac{150-32}{150} \times 100 \approx 79$

   d $\dfrac{225\pi - 25\pi}{225\pi} \times 100 \approx 89$

14 a no   **b** true

   c no   **d** true

15 3 blue, 2 red, 4 green, 1 yellow

16 2 strawberry, 3 caramel, 2 coconut, 4 nut, 1 mint

Exercise 9G

1 a common   **b** middle   **c** mean

2

	mean	median	mode
a	3	2	2
b	8	9	10
c	7	7	7
d	7	7	3
e	15	16	20
f	7	7	2

3

	mean	median	mode
a	6	7	8
b	8	6	5, 10
c	6	6	2
d	11	12	none
e	4	3.5	2.1
f	5	4.5	none
g	3	3.5	-3
h	0	2	3

4 a outlier = 33   mean = 12   median = 7.5

   b outlier = -1.1   mean = 1.075   median = 1.4

   c outlier = -4   mean = -49   median = -59

5 a yes   **b** no   **c** no   **d** yes

6 a 24.67 s   **b** 24.8 s

7 a 15   **b** 26

8 a 90   **b** 60

9 9

10 answers may vary

   a 1, 4, 6, 7, 7 is a set   **b** 2, 3, 4, 8, 8 is a set

   c 4, 4, 4, 4, 4 is a set   **d** 2.5, 2.5, 3, 7, 7.5 is a set

   e -3, -2, 0, 5, 5 is a set   **f** $0, \dfrac{1}{2}, 1\dfrac{1}{4}, 1\dfrac{1}{4}, 2$ is a set

11 a $1\ 700\ 000

   b ($354 500 and $324 000) drops $30 500

   c ($570 667 and $344 800) drops $225 867

12 An outlier has a large impact on the addition of all the scores and therefore significantly affects the mean. An outlier does not move the middle of the group of scores significantly.

13 a 15   **b** 1.2   **c** 1   **d** 1

   e No, as it will still lie in the 1 column.

14 a 2   **b** 3   **c** 7

15 a 76.75   **b i** 71.4, B⁺   **ii** 75, B⁺   **iii** 80.2, A

   c 81.4, he cannot get an A⁺

   d i 43   **ii** 93

   e $\dfrac{307+m}{5}$ **f** $m = 5M - 307$

Exercise 9H

1 a 9   **b i** 8 min   **ii** 35 min   **c** 21 min   **d** 21 min

2 a 26   **b i** 0 mm   **ii** 6 mm   **c i** 21 mm   **ii** 24 mm

   d i 8 mm   **ii** 15 mm   **e** skewed   **f** symmetrical

3 a i

stem	leaf
1	9 9
2	3 4 6 6 8 8 8
3	2 2 3 5
4	1
5	4

   ii 28   **iii** 28   **iv** skewed

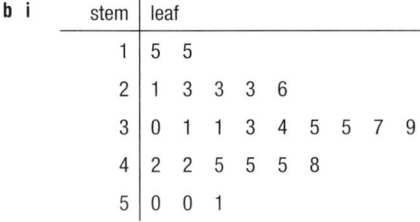

b i

stem	leaf
1	5 5
2	1 3 3 3 6
3	0 1 1 3 4 5 5 7 9
4	2 2 5 5 5 8
5	0 0 1

ii 35 **iii** 23, 45 **iv** almost symmetrical

c i

stem	leaf
32	0
33	3 7 8
34	3 4 5 5 7 8 9
35	2 2 4 5 8
36	1 3 5
37	0

ii 34.85 **iii** 35.2, 34.5 **iv** almost symmetrical

d i

stem	leaf
15	7 8 9 9 9 9
16	1 4 7 7 7
17	3 5 7 7
18	5 5 7 9
19	3 8
20	0 2

ii 173 **iii** 159 **iv** skewed

4 a

stem	leaf
0	5 6 6 8 8 9
1	0 1 1 2 2 2 4 4 5 6 7
2	0 1 2

b 9 **c** 12

5 a i

		Set A		Set B	
	3 2	3	1		
	9	3			
3 3 0	0	4	0 1 3 4 4		
8 7 6	5	4	6 7 8 8 9 9		
4 4	3	5	1 3		

ii Set A has values spread between 32 and 54 while Set B has most of its values between 40 and 53 with an outlier at 31.

b i

	Set A		Set B	
9 8 6 4 3 2 2 1	0	9		
7 7 6 1 1 0 0	1	8 9 9		
9 6 4 3 3 2	2	0 1 3 4 7 8		
7 6 6 5 0	3	1 7 7 8 9 9 9		
8 3 1	4	0 1 1 3 4 4 5 7		
0	5	0 0 1 3 3 4 4 5 6		

ii Set A has values between 1 and 50 with the frequency decreasing as the numbers increase whereas Set B has values between 9 and 56 with the frequency increasing as the numbers increase.

c i

	Set A		Set B	
8 7 4 3	0	1 1 1 2 3 6 6 9 9		
9 9 7 6 4	1	2 3 5 8 9		
6 5 3 1	2	1 5 6		
9 9 6 4 3 2	3	3 4 9		
7 3 1	4	3 7 8		
7 3 2	5	2 3 7		
2 1	6	1 2		
8 3	8	3 8		
1	9			

ii Set A and B are similar. The frequency decreases as the numbers increase.

6 a

	Collingwood		St Kilda	
	8 3	6	6 8 8	
8 7 2 1 0		7	8	
9 9 8 2 0		8	0 0 2 2 3 4 7 8	
8 7 5 1		9	0 4	
4 3 3 3		10	6 9	
9 8 5		11	1 3 7 8	
7		12	2 5 6	
		13	8	

b Collingwood $33\frac{1}{3}\%$ St Kilda $41\frac{2}{3}\%$

c Collingwood is almost symmetrical data and based on these results seem to be consistent. St Kilda has groups of similar scores and while less consistent, they have higher scores.

7 a 9 days **b** 18°C **c** 7°C

8 a 16.1 s **b** 2.3 s **c** yes 0.05 lower

9 a

Battery lifetime

	Brand A		Brand B	
	3	7	2 3 4	
		7	5 6 8 9 9	
	4 2	8	0 1 3	
9 8 7 5		8		
4 4 3 2 1		0	9 0 1 2 3 4	
9 9 8 7 6 5 5		9	5 6 8 8	

8 | 3 represents 8.3 hours

b Brand A, 12; Brand B, 8

c Brand A consistently performs better than Brand B.

10 a $c = 2$ **b** 0.02

c i 5, 6, 7 or 8 **ii** 0, 1, 2, 3, 4, 5 or 6

11 a 48% **b** 15%

c In general, birth weights of babies are lower for mothers who smoke.

12 In symmetrical data the mean is close to the median as the data is spread evenly from the centre with an even number of data values with a similar difference from the median above and below it.

13 a 52 **b** 17.8

14 a mean = 41.06 median = 43

    b median as more of the scores exist in the higher stems but a few low scores lower the mean.

    c the mean is higher for positively skewed data as the majority of the scores are in the lower stems however a few high scores increase the mean.

    d symmetrical data

Exercise 9I

1 a 3   **b** 360 000 – 370 000

2 a $a = 15$ $b = 2$ $c = 30\%$ $d = 40\%$
     $e = 20\%$ $f = 100\%$

    b $a = 50$ $b = 28\%$ $c = 12\%$ $d = 40$
     $e = 100\%$

3 a 2   **b** 20   **c i** 30%   **ii** 65%

4 a

Class	Frequency	Percentage frequency
0–9	23	46%
10–19	10	20%
20–29	6	12%
30–39	7	14%
40–49	4	8%
	50	100%

    b

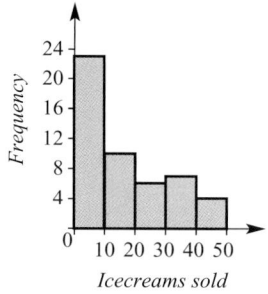

    c i 33   **ii** 11   **d** 34%

5 a

Class	Frequency	Percentage frequency
50–59	8	13.33%
60–69	14	23.33%
70–79	9	15%
80–89	25	41.67%
90–99	4	6.67%
	60	100%

b

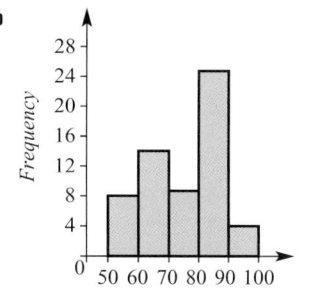

Exam mark

c i 22   **ii** 48.33%

6 a

Number of goals	Frequency
0–2	1
3–5	8
6–8	7
9–11	7
12–14	7
	30

b

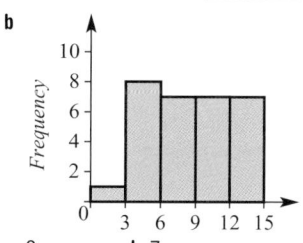

c 9   **d** 7

7 a symmetrical data   **b** skewed data

8 a $a = 6$ $b = 27.5$ $c = 17.5$ $d = 4$
     $e = 12$ $f = 30$ $g = 100$

    b $a = 1$ $b = 18$ $c = 8$ $d = 24$
     $e = 20$ $f = 40$ $g = 100$

9 a i 20%   **ii** 55%   **iii** 80%   **iv** 75%   **v** 50%

    b i 30   **ii** 45   **c i** 2   **ii** 22

10 85.5%

11 Because you only have the number of scores in the class interval not the individual scores

12 The number of data items within each class

13 a Student A

    b Make the intervals for their groups of data smaller so that the graph conveys more information.

14 a minimum wage: $204; maximum wage: $940

    b i

Weekly wages ($)	Frequency
200–	2
300–	7
400–	6
500–	6
600–	11
700–	11
800–	5
900–	2

ii

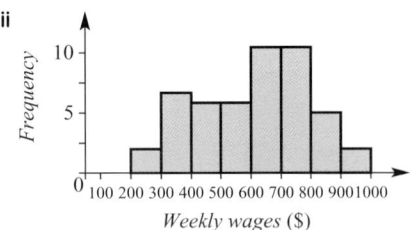

Weekly wages ($)

c i

Weekly wages	Frequency
200–	9
400–	12
600–	22
800–	7

ii

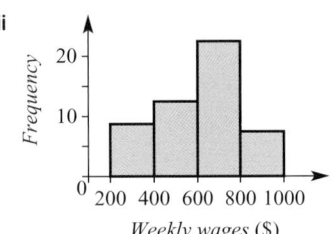

Weekly wages ($)

d More intervals shows greater detail. Since first graph has each pair of intervals quite similar, these two graphs are quite similar.

Exercise 9J

1 a 6   **b** 7
   c i 5   **ii** 8   **d** 3
2 a 12   **b** 5
   c i 3   **ii** 8   **d** 5

3

	Range	Q_2	Q_1	Q_3	IQR
a	11	6	2.5	8.5	6
b	23	30	23.5	36.5	13
c	170	219	181.5	284.5	103
d	851	76	28	367	339
e	1.3	1.3	1.05	1.85	0.8
f	34.98	10	0.1	23	22.9

4 a 110
   b i 119.5 min   **ii** 106 min
     iii 130 min   **iv** 24 min
   c The middle 50% of videos rented varied in length by 24 min
5 a i $12 000   **ii** $547 000
     iii $71 500   **iv** $46 000
     v $78 000   **vi** $32 000
   b The middle 50% of prices differs by less than $32 000
   c No effect on Q_1, Q_2 or Q_3 but the mean would increase.

6 a 17.5   **b** 2.1
7 a 2   **b** 2
   c No, only the many value has changed so no impact on IQR.
8 No, as the range is the difference in the highest and lowest score and different sets of two numbers can have the same difference (10 − 8 = 2, 22 − 20 = 2)
9 a Yes – the lowering of the highest price reduces the range
   b No – the middle price will not change
   c No; as only one value, the highest has changed, yet it still remains the highest, Q_1 and Q_3 remain unchanged.
10 a Yes (3, 3, 3, 4, 4, 4; IQR = 4 − 3 = 1; Range = 1)
   b Yes (4, 4, 4, 4, 4 has IQR = 0)
11 a i $Q_1 = 25$; $Q_2 = 26$; $Q_3 = 27$
     ii $Q_1 = 22$; $Q_2 = 24.5$; $Q_3 = 27$
   b 27 jelly beans   **c** 22 jelly beans
   d i IQR = 2   **ii** IQR = 5
   e Shop B is less consistent than shop A and its data is more spread out
   f Shop A

Exercise 9K

1 a minimum value   **b** lower quartile, Q_1
   c median, Q_2 **d** upper quartile, Q_3
   e maximum value   **f** scale
   g whisker   **h** box
2 a the minimum from the maximum
   b the lower quartile Q_1 from the upper quartile Q_3
3 D
4 a min = 35 cm   max = 60 cm   **b** 25 cm
   c 50 cm   **d** 10 cm
   e 50 cm   **f** 55 cm
   g 20 babies
5 a min = 0 rabbits, max = 60 rabbits
   b 60   **c** 25   **d** 25
   e 35   **f** 25   **g** 25
6 a i 2   **ii** 13   **iii** 8   **iv** 4   **v** 11
     vi

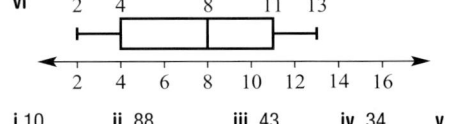

   b i 10   **ii** 88   **iii** 43   **iv** 34   **v** 56
     vi

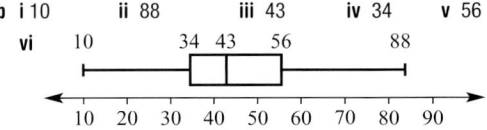

   c i 244   **ii** 933   **iii** 435   **iv** 255   **v** 674
     vi

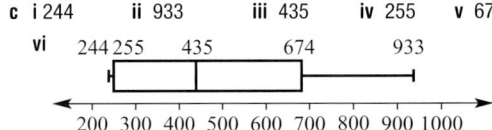

d i 0.1   ii 1.3   iii 0.6   iv 0.4   v 0.95

vi   0.1   0.4 0.6   0.95   1.3

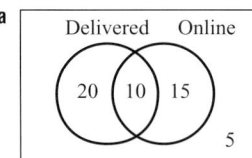

7 a

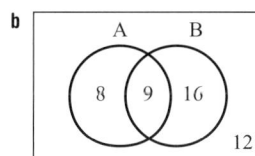

b i 100%   ii 50%   iii 75%   iv 25%

8 a Africa   **b** 10 kg   **c** yes, 25 kg

d i 50%   ii 75%   **e** African

9 a Mac   **b** 75%   **c** 50%

d They are the same. Mac has 100% of times within same range as middle 50% of PC start up times. Mac is more consistent.

10 a Waldren   **b** Yeng   **c** Yeng

d Yeng, smaller range and IQR

e Yeng, higher median

11 a 1, 3, 5, 6, 6   **b** 1, 4, 4, 4, 5, 6

12 No, the median is anywhere within the box, including at times at its edges.

13 Yes, one reason is if an outlier is the highest score then the mean $> Q_3$ [e.g. 1, 1, 3, 5, 6, 7, 256]

14 a $Q_1 = 4$
$Q_2 = 6$
$Q_3 = 8$

b yes, 17

c 9

d

```
   ┌──┬──┐
├──┤  │  ├──┤              ×
   └──┴──┘
──────────────────────────────→ x
  1  2  4  6  8 10 12 14 16 18
```

Challenges

1 a $2^5 = 32$ **b** $\dfrac{3}{16}$ **c** $\dfrac{31}{32}$

2 a $\dfrac{1}{6}$ **b** $\dfrac{1}{3}$

3 a i $\dfrac{1}{4}$ ii $\dfrac{1}{2}$ **b** $\dfrac{1}{6}$

c $\dfrac{1}{12}$ **d** $\dfrac{1}{3}$

4 a mean and median increase by 5, range unchanged

b mean, median and range all double

c mean and median double and decrease by 1, range doubles

5 $5m$

6 a 3, 5, 7, 8, 10 or 3, 5, 7, 9, 10   **b** 2, 2, 8, 12

7 1, 4, 6, 7, 7; 2, 3, 6, 7, 7 and 1, 2, 5, 6, 6

Multiple-choice questions

1 B   **2** A   **3** D   **4** B   **5** D

6 B   **7** E   **8** C   **9** B   **10** E

Short-answer questions

1 a $\dfrac{2}{3}$ **b** $\dfrac{5}{9}$ **c** $\dfrac{3}{5}$

2 a

```
┌─────────────────────────────────┐
│  Delivered      Online          │
│     ╱──────╲ ╱──────╲           │
│    │  20  │ 10 │ 15  │          │
│     ╲──────╱ ╲──────╱           │
│                         5        │
└─────────────────────────────────┘
```

b 15   **c** i $\dfrac{1}{5}$ ii $\dfrac{2}{5}$ iii $\dfrac{3}{10}$

3 a

	A	A′	Total
B	9	16	25
B′	8	12	20
Total	17	28	45

b

```
┌─────────────────────────────┐
│      A        B             │
│   ╱──────╲ ╱──────╲         │
│  │   8   │ 9 │ 16  │        │
│   ╲──────╱ ╲──────╱         │
│                    12        │
└─────────────────────────────┘
```

c i $\dfrac{4}{9}$ ii $\dfrac{1}{5}$ iii 8   iv 33

4 a 12 outcomes

	1	2	3	4
red	(red, 1)	(red, 2)	(red, 3)	(red, 4)
green	(green, 1)	(green, 2)	(green, 3)	(green, 4)
blue	(blue, 1)	(blue, 2)	(blue, 3)	(blue, 4)

b i $\dfrac{1}{6}$ ii $\dfrac{1}{6}$ iii $\dfrac{2}{3}$

5 a

```
           Coin 1    Coin 2    Outcomes
                      10ᶜ      ($1, 10ᶜ)
            $1 <
                      10ᶜ      ($1, 10ᶜ)
                      $1       (10ᶜ, $1)
          10ᶜ <
    <                 10ᶜ      (10ᶜ, 10ᶜ)
                      $1       (10ᶜ, $1)
          10ᶜ <
                      10ᶜ      (10ᶜ, 10ᶜ)
```

b $\dfrac{2}{3}$

6 a $\dfrac{48}{120} = \dfrac{2}{5}$ **b** 14

7 a 26   **b** 26.5   **c** 23, 31

8 a

Employee 1		Employee 2
9	1	7 7
5 3 1	2	0 4 8 9
9 8 6 5 5 4	3	2 7 7 8
6 5 0	4	0 1 2 5 8
3 1	5	

2 | 4 means 24

b i Employee 1: 36, Employee 2: 37

ii Employee 1: 36, Employee 2: 33

c Employee 1, they have a higher mean and more sales at the high end.

d Employee 1 symmetrical, employee 2 skewed

9 a

Class interval	Frequency	Percentage frequency
120–	1	4
130–	3	12
140–	4	16
150–	8	32
160–	7	28
170–180	2	8
Total	25	100%

b

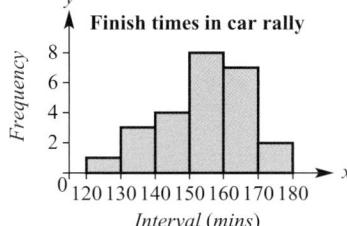

Finish times in car rally

c i 4 **ii** 60%

10 a 52 runs

b

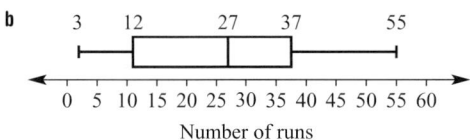

c 37 runs

Extended-response questions

1 a i

		1st spin				
		1	2	3	4	5
2nd spin	1	(1, 1)	(2, 1)	(3, 1)	(4, 1)	(5, 1)
	2	(1, 2)	(2, 2)	(3, 2)	(4, 2)	(5, 2)
	3	(1, 3)	(2, 3)	(3, 3)	(4, 3)	(5, 3)
	4	(1, 4)	(2, 4)	(3, 4)	(4, 4)	(5, 4)
	5	(1, 5)	(2, 5)	(3, 5)	(4, 5)	(5, 5)

ii $\dfrac{12}{25}$ **iii** $\dfrac{4}{25}$ **iv** 24 **v** $68

b i

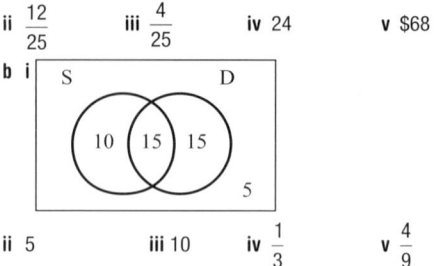

ii 5 **iii** 10 **iv** $\dfrac{1}{3}$ **v** $\dfrac{4}{9}$

vi $\dfrac{7}{9}$, the probability a person did not buy a sausage on its own

2 a Yes, 52 mins **b i** 12 **ii** 4 **iii** 15.5

c and **e**

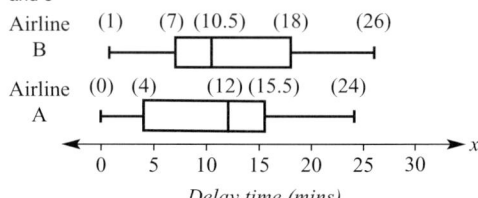

Delay time (mins)

d No, the median time is 12 mins so half the flights have less than 12 minute delay.

f Airline A: range = 24, IQR = 11.5

Airline B: range = 25, IQR = 11

Both airlines have a very similar spread of their data when the outlier is removed.

g There is not much difference when airline A's outlier is removed. It has a marginally better performance with 75% of flights delayed less than 15.5 mins compared with 18 mins for airline B.

Chapter 10

Pre-test

1 a i 0 **ii** 4 **iii** 1 **iv** 9

b i 0 **ii** 2 **iii** 5 **iv** 27

c i 3 **ii** -1 **iii** 2 **iv** -6

d i -1 **ii** 7 **iii** -2 **iv** 2

2 a yes **b** no **c** yes

3 a 0 **b** 3 **c** -5 **d** -3

e 4 **f** $\dfrac{4}{3}$

4 a $a^2 - 2a = 0$ **b** $a^2 - 3a + 1 = 0$

5 a $2x$ **b** x **c** $3x$ **d** $2x$

e 4 **f** 5

6 a $(x + 3)(x - 3)$ **b** $(x + 5)(x - 5)$

c $(x + 8)(x - 8)$ **d** $(x + 4)(x - 4)$

7 a $(x + 6)(x + 2)$ **b** $(x + 4)(x + 1)$

c $(x - 7)(x + 4)$ **d** $(x - 5)(x - 4)$

8 a $2x - 6$　　**b** $2x - x^2$　　**c** $x^2 - x - 2$
　　d $x^2 - 7x + 12$
9 a $A = x^2 + 2x$　　　　**b** $A = x^2 - 9$
　　c $A = x^2 + x - 2$
10 a $(2, 0), (0, -4)$　**b**　　$(4, 0), (0, 2)$
11 a $x = 5$　　**b** $x = 3$　　**c** $x = 1$　　**d** $x = 5.5$

Exercise 10A

1 a 12　　　**b** -4　　　**c** 6
　　d -1　　　**e** 20　　　**f** 4
　　g 72　　　**h** 0　　　**i** -27
2 a no　　　**b** no　　　**c** yes　　**d** yes
　　e yes　　**f** no　　　**g** no　　　**h** yes
　　i yes
3 a 1　　　　　**b** -3　　　　　**c** -11
　　d -2　　　　**e** 3　　　　　**f** -6
4 a $x - 5 = 0, x = 5$
　　b $2x + 1 = 0, 2x = -1$ or $x = 3, x = -\dfrac{1}{2}$ or $x = 3$
5 a $x^2 + 2x - 5 = 0$　　**b** $x^2 - 5x + 2 = 0$
　　c $x^2 - 4x + 1 = 0$　　**d** $x^2 - 7x - 2 = 0$
　　e $2x^2 + 2x + 1 = 0$　　**f** $3x^2 - 3x + 4 = 0$
　　g $3x^2 + 4 = 0$　　**h** $x^2 - 3x - 1 = 0$
　　i $2x^2 + 5x - 10 = 0$
6 a yes　　　**b** yes　　　**c** no
　　d no　　　**e** yes　　　**f** yes
　　g no　　　**h** no　　　**i** no
7 both are solutions　　**8** both are solutions
9 a 0, -1　　**b** 0, -5　　**c** 0, 2　　**d** 0, 7
　　e -1, 3　　**f** 4, -2　　**g** -7, 3　　**h** $-\dfrac{1}{2}, \dfrac{1}{2}$
　　i 0, -5　　**j** 0, $\dfrac{2}{3}$　　**k** 0, $-\dfrac{2}{3}$　　**l** 0, -2
10 a $\dfrac{1}{2}$, -2　**b** -2, $\dfrac{1}{3}$　**c** $-\dfrac{2}{5}$, -4　**d** 1, $\dfrac{1}{3}$
　　e -5, $-\dfrac{2}{7}$　**f** $\dfrac{2}{3}$, $-\dfrac{1}{5}$　**g** $\dfrac{7}{11}, \dfrac{13}{2}$　**h** $-\dfrac{9}{4}, \dfrac{7}{2}$
　　i $\dfrac{4}{3}, -\dfrac{1}{7}$
11 a 0, -3　　　**b** 0, 7　　　**c** 1, -4
　　d $\dfrac{1}{2}$, -6　　**e** $-\dfrac{3}{2}, \dfrac{1}{2}$
12 a $4x^2 + x + 1 = 0$　　**b** $3x^2 - 3x = 0$
　　c $3x^2 - x - 4 = 0$　　**d** $5x^2 + x - 2 = 0$
　　e $2x^2 - x - 3 = 0$　　**f** $3x^2 - 10x + 6 = 0$
　　g $x^2 - x - 5 = 0$　　**h** $4x^2 - 5x - 6 = 0$
13 a -1, 2　　**b** 1, 3　　**c** 0, 4　　**d** 0, -3
　　e -4, 1　　**f** -4, 4
14 a $(x + 2)(x + 2) = 0$　**b** both solutions are the same, $x = -2$
　　c i -3　　**ii** 5　　**iii** $\dfrac{1}{2}$　　**iv** $\dfrac{7}{5}$
15 a $(x - 1)(x + 2) = 0$　　**b** $x = 1, x = -2$
　　c multiplying by a constant doesn't change a zero value.
　　d i -2, 3　　**ii** 0, -2　　**iii** -1, 3

16 a i no　　**ii** no　　**iii** no　　**iv** no
　　b It has no solutions as $(x - 3)^2$ is always ≥ 0, so
　　$(x - 3)^2 + 1 \geq 1$
17 a Linear　　**b** Quadratic　**c** Quintic　**d** Cubic
　　e Quartic　　**f** Quintic
18 a -2, -1, 3　　**b** -11, 2, 5
　　c $-\dfrac{2}{3}, \dfrac{1}{5}, \dfrac{1}{2}$　　**d** $-\dfrac{10}{7}, -\dfrac{4}{5}, -\dfrac{2}{3}, 6\dfrac{1}{2}$

Exercise 10B

1 a 2　　　　**b** 5　　　　**c** 2　　　　**d** 8
　　e x　　　**f** x　　　**g** $3x$　　　**h** $3x$
2 a $2(x - 2)(x + 2)$　**b** $4(x - 3)(x + 3)$　**c** $3(x - 5)(x + 5)$
　　d $12(x - 1)(x + 1)$　**e** $x(x - 3)$　　**f** $x(x + 7)$
　　g $2x(x - 2)$　　**h** $5x(x - 3)$　　**i** $2x(3x + 2)$
　　j $9x(x - 3)$　　**k** $4x(1 - 4x)$　　**l** $7x(2 - 3x)$
3 a $x = 0, x = 3$　　**b** $x = 0, x = -1$　**c** $x = 0, x = -2$
　　d $x = -1, x = 1$　**e** $x = -5, x = 5$　**f** $x = -\dfrac{1}{2}, x = \dfrac{1}{2}$
4 a $x = 0, x = -3$　**b** $x = 0, x = -7$　**c** $x = 0, x = -4$
　　d $x = 0, x = 5$　　**e** $x = 0, x = 8$　　**f** $x = 0, x = 2$
　　g $x = 0, x = -\dfrac{1}{3}$　**h** $x = 0, x = \dfrac{1}{2}$
5 a $x = 0, x = 3$　　**b** $x = 0, x = 4$　　**c** $x = 0, x = -5$
　　d $x = 0, x = 3$　　**e** $x = 0, x = 3$　　**f** $x = 0, x = -4$
6 a $x = 0, x = 3$　　**b** $x = 0, x = 2$　　**c** $x = 0, x = 4$
　　d $x = 0, x = -3$　**e** $x = 0, x = -4$　**f** $x = 0, x = -3$
7 a $x = 3, x = -3$　　**b** $x = 4, x = -4$　　**c** $x = 5, x = -5$
　　d $x = 12, x = -12$　**e** $x = 9, x = -9$　**f** $x = 20, x = -20$
8 a $x = 2, x = -2$　　**b** $x = 3, x = -3$　　**c** $x = 5, x = -5$
　　d $x = 2, x = -2$　　**e** $x = 2, x = -2$　**f** $x = 2, x = -2$
　　g $x = 4, x = -4$　　**h** $x = 3, x = -3$
9 a $x = 2, x = -2$　　**b** $x = 5, x = -5$　**c** $x = 10, x = -10$
　　d $x = 0, x = -7$　**e** $x = 0, x = 7$　　**f** $x = -1, x = 1$
　　g $x = 0, x = \dfrac{2}{3}$　**h** $x = 0, x = \dfrac{3}{5}$　**i** $x = -\sqrt{3}, x = \sqrt{3}$
10 a $x = -2, x = 2$　**b** $x = -6, x = 6$　**c** $x = -1, x = 1$
　　d $x = -1, x = 1$　**e** $x = 0, x = -7$　**f** $x = 0, x = 4$
11 a 0 or 7　　　**b** 8 or -8　　　**c** 0 or -4
12 a $(x + 2)(x - 2) = x^2 - 4$ not $x^2 + 4$
　　b No, $\sqrt{-4}$ is not a real number
13 a $ax^2 + bx = x(ax + b) = 0, x = 0$ is always one solution
　　b $x = -\dfrac{b}{a}$
14 a $x = -\dfrac{4}{3}, x = \dfrac{4}{3}$　**b** $x = -\dfrac{6}{5}, x = \dfrac{6}{5}$　**c** $x = -\dfrac{1}{5}, x = \dfrac{1}{5}$
　　d $x = -\dfrac{9}{5}, x = \dfrac{9}{5}$　**e** $x = -\dfrac{8}{11}, x = \dfrac{8}{11}$　**f** $x = -\dfrac{12}{7}, x = \dfrac{12}{7}$
15 a $x = -1, x = 5$　**b** $x = -1, x = -9$　**c** $x = -1, x = 0$
　　d $x = -\dfrac{2}{5}, x = \dfrac{8}{5}$　**e** $x = 1, x = 7$　**f** $x = -1, x = \dfrac{13}{7}$

Exercise 10C

1 a 3, 2   **b** 4, 2   **c** -2, -1   **d** -5, -2
   e 2, -1   **f** 5, -1   **g** -4, 3   **h** -6, 2

2 a $(x + 5)(x + 4) = 0$ **b** $(x - 6)(x + 4) = 0$
    $x + 5 = 0$ or $x + 4 = 0$ $x - 6 = 0$ or $x + 4 = 0$
    $x = -5$ or $x = -4$ $x = 6$ or $x = -4$
   c $(x + 9)(x - 5) = 0$ **d** $(x - 8)(x - 2) = 0$
    $x + 9 = 0$ or $x - 5 = 0$ $x - 8 = 0$ or $x - 2 = 0$
    $x = -9$ or $x = 5$ $x = 8$ or $x = 2$

3 a -6, -2   **b** -8, -3   **c** -5, -2
   d -7, 2   **e** -6, 2   **f** -10, 3
   g 4, 8   **h** 3, 6   **i** 3, 7
   j -3, 5   **k** -2, 8   **l** -5, 9
   m 4, 6   **n** -6, 7   **o** -12, 7
   p -3, -1   **q** -3, 9   **r** 2, 10

4 a -3   **b** -2   **c** -7
   d -12   **e** 5   **f** 8
   g 6   **h** 9   **i** 10

5 a -2, 5   **b** 2, 5   **c** 3
   d -4, 1   **e** -7, 2   **f** 4
   g -6, 2   **h** -6, 1   **i** 3, 5
   j -8, 2   **k** -4, -2   **l** -9, 2

6 a -2, 3   **b** -5, -3   **c** -2, 8
   d 2, 3   **e** 2   **f** -1
   g 5   **h** -3   **i** -7, 1

7 a 2, 3   **b** 3   **c** -10, 2
   d -5, 7   **e** -1   **f** 2

8 a $x^2 - 3x + 2$ **b** $x^2 - x - 6$
   c $x^2 + 3x - 4$ **d** $x^2 - 7x - 30$
   e $x^2 - 10x + 25$ **f** $x^2 + 22x + 121$

9 11 am, 6 pm

10 a Equation is not written in standard form $x^2 + bx + c = 0$ so cannot apply Null Factor Law in this form.
   b $x = -2, x = 3$

11 It is a perfect square, $(x - 1)(x - 1)$, $(x - 1)^2 = 0$, $x = 1$

12 a $(x - a)(x - a) = 0$ or $(x - a)^2 = 0$
   b $(x - a)(x - b) = 0$

13 a $x = -3$ or $x = -\dfrac{1}{5}$ **b** $x = \dfrac{2}{3}$ or $x = -2$

   c $x = \dfrac{1}{3}$ or $x = -\dfrac{1}{2}$ **d** $x = \dfrac{1}{2}$ or $x = -1$

   e $x = \dfrac{3}{2}$ or $x = -5$ **f** $x = \dfrac{3}{2}$

   g $x = \dfrac{7}{3}$ or $x = -2$ **h** $x = \dfrac{3}{5}$ or $x = -4$

   i $x = -\dfrac{5}{3}$ **j** $x = \dfrac{1}{3}$ or $x = \dfrac{5}{2}$

Exercise 10D

1 a $x(x + 2) = 8$ **b** 2, -4
   c 2, width > 0   **d** $L = 4$ cm, $W = 2$ cm

---

2 a $x(x + 5) = 14$ **b** 2, -7
   c 2, width > 0   **d** $L = 7$ m, $W = 2$ cm

3 a -6, 3   **b** 5, -4   **c** 2, -5

4 -8, 6   **5** -5, 12   **6** -2, 15

7 $L = 9$ cm, $W = 4$ cm   **8** $L = 3$ m, $W = 23$ m

9 a $A = 100 - x^2$ **b** $x = 6$

10 $h = 5$

11 a $A = x^2 + 5x + 15$ **b** $x = 7$

12 a $x = 3$ (-4 not valid)   **b** $x = 12$ **c** $x = 25$

13 -8 not valid because dimensions must be > 0

14 $x = -2$ or $x = 3$ both valid as both are integers

15 a 10, 15, 21   **b i** 28   **ii** 210   **c i** 9   **ii** 15

16 a 9, 14   **b i** 8   **ii** 12

17 a $A = (20 + 2x)^2 = 4x^2 + 80x + 400$ **b** 10 cm

18 4 cm

Exercise 10E

1 a highest   **b** parabola   **c** intercepts
   d vertex   **e** lowest   **f** zero

2 a $x = 3$ **b** $x = 1$ **c** $x = -2$ **d** $x = -5$

3

	i axis of symmetry	**ii** turning point	**iii** type of turning point	**iv** x-intercepts	**v** y-intercept
a	$x = 2$	(2, -1)	minimum	(1, 0), (3, 0)	(0, 3)
b	$x = 0$	(0, -4)	minimum	(-2, 0), (2, 0)	(0, -4)
c	$x = 0$	(0, 3)	maximum	(-1, 0), (1, 0)	(0, 3)
d	$x = 0$	(0, 4)	maximum	(-2, 0), (2, 0)	(0, 4)
e	$x = 2$	(2, 1)	minimum	none	(0, 4)
f	$x = -1$	(-1, 7)	maximum	(-4, 0), (2, 0)	(0, 6)
g	$x = 0$	(0, 0)	minimum	(0, 0)	(0, 0)
h	$x = 0$	(0, -4)	minimum	(-2, 0), (2, 0)	(0, -4)
i	$x = 3$	(3, 4)	maximum	(1, 0), (5, 0)	(0, -5)
j	$x = 3$	$(3, -\frac{1}{2})$	minimum	(2, 0), (4, 0)	(0, 4)
k	$x = 0$	(0, 2)	maximum	(-1, 0), (1, 0)	(0, 2)
l	$x = -2$	(-2, -1)	maximum	none	(0, -4)

4

x	-2	-1	0	1	2
y	3	0	-1	0	3

$y = x^2 - 1$

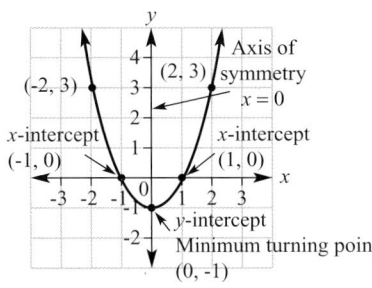

5

x	-3	-2	-1	0	1	2	3
y	0	5	8	9	8	5	0

$y = 9 - x^2$

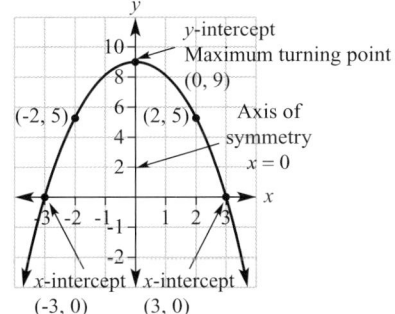

6

x	-4	-3	-2	-1	0	1	2
y	5	0	-3	-4	-3	0	5

$y = x^2 + 2x - 3$

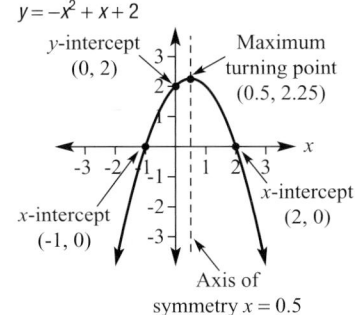

7

x	-2	-1	0	1	2	3
y	-4	0	2	2	0	-4

$y = -x^2 + x + 2$

y-intercept (0, 2)
Maximum turning point (0.5, 2.25)
x-intercept (-1, 0)
x-intercept (2, 0)
Axis of symmetry x = 0.5

8 a i 1 s, 3 s
  ii one time is on the way up and the other is on the way down

---

 b i 2 s **ii** 12 m **iii** 4 s
9 a 100 m **b** 155 m **c** 5 s
  d journey takes 1 s longer to go down to the ground
10 a $x = 1$
  b (1, -3)
11 a $x = 1$ **b** (2, 0)
12 a $y = x^2$ **b** $y = x^2 - 4$
  c $y = 1 - x^2$ **d** $y = x^2 - 2x + 1$
  e $y = -x^2 - 2x$ **f** $y = x^2 - 3x - 4$
13 a Yes **b** Yes

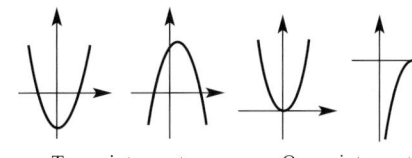

Two x-intercepts   One x-intercept

  c Yes

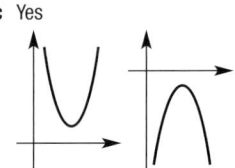

Zero x-intercepts

  d No
14 a $-2^2 = -1 \times 2^2 = -4$. It is not $(-2)^2 = 4$, so correct solution is
    $y = -2^2 + 2 \times 2 = -4 + 4 = 0$
  b $-(-3)^2 = -1 \times 9 = -9$. It is not $-3^2 = +9$, so correct solution
    is $y = -3 - (-3)^2 = -3 - 9 = -12$
15 a $x = -2, x = 2$ **b** $x = 0$
  c i infinite **ii** one **iii** none
16 a i $x = 0, x = 2$ **ii** $x = -1, x = 3$
  b two, a parabola is symmetrical
  c one, this is the minimum turning point
  d none, -1 is the minimum y-value so there are no values of
    y less than -1

Exercise 10F

1 a $y = 3x^2, y = x^2, y = \frac{1}{2}x^2$ **b** $y = -3x^2, y = -x^2, y = -\frac{1}{2}x^2$
  c (0, 0) **d** $x = 0$
  e i $y = 3x^2$ **ii** $y = \frac{1}{2}x^2$ **iii** $y = -3x^2$ **iv** $y = -\frac{1}{2}x^2$
  f i $y = -x^2$ **ii** $y = -3x^2$ **iii** $y = \frac{1}{2}x^2$
2 a positive **b** negative
3 a $y = -x^2$ **b** $y = 4x^2$ **c** $y = 5x^2$ **d** $y = \frac{1}{3}x^2$

4 a

x	-2	-1	0	1	2
y	4	1	0	1	4

x	-2	-1	0	1	2
y	12	3	0	3	12

x	-2	-1	0	1	2
y	$\frac{4}{3}$	$\frac{1}{3}$	0	$\frac{1}{3}$	$\frac{4}{3}$

b

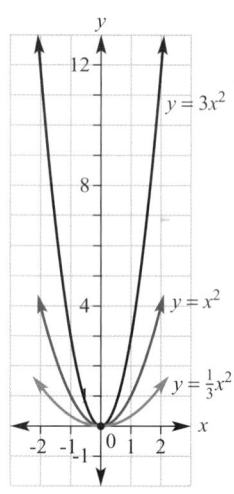

c For all 3 graphs, the turning point is a minimum at (0, 0) and the axis of symmetry is $x = 0$

d i narrower   **ii** wider

5 a i

x	-2	-1	0	1	2
y	16	4	0	4	16

ii

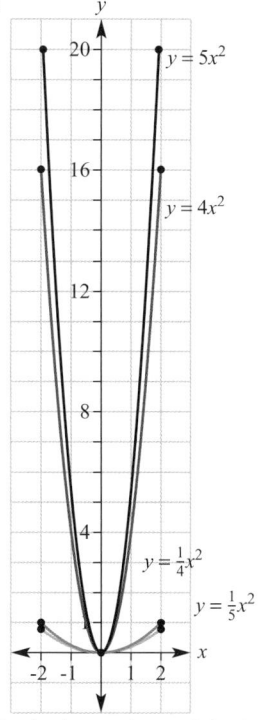

iii axis of symmetry: $x = 0$; turning point: (0, 0)

iv narrower

b i

x	-2	-1	0	1	2
y	20	5	0	5	20

iii axis of symmetry: $x = 0$; turning point: (0, 0); x- and y-intercept: (0, 0)

iv narrower

c i

x	-2	-1	0	1	2
y	1	$\frac{1}{4}$	0	$\frac{1}{4}$	1

iii axis of symmetry: $x = 0$; turning point: (0, 0)

iv wider

d i

x	-2	-1	0	1	2
y	$\frac{4}{5}$	$\frac{1}{5}$	0	$\frac{1}{5}$	$\frac{4}{5}$

iii axis of symmetry: $x = 0$; turning point: (0, 0)

iv wider

6 a i

x	-2	-1	0	1	2
y	-8	-2	0	-2	-8

ii

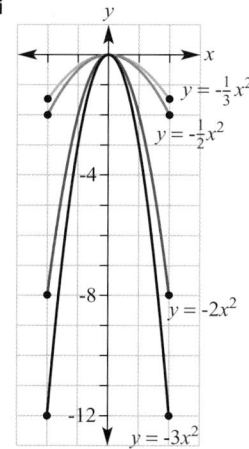

iii axis of symmetry: $x = 0$; turning point: (0, 0); x- and y-intercept: (0, 0)

iv narrower

b i

x	-2	-1	0	1	2
y	-12	-3	0	-3	-12

iii axis of symmetry: $x = 0$; turning point: (0, 0); x- and y-intercept: (0, 0)

iv narrower

c i

x	-2	-1	0	1	2
y	-2	$-\frac{1}{2}$	0	$-\frac{1}{2}$	-2

iii axis of symmetry: $x = 0$; turning point: (0, 0); x- and y-intercept: (0, 0)

iv wider

d i

x	-2	-1	0	1	2
y	$-\frac{4}{3}$	$-\frac{1}{3}$	0	$-\frac{1}{3}$	$-\frac{4}{3}$

iii axis of symmetry: $x = 0$; turning point: $(0, 0)$; x- and y-intercept: $(0, 0)$

iv wider

7 a A   **b** H

8 i d   **ii** c   **iii** a

   iv e   **v** f   **vi** b

9 a reflection in the x-axis, dilating by a factor of 3 from the x-axis

  b reflection in the x-axis, dilating by a factor of 6 from the x-axis

  c reflection in the x-axis, dilating by a factor of $\frac{1}{2}$ from the x-axis

  d reflection in the x-axis, dilating by a factor of 2 from the x-axis

  e reflection in the x-axis, dilating by a factor of 3 from the x-axis

  f reflection in the x-axis, dilating by a factor of $\frac{1}{3}$ from the x-axis

10 a $y = -4x^2$ **b** $y = \frac{1}{3}x^2$ **c** $y = -4x^2$ **d** $y = -\frac{4}{3}x^2$

11 No because both transformations are multiplying to 'a' and multiplication is commutative: $bc = cb$

12 $y = ax^2$, has y-axis as axis of symmetry so it is symmetrical about the y-axis

13 a $y = 5x^2$ **b** $y = 7x^2$ **c** $y = x^2$ **d** $y = \frac{7}{4}x^2$

  e $y = \frac{4}{25}x^2$ **f** $y = \frac{26}{9}x^2$ **g** $y = 5x^2$ **h** $y = -52x^2$

14 $y = \frac{67}{242064}x^2$

Exercise 10G

1 a i $(-2, 0)$ **ii** $(3, 0)$ **b i** $(0, 4)$ **ii** $(0, -9)$

  c left   **d** right

2 a i $(0, -3)$ **ii** $(0, 2)$ **b i** $(0, -3)$ **ii** $(0, 2)$

  c down   **d** up

3 a i $(2, 3)$ **ii** $(-1, -1)$ **b i** $(0, -1)$ **ii** $(0, 0)$

  c i one, left, one, down

    ii two, right, three, up.

4 a $(0, 3)$ **b** $(0, -4)$ **c** $(0, -4)$ **d** $(0, 25)$

5 a $y = x^2 + 1$ **b** $y = x^2 + 3$ **c** $y = x^2 - 2$

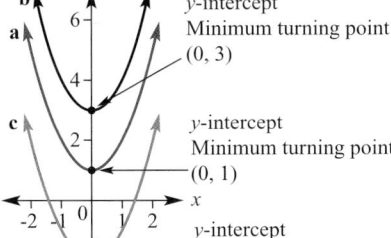

y-intercept
Minimum turning point
$(0, 3)$

y-intercept
Minimum turning point
$(0, 1)$

y-intercept
Minimum turning point
$(0, -2)$

d $y = -x^2 + 4$ **e** $y = -x^2 + 1$ **f** $y = -x^2 - 5$

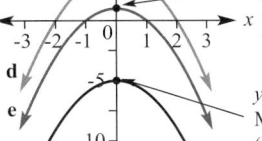

y-intercept
Maximum turning point
$(0, 4)$

y-intercept
Maximum turning point
$(0, 1)$

y-intercept
Maximum turning point
$(0, -5)$

6 a $y = (x - 2)^2$ **b** $y = (x - 4)^2$ **c** $y = (x + 3)^2$

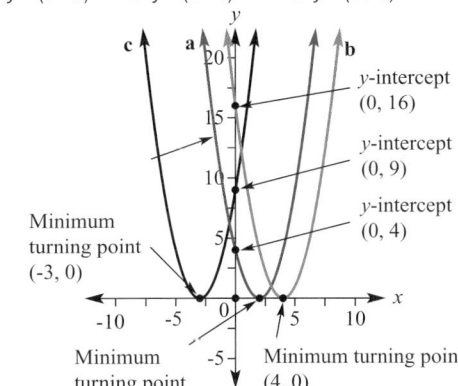

y-intercept
$(0, 16)$

y-intercept
$(0, 9)$

y-intercept
$(0, 4)$

Minimum turning point
$(-3, 0)$

Minimum turning point
$(2, 0)$

Minimum turning point
$(4, 0)$

d $y = -(x - 3)^2$ **e** $y = -(x + 2)^2$ **f** $y = -(x + 6)^2$

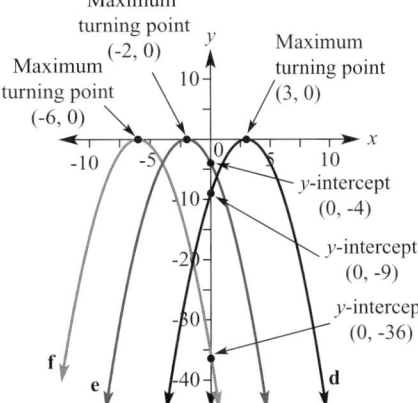

Maximum turning point
$(-2, 0)$

Maximum turning point
$(3, 0)$

Maximum turning point
$(-6, 0)$

y-intercept
$(0, -4)$

y-intercept
$(0, -9)$

y-intercept
$(0, -36)$

7 a $y = (x - 3)^2 + 2$

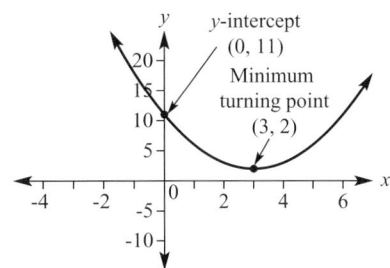

y-intercept
$(0, 11)$

Minimum turning point
$(3, 2)$

b $y = (x-1)^2 - 1$

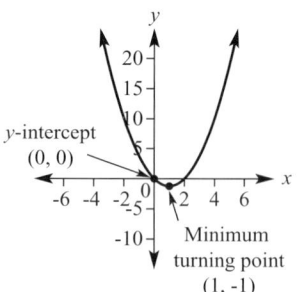

y-intercept (0, 0)

Minimum turning point (1, -1)

c $y = (x+2)^2 - 3$

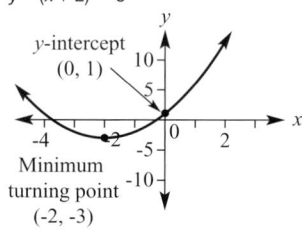

y-intercept (0, 1)

Minimum turning point (-2, -3)

d $y = (x+1)^2 + 7$

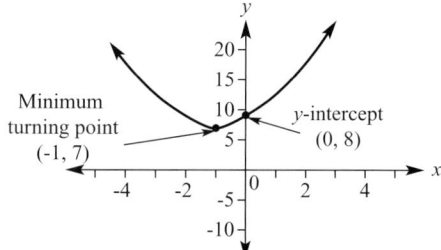

Minimum turning point (-1, 7)

y-intercept (0, 8)

e $y = -(x-2)^2 + 1$

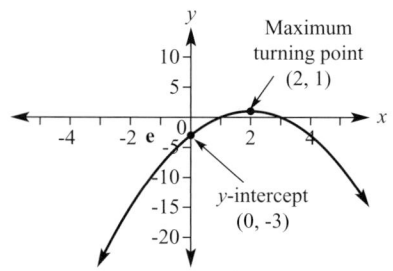

Maximum turning point (2, 1)

y-intercept (0, -3)

f $y = -(x-5)^2 + 3$

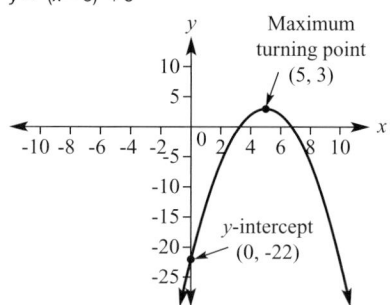

Maximum turning point (5, 3)

y-intercept (0, -22)

g $y = -(x+3)^2 - 4$

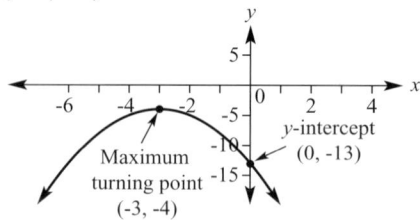

y-intercept (0, -13)

Maximum turning point (-3, -4)

h $y = -(x+1)^2 - 5$

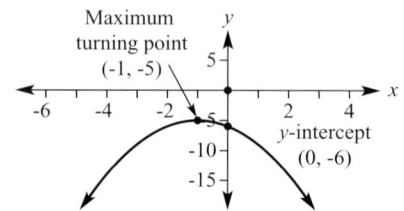

Maximum turning point (-1, -5)

y-intercept (0, -6)

i $y = -(x-3)^2 - 6$

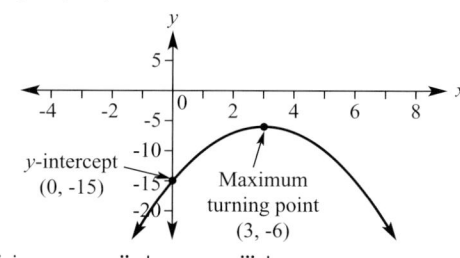

y-intercept (0, -15)

Maximum turning point (3, -6)

8 i j   **ii** d   **iii** b

   iv h   **v** k   **vi** g

   vii a   **viii** e   **ix** l

   x i   **xi** f   **xii** c

9 a $y = (x-1)^2 + 1$ **b** $y = (x+2)^2 + 2$

  c $y = (x+1)^2 - 3$ **d** $y = -(x-1)^2 + 4$

  e $y = -(x-2)^2 - 2$ **f** $y = -(x+2)^2 + 4$

10 a $y = -(x-2)^2 + 9$, turning point (2, 9)

    $y = (x-7)^2 - 4$, turning point (7, -4)

b

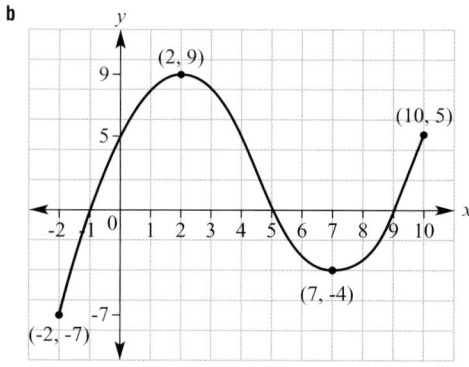

(2, 9)

(10, 5)

(7, -4)

(-2, -7)

11 a i $y = -(x+1)^2 + 3$ **ii** $y = (x+3)^2 + 4$

   iii $y = (x-1)^2 - 3$ **iv** $y = -(x-5)^2 - 7$

   v $y = -x^2 - 2$ **vi** $y = x^2 - 6$

  b i (-1, 3)   **ii** (-3, 4)   **iii** (1, -3)   **iv** (5, -7)

   v (0, -2)   **vi** (0, -6)

12 a (h, k) **b** $y = ah^2 + k$

13 a $(2 - x)^2 = (-1(x - 2))^2 = (-1)^2(x - 2)^2 = (x - 2)^2$, so graphs are the same

   b graphs are the same

14 a $y = x^2 + 3$ **b** $y = x^2 - 4$

   c $y = x^2 - 3$ **d** $y = x^2 - 5$

15 a $y = -x^2 + 4$ **b** $y = -x^2 + 4$

   c $y = -x^2 + 24$ **d** $y = -x^2 + 10$

16 a $y = (x + 3)^2$ or $y = (x - 5)^2$ **b** $y = (x - 2)^2$ or $y = (x - 4)^2$

   c $y = (x + 4)^2$ or $y = (x - 2)^2$ **d** $y = x^2$ or $y = (x - 6)^2$

17 a $y = -(x - 1)^2 + 1$ **b** $y = (x + 2)^2$

   c $y = -(x - 3)^2$ **d** $y = -(x + 3)^2 + 2$

   e $y = (x + 1)^2 + 4$ **f** $y = (x - 3)^2 - 9$

Exercise 10H

1 a $x(x + 2)$ **b** $x(x - 3)$ **c** $5x(x - 2)$

   d $(x + 3)(x - 3)$ **e** $(x + 1)(x - 1)$ **f** $(x + 7)(x - 7)$

   g $(x + 2)(x + 1)$ **h** $(x + 3)(x + 2)$ **i** $(x - 4)(x + 3)$

   j $(x - 7)(x + 4)$ **k** $(x - 2)(x - 2) = (x - 2)^2$

   l $(x + 5)(x + 5) = (x + 5)^2$

2 a 0   **b** 0   **c** -3

   d 8   **e** -1   **f** -1

   g -0.5   **h** 4.5   **i** 6

3 a -4   **b** -1   **c** -9

   d -1   **e** -9   **f** -9

4 a i (0, 0) (-7, 0)   **ii** (0, 0)   **b i** (0, 0) (-3, 0)   **ii** (0, 0)

   c i (0, 0) (-4, 0)   **ii** (0, 0)   **d i** (4, 0) (-2, 0)   **ii** (0, -8)

   e i (-2, 0) (5, 0)   **ii** (0, -10)   **f i** (-3, 0) (7, 0)   **ii** (0, -21)

   g i (-3, 0) (1, 0)   **ii** (0, -6)   **h i** (-4, 0) (-1, 0)   **ii** (0, 12)

   i i (2, 0) (3, 0)   **ii** (0, 6)

5 a $y = x(x - 5)$

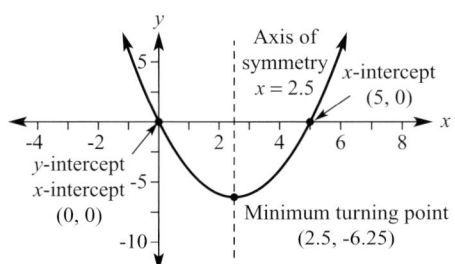

   b $y = x(x + 1)$

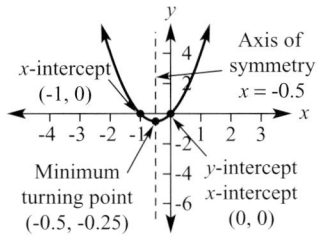

c $y = x(x - 3)$

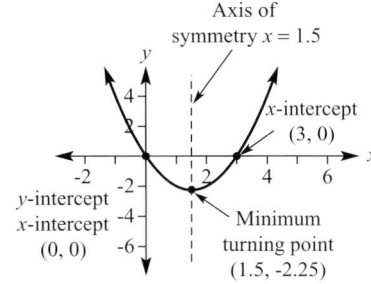

d $y = x(2 + x)$

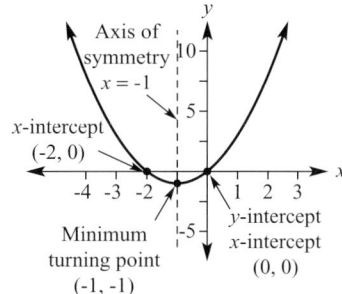

e $y = x(5 + x)$

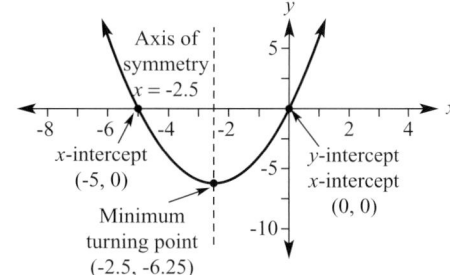

f $y = x(3 - x)$

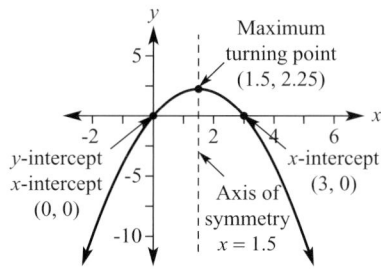

g $y = -x(x + 8)$

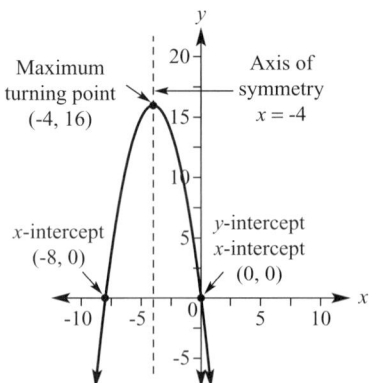

Maximum turning point (-4, 16)
Axis of symmetry $x = -4$
x-intercept (-8, 0)
y-intercept
x-intercept (0, 0)

h $y = -x(2 + x)$

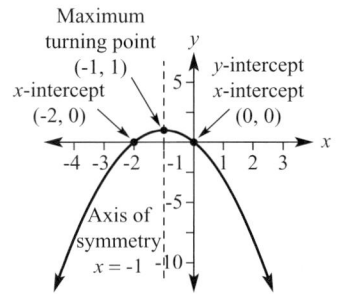

Maximum turning point (-1, 1)
x-intercept (-2, 0)
y-intercept
x-intercept (0, 0)
Axis of symmetry $x = -1$

i $y = -x(x - 1)$

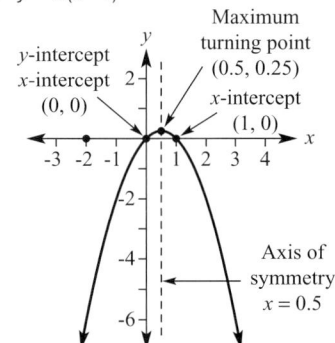

Maximum turning point (0.5, 0.25)
y-intercept
x-intercept (0, 0)
x-intercept (1, 0)
Axis of symmetry $x = 0.5$

6 a $y = (x - 2)(x - 1)$

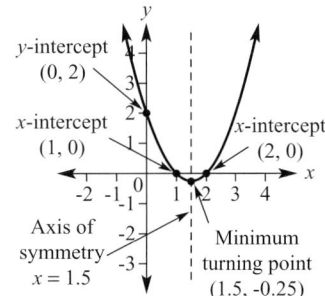

y-intercept (0, 2)
x-intercept (1, 0)
x-intercept (2, 0)
Axis of symmetry $x = 1.5$
Minimum turning point (1.5, -0.25)

b $y = (x - 3)(x - 1)$

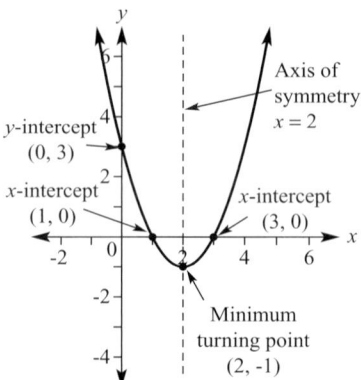

Axis of symmetry $x = 2$
y-intercept (0, 3)
x-intercept (1, 0)
x-intercept (3, 0)
Minimum turning point (2, -1)

c $y = (x + 3)(x - 1)$

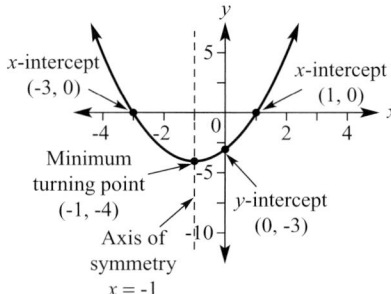

x-intercept (-3, 0)
x-intercept (1, 0)
Minimum turning point (-1, -4)
y-intercept (0, -3)
Axis of symmetry $x = -1$

d $y = (x + 2)^2$

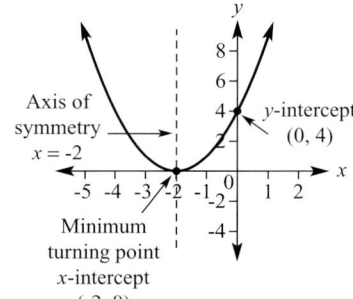

Axis of symmetry $x = -2$
y-intercept (0, 4)
Minimum turning point x-intercept (-2, 0)

e $y = (x + 1)^2$

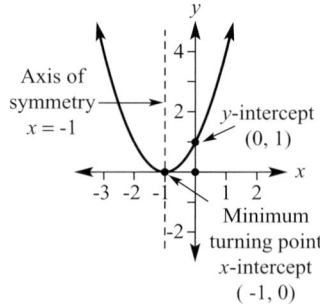

Axis of symmetry $x = -1$
y-intercept (0, 1)
Minimum turning point x-intercept (-1, 0)

f $y = (x + 4)(x - 2)$

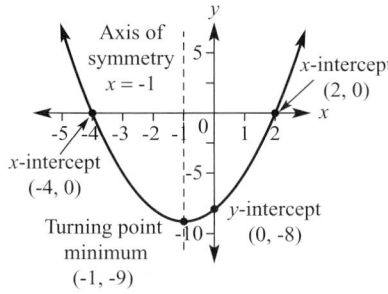

Axis of symmetry $x = -1$

x-intercept (2, 0)

x-intercept (-4, 0)

y-intercept (0, -8)

Turning point minimum (-1, -9)

7 a $y = x^2 - 1$

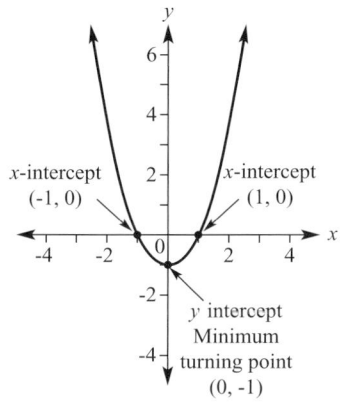

x-intercept (-1, 0)

x-intercept (1, 0)

y intercept Minimum turning point (0, -1)

b $y = 9 - x^2$

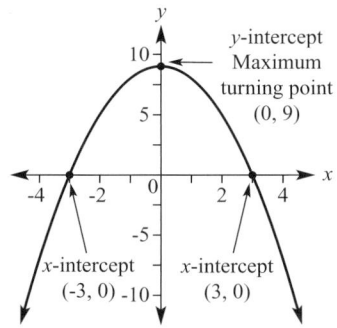

y-intercept Maximum turning point (0, 9)

x-intercept (-3, 0)

x-intercept (3, 0)

c $y = x^2 + 5x$

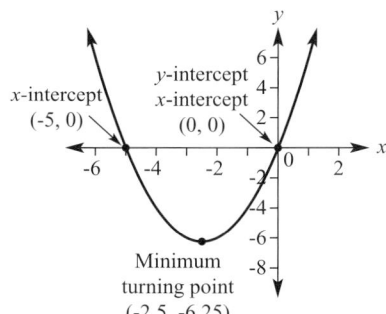

x-intercept (-5, 0)

y-intercept x-intercept (0, 0)

Minimum turning point (-2.5, -6.25)

d $y = 2x^2 - 6x$

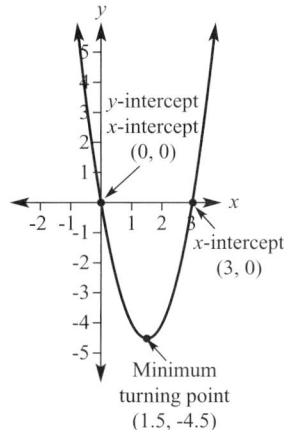

y-intercept x-intercept (0, 0)

x-intercept (3, 0)

Minimum turning point (1.5, -4.5)

e $y = 4x^2 - 8x$

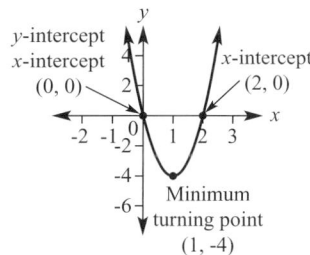

y-intercept x-intercept (0, 0)

x-intercept (2, 0)

Minimum turning point (1, -4)

f $y = x^2 - 3x - 4$

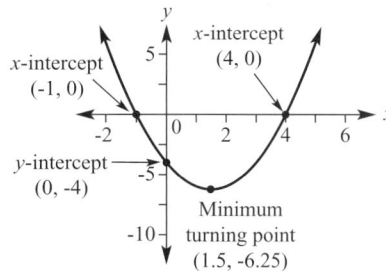

x-intercept (-1, 0)

x-intercept (4, 0)

y-intercept (0, -4)

Minimum turning point (1.5, -6.25)

g $y = x^2 + x - 12$

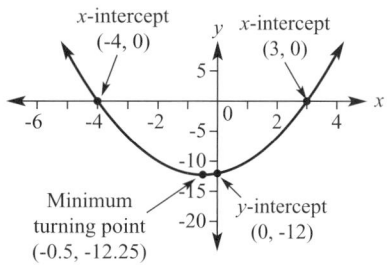

x-intercept (-4, 0)

x-intercept (3, 0)

Minimum turning point (-0.5, -12.25)

y-intercept (0, -12)

h $y = x^2 + 2x + 1$

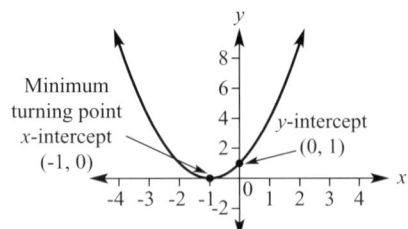

i $y = x^2 - 6x + 9$

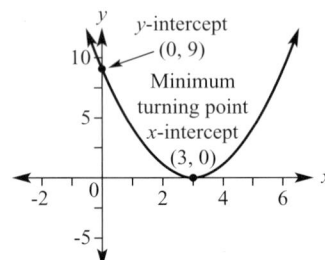

8 a -3 **b** 2 **c** 3 **d** -4 **e** -5 **f** 6

9 a 30 m **b** 225 m **10 a** 200 m **b** 1000 m

11 There is only one x-intercept so this must be the turning point

12 a $y = c$ **b** $y = ab$

13 a (1, -16) **b** (5, 0) (-3, 0) TP$\left(\dfrac{5 + -3}{2}, -16\right) = (1, -16)$

c $y = (x - 2)^2 - 49$, $h = 2$, $k = -49$

14 b $y = (x + 3)(x - 1)$ **c** $y = 2(x + 5)(x - 1)$

d $y = -(x + 1)(x - 5)$ **e** $y = -(x + 8)(x + 2)$

f $y = \dfrac{1}{2}(x + 8)(x - 2)$ **g** $y = -\dfrac{1}{3}(x + 3)(x - 7)$

Challenges

1 a they are square numbers; **b** $100^2 = 10\ 000$

2 a $\dfrac{5}{3}, -\dfrac{7}{2}$ **b** 2, -1 **c** $2^{\frac{2}{3}} + 1$

3 6 seconds **4** $\dfrac{n(n+1)}{2}$; $n = 11$ **5** $x = 2$

6 a 20 units, 21 units, 29 units

b 17 units

7 a $k < 0$ **b** $k = 0$ **c** $k > 0$

Multiple-choice questions

1 D **2** B **3** C **4** A **5** D
6 B **7** E **8** C **9** B **10** A

Short-answer questions

1 $y = x^2 - 2x - 3$

x	-3	-2	-1	0	1	2	3
y	12	5	0	-3	-4	-3	0

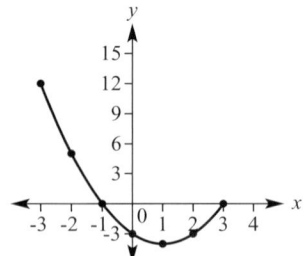

2 a 0, -2 **b** 0, 4 **c** -3, 7

d 2, -2 **e** -1, $\dfrac{2}{5}$ **f** $\dfrac{1}{2}, \dfrac{4}{3}$

3 a 0, -3 **b** 0, 4 **c** -5, 5

d -9, 9 **e** -2, 2 **f** -4, 4

g -3, -7 **h** -5, 8 **i** 4

4 a $x^2 - 5x = 0$; $x = 0, 5$ **b** $3x^2 - 18x = 0$; $x = 0, 6$

c $x^2 + 8x + 12 = 0$; $x = -6, -2$ **d** $x^2 - 2x - 15 = 0$; $x = -3, 5$

e $x^2 - 8x + 15 = 0$; $x = 3, 5$ **f** $x^2 + 3x - 4 = 0$; $x = -4, 1$

5 a $x^2 + 2x - 80 = 0$; $x = 8$ units **b** $x^2 + 5x - 24 = 0$; $x = 3$ units

c $x^2 + 3x - 28 = 0$; $x = 4$ units

6 a i $x = 3$ **ii** minimum (3, -2)

b i $x = -1$ **ii** maximum (-1, 3)

c i $x = 5$ **ii** minimum (5, 0)

7 a $y = 2x^2$ **b** $y = -x^2 + 2$ **c** $y = (x + 1)^2$

d $y = (x - 3)^2$ **e** $y = x^2 - 4$

8 a $y = x^2 + 2$

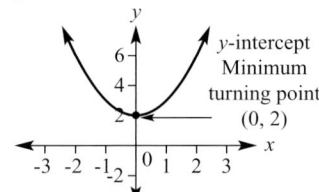

b $y = -x^2 - 5$

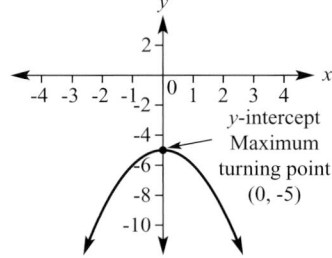

c $y = (x + 2)^2$

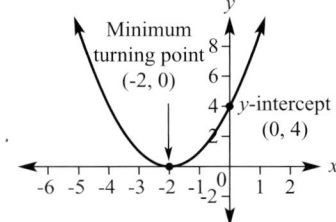

d $y = -(x-3)^2$

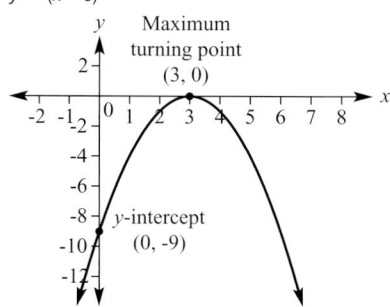

Maximum turning point (3, 0)

y-intercept (0, -9)

e $y = (x-1)^2 + 3$

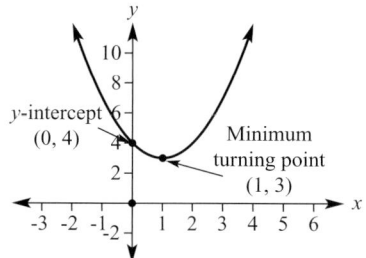

y-intercept (0, 4)

Minimum turning point (1, 3)

f $y = 2(x+2)^2 - 4$

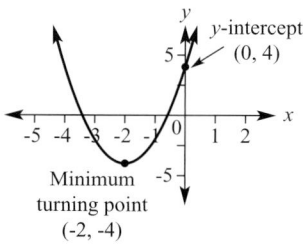

y-intercept (0, 4)

Minimum turning point (-2, -4)

9 a $y = x^2$ translated up 2 units

b $y = x^2$ reflected in the x-axis and translated down 5 units

c $y = x^2$ translated 2 units left

d $y = x^2$ reflected in the x-axis then translated 3 units right

e $y = x^2$ translated 1 unit right then 3 units up

f $y = x^2$ dilated by a factor of 2 from the x-axis, translated 2 units left and then down 4 units

10 a $y = x^2 - 8x + 12$

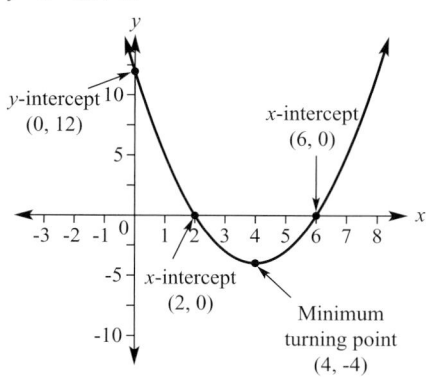

y-intercept (0, 12)

x-intercept (6, 0)

x-intercept (2, 0)

Minimum turning point (4, -4)

b $y = x^2 + 10x + 16$

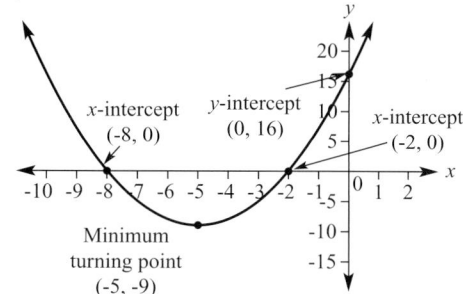

x-intercept (-8, 0)

y-intercept (0, 16)

x-intercept (-2, 0)

Minimum turning point (-5, -9)

c $y = x^2 + 2x - 15$

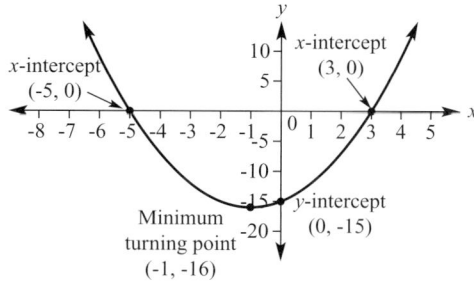

x-intercept (-5, 0)

x-intercept (3, 0)

y-intercept (0, -15)

Minimum turning point (-1, -16)

d $y = x^2 + 4x - 5$

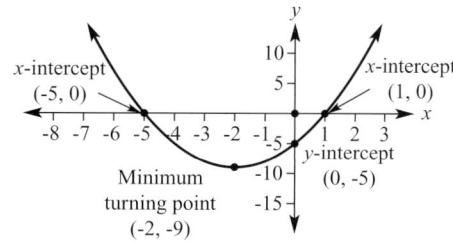

x-intercept (-5, 0)

x-intercept (1, 0)

y-intercept (0, -5)

Minimum turning point (-2, -9)

Extended-response questions

1 a $x + 5$ **b** $A = x^2 + 5x$ **c** $x = 2$ ($x = -7$ not valid as $x > 0$)

d Base = 4 m, Height = 7 m

2 a i (0, 0), (6, 0) **ii** Maximum at (3, 18)

iii

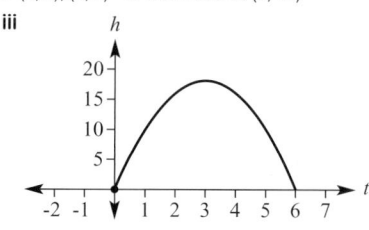

b i (0, 0) **ii** (4, 16) **iii** (0, 0), (8, 0)

iv

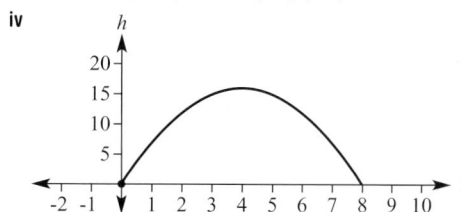

c i Connor's rocket, 8 s

ii Sam's rocket, 2 m higher

iii 16 m, the same height

Semester review 2

Indices and surds
Multiple-choice questions

1 C   2 B   3 D   4 E   5 C

Short-answer question

1 a $\dfrac{a^2 b}{2}$ b $2x^3 y^5$ c $8x^6 - 2$

2 a $5m^2$ b $\dfrac{2a^8}{3b^5}$ c $\dfrac{3x^2}{y}$

3 a 3.07×10^{-2} kg   b 4.24×10^6 kg

   c 1.22×10^4 seconds   d 2.35×10^{-7} seconds

4 a 12   b 3   c $\sqrt{3} + 7\sqrt{5}$ d $\sqrt{7}$

Extended-response question

a i 74 000 000 000

   ii 7.4×10^{10}

b 1.87×10^{17}

c 8.72×10^{-7}

Geometry
Multiple-choice questions

1 C   2 B   3 A   4 E   5 B

Short-answer questions

1 a $a = 100$, $b = 140$ b $a = 70$, $b = 55$

   c $x = 67$, $y = 98$ d $x = 35$

2 $85°$

3 $CB = CD$ (given equal sides)

   $\angle ACB = \angle ACD$ (given equal angles)

   AC is common

   $\therefore \triangle ABC \,|||\, \triangle ADC$ (SAS)

4 a AAA   b 2.4

Extended-response question

a $\angle ABD = \angle ECD$ (given right angles)

   $\angle ADB = \angle EDC$ (common angle)

   $\angle DAB = \angle DEC$ (corresponding angles in parallel lines are equal)

   $\therefore \triangle ABD \equiv \triangle ECD$ (AAA)

b 7.5 m   c 3.75 m   d 4.3 m

Algebra
Multiple-choice questions

1 E   2 D   3 B   4 A   5 D

Short-answer questions

1 a $x^2 - 9$ b $x^2 + 4x + 4$

   c $6x^2 - 17x + 12$

2 a $2ab(4 + a)$ b $(3m - 5)(3m + 5)$

   c $3(b - 4)(b + 4)$ d $(a + 4)(a + 10)$

   e $(x + 3)^2$ f $(x - 2)(x + 10)$

   g $2(x - 3)(x - 5)$ h $(2x - 3)(x - 4)$

   i $(2x - 1)(3x + 4)$

3 a $(x - 3a)(x - 1)$ b $(x + 2)(2a - 5b)$

4 a i $\dfrac{3}{2}$ ii $\dfrac{4}{x+3}$

   iii $\dfrac{13x+21}{14}$ iv $\dfrac{1}{3x}$

   v $\dfrac{11x - 10}{(x+1)(x-2)}$ vi $\dfrac{2x + 25}{(x - 5)(x + 2)}$

  b i $x = \dfrac{17}{12}$ ii $x = -11$

Extended-response question

a $10 - 2x$ and $8 - 2x$

b $(10 - 2x)(8 - 2x) = 80 - 36x + 4x^2$

c 48 m^2

d $4(x - 4)(x - 5)$

e Area of rug is 0 as it has no width

f $x = 2.5$

Probability and statistics
Multiple-choice questions

1 D   2 A   3 C   4 B   5 C

Short-answer questions

1 a

b i 24   ii 16

c i $\dfrac{1}{5}$ ii $\dfrac{1}{3}$

2 a

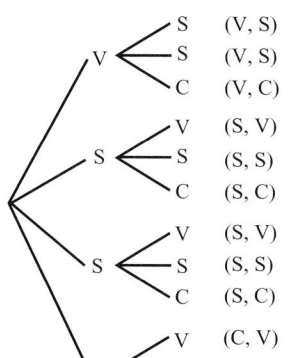

	Outcome
	S (V, S)
V	S (V, S)
	C (V, C)
	V (S, V)
S	S (S, S)
	C (S, C)
	V (S, V)
S	S (S, S)
	C (S, C)
	V (C, V)
C	S (C, S)
	S (C, S)

b i $\frac{1}{3}$ ii $\frac{1}{6}$ iii $\frac{1}{2}$

3 a

Stem	Leaf
1	0 1 1 2 3 5 7 8
2	2 5 5 5 6
3	1 2 2

1 | 3 means 13 aces

b mode = 25, median = 20

c skewed

4 a

Class interval	Frequency	Percentage Frequency
0–	2	6.7
50–	4	13.3
100–	5	16.7
150–	9	30
200–	7	23.3
250–	3	10
Total	30	100

b

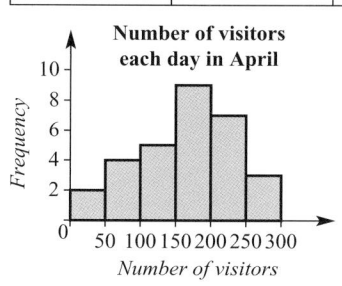

Number of visitors each day in April

c i 6   ii 60%

Extended-response question

a

		Red		
		1	2	3
Green	1	(1, 1)	(1, 2)	(1, 3)
	2	(2, 1)	(2, 2)	(2, 3)
	3	(3, 1)	(3, 2)	(3, 3)

b $\frac{4}{9}$

c i $\frac{1}{3}$ ii 18

d i (7)(11.5)(17)   (30)   (42)

Age (years)

ii 11.5 yrs   iii 90

Introduction to quadratic equations and graphs
Multiple-choice questions

1 B   **2** B   **3** E   **4** C   **5** E

Short-answer questions

1 a $x = -5, 3$ **b** $x = \frac{1}{2}, -\frac{5}{3}$ **c** $x = 0, -2$

d $x = -3, 3$ **e** $x = 2, 7$ **f** $x = -4$

2 15 m by 8 m

3 a translated 3 units up

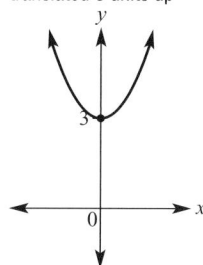

b reflected in the x-axis and translated 4 units left

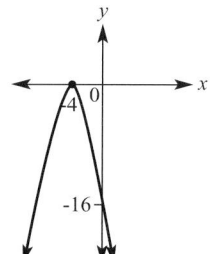

c translated 2 units right and 5 units up

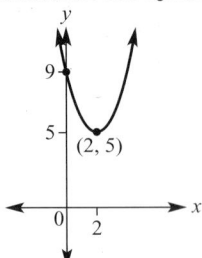

4 a $y = -12$

 b $x = -2, 6$

 c $(2, -16)$

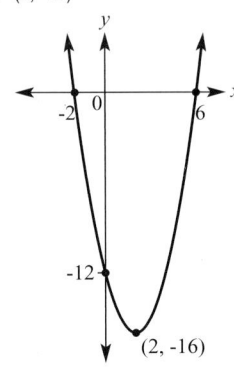

a Lands after 6 seconds.

b **i** 180 cm

 ii 3 seconds

c After 2 seconds and 4 seconds

d

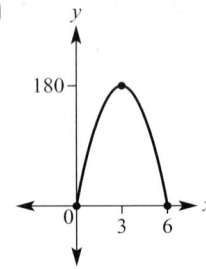